Central A

a Lonely Planet shoestring guide

Tom Brosnahan
Mark Honan
Nancy Keller
Rob Rachowiecki
Stephen Schwartz

Central America

2nd edition

Published by
  Lonely Planet Publications
  Head Office: PO Box 617, Hawthorn, Vic 3122, Australia
  Branches: PO Box 2001A, Berkeley, CA 94702, USA
                 10 Barley Mow Passage, Chiswick, London W4 4PH, UK
                 71 bis rue du Cardinal Lemoine, 75005 Paris, France

Printed by
  Singapore National Printers Ltd, Singapore

Photographs
  Front cover: Woman and woven goods, Guatemala (Daniel Hummel, The Image Bank)

First Published
  February 1992

This Edition
  September 1994

National Library of Australia Cataloguing in Publication Data

  Central America on a shoestring.

  2nd ed.
  Includes index.
  ISBN 0 86442 218 0.

  1. Central America – Guidebooks. I. Brosnahan, Tom.
  II. Keller, Nancy J. Central America
  (Series: Lonely Planet on a shoestring).

917.280453

Tom Brosnahan

Tom was born and raised in Pennsylvania, went to college in Boston, then travelled in Europe. He saw Mexico for the first time as part of the Peace Corps training programme, and then worked with them in Turkey. This whetted his appetite: after graduate school, he travelled throughout Mexico, Guatemala and Belize writing travel articles and guidebooks, and since then he has written 20 travel books. Tom contributed the Guatemala and Belize chapters of this edition, based on his research for *Guatemala, Belize & Yucatán: La Ruta Maya – a travel survival kit.*

Mark Honan

After a university degree in Philosophy opened up a glittering career as an office clerk, Mark decided 'the meaning of life' lay elsewhere and set off on a two-year trip around the world. As a freelance travel writer, he then went campervanning around Europe to write a series of articles for a London magazine. When the magazine went bust, Mark joined a travel agent, from which he was rescued by Lonely Planet. Mark wrote *Switzerland – a travel survival kit*, and is currently working on *Austria – a travel survival kit*. Mark coordinated the writing of this edition, and wrote the Honduras and El Salvador chapters.

Nancy Keller

Nancy was born and raised in northern California, and worked in the alternative press during the '70s, doing every aspect of newspaper work from editorial and reporting to delivering the papers. She returned to university to earn a master's degree in journalism, finally graduating in 1986 after many breaks for extended stays on the west coast of Mexico. Since then she's been travelling and writing. Nancy wrote the chapters on Honduras, El Salvador, Nicaragua and Panama for the first edition of this book.

Rob Rachowiecki

Born in London, Rob spent most of the 1980s in Latin America, travelling, teaching English, visiting national parks, and leading adventure tours for *Wilderness Travel*. With Hilary Bradt, he is co-author of *Backpacking in Mexico & Central America* (Bradt Publications). He has also written Lonely Planet travel survival kits for Ecuador and Peru, and contributed to *South America on a shoestring*. Rob wrote the Costa Rica chapter for this edition, based on research for *Costa Rica – a travel survival kit*. When not travelling, he lives in Arizona with his wife Cathy and daughters Julia and Alison.

Stephen Schwartz

Stephen was born in 1948. He has lived nearly all his life in San Francisco and has travelled widely in Asia, Latin America and Europe. He is a staff writer for the *San Francisco Chronicle* and contributor to many other periodicals. He has published four books on 20th-century political history, as well as poetry and translations. He was educated in linguistics and history, and was affiliated from 1984 to 1989 with the Institute for Contemporary Studies in San Francisco. His writing has been published in Spanish as well as English. Stephen co-authored the Albanian section of Lonely Planet's *Mediterranean Europe Phrasebook*. He updated the Panama and Nicaragua chapters for this edition.

From the Authors

From Tom My thanks to Andy Alpers of L Martinez Associates Inc in Miami; to Bibi Rubio, Roberto Woolfolk Saravia and the staff of the Instituto Guatemalteco de Turismo in Guatemala City for their valuable assistance and ever-cheerful support in many ways; and as always to Jane Fisher, my wife.

From Rob In Costa Rica, Michael Kaye, Amos Bien, Wolf Bissinger, and Richard Laval were major sources of help and information. In the USA, Bill Abbott made my travel arrangements. As always, my greatest debt is to my wife, Cathy Payson, who tolerates my absences with good humour, and provides a warm welcome on my return.

From Mark Various tourist offices were helpful, especially those in Tegucigalpa, San Pedro Sula and San Salvador (particularly Jorge Martínez). Bill Shorr and Tanya gave me some great information about El Salvador. Thanks also to Steve Collins of Journey Latin America, Chris Lee of the Latin America Bureau and Fiona Reeve of Iberia Airlines.

From Stephen In Nicaragua I am grateful to Adán Fletes Valle, Dr Bayardo García Nuñez, Gilda de Sacasa, Sandra Correa, Javier Llanes, Edgardo Buitrago, and, above all, Pablo Antonio; in Panama to Ariel Beliz, Liriola Pitti de Cordoba, Hernán Araúz, Gerry Kanelopulos, and Nick and María Consuelo; and in San Francisco to Luís Mauricio Chamorro, head of the mission at the Nicaraguan Consulate, and Creon Levit.

This Book

The first edition of this book was researched and written by Tom Brosnahan, Rob Rachowiecki and Nancy Keller. This second edition was researched and written by Mark Honan (who also coordinated the writing), Tom Brosnahan, Rob Rachowiecki and Stephen Schwartz.

From the Publisher

This second edition of *Central America on a shoestring* was edited at the Lonely Planet office in Australia by Miriam Cannell, David Meagher, Jenny Missen and Caroline Williamson. Samantha Carew took it through production. Matt King was responsible for the design and illustrations. He also coordinated the mapping and was assisted by Chris Lee-Ack, Jacqui Schiff, Louise Keppie and Sally Woodward. Thanks to Tamsin Wilson for the cover design.

Thanks

A special thanks to those readers who took the time and energy to write to us from places large and small all over the region. These people's names appear at the back of the book on page 630.

Warning & Request

Things change – prices go up, schedules change, good places go bad and bad places go bankrupt – nothing stays the same. So if you find things better or worse, recently opened or long since closed, please write and tell us and help make the next edition better!

Your letters will be used to help update future editions and, where possible, important changes will also be included as a Stop Press section in reprints.

All information is greatly appreciated and the best letters will receive a free copy of the next edition, or any other Lonely Planet book of your choice. We give away lots of books, but unfortunately not every letter/postcard receives one.

Contents

COSTA RICA 454

PANAMA 560

Map Legend

BOUNDARIES

............International Boundary
............Internal Boundary
............Marine Park Boundary

ROUTES

............Freeway
............Highway
............Major Road
............Unsealed Road or Track
............City Road
............City Street
............Railway
............Underground Railway
............Walking Track
............Walking Tour
............Ferry Route
............Cable Car or Chairlift

AREA FEATURES

............Park, Gardens
............National Park
............Forest
............Built-Up Area
............Pedestrian Mall
............Market
............Cemetery
............Reef
............Beach or Desert
............Rocks

HYDROGRAPHIC FEATURES

............Coastline
............River, Creek
............Intermittent River or Creek
............Lake, Intermittent Lake
............Swamp

SYMBOLS

✪ CAPITAL		............National Capital
◉ Capital		............State Capital
🌐 CITY		............Major City
● City		............City
● Town		............Town
● Village		............Village
■		............Place to Stay
▼		............Place to Eat
♟		............Pub, Bar
✉	☎	............Post Office, Telephone
❶	🅂	............Tourist Information, Bank
⊖	🅿	............Transport, Parking
🏛	⛪	............Museum, Youth Hostel
🚐	🅇	Caravan Park, Camping Ground
† 🚊 †		............Church, Cathedral
☪	✡	............Mosque, Synagogue
⚖	⚕	Buddhist Temple, Hindu Temple

✛	★	............Hospital, Police Station
✈	✞	............Airport, Airfield
◩	✿	............Swimming Pool, Gardens
❖	🐘	............Shopping Centre, Zoo
⋔	⛽	............Picnic Site, Petrol Station
←	A25	One Way Street, Route Number
∴		............Archaeological Site or Ruins
🏛	⏏	............Stately Home, Monument
♖	▣	............Castle, Tomb
⌒	⌂	............Cave, Hut or Chalet
▲	☀	............Mountain or Hill, Lookout
⛩	⚓	............Lighthouse, Shipwreck
)(	⌒	............Pass, Spring
		............Ancient or City Wall
		............Rapids, Waterfalls
		............Cliff or Escarpment, Tunnel
		............Railway Station

Note: not all symbols displayed above appear in this book

Introduction

Central America is a small region – its seven countries together have a land area less than a third the size of Mexico. Nevertheless, it is a remarkably varied and interesting part of the world, with attractions ranging from the ruins of ancient Mayan cities, to the Panama Canal, one of the engineering triumphs of the 20th century.

Central America draws visitors from all over the world, with the Mayan ruins being probably the best-known attractions. Then there are idyllic Caribbean islands off Honduras and Nicaragua, with waving palms and white sandy beaches, while Belize has the second largest coral reef in the world. Costa Rica's pristine national parks, several in tropical rainforest, are becoming an attraction for international scientists and visitors interested in the natural environment. Guatemala is known for the vibrant indigenous Mayan culture which still thrives there, for the beautiful Lake Atitlán, and for the old Spanish colonial city of Antigua Guatemala.

You can see mountain mining villages, vast wilderness areas, unusual wildlife, and ecological systems ranging from large Caribbean lagoons to high-altitude cloud forests. The landscapes can be spectacular – almost everywhere in El Salvador is within sight of a volcano, and some of them are still active. Away from these well-known highlights however, there are many places so rarely visited that the arrival of a foreigner is quite an event.

Central America has been making international newspaper headlines for years, not so much for its tourist attractions as for its volatile politics. For us, apprehension about travelling to the region was replaced by a great affection for the Central American people, and a greater understanding of the conditions they face today.

This is a fascinating part of the world. It's also compact, accessible, easy to travel in, and not expensive. All in all, it's a great place for travelling on a shoestring.

Facts about Central America

HISTORY

Early Human Settlement

Central America has been heavily populated for many thousands of years. Archaeologists and anthropologists trace the origins of the native American peoples to Asia. Their ancestors migrated across the Bering Strait from Siberia to Alaska at times when ice ages had caused an increase in polar ice and a consequent fall in sea levels, creating a land bridge between the two continents.

A major migration occurred between 20,000 and 25,000 years ago, with populations then fanning out over the North American continent, passing down through Central America and into South America, all the way to Tierra del Fuego. The Bering Strait land bridge was inundated by rising sea levels for the last time around 7000 BC.

Some speculate that there could also have been migrations, or at least contact, between the Americas and parts of Africa, particularly Egypt. The pyramids, sculptures, and many other ancient artefacts found in America have been cited as evidence of such a contact.

Native American Civilisations

Central America is not only a geographical bridge between North and South America; historically it has also been an intermediate region between North and South American cultures. The lowlands of Nicaragua and Costa Rica seem to have formed a very loose boundary between the overlapping cultures of indigenous Central and South American peoples.

South of this area were a number of tribes which had cultural contacts ranging into Colombia, Ecuador, and down to the Inca empire of Peru. The languages of these tribes are related to linguistic groups of South America.

Tribes living to the north of this intermediate region were more influenced by Mexican cultures, particularly that of the Maya, whose empire stretched through Guatemala, Belize, Chiapas, the Yucatán, and into the western parts of modern Honduras and El Salvador.

The Maya are counted as one of America's three great ancient civilisations, along with the Inca of Peru and the Aztec of Mexico. They left behind stone pyramids, sculptures, ceramics and ceramic art, and a hieroglyphic writing which has yet to be deciphered. They had a well-established religious and social structure, and traded throughout their large area of influence. Their architecture, agriculture, mathematics and astronomy were advanced, and they had an accurate calendar which was later adopted by the Aztec.

Though the history of the Maya can be traced back for over 4000 years, the Classic Period of more advanced Mayan civilisation actually began around the 3rd century AD and reached its height around the 6th to 8th centuries.

After this came a period of decline, but between the 10th and 11th centuries they experienced a renaissance under the influence of the Toltec from Mexico. There was also some cultural blending between the Maya and the Aztec.

The Maya were once again in a period of decline by the 14th century, and at the time of the Spanish arrival many of the Mayan cities were deserted. (See the Guatemala chapter for more about the Maya.)

European Contact & Colonisation

Christopher Columbus is recognised as the first European to 'discover' America, though his first landfall, in 1492, was actually on one of the Caribbean islands, Guanahanín in the Bahamas. It was not until his fourth and final voyage (1502-4), that he reached mainland Central America, exploring the Caribbean coast from present-day Honduras to Panama. Meanwhile, the north coast may have been visited by Alonso de Ojeda in 1499, and Rodrigo de Bastidas certainly sighted

Central America when making exploratory trips out from the Gulf of Venezuela in 1501.

Cristóbal Colón, as Columbus is known in Spanish, was not Spanish but Italian. He had unsuccessfully sought Portuguese support for his explorations, before the Spanish Queen Isabella finally agreed, after six years, to sponsor his voyage. He left Europe looking for a sea route for the spice trade with Asia, and at first he thought he had found it; when he landed in the Bahamas, he believed he had reached the Indies, that is, the East Indies. To this day, the native American peoples are called 'Indians' due to his massive geographical mistake.

The first Spanish settlement on the American mainland was on the east side of the Gulf of Urabá, near the present-day border between Colombia and Panama. The settlement was founded in 1509 but was moved the following year to Santa María de la Antigua del Darién. It was an important base for Spanish exploration.

In 1513 Vasco Nuñez de Balboa scaled the mountains of the Isthmus of Panama and became the first European to sight the Pacific Ocean. The Indians, of course, had known about it for a long time. Panama City was founded on the Pacific side in 1519 by Pedro Arias de Avila (also known as Pedrarias Dávila). The port on the Caribbean side was first located at Nombre de Dios in the Darién, but later moved to Portobelo, which had been explored and named by Columbus. These cities, and the isthmus between them, became vitally important to the Spanish.

In 1519, the same year that Panama City was founded, Hernán Cortés was beginning his invasion of Mexico. The Spanish conquest of Central America then radiated outwards, from Panama in the south and Mexico in the north.

From the Panama City base, Spanish exploration branched out into the Pacific. The Central American Indians had traded with the Inca, and the Spanish were attracted to Peru by the gold they saw coming from the south. After Pizarro's conquest of the Inca Empire in 1532, gold, pearls and other wealth from Peru began to pass across the isthmus from Panama City to Portobelo, headed for the treasuries of Spain.

Spanish Expansion

From Panama, the Spanish bypassed Costa Rica and pushed northward to the lowlands of Nicaragua. Two large Indian towns stood here on the banks of Lago de Managua and Lago de Nicaragua, where Managua and Granada are today.

These cities had also attracted the Spanish forces sent down from Mexico by Cortés. The two Spanish forces, meeting on the plains of Nicaragua, battled against one another. The third city of Nicaragua, León, was established in 1524 by Hernández de Córdoba. Costa Rica was settled later, in the latter half of the century, mostly by missionary and agricultural Spaniards.

Cortés had also sent his lieutenant, Pedro de Alvarado, out to conquer Guatemala. Alvarado's bloodthirstiness, and the bitter fighting between his forces and the Indians of Guatemala, matched the savagery of the Mexican conquest. Alvarado, accompanied by Aztec warriors, crossed the Isthmus of Tehuantepec in 1522, and the decisive battle occurred in the area around Quetzaltenango in 1524. From there, Alvarado went on to conquer all of present-day Guatemala and a good deal of El Salvador.

Honduras, which had been initially claimed for Spain by Columbus, was also conquered by one of Cortés' warriors. Cristóbal de Olid was sent from Mexico at around the same time as Alvarado started. He arrived on the Honduran coast, established a base near present-day Trujillo, and from there the Spanish invaded the area of present-day Honduras, and established settlements at Gracias a Dios, Comayagua, Olancho and Naca.

The Colonial Period

Under the Spanish, the region called Guatemala, which included all of Central America except Panama, was designated a part of the vice-royalty of Mexico, then called Nueva España (New Spain).

Though under Mexico, Guatemala

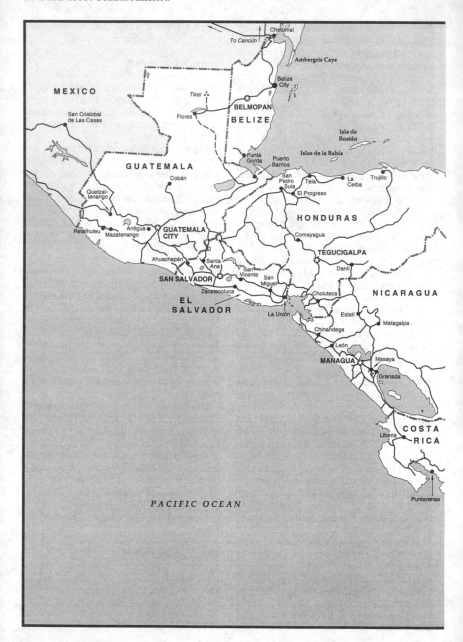

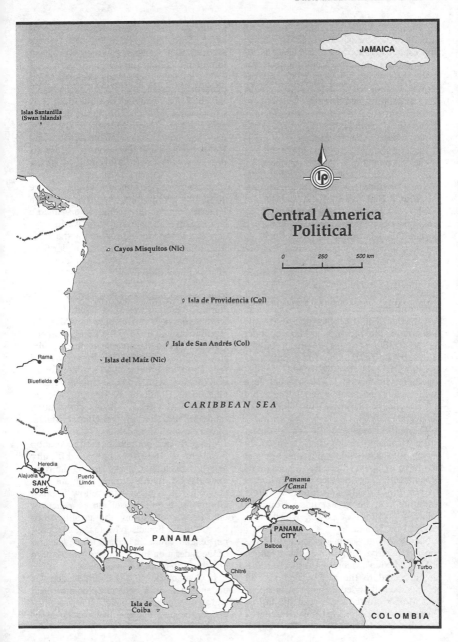

JAMAICA

Islas Santanilla
(Swan Islands)

Cayos Misquitos (Nic)

Central America
Political

0   250   500 km

Isla de Providencia (Col)

Isla de San Andrés (Col)

Rama

Islas del Maíz (Nic)

Bluefields

CARIBBEAN SEA

Heredia

Alajuela

SAN
JOSÉ

Puerto
Limón

Panama
Canal

Colón

Chepo

PANAMA CITY

PANAMA

Balboa

David

Santiago

Chitré

Turbo

Isla de
Coiba

COLOMBIA

became a Captaincy-General, reporting directly to the Spanish crown. Its capital was first established in 1527 at Santiago de los Caballeros de Guatemala, but the town was destroyed by mudslide in 1543 and the capital was moved to Antigua Guatemala. The capital remained here for over two centuries, until 1773 when Antigua was devastated by earthquake and the capital was moved again to Guatemala City.

Panama continued to be an important part of the Spanish empire throughout the colonial period. The rest of Central America was no great producer of wealth, and hence was not of such vital interest to the Spanish.

The colonial period lasted until 1821, by which time both Mexico and Guatemala had declared their independence from Spain. In the same year Colombia, including Panama, also became independent. Panama was a region of Nueva Andalucía, Nueva Granada and finally Colombia until 1903.

Independence

A rising tide of disaffection with Spanish rule first erupted into rebellion in Mexico, under the leadership of a parish priest, Miguel Hidalgo, in 1810. The following year another priest, José Matías Delgado, together with liberal leader Manuel José Arce, organised a revolt in San Salvador, but it was quickly suppressed by forces from Guatemala City.

The will for independence sprang almost entirely from the Creoles – those born locally of Spanish stock – and local business people frustrated by Spain's trade restrictions on its dependencies. Together they formed a home-grown middle class, united by their resentment at being excluded from the colony's positions of power, which were reserved for Spaniards.

Napoleon's invasion of Spain in 1812 boosted the drive for reform in the colonies. In 1821 Mexico's viceroy, Agustín de Iturbide, defected to the rebels, and shortly became the self-styled emperor of independent Mexico. In the same year, the last of Guatemala's conservative Captains General, Brigadier Don Gabino Gainza, was obliged to sign the first of several Acts of Independence. The link with Spain was forever severed, but Central America's political tumult had only begun.

The moment Guatemala declared independence, Iturbide sent his troops to annex the states of the fledgling republic to Mexico. Conservatives in many of the smaller states supported union with Mexico. El Salvador, however, under the leadership of Arce and Delgado, held out for months before its defences were finally broken down by the invaders.

In many respects the forces for change were fiercely divided. A political chasm yawned between the liberals who wanted a more egalitarian state, and the powerful conservatives who wanted essentially the same kind of authoritarian society but under their control. This made any clean political change impossible.

The Central American Federation

Iturbide's empire was short-lived. The following year he was overthrown by Mexican republicans and in 1823 the Central American states declared their independence again, this time from Mexico. They formed a loose federation, the Provincias Unidas del Centro de América, with five constituent states – Guatemala, Honduras, El Salvador, Nicaragua and Costa Rica – and a constitution modelled on that of the United States. Slavery was abolished.

General Arce became the first federation president in 1825, but he had difficulty asserting his authority and finding the right executives. In his home state he was embroiled in conflict with fellow liberals. Ultimately, he set himself up as a dictator until he was overthrown by an alliance of liberals under Francisco Morazán, a Honduran general. Morazán became the new leader of the federation in 1830. Like Arce before him, his grip on power was shaky.

In Guatemala, too, the liberal leader was under threat. As a cholera epidemic raged and an unpopular new penal code was introduced, the underclass – that vast mass of dispossessed to whom middle-class freedoms meant little – grew increasingly restive.

Under the leadership of the young, charismatic Rafael Carrera, a largely Indian mob marched on Guatemala City in 1837. An unlikely alliance formed between Carrera, the Church and the conservatives, and Carrera was installed as dictator. His victory signalled the end of the liberal era and thus of the federation.

In 1838, the congress passed a resolution permitting states to leave the federation. By 1839, El Salvador was the only state left. Regional rivalries between the now separate countries persisted, but from this moment they pursued their own courses. The modern history of each of the Central American republics is covered in the corresponding chapters of this book.

GEOGRAPHY

Because of this political history, the term 'Central America' is sometimes used to mean only the five states of the former federation, with Belize and Panama left out. But in recent years it has usually meant all the land between Mexico and Colombia. Central America covers only a small area – the seven countries together comprise around 544,700 sq km, about a quarter the size of Mexico. Nevertheless, Central America is a strategically important part of the world as it separates the Pacific Ocean from the Caribbean Sea and the Atlantic Ocean, and it also forms a bridge, or a barrier, between North and South America.

The dominant geographical features of Central America are its mountains and volcanoes and its long coastlines. Central America has 2379 km of Caribbean coast and 3287 km of Pacific coast, separated by a land mass that is 280 km wide at its widest point (around the border of Honduras and Nicaragua) but only about 60 km wide at its narrowest point (the isthmus of Panama).

This relatively narrow strip of land is primarily volcanic in origin, with over 100 major volcanoes and 150 minor ones. Several separate mountain chains (cordilleras) stretch for hundreds of km down

through this strip of land. The result is a pattern of mountain ranges and volcanoes, broken by valleys and basins with large, fertile areas of rich volcanic soil.

It may seem strange to find cities at the feet of giant volcanoes, where they are repeatedly endangered by eruptions and earthquakes. Some of the more famous destructions of major cities that have occurred in recent history include that of Antigua Guatemala in 1773, Guatemala City in 1917-18 and 1976, Managua in 1931 and 1972, and San Salvador in 1854 and 1986. Another major quake, 7.4 on the Richter scale, rocked Costa Rica and the northwestern corner of Panama in April 1991. There is, however, a good reason for this pattern of settlement – the volcanic soil is excellent for all types of agriculture and can support the greatest concentrations of agricultural people, so the population centres naturally developed in those areas.

A narrow plain runs along both coasts. In most places it's no more than a 15 to 40-km wide strip between the sea and the mountains. The coastal plain is also fertile, and in some areas there are large, flat plantations of export crops (for example, bananas and pineapples), close to the ports from which the produce is shipped to overseas markets, principally the USA.

CLIMATE

All of Central America is within the tropics, but there's a lot of variation in climate within this small region. The land rises from sea level to over 4000 metres, dividing the region into three primary temperature zones according to altitude, but there is little variation in temperature throughout the year.

The lowlands, from sea level to about 1000 metres, are the hottest zone; daytime temperatures are from 29°C to 32°C (85°F to 90°F), night temperatures around 21°C to 23°C (70°F to 75°F).

The temperate zone, from around 1000 to 2000 metres, has a pleasant, springlike climate, with daytime temperatures from 23°C to 26°C (75°F to 80°F) and night-time

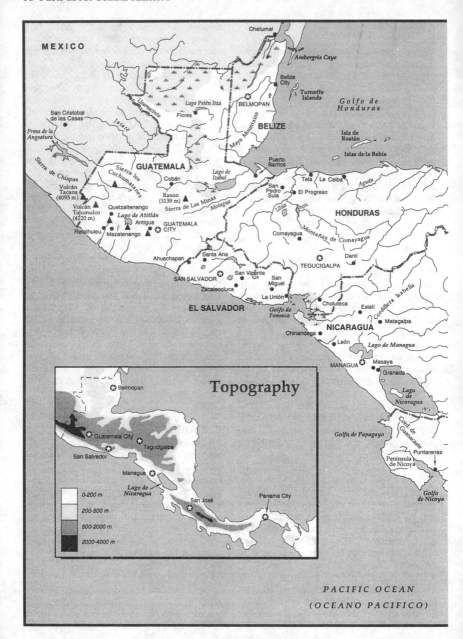

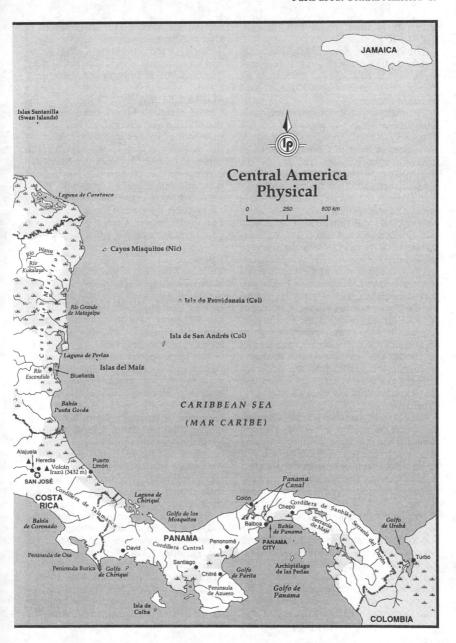

JAMAICA

Islas Santanilla
(Swan Islands)

Laguna de Caratasca

**Central America
Physical**

0   250   500 km

Río Wawa
Río Kukalaya

⌒ Cayos Misquitos (Nic)

Río Grande
de Matagalpa

⌒ Isla de Providencia (Col)

Isla de San Andrés (Col)

Laguna de Perlas

Islas del Maíz

Río Escondido   Bluefields

*Bahía
Punta Gorda*

CARIBBEAN SEA

(MAR CARIBE)

Alajuela
▲ Heredia   Puerto
▲ Volcán   Limón
Irazú (3432 m)
✹ SAN JOSÉ

Panamá
Canal

**COSTA
RICA**   *Cordillera de Talamanca*   *Laguna de
Chiriquí*   Colón

Cordillera de Sanblás   Serranía
Chepo   del Darién

*Bahía
de Coronado*   *Golfo de los
Mosquitos*   Balboa   Golfo
de Urabá

Bahía
de Panamá   Serranía
de Majé

Peninsula de Osa   David   **PANAMA**   Penonomé   **PANAMA
CITY**   Turbo

Peninsula Burica   *Golfo
de Chiriquí*   Santiago   Cordillera Central   *Archipiélago
de las Perlas*

Chitré ●   *Golfo
de Parita*

Peninsula
de Azuero   *Golfo de
Panama*

Isla de
Coíba

COLOMBIA

temperatures from around 15°C to 21°C (60°F to 70°F).

The cold zone, above 2000 metres, has similar daytime temperatures but is colder at night, around 10°C to 12°C (50°F to 55°F). The very few areas over 4000 metres have an alpine climate.

The main seasonal differences are not in temperature but in the amount of rainfall. The rainy season, from around April to November in most of Central America, is called *invierno* (winter). The dry season, from around November to April, is called *verano* (summer). Thus the seasons are, at least in name, the reverse of what they are in the rest of the northern hemisphere. There are some regional variations to the general rule – Panama, for instance, has only a three-month dry season, from January to mid-April.

The Caribbean side of Central America gets much more rainfall than the Pacific side – often more than twice as much. In Panama, the Caribbean side has around 3200 mm of rainfall annually, whereas the Pacific side, less than 100 km away, receives only about 1800 mm. The Caribbean coast receives a lot of rainfall all year round, and is always green. On the Pacific side, the landscape dries out and browns in the dry season, and the air can be dusty and smoky with burning vegetation.

Even during the rainy season, it's a rare day when the sun doesn't shine; a typical pattern is sun during the morning, clouding over later in the day, and a downpour that might last for an hour or so in the late afternoon or evening. But don't bank on it: it can rain any time of day, and if a tropical storm hits (most likely in September and October on the Caribbean coast) it can rain solidly for days at a time. In most places the rainy season doesn't interfere much with travel, but there are a few notable exceptions. It is too hazardous to go overland through the Darién Gap during the rainy season, and occasional flooding can impede travel on the Caribbean coast of Honduras at certain times from December to February. Travelling anywhere on dirt roads can be a thrill in the rainy season, but most of the main routes in Central America are paved.

Smog is a problem in most Central American cities, particularly Guatemala City, Tegucigalpa, San Salvador and Managua.

FLORA & FAUNA

Central America's flora & fauna are exceptionally rich and diversified, with tens of thousands of species represented. Much of the diversity is due to the region's 'in-between' location, between the North and South American continents – hundreds of plant and animal species from both continents spill into Central America. Costa Rica has probably the greatest range of accessible flora and fauna in Central America, and you'll find more details in that chapter.

Fauna

There are thousands of species of mammals, birds, insects, reptiles, amphibians and fishes in Central America. Costa Rica and Belize have the most abundant wildlife, El Salvador and Honduras have the least abundance. Around 900 species of birds have been recorded in Panama alone.

The many species of mammals include jaguars, pumas, ocelots and other cats; spider monkeys, howler monkeys, white-faced capuchin monkeys and squirrel (tití) monkeys; agoutis, capybaras, coatimundis, kinkajous, peccaries and tapirs; two species of armadillos and sloths; several species of anteaters, deer and squirrels; and scores of bat species. Panama is the only Central American country where there are bears (the spectacled bear). Manatees are found in some coastal waters, and the sea harbours dolphins and whales.

Fish are also abundant, in rivers and lakes, and along the Pacific and Caribbean coasts. Reptiles and amphibians include sea, river and land turtles (Costa Rica has some famous nesting sites), crocodiles, frogs (such as tree frogs and the colourful poison-arrow frog), iguanas and many others. There are many species of snake, including the boa constrictor, but only a few are poisonous, notably the tiny coral snake and the large fer-de-lance.

The famous and colourful quetzal is the national bird of Guatemala, and an often-used symbol of Central America. Quetzals are about 35 cm long, but the male has a very long tail which may be a further 60 cm, brilliantly plumed with bright green, red and white feathers. It lives in high-altitude forests all the way from southern Mexico to Panama, but unfortunately, as the forests become threatened, the bird is also endangered. Quetzals can only survive in the wild – they die in captivity. Other beautiful birds of the region include toucans, macaws, many species of parrots, hummingbirds, hawks, harpy eagles, doves and hundreds of others. Striking but common birds are motmots, jacamars, trogons, chacalacas, woodcreepers, puffbirds, manakins, oropendolas and tanagers. It's a rich field for bird watchers.

Not only the quetzal but many other species as well are endangered and may be facing extinction. Hunting takes a large toll, but even more critical is the destruction of the forest environments on which so many creatures depend.

Flora

Central America's geographical position, its varying altitudes, wet and dry climates and differing soil types all contribute to the wide variety of plant species found in Central America.

There are five major types of vegetation. On the Caribbean coastal plain, up to about 850 metres, there is tropical rainforest with a canopy of tall trees, a layer of medium-sized trees, and a lush ground cover of smaller plants.

The Pacific coastal plain and the northern lowlands of Belize are covered with tropical seasonal woodland and savanna, with deciduous trees and shrubs that are parched and brown during the dry season, and spring into green during the rainy season.

Higher up, at around 850 to 1650 metres, there's a cooler climate with a mixed upland forest of evergreen trees and pines, deciduous oaks and broadleaf trees, and a ground cover of shrubs, herbs, grasses and flowering plants.

Above 1650 metres is one of Central America's loveliest terrains, the cloud forest. With 100% humidity and a very cool climate all year round, the cloud forests are bathed in either clouds or rain so they never dry out. The canopy of high trees means that direct sunlight never reaches the forest floor, which is covered by herbs, ferns and mosses.

Only very small areas of Central America, at elevations over 3000 metres, have alpine vegetation, with short, coarse grasses, ferns, mosses and flowering herbs. But even at such high elevations there is regional variety, eg the Andean *páramo* found in Costa Rica and the North American bunchgrass landscape found in the Guatemala highlands above the treeline.

A walk through a tropical forest is very different from the temperate forests that many readers know. Temperate forests tend to have little variety. Tropical forests, on the other hand, have great variety. If you stand in one spot and look around, you'll see scores of different species of trees, but you often have to walk several hundred metres to find another example of any particular species.

This biodiversity is one of the reasons why biologists and conservationists are calling for a halt to the destruction of tropical forests.

Conservation

Deforestation is happening at such a rate that most of the world's tropical forests will have disappeared by early in the 21st century; loss of other habitats is a less publicised but equally pressing concern. Almost a million known species on earth live in tropical rainforests and scientists predict that millions more plant and animal species remain to be discovered in the world's remaining rainforests. This incredible array of plants and animals cannot exist unless the forest that they inhabit is protected – deforestation will result not only in the loss of the rainforest but in countless extinctions as well.

Tropical forests are vitally important for pharmaceutical purposes and as a source of genetic diversity in our increasingly monocultural forms of agriculture. In the event of a crop epidemic, scientists would look in the forests for disease-resistant wild strains to breed into the commercially raised crops. Deforestation leads not only to species extinction, but also to loss of the genetic diversity which may help species adapt to a changing world.

The rainforest is important to the indigenous peoples who survive within it. Miskitos in Honduras and Nicaragua, Bribris in Costa Rica and the Chocos of Panama are some of the indigenous groups that still live in the rainforest in a more or less traditional manner, practicing shifting agriculture, hunting, and gathering.

Rainforests are important on a global scale because they moderate climatic patterns worldwide. Destruction of the rainforests is a major contributing factor to global warming.

However, the point of view of the developing nations which own tropical forests must also be considered. The rainforest provides lumber, pastureland, and possible mineral wealth in the short term. Efforts are now under way to show that the economic value of the standing rainforest as a resource of biodiversity, genetic variation, and pharmaceutical wealth is greater than the quick profits realised by deforestation.

One way of making the tropical forest an economically productive resource is by protecting it in national parks and preserves and making it accessible to the public. 'Ecotourism' is becoming increasingly important for the economies of countries like Costa Rica and Belize. More people are likely to visit a tropical country to see monkeys in the forest than to see cows on pasture.

Other innovative projects for sustainable development of tropical forests are being developed on private reserves, especially in Costa Rica and Belize. One example is butterfly farming on the Rara Avis reserve in Costa Rica and the Shipstern reserve in Belize. Another project, developed in Panama and now continuing in Costa Rica, is the harvesting of the green iguana which is a traditional food in forested areas.

Deforestation in Central America Deforestation is taking place in every Central American country. In some places, the forests have been stripped for export timber. Elsewhere the native forest has been cleared for subsistence slash-and-burn agriculture, for grazing land, or for the planting of crops for export.

In 1950, about 60% of Central America was forested. Today, approximately 30% of Central America is covered by some form of tropical forest – with the notable exception of densely populated El Salvador, with less than 5% of the land forested. Sparsely settled Belize, with less population pressure, has about 40% of its land under forest.

The Petén region of Guatemala has that country's greatest variety of wildlife, but, despite the protected status of much of the region, it is being threatened by illegal logging. Much of the logging here is done to clear the land for agriculture, as has happened throughout much of Central America. This is the most wasteful form of logging – many of the trees are burnt or left to rot. One estimate of this kind of wasteful logging is that Honduras is losing over US$300 million annually in lost commercial timber.

Fortunately, as noted above, conservation is becoming an important priority in Central America, with government and private organisations dedicated to forest management and reforestation programmes.

Despite the deforestation, Central America still has some wilderness areas where the forests are largely unexplored. These include parts of Belize, the Mosquitia region of Honduras and Nicaragua, and the Darién region of Panama.

The 30% of Nicaragua which is covered by forest has been, ironically, protected by the protracted civil war and Sandinista/Contra hostilities which occurred at a time when deforestation was rampant elsewhere. Many remote areas are still mined (with bombs) which is discouraging potential settlers, and the wildlife here is prolific.

ECONOMY

Each Central American country has its particular economic structure. By and large this is not a 'developed' part of the world, but some countries are doing much better than others. The 1988 and 1992 World Bank figures for per capita GNP (in US dollars) were:

	1988	1992
Guatemala	880	980
Belize	1460	2210
Honduras	850	580
El Salvador	950	1170
Nicaragua	764	410
Costa Rica	1760	2000
Panama	1880	2440

The figures show that while most countries are improving economically (particularly Belize and Panama), Honduras and Nicaragua are moving backwards. Honduras appeared to have turned the corner in 1993, with the economy growing again, but Nicaragua was still struggling. At least Nicaragua now has inflation under control, down to an annual rate below 20%, compared to levels above 1000% annually a few years back. The lowest inflation rates are enjoyed by Panama with 1.3% and Belize with 3.2% (both figures are a seven-year annual average from 1985-92).

Agriculture is the most important part of the economy of every Central American country. In addition to basic subsistence crops, such as maize, beans, vegetables and fruits, several countries also produce export crops, including coffee, sugar cane, cotton, tobacco, bananas, citrus fruits, pineapples, and coconuts. Forestry and timber industries are important in some places.

Fishing, including catches of shrimp and lobster, is also important, especially on the Caribbean coast but also on the Pacific coast, and in the lakes and rivers.

Manufacturing industry is developed in some places. Panama has additional sources of income from the Panama Canal and from duty-free trade and offshore banking. Tourism is economically important in some parts of Central America.

The commencement of the North American Free Trade Agreement (NAFTA) on 1 January 1994 is expected to have a negative effect on Central American economies, with the USA diverting its trading links more towards Mexico, a co-signatory. In the longer term, it is envisaged that Central American countries may themselves join NAFTA. In the meantime, ways are being sought to improve trading links between the Central American economies.

POPULATION & PEOPLE

The majority of the population of Central America is *mestizo,* ie of mixed Indian and Spanish descent. Mestizos who speak Spanish are often called *ladinos.* Each country has its own particular mixture of peoples and cultures.

The Spanish-Indian mixture ranges from almost pure Indian to almost pure European. In Guatemala over half the population is Mayan Indian, and many mestizos are of predominantly Indian descent. On the other hand, over 95% of Costa Ricans are of wholly or predominantly European descent, with fewer than 1% being Indian – the Indians were almost completely wiped out by European diseases. In El Salvador there are very few Indians, less than 5% of the population, but Honduras, Nicaragua, and Panama all have important Indian tribes. Belize has mostly Blacks along the coast, but most of the people in the interior are either Mayan Indians or mestizos.

Native Americans

Before the Spanish conquest, Central America had many different groups of native peoples, and all the Central American countries still have groups, larger or smaller, of native Americans. The largest surviving groups are the Maya in Chiapas, the Yucatán, Belize and Guatemala. The Guatemalan areas around Chichicastenango, Lago de Atitlán, and Todos Santos Cuchamatán are particularly known for the colourfully dressed, traditional Maya Indians who live there.

In Honduras, and spilling over into Nicaragua are Jicaque, Paya, Sumo, Lenca, Chorti, and Miskito. Nicaragua also has

Rama Indians. El Salvador has small numbers of Izalco and Pancho Indians, descended from the Pipil. Costa Rica has very few Indians but they include Bribri, Boruca, Cabecar, Terraba and Guatuso. In Panama are significant groups of Guaymí, Chocó and Cuna Indians.

After five centuries of contact with the Spanish, the Indian groups vary in the extent of their assimilation into ladino society. On one end of the spectrum are traditional Indians, wearing traditional dress, maintaining traditional social and economic systems, and speaking only their own language with no Spanish. Even these groups may have been affected by the Spanish influence. For example, they may mix Catholicism with their traditional religious practices. At the other extreme, many Indians are assimilated into modern Central American society, speak only Spanish, and are indistinguishable from the mestizo populations around them.

In between are groups of varying degrees of assimilation. In some, the men wear Western dress and speak Spanish in addition to their Indian language, while the women, more sheltered, still wear traditional dress and speak only their Indian language. In some groups the older people are more traditional, while the young people are becoming more modernised, attending school, and learning Spanish.

Social distinctions are often more connected to these visible social factors than to actual bloodlines. People who observe the traditional Indian ways are called Indians, but those of Indian ancestry who speak Spanish and live and work in the towns are often called ladinos. Thus, in some places, the percentage of Indians in census figures seems to be declining, but this may be because fewer people are identifying themselves as Indians.

Blacks

All along the Caribbean coast of Central America there are Blacks, mostly descended from Africans brought to the West Indies (primarily Jamaica) as slaves. Some slaves were brought to the region by the Spanish,

especially to Panama, but most Blacks came to Central America from the Caribbean islands in the 19th century, not as slaves but as labourers, largely to work on agricultural (especially banana) plantations. Another large group of West Indian Blacks came to Panama to work on the canal early this century.

In many places these Blacks speak a Caribbean-accented English. In the countries bordering the Caribbean, Blacks form a majority in some coastal areas, though only a small proportion of the total population. In Belize, however, about 40% of the people are Blacks. In the past, Blacks often interbred with Europeans, especially the British, and their descendants are known as Creoles. (Note that in most of Latin America 'Creole', from the Spanish *criollo*, means someone of European parentage born in the Americas.)

Garífuna

Along the Caribbean coast is another group of Black people, the Garífuna, who are descended from West Africans and Carib Indians. The latter were brought by the British from the Caribbean island of St Vincent to the island of Roatán, off the coast of Honduras, in 1797. From there they spread out and established communities which still thrive on the coasts of Honduras, Nicaragua, Belize and Guatemala. (For more about the Garífuna people, refer to the Honduras chapter.)

ARTS

The arts of Central America correspond to the cultures of the various places. Music, poetry, literature (especially stories and legends), dance, theatre, painting and sculpture are found throughout Central America.

The innovative Nicaraguan poet Rubén Darío (1867-1916) was a prime influence in the development of modernism in Spanish literature. The literary tradition is still strong in Nicaragua (see the Nicaragua chapter for more information).

La Palma in Northern El Salvador and the Archipiélago de Solentiname in Southern

Nicaragua each has an artistic tradition with its own distinctive style.

Music on the Caribbean coast has a strong reggae influence, and some of the reggae bands in Nicaragua's Bluefields area have an international reputation. Punta is a percussion-based style of music and a shuffling, hip-swinging dance performed by the Garífuna people. A good place to see the Punta is in Trujillo, Northern Honduras.

Handicrafts *(artesanías)* are produced in every country and some are world-famous, especially the weaving and embroidery of Guatemala. Also commonly found throughout most parts of Central America are ceramics, woodcarving, leatherwork, basketry, jewellery, hammocks, musical instruments, and many other handicrafts (see Things to Buy in the country chapters).

CULTURE

Most countries of Central America have agrarian economies and cultures tied to the traditions of the land. The family, usually a large extended family, is the basic unit of society and is the most important thing in the lives of most people.

Though Central America remains primarily rural there is, in many places, a migration from the countryside to the cities. People come to the cities seeking education, employment, money and a more modern 'better life'. Even in the cities, though, there are hangovers from rural life – the family remains the principal social unit, and there are neighbourhood churches and large open-air markets just as you would find in the country.

Religion is important in Central America and much of the culture revolves around it. Every city, town and village has its patron saint, and the annual festival or fair on the saint's day is usually the most important local celebration of the year.

Semana Santa (Holy Week, the week before Easter) is the most important general holiday, with church services, processions through the streets, dramas, dances, fiestas, special foods, and other celebrations. Semana Santa is also the time when most people get a week-long holiday from work. People often take a trip somewhere for Semana Santa, going to the beach, a resort or to visit faraway family. Often this is the only time of the year they can do it, so it's a special holiday for secular as well as religious reasons.

Christmas *(Navidad)*, often celebrated not on Christmas Day but on the evening of 24 December, is another important holiday. It is celebrated in different ways in different places. In Tegucigalpa for example, lots of people get drunk and they set off fireworks at midnight. After a midnight mass, people may stay up all night long, visiting from house to house and having parties, then use Christmas Day to rest and recover.

The many ethnic groups of Central America all have their own distinct cultures. The mestizos are not only racially, but also culturally, a mixture of Spanish and Indian. As well as the Spanish traditions, the various Indian groups, the Blacks of the Caribbean coast, the small groups of immigrant Chinese, North American and other groups all have their own distinctive cultural features, making Central America a patchwork rather than a uniform cultural fabric.

The USA also has a significant influence on Central American life. It's a rare place where you won't find Coca Cola and Pepsi, blue jeans, mass-produced clothes (often second-hand from the USA), and radios and cassette tape recorders. TV stations from the USA come in by satellite. Many Central Americans have gone north to the USA to work, and many more dream of doing so.

All the Central American countries have radio and TV, and in many rural areas homes might have TV before they have running water. This can lead to some strange sights. For example, in a remote Garífuna fishing village you might see young men with flat-top haircuts. Ask why they wear their hair like that and they'll tell you, 'That's how they wear it in New York!' 'How do you know?' 'We saw it on television!'

RELIGION

Roman Catholicism, brought by the Spanish,

is the principal religion of Central America. In Caribbean areas that were influenced by the British, Protestant sects are predominant.

Against the background of Catholicism, however, there are many different religions and sects. Evangelical and Pentecostal Christian denominations have gained wide followings in many areas. Other religious sects include Baptists, Mormons and Seventh Day Adventists.

In addition, the Indian peoples and other ethnic groups still preserve their traditional religions, often mixed and blended with Catholicism. A notable example is the religion of the Mayan Indians of Guatemala. The Garífuna peoples continue to practise their traditional African-related religion, focusing on ancestral spirits, in addition to Christianity.

LANGUAGE

The language patterns of Central America follow the patterns of colonisation. Spanish is the primary language of most of the Central American countries, with the exception of Belize, which was colonised by the British and whose official language is English.

The patterns of British and US influence have left other English-speaking pockets in Central America, notably among the Blacks on the Caribbean coasts. English is an important language in Panama, not only because of the English-speaking descendants of Jamaican and West Indian settlers, but also because of the US influence in connection with the Canal, and the tendency of more affluent families to send their children to study in the USA.

Throughout Central America there are groups of people who speak native Indian languages and dialects – at least 20 languages and even more dialects are spoken. But in most of Central America, Spanish is the predominant language.

Hints for the Traveller

Fortunately, Spanish is a relatively easy language for an English speaker to learn. If you have no background in the language, you could begin by taking an evening class, or by borrowing a record/cassette course from the local library. Try to find a Spanish speaker to practise with.

There are a few places in Central America, notably Antigua Guatemala, that specialize in Spanish language courses. A few weeks spent studying Spanish in Antigua at the beginning of your trip could make an enormous difference in your experience of Central America, and any other Spanish-speaking countries you may ever visit.

A pocket-sized book of Spanish grammar and phrases can help you tremendously. Lonely Planet's *Latin American Spanish phrasebook* is very useful and compact.

Also be sure to take along a pocket-sized Spanish-English dictionary. Many are available, so you might want to compare several. It's best to bring your own as they are not widely available in Central America, though you might find one in an occasional bookstore, or in the gift shop of a major hotel.

Spanish-speakers often have a remarkable patience with those who are attempting to learn the language. Even if you feel like an idiot at first, your efforts to communicate in Spanish will most often be met with warm smiles and helpfulness by local people. So don't be shy.

Central American Spanish

As with Spanish everywhere, Central American Spanish has lots of regional variations in words and slang. Panamanian Spanish is spoken very fast, with a unique accent and many slang words which are used only in Panama. The bus station, for example, which is called the 'terminal' in most places, and the 'camionera' in Mexico, is called the 'piquera' in Panama. A soft drink is called a 'soda' in Panama, a 'fresco' or 'refresco' in Nicaragua, but a 'gaseosa' in El Salvador.

Since a lot of travel takes place between the small Central American republics, people are familiar with the various words used in different places, and most of the time there is no problem with understanding.

Pronunciation
Most of the sounds in Spanish have equivalents in English, and written Spanish is largely phonetic. Once you've learnt how to pronounce all the letters, and certain groups of letters, and you know which syllable to stress, you can read any word or sentence and pronounce it more or less correctly.

Vowels There is not much variation in the length of vowels in Spanish. Each vowel is consistently pronounced the same way except if it's in a specific vowel combination.

a	as the 'u' in nut or a shorter sound than the 'a' in 'art'
e	as the 'e' in 'met'
i	similar to the 'i' in 'marine' but not as strong or drawn out; between that sound and the 'i' in 'flip'
o	similar to the 'o' in 'hot'
u	as the 'oo' in 'fool'

Diphthongs Vowel combinations (diphthongs) are best pronounced by just running the two vowel sounds together.

ai	as the 'i' in 'hide'
au	as the 'ow' in 'how'
ei	as the 'ay' in 'hay'
ia	as the 'ya' in 'yard'
ie	as the 'ye' in 'yes'
oi	as the 'oy' in 'boy'

Consonants Many Spanish consonants are pronounced similarly to their English counterparts. The pronunciation of a consonant varies according to which vowel follows it and also according to what part of Central America you happen to be in.

c	a hard 'c' as in 'cat' when followed by 'a', 'o' or 'u'; as an 's' before 'e' or 'i'
ch	as 'ch' in 'choose'
d	in the initial position, as the 'd' in 'dog'; elsewhere as the 'th' in 'the'
g	before 'a', 'o', 'u', 'ua' or 'uo', as the 'g' in 'gate'; before 'e' or 'i' it is a throaty sound, like the 'h' in 'hit'; when 'g' is followed by 'ue' or 'ui', the

'g' is pronounced as the 'g' in 'gate' but the 'u' is silent, unless it's a ü

h	never pronounced, silent
j	similar to the 'ch' in the Scottish 'loch'
ll	as the 'y' in 'yes'
ñ	this is a nasal sound like the 'ni' in 'onion'
q	as the 'k' in 'kick'; 'q' is always followed by a silent 'u' and either 'e' or 'i'
r	a rolled 'r' sound, longer and stronger for a double 'r' or if it's at the start of the word
s	as the 's' in 'send', but not pronounced when it's at the end of the word
v	as the 'b' in 'book'
x	as the 'ks' in 'thinks' with a weaker 'k' sound
y	'y' is a semiconsonant, pronounced as the Spanish 'i' when it's by itself or in the middle of a word; at the start or end of a word it is pronounced between the 'y' in 'yonder' and the 'g' in 'beige'
z	as the 's' in 'sat'

Stress As a general rule the stress goes on the second last syllable of a word. Words ending in an 'r' (usually verbs) have the stress on the last syllable. If there is an accent on any vowel, the stress is on that syllable.

amigo – a-MI-go
comer – com-ER
aquí – a-QUI

Grammar
This section, though brief, aims to explain the basic rules and should enable you to construct your own sentences.

Word Order The word order of Spanish sentences is similar to English sentence word order, ie subject-verb-object. Where the subject of the sentence is a pronoun, it is usually omitted.

The girl works in a restaurant.
La chica trabaja en un restaurante.
She works in a restaurant.
Trabaja en un restaurante.

Central Americans speak Spanish.
Los Centroamericanos hablan español.
We speak English.
Hablamos inglés.

Verbs There are three types of verbs in Spanish, with infinitives ending in *-ar*, *-er* and *-ir*. They each have a standard set of endings for first, second and third person, singular and plural, and if you follow those you will manage very well. The verb *hablar*, 'to speak', is a regular *-ar* verb:

I speak	*(yo) hablo*
you speak (formal)	*(usted) habla*
you speak (familiar)	*(tú) hablas*
he/she/it speaks	*(él/ella) habla*
we speak	*(nosotros) hablamos*
you speak (plural)	*(ustedes) hablan*
they speak	*(ellos/ellas) hablan*

In addition there are quite a few irregular verbs, and the only way is to learn them by heart, but the verb endings are more or less common to all regular and most irregular verbs.

The familiar form of 'you' (singular), *tú*, and the verb forms which go with it, are used with family and friends, particularly amongst young people. The more formal *usted* should be used to address officials and to show respect to older or more senior people.

Nouns Spanish nouns are either masculine or feminine. Nouns ending in 'o', 'e' or 'ma' are usually masculine. Nouns ending in 'a', 'ión' or 'dad' are usually feminine.

masculine

book	*libro*
glass	*vaso*
bridge	*puente*
problem	*problema*
traveller	*viajero*

feminine

house	*casa*
song	*canción*
city	*ciudad*

reality	*realidad*
traveller	*viajera*

Plurals As a general rule you make a plural by adding 's' to the noun, or adding 'es' if the noun ends in a consonant.

house, houses	*casa, casas*
election, elections	*elección, elecciones*

Articles The definite article (the) and the indefinite article (a, some) must agree with the noun in gender and number, so there are four forms of each.

the boy	*el chico*
the boys	*los chicos*
the bed	*la cama*
the beds	*las camas*
a boy	*un chico*
some boys	*unos chicos*
a bed	*una cama*
some beds	*unas camas*

Adjectives An adjective follows the noun it describes and, like the definite or indefinite article, must agree with it in gender and number.

the pretty house	*la casa bonita*
some pretty rooms	*unos cuartos bonitos*
a good boy	*un chico bueno*
the good girls	*las chicas buenas*

Greetings & Civilities
Greetings are used more frequently in Latin America than in English-speaking countries. For example, it is polite to greet people when you walk into a shop or a bar.

Hello.	*Hola.*
Good morning.	*Buenos días.*
Good afternoon.	*Buenas tardes.*
Good evening or good night.	*Buenas noches.*

The last three are frequently shortened to *buenos/as*. This is used a lot in Central

America, accompanied by a slight nod of the head.

How are you?
¿Cómo está? (formal)
or *¿Cómo estás?* (informal)
How are things going?
¿Qué tal?
Well, thanks.
Bien, gracias.
Very well.
Muy bien.
Very badly.
Muy mal.
Goodbye.
Adiós (rarely used).
Bye, see you soon.
Hasta luego (sometimes just 'sta luego').

please	*por favor*
thank you	*gracias*
many thanks	*muchas gracias*
you're welcome	*de nada*
excuse me	*permiso*
sorry	*perdón*
excuse me, forgive me	*disculpe, discúlpeme*
Good luck!	*¡Buena suerte!*

Mr, Sir	*Señor* (formal)
Madam, Mrs	*Señora* (formal)
unmarried woman	*Señorita*
pal, friend	*compañero/a, amigo/a*

Small Talk
I'd like to introduce you to ...
Le presento a ...
A pleasure (to meet you).
Mucho gusto.
What is your name?
¿Cómo se llama usted? (formal)
¿Cómo te llamas? (informal)
My name is ...
Me llamo ...
Where are you from?
¿De dónde es usted? (formal)
¿De dónde vienes? (familiar)

I am from ...	*Soy de ...*
Australia	*Australia*
Canada	*Canadá*
England	*Inglaterra*
Germany	*Alemania*
Israel	*Israel*
Italy	*Italia*
Japan	*Japón*
New Zealand	*Nueva Zelanda*
Norway	*Noruega*
Scotland	*Escocia*
Sweden	*Suecia*
the United States	*los Estados Unidos*

What do you do?
¿Qué hace?
What's your profession?
¿Cuál es su profesión?

I am a ...	*Soy ...*
student	*estudiante*
teacher	*profesor/a*
nurse	*enfermero/a*
lawyer	*abogado/a*
engineer	*ingeniero/a*
mechanic	*mecánico/a*

Can I take a photo?
¿Puedo sacar una foto?
Of course/Why not/Sure.
Por supuesto/Cómo no/Claro.
How old are you?
¿Cuántos años tiene?
Do you speak English?
¿Habla inglés?
I speak a little Spanish.
Hablo un poquito de español.
I don't understand.
No entiendo.
Could you repeat that?
¿Puede repetirlo?
Could you speak more slowly please?
¿Puede hablar más despacio por favor?
How does one say ...?
¿Cómo se dice ...?
What does ... mean?
¿Que significa ...?

Families are very important in Central

America and people will generally ask you all about yours.

Are you married?
¿Es casado/a?
I am single.
Soy soltero/a.
I am married.
Soy casado/a.
Is your husband/wife here?
¿Está su esposo/a aquí?

If the conversation is more personal, the 'familiar' form is used:

How many children do you have?
¿Cuántos niños tienes?
How many brothers/sisters do you have?
¿Cuántos hermanos/hermanas tienes?
Do you have a boyfriend/girlfriend?
¿Tienes novio/a?

Feelings Spanish usually uses the irregular verb *tener* (to have) to express feelings.

I am …	*Tengo …*
cold	*frío*
hot	*calor*
We are …	*Tenemos …*
sleepy	*sueño*
thirsty	*sed*
hungry	*hambre*

Accommodation

Where is …?	*¿Dónde hay …?*
a hotel	*un hotel*
a boarding house	*una pensión*
a guesthouse	*un hospedaje*

I am looking for …	*Estoy buscando …*
a cheap hotel	*un hotel barato*
a good hotel	*un hotel bueno*
a nearby hotel	*un hotel cercano*
a clean hotel	*un hotel limpio*

Are there any rooms available?
¿Hay habitaciones libres?
Where are the toilets?
¿Dónde están los servicios/baños?

I would like a …	*Quisiera un …*
single room	*cuarto sencillo*
double room	*cuarto doble*
room with a bath	*cuarto con baño*

Can I see it?	*¿Puedo verlo?*
Are there others?	*¿Hay otros?*
How much is it?	*¿Cuánto cuesta?*
It's too expensive.	*Es demasiado caro.*

your name	*su nombre*
your surname	*su apellido*
your room number	*el número de su cuarto*

Getting Around

Where is …?	*¿Dónde está …?*
the central bus station	*la estación central de autobuses*
the railway station	*la estación de trenes*
the airport	*el aeropuerto*
the ticket office	*la boletería*
bus	*autobús/camión*
bus (long-distance)	*flota/bus*

When does the bus/train/plane leave?
¿Cuándo sale el autobus/tren/avión?
I want to go to …
Quiero ir a …
What time do they leave?
¿A qué hora salen?
Can you take me to …?
¿Puede llevarme a …?
Could you tell me where … is?
¿Podría decirme dónde está …?
Is it far?
¿Está lejos?
Is it close to here?
¿Está cerca de aquí?

I'm looking for …	*Estoy buscando …*
the post office	*el correo*
the … embassy	*la embajada de …*
the museum	*el museo*
the police	*la policía*
the market	*el mercado*
the bank	*el banco*

Stop!	*¡Pare!*
Wait!	*¡Espera!*

North	*norte*
South	*sur*
East	*este*
West	*oeste*

Money

I want to change some money.
Quiero cambiar dinero.
I want to change travellers' cheques.
Quiero cambiar cheques viajeros.
What is the exchange rate?
¿Cuál es el tipo de cambio?
How many colones/pesos/quetzales per dollar?
¿Cuántos colones/pesos/quetzales por dólar?

cashier	*caja*
credit card	*tarjeta de crédito*
the black market	*el mercado negro*
bank notes	*billetes de banco*
exchange houses	*casas de cambio*

Emergencies

Watch out!	*¡Cuidado!*
Help!	*¡Socorro!*
	¡Auxilio!
Fire!	*¡Fuego!*
Thief!	*¡Ladrón!*

I've been robbed.	*Me han robado.*
They took …	*Se llevaron …*
my money	*mi dinero*
my passport	*mi pasaporte*
my bag	*mi bolsa*
Where is …?	*¿Dónde hay …?*
a policeman	*un policía*
a doctor	*un doctor*
a hospital	*un hospital*

Leave me alone!	*¡Déjeme!*
Don't bother me!	*¡No me moleste!*
Get lost!	*¡Váyase!*

Days

Monday	*lunes*
Tuesday	*martes*
Wednesday	*miércoles*
Thursday	*jueves*
Friday	*viernes*
Saturday	*sábado*
Sunday	*domingo*

Months

January	*enero*
February	*febrero*
March	*marzo*
April	*abril*
May	*mayo*
June	*junio*
July	*julio*
August	*agosto*
September	*se(p)tiembre*
October	*octubre*
November	*noviembre*
December	*diciembre*

today	*hoy*
this morning	*esta mañana*
this afternoon	*esta tarde*
tonight	*esta noche*
yesterday	*ayer*
tomorrow	*mañana*
week/month/year	*semana/mes/año*
last week	*la semana pasada*
next month	*el próximo mes*
always	*siempre*
it's early/late	*es temprano/tarde*
now	*ahora*
before/after	*antes/después*

What time is it?
¿Qué hora es?
It is 1 o'clock.
Es la una.
It is 7 o'clock.
Son las siete.

Cardinal Numbers

0	*cero*
1	*uno, una*
2	*dos*
3	*tres*
4	*cuatro*
5	*cinco*
6	*seis*
7	*siete*
8	*ocho*
9	*nueve*
10	*diez*

11	*once*	500	*quinientos*
12	*doce*	600	*seiscientos*
13	*trece*	900	*novecientos*
14	*catorce*	1000	*mil*
15	*quince*	2000	*dos mil*
16	*dieciséis*	100,000	*cien mil*
17	*diecisiete*	1,000,000	*un millón*
18	*dieciocho*	2,000,000	*dos millones*
19	*diecinueve*		
20	*veinte*		
21	*veintiuno*		
22	*veintidós*		
30	*treinta*		
31	*treinta y uno*		

Ordinal Numbers

Masculine forms are given; the feminine form ends with an 'a' instead of an 'o'.

40	*cuarenta*		
50	*cincuenta*	first	*primero*
60	*sesenta*	second	*segundo*
70	*setenta*	third	*tercero*
80	*ochenta*	fourth	*cuarto*
90	*noventa*	fifth	*quinto*
100	*cien*, when followed by	sixth	*sexto*
	a noun, *ciento*	seventh	*séptimo*
101	*ciento uno*	eighth	*octavo*
102	*ciento dos*	ninth	*noveno, nono*
193	*ciento noventa y tres*	tenth	*décimo*
200	*doscientos*	eleventh	*undécimo*
300	*trescientos*	twelfth	*duodécimo*
		twentieth	*vigésimo*

Facts for the Visitor

PLANNING

When to Go

Any time is a good time to go to Central America. The seasons are defined, not by temperature but by rainfall, into *invierno* ('winter', the rainy season, roughly from April to November) and *verano* ('summer', the dry season, from November to April). Most travellers go during the dry season, and certain places do have their busier times – the Caribbean islands have more 'fun and sun' enthusiasts during the North American winter, for obvious reasons – but you can have a good trip any time of the year.

Verano tends to be hot, dry and dusty, invierno hot and humid, but the primary climate differences throughout the region depend on elevation (see Climate, in the Facts about Central America chapter). With just a few exceptions – for instance, it's too hazardous to hike the Darien Gap in the rainy season – you can travel practically anywhere in Central America regardless of the season.

You might want to plan to be in a certain place at a certain time to catch a festival; *Semana Santa* (Holy Week) in Antigua Guatemala, for example, is an unforgettable spectacle. This week is not only 'Holy Week' but also 'Holiday Week' all over Central America; beach resorts and other holiday spots will be packed at this time. This makes it great for meeting and partying with the locals, but not so good if you wanted the beach all to yourself.

Although Central America does not have a distinct 'tourist season', the airlines do have high season and off season rates. High season (more expensive) rates may occur around Christmas, Easter, and the North American winter or summer holiday seasons, but may vary from airline to airline. Flying just a day or two earlier or later could get you a tremendous saving.

How Much Does It Cost?

Looking through the prices in the country chapters of this book will give you a good idea of costs. (Prices are more likely to go up than down, so you may find some things more expensive.) An inexpensive hotel can cost anywhere from US$3 to US$10 a night for two people sharing a room, and will not be much cheaper for a single traveller. A meal in an inexpensive restaurant or in the outdoor market need cost only about US$1 or US$2, and if you buy your own fresh fruit and other food in the market you can eat even cheaper. Travelling on buses is cheap, and a good way to get around Central America – all the countries have good (or at least adequate) bus systems.

This book focuses on the cheapest ways to get around and have an enjoyable visit to Central America, but we do have some minimum standards of hygiene and comfort. If a place was too grotty we didn't include it in the book. And for the times when you do want to spend a little more, you'll find that the few extra dollars can get you a huge jump up in quality. There can be a great difference between a US$4 and US$7 hotel room.

How Long?

How long you plan to stay in Central America depends, of course, on what you want to do there. It is a small area of the world but it's incredibly rich and diverse. If you're just rushing through on buses between North and South America, you could pass through in a few days. Or you could stay for six months and still feel that you'd barely scratched the surface. Look at the Highlights section later in this chapter to get an idea of what the region has to offer.

What Kind of Trip?

Travellers are in Central America for many reasons. Many are en route between North and South America. Others come for special interests: to explore the Mayan pyramids and other ruins, to visit the Caribbean islands off the coast of Central America with their famous diving and snorkelling possibilities, or to study Spanish, particularly in Antigua Guatemala, where there are some of the best and cheapest language courses in the world. Nicaragua and El Salvador draw international visitors interested in the politics there. Other people come connected with church groups, the Peace Corps, or on agricultural projects.

'Ecotourism', with a focus on nature, is very popular, especially Costa Rica. The rainforests, with their abundant wildlife, are a particular attraction: just as interesting as those in the Amazon, and a lot more accessible for most people.

Many other Central American terrains are equally worth exploring, including mountains, cloud forests, volcanoes, coastal lands, river systems, and of course the beautiful Caribbean beaches and islands. Every country in Central America has national parks for the preservation of natural features and environments.

Then there are travellers who are in Central America not on any particular mission, but simply because it is a beautiful, diverse, inexpensive and fascinating part of the world.

What to Bring

Travel light. Most things you need can be bought along the way, often more cheaply than at home. Do be sure to bring insect repellent, something for water purification, and antimalarial pills (though Chloroquine is sold in many Central American pharmacies if you run out). If you need contraceptives or contact-lens solution, bring these along too. Tampons are available in the larger cities, but bring some with you anyway.

A torch (flashlight) will come in useful, for walking around at night and in case there is a power failure. During the rainy season, carry an umbrella. If you want to trek in rainforests any time of year you'll need water-resistant boots and decent raingear.

If you have a special interest, such as snorkelling, bird-watching, fishing etc, bring your own equipment with you. You may find it available in certain places but there are

some great snorkelling places where no gear is available locally.

Central America is not cold, so there's no need to load up with clothing – a medium or heavy sweater is necessary in the mountains, and should be warm enough for any time of year unless you plan on camping in the high-altitude cloud forests.

If you'll want to do any reading in any language besides Spanish, bring your own books with you. Bookstores with good books in English are few and far between, and it's even more rare to find books in any other language. Also, bring along a Spanish-English dictionary and possibly a Spanish grammar and phrasebook.

Then there are all the normal things you would take with you when travelling anywhere in the world: pocket knife, sewing kit, cord for clothesline, padlocks for your pack etc. A shortwave radio is useful for keeping in touch with world events, and nowadays they're small and light enough to fit in a pocket. If you don't already have one, Panama City is a very cheap place to buy.

Appearances & Conduct

Pay attention to your appearance when travelling in Central America. As a foreigner you're bound to generate attention anyway, so try to keep it positive.

Latin Americans on the whole are very conscious of appearance, grooming and dress; it's difficult for them to understand why a foreign traveller, who is naturally assumed to be rich, would go around looking scruffy when even poor people in Latin America do their best to look neat. Your relations with locals will be smoother if you try to present as clean an appearance as possible. This is especially true if you're dealing with officialdom (police, border officials, immigration officers etc), when it's a good idea to look not only clean, but also as conservative and respectable as possible.

Also think about safety in connection with your appearance. In many places in Central America, especially the capital cities, the locals will warn you against wearing even cheap imitation jewellery: you could be mugged for it. If you have any wealth, take care not to flaunt it.

Women Travellers Women in particular will get on much better if they dress conservatively. You may already be considered a 'loose woman', or fair game, simply because you are a foreign female; anything you can do with your personal appearance and demeanour to dispel that impression can only help you.

Shorts and swimsuits are OK at beaches, especially where there's a fair amount of international tourism, but not elsewhere. Even sleeveless shirts may be a bit on the risqué side in some places; sleeves are probably better, and skirts or pants should go below the knee. Most importantly, wear a bra, whether or not it's your usual custom, as not doing so in this part of the world is regarded as provocative. One good general rule is to watch carefully how the local women dress and behave, and follow their example.

The 'Madonna vs whore' mentality, which classifies every woman as 'good' or 'bad', and therefore worthy of respect or not, is a well-known principle of *machismo* – the exaggerated masculine pride of the Latin American male. It has many practical applications in everyday situations in Latin America. While the 'bad' woman is fair game for any type of treatment, the 'good' woman, on the other hand, is protected and treated with much more respect.

PAPERWORK
Passports
Before you start out, be sure your passport will be valid for a reasonable period: some countries will not let you in if your passport is about to expire. Six months' validity is the usual minimum requirement. Also be sure your passport has plenty of free space for visa stamps: if it fills up, you may have to get it replaced or have more pages added.

Take a photocopy of the first page of your passport and keep the copy in a separate place. This makes it much faster and easier to get a replacement from your embassy or consulate if your passport is lost or stolen. Memorising your passport number is also a good idea.

Visas
A visa is an endorsement in your passport, usually a stamp, permitting you to enter a country and stay there for a specified period of time. It is obtained from a foreign consulate or embassy of the country you want to visit. You can get all your visas before you set out on your trip, or get them as you go along at the consulates and embassies in neighbouring countries. Be sure to find out how long your visas are valid; typically they are good for entry into a country within three or six months of the date of issue, but regulations vary.

A country may have a number of consulates and embassies in various places, which may have different conditions for issuing visas. At some, you simply fill out your application, pay your money, have your passport stamped, and that's all there is to it. Others may take your application and passport and have you return in a few days. Still others may require one or more passport-size photos (always have some extra ones with you), or evidence of the amount of money you're planning to take into the country. You can learn a lot from fellow travellers about which consulates along the way are the easiest for obtaining visas.

Visa requirements – which nationalities need a visa and which ones don't – are different for each country, and may change at any time. Always be sure to double-check each country's visa and onward ticketing requirements before you get there. If you need a visa and don't have it, you will be turned back at the border if you're coming overland. If you're coming by air, you will not be allowed to board the plane without having your visa in order.

The amount of time you are given on a visa is usually standard, but occasionally you may be given less time for some reason, such as not having much money ('insufficient funds') or looking a bit suspicious.

Once you are inside a country, you can

always apply for an extension at the country's immigration office. Usually there is some limit on how many extensions you can receive; if you leave the country and re-enter, your time starts over again.

Onward Tickets

Some Central American countries, notably Costa Rica and Panama, require you to have a ticket out of the country (onward or return) before they will let you in. Belize also has such a law on the books, though the only time they enforce it is if they think you look suspicious for some reason and they're trying to keep you out. Panama enforces its onward ticket requirements for all travellers; Costa Rica has been less rigorous of late but it's still best not to take the risk of being turned back – see the chapters on Getting There & Away, Getting Around, and the individual countries for suggestions on how to satisfy these requirements.

If you're continuing south, note that several South American countries, including Colombia, Venezuela, Peru and Guyana, also have onward ticket requirements. So you can't, for example, just buy a one-way ticket from Central America to one of these countries and keep on going. It's a little more complicated than that.

The only way to avoid the onward ticket requirement altogether in countries which demand it is to enter the country by private rather than public transport. If you enter by private vehicle, whether your own or one that's picked you up hitchhiking, no onward ticket is required.

Other Documents

Several other documents are useful to have with you. An International Health Certificate listing the type and date of all your vaccinations and immunisations is a good idea any time you travel internationally. You can get one from the physician who vaccinates you, your doctor back home, or any government health department. Be sure to keep it up to date with all immunisations recorded.

An International Driving Permit is a good thing to have, even if you're not in your own

vehicle, just in case any opportunity or need to drive comes up. You can get one from your national automobile or motoring association. Just show them your local driving licence, give them two passport-size photos, and pay a fee of around US$5.

An International Student Identity Card (ISIC) is another useful document, entitling you to discounts on travel (airfares, tour packages, and so on) at student travel agencies around the world (see Useful Organisations), and to various discounts within countries. You must be a full-time student to qualify for an official ISIC card. The normal place to buy ISIC cards is at student travel agencies around the world. STA Travel is the big agency in Europe, Australia, New Zealand and the USA. Council Travel is also big in the USA.

Some 'bucket shop' ticket agencies will sell you an 'ISIC card' when you book a 'student' flight with them. In some places where travellers congregate there's a black market in fake ISIC cards, but be wary of this – it's been going on so much for so long that the bona fide ISIC card is defending itself against phonies by incorporating a magnetic strip. A fake card won't carry any of the insurance or other benefits of the real thing.

A Hostelling International membership card is not as useful in Central America as it is in some other parts of the world. There are only a couple of youth hostels or places where the card gets a discount in all Central America.

MONEY

The best currency to bring with you to Central America is US dollars. They can be exchanged everywhere in Central America. Other currencies will be impossible to exchange on any consistent basis, if at all.

In Panama City there is one *casa de cambio* (exchange house) that will exchange currency from just about anywhere on earth with a convertible currency, so if you do have some unusual banknotes, it might be worth going there. The US dollar is the national currency of Panama (it's called a 'Balboa' but it's exactly the same money). Several international banks in Panama City exchange the currency of their home country for dollars, though if they are overstocked with foreign currency they may not do so. Being a centre of international banking, Panama City does have more possibilities, but otherwise you'll need to have US dollars.

You can usually manage to exchange Central American currencies from one country to the next, though it's easier when you're close to the border. It's a good habit, though, to use up all your local money while you're in the country, and start changing dollars again when you get to the next country.

Travellers' Cheques

Take most of your money in travellers' cheques, since they can be refunded if they are lost or stolen. American Express and Visa are the most widely recognised cheques, and the easiest to exchange (you may have difficulty cashing other brands). American Express has offices in all the Central American capitals except Managua. Most banks and casas de cambio that change cheques at all will change American Express cheques. You can cash Visa cheques at any bank with Visa affiliation, though this is not every bank.

Keep an up-to-date record of cheque numbers and the original bill of sale in a safe, separate place. If your cheques go missing, you'll need to know the numbers of the missing cheques to get them replaced. Sometimes banks want to see the bill of sale before they'll cash your cheques.

Carry plenty of cheques in small denominations. US$20 or US$50 will last a long time in many places, and you don't want to get stuck with large amounts of a country's currency when you are about to leave.

Cash

You should also carry some money in US dollars cash. Small bills are best: they can be changed almost anywhere. It's especially useful to have cash for times when you can't change travellers' cheques – in remote places, or where there's no bank that will change the type of cheques you have, or when the banks are closed, or when the casa de cambio changes cash but not cheques. If there's a black market, you might get a better rate for cash, or you may not be able to change cheques at all. It's also useful to be able to change just a few dollars when you're about to leave a country. If you have to change a US$20 travellers' cheque to local currency and then cross a border, you will have to change most of that once again into the currency of the new country, and you lose a little every time you have to change currencies.

In some places you'll get the same exchange rate for travellers' cheques or cash, but often you'll get a better rate for cash. Banks may offer about a 4% higher rate for cash.

Credit Cards

A credit card is a wonderful thing to have when travelling. It acts as insurance against emergencies, can be used to obtain cash, allows you a little unexpected luxury somewhere along the way, and can also be useful if you're asked to demonstrate 'sufficient funds' when you enter a country. Some cards offer free insurance if you use the card when buying airline tickets or hiring a car. This can sometimes save you up to half the cost of hiring the car. Also, if you hire a car using a credit card, you don't have to pay a cash deposit.

You can take out money on your credit card and use it to buy travellers' cheques in US dollars, even in countries where you can only otherwise get local currency on your card (both American Express and Visa allow you to do this). Often, you can simply get your cash advance in US dollars cash. Branches of Creditomatic are a good place in most countries for Visa and MasterCard cash advances. Some travellers rely on cash advances to reduce the need for travellers' cheques, but enquire about transaction charges; for example, there's usually no charge in Honduras but in Guatemala you may be charged anything between 5% and 25%.

Of course you have to make the monthly payments on the bill you run up, and there's the interest charges to pay on your statement back home. But there are even ways of getting around this. You can pay a sum into your credit card account *before* you take off on your trip, so the money is already in there. Then, when you use your card it's just like taking money out of your own bank account, and you won't have to make any payments or incur any interest until you've used up your initial deposit.

If you have an American Express card, requiring full payment each month, you can use a personal cheque to pay your bill at any American Express office, then use your card to obtain cash or travellers' cheques. It's like being able to cash personal cheques in any country.

If you need more money on your travels, you could ask someone back home to put some into your credit card account rather than sending it by bank transfer. This might save you a lot of anxiety while you're waiting for the money to show up!

American Express, Visa and MasterCard are the most widely accepted credit cards in Central America. There are a couple of other types of credit card issued by banks in Central America, but stick to the big, internationally known ones.

Exchange Rates

Exchange rates can vary quite a bit, depending where you change your money. Always find out the going rates before you change any large amount. Usually hotels offer the worst rates of exchange. Casas de cambio may offer the same rate as banks, but sometimes it's better or worse, depending on whether you're changing cash or travellers' cheques. The exchange rate at a bank for cash advances on a credit card may be different from the rate for changing cash or travellers' cheques.

In some places there's a black market, and it may offer a better rate for your dollar but sometimes the difference is very small; occasionally it's actually worse. Usually only US dollars cash can be changed on the black market. If you do decide to patronise the black market, remember that it's illegal. You could get into big trouble if you get caught, though in some places it's very common to change money this way, and right out on the street at that. We're not telling you whether or not to use the black market, but if you do, be aware of the risks.

Crossing land borders, the black market may be your only way to get the next local currency and unload your excess from the country you're leaving. Make sure you know the correct *current* rate or you could be easily ripped off. If in doubt, change only enough to last you until you can get to a bank.

If you change money on the street, be as discreet about it as possible, and be alert. Always be sure to count out the money you're receiving carefully before you hand over your dollars. If there's any mistake in what you're given the first time, be sure to count the whole lot all together, all over again, to see it's correct before you give them your money. It's remarkably easy to be caught by sleight-of-hand tricks. Have the exact amount of dollars you want to change ready, to avoid fumbling around with them on the street or showing more of them than you need to.

Money Transfers

If you don't have a credit card, direct bank transfers are the most reliable way of having money sent to you while you're travelling.

Make sure you specify the city, the bank and the branch that you want the money sent to. It's best to make all the arrangements at the receiving bank, find out everything that should be done, then request the transfer from your home bank, and have them follow the instructions exactly.

Be sure to find out in advance what the policy of the receiving bank will be when your money does arrive. Can you take all or part of it in dollars, or buy travellers' cheques with it in dollars, or do you have to take all of it in the currency of the country you're in? If so, at what rate of exchange? Can you pick it up the same day, or if not, how long will it take? Will they charge you a service fee?

How much? Different banks may have different policies so check around.

Even though wiring money directly from bank to bank should go smoothly and be easily accomplished within a couple of days, a surprising number of technical complications and delays can arise. For example, your home bank might wire the money to the main office of the receiving bank and have it available there in hours, but it could take weeks for it to get from there to the branch where you're waiting for it. Or the transaction may be lost in a pile of paper, so the bank on your end tells you they haven't received it while the bank back home assures you it was sent days ago.

It's best to allow as much time as you can for bank transfers, rather than waiting until you're down to your last *centavo* before starting the process. You might ask your embassy how to send money reliably to wherever you are; they may deal with a certain bank or have some other helpful hint. With Western Union, you can get money within 15 minutes from the USA, but charges are high (10% or more in El Salvador).

Despite the problems, it's still better to have money transferred through a bank than to trust it to the mail. It's a fact of life that anything sent through the mail to Central America may disappear.

Security

Everyone has a preferred way to carry their money. For a few suggestions on carrying it safely, see the Dangers & Annoyances section later on in this chapter.

Bargaining

Bargaining is essential in some situations and not done in others. Bargaining is very common at outdoor markets, but in supermarkets or other indoor shops it isn't done. Bargaining is practically universal at handicrafts markets, where the first price you're told will often be double (or more) what they really expect to receive.

Bargaining definitely has a technique to it, indeed almost an art. If you're not used to it, you'll probably start to feel more comfortable and develop your own style and strategies with practice. Of course the object is to arrive at a price agreeable to both you and the seller. Remember that bargaining is not a fight to the death; be friendly about it, keep your sense of humour, and have patience.

It's important when bargaining not to succumb to the all-too-common 'ugly tourist' attitude. Surprisingly often, travellers who expect to be well paid for their jobs back home do not recognise that those they deal with when travelling have similar expectations. As a foreigner, you represent enormous wealth to local people, and your business may be one of their few opportunities to earn an income. In most Central American countries, the economy makes it almost impossible for many people to make a decent living, no matter how long or hard they work. It's great to bargain, but always do it with an attitude of respect, and don't expect to come away with something for nothing.

Aside from bargaining in markets, you can sometimes bargain for better rates at hotels and guest houses, especially at times when business is slow. From the hotelier's point of view it's better to rent a room for a cheaper price than to have it stand empty, but there's no reason to do so if another customer is likely to show up and pay the full price. Often you can get a discount off the nightly rate if you take the room for a few days or a week; ask about this at the time you take the room.

BOOKS & MAPS

Central America is a small area geographically, but it is an important and much-studied part of the world for a variety of reasons. Hundreds of books have been written about Central America in general and the various countries in particular. There are history books, books about the Maya and the Maya ruins, books on modern social and political developments, books on the relationship between the USA and Central America, books about nature, tropical rainforests and wildlife and more. The following books relate to the region as a whole; books about individual countries are mentioned in the country chapters.

It's a good idea to do some reading before your trip, but Central America will probably still surprise you when you get there. If you read too much about political problems, it might put you off going there!

If you don't read Spanish, bring some books with you. It's hard to find books in English (or any language other than Spanish). You might find some in the gift shops of luxury hotels, but they'll be expensive.

Ancient & Mayan History

Popol Vuh (Simon & Schuster, 1985, paperback). The sacred book of the ancient Quiché Maya, telling their history from the time of creation. This is believed to be the oldest book in the Americas.

The Maya by Michael D Coe (Thames and Hudson, 1987, paperback). Hundreds of books have been written about the Maya, but this is the best general introduction to their life and culture.

Modern Politics

The Inter-Hemispheric Education Resource Center, Box 4506, Albuquerque, New Mexico 87916 USA, publishes a paperback 'Country Guide' on each of the seven Central American countries, covering politics, institutions, the economy, the environment, international relations etc. The 1993 edition of *Honduras: A Country Guide* is called *Inside Honduras*; all the other country guides will eventually be similarly re-released and re-titled. You can get a discount if you order the whole set. The same people publish a number of other books about Central America; write for a free catalogue.

Central America Fact Book by Tom Barry & Deb Preusch (Grove Press, 1986, paperback). Examines the economic, political and military role of the USA in Central America, and other issues.

Inevitable Revolutions: The United States in Central America by Walter LaFeber (WW Norton & Co, 1983, paperback).

Roots of Rebellion: Land and Hunger in Central America by Tom Barry (South End Press, 1987, paperback).

Nature & Rainforests

Tropical Nature: Life and Death in the Rain Forests of Central and South America by Adrian Forsyth & Ken Miyata (Charles Scribners & Sons, 1984, paperback).

Life above the Jungle Floor: A Biologist Explores a Strange and Hidden Treetop World by Donald Perry (Don Perro Press, San José, Costa Rica, 1991, paperback).

A Neotropical Companion: An Introduction to the Animals, Plants, and Ecosystems of the New World Tropics by John C Kricher (Princeton University Press, 1989).

Travellers' Tales

Incidents of Travel in Central America, Chiapas & Yucatán by John L Stephens, illustrated by Frederick Catherwood (Century, 1988, paperback, one volume; or Dover, 1969, paperback, two volumes). Originally published in 1841, this book caused an international sensation with its descriptions and drawings of the Mayan ruins and many other things Stephens and Catherwood discovered in their explorations. A famous book, still widely read and enjoyed after 150 years. (Also look for *Incidents of Travel in Yucatán* by the same author.)

Time among the Maya: Travels in Belize, Guatemala, and Mexico by Ronald Wright (Weidenfeld & Nicolson, 1989, hardcover). Describes a number of recent journeys among the modern Maya people; gives a good feel for Maya culture.

So Far From God: A Journey to Central America by Patrick Marnham (Penguin, 1985, paperback). A vivid, entertaining book describing a modern overland journey from California to Nicaragua, including Mexico, Guatemala, El Salvador and Honduras.

The Old Patagonian Express: By Train through the Americas by Paul Theroux (Houghton Mifflin, 1979, paperback). Theroux went by train from a suburb of Boston all the way to Patagonia. Several interesting Central American train rides are included; sadly, some of the trains he took are no longer operating, but it's still a great book.

Tekkin a Waalk by Peter Ford (Flamingo, 1993, paperback). An entertaining and informative account of a trip by foot and boat along the Carribean coast from Belize to Panama, including negotiating the Mosquitia jungle in the dying days of the Contra-Sandinista War. Historical anecdotes and personal experiences are combined with insights into the culture of Garífuna and Miskito communities.

Literature

All the following books by local writers are translated into English:

And We Sold the Rain: Contemporary Fiction from Central America, ed Rosario Santos (FWEW, New York, 1988). 20 short stories by Central American writers.

*Clamor of Innocence: Central American Short
Stories*, ed Barbara Paschke & David
Volpendesta (City Lights Books, San Francisco,
1988). 31 short stories by Central American
writers.
*When New Flowers Bloomed: Short Stories by
Women Writers from Costa Rica & Panama*, ed
Enrique J Levi (Latin American Literary Review
Press, Pittsburgh, 1991).
There Never Was a Once Upon a Time by Carmen
Naranjo, trans Linda Britt (Latin American Lit-
erary Review Press, Pittsburgh, 1989). Short
stories by a major Costa Rican writer.
*Beyond the Border: A New Age in Latin American
Women's Fiction* ed Nora Erro-Peralta & Caridad
Silva-Nunez (Cleis Press, Pittsburgh, 1991).
Costa Rica: A Traveler's Literary Companion ed
Barbara Ras (Whereabouts Press, San Francisco,
1994). 26 short stories by Costa Rican writers.
Riverbed of Memory by Daisy Zamora, trans Barbara
Paschke (City Lights Books, San Francisco,
1993). An anthology of poems by a Nicaraguan
poet.

Other Guide Books

Lonely Planet publishes in-depth guide
books for several Central American coun-
tries in its travel survival kit series. Look for
*Guatemala, Belize & Yucatán: La Ruta
Maya – a travel survival kit*, by Tom
Brosnahan, a detailed 600-page guide to the
Mayan lands including the Yucatán penin-
sula, Chiapas, Guatemala and Belize, and
Costa Rica – a travel survival kit by Rob
Rachowiecki.

If you're heading north, there's the comprehensive *Mexico – a travel survival kit*. If
you're continuing south, *South America on
a shoestring* is the counterpart of this book,
and LP also publishes individual travel survival kits for nearly all the countries of South
America.

The *Mexico & Central American Handbook* (Trade & Travel Publications, Bath,
UK, updated annually, hardback) contains
excellent information, though its format and
style is something of an acquired taste. It also
has companion volumes, covering the Caribbean and South America.

Carl Franz's *People's Guide to Mexico*
(John Muir Publications, 8th edition, 1990,
paperback) is mostly about Mexico, but it
does venture into Central America and it still

makes delightful, humorous, informative
and useful reading for shoestring travellers
in this part of the world. It was first published
in 1972. You're missing something if you've
never seen this book.

Another travel guide, recommended more
for its entertaining style than for its practical
travel information, is *Central America by
Chicken Bus* by Vivien Lougheed (Reposi-
tory Press, Prince George, BC, Canada,
1988, paperback).

There are also guide books for those with
special interests, such as *The Rivers of Costa
Rica: A Canoeing, Kayaking, and Rafting
Guide* by Michael W Mayfield & Rafael E
Gallo (Menasha Ridge Press, 1988, paperback), and *Say Sí!* (Legal Assistance
Resource Centre of Connecticut, 1993,
paperback), a guide to Spanish language programs around the world, with extensive
sections on Guatemala and Costa Rica.

Bioyole Touring *Latin America On Bicycle*
by J P Panet (Passport Press, 1987, paperback) has chapters on Costa Rica, Guatemala
and a few other Latin American countries;
*Latin America By Bike: A Complete Touring
Guide* by Walter Sienko (The Mountaineers,
Seattle, Washington & Cordee, Leicester,
UK, 1993), covers all the Central American
countries except El Salvador.

Field Guides *A Field Guide to the Birds of
Mexico and Central America* by L I Davis,
(University of Texas Press, 1972); *Birds of
Guatemala* by H C Land (Livingston Pub-
lishing Co, Wynnewood, Pennsylvania,
1970); *A Guide to the Birds of Costa Rica* by
F Gary Stiles & Alexander F Skutch (Cornell
University Press, 1989, paperback); *A Guide
to the Birds of Panama* by R S Ridgely
(Princeton University Press, New Jersey,
2nd ed 1981); *Neotropical Rainforest
Mammals: A Field Guide* by Louise H
Emmons (University of Chicago Press,
Chicago & London, 1990, paperback).

Periodicals
Central America Bulletin Central America Research

Institute, Box 4797, Berkeley CA 94704, USA, monthly, in English.

Central America Report Inforpress Centroamericana, Guatemala City, weekly, in English.

NACLA Report on the Americas North American Congress on Latin America, 9th floor, 151 West 19th St, New York NY 10011, USA, bi-monthly, in English.

National Geographic has had some excellent articles on Central American countries, eg *La Ruta Maya* and related articles in the October 1989 issue (Vol 176, No 4).

South American Explorer South American Explorers Club, quarterly, in English. (See the entry on Useful Organisations for more information about this club.)

The Tico Times weekly English language newspaper published in Costa Rica on Fridays. It covers Costa Rica news in detail and has a page on Central America. Subscriptions available from Apartado 4632, San José, Costa Rica or Dept 717, P O Box 025216, Miami, FL 33102, USA.

Maps

The best map of Central America is the 1:1,800,000 map produced by Kevin Healey for International Travel Map Productions (ITM); it is map No 156 in their series of excellent maps on South and Central America. They also publish a map covering the Yucatán region of Mexico, Guatemala and Belize, one of Costa Rica and several on South America. They show national parks, nature reserves, archaeological sites, geographical features, roads and much more, and have legends in four languages.

ITM maps are often available in travel shops but if you can't find them, contact their distributors: World Wide Books and Maps, 736A Granville Street, Vancouver, BC, Canada V6Z 1G3 (☎ (604) 687 3320, fax (604) 687 5925. They will send you a complete list of available titles; new ones are coming out all the time. ITM maps are also available in the USA through the South American Explorers Club (see Useful Organisations) or through Map Link, 25 East Mason St, Santa Barbara, CA 93101 (☎ (805) 965-4402, fax (805) 962-0884). Both of these organisations have a variety of other maps of Central and South America. Map Link has maps on areas all over the world; they'll send you a free catalogue of

their top 1500 titles, but a complete listing of their maps is *The World Map Directory*, a 300-page volume. In Britain ITM maps are available from Bradt Publications, 41 Nortoft Rd, Chalfont St Peter, Bucks, SL9 0LA, UK (☎ (0494) 873 478).

The American Automobile Association (AAA) publishes a decent road map called *Mexico & Central America*; it's free for AAA members or members of other motoring organisations with reciprocal arrangements with AAA. Texaco and Esso also publish road maps for Central America and for individual Central American countries.

POST

Sending and receiving mail between Central America and other parts of the world sometimes goes without a hitch, but it can be a very uncertain business. Because many Central Americans go to the USA to work and send money back home to their families, often through the mail, there's a high rate of mail theft in many places. The mail simply 'disappears', never reaching its destination.

This is primarily true of mail sent from the USA to points in Central America, but it can also happen with mail coming in from other countries, or even with mail being sent out from Central America to other parts of the world. Mail going more locally, within or between the Central American countries, is not as likely to disappear.

Mail is most likely to reach its destination when it looks like there is no way it could contain money, or anything else of value, as with a fold-up aerogramme.

Sending Mail

Sending letters is a straightforward business. If you want something to arrive within a reasonable time, be sure to specify that you want air mail *(correo aéreo* or *por avión)*. Surface mail sent to other parts of the world, whether letters or packages, usually takes several months to get there.

If you want to send a package home, check with the post office first. Don't arrive with your parcel all wrapped for mailing – you may have to have the contents approved by customs officials first, or there may be particular wrapping requirements to comply with.

Receiving Mail

The poste restante (or general delivery) service is known as Lista de Correos. To receive mail at a post office, have it addressed to you like this:

Name
Lista de Correos
Correo Central
City, Country

It will be sent to the main post office in the city and held there, usually for up to 30 days. Remember that mail sent to Panama must be addressed 'República de Panamá', as calling the country simply 'Panama' can cause the mail to be returned. Most of the time there's no charge for the service, but occasionally it costs a few cents to pick up your mail.

In larger cities, the Lista de Correos mail will probably be separated into alphabetical order. In small town post offices, you may find all the mail in one box. Be sure to check every conceivable letter your name could be filed under – not only your surname, but your first name also and even titles, such as 'M' for Mr, Mrs, Miss or Ms, or 'S' for Señor (Sr), Señora (Sra) or Señorita (Srta). To minimise confusion, it's best to use no titles, and to underline the surname.

Other alternatives for picking up mail include having it sent care of your country's embassy, but check in advance to see if they offer this service, as some countries' embassies don't. If you have either an American Express credit card or American Express travellers' cheques, you can have mail sent to you at any American Express office, but there may be a fee for the service.

TELECOMMUNICATIONS

See the individual country chapters for details. Note that it is *not* possible to make collect (reverse-charge) calls to many countries from Central America; you can (usually) to the USA.

TIME

Cross a border in Central America and you could lose or gain an hour. Proceeding west to east, Guatemala, Belize, El Salvador and Honduras are all six hours behind Greenwich Mean Time (GMT), the same as USA's Central Time. At Nicaragua you leap forward to five hours behind GMT; at Costa Rica you're again at six hours behind GMT, and at Panama you return to five hours behind GMT. None of the countries has 'daylight saving' time.

ELECTRICITY

Electric current almost everywhere in Central America is 110 volts AC, 60 cycles, the same as in the USA, Canada and Mexico. Plugs are the same flat two-prong style as in these countries. It's rare to see a socket with three holes, so if your appliance has the third prong on it, you should bring an adapter.

There is, however, the occasional place in Honduras and Panama which has 220 volt current, as in Europe, Australia and New Zealand. If you use an electric appliance, always ask about the current first, just to be on the safe side. If you're using a delicate appliance such as a computer, be sure to use a surge protector, as current is often very uneven.

HEALTH

Travel health depends on your pre-departure preparations, your day-to-day health care while travelling and how you handle any medical problem or emergency that does develop. While the list of potential dangers can seem quite frightening, with a little luck, some basic precautions and adequate information few travellers experience more than upset stomachs.

Travel Health Guides

There are a number of books on travel health:

Staying Healthy in Asia, Africa & Latin America, Volunteers in Asia. Probably the best all-round guide to carry, as it's compact but very detailed and well organised.
Travellers' Health, Dr Richard Dawood, Oxford Uni-

versity Press. Comprehensive, easy to read, authoritative and also highly recommended, although it's rather large to lug around.

Where There is No Doctor, David Werner, Hesperian Foundation. A very detailed guide intended for someone, like a Peace Corps worker, going to work in an undeveloped country, rather than for the average traveller.

Travel with Children, Maureen Wheeler, Lonely Planet Publications. Includes basic advice on travel health for younger children.

Pre-Departure Preparations

Health Insurance A travel insurance policy to cover theft, loss and medical problems is a wise idea. There is a wide variety of policies and your travel agent will have recommendations. The international student travel policies handled by STA or other student travel organisations are usually good value. Some policies offer lower and higher medical expenses options, but the higher one is chiefly for countries like the USA which have extremely high medical costs. Check the small print:

1. Some policies specifically exclude 'dangerous activities' which can include scuba diving, motorcycling, even trekking. If such activities are on your agenda you don't want that sort of policy.
2. You may prefer a policy which pays doctors or hospitals direct rather than your having to pay on the spot and claim later. If you have to claim later make sure you keep all documentation. Some policies ask you to call back (reverse charges) to a centre in your home country where an immediate assessment of your problem is made.
3. Check if the policy covers ambulances or an emergency flight home. If you have to stretch out you will need two seats and somebody has to pay for them!

Medical Kit A small and straightforward medical kit is a wise thing to carry. A possible kit list includes:

1. Aspirin or Panadol – for pain or fever.
2. Antihistamine (such as Benadryl) – useful as a decongestant for colds, allergies, to ease the itch from insect bites or stings or to help prevent motion sickness.
3. Antibiotics – useful if you're travelling well off the beaten track, but they must be prescribed and you should carry the prescription with you.
4. Kaolin preparation (Pepto-Bismol), Imodium or Lomotil – for stomach upsets.
5. Rehydration mixture – for treatment of severe diarrhoea, particularly important if travelling with children.
6. Antiseptic, mercurochrome and antibiotic powder or similar 'dry' spray – for cuts and grazes.
7. Calamine lotion – to ease irritation from bites or stings.
8. Bandages and Band-aids – for minor injuries.
9. Scissors, tweezers and a thermometer (note that mercury thermometers are prohibited by airlines).
10. Insect repellent, sunscreen, suntan lotion, chap stick and water purification tablets.

Ideally antibiotics should be administered only under medical supervision and should never be taken indiscriminately. Overuse of antibiotics can weaken your body's ability to deal with infections naturally and can reduce the drug's efficacy on a future occasion. Take only the recommended dose at the prescribed intervals and continue using the antibiotic for the prescribed period, even if the illness seems to be cured earlier. Antibiotics are quite specific to the infections they can treat. Stop immediately if there are any serious reactions, and don't use them at all if you are unsure if you have the correct ones.

In many countries, if a medicine is available at all, it will generally be available over the counter and the price will be much cheaper than it is at home. However, be careful of buying drugs in developing countries, particularly where the expiry date may have passed or correct storage conditions may not have been followed. It's possible that drugs which are no longer recommended, or have even been banned, in your country are still being dispensed in many Central American countries.

Health Preparations Make sure you're healthy before you start travelling. If you are embarking on a long trip make sure your teeth are OK; there are lots of places where a visit to the dentist would be the last thing you'd want.

If you wear glasses take a spare pair and your prescription. Losing your glasses can be a real problem, although in many places you can get new spectacles made up quickly, cheaply and competently.

If you require a particular medication take an adequate supply, as it may not be available locally. Take the prescription, with the generic rather than the brand name (which may not be locally available), as it will make getting replacements easier. It's a wise idea to have the prescription with you to show you legally use the medication – it's surprising how often over-the-counter drugs from one place are illegal without a prescription or even banned in another.

Immunisations Vaccinations provide protection against diseases you might meet along the way. Although vaccinations are not strictly required for entry into any of the Central American countries, except if you are entering from an area infected with yellow fever, there are some diseases there that you wouldn't want to catch. The further off the beaten track you go the more necessary it is to take precautions. All vaccinations should be recorded on an International Health Certificate, which is available from your physician or government health department.

Plan ahead for getting your vaccinations: some of them require an initial shot followed by a booster, while some vaccinations should not be given together. Most travellers from Western countries will have been immunised against various diseases during childhood but your doctor may still recommend booster shots against measles or polio, diseases still prevalent in many developing countries. The period of protection offered by vaccinations differs widely and some should not be taken if you are pregnant.

In some countries immunisations are available from airport or government health centres. Travel agents or airline offices will tell you where. The list of possible vaccinations includes:

Smallpox Smallpox has now been wiped out worldwide, so immunisation is no longer necessary.

Cholera Vaccinations against cholera are not currently required in any Central American countries, but there are regular (if not widespread) outbreaks of the disease in places where sanitation is poor (eg Honduras). The vaccination is less than 50% effective and most Western doctors will advise that it's not worth bothering with; the best protection is taking care that what you eat and drink is hygienic. If you intend to cross land borders it's wise to get hold of a certificate just in case the odd truculent border guard demands to see one. A single injection is sufficient to get the certificate; your doctor at home may even give you the certificate without actually giving you the injection. If you have the vaccination it only lasts six months. It should not be taken if you're pregnant.

Polio A booster is recommended if you have not had one since childhood.

Tetanus & Diptheria Boosters are necessary every 10 years and protection is highly recommended.

Typhoid Protection lasts for three years (if injected) or five years (if taken orally) and is recommended for travel in Central America, especially if you are travelling for long in rural areas. You may get some side effects such as pain at the injection site, fever, headache and a general unwell feeling.

Yellow Fever Protection lasts 10 years and is recommended where the disease is endemic. In Central America this is only in Panama in the areas east of the Canal Zone, chiefly the San Blas Islands and Darién province; the disease is also present in parts of South America. All the Central American countries except Costa Rica and Panama require vaccinations if you are entering from an infected area, or if you have been in the infected area within the past six months to a year. To be immunised you usually have to go to a special yellow fever vaccination centre. Vaccination is contraindicated during pregnancy, for infants under six months, for anyone who is allergic to eggs or who has leukaemia, lymphoma, cancer, or who is taking chemotherapy or radiation treatments.

Infectious Hepatitis Gamma globulin is not a vaccination but a ready-made antibody which has proven very successful in reducing the chances of hepatitis infection. Because it may interfere with the development of immunity, it should not be given until at least 10 days after administration of the last vaccine needed. It should be given as close as possible to the date of departure because of its relatively short protection period – up to six months, though its efficacy drops off after about eight weeks. For those planning long-term travels, the injection to have is Havrix, though this is not routinely dispensed. The full course – two injections a month apart, followed by another after six months – provides protection for ten years.

There is a new vaccine against hepatitis B, but it is expensive, not widely available and does not guarantee immunity. A variant of hepatitis B, called hepatitis C, now also exists but fortunately it is not common. Its transmission and symptoms are similar to to those for hepatitis B, but there is no vaccine for hepatitis C.

Basic Rules

Care in what you eat and drink is the most important health rule; stomach upsets are the most likely travel health problem but the majority of these upsets will be relatively minor. Don't become paranoid: trying the local food is part of the experience of travel after all.

Water The number one rule is *don't drink the water* unless you know for sure that it's safe, and that includes ice. If you don't know for certain that the water is safe, always assume the worst, and don't even brush your teeth with unpurified water. Reputable brands of bottled water or soft drinks are generally fine, although in some places bottles refilled with tap water are not unknown. Take care with fruit juice, particularly if water may have been added. Tea or coffee can be OK, but only if the water has been boiled long enough to purify it.

Some places in Central America have safe water, some don't. In Panama and Nicaragua the water is safe to drink in all but the most remote rural areas. In Costa Rica it is safe in San José and in major towns, but should be purified elsewhere. Be sure to purify all water in Guatemala, Belize, El Salvador and Honduras. Even when the locals can drink the water safely, you should still exercise caution. Everywhere in the world, people's bodies tend to develop immunities to the germs in their own water supply, a protection that a traveller new to the area hasn't developed. Or it could be that the locals do in fact have chronic health problems from drinking their water. It's better to err on the side of caution.

Milk should be treated with suspicion, as it is often unpasteurised. Boiled milk is fine if it is kept hygienically, and yoghurt is always good.

Water Purification You can usually find bottled water in Central America, but it's still wise to carry a means of purification. The simplest way of purifying water is to boil it thoroughly. Technically this means boiling for around 20 minutes, something which happens very rarely! Remember that at high altitudes water boils at lower temperature, so germs are less likely to be killed.

Simple filtering will not remove all dangerous organisms, so if you cannot boil water it should be treated chemically. Chlorine tablets (Puritabs, Steritabs or other brand names) will kill many but not all pathogens. Iodine is very effective in purifying water and is available in tablet form (such as Potable Aqua), but follow the directions carefully and remember that too much iodine can be harmful.

If you can't find tablets, tincture of iodine (2%) or iodine crystals can be used. Five drops of tincture of iodine per litre or quart of clear water is the recommended dosage; if the water is cloudy, double the dosage, and if it is very cloudy it should be strained through a clean cloth before treatment. The treated water should be left to stand for 30 minutes before drinking. If the water is extremely cold, try to get it warmer before treating it and let it stand longer to purify.

Iodine crystals can also be used to purify water, but this is a slightly more complicated process as you have first to prepare a saturated iodine solution. Iodine loses its effectiveness if exposed to air or damp so keep it in a tightly sealed container. Flavoured powder will disguise the taste of treated water and is a good idea if you are travelling with children.

Food Salads and fruit should be washed with purified water or peeled where possible. Ice cream is usually OK if it is a reputable brand name, but beware of Third World street vendors and of ice cream that has melted and been refrozen.

Thoroughly cooked food is safest, but not if it has been left to cool or if it has been reheated. Take great care with shellfish or fish and avoid undercooked meat. If a place looks clean and well run and if the vendor also looks clean and healthy, then the food is probably safe. In general, places that are packed with travellers or locals will be fine, while empty restaurants are questionable.

Nutrition If your food is poor or limited in availability, if you're travelling hard and fast and therefore missing meals, or if you simply lose your appetite, you can soon start to lose weight and place your health at risk.

Make sure your diet is well balanced. Eggs, tofu, beans (especially soybeans), lentils and nuts are all safe ways to get protein. Mixing legumes (beans, peanuts, peas or lentils) with grains (rice, corn, wheat etc) results in a complete protein which can be substituted for meat in the diet; throughout Central America the most common meal of beans and rice, or beans and corn tortillas, is an excellent way to get complete protein and avoid questionable meat. Other complete protein combinations include legumes with seeds (sunflower or sesame), and grains with milk products.

Fruit you can peel (bananas, mangoes, pineapple, oranges or mandarins for example) is always safe and a good source of vitamins. Remember that although food is generally safer if it is cooked well, overcooked food loses much of its nutritional value. If your diet isn't well balanced or if your food intake is insufficient, it's a good idea to take vitamin and iron pills. In hot climates make sure you drink enough – don't rely on feeling thirsty to indicate when you should drink. Not needing to urinate, or passing very dark yellow urine, are danger signs. Always carry a water bottle with you on long trips. Excessive sweating can lead to loss of salt and therefore muscle cramping. Salt tablets are not a good idea as a preventative, but in places where salt is not used much, adding salt to food can help.

Everyday Health A normal body temperature is 37°C (98.6°F); more than 2°C higher is a 'high' fever. A normal adult pulse rate is 60 to 80 per minute (children 80 to 100, babies 100 to 140). You should know how to take a temperature and a pulse rate. As a general rule the pulse increases about 20 beats per minute for each °C rise in fever.

Respiration (breathing) rate is also an indicator of illness. Count the number of breaths per minute: between 12 and 20 is normal for adults and older children (up to 30 for younger children, 40 for babies). People with a high fever or serious respiratory illness (like pneumonia) breathe more quickly than normal. More than 40 shallow breaths a minute usually means pneumonia.

Many health problems can be avoided by taking care of yourself. Wash your hands frequently – it's quite easy to contaminate your own food. Clean your teeth with purified water rather than straight from the tap. Avoid climatic extremes: keep out of the sun when it's hot, dress warmly when it's cold. Avoid potential diseases by dressing sensibly. You can get worm infections through walking barefoot, or dangerous coral cuts by walking over coral without shoes. You can avoid insect bites by covering bare skin when insects are around, by screening windows or beds or by using insect repellents. Seek local advice: if you're told the water is unsafe due to jellyfish, crocodiles or strong currents, don't go in. In situations where there is no information, discretion is the better part of valour.

Medical Problems & Treatment
Potential medical problems can be broken

down into several areas. First there are the climatic and geographical considerations – problems caused by extremes of temperature, altitude or motion. Then there are diseases and illnesses caused by insanitation, insect bites or stings, and animal or human contact. Simple cuts, bites or scratches can also cause problems.

Self-diagnosis and treatment can be risky, so wherever possible seek qualified help. Although we do give treatment dosages in this section, they are for emergency use only. Medical advice should be sought before administering any drugs.

An embassy or consulate can usually recommend a good place to go for such advice. So can five-star hotels, although they often recommend doctors with five-star prices. (This is when that medical insurance really comes in useful!) In some places standards of medical attention are so low that for some ailments the best advice is to get on a plane and go somewhere else.

Climatic & Geographic Considerations
Sunburn In the tropics or at high altitude you can get sunburnt surprisingly quickly, even through cloud. Use a sunscreen and take extra care to cover areas which don't normally see sun – eg, your feet. A hat provides added protection, and you should also use zinc cream or some other barrier cream for your nose and lips. Calamine lotion is good for mild sunburn.

Prickly Heat Prickly heat is an itchy rash caused by excessive perspiration trapped under the skin. It usually strikes people who have just arrived in a hot climate and whose pores have not yet opened sufficiently to cope with greater sweating. Keeping cool but bathing often, using a mild talcum powder or even resorting to air-con may help until you acclimatise.

Heat Exhaustion Dehydration or salt deficiency can cause heat exhaustion. Take time to acclimatise to high temperatures and make sure you get sufficient liquids. Salt deficiency is characterised by fatigue, lethargy,

headaches, giddiness and muscle cramps and in this case salt tablets may be of some help. Vomiting or diarrhoea can deplete your liquid and salt levels. Anhydrotic heat exhaustion caused by an inability to sweat, is quite rare . Unlike the other forms of heat exhaustion it is likely to strike people who have been in a hot climate for some time, rather than newcomers.

Heat Stroke This serious, sometimes fatal, condition can occur if the body's heat-regulating mechanism breaks down and the body temperature rises to dangerous levels. Long, continuous periods of exposure to high temperatures can leave you vulnerable to heat stroke. You should avoid excessive alcohol or strenuous activity when you first arrive in a hot climate.

The symptoms are feeling unwell, not sweating very much or at all and a high body temperature (39°C to 41°C). Where sweating has ceased the skin becomes flushed and red. Severe, throbbing headaches and lack of coordination will also occur, and the sufferer may be confused or aggressive. Eventually the victim will become delirious or convulse. Hospitalisation is essential, but meanwhile get patients out of the sun, remove their clothing, cover them with a wet sheet or towel and then fan continuously.

Fungal Infections Hot weather fungal infections are most likely to occur on the scalp, between the toes or fingers (athlete's foot), in the groin (jock itch or crotch rot) and on the body (ringworm). You get ringworm (which is a fungal infection, not a worm) from infected animals or by walking on damp areas, like shower floors.

To prevent fungal infections wear loose, comfortable clothes, avoid artificial fibres, wash frequently and dry carefully. If you do get an infection, wash the infected area daily with a disinfectant or medicated soap and water, and rinse and dry well. Apply an antifungal powder like the widely available Tinaderm. Try to expose the infected area to air or sunlight as much as possible and wash all towels and underwear in hot water as well as changing them often.

Cold Too much cold is just as dangerous as too much heat, particularly if it leads to hypothermia. You're more likely to encounter too much heat than too much cold in Central America, but at higher elevations temperatures can be much chillier than you'd expect. While the lowlands are baking, night-time temperatures can drop below freezing at high altitudes. The effects of low temperatures are exacerbated by wind, rain or wetness. If you are trekking at high altitudes, or simply taking a long bus trip over mountains, particularly at night, be prepared.

Hypothermia occurs when the body loses heat faster than it can produce it and the core temperature of the body falls. It is surprisingly easy to progress from very cold to dangerously cold due to a combination of wind, wet clothing, fatigue and hunger, even if the air temperature is well above freezing. It is best to dress in layers; silk, wool and some of the new artificial fibres are all good insulating materials. A hat is important, as a lot of heat is lost through the head. A strong, waterproof outer layer is essential, as keeping dry is vital. Carry basic supplies, including food containing simple sugars to generate heat quickly and lots of fluid to drink.

Symptoms of hypothermia are exhaustion, numb skin (particularly toes and fingers), shivering, slurred speech, irrational or violent behaviour, lethargy, stumbling, dizzy spells, muscle cramps and violent bursts of energy. Irrationality may take the form of sufferers claiming they are warm and trying to take off their clothes.

To treat hypothermia, first get the patient out of the wind and/or rain, remove their clothing if it's wet and replace it with dry, warm clothing. Give them hot liquids – not alcohol – and some high-kilojoule, easily digestible food. This should be enough for the early stages of hypothermia, but if it has gone further it may be necessary to place the victim in a warm sleeping bag and get in with them. Do not rub the patient or place them near a fire. Do not remove their wet clothes in the wind. If possible, place a sufferer in a warm (not hot) bath.

Motion Sickness Eating lightly before and during a trip will reduce the chances of motion sickness. If you are prone to motion sickness try to find a place that minimises disturbance – near the wing on aircraft, close to midships on boats, near the centre on buses. Fresh air usually helps; stale air, cigarette smoke and reading make it worse. Looking far into the distance, rather than at your immediate surroundings, is also helpful. Commercial anti-motion-sickness preparations, which can cause drowsiness, have to be taken before the trip commences; when you're feeling sick it's too late. Ginger is a natural preventative and is available in capsule form.

Diseases of Insanitation

Diarrhoea Changes in drinking water, food or climate can all cause the runs; diarrhoea caused by contaminated food or water is more serious. Despite all your precautions you may still have a bout of mild travellers' diarrhoea, but a few rushed toilet trips with no other symptoms is not indicative of a serious problem.

Moderate diarrhoea, involving half-a-dozen loose movements in a day, is more of a nuisance. Dehydration is the main danger with any diarrhoea, particularly for children, so fluid replenishment is the number one treatment. Weak black tea with a little sugar, soda water, or soft drink allowed to go flat and diluted 50% with water are all good. With severe diarrhoea a rehydrating solution is necessary to replace minerals and salts. You should stick to a bland diet as you recover.

Lomotil or Imodium can be used to bring relief from the symptoms, although they do not actually cure the problem. Only use these drugs if absolutely necessary – that is, if you *must* travel. For children Imodium is preferable. Do not use these drugs if the patient has a high fever or is severely dehydrated. Pepto-Bismol and Kaopectate are other common medications for relief of mild or moderate diarrhoea symptoms, but if they persist for more than a few days, further treatment may be necessary.

Antibiotics can be very useful in treating severe diarrhoea especially if it is accompanied by nausea, vomiting, stomach cramps or mild fever. Ampicillin, a broad spectrum penicillin, is usually recommended. Two capsules of 250 mg each taken four times a day is the recommended dose for an adult. Children aged between eight and 12 years should have half the adult dose; younger children should have half a capsule four times a day. Note that if the patient is allergic to penicillin, ampicillin should not be administered.

Three days of treatment should be sufficient and there should be an improvement within 24 hours.

Giardia This intestinal parasite is present in contaminated water. The symptoms are stomach cramps, nausea, a bloated stomach, watery, foul-smelling diarrhoea and frequent gas. Giardia can appear several weeks after you have been exposed to the parasite. The symptoms may disappear for a few days and then return; this can go on for several weeks. Metronidazole, known as Flagyl, is the recommended drug, but it should only be taken under medical supervision. Antibiotics are of no use.

Dysentery This serious illness is caused by contaminated food or water and is characterised by severe diarrhoea, often with blood or mucus in the stool. There are two kinds of dysentery. Bacillary dysentery is characterised by a high fever and rapid development; headache, vomiting and stomach pains are also symptoms. It generally does not last longer than a week, but it is highly contagious.

Amoebic dysentery is more gradual in developing, has no fever or vomiting but is a more serious illness. It is not a self-limiting disease: it will persist until treated and can recur and cause long-term damage.

A stool test is necessary to diagnose which kind of dysentery you have, so you should seek medical help urgently. In case of an emergency, note that tetracycline is the prescribed treatment for bacillary dysentery, metronidazole for amoebic dysentery.

With tetracycline, the recommended adult dosage is one 250 mg capsule four times a day. Children aged between eight and 12 years should have half the adult dose; the dosage for younger children is a third of the adult dose. It's important to remember that tetracycline should be given to young children only if it's absolutely necessary and only for a short period; pregnant women should not take it at all.

With metronidazole, the recommended adult dosage is one 750 mg to 800 mg capsule three times daily for five days. Children aged between eight and 12 years should have half the adult dose; the dosage for younger children is a third of the adult dose.

Cholera Cholera vaccination is not very effective. However, outbreaks of cholera are generally widely reported, so you can avoid such problem areas. The disease is characterised by a sudden onset of acute diarrhoea with 'rice water' stools, vomiting, muscular cramps, and extreme weakness. You need medical help – but treat for dehydration, which can be extreme, and if there is an appreciable delay in getting to hospital then begin taking tetracycline. See the Dysentery section for dosages and warnings.

Viral Gastroenteritis This is caused not by bacteria but, as the name suggests, by a virus. It is characterised by stomach cramps, diarrhoea, and sometimes by vomiting and/or a slight fever. All you can do is rest and drink lots of fluids.

Hepatitis Hepatitis A is the more common form of this disease and is spread by contaminated food or water. The first symptoms are fever, chills, headache, fatigue, feelings of weakness and aches and pains. This is followed by loss of appetite, nausea, vomiting, abdominal pain, dark urine, light-coloured faeces and jaundiced skin; the whites of the eyes may also turn yellow. In some cases there may just be a feeling of being unwell or tired, accompanied by loss of appetite, aches and pains and the jaundiced effect. You should seek medical advice, but in general there is not much you can do apart from resting, drinking lots of fluids, eating lightly and avoiding fatty foods. People who have had hepatitis must forgo alcohol for six months after the illness, as hepatitis attacks the liver and it needs that amount of time to recover.

Hepatitis B, which used to be called serum hepatitis, is spread through sexual contact or by skin penetration – it could be transmitted via dirty needles or blood transfusions, for instance. Avoid having your ears pierced, tattoos done or injections where you have doubts about the sanitary conditions. The symptoms and treatment of type B are much the same as for type A, but gamma globulin as a prophylactic is effective against type A only. The new vaccine against hepatitis B is expensive, not widely available and does not guarantee immunity.

There is now also a variant of hepatitis B, called hepatitis C. Its transmission and symptoms are similar to to those for hepatitis B, but there is no vaccine for hep C. Fortunately, hepatitis C is not common, and is not a great concern for travellers in Central America.

Typhoid Typhoid fever is another gut infection that travels the faecal-oral route – ie, contaminated water and food are responsible. Vaccination against typhoid is not totally effective and it is one of the most dangerous infections, so medical help must be sought.

In its early stages typhoid resembles many other illnesses: sufferers may feel like they have a bad cold or flu on the way, as early symptoms are a headache, a sore throat, and a fever which rises a little each day until it is around 40°C or more. The victim's pulse is often slow relative to the degree of fever present and gets slower as the fever rises – unlike a normal fever where the pulse rate increases. There may also be vomiting, diarrhoea or constipation.

In the second week the high fever and slow pulse continue and a few pink spots may appear on the body; trembling, delirium, weakness, weight loss and dehydration are other symptoms. If there are no further complications, the fever and other symptoms will slowly go during the third week. However you must get medical help before this because acute infection of the lungs (pneumonia) or the abdominal cavity (peritonitis, typically caused by a burst appendix) are common complications, and because typhoid is very infectious.

The fever should be treated by keeping the victim cool and dehydration should also be watched for. Chloramphenicol is the recommended antibiotic but there are fewer side effects with ampicillin. The adult dosage is two 250 mg capsules, four times a day. Children aged between eight and 12 years should have half the adult dose; younger children should have one-third the adult dose.

Patients who are allergic to penicillin should not be given ampicillin.

Worms These parasites are most common in rural, tropical areas and a stool test when you return home is not a bad idea. They can be present on unwashed vegetables or in undercooked meat and you can pick them up through your skin by walking in bare feet. Infestations may not show up for some time, and although they are generally not serious, if left untreated they can cause severe health problems. A stool test is necessary to pinpoint the problem and medication is often available over the counter.

Diseases Spread by People & Animals
Tetanus This potentially fatal disease is found in undeveloped tropical areas. It is difficult to treat but is preventable with immunisation. Tetanus occurs when a wound becomes infected by a germ which lives in the faeces of animals or people, so clean all cuts, punctures and animal bites. Tetanus is known as lockjaw, and the first symptom may be discomfort in swallowing, or stiffening of the jaw and neck; this

is followed by painful convulsions of the jaw and whole body.

Rabies Rabies is found in many countries and is caused by a bite or scratch by an infected animal. Dogs are noted carriers, as are skunks, squirrels and bats. Any bite, scratch or even lick from a mammal should be cleaned immediately and thoroughly. Scrub with soap and running water, and then clean with an alcohol solution. If there is any possibility that the animal is infected medical help should be sought immediately. Even if the animal is not rabid, all bites should be treated seriously as they can become infected or result in tetanus. A rabies vaccination is now available and should be considered if you are in a high-risk category – eg if you intend to explore caves (bat bites could be dangerous) or work with animals.

Tuberculosis Although this disease is widespread in many developing countries, it is not a serious risk to travellers. Young children are more susceptible than adults and vaccination is a sensible precaution for children under 12 travelling in areas where it is endemic. TB is commonly spread by coughing or by unpasteurised dairy products from infected cows. Milk that has been boiled is safe to drink; the souring of milk to make yoghurt or cheese also kills the bacilli.

Diptheria Diptheria can be a skin infection or a more dangerous throat infection. It is spread by contaminated dust contacting the skin or by the inhalation of infected cough or sneeze droplets. Frequent washing and keeping the skin dry will help prevent skin infection. A vaccination is available to prevent the throat infection.

Sexually Transmitted Diseases Sexual contact with an infected sexual partner spreads these diseases. While abstinence is the only 100% preventative, using condoms is also effective. Gonorrhoea and syphilis are the most common of these diseases; sores, blisters or rashes around the genitals, discharges or pain when urinating are common symptoms. Symptoms may be less marked or not observed at all in women. Syphilis symptoms eventually disappear completely but the disease continues and can cause severe problems in later years. The treatment of gonorrhoea and syphilis is by antibiotics.

There are numerous other sexually transmitted diseases, for most of which effective treatment is available. However, there is no cure for herpes and there is also currently no cure for AIDS. AIDS (SIDA is its Spanish acronym) is common in parts of Central America and is becoming more widespread.

AIDS is a sexually transmitted disease for which the best preventatives are abstinence, monogamy or the use of condoms. It can also be spread through infected blood transfusions (most developing countries cannot afford to screen blood for transfusion) and by dirty needles. Vaccinations, acupuncture and tattooing can potentially be as dangerous as intravenous drug use if the equipment is not clean. Syringes can be effectively sterilised with chlorine bleach, but unless you do this yourself you may not be able to know for sure it's been done or done properly. If you do need an injection it may be a good idea to buy a new syringe from a pharmacy and ask the doctor to use it.

Insect-Borne Diseases

Malaria This serious disease is spread by mosquito bites. If you are travelling in areas where it is endemic it is extremely important to take malarial prophylactics. All of Central America is considered a risk area, except for the high-altitude central highlands of Guatemala and Costa Rica. The disease has been stamped out in Panama City, but in general if you're travelling in Central America, it's a good idea to get onto an antimalarial regimen and stay on it.

Malaria symptoms include headaches, fever, chills and sweating which may subside and recur. Malaria can be effectively treated early in the course of the disease, but delays in treatment can lead to more serious or even fatal consequences. For this reason it's important not to ignore malaria-like symptoms or assume that it's only a case of flu.

Symptoms of malaria can show up as early as eight days after initial exposure to the disease, or as late as several months or even years after leaving the malarial area. Keep this in mind if you should become ill later, and be sure to inform your physician that you may have been exposed to malaria, so that it can be kept in mind in making a diagnosis. Delays in correct diagnosis once you are back in a part of the world where malaria doesn't exist can be dangerous to your health or even fatal.

Also note that it is possible to contract malaria *even if you have correctly followed an antimalarial regimen*. Your chances of catching malaria will be far less but that doesn't mean it's impossible.

Antimalarial drugs do not prevent you from being infected but kill the parasites during a stage in their development. Chloroquine is the usual malarial prophylactic; a tablet is taken once a week for two weeks before arriving in an infected area, the whole time you're there, and for six weeks after you leave.

Unfortunately there is now a strain of malaria which is resistant to chloroquine and if you are travelling in an area infected with this strain an alternative drug is necessary. In Central America the only chloroquine-resistant area is east of the Canal Zone in Panama, including the San Blas Islands and Darién province. In these areas you should continue to take chloroquine but supplement it with a weekly dose of maloprim or a daily dose of Proguanil. Another possibility in this area is to use mefloquine or doxycycline instead of chloroquine.

Chloroquine is quite safe for general use; side effects are minimal and it can be taken by pregnant women. Maloprim can have rare but serious side effects if the weekly dose is exceeded and some doctors recommend a check-up after six months' continuous use. Mefloquine can produce transient side effects including gastrointestinal disturbance and dizziness; hallucinations and convulsions are very rare side effects but if they occur you should stop taking the drug and consult a physician.

Fansidar, once used as a Chloroquine alternative, is no longer recommended as a prophylactic as it can have dangerous side effects, but it may still be recommended as a treatment for malaria. Chloroquine is also used for malaria treatment but in larger doses than for prophylaxis. Doxycycline is another antimalarial for use where chloroquine resistance is reported; it causes hypersensitivity to sunlight, so sunburn can be a problem.

Malaria-carrying mosquitoes appear after dusk. Avoiding bites by covering bare skin and using an insect repellent will reduce the risk of catching malaria. Insect screens on windows and mosquito nets on beds offer protection, as does burning a mosquito coil or spraying with a pyrethrum-based insect spray. Mosquitoes may be attracted by perfume, aftershave or certain colours. Mosquitoes can bite you right through thin fabrics, or on any small part of your skin not covered by repellent. The risk of infection is higher in rural areas and during the wet season.

The most effective insect repellent is called DEET (N,N-Diethylmetatoluamide); it is an ingredient in many commercially available insect repellents. Buy your repellent before you arrive in the risk area, and look for one with at least a 28% concentration of DEET. Repellents are made which contain up to a 95% concentration; these are greasier on the skin and may smell unpleasant, but might be considered for a heavily infested area. DEET breaks down plastic and synthetic fabrics, so be careful what you touch after using it. It poses no danger to natural fibre fabrics.

If you can't get hold of insect repellent, kerosene mixed with coconut or vegetable oil is also effective, though smelly.

Dengue Fever There is no prophylactic available for this mosquito-spread disease; the main preventative measure is to avoid mosquito bites. Unlike malaria-carrying mosquitoes which bite from dusk to dawn, the mosquitoes which carry this disease bite during the daytime. A sudden onset of fever, headaches and severe joint and muscle pains are the first signs before a rash starts on the trunk of the body and spreads to the limbs and face. After a further few days, the fever will subside and recovery will begin. Serious complications are possible but not common.

Yellow Fever This viral disease is found in a number of South American countries, but in Central America it only occurs in Darién province in eastern Panama.

Yellow fever is transmitted to humans by mosquitoes; the initial symptoms are fever, headache, abdominal pain and vomiting. There may appear to be a brief recovery before the disease progresses to more severe complications, including liver failure. There is no medical treatment apart from keeping the fever down and avoiding dehydration, but yellow fever vaccination gives good protection for 10 years.

Vaccination is recommended (though not required) if you're travelling to eastern Panama. All the Central American countries except Panama and Costa Rica require proof of vaccination if you are entering from an infected area, or if you have been in an infected area within the past six to 12 months.

Chagas' Disease In remote rural areas of Central and South America this parasitic disease is transmitted by a bug called the *vinchuca* (called a reduviid bug or an assassin bug in English), which hides in crevices and palm fronds and often takes up residence in old buildings and in the thatched roofs of huts. The vinchuca is a smooth, oval-shaped, brownish-coloured insect with a long, narrow cone-shaped head, and two antennae curving under the head. The insect comes out to feed at night, sucking your blood for up to 20 minutes and usually defecating at the same time. The disease is caused by a protozoan, *trypanosoma cruzi*, present in the faeces of the infected insect and entering through the bite wound. A hard, violet-coloured swelling appears at the site of the bite in about a week. The trypanosomes invade internal organs such as the brain, heart, liver and spleen.

Usually the body overcomes the disease unaided, but it is important to seek immediate medical attention if you suspect you are infected. If it progresses it can take one of two forms. Symptoms of the acute form of Chagas' disease are fever, vomiting, and shortness of breath, proceeding to convulsions and stiffness of the neck. You could die within three months of being bitten. In the slower, chronic form of the disease, symptoms are acute at first but then subside. The trypanosomes continue to live in your body, however, weakening your organs and finally destroying them over a period of years.

Chagas' disease can be treated in its early stages, but it is best to avoid the insect in the first place. The vinchuca lives only at elevations under 1000 metres. Beware of sleeping in thatched-roof huts or old buildings, and of camping under palm trees. Sleep under a mosquito net, use insecticides and insect repellents, and check for hidden insects. If you do get a suspicious bite, especially on your face, seek medical attention. The disease is relatively uncommon and predominantly affects children under two years of age.

Typhus Typhus is spread by ticks, mites or lice. It begins as a bad cold, followed by fever, chills, headache, muscle pains and a body rash. There is often a large painful sore at the site of the bite and nearby lymph nodes are swollen and painful.

Tick typhus is spread by ticks. Seek local advice on areas where ticks pose a danger and always check yourself carefully for ticks after walking in a danger area. A strong insect repellent can help, and serious walkers in tick areas should consider having their boots and trousers impregnated with benzyl benzoate and dibutylphthalate.

Cuts, Bites & Stings
Cuts & Scratches Skin punctures can easily become infected in hot climates and may be difficult to heal. Treat any cut with an antiseptic solution and mercurochrome. Where possible avoid bandages and Band-aids, which can keep wounds wet. Coral cuts are

notoriously slow to heal, as the coral injects a weak venom into the wound. Avoid coral cuts by not touching or walking on reefs; irrespective of the risk of cuts, coral supports marine life and can be damaged by physical contact.

Bites & Stings Bee and wasp stings are usually painful rather than dangerous. Ammonia is an effective remedy for bee and other stings. Calamine lotion will also give relief; ice packs will reduce the pain and swelling.

Some spiders have dangerous bites but antivenins are usually available. Scorpion stings are notoriously painful and in Mexico can be fatal. Scorpions shelter in shoes or clothing, so if they're around, always shake out shoes and clothes before putting them on.

Various fish and other sea creatures can sting or bite dangerously, or are dangerous to eat. Take local advice.

Snakes To minimise your chances of being bitten always wear boots, socks and long, loose trousers when walking through undergrowth where snakes may be present. Don't put your hands into holes and crevices, and be careful when collecting firewood.

Central America has dozens of species of snakes but most are not poisonous. The most poisonous snake of all is the tiny coral snake, which is actually a land snake, brightly coloured with bands of red, yellow and black. Coral snakes are nocturnal and not aggressive. The large *fer-de-lance* is much more of a danger. It's called *barba armarilla* (yellow chin) in Central America, and it's also recognisable by its lance-shaped head and the diamond markings on its back. It is often encoutered in undergrowth and canefields, and sometimes comes out at night to lie on warm roads and trails. Its venom is extremely toxic. Rattlesnakes are also found in Central America.

Snake bites do not cause instantaneous death and antivenins are usually available. Keep the victim calm and still, wrap the bitten limb tightly, as you would for a sprained ankle, and then attach a splint to immobilise it. Then seek medical help, if possible with the dead snake for identification. Do not attempt to catch the snake if there is even a remote possibility that you will be bitten again. Tourniquets and sucking out the poison are now comprehensively discredited.

Jellyfish Local advice is the best way of avoiding contact with these sea creatures with their stinging tentacles. Stings from most jellyfish are quite painful. The most effective folk remedy for jellyfish stings, used all over the world, is to apply fresh urine to the stings as soon as possible. This is also useful if you touch fire coral, which causes a stinging skin reaction. Ammonia is also effective. Dousing in vinegar will de-activate any stingers which have not 'fired'. Calamine lotion, antihistamines and analgesics may reduce the reaction and relieve some of the pain.

Bedbugs & Lice Bedbugs live in various places, but particularly in dirty mattresses and bedding. Spots of blood on bedclothes or on the wall around the bed can be read as a suggestion to find another hotel. Bedbugs leave itchy bites in neat rows. Calamine lotion may help.

All lice cause itching and discomfort. They make themselves at home in your hair (head lice), your clothing (body lice) or in your pubic hair (crabs). You catch lice through direct contact with infected people or by sharing combs, clothing and the like, or from sheets or bedding where they are present. Powder or shampoo treatment will kill the lice and infected clothing should then be washed in very hot water.

Leeches & Ticks Leeches may be present in damp rainforest conditions; they attach themselves to your skin to suck your blood. Trekkers often get them on their legs or in their boots. Salt or a lighted cigarette end will make them fall off. Do not pull them off because the bite is then more likely to become infected. An insect repellent may keep them away.

Vaseline, alcohol or oil will persuade a tick to let go. You should always check your body if you have been walking through a tick-infested area, as they can spread typhus.

Women's Health
Gynaecological Problems Poor diet, lowered resistance because of the use of antibiotics for stomach upsets and even contraceptive pills can lead to vaginal infections when travelling in hot climates. Keeping the genital area clean, and wearing skirts or loose-fitting trousers and cotton underwear will help to prevent infections.

Yeast infections, characterised by a rash, itch and a discharge, can be treated with a diluted vinegar or lemon-juice douche or with yoghurt. Nystatin suppositories are the usual medical prescription. Cystitis, a common and very painful urinary infection, can be combatted by drinking a solution of bicarbonate of soda in water, although chronic sufferers would be advised to take sachets of a prescribed antibiotic with them. Trichomonas is a more serious infection; symptoms are a discharge and a burning sensation when urinating. Sexual partners must also be treated, and if a vinegar-water douche is not effective medical attention should be sought. Flagyl is the prescribed drug.

Pregnancy Most miscarriages occur during the first three months of pregnancy, so this is the most risky time to travel as far as your own health is concerned. Miscarriage is not uncommon, and can occasionally lead to severe bleeding. The last three months should also be spent within reasonable distance of good medical care. A baby born as early as 24 weeks stands a chance of survival, but only in a good modern hospital. Pregnant women should avoid all unnecessary medication, but vaccinations and malarial prophylactics should still be taken where possible. Additional care should be taken to prevent illness and particular attention should be paid to diet and nutrition.

Women travellers often find that their periods become irregular or even cease while they're on the road. Remember that a missed period in these circumstances doesn't necessarily indicate pregnancy. A simple urine test takes a few minutes and will determine whether you are pregnant or not.

DANGERS & ANNOYANCES
Civil War & Political Turmoil
Unless you have been to Central America and seen what it's like, there is a tendency to overestimate the amount of danger that the average traveller will encounter from political conflicts. This is especially true if you are coming from the USA, where you'll hear news stories of unstable politics, CIA activities, guerrilla warfare and economic catastrophes.

The Citizens Emergency Center of the US State Department offers a 24-hour telephone recording (☎ (202) 647-5225) with travel advisories on current conditions in various countries. The advisories usually pertain to civil unrest, natural disasters, or outbreaks of serious diseases, and they also offer current information on visa requirements for US citizens. It's best to call from a 'touch tone' phone, since the recording gives you a number of options in selecting what you want to hear by pushing the buttons.

In Britain, telephone the Foreign Office Consular Advice Unit (☎ (071) 270 4129), Monday to Friday from 9.30 am to 4 pm.

Central America does have political disturbances which can on occasion break out in armed conflict. The lengthy civil wars in El Salvador and Nicaragua are now over, but they remain the most volatile of the Central American countries: there's still the odd political killing and stand-off situation. Guatemala also has suffered, with many deaths and many 'disappeared' citizens.

As a traveller you're unlikely to come across any fighting. Conflicts that break out are between internal factions and tourists are not targets. But check with the local authorities for the latest information before travelling in a turbulent area. You can also check with your embassy or consulate. A short-wave radio is useful for keeping abreast of current affairs.

Encountering danger is certainly a possibility, but don't let exaggerated fears put you off from travelling to Central America.

Theft

Theft, on the other hand, is a greater possibility. It's much more likely in some places than others, major cities being the worst. The more poverty and economic problems an area has, the more you have to watch out. It's a good idea to develop the habit of being alert and doing things in such a way that you don't make yourself an easy target, no matter where you are. Thieves look for an easy mark. To some degree you are a target just because you're a foreigner, but you certainly don't have to make it easy for them.

This does not mean you should be paranoid; it's quite possible to travel for months in Central America and have no problem at all. It just means you should develop habitual, healthy awareness. You're much more likely to get ripped off if you're not paying attention – sometimes you're less likely to get robbed at the beginning of your journey, when you're most alert, than you are after you've been away a while, when you feel more secure and fail to take precautions.

Most theft in Central America is not open confrontational robbery, but sneak thievery of one kind or another. It is most likely for this sort of theft to occur in busy public places such as crowded buses, bus stations, markets, fiestas, and so on. Often the thieves work in pairs or groups to distract your attention. A 'fight' can break out, or someone can drop something in front of you, bump into you, or spill something on you. Before you realise what has happened, your bag has been slashed or your pocket picked. Pay attention.

Bag slashing is one of the most common forms of theft. They do it with a razor blade, and you don't feel a thing. They can also slit your pocket, which you won't feel either. Razor thieves are especially common on crowded buses, especially urban buses where lots of people are standing pushed together.

The best protection from this is to keep your bag where you can see it. In capital cities, a local would never wear a pack on their back while riding a bus or walking in the market or on city streets. Wear your pack on your chest instead. If you have a shoulder bag, make sure it is in front of you and the strap is across your body, not just hanging on one shoulder. Even then, the strap can be slashed, enabling the thief to make off with your whole bag.

A larger pack can also be slashed or snatched, while you are wearing it or when it is left unguarded, such as on a bus while you're sleeping. If you always keep moving while wearing your pack, it's harder for thieves to slash without you knowing it. Be aware of how you hold a bag when you carry one, and be especially conscious of putting things down in busy places. If you put your bag down by your feet in a bus station or market while you fumble for change, it can disappear amazingly quickly. At least keep your foot on it!

If you don't have much to carry, you may not need to have a bag at all, just use an inside pocket. If you do have to carry a bag, it's better to have one that looks like a common plastic shopping bag, not a cloth bag that looks like it contains valuables.

Snatchers are also attracted to cameras, watches and jewellery. It's obviously best not to go around in poor countries wearing jewels, but even a cheap brass chain can attract a thief who thinks that, if a foreigner is wearing it, it just might be gold. Locals in many parts of Central America will warn you against wearing any type of jewellery, but you can wear something obviously cheap, made of wood, thread or plastic. A US$2 plastic wristwatch (common in Central America) will usually keep time just as well as an expensive one, and not attract a problem.

Thieves can also spirit your pack off a long-distance bus. Always be sure you know where your pack is; it's best to keep it where you can see it. Some travellers carry a small padlock to lock their packs to a luggage rack, especially on long journeys where they might want to sleep. This is a good idea, but also remember the razor-blade artists.

Finally, picking pockets is one of the most common forms of theft, occurring in all the places already mentioned. The city bus routes of Managua are so famous for pickpockets that it's practically a cliché. Central America has some real professionals, but you can protect yourself by knowing what might be tried on you, and taking appropriate precautions.

There are many ways to protect yourself, and all of them can become good travelling habits which you do automatically. Most important is how you carry things. Obviously you shouldn't walk around with your wallet hanging out of your back pocket. Everyone has their own preferred way to carry money. Some carry it in a money belt, worn with the money in front, behind, under their jeans, or wherever. Some keep it in a strong leather pouch on their belts, or in a leather belt with a secret zippered compartment. A pouch worn round the neck is pretty obvious and not so safe; if you do this, be sure to sew a guitar string through the strap so it can't be slashed. You can tuck money under your hat, into your socks, into a bra, or into your underwear, in a spot where a thief won't find it, at least without your noticing. Some travellers sew extra pockets inside their clothes, sew money into the hem or lining of a garment, or make a pocket which they can safety-pin into the clothes they're wearing. Some keep it in a front pocket, with a handkerchief on top just in case, so the thief gets the handkerchief instead of the money.

Don't carry all your money with you in the same spot; have separate places for your long-term travelling money and your everyday change.

It may be safer not to carry everything around with you. Many hotels, even small ones, have safes or locked drawers, and will store valuables and extra luggage for you. If you know you're going to be coming back to a place, you can leave all but what you know you'll be using – as long as the hotel is trustworthy!

Unfortunately, petty pilfering from cheap hotel rooms can also be a problem. Some travellers alway lock their packs when they go out to limit this possibility. In basic places, use your own padlock to lock the door instead of the hotel's. Don't even assume your pack is safe on an airline. One traveller forgot to lock his pack when travelling by air in Guatemala, and stuff was stolen from inside; he felt all the more aggrieved because the airline had charged him to check-in his luggage!

Try not to take valuables to the beach. It couldn't be easier for a thief to take unattended belongings from a deserted beach while the owner is swimming or snorkelling. Stagger your swims if you're travelling with friends.

The most important things to protect are your long-term travelling money (travellers' cheques), your passport and your airline tickets. Carry these in the safest way possible, but as an extra precaution make a list of cheque numbers, passport information and airline ticket details, take one or two photocopies of the essential documents, and carry them in a separate place from the originals.

Travel insurance is also a good idea, and strongly recommended. In case of theft, be sure to get a police report – not because the police will get your things back, but because you'll need one for the insurance company.

Travelling with a friend can be good protection because you can watch out for one another. (I took a pickpocket's hand from the shirt of my travelling companion on a bus from Managua to León.) Unfortunately you can't always depend on strangers to help you as they may be afraid to (one man showed me a knife scar over his ribs, a souvenir of his helping a young female tourist who had been pickpocketed in Managua). Locals say it's dangerous to interfere in crimes, so usually they don't get involved.

Remember to be wise, but not paranoid. If you're careful and aware of what you're doing, it is perfectly possible to travel almost anywhere in Central America with no problems at all.

Women Travellers

Women travellers should encounter no special dangers, though you may receive unwanted attention from local men. This may be simply be in the form of a flirtatious comment or an appreciative hiss, and the best way to deal with it is to do what the locals do: ignore the comments completely and not look at the man making them. Some women have experienced problems with importunate men pressing against them in crowded buses. Try moving away, telling them to leave you alone, or manoeuvring your pack between you and them.

Health Risks
In many parts of Central America, malaria-carrying mosquitoes and microscopic organisms in the water are much more of a danger to you than other humans might be. See the Health section for tips on staying healthy.

Swimming Safety
Hundreds of people are drowned each year on Central American beaches – about 200 drownings are recorded annually from Costa Rica beaches alone. Of these, 80% are caused by rip-tides which are strong currents which pull the swimmer out to sea. They can occur in waist-deep water. Remember that rip-tides will pull you *out but not under*. Many deaths are caused by panicked swimmers struggling to the point of exhaustion.

If caught in a rip-tide, float, do not struggle. If you swim, do so parallel to the beach, not directly back in. You are unlikely to be able to swim against a rip-tide. If you are carried out beyond the breakers, the rip-tide will dissipate – it won't carry you out for miles. Then you can swim back in to shore at a 45° angle to avoid being caught by the current again.

If you feel a rip-tide whilst wading, try and come back in sideways to offer less body surface to the current, Walk parallel to the beach to get out of the rip-tide. Attract attention by waving your arms and calling for help. Ask about local conditions before entering the water.

The Environment
Although awareness about environmental issues is growing in Central America, the message hasn't really filtered down to the majority of the people. On every bus journey you take you see passengers casually throwing rubbish out of the window, whether in the city or the countryside. Discarded cartons, wrappings and plastic bags are a depressing fixture of every roadside. Try not to add to the collection.

On a more general point, don't undermine what you have come to see; eco-systems and indigenous cultures are very vulnerable to the effects of tourism. Treat the human and physical environment with respect, or you may end up being a danger and annoyance yourself.

ACTIVITIES
Hiking & Trekking
Possibilities for hiking are infinite in Central America. An avid hiker could tramp around here for years and never get bored. The pristine natural environments and the abundant wildlife are most impressive. Terrains include mountains, cloud forests, rainforests, lowland jungles, river trails, tropical islands, palm-lined beaches, lagoons full of wildlife, and dozens of volcanoes, often with natural hot springs. There are remote wilderness areas, national parks, and wildlife preserves, and also the less remote trails which link rural villages to one another.

Central America has hundreds of places, many close to cities and towns, where you can take simple day walks and see many of the natural features. Hardier backpackers and campers will find more challenging tramps that can last for days or weeks. This part of the world is a hiker's paradise.

Snorkelling & Diving
The reefs off the Caribbean coast of Central America, especially off Belize, but also extending down the Honduran coast, and including some of the Caribbean islands as far east as Panama, are magnificent for snorkelling and diving. This reef is the second largest in the world (after Australia's Great Barrier Reef) and has every kind of feature you could dream of, including ship-

wrecks from the pirate days. The reef attracts divers from all over the world, and the fishing is also fantastic.

The Bay Islands of Honduras are among the cheapest places in the world to take a PADI scuba diving course; even travellers on the most threadbare of shoestrings take the opportunity to learn to dive.

Surfing

The Pacific coast has several surf breaks which enjoy an international reputation, and each country with a Pacific coastline has its own famous spots. International surfing competitions are held at some of them, notably at Zunzal in El Salvador.

Language Courses

Antigua Guatemala is famous for its Spanish language courses. The town has many schools and provides total immersion teaching. Students come here from all over the world and live in the homes of local families, becoming familiar with the culture as well as living with the language 24 hours a day. Spanish can also be studied in other parts of Central America, but Antigua has the best reputation and is the most widely known. Many language schools are listed in the country chapters, or refer to *Say Sí!*, mentioned in the Books section.

HIGHLIGHTS
Walks

Simple walks in out-of-the-way places can be what you'll remember most, not only scaling volcanoes and visiting magnificent national parks, but just walking around wherever you happen to be – to the other side of an island, to the top of a hill at sunset, down a long stretch of beach, and so on.

Wilderness

There are a number of real wilderness areas, like the Mosquitia region of Honduras, Darién province in Panama, and the less accessible national parks and wildlife sanctuaries of Costa Rica. These areas can offer unforgettable wilderness experiences.

Backroads

In rural areas it's common for someone who has a vehicle (usually a dusty diesel pick-up truck) to stop for anyone they see hitching. Be sure to offer to pay something for your ride, since this is the local custom. Riding through the wilds of Central America, in the back of a pick-up with the wind in your hair, is a marvellous feeling. Riding the backroads on the roof of a bus is a similar thrill – though the bus may be stuffed to overflowing with women, children and old people, you can sometimes get on top with the boys and the big round baskets of produce being brought back from market.

Markets

The large open-air markets and the handicraft markets in Central America are always interesting. It's great eating a meal at a table set up in a marketplace, amidst all the activity.

Food

Eating and drinking new and unusual things is a joy, and you'll discover some wonderful treats. Try the seafood soups and coconut bread along the Caribbean coast; the strong hot coffee in Costa Rica; the shaved ice with sweet fruit syrup from street stands in the hot sun of Panama City; the odd little vegetarian restaurant, like Todo Rico in Tegucigalpa; chicken, barbecued outdoors; and tropical fruits that you've never seen before.

Fiestas & Celebrations

Town fairs, annual celebrations, Carnaval, saints' days etc are magnificent occasions. Some of the more famous ones are Semana Santa (Holy Week) in Antigua Guatemala; Carnaval in Panama City, or the much smaller Carnaval in La Ceiba, on the Caribbean coast of Honduras; and Corpus Christi in Las Tablas, Panama. The celebrations on the anniversary of the 19 July revolution are a big event in Managua. Then there are religious pilgrimages attracting throngs of participants, such as the day of the Virgen de Suyapa (patron saint of Honduras) at the Suyapa cathedral near Tegucigalpa on 3 February, or the day of the Virgen de Fátima at the Virgin's grotto outside Cojutepeque (El Salvador) on 13 May.

Every city, town and village has its annual celebration and fair. Sometimes they are not big or famous, but celebrations in small places, where the presence of a foreigner is an event, are often the best. For example, in tiny towns in Guatemala's highlands the *cofradías* (religious brotherhoods) hold street processions on saints' days and festival Sundays, accompanied by a ragtag assortment of drums, trumpets, firecrackers and incense. The re-populated communities in Northern El Salvador usually have a celebration on the anniversary of the return of the villagers after the civil war.

Ethnic Cultures

Cultural events of the many and diverse ethnic groups of Central America are fascinating; if you get a chance to see one, don't miss it. In Honduras you may see a Garífuna music or dance performance. Garífuna Settlement Day (19 November) celebrates the arrival of the Garífuna in Belize in 1828. Panama's Cuna Indians do some wonderful music and dance, and there are many others.

Theatres

Some cultural events are a thrill, as much for the venue as for the event. Don't miss seeing the national theatres in San José (Costa Rica), San Salvador, and Panama City, and catch a performance of anything there if you can. These theatres, built around the turn of the century, have tiered seating and lush decorations of velvet and gold.

Plazas, Parks & Picnics

Go to places where the locals go and just hang out. In Tegucigalpa, be sure to spend one sunset sitting in the central plaza in front of the cathedral. People go in and out of the cathedral, catch buses on the sides of the plaza, stroll or rush past and watch the other people, while all around is the din of a thousand birdsongs in the trees. For a few cents you can get a little bag of crispy banana chips with lime, salt and hot sauce, and spend a sublime hour. Another place where locals

throng is Balboa Park, outside San Salvador. On a Sunday the townspeople come to stroll in the park, let the children play, hear wandering musicians, and eat in the many little outdoor cafés. In Guatemala, have a picnic at El Baúl near Santa Lucía Cotzumalguapa, where locals come to worship at a thousand-year-old Mayan idol. The Fuentes Georginas hot springs are an idyllic jungle retreat near Quetzaltenango, popular with Guatemalans but relatively untouched by tourists.

People

The people you meet and interact with should be the highlight of any journey, but this is especially true in Central America. As Rob writes in this book, 'Two major Costa Rican products worth sampling are the coffee, and the friendliness of the local people. Ticos always seem to have a ready smile and a helping hand for the inquisitive visitor.'

In Nicaragua, you can get an interesting discussion going with almost anyone you meet – just ask them to tell you about the revolution and the many events since then. Nicaraguans have a variety of opinions on political issues, all strongly held and eloquently expressed. The many regional and ethnic groups also provide a wealth of possibilities for conversation and cultural exchange. In El Salvador, especially in the re-populated communities, you can hear hair-raising stories about the recent civil war.

And then there are your fellow travellers. Most parts of Central America are not overrun with foreign travellers but those you do meet are often interesting and memorable characters.

Mayan Ruins

The stone pyramids, temples, hieroglyphics, statues, stone carvings, artwork and mysteriously abandoned cities of the Maya rank them as one of the great ancient civilisations of the world. Tikal in Guatemala is the most recognised and spectacular Mayan site in Central America, followed closely by Copán in Honduras.

Caribbean Islands

Several islands off the coast of Central America are wonderful for diving, snorkelling, swimming and fishing, with sunny, palm-lined, white sand beaches for lazing around on – you get the idea. The barrier reef off the coast of Belize is the second largest in the world, after Australia's Great Barrier Reef, and diving in the Caribbean has the extra attraction of the many shipwrecks from the colonial era.

In Belize, Caye Caulker and Ambergris Caye are the two islands to visit. Off the coast of Honduras, visitors go to all three Bay Islands but Roatán is most people's favourite. The San Blas Islands – over 365 of them spread along Panama's Caribbean coast almost all the way to Colombia – are famous for the Cuna Indians, who live here as they have for centuries.

Volcanoes

Central America has hundreds of volcanoes, some dormant and some active. In several places you can climb them and look right into the craters; some even have roads right up to the top to make it easy.

Two of the best volcanoes to see are the Poás and the Irazú, both in national parks in Costa Rica which can be visited as day trips from the capital. Also in Costa Rica is Volcán Arenal, in a state of constant eruption and easily visited from nearby Fortuna, and Rincón de la Vieja National Park, which is a little less accessible but great for hikers and campers.

El Salvador has a couple of magnificent volcanoes. Boquerón ('big mouth') is the deep crater of the San Salvador volcano which towers over the capital. It's a good day trip from the city. You can also climb the Izalco volcano in the west of the country, known for over a century as 'the lighthouse of the Pacific' and now a dark cone on the landscape.

In Nicaragua, the Volcán Masaya National Park can easily be visited as a day trip from Managua. In Guatemala, perhaps the most famous volcano views in all of Central America are those from Lake Atitlán and Antigua.

National Parks

Central America has some of the richest natural beauty on earth, with a variety of ecosystems including tropical rainforests, cloud forests, jungle river systems, lagoons and coastal wildlife preserves, just to name a few. Thousands of species of wildlife and tropical plants attract visitors, scientists and bird-watchers from all over the world. National parks have been set up in all the countries to preserve the natural wonders; Costa Rica's national park system is one of the most advanced in Latin America.

A few of the best-known national parks and nature reserves are listed below, but many others are also worth visiting (see the country chapters for details).

Costa Rica
  Corcovado, on the Osa Peninsula, Manuel Antonio, on the Pacific coast, Santa Rosa, on the northern Pacific coast, and Tortuguero, on the north-eastern coast, all have magnificent wildlife. Tortuguero is the most important nesting area in the western Caribbean for thousands of green turtles, and is also a great place for river trips to see exotic birds, crocodiles, caymans, lizards, monkeys, and frogs weighing up to a kg.
Guatemala
  Tikal is much more than just the ruins. Its national park covers the entire north and central portions of El Petén province.
Belize
  Mountain Pine Ridge, in the Maya Mountains.
Honduras
  La Tigra Cloud Forest, near Tegucigalpa; Río Plátano Nature Reserve, in the Mosquitia.
El Salvador
  Montecristo Cloud Forest, at the border of three countries, is shared by Guatemala, Honduras and El Salvador. It's most easily reached from the El Salvador side, but it's still very remote.
Panama
  Isla Barro Colorado, in the Panama Canal.

Lake Atitlán

This beautiful Guatemalan mountain lake is ringed by volcanoes and surrounded by villages of colourfully dressed traditional Maya Indians.

Antigua Guatemala

This is among the prettiest and best-preserved colonial cities in Latin America; Semana Santa is an unforgettable spectacle here.

Chichicastenango

This picturesque, traditional Guatemalan mountain town has been famous for centuries for its traditional Mayan market on Sunday and Thursday that sells colourful woven cloth, wooden masks (carved and painted, still used in fiestas), pottery and other crafts. Sololá, near Lake Atitlán, has a Friday market day just as colourful, but with fewer tourists.

Panama Canal

The more you learn about this engineering wonder, the more interesting it gets. It has locks where you can observe how the ships pass through, a national park and nature trail beside it, the Barro Colorado Island nature preserve right in it, the graceful Bridge of the Americas over it and an impressive line-up of ships waiting at either end.

Journeys

There are several famous journeys which you can make within Central America.

Río Dulce Boat Trip
This one-day trip, departing from Lívingston on Guatemala's Caribbean coast, passes up the Río Dulce through tropical jungle to El Golfete, a small gulf with a reserve for manatee (sea-cow) and other wildlife, and on to the Castillo de San Felipe, an old Spanish fort on the shores of the Lago de Izabal.

To Bluefields
In Nicaragua, you can make a relaxing two-day journey to Bluefields on the Caribbean coast: one day on land from Managua to Rama, a small river town on the Río Escondido, and the next day by boat down the river to Bluefields. Bluefields itself isn't so remarkable, but it's a fine trip to get there.

Río San Juan Río
San Juan is the river which forms the eastern part of the border between Nicaragua and Costa Rica. Boat trips on this river depart from San Carlos on Lake Nicaragua and travel through the jungle to Castillo Viejo, another old Spanish fort.

Darién Gap
The Interamerican (or Pan American) Highway does not go straight through from Central to South America. At the border between Panama and Colombia is an extensive wilderness area known as the Darién, where the road gives way to jungle – hence the name 'Darién Gap'. Travellers wishing to go overland all the way to (or from) South America can get through here on foot and river boat, as do the local Indians. It takes several days and is a demanding trip, not to be taken lightly; it is becoming more dangerous by the year.

WORK

Central America is an economically depressed region so there's little casual work available for travellers. Some of the countries have a huge unemployment problem among their own citizens, and wage levels are low by European or North American standards.

During the Sandinista years, Nicaragua hosted international volunteer brigades coming to pick coffee and do many other things to assist the revolution. This came to a halt with the 1990 change of government. If you're interested, though, the Sandinista organisations can still direct you to schools and other places where you can volunteer. Pay, if any, will not be much.

Various foreign aid organisations, such as the USA's Peace Corps and Australia's Overseas Service Bureau send volunteers to Central America. They usually want people with skills that are in short supply locally.

You're most likely to find work as an English teacher – the USA is of course influential in the region, and a lot of Central Americans go to the USA to work, so learning English is seen as desirable. Bilingual schools are becoming common in many places, or there may also be private tutoring work available.

In Panama you can sometimes get work as a linehandler (deckhand) on yachts passing through the canal. Last we heard, the pay was US$30 for two days of work, but you had to be lucky to land a job.

With the economy in most of Central America being what it is, it's far better to have enough money so you won't have to look for work there.

USEFUL ORGANISATIONS
Tourist Offices
There is a tourist office in the capital city of each country; some countries have them in outlying towns as well. They can be good sources of information for travellers.

Student Organisations
Student travel agencies are in the capital cities of Guatemala, Costa Rica and Panama. If you have your International Student Identity Card (ISIC) you can get discounted airfares, tours and other travel services, and find out about other student bargains. Discount fares are only offered on particular flights.

American Express
Amex has offices in all the Central American capital cities except Managua; Honduras has an office in San Pedro Sula as well. You can buy or cash American Express travellers' cheques, get cash advances on your card if you have one, get refunds on lost or stolen cheques, or have mail sent to you at all of these offices.

Hostelling International
HI membership is not particularly useful in Central America: there are very few hostels and they are no cheaper than other types of budget accommodation.

South American Explorers Club
This club has long been a favourite with travellers to South America, and due to repeated requests from members they have now branched out to cover Mexico and Central America as well. The club is probably the most comprehensive source of information for travellers to Latin America. They sell maps, books, and guide books and publish a free catalogue (members get a substantial discount). Members have submitted hundreds of practical reports on trips they've made, and these are also available. As a member, you can request information on virtually anything having to do with travelling in Latin America and, for a small copying fee, they will send you trip reports and articles culled from magazines, books and other sources.

The information available through the club covers a wide range of interests, not just 'exploring' in the sense of tramping through tropical jungles (though they have plenty on that). Other topics include scientific research, archaeology, working on digs, scuba diving, child adoption, retiring in Costa Rica, volunteer programmes, driving through Latin America, bicycling, discount airfares, and much more. They have information on Honduras' 'lost city' of Ciudad Blanca, and a whole file on the Darién Gap, including entries on bicycling through it and taking a motorcycle through it.

Other services include expedition planning; connecting with exploring or travelling partners; linking members for scientific and other purposes; and an informative quarterly magazine, the *South American Explorer*. Their offices in Lima (Peru) and Quito (Ecuador) offer other services, like luggage storage and mail holding.

Annual membership costs US$30 a year for an individual or US$40 for a couple. You can become a member or get more information about this nonprofit organisation by contacting its United States office, 126 Indian Creek Road, Ithaca, NY 14850, (☎ (303) 277-0488). The European agent is Bradt Publications, 41 Nortoft Road, Chalfont St Peter, Bucks, SL9 0LA, England, (☎ (0494) 873 478).

Latin American Bureau
Based in London, LAB is a nonprofit organisation engaged in research and publishing on Latin America and the Caribbean. It is a good source of information and has extensive library facilities (access by arrangement). Many useful publications are available by mail order; for the books catalogue write to Latin America Bureau, 1 Amwell St, London EC1R 1UL, UK (☎ (071) 278 2829).

ACCOMMODATION

In most Central American countries you can find a roof over your head for around US$2 to US$5 a night. Often the difference in price between a single and a double room is negligible, so if you're sharing with someone else the price per person can drop considerably. Since Latin American families tend to be large, most hotels also have at least a couple of rooms for up to six people, which are even cheaper per person.

The cheapest places to stay are the *hospedajes* or *casas de huespedes* (guest houses). Often, the same establishment will have a variety of rooms at a variety of prices, or rooms of widely varying quality all at the same price. There may be a choice of rooms – some with private bathrooms, others with a shared (communal) bathroom between several rooms. Some rooms may have one double bed while others have two singles, and so on. You might get in the habit of asking *¿Hay algo mas barato?* (Is there anything cheaper?), no matter what price you're quoted at first, since often the management will assume a foreign tourist would want the most expensive room in the house.

Always ask to see a room, or a few rooms, before you say you'll take one. This is a perfectly legitimate request. If you don't like the first room they show, you can ask to see another; if you don't like any of the rooms, you can thank them politely and go somewhere else. Don't be shy about asking to have the sheets changed if they look dirty.

This book describes rooms as being with or without private bath *(baño)*; this means there's a bathroom with a shower and (usually) a WC, but not an actual bathtub. Note that in many cheap hotels, used toilet paper should be placed in the receptacle provided, as the plumbing can't handle the paper.

Most places you'll stay will have cold water showers; this is what people in Central America use. You'll only see hot water showers in cool mountain areas, or in more expensive hotels catering to foreign tourists.

When you do run into a place with hot showers, the mechanism for heating the water might be an electric device attached to the shower head. Try not to touch anything metal while taking a shower under one of these things or you could get an electric shock. It probably won't kill you but it could be pretty uncomfortable.

As a rule, breakfast is *not* included in the overnight rate, though it may sometimes be available on the premises.

Camping

Camping as a form of cheap accommodation is not common in Central America. Going camping is not a local custom. Only in Costa Rica, where travellers and naturalists from all over the world camp in the many national parks, is the idea of camping starting to catch on with local people. In most of Central America, anyone with a tent, sleeping bag, and portable stove is an oddity.

It is recommended that you camp only in the official camping areas of national parks, in very remote wilderness areas, or on someone's land with their permission.

Most national parks in Central America do not have facilities for camping; you're allowed to camp, but you need to take care of all your own needs. In Costa Rica, some national parks have organised camping grounds. The facilities are nothing fancy by international standards, but they have drinking water on tap, fire pits, latrine toilets, cold showers and so on. They charge a very small nightly fee. Some national parks in Costa Rica and other countries offer basic accommodation, such as in dorms at the ranger station.

If you want to camp in a wilderness area, on an isolated stretch of beach, or somewhere there is no human settlement, be very aware of your surroundings. There are people living in some remarkably remote regions of Central America – you may think you're the only person around, but you could be quite mistaken. Also, if you camp in wilderness areas, be sure you know everything you should about local animals, insects, snakes etc, so that you won't have any unpleasant surprises.

In sparsely settled rural areas, it's best to

camp on private land, with the permission of the owner. The fact the owner knows you are there gives you some security. Around cities and towns, indoor accommodation is so cheap and so much safer that it's a much better idea to use it than to risk setting up camp.

Be sure not to leave anything you would mind losing in your tent when you're not there. People have been ripped off even when they're *in* their tent – someone quietly cuts the tent with a razor blade, sticks in their hand and gets what they can reach, and the sleeping camper finds out in the morning. This has happened more than once.

If you leave things unattended in your tent, you're asking to get ripped off. People might assume that you're a rich foreigner who can afford to leave your belongings unguarded, and can certainly afford to lose them.

FOOD

Lunch is the big meal of the day in Central America. It is also usually the cheapest meal; most cafés and restaurants offer a *comida corrida* set meal at lunchtime for around US$1 to US$3. Typically it will include rice, beans, eggs or meat (usually chicken, beef or fish), cheese or a dollop of cream, a small salad and a cold drink. It may also include soup and a dessert. If you make a habit of eating this for your main meal of the day, you can get by with a small snack in the morning and evening. This is the way the local people eat.

A *comida típica* or *comida corriente* is a typical meal of local food. It usually consists of a combination of the foods mentioned above, and it's usually the cheapest option on any menu. Other meals may cost double or more. Though great for nutrition and protein, and for filling you up, you might get very tired of rice and beans. Make a point of varying your diet.

Each country has its own specialities that can be a diet staple and a way to eat cheaply. In El Salvador, for example, a *pupusa*, a hot corn tortilla stuffed with sausage or cheese, costs about US$0.25, and two or three of them with a soft drink make a light meal. On the north coast of Honduras, the seafood soups and stews, made with coconut milk, are an inexpensive but magnificent dish. Make a point of trying the local food speciality wherever you are.

If you can't do without a taste of home, fast food joints – burger and pizza places – are found in most Central American cities nowadays.

Eating Cheaply

The cheapest places for a meal are the markets *(mercados)* in every city and town. You can buy ingredients to make your own meals with, you'll find fresh fruit, vegetable and tortilla stalls, and there are usually several small kitchens where food is cooked and served at tables. Take a look at the cleanliness of the kitchen before you sit down to eat, and beware of food that is cooked and then left out waiting to be served; bacteria can multiply quickly in a warm climate, and there may be many flies around. It is possible to eat in markets without ill effects in the places with good standards of cleanliness.

Meat in markets is especially suspicious if it is not properly refrigerated (it seldom is) and if flies can get to it. Many travellers avoid eating meat altogether, or eat it only at better restaurants where refrigeration and cleanliness standards are higher.

A step up from eating in markets is to eat in the small restaurants and cafés where the local people eat. They are not much more expensive than market kitchens, but the atmosphere is usually more peaceful. Chinese restaurants are found in every city and in most towns, and are another good option for eating fairly cheaply, as are bakeries. Apart from these, you have to get into the larger cities before you'll find much variety in food.

Vegetarian Food

Vegetarians have no trouble finding something healthy to eat in Central America. Beans and rice, or beans and tortillas, are good sources of protein, which can be supplemented with eggs and dairy products. If you want to avoid red meat, chicken is available everywhere, and seafood is also common. If you go into a restaurant, café or market stall and say you want a meal with no meat *(No como la carne* – I don't eat meat), it's very rarely a problem.

Most larger cities have vegetarian restaurants, with a wide variety of dishes. They often serve delicious food and they can be amongst the cheapest restaurants in town.

There's something of a movement in Central America to educate the public about the benefits of soy protein. It hasn't quite caught on yet, but you will usually find soy dishes served in vegetarian restaurants.

DRINKS

With the wide variety of tropical fruits found in Central America, you'll probably see kinds of fruit juice you haven't seen before; small fruit juice places are common and it's not unusual to see a dozen or even 20 kinds of fruit juices listed on the wall. If the local water isn't safe to drink, be sure that the juice doesn't get mixed with water. They often blend the juice with water or milk and sugar; eggs can be added for extra protein.

Soft drinks are found everywhere in Central America and make another alternative to drinking the water. Coca-Cola and Pepsi are the two big brands, but there is a host of local varieties and flavours, including apple, banana, grape, orange, strawberry, and pineapple. They are sometimes very sweet, tasting more like syrup or a chemical than fruit, but sometimes you'll hit on a good one. Some people delight in seeking out obscure and garish-coloured concoctions in the perverse hope of experiencing an eldritch, artificial mixture that even Dr Jekyll would hestitate to consume.

Asking for *agua mineral* (mineral water) or *soda* (soda water, club soda) might get you a cold drink without the sugar. Squeeze some lime into it and it's very refreshing.

A lot of coffee is grown in Central America, but the good stuff might not be as easy to find as you'd expect – a lot of places serve instant coffee!

As for alcoholic drinks, each country brews its own brand of beer, always costing much less than imported beers. Beer is very popular in Central America. Stronger spirits, including rum, are also manufactured in some countries. *Aguardiente*, also sometimes called *vino*, is a clear firewater made from sugar cane. It has an alcohol content even higher than vodka and will destroy your brain cells at a remarkable rate – it may make you feel like a rabid pit bull. Nonetheless it is popular stuff.

See the previous Health section for tips on how to drink water and milk without having it kill you. Never assume that water is OK to drink unless you know for sure it is safe. You can usually find bottled water for sale – or get into the habit of filling your own bottle when you stay somewhere that has a purified supply.

Getting There & Away

AIR

Central America has eight international airports: Guatemala City (Guatemala); Belize City (Belize); Tegucigalpa (Honduras); San Pedro Sula (Honduras); San Salvador (El Salvador); Managua (Nicaragua); San José (Costa Rica); and Panama City (Panama).

The island of Roatán, off the north coast of Honduras, also receives direct international flights but services are limited to one flight a week from Miami, one from New Orleans and one from Houston (all on TAN/SAHSA airline).

Buying a Ticket

What you pay for a ticket will depend on a number of factors, including: where you fly from; which airport you fly into; what travel agencies you have access to; whether you buy your ticket in advance; how long you want to stay; how flexible you can be with your travelling arrangements; what time of year you travel; how old you are (it can be to your advantage to be 26 years old or under); and whether you have an ISIC student card.

A good source of information about cheap fares is the travel section of newspapers, especially the Sunday edition.

Ticket Options

A number of different types of discount air tickets are available. The main ones are:

Advance Purchase These tickets must be bought at least 21 days in advance and are usually only available for return trips. There are minimum and maximum stay requirements (usually four and 180 days respectively), no stopovers are allowed and there are cancellation charges.

Excursion Fares These are priced midway between Advance Purchase and full economy fares. There are no advance booking requirements but a minimum stay abroad is often obligatory. Their advantage over Advance Purchase tickets is that you can change your bookings and/or stopovers without surcharge.

Point-to-Point This is a discount ticket offered on some routes to passengers who waive their stopover rights.

Stand-By This can be one of the cheapest ways of flying. You simply turn up at the airport or at an airline's city terminal, and if there are spare seats on the flight you want, you can get them at a considerable discount. It's become so common that many airline counters now have a special stand-by section. To give yourself the best possible chance of getting on the flight you want, get there early and have your name placed on the waiting list. It's first come, first served.

Round-the-World RTW tickets can be a cheap way of travelling. There are some excellent deals available and you may well pick one up for less than the cost of a return excursion fare. You must travel round the world in one direction and you cannot backtrack; you are usually allowed from five to seven stopovers.

Economy Class Symbolised by 'Y' on the airline ticket, this is the full economy fare. Tickets are valid for 12 months.

Budget Fares These can be booked at least three weeks in advance, but the actual travel date is not confirmed until seven days prior to travel. There are cancellation charges.

Open Jaw Returns This enables you to fly into one country and fly out from somewhere else, eg flying into Panama City on the first leg, and out of Guatemala City on the return leg. It needn't cost more than a normal budget return ticket and can meet the problematic 'onward ticket' requirement.

Courier Fares Some courier firms require people to accompany urgent documents through customs and will offer very low fares for someone to act as a 'courier'. You may be required to surrender all your baggage allowance for the use of the courier company (though you can take carry-on luggage) and there are sometimes dress codes. To Central America, courier flights are more common from the USA than from Europe.

Student Fares You can get up to 50% off regular fares by getting a student fare. Usually you must have an ISIC (International Student Identity Card) to get these fares, and buy your ticket from a special student travel agency.

Youth Fares Youth fares, for travellers aged 26 or under, are often available at student travel agencies, whether or not you're a student.

Miscellaneous Charges Order An MCO is a voucher which looks like an airline ticket but has no destination or date on it. It is exchangeable with any IATA airline for credit on a specific flight. Its principal use for travellers is as an alternative to an onward ticket, though MCOs are becoming less acceptable for this purpose. For entering those countries which demand an onward ticket (such as Costa Rica and Panama, and possibly Belize) it's obviously much more flexible than a ticket for a specific flight, but check first to be sure they will accept an MCO.

'Bucket Shop' Tickets In addition to the official ticket structure there are unofficially discounted tickets available through certain travel agents. These are known in the UK as 'bucket shops', and in the USA as 'consolidators'. The practice is more widespread in Europe than the USA.

These agencies have contracts with airlines, getting tickets at a discount in exchange for selling high volumes. Some agencies specialize in student and youth fares; others simply sell great volumes of cheap tickets. You go on regularly scheduled flights on regular airlines, but at a cheaper price.

Generally bucket shop tickets cost less than Advance Purchase tickets, but they don't have the advance purchase requirements or cancellation penalties (though they often have their own set of restrictions or cancellation penalties). Most bucket shops are well established and scrupulous, but it's not unknown for fly-by-night operators to set up office, take money and then disappear without issuing any tickets, or after issuing invalid or unusable tickets. Check carefully what you are buying before handing over the money.

Stopover Options Extensive stopover options are common on flights to and within Central America. Whether originating outside Central America or within it, air routes usually stop at more than one airport in the region. This often means you can visit extra countries at no extra cost; usually the fare is the same whether you pick up the next leg of the journey at a later date, or continue on immediately. If you would like to visit a few countries, be sure to check the stopover options before you buy your ticket.

Different airlines will have stopovers scheduled at different places, even on flights between the same two points. All the Central American national airlines schedule transfers through the international airports in their home countries, and may offer stopovers in other countries as well.

Onward Ticket Requirements

Costa Rica and Panama have onward ticket requirements; that is, you cannot enter the country unless you already have an onward ticket to another destination. This can be a return ticket, a ticket continuing to next country, or even a ticket out of a nearby country. It can be by any means of transport, whether by air or land; the object is simply to be sure that you won't stay in the country indefinitely.

An open jaw ticket (see Ticket Options) will suffice, but it may not be accepted by the border guards if you're travelling in the 'wrong' direction (eg ultimately flying from a point north but travelling south).

Many travellers have recently reported not being asked to show any sort of ticket when entering Costa Rica or Panama, but officially it is a requirement so you can't take it for granted. Belize also has an onward ticket requirement which is practically never enforced.

However, if you are aiming to fly into one of these countries but you don't have your ticket out, the airline will not even let you board the plane. If you arrive in a country and are refused entry, the airline is responsible for flying you back out again, so they make sure you have the necessary papers and tickets before you board.

A bus ticket is sufficient as an onward ticket, but if you are flying in, or if you are coming from Colombia into Panama, you won't have a chance to buy a bus ticket before you arrive so you'll need an airline ticket. If you do indeed want to fly out of the country, this is no problem. If, however, you plan to continue overland, the onward ticket requirement can be a drag.

If you have to buy a ticket simply to meet this requirement, consider getting a Miscellaneous Charges Order (MCO, see Ticket Options), which you can use later to buy a ticket for any flight with any IATA airline. Otherwise, you'll want to get a refund on the ticket, so check the refund policy carefully to be sure you can do it.

Sometimes there are restrictions on refunds, such as giving refunds only at the

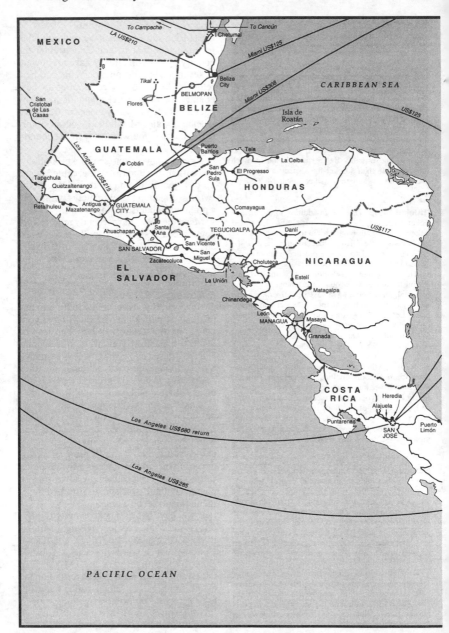

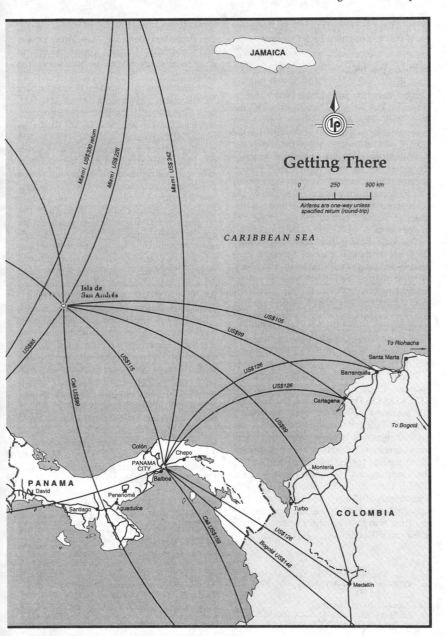

JAMAICA

Miami US$330 return
Miami US$226
Miami US$342

Getting There

0   250   500 km

Airfares are one-way unless
specified return (round-trip)

CARIBBEAN SEA

Isla de
San Andrés

US$105

US$99

US$85

Cali US$99

US$115

US$126

US$126

US$69

To Riohacha
Santa Marta
Barranquilla
Cartagena

To Bogotá

PANAMA
David

Colón
Chepo
PANAMA
CITY
Balboa

Penonomé

Santiago
Aguadulce

Montería

Turbo

COLOMBIA

Cali US$59

US$126

Bogotá US$148

Medellín

office where you bought the ticket – impossible if you're not going back that way.

To/From the USA

The major gateway cities for flights to Central America are Miami, New Orleans, Houston, Los Angeles, Washington DC and New York. Flights do originate from a few other places, but generally if you fly from the USA it will be through one of these airports.

The cheapest flights to Central America from the USA are those from Miami, though occasionally Houston has equivalent fares. If you're coming from some other part of the USA, your travel agent can arrange a discounted 'add-on' fare to get you to the city of departure.

The easiest way to get a cheap airfare from the USA is through a travel agency selling discounted fares. The Sunday travel sections of some major newspapers have advertisements from many such agencies; the *New York Times*, the *Los Angeles Times* and the *San Francisco Chronicle-Examiner* are all good ones to check. Even if you don't live in these areas, you can have the tickets sent to you by mail. Charter flights are another possibility.

Two of the most reputable discount travel agencies in the USA are STA Travel and CIEE/Council Travel Services. Both of these are international travel agencies with a number of offices throughout the USA and in other countries. Both started out as student travel agencies. While they both still specialize in student travel, honouring and selling the International Student Identity Card (ISIC), they also offer discount tickets to nonstudents of all ages. You can contact their national head offices to ask about prices, find an office near you, purchase tickets by mail or buy an ISIC card.

STA has offices in Los Angeles, San Diego, San Francisco, Berkeley, New York, Boston and Cambridge. Council Travel has offices in all these cities and in 20 others around the country.

When shopping around for tickets, be sure to ask about any restrictions on the fare, including cancellation fees, refund policies, replacement for lost tickets, advance purchase requirements, and the policies on making date or route changes once you've purchased the ticket. Tickets bought using an ISIC card carry an excellent free insurance policy and are among the cheapest tickets you'll find.

Airline prices change faster than the weather, so it's practically pointless to specify fares, especially with all the variables pertaining to the purchase of tickets. But to give you an idea, a return (round-trip) ticket to San José, Costa Rica, valid for up to 30 days, costs around US$680 from Los Angeles, US$430 from New Orleans, Houston or Dallas, and US$330 from Miami – these flights depart on Mondays to Thursdays and cost about US$50 more for weekend departures. If you want to stay more than 30 days you end up paying about US$200 more per ticket. Student and youth fares (under 26 years old) are usually US$30 to US$100 cheaper than the fares quoted above and don't necessarily have a 30-day limit – many are valid for up to a year. Fares to other destinations in Central America shouldn't vary too much: the standard TAN/SASHA one way fare from Miami to Guatemala City is US$308 as compared to US$342 for Miami to Panama City.

All the Central American airlines have offices in the USA, and they all have toll-free telephone numbers on which you can ask about their services from the USA or within Central America:

STA Travel
    5900 Wiltshire Boulevard, Los Angeles, CA 90036 (☎ 800-777-0112, (213) 937 8722; fax (213) 937-2739)
CIEE/Council Travel Services
    205 East 42nd St, New York, NY 10017 (☎ (212) 661-1414/50; fax (212) 972-3231)

Aviateca	(Guatemala)	800-327-9832
TAN/SAHSA	(Honduras)	800-327-1225
TACA	(El Salvador)	800-535-8780
Nica	(Nicaragua)	800-323-6422
LACSA	(Costa Rica)	800-225-2272
COPA	(Panama)	800-359-2672

Other airlines, such as American, Continental and United, have toll-free numbers and fly to Central America. Note that US airports charge an airport security tax which is not included in the ticket – about US$30 for international departures from Los Angeles and Miami, less from some other cities.

Travel Unlimited (PO Box 1058, Allston, MA 02134) publishes monthly listings of courier and cheap flights to Central America and many other countries. A one-year subscription costs US$25.

Don't overlook the possibility of flying to Mexico first and then travelling overland to Central America. Travel agents and discount houses frequently offer special airfares to Mexico, or package tours at very reasonable prices; ask if you can take the return portion of the ticket at a later date. You can sometimes buy a package tour for less than it would cost you for a simple airfare. Ask the travel agent if you can purchase it 'airfare only': this is sometimes possible, though the reduction may be minimal.

To/From Canada

Flights from Canada to Central America will transfer through one of the USA's gateway cities.

In Canada, the student and discount agency is Travel CUTS, which has about 20 offices around Canada. Once again, you don't have to be a student to use their services. Their national head office will give you the address of their office nearest you:

Travel CUTS
171 College St, Toronto, Ontario M5T 1P7
(☎ (416) 977-3703; fax (416) 977-4796)

As mentioned in the USA section, you can frequently get a good deal by buying a package tour to Mexico and then setting off from there.

To/From South America

Panama to Colombia The shortest and cheapest way to fly from Central to South America is between Panama and Colombia. The cheapest routes are between Panama City and Cartegena (with COPA), Barranquilla (COPA or LACSA) or Medellín (COPA or SAM), each costing under US$120 one way. Avianca has more expensive flights from Panama City to Bogotá (US$146) and Cali (US$159).

Another option, even cheaper, would be to fly from Panama City to Puerto Obaldía for US$21, cross by land to Capurganá on the Colombian side, and then fly on to Medellín (US$50), or take the boat to Turbo. See Along the North Coast, in the Darien Gap section of this chapter for details.

Via San Andrés If you're flying from anywhere in Central America besides Panama, the cheapest way to reach South America is to fly to Colombia via the town of San Andrés, on Isla de San Andrés, which is off the coast of Nicaragua though it belongs to Colombia. San Andrés has an international airport and is a hub for flights between South America, Central America and the USA.

There are direct flights between San Andrés and Tegucigalpa (TAN/SAHSA, US$117 one way), Panama City (COPA, US$115 one way), Guatemala City (MM, US$125) or San José, Costa Rica (LASCA, US$85 one way). From other Central American airports, you'll have to transfer at one of these places, usually San José, which will involve paying for two separate legs of travel. Tan/SAHSA flights from San Pedro Sula go via Tegucigalpa (US$110).

It is cheaper to buy two separate tickets (one from Central America to San Andrés and another on a Colombian airline from San Andrés to mainland South America) than it is to buy one ticket all the way through. The same applies in the opposite direction, coming up from South America. Avianca, Sam and Aces have flights from San Andrés to all the major Colombian cities for around US$100, which you can buy from Central America. You might get a cheaper fare if you wait until you arrive at San Andrés to buy your ticket.

Once you're at San Andrés, there are a couple of other cheap ways to get to the mainland. Aerosucre has two or three cargo flights weekly, mainly to Barranquilla, but also to Medellín, Bogotá and some other places. They usually take passengers and charge about half the commercial fare. Enquire in the Aerosucre office near the passenger terminal. It's in the green-roofed building next to the building with the Marlboro cowboy advertisement on top. The entrance is on the right side, not at the front.

Another way is to fly with Satena. They have irregular noncommercial passenger flights to Bogotá, usually around once a month, and they're very cheap: it was US$60, and though the price will probably rise, it's still a lot less than the commercial airlines. The Satena flights are heavily booked, but there is always a chance – just go to the airport before the flight and try your luck.

Cargo ships run from San Andrés to Cartagena, and they sometimes take passengers. The trip takes two to three days and costs about US$35, including food.

Colombia has an onward ticket requirement wherever you enter the country, including San Andrés. This is a hassle if you want to continue to the mainland on a domestic Colombian airline. Consequently San Andrés has something of a black market in the return portions of tickets from Central America. Travellers buy a return ticket from Central America to San Andrés, then sell the return portion to another traveller coming up from South America. The return portions of the tickets are usually sold for about half their face value, and the buyers will obviously expect you to cooperate in getting them on the plane. Remember that both Costa Rica and Panama also have onward ticket requirements to contend with.

You can't get a refund on return portions of tickets from the airline offices in San Andrés, but you may be able to in their offices on the mainland. If you're planning to get a refund on the return portion later on, check the refund policy carefully when you buy your ticket.

San Andrés This is a pleasant little island covered with coconut palms: not a bad place to hang around for a few days while you're making your travel arrangements. Because it's a transport hub, a lot of tourists come through, and it has banks and places to stay. Panama, Costa Rica, Honduras and Guatemala all have consulates here. The island has only one town, also called San Andrés but locally known as 'El Centro'.

The town has a pretty good beach and there are a few other things to see and do around the island. You can try snorkelling on Johnny Cay; Acuario Cay and Haynes Cay off the east coast are even better and not as crowded. Take buses or a bicycle around the island to visit the villages and see the blowhole.

The best place to stay for those on a shoestring is the *Hotel Restrepo*, on the opposite side of the runway from the airport terminal; rooms are US$3 per person and they also serve meals. It's a popular congregating place for travellers.

To/From Australasia

Coming from Australia or New Zealand, the cheapest and easiest way is to fly first to Los Angeles or Miami, then fly south from there. They are both good places to get cheap flights to Central America, or you could go overland, but it's a long way south through Mexico to Central America.

STA Travel is one agency which has student and youth airfares, and it's worth checking their deals. You don't have to be a student to use their services. In Australia, STA has offices in Adelaide, Brisbane, Canberra, Melbourne, Perth, and Sydney. Contact their national headquarters for the address of a branch close to you:

STA Travel
    220 Faraday St, Carlton, Melbourne, Victoria 3053 (☎ (03) 3474711; fax (03) 3470608)

In New Zealand, STA has offices in Auckland, Christchurch, Dunedin, Hamilton, Palmerston North, and Wellington. Again, contact the national office for the address of a branch close to you:

STA Travel
    1st floor, 10 High St, Auckland (☎ (09) 309-9723; fax (09) 309-9829)

To/From the UK

The cheapest fares to Central America are from London, where there are numerous 'bucket shops' selling discount tickets. Their prices are well advertised in publications such as *Time Out* and the *Evening Standard*, both widely available in London. The best choice is in *TNT*, London's free weekly magazine for entertainment, travel and jobs, available at some London underground stations or ring (☎ (081) 244 6529 for details of the nearest pick-up points. The *Sunday Times* has the best choice of the national newspapers. Before you buy a ticket, note whether the ticket vendor is 'bonded' (ie affiliated with ABTA, ATOL or AITO), which gives you protection if they go bankrupt.

Apart from the bucket shops, there are four other agencies worth trying. STA Travel and Council Travel are both excellent organisations specialising in both student and budget travel, but many of the cheapest fares are only available to students, academics and those under 26 years old. Trailfinders has low fares and regional branches in Manchester, Bristol and Glasgow. Journey Latin America (JLA) specializes in travel from the UK to Central and South America, and they're particularly helpful. They can make travel arrangements over the phone, and can arrange itineraries for both independent and escorted travel. JLA and Trailfinders both produce a free magazine.

STA Travel
    74 Old Brompton Rd, London, SW7 3LQ (☎ (071) 937 9962)
    117 Euston Rd, London NW1 2SX (☎ (071) 465 0484)
Council Travel
    28a Poland St, London W1 (☎ (071) 437 7767)
Trailfinders
    194 Kensington High St, London W8 7RG (☎ (071) 938 3939)
JLA
    14-16 Devonshire Rd, Chiswick, London W4 2HD (☎ (081) 747 3108; fax (081) 742 1312)

There is a great variety of fares to Central America, many with complicated restrictions, conditions and dates of availability. The following sample fares from London are the cheapest ones quoted by JLA for each route, but they are subject to restrictions and they can change at any time, so you'll have to check yourself to find a cheap fare that suits your plans.

	One way	Return
Guatemala City	£325	£503
Belize	£301	£503
Managua	£341	£503
Panama City	£325	£503

The cheapest airline is usually Continental, on which low-season, mid-week return fares to Central America can be as low as £469; an overnight stop in Houston may be necessary, with attendant hotel costs. Iberia is more expensive, but the hotel is included if a stopover is necessary in Madrid.

To/From Europe

In mainland Europe, Amsterdam has lots of bucket shops, and is probably the best place to buy tickets to Central America. Frankfurt, Brussels and Athens are also places to look for cheap fares. Depending on where you are, it may be cheaper to fly to London first and then seek a cheap ticket. Apart from the bucket shops, STA and Council Travel have offices in Europe:

STA Travel
    c/o Voyages Decouvertes, 21 Rue Cambon, 75001 Paris, France (☎ 142-61-00-01)
    c/o Srid Reisen, Berger Strasse 118, 6000 Frankfurt 1, Germany (☎ 49-69-43-01-91)
Council Travel
    31 Rue St Augustin, 75002 Paris, France (☎ 142-66-20-87)
    18 Graf Adolf St, 4000 Dusseldorf 1, Germany (☎ 211-32-90-88)

At the time of writing, the best deal from Germany was with United Airlines: Frankfurt to San José return was DM1420 (US$830). This was a limited offer; the next cheapest were Iberia and Continental. Surprisingly, although Iberia's flights from

Europe are routed through Madrid, it is not necessarily cheaper to commence your journey in that city; fares starting from London are usually lower. In Italy, KLM offered the lowest fares.

Aeroflot, the Soviet airline, flies from Moscow to Managua (Nicaragua), with a stopover in Havana, Cuba. All flights from Europe transfer through Moscow; the average price starting in Western Europe is around US$850 return. However, you may have to spend one or more nights in Moscow waiting for your flight, entailing staying at a specified hotel which costs around US$50 a night! The flight is also long and uncomfortable. It might still be worthwhile price-wise if you're planning a long trip in Central America: tickets are valid for one year, rather than the usual three months for the cheapest tickets on other airlines. However, think carefully before choosing to fly with Aeroflot, as safety standards have been very poor of late.

LAND
To/From the USA & Canada
Coming to Central America overland from the USA or Canada means coming through Mexico. It's a long trip that will take at least several days, whether you do it by bus, train or driving. If you fall in love with Mexico, though, it could take months to cross that fascinating country. (See Lonely Planet's *Mexico – a travel survival kit.*)

Bus Mexico has an excellent system of long-distance buses, both first and second class. Often there's not much difference between the two. Buses cover Mexico all the way from the US border to the borders of Guatemala and Belize, and from there you change buses and continue into Central America.

Train Mexico has an extensive rail transport system, but the quality of the trains ranges from some of the best in the world to some of the worst. Take the best class of train you can afford in Mexico, and avoid those in Yucatán. Trains run as far south as Tapachula, on the Guatemalan border.

Bringing your own Vehicle If you bring your own vehicle from the USA, you'll have to obtain Mexican car insurance and a permit to bring your vehicle into the country. These are easily obtained at the border.

If your vehicle uses unleaded fuel, you will have to change the catalytic converter, so it can run on regular (see the Getting Around chapter for details). In Mexico and Central America, the only fuels commonly available are regular leaded, super leaded, and diesel (though unleaded is becoming increasingly available in Mexico). Diesel is cheaper and is therefore the favourite in this region. If you're buying a vehicle in the USA to take you to Mexico and Central America, consider buying one with a diesel engine.

To/From South America via the Darién Gap
The Interamerican Highway does not go all the way through Panama, but terminates in the middle of the jungle in a vast wilderness region called the Darién. There is, therefore, a transport gap between Central and South America, known to travellers as the Darién Gap.

Notwithstanding the occasional recent announcements by Panamanian and international authorities, who have promised funding and other support for its extension, it is extremely unlikely that the Highway will be pushed through the Darién. In addition to ecological concerns, Panama is extremely fearful of foot-and-mouth disease in cattle, which is presently limited to South America.

Darién is a region of pristine tropical rainforest which UNESCO has declared a World Heritage Site. It is also designated a Biosphere Reserve. Panama has established a national park, Parque Nacional Darién, to protect both the natural and human resources of the region. This park covers 90% of the border between Panama and Colombia, and at 5750 sq km it is the largest national park in all of Central America. On the Colombian side, that government has also established a national park for protection of the wilderness, the Parque Natural Nacional Los Katíos.

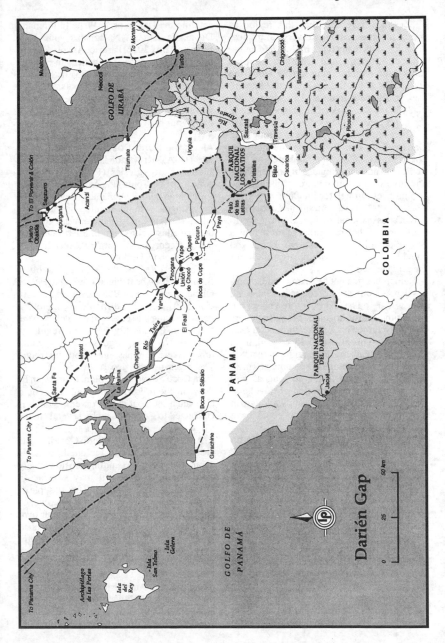

Darién Gap

Scientists have described this region as one of the most naturally diverse in tropical America, with many types of flora and fauna. Chocó, Emberá, and Uainana peoples inhabit the region, living mostly along the rivers. The Cuna Indians are better known; they still have a traditional lifestyle, especially in the San Blas archipelago and along the north coast of the Darién.

There are basically two ways through the Darién Gap. The first skirts the northern coast via the San Blas archipelago and Puerto Obaldía, making use of boat services and involving a minimum of walking. The second goes through the jungle from Yaviza (Panama) to the Río Atrato in Colombia's Los Katíos national park, and you have to walk most of the way. Either of these routes can be done in as little as a week, but you should allow twice this time, especially for the jungle route.

Remember that both Panama and Colombia demand onward tickets, so get one, and your visa if you need one, before you set out from either north or south. Many travellers have been turned back at the borders for lack of an onward ticket, especially coming from Colombia to Panama. Rumour has it that you *might* be able to get into Colombia at Turbo without an onward ticket, so long as you have an impressive collection of travellers' cheques. Don't count on it – it's a long trip back to buy a ticket that you could have easily bought in the first place.

Take dried food with you, especially on the jungle route. There are very few places where you can buy food. Be sure you have plenty of water and drink lots of it – this is a very hot region. You'll need to carry some drinking water, and be equipped to purify more as required. A compass and a machete are essential equipment on the jungle route. Whichever way you go, some fluency in Spanish is desirable – almost essential – to minimalise the risk of getting lost and to avoid misunderstandings with the locals in this isolated area.

If using the jungle route, you are required by Panama's environmental agency, Inrenare, to obtain written permission before entering the Darién park. Write to Inrenare, Depto. de Parques Nacionales y de Vida Silvestre, Box 2016, Paraiso, Ancón, Republic of Panama, or visit its offices in Panama City (☎ 32-4325, fax 32-4083) or El Real. Inrenare will arrange guides, boats, and pack animals as needed; lodging is free, whether you use their guides or not, but you must still bring your own food.

Along the North Coast Thanks to Carlton Lee (USA), Krzysztof Dydynski (Poland), Juan Amado Iglesias (Panama), Hernán Araúz of Eco-Tours (Panama), and various Colombian and Panamanian travellers for providing us with information on this route, which starts at Colón (Panama) and goes via the San Blas archipelago to Puerto Obaldía, then to Capurganá (Colombia), Acandí, Titumate and on to Turbo.

The first leg of the journey involves finding a cargo boat which is going to Puerto Obaldía, via the San Blas archipelago, from Colón. This is not difficult, as merchant boats carrying passengers and supplies to the San Blas Islands ply the route regularly. Guardia Nacional cargo ships also sometimes take a few passengers on this route. The boats usually depart around midnight from Coco Solo pier in Colón, to arrive in El Porvenir the following morning. You could also catch the boat at El Porvenir, which is connected to Panama City by several flights a day.

A boat from Colón to Puerto Obaldía costs around US$25, meals included. It takes about five days, depending on how many stops the boat makes; it may stop at 48 islands along the way, staying for a couple of hours or so at each one, so you'll get a chance to visit many small islands. Make your own sleeping arrangements on deck – a hammock is very useful. You might also spend a night or two on islands along the way.

It is also possible to fly between Panama City and Puerto Obaldía; it costs US$42 round trip with Ansa airline (☎ 26-7891, 26-6898 in Panama City), twice as much with Aerotaxi. Puerto Obaldía is a small tropical waystation for traffic between Colombia and

Panama. It has good beaches, palms and clear blue sea. If you're on a tight budget you can sleep on the beach south of the town, though there are a few hotels if you'd prefer. If you're heading south you need to check with the immigration inspector here for an exit stamp or, if you're heading north, an entry stamp. Make sure you have all the necessary papers, visas and onward tickets, as well as sufficient funds.

There are occasional launches and boats from Puerto Obaldía to Capurganá and Acandí in Colombia, but they're infrequent and quite expensive – it's about US$17 for the one-hour trip. Some of these boats, which may be crowded and unsafe, are used by drug and other smugglers. It's better to walk. There's a well-defined (though often muddy) trail all the way to Acandí, and it's almost impossible to get lost. If in doubt, ask somebody en route. The region is inhabited and you will pass many farmhouses along the way.

The first part of the trail goes from Puerto Obaldía to La Miel, the last Panamanian village, a two-hour walk away. From there you climb a small hill, pass the border marker on the top and descend to Sapzurro – all that in half an hour.

Sapzurro is a small, pleasant fishing village, beautifully set on the shore of a bay. There are a couple of hospedajes and several restaurants, and a Panamanian consulate – your last chance to get a visa for Panama if you're heading north. From Sapzurro the footpath climbs again, then drops to the next coastal village, Capurganá. This portion can be easily done in 1½ hours. Capurganá is the most touristy place of the whole area and gets pretty crowded from mid-December to the end of January (the Colombian holiday season), but at other times it's quiet and easy-going. It has a choice of budget hotels and restaurants and is a pleasant place to hang around for a day or two. If you want to get out quickly, you can fly from Capurganá to Medellín for about US$50.

From Capurganá you can take a boat to Acandí (US$6, one hour) and continue on another boat to Turbo. If you are not in a hurry, though, it's worthwhile to continue from Capurganá to Acandí on foot. It's a lovely walk; allow yourself the best part of a day.

Start along the beach and follow the path, which doesn't always stick to the coast. Sometimes it goes a bit inland, climbing the hills to avoid the high rocky cliffs. An hour's walk brings you to Aguacate, which is nothing more than several huts with a local-style house functioning as a hospedaje. Follow the footpath for a bit more than an hour to Rufino, a cluster of houses (one was painted a conspicuous yellow). From there the path continues inland. It climbs the extensive coastal ridge, passes it, and drops into the valley of the Acandí River (another hour to get to this point). Follow the river downstream; it is a leisurely three-hour walk to Acandí. The path does not always follow the river and includes several crossings; be prepared to wet your shoes. This part of the track is often muddy.

Acandí is a fair-sized village with a church, two or three hotels, a few cafés and several small *tiendas* selling mostly bottled and canned goods of limited variety and quantity. Some of the shops here will change your dollars into Colombian pesos, and will probably give a better rate than you'll get in Capurganá, or even in Turbo, your next stop.

From Acandí there is a launch every morning to Turbo via Titumate. The journey takes three to four hours and costs around US$10. The boat service is only reliable during the first six months of the year, when the sea is not too rough; at other times you might have to wait for good weather before the boat will go. It is never a very smooth journey though; be prepared to get soaked through unless you have waterproof clothing. Anything you want to keep dry should be wrapped up in plastic. Try to get one of the seats in the rear of the boat.

Capurganá and Acandí are also jumping off points for inland, east-west trekking through Darién to the Interamerican Highway.

Turbo is an uninteresting and unsafe port on the Golfo de Urabá. There's a variety of fresh and canned foods available, so if you're heading north then this is a good place to stock up.

Whether you're heading north or south, you need to call at the Policía Distrito Especial, two blocks down from the harbour in Turbo, to obtain an exit or entry stamp. It's very informal and quick as long as your papers are in order. Travellers have been fined for entering Colombia via Turbo without an entry stamp, intending to get one in Cartagena.

There's no bank in Turbo to change either cash or travellers' cheques, but many shops and the more expensive hotels will exchange cash dollars. They usually give a poor rate so only change enough to get to Medellín or Cartagena. If you need to spend the night in Turbo, try the *Hotel Marcela*, one block from the church, with comfortable rooms for US$2.50 per person. If they're full you could try the *Turbo* next door or the *El Viajero* just round the corner, also around US$2.50 per person.

There are several buses daily from Turbo to Medellín (US$7, 13 hours). If you head for Cartagena, take a jeep from the market square to Montería (US$7, seven hours) and then continue by bus to Cartagena.

There is no Panamanian consulate in Turbo, so if you're heading north, get your visa beforehand if you need one. You still have a chance to get one in Sapzurro, but if the consulate there is closed for some reason, you will have to go a long, long way back to Medellín or Barranquilla. Be sure you already have your onward ticket to enter Panama as well; many travellers have been forced to backtrack to Medellín to get one.

The whole journey between Colón and Turbo can be done in as little as a week, but you could easily take double that or even longer, especially if you have to wait around for boats between Colón and Puerto Obaldía, or if you stay a while somewhere on the way. The San Blas archipelago, Sapzurro and Capurganá are the most pleasant places to break the journey.

Through the Jungle The original informa-tion about this journey comes from Lilian Wordell (Ireland), updated with recent advice from, amongst others, David Wilson (England), eleven Peruvians, two Swiss bikers, and a Panamanian who has made the journey many times.

Warning In addition to such natural hazards as high rivers and mudslides (the Darién is a zone of serious seismic activity), the human dangers to the low-budget traveller in the area must not be underestimated. Though the Darién is still a wilderness, it is not unpopulated; there are a fair number of people crossing the region by small boat and on foot.

The indigenous inhabitants get around on the trails and by river, and there's a mine in the Darién to which miners walk from both the Panamanian and Colombian sides. The mine is controlled by the Panamanian government environmental agency, ANCON. Many freelance miners are undocumented immigrants, and are subject to arrest by the indigenous Cuna authorities. There are also a lot of Peruvians heading north to the USA, as well as the smugglers of drugs and other contraband. As a result, the route is getting more dangerous.

Indispensable incidentals include as good a knowledge of Spanish as possible, a compass, and a sharp machete, as well as some source for replenishment of salt lost from the body.

Several people who have made the journey recently definitely recommend that foreign travellers hire a guide, not just to find the right trail (though this is part of it) but also for safety. Inrenare will arrange for a guide, as noted above. In addition, local guides should be available as far south as Boca de Cupe. The Eco-Tours firm (☎ 36-3076, 36-3575, 36-4494; fax 26-3550, Apartado 465) in Panama City, is worth a preliminary visit. If they do not arrange a guide they will certainly help a prospective traveller through the area to get oriented. An unaccompanied foreigner travelling in this area might be assumed to be either a drug trafficker or a US Drug Enforcement Agency operative. There are also bandits who prey on jungle travellers.

In addition, the Darién has become a major area of activity for guerrillas operating across the frontier from the neighbouring Colombian province of Antioquia. In January 1993, three US Protestant missionaries, who had been working among the Cuna and who were known for their aid to travellers through the region, were kidnapped from the town of Púcuro by Colombian guerrillas, reportedly affiliated with the Revolutionary Armed Forces (FARC). Ten months later they still had not been ransomed or released. The guerrillas are said to have a camp in the Altos de Limón mountain area on the Panama-Colombian border, due east of Púcuro overlooking the trail from Yaviza to Palo de las Letras, and to dominate the entire area.

Local Indian guides are reportedly willing to conduct travellers to but not across the Colombian border, for fear of kidnapping by guerrillas for forced labor. In the most recent disturbing incident, a young Canadian hiker who attempted to cross the Darién alone disappeared, and his body was found after a search. He was shot to death, apparently by guerrillas.

Having said all that, many people complete this route without major problems; those who have done so describe it as a unique and rewarding experience.

When to Go This trip should only be undertaken in the dry season, from December to March (or possibly in July and August if little rain has fallen) and never without preparation. The rest of the time the trails are almost impossibly waterlogged and the rivers are raging torrents full of broken trees and the like. On the other hand, towards the end of the dry season the rivers get low and it's often difficult to find boats.

Ideally you need camping gear and decent hiking boots, but otherwise keep your baggage to a minimum. You might make it in eight days but it's best to plan for a longer trek. A tent isn't necessary according to quite a few travellers who have done the trek.

What *is* necessary is a light pack. The total cost won't be any less than flying from Panama to Colombia, by the time you add up the cost of buses, boats, accommodation, food and a guide, but the experience will be incomparable.

From Panama City there are two ways to start the trek: via Yaviza or via El Real.

To Boca de Cupe via Yaviza You get to Yaviza from Panama City by bus on the Interamerican Highway (US$14, 10 hours). It's a long, hard bus trip on a dirt road, and even the bus trip can only be accomplished in the dry season; the rest of the year the last stretch of the road becomes impassable and the bus can't make it all the way to Yaviza, but only as far as Canglón (US$11, eight hours). Alternatively you can fly with Parsa (☎ 26-3883, 26-3803 in Panama City) between Panama City and Yaviza (Tuesday, Thursday, and Saturday, US$33.50 one way). There's one hotel in Yaviza.

To continue from Yaviza you first have to trek to Unión de Chocó on the Río Tuira, which will take about a day. To get there, first cross the river by canoe (US$0.25), then walk 1½ hours to Pinogana. Wade through the river here or cross by dugout (US$1) and then walk for three to four hours along a jeep track to Aruza. Chocó Indians live in the area, and you'll encounter quite a few along the way. Cross the river at Aruza by wading through it again and then walk for about 45 minutes to Unión de Chocó. From there, continue on the same side of the river to Yape, Capetí and finally cross the river to Boca de Cupe. It's a very pleasant walk which will take about five hours. Alternatively, you may be able to find a boat going from Yaviza to Boca de Cupe. It never hurts to ask around.

To Boca de Cupe via El Real You get to El Real from Panama City by banana boat. The boats depart from the Muelle Fiscal and take between 12 and 36 hours. They cost about US$12 per person, including the simple meals which are provided on board. There's no fixed schedule for these boats but, if possible, try to get a passage on a larger and more comfortable one.

The port at El Real is some distance away from the town itself, so you first have to go about five km upstream to the Mercadero, where you pick up a boat to Boca de Cupe. The best place to inquire about these is the general store; most provisions arrive by boat so the owner is generally clued up about what's going on. Prices for the two to four-hour boat trip to Boca de Cupe are negotiable, as are all the boat trips on this route, but should be no more than around US$5 per person. You can camp either at the port or at the Mercadero.

Boca de Cupe to Púcuro Boca de Cupe is the last town of any size you'll see until you're near the end of the trail. It's here that you must get your Panama exit stamp from a shop alongside the river. If you're heading north, you'll need an entry stamp from the same place. You can stay overnight with a local family and buy food here. Try María's place, which also serves meals.

From Boca de Cupe you must find a boat going to Púcuro. You may have to wait two or three days for a boat, then it's a five or six-hour trip (US$30). Or you may be able to arrange a motorised dugout via the school-teacher (three hours, US$7.50 per person). Púcuro is an interesting place, and the first Indian village you'll encounter. However, as noted, it is also the site of recent guerrilla activity.

When the river is high you'll find yourself landing right at the village but otherwise it takes about half an hour to walk there. Ask someone where you can stay for the night; the village chief may let you sleep in the meeting hall for a fee (with all the village taking an interest in you), but there are other possibilities. If you want to keep moving, ask where the trail to Paya starts.

Púcuro to Paya The 18-km walk to Paya, the next village, can be done in a day and involves four river crossings (all the rivers are fordable). You need to look hard for the trail after the third crossing. There are good camping sites just before the third crossing and just after the last. Guides can be hired in Púcuro for this section of the trail for about US$20, but don't pay in advance. The walk should take you six to nine hours.

When you get to Paya you will probably meet the chief's son, who will have you taken either to the military barracks about two km away, where you can stay for the night but where no food is available, or to the house of any gringo who is staying there on a study programme.

Paya was once the site of the Cuna 'university' to which Cunas from all over the area came to study the traditional arts of magic, medicine and history. It fell on hard times about 100 years ago as European technology and European diseases gradually penetrated the area, but it's still a very interesting place. Be discreet with your camera, and ask permission before you take photographs. In Paya there's a foot-and-mouth disease control station where, if you're coming up from Colombia, your baggage will be inspected and anything made of leather, or even vaguely resembling leather, will be dipped in a mild antiseptic to kill any pathogens.

Paya to Cristales The next part of the trail goes to Cristales via Palo de Letras (the border marker between Panama and Colombia). It is the most difficult stage and usually takes one or two days, though you can do it in eight to 10 hours under the right conditions. It's also the part where you're most likely to get lost, so you'll appreciate a guide. In 1992, a party of six were lost here for nine days, according to rangers.

The first part of the trail to Palo de Letras is uphill and well marked; a British Army expedition came through here in 1972 and cut the trail, which is still about three metres wide. Local Indians use it constantly so you'll have no difficulty following it. From the border marker it's downhill about 30 km to Cristales; it should take about seven hours. There are several river crossings where the trail becomes indistinct or confusing. After the last crossing you come into cultivated areas and must keep to the left whenever the trail forks. Quite a few travellers have had adventures (some would call them ordeals) near the end of this leg of the journey, when they got lost at night and had to wade down the river for an hour to Cristales.

Cristales is the next stop but you're advised to carry on another half an hour downstream to the headquarters of the Parque Natural Nacional Los Katíos, where bed and board is available at very reasonable rates. At the Cristales ranger station, shout to be taken across the river, which is quite deep, to the HQ itself. The staff are very friendly and helpful. They may let you sleep on the porch free of charge.

Cristales to Turbo The last part of the trip from Cristales to Turbo is by a combination of motorised dugouts and banana boats. If the park workers are going for supplies in Turbo then it can be done in one haul, but if not you'll first have to find a boat to Bijao and then, possibly, another to Travesía, also known as Puente América, on the Río Atrato. A regular boat from Cristales to Bijao will cost about US$40; you can walk instead in five hours but getting lost is highly likely unless you hire someone to guide you. The best person to ask about boats in Bijao is the store owner. You may have to wait a few days before a boat turns up. Hiring a motorised dugout from Bijao to Travesía should cost about US$45 (three hours). There is a shop in Travesía with expensive food, soft drinks and beer.

Once at Travesía you'll have no difficulty finding transport to Turbo. There are fast passenger motorboats coming through from Riosucio every morning, which continue on to Turbo (US$6, two hours). If you decide to take one of the cargo boats which ply up and down the Río Atrato, allow a whole day for the journey; your boat may stop en route several times to load, unload, fix the engine, fish, rest, fix the engine, visit the family, fix the engine, or for a hundred other unexpected reasons. For information about Turbo see the previous section, Along the North Coast.

The out of print *Backpacking in Mexico &* *Central America* by Hilary Bradt & Rob Rachowiecki would help on the jungle route if you can find a second-hand copy.

SEA

If you don't mind roughing it, there are many possibilities for getting to/from Central America by sea. Having your own yacht would, of course, make it much easier, but there are other options.

On the Caribbean side, boats are continually coming and going between all the Central American countries, the Caribbean islands, Mexico, the USA, and the north coast of South America. Though there are virtually no regular passenger liners, you might get on to a cargo ship, fishing boat, yacht, or other vessel.

Sailing times are short in this region – for example, it's only a two-day voyage from New Orleans to the north coast of Honduras – so it's possible to make informal arrangements to get a ride on a boat. These informal arrangements require luck and good timing, and they are difficult to plan in advance. Probably the best strategy is simply to ask around the docks at every port you come to. You may come up with nothing, but it's worth a try. Also try at yacht marinas: boat owners may have space for a hitch-hiker or willing helper.

There is less sea traffic along the Pacific coast. Most of the boats are larger vessels on defined schedules, so they're less willing to pick up the stray traveller.

The Panama Canal, one of the shipping crossroads and bottlenecks of the earth, is a sure place to encounter sea traffic. It's not easy to make contact with the boats however; they simply pass through the canal and usually don't even pull up to a dock. Most are huge ocean-going vessels, but yachts pass through the canal on Tuesdays and Thursdays. Check at the yacht clubs on both sides of the canal if you want to contact a passing yacht.

If you arrive or depart from any country by sea, be sure to have your exit/entry stamps correctly registered into your passport at the first opportunity.

SHIPPING A VEHICLE

If you are in a private vehicle and want to travel between Central and South America, you will have to figure out a way to get the vehicle around the Darién Gap.

Usually this means shipping it from Panama to Colombia. This is neither cheap nor easy, but people do it. There is a lot of cargo traffic between the two countries so you can get almost anything shipped. It will involve a lot of paperwork on both sides, and will require investigation, time, money and patience. Basically your choices are shipping the vehicle by boat or by air. Air cargo planes do have size limits, but a normal car, or even a Land Rover, can fit. If you have a motorcycle, air is probably the easiest option. You may be able to get a special rate for air cargo if you are also flying with the same airline; you could start by asking the cargo departments of the airlines that fly there (like COPA), or at the cargo terminal at Tocumen international airport in Panama City. Travel agents can sometimes help.

Going to mainland Colombia, the options are the port of Buenaventura on the Pacific side, or either Cartagena or Barranquilla on the Caribbean side. Most people find it easier to go to a Caribbean port. To find a cargo boat heading that way, go to the docks in Colón and ask what ships are going. You'll come up with many options, some better than others.

Smaller cargo vessels depart from Coco Solo pier in Colón. They may offer you the best price, but may not be able to help you with the paperwork you need to enter Colombia. These smaller vessels are sometimes contraband boats, and their service is probably the most risky and uncomfortable, but also the cheapest. Prices are very negotiable; they might start out asking US$1500 and come down to half that. You might feel it's better to go with a more established shipper. As a general rule, you might expect to pay a minimum of about US$700 to ship a vehicle from Colón to Cartagena or Barranquilla; it could easily cost US$1000 or more. Prices are extremely variable.

Another option is to go first to the Colom-bian island of San Andrés, and then on to the mainland. Expect to pay at least US$1000 for the combined fare, and allow a week or so wait in San Andrés for the connecting boat. This option has worked out in the past, but of late people have experienced difficulties in doing this. Contact the South American Explorers Club (see Useful Organisations) for advice if you are considering doing this.

There are alternatives to shipping the vehicle to Colombia. Some travellers have come upon equally good deals shipping to Venezuela, Ecuador or even Chile. It all depends on your luck and what cargo ships are leaving at the time you're asking.

One couple, after taking their vehicle through Central America and into South America, said that it would have been easier and cheaper to ship their car from Miami to Caracas (the easiest way of shipping a vehicle directly from the USA to South America), or to buy a car in South America and sell it again before leaving. But they also said they wouldn't have missed Central America for anything, and were glad they'd come through that way.

Safety

If you cannot stay with your vehicle every minute, you can expect that something will be stolen from it. Stealing from vehicles being shipped is a big business. If you ship the vehicle with all your worldly belongings in it take every precaution, and even then don't be surprised if thieves get your stuff. Remove everything removable (hubcaps, wipers, mirrors etc) and take everything visible out of the interior. Camper vans are a special target – seal off the living area from the driving compartment, double-lock the living area, cover the windows so no one can see inside, and double-lock your possessions *again* inside the cabinets.

Carnet de Passage

If you're taking a vehicle to South America you'll need a *carnet de passage* in addition to the customs, shipping, and other paperwork. The carnet ('Libreta de Pasos por Aduana' in Spanish) is a bond guaranteeing that you won't sell your vehicle in South America – you post a bond to get the carnet, and it's partly refunded when you get back and show that you still have the vehicle.

You don't need the carnet for travel in Central America, but you will need it as soon as you arrive on South American soil. You should arrange it before you arrive in South America. If you don't have a carnet, you and your vehicle could be halted and refused admission at any border in South America.

According to several travellers, the best way to obtain a carnet is through the Venezuelan Automobile Association, where it costs only US$300, with US$150 of that being refundable. The number for the Caracas office is ☎ 91-48-79. It may be better to get the carnet here than in your home country, not only because it will be thousands of dollars cheaper, but also because it will be issued by a South American country, and the documents will be in Spanish and thus more easily recognised and accepted throughout South America.

You can arrange a carnet through the Automobile Association in either Canada or the UK, but it is very expensive: travellers have had to post bonds for more than the full value of their vehicle, coming to thousands of dollars.

In the USA, the American Automobile Association (AAA) used to issue the carnet but they no longer do so. Don Montague at the South American Explorers Club (see Useful Organisations) in the USA has some information on carnets, and his most recent advice was to go through the Venezuelan Automobile Association. (If you find a way to get a carnet de passage in the USA, please let him, and us, know.)

Motorcycles

Some travellers have had horrendous experiences when taking vehicles, especially motorcycles, from Panama to South America without the carnet de passage.

In Panama we met Pat, a Kiwi biker coming north from Colombia, who related some experiences of foreign bikers going the other way. He told us of one who had air-freighted his bike to Bogotá, where it took him four weeks and several hundred dollars in bribes to get it out of customs. When he did get it, they made him go straight to the Ecuadorean border. The authorities there made him pay US$50 and go straight on to the Peruvian border, accompanied by a policeman on the back of his bike!

Another biker air-freighted his machine to Colombia but never did get it out of customs – he had to air-freight it straight on to Ecuador which was very expensive.

Pat, having experienced various South American scenes himself, stored his bike in Panama when he went to Colombia.

These are just a couple of the many unfortunate experiences bikers have encountered. Apparently some South American officials don't take kindly to long-haired foreign bikers. On the other hand, travellers with their own vehicle and a carnet de passage were getting through smoothly with no trouble at all. Pat urged us to let people know about the carnet de passage, and to warn bikers about the problems they may face.

Getting Around

The Central American countries are small; getting around is usually easy in this part of the world. Distances are short, highways are mostly good, and there are adequate bus services and other means of transport. Most travellers enjoy travelling through Central America and have no problems.

AIR – INTERNATIONAL

All the Central American countries except Belize have their own international airlines. Most of them make stops at all of Central America's international airports and others stop further afield, particularly in the USA.

The Central American airlines are:

Guatemala	Aviateca
Honduras	Tan/SAHSA
El Salvador	TACA
Nicaragua	Nica
Costa Rica	LACSA
Panama	COPA

Considering the short distances, flights among the various Central American countries tend to be quite expensive. A half-hour flight can easily cost around US$75.

You can get at least one free stopover on many of the Central American airlines' international routes, whether they originate within or outside Central America. If you fly between Central American countries, this can be an easy way to visit extra countries at no extra cost. It usually makes no difference to the price whether you stop for a couple of hours or a couple of weeks between flights.

Buying Air Tickets

Unlike flights from some other parts of the world, which have complicated price options, airfares in Central America are straightforward. There are three categories of ticket: economy class, business class, and first class. Most travellers use economy class.

The governments regulate airfares, so all the airlines charge the same prices for the same routes within Central America. There are no advance purchase, length of stay or other requirements; you simply go to an airline office or travel agent, see when a flight is going, pay your money, and go. Often you can go the same day or the next day – the only exception is at busy flying times, especially around Easter, when the entire region goes on holiday. Some flights may fill up, but this is generally not a region where you have to book all your tickets far in advance.

If you do have reservations on a Central American airline, be sure you find out the procedure for reconfirming your flight. Usually you must reconfirm, by phone or in person, 72 hours before the flight departs. It's not a bad idea to check once again, to be sure your seat has in fact been confirmed.

If you buy any type of airline ticket in Central America, pay attention to the currency exchange rate the airline is using. Often you can pay for the ticket in either the local currency or in US dollars (cash, travellers' cheques or credit card). Check the difference between the price quoted in dollars and the price in the local currency – paying in one currency or the other can sometimes make a difference to the cost.

AIR – DOMESTIC

Each country also has domestic air services within its borders. Many of the domestic airlines use small planes with about 10 seats. Flying these can be an adventure.

Prices for most domestic flights can be fairly reasonable. In Honduras they're a real bargain: most flights are under US$17 and can save a whole day's travel on an uncomfortable bus or boat, as well as providing a bird's eye view of the country into the bargain. In Costa Rica, on the other hand, domestic air fares have almost doubled in the last three years.

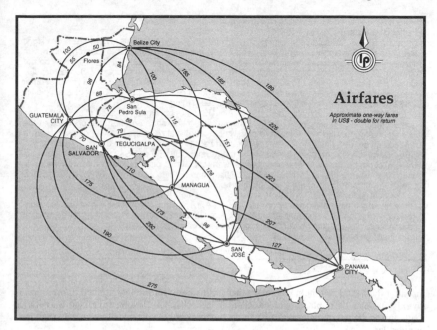

Airfares

Approximate one-way fares
in US$ - double for return

Student Travel Agencies

Costa Rica and Panama have student travel agencies where you can use an International Student Identity Card (ISIC) to obtain discounts on airfares, tours and other travel services. If you have an ISIC card it's worth contacting these offices to see what they're offering.

They do not offer the vast range of discounted airfares that are available at student travel agencies in, for example, the USA or Europe, but you can get discounted airfares on a few routes. (You might get the discounts even if you aren't a student!)

The offices are:

OTEC
   Avenida 3, Calle 3, Edificio Ferencz, 275 Norte del Teatro Nacional, San José, Costa Rica (☎ (506) 222-0866; fax (506) 233-2321)
APTE
   Calle 50 y Calle 46, Bella Vista, Panama City, Panama (☎ 25-4721, 25-2356; fax 64-2148)

BUS

It is quite easy to bus all through Central America. All the countries have adequate bus systems. Some have notorious problems of one kind or another, particularly Nicaragua (pickpockets in Managua buses), but in general you can get almost anywhere in Central America by bus. By local standards it's very expensive to buy and operate your own vehicle, so buses are the principal means by which most people in Central America get around.

On both local and long-distance routes, the first bus of the day usually departs very early in the morning, around 5 am. Often there will be many people taking a bus in the morning, but a lot fewer in the afternoon. Buses may run every few minutes, half-hourly, hourly, or only once or twice a day, depending on the route.

With just a few exceptions, night buses are rare. Sometimes the last bus of the day is scheduled to reach its destination before or

Land Borders
Crossing land borders can sometimes present its own special problems. There are rarely signs telling you at which window or building you are to present yourself, but fortunately children or money-changers are usually on hand to help out. A greater pitfall is the fees demanded by border officials. These can vary from crossing to crossing, let alone country to country. Sometimes it is clearly an official fee (eg the 75 colones ticket in your passport when leaving Costa Rica); at other times you can be fairly sure the money is just going into the guards' pockets. Charges are typically US$2 or less, but occasionally you won't be charged a thing.

Entering Honduras normally costs US$0.70 or US$1.40, but when I crossed at Las Manos the guard demanded 50 lempiras (US$7); coincidentally, the exact sum I had just changed at the money-changer's window. I refused to pay without an official receipt, at which point she backed down and I got in for nothing. Going the other way at the same crossing a traveller was charged US$4.50 by the Nicaraguans, in addition to the normal US$1.50 or US$2.25. This, he was told, was an 'overtime' payment for crossing at the weekend after 1 pm on Saturday. Another traveller wrote that when crossing from Honduras to Nicaragua he was asked for US$20; he refused to pay, and was eventually charged the usual amount.

The best policy is to pay up if the sum demanded is small, to ensure a smooth passage (though some travellers have successfully argued against even minimal fees). If the fee seems too high, seek confirmation of the amount, either from written documentation, the official in charge, or from other people crossing the border. You could refuse to pay; if there seems no option but to pay, at least insist on an official receipt. ■

just after dark. The few night bus routes that do exist are usually in places with excellent roads and no danger of violence from bandits or guerillas.

Buses in Central America range from decrepit, round-fendered models to modern, air-conditioned Mercedes Benzes. Many are yellow, ex-school buses from the USA. Luggage may go in a lower compartment, or be piled on the roof. Since buses are the principal means of transport, people carry anything and everything by bus: goods to sell at the market, produce bought at the market, even small farm animals.

Regardless of their state of newness or decrepitude, buses in Central America are rarely the monotonous, uniform and impersonal transport they can be elsewhere. A bus driver typically has his own bus to drive, and it's usually done up with bright decoration inside and out – stickers, slogans, pictures of Jesus and the Virgin Mary, names of girlfriends written all over the windows, fringes over the windscreen etc. Often the buses have a radio or cassette player; you can bring along your own cassettes and ask the driver to play them.

Don't take bus departure times listed in

this book for granted as such information is particulary vulnerable to change. Sometimes buses only leave once there are enough passengers.

Bus Stations
Bus stations vary greatly in size, location and in the facilities they offer. In some places, all the buses arrive and depart from the same bus station. These can be large, hectic and crowded, but they're the most convenient because you know you can get the bus you want from that bus station.

In other places, such as San Salvador and Managua, different bus stations serve routes for different directions; all the westbound buses come and go from one bus station, while all the eastbound buses come and go from another. If you are just passing through the city, you will have to take a local bus between the two stations.

In still other cities, such as Tegucigalpa and San Pedro Sula, each bus company has its own station. Where this is the case, all the major bus stations are listed in this book, and shown on the city maps where possible. Where the bus stations are spread out like this, the best way to find the one you need is to ask a taxi driver which station has the buses going to your destination.

You can almost always get food at bus stations, and soft drinks will be sold in plastic bags to take on the bus. It is also quite common for food to be available along the way, with crowds of people running up to sell snacks and drinks through the bus windows at every stop. This is a sight to behold; a pack of these determined vendors could easily take on the average American football team. Bring your own toilet paper for bus station toilets as it will never be provided.

Safety & Hassles
Always keep an eye on your luggage on bus trips, wherever it is stored for the journey – it's easy for things to disappear. Also watch out for pickpockets, which are notorious in some places.

Nicaragua is one of the bus rip-off centres of the world. The local buses in Managua are famous for pickpockets, but the long-distance buses have pickpockets too, along with bag slashers, purse snatchers and, of course, the many honest people who also travel by bus.

International Buses
For international bus trips, the normal procedure is to take a bus to the border, get off, go through customs, and board another bus on the other side. Most border stations are open every day from around 7 am to 5 pm, with a couple of hours off for lunch, but it's best to arrive early in the day.

Some international buses will carry you across the border. For example, Costa Rica's Tica Bus company has direct express buses between all capital cities in Central America (except Belize). Of course you can't stop and visit other places in between, and a direct express bus will cost more than taking two or more separate buses. There can also be delays at borders as you have to wait while the whole busload of people goes through customs.

Both Costa Rica and Panama have an onward ticket requirement, and Tica Bus can sell you an international onward or return

bus ticket. If you don't plan to use the onward or return portion of the ticket, be sure to check the refund policy when you buy the ticket.

TRAIN
Unfortunately, train services have been contracting, and it is not possible to get around Central America by train. A few countries still have trains running within their own borders.

CAR
Central America is easy to get around by private vehicle. Taking your own car is more expensive than taking the bus, however, and there are various hassles involved. Roads vary greatly in quality. Most major transport routes are good, paved, two-lane roads, but back country roads are often unpaved, making for much slower travel. Dirt roads are a thrill at any time of year – dusty in the dry season and muddy in the rainy season.

All the Central American countries honour the International Driving Permit, issued at automobile associations all over the world. All you need to do to get one is to present your valid driver's licence, one or two passport-size photos, and a small fee (usually around US$5). It's a good idea to have this permit with you even if you don't have your own vehicle, just in case the opportunity to drive or hire a car presents itself.

Taking your own Vehicle
There are many things to consider when deciding whether to bring a vehicle with you to Central America. If your intention is to travel from North to South America, or vice versa, don't forget the Darién Gap – as noted in the previous chapter, you'll have to ship your vehicle around it.

If you plan simply to travel around Central America, there are various advantages and disadvantages to taking your own vehicle. On the positive side, it makes it easy to stop and see anything you want (including things the bus whizzes past), take as long as you like to do it and go any time you want – you're not tied to bus routes or schedules. It allows you to stay in more remote places. You can do more travelling in less time with your own vehicle than you could on buses, which might be an important consideration if time is limited.

On the other hand, bringing your own vehicle does have certain drawbacks. There are a number of expenses: *gasolina* (petrol, gasoline) costs around US$2 a US gallon (US$0.50 a litre) in Central America. Diesel fuel costs significantly less than regular or premium grades, and is available practically everywhere. Because of this, diesel-run vehicles (especially the new, small pick-ups) are among the most common vehicles in Central America.

When calculating costs, take everything into account. If you bring your own vehicle, will you be camping, thus saving on hotel bills? There are insurance costs to consider: some countries require insurance and some don't, but you should definitely have it when driving in a foreign country.

It can take a long time (sometimes hours) to cross borders with a vehicle. The law may require that the vehicle be fumigated when passing from one country to another, and a fee will be charged for this. The vehicle may be rigorously searched.

Then there is the paperwork. As a rule, Central American countries require a lot of it for any vehicle brought within their borders. There are forms to fill out at the border, more fees to pay, and then there is continuing paperwork once you're inside the country. In some places you may be given a 30-day visa for yourself, but only a 10-day permit for your vehicle! You'll then have to re-register your vehicle at the transport department every 10 days you stay there, and after a month they might require you either to pay a hefty import duty tax on the vehicle or to remove it from the country. Rules vary between countries.

When carrying all your belongings in a vehicle, you must be careful how and where you leave it. In some places theft from vehicles is commonplace, and a foreign licence plate naturally attracts extra attention. At night, you'll have to find a safe place not only for yourself, but also for your vehicle.

Then there's the matter of people. When you travel by public transport or hitchhike, you get closer to the people and culture. You meet people all along the way, buy tacos through bus windows, and a million other things that you could never do if you were insulated in the privacy of your own vehicle.

Catalytic Converters If you are bringing a vehicle from the USA, unless it is over 20 years old it will have a catalytic converter, enabling it to run on unleaded fuel. This is required by law in the USA. In Mexico and most Central American countries, however, unleaded fuel may be unavailable so you'll have to use regular, premium, or diesel fuel.

If your car normally requires unleaded fuel, you can modify it simply by taking off the catalytic converter and replacing it with a straight piece of exhaust pipe. It will then be able to run on regular fuel. Just be sure to re-install the catalytic converter when you return to the USA. Workshops in Mexico, just south of the US border, will remove and re-install catalytic converters, but it's illegal to do it in the USA.

Rental

Hiring a vehicle provides many of the advantages of having your own transport, and eliminates many of the disadvantages. When you hire a car, you're not stuck with it; you get it just for the time you want, make a special trip or two, then take it back and you're finished with it. You can take the vehicle anywhere within the country where you hire it, but you cannot cross any borders.

Hiring is expensive but there are several things you can do to mitigate the cost. The most effective is to get a group of people to share the expense. You can usually drum up four or five people by going around to the budget hotels and proposing a trip.

Ring around and ask the rates for the cheapest available cars at every agency in town. *'Alquiler de Automóviles'* and *'Renta de Automóviles'* in the yellow pages of the telephone directory will list a score of agencies in any capital city. Some other towns may have agencies, too. The big international companies (Avis, Budget, Hertz etc) are represented in Central America but the small local operators usually have the best prices. Car hiring costs at airports can be inflated; you often get much better prices by taking the airport transport into town and hiring a car from an agency there.

When you phone agencies, be sure they understand that you want to hire a vehicle as cheaply as possible. Ask about special deals, and be as flexible as possible with your plans. Often you'll run into a bargain: three days for the price of two, discounts during a particular month, and so on. Weekend prices are frequently lower than weekday prices, and the longer you keep the car, the less the daily rate will be. It can be cheaper to hire a car for seven days than for six, as it knocks you up into the weekly rate. Compare the rate for unlimited km with per km rate, and consider the distance you intend to drive; sometimes one rate will suit your purpose much better than the other.

Many agencies will have 4WD vehicles, including jeeps, pick-up trucks and others, as well as regular cars. Sometimes 4WDs are cheaper to hire than cars, and they're great for getting off the beaten track.

One of the best ways to save money on hiring vehicles is to have a credit card that provides free insurance when you use it to pay for travel. Check the details of the insurance your card includes. If you want to hire a car from time to time, it can be worth getting a card like this before you set off on your trip: it can save you as much as half the hiring cost.

Whenever you hire, particularly from a cheaper, local operator, always ask about your liability in the event an accident or breakdown. Some travellers have been faced with big bills for damage that wasn't necessarily their fault.

Buying & Selling

You can buy a car anywhere in Central America, but some places are better than others. Honduras, for example, has an import tax which raises the price of cars out of sight; the same vehicle will be much cheaper in Panama. It might be even cheaper in the USA.

Travellers used to make money buying used vehicles in the USA, driving them to Central America and selling them there. These days, reports on this kind of venture vary. One Central American, now living in New York, does it every couple of years. He said he wouldn't make a lot of money on any sale, but it would be enough to pay for the trip and, of course, he had the car for getting around the country in the meantime. An Englishman pays for his trips by bringing merchandise down from the USA and selling it out of the boot of his car before selling the car itself.

It is said, however, that it is getting more difficult to do this kind of thing. Central American governments levy substantial taxes on car sales, hence all the paperwork to bring a private vehicle into these countries. If you sell your car privately, the government still wants its cut. Any local who buys a car from you will have to pay a large import tax before the car can be registered. This additional cost reduces the amount you can expect to get when you sell the car. You, for your part, will have to present documents to show why you no longer have your vehicle, and what happened to it.

As with buying, some places in Central America are probably better for selling cars than others. It is definitely *not* possible to bring a car into Panama and sell it there. If it were, Panama would soon find itself piled with used vehicles from border to border, with all the travellers wanting to sell cars there before going to Colombia.

If you want to try your luck selling a vehicle in Central America, you should consider it as a possible way to subsidise your trip, rather than as a big money-making venture. Probably the easiest kind of vehicle to sell is a small Japanese diesel pick-up truck (a Toyota or Suzuki, for example). In rural areas a pick-up truck is about the only kind of vehicle anyone wants. A 4WD pick-up truck would probably be best.

Whether you're buying or selling, be sure all the paperwork is in order, or you could be in serious trouble.

BICYCLE

There aren't many foreign cyclists pedalling through Central America, but it can be done. *Latin America on Bicycle* and *Latin America by Bike: a Complete Touring Guide* (see Books & Maps in the Facts for the Visitor chapter) are both helpful.

If you try it, be sure to cycle extremely defensively; drivers in Central America are not expecting to come upon a cyclist on the road. Central American highways are often very narrow. There are plenty of drivers who are speeding along like maniacs and won't have a chance to avoid hitting you if you're in their way.

Be sure to bring with you any spare parts you might need, or you could be stuck for a very long time waiting for a replacement part to be sent to you.

The biggest drawback to cycling through Central America might be the heat. Temperatures are cooler in the highlands (though even there it can still be quite warm in the daytime, cooling off at night), but in the flat lowlands the heat can be brutal. Be sure to drink enough water, possibly taking salt so your body will retain moisture, and avoid cycling during the heat of the day.

If you're planning a cycling trip, consider the rainy and dry seasons. It usually doesn't rain all day long even in the rainy season, so you won't be slogging through rain day after day, but dirt roads in the more remote areas will be very muddy. Remember that the rainy season is very humid as well as hot.

Rental

There aren't many places to hire a bicycle in Central America; you'll find a few mentioned in this book. If you plan to do any serious cycling, you should plan to bring your own bike, gear and spare parts.

HITCHING

Hitching is never entirely safe in any country in the world, and we don't recommend it.

Travellers who decide to hitch should understand that they are taking a small but potentially serious risk. However, many people do choose to hitch, and the advice that follows should help to make their journeys as fast and safe as possible.

It's pretty easy to hitchhike around Central America. In many rural areas, where the bus comes infrequently and few people have private vehicles, hitchhiking is a recognised form of transport. Someone may pull up in a pick-up truck and load up all the walkers along the road.

The hitching custom in Central America is that you should offer to pay for your ride (*¿Quanto le debo?* – What do I owe you?). It never costs much, usually less than the bus fare. It's quite likely that the driver will say you owe nothing, but don't expect a free ride. Petrol is very expensive for locals, and someone who gets a lift will usually contribute something.

All the usual common-sense hitchhiking rules of the road apply here. Hitching is much easier in the daytime than after dark. Make sure you stand in a spot where you can be easily seen, and where the driver can pull over safely. Be aware of how you look – you don't want to look so grubby that nobody would want you in their car, but you don't want to look too rich either.

Hitching is difficult in cities and populated areas; the best hitching spots are usually on major highways or roads on the outskirts of towns, where drivers will be heading out. Leaving a city, it's often worth paying a few cents to take a local bus to a good hitching spot on the outskirts.

Two or three people hitchhiking together are safer than one person alone; women in particular should be very cautious about hitchhiking alone. In many countries it can be difficult for groups of two or more people (particularly males) to get a lift, but in Central America, three or four travellers can often successfully hitch together because of the prevalence of trucks, both large and small.

Use your instincts, and don't get into a car that seems suspicious for any reason – or even for no reason. You can always wait for another ride, but once you're in a car it might not be so easy to get out again.

BOAT

Central America has extensive coastlines on both the Caribbean and Pacific sides, hundreds of sea islands, thousands of km of rivers, and the Panama Canal, one of the world's most important waterways. There are plenty of options for getting around by boat within the various countries, between different countries, and from Central America to other parts of the world.

Boat travel within each country is described in the individual country chapters. Some of the more famous boat trips include the journey up the Río Dulce from Lívingston in Guatemala, the Río Plátano in Honduras, the trip from Rama to Bluefields in Nicaragua, various trips on the Río San Juan on the Nicaragua/Costa Rica border, and crossings of the Panama Canal.

Other boat trips include those to the Bay Islands on the Caribbean coast of Honduras, to the Corn Islands of Nicaragua, to the islands of Ometepe, Solentiname and others in Lake Nicaragua, and between the hundreds of islands of the San Blas archipelago of eastern Panama.

There are no regularly scheduled passenger lines between the Central American countries, but all kinds of boats ply the coasts all the time. If you're lucky, if you look like you wouldn't be too much trouble to take along, if you could pitch in with the work, and especially if you can pay for your passage, you might be able to catch a ride on something. The more flexible you can be, the better chance you'll have, whether on a fishing boat, a cargo vessel, a smaller boat taking supplies to coastal villages, or a sailing yacht making coastal hops. The best way to catch one of these is to go to a port and ask around the docks or yacht marinas. There's a lot more small boat traffic on the Caribbean coast than on the Pacific. Even so, you might have to wait a couple of days for the right boat to come along.

TOURS

Green Tortoise, Box 24459, SF CA 94124 (☎ (415) 821 0803, 1 800 227 4766) has offices in New York, Boston, Los Angeles, Seattle, Portland, Eugene, Santa Cruz, Santa Barbara in the USA and Vancouver in Canada. They have budget tours to Central America which usually run during the dry season, including a 'Language School on Wheels', a 17-day tour all over Costa Rica with Spanish lessons included, starting and ending in San José.

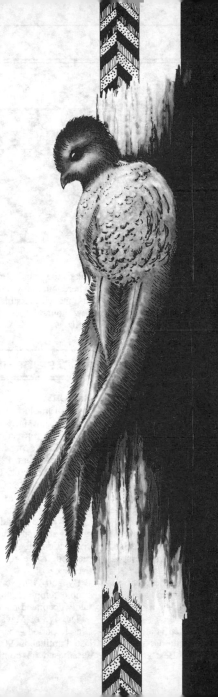

GUATEMALA

Guatemala

Guatemala is Central America in an exaggerated form. Its volcanoes are the highest and most active, its Mayan ruins the most impressive, its population the largest, its manufacturing base the most developed, its earthquakes the most devastating. It has the largest indigenous population, and the Maya of Guatemala cling most tenaciously to their traditional way of life. Under Spain's rule, what we know as Central America was the Captaincy-General of Guatemala. When independence arrived, it was Guatemala which led the short-lived and ill-fated Central American Republic.

The country offers a lot to travellers. Guatemala City is the largest and richest in the region; nearby, the old capital of Antigua Guatemala is among the most charming colonial cities in all of Latin America.

The highlands of western Guatemala have perfect Fuji-like volcanoes, clear lakes, cool pine forests and tawny cornfields. In town after town the Maya inhabitants cling to their ancient modes of dress, daily life and religious worship. The colourful, intricately woven costumes, the mysterious native prayer-leaders swathed in clouds of incense, the vast and vibrant weekly markets are familiar from magazine articles and travel videos, but all are authentic and accessible.

The Pacific Slope, though lined with broad beaches of volcanic sand, is mostly visited for its archaeological sites such as La Democracia, Santa Lucía Cotzumalguapa, and Abaj Takalik.

Dinosaurs once roamed in central and eastern Guatemala. Today it's tourists, ascending to the cool forests of Alta Verapaz, exploring the hot, dry tropics of the Río Motagua valley, peering into the great pilgrimage church at Esquipulas, and admiring the huge, intricately carved Maya stelae at Quiriguá.

The vast jungle of El Petén is alive with exotic flora & fauna, and littered with the ruins of rich Maya cities. Best-known is

Tikal, the grandest restored Maya city anywhere, but many others are being excavated and made accessible. From Tikal, it's only a few hours by bus through the jungle to Belize.

Facts about the Country

HISTORY
Pre-Columbian
Fishing and farming villages producing primitive crops emerged here as early as 2000 BC. The 'pre-Maya' Olmec civilisation flourished from 1200 to 900 BC at San Lorenzo, Veracruz (Mexico) about the same time as Teotihuacán (outside present-day Mexico City) was becoming a powerful kingdom.

Between 800 and 300 BC, Maya towns grew in size and population just as the Olmec civilisation, on which the Maya would build, reached its height at La Venta, Tabasco (Mexico).

By 250 AD, Maya cities had large but simple temples and pyramids, and elaborately decorated pottery.

The age of Maya greatness – called the Classic period – began about 250 AD, and lasted until about 900 AD. The Maya calendar, based on complex mathematics and

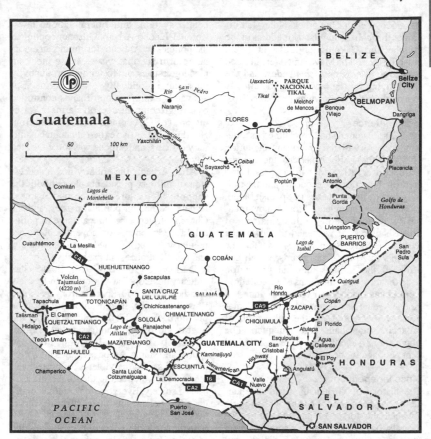

sophisticated astronomical observation, became the basis of Maya religion. Great temples of aesthetic, architectural and engineering excellence were built around spacious plazas. The Maya lands were ruled not as an empire but as a collection of independent but also interdependent city-states. Each city-state had its noble house, headed by a king who was the social, political and religious centre of the city's life.

Though high Maya civilisation flourished in the western highlands, the culture's power and wealth moved to the lowlands of El Petén and Mexico's Yucatán in the 9th and

10th centuries. By 900, the great Maya cities of Tikal, Copán, Quiriguá, Piedras Negras and Caracol had reverted to little more than minor towns.

No one knows why this great civilisation collapsed after 900, but collapse it did. Population growth, food shortages, decline in trade, military campaigns, revolutions and migrations have all been given as reasons.

Spanish Conquest

When Pedro de Alvarado (1485-1541) came to conquer Guatemala for the king of Spain, he found an assortment of warring tribes.

Alvarado, a clever but cruel soldier, led his armies through the highland kingdoms of the Quiché and Cakchiquel Maya in 1523, crushing them. The Maya lands were divided into large estates or *encomiendas*, and the Maya living on the lands were mercilessly exploited by the landowning *encomenderos*.

Independence

By 1821 Guatemala had proclaimed its independence. As with the American Revolution of 1776, the Latin American movements were conservative in nature, preserving control of politics, the economy and the military for the upper classes of Spanish blood.

Though independence brought new prosperity to the creoles (Guatemalans of Spanish blood), it worsened the lot of the Maya. The end of Spanish rule meant that the Crown's few liberal safeguards, which had afforded the Indians minimal protection from the most extreme forms of exploitation, were abandoned. Maya claims to ancestral lands were largely ignored and huge plantations were created for the cultivation of tobacco, sugar cane and henequen. The Maya, though legally free, were enslaved by debt peonage to the great landowners.

Since Independence

The history of Guatemala since independence has been one of rivalry and struggle between the forces of left and right. The liberals have historically wanted to turn backward Guatemala into an enlightened republic of political, social and economic progress. The conservatives hoped to preserve the traditional verities of colonial rule, with a strong Church and a strong government. Their motto might have been 'power must be held by those with merit, virtue and property'. Historically, both movements have benefited the social and economic elites and disenfranchised the people of the countryside, mostly Maya.

There have been a few exceptional leaders. Juan José Arévalo, in power from 1945 to 1951, established the nation's social security system, a government bureau to look after Indian concerns, a modern public health system, and liberal labour laws. Colonel Jacobo Arbenz Guzmán continued the policies of Arévalo, instituting an agrarian reform law that was meant to break up the large estates and foster high productivity on small individually owned farms. But Arévalo's expropriation of lands controlled by foreign companies set off alarms in Washington. The CIA organised an invasion from Honduras led by two exiled Guatemalan military officers, and Arbenz was forced to step down.

After Arbenz, the country had a succession of military presidents elected with the support of the officers' corps, business leaders, compliant political parties, and the Church. Violence became a staple of political life. Opponents of government power regularly turned up dead, not immediately, and not all at once, but eventually.

During the 1960s and 1970s, Guatemalan industry developed at a fast pace, and society felt the effects. Most profits from the boom flowed upwards, labour union organisation put more stresses on the political fabric, and migration from the countryside to the cities, especially the capital, produced urban sprawl and slums. As the pressures in society increased so did the violence of protest and repression, which led to the total politicisation of society. Everyone took sides, usually the poorer classes in the countryside versus the richer population of the cities.

In the early 1980s the military suppression of antigovernment elements in the countryside reached a peak. Alarming numbers of people, usually Indian men, were killed in the name of anti-insurgency, stabilisation and anticommunism. The bloodbath led to a cutoff of US military assistance to the Guatemalan government, which led in turn to the election in 1985 of a civilian president, Marco Vinicio Cerezo Arévalo, the candidate of the Christian Democratic Party. Before turning over power to the civilians, the military ensured that its earlier activities would not be examined or prosecuted, and it established formal mechanisms for the military control of the countryside. There was hope that Cerezo's administration would temper the excesses of the powerful elite and the military and establish a basis for true democracy. When Cerezo's term ended in 1990, however, many people wondered if any real progress had been made.

In 1992 a Guatemalan Maya woman, Rigoberta Menchú Tum, was awarded the Nobel Peace Prize. Menchú had lost many members of her family (mostly male) in the bloodbath which engulfed the countryside during the early 1980s. She responded without bitterness, dedicating herself to the cause of social and political progress for the Maya. Guatemalan conservatives, however, were uneasy with the award, regarding Menchú as a rabble-rouser.

President Cerezo was succeeded by Jorge Serrano Elías (1990-1993), an evangelical Christian who ran as the candidate of the conservative Movimiento de Acción Solidaria (Solidarity Action Movement). Serrano opened a dialogue with the URNG, the main guerrilla organisation, with the aim of bringing the decades-long civil war to an end. When the talks collapsed, the mediator from the Catholic church blamed both sides for intransigence.

As Serrano's popularity declined, he came to depend more on the army for support. On 25 May 1993, after a series of student demonstrations and public protests over price rises and cuts in subsidies, Serrano carried out an *autogolpe* ('auto-coup'). Complaining that the country was sliding into chaos and that the Guatemalan congress was corrupt and infiltrated with narcotics traffickers, he dissolved congress and the Supreme Court of Justice and assumed extraordinary emergency powers.

While Guatemala is indeed a transshipment point for cocaine and heroin from Colombia bound for Mexico and the USA, this is nothing new; and some sources suspect the army of involvement in the drug trade.

The auto-coup was short-lived, however, as popular sentiment was against the move. After a tense few days Serrano was forced to flee into exile. Congress elected Ramiro de León Carpio, the Solicitor for Human Rights

and an outspoken critic of the army's strong-arm tactics, as the country's new president.

GEOGRAPHY

The western highlands are the continuation of Mexico's Sierra Madre range, volcanic formations reaching heights of 3800 metres in the Cuchumatanes range north-west of Huehuetenango. Land that has not been cleared for Maya *milpas* (cornfields) is covered in pine forests. Many of the volcanoes are active or dormant, and you should not be surprised to see, some dark night, the red glow of volcanic activity above a distant mountaintop. All this volcanic activity means that this is an earthquake area as well. Major quakes struck in 1773, 1917 and 1976, and there are more to come.

The Pacific Slope has rich coffee, cacao, fruit and sugar plantations. Down along the shore the volcanic slope meets the sea, yielding vast beaches of black volcanic sand in a sweltering climate.

South and east along the Interamerican Highway the altitude decreases to about 1500 metres at Guatemala City.

North of Guatemala City the highlands of Alta Verapaz gradually decline to the lowland of El Petén. The climate is hot and humid or hot and dry, depending upon the season. To the south-east of Petén is the Motagua valley, dry in some areas, moist in others. It's rich in dinosaur bones, and is wonderful for growing bananas, as you'll see when you visit Quiriguá.

CLIMATE

Temperatures can get down to freezing at night in the mountains, and days in the highlands can be dank and chill during the rainy season, though warm and positively delightful in the dry season from October to May. Guatemala's Pacific coast is tropical, rainy and hot, as is its Caribbean coast, with temperatures often reaching 32°C to 38°C (90°F to 100°F), and almost constant high humidity, abating only a little in the dry season. The vast jungle lowland of El Petén is hot and humid or hot and dry, depending upon the season.

GUATEMALA

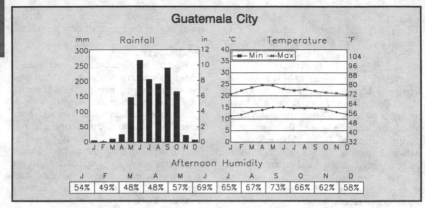

ECONOMY

The Guatemalan highlands are given over completely to agriculture, particularly corn, with some mining and light industry around the larger cities. The Pacific Slope has large coffee, citrus and sugar cane plantations worked by migrant labour from the highlands, and the Pacific coast has cattle ranches and some fishing villages.

Guatemala City, the industrial and commercial centre of the country, has problems of immigration, pollution and congestion arising from its near-monopoly on the commercial life of the country.

The Motagua Valley has some mining, but agriculture is most important here, with vast banana plantations. In the hills of Alta Verapaz, dairy farming, agriculture and forestry are important.

El Petén depends upon tourism and farming for its livelihood, and the two are not happy together. The rapid growth of agriculture and cattle farming is a serious threat to the ecology of Petén, a threat that will have to be controlled if the forests are to survive.

POPULATION & PEOPLE

In Guatemala's population of eight million people, the division between Maya and Spanish descent is fairly strict. Though traditional life thrives in the highlands, during colonial times Maya culture around Guate-

mala City was largely replaced by a hybrid culture that was neither Maya nor strictly Hispanic. Interrelations produced a mestizo population known as *ladinos*, who had abandoned their Maya traditions to adopt the Spanish ways, but who were not accepted into White Spanish society.

Many of the Maya you meet today are the direct descendants of the people who built the marvellous temples and pyramids. To confirm this, all you need to do is compare their appearance with that of the ancient Maya shown in inscriptions and drawings.

Today, Guatemala's Maya are proud of their Maya heritage, and keep alive the ancient traditions and community practices that give meaning to their lives. Guatemalans of European blood are proud of their ancestry as well; they form the elite of the modern commercial, bureaucratic and military upper classes. Ladinos fill in the middle ground between the Old Guard White Hispanic, European and North American elite and the Maya farmers and labourers. Ladinos are shopkeepers, merchants, traders, administrators, bureaucrats and – especially – politicians.

CULTURE
Traditional Dress

One of the most intriguing aspects of Indian life in Guatemala is the colourful, usually handmade, traditional clothing. This comes in infinite and exotic variety, often differing dramatically from village to village. Under the onslaught of modernity, such clothing is less common in everyday use than a few decades ago, but in some areas it's actually becoming more popular as Maya pride reasserts itself and the commercial potential of handicrafts is developed. In general, Maya women have kept to traditional dress longer than men.

Some styles still in common use go back to precolonial times. Among these (all worn by women) are the *huipil*, a long, sleeveless tunic; the *quechquémitl*, a shoulder cape; and the *enredo*, a wraparound skirt. Blouses are colonial innovations. Maya men's garments owe more to Spanish influence; nudity was discouraged by the church, so shirts, hats and *calzones*, long baggy shorts, were introduced.

What's most eye-catching about these costumes is their colourful embroidery often entire garments are covered in a multi-coloured web of stylised animal, human, plant and mythical shapes which can take months to complete. Each garment identifies the group and village from which its wearer comes. *Fajas*, waist sashes, which bind the garments and also hold what we would put in pockets, are also important in this respect.

The designs often have multiple religious or magical meanings. In some cases the exact significance has been forgotten, but in others the traditional associations are still alive.

Music & Dance

You're likely to hear live music at any time on streets, plazas, or even buses. The musicians are playing for their living and range from marimba teams to lone buskers. Marimbas are particularly popular in the highlands.

Music and traditional dance are important parts of the many colourful festivals on the Maya calendar. There are many traditional dances, some of which can be seen only in a single town or village. Nearly all feature special costumes, often including masks.

Facts for the Visitor

VISAS & EMBASSIES

You need only a tourist card or passport stamp if you are a citizen of Austria, Belgium, Canada, Denmark, Finland, France, Germany, Holland, Italy, Israel, Japan, Luxembourg, Norway, Spain, Sweden, Switzerland or the USA. The Guatemalan tourist card is valid for three months from the date of entry to Guatemala. It carries a fee of US$5, payable when you receive the form; anything else is a bribe.

If you are a citizen of Australia, the UK, New Zealand or another British Commonwealth country, you should obtain a visa in advance from a Guatemalan consulate before you arrive at the Guatemalan border or airport.

Foreign embassies in Guatemala are listed under Guatemala City.

Some Guatemalan embassies are:

Australia
    No embassy maintained, contact the embassy in Tokyo, Japan
Canada
    100 Goulburn St, Ottawa, Ontario (☎ (613) 237 3941/2; fax 237 0492)
El Salvador
    15 Avenida Norte 135, San Salvador (☎ 22 29 03, 71 22 25; fax 21 30 18)
Japan
    KOWA 38 Building Room 905, 12-24 Nishi Azabu, 4-Chome, Minato-Ku, Tokyo 105 (☎ (03) 400 1830, 400-1820)
Mexico
    Colonia Lomas de Virreyes II, Mexico, DF (☎ (5) 540 7520, 520 9249; fax 202 1142)
UK
    13 Fawcett St, London SW 10 (☎ (071) 351 3042; fax 376 5708)
USA
    2220 International Drive NW, Suite 2-J, Washington DC 20008-3098 (☎ (202) 363 4505; fax (202) 362 7468)
    There are consulates in Los Angeles, Chicago, Denver, Miami, San Francisco and New Orleans – consult the telephone directory.

Minors Travelling Alone

If you are under 18 years of age and travelling alone, technically you must have a letter of permission signed by both your parents and witnessed by a Guatemalan consular official in order to enter Guatemala. Call a Guatemalan consulate if you have questions about this.

MONEY

The Guatemalan quetzal (Q) is divided into 100 centavos. There are coins of one, five, 10 and 25 centavos, and bills (notes) of 50 centavos, one, five, 10, 20, 50 and 100 quetzals.

US dollars are the currency to take to Guatemala, as any other currency, even Canadian dollars, can cause delays and problems when being exchanged for quetzals.

Many establishments will accept US dollars instead of quetzals, usually at the bank exchange rate or even better, but sometimes worse.

There's a healthy unofficial exchange market for dollars, paying slightly better than the bank rate. At most border crossing points you may find yourself buying quetzals unofficially as there are no banks; at the airport, the bank exchange desks are usually open only during banking hours, and you may find yourself buying your first quetzals (or your last, to pay the US$10-equivalent exit tax) at a shop in the terminal.

Foreign		Guatemala
A$1	=	Q4.15
C$1	=	Q4.20
DM1	=	Q3.45
NZ$1	=	Q3.35
UK£1	=	Q8.70
US$1	=	Q5.80

Costs

For the budget traveller, Guatemalan prices are fairly good: beds in little pensions for US$3 to US$5 per person in a double, camping places for less, elaborate markets selling fruits and snacks for pennies, cheap eateries called *comedores* offering one-plate meals for US$2 or US$3, and bus trips at less than US$2 per hour. If you want a bit more comfort, you can readily move up to rooms with private showers and meals in nicer restaurants, and still pay only US$20 per day for a room and two – or even three – meals.

Guatemala's IVA (VAT) tax is 7%, and there's also a 10% tax on hotel rooms to pay for the activities of the Guatemala Tourist Commission (INGUAT), so a total tax of 17% will be added to your hotel bill. The very cheapest places usually ignore the tax and don't collect it from you.

A departure tax equivalent to approximately US$10 is levied on travellers departing by air to foreign destinations.

WHEN TO GO

The dry season, from October to May, is the best time to visit the highlands. See the Climate section in the Facts About the Country chapter for details.

BUSINESS HOURS & HOLIDAYS

Banks are open from 8.30 or 9 am to 2 pm Monday to Thursday, 8.30 am to 2.30 pm on Friday. A few banks in Guatemala City may have longer hours, until 3 pm, with a few walk-up teller windows open until 4.30 pm. Shops open at about 9 am and close for lunch around 12.30 or 1 pm, reopening an hour or so later, and remaining open until about 6 pm, Monday to Friday; on Saturday many shops close for the day at 12.30 or 1 pm. Government office hours are officially 7.30 am to 3.30 pm, though there's some absenteeism around lunchtime.

Semana Santa (Holy Week) is the biggest holiday festival, with processions and celebrations in many towns and villages. (See individual entries for details.)

1995: Semana Santa begins on Palm Sunday (the Sunday before Easter) 9 April, and runs until 16 April (Easter Sunday)
1996: 31 March to 7 April
1997: 23 March to 30 March.

POST & TELECOMMUNICATIONS
Post

An air-mail letter sent from Guatemala to Canada or the USA may take anywhere from four to 14 days. Air-mail letters to Europe can take anywhere from one to three weeks.

Telephone

Local and domestic long-distance calls are quite cheap in Guatemala, and international direct calls much more expensive. The local phone company is called Guatel. A local call costs about US$0.06 per minute, an adjacent-zone call about US$0.08 per minute, and a call across the country about US$0.10 per minute.

International direct calls (called *discado internacional automática*, or DIA) can be made from coin phones if you have a heavy pocketful of Guatemalan 25-centavo pieces and don't mind feeding them fast. But your best bet is to make a short call, inform the other person of a time and telephone number at which you may be reached, then end the call.

Collect (reverse-charge) calls may be made from Guatemala to the following countries only: Canada, Central America, Mexico, Italy, Spain, Switzerland and the USA.

To place an international direct call, dial the international prefix '00' (that's zero zero), then the country code, area or city code, and local number.

For semi-automatic (operator-assisted) calls, dial 171. The minimum call period is three minutes, and thus the minimum charge to the USA or Canada is about US$6; to countries overseas (ie, outside the western hemisphere), the minimum charge is about US$20.

There are also numerous 'direct line' services, such as AT&T's *USADirect*: dial 190 and you will be connected with an AT&T operator in the USA who will complete your collect or credit card call. Here are the direct line numbers:

National Police	120
Inter-City Long Distance Calls	121
Fire	123
Directory Assistance	124
Red Cross	125
Correct Time	126
Ambulance	128
International Calls (by Operator)	171
MCI Call USA	189
USADirect (AT&T)	190

España Directo	191
Italia Directo	193
Sprint Express	195
Costa Rica Directo	196
Canada Directo	198

BOOKS & MAPS

Other guidebooks published by Lonely Planet cover areas adjacent to and overlapping Guatemala. *Guatemala, Belize & Yucatán: La Ruta Maya – a travel survival kit* covers these areas in detail, with lots of background information on Maya life and culture. The encyclopaedic *Mexico – a travel survival kit* covers that entire country in great detail.

The Maya, by Michael D Coe (New York and London: Thames & Hudson, 1987, 4th revised edition; paperback), is the best general introduction to Maya life and culture by an eminent scholar.

Tikal: A Handbook of the Ancient Maya Ruins, by William R Coe (Philadelphia: The University Museum of the University of Pennsylvania, 1967; paperback) is available at Tikal, but may be cheaper if you buy it at home before you leave.

Most important of the travelogues are the delightful books by John L Stephens, illustrated by Frederick Catherwood. Stephens, a New York lawyer, and Catherwood travelled extensively in the Maya lands in the mid-19th century. *Incidents of Travel in Central America, Chiapas and Yucatan*, in two volumes (1969 reprint of 1841 edition), by John L Stephens, is available in paperback at some bookshops in Guatemala, from many bookshops in the USA, and also directly from the publisher, Dover Publications, 31 East Second St, Mineola, NY 11501-3582 USA.

Time Among the Maya: Travels in Belize, Guatemala and Mexico, by Ronald Wright (New York: Weidenfeld & Nicolson, 1989; hardback) is a thoughtful account of numerous journeys made in recent years among the descendants of the ancient Maya.

The basic text of Maya religion is the Popol Vuh (or Popol Wuh), which recounts the Maya creation myths. A version easily available in Guatemala is *Popol Wuh: Ancient Stories of the Quiche Indians of Guatemala*, by Albertina Saravia E (Guatemala City: Editorial Piedra Santa, 1987; paperback).

Maps

International Travel Map Productions, PO Box 2290, Vancouver, BC V6B 3W5, Canada, publishes a series of travellers' reference maps. Titles include *Guatemala-El Salvador* (1:500,000), which also covers neighbouring portions of Chiapas, Tabasco, Belize and Honduras; *Yucatán Peninsula* (1:1 million), which includes Tabasco, Chiapas, Guatemala's Petén and Belize; and *Belize* (1:350,000).

A letter to the Instituto Guatemalteco de Turismo (INGUAT, 7 Avenida 1-17, Zona 4, Guatemala City), sent well in advance of your departure, will yield a useful map of the country with city street plans, but the scale is fairly small. The same map, called the *Mapa Vial Turístico*, may be bought in Guatemala at shops or from street vendors for several dollars.

DANGERS & ANNOYANCES
Safety

Certain Guatemalan regions have been and may still be the scene of political and military conflict, and even occasional attacks on foreign tourists. These incidents occur at random and are unfortunately not predictable.

Don't let vague fears or rumours of trouble scare you off, as these areas offer exceptional travel experiences which you should not miss. Your best defences against trouble are up-to-date information and reasonable caution. You should take the trouble to contact your government and enquire about current conditions and trouble spots, and follow the advice offered. Up-to-date travel advice is available from the US Department of State's Citizens Emergency Center (☎ (202) 647-5225), and the UK Foreign Office's Travel Advisory Service (☎ (071) 270-3000).

If you plan to travel by road in the Guate-

malan highlands or El Petén, you should also ask as many other travellers as possible about current conditions. Don't rely on local newspapers, government officials or business people as your sole sources of information, as they often cover up 'unpleasant' incidents which might result in the loss of tourist revenues. Your home country's government, on the other hand, has an interest in protecting the lives of its citizens. If you speak Spanish, you can also ask local children, who tend to tell the truth about unpleasant incidents they've heard about.

Warning

Guatemala has been the scene of antigovernment insurgent activity for a century or so. The guerrillas believe themselves to be fighting for the rights of the common people, and dream of overthrowing the government to establish a populist state. The government sees the guerrillas as a danger to public order and to its own legitimacy, and it has been attempting to suppress insurgent activity with great severity.

Whatever your opinion on the matter, you should avoid clashes between government soldiers and guerrillas. Don't go wandering about the countryside at night. Chances are very small that you will have any serious encounter with either group. If you do, don't panic – chances are that you'll be on your way again in a few minutes with no harm done.

LANGUAGE COURSES

Courses in Spanish are offered in several different parts of Guatemala. See entries under Antigua and Quetzaltenango for details of where to write or telephone for information.

ACCOMMODATION

Most Guatemalan cities have good selections of cheap hotels and pensions. In the back country, however, lodgings may be primitive or nonexistent, and you should be prepared to camp. If and when you camp, be *very* sensitive to safety concerns. It's wise to camp only with other campers nearby. Wherever facilities are available for campers, expect to pay from US$1 to US$10 per night, depending upon the facilities and the location.

As the country is becoming a more popular destination for travellers, hotels and pensions are raising prices to meet demand, and the days of the US$2 bed may be numbered.

FOOD
When it comes to cuisine, Guatemala is the poorer cousin to the more elaborate cuisines of Mexico, the USA and Europe. You can find a few Mexican standards such as tortillas topped with beans, meat or cheese; enchiladas; *guacamole*, a salad of mashed or chopped avocados, onions and tomatoes; and *tamales*, steamed corn dough rolls, perhaps with a meat or other stuffing. But mostly you will encounter *bistec*, tough grilled or fried beef, *pollo asado*, grilled chicken, *chuletas de puerco*, pork chops, and lighter fare such as *hamburguesas*, hamburgers, and *salchichas*, sausages like hot dogs. Of the simpler food, *frijoles con arroz*, beans and rice, is cheapest and often best.

US-style breakfasts are always available: bacon or sausage and eggs, pancakes *(panqueques)*, cold cereal such as corn flakes or hot cereal such as cream of wheat (semolina), fruit juice and coffee.

Virtually any city or town of any size has at least one Chinese eatery, usually small and not overly authentic, but cheap and good for a change of scene.

DRINKS
Nonalcoholic Drinks
The Pacific Slope of Guatemala has many large coffee plantations which produce excellent beans. Some hotels in Antigua have coffee bushes growing right on their grounds. Coffee is available everywhere, but it's often surprisingly weak and sugary in some parts of Guatemala.

Hot chocolate or cocoa was the royal stimulant during the Classic period of Maya civilisation, being drunk on ceremonial occasions by the kings and nobility. Their version was unsweetened, and dreadfully bitter. Today it's sweetened and, if not authentic, at least more palatable.

Alcohol
Breweries were first established in Guatemala by German immigrants in the late 19th century. Guatemala's two nationally distributed beers are Gallo (GAH-yoh, rooster) and Cabro (goat). The distribution prize goes to Gallo – you'll find it everywhere. These two beers are light lagers, served cold from bottles or cans, but there is also the flavourful dark beer named Moza.

Rum and *aguardiente* (sugar cane liquor) are the favourite strong drinks in Guatemala, and though most are of low price and matching quality, some local products are exceptionally fine. The cheaper rums and brandies are often mixed with soft drinks to make potent but cooling drinks like the *Cuba libre* of rum and Coke.

THINGS TO BUY
Most *artesanías* (handicrafts) originated in objects made for everyday use or for specific occasions such as festivals. Today many objects are made simply to sell as 'folk art' – some purely decorative, others with a useful function – but that doesn't necessarily reduce their quality.

There's a flourishing trade in artesanías, and you'll often find a better selection in shops and markets in towns and cities than in the original villages. The artisans who make these crafts have learned that the most profitable markets for their wares are in Panajachel and Antigua, where there are lots of appreciative tourists interested in buying.

Colourful handwoven and embroidered Indian costumes come in a number of basic shapes and as many designs as there are weavers.

Ceremonial masks are fascinating, eye-catching, and still in regular use. You'll see them in the markets in Panajachel, Sololá, Chichicastenango and Antigua.

Getting There & Away

AIR

To/From North & Central America

Virtually all flights to Guatemala from the rest of the world pass through the 'hub' cities of Dallas/Fort Worth, Houston, Los Angeles, Miami, Mexico City or San Salvador. You can fly to Guatemala City directly from these places:

Belize City – Aerovías has three flights weekly via Santa Elena (Tikal); TACA has daily flights via San Salvador

Cancún – Aerocaribe (Mexicana) and Aeroquetzal have daily flights

Houston – Continental has direct flights daily, and Aviateca three flights per week via Mérida

Los Angeles – daily flights are by American, Aviateca, Mexicana and TACA; most of these flights make at least one stop along the way

Mérida – three flights weekly by Aviateca (see Houston)

Mexico City – Mexicana and Aviateca have daily nonstop flights

Miami – lots of daily flights by American, Aviateca and TACA; many European airlines connect through Miami

New York (JFK) – there is one direct flight by TAN; all other flights connect through Miami, Houston or Dallas/Fort Worth

San José (Costa Rica) – daily nonstops by American, Continental and Medellín, and a direct flight with one stop by LACSA three times per week

San Salvador (El Salvador) – daily nonstops by COPA and TACA

Santa Elena (near Tikal) – Aerocaribe, Aeroquetzal, Aerovías, Aviateca and TAPSA operate daily flights. Note that some flights to Santa Elena (Tikal) depart from Avenida Hincapié on the east side of the airport (the main terminal is on the west side); to reach the TAPSA terminal, for instance, you must take a taxi to the east side.

To/From Europe

Few European airlines fly directly to Guatemala City. Most take you to one of the hub cities, where you change to a US, Mexican, Guatemalan or other Central American airline.

To/From Australasia

There are no direct flights from Australia to Guatemala. The cheapest way of getting there is via the USA – often Los Angeles. Discount returns from Sydney to Los Angeles cost from A$1300. Cheap flights from the USA to Guatemala are hard to find in Australia. Regular Los Angeles/Guatemala City fares are US$360 one way, US$470 return – but you may be able to pick up cheaper tickets if you are stopping for a day or two in Los Angeles.

LAND

Getting to Central America from the north means going through Mexico.

Bus

It doesn't make sense to get to Central America by bus unless you plan to stop and see the USA or Mexico along the way. The distances are great, and when you add up the cost of bus tickets, meals, hotel nights and incidentals, a bus trip can be almost as expensive as a flight. It's almost 6000 km from New York to Guatemala City, and more than 5000 km from Los Angeles. At an average of 70 km/h, these trips would take three or four days of constant travel, not counting border formalities or nights in hotels.

Once you've reached Mexico City, Oaxaca, San Salvador or Tegucigalpa (Honduras), taking the bus to Guatemala makes sense.

Train

As with bus travel, you must plan to tour the USA and Mexico to make it worthwhile. Plan to use trains in the USA and in Mexico west of the Isthmus of Tehuantepec if you like, but avoid trains in Yucatán and Guatemala.

Trains run from the USA/Mexican border to Mexico City and beyond to Yucatán and Chiapas via Veracruz to Juchitan and along the Pacific coast of Chiapas to Tapachula. From Ciudad Tecún Umán, across the border from Tapachula in Guatemala, trains run to Guatemala City. There is sometimes service from Guatemala City to Puerto Barrios on the Gulf of Honduras as well.

All of these trains are very cheap, all are slow and unreliable, most are quite uncomfortable. Some are unsafe as sneak thieves and muggers work with train crew members to relieve foreign tourists of wallets and cameras. You may want to take the train as far as Mexico City, Veracruz or Oaxaca, but switch to bus to continue south and eastward. Trains in Guatemala are a source of adventure more than a means of transport.

Car
The major roads are easily passable by any sort of car, and border crossings are fairly easy.

The most apparent difficulty in driving from the USA is that most North American cars now have catalytic converters which require unleaded fuel. At the time of writing, unleaded fuel was available in many parts of Mexico, but not in Guatemala or Belize. You can arrange to have your catalytic converter disconnected, and replaced with a straight piece of exhaust pipe soon after you cross into Mexico (it's illegal to have it done in the USA). Save the converter, and have it replaced before re-crossing the border into the USA.

Coming from overseas, you may want to buy a used car or van in the USA, where they're relatively cheap, drive through the USA to Mexico, and through Central America.

Sea
It's possible to travel by sea. There's only one route: from Punta Gorda, Belize, to Puerto Barrios, Guatemala.

Getting Around

AIR
Besides its international connections, Guatemala City has flights to Flores (Santa Elena) near Tikal. It's tedious (and sometimes dangerous) to reach Flores by road (bus or car), so if your budget will allow, you might want to fly there from Guatemala City or Belize City. Aerocaribe, Aeroquetzal, Aerovías, Aviateca and TAPSA operate daily flights between Guatemala City and Flores for US$55 one way. Four days a week, Aerovías flies between Flores and Belize City for US$50 one way.

BUS
For a list of schedules and fares covering all of Guatemala, see Getting There & Away in the Guatemala City section later.

In general, bus traffic is most intense in the morning (beginning as early as 4 or 5 am), tapering off by mid or late afternoon. In many places there are no buses in the late afternoon or evening.

Among Guatemala's many bus companies, by far the most popular sort of bus is the second-hand American school bus (usually a 'Blue Bird'), often with the original seats which allow room enough for school children but are very cramped for adults of European or North American stature.

In addition to the school buses, several Guatemalan lines run more comfortable passenger buses on long-distance routes between Guatemala City and the Mexican and Salvadoran borders, and to Puerto Barrios on the Gulf of Honduras.

HITCHING
You should be exceptionally cautious about – and while – hitching in Guatemala. Many people do hitch along certain stretches in Guatemala, and often it is necessary because bus services are infrequent or nonexistent, particularly to the fairly remote Maya archaeological sites. However, hitchhiking is not necessarily free transport. In most cases, if you are picked up by a truck, you will be expected to pay a fare similar to that charged on the bus (if there is one). In some areas, pickup and flatbed stake trucks *are* the 'buses' of the region, and every rider pays. Your best bet for free rides is with other foreign tourists who have their own vehicles.

STREET GRID SYSTEM
All Guatemalan towns are laid out according

to a street grid system which is logical and fairly easy to use. Avenidas run north-south; Calles run east-west. Streets are usually numbered from north and west (lowest) to south and east (highest); building numbers run in the same directions, with odd numbers on the left-hand side and even on the right as you head south or east. Larger cities and towns are divided into *zonas* (zones); each zona has its own separate version of this grid system.

Addresses are given in this form: '9a Avenida 15-12, Zona 1', which is read '9th Ave above 15th St, No 12, in Zone 1'. The building you're looking for will be on 9th Ave between 15th and 16th Sts, on the right-hand side as you walk south.

Short streets may be numbered 'A', as in 14 Calle A, a short street running between 14 Calle and 15 Calle.

Guatemala City

Population: 2 million

Guatemala's capital city, the largest urban agglomeration in Central America, sprawls across a range of flattened mountains (altitude 1500 metres), scored by deep ravines. Founded in 1775, it has expanded to cover the entire great plain of flattened mountains, even tumbling into the valleys which surround it.

Many things are typically Latin. There's the huge and chaotic market, colourful and disorganised as though Guatemala City was just a gigantic village. There are the ramshackle city buses, without windows, without lights, without paint, sometimes without brakes, which trundle citizens about with surprising efficiency. And there are the thousands of guards in blue clothing carrying very effective-looking firearms.

History

On 29 July 1773 a *temblor* (earthquake) destroyed much of Guatemala's capital at Antigua, and the colonial government decided to move its headquarters to the present site of Guatemala City, hoping to escape any further such terrible destruction. On 27 September 1775 King Carlos III of Spain signed a royal charter for the founding of La Nueva Guatemala de la Asunción, and Guatemala City was officially born.

The fervent hopes for a quakeless future were shaken in 1917, 1918 and 1976 as temblors did major damage to buildings in the capital – as well as in Antigua. The city's comparatively recent founding and its history of earthquakes have left little to see in the way of grand churches, palaces, mansions, or quaint old neighbourhoods. What you see here is mostly concrete.

Orientation

Because of its size and uneven topography, Guatemala City's street grid has a number of anomalies as well: diagonal streets called *rutas* and *vías*, wandering boulevards called *diagonales* etc.

The ceremonial centre of Guatemala City is the Plaza Mayor (sometimes called the Parque Central) at the heart of Zona 1, surrounded by the Palacio Nacional, the Catedral Metropolitana and the Portal del Comercio. Beside the Plaza Mayor to the west is the large Parque Centenario, the city's central park. Zona 1 is also the retail commercial district, with shops selling clothing, crafts, film, and a myriad other things. The Mercado Central, a market selling lots of crafts, is behind the cathedral. Most of the city's good cheap hotels are in Zona 1. The major thoroughfares which connect Zona 1 with other zonas are 6a Avenida running south and 7a Avenida running north.

Zona 4, south of Zona 1, holds the modern Centro Cívico (Civic Centre) with various government buildings. In south-western Zona 4 are the city's major market district and chaotic bus terminals.

Zona 9 (west of Avenida La Reforma) and Zona 10 (east of Avenida La Reforma), are south of Zona 4; Avenida La Reforma is the southerly extension of 10a Avenida. These are the fancier residential areas of the city, also boasting several of the most interesting small museums. Zona 10 is the poshest, with the Zona Viva (Lively Zone) arrayed around the deluxe Camino Real Guatemala and Guatemala Fiesta hotels.

Zona 13, just south of Zona 9, has the large Parque Aurora, several museums, and the Aeropuerto Internacional La Aurora (La Aurora international airport).

Information

Tourist Office The tourist office is in the lobby of the INGUAT headquarters (Guatemalan Tourist Commission), (☎ (2) 311333 to 47; fax 318893), 7a Avenida 1-17, Centro Cívico, Zona 4. Look for the blue-and-white sign with the letter 'i' on the east side of the street, next to a flight of stairs a few metres to the south of the railway viaduct that crosses above 7a Avenida. Opening hours on weekdays are from 8 am to 4.30 pm, and on Saturday from 8 am to 1 pm. It's closed Sunday. Staff here are friendly and helpful, with lots of good information at their fingertips.

Money Normal banking hours are 8.30 am to 2 pm (until 2.30 pm on Friday), closed weekends, but several banks have *ventanillas especiales* (special teller windows) open longer; ATM cash machines are also making their appearance. Most banks give a maximum of US$100 for an ATM withdrawal, but Banco Credomático, 7a Avenida at 6 Calle, Zona 1, allows US$500 from a MasterCard. Banquetzal has an office (☎ (2) 512153/055), at 10 Calle 6-28, Zona 1, near the Hotel Ritz Continental, that's open from 8.30 am to 8 pm Monday to Friday, and on Saturday from 9 am to 1 pm.

The airport terminal office of Banco de Guatemala is open 7.30 am to 6.30 pm, Monday to Friday.

American Express is represented in Guatemala by Banco del Café S A (☎ (2) 311311, 340040; fax 311418), Avenida La Reforma 9-00, Zona 9.

Post The city's main post office (☎ (2) 26101/2/3/4/5) is at 7a Avenida 12-11, Zona 1, in the huge pink building. There's no sign,

but by the racks of postcards shall ye know it. It's open from 8 am to 7 pm on weekdays, 8 am to 3 pm on Saturday, closed Sunday. Don't expect much from the mail here. The service is distinctly unreliable, especially when you're sending urgent messages or valuable items, and local citizens and businesses often use private courier companies instead.

Telephone If you are calling Guatemala City from outside the country, the country code is 502, the city code is 2; for any other Guatemalan city or town it's 9. Most telephone numbers in Guatemala City have six digits, but a few old ones have only five.

A coin-operated telephone in Guatemala is called a *teléfono monedero*.

Embassies Remember that embassies *(embajadas)* and their consular sections *(consulados)* often have strange, short working hours. Call ahead to be sure the place will be open before you venture out to find it.

Austria
  Embassy, 6a Avenida 20-25, Zona 10, Edificio Plaza Marítima (4th floor) (☎ (2) 681134, 682324; fax 336180)
Belgium
  Embassy & Consulate, Avenida La Reforma 13-70, Zona 9, Edificio Real Reforma (2nd floor) (☎ (2) 316597, 315608; fax 314746)
Canada
  Embassy & Consulate, 7a Avenida 11-59, Zona 9, Edificio Galerías España (☎ (2) 321411/12/13; fax 321419)
Costa Rica
  Embassy, Avenida La Reforma 8-60, Zona 9, Edificio Galerías Reforma offices 320 and 902 (☎ & fax (2) 320531)
Denmark
  Consulate-General, 7a Avenida 20-36, Zona 1 (☎ (2) 81091, 514547; fax 513087)
El Salvador
  Embassy, 12 Calle 5-43, Zona 9 (☎ (2) 325848, 362421; fax 343947)
France
  Embassy & Consulate, 16 Calle 4-53, Zona 10, Edificio Marbella (☎ (2) 374080, 373639)
Germany
  Embassy, 20 Calle 6-20, Zona 10, Edificio Plaza Marítima (☎ (2) 370028/29; fax 370031)

GUATEMALA

Guatemala
City
(North)

0   250   500 m

To Parque
Minerva

■ PLACES TO STAY		11	Restaurant Bologna	6	Mercado Central
		16	Restaurant Piccadilly	18	Correos (Main Post
1	Hotel Centenario	17	Los Tilos		Office)
8	Hotel Pan American	19	Café Bohemia	20	Guatel (Telephone
12	Hotel Ritz Continental	21	El Gran Pavo		Office Long-
13	Pensión Meza	23	Restaurant Altuna		Distance)
14	Hogar del Turista &	31	Restaurant Cantón	25	Iglesia Santa Clara
	Hotel Casa Real	32	Restaurant El Gran	27	Iglesia San Francisco
15	Hotel Lessing House		Emperador	28	Policia Nacional
22	Hotel Del Centro	33	Hotel Colonial	30	Parque Concordia
24	Hotel-Apartamentos		Restaurant		(Parque Gómez
	Guatemala	34	Delicadezas		Carrillo)
	Internacional		Hamburgo	39	FEGUA Railway
26	Spring Hotel	35	Pollo Campero		Station
29	Posada Belén	38	Cafetín El Rinconcito	40	Centro Cultural
36	Hotel Ajau				Miguel Ángel
37	Hotel Excel	**OTHER**			Asturias
				41	Centro Cívico
▼ PLACES TO EAT		2	Palacio Nacional	42	INGUAT Tourist Office
		3	Parque Centenario		
7	Pollo Campero	4	Plaza Mayor		
9	Pollo Campero	5	Catedral		
10	Cafetería El Roble		Metropolitana		

Honduras
Embassy, 16 Calle 8-27, Zona 10 (☎ (2) 373919, 371921; fax 334629)

Italy
Embassy & Consulate, 5 Avenida 8-59, Zona 14 (☎ (2) 374578/88; fax 374538)

Mexico
Embassy, 13 Calle 7-30, Zona 9 (☎ (2) 319573, 325249; fax 344124);
Chancellery, 15 Calle 3-20, Zona 10 (7th floor), Edificio Centro Ejecutivo
(☎ (2) 337254/55/56/57/58)

Nicaragua
Embassy, 10 Avenida 14-72, Zona 10 (☎ (2) 336434, 680785; fax 374264)

Panama
Embassy, Vía 5 No 4-50, Zona 4, Edificio Maya (7th floor) (☎ (2) 320763; fax 347161)

South Africa
Consulate, 10a Avenida 30-57, Zona 5 (CIDEA) (☎ (2) 362890, 341531/35; 365291)

Spain
Consulate, 6 Calle 6-48, Zona 9 (☎ (2) 343787)

UK
Embassy, 7a Avenida 5-10, Zona 4, Edificio Centro Financiero Torre II (7th floor) (☎ (2) 321601/02/04; fax 341904)

USA
Embassy & Consulate, Avenida La Reforma 7-01, Zona 10 (☎ (2) 311541; fax 318885)

Immigration Office If you need to extend your tourist card for a longer stay, you should contact the Dirección General de Migración (☎ (2) 714682; fax 714678), 41 Calle 17-36, Zona 8, one block off Avenida Castellana.

Medical Services Guatemala City has a range of private hospitals and clinics. One such is the Centro Médico (☎ (2) 323555), 6a Avenida 3-47, Zona 10; another is Hospital Herrera Llerandi (☎ (2) 366771/75, 320444/48), 6a Avenida 8-71, Zona 10. For the names and addresses of others, consult your embassy or consulate, or the yellow pages of the telephone directory under Hospitales.

The Guatemalan Red Cross (☎ (2) 125) is at 3 Calle 8-40, Zona 1.

Guatemala City uses a duty-chemist (*farmacia de turno*) system with designated pharmacies remaining open at night and weekends. Ask at your hotel for the nearest farmacia de turno, or consult the farmacia de turno sign in the window of the closest chemist/pharmacy.

Things to See – Zona 1
Most of what you'll want to see is in Zona 1 near the Plaza Mayor, bounded by 6 and 8 Calles and 6a and 7a Avenidas.

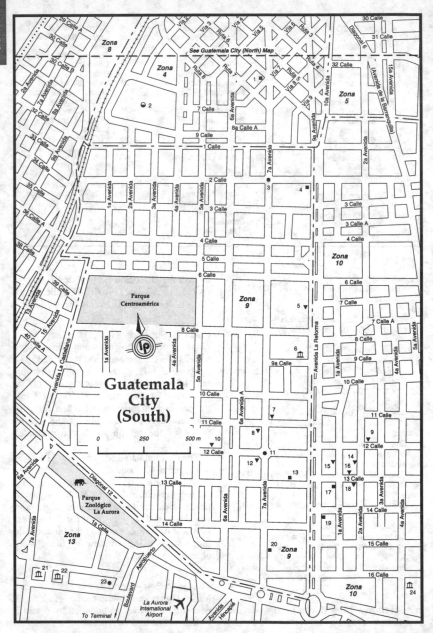

Zona 8

Zona 4

See Guatemala City (North) Map

Zona 5

Zona 10

Zona 9

Parque Centroamérica

Guatemala City (South)

0   250   500 m

Parque Zoológico La Aurora

Zona 13

Zona 9

Zona 10

La Aurora International Airport

To Terminal

Plaza Mayor According to the Spanish colonial town-planning scheme, every town in the New World had to have a large plaza for military exercises, reviews and ceremonies. On the north side of the plaza was to be the *palacio de gobierno*, or colonial government headquarters. On another side, preferably the east, there was to be a church (if the town was large enough to merit a bishop then it was a cathedral). On the other sides of the square there could be other civic buildings, or the large and imposing mansions of wealthy citizens. Guatemala's Plaza Mayor is a good example of the classic town plan.

To appreciate the Plaza Mayor, you've got to visit it on a Sunday when it's thronged with thousands of citizens who have come to stroll, lick ice-cream cones, play in the fountains, take the air, smooch on a bench, listen to *salsa* music on boom-boxes, and ignore the hundreds of trinket vendors.

Palacio Nacional On the north side of the Plaza Mayor is the country's Palacio Nacional, built during the dictatorial presidency of General Jorge Ubico (1931-44) at enormous cost. It replaced an earlier palace called El Centenario, which burnt down in 1925. El Centenario had replaced an even earlier palace which was destroyed in the earthquake of 1917.

The palace is where the President of Guatemala has his executive offices. Visit is by free guided tour (Monday to Friday, 8 am to 4.30 pm). The tour takes you through a labyrinth of gleaming brass and polished wood, carved stone and frescoed arches. The frescoes are by Alberto Gálvez Suárez.

Catedral Metropolitana Built between 1782 and 1809 (the towers were finished later, in 1867), the Catedral Metropolitana has survived earthquake and fire much better than the Palacio Nacional, though the quake of 1917 did a lot of damage, and that of 1976 did even more. All has been restored. It's not a particularly beautiful building, inside or out. Heavy proportions and spare ornamentation make it look severe, though it does have a certain feeling of stateliness. The cathedral is supposedly open every day from 8 am to 7 pm, though you may find it closed, especially at siesta time.

Mercado Central Reconstructed after the earthquake of 1976, this modern market specializes in tourist-oriented items such as cloth (handwoven and machine-woven), carved wood, worked leather and metal, basketry and other handicrafts. Necessities have been moved aside to the streets surrounding the market. You should take a stroll through here, though there are better places to buy crafts. Market hours are 6 am to 6 pm Monday to Saturday, 9 am to noon Sunday. The city's true 'central' food market is in Zona 4.

Things to See – Zona 2
Parque Minerva Zona 2 is north of Zona 1. Though mostly a middle-class residential

district, it holds the large, shady, restful Parque Minerva.

Minerva, goddess of wisdom, technical skill and invention, was a favourite of President Manuel Estrada Cabrera (1898-1920), who fancied himself the country's 'Great Educator'. He accomplished little in the way of educating Guatemala's youth, but he built lots of sylvan parks named for the goddess and quaint little temples in her honour. Otherwise, his presidency is notable for the amount of Guatemalan territory he turned over to the gigantic United Fruit Company for the cultivation of bananas.

Be on the alert for pickpockets, pursesnatchers and other such types, who look especially for tourists.

The prime sight to see in the Parque Minerva is the Relief Map of Guatemala, called simply the **Mapa En Relieve**. Constructed in 1904 under the direction of Francisco Vela, the map shows the country at a scale of 1:10,000, but the height of the mountainous terrain has been exaggerated to 1:2000 for dramatic effect. Little signs indicate major towns and topographical features. Viewing towers afford a panoramic view. This place is odd but fun, and costs only a few centavos for admission (free on Sunday); hours are 8 am to 5 pm every day.

The Mapa En Relieve and Parque Minerva are two km north of the Plaza Mayor along 6a Avenida, but that street is one-way heading south. To get there you can catch a northbound bus (No 1, 45 or 46) on 5a Avenida in Zona 1.

Things to See Zona 4

Zona 4 is known mostly for its markets and its bus stations, all thrown together in the chaotic south-western corner of the zona near the railway.

Pride of Zona 4 however is the **Centro Cívico**, constructed to the north of the zona in the 1950s and '60s. Here you'll find the Palace of Justice, the headquarters buildings of the Guatemalan Institute of Social Security (IGSS), the Banco de Guatemala, the city hall, and the headquarters of INGUAT. The **Banco de Guatemala** building bears high-relief murals by Dagoberto Vásquez depicting the history of his homeland; in the city hall is a huge mosaic by Carlos Mérida completed in 1959.

Behind INGUAT is the **Ciudad Olímpica sports grounds**, and across the street from the Centro Cívico on a hilltop are the **Centro Cultural Miguel Ángel Asturias** (the national theatre, chamber theatre, open-air theatre and a small museum of old armaments).

Things to See – Zona 10

Lying east of Avenida La Reforma, Zona 10 is the up-market district of posh villas, luxury hotels, embassies, and several important museums.

Museo Popol Vuh If you're interested in Maya and Spanish colonial art you must make a visit to this museum (☎ (2) 347121), named for the famous mythic chronicle of the Quiché Maya. Well-chosen polychrome pottery, figurines, incense burners, burial urns, carved wooden masks and traditional textiles fill several exhibit rooms. Others hold colonial paintings, gilded wood and silver objects. A faithful copy of the Dresden Codex, one of the precious 'painted books' of the Maya, is among the most interesting pieces.

The collection is housed on the 6th level of the Edificio Galerías Reforma, Torre 2, Avenida La Reforma 8-60, Zona 9. Opening hours are 9 am to 4.30 pm, Monday to Friday; 9 am to 1 pm Saturday (closed Sunday); admission costs US$1 for adults, US$0.25 for students, US$0.10 for children.

Museo Ixchel (Indian Costumes) The Museo Ixchel del Traje Indígena (☎ (2) 680713) is named for Ixchel, wife of Maya sky god Itzamná and goddess of the moon and of women in childbirth, among other things. As you approach the museum at 4a Avenida 16-27, Zona 10, you'll see groups of village women in their wonderful traditional dress with their woven artwork spread out around them for sale. Within the museum, photographs and exhibits of textiles and other village crafts show the richness of traditional arts in Guatemala's highland towns.

The museum is open Monday to Friday from 8.30 am to 5 pm, Saturday 9 am to 1 pm, and is closed Sunday. Admission costs US$1 for adults, US$0.25 students, and US$0.10 for children.

A new, larger building is being built to house the museum on the campus of the Universidad Francisco Marroquín, at the end of 6 Calle, Zona 10. For now, though, you can walk to the Museo Ixchel from the Museo Popol Vuh. Walk south along Avenida La Reforma for seven blocks; you'll pass the Hotel Camino Real on the left. At 16 Calle turn left and walk a few blocks to 4a Avenida, turn right (south) and the museum is only a few metres further along.

Things to See – Zona 13

The major attraction in the southern reaches of the city is the **Parque Aurora** with its zoo, children's playground, fairgrounds, and several museums offering free admission.

The Moorish-looking **Museo Nacional de Arqueología y Etnología** (☎ (2) 720489) has a collection of Maya sculptures, ceramics and jade, plus some displays of traditional handicrafts. Facing the Museo Nacional de Arqueología y Etnología is the **Museo Nacional de Arte Moderno** (☎ (2) 720467), with a collection of 20th-century Guatemalan art, especially painting and sculpture. Opening hours at both museums are Monday to Friday from 9 am to 4 pm, Saturday and Sunday from 9 to noon and 2 to 4 pm.

Several hundred metres east of the museums is the city's official handicraft market, the **Mercado de Artesanía** (☎ (2) 720208), on 11a Avenida, just off the access road to the airport. Like most official handicraft markets, it livens up only when a tour bus rolls in. Hours are officially 9 am to 6 pm Monday to Saturday, 9 am to 1 pm Sunday.

Kaminaljuyú

Several km west of the centre lie the extensive ruins of Kaminaljuyú, an important Late Pre-Classic/Early Classic Maya site. Unfortunately, much of Kaminaljuyú has been covered by urban sprawl. What has not been covered is presently being excavated. Though you are allowed to visit from 8 am to 6 pm daily, your time would be better spent in the city's museums.

Places to Stay

There are at least a dozen decent hotels about eight blocks south of the Plaza Mayor near the Policía Nacional (National Police Headquarters) and the Correos (post office), in the area bounded by 6a Avenida 'A' and 9a Avenida, and 14 and 16 Calles. Keep street noise in mind as you search for a budget room.

Spring Hotel (☎ (2) 514207/876), 8a Avenida 12-65, Zona 1, is often *completo* (full up) because the location is good, the 28 rooms presentable, the courtyard sunny, and the price right. US$12/16/23 a single/double/triple with private shower. Bathless rooms are 25% to 30% cheaper.

Hotel Lessing House (☎ (2) 513891), 12 Calle 4-35, Zona 1, is run by an efficient señora who offers seven tidy rooms for rent. Rooms can accommodate one (US$7.50), two (US$12), three (US$14.50) or four (US$19). The larger rooms have private showers.

Hogar del Turista (☎ (2) 25522), 11 Calle 10-43, Zona 1, has two narrow courtyards which allow in some sun. Most of the 14 rooms have windows, but a few do not. Prices are high: US$16 a single, US$20 a double with shower. Breakfast is too expensive, but there's free parking.

Right next door is the *Hotel Casa Real* (☎ (2) 21142), 11 Calle 10-57, Zona 1. None of the eight rooms has any plumbing, but some are quite large, with skylights. There's a tidy garden courtyard. Rate is US$6.50 per person.

Hotel Chalet Suizo (☎ (2) 513786), 14 Calle 6-82, Zona 1, has 25 rooms around a plant-filled courtyard. The rooms are clean, though some are dark and claustrophobic. The Café Suizo provides meals. Rates are

US$12/15 a single/double with shared bath, or US$20/25 with private bath.

Hotel Excel (☎ (2) 532709), 9a Avenida 15-12, Zona 1, is a modern place with 17 rooms on three levels. Rooms with bath go for US$15/18/22 a single/double/triple. Most rooms have colour TVs.

Hotel Ajau (☎ (2) 20488), 8a Avenida 15-62, Zona 1, is fairly clean, somewhat cheaper, and a lot quieter than many 9a Avenida hotels. You pay US$7 a double without private shower, US$9 with.

Pensión Meza (☎ (2) 23177), 10 Calle 10-17, Zona 1, is drab and beat-up but busy with international budget travellers who like the camaraderie and the low price of US$6 per person; shared baths only. The restaurant serves cheap meals.

Hotel Colonial (☎ (2) 26722, 22955; fax 28671), 7a Avenida 14-19, Zona 1, is a large old city house converted to a hotel with heavy colonial decor. The covered interior court is pleasant, the 47 rooms clean, all with bath. Rates are US$22/28 a single/double. The hotel has a restaurant.

Posada Belén (☎ (2) 29226, 534530), 13 Calle 'A' 10-30, Zona 1, is on a quiet side street. A charming hostelry, the Belén consists of three neighbouring houses, each with a sunny courtyard. The price is US$28/36 a single/double, with bath. Children under five are not accepted.

Places to Eat

The west side of the Parque Concordia, bounded by 4a and 5a Avenidas and 14 and 15 Calles in Zona 1, is lined with little open-air food stalls serving sandwiches and snacks at rock-bottom prices from early morning to late evening. A meal for US$1 is the rule here.

Delicadezas Hamburgo (☎ 81627), 15 Calle 5-34, Zona 1, on the south side of Parque Concordia, provides a long list of sandwiches at lunch and dinner, as well as German, Guatemalan and American platters at moderate prices. Full meals cost US$4 to US$10. Opening hours are from 7 am to 10 pm every day.

Restaurant Cantón (☎ 516331), 6a Avenida 14-20, Zona 1, facing the park on its east side, is the place to go for cheap Chinese food. Prices seem high at US$5 to US$8 per platter, but platters are meant to be shared by two or more. The Canton is open from 9 am to 5 pm and from 5.30 pm to midnight every day of the week.

There are numerous other Chinese restaurants near the corner of 6a Avenida and 14 Calle, Zona 1. The city's other rich concentration of Chinese restaurants is in the blocks west of the Parque Centenario along 6 Calle, where you'll find the *Restaurant Long Wah* (☎ 26611), 6 Calle 3-70, Zona 1, along with several other places such as *Felicidades, Palacio Real* and *China Hilton*.

Restaurante El Gran Emperador, 14 Calle 6-74, Zona 1, next door to the Chalet Suizo, serves both meat-based and vegetarian meals. The set-price meals go for US$1.50 and US$3.

Los Tilos, 11 Calle 6-54, Zona 1, is the place to go for Central European pastries and baked goods. It's appropriately Tirolean with dark wood and a menu of pastries, wholegrain breads and light meals. A cup of coffee and a pastry cost only US$1 or so. *Café Bohemia* (☎ 82474), 11 Calle 8-48, Zona 1, is a nearby alternative.

On 6a Avenida between 10 and 15 Calles there are dozens of restaurants and fast-food shops of all types: hamburgers, pizzas, pasta, Chinese, fried chicken. You'll have no trouble eating well for US$3 to US$4.

In the midst of the cheap hotel area between 15 and 16 Calles, 9a Avenida has several good little restaurants. There's the *Cafetín El Rinconcito*, 9a Avenida 15-74, facing the Hotel Capri, which is good for tacos, and the restaurant in the Hotel Capri itself, 9a Avenida 15-63, Zona 1, for more substantial meals. The Hotel Colonial, 7a Avenida 14-19, Zona 1, has a slightly better and pricier restaurant.

You might also want to try the *Cafetería El Roble*, 9 Calle 5-46, Zona 1, facing the entrance to the Hotel Pan American. This clean little café is very popular with local office workers who come for breakfast (US$1.75), lunch and dinner (US$3.50).

Pollo Campero (Country Chicken) is the name of Guatemala's Kentucky Fried Chicken clone. You can find branches of the chain on the corner of 9 Calle and 5a Avenida, at 6a Avenida and 15 Calle, and at 8 Calle 9-29, all in Zona 1. Cheerful chicken colours of orange and yellow predominate in these bright, clean places. Two pieces of chicken, French fries (chips), and a soft drink or coffee costs US$3.

El Gran Pavo (The Big Turkey, ☎ 29912, 510933), 13 Calle 4-41, Zona 1, is a big place just to the left (west) of the Hotel Del Centro's entrance. The menu seems to include every Mexican dish imaginable. The birria, a spicy-hot soup of meat, onions, peppers and cilantro (coriander leaf), served with tortillas, is a meal in itself at US$2.75. The Big Turkey is open seven days a week from 11.30 am to 1 am. There's another branch (☎ 325693) at 12 Calle 5-54, Zona 9.

Restaurant Altuna (☎ 20669, 517185), 5a Avenida 12-31, Zona 1, is a large restaurant with the atmosphere of a private club, located just a few steps north of the Hotel Del Centro. Specialities are seafood and Spanish dishes. Full cost for a meal is about US$12 per person; it's open for lunch and dinner every day except Monday.

Restaurant Piccadilly (☎ 514268, 539 223), 6a Avenida 11-01, Zona 1, is among the capital's most popular eateries, with a multinational menu that might have from the UN cafeteria. Most main courses cost US$3 or less. There's another branch of the Piccadilly on the Plazuela España, 7a Avenida 12-00, Zona 9.

Entertainment

Many visitors wine and dine the night away in the Zona Viva, but this is expensive. Instead, take in a movie at one of the cinemas along 6a Avenida between the Plaza Mayor and Parque Concordia; walk along the street to see what's playing. Tickets sell for about US$1.25.

Getting There & Away

Air Flights are expensive, of course, but you might want to at least consider the flight to Flores (Santa Elena) to get to Tikal. The alternative is the bus, a 14-hour grind subject to attacks by robbers.

Belize City – Aerovías flies on Tuesday, Saturday and Sunday via Flores; Aviateca has two flights daily via Flores.

Cancún – Aerocaribe (Mexicana), Aeroquetzal and Aviateca have daily flights.

Chetumal (Mexico) – Aerovías has a nonstop morning flight on Monday, and flights via Belize City on Wednesday and Friday.

Flores, Petén (for Tikal) – Aerocaribe, Aeroquetzal, Aerovías, Aviateca and several smaller airlines (Aviones Comerciales, TAPSA, Tikal Jets) operate daily (some twice-daily) flights. Fares range from US$55 to US$95 one way.

Houston – Continental has direct flights daily, and Aviateca three flights per week via Mérida

Los Angeles – daily flights are by American, Aviateca, Mexicana and TACA; most of these flights make at least one stop along the way.

Mexico City – Mexicana and Aviateca have daily nonstop flights. Aviacsa has flights on Tuesday, Thursday and Saturday.

Mérida – Aviateca has a morning flight three days per week.

Miami – lots of daily flights by American, Aviateca and TACA; many European airlines connect through Miami.

New York – all flights connect through Miami, Houston or Dallas/Fort Worth.

Oaxaca (Mexico) – Aviacsa has flights on Tuesday, Thursday and Saturday.

San José (Costa Rica) – There are daily nonstops by American, Continental and Medellín, and a direct flight with one stop by LACSA three times per week.

San Salvador (El Salvador) – Aviateca, COPA and TACA have daily nonstops.

Tapachula (Mexico) – Aviacsa has flights on Sunday, Tuesday, Thursday and Saturday.

Tuxtla Gutiérrez (Mexico) – Aviacsa has flights Tuesday, Thursday and Saturday.

Airlines based in Guatemala City are listed here:

Aeronica, 10 Calle 6-20, Zona 9, Nicaragua's national airline (☎ (2) 325541, 316759; fax 325649)

Aeroquetzal, 5 Avenida 15-45, Zona 10, Centro Empresarial, Torre 1, office 1007, a Guatemalan regional carrier (☎ (2) 373467/68/69, 337131; fax 347689)

Aerovías, Avenida Hincapié at 18 Calle, Zona 13, a Guatemalan regional carrier (☎ (2) 347935, 319663; fax 325686)

GUATEMALA

Air France, Avenida La Reforma 9-00, Zona 9, Edificio Plaza Panamericana, 8th floor, Guatemala City (☎ (2) 367371, 367667)

Aviacsa, 12 Calle 7-42, Zona 9, Local A, a Mexican regional airline (☎ (2) 319708, 325381; fax 312516)

Aviateca, Avenida Hincapié 12-22, Zona 13, Guatemala's national airline (☎ (2) 318222, 31-8227; fax 347401)

British Airways, Avenida La Reforma 8-60, Zona 9, Edificio Galerías Reforma, Torre II, Guatemala City (☎ (2) 312555)

Continental, La Aurora International Airport (☎ (2) 312051/52/53/54/55)

COPA (Compañía Panameña de Aviación), 7 Avenida 6-53, Zona 4, Edificio El Triángulo, the Panamanian national airline (☎ (2) 313376, 318443; fax 318314)

Iberia, Avenida La Reforma 8-60, Zona 9, Edificio Galerías Reforma (☎ (2) 373914/15, 536555)

Japan Air Lines, 7a Avenida 15-45, Zona 9, Guatemala City (☎ (2) 318597; fax 318531)

KLM Royal Dutch Airlines, 6a Avenida 20-25, Zona 10, Edificio Plaza Marítima, Guatemala City (☎ (2) 370222)

LACSA (Líneas Aereas Costariquenses), 7 Avenida 14-44, Zona 9, Edificio La Galería, Oficina 3, the Costa Rican national airline (☎ (2) 323907, 310906; fax 312284)

Lufthansa German Airlines, 6a Avenida 20-25, Zona 10, Edificio Plaza Marítima, Guatemala City (☎ (2) 370113/14/15/16)

Mexicana, 13 Calle 8-44, Zona 10, Plaza Edyma, Oficina 104, a Mexican international airline (☎ (2) 336001, 312697; fax 336096)

SAHSA, 12 Calle 1-25, Zona 10, Edificio Géminis 10, office 208, the Honduran national airline (☎ (2) 352958/671; fax 353257)

TACA International Airlines, 7 Avenida 14-35, Zona 9, El Salvador's national airline (☎ (2) 322360, 319172; fax 342775)

Bus Unfortunately, Guatemala City has no central bus terminal, even though many Guatemalans talk about the Terminal de Autobuses. Ticket offices and departure points are different for each company. Many are near the huge and chaotic market in Zona 4. If the bus you desire is one of these, the only thing to do is go to the market and ask around until you find the bus.

Here is bus route information for most of Guatemala:

Antigua – 45 km, one hour; Transportes Unidos, 15 Calle 3-65, Zona 1, makes the trip every half-hour for US$0.50 from 7 am to 7 pm stopping in San Lucas Sacatepéquez (☎ (2) 24949).

Chichicastenango – 146 km, 3½ hours; Veloz Quichelense, Terminal de Buses, Zona 4, runs buses every half-hour from 5 am to 6 pm, stopping in San Lucas, Chimaltenango and Los Encuentros for a fare of US$2.25.

Chiquimula – 169 km, three hours; Rutas Orientales, 19 Calle 8-18, Zona 1, runs buses via El Rancho (San Jerónimo), Río Hondo and Zacapa to Chiquimula every 30 minutes from 4 am to 6 pm, for US$2.50 to US$3, depending on the bus. If you're heading for Copán, Honduras, change to a Vilma bus at Chiquimula; see El Florido for details (☎ (2) 537282, 512160).

Cobán – 219 km, four hours; Escobar Monja Blanca, 8a Avenida 15-16, Zona 1, has buses at 4, 5, 7, 8, 9, 10 am, noon, 2, 2.30, 4, 4.30 and 5 pm stopping at the Biotopo del Quetzal, Purulhá, Tactic and San Cristóbal for US$2 to US$3 (☎ (2) 511878).

Copán (Honduras) – see El Florido

El Carmen/Talismán (Mexico) – 278 km, five hours; Transportes Galgos, 7a Avenida 19-44, Zona 1, runs buses along the Pacific Slope road to this border-crossing point, stopping at Escuintla (change for Santa Lucía Cotzumalguapa), Mazatenango, Retalhuleu and Coatepeque, at 5.45 and 10 am, noon, 3.30 and 5.30 pm, for US$4.50 (☎ (2) 534868, 23661).

El Florido/Copán (Honduras) – 280 km, seven hours; Rutas Orientales, 19 Calle 8-18, Zona 1, runs buses via El Rancho (San Jerónimo), Río Hondo and Zacapa to Chiquimula every 30 minutes from 4 am to 6 pm, for US$3. In Chiquimula you transfer to a Vilma bus for the remaining 58-km, 2½-hour trip. Refer to the Central & Eastern Guatemala section for details (☎ (2) 537282, 512160).

Esquipulas – 222 km, four hours; Rutas Orientales, 19 Calle 8-18, Zona 1, has buses departing every half-hour from 4 am to 6 pm, with stops at El Rancho (San Jerónimo), Río Hondo, Zacapa and Chiquimula. The trip costs US$3 (☎ (2) 537282, 512160).

Flores (Petén) – 506 km, 14 or 15 hours, US$12; Petenero, at 17a Avenida 10-25 in Guatemala City, is the favoured company at the moment, with newish buses making the run three times daily (4, 6 and 8 pm from Guatemala City). Others operating this route are:
Maya Express, 17a Avenida 9-36, Zona 1 in Guatemala City) (☎ (2) 539325)
Fuentes del Norte, 17 Calle 8-46, Zona 1 in Guatemala City, runs buses departing from the capital at 1, 2, 3 and 7 am, and 11 pm, with stops at Morales, Río Dulce, San Luis and Poptún. Buses usually depart Guatemala City and Santa Elena full, and riders getting on midway must stand (☎ (2) 86094, 513817).

Huehuetenango – 270 km, five hours; Los Halcones, 7a Avenida 15-27, Zona 1, runs two buses a day (7 am and 2 pm) up the Interamerican Highway to Huehue, stopping at Chimaltenango, Patzicía, Tecpán, Los Encuentros, and San Cristóbal Totonicapán. The fare is US$3.50 (☎ (2) 81979).

La Democracia – 92 km, two hours; Chatia Gomerana, Muelle Central, Terminal de Buses, Zona 4, has buses every half-hour from 6 am to 4.30 pm, stopping at Escuintla, Siquinalá (change for Santa Lucía Cotzumalguapa), La Democracia, La Gomera and Sipacate. The fare is US$1.

La Mesilla/Ciudad Cuauhtémoc (Mexico) – 380 km, seven hours; El Condor, 19 Calle 2-01, Zona 1, goes to La Mesilla, on the Interamerican Highway at the border with Mexico, at 4, 9, 10 and 11 am, and 1 and 5 pm daily for US$4 (☎ (2) 28504).

Panajachel – 147 km, three hours; Rebuli, 21 Calle 1-34, Zona 1, departs for Lago de Atitlán and Panajachel every hour from 7 am to 4 pm, stopping at Chimaltenango, Patzicía, Tecpán Guatemala (for the ruins at Iximché), Los Encuentros, and Sololá, for US$1.75 (☎ (2) 513521).

Puerto Barrios – 307 km, six hours; Litegua, 15 Calle 10-42, Zona 1, has regular buses and also more comfortable Pullman buses every hour from 6 am to 5 pm. Stops are at El Rancho (San Jerónimo), Teculután, Río Hondo and Los Amates (Quiriguá); fare is US$4.50 or US$6 (☎ (2) 27578, 538169).

Puerto San José – 110 km, 1½ hours; Transportes Unidos, 4 Avenida and 1 Calle, Zona 9, runs buses every 30 minutes from 5.30 am to 6 pm, for US$1.50.

Quetzaltenango – 203 km, four hours; Transportes Galgos, 7a Avenida 19-44, Zona 1, makes this run at 5.30, 8.30 and 11 am, and 2.30, 5, 7 and 9 pm, stopping at Chimaltenango, Los Encuentros and Totonicapán, for US$3 (☎ (2) 23661).

Quiriguá – see Puerto Barrios

Retalhuleu – see El Carmen and Tecún Umán

Río Dulce – see Flores

Río Hondo – see Chiquimula, Esquipulas and Puerto Barrios

San Salvador (El Salvador) – 268 km, five hours; Melva Internacional, 3 Avenida 1-38, Zona 9, runs buses from Guatemala City via Cuilapa, Oratorio and Jalpatagua to the Salvadoran border at Valle Nuevo and onward to San Salvador every hour from 5.30 am to 4.30 pm, for US$6 (☎ (2) 310874).

San Vicente Pacaya – 46 km, two hours; Cuquita, Muelle Central, Terminal de Buses, Zona 4, leaves for this volcano village south-west of the capital at 7 am and 4 pm daily, stopping at Amatitlán, for US$1.

Santa Lucía Cotzumalguapa – see El Carmen, La Democracia and Tecún Umán

Tecún Umán/Ciudad Hidalgo (Mexico) – 253 km, five hours; Fortaleza, 19 Calle 8-70, Zona 1, has hourly buses from 1 am to 7 pm, stopping at Escuintla (change for Santa Lucía Cotzumalguapa), Mazatenango, Retalhuleu and Coatepeque (☎ (2) 517994).

Tikal – see Flores

Tourist Minibuses TURANSA (Servicios Turísticos Antigua S A (☎ (2) 953574/75/78/82; fax 953583), Supercentro Molino, Local 58-59, Carretera Roosevelt Km 15, Zona 11) operates tourist minibus shuttle and tour services to various sites in the highlands.

TURANSA minibuses make trips (US$10) in early morning (7.15 am) and late afternoon (6.15 pm) to Antigua, stopping to pick up passengers at major hotels in Guatemala City and at the airport. Similarly, a minibus circulates among Antigua hotels (4.30 to 5 am and 2.50 to 3.20 pm) before heading for La Aurora airport, arriving at 5.40 am and 4 pm.

A similar service is offered by Econo Shuttle (☎ (2) 323434).

Getting Around

To/From the Airport La Aurora international airport is in Zona 13, half an hour or more by bus from Zona 1. If you arrive by air, go up the stairs from the arrivals level to the departures level and walk outside to the small park in front of the terminal. The No 5-Aeropuerto bus will take you through Zonas 9 and 4 to Zona 1, though you may have to wait a half-hour or so for it. The fare is less than one quetzal. See also the Tourist Minibus section earlier.

Bus & Jitney City buses often lack the comforts of windows, paint and seats, but they work, they're cheap, they're frequent, and though often very crowded, they're useful. They are not always safe, however. Theft and robbery are not unusual; there have even been incidents of rape. *Preferencial* buses are newer, safer, not as crowded, and more expensive at about US$0.20 per ride.

In Zona 9, 6a Avenida (southbound) and 7a Avenida (northbound) are loaded with buses traversing the city; in Zona 1 these buses tend to swing away from the commercial district and travel along 4a, 5a, 9a and 10a Avenidas. The most useful north-south buses are Nos 2, 5 and 14. Note that modified numbers (2A, 5-Bolívar etc) follow different routes, and may not get you where you expect to go. Any bus with 'Terminal' in the front window stops at the inter-city bus 'terminal' near the market in Zona 4.

City buses stop running about 10.30 pm, and jitneys *(ruleteros)* begin to run up and down the main avenues. The jitneys run all night, until the buses resume their rattling rides at 4 am; hold up your hand as the signal to stop a jitney.

Taxi Taxis are expensive, US$4 or US$6 for a normal ride – even a short one – within the city. Be sure to agree on the fare before entering the cab; there are no meters.

Western Guatemala

The highlands, stretching from Antigua to the Mexican border north-west of Huehuetenango, are Guatemala's most beautiful region. The verdant hills are clad in lush carpets of emerald green grass, fields of tawny corn and towering stands of pine. All of this lushness comes from the abundant rain which falls between May and October. If you visit during the rainy season, be prepared for some dreary, chilly, damp days. But when the sun comes out, this land is glorious.

Highlights of the region include: graceful Antigua, Guatemala's beautiful colonial city; Lago de Atitlán, a perfect mirror of blue surrounded by Fuji-like volcanoes; the town of Chichicastenango, where traditional Maya religious rites blend with the Catholicism introduced by the Spanish; Quetzaltenango, the commercial and market centre of the south-west; and Huehuetenango, jumping-off place for the cross-border journey to Comitán and San Cristóbal de las Casas in Mexico.

The age-old culture based on maize is still alive; a sturdy cottage set in the midst of a thriving milpa (field of maize) is a common sight, a sight as old as Maya culture itself. Each highland town has its own market and festival days. Life in a highland town can be *muy triste* (sad, boring) when there's not a market or festival going on, so you should try to visit on those special days.

Guatemala's Pacific Slope, descending from the highlands to the ocean, is a lush, humid region of tropical verdure. The volcanic soil is rich and good for growing coffee at the higher elevations, palm-oil seeds and sugar cane at the lower. Vast *fincas* (plantations) exploit the land's economic potential, drawing seasonal workers from the highland towns and villages where work is scarce. Along the Pacific shore stretch endless beaches of dark volcanic sand. The temperature and humidity along the shore are always uncomfortably high, day and night, rainy season and dry. The few small resorts attract mostly local – not foreign – beachgoers.

To travellers, the Pacific Slope is mostly the fast highway called the Carretera al Pacífico (CA2) which runs from the border crossings at Ciudad Hidalgo/Tecún Umán and Talismán/El Carmen to Guatemala City. The 275 km between the Mexican border at Tecún Umán and Guatemala City can be covered in about four hours by car, five by bus, much less than the 342 km of the Interamerican Highway (CA1) through the south-western highlands between La Mesilla and Guatemala City, which takes seven hours. If speed is your goal, the Pacific Slope is your route.

A NOTE ON SAFETY
Though most visitors never experience any trouble, there have been some incidents of robbery, rape and murder of tourists in the highlands. Incidents have occurred on trails up the volcanoes, on the outskirts of Antigua and Chichicastenango, and at lonely spots along country roads. Incidents happen at random and are not predictable. Use caution and common sense, don't do much roaming or driving at night, and you should have a fine time in this beautiful region.

Before you travel in the highlands, contact your embassy or consulate in Guatemala City and get information on the current situation, and advice on how and where to travel in the highlands. Don't rely on local authorities for safety advice as they may downplay the dangers. For embassy phone numbers, see the Guatemala City section earlier.

GETTING AROUND

Guatemala City and the Guatemalan/ Mexican border station at La Mesilla are connected by the Interamerican Highway, known also as the Carretera Interamericana or as Centroamérica 1. The 266-km bus trip between Guatemala City and Huehue- tenango can take over five hours, on this curvy mountain road, but the time passes pleasantly amidst the beautiful scenery. The Carretera al Pacífico via Escuintla and Retalhuleu is straighter and faster, and is the better route to take if your goal is to reach Mexico as quickly as possible.

Many buses of different companies rumble up and down the highway; for an idea of the service, refer to Getting There & Away in the Guatemala City section. As most of the places you'll want to reach are some distance off the Interamerican Highway, you may find yourself waiting at major highway junctions such as Los Encuentros and Cuatro Caminos in order to connect with the right bus. Travel is easiest on market days and in the morning. By mid or late afternoon buses may be difficult to find, and all short-distance local traffic stops by dinner time.

ANTIGUA GUATEMALA

Altitude 1530 metres
Population 28,000
La muy Noble y muy Leal Ciudad de Santiago de los Caballeros de Goathemala, as it was first known, is among the oldest and most beautiful cities in the Americas. Its setting is superb, amidst three magnificent volcanoes named Agua, Fuego and Acatenango. Fuego (Fire) is easily recognisable by its plume of smoke and – at night – by the red glow it projects against the sky.

Founded in 1542, Antigua Guatemala has weathered 16 damaging earthquakes, floods and fires. The handsome, sturdy colonial buildings that survive have proved their worth over and over again, and Antigua today might be said to be the result of Darwinian architecture: survival of the fittest buildings. The survivors continue to be strengthened (nowadays with steel beams and reinforced concrete); the rubble of the weakest has long since been swept away.

If you have the opportunity to be in Antigua during Semana Santa (Holy Week) – especially on Good Friday – seize it; but make your hotel reservations months in advance, as all hotels will be full.

Orientation

Volcán Agua is south-east of the city and visible from most points within it; Volcán Fuego is south-west, and Volcán Acatenango is to the west. The three volcanoes, which appear on the city's coat of arms, provide easy reference points.

Antigua's street grid uses a modified version of the numbering system used in Guatemala City. (For details of that system, see the Street Grid System under the Getting Around section earlier in this chapter) In Antigua the city is divided into quadrants by 4a Avenida and 4 Calle, and compass points – *norte* (north), *sur* (south), *oriente* (east) and *poniente* (west) – are added to the avenidas and calles. Calles run east-west, and so 4 Calle west of the Parque Central is 4 Calle Poniente; avenidas run north-south, and 3a Avenida north of the Parque Central is 3a Avenida Norte. The central point is the north-east corner of the city's main plaza, the Parque Central.

The old headquarters of the Spanish colonial government, called the Palacio de los Capitanes, is on the south side of the plaza; you'll know it by its double (two-storey) arcade. On the east side is the cathedral; on the north side is the Palacio del Ayuntamiento (Town Hall); and on the west side are banks and shops.

The Arco de Santa Catalina (Arch of St Catharine), spanning 5a Avenida Norte between 1 Calle and 2 Calle, is another famous Antigua landmark.

Intercity buses arrive at the Terminal de Buses, a large open lot just north of the market, four blocks west of the Parque Central along 4 Calle Poniente. Buses serving towns and villages in the vicinity leave from the terminal as well, or from other points around the market.

Information

Tourist Information Antigua's INGUAT tourist office (☎ (9) 320763) is in the Palacio de los Capitanes, at the south-east corner of the Parque Central, next to the intersection of 4a Avenida Sur and 5 Calle Oriente. It's open 8 am to 5 pm, seven days a week.

Check the bulletin board at Doña Luisa Xicotencatl restaurant, the informal social centre for travellers, which is described under the Places to Eat section below. It has noticeboards which are good for all kinds of information: on renting houses and rooms, bikes or horses; for Spanish lessons, rides to the airport or tours to Tikal and other sites; and even video bar film schedules.

Another good source of information on

Antigua
Guatemala

places for rent is *The Classifieds*, a free weekly booklet distributed in hotels and the tourist office.

Money Banks in Antigua, as elsewhere in Guatemala, tend to be open from 9 am to 2 pm Monday to Thursday (until 2.30 pm Friday) but the Banco del Agro, on the north side of the Parque Central, has a *ventanilla especial* (special teller window) open longer hours, and on Saturday. Lloyd's Bank is at the north-east corner of the Parque Central, on the corner of 4a Avenida and 4 Calle.

Post & Telecommunications The post office (Correos) is at 4 Calle Poniente and Alameda de Santa Lucía, west of the Parque Central near the market. It's open Monday to Saturday from 8 am to noon and from 2 to 8 pm, and is closed on Sunday.

The Guatel (telephone office) is just off the south-west corner of the Parque Central, at the intersection of 5 Calle Poniente and 5a Avenida Sur. Hours are 7 am to midnight daily.

See Post & Telecommunications in the Facts for the Visitor section earlier in this chapter for information on using special services which connect you to an operator in your home country.

For phone, fax, electronic mail and telex messages, try Conexión Telecommunications (☎ (9) 323316; fax 320602; Internet 5385706@MCImail.com, 5 Calle Poniente 11-B. Prices for sending are fairly high; receiving is cheap. They're open every day.

■	PLACES TO STAY	20	Pizzería Martedino & Pollo Campesino		Palacio del Ayuntamiento
2	Pensión Ruiz 1	21	Cenicienta	28	Chevron Fuel Station
3	Ponción El Arco	22	Asados de la Calle del Arco, El Fondo de la Calle Real & Sueños del Quetzal	29	Cementerio General
4	Hotel Convento Santa Catalina			30	Mercado (Market)
5	Posada Asjemenou			31	Monumento a Landívar
9	Pensión Ruiz 2	25	Restaurant Doña Luisa Xicotencatl	32	Correos (Main Post Office)
11	Posada de Don Rodrigo	36	Restaurant Italiano El Capuchino	35	Iglesia de San Agustín
13	Hotel Casa Santo Domingo	39	Doña María Gordillo Dulces Típicos	37	Parque Central
17	Posada Refugio	40	Mistral	38	Catedral de Santiago
21	Hotel El Descanso	45	El Sereno & Rainbow Reading Room	46	Conexión Telecommunications
24	Hotel El Carmen			47	Guatel Telephone Office
26	Hotel Aurora		OTHER	48	Cinema
27	Posada San Francisco			49	Palacio de los Capitanes
33	Posada Doña Angelina	1	La Merced	50	INGUAT Tourist Office
34	Hotel Posada Don Valentino	6	Arco de Santa Catalina	51	Museo de Arte Colonial & Universidad de San Carlos
41	Hotel El Confort de Antigua	7	Convento de Santa Teresa	52	Casa Popenoe
42	La Quinta	8	Convento de las Capuchinas	53	Iglesia del Espíritu Santo
43	Casa de Santa Lucía	10	TURANSA-Avis Rent a Car Office	54	Iglesia de Santa Lucía
44	Hotel El Pasaje	12	El Carmen	55	Hospital de San Pedro
58	Hotel Santa Clara	14	Casa K'ojom	56	Park & Handicrafts Market
61	Hotel Antigua	15	Terminal de Buses	57	Iglesia y Convento de Santa Clara
62	Hotel San Jorge	16	Mercado (Market)	59	Iglesia de San Francisco
63	Ramada Hotel Antigua	18	Convento de la Compañía de Jesús & Handicrafts Market		
64	Mesón Panza Verde			60	Iglesia de San José
		23	Museo de Santiago &	65	Escuela de Cristo
▼	PLACES TO EAT				
19	Capri Antigua Cafetería				

Slightly cheaper rates are charged at Guisela Fax (☎ & fax 323091), 2 Calle Poniente 19.

Bookshops Rainbow Reading Room, 7a Avenida Sur No 1, at 6 Calle Poniente, has thousands of used books in English and Spanish. They serve cheap, healthy food and sponsor musical programs in the evenings. The opening hours are 8 am to 10 pm (until 11 pm on Friday and Saturday).

Un Poco de Todo, at the north-west corner of the Parque Central, has English and Spanish books. It's open Monday to Friday from 9.30 am to 1 pm and 3 to 6 pm.

Casa Andinista, 4 Calle Oriente No 5, just a few steps off the Parque Central, sells Spanish books, postcards and maps.

Librería del Pensativo (☎ 320729), 5a Avenida Norte 29 between 1 and 2 Calle, just north of the arch on the right-hand side, has some English books among the Spanish ones.

Emergency The local hospital is named for Pedro de Betancourt, Antigua's great healer: Hospital de San Pedro (☎ (9) 320301) is at 3a Avenida and 6 Calle.

Laundry Wash & Wear Antigua, Alameda de Santa Lucia 52, is a few steps south of the Hotel El Pasaje near 6 Calle Poniente, open 7 am to 7 pm (Sunday 8 am to noon). Another laundry is to the left of the Posada Refugio, 4 Calle Poniente No 30.

Toilets Public toilets are at 4a Avenida and 4 Calle, at the north-east corner of the Parque Central.

Semana Santa

By far the most interesting time to be in Antigua is during Semana Santa (Holy Week), when the city celebrates by dressing up hundreds of its people in deep purple robes as pseudo-Israelites to accompany daily religious processions in remembrance of the Crucifixion. Streets are covered in elaborate and colourful *alfombras* (carpets) of coloured sawdust and flower petals. These beautiful but fragile works of art are destroyed as the processions shuffle through them, but recreated the next morning for another day.

If you don't pin down a room in advance, you may have to stay in Guatemala City, and commute to the festivities.

Pick up a schedule of events at the tourist office. Traditionally, the most interesting days are Palm Sunday, when a procession departs from La Merced (see under Churches) in mid-afternoon; Holy Thursday, when a late afternoon procession departs the Iglesia de San Francisco; and Good Friday, when an early morning procession departs from La Merced, and a late afternoon one from the Escuela de Cristo.

On a secular note, beware of pickpockets. In the press of the emotion-filled crowds lining the processional routes, razor blades silently slice pocket and bag, and gentle hands remove contents seemingly without sound or movement.

Parque Central

Antigua's Central Park is the gathering place for citizens and foreign visitors alike. On most days the periphery is lined with villagers who have brought their handicrafts – cloth, dolls, blankets, pottery – to sell to tourists; on Sunday the parque is mobbed with marketeers, and the streets on the east and west sides of the parque are closed to traffic in order to give them room. The best prices are to be had late on Sunday afternoon, when the market is winding down.

The **Palacio de los Capitanes**, built in 1543 as the Palace of the Royal Audiencia & Captaincy-General of Guatemala, has a stately double arcade on its façade which marches proudly across the southern extent of the parque. The façade is original, but most of the rest of the building was reconstructed a century ago. From 1543 to 1773, this building was the governmental centre of all Central America.

The **Catedral de Santiago**, on the east side of the parque, was founded in 1542, damaged by earthquakes many times, badly ruined in 1773, and only partially rebuilt between 1780 and 1820. In the 16th and early

17th centuries, Antigua's churches had lavish Baroque interiors, but most lost this richness when they were rebuilt after the earthquakes. The cathedral shares this fate. Its chief distinction today is as the resting place (in the crypt) of Bernal Díaz del Castillo, historian of the Spanish conquest, who died in 1581.

On the north side of the parque stands the **Palacio del Ayuntamiento**, Antigua's town hall, which dates mostly from 1743. In addition to town offices, it holds the Museo de Santiago, which houses a collection of colonial furnishings, artefacts and weapons. Opening hours are from 9 am to 4 pm Tuesday to Friday, 9 am to noon and 2 to 4 pm on Saturday and Sunday, closed Monday; admission costs US$0.20. Next door is the **Museo del Libro Antiguo** (Old Book Museum), which has exhibits of colonial printing and binding; opening hours are the same.

The **Universidad de San Carlos** was founded in 1676, but its main building (built in 1763) at 5 Calle Oriente No 5, half a block east of the parque, now houses the Museo de Arte Colonial (same hours as the Museo de Santiago).

Churches

Once glorious in their gilded Baroque finery, Antigua's churches have suffered indignities from both nature and humankind. Rebuilding after earthquakes gave the churches thicker walls, lower towers and belfries, and unembellished interiors; and moving the capital to Guatemala City deprived Antigua of the population needed to maintain the churches in their traditional richness. Still, they are impressive.

From the parque, walk three long blocks up 5a Avenida Norte, passing beneath the arch of Santa Catalina (Arco de Santa Catalina), built in 1694 and rebuilt in the 19th century. At the northern end of 5a Avenida is the Iglesia y Convento de Nuestra Señora de La Merced (Church & Convent of Our Lady of Mercy), known simply as **La Merced**, Antigua's most striking colonial church. Its

Baroque façade dates from the mid 19th century.

The next most notable church is the **Iglesia de San Francisco**, on the corner of 7 Calle Oriente and Calle de los Pasos. Dating from the mid-16th century, little of the original building remains. All that remains of the original church is the Chapel of Hermano Pedro, resting place of Fray Pedro de Betancourt, a Franciscan monk. Hermano Pedro (Brother Peter) arrived in Antigua in the mid-17th century, promptly founded a hospital for the poor, and earned the gratitude of generations. His intercession is still sought by the ill, who pray fervently by his casket.

The **Convento de las Capucinas**, 2a Avenida Norte and 2 Calle Oriente, was a convent founded in 1736 by nuns from Madrid. Destroyed repeatedly by earthquakes, it is now a museum, with exhibits of the religious life in colonial times.

Casa K'ojom

Guatemala's rich traditional Maya culture is changing, giving way before the onslaught of modernity as portrayed by tourists and the mass media. In 1984, Sr Samuel Franco Arce began photographing the Maya ceremonies and festivals, and recording their music on audio tape. By 1987 he had enough to found Casa K'ojom ('house of music'), a museum of Maya music and the ceremonies in which it was used.

Some visitors to Guatemalan towns and villages are lucky enough to witness a parade of the *cofradías*, or some other age-old ceremony. But lucky or not, you can experience some of the fascination of the culture in a visit to Casa K'ojom, Calle de Recoletos, a block west of the bus station, open 9.30 am to 12.30 pm, and 2 to 5 pm (till 4 pm on Saturday); closed Sunday. Admission costs US$0.40, or US$1 including the audiovisual show.

Besides the fine collection of photographs of ceremonies, musicians and festivals, Sr Franco has amassed a wealth of objects: musical instruments, tools, masks and figures. Don't miss the exhibit featuring

Maximón, the evil folk-god venerated by the people of several highland towns.

Casa Popenoe

At the corner of 5 Calle Oriente and 1a Avenida Sur stands this beautiful mansion, built in 1636 by Don Luis de las Infantas Mendoza y Venegas. Ruined by the earthquake of 1773, the house stood desolate for 1½ centuries until it was bought in 1931 by Dr and Mrs Popenoe. The Popenoes' painstaking and authentic restoration yields a fascinating glimpse of how the family of an important royal official (Don Luis) lived in 17th-century Antigua. The house is open Monday to Saturday from 2 to 4 pm; the guided tour costs US$0.50.

Market & Monumento a Landívar

At the western end of 5 Calle Poniente is the Monumento a Landívar, a structure of five colonial-style arches set in a little park. Rafael Landívar, an 18th-century Jesuit priest and poet, lived and wrote in Antigua for some time.

Around the Monumento a Landívar on the west side of Alameda de Santa Lucía sprawls the Mercado – chaotic, colourful and always busy. Morning, when all the village people from the vicinity are actively buying and selling, is the best time to come.

Spanish Schools

Antigua is the nicest place in the country to study Spanish, and there are many schools to choose from.

Reports from travellers indicate that price, quality of teaching and satisfaction of students varies greatly from one to another. Often the quality of the class depends upon the particular instructor, and thus may vary even within a single school. Instructors tend to move around from one school to another to improve their own incomes and teaching conditions, so it is difficult to recommend particular schools at any given time. If possible, ask for references and talk to someone who has studied at your chosen school recently.

Many of Antigua's Spanish schools are organised into two loose groupings, the Asociación de Academias de Español, Apdo Postal 76, Antigua Guatemala; and the Escuelas Unidas de Español. Both claim to be approved by the Guatemalan Ministry of Education and INGUAT (Institute of Tourism).

Asociación de Academias de Español

Academia Centroamérica, Abel Alfredo Aquino Cuellar, 1 Calle del Chajón No 19-A (☎ 323297)

Academia Cervantes, Carlos René Aguilar López, 5 Calle Poniente No 42-A; I've had a good report on this school (☎ 320635).

Academia de Español Cristiana, Franklin Romeo Contreras, 6a Avenida Norte No 15 (☎ 320367)

Academia Landívar, Héctor Haroldo Pérez Estrada, 2 Calle Oriente No 4

Academia Pedro de Alvarado, Catalina Galindo de Le-cunff, 1 Calle Poniente No 24 (☎ 322266)

Centro Dinámico, Marta Elisa Gaytán, 6a Avenida Norte No 63 (☎ 322440)

Centro Lingüístico Maya, Angel Arturo Miranda Baeza, 5a Calle Poniente No 20; I've had good reports on this school as well (☎ 320656).

Instituto Antigüeño, José Mario Valle García, 1 Calle Poniente No 33 (☎ 322682)

Proyecto Lingüístico Francisco Marroquín, 4a Avenida Sur No 4 (☎ & fax 320406)

Escuelas Unidas de Español

Arcoiris, 7 Calle Oriente No 19 (☎ 322933)

Cabaguil, 7 Calle Oriente No 3

Colonial, Calzada Santa Lucía Sur y Pasaje Matheu No 7

Donquijote, 9 Calle Poniente No 7 (☎ 320651)

Tecún Umán, 6 Calle Poniente No 34 (☎ 322792)

Independent

Quiché College Level Spanish, 8a Avenida No 15-A (☎ & fax 320575)

Places to Stay

Foreign students at Spanish-language schools usually stay in cheap family pensions at low prices – about US$40 per week. The tourist office has information on how to get in touch with willing families.

Casa de Santa Lucía, at No 9, between 5 and 6 Calles Poniente, is exceptionally attractive and well kept, and charges US$8/10 a single/double with shower and pseudo-colonial atmosphere; ring the bell to the left of the door; there's a car park. The friendly *Hotel El Pasaje*, Alameda de Santa Lucía Sur 3, charges US$6 a double without bath, US$8 with.

Nearby, the *Posada Doña Angelina*, 4 Calle Poniente 33, is actually two hotels in one. The older section on 4 Calle, a few steps off the Alameda de Santa Lucía, charges US$5/9/11 a single/double/triple in waterless rooms arranged around a bare courtyard. The newer section of the hotel, also around a courtyard, charges US$10/14/18 for a room with shower.

La Quinta, 5 Calle Poniente 19, is clean, friendly, and near the bus station. Rooms are OK at US$5/7/9 a single/double/triple, without running water.

Posada San Francisco, 3 Calle Oriente 19-A, is good, simple, quiet, and family-run, with double rooms for US$6/8 without/with private bath.

Despite its popularity with budget travellers, only parts of the *Posada Refugio*, 4 Calle Poniente 30, are comfortable or clean. The price is US$6/8 a double without/with bath.

Hotel El Descanso (☎ (9) 320142), 5a Avenida Norte 9, '50 steps from the central parque', has 14 small rooms in the building facing the restaurant called Café Café. It's clean and convenient at US$12 to US$16 a double with bath.

Pensión El Arco, 5a Avenida Norte 32, just north of the Santa Catalina arch, rents plain and sometimes claustrophobic but nevertheless tidy rooms without bath for US$3.50 per person. It's worth looking at the room before you say yes.

Pensión Ruiz 2 2 Calle Poniente 25, is slightly cleaner, pleasanter and more expensive (at US$3.50 per person) than its sister establishment, the *Pensión Ruiz 1*, Alameda de Santa Lucia north of 2 Calle Poniente.

Hotel El Confort de Antigua (☎ (9) 320566), 1 Avenida Norte No 2, is clean and beautifully kept. The five rooms share two baths, and cost US$15/20 a single/double.

Hotel Posada Don Valentino (☎ (9) 320384), 5 Calle Poniente No 28, has tiny rooms that are bright and clean, and a nice patio and garden, for US$9/14 a single/

double without bath, US$11/16 with. They have a car park one block away.

Hotel Santa Clara (☎ (9) 320342), 2 Avenida Sur No 20, is quiet, proper and clean, with a small garden and some large rooms with two double beds. Rates are US$10 to US$15 a single, US$13 to US$18 a double, with bath.

Posada Asjemenou (☎ (9) 322670), 5 Avenida Norte No 31, just north of the arch, is a beautifully renovated house built around a grassy courtyard with a fountain. At the time of writing, its prices of US$12/18 a double without/with bath make it the best value for money in town. Prices will no doubt rise, though. There's a pay car park nearby.

Hotel Convento Santa Catalina (☎ & fax 9-323080), 5 Avenida Norte No 28, just south of the arch, is a nicely renovated convent around a courtyard, with large rooms very reasonably priced at US$22 to US$28 a single, US$28 to US$34 a double, with bath.

Places to Eat
Not far from the market and bus terminal on 4 Calle Poniente between the Alameda de Santa Lucía and 7a Avenida Sur are several *comedores*, family-run cookshops specialising in simple food at rock-bottom prices. There's the *Comedor Antigua* at No 21, and the *Cafetería y Comedor San José* at No 30.

The richest concentration of restaurants is on 5 Avenida Norte. *Asados de la Calle del Arco*, just off the parque on the right, serves grilled meats and Tex-Mex food. Try the burritos for US$3.

Right next door to the red-meat place is *Sueños del Quetzal* (☎ (9) 322676), 5 Avenida Norte No 3, a full-service vegetarian restaurant open 7 am to 10 pm every day. Most of the tables are upstairs.

Half a block north from the parque is *Cenicienta*, 5a Avenida Norte 9, mostly for cakes, pastries, pies and coffee, but the blackboard menu often features quiche lorraine and quiche chapín (Guatemalan-style), yoghurt and fruit as well. A slice of something and a hot beverage cost less than US$2.

El Fondo de la Calle Real, 5a Avenida Norte 5, appears to have no room for diners, but that's because all the tables are upstairs. The menu is good and varied, for all tastes and appetites. The speciality, caldo real (hearty chicken soup), for US$2.50 makes a good lunch. Roast chicken, sandwiches, tacos and fondues are priced from US$2.50 to US$5.

Pollo Campesino, 4 Calle Poniente 18, half a block west of the parque, provides cheap roast chicken in modern surroundings.

Restaurant Pizzería Martedino, also at 4 Calle Poniente 18, sells good pizzas for US$2 to US$5 depending upon size and ingredients; dishes of pasta are less. The almuerzo del día (daily set-price lunch) is a bargain at US$2.50. *Restaurant Gran Muralla*, next door, serves a Guatemalan highland version of Chinese food.

Capri Antigua Cafetería, 4 Calle Poniente 24, near the corner with 6a Avenida Norte, is a simple, modern place that's very popular with younger diners and budget travellers. They usually fill its little wooden benches and tables, ordering soup for less than US$1, sandwiches for only slightly more, and platos fuertes (substantial platters) for US$2.20 to US$3.25.

Rainbow Reading Room, at 7a Avenida and 6 Calle Poniente, is a lending library, bookshop, travellers' club and restaurant all in one. Healthy vegetarian dishes are a speciality, as is close camaraderie.

Perhaps the best bargain in a full restaurant is the *Restaurant Italiano El Capuchino* (☎ 320613), 6a Avenida Norte 10, between 4 and 5 Calles Poniente. The daily four-course set-price lunch costs about US$4 or US$5. There's a well-stocked bar.

The social centre of travelling gringos and gringas in Antigua is *Restaurant Doña Luisa Xicotencatl*, 4 Calle Oriente No 12, 1½ blocks east of the parque. A small central courtyard is set with dining tables, with more dining rooms on the upper level. The menu lists a dozen sandwiches made with Doña Luisa's own bread baked on the premises, as well as yoghurt, chilli, cakes and pies, and heartier meat dishes, all priced from about US$2.50 to US$5. Alcoholic beverages are served, as is excellent Antigua coffee.

Mistral, 4 Calle Oriente 7, across the street from Doña Luisa, serves freshly squeezed fruit and vegetable juices, good coffee and sandwiches, with most items priced at US$1 or less.

Entertainment
Dinner, drinks with friends, a video movie in the bar at Mistral, 4 Calle Oriente 7, a stroll through Antigua's colonial streets – these are the pleasures of the evening here. Bars for music and dancing open and close frequently. Current trendy favourite is the *Macondo Pub*, 5 Avenida at 2 Calle Poniente, just south of the arch. The *Rainbow Reading Room* has singalongs and similar informal entertainment most evenings.

The cinema half a block south of the Parque Central on 5a Avenida Sur mostly has movies in Spanish, but occasionally has something with subtitles.

Getting There & Away
Bus connections with Guatemala City are frequent, and there are direct buses several times daily to Panajachel on Lago de Atitlán. To go directly to other highland towns such as Chichicastenango, Quetzaltenango and Huehuetenango you may have to take one of the frequent minibuses to Chimaltenango (US$0.40), on the Interamerican Highway, and catch an onward bus from there.

Guatemala City – 45 km, one hour; Transportes Unidos, 15 Calle 3-65, Zona 1, in Guatemala City, makes the trip every half an hour from 7 am to 7 pm stopping in San Lucas Sacatepéquez, for US$0.80 (☎ 2-24949).

Izabal, Río Dulce – 352 km, eight hours; Río Dulce Shuttle, 7 Avenida 14-44, Zona 9 in Guatemala City, operates tourist minibuses between Antigua and Izabal, on the Río Dulce, on Wednesday, Friday and Sunday, for US$32 one way. The trip includes a 45-minute stop at Quiriguá to see its famous stelae (☎ 2-340323/4; fax 340341).

Panajachel (Lago de Atitlán) – 80 km, two hours; several buses daily from Antigua's Terminal de Buses, even more from Chimaltenango.

Getting Around

Buses to outlying villages such as Santa María de Jesús (US$0.25, 30 minutes) and San Antonio Aguas Calientes (US$0.20, 25 minutes) depart from the Terminal de Buses west of the market. It's best to make your outward trip early in the morning, and your return trip by mid-afternoon, because services drop off dramatically as late afternoon approaches.

Bicycles and motorbikes are available for hire at several places in Antigua for US$25 per day. Try the Hotel Los Capitanes, next to the Los Capitanes cinema, 9a Avenida Sur. Read 'A Note on Safety' at the beginning of this section before venturing out of town on a motorbike.

AROUND ANTIGUA GUATEMALA
Horse Riding

Several stables in Antigua rent horses and arrange for day or overnight tours into the countryside. Ask at the tourist office, or contact R Rolando Pérez (☎ (9) 322809), San Pedro El Panorama No 28.

Ciudad Vieja & San Antonio Aguas Calientes

Six and a half km south-west of Antigua along the Escuintla road is Ciudad Vieja (Old City), site of the first capital of the Captaincy-General of Guatemala. Founded in 1527, it was destroyed in 1541 when the aptly named Volcán Agua loosed a flood of water pent up in its crater. There is little to see today.

Past Ciudad Vieja, turn right at a large cemetery on the right-hand side; the unmarked road takes you through San Miguel Dueñas to San Antonio Aguas Calientes. (In San Miguel Dueñas, take the first street on the right – between two houses – after coming to the concrete-block paving; this, too, is unmarked. If you come to the Texaco station in the centre of San Miguel, you've missed the road.)

The road winds through *fincas* coffee, little vegetable and cornfields and hamlets of farmers to San Antonio Aguas Calientes, 14 km from Antigua. As you enter San Antonio's plaza, you will see that the village is noted for its weaving. Market stalls in the plaza sell local woven and embroidered goods, as do shops on side streets (walk to the left of the church to find them). Bargaining is expected.

Volcanoes

Climbing the volcanoes that loom above Antigua is exciting in more ways than one. In recent years robbers have intercepted groups of foreigners from time to time, relieving them of all their goods (including clothing). There have been incidents of rape and murder as well. Still, many visitors take their chances and join a group with an armed guard in return for the exhilaration and the beauty of the view.

Check with your embassy in Guatemala City regarding safety before you climb. If you decide to go, it's easy to find a guide. Ask at the tourist office in Antigua, or at your hotel.

Take sensible precautions. Have warm clothing and, in the rainy season, some sort of rainproof gear. Carry a torch (flashlight) in case the weather changes – it can get night-dark in rain on the mountain. Carry some candy or snacks and water as well.

Various agencies operate tours up **Volcán Pacaya** for about US$25 per person, including a 1½-hour bus ride to the head of the trail followed by a two-hour trek to the summit.

For treks up the slopes of **Volcán Agua** (3766 metres), follow 2a Avenida Sur or Calle de los Pasos south toward El Calvario (two km), then continue onward via San Juan del Obispo (another three km) to Santa María de Jesús, nine km south of Antigua. The volcano rises dramatically right behind the village.

Santa María (altitude 2080 metres, population 11,000) is a village of unpaved streets, bamboo fences, a church and Municipalidad on the main plaza, which is also the bus terminal. Down the street from the church towards the white church in the distance is the *Comedor & Hospedaje El Oasis*, a tidy little pension where you can get a meal or a bed for the night.

Various outfitters in Antigua can furnish details about the climb. Start very early in the morning, as it can take five hours to reach the summit. If you are not an experienced hiker in good physical condition, don't plan to go all the way. You'll need water, warm clothing and good lungs as the air gets mighty thin at 3766 metres.

CHIMALTENANGO

The road westward from Antigua makes its way 17 km up to the ridge of the Continental Divide, where it meets the Interamerican Highway at Chimaltenango, capital of the department (province) of Chimaltenango. This was an old town to the Cakchiquel Maya when the conquistadors arrived in 1526, but today there is little to detain you.

Westward 32 km along the highway takes you past the turning for the back road to Lago de Atitlán via Patzicía and Patzún. The area around these two towns has been notable for high levels of guerrilla activity in recent years. The road is in poor condition in any case, so it's just as well that your bus stays on the Interamerican Highway to Tecpán Guatemala, the turning-point for a visit to the ruined Cakchiquel capital city of Iximché.

IXIMCHÉ

Set on a flat promontory surrounded by steep cliffs, Iximché, founded in the late 15th century, was well sited to be the capital city of the Cakchiquel Maya. The Cakchiquels were at war with the Quiché Maya, and the city's natural defences served them well. When the conquistadors arrived in 1524, the Cakchiquels made an alliance with them against their enemies, the Quichés and the Tzutuhils. The Spaniards set up their headquarters right next door to the Cakchiquel capital at Tecpán Guatemala. But Spanish demands for gold and other loot soon put an end to the alliance. In the ensuing battles the Cakchiquels went down in defeat.

As you enter Tecpán you will see signs pointing to the unpaved road leading through fields and pine forests to Iximché, less than six km to the south. If you don't have your own vehicle, you can walk the distance in

about an hour, see the ruins and rest (another hour), then walk back to Tecpán, for a total of three hours. If you're going to walk, it's best to do it in the morning so that you're back at the highway by early afternoon. Bus traffic dwindles by late afternoon.

Enter the archaeological site (open 9 am to 4 pm daily), pass the small museo (museum) on the right, and you come to four ceremonial plazas surrounded by grass-covered temple structures and ball courts. Some of the structures have been cleaned and maintained; on a few the original plaster coating is still in place, even with some traces of the original paint.

Getting There & Away

Transportes Poaquileña, runs buses from Tecpán Guatemala to Guatemala City (87 km, 1½ hours) every half hour from 3 am to 5 pm. From Guatemala City to Tecpán, buses run as frequently, from 5 am to 7.30 pm.

LOS ENCUENTROS

Another 40 km westward along the Interamerican Highway from Tecpán brings you to the highway junction of Los Encuentros. There is no real town here, just a lot of people waiting to catch buses. The road to the right heads north to Chichicastenango and Santa Cruz del Quiché; the road to the left descends 12 km to Sololá, capital of the department of the same name, and then to Panajachel on the shores of Lago de Atitlán.

SOLOLÁ

Population 9000

Though the Spaniards founded Sololá (altitude 2110 metres) in 1547, there was a Cakchiquel town called Tzoloyá here before they came. Sololá's importance comes from its geographic position on trade routes between the Tierra Caliente (hot lands of the Pacific Slope) and Tierra Fría (the chilly highlands). All the traders meet here, and Sololá's Friday market is one of the best in the highlands.

On market days, the plaza next to the cathedral is ablaze with the colours of costumes from a dozen surrounding villages and towns. On Sunday mornings the officers of the cofradías (traditional religious brotherhoods) parade ceremoniously to the cathedral for their devotions. On other days, Sololá sleeps.

Sololá to Panajachel
The road from Sololá descends more than 500 metres through pine forests in its eight-km course to Panajachel. You should try to get a seat on the right-hand side of the bus because all of the sights and views are on your right.

Along the way the road passes Sololá's colourful cemetery, and a Guatemalan army base. The fantastic guard post by the main gate is in the shape of a huge helmet resting upon a pair of soldier's boots.

PANAJACHEL
Nicknamed Gringotenango ('place of the foreigners') by locals and foreigners alike, 'Pana' has long been discovered by tourists. In the hippy heyday of the 1960s and '70s it was crowded with laid-back travellers in semi-permanent exile. In recent years the town's tourism has boomed again.

There is no notable colonial architecture in this town, no colourful indigenous market. The lake, however, is absolutely gorgeous, still and beautiful early in the day, the best time to swim. By noon the Xocomil, a south-easterly wind, may have risen to ruffle the lake's surface. The lake is a caldera (collapsed volcanic cone) more than 320 metres deep, and the land drops off sharply very near the shore.

The volcanoes surrounding the lake are: Volcán Tolimán (3155 metres), due south of Panajachel; Volcán Atitlán (3505 metres), also to the south; and Volcán San Pedro (3025 metres) to the south-west.

Panajachel is the starting point for excursions to the smaller, more traditional indigenous villages on the western and southern shores of the lake. These, too, have been touched by tourism, but retain their charm nonetheless.

Orientation & Information
The geographic centre of town, and the closest thing it has to a bus station, is the intersection of Calle Real and Calle Santander, where you will see the Banco Agricola Mercantil, as well as the INGUAT tourist office and the Maya Palace Hotel. Calle Santander, lined with stands selling handicrafts, is the main road to the beach. Along it are many of the town's cheapest lodgings.

North-east along Calle Real are more hotels, restaurants and shops; finally at the north-eastern end of town you come to the town's civic centre with the post and telegraph offices, the church, town hall, police station and market (busiest on Sunday and Thursday, but with some activity on other days from 9 am to noon).

Tourist Office The INGUAT tourist office (☎ (9) 621392) is open from 8 am to noon and 2 to 6 pm, Wednesday to Sunday, 8 am to noon Monday, closed Tuesday. Bus and boat schedules are posted on the door.

Money Banco Inmobiliario on Calle los Arboles is open Monday to Friday 9 am to 8 pm, Saturday and Sunday 10 am to 2 pm. Banco Agricola Mercantil (BAM), at the intersection of Calle Real and Calle Santander, is open Monday to Friday from 9 am to 3 pm (till 3.30 pm on Friday), but currency exchange services are provided from 9 am to noon only.

Post & Telecommunications The post office next to the church is open from Monday to Friday from 8 am to 4.30 pm. The Guatel telephone office on Calle Santander is open from 7 am to midnight every day. Fax service is available at the Gallery Bookstore on Calle los Arboles, at the shop called Que Hay de Nuevo, on Calle Real to the left of the Hotel Galindo, and at numerous other establishments. Get Guated Out (☎ & fax 9-622015), next to the Gallery Bookstore, can ship your important letters and parcels by international courier.

GUATEMALA

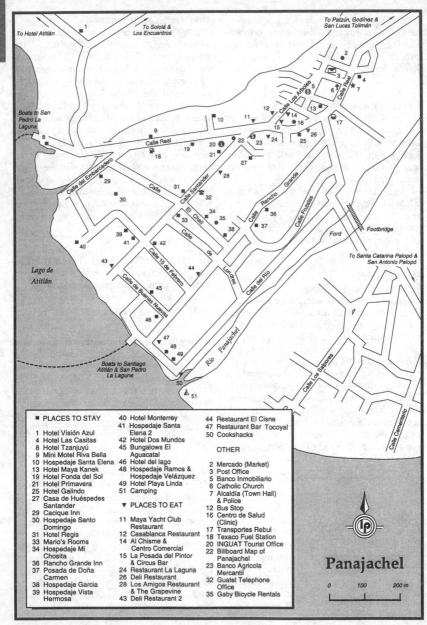

Panajachel

■ PLACES TO STAY

1 Hotel Visión Azul
4 Hotel Las Casitas
8 Hotel Tzanjuyú
9 Mini Motel Riva Bella
10 Hospedaje Santa Elena
13 Hotel Maya Kanek
19 Hotel Fonda del Sol
21 Hotel Primavera
25 Hotel Galindo
27 Casa de Huéspedes Santander
29 Cacique Inn
30 Hospedaje Santo Domingo
31 Hotel Regis
33 Mario's Rooms
34 Hospedaje Mi Chosita
36 Rancho Grande Inn
37 Posada de Doña Carmen
38 Hospedaje Garcia
39 Hospedaje Vista Hermosa
40 Hotel Monterrey
41 Hospedaje Santa Elena 2
42 Hotel Dos Mundos
45 Bungalows El Aguacatal
46 Hotel del lago
48 Hospedaje Ramos & Hospedaje Velázquez
49 Hotel Playa Linda
51 Camping

▼ PLACES TO EAT

11 Maya Yacht Club Restaurant
12 Casablanca Restaurant
14 Al Chisme & Centro Comercial
15 La Posada del Pintor & Circus Bar
24 Restaurant La Laguna
26 Deli Restaurant
28 Los Amigos Restaurant & The Grapevine
43 Deli Restaurant 2
44 Restaurant El Cisne
47 Restaurant Bar Tocoyal
50 Cookshacks

OTHER

2 Mercado (Market)
3 Post Office
5 Banco Inmobiliario
6 Catholic Church
7 Alcaldía (Town Hall) & Police
12 Bus Stop
16 Centro de Salud (Clinic)
17 Transportes Rebul
18 Texaco Fuel Station
20 INGUAT Tourist Office
22 Billboard Map of Panajachel
23 Banco Agricola Mercantil
32 Guatel Telephone Office
35 Gaby Bicycle Rentals

0   100   200 m

Bookshops The Gallery Bookstore (☎ & fax 9-622015) on Calle los Arboles offers new and used books for sale, fax service, and travel and ticket sales. Opening hours are 8.45 am to 6 pm Monday to Saturday, closed Sunday.

Places to Stay

There's a public camping ground on the beach on the east side of the Río Panajachel's mouth in Jucanyá. Safety can be a problem here. A safer but more expensive alternative is the one at the Hotel Visión Azul on the western outskirts of town. This one has electrical and water hook-ups for campervans and caravans.

Panajachel has numerous little family-run *hospedajes* (pensions). The best of the hospedajes provide clean toilets, hot showers and even perhaps some meals at a patio comedor. Prices average US$5 for a double, with a US$0.60 charge for a hot shower. The first place to look for hospedajes is along Calle Santander midway between Calle Principal and the beach.

Hospedaje Santa Elena 2, off Calle Santander, is tidy, and typical of Pana's hospedajes. The little courtyard is planted with bananas and noisy with macaws; the showers provide cold water only. The original *Hospedaje Santa Elena* is in an alley off Calle Real opposite the INGUAT tourist office, closer to the centre but farther from the beach.

Hospedaje Vista Hermosa is a friendly place with simple rooms on two levels around a small, pretty courtyard. There are hot showers in the morning only for a quetzal or so. *Hospedaje Santo Domingo* is a step up in quality but a few steps off the street; follow the road toward the Hotel Monterrey, then follow signs along a shady path. This backpackers' motel has rough timber rooms built around a nice yard that's quiet, being well away from the noise on Calle Santander. Cold showers, laundry sinks and toilets are available; the price, as usual, is US$5 a double.

Posada de Doña Carmen (☎ (9) 622085), Calle Rancho Grande, is very simple but tidy, family-run and quiet with a big garden. Stark rooms without running water cost US$4 a double.

Casa de Huéspedes Santander, in an alley off Calle Santander, has clean beds in tidy, bare rooms around a verdant garden for US$3/5/6 a single/double/triple.

Mario's Rooms (☎ (9) 621313), just south of the Guatel office on Calle Santander, is popular with young, adventurous travellers, and is among the best of the hospedajes. Rates for each of the 20 rooms are US$3.25/5 a single/double, and there's a tiny little restaurant-bar. *Hospedaje Mi Chosita*, on Calle El Chali (turn at Mario's Rooms), is tidy and quiet, at US$5 a double. *Hospedaje Garcia* (☎ (9) 622187), 4 Calle 2-24, Zona 2, farther east along the same street toward Calle Rancho Grande, charges US$3/4.

Moving upscale in both price and comfort, *Hotel Las Casitas* (☎ (9) 621224), across from the market near the church and town hall, rents little brick bungalows with tile roofs. Señora Dalma Gutiérrez is always smiling, cleaning or cooking (all three meals) to keep her guests happy. Rooms cost US$6.50/10/13.50 a single/double/triple with private (hot) shower.

Hotel Maya Kanek (☎ (9) 621104), Calle Real just down from the church, is a motel-style hostelry with rooms facing a cobbled court with a small garden; the court doubles as a secure car park. The 20 rooms, though simple, are a bit more comfortable than at a hospedaje, and cost US$8.50/12 a single/double. It's quiet here.

Bungalows El Aguacatal (☎ (9) 621482), Calle de Buenas Nuevas, is aimed at weekenders from the capital. Each modern bungalow has two bedrooms, equipped kitchen, bath and salon for US$25 a double Sunday to Thursday, US$30 on Friday and Saturday.

Mini Motel Riva Bella (☎ (9) 621348, 621177; fax 621353), Calle Real, is a collection of neat two-room bungalows, each with its own parking place. Señora María Gertraude E de Benini oversees maintenance and management. The location is convenient and the price US$26 a double.

Rancho Grande Inn (☎ (9) 621554, 622255; fax 622247), Calle Rancho Grande, has seven perfectly maintained German country-style villas in a tropical Guatemalan setting amidst emerald-green lawns. Marlita Hannstein, the congenial owner, charges a very reasonable US$30 a single, US$40 to US$60 a double, full breakfast and tax included. In my opinion, this is Pana's best place to stay.

Places to Eat

The cheapest places to eat are down by the beach at the mouth of the Río Panajachel. Right by the river's mouth are crude cookshacks with very low prices. The little food stands around the car park cost only a bit more. Then there are the little restaurants just inland from the car park with names such as *El Xocomil, El Pescador, Los Pumpos, Brisas de Lago* and *Los Alpes*. Not only is the food cheap (US$3 for a fill-up), but the view of the lake is a priceless bonus.

The Grapevine, on Calle Santander, has a ground-floor restaurant serving plates of fish and beef for US$3 to US$5. Upstairs is the video bar, which serves up popcorn, beer and drinks, and a good selection of American and European films.

On Calle los Arboles is *Al Chisme* (The Gossip), a favourite with regular Pana foreign visitors and residents, with its shady streetside patio. Breakfasts of English muffins, Belgian waffles and omelettes cost US$2 to US$3. For lunch and dinner Al Chisme offers lots of sandwiches, soups, salads, crepes and chicken pot pie for US$2.75 to US$5. Alcoholic beverages are served.

Next door in the Centro Comercial complex on Los Arboles is *Sevananda Vegetarian Restaurant*, offering sandwiches and vegetable plates for US$2 to US$4. It's open Monday to Saturday from 11 am to 10 pm; closed on Sunday.

Deli Restaurant, on Calle Real next to the Hotel Galindo, has nice gardens with lots of roses, simple tables and chairs, and breakfasts of whole-wheat pancakes and other good things for US$1.50 to US$2.50. For lunch and dinner there are many tofu dishes, sandwiches and big salads for US$2 to US$5. Opening hours are 8 am to 6.45 pm; closed Wednesday. The *Deli Restaurant 2*, in a quiet garden at the lake end of Calle Santander, sells sandwiches, cakes and the like to the sounds of soft classical music.

At the *Maya Yacht Club*, near the intersection of Calle Real and Calle Santander, the pizzas (US$3.50 to US$8) have a good reputation. Opening hours are 1 to 10 pm daily.

Los Amigos Restaurant on Calle Santander is open only for dinner from 6 to 9.30 pm (closed Monday) but usually fills up for that meal. One low darkish room is lit by candles and the glow of good conversation. Soup, a huge burrito and a beer cost about US$6; a 10% service charge is added to the bill.

La Posada del Pintor on Calle los Arboles has walls hung with old circus posters, and quiet jazz and rock as background music. Pizzas, boeuf bourguignon, potato salads, steaks, pastas and desserts all share space on the menu. You can expect to spend US$6 to US$12 for a full dinner. Portions tend to be small.

Getting There & Away

The town's main bus stop is where Calle Santander meets Calle Real, but buses leave from other parts of the town as well, depending upon the company.

Antigua – 80 km, two hours; several direct buses daily, even more if you take any bus stopping at Chimaltenango, and change to an Antigua-bound minibus there. TURANSA shuttle minibuses operate as well.

Chichicastenango – 29 km, one hour; buses (US$1) depart Panajachel at 6.45, 7.45, 8.45 and 9.45 am. Panajachel Tourist services run minibuses from Pana to Chichi each Thursday and Sunday at 8 am, returning at 1 pm, for US$20 round-trip (☎ & fax 9-621474).

Guatemala City – 147 km, three hours; Rebuli, 3a Avenida 2-36, Zona 9, departs for Lago de Atitlán and Panajachel every hour from 7 am to 4 pm, stopping at Chimaltenango, Patzicía, Tecpán Guatemala (for the ruins at Iximché), Los Encuentros, and Sololá, for US$1.75. Departures from Panajachel are at 5, 5.30, 7, 8, 9.30, 11.30 am and 1 and 2.30 pm; on Saturday there's also an 11 am bus (☎ 2-516505).

Panajachel Tourist Services, on Calle los Arboles, run tourist minibuses between Pana and Guatemala City several times per week for US$20 (☎ & fax 9-621474).

Huehuetenango – 159 km, 3½ hours; catch a bus or minibus to Los Encuentros, and wait for a Huehue-bound bus there; see Getting There & Away under the Guatemala City section for a schedule of Huehue-bound buses; or catch a Morales bus from Panajachel to Quetzaltenango, get out at Cuatro Caminos, and wait for a Huehue bus.

La Mesilla (Mexican border) – 241 km, five hours; see Huehuetenango

Quetzaltenango – 99 km, two hours; buses run by Morales or Rojo y Blanco depart at 5.30, 5.45 and 11.30 am and 2.30 pm, for US$1.75

Getting Around

You can rent bicycles from Alquiler de Bicicletas Gaby, on Calle el Chali between Calle Santander and Calle Rancho Grande. Otherwise, most people get around on foot.

AROUND LAGO DE ATITLÁN

Various lakeside villages, which can be reached on foot, by bus or motor launch, are interesting to visit. The most popular destination for day trips is Santiago Atitlán, directly across the lake south of Panajachel, but there are others. Some villages even have places for you to stay overnight. A launch tour to three villages with an hour spent in each costs US$7. The launch leaves from the public beach at the foot of Calle Rancho Grande.

Santa Catarina Palopó to San Lucas Tolimán

Four km east of Panajachel along a winding, unpaved road lies the village of Santa Catarina Palopó. Narrow streets paved in stone blocks and adobe houses with roofs of thatch or corrugated tin huddled around a gleaming white church: that's Santa Catarina. Except for exploring village life and enjoying views of the lake and the volcanoes, there's little in the way of 'sightseeing'. For refreshments, there are several little comedores on the main plaza, one of which advertises 'Cold beer sold here'.

The road continues past Santa Catarina

five km to **San Antonio Palopó**, a larger but similar village. High up on the steep hillside east of these villages is the town of Godínez.

Beyond San Antonio and Godínez lies **San Lucas Tolimán**, busier and more commercial than most lakeside villages. Set at the foot of the dramatic Volcán Tolimán, San Lucas is a coffee-growing town and a transport point on the route between the Interamerican Highway and the Pacific Slope Highway. Market days are Monday, Tuesday, Thursday and Friday.

Getting There & Away A bus leaves daily at 9 am (except Saturday) for Guatemala City via Santa Catarina (four km) and San Antonio (11 km), but returns by another route. Buses leave Panajachel daily for San Lucas Tolimán via Santa Catarina and San Antonio at 6.30 am and 4 pm.

Santiago Atitlán

South across the lake from Panajachel, on the shore of a lagoon squeezed between the towering volcanoes of Tolimán and San Pedro, lies the small town of Santiago Atitlán. Though it is the most visited village outside Panajachel, it clings to the traditional lifestyle of the Tzutuhil Maya. The women of the town still weave and wear huipiles with brilliantly coloured flocks of birds and bouquets of flowers embroidered on them. The best day to visit is market day (Friday, with a lesser market on Tuesday), but in fact any day will do.

Santiago is also a curiosity because of its reverence for Maximón (MAH-shee-MOHN), a local deity who is probably a blend of ancient Maya gods, Pedro de Alvarado the fierce conquistador of Guatemala, and the biblical Judas. Despised in other highland towns, Maximón is revered in Santiago Atitlán, and his effigy with wooden mask and huge cigar is paraded triumphantly during Holy Week processions (see 'Business Hours & Holidays' in the Facts for the Visitor section at the start of this chapter for the dates of Holy Week).

Walk to the left from the dock along the shore to reach the street into town. This is the main commercial street. As every tourist who's come to visit walks up and down it between the dock and the town, it's lined with shops selling woven cloth, other handicrafts and souvenirs.

At the top of the slope is the main square, with the town office and huge church, which dates from the time, several centuries ago, when Santiago was an important commercial town. Within the stark, echoing church are some surprising sights. Along the walls are wooden statues of the saints, each of whom gets a new shawl embroidered by local women every year. On the carved wooden pulpit, note the figures of corn (from which humans were formed, according to Maya religion), of a quetzal bird reading a book, and of Yum-Kax, the Maya god of corn.

Places to Stay & Eat Best in town is *Hotel Chi-Nim-Yá*, a simple, basic place with several advantages. The best room in the place is No 106, large and airy, with lots of windows and excellent lake views, for US$8 a double. Smaller, less desirable rooms cost only half that much.

Pensión Rosita, to the right of the school

Lago de Atitlán

and behind the basketball court off the main plaza, has very stark, bare rooms for US$3 per person. The plumbing is primitive.

Restaurant Santa Rita, a few steps from the north-east corner of the plaza past Distribuidor El Buen Precio, boasts deliciosos pays (delicious pies).

The most comfortable and charming place is the *Posada de Santiago* (☎ & fax 9-627167), one km from the village centre, with six stone bungalows and an excellent dining room on grounds sloping down to the lake. Cost is US$23/30/36/45 a single/double/triple/quad.

Getting There & Away An unpaved road in bad repair connects Santiago and San Lucas Tolimán (16 km), but most visitors reach Santiago by motor launch from Panajachel, which is the safer method. Motor launches depart from the public beach at the foot of Calle Rancho Grande, near the Hotel del Lago. The voyage takes 1¼ to 1½ hours each way, depending upon the winds, and costs US$3.50 return.

Naviera Santiago departs from Panajachel at 8.45 and 10 am and 4 pm, returning from Santiago at 11.45 am and 1 pm. Naviera Santa Fe leaves Panajachel at 9 and 9.30 am, returning from Santiago at 12.30 and 1 pm.

San Pedro La Laguna

Perhaps the next most popular lakeside town to visit, after Santiago, is San Pedro La Laguna.

Places to Stay & Eat Right near the boat dock is *Hospedaje Chuasinahu*, the best place in town, with beds for US$2 per night. The *Ti-Kaaj* next door is not quite as good, but takes the overflow if the Chuasinahu is full. *Villa San Pedro*, next door, is an even better choice at US$3 per person. The *Pensión Johanna*, on the other side of the village near another dock, has similar rates.

Getting There & Away The rough road from San Lucas Tolimán to Santiago Atitlán continues 18 km to San Pedro, making its way around the lagoon and Volcán San Pedro.

Coming from Panajachel, you should take a motor launch, of which there are two. Naviera Pato Poc departs from the public beach in Panajachel, at the foot of Calle Rancho Grande near the Hotel del Lago, at 10 am, 1 and 5 pm, returning from San Pedro at 11.30 am and 3 pm. Naviera Santa María departs from a dock near the Hotel Tzanjuyú, at the western edge of Panajachel, each day at 9.30 am and 2.30 pm, returning from San Pedro at 1 pm only. The voyage costs US$4 return.

CHICHICASTENANGO

Population 8000

Surrounded by valleys, with nearby mountains looming overhead, Chichicastenango (altitude 2030 metres) seems isolated from the rest of Guatemala. It can also seem magical when its narrow cobbled streets and red-tiled roofs are enveloped in mists, as they often are.

If you have a choice of days, come for the Sunday market rather than the Thursday one, as the *cofradías* (traditional religious brotherhoods) often hold processions on Sunday. It's best to arrive in town the day before market day to find a room.

Besides the famous market, Masheños (citizens of Chichicastenango) are famous for their adherence to pre-Christian religious beliefs and ceremonies. You can readily see survivals of these old rites in and around the church of Santo Tomás and at the shrine of Pascual Abaj on the outskirts of town.

History

Once called Chaviar, this was an important Cakchiquel trading town well before the Spanish conquest. Not long before the conquistadors arrived, the Cakchiquels and the Quichés (based at K'umarcaaj near present-day Santa Cruz del Quiché, 20 km north) went to war. The Cakchiquels abandoned Chaviar and moved their headquarters to Iximché, which was easier to defend. The conquistadors came and conquered K'umarcaaj, and many of its residents fled to Chaviar, which they renamed Chugüilá (Above the Nettles) and Tziguán Tinamit

GUATEMALA

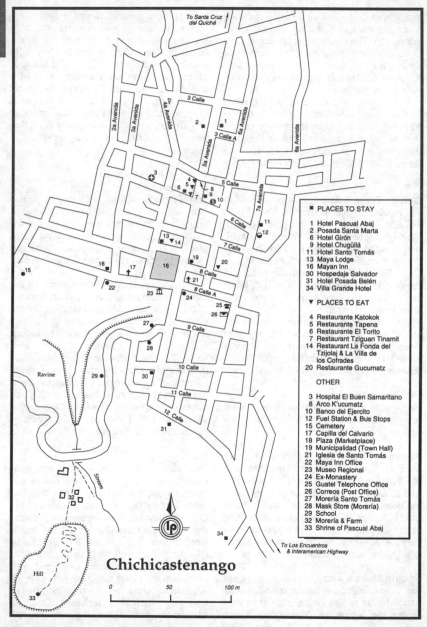

PLACES TO STAY

1 Hotel Pascual Abaj
2 Posada Santa Marta
6 Hotel Girón
9 Hotel Chugüilá
11 Hotel Santo Tomás
13 Maya Lodge
16 Mayan Inn
30 Hospedaje Salvador
31 Hotel Posada Belén
34 Villa Grande Hotel

▼ PLACES TO EAT

4 Restaurante Katokok
5 Restaurante Tapena
6 Restaurante El Torito
7 Restaurant Tziguan Tinamit
14 Restaurant La Fonda del
   Tzijolaj & La Villa de
   los Cofrades
20 Restaurante Gucumatz

OTHER

3 Hospital El Buen Samaritano
8 Arco K'ucumatz
10 Banco del Ejercito
12 Fuel Station & Bus Stops
15 Cemetery
17 Capilla del Calvario
18 Plaza (Marketplace)
19 Municipalidad (Town Hall)
21 Iglesia de Santo Tomás
22 Maya Inn Office
23 Museo Regional
24 Ex-Monastery
25 Guatel Telephone Office
26 Correos (Post Office)
27 Morería Santo Tomás
28 Mask Store (Morería)
29 School
32 Morería & Farm
33 Shrine of Pascual Abaj

Chichicastenango

0   50   100 m

To Los Encuentros
& Interamerican Highway

(Surrounded by Canyons). These are the names still used by the Quiché Maya, although everyone else calls the place Chichicastenango, a foreign name given by the conquistadors' Mexican allies.

Government

Chichi has two religious and governmental establishments. The Catholic Church and the Republic of Guatemala appoint priests and town officials to manage their interests, but the local people elect their own religious and civil officers to deal with local matters.

The Indian town government has its own council, mayor and deputy mayor, and court which decides cases involving local Indians exclusively. Chichi's religious life is centred in the cofradías. Leaders are elected periodically, and the man who receives the honour of being elected must provide banquets and pay for festivities for the cofradía throughout his term. Though it is very expensive, a *cofrade* (member of the brotherhood) happily accepts the burden, even going into debt if necessary.

The cofradías march in procession to church on Sunday morning and during religious festivals, the officers dressed in costumes showing their rank. Before them is carried a ceremonial staff topped by a silver crucifix or sun-badge which signifies the cofradía's patron saint. During major Church festivals, effigies of the saints are brought out and carried in grand processions, and richly costumed dancers wearing the traditional carved wooden masks act out legends of the ancient Maya and of the Spanish conquest.

Information

There is no official tourist information office. Ask your questions at the museum on the main square, or at one of the hotels.

Money The Banco del Ejercito, across from the Restaurant El Mash on 6 Calle, is open Monday to Friday 9 am to noon and 2 to 5 pm, on Saturday 9 am to 3 pm, and on Sunday 9 am to 2 pm.

Post & Telecommunications The post office (Correos) is at 7a Avenida 8-47, two blocks south-west of the Hotel Santo Tomás on the road into town. Near it is the Guatel telephone office, at 7a Avenida 8-21, on the corner of 8 Calle.

Market Day

Between dawn and about 8 or 9 am on Sunday and Thursday, stacks of poles are erected into stalls and hung with cloth, furnished with tables and piled with goods for sale, and Chichi's famous Indian market begins yet again. In general, the tourist-oriented stalls selling carved wooden masks, lengths of embroidered cloth and garments are around the outer edges of the market in the most visible areas. Behind these very visible ranks of stalls, the centre of the square is devoted to things that the villagers want and need: vegetables and fruit, baked goods, macaroni, soap, clothing, spices, sewing notions and toys. Cheap cookshops provide lunch for buyers and sellers alike.

The market continues into the afternoon; most of the stalls are taken down by late afternoon. Prices are best just before the market breaks up, as traders would rather sell than carry goods away with them.

Iglesia de Santo Tomás

This simple colonial church dates from about 1540. Though dedicated to the Catholic rite, it is more often the scene of rituals which are slightly Catholic and highly Maya.

The front steps of the church serve much the same purpose as did the great flights of stairs leading up to Maya pyramids. Much of the day (especially on Sunday) the steps smoulder with incense of copal resin, while indigenous prayer leaders swing censers containing incense and chant magic words in honour of the ancient Maya calendar and of their ancestors.

It's customary for the front steps and door of the church to be used only by important church officials and by the prayer leaders, so you should go around to the right and enter by the side door.

Inside, the floor of the church may be

spread with pine boughs and dotted with offerings of maize kernels, bouquets of flowers, bottles of liquor wrapped in corn husks, and candles, candles everywhere. Many local families can trace their lineages back centuries, some even to the ancient kings of Quiché. Many of their ancestors are buried beneath the church. The candles and offerings on the floor are in remembrance of the ancestors lying directly beneath.

On the west side of the plaza is another little whitewashed church, the Capilla del Calvario, which is similar in form and function to Santo Tomás, but smaller.

Museo Regional

In the arcade facing the south side of the square is the Museo Regional (Regional Museum), open from 8 am to noon and 2 to 5 pm (closed Tuesday). In the two large rooms of the museum you can see ancient clay pots and figurines, arrowheads and spearheads of flint and obsidian, copper axeheads, and *metates* (grindstones for maize). The museum also holds the Rossbach jade collection with several beautiful necklaces, figurines and other objects. Ildefonso Rossbach served as Chichi's Catholic priest for many years until his death in 1944.

Shrine of Pascual Abaj

Before you have been in Chichi very long, some village lad will offer to guide you (for a tip) to a hilltop on the outskirts to have a look at Pascual Abaj (Sacrifice-Stone), the local shrine to Huyup Tak'ah (Mountain-Plain), the Maya earth god. Said to be hundreds – perhaps thousands – of years old, the stone-faced idol has suffered numerous indignities at the hands of outsiders, but local people still revere it. *Chuchkajaues* (prayer leaders) come here regularly to offer incense, food, cigarettes, flowers, liquor and Coca-Cola to the earth god, and perhaps even to sacrifice a chicken. The offerings are thanks and hope for earth's continuing fertility.

Sacrifices do not take place at regular hours. If you're in luck, you can witness one. The worshippers will not mind if you watch, and some (but not all!) won't mind if you take photographs, though they may ask if you want to make an offering (of a few quetzals) yourself. If there is no ceremony, you can still see the idol and enjoy the walk up to the pine-clad hilltop and the views of the town and valley.

There have been some incidents of robbery of tourists walking to visit Pascual Abaj, so the best plan is to go with others in a large group.

Walk down the hill on 5a Avenida from the Santo Tomás church, turn right onto 9 Calle and continue downhill along this unpaved road, which bends to the left. At the bottom of the hill, bear left and follow a path through the cornfields. Signs mark the way.

Walk through the farm buildings to the hill behind, and follow the switchback path to the top and along the ridge of the hill, called Turukaj, to a clearing in which you will see the idol in its rocky shrine.

The squat stone crosses near the idol have many levels of significance for the Maya, only one of which pertains to Christ. The area of the shrine is littered with past offerings. The bark of the pines here has been stripped away in places to be used as fuel in the incense fires.

Places to Stay

Chichi does not have a lot of accommodation, and most of what it has is in the higher price range.

Hotel Pascual Abaj (☎ (9) 561055), 5a Avenida 3-38, Zona 1, is a clean little place one long block north downhill from the Arco K'ucumatz. Rooms with shower cost US$8/10 a single/double. The *Posada Santa Marta* across the street is much simpler.

Hotel Girón (☎ (9) 561156), on 6 Calle next to the Restaurant Tziguan Tinamit, is at the rear of the commercial Girón building; walk through to the back. Recently renovated, the 16 rooms are clean and cost US$10 a double with shower.

Of the cheap hotels, *Hospedaje Salvador*, two blocks south-west of the Santo Tomás church along 5a Avenida, is the biggest. This maze-like warren of red bricks, tiles and white stucco has 35 rooms on three floors reached by obscure routes. Rooms without bath offer the better value as the private baths – particularly those on the lower floors – smell quite strongly. Doubles cost US$7 without running water, US$10.50 with private bath.

Hotel Posada Belén (☎ (9) 561244), 12 Calle 5-55, Zona 1, is quite expensive at US$12/16 a double without/with shower, but will do if all else is full.

Chichi's other hostelries are more expensive. *Hotel Chugüilá* (☎ & fax 9-561134), 5a Avenida 5-24, just south of the Arco K'ucumatz, is charming, and affordable if you get a bathless room at US$12/16/21 a single/double/triple. Rooms with bath cost US$27/32/36.

Maya Lodge (☎ (9) 561167), in the main plaza, has 10 rather dark rooms with clean add-on showers in the very midst of the market. Fairly plain despite some colonial touches, it is comfortable but overpriced at US$25/30 a single/double.

Places to Eat

On Sunday and Thursday, eat where the marketers do – at the cookshops set up in the centre of the market. These are the cheapest in town. On other days, look for the little comedores near the post office and Guatel telephone office on the road into town (7a Avenida).

Next cheapest places to eat are the *Restaurante Katokok* and *Restaurante Tapena*, two little *cocinas económicas* on 5a Avenida facing the Hotel Chugüilá just south of the Arco K'ucumatz.

Restaurant La Fonda del Tzijolaj, upstairs in the Centro Comercial Santo Tomás on the north side of the square, has everything: good views, nice décor, decent food, and prices of US$2 to US$3 for breakfast, twice that for lunch or dinner. It's closed on Tuesday. There are several other restaurants with portico tables in the Centro Comercial. At *La Villa de los Cofrades* you can while away the hours with checkers (draughts) and backgammon. The courtyard of the Centro Comercial is a vegetable market.

Similar in feeling and price is the *Restaurante El Torito*, upstairs in the Hotel Girón building. Platos fuertes of soup, main course, rice and dessert cost US$3 to US$5. It's open every day for all three meals.

Restaurante Gucumatz, on the corner of 6a Avenida and 8 Calle, is tidy and pleasant, with local foods at low prices.

Restaurant El Mash, 6 Calle near 5a Avenida, at the back of a little flowered courtyard, has declined since my last visit there, but is still serviceable. There's music some evenings.

Restaurant Tziguan Tinamit, situated on the corner of 6 Calle and 5a Avenida, takes its name from the Quiché Maya name for Chichicastenango. It's popular with locals and foreigners, and open all day every day.

Getting There & Away

The road to Chichi leaves the Interamerican Highway at Los Encuentros, winding its way through pine forests and cornfields, down into a steep valley and up the other side. You cover the 17 km in half an hour.

Chichi has no bus station. The closest thing to a bus stop is the corner of 7a Avenida and 6 Calle, but buses depart from various points around the market, particularly near the Hotel Santo Tomás and the Hotel Chugüilá. Ask any bus driver or police officer by naming your destination, and you'll be directed to the proper spot.

Any bus heading south can drop you at Los Encuentros, where you can catch a bus to your final destination. There are direct buses to Quetzaltenango (94 km, two hours, US$1.25) and to Guatemala City (Veloz Quichelense, 146 km, 3½ hours, US$2.25).

SANTA CRUZ DEL QUICHÉ

Population 13,000

The capital of the department of Quiché (altitude 2020 metres) is 19 km north of Chichicastenango.

Without the bustle of the big market and the big tourism buses, Santa Cruz – which is usually called 'El Quiché' – is quieter and more typical of the Guatemalan countryside than is Chichi. If you visit El Quiché, it is probably because you want to visit the ruins of K'umarcaaj (Utatlán). This is best done early in the morning, as you may have to walk to the ruins and back.

K'umarcaaj

The ruins of the ancient Quiché Maya capital are three km (a half-hour walk) west of El Quiché along an unpaved road. Start out of town along 10 Calle and ask the way frequently. No signs mark the way, and no transport runs regularly. Admission to the site costs a few pennies.

The kingdom of Quiché was established in Late Post-Classic times (about the 14th century). Around 1400, King K'ucumatz founded his capital at K'umarcaaj and conquered many neighbouring cities. During the long reign of his successor Q'uikab (1425-75), the kingdom of Quiché grew in size and power.

Pedro de Alvarado led his conquistadors into Guatemala in 1524, and it was the Quichés, under their king, Tecún Umán, who organised the defence of the country. In the decisive battle fought near Quetzaltenango on 12 February 1524, Alvarado and Tecún found one another and locked in mortal combat. Alvarado won, and Tecún was killed. The defeated Quiché invited the victorious Alvarado to visit their capital, where they secretly planned to kill him. Smelling a rat, Alvarado, with the aid of his Mexican auxiliaries and the anti-Quiché Cakchiquels, captured the Quiché leaders instead, burnt them alive, took K'umarcaaj (called Utatlán by his Mexican allies) and destroyed it.

The history is more interesting than the ruined city, of which little remains but a few grass-covered mounds. Of the 100 or so large structures identified by archaeologists, only half a dozen are at all recognisable by us mere mortals, and these are uninspiring. The site itself is a beautiful place for a picnic, shaded by tall trees and surrounded by its defensive ravines, which failed to save the city from the conquistadors. Local prayermen keep the fires of ancient Quiché burning, so to speak, by using ruined K'umarcaaj as a ritual site. A long tunnel *(cueva)* beneath the plaza is a favourite spot for prayers and chicken sacrifices.

Places to Stay & Eat

Near the bus station there are cheap lodging places such as *Hospedaje Tropical* and *Hospedaje Hermano Pedro*, charging US$2 per bed; look at the room first and decide if you think it's worth it.

Hotel San Pascual (☎ (9) 55-1107), 7 Calle 0-43, 1½ blocks south-east of the plaza, has 40 rooms for US$5 to US$8 a double; the more expensive rooms have private bath. The newest rooms have TVs as well as private baths, and cost a bit more.

Restaurant 2000 No 2, two blocks west of the square, is simple and cheap. *Restaurant Lago Azul* is second best.

Getting There & Away

Many buses from Guatemala City to Chichicastenango continue to El Quiché (look for 'Quiché' on the signboard); on market days (Sunday and Thursday) there may be a bus every hour in the morning. The last bus from El Quiché to Chichicastenango and Los Encuentros leaves mid-afternoon.

El Quiché is the transport point for the sparsely populated and somewhat remote reaches of northern Quiché, which extends all the way to the Mexican border. Ask at the bus station for details. The bus trip over a rough road to Sacapulas, for instance, takes five hours.

NEBAJ

High among the Cuchumatanes lies the Ixil Maya village of Nebaj. The scenery is breathtakingly beautiful, and the local people, remote from the cultural influences of TV and modern urbanity, proudly preserve their ancient way of life.

Nebaj's location in this mountain fastness has been both a blessing and a curse. The conquistadors found it difficult to conquer, and wreaked destruction on the inhabitants when they did. In recent years guerrilla forces made the area a base of operations, and the army took strong measures to dislodge them. Many small villages were destroyed, with their surviving inhabitants being herded into 'strategic hamlets'.

Today the area around Nebaj is still troubled, but travellers continue to come here for the scenery, the local culture, the excellent handicrafts, the market (Thursday and Sunday) and, during the second week in August, the annual festival.

Places to Stay & Eat

Pensión Las Tres Hermanas is the best-known lodging, charging US$1 for a bed, the same price for a meal. The shower is hot. If the 'Three Sisters' is full, alternatives include the *Pensión Las Gemelitas* and the *Hotel Ixil*.

Getting There & Away

Much of the transport to Nebaj from Sacapulas, Santa Cruz del Quiché and Cobán is by truck, charging a fare equivalent to that of the bus. There is a daily market bus departing Nebaj for Santa Cruz del Quiché about 3 am, returning from El Quiché by mid-morning, a five-hour trip.

CUATRO CAMINOS

Westward from Los Encuentros, the Interamerican Highway twists and turns ever higher into the mountains, bringing still more dramatic scenery and cooler temperatures. After 58 km you come to another important highway junction known as Cuatro Caminos (Four Roads). The road east leads to Totonicapán (12 km); west to Quetzaltenango (13 km); and north (straight on) to Huehuetenango (77 km). Buses shuttle from Cuatro Caminos to Totonicapán and Quetzaltenango about every 30 minutes from 6 am to 6 pm.

TOTONICAPÁN

Population 9000

If you want to visit a pleasant, pretty Guatemalan highland town with decent services for the traveller but with few other tourists in sight, Totonicapán (altitude 2500 metres) is the place to go. Buses shuttle into the centre of town from Cuatro Caminos frequently throughout the day.

Totonicapán's main plaza has the requisite large colonial church, and also a municipal theatre in neoclassical style, which has recently been restored. Buses go directly to the parque, as the plaza is called, and drop you there.

Places to Stay

As you make your way into town, one block before coming to the parque on the left, stands the *Hospedaje San Miguel* (☎ (9) 661452), 3 Calle 7-49, Zona 1. It's a tidy place, not what you'd call Swiss-clean, but good for the price, which is US$4 a double with common bath, US$5.50 with private shower. The rooms with showers tend to be larger, with three beds. Flash heaters provide the hot water, which is thus fairly dependable.

QUETZALTENANGO

Population 100,000

Called Xelajú or simply Xela by its Quiché Maya citizens, Quetzaltenango (altitude 2335 metres) is the commercial centre of south-western Guatemala. Its good selection of hotels in all price ranges makes it an excellent base for excursions to the nearby towns and villages noted for their handicrafts and hot springs.

History

Quetzaltenango came under the sway of the Quiché Maya of K'umarcaaj when they began their great expansion in the 14th century. Before that it had been a Mam Maya town. Tecún Umán, the powerful leader of the Quiché, met Pedro de Alvarado on the field of battle near Quetzaltenango on 12 February 1524. The prize was Guatemala, much of which Tecún controlled, all of which the conquistadors wanted. Alvarado struck a mortal blow, Tecún Umán fell dead, and Guatemala was open to the Spaniards.

In the mid-19th century, when the Central American Federation was founded, Quetzaltenango initially decided on federation with Chiapas and Mexico instead of with Central America. Later changing its mind, the city joined the Central American

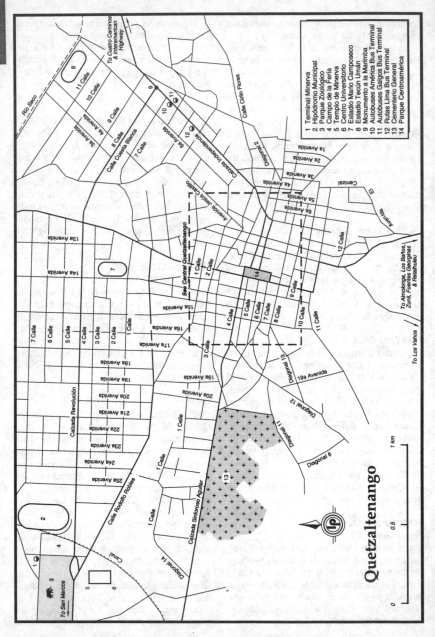

Quetzaltenango

1 Terminal Minerva
2 Hipódromo Municipal
3 Parque Zoológico
4 Campo de la Feria
5 Templo de Minerva
6 Centro Universitario
7 Estadio Mario Camposeco
8 Estadio Tecún Umán
9 Monumento a la Marimba
10 Autobuses América Bus Terminal
11 Autobuses Galgos Bus Terminal
12 Rutas Lima Bus Terminal
13 Cementerio General
14 Parque Centroamérica

Federation, and became an integral part of Guatemala in 1840.

With the late 19th-century coffee boom, Quetzaltenango's wealth increased. This is where the finca (plantation) owners came to buy supplies and where the coffee brokers had their warehouses. Things went along fine with the city getting richer and richer until a dual calamity – an earthquake and a volcanic eruption – brought mass destruction and an end to the boom.

The city's position at the intersection of the roads to the Pacific Slope, Mexico and Guatemala City guarantees it some degree of prosperity. Today it's busy again with commerce, both Indian and ladino.

Orientation

The heart of Xela is the Parque Centroamérica, shaded by old trees, graced with neoclassical monuments, and surrounded by the town's important buildings: cathedral, banks, tourist office, government headquarters, museum, Guatel telephone office, and one of the best hotels.

Terminal Minerva, the second-class bus station, is on the western outskirts near the Parque Minerva on 6 Calle in Zona 3, next to the market. City bus Nos 2 and 6 run between the terminal and Parque Centroamérica – look for 'Terminal' and 'Parque' in the front window of the bus.

First-class bus lines have their own terminals separate from the common ones. For locations, see Getting There & Away later.

Information

Tourist Office The tourist office (☎ (9) 614931) is in the right-hand wing of the Casa de la Cultura (also called the Museo de Historia Natural) at the lower (southern) end of the Parque Centroamérica. It's open Monday to Friday from 8 am to 1 pm, and from 2 to 5 pm, on Saturday from 8 am to noon and closed on Sunday.

Money The Parque Centroamérica is surrounded by banks. Opening hours for most are 8.30 am to 2.30 pm Monday to Friday. Banco del Café, on the parque at 6 Calle, is open Monday to Thursday 8.30 am to 8 pm, Friday 8 am to 8 pm, and Saturday 10 am to 2 pm.

Post & Telecommunications The post office is at 15a Avenida and 4 Calle, Zona 1. The Guatel telephone office is on 12a Avenida between 7 and 8 Calles, at the southwestern corner of the Parque Centroamérica, only steps from the tourist office.

Mexican Consulate The consulate (☎ (9) 612547) is at 9a Avenida 6-19, Zona 1, open Monday to Friday from 9 to 11 am.

Laundry Lavandería Mini-Max, 14a Avenida C-47, at 1 Calle, faces the neoclassical Teatro Municipal, five blocks north-west of the parque.

Parque Centroamérica

Start your tour at the southern (lower) end and walk around the square anticlockwise. The Casa de la Cultura holds the Museo de Historia Natural, with some Maya exhibits and others focusing on the liberal revolution in Central American politics and on the Estado de Los Altos, of which Quetzaltenango was the capital. Marimbas, the weaving industry and other local lore all claim places here.

Just off the south-eastern corner of the parque is a small market devoted largely to handicraft items and daily necessities, a convenient spot for a little shopping.

The once-crumbling cathedral has been rebuilt in the last few decades. The façade of the colonial building was preserved, and a modern sanctuary built behind it.

The city's town hall, or Municipalidad, at the north-eastern end of the parque, follows the grandiose neoclassical style so favoured as a symbol of culture and refinement in this wild mountain country. To its right is the Pensión Bonifaz, the best hotel in the centre.

On the west side of the parque between 4 and 5 Calles is the palatial Pasaje Enriquez, built to be lined with elegant shops, but as Quetzaltenango has few elegant shoppers, it has suffered decline. One of the local tourism brochures defined it well by means of a malapropism: 'The outstanding characteristic of the western arch is its graffiti'.

Other Sights

Walk north on 14a Avenida to 1 Calle, to see the impressive neoclassical **Teatro Municipal**. Inside are three tiers of seating, the lower with private boxes for prominent families; each box is equipped with a vanity for the ladies.

Mercado La Democracia, in Zona 3, is about 10 blocks north-west of the Parque Centroamérica. Walk along 14a Avenida to 1 Calle (to the Teatro Municipal), turn left, turn right onto 16a Avenida, cross the major street called Calle Rodolfo Robles, and the market is on your right. It's an authentic Guatemalan city market with fresh produce and meat, foodstuffs and necessities for city dweller and villager alike.

Less than a km west of the Parque Centroamérica near the Terminal Minerva is the **Parque Minerva** with its neoclassical Templo de Minerva, built to honour the classical goddess of education and to inspire Guatemalan youth to new heights of learning. Many historians note that lots of

Central Quetzaltenango

Minerva temples got built during the presidency of Manuel Estrada Cabrera (1898-1920), but few schools.

Spanish Schools

Quetzaltenango has several schools where you can study Spanish with native speakers. I have not attended classes at any of these, and would be grateful for reports on the quality of programmes.

Academia Latinoamericana Mayanse, 15a Avenida 6-75, (PO Box 375) Zona 1 (☎ (9) 612707)
 For information in the USA, c/o Max Kintner and Mary Pliska, 3314 Sherwood Lane, Wichita Falls, TX 76308 (☎ 817-696 3319).
Guatemalensis Spanish School, 19a Avenida 2-14, Zona 1
 For information in the USA, c/o Elizabeth Oudens, 644 33rd Avenue, San Francisco, CA 94121 USA (☎ 415-221 8965).
Instituto Central America, 1 Calle 16-93, Zona 1 (☎ (9) 611871)
 For information in the USA, c/o RR 2, Box 101, Stanton, NE 68779 (☎ 402-439 2943).
Kie-Balam Spanish School, 9a Avenida 0-55, Zona 1, uses income from its classes to support community projects (☎ (9) 614640).
 For information in USA, contact Martha Mora, 1816 N Wells, Chicago, IL 60614 (☎ 708-888 2514 or 312-642 8019).

Places to Stay

Two concentrations of cheap hostelries are at the northern end of the Parque Centroamérica along 12a Avenida and south of the parque more or less behind the Casa de la Cultura.

Walk up 12a Avenida from the parque with the Municipalidad on your right and the Cantel textile shop on your left to find the *Pensión San Nicolás*, on the left between 4 and 3 Calles. No one would call it beautiful, but it has a courtyard with plants, a car park, and decent rooms for US$1 to US$1.50 a single, US$2 to US$3 a double, US$3.50 a triple. Look at the room before you pay.

At 2 Calle there are nicer places. Turn right for the *Hotel Horiani*, officially at 12a Avenida 2-23, though you enter on 2 Calle. This place charges US$2 a single, US$4 a double.

Turn left (west) at 2 Calle to find the *Hotel Río Azul* (☎ (9) 63-0654), 2 Calle 12-15, Zona 1, which offers luxury compared to its neighbours. All rooms here have private showers with hot water, and some even have colour TVs. Prices are excellent for what you get: US$8.50/12/16 a single/double/triple. There's even a car park.

Two more places are on 13a Avenida. Follow 2 Calle westward half a block from the Hotel Río Azul and turn left to find the *Casa Kaehler* (☎ (9) 612091), 13a Avenida 3-33, Zona 1, an old-fashioned European-

■	PLACES TO STAY	6	Pizza-Pastelería Bombonier	25	Banco Nacional de Desarrollo Agrícola
4	Casa Suiza	7	Pizza Ricca	26	Banco del Café
5	Hotel Modelo	16	El Rincón de los	27	Parque
8	Hotel Río Azul		Antojitos		Centroamérica
9	Hotel Horiani	17	Restaurant El Kopetin	28	Museo & Banco
10	Hotel Quetzalteco	18	Restaurant Shanghai		Industrial
11	Casa Kaehler	21	Restaurant Bonifaz	29	Guatel Telephone
12	Pensión San Nicolás	36	Restaurant Capri		Office
13	Hotel Radar 99			30	Construbanco
14	Hotel Casa Florencia		OTHER	32	Cathedral
19	Hotel Villa Real Plaza			33	Casa de la Cultura
21	Pensión Bonifaz	1	Cine Teatro Roma		(Museo de
31	Hotel Kiktem-Ja	2	Teatro Municipal		Historia Natural)
36	Hotel Capri	3	Lavandería Mini-Max	34	Tourist Office
		15	Post Office	35	Small Market
▼	PLACES TO EAT	20	Municipalidad		
		22	Pasaje Enriquez		
5	Restaurant Modelo	23	Taxis		
		24	Banco de Guatemala		

style family pension with seven rooms of various shapes and sizes. Room 7 is the most comfortable. Prices here are US$7/11/14/17 a single/double/triple/quad for rooms with private bath. Rooms without bath are a bit cheaper. This is an excellent, safe place for women travellers; ring the bell to gain entry. The *Hotel Radar 99* next door is for dire emergencies only.

Two streets west of Casa Kaehler is *Casa Suiza* (☎ (9) 614350), 14a Avenida 'A' 2-36, Zona 1, with 18 basic rooms grouped around a big courtyard in a fairly convenient location. There's a cheap comedor, and a dozen rooms priced at US$5.50 to US$7 a single, US$10 to US$12 a double, US$14 to US$17 a triple. Bathless rooms have sinks for your morning splash; the more expensive rooms have private showers. Some readers have complained of noise and brusque management.

South-west of the parque is the huge old *Hotel Kiktem-Ja* (☎ (9) 614304), a colonial-style building at 13a Avenida 7-18, Zona 1. The 20 rooms are on two levels around the courtyard, which also serves as car park. Fireplaces are available in each room for a comforting blaze. Rooms cost US$9/11/13 a single/double/triple with private hot shower.

Hotel Capri (☎ (9) 614111), 8 Calle 11-39, Zona 1, a block from the Parque Centroamérica behind the Casa de la Cultura, offers rooms in a convenient location for US$3 per person with common bath. Many are filled by foreign students attending local Spanish language courses.

If you want to spend a little more for a lot more comfort, head straight for the family-run *Hotel Modelo* (☎ (9) 630216, 612529; fax 631376), 14a Avenida 'A' 2-31, Zona 1. Pleasant small rooms with tiled showers rent for US$25/30 in the main hotel, US$14/18 in the simpler annexe. The hotel's good dining room serves breakfast (7.15 to 9.30 am), lunch (noon to 2 pm) and dinner (6 to 9 pm) daily.

Hotel Casa Florencia (☎ (9) 612326), 12a Avenida 3-61, Zona 1, is a relatively new place with good big rooms with double beds for US$18/25 a single/double.

Places to Eat

Cheapest places are the food stalls in and around the small market to the left of the Casa de la Cultura, where snacks and substantial main-course plates are sold for US$1 or less.

A very popular place with good food at good prices is *El Rincón de los Antojitos*, 15a Avenida at 5 Calle, Zona 1. The menu is mostly Guatemalan, with a few concessions to international tastes. All three meals, and vegetarian dishes, are served for US$3 to US$6.

Try also *La Góndola* (☎ 612148), at 10a Avenida beneath the Palacio Municipal, for pizza and Italian specialities.

For sit-down eateries serving everything from tacos to pizza and back, go to the corner of 14a Avenida and 3 Calle, then walk north (uphill) along 14a Avenida to find the following places.

Restaurant El Kopetin (☎ 612401), 14a Avenida 3-31, is pleasant and modernish. The long and varied menu ranges from hamburgers to Cuban-style sandwiches to filet mignon. Full meals may cost as much as US$4. Alcoholic drinks are served.

Pizza Ricca (☎ 618162), 14a Avenida 2-52, has a busy white-coated staff baking pizzas in a wood-fired oven and serving them to hungry customers waiting patiently in comfy booths. Pizzas come in various sizes and prices from US$1.75 to US$6; hamburgers and plates of spaghetti cost US$1.50 to US$2. Beer is served.

Pizza-Pastelería Bombonier (☎ 616225), 14a Avenida 2-20, serves more pizzas and hamburgers than bonbons despite its name; many customers order to take away, as there are only a few tables. Both the burgers and pizzas here are cheaper than at Pizza Ricca.

Restaurant Shanghai (☎ 614154), 4 Calle 12-22, Zona 1, is the most convenient Chinese place to the parque. The food is Guatemalan Oriental: pato (duck), camarones (shrimp) and other Chinese specialities for about US$2.50 to US$3.50 per plate. The Shanghai is open from 8 am to 9:30 pm, seven days a week.

The dining room of the *Hotel Modelo*, 14a

Avenida 'A' 2-31, has good set-price lunches and dinners for US$5.

Entertainment

Evening entertainment possibilities are limited, as you might expect. It gets chilly when the sun goes down, so you won't want to sit out in the Parque Centroamérica enjoying the balmy breezes – there aren't any.

The *Teatro Roma*, on 14a Avenida 'A' facing the Teatro Municipal, might be playing an interesting movie – perhaps even in English with Spanish subtitles. The bars at the Pensión Bonifaz and Hotel Modelo are good for a drink, a chat and a snack. The Bonifaz features delicious cakes and pastries to go with your coffee or drink.

Getting There & Away

For 2nd-class buses, head out to the Terminal Minerva on the western outskirts near the Parque Minerva on 6 Calle in Zona 3, next to the market. City bus Nos 2 and 6 run between the terminal and Parque Centroamérica (look for 'Terminal' and 'Parque' in the front window of the bus). You can catch the city bus (US$0.10) to the terminal from 8 Calle at 12a Avenida or 14a Avenida in the centre. The busy Terminal Minerva has almost hourly buses to many highland destinations.

Rutas Lima, Autobuses América and Autobuses Galgos, three 1st-class lines, have their own terminals on Calzada Independencia, the wide boulevard which is the north-easterly continuation of Diagonal 3 (Zona 1) leading out of town to the Cuatro Caminos road; in Zona 2 it is called 7a Avenida.

Autobuses Galgos (☎ (9) 612248) also has an office at Calle Rodolfo Robles 17-43, Zona 1, about a dozen blocks north-west of the parque.

Chichicastenango – 94 km, two hours; direct buses on market days cost US$1.25. If you don't get one of these, change at Los Encuentros.

Guatemala City – 203 km, four hours; lots of companies have plenty of buses departing frequently from Terminal Minerva. Transportes Galgos has seven 1st-class buses daily (US$2.50) stopping at Totonicapán, Los Encuentros (change for Chichicastenango or Panajachel) and Chimaltenango (change for Antigua).

Huehuetenango – 90 km, two hours, US$2.50; hourly buses from Terminal Minerva; for first class, see La Mesilla

La Mesilla (Mexican border) – 170 km, four hours; Rutas Lima has two first-class buses daily to Huehuetenango (US$2.75) and La Mesilla (US$4) departing from Quetzaltenango at 5 am and 6.30 pm. Or, get a 2nd-class bus from Terminal Minerva to Huehuetenango and change there.

Panajachel – 99 km, two hours; direct buses run by Morales or Rojo y Blanco depart four times daily for US$1.25, or you can take any bus bound for Guatemala City and change at Los Encuentros. Transportes Higueros has Guatemala City-bound buses which stop at Panajachel as well.

Retalhuleu – 67 km, two hours; hourly buses from Terminal Minerva (US$1). Rutas Lima has one daily bus to the border station at Talisman which will drop you in Retalhuleu.

AROUND QUETZALTENANGO

The beautiful volcanic countryside around Quetzaltenango has numerous possibilities for outings. Take note of the market days: Sunday in Momostenango, Monday in Zunil, Tuesday and Saturday in Totonicapán, Friday in San Francisco El Alto.

Buses from Quetzaltenango to Almolonga, Los Baños and Zunil depart several times per hour from Terminal Minerva; some buses stop on the corner of 10a Avenida and 10 Calle, Zona 1, to take on more passengers.

Los Vahos

If you're a hiker and if the weather is good you might enjoy a trip to the rough-and-ready steam baths at Los Vahos (The Vapours) which are 3½ km from Parque Centroamérica. Take a bus headed for Almolonga, and ask to get out at the road to Los Vahos. If you're driving, follow 12a Avenida south from the parque to its end, turn left, go two blocks and turn right up the hill; this turn is 1.2 km from the parque. The remaining 2.3 km of unpaved road is steep and rutted, a thick carpet of dust in the dry season, of mud in the rainy season.

The first turn along the dirt road is a sharp right (unmarked); at the second you bear left (this is badly marked). Views of the city on a clear day are remarkable. The road ends at Los Vahos, where you can have a steam bath for only a few quetzals and, if you've brought food with you, a picnic.

Zunil

Zunil is a pretty market town in a lush valley framed by steep hills and dominated by a towering volcano. On the way to Zunil the road passes by **Almolonga**, a vegetable-growing town four km from Quetzaltenango. Just over one km beyond Almolonga, on the left side of the road, is **Los Baños**, with natural hot springs. The bath installations are quite decrepit, but if a hot bath at low cost is your desire you may want to stop.

Winding down the hill from Los Baños, the road skirts Zunil and its fertile gardens on the right side before intersecting the Cantel-El Zarco road. A bridge crosses a stream to lead into the town; it's one km from the bridge to the plaza.

Zunil is a perfectly typical Guatemalan country town with a particularly pretty church. The church's ornate façade, with eight pairs of serpentine columns, is echoed inside by a richly worked altar of silver. On market day (Monday) the plaza in front of the church is bright with the predominantly red traditional garb of local people buying and selling.

From Zunil, which is 10 km from Quetzaltenango, you can continue to Fuentes Georginas (nine km), return to Quetzaltenango via the Cantel road (16 km), or take the jungle-bound toll road down the mountainside to El Zarco junction and the Pacific Slope Highway. Buses depart every half hour or so on the return trip to Quetzaltenango.

Fuentes Georginas

Imagine a steep, high wall of tropical verdure – huge green leaves, ganglions of vines, giant ferns, spongy moss, profusions of tropical flowers – at the upper end of a lush mountain valley. At the base of this wall of greenery is a limpid pool of naturally warm mineral water. This is Fuentes Georginas, the prettiest spa in Guatemala.

The pools were built during the presidency of General Jorge Ubico (1931-44) and named in his honour. Unfortunately, a major construction project nearby has in recent years robbed Fuentes Georginas of much of its naturally warm water. Enquire about the current condition of the pools before making the trek out here.

Besides the restaurant, there are three sheltered picnic tables with cooking grills (bring your own fuel). Down the valley a few dozen metres are seven cottages for rent at US$12 per night. Each cottage has a hot shower and a fireplace. Admission to the site costs US$0.50, the same again to park a car. Bring a bathing suit, which is required.

Getting There & Away A half-day tour to Fuentes Georginas using one of the taxis parked in the Parque Centroamérica in Quetzaltenango costs US$15 per carload (US$3 to US$5 per person), and includes a visit to Zunil as well as two hours' swimming time at the spa. This is not a bad price, but it doesn't give you much time there. You might want to take the taxi to the baths, bring a picnic, and walk back to Zunil to catch a late afternoon bus. Hitching is not good on the Fuentes Georginas access road. The best days to try for a ride are Saturday and Sunday, when the baths are busiest.

If you're driving or hitching, go uphill from Zunil's plaza to the Cantel road (about 60 metres), turn right and go downhill 100 metres to a Pepsi sign ('Baños Georginas'). On the left, an unpaved road heads off into the mountains; the baths are nine km from Zunil's plaza. Walking uphill takes two hours, 1½ to walk back down.

San Francisco El Alto

High on a hilltop (2610 metres) overlooking Quetzaltenango (17 km away) stands the market town of San Francisco El Alto. Six days a week it's a sleepy sort of place, but on Friday it explodes with activity as thousands of country people pour into the sloping plaza for the huge market.

San Francisco's market is not heavy with handicrafts as are those in Chichicastenango and Antigua, though you will find some nice crafts here, such as Momostenango blankets. Rather, this is a real people's market at which you'll find anything and everything needed by a Guatemalan highland villager.

Places to Stay & Eat The lodging and eating situation here is dire. If you're in need of a bed you'll have to suffer the *Hotel y Cafetería Vista Hermosa* (☎ 9-661030), 3a Avenida 2-22, Zona 1. Rates are US$4 a double with common bath, US$5.50 to US$7.50 with private shower, too expensive for what you get.

As for eating, the *Comedor San Cristóbal*, near the Hospedaje San Francisco de Assis, may be your best bet, but that's not saying much.

Momostenango

Beyond San Francisco El Alto, 22 km from Cuatro Caminos (35 km from Quetzaltenango) along a fairly rough unpaved country road is this village in a pretty mountain valley. Momostenango is Guatemala's famous centre for the making of *chamarras*, the thick, heavy woollen blankets which will you have no doubt already used to protect yourself from the chill of a highland night. They also make ponchos and other woollen garments.

As you enter the village square after an hour of bashing over the bad road, you will see signs inviting you to inspect blanket-making as it happens, and to purchase the finished products. The best time to do this is on Sunday, which is market day; haggle like mad. You might also want to hike three km north to the hot springs of Pala Chiquito, where the blankets are washed and the dyes fixed.

Momostenango is also noted for its adherence to the ancient Maya calendar, and for observance of traditional rites. Hills about two km west of the plaza are the scene of these ceremonies, coordinated with the important dates of the Maya calendar. Unfortunately, it's not as easy to witness these rites

as it is to visit the Shrine of Pascual Abaj at Chichicastenango.

Places to Stay & Eat For comfort and price, it's best to catch the mid-afternoon bus back to Quetzaltenango. If you miss it, *Casa de Huéspedes Paclom* charges US$6 for a bare double room; water to the toilets is shut off at night, there is no shower in the hotel, and the food is no treat. *Hospedaje Roxana*, on the plaza, is marginally better. There are several basic comedores on the plaza as well.

Getting There & Away Catch an early bus from Quetzaltenango's Terminal Minerva, or at Cuatro Caminos, or at San Francisco El Alto. There are five or six buses daily, the last one returning from Momostenango by about 3 pm.

HUEHUETENANGO
Population 40,000

Separated from the capital by mountains and a twisting road, Huehuetenango (altitude 1902 metres) has that self-sufficient air exuded by many mountain towns. Coffee growing, mining, sheep raising, light manufacturing and agriculture are the main activities in this region. The lively Indian market is filled daily with traders who come down from the Sierra de los Cuchumatanes, the mountain range (highest in Central America) which dominates the department of Huehuetenango.

For travellers, Huehuetenango is usually a stage on the journey to and from Mexico. It's a good introduction to Guatemalan highland life: a pleasant town with good cheap hotels, an interesting market and the ruins of ancient Zaculeu on the outskirts.

History

Huehuetenango was a Mam Maya region until the 15th century when the Quiché, expanding from their capital at K'umarcaaj near present-day Santa Cruz del Quiché, pushed them out. Many Mam fled into neighbouring Chiapas, which still has a large Mam-speaking population near its border with Guatemala. In the late 15th century, the weakness of Quiché rule brought about civil war, which engulfed the highlands and provided a chance for Mam independence. The troubles lasted for decades, coming to an end in the summer of 1525 after the arrival of Gonzalo de Alvarado, brother of Pedro, who conquered the Mam capital of Zaculeu for the king of Spain.

Orientation & Information

The town centre is five km north of the Interamerican Highway. The new bus station and new market are three km from the highway along the road to the centre (6 Calle), on the east side. The bus station is little used, and most buses continue right into the centre.

Almost every service of interest to tourists is in Zona 1 within a few blocks of the plaza. The old market, bordered by 1a and 2a Avenidas and 3 and 4 Calles in Zona 1, is still the busy one, especially on Wednesday, which is market day. Four blocks west of the market on 5a Avenida between 2 and 3 Calles is the main plaza, called the parque. Hotels and restaurants are mostly near the parque, except for one or two small hotels near the new bus station.

The post office is at 2 Calle 3-54, right next to the Guatel telephone office across the street from the Hotel Mary, half a block east of the plaza. The Mexican Consulate is in the Farmacia Del Río on the corner of 5a Avenida and 4 Calle. Town-operated *servicios sanitarios* (toilets) are on 3 Calle between 5a and 6a Avenidas, only a few steps west of the plaza. Farmacias (chemists) and banks are dotted around the centre.

Parque Central

Huehuetenango's main plaza is shaded by nice old trees and surrounded by the town's imposing buildings: the Municipalidad, with its band shell on the upper floor; and the huge colonial church. The plaza has its own little relief map of the department of Huehuetenango, which is interesting because of the Cuchumatanes Mountains.

Zaculeu

Surrounded by natural barriers – ravines and a river – on three sides, the Late Post-Classic religious centre of Zaculeu occupies a good defensive location which served its Mam Maya inhabitants well. It only failed in 1525 when Gonzalo de Alvarado and his conquistadors laid siege to the site. Good natural defences are no defence against starvation, and it was this that defeated the Mam.

The current wisdom about Zaculeu is that it is boring; a bad restoration left its pyramids, ball courts and ceremonial platforms covered in a thick coat of greying plaster.

Though some of the construction methods used in the restoration were not authentic to the buildings, the work goes further than others in making the site look as it might have to the eyes of Mam priests and worshippers when it was still an active religious centre. We have become so used to seeing ruddy bare stones and grass-covered mounds that the tidiness of Zaculeu is unsettling.

When Zaculeu flourished, its buildings were coated with plaster, as they are now. What is missing is the painted decoration that must have been applied to the wet plaster. Imagine some painted figures on the walls, and you can almost see the Mam priests mounting the steep staircases.

The park-like archaeological zone of Zaculeu is four km north of Huehuetenango's main plaza. It's open daily from 8 am to 6 pm; admission is US$0.20 after you sign the register. Cold soft drinks are available. The small, modern museum has drawings of scenes from the Spanish conquest, a Mam burial urn and potsherds. Visitors are allowed to climb on the restored structures, but it's strictly forbidden to climb the grassy mounds which have not yet been excavated.

Jitney trucks and vans depart from the corner of 3a Avenida and 4 Calle (between the church and the market) near Rico Mac Pollo heading north along 5a Avenida toward Zaculeu. 'Esperanza' buses travel this route as well. Some go fairly close to the ruins, others do not, so ask. Another route goes west via 3 Calle and out past the Campo de

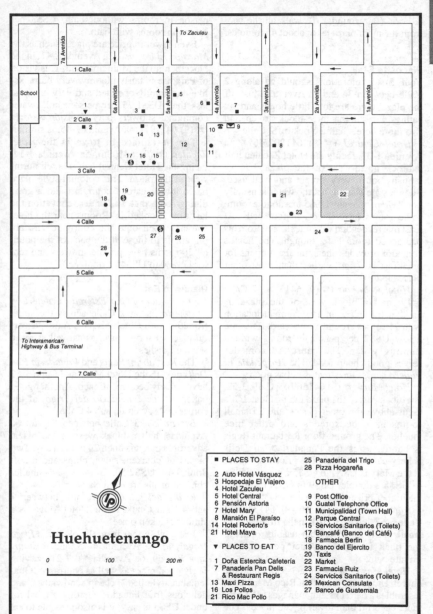

Huehuetenango

0   100   200 m

■ PLACES TO STAY

2 Auto Hotel Vásquez
3 Hospedaje El Viajero
4 Hotel Zaculeu
5 Hotel Central
6 Pensión Astoria
7 Hotel Mary
8 Mansión El Paraíso
14 Hotel Roberto's
21 Hotel Maya

▼ PLACES TO EAT

1 Doña Estercita Cafetería
7 Panadería Pan Delis
   & Restaurant Regis
13 Maxi Pizza
16 Los Pollos
21 Rico Mac Pollo
25 Panadería del Trigo
28 Pizza Hogareña

OTHER

9 Post Office
10 Guatel Telephone Office
11 Municipalidad (Town Hall)
12 Parque Central
15 Servicios Sanitarios (Toilets)
17 Bancafé (Banco del Café)
18 Farmacia Berlin
19 Banco del Ejercito
20 Taxis
22 Market
23 Farmacia Ruiz
24 Servicios Sanitarios (Toilets)
26 Mexican Consulate
27 Banco de Guatemala

la Feria (fairgrounds). To walk all the way from the main plaza takes about 45 minutes.

Places to Stay

Your first explorations should be along 2 Calle between 3a and 7a Avenidas, just off the plaza; there are four little hotels and six eating-places in this three-block stretch, and two more hotels half a block off 2 Calle.

Hotel Central (☎ (9) 641202/467), 5a Avenida 1-33, facing the Hotel Zaculeu half a block north-west of the plaza, has 17 largish rooms, very simple and well used. Showers are shared, but the water is usually hot. Two people pay US$5 in a double room; some rooms have three and four beds. At least one reader had valuables stolen from his padlocked room here, though. The hotel's comedor provides cheap meals. It opens for breakfast at 7 am, earlier than most other places in town.

Hotel Roberto's (☎ (9) 641526), 2 Calle 5-49, half a block west of the plaza, is another tidy place in a convenient location with 21 rooms around a courtyard. Rates are a low US$2 per person in rooms without running water. The courtyard comedor serves good cheap food. The *Hospedaje El Viajero* across the street is not as good.

Hotel Mary (☎ (9) 641569), 2 Calle 3-52, is a block east of the plaza facing Guatel. It's a cut above the other places: the 25 small rooms have bedspreads and other nice touches. The ground-floor Restaurant Regis is handy, as is the Panadería Pan Delis bakery-café next door. The price for a room at the Mary is US$4 to US$5 a single, US$6 to US$8 a double, US$9 to US$11 a triple; the higher priced rooms have private baths.

Auto Hotel Vásquez (☎ (9) 641338), 2 Calle 6-67, has a car park in the front, and 20 small, fairly cheerless but usable rooms at the back for US$2.50 per person, with private bath.

Hotel Maya, 3a Avenida 3-55, behind the church and just to the left of Rico Mac Pollo, resembles a barracks, but manages to be a bit more cheerful than lower priced places. The location is convenient. Rates are US$2 per

person in rooms without bath, US$3 per person in rooms with bath.

Even lower in price are places such as the *Mansión El Paraíso*, 3a Avenida 2-41, in the block behind the Municipalidad. This vision of Paradise is fairly gloomy, very barracks-like, but family operated and very cheap at less than US$1.75 per person; cold water communal showers only. *Pensión Astoria* (☎ (9) 641197), 4a Avenida 1-45, is similar.

The best place in town is the *Hotel Zaculeu* (☎ (9) 641086), 5a Avenida 1-14, facing the Hotel Central half a block north-west of the plaza. This colonial-style place has a lovely garden courtyard and a good dining room that was under renovation the last time I looked in. Rooms near the hotel entrance open onto the courtyard and are preferable to those at the back of the hotel; all 20 rooms have private showers and rent for US$20 to US$45 a double.

Places to Eat

Especialidades Doña Estercita Cafetería y Pastelería, is on 2 Calle across the street from the Auto Hotel Vásquez. A tidy, cheerful place, it serves pastries as well as more standard dishes.

The *Restaurant Regis* and *Panadería Pan Delis* next to the Hotel Mary at 2 Calle 3-52 have already been mentioned. Another good bakery is the *Panadería del Trigo*, at the corner of 4a Avenida and 4 Calle.

Los Pollos, 3 Calle between 5a and 6a Avenidas, half a block west of the plaza, advertises that it is open 24 hours a day. Two pieces of chicken, salad, chips and a soft drink cost US$2.50. Burgers and smaller chicken meals are even cheaper.

Rico Mac Pollo, 3a Avenida between 3 and 4 Calles, next to the Hotel Maya, is a similar chicken place.

Just a bit farther from the plaza are *Pizza Hogareña*, 6a Avenida 4-45, and *Restaurante Rincón*, 6a Avenida 'A' 7-21, serving fairly good pizza as well as churrasco (Guatemalan-style beef), cheap sandwiches, and delicious fruit licuados. Getting a meal for under US$3 is easy; it is also possible to eat for US$2.

Probably the best restaurant in town is the *Steak House*, at the intersection of 4a Avenida and 2 Calle, where a full meal of Chinese food or steak should cost no more than US$5 or so.

Getting There & Away

The new bus terminal is in Zona 4, two km south of the plaza along 6 Calle, but most buses still depart from 1a Avenida between 2 and 3 Calles. Second-class buses run between the terminal and the Guatemalan border post at La Mesilla (84 km, 1½ hours, US$1.25) about every hour between 5 am and 4 pm. There are also a few 1st-class buses for slightly more money. Hourly buses head down the Interamerican Highway to Cuatro Caminos (74 km, 1¾ hours, US$2) and Quetzaltenango's Terminal Minerva (90 km, two hours, US$2.50). Los Halcones (☎ (2) 81979), 7a Avenida 15-27, Zona 1 in Guatemala City, runs two buses a day on the 270-km, five-hour run down the Interamerican Highway to Guatemala City. The fare is US$3.50.

LA MESILLA

There is a distance of four km between the Mexican and Guatemalan immigration posts at La Mesilla/Ciudad Cuauhtémoc, and you must take a collective taxi for US$1. There is no bank on either the Guatemalan or Mexican side, but moneychangers will do the deal at a worse rate.

TODOS SANTOS CUCHUMATÁN

Population 2000

If you are keen for a trek into the Cuchumatanes, two buses daily depart at 4 am and 11 am from the corner of 1a Avenida and 4 Calle, near the Pensión San Jorge in Huehuetenango on the 40-km ride to Todos Santos Cuchumatán. The road is rough, the mountain air cold, the journey slow, but the scenery is spectacular. Return buses depart Todos Santos at 5.30 and 11.30 am and 1 pm for Huehue.

The picturesque town of Todos Santos Cuchumatán (altitude 2450 metres) is one of the few in which the traditional Maya tzolkin calendar is still remembered and (partially) observed. Saturday is market day. It's possible to take some vigorous treks from the town into the mountains, and to rejuvenate in the traditional Mam sauna.

Accommodation consists of two primitive, cheap hospedajes, *Tres Olguitas* and *La Paz*. There are also rooms in private homes. People with rooms to rent will probably solicit your business as you descend from your bus, and charge US$1 per person. Try the house attached to the café and shop *Ruinas de Tecumanchun*.

A few small comedores provide food; *Comedor Katy* is perhaps the best. You'll need these places because the buses – which are run to take villagers into Huehue for shopping and then home again – don't return there until early the next morning.

The Pacific Slope

Most of the towns along the Pacific Slope are muggy, chaotic, and hold little of interest for travellers. The beach villages are worse – unpleasantly hot, muggy and dilapidated. There are exceptions, though. Retalhuleu, a logical stopping-place if you're coming from the Mexican border, is pleasant. Nearby is the archaeological dig at Abaj Takalik. The pre-Olmec stone carvings at Santa Lucía Cotzumalguapa, eight km west of Siquinalá, and those at La Democracia nine km south of Siquinalá, are unique, and if you travel on the Carretera al Pacífico you must stop to see them. The port town of Iztapa and its beach resorts of Likín and Monterrico can fill the need if you simply must get to the beach. Near Guatemala City, Lago de Amatitlán is the citified version of the more beautiful Lago de Atitlán.

The Carretera al Pacífico is good and very fast, which is exactly how the 1st-class buses drive it.

CIUDAD TECÚN UMÁN

This is the preferable and busier of the two Pacific Slope border-crossing points, with a

GUATEMALA

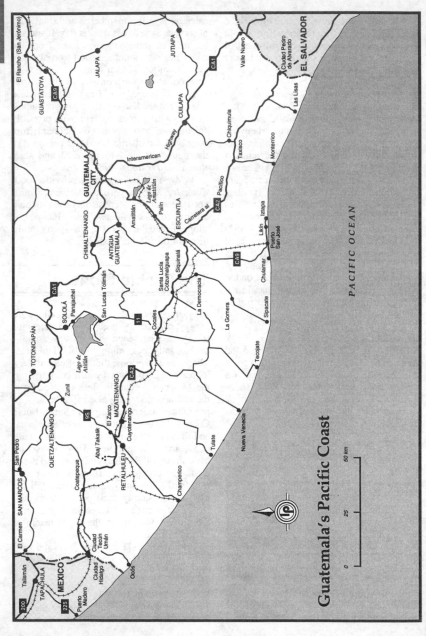

Guatemala's Pacific Coast

bridge linking Ciudad Tecún Umán, Guatemala with Ciudad Hidalgo, Mexico. The border posts are open 24 hours a day. There are basic hotels and restaurants, but you'll want to get through the border and on your way as soon as possible.

Minibuses and buses run frequently between Ciudad Hidalgo and Tapachula, 38 km to the north. From Ciudad Tecún Umán there are frequent buses heading east along the Carretera al Pacífico, stopping at Coatepeque, Retalhuleu, Mazatenango and Escuintla before climbing into the mountains to Guatemala City. If you don't find a bus to your destination, take any bus to Coatepeque or, preferably, Retalhuleu, and change buses there.

EL CARMEN
Though you can cross at El Carmen, you will encounter much less hassle and expense if you cross at Tecún Umán.

A toll bridge across the Río Suchiate connects Talismán, Mexico and El Carmen, Guatemala. The border-crossing posts are open 24 hours every day. Minibuses and trucks run frequently between Talismán and Tapachula, half an hour (20 km) away.

There are few services at El Carmen, and these are very basic. There is a good bus service from El Carmen to Malacatán, on the San Marcos-Quetzaltenango road, and to Ciudad Tecún Umán 39 km to the south. There are also fairly frequent 1st-class buses to Guatemala City along the Carretera al Pacífico (278 km, five hours, US$4). Transportes Galgos (☎ (2) 534868, 23661), 7a Avenida 19-44, Zona 1, Guatemala City, is only one company operating along this route. It runs five buses daily from El Carmen stopping at Ciudad Tecún Umán, Coatepeque, Retalhuleu, Mazatenango and Escuintla (change for Santa Lucía Cotzumalguapa). Rutas Lima has a daily bus to Quetzaltenango via Retalhuleu and El Zarco junction.

COATEPEQUE
Set on a hill in the midst of lush coffee plantations, Coatepeque is a brash, fairly ugly and chaotic commercial centre, noisy and humid at all times. The town is several km north of the Carretera al Pacífico, and there is no reason to stop here unless you're a coffee broker or you have an emergency.

EL ZARCO JUNCTION
About 40 km east of Coatepeque and nine km west of Retalhuleu on the Carretera al Pacífico is El Zarco, the junction with the toll road north to Quetzaltenango. The road winds up the Pacific Slope, carpeted in tropical jungle, rising more than 2000 metres in the 47 km from El Zarco to Quetzaltenango. The toll is less than US$1. Just after the upper toll booth the road divides at Zunil: the left fork goes to Quetzaltenango via Los Baños and Almolonga (the shorter route); the right fork via Cantel. For information on these places and the beautiful Fuentes Georginas hot springs near Zunil, see the Around Quetzaltenango section earlier.

RETALHULEU
Population 40,000
The Pacific Slope is a rich agricultural region, and Retalhuleu (altitude 240 metres) is its clean, attractive capital – and proud of it. Most Guatemalans refer to Retalhuleu simply as Reu (RAY-oo).

If Coatepeque is where the coffee traders trade, Retalhuleu is where they come to relax, splashing in the pool at the Posada de Don José and sipping a cool drink in the bar. You'll see their expensive Range Rovers and big 4WD vehicles parked outside. The rest of the citizens get their kicks strolling through the plaza between the whitewashed colonial church and the wedding-cake government buildings, shaded by royal palms.

The balmy tropical air and laid-back attitude are restful. In the evening the parque (plaza) is alive with strollers and noisy with blackbirds. Tourists are something of a curiosity in Reu, and are treated well.

Orientation
The town centre is four km south-west of the Carretera al Pacífico along a grand boulevard lined with towering palm trees. The bus

station is near the market and the fairgrounds, 700 metres south-west of the plaza along 5a Avenida 'A'. To find the plaza, look for the twin church towers and walk towards them. The railway station is two blocks north-west of the plaza very near the Posada de Don José.

Most of the services you may need are within two blocks of the plaza, including banks, public toilets, cinemas, hotels and restaurants. There is no official tourist office, but people in the Municipalidad, on 6a Avenida facing the east side of the church, will do their best to help with vexing problems.

Places to Stay

There are few rock-bottom low-end places to stay in Reu, though there are several low-priced central hotels. Two of the most convenient are just half a block west of the plaza. The better of the two is the *Hotel Astor*

(☎ (9) 710475), 5 Calle 4-60, Zona 1, with a pretty courtyard, nine well-kept if simple rooms with showers, and its own parking lot. Rates are US$7/12/15 a single/ double/triple with private shower, US$4.75 per person in bathless rooms. *Hotel Modelo* (☎ (9) 710256), 5 Calle 4-53, Zona 1, just across 5 Calle from the Hotel Astor, is a similar big old place with seven shower-equipped rooms on two floors around a cavernous central court. Prices are the same as at the Astor.

For even cheaper rooms, look at the *Hospedaje San Francisco*, 250 metres along 6a Avenida from the church on the right-hand side, at 8 Calle.

The nicest place in town is the 35-room *Hotel Posada de Don José* (☎ (9) 710180/41), 5 Calle 3-67, Zona 1, across the street from the railway station and two blocks north-west of the plaza. On weekends the Don José is often filled with finca owners in town for relaxation; at other times you can

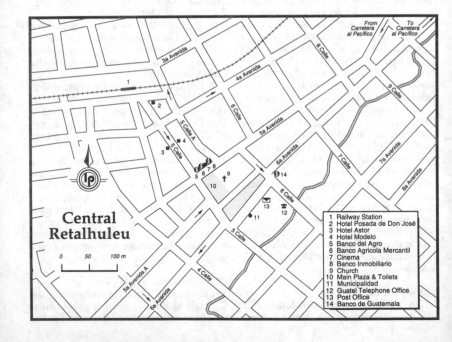

Central Retalhuleu

0   50   100 m

1 Railway Station
2 Hotel Posada de Don José
3 Hotel Astor
4 Hotel Modelo
5 Banco del Agro
6 Banco Agrícola Mercantil
7 Cinema
8 Banco Inmobiliario
9 Church
10 Main Plaza & Toilets
11 Municipalidad
12 Guatel Telephone Office
13 Post Office
14 Banco de Guatemala

get an air-con room with private bath for US$18/28/36 a single/double/triple.

Places to Eat
Several little restaurants facing the plaza – *Cafetería Nuevos Horizones, Restaurant El Patio* etc – provide meals at cheap prices (under US$3). For the best meal in town, head for the *Hotel Posada de Don José*, where the pleasant restaurant serves beef and chicken plates for US$4 to US$6, and a big, full meal can be had for US$7 to US$10. Breakfast is served here as well.

Getting There & Away
As Reu is the most important town on the Carretera al Pacífico, transport is easy. Most buses travelling along the highway stop at the city's bus station, so you can catch a bus to Guatemala City (186 km, four hours, US$3 to US$4), Quetzaltenango (67 km, two hours, US$2) or the Mexican border at Ciudad Tecún Umán (78 km, 1½ hours, US$1.75) almost every hour from about 7 am to 5 pm.

Around Retalhuleu
Abaj Takalik There's nothing to see in Retalhuleu proper, but about 30 km to the west is the active archaeological dig at Abaj Takalik (ah-BAH tah-kah-LEEK), where exciting finds have already been made. Large 'Olmecoid' stone heads have been discovered, along with many other objects, which date the site as one of the earliest in all of the Maya realm. The site has yet to be restored and prettified for tourists, so don't expect a Chichén Itzá or Tikal. But if you're truly fascinated with archaeology and want to see it as it's done, make a visit.

It's difficult to reach Abaj Takalik without your own vehicle; you may have to hire a taxi from Retalhuleu (US$20 to US$30). To do it by bus, early in the morning take any bus heading west towards Coatepeque, go about 15 km west along the Carretera al Pacífico and get out at the road, on the right, to El Asintal. It's five km to El Asintal (you may have some luck hitching); Abaj Takalik is

four km beyond El Asintal along an unpaved road.

CHAMPERICO
Built to serve as an exit route for shipments of coffee during the boom of the late 19th century, Champerico, 38 km south-west of Retalhuleu, is a tawdry, sweltering, dilapidated place that sees few tourists – and with good reason. Though there are several cheap hotels and restaurants, you would do better to reserve your seaside time for more attractive towns.

MAZATENANGO
Population 38,000
East of Retalhuleu 26 km along the Carretera al Pacífico, is Mazatenango (altitude 370 metres), capital of the department of Suchitepéquez. It's a centre for farmers, traders and shippers of the Pacific Slope's agricultural produce. There are a few serviceable hotels if you need to stop in an emergency.

SANTA LUCÍA COTZUMALGUAPA
Population 20,000
Another 71 km eastward from Mazatenango brings you to Santa Lucía Cotzumalguapa (altitude 356 metres), an important stop for anyone interested in Maya art and culture. In the sugar cane fields and fincas near the town stand great stone heads carved with grotesque faces, fine relief scenes in stone, and a mystery: who carved these ritual objects, and why?

The town itself, though pleasant, is unexciting, with little to keep you except the mysterious carved stones with beautiful reliefs, still not fully understood by archaeologists.

Orientation
Santa Lucía Cotzumalguapa is north-west of the Carretera al Pacífico. In its main square (el parque), several blocks from the highway, are copies of some of the famous carved stones to be found in the region.

There are three main archaeological sites to visit: Bilbao, a finca right on the outskirts of Santa Lucía; Finca El Baúl, a large plantation farther from the town, at which there are two sites, a hilltop site and the finca headquarters; and Finca Las Ilusiones, which has collected most of its findings into a museum near the finca headquarters. Of these sites, Bilbao and the hilltop site at El Baúl are by far the most interesting. If time and energy are short, make for these.

If you don't have your own transport and you want to see the sites in a day, haggle with a taxi driver in Santa Lucía's main square for a visit to the sites. It's hot and muggy, the sites are several km apart, and you will really be glad you rode at least part of the way. If you do it all on foot and by bus, pack a lunch so you won't have to return to town. The perfect place to have a picnic is the hilltop site at El Baúl.

Bilbao

This site was no doubt a large ceremonial centre which flourished about 600 AD. Ploughs have unearthed (and damaged) hundreds of stones during the last few centuries; thieves have carted off many others. In 1880 many of the best stones were removed to museums abroad, including nine stones to the Dahlem Museum in Berlin.

Known locally as simply *las piedras* (the stones), this site actually consists of several separate sites deep within tall stands of sugar cane. The fields come right to the edge of the town. From Santa Lucía's main square, go north uphill on 3a Avenida to the outskirts of town. Pass El Calvario church on your right, and shortly thereafter turn sharp right. A hundred metres along, the road veers to the right but an unpaved road continues straight on; follow the unpaved road. The canefields are on your left, and you will soon see a path cut into the high cane.

At times when the cane is high, finding your way around would be very difficult if it weren't for the swarms of local boys that guide you in exchange for a tip.

The boys may lead you to the sites in a different order from that which follows. The first stone is flat with three figures carved in low relief; the middle figure's ribs show

prominently, as though he were starving. A predatory bird is in the upper left-hand corner. Holes in the middle-right part of the stone show that thieves attempted to cut the stone apart in order to make it more easily portable.

Next is an elaborate relief showing players in a ball game (an obsession of the Pipils), fruit, birds, animals and cacao bean pods, for which this area was famous and which made it rich.

Farther into the fields are more stones, several of which are badly weathered and worn so that the figures are difficult to make out. The last stones the boys show you are a 10-minute walk from the starting-point. These bear Mexican-style circular date glyphs and other mysterious patterns which resemble closely those used by people along the Gulf coast of Mexico near Villahermosa. These two peoples must have had close relations, but just how they did so is a mystery.

Finally, the boys lead you along a broad unpaved track in the canefields back to the dead end of the unpaved road from which you began. If you go south from this point you can join 4a Avenida and continue to the main square.

To go on to El Baúl, however, you can save time by backtracking to the point where you turned sharp right just beyond El Calvario church. Buses heading out to El Baúl pass this point every few hours; or you can hitch with any other vehicle. If you're driving, you'll have to return to the centre along 4a Avenida and come back out along 3a Avenida, as these roads are one way.

Finca El Baúl

Just as interesting as las piedras is the hilltop site at El Baúl, which has the additional fascination of being an active place of pagan worship for local people. This is an excellent place for a picnic. Some distance from the hilltop site on another road, next to the finca headquarters, is the finca's private museum of stones uncovered on the property.

The hilltop site at El Baúl is 4.2 km northwest of El Calvario church. From the church (or the intersection just beyond it), go 2.7 km

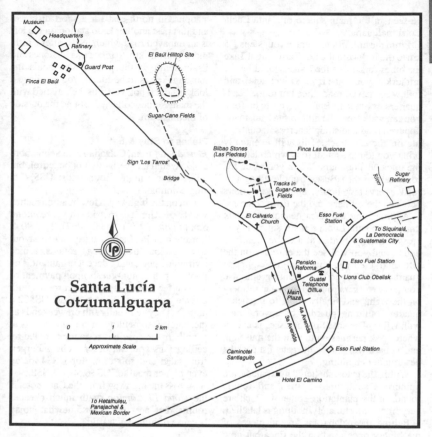

Santa Lucía
Cotzumalguapa

0   1   2 km
Approximate Scale

to a fork in the road just beyond a bridge; the fork is marked by a sign reading Los Tarros. Take the right-hand fork, an unpaved road. From the Los Tarros sign it's 1.5 km to the point where a dirt track crosses the road; on your right is a tree-covered 'hill' in the midst of otherwise flat fields. The 'hill' is actually a great ruined temple platform which has not been restored. Make your way across the field and around the south side of the hill, following the track to the top.

If you visit on a weekend, you may find several worshippers paying their respects to the idols here. They will not mind if you visit

as well, and are usually happy to pose with the idols for photographs in exchange for a small 'contribution'.

Of the two stones here, the great grotesque half-buried head is the most striking. The head is stained with wax from candles, with liquor and other drinks, and with the smoke and ashes of incense fires built before it, all part of worship. The idol may have reason to be happy. People have been coming here to pay homage for over 1400 years.

The other stone is a relief carving of a figure surrounded by circular motifs which may be date glyphs. A copy of this stone may be seen in the main square of Santa Lucía Cotzumalguapa.

From the hilltop site, retrace your steps 1.5 km to the fork with the Los Tarros sign. Take the other fork this time (what would be the left fork as you come from Santa Lucía), and follow the paved road three km to the headquarters of Finca El Baúl. (If you're on foot, you can walk from the hilltop site back to the unpaved road and straight across it, continuing on the dirt track. This will eventually bring you to the asphalt road which leads to the finca headquarters. When you reach the road, turn right.) Buses trundle along this road every few hours, shuttling workers between the refinery and the town centre.

Approaching the finca headquarters (six km from Santa Lucía's main square), you cross a narrow bridge at a curve, continue uphill, and you will see the entrance on the left, marked by a machine-gun-equipped guard post. Beyond this daunting entrance you pass workers' houses, a sugar refinery on the right, and finally come to the headquarters building guarded by several men with rifles. The smell of molasses is everywhere. Ask permission to visit the museum, and a guard will unlock the gate just past the headquarters building.

Within the gates, sheltered by a palapa, are numerous sculptured figures and reliefs found on the plantation, some of which are very fine. Unfortunately, nothing is labelled.

Behind the palapa are several pieces of machinery once used on the finca but now retired. One of these is a small Orenstein & Kopdel steam locomotive manufactured in Berlin in 1927.

Finca Las Ilusiones

The third site is very close to Bilbao – indeed, this is the finca which controls the Bilbao canefields – but, paradoxically, access is more difficult. Your reward is the chance to view hundreds of objects, large and small, which have been collected from the finca's fields over the centuries.

Leave the town centre by heading east along Calzada 15 de Septiembre, the boulevard which joins the highway at an Esso fuel station. Go north-east for a short distance, and just past another Esso station on the left is an unpaved road which leads, after a little more than one km, to Finca Las Ilusiones and its museum. If the person who holds the museum key is to be found, you can have a look inside. If not, you must be satisfied with the many stones collected around the outside of the museum.

Places to Stay & Eat

Pensión Reforma, Calzada 15 de Septiembre at 4a Avenida, is certainly not beautiful, but will do for a night. Rooms cost US$3/5 a single/double.

Out on the highway, a few hundred metres west of the town, is the *Caminotel Santiaguito* (☎ (9) 845435/6/7), Km 90.4, Carretera al Pacífico, a fairly lavish layout with spacious tree-shaded grounds, a nice swimming pool, and a decent restaurant. The pool is open to non-guests upon payment of a small fee. Motel-style air-con rooms with private baths cost US$16 a single, US$22 a double. They're usually full on weekends as the hotel is something of a resort for local people. In the spacious restaurant cooled by ceiling fans you can order a cheeseburger, fruit salad and soft drink for US$4, or an even bigger meal for US$6.50 to US$8.

Across the highway from the Caminotel is the *Hotel El Camino*, with much cheaper rooms that are hot and somewhat noisy because of highway traffic.

Getting There & Away

Esmeralda 2nd-class buses shuttle between Santa Lucía Cotzumalguapa and Guatemala City (4a Avenida and 2 Calle, Zona 9) every half an hour or so between 6 am and 5 pm, charging US$1.50 for the 90-km, two-hour ride. You can also catch any bus travelling along the Carretera al Pacífico between Guatemala City and such points as Mazatenango, Retalhuleu or the Mexican border.

To travel between La Democracia and Santa Lucía, catch a bus running along the Carretera al Pacífico between Santa Lucía and Siquinalá (eight km); change in Siquinalá for a bus to La Democracia.

Between Santa Lucía and Lago de Atitlán you will probably have to change buses at Cocales junction, 23 km west of Santa Lucía and 58 km south of Panajachel.

LA DEMOCRACIA

Population 4200

South of Siquinalá 9.5 km along the road to Puerto San José is La Democracia (altitude 165 metres), a nondescript Pacific Slope town that's hot both day and night, rainy season and dry. Like Santa Lucía Cotzumalguapa, La Democracia is in the midst of a region populated from early times with – according to some archaeologists – mysterious cultural connections to Mexico's Gulf coast.

At the archaeological site called **Monte Alto**, on the outskirts of the town, huge basalt heads have been found. Though cruder, the heads resemble those carved by the Olmec near Veracruz several thousand years ago. The Monte Alto heads could be older than, as old as, or not as old as the Olmec heads. We just don't know.

Today these great 'Olmecoid' heads are arranged around La Democracia's main plaza. As you come into town from the highway, follow signs to the *museo*, which will cause you to bear left, then turn left, then turn left again.

Facing the plaza, along with the church and the modest Palacio Municipal, is the small, modern Museo Rubén Chevez Van Dorne with other fascinating archaeological finds. The star of the show is an exquisite jade mask. Smaller figures, 'yokes' used in the ball game, relief carvings and other objects make up the rest of this important small collection. On the walls are overly dramatic paintings of Olmecoid scenes; there's more drama than meaning or accuracy. The museum is open from 8 am to noon and 2 to 5 pm; admission costs US$0.50.

The road south continues 42 km to **Sipacate**, a small and very basic beach town. The beach is on the other side of the Canal de Chiquimulilla, an intra-coastal waterway. Though there are a few scruffy, very basic places to stay there, you'd be better off

saving your beach time for Puerto San José, 35 km farther to the east, reached via the road from Escuintla.

Places to Stay & Eat

La Democracia has no places to stay and few places to eat. The eateries are very basic and ill-supplied, and it's best for you to bring your own food and buy drinks at a place facing the plaza. *Café Maritza*, right next to the museum, is a picture-perfect hot-tropics hangout with a *rockola* (jukebox) blasting music, and a small crew of semi-somnolent locals sipping and sweltering.

Getting There & Away

Chatia Gomerana, Muelle Central, Terminal de Buses, Zona 4, Guatemala City, has buses every half hour from 6 am to 4.30 pm on the 92-km, two-hour ride between the capital and La Democracia. Buses stop at Escuintla, Siquinalá (change for Santa Lucía Cotzumalguapa), La Democracia, La Gomera and Sipacate. The fare is US$1.50.

ESCUINTLA

Set amidst lush tropical verdure, Escuintla should be an idyllic place where people swing languidly in hammocks and concoct pungent meals of readily available exotic fruit and vegetables. But it's not.

Escuintla is a hot, dingy, dilapidated commercial and industrial city that's very important to the Pacific Slope's economy, but not important to you. It is an old town, inhabited by Pipils before the conquest, but now solidly ladino. Though it does have some fairly dingy hotels and restaurants, it provides no reason why you should use them.

You may have to change buses in Escuintla. The main bus station is in the southern part of town; this is where you catch buses to Puerto San José. For Guatemala City, you can catch one of the frequent buses from the main plaza.

PUERTO SAN JOSÉ, LIKÍN & IZTAPA

Guatemala's most important seaside resort leaves a lot to be desired, even when compared to Mexico's smaller, seedier places. But if you're eager to get into the Pacific surf, head south from Escuintla 50 km to Puerto San José and neighbouring settlements.

Puerto San José (population 14,000) was Guatemala's most important Pacific port in the latter half of the 19th century and well into the 20th. Now superseded by the more modern Puerto Quetzal to the east, Puerto San José languishes and slumbers; its inhabitants languish, slumber, play loud music and drink. The beach, inconveniently located across the Canal de Chiquimulilla, is reached by boat.

A smarter thing to do is to head west along the coast five km (by taxi or private car) to Balneario Chulamar, which has a nicer beach and also a suitable hotel or two.

About five km to the east of Puerto San José is Balneario Likín, Guatemala's only up-market Pacific resort. Likín is much beloved by well-to-do families from Guatemala City who have seaside houses on the tidy streets and canals of this planned development.

About 12 km east of Puerto San José is Iztapa, Guatemala's first Pacific port, first used by none other than Pedro de Alvarado in the 16th century. When Puerto San José was built in 1853, Iztapa's reign as the port of the capital city came to an end, and it relaxed into a tropical torpor from which it has yet to emerge. Having lain fallow for almost a century and a half, it has not suffered the degradation of Puerto San José.

Iztapa is comparatively pleasant, with several small, easily affordable hotels and restaurants on the beach. The bonus here is that you can catch a Transportes Pacifico bus from the market in Zona 4 in Guatemala City all the way to Iztapa (four hours), or pick it up at Escuintla or Puerto San José to take you to Iztapa.

MONTERRICO

Similar in many ways to the rest of Guatemala's Pacific coast, Monterrico has three things to attract you.

The first is the Biotopo Monterrico-Hawaii, a 20-km-long nature reserve comprising coastal mangrove swamps filled with bird and aquatic life. Its most famous denizens are perhaps the endangered leatherback and Ridley turtles which lay their eggs along the beach. Boat tours of the reserve can be had for only a few dollars.

The second attraction is the beach, the dramatic black volcanic sand crashing with surf.

The third is the *Hotel El Baule Beach*, a cosy ten-room hotel run by former Peace Corps Volunteer Nancy Garver. Rooms are right on the beach, and cost US$5 to US$10 per person with private bath and shower. Meals are reasonably priced as well. As there is little other accommodation, reserve in advance by telegram to Hotel Baule Beach, Monterrico, Taxisco, Santa Rosa 06024. The hotel is reached by a half-hour ferry ride from the village of La Avellana. Buses reach La Avellana via Taxisco and Escuintla from Guatemala City.

LAGO DE AMATITLÁN

A placid lake backed by a looming volcano, situated a mere 25 km south of Guatemala City – that's Amatitlán. It should be a pretty and peaceful resort, but unfortunately it's not. The hourglass-shaped lake is divided by a railway line, and the lake shore is lined with industry at some points. On weekends people from Guatemala City come to row boats on the lake (its waters are too polluted for swimming), or to rent a private hot tub for a dip.

There's little reason for you to spend time here. If you want to have a look, head for the town of Amatitlán, just off the main Escuintla-Guatemala City highway. Amatitlán has a scruffy public beach area where you can confirm your suspicions.

Central & Eastern Guatemala

North and east of Guatemala City is a land of varied topography, from the misty, pine-

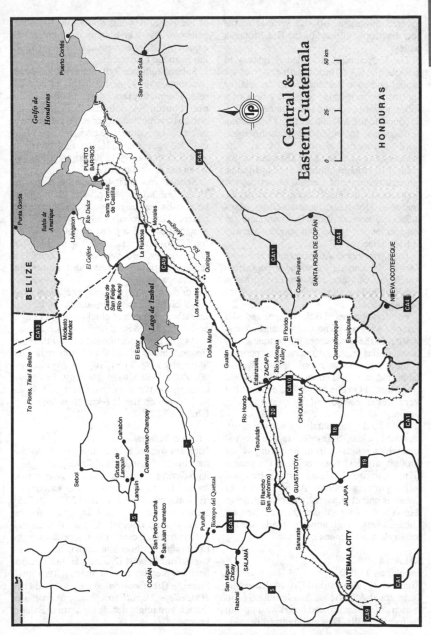

Central &
Eastern Guatemala

covered mountains of Alta Verapaz to the hot, dry-tropic climate of the Río Motagua Valley.

The Carretera al Atlantico (Highway to the Atlantic, CA-9) heads north-east from the capital and soon descends from the relative cool of the mountains to the dry heat of a valley where dinosaurs once roamed. Along its course to the Atlantic are many interesting destinations, including the beautiful highland scenery around Cobán; the palaeontology museum at Estanzuela; the great pilgrimage church at Esquipulas, famous throughout Central America; the first-rate Maya ruins at Copán, just across the border in Honduras; the marvellous Maya stelae and zoomorphs at Quiriguá; and the tropical lake of Izabal and jungle waterway of Río Dulce.

The Carretera al Atlantico ends at Puerto Barrios, Guatemala's Caribbean port, from which you can take a boat to Lívingston, a laid-back hideaway peopled by Black Afro-Guatemalans.

The departments of Baja Verapaz and Alta Verapaz were once known for their bad hospitality. In the time before the conquest, this mountainous highland region was peopled by the Rabinal Maya, noted for their warlike habits and merciless conquests. They battled the powerful Quiché Maya for a century, but were never conquered by that imperial nation.

The two departmental capitals are easily accessible along a smooth, fast, asphalted road which winds up from the hot dry valley through wonderful scenery into the mountains, through long stretches of coffee-growing country. Along the way to Cobán is one of Guatemala's premier nature reserves, the Biotopo del Quetzal. Beyond Cobán, along rough unpaved roads, are the country's most famous caverns.

SALAMÁ
Population 11,000
Highway 17, also marked CA-14, leaves the Carretera al Atlantico at San Jerónimo (also known as El Rancho) and heads west up into the forested hills. Descending the other side

of the ridge, it winds down into the broad valley of the Río Salamá, and enters the capital of the department of Baja Verapaz, 20 km from the Carretera.

Salamá (altitude 940 metres) is an attractive town with some reminders of colonial rule. The main plaza boasts an ornate colonial church. A colonial bridge on the outskirts, which once carried all the traffic to this rich agricultural region, is used today only by pedestrians. If you find reason to stop in Salamá, try to do so on a Sunday, when the market is active.

Should you want to stay the night, the *Hotel Tezulutlán*, just off the main square behind the Texaco fuel station, is simple and cheap. Fifteen rooms with private showers, arranged around a pleasant courtyard, rent for US$6 a single, US$10 a double. The *Hotel Juárez*, 10a Avenida 5-55, Zona 1, is larger, with 26 rooms, and somewhat cheaper as well.

For food, try the *Restaurant El Ganadero*, a half block off the main square on the road into town. A lunch of chicken or beef might cost US$4 to US$6, a sandwich much less.

As this is a departmental capital there are frequent buses to and from Guatemala City. Salamateca (☎ (2) 81716), 9a Avenida 19-00, Zona 1 in Guatemala City, has buses running about every two hours from 5.45 am to 4.45 pm on the 151-km, three-hour trip. Fare is US$2.

Around Salamá
Nine km west of Salamá along Highway 5 is the village of **San Miguel Chicaj**, known for its weaving. Continue along the same road for another 18 km to reach the colonial town of **Rabinal**, founded in 1537 by Fray Bartolomé de las Casas as a base for his proselytising. Rabinal has gained fame as a pottery-making centre (look especially at the hand-painted chocolate cups), and for its citrus fruit harvest (November and December). Market day here is Sunday. Two small hotels, the *Pensión Motagua* and the *Hospedaje Caballeros*, can put you up, though you might decide to return to Salamá instead.

BIOTOPO DEL QUETZAL

Stay on the main highway instead of turning left for Salamá, and another 34 km brings you to the Mario Dary Rivera Nature Reserve, commonly called the Biotopo del Quetzal, Guatemala's quetzal reserve at Km 161, just east of the village of Purulhá.

If you stop here intent on seeing a quetzal, Guatemala's national bird, you may be disappointed, because the birds are rare and elusive. Stop instead to explore and enjoy the lush high rainforest ecosystem which is preserved here, and which is the natural habitat of the quetzal. The reserve, founded in 1977, is open daily from 6 am to 4 pm (you must leave the grounds by 5 pm). Drinks are available at the site, but no food. Guides may be hired to explain the rainforest to you.

Two nature trails wind through the reserve, the 1800-metre **Sendero los Helechos** (Fern Trail), and the **Sendero los Musgos** (Moss Trail), which is twice as long. As you wander through the dense growth, treading on the rich, dense, spongy humus and leaf-mould, you'll see many varieties of epiphytes (air plants) which thrive in the humid jungle atmosphere: lichens, ferns, liverworts, bromeliads, mosses and orchids. The Río Colorado cascades through the forest along a geological fault. Deep in the forest is Xiu Ua Li Che (Grandfather Tree), some 450 years old, which was alive when the conquistadors fought the Rabinals in these mountains.

The village of **Purulhá**, slightly less than five km west of the Biotopo, has a very basic medical clinic and a small market, but no other services.

Places to Stay

The reserve has its own camping places, so if you have the equipment, this is the best place to stay. Officially, you are supposed to obtain permission to camp from CECON (Center for Conservation Studies of the University of San Carlos; ☎ (2) 310904), Avenida La Reforma 0-63, Zona 10, Guatemala City.

There are two lodging places within a short distance of the Biotopo. Just beyond the Biotopo, another 200 metres up the hill toward Purulhá and Cobán, is the *Pensión y Comedor Ranchito del Quetzal*, a convenient rustic hospedaje. Being the only lodging right by the Biotopo keeps the Ranchito's rates high for what you get: US$12 for a double with shower. In fact, you must pay US$0.40 just to set foot on the Ranchito's grounds. Meals are equally pricey, but convenient.

Should you be looking for more comfort, the *Posada Montaña del Quetzal* (☎ (2) 351805 in Guatemala City during business hours), Carretera a Cobán Km 156, is five km back along the road towards the Carretera al Atlantico. This attractive hostelry has 18 little, white stucco tile-roofed cabins, each with a sitting room and fireplace, a bedroom with three beds, and a private bathroom for US$25/35 a single/double.

Biotopo del Quetzal to Cobán

The asphalt road is good, smooth and fast, though curvy, with light traffic. As you ascend into the evergreen forests, tropical flowers are still visible here and there. Signs by the roadside advertise the services of brokers willing to buy farmers' harvests of cardamom and coffee and dairy cattle. As you enter the town, a sign says 'Bienvenidos a Cobán, Ciudad Imperial', referring to the charter granted in 1538 by Emperor Charles V. About 126 km from the Carretera al Atlantico, you enter Cobán's main plaza.

COBÁN

Population 20,000

Cobán (altitude 1320 metres) was once the centre of Tezulutlán (Tierra de Guerra in Spanish), the Land of War. Alvarado's conquistadors overran western Guatemala in short order, but the Rabinal Maya of Verapaz fought them off until Fray Bartolomé and his brethren came and conquered them with religion.

A later conquest came in the 19th century, when German immigrants moved in and founded vast coffee fincas. Cobán took on the aspect of a German mountain town as the finca owners built town residences with

GUATEMALA

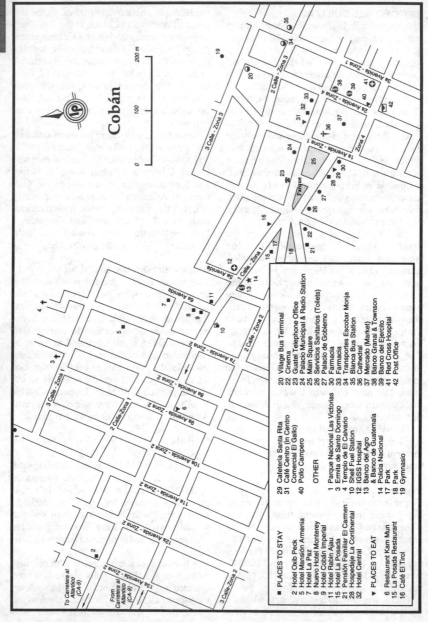

Cobán

PLACES TO STAY

2 Hotel Oxib Peck
5 Hotel Mansión Armenia
7 Hotel La Paz
8 Nuevo Hotel Monterey
9 Hotel Cobán Imperial
11 Hotel Rabin Ajau
15 Hotel La Posada
21 Pensión Familiar El Carmen
28 Hospedaje La Continental
32 Hotel Central

▼ PLACES TO EAT

6 Restaurant Kam Mun
15 La Posada Restaurant
16 Café El Tirol
29 Cafetería Santa Rita
31 Café Centro (in Centro
    Comercial El Gallo)
40 Pollo Campero

OTHER

1 Parque Nacional Las Victorias
3 Ermita de Santo Domingo
4 Templo de El Calvario
10 Shell Fuel Station
12 IGSS Hospital
13 Banco del Agro
    & Banco de Guatemala
14 Policía Nacional
17 Park
18 Park
19 Gymnasio
20 Village Bus Terminal
22 Cinema
23 Guatel Telephone Office
24 Palacio Municipal & Radio Station
25 Main Square
26 Servicios Sanitarios (Toilets)
27 Palacio de Gobierno
30 Farmacia
33 Farmacia
34 Transportes Escobar Monja
35 Blanca Bus Station
36 Cathedral
37 Mercado (Market)
38 Banco Granai & Townson
39 Banco del Ejército
41 Red Cross Hospital
42 Post Office

To Carretera al
Atlántico (CA-9)

From
Carretera al
Atlántico (CA-9)

steeply pitched roofs, elaborate gingerbread bargeboards and other decoration, and gathered to exchange the morning's news in Central European-style cafés.

The era of German cultural and economic domination ended during WW II, when the USA prevailed upon the Guatemalan government to deport the powerful finca owners, many of whom actively supported the Nazis.

Today Cobán can be a pleasant town to visit, though much depends upon the season. During most of the year it can be overcast, dank, chill and cheerless; in the midst of the dry season (January to March) it can be misty, or bright and sunny with marvellous clear mountain air. The departmental festival is held in Cobán during the first week of August.

Orientation

The main plaza (el parque) bears a modern concrete bandstand. Most of the services you'll need – banks, hotels, restaurants, bus stations – are within a few blocks of the plaza and the cathedral, as shown on our map. The shopping district is around and behind the cathedral.

Places to Stay

The *Pensión Familiar El Carmen* (☎ (9) 511750), near the main plaza, is very simple and fairly beat-up, but the price is good at US$6 a double, with shared baths. There's a small, cheap café attached. *Hotel La Paz*, 6a Avenida, Zona 1, 1½ blocks north of the plaza, charges US$3 per person, which is too expensive. To get a room, ask at the shop to the right of the hotel. At this writing, the *Hospedaje La Continental*, facing the main plaza, is the most basic lodging of them all.

A step up in quality and price is the *Hotel Oxib Peck* (☎ (9) 511039), 1 Calle 12-11, Zona 1, six blocks (750 metres) west of the plaza on the road out of town. By Guatemalan standards it's clean and bright, with a nice little garden in front, plus a dining room. The 11 rooms are tidy, with clean tiled showers, but plain, with no windows to the outside. Rates are US$6.50 per person.

Hotel Cobán Imperial (☎ (9) 511131), 6a Avenida 1-12, Zona 1, 250 metres from the plaza, is administered along with the adjoining *Nuevo Hotel Monterey*. Most rooms have add-on tiled baths, and also TVs, which are necessary for a 'view' as few rooms have windows. It's popular with Guatemalan families for the price of US$6 to US$8 a single, US$8 to US$12 a double.

Hotel Rabin Ajau (☎ (9) 512296), 1 Calle 5-37, Zona 1, two blocks north-west of the main plaza, is old-fashioned, well located and fairly well kept, but its disco is noisy. There's a restaurant and parking. Rooms with private shower cost US$8/10/12 a single/double/ triple.

Hotel Central (☎ (9) 511442), 1 Calle 1-79, Zona 4, is tidy, run by women, arranged around a flowered courtyard, and decently priced at US$10 a double.

Hotel Mansión Armenia (☎ (9) 512284), 7a Avenida 2-18, Zona 1, one block from Templo de El Calvario, is clean, fairly new and quiet. Rooms are cell-like, as usual, but equipped with private baths and cable TV for US$17/22 a single/double.

Best in town is the *Hotel La Posada* (☎ (9) 511495), 1 Calle 4-12, Zona 2, just north-west of the main plaza in the very centre of town. Colonial in style, its colonnaded porches are festooned with tropical flowers and furnished with easy chairs and hammocks from which to enjoy the mountain views. The rooms have nice old furniture, fireplaces, and wall hangings of local weaving. They rent for US$28/34/42 a single/double/triple with private bath.

Places to Eat

Virtually all of Cobán's hotels have their own restaurants.

Café El Tirol, near the Hotel La Posada, advertises 'the best coffee' in four languages. Facing a bust of Fray Bartolomé de las Casas is a cosy room in which to take pastries and coffee for US$1 to US$2. Breakfast and light meals are served as well. It's closed on Monday.

Cafetería Santa Rita, facing the main square, is small, modern, tidy, and popular with locals. The reason why is no secret:

good breakfasts for US$1 to US$2, lunches and dinners for US$2.50 to US$4.

Café Centro (☎ (51) 2192), 1 Calle between 1a and 2a Avenidas, opposite the cathedral, has a varied lunch and supper menu (no breakfast), and a dining room with views through large windows. Substantial plates of chicken (US$2.75) and beef (US$4) are offered along with a variety of sandwiches (US$1 to US$2).

Pollo Campero, the Guatemalan fried chicken franchise, has an outlet across from the post office on 2a Avenida at 2 Calle. The gilded youth of Cobán gather here for three meals a day.

You have to walk almost 500 metres from the plaza to reach the *Restaurant Kam Mun*, 1 Calle at 9a Avenida, on the road out of town. When you reach the restaurant you can sample Chinese food in a pleasant, clean little place and pay US$5 to US$8 for a full meal.

Getting There & Away
Transportes Escobar Monja Blanca (☎ (2) 511878), 8a Avenida 15-16, Zona 1 in Guatemala City, runs about 10 buses a day from 4 am to 4 pm on the 219-km, four-hour trip to Guatemala City, stopping at the Biotopo del Quetzal, Purulhá and Tactic, for US$2 to US$3. You can catch these buses at El Rancho (San Jerónimo), at the intersection of the Carretera al Atlantico and the highway to Cobán.

AROUND COBÁN
Cobán is becoming a base for organised excursions to sites in the surrounding mountains. For example, Marcio & Ashley Acuña (☎ (9) 511268) run eco-tours from Cobán to Semuc-Champey and also to many Maya jungle sites such as La Candelaria, Ceibal, Aguateca, Dos Pilas, Yaxchilán, Yaxhá, Nakun, Tikal, Uaxactún and Río Azul. No doubt other operators will start up by the time you visit Cobán.

San Juan Chamelco
About 16 km south-east of Cobán is the village of San Juan Chamelco, with swim-

ming at the Balneario Chio. In Aldea (district) Chajaneb, Jerry Makransky rents comfortable, simple bungalows for US$10 per person per day, vegetarian meals included. If you need to get away from it all, this may be just the place.

San Pedro Carchá
Six km east of Cobán on the way to Lanquín, this spot offers swimming at the Balneario Las Islas, as well as transport by bus farther along to Lanquín.

Grutas de Lanquín
If you don't mind bumping over bad and/or busy roads, the best excursion to make from Cobán is to the caves near Lanquín, a pretty village 61 km to the east.

The Grutas de Lanquín are a short distance north-west of the town, and extend for several km into the earth. Have a powerful torch (flashlight) or two, pay the US$2 admission fee at the Municipalidad (town hall) in Lanquín, and make sure that the attendant is on duty at the caves to turn on the lights for you.

Though the first few hundred metres of cavern has been equipped with a walkway and electric lights powered by a diesel generator, the major extent of this subterranean system is untouched. If you are not an experienced spelunker you should think twice about wandering too far into the caves.

The Río Lanquín runs through the caves before coming above ground to run down to Lanquín, offering swimming possibilities at several points. If you have camping equipment you can spend the night near the cave entrance. Otherwise, there are a few simple hostelries in Lanquín.

Semuc-Champey
Ten km south of Lanquín along a rough, bumpy, slow road is Semuc-Champey, famed for a natural wonder: a great limestone bridge 300 metres long on top of which is a series of pools of cool, flowing river water good for swimming. The water is from the Río Cahabón, most of which passes beneath the bridge underground. Though this bit of

paradise is difficult to reach, the beauty of its setting and the perfection of the water make it all worth it.

Getting There & Away
From Cobán, take a bus to San Pedro Carchá, six km to the east along the Lanquín-Cahabón road; buses leave very frequently from the village bus terminal down the hill behind the town hall in Cobán. From San Pedro Carchá, buses leave three times daily (starting at 5.30 am) on the three-hour ride to Lanquín. The last of three return buses departs Lanquín for San Pedro Carchá in the early afternoon, so you should probably plan to stay the night, either camping at Grutas de Lanquín or Semuc-Champey, or staying in a small hospedaje in Lanquín.

There are occasional buses and trucks to Semuc-Champey. Otherwise, it's a longish, hot walk unless you have your own vehicle, in which case it's a slow, bumpy drive.

ESTANZUELA
Travelling south along CA-10 from Río Hondo on the Carretera al Atlantico, you are in the midst of the Río Motagua Valley, a hot expanse of dry tropic which once supported a great variety of dinosaurs.

In the small town of Estanzuela is the Museo de Paleontología filled with dinosaur bones. The museum is open from 9 am to 5 pm every day except Monday; admission is free. To find the museum, go west from the highway directly through the town for one km, asking along the way for el museo. Next door to the museum is a small shop selling cold drinks and snacks.

Within the museum are most of the bones of three big dinosaurs, including those of a giant ground sloth some 30,000 years old, and a prehistoric whale. Other exhibits include early Maya artefacts.

ZACAPA
Population 18,000
Capital of the department of the same name, Zacapa (altitude 230 metres) is several km east of the highway. It offers little to travel-lers, though the locals do make cheese, cigars, and superb old rum.

CHIQUIMULA
Population 24,000
Another departmental capital set in a mining and tobacco-growing region, Chiquimula (altitude 370 metres) is a major market town for all of eastern Guatemala. It's also a transportation point and overnight stop for those making their way to Copán in Honduras.

Chiquimula is easy to get around on foot. Banco del Café, on the main plaza (called the Parque Ismael Cerna) has long hours: 8.30 am to 8 pm Monday to Thursday, 8 am to 8 pm Friday, 10 am to 2 pm on Saturday. Banco del Agro's opening hours are 9 am to 3 pm Monday to Friday, 9 am to 1 pm on Saturday.

Places to Stay
Hotel Chiquimulja (☎ (9) 420387), 3 Calle 6-51, on the north side of the plaza between two Chinese restaurants, is the best in town. Rooms come with private showers, with fan or with air-con, and range in price from US$5 to US$8 a single, US$8 to US$12 a double.

Hotel Victoria (☎ (9) 422238), 2 Calle at 10a Avenida, is convenient to the bus station, offering small rooms with fan, TV and add-on showers for US$9 a double. The restaurant is good and cheap, with big breakfasts for US$2.

A block east of the Chiquimulja, downhill on the same street (3 Calle), are several even cheaper places. *Hotel Hernández* is clean, simple and quietish, renting rooms without running water for US$3 per person, or US$4 per person for a room with private shower. The neighbouring *Pensión España* is even more basic, with closet-like rooms, but it has gardens and it's cheaper. *Hospedaje Río Jordan* (☎ (9) 420887), 3 Calle 8-91, a block further east, charges US$2 to US$3.50 a single, US$4 to US$6 a double, the higher price being for rooms with fans. You can park your vehicle in the courtyard.

Hotel Posada de Don Adán (☎ (9) 420549), 8a Avenida 4-30, Zona 1, is new, clean, proper, run by an efficient señora who

Chiquimula

0   50   100 m

■ PLACES TO STAY	OTHER
4 Hotel Victoria	1 Transportes Vilma Bus Station
9 Hotel Chiquimulja	
11 Hotel Hernández	2 Bus Terminal
12 Pensión España	3 Correos y Telegraphos (Post & Telegraph Office)
14 Hospedaje Río Jordan	
15 Hotel Posada Perla de Oriente	6 Banco de Guatemala
21 Hotel Posada de Don Adán	7 Banco del Café
	8 Banco del Agro
	10 Cinema Liu
▼ PLACES TO EAT	13 Chevron Fuel Station
	16 Palacio de Gobierno
5 Restaurant El Dorado	17 Guatel Telephone Office
10 Restaurant El Tesoro	
18 Pupucería Guanachapi	19 Market
20 Restaurant Las Vegas	

charges US$17 for a double with fan, shower and TV.

The best in town is the *Hotel Posada Perla de Oriente* (☎ (9) 420014/152),12a Avenida 2-30, with extensive grounds but simple rooms with fan, shower and TV for US$12. There's a small swimming pool. This place may be upgraded – and the prices raised substantially – soon.

Places to Eat

Eating in Chiqui is easy as there are lots of cheap little places. Try the *Pupucería Guanachapi*, across the street from the Pensión España. Sit at the long counter, watch the cooks at work, and fill up for only a few quetzals.

Restaurant El Tesoro, on the main square, serves Chinese food at reasonable prices.

For a step up in quality, try the *Restaurant El Dorado*, 3 Calle between 5a and 6a Avenidas, where you can dine on the shady terrace around the rear courtyard. Full meals cost US$5 to US$8.

Also good is the *Restaurant Las Vegas*, on 7a Avenida off 4 Calle, perhaps Chiquimula's best with fancy plants, jazzy music, a well-stocked bar, and full meals for US$6 to

US$10. Appropriate to its name, the Las Vegas claims to be open 24 hours a day.

Getting There & Away

Rutas Orientales (☎ (2) 537282, 512160), 19 Calle 8-18, Zona 1 in Guatemala City, runs buses via El Rancho (San Jerónimo), Río Hondo and Zacapa to Chiquimula every 30 minutes from 4 am to 6 pm, for US$3 to US$4, depending on the bus; the 169-km journey takes three hours.

It's easy to get back to Río Hondo junction (35 km) from Chiquimula; just hop on any bus heading north. From Río Hondo you can catch buses eastward to Quiriguá and Puerto Barrios.

You can also easily catch a bus from Chiquimula's busy bus terminal southward to Esquipulas (55 km, one hour, US$1.25).

TO COPÁN (HONDURAS)

The ancient city of Copán in Honduras, 12 km from the Guatemalan border, is one of the most outstanding Maya achievements, ranking with Tikal, Chichén Itzá and Uxmal in splendour. For information on the archaeological site and the nearby town of Copán Ruinas, see the Honduras chapter.

You can visit Copán from Chiquimula or Esquipulas, then return to Guatemala or continue into Honduras. If you need a Honduran visa in advance, you can obtain it at the Honduran Consulate in Esquipulas.

The Road to Copán

Go south from Chiquimula 10 km, north from Esquipulas 48 km, and turn eastward at Vado Hondo (Km 178.5 on CA-10). A sign marked 'Vado Hondo Ruinas de Copán' marks the way on the two-hour, 50-km drive from this junction to El Florido.

The road is unpaved but usually in good repair and fairly fast (an average of 40 km/h). Twenty km north-east of Vado Hondo are the Chorti Maya villages of **Jocotán** and **Camotán** set amidst mountainous tropical countryside dotted with thatched huts in lush green valleys.

Jocotán has a small Centro de Salud (medical clinic) and the *Hotel/Pension Ramirez*, a half-block north of the hilltop church and main square. You can stay in a room with shower for US$3.50 per person, less for a bathless room. There's a small restaurant as well.

Along the road you may have to ford several small streams. This causes no problem unless there has been an unusual amount of rain on previous days.

El Florido

The village of El Florido, which has no services beyond a few soft-drink stands, is 1.2 km west of the border. At the border-crossing proper are a few snack stands and the very basic *Hospedaje Las Rosas*, which can put you up in an emergency.

Allow at least 45 minutes (one to 1½ hours with a car) for border formalities; the border is open from 7 am to 6 pm.

Moneychangers will approach you on both sides of the border, willing to change Guatemalan quetzals for Honduran lempiras or either for US dollars. You might want to change at least US$20 into lempiras to pay for customs fees, the minibus ride to the town

and return, lunch, and the entrance to the ruins and the museum. If you plan to stay the night, change more.

You must present your passport and tourist card to the Guatemalan immigration and customs authorities, pay fees (some of which are unauthorised) of US$6, then cross the border and do the same thing with the Honduran authorities.

If you just want a short-term permit to enter Honduras and plan to go only as far as Copán, tell this to the Honduran immigration officer and he will charge you a fee of US$3. With such a permit you cannot go farther than the ruins and you must leave Honduras by the same route.

If you want to travel farther in Honduras, ask for a standard visa, which costs US$10 and may take a bit more time.

When you return through this border point you must again pass through both sets of immigration and customs and pay fees (lower this time). The Guatemalan immigration officer should give you your old tourist card back without charging the full fee for a new one.

Getting There & Away

Catch a Transportes Vilma bus (pronounced BEEL-mah) at Chiquimula for the 58-km, 2½-hour trip (US$2) via Jocotán and Camotán to El Florido on the Guatemalan side of the border.

On the Honduran side, Etumi minibuses depart the border every 40 minutes throughout the day, charging US$1 for the 12-km, 30-minute ride.

ESQUIPULAS

From Chiquimula, CA-10 goes south into the mountains where it's cooler and a bit more comfortable. After an hour's ride through pretty country the highway descends into a valley ringed by mountains. The reason for a trip to Esquipulas is evident as soon as you catch sight of the town: the great Basílica de Esquipulas towers above the town, its whiteness shining in the sun.

History

This town may have been a place of pilgrimage even before the Spanish conquest. Legend has it that the town takes its name from a noble Maya lord who ruled this region when the Spanish arrived, and who received them in peace rather than going to war.

With the arrival of the friars, a church was built, and in 1595 an image of Christ carved from black wood was installed in it. The steady flow of pilgrims to Esquipulas became a flood after 1737, when Pedro Pardo de Figueroa, Archbishop of Guatemala, came here on pilgrimage and went away cured of a longtime ailment. Delighted with this development, the prelate commissioned a huge new church to be built on the site. It was finished in 1758, and the pilgrimage trade has been the town's livelihood ever since.

Orientation

The church is your landmark in Esquipulas, the centre of everything. Most of the good cheap hotels are within a block of it, as are numerous small restaurants. There's a Honduran consulate in the Hotel Payaquí, facing the park.

The Basilica

A grand, massive pile of stone which has resisted earthquakes for almost 2½ centuries, the basilica is approached through a pretty park and up a flight of steps.

Inside, the devout approach El Cristo Negro with great reverence, many on their knees. Incense, the murmur of prayers and the shuffle of sandalled feet fill the air. To get a close view of the famous Black Christ you must enter the church from the side. Shuffling along quickly, you may get a good glimpse or two before being shoved onwards by the press of the crowd behind you. On Sunday, religious holidays, and especially during the festival around 15 January, the press of devotees is intense.

Places to Stay

On holidays and during the annual festival every hotel in town is filled, whatever the price; weekends are fairly busy as well, and prices substantially higher. On weekdays when there is no festival, ask for a *descuento* (discount) and you'll probably get it.

The family-run *Pensión Santa Rosa* is typical of the small back-street places, charging US$7 a double in a waterless room. *Pension La Favorita* nearby is similar, and there are several others on this street.

Hotel Los Angeles (☎ (9) 431254), 2a Avenida 11-94, on the south-west corner of the park, has 39 rooms arranged around a bright inner courtyard. Doubles with shower cost US$11 on weekdays, US$15 on weekends.

Hotel San José, on1 the north-east corner of the park, is typical, renting tiny waterless rooms for US$2.75 per person weekdays, US$3.50 weekends, or rooms with showers for US$4/5. *Hotel San Pablo*, on the north side of the park, is similar, as are the *Hotel El Ángel* and *Hotel Lucam*.

Hotel Monte Cristo (☎ (9) 431453), 3a Avenida 9-12, has 34 quite good rooms with bath for US$18 a double – good value for money.

Hotel El Peregrino (☎ (9) 431054) has two kinds of rooms, all with private bath. Older rooms cost US$13 a double, newer ones with TV are US$25.

Hotel Payaquí (☎ (9) 431143; fax 431371), 2a Avenida 11-56, facing the park, has 40 rooms with bath, a swimming pool, a car park and a restaurant with a view of the park. It's priced high (for what you get) at US$29 a double.

Places to Eat

Low-budget restaurants are clustered at the north end of the park where hungry pilgrims can find them readily. It is very important to ask in advance the price of each food item you order, and to add up your bill carefully.

The street running north opposite the church has many small eateries. At some point I predict that it will be closed to all but pedestrian traffic, and the restaurants will be able to have sidewalk dining areas.

Comedor Rosy, on the street opposite the park, is tidy and cheerful, with big bottles of pickles on the tables. Sandwiches go for US$2 or so. *Restaurante y Cafetería Victoria* across the street is a bit fancier, with tablecloths and plants, but prices are about the same.

Comedor y Cafetería Beato Hermano Pedro realises what the dining situation is in this town, and advertises 'Coma bien y pague menos!' (Eat well and pay less!) Set prices for full meals are around US$2. 'Come on in and convince yourself!'

All of the middle-range and top-end hotels have their own dining rooms; look here for somewhat fancier fare.

Getting There & Away

Rutas Orientales (☎ (2) 53-7282, 51-2160), 19 Calle 8-18, Zona 1 in Guatemala City, has buses departing every half an hour from 4 am to 6 pm, with stops at El Rancho (San Jerónimo), Río Hondo, Zacapa and Chiquimula. The 222-km, four-hour trip costs US$3. If you're going to Copán, take any bus as far as Chiquimula and switch to a Transportes Vilma bus there. See the Chiquimula section earlier for details.

QUIRIGUÁ

Like Copán, Quiriguá is famed for its intricately carved stelae. Unlike Copán, the gigantic brown sandstone stelae at Quiriguá rise as high as 10.5 metres.

From Río Hondo junction it's 67 km along the Carretera al Atlantico to the village of Los Amates, where there is a hotel and restaurant. The village of Quiriguá is 1.5 km east of Los Amates, and the turnoff to the ruins is another 1.5 km to the east. Following the access road south from the Carretera al Atlantico, it's 3.4 km through banana groves to the archaeological site.

History

Quiriguá's history parallels that of Copán, of which it was a dependency during much of the Classic period. The location lent itself to the carving of giant stelae. Beds of brown sandstone in the nearby Río Motagua had cleavage planes suitable for cutting large pieces. Though soft when first cut, the sandstone dried hard in the air. With Copán's expert artisans nearby for guidance, Quiriguá's stonecarvers were ready for greatness. All they needed was a great leader to inspire them – and to pay for the carving of the huge stelae.

That leader was Cauac Sky (725-784), who decided that Quiriguá should no longer be under the control of Copán. In a war with his former suzerain, Cauac Sky took King 18 Rabbit of Copán prisoner in 737 and later had him beheaded. Independent at last, Cauac Sky commissioned his stonecutters to go to work, and for the next 38 years they turned out giant stelae and zoomorphs dedicated to the glory of King Cauac Sky.

Cauac Sky was followed by his son Sky Xul (784-800), who lost his throne to a usurper, Jade Sky. This last great king of Quiriguá continued the building boom initiated by Cauac Sky, reconstructing Quiriguá's Acropolis on a grander scale.

Quiriguá remained unknown until John L Stephens arrived in 1840. Between 1881 and 1894 excavations were carried out by Alfred P Maudslay. In the early 20th century all the land around Quiriguá was sold to the United Fruit Company and turned into banana groves.

The Ruins

The beautiful park-like archaeological zone is open from 7 am to 5 pm daily; admission costs US$1. There's a small stand selling cold drinks and snacks near the entrance. You'd do well to bring your own picnic.

Despite the sticky heat and (sometimes) the bothersome mosquitoes, Quiriguá is a wonderful place. The giant stelae on the Great Plaza are all much more worn than those at Copán. To impede their further deterioration, each has been covered by a thatched roof.

Seven of the stelae, designated A, C, D, E, F, H and J, were built during the reign of Cauac Sky and carved with his image. Stela E is the largest Maya stela known, standing some eight metres above ground, with another three metres or so buried in the earth. It weighs almost 60,000 kg. Note the exuberant, elaborate headdresses, the beards on some of the figures (an oddity in Maya art), the staffs of office held in the kings' hands, and the glyphs on the stelae's sides.

At the far end of the plaza is the Acropolis, far less impressive than the one at Copán. At its base are several zoomorphs, blocks of stone carved to resemble real and mythic creatures. Frogs, tortoises, jaguars and serpents were favourite subjects.

Places to Stay & Eat
In the village of Quiriguá, 700 metres south of the highway, is the tidy *Hotel Royal*, a Caribbean-style wooden structure with numerous large rooms with four or five beds each, a cold-water washbasin and shower, and a toilet. Beds cost US$4 each; doubles with private shower cost US$14. A little comedor serves meals.

Getting There & Away
The turnoff to Quiriguá is 205 km (four hours) east of Guatemala City, 70 km east of the Río Hondo junction, 43 km west of the road to Flores in El Petén, and 90 km west of Puerto Barrios.

Transportes Litegua (☎ 2-27578), 15 Calle 10-42, Zona 1 in Guatemala City, has regular buses from the capital to Puerto Barrios every hour from 6 am to 5 pm, and several Pullman express buses (faster and more comfortable) as well. Stops are at El Rancho (San Jerónimo), Teculután, Río Hondo and Los Amates (Quiriguá). The fare is US$4.50 or US$6 if you go all the way to Puerto Barrios. The driver will usually oblige if you ask to be dropped off at the access road to the archaeological site rather than three km west at Los Amates.

The transport centre in this area is Morales, about 40 km north-east of Quiriguá. This is where it's easiest to catch a bus for Río Dulce.

Getting Around
Waiting at the junction of the Carretera al Atlantico and the Quiriguá access road are men on motorbikes. They run a primitive shuttle service from the highway to the archaeological site and the banana company headquarters, charging a quetzal or two for the 3.4 km ride. You cannot depend upon them to take you back from the archaeological site to the highway unless you establish a time in advance.

LAGO DE IZABAL
The large lake to the north-west of the Carretera al Atlantico has hardly been developed for tourism at all. Head north-west from Morales and La Ruidosa junction (Carretera al Atlantico Km 245) along the road to Flores in El Petén, and after 34 km you reach the village of **Río Dulce**, also known as El Relleno.

From beneath the bridge you can hire a motorboat (you must bargain for a price) to take you to the Castillo de San Felipe, the region's major tourist attraction. It's also reachable on foot. Boat owners can also take you downriver to El Golfete, Chocón-Machacas Nature Reserve and Lívingston. For details of the trip, see the Lívingston section. Many people prefer to do the trip from Río Dulce rather than from Lívingston.

Castillo de San Felipe
The fortress of San Felipe de Lara, about one km west of the bridge, was built in 1652 to keep pirates from looting the villages and commercial caravans of Izabal. Though it deterred the buccaneers a bit, a pirate force captured and burnt the fortress in 1686. By the end of the next century, pirates had disappeared from the Caribbean and the fort's sturdy walls served as a prison. Then it became a tourist attraction.

Places to Stay & Eat
In Río Dulce near the bridge are several cheap hotels. *Café El Sol* is typical, charging US$4 per person in rooms with private bath. More expensive and comfortable resort hotels are just a few km east on the shores of the river.

Near the Castillo, the *Hotel Don Humberto* can put you up for US$4 per person if you don't have your own camping equipment.

El Estor

The major settlement on the north-western shore is El Estor, once a nickel mining town, but now growing in popularity as a way-station for intrepid travellers on the Cobán-Lago de Izabal route through the Panzós Valley. Three buses make the seven-hour, US$3 run each day, departing Cobán at 5, 8 and 11 am, and El Estor at 5, 7 and 8.30 am.

The link from El Estor to the Carretera al Atlantico is completed by the El Estor-Mariscos ferry, which departs El Estor at 5 am, and departs Mariscos for the return journey at 1 pm. Buses run from Mariscos down to the highway.

There's nothing to do in El Estor, but there are a few small lodging-places, including the *Hotel Vista del Lago*, with rooms for US$3/6 a single/double. There are even cheaper places as well.

RÍO DULCE TO FLORES

North across the bridge is the road into El Petén, Guatemala's vast jungle province. It's 208 km to Santa Elena and Flores, and another 65 km to Tikal.

The road from the Carretera al Atlantico to Modesto Méndez is not bad, but from Méndez to Santa Elena it's in terrible condition. It's a bone-jangling ride of at least six hours to Flores.

Poptún

Along the way to Flores there are only small jungle hamlets at which simple meals are sometimes available. The best facilities are at Carole DeVine's Finca Ixobel (☎ (9) 507363) in Poptún. For several decades Carole has offered travellers tent sites, palapas for hanging hammocks, beds and good home-cooked meals with or without meat. Camping (with cold-water showers) costs US$2 to US$3 per person. Beds are US$4 in dormitories, or US$8/10/12 a single/double/triple for rooms with hot showers. Bread, granola, yoghurt and pastries are made fresh daily. Meals offer excellent value, right up to the eat-all-you-like buffet dinner for US$6.

Getting There & Away

See Getting There & Away in the sections on Flores or Guatemala City for bus details. The buses reach Río Dulce about five hours after leaving Guatemala City, and are usually packed full by the time they reach get there. You'll have a better chance trying to board at Morales.

PUERTO BARRIOS

Population 35,000

The United Fruit Company built railways to ship its bananas to the coast, and it built Puerto Barrios to load the bananas onto ships sailing for New Orleans and New York. Laid out as a company town, Puerto Barrios has wide streets arranged neatly on a grid plan, and lots of Caribbean-style wood-frame houses, many on stilts. In the 1960s, a new port was built a few km to the south-west at Santo Tomás de Castilla, and Puerto Barrios settled into tropical torpor.

For foreign visitors, Puerto Barrios is little more than the jumping-off point for a visit to Lívingston. As the boats for Lívingston leave at odd hours, you may find yourself staying the night in Puerto Barrios.

Orientation

It's 800 metres from the bus terminal by the market to the Muelle Municipal (Municipal Boat Dock) at the foot of 12 Calle, from which boats depart for Lívingston.

Places to Stay & Eat

Motel Miami (☎ (9) 480537), 3a Avenida at 12 Calle, is a relatively new place one block from the dock. Rooms are arranged around a central courtyard used as a safe car park. Rates are US$10 a double with private bath, US$14 a double if you want air-con (which you might).

Hotel Europa 2 (☎ (9) 481292), next to the Miami, is similar to the Miami in accommodation and price. The original *Hotel Europa 1* (☎ (9) 480127), on 8a Avenida between 8 and 9 Calles, is fairly clean, pleasant and quiet, they charge US$8 for one of their 28 double rooms with shower. *Hotel Xelajú*, nearby at 7a Avenida and 9 Calle,

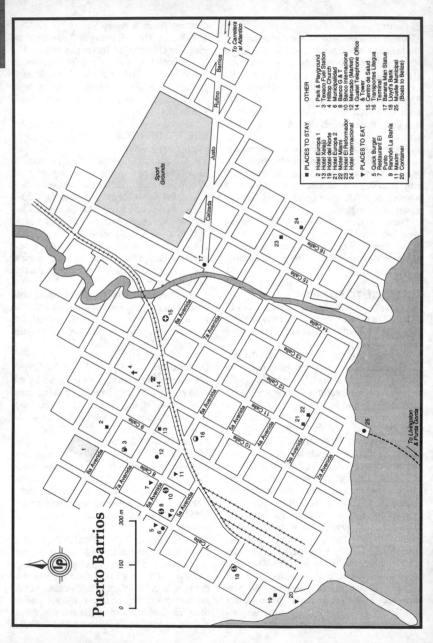

Puerto Barrios

■ PLACES TO STAY

2 Hotel Europa 1
13 Hotel Xelajú
19 Hotel del Norte
21 Hotel Europa 2
22 Motel Miami
23 Hotel El Reformador
24 Hotel Internacional

▼ PLACES TO EAT

5 Quick Burger
7 Restaurant El
   Punto
9 Ranchón La Bahía
11 Maxim
20 Container

OTHER

1 Park & Playground
3 Texaco Fuel Station
4 Hilltop Church
6 Municipalidad
8 Banco G & T
10 Banco Internacional
12 Mercado (Market)
14 Guatel Telephone Office
   & Tower
15 Centro de Salud
16 Transportes Litegua
   Terminal
17 Banana Man Statue
18 Lloyd's Bank
25 Muelle Municipal
   (Boats to Belize)

To Carretera
al Atlántico

Barrios

Rufino

Justo

Calzada

Sport
Grounds

To Livingston
& Punta Gorda

0   150   300 m

charges a bit less for bathless rooms and provides safe parking in its courtyard.

In a class by itself is the old *Hotel del Norte* (☎ (9) 480087), 7 Calle at 1a Avenida, at the waterfront end of 7 Calle, 1200 metres from the dock (you must walk around the railway yard). In its airy dining room overlooking the Bahía de Amatique you can almost hear the echoing conversation of turn-of-the-century banana moguls, and smell their pungent cigars. Spare, simple and agreeably dilapidated, this is a real museum piece with 31 rooms renting for US$12 a double with shared bath, or US$18 a double with private bath. Meals are served in the dining room. Service is refined, careful and elegantly old-fashioned, but the food can be otherwise.

For fancier lodgings you must head out of town. East of the streambed and south of the main road, Calle Rufino Barrios, are two more comfortable hotels. The 36-room *Hotel El Reformador* (☎ (9) 480533), 16 Calle and 7a Avenida No 159, is a modern building offering rooms with private bath for US$11 a double. *Hotel Internacional*, around the corner, is similar.

Quick Burger, on 7 Calle next to the Municipalidad, is modern, clean, cheap and not far from the centre of the town. Full meals can be had for US$3 or less.

Ranchón La Bahía, across the street from the Municipalidad on 7 Calle, is a Caribbean-style thatch-and-bamboo cottage with Latin music playing. Come here for beans and rice, fried bananas and other regional specialities for US$5 or less.

Maxim (☎ 482258) is a funky Chinese place at the corner of 6a Avenida and 8 Calle. Chop suey and beer at US$6 is typical.

Among the tidier, modern places is *Restaurant El Punto*, beneath the arches on the corner of 6a Avenida and 8 Calle, where full meals cost US$6 or so.

Perhaps the oddest eatery in town is *Container*, a café and drinks stand at the foot of 7 Calle near the Hotel del Norte. It's made of two steel shipping containers with chairs and tables set out in the street, and has a fine view of the bay.

Getting There & Away
Bus Transportes Litegua (☎ (2) 27578), 15 Calle 10-42, Zona 1 in Guatemala City, has regular buses along the Carretera al Atlantico to Puerto Barrios every hour from 6 am to 5 pm, and Pullman express buses (faster and more comfortable) at 10 am and 5 pm. The 307-km journey takes six hours, with stops at El Rancho (San Jerónimo), Teculután, Río Hondo and Los Amates (Quiriguá); fare is US$4.50 or US$6.

The Litegua terminal in Puerto Barrios will store your luggage for about US$0.20 per day.

Boat Boats to Lívingston depart from the Muelle Municipal at the foot of 12 Calle in Puerto Barrios at 10.30 am and 5 pm daily, arriving in Lívingston 1½ hours later; on busy days there may be a 3 pm boat as well. Return trips from Lívingston depart at 5 am and 2 pm, with a 7 am boat on some busy days. The one-way fare is US$1. Get to the dock at least 30 minutes prior to departure (45 is better) in order to get a decent seat; otherwise you could end up standing the whole way.

Twice-weekly boats from Puerto Barrios to Punta Gorda in southern Belize depart at 7.30 am on Tuesday and Friday. They used to stop in Lívingston, but no longer do so. Inquire at the dock at the foot of 12 Calle for details. If you take this boat, you must pass through Guatemalan Immigration (Migración) & Customs (Aduana) before boarding the boat. Allow some time, and have your passport and tourist card handy.

LÍVINGSTON

The Garífuna (Garinagu, or Black Carib) people of Lívingston and southern Belize are the descendants of Africans brought to the New World as slaves, who escaped or were shipwrecked in the Caribbean. Intermarrying with shipwrecked sailors of other races and with the indigenous Maya, they developed a distinctive culture and language incorporating African, Maya and European elements. They trace their roots through legend to the Honduran island of Roatán, where they were settled by the British after the Garífuna revolt of 1795.

As you come ashore in Lívingston, you will be surprised to meet Black Guatemalans who speak Spanish as well as their traditional language; some speak the musical English of Belize and the islands as well. The village of Lívingston is an interesting anomaly with a laid-back, Belizean way of life, groves of coconut palms, gaily painted wooden buildings, and an economy based on fishing and tourism.

Orientation

Walk up the hill from the dock along the village's main street. The fancy Hotel Tucán Dugú is on your right, several small restaurants on your left. The street off to the left at the base of the hill goes to the Casa Rosada and several other hotels. At the top of the hill another street goes left to several hotels and restaurants. There is no bank in Lívingston, and the rate of exchange for dollars offered in the shops and hotels is not particularly good, so you should come with enough quetzals to cover your stay.

Río Dulce Cruises

Lívingston is the starting point for boat rides on the Río Dulce to enjoy the tropical jungle scenery, have a swim and a picnic, and explore the Biotopo Chocón-Machacas, 12 km west along the river. The 7200-hectare reserve was established to protect the beautiful river landscape, the valuable mangrove swamps, and especially the manatees, or seacows, which inhabit the waters (both salt and fresh) of the Río Dulce and El Golfete.

There are several ways to make the voyage up the Río Dulce. A mail launch departs from Lívingston for the trip upriver every Tuesday and Friday at about 11 am, charging US$5 per passenger. Motorised dugout canoes called *cayucos* act as tour boats, taking groups of travellers upriver for about US$10 per person. If you hire a native canoe for the trip, the cost could be higher. Almost anyone in Lívingston – your hotel clerk, a shopkeeper, a restaurant waiter – can tell you who's currently organising trips up the river.

Shortly after you leave Lívingston, the river enters a steep-walled gorge, its walls hung with great tangles of jungle foliage and bromeliads, the humid air noisy with the cries of tropical birds. A hot spring forces sulphurous water out at the base of the cliff, providing a delightful place for a swim.

Emerging from the gorge, the river eventually widens into El Golfete, a lake-like body of water. On the northern shore of El Golfete is the Biotopo Chocón-Machacas. The nature reserve's boat dock is good for swimming. A network of 'water trails' (boat routes around several jungle lagoons) provide ways to see the bird, animal and plant life of the reserve. A nature trail begins at the Visitors' Centre and winds its way through forests of mahogany, palm trees, and rich tropical foliage.

From El Golfete and the nature reserve, some boats will continue upriver to the village of Río Dulce, where the road into El Petén crosses the river (see the Lago de Izabal section earlier). If you didn't stop to visit the Castillo de San Felipe before, now's your chance.

Las Siete Altares

Beaches in Lívingston are mostly disappointing, as the jungle comes right down to the water's edge in most places. Those beaches which do exist are often clogged with vegetation as well. The Seven Altars is a series of freshwater falls and pools about five km north-west of Lívingston along the shore of the Bahía de Amatique. It's a pleasant goal for a walk along the beach and a good place for a picnic and a swim. Follow the shore northwards to the mouth of a river. Ford the river, and a path into the woods leads to the falls. If you'd rather not do the ford, the ferries at the mouth of the river charge only a few quetzals.

Places to Stay

Up the hill from the boat dock, on the left side of the main street is the *Hotel Río Dulce*. It is an authentic two-storey wood-frame

Caribbean place painted blue. Bare rooms without running water cost US$6. A bit farther along, turn left down the side street to reach the *Hotel Marina*, which is also cheap. *Hotel Garífuna* is good at US$11 a double with private bath.

Hotel Caribe, a minute's walk along the shore to the left as you come off the boat dock, is a simple, family-run place right on the water offering double rooms for US$5 a double (shared bath).

Turn right at the Catholic church to find the *Parador Flamingo*, on the shore of the Bahía de Amatique, with eight tidy rooms in a walled compound going for US$10 a double. The *African Place*, a restaurant with several rooms to rent, will put you up for US$9 a double with common bath.

Casa Rosada (☎ (9) 171121), another 700 metres (a five-minute walk) along the shore just past the auxiliary electric generating plant, has nice little bungalows in a private compound right on the water going for US$20 a double. All three meals are served. It's a good idea to reserve in advance by phone, mail or telegram as there are only five rooms and they're often full.

Places to Eat

The main street is lined with little comedors, *tiendas* (shops) and *almacenes* (stores). Your best plan may be to choose the place which is currently the most popular. *Restaurant El Malecón*, just up the hill from the boat dock on the left, is airy and rustic, has good views of the water and a loyal local clientele. A full meal of Caribbean-inspired fare can be had for US$6.

A bit farther up the hill, the *Tropic*, on the right-hand side, is half restaurant and half shop, with some of the lowest prices in town.

Turn left just beyond the ice plant (Fábrica de Hielo) to find the *Restaurant Saby*, on the left, a typical Caribbean bamboo eatery with local music playing and meals of rice and beans and similar fare for US$2 to US$3. The fancier *Restaurant Margoth*, beyond it, was empty at my last visit.

The very funky *African Place*, on the way to the Hotel Flamingo, looks like a miniature Moorish palace and serves a variety of exotic and local dishes; full meals are available for US$5 or less.

Entertainment

Some nights of the week, the busiest place in town, with the loudest music, is the Templo Evangélico Iglesia del Nazareno (Evangelical Church of the Nazarene), opposite the Restaurant Margoth. If Caribbean Christianity is not your idea of nightlife, check out any of the numerous bars with loud reggae and cheap drinks.

Getting There & Away

The only way to get to Lívingston is by boat. For details, see the Puerto Barrios section.

El Petén

In the dense jungle cover of Guatemala's vast north-eastern department of El Petén you may hear the squawk of parrots, the chatter of monkeys and the rustlings of strange animals moving through the bush. The landscape here is utterly different from that of Guatemala's cool mountainous highlands or its steamy Pacific Slope.

There are three reasons to penetrate the forests of El Petén: to visit Tikal (and perhaps other sites such as ruins of Uaxactún and Ceibal), to enjoy the great variety of bird life, and to see a different Guatemala, one of small farming villages and jungle hamlets, without paved roads or colonial architecture.

For information on the road from the Carretera al Atlantico to Flores via Poptún, see Rio Dulce to Flores in the Central & Eastern Guatemala section.

FLORES & SANTA ELENA

The town of Flores (population 2000) is built on an island on Lago de Petén Itzá. A causeway 500 metres long connects Flores to her sister town of Santa Elena (altitude 110 metres, population 17,000) on the lake shore. Adjoining Santa Elena to the west is the town of San Benito (population 22,000).

Flores, being the departmental capital, is dignified, with its church, small government building and municipal basketball court arranged around the main plaza atop the hill in the centre of the island. The narrow streets of Flores, paved in cement blocks, hold numerous small hotels and restaurants.

Santa Elena is a disorganised town of dusty, mostly unpaved streets, open drainage ditches, small hotels and restaurants. San Benito is even more disorganised, but lively with its honky-tonk bars. The three towns actually form one large settlement. Most of the time it's referred to simply as Flores.

History

Making their way southwards after being driven out of Chichén Itzá (Yucatán) in the 15th century, a group of Itzá Maya settled on an island in Lago de Petén Itzá, at what is now the town of Flores. They founded a city named Tayasal, and enjoyed independence for over a century after the fall of Yucatán. The intrepid Cortés visited Tayasal in 1524 while on his way to conquer Honduras, but did not make war against King Canek, who greeted him peacefully. Only in the latter years of the 17th century did the Spanish decide that this last surviving Maya state

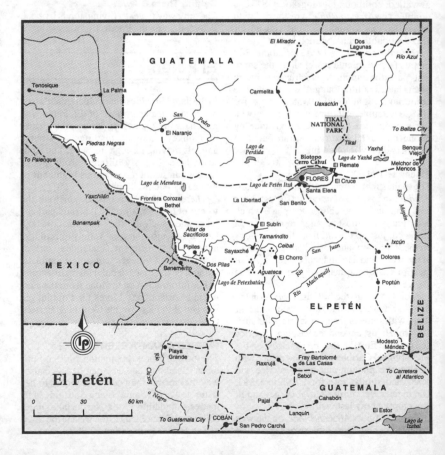

must be brought within the Spanish Empire, and in 1697 Tayasal fell to the latter-day conquistadors, some 2000 years after the founding of the first important Maya city-states in the highlands.

At the time of its conquest, Tayasal (Flores) was perhaps the last major functioning Maya ceremonial centre, covered in pyramids and temples, with idols in evidence everywhere. The God-fearing Spanish soldiers destroyed these 'pagan' buildings. Today when you visit Flores you will see not a trace of them, although the modern town is doubtless built on the ruins and foundations of Maya Tayasal.

Orientation

The airport is on the eastern outskirts of Santa Elena, about one km from the causeway connecting Santa Elena and Flores. Each bus company has its own terminal, near the market in Santa Elena.

Information

There is an INGUAT tourist information desk at the airport, open generally from 8 am to 5 pm.

Money Banco Hipotecario in Flores is open from 8.30 am to 2.30 pm, Monday to Friday (till 3.30 pm on Friday). Banco de Guatemala in Flores is open during the same hours. You may also be able to change dollars to quetzals at your hotel.

Post & Telecommunications The Post & Telegraph office (Correos y Telégrafos) is just west of the Hotel del Patio in Santa Elena.

Grutas Actun-Can

The caves of Actun-Can, also called La Cueva de la Serpiente ('the cave of the serpent'), are of the standard limestone variety. No serpents are in evidence, but the cave-keeper will turn on the lights for you after you've paid the admission fee (US$1.75, 8 am to 5 pm daily), and may give you the rundown on the cave formations, which suggest animals, humans and various scenes. Bring a torch (flashlight) if you have one.

At the cave entrance is a shady picnic area. Actun-Can makes a good goal for a walk from Santa Elena. To find it, walk south on 6a Avenida past the Guatel telephone office. About one km from the centre of Santa Elena, turn left, go 300 metres and turn right at the electricity generating plant. Go another km to the site.

Lago de Petén Itzá

Boat rides on the lake are a major activity. The people at the bus ticket desk in the Hotel San Juan can make the arrangements for you, or your hotel may be willing to do it, or you can haggle with a boat owner yourself. Stops on a tour might include the lagoons at La Guitarra and Petencito, the settlements of San Andrés and San José, and of course the Biotopo Cerro Cahuí.

Places to Stay

The only really cheap hotels are in Santa Elena.

Santa Elena *Hotel Don Quijote*, not far from the causeway to Flores, is cheap, though the rooms are nothing special. Rates are US$2.50 to US$4 a single, US$4.50 to US$7.50 a double; more expensive rooms have running water.

Hotel Jade, even nearer to the causeway, is a longtime favourite with backpackers because of its handy location, washbasin and clothesline for laundry, and its low prices: US$2 a single, US$6 a double. Renovation and expansion is raising the comfort level – and the prices – here, though.

Hotel Leo Fu Lo, next door, was still abuilding at my last visit, but should be similar to the Jade.

Hotel San Juan (☎ (9) 811562) has fan-equipped rooms that are musty, beat-up and a bit overpriced at US$7 for a waterless double. Doubles with private bath cost US$14, or US$25 with air-con. Some rooms have little TVs. The hotel's travel agency sells bus and air tickets, but there have been some complaints about service and price.

GUATEMALA

Hotel El Diplomático, a biggish three-storey building in the southern part of town near the market, is very beat-up by the marketeers who use it regularly, but it is certainly cheap at US$2 to US$2.50 per person.

Hotel Jaguar Inn (☎ (9) 500002; fax 500662), Calzada Rodríguez Macal 8-79, Zona 1, is comfortable without being fancy, but slightly inconveniently located 150 metres off the main road near the airport. It's good if you have a vehicle. Rooms cost US$22 a double with private bath and fan.

Flores *Hotel Casablanca* (☎ (9) 501467) is very plain, but some rooms have lake views, and all cost US$9/11 a double without/with shower.

Hotel Santa Rita (☎ (9) 501266) is clean, family-run, and excellent value at US$10/13 a single/double with private shower.

Hotel Mesa de los Mayas (☎ & fax (9) 501240) has a few quite comfortable rooms above the restaurant for US$10/14/26 a single/double/triple with private shower and fan.

Hotel Villa del Lago (☎ (9) 501446) is cheerful, family-run and very tidy as Petén hotels go, with clean common showers, some lake views, and waterless rooms priced at US$9/11/13 a single/double/triple.

Posada El Túcan, next door, has forgettable rooms at US$8 a double without running water.

Hotel Yum Kax (☎ (9) 811386/68), to the left as you arrive on the island along the causeway, is named for the Maya god of maize (pronounced yoom-KASH). It's often flooded by a rise in the lake's water level, but when it's not, it offers 43 plainish rooms with private bath and either fan or air-con for US$18 to US$24 a double. *Hotel La Jungla*, across the street, is a bit cheaper.

Hotel El Itzá 2 (☎ (9) 500686) is dumpy, but may improve with time. Rooms cost US$9 with private shower.

Hotel Petén (☎ & fax (9) 500662), has a small courtyard with tropical plants and a pleasant roof terrace. The 14 comfy if plain double rooms rent for US$22 with private shower, electric hot water showerhead, and fan. Try to get a room on the top floor (Nos 33, 34 etc) with a view of the lake; these cost US$26 a double. The adjoining *Hotel Santana* is similar, though less attractive.

Hotel Casona de la Isla (☎ & fax (9) 501663) was constructing a small swimming

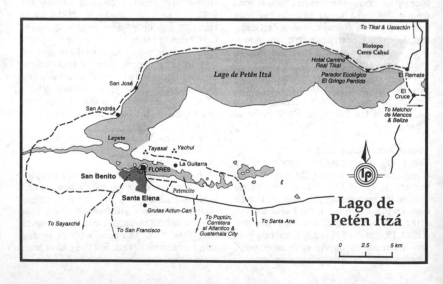

Lago de Petén Itzá

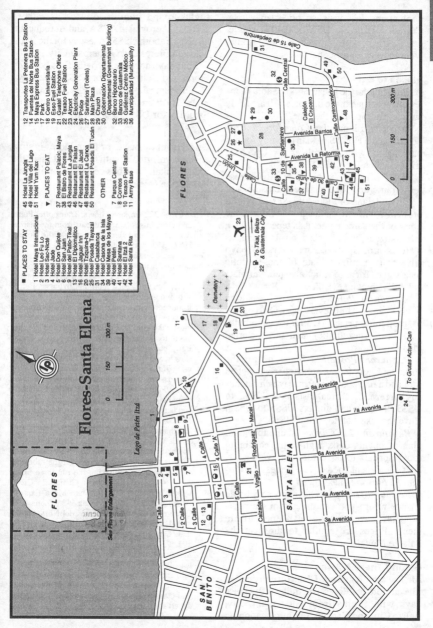

Flores-Santa Elena

PLACES TO STAY

1 Hotel Maya Internacional
2 Hotel Leo Fu Lo
3 Hotel Sac-Nicté
4 Hotel Jade
5 Hotel Don Quijote
6 Hotel San Juan
9 Hotel del Patio-Tikal
13 Hotel El Diplomático
16 Hotel Jaguar Inn
20 Hotel Itzquina-ha
25 Hotel Posada Tayazal
31 Hotel Casablanca
34 Hotel Casona de la Isla
39 Hotel Mesa de los Mayas
40 Hotel Petén
41 Hotel Santana
42 Hotel El Itzá 2
44 Hotel Santa Rita
45 Hotel La Jungla
49 Hotel Villa del Lago
51 Hotel Yum Kax

▼ PLACES TO EAT

37 Restaurant Palacio Maya
38 El Bistro de Flores
43 Restaurant La Jungla
46 Restaurant El Faisan
47 Restaurant El Jacal
48 Restaurant La Canoa
50 Restaurant Posada El Tucán

OTHER

7 Parque Central
8 Correos
10 Texaco Fuel Station
11 Army Base
12 Transportes La Petenera Bus Station
14 Fuentes del Norte Bus Station
15 Maya Express Bus Station
17 Park
18 Centro Universitaria
19 Esso Fuel Station
22 Guatel Telephone Office
22 Texaco Fuel Station
23 Airport
24 Electricity Generation Plant
26 Police
27 Sanitarios (Toilets)
28 Main Plaza
29 Church
30 Gobernación Departamental
   (Departmental Government Building)
32 Banco Hipotecario
33 Banco de Guatemala
35 Gutiérrez Centro Médico
36 Municipalidad (Municipality)

pool at my last visit, so prices may rise. Currently they are US$20/30/40 a single/double/triple with shower and fan, somewhat more with air-con.

Places to Eat

As with hotels, the restaurants in Santa Elena are cheaper than those in Flores. All are fairly simple, and open all the time.

In Santa Elena, the *Comedor El Caracolito* in the Hotel San Juan is handy for bus passengers, with fruit plates for US$2.25, fried chicken for US$3.50.

Hotel Leo Fu Lo has a small Chinese restaurant good for a change of cuisine.

On the island of Flores, the *Restaurant La Mesa de los Maya*, on the ground floor of the hotel of the same name, lists tepezcuintle, a rabbit-sized jungle rodent, on its menu, as well as armadillo and wild turkey (pavo silvestre). A mixed plate of these exotic meats goes for US$9, but a vegetarian plate is US$5, chicken even less.

Restaurant Palacio Maya is open long hours (7 am to 11 pm every day), charges low to moderate prices (US$3 for spaghetti, US$6 for tepezcuintle), and has a varied menu.

Restaurant Posada El Túcan, next to the Villa del Lago, has an atmospheric thatched roof and a fine lakeside terrace which catches any breeze. Set breakfasts cost US$2 to US$3, lunches and dinners US$5 to US$8. Have the lake fish for about US$6.

Restaurant La Canoa is cheaper and plainer, but its dark, high-ceilinged dining room appeals to adventurous travellers, as does the decent food at low prices. *Restaurant El Faisan* is also cheap.

Restaurant La Jungla has a tiny street-side terrace where you can dine from the now-familiar burgers-spaghetti-tepezcuintle menu. Prices are similar to those at the Palacio Maya.

Getting There & Away

Air The airport at Santa Elena (usually called 'the airport at Flores') is quite busy these days with flights from Guatemala City, Belize City and Cancún. For information on

flights to and from these places, see those sections. Aerovías, TAPSA, and Aeroquetzal all charge about US$55 one way for the flight between Flores and Guatemala City.

Four days a week, Aerovías flies between Flores and Belize City for US$50 one way.

Aeroquetzal flies from Flores to Guatemala City, then on to Cancún on Tuesday and Saturday for US$175 one way.

Bus Travel by bus to or from Flores is slow and uncomfortable, with the exception of the road to Tikal. Each bus company has its own bus station (see map).

Belize City – 222 km, seven hours; Transportes Pinita 2nd-class buses (US$8) depart from the market daily at 5, 8 and 10 am, connecting with a Novelo bus (US$3) at the Belizean border.
Ceibal – see Sayaxché, later
Chetumal (Mexico) – 350 km, nine hours; a special direct 1st-class bus (US$35) departs from the Hotel San Juan each morning, bypasses Belize City and goes straight to Chetumal. At Chetumal it connects with an ADO bus heading north along the coast to Cancún at 2 pm. To go 2nd class you must take the Transportes Pinita and Novelo buses to Belize City (see Belize City), then a Batty bus (US$5) to Chetumal. It's somewhat slower, and less convenient, but less than half the price of the special 1st-class bus.
El Naranjo – see 'From El Petén to Mexico'.
El Remate/Puente Ixlu – 35 km, 45 minutes; Tikal-bound buses and minibuses (see Tikal) will drop you here; buses running to and from Melchor de Mencos will drop you at Puente Ixlu/El Cruce, less than two km south of El Remate.
Guatemala City – 506 km, 14 or 15 hours, US$12; Petenero, at 17a Avenida 10-25 in Guatemala City, is the favoured company at the moment, with newish buses making the run three times daily (4, 6 and 8 pm from Guatemala City). Others operating this route are Maya Express (☎ (2) 539325), 17a Avenida 9-36, Zona 1 in Guatemala City), and Fuentes del Norte (☎ (2) 86094, 513817), 17 Calle 8-46, Zona 1 in Guatemala City, runs buses departing from the capital at 1, 2, 3 and 7 am, and 11 pm, with stops at Morales, Río Dulce, San Luis and Poptún. Buses usually depart Guatemala City and Santa Elena full, and riders getting on midway must stand.
Melchor de Mencos – 101 km, three or four hours; 2nd-class Transportes Pinita buses (US$2.50) depart from the market at 5, 8 and 10 am for this town on the Belizean border. Buses (US$0.50)

and shared taxis (US$2) take you to Benque Viejo and San Ignacio every hour or so.

Palenque (Mexico) – see the From El Petén to Mexico section

Sayaxché – 61 km, two hours; 2nd-class buses (US$2) run by Transportes Pinita depart at 6 am and 1 pm, returning from Sayaxché at these same times. There are also tours from Santa Elena via Sayaxché to the Maya ruins at Ceibal for about US$30 per person, round trip.

Tikal – 71 km, two hours or more by bus, one to 1½ hours by minibus, one hour by car; buses (US$2.50) depart from the market daily at 7 am and noon; return trips from Tikal are at similar times, making it necessary to stay overnight or find other means of returning to Flores.

Minibuses depart each morning from various hotels (6, 8 and 10 am), the Flores airport (meeting all flights), and various middle-range hotels in Flores and Santa Elena for the ride to Tikal. The fare is US$9 round trip. Return trips are made at 2, 4 and 5 pm for the same fare. Your driver will anticipate that you'll want to return to Flores in his minibus that same afternoon; if you tell him which return trip you plan to be on, he'll hold a seat for you, or arrange a seat in a colleague's minibus.

A taxi for up to four people, from the town or the airport to Tikal, costs $40 round trip.

Uaxactún – 25 km, one hour, US$2; a bus departs Flores at 8 am, returning from Uaxactún at 11.30 am or noon, allowing enough time for a quick visit to the ruins.

Getting Around

For destinations to small villages around the lake and in the immediate vicinity, there are sometimes seats available in the minibuses which depart from the market area in Santa Elena.

It is often possible to hire a cayuco (local boat) for cruises and tours on Lago de Petén Itzá. Any hotel clerk can help you with this.

FROM EL PETÉN TO CHIAPAS

There are currently three routes through the jungle from Flores (Guatemala) to Palenque (Mexico).

Via El Naranjo

The traditional route is via bus to El Naranjo, then by boat down the Río San Pedro to La Palma, then by bus to Tenosique and Palenque.

Buses to El Naranjo (seven hours, US$3),

on the Río San Pedro, depart from the market daily at 5 am and 12.30 pm on the rough, bumpy 125-km, six-hour, US$4.50 ride. El Naranjo is a hamlet with a few thatched huts, large military barracks, an immigration post, and a few basic lodging places. From El Naranjo you must catch a boat on the river and cruise for about four hours to the border town of La Palma. From La Palma you can go by bus to Tenosique (1½ hours), then to Emiliano Zapata (40 km, one hour), and from there to Palenque.

Via Bethel & Frontera Corozal

The newer route is by bus from Flores via El Subín crossroads to the hamlet of Bethel (four hours), on the Río Usumacinta. Frequent cargo boats make the two-hour trip downriver to Frontera Corozal in Mexico, charging a few dollars for the voyage. There are no services in Bethel except a small shop.

At Frontera Corozal there is a restaurant but no lodging. From Frontera, a chartered boat to Yaxchilán might cost US$50, but sometimes you can hitch a ride with a group for US$10 or so. The one bus per day takes six hours (US$5) to reach Palenque.

Via Pipiles & Benemerito

From Sayaxché, you can negotiate with one of the cargo boats for the trip down the Río de la Pasión via Pipiles (the Guatemalan border post) to Benemerito, in the Mexican state of Chiapas. From Benemerito you can proceed by bus or boat to the ruins at Yaxchilán and Bonampak, and then onward to Palenque.

SAYAXCHÉ & CEIBAL

The town of Sayaxché, 61 km south of Flores through the jungle, is the closest settlement to a half-dozen Maya archaeological sites, including Aguateca, Altar de Sacrificios, Ceibal, Dos Pilas, El Caribe, Itzán, La Amelia and Tamarindito. Of these, Ceibal is currently the best-restored and most interesting, partly because of its Maya monuments, and partly because of the river voyage and jungle walk necessary to reach it.

Sayaxché itself is of little interest, but its

few basic services allow you to eat and to stay overnight in this region.

Orientation

The bus from Santa Elena drops you on the north bank of the Río de la Pasión. The main part of the town is on the south bank. Frequent ferries carry you over the river for a minimal fare.

Ceibal

Unimportant during the Classic period, Ceibal grew rapidly thereafter, attaining a population of perhaps 10,000 by 900 AD. Much of the population growth may have been due to immigration from what is now Chiapas, in Mexico, because the art and culture of Ceibal seems to have changed markedly during the same period. The Post-Classic period saw the decline of Ceibal, after which its low ruined temples were quickly covered by a thick carpet of jungle.

Today Ceibal is not among the most impressive of Maya sites, but the journey to Ceibal is among the most memorable. A two-hour voyage on the jungle-bound Río de la Pasión brings you to a primitive dock. After landing, you clamber up a narrow, rocky path beneath gigantic ceiba trees and ganglions of jungle vines to reach the archaeological zone.

Smallish temples, many of them still (or again) covered with jungle, surround two principal plazas. In front of a few temples, and standing seemingly alone on paths deeply shaded by the jungle canopy, are magnificent stelae, their intricate carvings still in excellent condition.

Getting There & Away Day trips to Ceibal are organised by various agencies and drivers in Santa Elena and Flores for about US$30 to US$50 per person, round trip. It can be done cheaper on your own, but is significantly less convenient.

Buses depart Santa Elena at 6 am and 1 pm (US$2.50) on the two-hour ride to Sayaxché, where you must strike a deal with a boatman to ferry you up the river – a two-hour voyage – and back. The boat may

cost anywhere from US$30 to US$60, depending upon its size and capacity. From the river, it's less than 30 minutes' walk to the site. You should hire a guide to see the site, as some of the finest stelae are off the plazas in the jungle.

Other Ruins

Of the other Maya sites near Sayaxché, none is currently as interesting or as well restored as Ceibal. Dos Pilas is presently under excavation, but not equipped to receive visitors without their own camping gear. From Dos Pilas, the minor sites of Tamarindito and Aguateca may be reached on foot and by boat, but they are unrestored, covered in jungle, and of interest only to the very intrepid.

Places to Stay & Eat

Hotel Guayacan, just up from the dock on the south side of the river in Sayaxché, is basic and serviceable for US$8 in a waterless double, US$11 in a double with cold shower. The *Hotel Mayapan*, up the street to the left, has cell-like rooms for US$5 a double. *Restaurant Yaxkin* is typical of the few eateries in town: basic, family-run, and cheap.

EL REMATE

Once little more than a few thatched huts, 35 km north-east of Santa Elena on the Tikal road, the village of El Remate has recently grown into a small town thanks to the tourist trade. From El Remate an unpaved road snakes its way around the north-east shore of the lake to the Biotopo Cerro Cahuí and the luxury Camino Real hotel.

El Remate is less than two km north of Puente Ixlu, also called El Cruce, the settlement right at the junction of the Flores-Tikal-Melchor de Mencos roads.

With their newfound prosperity, Rematecos have constructed a Balneario Municipal (Municipal Beach) just off the highway, and have opened several cheap pensions and small hotels.

Biotopo Cerro Cahuí

At the north-east end of Lago de Petén Itzá,

about 43 km from Santa Elena (1½ km west of El Remate), the Biotopo Cerro Cahuí covers 651 hectares of hot, humid, subtropical forest. Within the reserve are mahogany, cedar, ramón, broom, sapodilla and cohune palm trees, as well as many species of lianas (climbing plants), bromeliads (air plants), ferns and orchids.

Animals in the reserve include spider monkeys, howler monkeys, ocelots, bears, white-tailed deer, raccoons, armadillos, and some 21 other beasts. In the water there are 24 species of fish, turtles, snakes, and *Crocodylus moreletti*, the Petén crocodile. The bird life, of course, is rich and varied.

The reserve is open daily from 7 am to 5 pm for walking along its nature trails.

Places to Stay & Eat
There are several small hotels and pensions abuilding right in El Remate, and more are opening all the time.

The traditional lodging-place in the area is the *Parador Ecológico El Gringo Perdido* (The Lost Gringo Ecological Inn; ☎ in Guatemala City (2) 363683) on the north-eastern shore of the lake three km west of El Remate. Shady, rustic hillside gardens hold a little restaurant, a bucolic camping area, and simple but pleasant bungalows and dormitories. Rates range from US$3 for a camping place through US$14 for a dorm bunk to US$20/24 a single/double. Meals cost US$6 for breakfast, US$10 for lunch or dinner. As there are no other eating places nearby, a bed and three meals starts at US$40 per person per day.

Getting There & Away
Any bus or minibus going north from Santa Elena to Tikal can drop you at El Remate.

TIKAL
Towering pyramids rise above the jungle's green canopy to heights of more than 44 metres, catching the sun. Howler monkeys swing noisily through the branches of ancient trees as brightly coloured parrots dart, squawking, from perch to perch. When the complex warbling song of some mysterious jungle bird is not filling the air, the buzz of tree frogs provides background noise. There is nothing like Tikal.

If you visit from December to February, expect some cool nights and mornings. March and April are the hottest months, and water is scarcest then. The rains begin in May or June, and with them come the mosquitos – bring along repellent and, for camping, a mosquito net. July to September is muggy and buggy. October and November see the end of the occasional rains, and a return to cooler temperatures. Tikal is so big that one needs at least two days to see even the major parts thoroughly.

History
Tikal is set on a low hill, a fact which is evident as you walk up to the Great Plaza from the entry road. The hill, affording relief from the surrounding low-lying swampy ground, may be why the Maya settled here around 700 BC. Another reason was the abundance of flint, the valuable stone used by the ancients to make clubs, spearpoints, arrowheads and knives.

Within 200 years the Maya of Tikal had begun to build stone ceremonial structures, and by 200 BC there was a complex of buildings on the site of the North Acropolis.

By the time of Christ, the Great Plaza was beginning to assume its present shape and extent. With the dawn of the Early Classic period about 250 AD, Tikal was an important religious, cultural and commercial city with a large population.

By the middle of the 16th century, Tikal's military prowess and its alliance with Teotihuacán allowed it to grow until it sprawled over 30 sq km and had a population of perhaps 100,000.

In 553, Lord Water came to the throne of Caracol (in south-western Belize), and by 562, using the same warfare methods learned by Tikal, had conquered Tikal's king and sacrificed him.

Around 700 a new and powerful king named Ah-Cacau (Lord Chocolate, 682-734), 26th successor of Yax-Moch-Xoc, ascended the throne of Tikal. Ah-Cacau

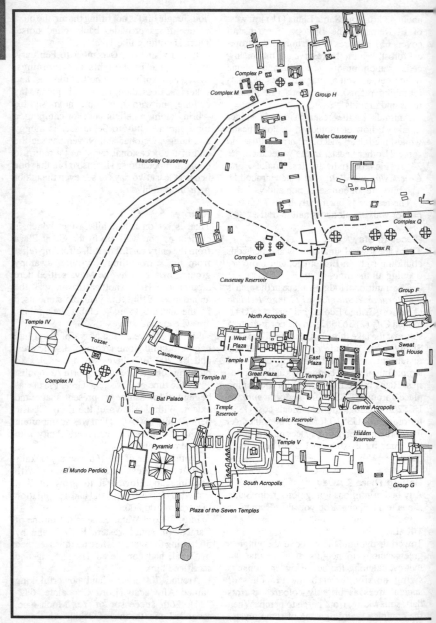

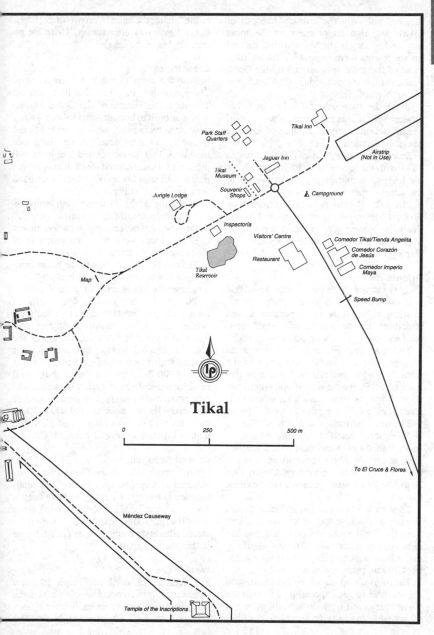

Park Staff Quarters

Tikal Inn

Jaguar Inn

Airstrip (Not in Use)

Tikal Museum

Souvenir Shops

Jungle Lodge

Campground

Inspectoría

Comedor Tikal/Tienda Angelita

Visitors' Centre

Comedor Corazón de Jesús

Restaurant

Comedor Imperio Maya

Tikal Reservoir

Map

Speed Bump

Tikal

0   250   500 m

To El Cruce & Flores

Méndez Causeway

Temple of the Inscriptions

restored not only the military strength of Tikal, but also its primacy as the most resplendent city in the Maya world. He and his successors were responsible for building most of the great temples around the Great Plaza, which survive today. Ah-Cacau was buried beneath Temple 1.

When the greatness of Tikal collapsed in around 900, it was not alone; it was part of the mysterious general collapse of lowland Maya civilisation.

Scientific exploration of Tikal began in 1881 with the arrival of Alfred P Maudslay, the English archaeologist, who travelled to the site by the only means available – on horseback. His work was continued by Teobert Maler, a German sponsored by the Peabody Museum at Harvard University. Maler was succeeded in Peabody sponsorship by Alfred M Tozzer and R E Merwin.

Orientation

Tikal is located in the midst of the vast Tikal National Park, a 575-sq-km preserve containing thousands of separate ruined structures. The central area of the city occupied about 16 sq km with 3000 buildings.

The road from Flores enters the national park boundaries about 15 km south of the ruins. When you enter the park you must pay a fee of US$6 for the day; if you enter after about 3 pm, you can have your ticket validated for the following day as well.

The area around the Visitors' Centre includes three hotels, a camping area, three small comedores, a tiny post office, a police post, an excellent little museum, and a rarely used airstrip. From the Visitors' Centre it's a 20 to 30-minute walk south-west to the Great Plaza.

The walk from the Great Plaza to the Temple of the Inscriptions is over one km, from the Great Plaza to Complex P one km in the opposite direction. To visit all of the major building complexes you must walk at least 10 km, probably more.

The ruins are open from 6 am to 5 pm; you may be able to get a special pass to visit the Great Plaza until 8 pm on moonlit evenings by applying to the Inspectorería to the west

of the Visitors' Centre. Carry a torch (flashlight) if you stay after sunset. There are no street lights in the jungle!

Great Plaza

Follow the signs to reach the Great Plaza. The path comes into the Great Plaza around Temple I, the Temple of the Grand Jaguar. This was built to honour – and to bury – King Ah-Cacau by his son, who succeeded to the throne in 734. Ah-Cacau's rich burial goods included 180 beautiful jade objects, 90 pieces of bone carved with hieroglyphs, pearls, and stingray spines which were used for ritual bloodletting.

At the top of the 44-metre-high temple is a small enclosure of three rooms covered by a corbelled arch. The zapote-wood lintels over the doors were richly carved; one of them is now in a Basel museum.

Temple II, directly across the plaza from Temple I, was once almost as high, but now measures 38 metres without its roofcomb.

The North Acropolis, while not as immediately impressive as the twin temples, is of great significance. Archaeologists have uncovered about 100 different structures, the oldest of which dates from before the time of Christ, with evidence of occupation as far back as 400 BC. Look for the two huge wall masks uncovered in an earlier structure, and now protected by roofs. The final version of the Acropolis, as it stood around 800 AD, had more than 12 temples atop a vast platform, many of them the work of King Ah-Cacau.

Central Acropolis

On the south side of the Great Plaza, this maze of courtyards, little rooms and small temples is thought by many to have been a palace where Tikal's nobles lived. Others think the tiny rooms may have been used for sacred rites and ceremonies, as graffiti found within them suggest.

West Plaza

The West Plaza, north of Temple II, has a large Late Classic-period temple on its north side. To the south, across the Tozzer Causeway, is Temple III, 55 metres high. Yet to be uncovered, it allows you to see a temple the way the last Tikal Maya and first European explorers saw them.

South Acropolis & Temple V
Due south of the Great Plaza is the South Acropolis. Excavation has hardly even begun on this huge mass of masonry covering two hectares. The palaces on top are no doubt from the time of King Ah-Cacau, but earlier constructions probably go back 1000 years.

Temple V, just east of the South Acropolis, is 58 metres high, and was built around 700 AD (again, in the reign of Ah-Cacau). Unlike the other great temples, this one has rounded corners and one very tiny room at the top. The room is less than a metre deep, but its walls are up to 4½ metres thick.

Plaza of the Seven Temples
On the other side of the South Acropolis is the Plaza of the Seven Temples. The little temples, all quite close together, were built in Late Classic times, though the structures beneath must go back a millennium at least. On the north side of the plaza is an unusual triple ball court; another, larger version in the same design stands just south of Temple I.

El Mundo Perdido
About 400 metres south-west of the Great Plaza is El Mundo Perdido, the Lost World, a large complex of 38 structures with a huge pyramid in its midst. Unlike the rest of Tikal, where Late Classic construction overlays work of earlier periods, El Mundo Perdido exhibits buildings of many different periods. The pyramid, 32 metres high and 80 metres along the base, has a stairway on each side, and had huge masks flanking each stairway, but no temple structure at its top. Each side of the pyramid displays a slightly different architectural style. Tunnels dug into the pyramid by archaeologists reveal four similar pyramids beneath the outer face, the oldest (Structure 5C-54 Sub 2B) dating from 700 BC, making the pyramid the oldest Maya structure at Tikal.

Temple IV & Complex N
Complex N, near Temple IV, is an example of the 'twin-temple' complexes popular among Tikal's rulers near the end of Maya greatness. This one was built in 711 by King Ah-Cacau. The king himself is portrayed on Stela 16, one of the finest stelae found at Tikal.

Temple IV, at 64 metres, is the highest building at Tikal, and the highest Indian building known in the western hemisphere. It was completed about 741, in the reign of Ah-Cacau's son. From the base it looks like a steep little hill. Clamber up the path, holding onto trees and roots, to reach the metal ladder which will take you to the top. Another metal ladder, around to the side, lets you climb to the base of the roofcomb. The view is almost as good as from a helicopter, a panorama across the jungle canopy. If you stay up here for the sunset, climb down immediately thereafter as it gets dark on the path very quickly.

Temple of the Inscriptions
Compared to Copán or Quiriguá, there are relatively few inscriptions on buildings at Tikal. The exception is this temple, 1200 metres south-east of the Great Plaza. On the rear of the 12-metre-high roofcomb is a long inscription; the sides and cornice of the roofcomb bear glyphs as well. The inscriptions give us the date 766 AD. Stela 21 and Altar 9, standing before the temple, date from 736 AD. Note that there have been some robberies near this temple, as it is distant from the others.

Tikal Museum
The museum in the Visitors' Centre is small but has some fascinating exhibits, including the burial goods of King Ah-Cacau, carved jade, inscribed bones, shells, stelae, and other items recovered from the excavations. There is no extra charge for admission.

Places to Stay
Some intrepid visitors sleep atop Temple IV, convincing the guards to overlook this illegal activity for a consideration of US$6 per

person, but this is not to be recommended. Safety is a major concern.

Otherwise, there are only four places to stay at Tikal. Most are booked in advance by tour groups. In recent years I have had numerous complaints by readers of price gouging, unacceptable accommodation and 'lost' reservations at these hotels. It is probably best if you plan to stay in Flores or El Remate and visit Tikal on day trips.

Cheapest of Tikal's lodgings is the official camping area by the entrance road and the disused airstrip. Set in a nice lawn of green grass with some trees for shade, it should be an idyllic camping ground, but it's not. Often the toilets and showers do not work, and the charge for tent space is US$6 per person.

The 32-room *Jungle Lodge* (☎ (2) 760294 in Guatemala City, 29 Calle 18-01, Zona 12), was built originally to house the archaeologists excavating and restoring Tikal. Rooms without bath in the original building cost US$18 a double; with bath (no hot water), the cost is US$40.

Jaguar Inn, to the right of the museum as you approach on the access road, has only two rooms. The price is US$32. Four tents rent for US$12 a double.

Tikal Inn charges US$40 a double in the main building, US$50 in its bungalows.

Places to Eat

As you arrive in Tikal, look on the right side of the road to find the three little comedors: *Comedor Imperio Maya, Comedor Corazón de Jesus, Comedor Tikal* and *Tienda Angelita*. The Comedor Imperio Maya, first on the way into the site, seems to be the favoured one. You can buy cold drinks and snacks in the tienda (shop) adjoining. All three comedores are similar in comforts and style (there are none), all are rustic and pleasant, all are run by local people, and all serve huge plates of tasty food at low prices. The meal of the day is almost always a piece of roast chicken, rice, salad, fruit and a soft drink for US$4.

Picnic tables beneath shelters are located just off Tikal's Great Plaza, with itinerant soft-drink pedlars standing by, but no food is sold. If you want to spend all day at the ruins without having to make the 20 to 30-minute walk back to the comedors, carry food with you.

Getting There & Away

For details of transport to and from Flores/Santa Elena, see that section. Coming from Belize, you can get off the bus at El Cruce/Puente Ixlu. Wait for a northbound bus or minibus – or hitch a ride with an obliging tourist – to take you the remaining 35 km to Tikal. Note that there is very little northbound traffic after lunch. If you come to El Cruce in the afternoon, it's probably best to continue to Flores or El Remate for the night rather than risk being stranded at El Cruce.

Warning Occasionally, armed guerrillas or robbers stop a bus or minibus on the Tikal-Flores road, take their valuables, then release them. The few incidents so far have not resulted in physical harm.

Ask at your embassy in Guatemala City, or ask the locals in Flores for news on the current situation.

UAXACTÚN

Uaxactún (pronounced 'wah-shahk-TOON'), 25 km north of Tikal along a poor unpaved road through the jungle, was Tikal's political and military rival in Late Pre-Classic times. It was conquered by Tikal's King Great-Jaguar-Paw in the mid-4th century, and was subservient to its great sister to the south for centuries thereafter.

During the rainy season from May to October, you will find it difficult to get to Uaxactún. A bus leaves Tikal daily around 8 am if road conditions allow, returning from Uaxactún around noon, for US$2. You might want to pack some food, though drinks are on sale at Uaxactún.

When you arrive at Uaxactún, sign your name in the register at the guard's hut. About halfway down the disused airstrip, roads go off to the left and to the right to the ruins. There are plenty of places to camp if you have your own equipment.

The Ruins

Turn right from the airstrip to reach Group E and Group H, a 10 to 15-minute walk. Perhaps the most significant temple here is E-VII-Sub, among the earliest intact temples excavated, with foundations going back perhaps to 2000 BC. It lay beneath much larger structures, which have been stripped away. On its flat top are holes, or sockets, for the poles which would have supported a wood-and-thatch temple.

About a 20-minute walk to the north-west of the runway are Group A and Group B. At Group A, early excavators sponsored by Andrew Carnegie simply cut into the sides of the temples indiscriminately, looking for graves. Sometimes they used dynamite. This unfortunate work destroyed many of the temples, which are now in the process of being reconstructed.

FLORES TO BELIZE

It is 101 km from Flores eastwards to Melchor de Mencos, the Guatemalan town on the border with Belize.

Transportes Pinita buses depart for Melchor at 5 am. The road from Flores to El Cruce is good, fast asphalt. If you're coming from Tikal, start early in the morning and get off at El Cruce to catch a bus or hitch a ride westward. For the fastest, most reliable service, however, it's best to be on that 5 am bus.

East of El Cruce the road reverts to what's usual in El Petén – unpaved mud in bad repair. The trip to Melchor takes three or four hours. There is guerrilla activity along this road, and a remote chance that your bus will be stopped (see Warning under the earlier Tikal section).

At the border you must hand in your Guatemalan tourist card before proceeding to Benque Viejo in Belize, about two km from the border. See the section on Benque Viejo for transport information to Benque Viejo, San Ignacio, Belmopan and Belize City (see Western Belize in the Belize chapter).

BELIZE

Belize

An English-speaking tropical country with a democratic government and a highly unlikely mixture of peoples and cultures – that's Belize.

Belize is tiny. The 23,300 sq km of land within its borders is slightly more than that of Massachusetts or Wales.

Belize is English-speaking, officially. But the Black Creoles, its largest ethnic group (over half of the population) speak their own dialect as well as standard English. Spanish is a popular second language, and you may also hear Maya, Chinese, Mennonite German, Lebanese Arabic, Hindi and Garífuna, the language of the Garinagu people of the southern townships.

Belize is a democracy. It has never had a coup; indeed, it does not have an army, only the tiny Belize Defence Force.

Belize is many other things. It is friendly, laid-back, beautiful, proud, poor, and hopeful for the future.

Belize has been discovered, but it is not prepared to receive lots of visitors. Services are few, far between and basic. Hotels may be full when you arrive. There are only two paved roads in the whole country, so transport is slow. If you expect convenience, comfort and ultra-cheapness, you're in for a surprise. But if you are adaptable and adventurous, you'll love Belize.

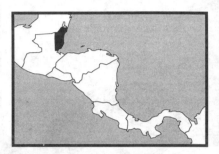

Facts about the Country

HISTORY

In the opinion of its Spanish conquerors, Belize was a backwater good only for cutting logwood to be used for dye. It had no obvious riches to exploit, and no great population to convert for the glory of God and the profit of the conquerors. Far from being profitable, it was dangerous, because the barrier reef tended to tear the keels from Spanish ships that attempted to approach the shore. So the Spaniards left Belize alone.

The lack of effective government and the safety afforded by the barrier reef attracted English and Scottish pirates to Belizean waters during the 17th century. In 1670, however, Spain convinced the British government to clamp down on the pirates' activities. The pirates, now unemployed, mostly went into the logwood business.

During the 18th century, British interests in the Caribbean countries increased, so did British involvement in Belize. Towards the end of the 18th century, Belize was already British by tradition and sympathy, and it was with relief and jubilation that Belizeans received the news, on 10 September 1798, that a British force had defeated the Spanish armada off St George's Caye. Belize had been delivered from Spanish rule, a fact that was ratified by treaty some 60 years later.

In 1862, while the USA was embroiled in its Civil War and unable to enforce the terms of the Monroe Doctrine, Great Britain declared Belize to be the colony of British Honduras. The declaration encouraged people from numerous parts of the British Empire to come and settle in Belize, which accounts in part for the country's present-day ethnic diversity.

After WW II the Belizean economy worsened, which led to agitation for inde-

BELIZE

Belize

pendence from the UK. Democratic institutions and political parties were formed over the years, self-government became a reality, and on 21 September 1981 the colony of British Honduras officially became the independent nation of Belize.

Guatemala, which had claimed Belize as part of its national territory, feared that Belizean independence would kill forever its hopes of reclaiming it. The Guatemalans threatened war, but British troops stationed in Belize kept the dispute to a diplomatic squabble. In 1992 a new Guatemalan government recognised Belize's independence and territorial integrity, and signed a treaty relinquishing its claim.

GEOGRAPHY

Belize is tropical lowland, though in the western part of the country the Maya Mountains rise to almost 1000 metres. The mountain country is lush and well watered, humid even in the dry season, but more pleasant than the lowlands.

Northern Belize is low tropical country, very swampy along the shore. The southern part of the country is similar, but even more rainy and humid.

Offshore, the water is only about five metres deep all the way out to the islands, called *cayes*. Just east of the cayes in the Caribbean is the barrier reef, a mecca for snorkellers and scuba divers.

CLIMATE

Though it is comfortably warm during the day in the mountains, cooling off a bit at night, the rest of the country is hot and humid day and night most of the year. In the rainforests of southern Belize the humidity is very high because of the large amount of rainfall (almost four metres per year). Out on the cayes, tropical breezes waft through the shady palm trees constantly, providing natural air-con; on the mainland, you swelter. The dry season from October to May is the better time to travel, but prices are lower and lodgings on the cayes easier to find if you avoid the busy winter season from mid-December to April.

Hurricane season in the Caribbean, including all of the Belizean coast and its cayes, is from June to November, with most of the activity from mid-August to mid-September. Normally there are at least a few tropical storms, which may or may not affect your travel plans. About once every decade, somebody gets clobbered. Belize City was badly damaged by hurricanes, with heavy loss of life, in 1931, 1961 and 1978. If there's a full-blown hurricane predicted for where you are, go somewhere else – fast!

ECONOMY

Farming and ranching are important in the lands west and south of Belize City, and forestry in the Maya Mountains. In the north are large sugar cane plantations and processing plants. The cayes (islands) offshore depend on tourism and fishing for their income, but these two pursuits are sometimes in conflict. The spiny lobster and some types of fish have been seriously over-exploited.

POPULATION & PEOPLE

The population of the entire country is less than 200,000, the size of a small city in Mexico, Europe or the USA.

The largest segment of Belizeans is Creole, descendants of the African slaves and British pirates who first settled here to exploit the country's forest riches. Racially mixed and proud of it, Creoles speak a dialect of English which, though it sounds familiar at first, is utterly unintelligible to a speaker of standard English. Most of the people you meet and deal with in Belize City and Belmopan are Creole.

Pure-blooded Maya make up only about 10% of Belize's population, while fully one-third of Belize's people are mestizos, some of whom migrated from Yucatán during the 19th century.

Southern Belize is the home of the Garinagus (or Garífunas, also called Black Caribs), who account for less than 10% of the population. The Garinagus are of South American Indian and African descent. They look more African than Indian, but they

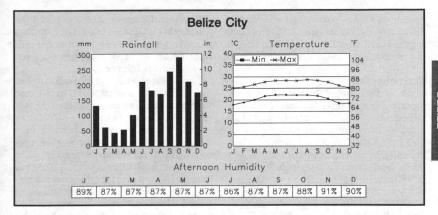

BELIZE

speak a language that's much more Indian than African, and their unique culture combines aspects of both peoples.

Belize also has small populations of Chinese restaurateurs and merchants, Lebanese traders, German-Swiss Mennonite farmers, Indians from the subcontinent, Europeans and North Americans.

Facts for the Visitor

VISAS
British subjects and citizens of Commonwealth countries, citizens of the USA, and citizens of Belgium, Denmark, Finland, Greece, Holland, Mexico, Norway, Panama, Sweden, Switzerland, Tunisia, Turkey and Uruguay who have a valid passport and an onward or return airline ticket from Belize do not need to obtain a Belizean visa in advance. If you look young, or grotty, or poverty-stricken, the immigration officer may demand to see your airline ticket out, and/or a sizeable quantity of money or travellers' cheques before you're admitted.

MONEY
The Belizean dollar (BZ$) is divided into 100 cents. Coins are of one, five, 10, 25 and 50 cents, and one dollar; notes (bills) are of one, two, five, 10, 20, 50 and 100 dollars. You can exchange US and Canadian dollars and pounds sterling at any bank; other currencies are difficult to exchange. Cash US dollars are accepted virtually everywhere, and many establishments will also accept US dollar travellers' cheques.

The Belizean dollar's value has been fixed for many years at US$1 = BZ$2, but recently there has been talk about devaluation.

Belizeans quote prices in 'dollars', but it may be Belizean or US. You'll find yourself asking 'US or Belize?' dozens of times each day. Often people will quote prices as '20 dollars Belize, 10 dollars US' just to make it clear.

Foreign		Belize
A$	=	BZ$1.38
CN$	=	BZ$1.56
DM	=	BZ$1.18
L100	=	BZ$1.25
NZ$	=	BZ$1.10
UK£	=	BZ$2.96
US$	=	BZ$2.00

Costs
Belize is surprisingly expensive. That fried chicken dinner which cost US$3 in Guatemala costs US$5 in Belize, and is no better. That waterless pension room, cheap in Guatemala and Mexico, costs US$7 to US$9 per

person on Caye Caulker. You may find it difficult to live for less than US$15 per day for room and three meals in Belize; US$20 is a more realistic bottom-end figure.

Consumer Taxes
A tax of 5% is added to your bill for hotel room, meals and drinks, but there is no value-added tax. A departure tax of BZ$20 (US$10), and an airport security fee of BZ$2.50 (US$1.25), are levied on travellers departing by air to foreign destinations. Exit tax at land border crossing points is BZ$1 (US$0.50).

TOURIST OFFICES
The Belize Tourist Board (☎ (02) 77213, 73255), 53/76 Regent St, Belize City, is staffed by very friendly and helpful people. It is open from 8 am to noon and 1 to 5 pm Monday to Thursday and until 4.30 pm Friday.

BUSINESS HOURS
Most banks and many businesses and shops are closed on Wednesday afternoon. Banking hours depend upon the individual bank, but most are open Monday to Friday from 8 am to noon or 1 pm; some are also open from 1 to 3 pm, and many have extra hours on Friday from 3 to 6 pm. Shops are usually open from 8 am to noon Monday to Saturday, and from 1 to 4 pm on Monday, Tuesday, Thursday and Friday. Some shops have evening hours from 7 to 9 pm on those days as well.

POST & TELECOMMUNICATIONS
Post
An air-mail letter sent to Canada or the USA may take anywhere from four to 14 days. Air-mail letters to Europe can take anywhere from one to three weeks.

To claim Poste Restante mail, present your passport or other identification; there's no charge.

Telephone
The telephone system is operated by Belize Telecommunications Ltd (BTL), with

offices (open 8 am to noon and 1 to 4 pm Monday to Friday, 8 am to noon on Saturday) in major towns. Rates for international calls from Belize are more expensive than you may be used to at home.

Local calls cost BZ$0.25. To call from one part of Belize to another, dial 0 (zero), then the one or two-digit area code, then the four or five-digit local number.

Calls dialled direct (no operator) from Belize to other western hemisphere countries cost BZ$3.20 per minute; to Europe, BZ$6 per minute; to all other countries, BZ$8 per minute. The best plan for calling internationally from Belize is to dial your call direct from a telephone office; or you can call reverse charge (collect) from your hotel. Be sure to ask before you call what the charges (and any hotel surcharges) may be. Here are some useful numbers:

Directory Assistance	113
Local & Regional Operator	114
Long-Distance (trunk) Operator	110
International Operator	115
Fire & Ambulance	90
Police	911

To place a reverse charge (collect) call, dial the international operator (115), give the number you want to call and the number you're calling from; the operator will place the call and ring you back when it goes through. Rates for operator-assisted calls are the same as for direct-dial calls, but the minimum initial calling period is three minutes.

The large US long-distance companies provide international service as well. Rates for these services may be higher than calling directly via BTL lines, however. To reach AT&T's *USADirect* service, dial 555; this service is not available from coin-operated telephones. For Sprint Express, dial 556; from coin-operated telephones, dial *4 (that's asterisk-4). MCI Call USA service is not yet available from Belize.

BOOKS & MAPS
International Travel Map Productions, PO Box 2290, Vancouver, BC V6B 3W5,

Canada, publishes a series of detailed, quite accurate Travellers' Reference Maps. Titles include *Belize* (1:350,000).

FOOD

Belizeans are justly proud of all the fresh fish and lobster (sometimes called 'crawfish') available from their coastal waters. Grilled or fried fish is always a good bet on the cayes and in coastal towns. By all means have lobster if it's in season when you're on the cayes or in Belize City.

Beef and chicken are the usual main courses, often served with fried potatoes, often greasy. But the traditional staple of the Belizean diet is certainly rice and beans, often with other ingredients – chicken, pork, beef, vegetables, even lobster – plus some spices and condiments like coconut milk.

More exotic traditional foods include *gibnut* or *paca*, a small brown-spotted rodent similar to a guinea pig. Armadillo and venison are served also, but their value is more as a curiosity than as a staple of the diet.

Belikin beer is the cheapest, most popular local brew. Belikin Export, the premium version, comes in a larger bottle, is much tastier, costs more, and is worth it.

Getting There & Away

AIR

American Airlines, Continental, TACA and TAN-SAHSA serve Belize City from North America. Most routes – both North American and European – connect through Miami or New Orleans. Fares are surprisingly high, about US$250 round-trip (return) from Miami, US$500 or more from any other point.

LAND

For information on reaching Belize by land from the USA, see the beginning of this book, and also Getting There in the Guatemala chapter.

Bus

For information on buses from Flores (and Tikal) in Guatemala, see that section in the Guatemala chapter.

To/From Chetumal, Mexico There are two lines, Venus Bus Line and Batty's Bus Service, with ticket offices right in the Chetumal bus station, and very frequent service. Note that departures are from near the corner of Calle Mahatma Gandhi and Avenida de los Héroes, however, not from the bus terminal.

Other companies run between Belize City and Benque Viejo del Carmen on the Guatemalan border, connecting with Guatemalan buses headed for Flores (near Tikal). Some of these lines arrange connections so that you can travel between Flores and Chetumal directly, with only brief stops to change buses.

Belize City, 160 km, four hours (express 3¼ hours); Venus has buses every hour on the hour from 4 am to 10 am for US$3.50; Batty's has buses every two hours on the hour from 4 am to 6 pm for the same price. The one express bus departs Chetumal at 2 pm.

Corozal (Belize), 30 km, one hour with border formalities; see Belize City schedule, or catch a minibus for the 12-km ride to the border at Subteniente López. Minibus departure and arrival point in Chetumal is the intersection of Primo de Verdad and Hidalgo, two blocks east of Héroes (four blocks north-east of the market).

Driving

Liability insurance is required in Belize, and you must have it for the customs officer to approve the temporary importation of your car. It can be bought at booths just across the border in Belize for about US$1 per day; the booths are closed on Sunday.

Getting Around

AIR

There are two main domestic air routes which the small planes follow from Belize City: Belize City-Caye Chapel-Caye

Caulker-San Pedro-Corozal and return along the reverse route; and Belize City-Dangriga-Placencia/Big Creek-Punta Gorda and return along the reverse route.

The following are the main Belizean airline companies:

Tropic Air, PO Box 20, San Pedro, Ambergris Caye, is the largest and most active of Belize's small airlines (☎ (26) 2012; fax (26) 2338).

Maya Airways, 6 Fort St (PO Box 458), Belize City, has a similar schedule of flights to points in Belize (☎ (2) 77215; fax 30585).

Island Air flies between Belize City and San Pedro via Caye Chapel and Caye Caulker (☎ (2) 31140 in Belize City, (26) 2435 in San Pedro, Ambergris Caye).

Aerovías, the Guatemalan regional airline, operates several flights per week between Belize City's Goldson Airport and Flores (near Tikal) in Guatemala (US$50 one way), with onward connections to Guatemala City (☎ (2) 75445).

BUS

Belizean buses are usually used US school buses running on marketeers' schedules. Fares are higher than in Guatemala. Outside routes connecting the major towns, trucks willing to take on passengers connect some remote sites, travelling on rough roads.

SEA

Fast motor launches connect Belize City, Caye Caulker and Ambergris Caye several times daily. See the Belize City section for details. There is a twice-weekly boat service connecting Punta Gorda, in southern Belize, with Puerto Barrios in Guatemala. Details are in the Punta Gorda section.

Belize City

Population 80,000
Ramshackle, funky, fascinating, daunting, homely – these are only a few of the words that can be used to describe the country's biggest city and former capital. The tropical storms which periodically razed the town in the 19th and early 20th centuries still arrive to do damage to its ageing wooden buildings,

but they also flush out the open drainage canals, redolent with pollution, which criss-cross the town. When there's no storm, Belize City bustles and swelters.

Orientation

Haulover Creek, a branch of the Belize River, runs through the middle of the city, separating the commercial centre (Albert, Regent, King and Orange Sts) from the slightly more genteel residential and hotel district of Fort George to the north-east.

Albert St in the centre and Queen St in the Fort George and King's Park neighbourhoods are joined by the Swing Bridge across Haulover Creek.

Each of Belize's bus companies has its own terminal. Most are near the Collett Canal, off Cemetery Rd. See Getting There & Away for details.

Information

Tourist Office The Belize Tourist Board (☎ (02) 77213, 73255), 83 North Front St (PO Box 325), just a few steps south of the post office, is open from 8 am to noon and 1 to 5 pm Monday to Thursday and until 4.30 pm on Friday; it's closed on weekends.

Money The Bank of Nova Scotia (☎ (02) 77027/8/9), on Albert St, is open Monday to Friday from 8 am to 1 pm and Friday afternoon from 3 to 6 pm.

The Atlantic Bank Limited (☎ (02) 77124), 6 Albert St, is open Monday, Tuesday and Thursday from 8 am to noon and 1 to 3 pm, Wednesday from 8 am to 1 pm and Friday from 8 am to 1 pm and from 3 to 6 pm.

Also on Albert St is the prominent Belize Bank (☎ (02) 77132/3/4/5), 60 Market Square (facing the Swing Bridge), and Barclay's Bank (☎ (02) 77211), 21 Albert St.

Post & Telecommunications The main post office is at the northern end of the Swing Bridge, at the intersection of Queen and North Front Sts. Hours are 8 am to noon and 1 to 5 pm daily. If you want to pick up mail at the American Express office, it's at Belize

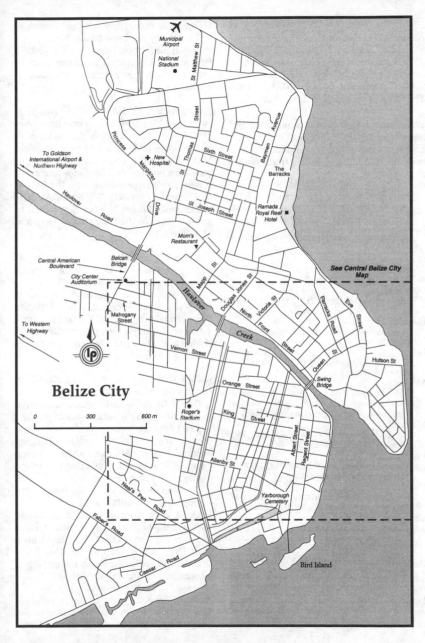

BELIZE

Belize City

Global Travel Service (☎ (02) 77363/4), 41 Albert St (PO Box 244).

Belize Telecommunications Limited (BTL for short; ☎ (02) 77085), 1 Church St, runs all of Belize's telephones. They have a public fax machine (☎ (02) 45211) as well. The office is open daily 8 am to 9 pm.

Embassies & Consulates Some embassies are in Belmopan, Belize's official capital. Embassies and consulates in Belize City tend to be open Monday to Friday from about 9 am to noon.

Canada
    Canadian Consulate (☎ (2) 31060), 83 North Front St, Belize City
France
    Honorary Consul (☎ (2) 32708), 9 Barracks Rd, Belize City
Germany
    Honorary Consul (☎ (2) 73343), 123 Albert St, Belize City
Guatemala
    Guatemalan Embassy (☎ (25) 2634, 2612), Mile 6, Northern Highway, Ladyville
Honduras
    Honduran Consulate (☎ (2) 45889), 91 North Front St, Belize City
Italy
    Consular Representative (☎ (2) 73086), 18 Albert St, Belize City
Mexico
    Mexican Embassy (☎ (2) 30193/4), 20 North Park St, Belize City (Note: the new Mexican Embassy is under construction in Belmopan)
Nicaragua
    Honorary Consul (☎ (2) 44232), Mile 2½, Northern Highway, Belize City
Panama
    Panamanian Consulate (☎ (2) 44941), 5481 Princess Margaret Drive, Belize City
UK
    British High Commission (☎ (8) 22146/7), 34-36 Half Moon Ave, Roseapple St, Belmopan
USA
    United States Embassy (☎ (2) 77161), 29 Gabourel Lane, Belize City

Bookshops The Book Center (☎ (02) 77457), 114 North Front St, just a few steps north-west of the Swing Bridge, has English-language books, magazines and greeting cards. Hours are Monday to Friday 8 am to noon, 1 to 5 and 7 to 9 pm; Saturday hours are the same except they're closed from 4.30 to 7 pm.; they're closed all day Sunday.

The Belize Book Shop (☎ (02) 72054), Regent St and Rectory Lane, across from the Mopan Hotel, has a smaller selection of books.

Emergency The Belize City Hospital (☎ (02) 77251) is on Eve St near the corner of Craig St in the northern part of town. A new, modern hospital is under construction. Many Belizeans with medical problems travel to Chetumal or Mérida for treatment. A new, modern, private clinic is the Clinica de Chetumal (☎ (983) 26508), on Avenida Juárez near the city's other hospitals. For serious illnesses, Belizeans fly to Houston, Miami or New Orleans.

Laundry Try the Belize Laundromat (☎ (02) 31117), 7 Craig St near Marin's Travel Lodge, open Monday to Saturday from 8 am to 5.15 pm, closed Sunday. A wash costs US$5 per load, detergent, fabric softener, bleach and drying included. A similar establishment is Carry's Laundry, situated at 41 Hyde Lane. It's open Monday to Saturday from 8 am to 5.30 pm.

Safety There is petty crime in Belize City, so follow some commonsense rules:

Don't flash wads of cash, expensive camera equipment or other signs of wealth.

Don't change money on the street, not because it's illegal, but because changing money forces you to expose where you keep your cash. Muggers will offer to change money, then just grab your cash and run off.

Don't leave valuables in your hotel room.

Don't use or deal in illicit drugs.

Don't walk alone at night. It's better to walk in pairs or groups and to stick to major streets in the centre, Fort George and King's Park. Especially avoid walking along Front St south and east of the swing Bridge; this is a favourite area for muggers.

Walking Tour
City Centre Start at the Swing Bridge and walk along Regent St, one block inland from

the shore. The large, modern **Commercial Center** to the left just off the Swing Bridge replaced a ramshackle market dating from 1820. The ground floor holds a food market; offices and shops are above.

As you start down Regent St, you can't miss the prominent **Court House** built in 1926 to be the headquarters of Belize's colonial administrators. It still serves its administrative and judicial functions.

Battlefield Park is on the right just past the Court House. Always busy with vendors, loungers, con men and other slice-of-life segments of Belize City society, it offers welcome shade in the sweltering midday heat.

Turn left just past the Court House and walk one block to the waterfront street, called Southern Foreshore, to find the **Bliss Institute**. Baron Bliss was an Englishman with a happy name and a Portuguese title who came to Belize on his yacht to fish. He seems to have fallen in love with Belize without ever having set foot on shore. When he died – not too long after his arrival – he left the bulk of his wealth in trust to the people of Belize. Income from the trust has paid for roads, market buildings, schools, cultural centres and many other worthwhile projects over the years.

The **Bliss Institute** (☎ (02) 77267) is open Monday to Friday from 8.30 am to noon and from 2 to 8 pm, and on Saturday from 8 am to noon; closed Sunday. Belize City's prime cultural institution, it is home to the **National Arts Council**, which stages periodic exhibits, concerts and theatrical works. There's a small display of artefacts from the Maya archaeological site at Caracol and, upstairs, the National Library.

Continue walking south along Southern Foreshore to the end to reach **Government House** (1814), the former residence of the governor-general. Belize attained independence within the British Commonwealth in 1981, and since that time the job has been purely ceremonial.

Down beyond Government House is **Bird Island**, a recreation area accessible only on foot. A sign above the gateway declares that it offers 'entertainment for all except trouble-makers'.

Inland from Government House, at the corner of Albert and Regent Sts, is **St John's Cathedral**, the oldest and most important Anglican church in Central America, dating from 1847.

A block south-west of the cathedral is **Yarborough Cemetery**, with gravestones outlining the turbulent history of Belize back to 1781.

Walk back to the Swing Bridge northward along Albert St; it is the main commercial thoroughfare.

Northern Neighbourhoods Cross the Swing Bridge heading north and you'll come face-to-face with the wood-frame **Paslow Building**, which houses the city's main post office. Go straight along Queen St to see the city's quaint wooden police station and, eventually, the US Embassy, in a' neighbourhood with some pretty Victorian houses.

Make your way to the southern tip of the peninsula. You pass through the luxury hotel district and emerge at the Baron Bliss Memorial, next to the **Fort George lighthouse**. There's a small park here and a good view of the water and the city.

Walk north around the point, pass the Radisson Fort George Hotel on your left and walk up Marine Parade to **Memorial Park**, next to the Chateau Caribbean hotel and the Mexican Embassy. The park's patch of green lawn is a welcome sight.

Places to Stay

The cheapest hotels in Belize City are often not safe because of break-ins and drug dealing. I've chosen the places below for relative safety as well as price.

Best all round, and often full, is the six-room *Sea Side Guest House* (☎ (2) 78339), 3 Prince St, on the upper floor, between Southern Foreshore and Regent St. Bunks in shared rooms cost US$9, US$14/19 for a single/double. Meals are good; book in advance.

BELIZE

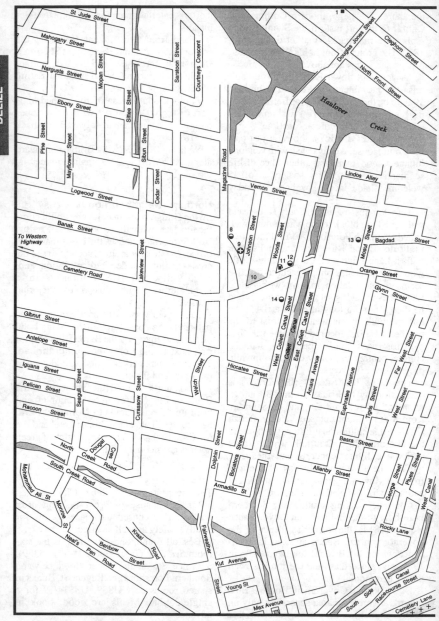

BELIZE

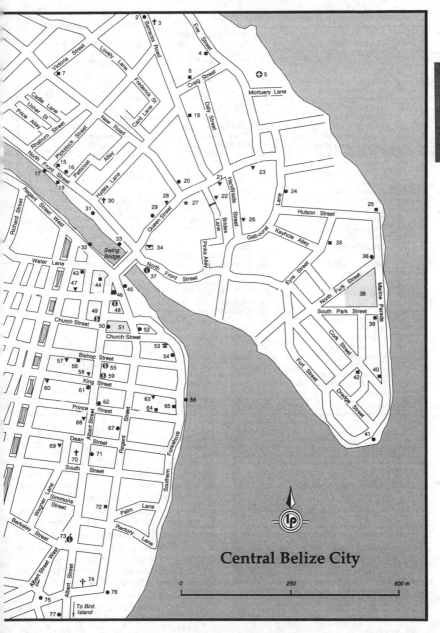

Central Belize City

0   250   500 m

■ PLACES TO STAY

1 Bakadeer Inn
4 Freddie's Guest House
6 Marin's Travelodge
7 Royal Orchid Hotel
15 North Front Street Guest House
16 Bon Aventure Hotel
17 Mira Rio Hotel
18 Riverside Hotel
19 Glenthorne Manor
25 Belize Guest House
35 Eyre Street Guest House
39 Chateau Caribbean Hotel
40 Radisson Fort George Hotel
42 Colton House
43 Bliss Hotel
44 Isabel Guest House
56 Hotel El Centro
64 Sea Side Guest House
65 Bellevue Hotel
72 Hotel Mopan

▼ PLACES TO EAT

21 Kee's Bakery
22 Golden Dragon Restaurant
23 Pete's Pastries
26 Pearl's Pizzería
28 Celebrations
40 Radisson Fort George Restaurant
47 Holiday Ice Cream Parlour
57 Macy's
58 Bluebird Ice Cream Parlour
60 Dit's Restaurant
63 GG's Café & Patio
68 Pete's Pastries
69 New Horizon Restaurant

OTHER

1 Bike Belize
2 Clock Tower
3 Methodist Church
5 Old Belize City Hospital
8 Venus & Z-Line Bus Station
9 Matron Roberts Health Centre
10 Constitution Park
11 Esso Fuel Station
12 Urbina's Bus Stop
13 Batty Brothers Bus Station
14 Novelo's Bus Station
20 American Airlines & TAN-SAHSA
24 US Embassy
27 Police Headquarters
29 Upstairs Café
30 Catholic Church
31 Boats to Caye Caulker & Ambergris Caye
32 Thunderbolt & Libra Express (Boats to Caye Caulker & Ambergris Caye)
33 Triple J Boat Dock
34 Post Office (Paslow Building)
36 Mexican Embassy
37 Belize Tourist Board & Canadian Consulate
38 Memorial Park
41 Baron Bliss Memorial
45 Commercial Centre
46 Market Square
48 Belize Bank
49 Barclays Bank
50 Taxi Stand
51 Battlefield Park
52 Court House
53 Belize Telecommunications Ltd Telephone Office
54 Bliss Institute
55 Bank of Nova Scotia
59 Atlantic Bank
61 Belize Global Travel Service
62 Italian Consular Agency
66 Andrea Boat to Ambergris Caye
67 Belize Air Travel Service
70 Methodist Church
71 Continental Airlines
73 Belize Tourism Industry Association
74 St John's Cathedral
75 Playground
76 Government House
77 German Consulate

Isabel Guest House (☎ (2) 73139), PO Box 362, is above Matus Store overlooking Market Square, but is entered by a stairway at the back: walk around the Central Drug Store to the back and follow the signs. Clean and family-run, it offers double rooms with shower for US$22.

Eyre Street Guest House (☎ (2) 77724), 7 Eyre St, is simple and homey, with waterless rooms priced at US$14/22 a single/double, or US$32 with private shower.

Freddie's Guest House (☎ (2) 44396), 86 Eve St, is the tidiest guest house in Belize. Two rooms share one bath, US$19 a double; the room with private bath costs US$22.

North Front Street Guest House (☎ (2) 77595), 124 North Front St just east of Pickstock St, has seen better days, but is still a favourite of low-budget travellers despite the noisy street and nightclub nearby. Bathrooms are shared, and bunks in the eight rooms cost US$6 to US$7.50. Double rooms cost US$13. Breakfast and dinner are served if you order ahead. Check out the bulletin board.

There are other cheap hotels in this area, including the *Riverside Hotel* and the *Mira Rio Hotel* (☎ (2) 44970), 59 North Front St. The seven rooms here are slightly more expensive, but they come with sink and

toilet. The bar overlooks Haulover Creek.
Bon Aventure Hotel (☎ (2) 44248, 44134;
fax 31134), 122 North Front St, right next to
the North Front St Guest House, has nine
rooms at US$12 a double (shared bath) and
US$22 a double (private bath).

Marin's Travelodge (☎ (2) 45166), 6
Craig St, is a yellow wooden Caribbean
house with seven rooms for rent. Shared
showers are clean, and the rooms cost
US$6/8 a single/double.

Hotel Mopan (☎ (2) 73356, 77351; fax
75383), 55 Regent St, is a big old Caribbean-
style wood-frame place with very basic
rooms that are quite expensive for what you
get, but the ambience is pure Belize. Rooms
cost US$27/37/43 a single/double/triple
with fan, or US$37/48/51 with air-con.
Meals are served, and there's a congenial bar.

The *Colton House* (☎ (2) 44666), 9 Cork
St, near the Radisson Fort George Hotel, is a
gracious 60-year-old wooden colonial house
beautifully restored. The large, airy, cheerful
rooms cost US$32/37 a single/double with
shared bath, US$37/42 with private bath;
add US$5 for air conditioning. Morning
coffee is served, but no meals.

Glenthorne Manor (☎ (2) 44212), 27 Barracks Rd (PO Box 1278), is a nice Victorian
house with a small garden, high ceilings and
eclectic furnishings. There are only four
rooms, all rented with breakfast included:
US$32/42/47 for a triple. Get the suite with
its own verandah if it's available.

Bliss Hotel (☎ (2) 72552, 73310), 1 Water
Lane, doesn't look like much from the
outside, but the inside is better. It has 20
rooms, all with private baths, which can be
dark and musty, but are clean and usable.
There's also a little kidney-shaped swimming pool, and the family management is
good. Rates are US$27.50 a double with fan,
US$40 with air-con.

Places to Eat

Belize City is not noted for its cuisine, but
there is some decent food.

GG's Café & Patio (☎ 74378), 2-B King
St, may be the tidiest little eatery in the city.
Arched windows and a tiled floor give it a
modern feel, and the pretty patio to the left
of the café is the place to eat in good weather.
'The best hamburgers in town' cost less than
US$3 to US$4. Big plates of rice and beans
with beef, chicken or pork are just US$3.50.
GG's is open from 11.30 am to 2.30 pm and
5.30 to 9 pm (10 pm on Friday and Saturday)
and closed Sunday.

Pearl's Pizzeria, 13 Handyside St, serves
quite good pizza and cold Belikin beer for
US$6 or so. They'll pack pizza to take away.

Macy's (☎ 3419), 18 Bishop St, has consistently good Caribbean Creole cooking,
friendly service, and decent prices. Fish fillet
with rice and beans costs about US$4, arma-
dillo or wild boar a bit more. Hours are 11.30
am to 10 pm, closed Sunday.

Dit's Restaurant (☎ 33330), 50 King St, is
a homey place with powerful fans and a loyal
local clientele who come for huge portions
and low prices. Rice and beans with beef,
pork or chicken costs US$3, and burgers are
half that. Cakes and pies make a good dessert
at US$1 per slice. Dit's is open from 8 am to
9 pm every day.

Ice cream parlours serving sandwiches
and hamburgers are also good places for
cheap meals. The menu may be limited, but
the prices are usually good and the surroundings pleasant.

Bluebird Ice Cream Parlour (☎ 73918),
35 Albert St, facing the Atlantic Bank, is a
very popular place in the commercial centre
of town. Besides ice cream there are sandwiches and burgers (US$1 to US$2), and
fried chicken for twice as much.

Celebrations (☎ 45789), 16 Queen St, not
far beyond the post office on the opposite
side of the street, is a clean, cheerful and
convenient ice cream parlour serving rice
and beans for US$2, sandwiches for US$1
and ice cream sundaes for just slightly more.

Pete's Pastries (☎ 44974), 41 Queen St
near Handyside St, serves good cakes, tarts,
and pies of fruit or meat. A slice and a soft
drink costs US$1; my favourite is the raisin
pie. You might try Pete's famous cowfoot
soup, served on Saturday only, for US$1.50;
or a ham and cheese sandwich for US$1.
Pete's is open 8.30 am to 7 pm (8 am to 6 pm

212 Belize – Belize City

Sunday). There's another shop at 71 Albert St, near Dean St, in the centre of town.

Kee's Bakery, 53 Queen St at Barracks Rd, is where all Belize City buys its fresh bread and rolls.

Mom's Restaurant, a Belize City institution for many years, has moved to a new location at 7145 Slaughter House Rd, near the Technical College.

Entertainment
There's lots of interesting action at night in Belize City, but most of it is illegal. Clubs and bars that look like dives probably are. If drugs are in evidence, clear out quick.

Clubs The Upstairs Café on Queen St a half block north-east of the Swing Bridge has cheap beer and is often fun, though on some evenings it gets rowdy. The lounges at the upscale hotels – Radisson Fort George, Ramada Royal Reef – are sedate, respectable and safe. The Belize Biltmore Plaza Hotel, 4.5 km from the centre on the Northern Highway, has karaoke many nights, live music on others. The club called The Big Apple, across from the North Front Street Guest House two blocks north-west of the Swing Bridge, has been here for years. The action depends upon the crowd, of course.

Getting There & Away
Air Belize City has two airports. Philip S W Goldson International Airport (BZE), at Ladyville, 16 km north-west of the centre, handles all international flights. The Municipal Airport (TZA) is 2.5 km north of the city centre, on the shore. Most local flights will stop and pick you up at either airport, but fares are almost always lower from Municipal, so if you have a choice use that one.

International airlines serving Belize City have offices at Goldson; some have offices or agents in the centre of town as well.

American Airlines (☎ (2) 32522/3/4/5/6; fax 31730), is at the corner of New Rd and Queen St
Continental (☎ (2) 78309, 78463; fax 78114)); is at 32 Albert St between Dean and South
SAHSA (☎ (2) 77080, 72057; fax 30795), the Hon-

duran airline, is at the corner of New Rd and Queen St
TACA (☎ (2) 77363, 77185; fax 75213), the Costa Rican airline, is at 41 Albert St (Belize Global Travel)

Bus Each major bus company has its own terminals. Belize City's bus terminals are near the Collett Canal. This is a rundown area not good for walking at night. Take a taxi.

Batty Brothers Bus Service (☎ (2) 77146), 54 East Collett Canal, operates buses along the Northern Highway to Orange Walk, Corozal and Chetumal (Mexico).
Venus Bus Lines (☎ (2) 73354, 77390), Magazine Rd, operates buses along routes similar to those of Batty Brothers.
Urbina's Bus Service runs between Belize City and Chetumal via Orange Walk and Corozal.
Escalante's Bus Service runs between Belize City and Chetumal via Orange Walk and Corozal.
Novelo's Bus Service (☎ (2) 77372), 19 West Collett Canal, is the line to take to Belmopan, San Ignacio, Xunantunich, Benque Viejo and the Guatemalan border at Melchor de Mencos.
Z-Line Bus Service (☎ (2) 73937) runs buses south to Dangriga, Big Creek (for Placencia) and Punta Gorda, operating from the Venus Bus Lines terminal on Magazine Rd in Belize City.

Pilferage of luggage is a problem, particularly on the Punta Gorda route. Give your luggage only to the bus driver or conductor, and watch as it is stored. Be there when the bus is unloaded to retrieve your luggage at once.

Here are the details on buses from Belize City to major destinations:

Belmopan – 84 km, 1½ hours, US$2; see Benque Viejo
Benque Viejo – 131 km, four hours, US$3; Novelo's operates buses from Belize City to Belmopan, San Ignacio and Benque Viejo every hour on the hour daily from 11 am to 7 pm (noon to 5 pm on Sunday). Batty Bros operates six morning buses westward between 5 and 10.15 am. Several of these go all the way to Melchor de Mencos in Guatemala. Returning from Benque/Melchor, buses to San Ignacio, Belmopan and Belize City start at 6 am and the last bus leaves at 3.30 pm.
Chetumal (Mexico) – 160 km, four hours (express 3¼ hours), US$5; Venus has buses departing from Belize City every hour on the hour from

noon to 7 pm; departures from Chetumal are hourly from 4 to 10 am. Batty's has buses every two hours on the hour for the same price. Urbina's and Escalante's also have frequent services.

Corozal – 155 km, 3½ hours, US$4; virtually all Batty's and Venus buses to and from Chetumal stop in Corozal, and there are several additional buses. There are frequent southbound buses in the morning but few in the afternoon; almost all northbound buses depart from Belize City in the afternoon.

Dangriga – 170 km, five hours, US$5.50; Z-Line has five buses daily (four on Sunday).

Flores (Guatemala) – 235 km, five hours, US$20; a minibus departs the Texaco station on North Front St near the north-east end of the Swing Bridge at 10 am for Flores. Some boats from the cayes can get you back to Belize City in time to catch it. Otherwise, take a bus to Melchor de Mencos (see Benque Viejo), and transfer to a Guatemalan bus.

Independence – 242 km, seven hours, US$7; buses bound for Punta Gorda stop at Independence, from whence you may be able to find a boat over to Placencia; but the boats can be expensive or difficult to find; the shuttle bus from Dangriga direct to Placencia along the peninsula is cheaper and more dependable.

Placencia – 260 km, eight hours, US$9; take a Z-Line bus to Dangriga, then the shuttle bus from The Hub guest house (Monday, Wednesday, Friday and Saturday at 2 pm) to Placencia.

Melchor de Mencos (Guatemala) – 135 km, 4¼ hours, US$3; see Benque Viejo

Orange Walk – 94 km, two hours, US$3; same schedule as Chetumal

Punta Gorda – 339 km, eight hours, US$8; Z-Line has two buses daily at 8 am and 3 pm. Return buses from Punta Gorda via Independence to Belize City depart at 5 and 11 am.

San Ignacio – 116 km, three hours, US$2.75; see Benque Viejo

Boat Fast motor launches zoom between Belize City and the cayes – particularly Caye Caulker – every day. Launches tie up by the A & R Texaco fuel station on North Front St, two blocks north-west of the Swing Bridge. Most boats leave Belize City between 8 and 10 am, and stop at Caye Chapel on the way to Caye Caulker; a few go on to San Pedro on Ambergris Caye. After 10 am, outbound boats are more difficult to find. It is preferable to take a morning boat, as these are the ones in better condition.

The fare for the voyage to Caye Caulker is usually US$8 to US$10 one way, but may be a bit higher depending upon the craft, the season, the number of people, or any of a dozen other factors. The trip against the wind takes from 40 minutes to one hour, depending upon the speed of the boat. Ask the price before you board the boat, and don't pay until you're safely off the boat at your destination.

Across Haulover Creek from the Texaco station, just west of the Swing Bridge on Regent St West, is the dock for the Thunderbolt Express and Libra Express boats (☎ in San Pedro (026) 2217, 2159) which make the run between San Pedro on Ambergris Caye and Belize City, stopping at Caye Caulker and Caye Chapel along the way.

Triple J ties up right at the north-eastern end of the Swing Bridge. It departs Belize City at 9 am for the trip to San Pedro (Ambergris), and departs San Pedro for Belize City at 3 pm.

Andrea I and *Andrea II* (☎ (2) 74988) departs from Belize City from Southern Foreshore by the Bellevue Hotel for San Pedro, Ambergris Caye (☎ (26) 2578), Monday to Friday at 4 pm (1 pm on Saturday, no boat on Sunday); the return trip to Belize City leaves San Pedro at 7 am. Fare is US$14 one way, US$20 round trip, and the voyage takes 1¼ to 1½ hours.

Getting Around
To/From the International Airport An airport shuttle service (☎ (2) 34367, 73977) operates between Goldson International Airport and Belize City daily, departing the airport at 6 and 8 am, noon, 4 and 6 pm, and stopping at Pallotti High School, the corner of Central American Boulevard and Vernon St, the corner of Central American Boulevard and Cemetery Rd, and Pound Yard Bridge near all the city's bus terminals. One way fare is US$2.50.

Shuttles run from Belize City to the airport at 5.30, 7.15 and 11.15 am and 3.30 and 5.30 pm.

It takes about 30 minutes to walk from the air terminal three km out along the access road to the Northern Highway, from whence it's easy to catch a bus going either north or south.

Taxi Trips by taxi within Belize City cost US$2.50 for one person, US$0.50 for each extra person. The taxi fare to or from the international airport is US$15.

Going to Municipal Airport, normal city taxi fares apply: US$2.50 for one person.

The Cayes

Belize's 290-km-long barrier reef, the longest in the western hemisphere, is the eastern edge of the limestone shelf which underlies most of Yucatán. To the west of the reef the water is very shallow – usually not much more than four or five metres deep – which allows numerous islands called cayes (pronounced 'keys') to bask in warm waters.

Of the dozens of cayes, large and small, which dot the blue waters of the Caribbean off the Belizean coast, the two most popular with travellers are Caye Caulker and Ambergris Caye. Caulker is commonly thought of as the low-budget island, where hotels and restaurants are considerably less expensive than on resort-conscious Ambergris.

CAYE CAULKER
Population 800
Caye Caulker lies about 33 km north of Belize City and 24 km south of Ambergris Caye. The island is about seven km long north to south, and only about 600 metres wide at its widest point. Mangroves cover much of the shore, coconut palms provide shade. The village is on the southern portion of the island. Actually Caulker is now two islands, ever since Hurricane Hattie cut the island in two just north of the village. The cut is called, simply, The Cut. It marks the northern limits of the settlement.

Orientation
The village has two principal streets, Front St to the east and Back St to the west. The distance from The Cut in the north to the cabañas at the southern edge of the village is a little more than one km.

The Belize Telecommunications telephone office is open from 8 am to noon and 1 to 4 pm, Monday to Friday, 8 am to noon on Saturday, closed Sunday.

Water Sports
The surf breaks on the barrier reef, easily visible from the eastern shore of Caye Caulker. Don't attempt to swim out to it, however. The local boaters speed their powerful craft through these waters and are completely heedless of swimmers. Several foreign visitors have died from boat propeller injuries. Swim only in protected areas.

A short boat ride takes you out to the reef to enjoy some of the world's most exciting snorkelling, diving and fishing. Virtually all of the island residents are trustworthy boaters, but it's still good to discuss price, duration, areas to be visited, and the seaworthiness of the boat. The cost is usually around US$10 to US$13 per person; sometimes lunch is included.

Underwater visibility is up to 60 metres. The variety of underwater plants, coral and tropical fish is wonderful. Be careful not to touch the coral, both to prevent damage to it and to yourself; coral is sharp, and some species sting or burn their assailants.

Beachgoers will find the water warm, clear and blue, but they won't find much in the way of beach. Though there's lots of sand, it doesn't seem to arrange itself in nice long, wide stretches along the shore. Most of your sunbathing will be on docks or in deck chairs at your hotel. Caulker's public beach, at The Cut to the north of the village, is tiny, crowded, and nothing special.

Places to Stay
A shady camping area adjoining the Vega Inn is just the place to pitch your tent, for US$6 per person.

Lena's Hotel (☎ (22) 2106) has 11 rooms in an old building right on the water, with no grounds to speak of. Rates are fairly good for

BELIZE

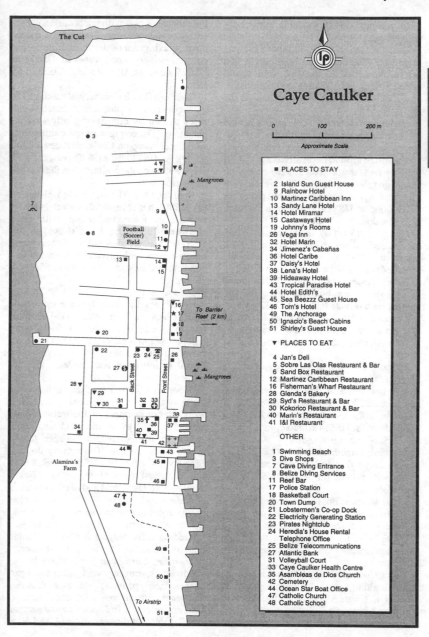

Caye Caulker

0   100   200 m

Approximate Scale

■ PLACES TO STAY

2 Island Sun Guest House
9 Rainbow Hotel
10 Martinez Caribbean Inn
13 Sandy Lane Hotel
14 Hotel Miramar
15 Castaways Hotel
19 Johnny's Rooms
26 Vega Inn
32 Hotel Marin
34 Jimenez's Cabañas
36 Hotel Caribe
37 Daisy's Hotel
38 Lena's Hotel
39 Hideaway Hotel
43 Tropical Paradise Hotel
44 Hotel Edith's
45 Sea Beezzz Guest House
46 Tom's Hotel
49 The Anchorage
50 Ignacio's Beach Cabins
51 Shirley's Guest House

▼ PLACES TO EAT

4 Jan's Deli
5 Sobre Las Olas Restaurant & Bar
6 Sand Box Restaurant
12 Martinez Caribbean Restaurant
16 Fisherman's Wharf Restaurant
28 Glenda's Bakery
29 Syd's Restaurant & Bar
30 Kokorico Restaurant & Bar
40 Marin's Restaurant
41 I&I Restaurant

OTHER

1 Swimming Beach
3 Dive Shops
7 Cave Diving Entrance
8 Belize Diving Services
11 Reef Bar
17 Police Station
18 Basketball Court
20 Town Dump
21 Lobstermen's Co-op Dock
22 Electricity Generating Station
23 Pirates Nightclub
24 Heredia's House Rental
    Telephone Office
25 Belize Telecommunications
27 Atlantic Bank
31 Volleyball Court
33 Caye Caulker Health Centre
35 Asambleas de Dios Church
42 Cemetery
44 Ocean Star Boat Office
47 Catholic Church
48 Catholic School

what you get: US$12 a double in the busy winter season.

Daisy's Hotel (☎ (22) 2123) has 11 rooms in several blue-and-white buildings which get full sun most of the day. Rooms with table or floor fans, sharing common baths, cost US$11 a double; with private shower the rate is US$18.

Hideaway Hotel (☎ (22) 2103), behind the Asambleas de Dios Church, is a hot two-storey cement-block building with six bare rooms on the ground floor; all have table fans (ceiling fans are preferable). No beach, no shade, no grounds, and the church rocks with up-tempo hymns some nights, but prices are fairly good at US$11 a double in summer, US$13 a double in winter.

Hotel Edith's is tidy and proper, with tiny rooms, each of which has a private shower, priced at US$15 a single, US$18 a double (one bed) or US$22 a double (two beds).

Hotel Miramar (☎ (22) 2157) has rooms on two floors in a building facing the sea. Rooms with private bath cost US$22.50.

Castaways (☎ (22) 2294) has six rooms that are quite clean, and cost a reasonable US$13 a double. There's a restaurant and bar as well.

Sylvano and Kathy Canto's *Island Sun Guest House* (☎ (22) 2215) has only two rooms, but both have fans and private baths, and cost US$30 or US$40 a double.

Johnny's Rooms (☎ (22) 2149) has clean hotel rooms for US$14 a double, and cabañas for US$26 with private bath.

Martinez Caribbean Inn (☎ (22) 2113) is a two-storey wood-and-masonry building of rooms with private showers for US$20/25 a single/double.

Hotel Marin is not on the shore but it has some trees and gardens. Prices are good: US$12 a double with common bath in summer, US$18 in winter; with private shower prices are US$22 in summer, US$28 in winter.

Tom's Hotel (☎ (22) 2102) has nice, tidy, white buildings with 20 rooms priced at US$10 a single, US$12 a double with common bathrooms.

Jimenez's Cabañas (☎ (22) 2175) has little thatched huts with walls of sticks, each with a private shower. The place is quaint, quiet, relaxing, atmospheric, family-run, and constitutes very good value at US$18 to US$25 a double, US$28 a triple, US$33 for four.

Ignacio's Beach Cabins, just south of The Anchorage, is a collection of thatched cottages shaded by dozens of gently swaying palm trees. The cottages are quite simple, but who needs more on Caulker? Rates are satisfying at US$12 to US$20 per hut, with private shower, depending upon the hut and the season.

Vega Inn (☎ (22) 2142; fax in Belize City (2) 31580), has several tidy waterless rooms upstairs in a wooden house, with clean showers down the hall; these go for US$20/24 a single/double. Other much bigger rooms with private showers are in a concrete building and cost US$45/55.

Places to Eat

Prices are not dirt cheap because much food must be brought from the mainland. Do your part to avoid illegal lobster fishing: don't order lobster off-season (mid-March to mid-July), and complain if they serve you a 'short' (a lobster below the legal size for harvest).

Sobre las Olas, north of the centre on the water, is a simple, tidy open-air place with a wooden dock, bar and umbrella-topped tables, as well as an indoor dining room across the road. Standard Belizean fare is served from 7 am to 10 pm every day but Monday. Expect to pay US$5 to US$8 for a full meal. Just to the north, the *Sand Box* is similar, with tasty food and decent prices.

Fisherman's Wharf Restaurant also has shady tables out by the water, and a 'breakfast nook' upstairs. Prices are low: burgers (including a fishburger) for US$2, Belikin beer for US$1.50. This is a popular place.

Martinez Caribbean Inn features lots of sandwiches, burgers and antojitos (garnaches, tacos, panuchos etc) as well as rice and beans with chicken or lobster. For breakfast, coffee and a fruit plate costs less than US$4. Lunch or dinner can cost US$3.50 to

US$8. They concoct a tasty rum punch that's sold by the bottle or the glass.

Marin's Restaurant, a block west of the Tropical Paradise, serves up fresh seafood in its outdoor garden and mosquito-proof screened dining room. Try the whole grilled catch-of-the-day for about US$5.

Nearby is the *I & I Restaurant* upstairs in a frame building with a dining deck overlooking the street. The reggae, playing constantly, sets the proper island mood. The food is a bit fancier than normal, and moderate in price.

Entertainment

After one evening on the island, you'll know what there is to do in the evening. The Reef Bar has a sand floor and tables holding clusters of bottles (mostly beer) as semi-permanent centrepieces. This is the locals' gathering, sipping and talking place.

Getting There & Away

See Getting There & Away in the Belize City section.

AMBERGRIS CAYE

Population 2000

The largest of Belize's cayes, Ambergris (pronounced am-BER-griss) lies 58 km north of Belize City. It's over 40 km long, and connected to Mexican land on its northern side. Most of the island's population lives in the town of San Pedro near the southern tip. The barrier reef is only one km east of San Pedro.

Like Caye Caulker, Ambergris has an engaging laid-back atmosphere. (A sign in a local restaurant has it right: 'No shirt, no shoes – *no problem!*') But the holiday condos are abuilding, and the island is even more expensive than Caulker.

Orientation

It's about one km from the Paradise Hotel in the northern part of town to the airport in the south, so everything is within easy walking distance.

San Pedro has three main north-south streets which used to be called Front St (to the east), Middle St and Back St (to the west). Now these streets have tourist-class names: Barrier Reef Drive, Pescador Drive and Angel Coral Drive, but some islanders might still use the old names.

Information

Money You can change money easily in San Pedro, but keep in mind that US dollars are accepted in many establishments.

Both the Atlantic Bank and the Belize Bank are near the Spindrift Hotel. The Atlantic Bank (☎ (026) 2195) is open Monday, Tuesday and Thursday from 8 am to noon and 1 to 3 pm; Wednesday 8 am to 1 pm; Friday 8 am to 1 pm and 3 to 6 pm; Saturday from 8.30 am to noon.

Belize Bank is open Monday to Thursday from 8 am to 3 pm, Friday 8 am to 1 pm and 3 to 6 pm, Saturday from 8.30 am to noon.

Post San Pedro's post office is on Buccaneer St between Barrier Reef and Pescador Drives. Hours are 8 am to noon and 1 to 5 pm (4.30 pm on Friday), closed Saturday and Sunday.

Telephone The Belize Telecommunications telephone office, up north on Pescador, is open Monday to Friday from 8 am to noon and 1 to 4 pm, Saturday from 8 am to noon; closed Sunday.

Water Sports

Ambergris is good for all water sports: scuba diving, snorkelling, sailboarding, boating, swimming, deep-sea fishing and sunbathing. Many island hotels have their own dive shops to rent equipment, provide instruction and organise diving excursions. Among the favourite seafaring destinations for diving and snorkelling are these:

Blue Hole, a deep sinkhole of vivid blue water where you can dive to 40 metres, observing the cave with diving lights

Caye Caulker North Island, the relatively uninhabited northern part of Caulker, with good snorkelling, swimming, and places for a beach barbecue

Glovers Reef, about 50 km east of Dangriga, is one of only three coral atolls in the western hemisphere;

BELIZE

BELIZE

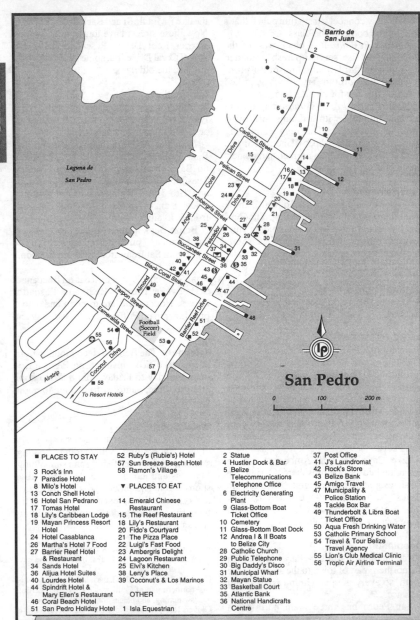

San Pedro

0   100   200 m

PLACES TO STAY

3 Rock's Inn
7 Paradise Hotel
8 Milo's Hotel
13 Conch Shell Hotel
16 Hotel San Pedrano
17 Tomas Hotel
19 Lily's Caribbean Lodge
19 Mayan Princess Resort
   Hotel
24 Hotel Casablanca
26 Martha's Hotel 7 Food
27 Barrier Reef Hotel
   & Restaurant
34 Sands Hotel
36 Alijua Hotel Suites
40 Lourdes Hotel
44 Spindrift Hotel &
   Mary Ellen's Restaurant
46 Coral Beach Hotel
51 San Pedro Holiday Hotel

52 Ruby's (Rubie's) Hotel
57 Sun Breeze Beach Hotel
58 Ramon's Village

PLACES TO EAT

14 Emerald Chinese
   Restaurant
15 The Reef Restaurant
18 Lily's Restaurant
20 Fido's Courtyard
21 The Pizza Place
22 Luigi's Fast Food
23 Ambergris Delight
24 Lagoon Restaurant
25 Elvi's Kitchen
38 Leny's Place
39 Coconut's & Los Marinos

OTHER

1 Isla Equestrian

2 Statue
4 Hustler Dock & Bar
5 Belize
  Telecommunications
  Telephone Office
6 Electricity Generating
  Plant
9 Glass-Bottom Boat
  Ticket Office
10 Cemetery
11 Glass-Bottom Boat Dock
12 Andrea I & II Boats
   to Belize City
28 Catholic Church
29 Public Telephone
30 Big Daddy's Disco
31 Municipal Wharf
32 Mayan Statue
35 Basketball Court
35 Atlantic Bank
36 National Handicrafts
   Centre

37 Post Office
41 J's Laundromat
42 Rock's Store
43 Belize Bank
45 Amigo Travel
47 Municipality &
   Police Station
48 Tackle Box Bar
49 Thunderbolt & Libra Boat
   Ticket Office
50 Aqua Fresh Drinking Water
53 Catholic Primary School
54 Travel & Tour Belize
   Travel Agency
55 Lion's Club Medical Clinic
56 Tropic Air Airline Terminal

the other two, Lighthouse Reef and the Turneffe Islands, are also in Belize

Half Moon Caye, a small island on Lighthouse Reef, 113 km east of Belize City, has a lighthouse, excellent beaches, and spectacular submerged walls teeming with marine flora and fauna. Underwater visibility can extend over 60 metres. The caye is a bird sanctuary and home to the rare Pink-footed Booby.

Hol Chan Marine Reserve, with submerged canyons 30 metres deep busy with large fish; the canyon walls are covered with colourful sponges

Lighthouse Reef, which includes Half Moon Caye, is one of three coral atolls in the western hemisphere, lying 100 km east of Belize City

Mexico Cave, filled with colourful sponges, lobsters and shrimp

Palmetto Reef, with lots of canyons, surge channels, and many varieties of coral (hard and soft) as well as sponges and fish

Punta Arena, an area of underwater canyons and sea caves teeming with fish, rays, turtles, sponges and coral

San Pedro Cut, the large break in the barrier reef used by the larger fishing and pleasure boats

Tres Cocos Cut, a natural break in the barrier reef which attracts a variety of marine life

Turneffe Islands, a large atoll 30 km east of Belize City teeming with coral and alive with fish and large rays

Glass-bottom boat tours are run by several companies. About the cheapest is the two-hour tour (9 to 11 am or 2 to 4 pm) for US$10. Buy your tickets in the house to the left of Milo's Hotel at the northern end of Barrier Reef Drive, and board the boat at the dock due east of there.

Swimming is best off the pier at the Paradise Hotel. All beaches are public and you can probably use their lounge chairs if it's a slow day.

Places to Stay

Milo's Hotel (☎ (26) 2033), PO Box 21, on Barrier Reef Drive, has nine small, dark, fairly dismal rooms above a shop in a blue-and-white Caribbean-style building. It's quiet, cheap, and often full for those reasons. Rooms using common showers go for US$8/11/14 a single/double/triple. Newer rooms with private shower and air-con are much more expensive.

Tomas Hotel (☎ (26) 2061), Barrier Reef

Drive, offers very good value for money. This family-run place charges US$21 (summer) or US$28 (winter) for eight light, airy double rooms with private baths (some with tubs).

Martha's Hotel (☎ (26) 2053), corner of Ambergris St and Pescador Drive, has 16 rooms. All have private bath. Rates are US$20 to US$28 a single, US$32 to US$38 a double, US$42 to US$48 a triple, US$55 for four; the higher prices apply during the busy winter season.

Ruby's (or Rubie's) Hotel (☎ (26) 2063; fax 2434), PO Box 56, at the south end of Barrier Reef Drive, is right on the water. Five of the nine rooms here have private showers. Rates are US$11/14 a single/double with common bath, US$29 to US$38 a double with bath.

Lourdes Hotel (☎ (26) 2066) on Pescador Drive is very plain and well used – no one would call it beautiful, few would call it pleasant but cheap at US$12/20 a single/double with private shower.

Places to Eat

Perhaps the first place you'll wander into is *Fido's Courtyard* on Barrier Reef Drive. Walk past The Pizza Place (see below) and you'll find several eating places, an art gallery and a travel agency around a shady deck area overlooking the sea. The bar serves drinks such as rum and Coke or beer for US$1.75. The *Island Grill*, open from 6 am to 6 pm (closed Wednesday), serves sandwiches, burgers, steaks and fish for prices ranging between US$5 and US$14.

The Pizza Place (☎ 2444) serves breakfast as well as pizzas (US$10 to US$17), sandwiches and ice cream concoctions. They'll deliver pizzas within San Pedro town.

Elvi's Kitchen (☎ 2176), on Pescador Drive near Ambergris St, is the old reliable here. A big plate of fish and chips is yours for US$7; rice and beans with fish for US$5. You can spend as little as US$1.75 for a ham and cheese sandwich.

Ambergris Delight, on Pescador Drive near Pelican St, serves fried chicken, burgers and pies as well as the inevitable rice and

BELIZE

beans, for low prices: it's inland, not on the beach. It's closed Wednesday.

Emerald Restaurant on Barrier Reef Drive is one of San Pedro's several Chinese restaurants, with a long menu and low prices. Filling Chinese platters cost US$4 to US$9; burgers are even cheaper at US$3. Food can be packed to take away. It's open every day. The other good Chinese restaurant is the *Jade Garden*, a five-minute walk south of Ramon's Village.

Luigi's Fast Food, across from the Hotel Casablanca on Pescador Drive, has cheap luncheon specials of rice and beans with chicken, fish or meat.

Barrier Reef Hotel on Barrier Reef Drive has a small restaurant on its ground floor specialising in pizza: nine, 12 and 16-inch pizzas priced from US$7.50 to US$17, depending upon ingredients. They also serve a few sandwiches, nachos and shrimp cocktails.

Mary Ellen's Little Italy Restaurant (☎ 2866), in the Spindrift Hotel, is a step up in comfort and quality, with indoor, patio and beachside dining. Spaghetti plates and Italian main courses cost US$5 to US$15; sandwiches are less. It's closed from 2 to 5.30 pm.

Entertainment
Sipping, sitting, talking and dancing are part of everyday life on Ambergris. Many hotels have comfortable bars, often with appropriate sand floors, thatched roofs and reggae music.

Tackle Box Bar, on a wharf at the eastern end of Black Coral Drive, is a San Pedro institution. Very popular with divers and boat owners, it's a good place to get the latest info on diving trips and conditions, boat rentals and excursions.

Fido's, on Barrier Reef Drive near Pelican St, always has a lively crowd in the evenings, sometimes playing bingo.

Big Daddy's, located right next to San Pedro's church, is the town's hot night spot, often featuring live reggae, especially during the winter.

To drink with the locals in a real cantina

at lower prices, head for Los Marinos, on the corner of Pescador Drive and Bucaneer St. Don't expect a beautiful place, expect a real Mexican-style cantina; women, therefore, may not find the atmosphere particularly welcoming or comfortable.

Getting There & Away
Air A one-way flight between San Pedro and Belize City's Municipal Airport costs US$30 to US$35. See Getting Around in the beginning of the Belize chapter.

Boat See Getting There & Away in the Belize City section.

Getting Around
San Pedranos get around on foot, by bicycle, dune buggy, golf cart and pick-up truck. A few huge slab-sided Ford station wagons act as taxis, charging US$2 for any trip in town. You can rent bicycles, motor bikes and golf carts at several locations.

Northern Belize

Low-lying, often swampy, cut by rivers and lagoons, northern Belize is farming country. Sugar cane is a major crop, but many farmers are branching out to different crops (including marijuana) rather than be held hostage to the fluctuations of the commodities markets. The shoreline in the north is often vague, a wide band of marshy land edged in dense mangrove.

The ancient Maya prospered in northern Belize, scooping up the rich soil and piling it on raised fields, and at the same time creating drainage canals.

BERMUDIAN LANDING COMMUNITY BABOON SANCTUARY
There are no real baboons in Belize, but locally the black howler monkey is given that name. Though there are howler monkeys throughout the Maya areas, the black howler, an endangered species, exists only in Belize, and like so much wildlife in the rapidly

developing Maya lands, its existence is threatened.

In 1985 a group of local farmers were organised to help preserve the black howler and to protect its habitat by harmonising its needs with their own. Care is taken to leave the forests along the banks of the Belize River where the black howler feeds, sleeps, and – at dawn and dusk – howls loudly and unmistakably. You can learn all about the black howler, and the other 200 kinds of animals and birds to be found in the Reserve, at the Visitors Center (☎ (2) 44405) in the village of Bermudian Landing.

You must tour the sanctuary with a guide, at US$3 per hour, US$11 per half day. For more information about the sanctuary, check with the Belize Audubon Society (☎ (2) 77369), 49 Southern Foreshore, Belize City.

Places to Stay & Eat
Camping is allowed at the visitors' centre for US$2. There are also simple rooms for US$12 a double, and simple, inexpensive meals.

Getting There & Away
Private buses leave Orange St in Belize City (one from the corner of Mussel St, the other the corner of George St) after lunch, Monday to Saturday, for the hour-long ride to Bermudian Landing. Departures from Bermudian Landing for Belize City are at 5.30 am, meaning that if you take the bus, you must plan to stay the night. The return fare is US$3.50.

ALTUN HA
Northern Belize's most famous Maya ruin is at Altun Ha, 55 km north of Belize City along the Old Northern Highway near the village of Rockstone Pond, 16 km south of Maskall.

The Old Northern Highway is narrow, potholed and broken in places, passing through jungle and the occasional hamlet. There is little transport. If you plan to hitch, start very early.

Altun Ha (Maya for Rockstone Pond) was undoubtedly a small (population about 3000) but rich and important Maya trading

town, with agriculture also playing an important role in its economy. Altun Ha had formed as a community by at least 600 BC, perhaps several centuries earlier, and the town flourished until the mysterious collapse of Classic Maya civilisation in around 900 AD. Most of the temples you see here date from Late Classic times, though burials indicate that Altun Ha's merchants were trading with Teotihuacán in Preclassic times.

Altun Ha is open daily from 9 am to 5 pm; admission costs US$1.50. There are toilets and a drinks shop at the site, but no accommodation.

Of the grass-covered temples arranged around the two plazas here, the largest and most important is the Temple of the Masonry Altars (Structure B-4), in Plaza B. The restored structure you see dates from the first half of the 7th century AD, and takes its name from altars on which copal resin was burnt and beautifully carved jade pieces were smashed in sacrifice. Excavation of the structure in 1968 revealed many burials of important officials. Most burials had been looted or desecrated, but two were intact. Among the jade objects found in one of these was a unique mask sculpture portraying Kinich Ahau, the Maya sun god, the largest known well-carved jade object from the Maya area.

In Plaza A, Structure A-1 is sometimes called the Temple of the Green Tomb. Deep within it was discovered the tomb of a priest/king dating from around 600 AD. Tropical humidity had destroyed the king's garments and the paper of the Maya 'painted book' which was buried with him, but many riches were intact: shell necklaces, pottery, pearls, stingray spines used in bloodletting rites, jade beads and pendants, and ceremonial flints.

CROOKED TREE WILDLIFE SANCTUARY
Midway between Belize City and Orange Walk Town, three km west of the Northern Highway, lies the fishing and farming village of Crooked Tree. In 1984 the Belize Audubon Society succeeded in having 12 sq

km around the village declared a wildlife sanctuary, principally because of the wealth of birdlife. Migrating birds flock to the rivers, swamps and lagoons here each year during the dry season (November to May – winter up north).

For details about the sanctuary, check with the Belize Audubon Society (☎ (2) 77369), 49 Southern Foreshore (PO Box 1001), Belize City.

Places to Stay & Eat
Bird's Eye View Lodge (☎ (2) 44101, PO Box 1976, Belize City), is located in Crooked Tree Village near the lagoon. Rooms cost US$60/75 a single/double, but they also have sites for camping.

Getting There & Away
Two buses run from Belize City to Crooked Tree daily; ask at the Belize Audubon Society, or the Batty or Venus bus stations, for current times. If you start early from Belize City, Corozal Town or Orange Walk Town, you can bus to Crooked Tree Junction and walk in to the village.

LAMANAI
By far the most impressive site in this part of the country is Lamanai, in its own archaeology reserve on the New River Lagoon near the settlement of Indian Church. Though much of the site remains unexcavated and unrestored, the trip to Lamanai, by motorboat up the New River, is an adventure in itself.

Figuring 90 minutes' boat travel each way, and somewhat over two hours at the site, the excursion to Lamanai takes most of a day.

History
As with most sites in northern Belize, Lamanai (Submerged Crocodile, the original Maya name of the place) was occupied as early as 1500 BC, with the first stone buildings appearing between 800 and 600 BC. Lamanai flourished in Late Preclassic times, growing to be a major ceremonial centre with immense temples long before most other Maya sites.

Unlike many other sites, Maya lived here until the coming of the Spaniards in the 16th century. The ruined Indian church (actually two of them) to be found nearby attests to the fact that there were Maya here for the Spanish friars to convert. Convert them they did, but by 1640 the Maya had reverted to their ancient forms of worship. British interests later built a sugar mill, now in ruins, at Indian Church. The archaeological site was excavated by David Pendergast in the 1970s and '80s.

New River Voyage
You motor for 90 minutes up the New River from the Tower Hill toll bridge south of Orange Walk, between river banks crowded with dense jungle vegetation. Along the way, your boatman/guide points out the many local birds and will almost certainly spot a crocodile or two. Along the way you pass the Mennonite community at Shipyard. Finally the river opens out into the New River Lagoon, a broad and very long expanse of water which can be choppy during the frequent rainshowers.

Touring Lamanai
Landing at Lamanai settlement (open from 9 am to 5 pm daily), you sign the visitor's book, pay the admission fee of US$1.50, and wander into the dense jungle, past gigantic guanacaste, ceiba and *ramón* (breadnut) trees, strangler figs, allspice, epiphytes and black orchids, Belize's national flower. In the canopy overhead one can sometimes see one of the five groups of howler monkeys resident in the archaeological zone.

A tour of the ruins takes 90 minutes minimum, more comfortably two or three hours.

Of the 60 significant structures identified here, the grandest is Structure N10-43, a huge Late Preclassic building rising more than 34 metres above the jungle canopy. Other buildings along La Ruta Maya are taller, but this one was built well before the others. It's been partially uncovered and restored.

Not far from N10-43 is Lamanai's ball court, a smallish one, partially uncovered.

To the north along a path in the jungle is Structure P9-56, built several centuries later, with a huge stylised mask of a man in a crocodile-mouth headdress four metres high emblazoned on its south-west face. Archaeologists have dug deep into this structure (from the platform level high on the east side) to explore for burials and to document the several earlier structures which lie beneath.

Near this structure is a small temple and a very fine ruined stela.

There is a small museum near the boat landing with quite interesting figurative pottery, and some large flint tools.

Places to Stay & Eat
Lamanai Outpost Lodge, a 15-minute walk south of the archaeological zone, has rooms for US$77/101 a single/double, but meals can be had for US$8 or so.

Getting There & Away
Lamanai can be reached by road (58 km) from Orange Walk via San Felipe except when heavy rains mire the road, but there is no regular bus service, and the bumpy road trip is just as long but not nearly so enjoyable as the river trip.

The main base for river departures is the Tower Hill toll bridge seven km south of Orange Walk on the Northern Highway. The Novelo brothers, Antonio and Herminio, run Jungle River Tours (☎ (3) 22293; fax 23749), 20 Lovers' Lane (PO Box 95), Orange Walk Town, and have excellent reputations as guides and naturalists. Contact them at the bridge, or at the Lovers' Café near the south-east corner of the central park in Orange Walk Town, or make a reservation by phone or fax. Be at their boat dock on the north-west side of the Tower Hill toll bridge by 9 am for the day-long trip (back by 4 pm), which includes lunch, beverages and the guided tour along the river and at Lamanai for US$50 per person (minimum of four persons).

The *Lamanai Lady* motorboat departs Jim's Cool Pool, just north of the toll bridge (by Novelo's), at 9 am daily (be there by 8.30 am) for the river tour to Lamanai. The boat ride and guided tour costs US$28 per person, a box lunch is another US$7. You can book your tour at the Batty's bus terminal in Belize City (☎ (2) 72025; fax 78991).

It's possible to take the 6 am Batty bus from Belize City to Orange Walk, get out at the Tower Hill toll bridge, and be in time for the 9 am departure of the boats for Lamanai. Boats return to the bridge before 4 pm, allowing you to catch the 4 pm Batty's bus southward back to Belize City. An entire tour from Belize City to Lamanai via the *Lamanai Lady*, and return to Belize City, costs US$52. Book at Batty's in Belize City.

ORANGE WALK
The agricultural and social centre of northern Belize is this town of some 10,000 people, 94 km north of Belize City. It's important to the farmers (including many Mennonites) who till the soil of the region, raising sugar cane and citrus fruits. Another important crop is said to be marijuana.

Orange Walk is not very important to visitors unless you're bound for one of the archaeological sites or wildlife reserves nearby, in which case its modest hotels and many Chinese restaurants are useful.

The centre of town is the shady central park on the east side of the main road, called Queen Victoria Ave. The town hospital is in the northern outskirts readily visible on the west side of the road.

Cuello & Nohmul Archaeological Sites
Near Orange Walk is Cuello, a Maya site with a 3000-year history, but little to show for it. Archaeologists have found plenty here, but you will find only a few grassy mounds. The site is on private property, that of the Cuello Brothers Distillery (☎ (3) 22141), four km west of Orange Walk along Yo Creek Rd. Call and ask for permission before you tramp around the site.

Nohmul, near the village of San Pablo (12 km north of Orange Walk), was a much more important site, with a lofty acropolis looming

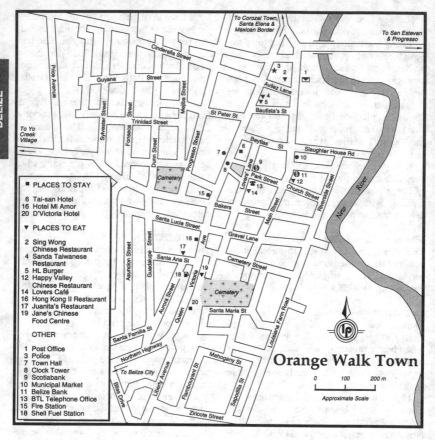

PLACES TO STAY

6 Tai-san Hotel
16 Hotel Mi Amor
20 D'Victoria Hotel

PLACES TO EAT

2 Sing Wong
    Chinese Restaurant
4 Sanda Taiwanese
    Restaurant
5 HL Burger
12 Happy Valley
    Chinese Restaurant
14 Lovers Café
16 Hong Kong II Restaurant
17 Juanita's Restaurant
19 Jane's Chinese
    Food Centre

OTHER

1 Post Office
3 Police
7 Town Hall
8 Clock Tower
9 Scotiabank
10 Municipal Market
11 Belize Bank
13 BTL Telephone Office
15 Fire Station
18 Shell Fuel Station

Orange Walk Town

0   100   200 m

Approximate Scale

over the surrounding countryside. Though a vast site, most of it is now covered in grass and sugar cane. To take a look at what there is, walk two km west of San Pablo. You may need a guide to find it.

Places to Stay

Hotel Mi Amor (☎ (3) 22031; fax 23462), 19 Queen Victoria Ave (PO Box 117), is perhaps the best choice: simple and clean, its rooms cost US$22 with one bed, US$30 with two, US$38 with air-con.

Tai-san Hotel (☎ (3) 22752), 30 Queen Victoria Ave, north of the plaza, is seven bathless rooms above a fairly noisy Chinese restaurant, each going for US$11 a single, US$15 a double.

Best in town is the *D'Victoria Hotel* (☎ (3) 22518; fax 22847), 40 Queen Victoria Ave (PO Box 74), which boasts a swimming pool and discotheque as well as guest rooms priced at US$22 to US$25 with private bath, US$38 to US$55 with air-con.

Places to Eat

Locals favour *Juanita's*, on Santa Ana St near the Shell fuel station, a simple place with local fare at low prices.

HL Burger, three blocks north of the park on the main road, has good cheap burgers (US$2), rice and bean plates and ice cream.

When it comes to Chinese restaurants, Orange Walk has them. *Happy Valley* on the corner of Church and Main Sts, and *Sing Wong* at the corner of Main and Avilez Sts are about the nicest, along with the *Sanda Taiwanese Restaurant* to the left of HL Burger. The *Hong Kong II* restaurant right next to the Hotel Mi Amor is favoured by locals. *Jane's Chinese Food Center* is about three blocks down the main street from it.

The Diner is also a favourite local place, located on the northern outskirts to the west of the hospital (follow the signs).

Getting There & Away
Southbound buses pass through town at least every hour (usually on the hour, and sometimes on the half-hour as well) from 4.30 am to about 12.30 pm, with a few later buses. Northbound buses pass through at 15 minutes before the hour from 1.45 pm to 8.45 pm. It's 61 km to Corozal Town (1½ hours, US$2), and 94 km to Belize City (two hours, US$2.50).

COROZAL TOWN
Corozal is a farming town of some 9000 people. Several decades ago the countryside was given over completely to sugar cane (there's a refinery south of the town). Today, though sugar is still important, crops are diversified. The land is fertile, the climate good for agriculture and the town is prosperous. Many of those who do not farm commute to Orange Walk or Belize City to work.

History
Corozal's Maya history is long and important. On the northern outskirts of the town are the ruins of a Maya ceremonial centre once called Chetumal, now called Santa Rita. Across the bay at Cerros is one of the most important Late Preclassic sites yet discovered. Maya have been living around Corozal since 1500 BC.

Modern Corozal Town dates from only 1849, however. In that year, refugees from the War of the Castes in Yucatán fled across the border to safe haven in British-controlled Belize. They founded a town, and named it after the cohune palm, a symbol of fertility. For years it had the look of a typical Caribbean town, but Hurricane Janet roared through in 1955 and blew away many of the old wooden buildings on stilts. Much of Corozal's cinder-block architecture dates from the late '50s.

Orientation
Though founded by Maya, Corozal resembles a Mexican town with its plaza, its Palacio Municipal and its large church. The bright chimes of the clock tower keep everyone on schedule. You can walk easily to anywhere in town.

The Belize Bank on the north side of the plaza is open for currency exchange Monday to Friday from 8 am to 1 pm, and also Friday afternoon from 3 to 6 pm.

Santa Rita Archaeological Site
A small, nicely kept park with one small restored Maya temple: that's Santa Rita, just over one km north-west of the Venus bus terminal in Corozal. Go north on the main highway; after 700 metres bear right, just before the statue; after another 100 metres turn left at the Restaurant Hennessy and go straight on for 300 metres to the site. The 'hill' on the right is actually a temple. The site is open during daylight hours and entry is free.

Called Chetumal by the Maya, this city sat astride important riverine trade routes, and had its share of wealth. The jade and pottery artefacts found here have been dispersed to museums, and the important frescoes destroyed.

Cerros Archaeological Site
There is more to see at Cerros (also called Cerro Maya) than at Santa Rita, namely a temple more than 20 metres high, but the site is mostly a mass of grass-covered mounds. Cerros flourished in Late Preclassic times, and has yielded important artefacts.

BELIZE

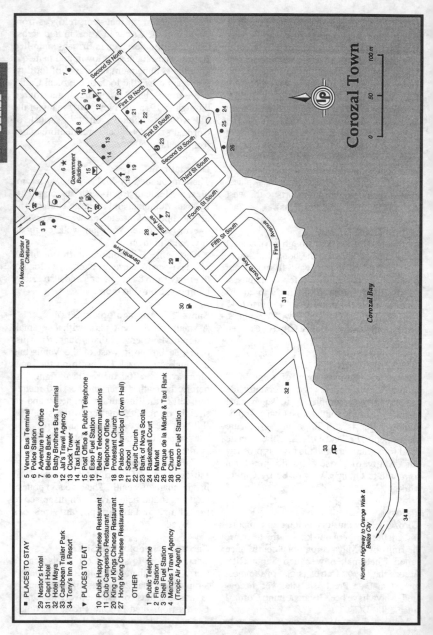

Corozal Town

PLACES TO STAY
29 Nestor's Hotel
31 Capri Hotel
32 Hotel Maya
33 Caribbean Trailer Park
34 Tony's Inn & Resort

PLACES TO EAT
10 Public Happy Chinese Restaurant
11 Club Campesino Restaurant
20 King of Kings Chinese Restaurant
27 Hong Kong Chinese Restaurant

OTHER
1 Public Telephone
2 Fire Station
3 Shell Fuel Station
4 Menzies Travel Agency
   (Tropic Air Agent)
5 Venus Bus Terminal
6 Police Station
7 Adventure Inn Office
8 Belize Bank
9 Batty Brothers Bus Terminal
12 Jal's Travel Agency
13 Clock Tower
14 Taxi Rank
15 Post Office & Public Telephone
16 Esso Fuel Station
17 Belize Telecommunications
   Telephone Office
18 Protestant Church
19 Palacio Municipal (Town Hall)
21 School
22 Jesuit Church
23 Bank of Nova Scotia
24 Basketball Court
25 Market
26 Parque de la Madre & Taxi Rank
28 Church
30 Texaco Fuel Station

Negotiate with a boat owner to ferry you from Corozal across Corozal Bay and back.

Places to Stay

Caribbean Trailer Park (☎ (4) 22045), PO Box 55, about 500 metres south of the plaza, has large swaths of lush grass shaded by coconut palms, usable toilets and mouldy showers, and all hook-ups. Rates are US$3.50 per person for a tent, US$7 in a camper van (RV). Talk to Jim or Donna, who live at the north end of the park.

Hotel Maya (☎ (4) 22082), PO Box 112, on 7th Ave (the main road) about 400 metres south of the plaza is somewhat dilapidated, but run by nice people. The 17 aged rooms are clean. Cheap meals are served in the adjoining eatery. Rates are a bit expensive at US$19 for a room with one double bed, US$24 with two beds; all have private showers.

Nestor's Hotel (☎ (4) 22354), 125 5th Ave South, used to be the budget travellers' favourite, but the bar downstairs is now patronised mostly by Corozal's cool youth who come to drink beer by the pitcher. Rooms are cheap at US$11 a single, US$14 to US$19 a double.

Capri Hotel (☎ (4) 22042), at the southern end of 4th Ave, has 30 small, fairly dingy rooms, some with private bath, priced a bit lower than Nestor's.

Places to Eat

The *Hotel Maya* has a serviceable restaurant, where sandwiches cost about US$2, burgers a bit more, and a full fried chicken dinner US$6. Otherwise, there are many small Chinese restaurants like the *Public Happy Restaurant* on the corner of 4th Ave and 2nd St North. Chow mein, chop suey, lobster or fish with rice, and many other items are listed on the menu. Portions cost US$1.75 to US$5, depending upon the ingredients and the size of the portion.

The *Club Campesino* has grilled meats, chicken and the like, but it doesn't open until 6.30 pm for dinner, drinks and late-night socialising.

Getting There & Away

Air Corozal Town has its own little airstrip (code: CZL) several km south of the centre, reached by taxi (US$4 – you can share the cost with other passengers). Tropic Air has two flights daily between Corozal Town and Ambergris Caye; the 20-minute flight costs US$30 one way.

Bus Venus Bus Lines (☎ (4) 22132) and Batty Brothers Bus Service operate frequent buses between Chetumal (Mexico) and Belize City, stopping at Corozal Town. Buses leave Corozal Town and head for Belize City at least every hour from 3.30 am to 11.30 am, with extra buses on the half-hour during busy times. From Belize City to Corozal, departures are on the hour between noon and 7 pm.

Belize City – 155 km, 3½ hours; many Venus & Batty
  Bros buses daily, US$4
Chetumal – 30 km, one hour with border formalities;
  many Venus & Batty Bros buses daily, US$1
Orange Walk – 61 km, 1½ hours; many Venus &
  Batty Bros buses daily, US$2

CROSSING THE BORDER

Corozal Town is 13 km south of the border-crossing point at Santa Elena/Subteniente López. Most of the Venus and Batty Brothers buses travelling between Chetumal and Belize City stop at Corozal Town. Otherwise, hitch a ride or hire an expensive taxi (US$12) to get you to Santa Elena. From Subteniente López, minibuses shuttle the 12 km to Chetumal frequently all day.

Santa Elena border station has the requisite government offices and one or two very basic restaurants, nothing more.

Western Belize

The bus departs Belize City heading westward along Cemetery Rd to reach the Western Highway. The road is paved and fairly good all the way to the Guatemalan border.

BELIZE

BELIZE ZOO

The Belize Zoo and Tropical Education Center (☎ (92) 3310), PO Box 474, Belize City, is home to a variety of indigenous Belizean cats and other animals kept in natural surroundings. The zoo's terrain, 46 km west of Belize City (Mile 29), hasn't been cleared; it's as if cages just appeared from nowhere and then paths were cleared for tourists. A sign marks the turning for the zoo, on the north side of the road; the entrance is less than one km off the highway. Hours are 9.30 am to 4 pm daily; admission costs US$5, and it goes to a worthy cause. The zoo is closed on major Belizean holidays.

In 1983, Ms Sharon Matola was in charge of 17 Belizean animals during the shooting of a wildlife film entitled *Path of the Raingods*. By the time filming was over, her animals were partly tame, and thus might not have survived well in the wild. With the movie budget exhausted, there were no funds to support the animals. So Ms Matola founded the Belize Zoo.

In 1991 the zoo was substantially enhanced with spacious natural enclosures for the inhabitants and a modern visitors centre.

The self-guided tour takes from 45 minutes to an hour. You'll see Baird's tapir, Belize's national animal, and the gibnut or paca (tepezcuintle). Jaguar, ocelot, howler monkey, peccary, vulture, stork, even a crocodile appear during the fascinating tour.

Getting There & Away

See Getting Around in the introduction to the Belize section for details on buses running along the Western Highway between Belize City and San Ignacio. Just ask to get out at the Belize Zoo. Look at your watch when you get out; the next bus will come by in about an hour.

GUANACASTE PARK

A few metres north of the junction of the Western and Hummingbird Highways is Guanacaste National Park. This small (21 hectare) nature reserve at the confluence of Roaring Creek and the Belize River holds one giant guanacaste tree which survived the axes of canoe makers and still rises majestically in its jungle habitat. The great tree supports a whole ecosystem of its own, festooned with bromeliads, epiphytes, ferns and dozens of other varieties of plants. Wild orchids flourish in the spongy soil among the ferns and mosses, and several species of 'exotic' animals pass through. Birdlife is abundant and colourful.

Admission is free (donations are accepted). The reserve is open every day from 8 am to 4.30 pm. Stop at the information booth to learn about the short nature trails in the park.

Just west of the highway junction across the bridge is the village of Roaring Creek, with several small restaurants.

BELMOPAN

In 1961, Hurricane Hattie all but destroyed Belize City, and the government resolved to build a new, modern capital city in a more central location, well away from hurricane danger.

Two decades after its founding, Belmopan has begun to come to life. Its population, now over 4000, is growing slowly, some embassies have moved here and when, inevitably, the next killer hurricane arrives, the new capital will no doubt get a population boost.

Orientation

The bus stops are near the post office, police station, the market and telephone office (see the Belmopan map). Unless you need to visit the British High Commission (☎ (08) 22146/7), 34/36 Half Moon Ave, or the US Embassy's Belmopan office (☎ (08) 22617), you'll probably only stay long enough to have a snack or a meal at one of the restaurants near the bus stops.

Things to See

There is one thing to do in Belmopan if you're excited about Maya ruins – examine the archaeological treasures preserved in the vault at the Archaeology Department (☎ (8) 22106). There is no museum yet, but if you

BELIZE

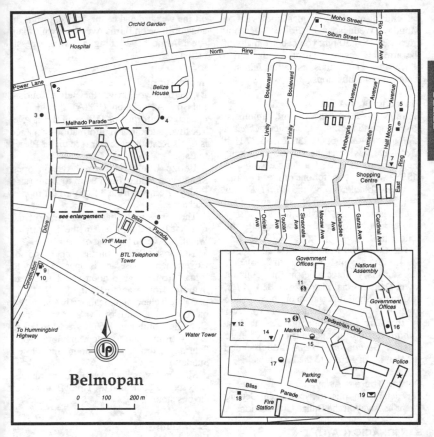

Belmopan

0   100   200 m

call and make an appointment for a visit on Monday, Wednesday or Friday afternoon from 1.30 to 4.30 pm, you can see many of the artefacts recovered from Belize's rich Maya sites. The vault is only a few minutes' walk from the bus stops.

Places to Stay & Eat
Belmopan is a bureaucrats' and diplomats' town, not one for budget travellers. *Circle A Lodge* (☎ (8) 22296; fax 23616), 35-37 Half Moon Ave, has seen better days, but is among the cheapest at US$34 a double with fan, US$39 with air-con, for one of its 14 rooms.

A few blocks away, the *Hotel El Rey* (☎ (8) 23438), 23 Moho St, is cheapest of all but cheerless and basic at US$20/25 a single/double for a room with bath and ceiling fan.

The *Caladium Restaurant* (☎ 22754), on Market Square just opposite the Novelo's bus stop, is your best bet in the centre of town. Daily special plates cost US$4. *Yoli's*, next to the Shell fuel station on the road into town, is a less convenient alternative. Over by the Circle A Lodge there's the *New Capital Restaurant* specialising in Chinese cuisine. *China Restaurant*, though much simpler, is very close to the bus stops.

Getting There & Away
For details on bus transport, see Getting There & Away in the Belize City section.

SAN IGNACIO (CAYO)
San Ignacio, also called Cayo, is a prosperous farming and holiday centre in the lovely tropical Macal River valley. In general it's a quiet place of about 8000 people (counting the population of neighbouring Santa Elena on the east side of the river). It's a good base from which to explore the natural beauties of Mountain Pine Ridge and to visit the Maya ruins of Xunantunich.

Orientation
San Ignacio is west of the river, Santa Elena to the east. The two are joined by the one-lane Hawkesworth Bridge, San Ignacio's landmark suspension bridge. As you come off the western end of the bridge, turn right and you'll be on Burns Ave, the town's main street. Almost everything in town is accessible on foot.

Information
By the time you arrive, the Belize Tourism Industry Association (BTIA) should have opened its Information Office on Burns Ave. The town's traditional information exchange is Eva's Restaurant & Bar (see under Places to Eat).

Belize Bank, on Burns Ave, is open Monday to Friday from 8 am to 1 pm (also Friday afternoon from 3 to 6 pm) for money exchange.

The very simple, basic San Ignacio Hospital (☎ (92) 2066), is up the hill off of Waight's Ave, to the west of the centre.

The post office is on the upper floor of Government House and is open Monday to Friday from 8 am to noon and 1 to 5 pm, Saturday from 8 am to 1 pm.

Belize Telecommunications has an office on Burns Ave north of Eva's in the Cano's Gift Shop building. Hours are Monday to Friday from 8 am to noon and 1 to 4 pm, Saturday from 8 am to noon and closed Sunday.

Market day is Saturday, with the marketeers setting up behind the Hotel Belmoral at the bus station.

Excursions
Every hotel and most restaurants in town will want to sign you up. Compare offerings, shop around, and talk to other travellers before making your choice. Most of the trips offered give good value for money, but are not cheap.

Many guides and excursion operators advertise their services at Eva's Restaurant (☎ & fax (92) 2267). Drop by and see what's available.

Among the favourite trips are these:

Voyages by boat or canoe along the Macal, Mopan and Belize Rivers; a favourite goal on the Macal is the Pantí Maya Medicine Trail at Ixchel Farm
A visit to a Mennonite community, usually combined

BELIZE

San Ignacio

0   75   150 m

■ PLACES TO STAY	▼ PLACES TO EAT	OTHER
1 Snooty Fox Guest House	3 Serendib Restaurant	10 Atlantic Bank
2 Venus Hotel	5 Eva's Restaurant & Bar	12 Bus Station
4 Central Hotel & Farmers' Emporium	6 Red Rooster Restaurant	13 Esso Fuel Station
7 Hi Et Hotel	9 Ice Cream Paradise	16 Belize Bank
8 24A West Street Guest House	11 Tai San Chinese Restaurant	21 Market Building
11 New Belmoral Hotel	15 Maxim's Chinese Restaurant	22 Shell Fuel Station
14 Martha's Guest House	17 New Lucky Restaurant	23 Taxi Rank
18 Maxima Hotel	20 Oriental Restaurant & Bar	24 Town Hall, Library & Toilets
19 Hotel Plaza	25 Rosy's Nice Food	27 Government House, Police Station & Post Office
30 Hotel San Ignacio	26 Roots Restaurant	28 Fire Station
31 Hotel Piache		29 Electricity Generating Plant

with a tour of the Hershey chocolate company's cacao plantation

An overland excursion to the caves at Río Frio

A picnic and swim in the pools at Río On

A walk to the 300-metre waterfall at Hidden Valley (which is less than spectacular at dry times of the year)

An overland trip to the Maya ruins at Caracol

A stop at the Tanah Maya Art Museum and Maya slate-carving workshop of the Garcia sisters, just north of San Antonio

A trip to Chechem Ha's Maya ceremonial cave and a picnic at Vaca falls

Tubing through caves along the Chiquibul River

An excursion to Tikal (Guatemala), either for the day or overnight

Cahal Pech

The best way to visit the hilltop Maya site of Cahal Pech is to take a picnic. It's less than two km uphill from Hawkesworth Bridge. Follow the Buena Vista Rd for a km, uphill and past the San Ignacio Hotel, until you see a large thatched structure (a nightclub) and a radio antenna atop a hill. Turn left and follow the signs uphill to Cahal Pech.

The site is open from 9 am to 4.30 pm; admission costs US$1.50.

From the site headquarters building, follow the path down, then up, for 150 metres to the small collection of temples arranged around a plaza. These have been partially restored, and in some places stuccoed, as they would have been in Classic Maya times.

Places to Stay – bottom end

Martha's Guest House (☎ (92) 2276), 10 West St, above the August Meat Market, is a modern home offering two spare rooms which share a bath for US$14 and US$16 a double. If you like family atmosphere, you'll love it here.

Central Hotel (☎ (92) 2253), 24 Burns Ave, is among the town's cheapest hotels, and a bargain at US$10 a single, US$14 a double in rooms without running water. *Jaguar Hotel*, across the street at 19 Burns Ave, is plain, basic and well used, though not as well kept as its neighbour. Prices are US$6 per person with shared bath.

Hi-Et Hotel (☎ (92) 2828), 12 West St at the corner of Waight's Ave, is a family-run place, and when you stay here you have the feeling that you're part of that family. Two people pay US$11 for a room with shared bathroom. Across the street at 24-A West St, José Espat rents rooms for the same price.

New Belmoral Hotel (☎ (92) 2024), 17 Burns Ave at the corner of Waight's Ave, has 15 good rooms with bath and cable TV for US$18/23 a single/double.

Venus Hotel (☎ (92) 3203), 29 Burns Ave, newish, clean and bright. Of its 25 clean rooms, most are without private shower and cost US$11/14 a single/double; the common showers are new and clean, if cramped. Rooms with private shower cost US$18/23. All rooms have ceiling fans, and some (especially rooms 10 and 16) have views of the football fields and the river.

Maxima Hotel (☎ (92) 3993), on Missiah St, is new, clean, good, and reasonably priced at US$25 a double with private bath and fan, US$5 more with air-con. *Hotel Plaza* (☎ (92) 3332), 4-A Burns Ave, is similarly nice and new, at identical prices. Many rooms here have TV sets.

Places to Eat

Eva's Restaurant & Bar (☎ & fax (92) 2267) is the information and social centre of the expatriate set – temporary and permanent – in San Ignacio. Daily special plates at US$3 to US$5 are the best value.

Maxim's Chinese Restaurant, at the corner of Far West and Bullet Tree Rds, serves fried rice, sweet-and-sour dishes, and vegetarian plates which range in price from US$2 to US$4. The restaurant is small, dark, and open from 11.30 am to 2.30 pm and from 5 pm until midnight.

Across Burns Ave and north a few metres from Eva's is the *Serendib Restaurant*, serving – of all things – Sri Lankan dishes, here in the Belizean jungle. Service is friendly, the food is good, and prices are not bad, ranging from US$3.50 for the simpler dishes, up to US$10 for steak or lobster. Lunch is served from 9.30 am to 3 pm, dinner from 6.30 to 11 pm.

Ice Cream Paradise, on Burns Ave across

from the Belmoral Hotel, serves sandwiches and light meals as well as ice cream in clean, attractive surroundings.

Red Rooster Restaurant on Far West St is noted for its good, cheap pizza.

Getting There & Away
Buses operate to and from Belize City (116 km, three hours, US$2.75), Belmopan (32 km, 45 minutes, US$1.50), San Ignacio, and Benque Viejo (15 km, 20 minutes, US$0.50). For details, see Getting There & Away in the Belize City section.

MOUNTAIN PINE RIDGE
Western Belize has lots of beautiful, unspoiled mountain country dotted with waterfalls and teeming with wild orchids, parrots, keel-billed toucans and other exotic flora and fauna. Almost 800 sq km to the south and east of San Ignacio has been set aside as the Mountain Pine Ridge Forest Reserve.

The rough forest roads in the reserve are often impassable in the wet season, and not easily passable even when it's dry. Inaccessibility is one of Mountain Pine Ridge's assets, for it keeps this beautiful land in its natural state for visitors willing to see it on horseback, on foot or along its rivers in canoes.

Pantí Medicine Trail
Among the most fascinating excursions is the one to the Pantí Medicine Trail at Ix Chel Farm (fax (92) 2267), located right next to Chaa Creek Cottages, 13 km south-west of San Ignacio. Named for Dr Eligio Pantí, a healer in San Antonio village who uses traditional Maya herb cures, the Trail was established by Dr Rosita Arvigo. Dr Arvigo, an American, studied medicinal plants with Dr Pantí, then began several projects to spread the wisdom of traditional healing methods and to preserve the rainforest habitats which harbour an incredible 4000 species of plants.

The Pantí Medicine Trail is the first of her efforts, a self-guiding path among the jungle's natural cures. Admission costs US$5; it's open every day from 8 am to noon and 1 to 5 pm.

Chechem Ha Maya Cave
At Chechem Ha, south of Benque Viejo, is a recently discovered Maya cave complete with ceremonial pots. Members of the Morales family, who discovered the cave, act as guides, leading you up the steep slope to the cave mouth, then down inside, walking and sometimes crouching, to see what the Maya left. A fee of US$25 pays for one to three people. Take water and a torch. You can also camp at Chechem Ha, or sleep in one of the recently built cabañas. Bob at Eva's Restaurant can provide further details.

Caracol
In the southern reaches of the reserve lies Caracol, a vast Maya city still engulfed by jungle. The archaeologists are still at work here, and nothing has been restored, but Caracol is obviously of major importance to studies of Maya archaeology, culture and history.

The vast site encompasses some 88 sq km, with 36,000 structures marked so far. Among the most impressive are the Acropolis and the Canaa temple complex, the largest and most massive yet to be found in Belize. There is also a good ball court, and the Temple of the Wooden Lintel, a very old structure dating back some 2000 years.

Caracol can be reached on an overnight trip in a good 4WD vehicle. The best way is to sign up for a tour in San Ignacio or at one of the lodges. There are no services at the site beyond those offered by the archaeologists.

Other Sites
Other suitable goals for forest trips include Hidden Valley Falls, a silver cascade which plunges 300 metres into a misty valley; Río On's pools and waterfalls; and Río Frio Caves, near Augustine. Camping here is allowed only with prior permission from the Department of Forestry, and only at Augustine and near the settlement of San Antonio.

BELIZE

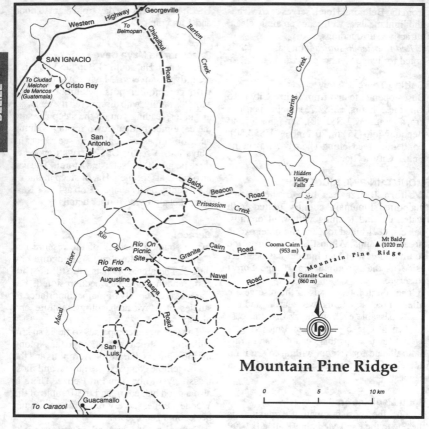

Mountain Pine Ridge

0   5   10 km

XUNANTUNICH

Set on a levelled hilltop overlooking the Mopan (or Belize) River, Xunantunich controlled the riverside track which led from the hinterlands of Tikal down to the Caribbean. During the Classic period, a ceremonial centre flourished here. Other than that, not a great amount is known. Archaeologists have uncovered evidence that an earthquake damaged the city seriously about 900 AD, after which it may have been largely abandoned.

Though it is an interesting site, and its tallest building, El Castillo, is impressive as it rises some 40 metres above the jungle floor, Xunantunich will perhaps disappoint you if you've already seen Tikal or Copán. It has not been extensively restored, as those better known sites have, and the jungle has grown around and over the excavated temples.

Xunantunich is open from 9 am to 5 pm; admission costs US$1.50. In the rainy season (June to October), bugs can be a problem; you may need your repellent.

The path from the guardian's hut leads to Plaza A-2, surrounded by low, bush-covered buildings and then on to Plaza A-1, dominated by Structure A-6: El Castillo. The stairway on the north side of El Castillo – the side you approach from the courtyard – goes only as far as the temple building. To climb to the roofcomb you must go around to the south side and use a separate set of steps. On the east side of the temple a few of the masks which once surrounded this structure have been restored.

Getting There & Away

The ferry to Xunantunich is opposite the village of San José Succotz, 8.5 km west of San Ignacio, 1.5 km east of Benque Viejo. From the ferry it's a walk of two km uphill to the ruins.

Novelo's buses on their way between San Ignacio and Benque Viejo will drop you at the ferry (US$0.35). There are also jitney taxis shuttling between San Ignacio and Benque Viejo which will take you for US$1. Make your excursion to Xunantunich in the morning to avoid the ferryman's lunch break. Ferry hours are 8 am to noon and 1 to 5 pm; the ferry crosses on demand. There is no fee for passengers or cars, except on weekends, when cars pay US$0.50 each way.

When you return, cross on the ferry and have a cold drink at the Xunantunich Hotel & Saloon across the road. You can wait for the bus to San Ignacio here. If your goal is Benque Viejo, you can walk there from the ferry in about 15 minutes.

BENQUE VIEJO DEL CARMEN

A foretaste of Guatemala just two km east of the border – that's Benque Viejo del Carmen. The name and lingua franca are Spanish, the people Spanish-speaking Maya or ladinos. Hotels and restaurants are very basic. You're better off staying and eating in San Ignacio if you can.

Places to Stay & Eat

Maya Hotel y Restaurante (☎ (93) 2116), 11 George St, is a dreary, family-run lodging near the bus terminal. The 10 rooms have lots of bunks. The restaurant serves all three meals. Rates are US$8/12 a single/double without bath, US$14/19 with private shower.

Next best is the *Hospedaje Roxy*, on Church St at the south-western end of town. It's family-run, and charges US$7 per person.

Oki's Hotel (☎ (93) 2006), 47 George St, has 11 very basic rooms in a converted village house, some of which are very cramped and dark. The communal showers and toilets are usable, the price US$6 per person.

Da Xin Chinese restaurant is currently the town favourite for both eating and drinking. *Oki's New restaurant* is the fanciest place in town, which isn't saying much.

Getting There & Away

There are frequent jitney taxis (US$2) and hourly buses (US$0.35) between San Ignacio and Benque, and a few buses go all the way to Melchor in Guatemala.

From Benque, taxis shuttle back and forth from the border charging a high US$4 for the three-km ride, so the energetic may choose to walk instead – the journey will take about 35 minutes.

Crossing the Border Cross early in the morning so as to have the best chance of catching buses onward. The border station is supposedly open 24 hours a day, but officers are usually only on duty from 6 am to midnight.

If you need a Guatemalan visa, as citizens of most British Commonwealth countries do, you should obtain it before you reach the border.

Guatemalan tourist cards (US$5) are obtainable at the border. There are also two banks at the border for changing money.

The Guatemalan town of Melchor de Mencos has several cheap hotels and restaurants. If you've crossed the border in the morning, you'll be able to catch a Transportes Pinita bus westward to El Cruce (Puente Ixlu) and Flores or Tikal. See the Guatemala chapter for details.

BELIZE

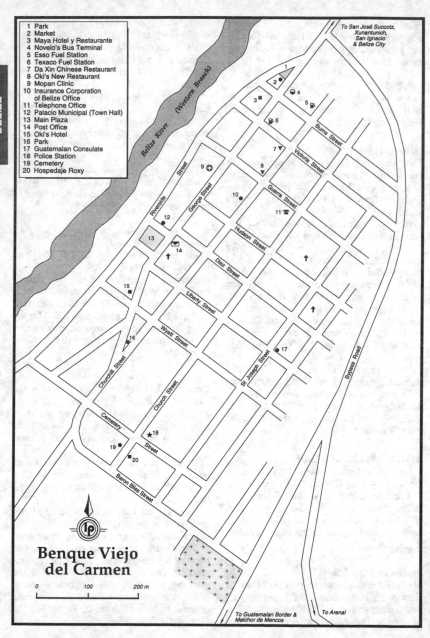

1 Park
2 Market
3 Maya Hotel y Restaurante
4 Novelo's Bus Terminal
5 Esso Fuel Station
6 Texaco Fuel Station
7 Da Xin Chinese Restaurant
8 Oki's New Restaurant
9 Mopan Clinic
10 Insurance Corporation
   of Belize Office
11 Telephone Office
12 Palacio Municipal (Town Hall)
13 Main Plaza
14 Post Office
15 Oki's Hotel
16 Park
17 Guatemalan Consulate
18 Police Station
19 Cemetery
20 Hospedaje Roxy

To San José Succotz,
Xunantunich,
San Ignacio
& Belize City

Belize River (Western Branch)

Riverside Street
George Street
Burns Street
Victoria Street
Guerra Street
Hudson Street
Diaz Street
Liberty Street
Wyatt Street
Churchill Street
Church Street
St Joseph Street
Bypass Road
Cemetery Street
Baron Bliss Street

Benque Viejo del Carmen

0   100   200 m

To Guatemalan Border &
Melchor de Mencos

To Arenal

Southern Belize

The roads to southern Belize are long and usually in bad condition, the towns small, and access to archaeological sites requires time, energy and – sometimes – money. If you want to explore off the tourist track, southern Belize is the place to do it.

Among the places to visit are Dangriga, main town of Stann Creek District, centre of the Black Carib Garinagu (or Garífuna) culture; the Cockscomb Basin Jaguar Preserve; Placencia, where life is similar to that on the cayes, but cheaper; and Punta Gorda, near several unrestored Maya sites. From Punta Gorda there are boats across the bay to Puerto Barrios in Guatemala.

THE HUMMINGBIRD HIGHWAY

Heading south from Belmopan, the Hummingbird Highway is well paved as far as the Caves Branch River (19 km), but then degenerates as it bumps and grinds its way south and east to Dangriga.

Blue Hole National Park

Just under 20 km south of Belmopan is Blue Hole National Park, where underground tributaries of the Sibun River bubble to the surface and fill a deep limestone sinkhole about 33 metres deep and 100 metres in diameter. After running out of the sinkhole and down a short distance, the stream cascades into a domed cavern. Deliciously cool on the hottest days, the cavern makes an excellent swimming hole. The park is open daily from 8 am to 4 pm.

A rugged nature trail leads 2½ km from the Blue Hole to St Herman's Cave. For an easier walk, follow the Hummingbird Highway north to a separate path to St Herman's 400 metres off the highway. The cave is entered from the bottom of a large limestone sinkhole. Maya artefacts dating from the Classic Period have been found in the cave. As there is no electric lighting, you must bring a torch (flashlight) to penetrate the cave to any distance.

DANGRIGA

Population 10,000

Once called Stann Creek Town, this is the largest town in southern Belize. It's much smaller than Belize City but friendlier and quieter.

There's not much to do here except spend the night and head onwards – unless it's 19 November. Read on.

History

Dangriga's citizens are descendants of the Black Caribs, people of mixed South American Indian and African blood, who inhabited the island of St Vincent as a free people in the 17th century. By the end of the 18th century, British colonisers had brought the independent-minded Caribs under their control and transported them from one island to another in an effort to subdue them. In the early 19th century, oppression and wandering finally brought many of the Black Caribs to southern Belize. The most memorable migration took place late in 1832, when on 19 November a large number of Caribs reached Belize from Honduras in dugout canoes. The event is celebrated annually in Belize as Garífuna Settlement Day. Dangriga is the place to be on 19 November as the town explodes in a frenzy of dancing, drinking and celebration of the Garífuna heritage.

Orientation

North Stann Creek (also called the Gumaragu River) empties into the Gulf of Honduras at the centre of the town. Dangriga's main street is called St Vincent St south of the creek and Commerce St to the north. The bus station is on St Vincent St at the southern end of the bridge over the creek. The airstrip, two km north of the centre near the Pelican Beach Resort, has a café and a small airline building.

Though there is no government tourist office, the Belize Tourism Industry Association has an office of sorts at PJ's Gift Shop (☎ (5) 22266) just south of the bridge at 21 St Vincent St.

The Affordable Corner Store and Laundromat is open from 9 am to noon and also

BELIZE

BELIZE

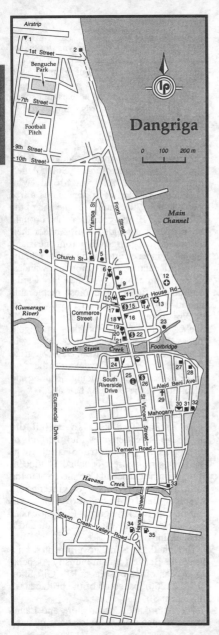

■ PLACES TO STAY

2   Pelican Beach Resort
17 Cameleon Central Hotel
21 Riverside Hotel
24 The Hub (Guest House)
27 Soffie's Hotel
28 Río Mar Hotel
31 Bonefish Hotel
33 Pal's Guest House

▼ PLACES TO EAT

1   Airport Café
6   Silver Garden
9   Relis Chinese Restaurant
16 Sunrise
18 Starlight
20 Burger King
24 The Hub Restaurant
27 Soffie's Restaurant
28 Río Mar Restaurant

    OTHER

3   BTL Telephone Towers
4   Water Tower ('Reservoir')
5   Ice Factory
7   Affordable Corner Store &
    Laundromat
8   Treasure House Travel Agency
10 Police
11 BTL Telephone Office
12 Public Health Center
13 Hospital
14 Courthouse
15 Barclay's Bank
19 Chemist's/Pharmacy
22 Scotiabank
23 Fish Market
25 BTIA Tourist Information
    (PJ's Gift Shop)
26 Belize Bank
29 Baptist Church
30 Post Office
32 B Nicholas, Artist
34 Shell Fuel Station
35 Texaco Fuel Station

2 to 8 pm. The last wash is at 5 pm, and it's closed Thursday afternoon, and Sunday.

Places to Stay

Among the cheapest places is the *Cameleon Central Hotel* (☎ (5) 22008), 119 Commerce St, which advertises itself as 'safe, clean and economical'. Rates are US$6.50 per person in waterless rooms.

The Hub (☎ (5) 23064; fax 22813), 573

South Riverside (PO Box 56), is a congenial place with a shady front terrace and six rooms (some with private showers) going for US$7/12 a single/double with common bath, or US$12/17 with bath.

On the south bank of North Stann Creek at the creek's mouth are two good choices. The *Río Mar Hotel* (☎ (5) 22201), 977 Southern Foreshore at the corner of Waight's St, with nine tidy, clean rooms, all with bath, most with TV, going for US$18 to US$28, a single or double. The upstairs rooms are preferable. The restaurant and bar serve good cheap meals and drinks.

Nearby is *Soffie's Hotel* (☎ (5) 22789), 970 Chatye St, which has 10 serviceable rooms ranging in price from US$22 to US$33, the most expensive having air-con; all have private baths. There's a restaurant on the ground floor, and good views of the water from upstairs.

Riverside Hotel (☎ (5) 22168; fax 22296), 5 Commerce St, at the north end of the bridge, has 12 rooms with clean common showers going for US$11 per person.

Pal's Guest House (☎ (5) 22095), 868-A Magoon St, is spartan but clean, with a sea breeze and the sound of the surf. You pay US$17 a double in a room with shared bath, US$23 with private bath and TV.

Places to Eat

The Hub, the Río Mar, and Soffie's hotels have good, cheap restaurants. The *Bonefish* and *Pelican* are the upscale places.

Otherwise, the locals favour *Burger King*, a tidy lunchroom on Commerce St with a long and varied menu from burgers to fish fillet and chicken. Their breakfast special of eggs, refried beans, toast and coffee is good at US$2.75.

Most of the other restaurants along Commerce St are Chinese: the *Sunrise*, *Starlight*, *Silver Garden* and *Relis* serving full meals for about US$6.

Getting There & Away

Air Maya Airways serves Dangriga. For details, see Getting Around in the introduction to the Belize chapter.

Bus Z-Line has five buses daily from Belize City (170 km, five hours, US$5.50) via Belmopan. Return buses depart Dangriga at 5, 6 and 9 am for Belize City; on Sunday, departures are at 10 am and 3 pm.

Two of the buses from Belize City continue southward to Independence (for Placencia, 85 km, 2½ hours, US$3) and Punta Gorda (169 km, six hours, US$5.50), departing Dangriga at noon and 7 pm (on Sunday, at 2 pm only).

A faster, better way to Placencia is via the shuttle van (☎ (5) 22702; in Belize City ☎ (2) 73977, 77811) which departs The Hub hotel in Dangriga at noon on Monday, Wednesday, Friday and Saturday, stopping at Hopkins village, arriving in Placencia at 2 pm, for US$4.

GLOVER'S ATOLL

Glover's Atoll Resort (☎ (8) 22149, 23180; fax 23505, 23235), PO Box 563, Belize City, has simple beachfront cabañas candles for light, rainwater to drink, outhouse etc – on one of the outer cayes, a five-km, six-hour boat trip from Sittee River Village near Hopkins (south of Dangriga). You must take some supplies, including food and towels, as this is a very simple place. But there's lots of watersports equipment for rent, excellent diving, and very few other people to disturb the tranquillity. Basic cost is US$55 per person per week for lodging (US$30 if you camp), plus US$40 per person for round-trip transport by boat. The boat departs Sittee River every Sunday morning at 8 am.

SOUTHERN HIGHWAY

The Southern Highway, south of Dangriga, is unpaved and can be rough going, especially in the rainy months, but along the way are some good opportunities for experiencing untouristy Belize.

Hopkins

The farming and fishing village of Hopkins (population 1100) is seven km east of the Southern Highway, on the coast. Most of its people are Garinagus, living as the coastal inhabitants of Belize have lived for centuries. If you're interested in simple living and Garinagu culture, visit Hopkins and stay at the *Sandy Beach Lodge*, at the southern end of the village. The lodge has six simple thatched rooms renting for US$13/20 a single/double with shared bath, or US$20/27 with private bath. Meals cost US$5 for breakfast or dinner, US$7 for lunch. For reservations in Dangriga, contact Gasper Martin at The Hub or Janice Lambert at PJ's Gift Shop; or call the Hopkins community telephone at (5) 22033.

Sittee River
Another small coastal village where you can get away from it all is Sittee River. *Prospect Cool Spot Guest House and Camp Site* (☎ (5) 22006, 22389; ask for Isaac Kelly Sr) will put you up in adequate simplicity for US$10/15 a single/double (US$2.50 in a tent). Simple, inexpensive meals are served.

Cockscomb Basin Wildlife Sanctuary
Almost halfway between Dangriga and Independence is the village of Maya Center, where a track goes 10 km west to the Cockscomb Basin Wildlife Sanctuary, sometimes called the Jaguar Reserve.

Created in 1984, the Sanctuary now covers over 40,000 hectares (100,000 acres). The varied topography and lush tropical forest make this an excellent place to observe Belizean wildlife.

There's no public transport to the reserve, but the walk through the lush forest is a pretty one. At the reserve is a campsite (US$2 per person), several simple shared cabins available for rent (US$10 per person), a visitors centre, and numerous hiking trails.

PLACENCIA
Perched at the southern tip of a long, narrow sandy peninsula, Placencia (population 600) is 'the caye you can drive to'. Activities here are the same as on the cayes: swimming, sunning, lazing, water sports, and excursions to cayes and to points inland.

Orientation
The village of Placencia is at the southern tip of the narrow peninsula. The village's main north-south 'street' is actually a narrow concrete footpath less than a metre wide which threads its way 1½ km among simple wood frame houses (some on stilts) and beachfront lodges.

Beaches & Excursions
Unlike most of the cayes, Placencia has good palm-lined beaches on its east side. When you're tired of the beach, contact a member of the Placencia Tourist Guide Association (there are 16) and arrange for some sailing, snorkelling, scuba diving, fly and sport fishing, bird and manatee watching, overnight camping on remote cayes, and excursions to jungle rivers and the Cockscomb Basin Reserve.

Places to Stay
Placencia's camping area is at the northern edge of the village on the beach. Pitch your tent or hang your hammock among the coconut palms for US$2 per person. Services are primitive.

Most houses in the village rent rooms, whether they call themselves a 'hotel' or not. Good places for lodging references are the Kingfisher Restaurant, Ranguana Lodge, D & L Resort, and Lydia's Rooms.

Lydia's Rooms (☎ (6) 23117), sometimes called Conrad & Lydia's Rooms, has simple rooms which share baths for US$8/12 a single/double. They also have a house for rent.

Paradise Vacation Hotel is a tidy white board structure with bathless rooms renting for US$13 to US$22 a double. *Jamie's* is similar.

Sun Rider Guest House (☎ (6) 23236) has good, clean rooms fronting on a beach with shady palms for US$23 a double. One room has two beds and a kitchenette, for US$39.

Julia's Budget Hotel is central, clean enough, and certainly cheap at US$8/11/17 a single/double/triple without bath.

Sea Spray Hotel, right in the centre of the village, has a variety of rooms, from those which share baths at US$15 to rooms with bath for US$20 to US$38.

BELIZE

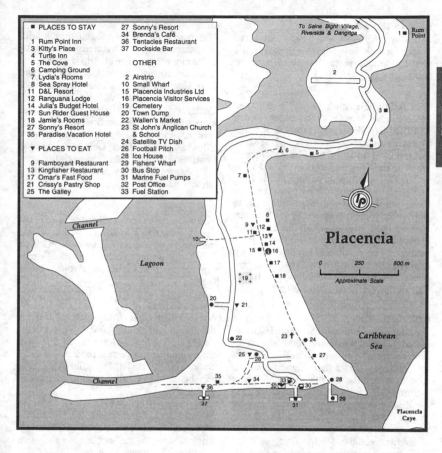

PLACES TO STAY

1 Rum Point Inn
3 Kitty's Place
4 Turtle Inn
5 The Cove
6 Camping Ground
7 Lydia's Rooms
8 Sea Spray Hotel
11 D&L Resort
12 Ranguana Lodge
14 Julia's Budget Hotel
17 Sun Rider Guest House
18 Jamie's Rooms
27 Sonny's Resort
35 Paradise Vacation Hotel

PLACES TO EAT

9 Flamboyant Restaurant
13 Kingfisher Restaurant
17 Omar's Fast Food
21 Crissy's Pastry Shop
25 The Galley
27 Sonny's Resort
34 Brenda's Café
36 Tentacles Restaurant
37 Dockside Bar

OTHER

2 Airstrip
10 Small Wharf
15 Placencia Industries Ltd
16 Placencia Visitor Services
19 Cemetery
20 Town Dump
22 Wallen's Market
23 St John's Anglican Church & School
24 Satellite TV Dish
26 Football Pitch
28 Ice House
29 Fishers' Wharf
30 Bus Stop
31 Marine Fuel Pumps
32 Post Office
33 Fuel Station

Places to Eat

A social centre of the village is the *Flamboyant Restaurant* (formerly Jene's), with indoor and outdoor tables and the usual list of sandwiches, rice and beans, and fish dishes for US$3 to US$6.

Kingfisher Restaurant, in the centre, has a fine view of the sea, and a menu stretching from the lowly cheese sandwich (US$1.50) to a shrimp or lobster dinner for US$12. This is another of Placencia's social centres. Neighbouring *Sonny's Resort* also has a good restaurant and bar.

Omar's Fast Food, in the Sun Rider Guest

House, has home-cooked food and low prices, with views of the beach.

Brenda's Café is a cosy thatched eatery down on the southern shore, with cheap, delicious daily specials for about US$3 or US$4.

The Galley, west of the main part of the village, is a favourite for long dinners with good conversation. A full meal with drinks costs about US$9 to US$12.

Tentacles Restaurant is another evening favourite, a breezy, atmospheric place with its popular Dockside Bar built on a wharf out in the water.

Getting There & Away

Air Maya Airways and Tropic Air serve Placencia with daily flights. For details, see Getting Around in the introduction to the Belize chapter.

Bus Shuttle buses run between Dangriga and Placencia on Monday, Wednesday, Friday and Saturday, departing Placencia at 6 am, Dangriga at noon on the two-hour, US$4 trip. For more information, see Getting There & Away in the Dangriga section.

The Z-Line buses running south from Dangriga to Independence can drop you there, whence it is possible in principle to find a boat going across the bay to Placencia. However, this may not be all that simple (or cheap) in fact, so if you travel this way, do so as early as possible in the day. To return northward, Z-Line buses depart Independence for Dangriga (2½ hours) and Belize City at 5 and 7.30 am, and 1.30 pm.

PUNTA GORDA

At the southern end of the Southern Highway is Punta Gorda (population 3000), the southernmost town of any size in Belize. Rainfall and humidity are at their highest, and the jungle at its lushest, in the Toledo District which surrounds Punta Gorda. Punta Gordians endure over four metres of rain per year, so be prepared for at least a short downpour almost every day.

Known throughout Belize simply as 'PG', this sleepy town was founded for the Garinagus who emigrated from Honduras in 1823. In 1866, after the American Civil War, some Confederate veterans received land grants from the British government and founded a settlement here, but it didn't endure.

Fishing was the major source of livelihood for almost two centuries, but now farming is important as well. There is also an increasing tourist trade, as PG is the base for excursions inland to the Maya archaeological sites at Lubaantun and Nim Li Punit, the Maya villages of San Pedro Colombia and San Antonio, and the Blue Creek Cave.

Orientation & Information

The town centre is the triangular park with bandstand and the distinctive blue-and-white clock tower. The airstrip is 350 metres to the north-west, the dock for boats to and from Guatemala even closer. Near the boat dock is the Toledo Visitors Information Center (☎ (7) 22470), PO Box 73, also known as the Belize Tourism Industry Association, supervised by Antonio and Yvonne Villoria of Dem Dats Doin (see Around Punta Gorda later in this chapter). It's open daily except Thursday and Sunday from 9 am to 1 pm.

Excursions

You will have experienced virtually all of the thrills Punta Gorda offers within a few minutes of your arrival. However, PG is an excellent base for excursions to more exciting places. For ideas, see Around Punta Gorda.

Places to Stay

Nature's Way Guest House (☎ (7) 22119) is the intrepid travellers' gathering-place. This converted house charges US$9/14 a single/double in waterless rooms with clean common showers. Trips by minibus and boat can be arranged to all points of interest around PG.

Mahung's Hotel (☎ (7) 22044), 11 North Main St, has an older section at the front with waterless rooms sharing a bath at US$8/13 a single/double. At the back are more modern rooms with private bath for US$14/20 a single/double.

Pallavi's Hotel, also on North Main St, is similar, now adding a new section of more modern rooms at the back which should be open by the time you arrive.

Dorl's Seabreeze Hotel (☎ (7) 22243), 6 Front St, is good and cheap at US$9/14 a single/double for a room with fan and private bath, but beware the noise from the ground-floor bar here.

Verde's Guest House (☎ (7) 22069), on Back St, is the standard frame barracks construction, okay at US$11 a double in a waterless room.

G & G's Inn (☎ (7) 22680), facing the main square, has good prices of US$20 a double in a room with private shower, fan and cable TV. On the ground floor there's a small restaurant-bar.

St Charles Inn (☎ (7) 22149), 23 King St, offers outstanding value for money. Clean, well kept – even stylish, for PG – it has comfy rooms with private bath and fan for US$17/23 a single/double. Small groups sometimes fill it.

Punta Caliente Hotel (☎ (7) 22561), 108 José Maria Nuñez St, is fairly new, with a good restaurant on the ground floor and rooms above. Each room has good cross-ventilation as well as *two* fans, and private bath. Prices are good: US$22 to US$28 a double. If you don't stay, at least come here for dinner, which is among the best in town.

Mira Mar Hotel (☎ (7) 22033), 95 Front St near the boat dock, is among PG's fancier places, with a Chinese restaurant occupying the ground floor and a porch for watching passers-by. Rooms can be simple, at US$14/26 a single/double with private bath, or more elaborate at US$59 with bath, TV and air-conditioning.

BELIZE

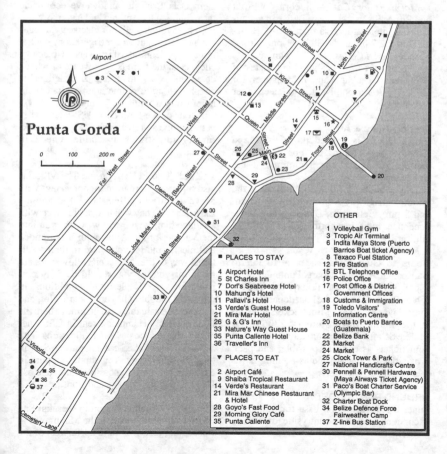

Punta Gorda

0   100   200 m

■ PLACES TO STAY

4   Airport Hotel
5   St Charles Inn
7   Dorl's Seabreeze Hotel
10 Mahung's Hotel
11 Pallavi's Hotel
13 Verde's Guest House
21 Mira Mar Hotel
26 G & G's Inn
33 Nature's Way Guest House
35 Punta Caliente Hotel
36 Traveller's Inn

▼ PLACES TO EAT

2   Airport Café
9   Shaiba Tropical Restaurant
14 Verde's Restaurant
21 Mira Mar Chinese Restaurant
    & Hotel
28 Goyo's Fast Food
29 Morning Glory Café
35 Punta Caliente

OTHER

1   Volleyball Gym
3   Tropic Air Terminal
6   Indita Maya Store (Puerto
    Barrios Boat ticket Agency)
8   Texaco Fuel Station
12 Fire Station
15 BTL Telephone Office
16 Police Office
17 Post Office & District
    Government Offices
18 Customs & Immigration
19 Toledo Visitors'
    Information Centre
20 Boats to Puerto Barrios
    (Guatemala)
22 Belize Bank
23 Market
24 Market
25 Clock Tower & Park
27 National Handicrafts Centre
30 Pennell & Pennell Hardware
    (Maya Airways Ticket Agency)
31 Paco's Boat Charter Service
    (Olympic Bar)
32 Charter Boat Dock
34 Belize Defence Force
    Fairweather Camp
37 Z-line Bus Station

Places to Eat

Punta Caliente serves stew pork, fish fillet, beans and rice with chicken, and similar dishes for US$3.50 to US$5, and it's all good.

Mira Mar is the place to go for Chinese at only slightly more.

Goyo's Fast Food is cheap and convenient to the main square.

Shaiba Tropical Restaurant on Front St is open only for dinner (at 6.30 pm), but enjoys a good reputation for its food, mood, conversation and prices. Expect to spend about US$6 to US$10 for a full meal.

Morning Glory Café, at the corner of Front and Prince Sts, is a standard Belizean restaurant-bar, more attractive than many. Hours are 7 am to 2 pm and 6.30 to 11 pm; closed Monday. *Sylvia's Restaurant* is similar.

The *Airport Café* has good big plates of rice, beans, cabbage and red snapper for US$3.75. It's a good place to meet other travellers.

Getting There & Away

Punta Gorda is served daily by Maya Airways and Tropic Air. For details see Getting Around at the beginning of the Belize chapter.

Z-Line buses (☎ (7) 22165) roll down the Southern Highway from Belize City (8 am and 3 pm), Belmopan, Dangriga and Independence, returning northward at 5 and 11 am, for US$8.

Boats to Guatemala The boat to Puerto Barrios, Guatemala, departs Punta Gorda at 2 pm on Tuesday and Friday, for US$10. (From Puerto Barrios, the boat departs on the same days at 7.30 am.) Boat tickets are sold at the Indita Maya store (☎ 22065), 24 Middle St, after 9.30 am on sailing days. Buy your tickets as early as possible, and pack provisions for the voyage as nothing is for sale on board.

AROUND PUNTA GORDA

Punta Gorda is a good base for numerous excursions into the countryside of Toledo district.

San Pedro Columbia

North-west of Punta Gorda 41 km lies San Pedro Columbia, a Kekchi Maya village with several reasons to visit. The first is to observe the Guatemalan lifestyle of the inhabitants, whose ancestors fled the tedious life of the coffee fincas in Alta Verapaz to find freedom in Belize. Their Guatemalan highland customs, traditions and dress have been preserved to a remarkable degree, and differ markedly from those of the lowland Mopan or 'Belizean' Maya.

Dem Dats Doin The second reason is to tour Dem Dats Doin, an innovative ecological farm founded by Antonio and Yvonne Villoria. Photovoltaic cells for electricity, biogas methane for light and refrigeration, natural insect repellents and fertilisers in place of chemicals: the farm is a showcase of what a determined, sensitive and knowledgeable couple can do to promote appropriate technology and sustainable farming.

A tour of the farm costs US$5 and takes between one and two hours. Bed and breakfast is sometimes available; check in advance.

The Indigenous Experience The Villorias also supervise a program for homestays with Maya families called 'The Indigenous Experience'. They will put you in touch with a village family who will welcome you into their home, provide you with a hammock and meals, and let you share in their traditional way of life. No special allowances are made for you, so you should be fully prepared for very simple living conditions. In return for roughing it, you'll learn a lot, and will provide valuable cash income to help the family get by. Hammock rent is US$4 per night; meals cost US$1.50 each. The Villorias ask a US$5 fee for putting you in touch with a family. You should enquire in advance by mail if possible, and enclose US$2 to pay for postage and printing.

Lubaantun Another reason to seek out San Pedro Columbia is to visit the Maya ruins at Lubaantun, just over a km north-west of the village. Aptly named, Lubaantun ('fallen stones') has been excavated to some extent, but not restored. The temples are still mostly covered with jungle, so you will have to use your imagination to reconstruct the great city which once stood here.

The archaeologists have found evidence that Lubaantun flourished until the late 8th century, after which little was built. In its heyday, the merchants of Lubaantun traded with people on the cayes, in Mexico and Guatemala, and perhaps beyond.

The principal temple at Lubaantun, built like its neighbours along a ridge of hills, is 12 metres high and 30 metres long. The precision stonework of this city seems to have been erected without benefit of mortar.

Getting There & Away San Pedro Columbia is 41 km north-west of Punta Gorda off the Southern Highway. A bus can drop you at the fuel station on the highway, from which it's almost a six km walk to the village. If you catch a San Antonio bus from the main plaza in PG, it will get you 2½ km closer to San Pedro.

More expensive, but also quicker and more dependable, are the minibus tours. Nature's Way Guest House will take up to six persons on a tour to San Pedro and Lubaantun for US$88, or about US$15 per person. This tour can be combined with a visit to Blue Creek Cave (see below) at a total cost of US$113, or US$19 per person.

Nim Li Punit

About 36 km north-west of Punta Gorda, just north of Big Falls and less than a km west of the Southern Highway, stand the ruins of Nim Li Punit, a less impressive site than Lubaantun. Nim Li Punit ('big hat') may in fact have been a tributary city to larger, more powerful Lubaantun.

Today, Nim Li Punit's distinction lies in its stelae, some of which are very large. Discovered by oil prospectors in 1974, it was soon looted by antiquities thieves. Later the archaeologists came and did some excavation and preliminary studies, but little restoration or stabilisation. Nim Li Punit, named for the headgear to be seen on one of its prominent stelae, is still mostly covered by jungle.

San Antonio & Blue Creek

The Mopan Maya of San Antonio are descended from former inhabitants of the Guatemalan village of San Luis Petén, just across the border. As have unfortunate Guatemalans for centuries, the San Antonians fled oppression in their home country to find freedom in Belize. They brought their ancient customs with them, however, and you can observe a traditional lowland Maya village on a short visit here. If you're fortunate enough to visit during a festival, your visit will be much more memorable.

About six km west of San Antonio, near the village of Santa Cruz, is the archaeological site of Uxbenka, which has numerous carved stelae.

South of San Antonio about 20 km lies the village of Blue Creek, and beyond it the nature reserve of Blue Creek Cave. Hike into the site (less than a km) along the marked trail and enjoy the rainforest around you, and the pools, channels, caves and refreshingly cool waters of the creek system.

Getting There & Away The San Antonio bus runs for the convenience of San Antonio villagers going into the big city, departing the village each morning at 5 am for Punta Gorda, and returning from PG at 4 pm. There is one small hotel in San Antonio, *Bol's Hilltop Hotel*, with beds for US$5. If you'd prefer not to stay the night, arrange a day excursion from Punta Gorda. Nature's Way Guest House runs minibus excursions to Blue Creek Cave: US$100 for up to six persons, or about US$17 per person.

BELIZE

HONDURAS

Honduras

Second-largest of the Central American countries, Honduras is a land of contrasts, with a cool, mountainous interior and a long, warm Caribbean coastline. Travel is easy, enjoyable and inexpensive.

Among the better known Honduran attractions are the spectacular Maya ruins at Copán, near the Guatemalan border, with pyramids, temples and intricately carved statues. Also popular with travellers are the Bay Islands, the idyllic Caribbean islands just off the north coast. Roatán is the most popular and probably most beautiful of the islands, but the smaller Utila also has its aficionados.

Several of the Caribbean beach towns, most notably Tela and Trujillo, have fine beaches, plenty of coconut palms, lots of opportunity for walking, interesting places to visit nearby, and wonderful seafood. The capital city, Tegucigalpa, in the central highlands, is surrounded by pine-treed mountains and has a temperate climate.

Less well known are the national parks and nature reserves. La Tigra, just a few km from the capital, is a lush, cool cloud forest. The Río Plátano nature reserve protects a pristine river system flowing through tropical rainforest in the Mosquitia region, one of Central America's large wilderness areas. Coastal and marine parks protect coastlands, wetlands and lagoons inhabited by manatees and other wildlife. On the Bay Islands they also protect coral reefs that are a continuation of the barrier reef off Belize, the second-largest barrier reef in the world, making them attractive for diving and snorkelling. A number of other national parks are more remote.

Facts about the Country

HISTORY
One of the earliest examples of civilisation

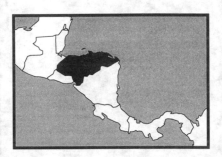

is the ruins at Copán, in western Honduras, indicating Maya settlement there since at least 1000 BC. Around 900 AD, Copán, like other Maya city-states, was mysteriously abandoned.

Spanish Colonisation
Columbus, on his fourth and final voyage, sailed from Jamaica and first landed on American mainland soil near Trujillo, Honduras, on 14 August 1502. He named the place 'Honduras' (meaning 'depths' in Spanish) after the deep waters off the north coast.

The town of Trujillo, founded in 1525 near where Columbus landed, was the first capital of the Spanish colony of Honduras, but the Spanish soon became more interested in colonising the cooler highlands of the interior. In 1537, Comayagua, in the geographical centre of Honduras, replaced Trujillo as capital. Comayagua remained the political and religious centre of Honduras for over three centuries, until the capital was transferred to its present location at Tegucigalpa in 1880.

In the early days there was a lot of fighting in the colony as a result of various Spaniards trying to establish power and also because of Indian resistance against the Spanish invaders. By some accounts the Indians nearly succeeded in driving the Spanish from their

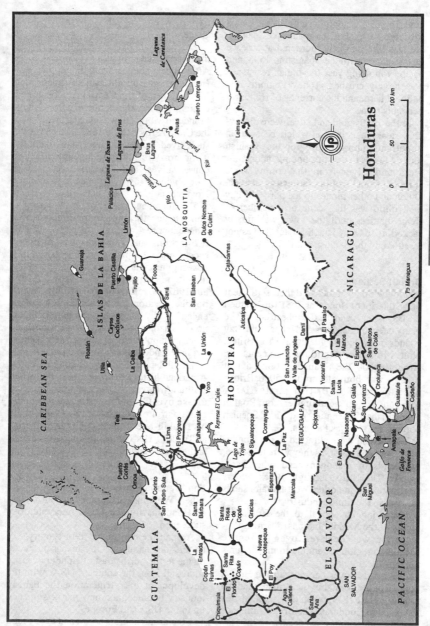

HONDURAS

land. In 1537, Lempira, a chief of the Lenca tribe, led 30,000 Indians against the Spanish. He was treacherously murdered at a peace talk arranged with the Spanish in 1538, and by the following year the Indian resistance was largely crushed. Today Lempira is a national hero, and the currency of Honduras bears his name.

In the 1570s gold and silver were discovered near Tegucigalpa, which became an important mining centre for the Spanish mining towns in the surrounding mountains. Gold and silver from the colony were shipped from Trujillo, attracting British, Dutch and other pirates to the port. The bay of Trujillo was the scene of a number of fierce battles, until the town was finally sacked in 1643 by Dutch pirates. It was not resettled by the Spanish until 1787.

British Settlement
While the Spanish focussed their settlement in the interior of Honduras, the British settled the Bay Islands and the Caribbean coast. The many deep, hidden bays and inlets of the Bay Islands provided an ideal base for British pirates from the 16th to the 18th centuries. Around 1600 the Spanish estimated that Roatán was home to around 5000 British buccaneers. The British pirate Henry Morgan set up headquarters on Roatán Island in the 17th century and raided Spanish ports as far away as Panama.

The British were attracted to the Honduran Caribbean coast, as they were to Belize, by stands of mahogany and other hardwoods. The British brought Black settlers from Jamaica and other West Indian islands to work in the timber industry.

Following an appeal to the British by chiefs of the Miskito Indians, a British Protectorate was declared over the entire Mosquitia region, extending from Honduras far into Nicaragua.

Spain was never happy with the British control of the coast, but the British ruled the territory until 1859, when they relinquished the lands to Honduras. The British influence is still evident today, especially on the Bay Islands, where English is the principal language.

Independence
After independence from Spain in 1821, Honduras was briefly part of independent Mexico, then of the Central American Federation. The Honduran liberal hero, General Francisco Morazán, was elected president of the United Provinces in 1830. The union was short-lived, however, largely due to continuing conflicts between liberals and conservatives, and Honduras declared its independence as a separate nation on 5 November 1838.

The liberal and conservative factions continued to wrestle for power in Honduras after independence. Power alternated between the two factions, and Honduras was ruled by a succession of civilian governments and military regimes. The country's constitution was rewritten 17 times in the years between 1821 and 1982. Government has officially been by popular election but Honduras has experienced literally hundreds of coups, rebellions, power seizures, electoral 'irregularities' and other manipulations of power since achieving independence.

Trujillo gained the spotlight in Central American history once again in 1860 when William Walker, an American who attempted to take over Central America and in fact did gain control of Nicaragua for a time, made his final ill-fated attack on Central America at Trujillo. His campaign ended in defeat, and he was captured and executed by firing squad.

The 'Banana Republic'
Where William Walker failed to gain control of Honduras for the USA, free enterprise succeeded.

Around the end of the 19th century, US traders took an interest in bananas produced on the fertile north coast of Honduras, just a short sail from the southern USA. With the development of refrigeration the banana industry boomed, and new markets opened up in the USA and Europe.

US entrepreneurs who wanted to buy land

for growing bananas were offered generous incentives to do so by a succession of Honduran governments. The three major companies were the Vaccaro brothers (later to become Standard Fruit) which operated around La Ceiba; the Cuyamel Fruit Company near the Cuyamel River and Tela; and after 1912, United Fruit, to the east, which by 1929 had swallowed up Cuyamel. The three companies owned a large part of northern Honduras, and by 1918, 75% of all Honduran banana lands were held by US companies.

Bananas provided 11% of Honduras's exports in 1892, 42% in 1903 and 66% in 1913. The economic success of the banana industry made the banana companies extremely powerful within Honduras, with policy and politicians controlled by banana company interests. Cuyamel allied itself with the Liberal Party, United Fruit with the National Party, and the rivalries between banana companies shaped Honduran politics.

Honduras failed to develop an indigenous landholding elite, unlike Guatemala, El Salvador and Nicaragua. Instead the economy and politics of the country became controlled by US banana interests.

20th-Century Politics

Along with economic involvement came increasing influence from the USA in various sectors of Honduran affairs, especially in the military. In 1911 and 1912, when it appeared the US banana interests were threatened by political developments, US President William Howard Taft sent US Marines into Honduras to 'protect US investments'.

During the worldwide economic depression of the 1930s, in the midst of civil unrest, General Tiburcio Carías Andino was elected president, establishing a virtual dictatorship that lasted from 1932 until 1949.

In 1954 the USA and Honduras signed a military pact that promised military training and equipment to Honduras in return for unlimited US access to raw materials if the need should arise. In 1957 a new constitution

put the military officially out of the control of civilian government, and the military then entered politics as an independent power.

Various elections and coups have come and gone, but whether the government has been civilian or military, the military has maintained much control. In 1963 Colonel Osvaldo López Arrellano led a military coup and ruled as president until he was forced to resign because of a scandal involving his acceptance of US$1.25 million in bribes from a US company, United Brands. He was replaced by Colonel Juan Alberto Melgar Castro, but he in turn was ousted by another military coup in 1978, led by General Policarpo Paz García.

The 'Football War'

In 1969, during the rule of Arrellano, Honduras and El Salvador had a brief war known as Guerra de Fútbol, the 'Football War' or 'Soccer War'.

In the 1950s and 1960s El Salvador's severe overpopulation and economic crisis led to 300,000 Salvadorans illegally crossing the border into Honduras. In 1969, 500 Salvadorans were sent back to El Salvador, and they were followed by a wave of 15,000 Salvadoran refugees alleging mistreatment at the hands of the Hondurans.

In the midst of this, in June 1969, the two countries were competing in World Cup qualifying soccer matches. At the game in San Salvador, visiting Honduran fans were attacked by Salvadorans. Angered, Honduras evicted thousands more Salvadoran immigrants. El Salvador closed off its borders, and amidst more allegations of abuse against Salvadorans in Honduras, El Salvador invaded Honduran territory on 14 July and bombed Honduran airports.

The war lasted only 100 hours, but the two countries were at odds for over a decade until a peace treaty was signed in 1980. However, relations between the two countries remained strained, especially during the 1980s when El Salvador erupted into civil war, sending fresh waves of refugees across the border into Honduras.

HONDURAS

The 1980s

During the 1980s Honduras was surrounded by the turmoil of Central American political developments. In July 1979, the revolutionary Sandinista movement in Nicaragua overthrew the Somoza dictatorship, and Somoza's National Guardsmen fled into Honduras. Civil war broke out in El Salvador in 1980, and was continuing in Guatemala.

Though Honduras experienced some unrest, Honduran politics were far more conservative. This can be attributed largely to the strong US influence, which help direct the course of Honduran politics and created a strong Honduran military capable of crushing any armed insurrection. Honduran government land reforms between 1962 and 1980 also showed that reform was possible through established channels.

With revolutions erupting on every side, and especially with the success of the Nicaraguan revolution in 1979, Honduras became the focus of US policy and strategic operations in the region.

The USA pressured the government to hold elections after 17 years of military rule. A civilian, Dr Roberto Suazo Córdova, was elected president, but real power rested with the commander-in-chief of the armed forces, General Gustavo Alvarez, who supported an increasingly military US policy in Central America.

With Ronald Reagan's election to the presidency of the USA in January 1981, US military involvement increased dramatically. The USA funnelled huge sums of money and thousands of US troops into Honduras as it conducted provocative manoeuvres clearly designed to threaten Nicaragua. Nicaraguan refugee camps in Honduras were used as bases for a US-sponsored undeclared covert war against the Nicaraguan government, which became known as the Contra war. At the same time the USA was training the Salvadoran military at Salvadoran refugee camps inside Honduras near the border of El Salvador.

Public alarm and opposition to the US militarisation of Honduras increased in the country during 1983, creating problems for the Honduran government. In March 1984, General Alvarez was toppled in a bloodless coup by his fellow officers. General Walter López Reyes was appointed his successor, and before long it was announced that Honduras was planning to re-examine its role as the military base of the USA in the region. In August the Honduran government suspended US training of Salvadoran military within its borders.

The 1985 presidential election, beset by serious irregularities, was won by José Simeón Azcona del Hoyo, who had obtained only 27% of the votes, while Rafael Leonardo Callejas had obtained 42% of the votes.

Despite growing disquiet in Washington after the revelations of the Iran-Contra affair in 1986, the Contra war escalated. In 1988 around 12,000 Contras operated from Honduras. Public anger in Honduras increased – anti-US demonstrations drew 60,000 demonstrators in Tegucigalpa and 40,000 in San Pedro Sula – forcing the Honduran government to declare a state of emergency. Finally, in November 1988, the Honduran government refused to sign a new military agreement with the USA, and President Azcona said the Contras would have to leave Honduras. With the election of Chamorro as president of Nicaragua in 1990, the Contra war ended and the Contras were finally out of Honduras.

Elections in 1989 brought Rafael Leonardo Callejas Romero of the National Party to the presidency in Honduras; he assumed office in January 1990. Callejas presided over an economically difficult time for Honduras – falling exports, a growing foreign debt and a shrinking GNP per capita. In the elections of November 1993 the Partido Nacional (National Party) candidate was convincingly beaten by Carlos Roberto Reina of the centre-right Partido Liberal (Liberal Party). No great change of course was expected of the new president, though he did pledge to attack government corruption and reform state institutions.

GEOGRAPHY

Honduras is the second-largest country in Central America (after Nicaragua), with an area of 112,492 sq km. This includes 288 sq km of territory formerly disputed with El Salvador, added to Honduras in the September 1992 judgement of the International Court of Justice. Honduras is bordered on the north by the Caribbean Sea, on the west by Guatemala, on the south by El Salvador and the Golfo de Fonseca, and on the east and south-east by Nicaragua. The Caribbean coast is 644 km long, but the Pacific coast on the Golfo de Fonseca is only 124 km. Honduras possesses many islands, including the Bay Islands and Swan Islands in the Caribbean and a number of islands in the Golfo de Fonseca.

This is a mountainous country; around 65% to 80% of the total land area is composed of rugged mountains from 300 to 2850 metres high, with many highland valleys. Lowlands are found only along both coasts and in several river valleys. Deforestation proceeds at a rate of 300,000 hectares (3000 sq km) a year; at this rate the country could become a desert within 20 years.

The highlands are relatively cool and the lowlands are hot. The Caribbean coast receives high rainfall all year.

GOVERNMENT

The government of Honduras is a constitutional democracy with three tiers: executive, legislative and judicial. All citizens over 18 can vote.

The president is elected by popular vote to a four-year term which cannot be renewed. The legislature consists of the National Congress with 132 elected legislators. The judiciary consists of a Supreme Court, appointed by the president, which controls all branches of the lower courts, including the appointment of justices.

Honduras is divided into 18 departments, each with a governor appointed by the president. The departments are divided into municipalities, which are further divided into *aldeas* or villages. Rural areas have *caserios*, which are subdivisions of aldeas.

Each locality can elect its own council, legal representative and mayor.

Honduras has several political parties but the two major ones are the Partido Liberal and the Partido Nacional.

ECONOMY

Honduras is a poor country, with one of the lowest gross national products in Latin America. Close to 50% of the workforce is unemployed or underemployed, the country has a large foreign debt, and it imports more than it exports. Inflation in 1993 was around 12%, double that of 1992 but much lower than in 1991.

Agriculture employs 60% of the workforce, and provides 80% of the country's exports. The main products are corn, bananas, coffee, cattle, dry beans, sugar cane, cotton, sorghum and tobacco. The other main industries, listed here in descending order, are: forestry, hunting, fishing, manufacturing, trade, services, transport and communications.

In 1993 coffee provided the largest export income, followed by bananas. The European Union was the biggest purchaser of Honduran products (around 65%, twice as much as the USA), particularly of bananas, meaning that the new European banana quota is bound to affect Honduras adversely. Non-traditional Honduran exports such as melon and shrimp are expanding, but the nations remains particularly vulnerable to the volatile prices of bananas and coffee.

The USA was traditionally Honduras's principal trading partner, and economic ties remain very strong. Two giant US companies, United Fruit and Standard Fruit, hold a large part of the country's agricultural land and grow the majority of the banana crop. Aid from the USA also forms a large part of the Honduran economy, though it's much less than in the 1980s when the USA needed Honduras's cooperation for its intrigues in Nicaragua. Aid earmarked by the USA in 1993 totalled US$43.5 million, over half going towards development projects and only about 5% going to the military.

HONDURAS

POPULATION & PEOPLE

The population of Honduras grew by about 3.4% per annum in the 1980s. Estimates in 1993 put the total population at close to 5.5 million. Honduras is experiencing the most rapid urbanisation in Central America: the urban population was 44% in 1990 and is expected to hit 59% in 2010.

About 90% of the population is mestizo, a mixture of Spanish and Indian. Another 7% or so are pure Indians living in pockets around the country, each group with its own language and culture. The Jicaque, or Xicaque, live in a swath of territory sweeping from San Pedro Sula south-east to Montaña de la Flor. The Lenca live in south-western Honduras; they hold markets in the towns of La Esperanza, Marcala and Tutule. Chorti live near the Guatemala border, about a quarter of the way up from the border's southern point.

Miskito live in the Mosquitia region in north-eastern Honduras, on the coast and along the Río Coco, which forms the border between Honduras and Nicaragua. A dark people, Miskito are believed to be a mixed race of indigenous Indians and black Caribs, themselves a mixture of African and Carib Indians.

Paya live in the interior river regions of the Mosquitia. Sumo also live in the interior of the Mosquitia, in the area around the Río Patuca.

Garífuna are a mixture of African and Carib Indians and make up around 2.5% of the population. They were transported by the British to the island of Roatán from the Caribbean island of St Vincent in 1797. Today, Garífuna settlements are all along the northern coast of Honduras.

Other Black people on the north coast and in the Bay Islands are descendants of Jamaicans and other West Indians who came to Honduras with the British, or to work on the banana plantations. They often speak Caribbean-accented English in addition to Spanish, and are Protestant rather than Catholic.

RELIGION

Roman Catholicism is the predominant religion of Honduras, but the country has freedom of religion and there are many other Christian sects, including Mormons, Jehovah's Witnesses, Seventh Day Adventists, Baptists, Pentecostals, Assemblies of God, Evangelicals, and so on.

The indigenous groups have their own religions, often existing alongside Christianity, including elements of African and Indian animism and ancestor worship.

LANGUAGE

Spanish is the principal language and is spoken throughout the country. The various ethnic groups also have their own languages, which they speak among themselves.

In the Bay Islands the language of choice is English, spoken with a broad Caribbean accent; the locals can also speak Spanish, since it is taught in the schools, though some of the older people cannot speak it. Their accent is reminiscent of the Old English and Scots who settled the islands centuries ago.

Facts for the Visitor

VISAS & EMBASSIES

Citizens of most Western European countries, Australia, Canada, Japan, New Zealand, the UK and the USA can stay for up to 30 days without a visa if they are visiting as tourists. Once inside Honduras, you can apply for an extension, for a total stay of up to 90 days. After that you may have to leave the country and re-enter. To extend your stay, take your passport to an immigration office; there may be a small fee.

The regulations seem to change quite frequently, so check the current situation before you arrive at the border.

Practically every city and town in Honduras has its own immigration office (migración). The immigration offices in Tegucigalpa and San Pedro Sula are open Monday to Friday from 7.30 am to 3.30 pm; the others are open Monday to Friday from 8 am to noon and 2 to 5 pm.

Honduran Embassies

Honduran embassies are listed below. Visas can be obtained at these embassies and at consulates. In the USA, Honduras has consulates in Chicago, Houston, Los Angeles, Miami, New Orleans, New York, San Francisco, Tampa and other places, in addition to their embassy in Washington DC.

Honduran embassies in other countries include:

Australia
    (consulate only) 19/31 Pitt St, Sydney (☎ 02-252-3779)
Belize
    91 North Front St, Belize City (☎ 45889)
Canada
    151 Slater St, Suite 300, Ottawa, Ontario KIP 5H3 (☎ 613-233-8900)
Colombia
    Carretera 21, No 93-40, Apartado Aereo No 090566, Santa Fe (☎ 236-3753)
Costa Rica
    300 Este and 200 Norte of ITAN, Los Yoses Sur, San José (☎ 234 9502)
El Salvador
    67a Avenida Sur, No 530, Colonia Flor Blanca, San Salvador (☎ 712139, 212234)
Guatemala
    16a Calle 8-27, Zona 10, Guatemala City (☎ 373919, 371921)
Mexico
    Alfonso Reyes No 220, Colonia Condesa, México DF 06140 (☎ 211-5747)
Nicaragua
    Planes de Altamira, No 64, Carretera a Masaya, Apdo P321, Managua (☎ 670105)
Panama
    Avenida Justo Arosemena and Calle 31, Edificio Tapia, 2nd floor, Panama City (☎ 258200)
UK
    115 Gloucester Place, London W1H 3PJ (☎ 071-486-4880)
USA
    3007 Tilden St NW, Washington DC 20008 (☎ 202-966-7702)

Foreign Embassies in Honduras

Foreign embassies and consulates in Honduras are in Tegucigalpa and San Pedro Sula; see those cities for particulars.

CUSTOMS

Customs regulations are the usual 200 cigarettes, 100 cigars or half a kg of tobacco, and two litres of alcohol.

MONEY
Currency

The unit of currency is the lempira. Notes are of one, two, five, 10, 20, 50 and 100 lempiras. There are 100 centavos in a lempira; coins are of one, two, five, 10, 20 and 50 centavos.

Foreign		Honduras
A$1	=	L5.40
C$1	=	L5.50
DM1	=	L4.50
NZ$1	=	L4.35
UK£1	=	L11.40
US$1	=	L7.55

The US dollar is the only foreign currency that is easily exchanged in Honduras; away from the borders it's even difficult to change the currencies of Guatemala, El Salvador or Nicaragua.

Cash gets a slightly better rate than travellers' cheques in some places (about 10 centavos' difference), the same rate in others. The black market rate for cash and travellers' cheques is only slightly higher or even the same as the official rate. Some banks don't exchange travellers' cheques so it's best to stock up in the cities.

Cash advances on Visa and MasterCard are available at Credomatic offices, and at Futuro and Ficenza banks. Some other banks will take Visa, which is more widely accepted than MasterCard. Check the credit card exchange rate as it can be unfavourable compared to that for cash or travellers' cheques. There's no transaction charge at the Honduran end for Visa or MasterCard cash advances.

Tipping

Most Hondurans do not tip. In places with a lot of tourist and foreign influence, tipping is more common, from a little loose change up to 10% of the bill.

Bargaining
Watch to see what the local people are doing. Bargaining is not as common in Honduras as in some other places in Central America. Usually you should bargain at open markets and on the streets; prices at indoor stores are fixed. Even taxis often have a fixed rate, which you can sometimes bargain down a lempira or two.

CLIMATE & WHEN TO GO
The mountainous interior is much cooler than the coastal lowlands. Tegucigalpa, at an elevation of 975 metres, has a temperate climate, with maximum/minimum temperatures varying from 25/14°C in January to 30/18°C in May. The coastal lowlands are much warmer and more humid, the Pacific coastal plain near the Golfo de Fonseca being hot indeed. December and January are the coolest months.

The rainfall also varies in different parts of the country. The rainy season is from around May to October. On the Pacific side and in the interior this means a relatively dry season from around November to April. However, the amount of rain and when it falls varies considerably from year to year.

On the Caribbean coast it rains all year round, but the wettest months are from around September or even November to January or February. During this time floods can occur on the north coast, impeding travel and occasionally causing severe damage (400 people died in floods in November 1993).

The most popular time to visit Honduras, especially the beach areas on the Caribbean coast and the Bay Islands, is around February to April, during the North American winter but after the rainy season. This is an excellent time to visit but outside this time you will find fewer tourists and prices may be lower.

WHAT TO BRING
On the north coast, the Bay Islands and in the Mosquitia, be sure to bring insect repellent against the mosquitoes and sandflies. A mosquito net is also a good idea. Be sure to bring anti-malaria pills as malaria is endemic in the region (chloroquine is easily available in most Honduran cities).

Since tap water is not safe to drink, and bottled water is sometimes hard to find, carry your own means of purifying water.

TOURIST OFFICES
The Instituto Hondureño de Turismo has offices in Tegucigalpa, San Pedro Sula, La Ceiba, Roatán and Copán Ruinas. They expect to open another one sometime soon at Agua Caliente, on the border with Guate-

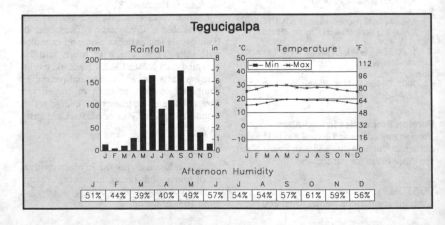

mala. In 1994 the tourist office achieved autonomy from the government, so there may be some re-organisation.

BUSINESS HOURS & HOLIDAYS

Business hours are normally Monday to Friday from 9 am to noon and 2 to 6 pm, and on Saturday from 9 am to noon. Bank hours are Monday to Friday from 9 am to 3 pm. Most government offices are open Monday to Friday from 7.30 am to 3.30 pm, sometimes with a lunch break that may last from noon to 12.30 pm, or 1 pm, or 2 pm.

Public holidays are:

1 January
  New Year's Day
14 April
  Day of the Americas
March/April
  Holy Week: Thursday, Friday and Saturday before Easter Sunday
1 May
  Labour Day
15 September
  Independence Day
3 October
  Francisco Morazán Day
12 October
  Columbus Day
21 October
  Army Day
25 December
  Christmas Day

In addition, a number of Catholic holy days are celebrated.

CULTURAL EVENTS

If you get a chance to attend a fair or presentation of any of Honduras's indigenous groups, do so. Several Garífuna music and dance troupes give presentations throughout the country, including the excellent Ballet Folklórico Garífuna.

The Feria Centroamericana de Turismo y Artesanía (FECATAI), an all-Central-American international artisans' and tourism fair, is held every year from 6 to 16 December in Tegucigalpa. Another annual all-Honduras artisans' and cultural fair is held in Copán Ruinas from 15 to 21 December.

As elsewhere in Central America, just about every city, town and village in Honduras has a patron saint and celebrates an annual festival or fair in the days around their saint's day. Some are big events, attracting crowds from far and wide.

One such fair is the Carnaval at La Ceiba, celebrated during the third week in May; the third Saturday is the biggest day, with parades, costumes, music and celebrations in the streets. The fair at San Pedro Sula, held in the last week of June, is another popular one. The fairs at Tela (13 June), Trujillo (24 June), Danlí (last weekend in August) and Copán Ruinas (15 to 20 March) are also good, and there are many others.

The fair for the Virgen de Suyapa, patron saint of Honduras, is celebrated in Suyapa, near Tegucigalpa, from around 2 to 11 February; 3 February is actually the saint's day. The services and festivities bring pilgrims and celebrants from all over Central America.

POST

The postal service in Honduras is not the best, but the rates and theoretical delivery times are:

to the USA	US$0.12	one week
to Europe	US$0.14	one week
to Australia	US$0.15	10 days

You can receive poste restante mail at any post office; have it directed to you at 'Lista de Correos, (town and department), República de Honduras, Central America'.

Honduras is notorious for problems with receiving incoming mail from the USA; since Hondurans working there send money to their families back home, a certain amount of the mail arriving from that country somehow never reaches its destination. Other times there can be inexplicable delays. Most mail, however, does manage to get through. It seems to have a better chance if there is no way it could even *appear* to have money in it; use aerograms which can't contain enclosures. Outgoing post is more reliable.

HONDURAS

TELECOMMUNICATIONS

International telephone, telegraph, telex and fax services are offered at Hondutel offices in every city and town. The country code when calling Honduras from abroad is 504. Long-distance and international calls are expensive: a minimum three-minute call costs about US$17 to Europe or US$4.60 to the USA. National and international calls from Honduras are cheaper after 10 pm.

Phone boxes for local calls are painted red and are found outside Hondutel offices. You can also sometimes find them in public places such as parks and on busy corners. You need a 10 centavo coin for a three-minute call; keep putting in coins, or you'll get cut off after three minutes.

TIME

Honduras is six hours behind GMT.

LAUNDRY

Most hotels have somewhere you can do your laundry; ask to use the *lavadero*. Expensive hotels usually have an expensive laundry service, but in cheaper places you can offer chamber staff a few lempiras to wash your clothes for you. Service or self-service laundries in town are cheap – about US$0.17 per pound ($US0.40 per kg).

WEIGHTS & MEASURES

The metric system of weights and measures is used. Other measurements used are the *vara* (838 mm) and the *manzana* (0.7 hectare). The US gallon is used for fuel.

ELECTRICITY

Honduras has both 110 and 220 volt electricity supplies; find out which it is in your hotel before you plug in any appliance.

BOOKS

Some good books for understanding social, political and economic developments in Honduras include *Honduras: The Making of a Banana Republic* by Alison Acker (South End Press, Boston, 1988, paperback); *Honduras: State for Sale* by Richard Lapper (Latin America Bureau, London, 1985,

paperback); *Honduras: Portrait of a Captive Nation* edited by Nancy Peckenham & Annie Street (Praeger Publishers, New York, 1985, paperback); and *Inside Honduras* by Tom Barry & Kent Norsworthy (Inter-Hemispheric Education Resource Center, Albuquerque, 1993, paperback).

Prisión Verde by Ramón Amaya Amador (1950, paperback, in Spanish) is a famous book about the Honduran banana industry.

On a lighter note, Guillermo Yuscarán (William Lewis, in his former incarnation as a professor of Hispanic studies in Santa Barbara, California), who writes in Spanish and English and now lives near Tegucigalpa, is one of Honduras's most wonderful painters and writers. His books, all in paperback – *Points of Light: Honduran Short Stories* (1990) in English, *Conociendo a la Gente Garífuna (The Garífuna Story)* (1990) in Spanish and English, and *Blue Pariah* (1989), also in English – are available at Book Village in Tegucigalpa. He's also written *Beyond Honduras: Tales of Tela, Trujillo and Other Places.*

Footloose in Honduras by Robert Millar (paperback, 1987), available in both English and Spanish *(Aventureros en Honduras)*, a novel by a long-time resident and lover of Honduras, is also available at Book Village.

MAPS

The Instituto Hondureño de Turismo in Tegucigalpa has maps for sale at US$1.70, but they're not very good. Tourist maps are also available from some petrol stations for about the same price. The Instituto Geográfico Nacional, whose office is in SECOPT in Tegucigalpa, has excellent coloured topographical and regional maps, but you have to apply in writing to the head of the armed forces to get them.

MEDIA

Honduras has four daily newspapers: *El Heraldo* and *La Tribuna* are published in Tegucigalpa, *La Prensa* and *El Tiempo* in San Pedro Sula. *Honduras This Week* is a small weekly English-language newspaper published in Tegucigalpa.

More than 150 radio stations and around six television stations broadcast in Honduras. Movies and news in English come from the USA by cable TV.

FILM & PHOTOGRAPHY
Film costs around US$3 for a roll of 24 colour prints and US$3.80 for a roll of 36 colour slides. Both Kodak and Fuji film are sold.

Larger cities have one-hour photo processing shops. In general, you're safer to wait for processing until you get to a more developed country.

HEALTH
Tap water is not safe to drink in Honduras. Many restaurants and hotels provide purified drinking water but be sure it really is purified before you drink it, and of course, watch out for ice cubes. Carry your own method of purifying water. Raw salads (lettuce, cabbage etc) are suspect if they have been washed with unpurified water. In 1994 millions of dollars were being invested in Tegucigalpa's water supply, which should eventually improve the quality.

Malaria-carrying mosquitoes are a problem on the north coast and in the aptly named Mosquitia; be sure to follow a regimen of anti-malarial medication. No vaccinations are required to enter the country, but you should be vaccinated against typhoid and tetanus. Over 1000 cases of cholera (resulting in 49 deaths) have been diagnosed in Honduras in the two years since an epidemic broke out in October 1991. The most recent cases were reported in Tegucigalpa and in the departments of Choluteca, Cortés, Santa Bárbara, Valle and El Paraíso. Be vigilant about the hygiene standards of what you eat and drink everywhere in Honduras. Don't rely on a cholera vaccination to protect you, as it is ineffective.

Digestive problems such as stomach ache and diarrhoea are likely, especially if you eat from street stands; pharmacies are well-equipped with medicines and can often cure whatever ails you. In larger towns there is usually a *farmacia de turno* open at all hours.

Over 3000 cases of AIDS have been diagnosed in Honduras since 1985, and the World Health Organisation estimates that one in 25 Hondurans has the HIV virus. Don't have sex with a local without using a condom.

WOMEN TRAVELLERS
Honduras is a good country for women travellers, but be sure to dress modestly: no shorts, except on the beach; skirts below the knee; and preferably sleeves (though they can be short sleeves). Be sure to wear a bra, as not wearing one brands you as a 'loose woman' and will invite problems. On the Bay Islands, where there are a lot of beach-going foreign tourists, standards of modesty in dress are much more relaxed.

DANGERS & ANNOYANCES
Honduras is safe for the most part, but use normal caution. Beware of bag-slashing on crowded buses, walking alone through cities in the middle of the night etc – the usual stuff.

If you go hiking through wild places, beware of poisonous snakes, especially the *barba amarilla* (fer-de-lance); the coral snake is also present. There are alligators in the waterways of the Mosquitia, in addition to the peaceful manatee and much other wildlife. Honduras also has scorpions (not lethal), wasps and other stinging insects. You probably will never see a dangerous animal but do be aware that they exist and know what to do if you encounter them.

Malaria-carrying mosquitoes and biting sandflies on the north coast, the Bay Islands and the Mosquitia are definitely an annoyance, and along with unpurified water can be the greatest threat to your well-being.

FOOD
The typical meal *(plato típico)* in Honduras usually includes beans, rice, tortillas, fried bananas, meat, potatoes or yucca, cream, cheese, and a cabbage and tomato salad, or some combination (not necessarily all) of these. Most restaurants have the plato típico on the menu, and it's usually the cheapest and most filling meal, whether for breakfast, lunch or dinner.

Most places also offer a *comida corrida* or *plato del día* at lunchtime – usually a good, large, cheap meal.

At markets and street stands or shacks, you can get *(baleadas)* – white flour tortillas folded over a filling of refried beans, cream and crumbled cheese. They usually cost around US$0.20; a couple of them with a soft drink for another US$0.25 will fill you up for a while. Be cautious, however, about the cleanliness of preparation of baleadas on the street, or you could end up with an amoebic illness.

Another good street snack is *tortillas con quesillo*, two crisp fried corn tortillas with melted white cheese between them. Fried chicken is also a common, favourite dish in Honduras. *Tajaditas*, crispy fried banana chips, are sold in little bags on the streets, as are sliced green mangos sprinkled with a mixture of salt and cumin.

On the coasts and around the Lago de Yojoa, the fish is fresh and cheap. Most common is fried fish; fish and seafood soups, including *sopa de caracol* (conch soup made with coconut), are delicious. On the Caribbean coast, *pan de coco* (coconut bread) is also very tasty.

DRINKS

Soft drinks are found everywhere, with all the regulars plus a few local flavours including banana. *Licuados* (milk blended with fruit) are always good; watch out for added ice, which might not have been purified. Fruit drinks blended with water could be made with unpurified water.

Four brands of beer are made in Honduras: Salva Vida, Port Royal Export, Nacional and Imperial.

THINGS TO BUY

Honduras produces a number of typical *artesanías*, including woodcarving and wooden musical instruments, woven *junco* basketry, embroidery and textile arts, leather goods and ceramics. Brightly painted ceramics (especially depicting roosters) can be bought along the road from El Amatillo to Nacaome.

Paintings of typical mountain villages, with cobblestoned lanes winding among houses with white adobe walls and red tile roofs, can be found in many places, including Tegucigalpa, Valle de Angeles and San Pedro Sula.

Getting There & Away

AIR

American, Continental, Taca, and Tan/Sahsa airlines have international flights to and from Honduras, all with connections at both Tegucigalpa and San Pedro Sula. Lacsa and Iberia have flights to/from San Pedro Sula, but not Tegucigalpa. Tan/Sahsa is the national airline of Honduras.

Frequent direct flights connect Honduras to all the other Central American capitals and many destinations in North America, including Mexico City, Miami, New Orleans, Houston, New York, Los Angeles and San Francisco.

If you fly out of Honduras you must pay a departure tax at the airport. The tax is L95 (about $US13.35) if you pay in Honduran currency, or US$16 if you pay in US dollars.

LAND

Honduran border crossings are open daily from around 7 am to 5 pm (6 pm on weekends). US$0.70 or US$1.40 is usually charged to enter or leave. In theory this is an overtime payment only applicable between noon and 2 pm and on the weekends after noon on Saturday; in practice it's charged almost any time. It's best to pay up unless the amount demanded is excessive.

Remember when heading south that Nicaragua is one hour ahead of Honduras, meaning you have one hour less in the day to get where you're going.

To Guatemala, the main crossings are at El Florido and Agua Caliente. To El Salvador, the crossings are El Poy and El Amatillo. There is also a crossing at Sabanetas, southwest of Comayagua. Tourists are expected to be able to start using this crossing in 1994, though it is not currently possible to proceed by bus on the El Salvadoran side. Check on the current situation before heading down there.

The crossings to Nicaragua are at El Espino, Las Manos and Guasaule. Frequent buses serve all of these border crossings (except Sabanetas). Most buses do not cross the border, meaning you have to cross on foot and pick up another bus on the other side. The exceptions are international buses. Tica Bus (☎ 387040, 386587), 17a Calle between 7a and 8a Avenida, Tegucigalpa, has buses leaving the capital at 9 am; to Guatemala City (via San Salvador) costs US$23 and to Panama City (via Managua and San José) costs US$60.

If you're driving, there is a lot of paperwork, fees and red tape involved in bringing a car into Honduras; you will be issued a special permit for your vehicle that must be renewed at regular intervals.

Jungle Trail

The Jungle Trail is the name given to the route between Puerto Cortés in Honduras and Puerto Barrios in Guatemala. Allow two days for the trip, and get your exit stamp from one of those towns before you leave. Corinto is the last place to stay and eat on the Honduran side and marks the end of the road. From there the trail bordering the jungle leads to Sujade Frontera (two hours), where you cross the river. From here the trail gets muddy and less defined. After two hours turn right beyond the gate (you're now in Guatemala) and continue for an hour to the next gate and a small settlement. Here you can either walk to the immigration office at El Cinchado (two hours) or hire a dugout to Finca Chinook (on the west side of the Río Motagua), where you can pick up a half-hourly bus to Puerto Barrios. You should be able to get from Corinto to Puerto Barrios on the same day. (The above itinerary is based on information supplied by John Peluso of the USA.)

Don't embark on this crossing without adequate preparation; if you lose your way you may have to spend the night in the open.

Hiring a guide would avoid this possibility, and should also provide some measure of protection against bandits who have been know to operate in the area. One traveller warned of quicksand. Take water, food, good hiking boots and a compass.

Another off-the-beaten-track crossing is through the Mosquitia to Nicaragua, but it's not without its own problems (see the Mosquitia section for details).

SEA

Though there are no regular passenger ship services to or from Honduras, it is often possible to arrange passage with fishing and cargo vessels if you pay your way. Don't waste time negotiating with an ordinary crew member: speak to the captain. On the Caribbean coast you can try to find a boat around Puerto Cortés, La Ceiba, Puerto Castilla (near Trujillo), Tela or the Bay Islands. The most common international destinations for these boats would be Puerto Barrios (Guatemala), Belize, Puerto Cabezas (Nicaragua), the Caribbean islands, and New Orleans and Miami in the USA.

On the Pacific side, the Golfo de Fonseca is shared by Nicaragua, Honduras and El Salvador, so you may be able to get a ride on boats sailing between the three countries. San Lorenzo is the main Honduran port town in the gulf.

If you arrive or depart from Honduras by sea, be sure to clear your paperwork (entry and exit stamps etc) immediately with the nearest immigration office.

LEAVING HONDURAS

See the preceding Air and Land entries for information on exit charges. Be sure that your exit stamp is stamped into your passport.

Getting Around

AIR

Tan/Sahsa, Honduras's national airline, offers domestic flights between Tegucigalpa,

San Pedro Sula, La Ceiba and Roatán. One-way fares (double for return) are:

Tegucigalpa-San Pedro Sula	US$13.00
Tegucigalpa-La Ceiba	US$16.50
Tegucigalpa-Roatán	US$22.30
San Pedro Sula-La Ceiba	US$13.00
San Pedro Sula-Roatán	US$15.65
La Ceiba-Roatán	US$12.00

Isleña and Sosa airlines, based in La Ceiba, offer flights from La Ceiba to the Bay Islands and various points in the Mosquitia (see the La Ceiba section for details).

BUS
Buses are an easy and cheap way to get around in Honduras, as buses run frequently to most places in the country. The first buses of the day often start very early in the morning; the last bus often departs in the late afternoon.

TRAIN
The only passenger train services in Honduras are in the north, running between San Pedro Sula, Puerto Cortés and Tela. The trains are rudimentary, slow, and very cheap. Services were disrupted in 1993 – check whether they're operating again before planning to use the train.

TAXI
There are numerous taxis in most towns in Honduras. Fares can start as low as US$0.35, charged either as a flat rate for the destination or per person. Longer journeys in town can cost around US$1.80. *Colectivos* (shared) taxis are also available.

Taxis are not metered in Honduras, so be sure to negotiate the fare before you take off.

CAR & MOTORBIKE
The main highways are all excellent paved roads. Away from the highways the roads may be paved or unpaved, with their condition ranging from excellent to disastrous. Travel on unpaved roads can be dusty in the dry season, and muddy and slippery in the rainy season.

Rental cars are available in Tegucigalpa, San Pedro Sula, La Ceiba and on the island of Roatán, but they are not cheap.

HITCHING
While not recommended, hitching is generally easy in Honduras, especially in the rural areas where not many people have private vehicles. It is normal in rural areas for pick-up trucks to stop to take on passengers.

BOAT
Boat transport in Honduras is common for getting around on the Caribbean coast, between the Bay Islands and from them to the mainland, though land travel on the coast and air travel to the islands is more convenient and very reasonably priced. In the Mosquitia, where there is just one road, almost all transport is along the waterways.

Tegucigalpa

Population 670,100
Tegucigalpa, capital of Honduras, is a busy, noisy city nestled into a bowl-shaped valley, surrounded by a ring of mountains. At an altitude of 975 metres, it has a fresh and pleasant climate, and is much cooler than the coasts. The surrounding mountainous region is covered in pine trees.

The name Tegucigalpa is a bit of a mouthful; Hondurans often call the city 'Tegus' (TEH-goos) for short. The name, meaning 'silver hill' in the original local dialect, was bestowed when the Spanish founded the city as a silver and gold mining centre in 1578, on the slopes of Picacho. Tegucigalpa became the capital of Honduras in 1880, when the government seat was moved from Comayagua, 82 km to the north-west.

In 1938 Comayagüela, on the opposite side of the river from Tegucigalpa, became part of the city.

Orientation
The city is divided by the Río Choluteca. On the east side is Tegucigalpa, with the city

centre and the more affluent districts. Plaza Morazán, usually called Parque Central, with its beautiful cathedral, is at the heart of the city and most local bus lines stop there or nearby.

Across the river is Comayagüela, generally poorer and dirtier, with a sprawling market area, lots of long-distance bus stations, cheap hotels and comedores. The two are connected by a number of bridges.

Information

Tourist Office The main office of the Instituto Hondureño de Turismo (☎ 383974/5) is situated on the 3rd floor, Edificio Europa, Avenida Ramon Ernesto Cruz. It is open Monday to Friday from 8.30 am to 4.30 pm.

More centrally located is their small kiosk office on Parque Central, due to reopen some time in 1994 and with similar hours to the main office. Staff at both offices can answer questions, and sell postcards, posters and maps. (Their city map, however, has no street names marked on it!)

They also operate a tourism office at Tegucigalpa's Toncontín airport; it is open every day from 6 am to 6 pm.

Money Not all banks in Tegucigalpa change money; those that do will change only US dollars cash or travellers' cheques, giving the same rate for both. Try Banco de Honduras, in the Edificio Soto on Parque Central; Banco de Londres y Montreal, on Avenida Cristobal Colón; or Banco Atlántida, which has several branches around town, including one by the Parque Central, one at Mercado San Isidro in Comayagüela, and another at the Hotel Honduras Maya. All are open Monday to Friday from 9 am to 3 pm.

The *casa de cambio* diagonally opposite the post office, on the corner of Avenida Miguel P Barahona and Calle El Telégrafo, changes US dollars cash at the same rate as the banks, and it's open daily.

Black-market moneychangers operate all along Avenida Miguel Barahona. For US dollars cash they give you about 10 centavos more than the banks (bargain for a good

rate); for travellers' cheques they might give you less than the banks! They will also change money from Guatemala, Nicaragua and El Salvador (but you'll get a better rate at the respective border) and even sell dollars.

At the airport, private entrepreneurs change US dollars at the same rate as the banks; they won't change any other currency.

Post & Telecommunications The central post office, on the corner of Avenida Miguel P Barahona and Calle El Telégrafo, is open Monday to Friday from 7 am to 9 pm, and on Saturday from 7 am to 3 pm. Poste restante mail is held for 30 days and costs a few cents to collect.

The Hondutel office is a short block away, at the corner of Avenida Cristobal Colón and Calle El Telégrafo. It is open 24 hours, every day. Services include international telephone, telegraph, telex and fax.

On the Comayagüela side, the Hondutel and post offices are in the same building, on 6a Avenida between 7a and 8a Calle. The Hondutel office is open Monday to Saturday from 7 am to 9 pm, and the post office is open the same hours as the one in Tegucigalpa, except it closes at noon on Saturday.

Warning Telephone numbers in some districts were altered in 1994.

Immigration Office You can extend your visa at the immigration office (Migración) (☎ 227711), on Avenida Máximo Jeréz between Calle Las Damas and Calle Dionicio Gutierrez, in the large office building beside the Hotel Rondo. It's open Monday to Friday from 7.30 am to 3.30 pm.

If you bring your passport in the morning before 10 am, you can usually get it back the same afternoon; otherwise pick it up the following day.

Foreign Embassies Foreign embassies, and a number of consulates, are in Tegucigalpa. Several countries also have

HONDURAS

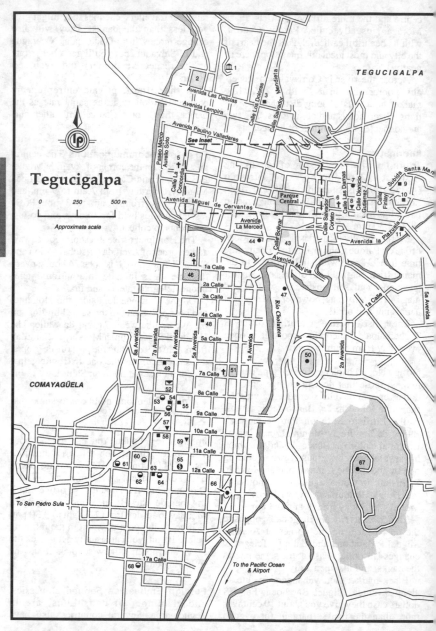

Tegucigalpa

0   250   500 m

Approximate scale

HONDURAS

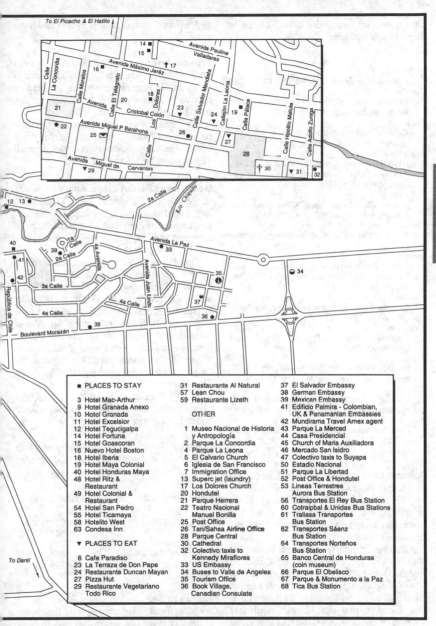

PLACES TO STAY	31 Restaurante Al Natural	37 El Salvador Embassy
	57 Lean Chou	38 German Embassy
3 Hotel Mac-Arthur	59 Restaurante Lizeth	39 Mexican Embassy
9 Hotel Granada Anexo		41 Edificio Palmira - Colombian,
10 Hotel Granada	OTHER	UK & Panamanian Embassies
11 Hotel Excelsior		42 Mundirama Travel Amex agent
12 Hotel Tegucigalpa	1 Museo Nacional de Historia	43 Parque La Merced
14 Hotel Fortuna	y Antropología	44 Casa Presidencial
15 Hotel Goascoran	2 Parque La Concordia	45 Church of Maria Auxiliadora
16 Nuevo Hotel Boston	4 Parque La Leona	46 Mercado San Isidro
18 Hotel Iberia	5 El Calvario Church	47 Colectivo taxis to Suyapa
19 Hotel Maya Colonial	6 Iglesia de San Francisco	50 Estadio Nacional
40 Hotel Honduras Maya	7 Immigration Office	51 Parque La Libertad
48 Hotel Ritz &	13 Superc jet (laundry)	52 Post Office & Hondutel
Restaurant	17 Los Dolores Church	53 Lineas Terrestres
49 Hotel Colonial &	20 Hondutel	Aurora Bus Station
Restaurant	21 Parque Herrera	56 Transportes El Rey Bus Station
54 Hotel San Pedro	22 Teatro Nacional	60 Cotraipal & Unidas Bus Stations
55 Hotel Ticamaya	Manuel Bonilla	61 Traliasa Transportes
58 Hotelito West	25 Post Office	Bus Station
63 Condesa Inn	26 Tan/Sahsa Airline Office	62 Transportes Sáenz
	28 Parque Central	Bus Station
PLACES TO EAT	30 Cathedral	64 Transportes Norteños
	32 Colectivo taxis to	Bus Station
8 Cafe Paradiso	Kennedy Miraflores	65 Banco Central de Honduras
23 La Terraza de Don Pepe	33 US Embassy	(coin museum)
24 Restaurante Duncan Mayan	34 Buses to Valle de Angeles	66 Parque El Obelisco
27 Pizza Hut	35 Tourism Office	67 Parque & Monumento a la Paz
29 Restaurante Vegetariano	36 Book Village,	68 Tica Bus Station
Todo Rico	Canadian Consulate	

consulates in San Pedro Sula. Those in Tegucigalpa include:

Belize
Colonia 15 de Septiembre, No 1703 (☎ 331423)

Canada
(consulate only) Edificio El Castaño, 6th floor, Boulevard Morazán (☎ 314538)

Colombia
Colonia Palmira, Edificio Palmira, 4th floor, opposite Hotel Honduras Maya (☎ 329709)

Costa Rica
Blvd Morazán, Costado Oeste de Reasa, Apartado 512, Colonia Lomas del Guijarro, east Tegucigalpa (☎ 321768, 321054)

El Salvador
Colonia San Carlos, No 205, one block from Boulevard Morazán (☎ 325045, 321344)

Germany
Boulevard Morazán, Edificio Paysen, 3rd floor (☎ 323161/2)

Guatemala
Colonia Las Minitas, No 1374, 4a Calle, between 1a Avenida and Avenida Juan Lindo (☎ 329704, 321580)

Mexico
Colonia Palmira, Paseo República del Brasil (☎ 326471, 324039)

Nicaragua
Colonia Lomas del Tepeyac, Bloque M-1 (☎ 324290, 329025)

Panama
Colonia Palmira, Edificio Palmira, 2nd floor, opposite Hotel Honduras Maya (☎ 315441)

UK
Colonia Palmira, Edificio Palmira, 3rd floor, opposite Hotel Honduras Maya (☎ 325429/80)

USA
Edificio Embajada Americana, Avenida La Paz (☎ 323120/4)

Cultural Centres The Instituto Hondureño de Cultura Interamericana (IHCI) (☎ 377539) on Calle Real de Comayagüela offers cultural events relating to all the Americas, and they have a small English-language library.

Alliance Française (Alianza Francesa) (☎ 370445), on the corner of Calle El Telégrafo and Avenida Lempira, in Barrio Abajo, Tegucigalpa, offers cultural events, French classes, and weekly French films. The German institute, Centro Cultural Alemán (☎ 371555), on Calle La Fuente, No 717, offers German cultural events and literature.

Travel Agencies Mundirama Travel (☎ 378181) on Avenida Republic Panama is an agent for American Express; for card or cheque holders they will hold mail for six months and cash travellers' cheques.

Check in the telephone directory yellow pages under 'Viajes, Agencias de' for other travel agencies. Some offer tours around Tegucigalpa and Honduras.

Bookshops Book Village, situated upstairs in the Centro Comercial Los Costeños on Boulevard Morazán, is an excellent English-language bookshop with a large selection of new and used books, as well as magazines and US newspapers.

The Percy Soto bookshop, also called Librería Panamericana, on Callejón La Leona between Avenidas Cristobal Colón and Jeréz, has a very small selection of books in English, but it also carries the *New York Times*, the *Wall Street Journal*, the *Miami Herald*, and *Diario de las Américas*, the Spanish-language newspaper published in Miami. Both bookshops sell the Tegucigalpa English-language newspaper, *Honduras This Week*.

The gift shop of the Hotel Honduras Maya also carries newspapers and paperback books in English.

Laundry Superc Jet on Avenida Juan Gutemberg will wash, dry and fold laundry for L1.20 per pound (about L2.60 per kg).

Emergency Emergency phone numbers are:

Police (FUSEP)	199, 228977 or 227924
Policía Femenina	228230
Ambulance (Red Cross)	378654
Hospital	326234
Fire	198

Things to See
Walking Tour – Tegucigalpa At the centre of the city is the fine **cathedral** and, in front

of it, the **Parque Central**. The domed 18th-century cathedral has an intricate Baroque altar of gold and silver, and lots of other fine art. Parque Central, with its statue of Morazán on horseback, is the hub of the city. Most local buses stop here or nearby. On the south side of the cathedral is the Palacio del Distrito Central (City Hall).

Two blocks south is another major plaza, **Parque La Merced**. The unusual modern building on stilts is the **Palacio Legislativo**, where Congress meets. Standing next to it in striking contrast is the old university, established in 1847, which is now a museum of art called the **Antiguo Paraninfo Universitaria**. It's open Monday to Friday from 8 am to 8 pm, and on weekends 10 am to 6 pm (free admission), with art exhibitions and performances.

Standing on this plaza in front of the Palacio Legislativo you can look a block to the west and see the **Casa Presidencial**, the Presidential Palace.

Back at Parque Central, Avenida Miguel P Barahona has a lively pedestrian-only section with many street vendors. Three blocks east of the cathedral on this avenue is the **Iglesia de San Francisco**, the first church in Tegucigalpa, founded in 1592 by the Franciscans. The building beside it was formerly the **Spanish Mint**.

Heading west from Parque Central on Avenida Miguel P Barahona, after two blocks turn up Calle Los Dolores to another walking mall full of market stalls; further north is another fine colonial church, **Los Dolores**, with a plaza out front and lots of art inside.

On Avenida Barahona, two blocks west past the post office, is **Parque Herrera**, another pleasant plaza, with the national theatre, **Teatro Nacional Manuel Bonilla**, dating from 1912, and a peaceful old church, **El Calvario**.

Walking north for four long blocks from El Calvario on Calle La Concordia, you reach **Parque La Concordia**, an interesting park full of reproductions of the Maya ruins at Copán, including a pyramid and many stone carvings.

A couple of blocks north-east, way up on a hill, is the **Museo Nacional**, the national museum of anthropology and history. The grand blue building was the personal home of Lozano, one of Honduras's past presidents. It now contains salons with displays on anthropology, archaeology and the pre-Hispanic history of Honduras, the 'moment of contact' when the Spanish arrived, the colonial period, and an interesting section on ethnography, with displays on Honduras's eight indigenous groups (the Jicaques, Lencas, Chortis, Miskitos, Payas, Sumos, Isleñas and Garífunas), showing where and how they live. The museum is open Wednesday to Sunday from 8.30 am to 3.30 pm. Admission is US$1.40.

Farther east is **Parque La Leona**, an attractive lookout park with a fine view over the city, from where you can make your way down the steep streets to the city centre.

Walking Tour – Comayagüela

Just across the Río Choluteca (also called Río Grande) is Comayagüela, about a five-minute walk from central Tegucigalpa.

If you cross the bridge leading to 6a Avenida in Comayagüela, you immediately come to Comayagüela's famous market, **Mercado San Isidro**, which sprawls for many blocks. Here you can buy anything you can think of. The leather shops have some good handcrafted leatherwork and saddles, and also sell handwoven hats.

The copper-domed church of **Maria Auxiliadora**, on the corner of 1a Calle and 5a Avenida, has a statue of the Virgin and Child on its tower overlooking the market area.

Comayagüela is more a commercial centre and has fewer old buildings and plazas than Tegucigalpa. On Parque La Libertad there's the old **Escuela Nacional de Bellas Artes**, the national school of fine arts with its white statues out front, but it's been closed for renovations for years.

Several blocks south on 2a Avenida is the **Parque El Obelisco**, with an obelisk commemorating the centennial of Central American independence. Nearby is the towering **Banco Central de Honduras**. Inside is a coin museum, open Monday to Thursday from noon to 4 pm. Aside from valuable notes and coins (one 1888 Honduran gold coin is worth US$12,000), there's an interesting exhibit on the idealised Indian face chosen to represent Lempira on the one lempira note. Look out also for the 1993 banknote issued by Kuwait to thank nations who provided military assistance in the Gulf War; Honduras's name appears on the note, despite the denials of the Honduran government that they sent any soldiers!

Parque y Monumento a la Paz Near the river, opposite the Parque El Obelisco, is Parque a la Paz, a wooded hill with a large monument to peace at its summit, which commands a sweeping view of the entire city. Nearby is the giant **National Stadium** where soccer matches are played.

Banco Atlantida The headquarters of this bank on Boulevard Centroamerica, southeast of the centre in Miraflores, has an interesting **Salon Cultural**. Inside is a coin collection and an archaeological collection; the latter has Maya statues, vessels and artefacts from Copán and other sites, plus explanatory maps and photos. It's free and open Monday to Friday from 9 am to 3 pm, and on Saturday from 9 am to noon.

The bank is a few hundred metres down the road from the RENARE office (where you get permission to stay in La Tigra); bus No 5 (Carrizal-Miraflores) runs from the centre and stops outside.

El Picacho On this peak on the north side of Tegucigalpa is the United Nations Park (Parque de las Naciones Unidas), established to commemorate the UN's 40th anniversary. There's also a soccer field where games are held on Sundays, several lookout points for excellent views over the city, and a zoo. You can get food and drink up here.

The zoo is not extravagant but it does have some interesting local wildlife. The sign at the entrance announces the zoo is open on Saturday from 9 am to 4 pm, and on Sunday from 9 am to 5 pm (admission US$0.30). The

caretakers say that you can also come during the week; enter at the gate about 20 metres to the right (east) of the main entrance, which is always open.

Buses to Picacho run only on Sunday; take the light blue bus No 9 from outside the Farmacia Santa Barbara behind the Los Dolores church. Be sure you get the right bus; several other No 9 buses also stop here. Or you could come from the same bus stop in a colectivo taxi – about US$2.20 for the whole taxi.

Festivals

The Feria Centroamericana de Turismo y Artesanía (FECATAI) is an all-Central American international artisans' and tourist fair. It's held from 6 to 16 December; the location changes, so check with the tourist office.

The Feria de Suyapa, from 2 to 11 February, is held in Suyapa, seven km south-east of Tegucigalpa, every year to honour the Virgen de Suyapa, Honduras's patron saint. Her day is 3 February, but the fair lasts for an entire week, attracting pilgrims and celebrants from all over Central America.

Places to Stay

There are many places to stay on the Tegucigalpa side or across the river in Comayagüela. Comayagüela has the central market area and lots of bus stations; the Tegucigalpa side is cleaner, safer and more pleasant. Everyone says it is cheaper to stay in Comayagüela, but it all depends which hotel you pick. Neither side has to be expensive.

If you do stay in Comayagüela, remember that it is *definitely not safe* to walk through the market area at night. The hotels mentioned here are away from the market. If you have to pass through the market area after dark, take a bus or taxi.

Tegucigalpa On the Tegucigalpa side, a good deal for the price is the *Hotel Granada* (☎ 372381) at Avenida Juan Gutemberg, No 1401, Barrio Guanacaste. Lots of Peace Corps and other volunteers stay here. Rooms with shared bath are US$3.35/4.20 for singles/doubles or US$6.70 for a three-person room with two beds; add around US$2.50 for a private bath.

A block away, at the *Hotel Granada Anexo* (☎ 220597), Subida Casa Marta, No 1326, all the rooms have a telephone and private bath. Cost is US$5.60/7 for singles/doubles or US$8.45/9.85 for two/three beds. Parking in the enclosed garage is US$0.70 extra. Both *Granadas* have hot water and are large (48 rooms), clean, modern and a bit impersonal, but a good deal. They are in a district with restaurants, movies and stores, not too far from the city centre.

Hotel Tegucigalpa (☎ 373847) at Avenida Juan Gutemberg, No 1645, a couple of blocks east of the Hotel Granada, is much simpler and not as clean, but it's cheaper, with rooms at US$1.70/2.25 with shared bath, or US$3.65 with private bath, and they do have hot water.

Another cheapie is the *Hotel Fortuna*, in a row of basic *hospedajes* beside the Los Dolores church. Rooms with shared cold bath are US$2.10/4.20 for singles/doubles. *Hotel Goascoran*, a couple of doors down, has rooms with double beds for US$3.10.

The *Nuevo Hotel Boston* (☎ 379411) at Avenida Máximo Jeréz, No 321, Barrio Abajo, is an excellent place to stay, very clean and well kept, with a comfortable sitting room and free coffee and purified water always available. Street-facing rooms, though noisy, are especially large and have doors opening onto a small balcony; these are US$6.30/7.75 for singles/doubles. The quieter interior rooms are US$5.60/7.00. All have private hot baths. If this is full, *Hotel Iberia* (☎ 379267) on the Calle Los Dolores walking street is clean, quiet, secure and has hot water. Rooms are smallish: singles/doubles with private bath are US$6.70/7.50, or about US$1.40 less with a shared bath.

Hotel Maya Colonial (☎ 372643) at Calle Pálace, No 1225, has a courtyard sitting area and a free pool table for guests. All the rooms have private hot baths; singles/doubles are US$7.30/11.15.

Hotel Excelsior (☎ 372638) at Avenida Cervantes, No 1515, has singles/ doubles for US$7.60/9.85. It's a well-kept place; all the rooms have good beds, fans and private hot-water bath, and there's a lawn at the back. The owner speaks English.

A more up-market choice is *Hotel Mac-Arthur* (☎ 379839), Avenida Lempira, No 454. It has large, attractive, clean singles/doubles for US$13.50/17.30, including tax and private hot bath. Rooms for US$18.55/22.10 have air-con and cable TV.

Comayagüela The most popular hotel with travellers on the Comayagüela side is the 90-room *Hotel San Pedro* (☎ 228987), on 6a Avenida between 8a and 9a Calles. It's clean and there are a couple of parking spaces out front. Singles/doubles are US$2.25/3.50, or US$4.90 with private bath. It's handy to the El Rey and Aurora bus stations for buses to San Pedro Sula or Juticalpa, and has an inexpensive café.

Opposite this is the *Hotel Ticamaya* (☎ 370084), where rates are US$2.50/4.20/5.90 for singles/doubles/triples, or US$4.20/7.30/10.55/12.95 for one to four people with private bath (plus 7% tax).

Hotelito West (☎ 379456), 10a Calle, No 635, between 6a and 7a Avenida, is a small place with plants on the landing and hot water. Small but pleasant rooms with a double bed are US$2.80. *Hotel Colonial* (☎ 375785), four blocks north, is another good place, very clean and modern, with 15 rooms where singles/doubles with private hot baths are US$4.90/5.60. The clean and inexpensive Cafe Colonial is on the ground floor.

The *Hotel Ritz* (☎ 222769) on 4a Calle at 5a Avenida, is unremarkable in most respects but it has a 3rd-floor rooftop terrace and restaurant. You can have meals out on the terrace, or sunbathe in a lounge chair and enjoy a good view of the city. Singles/doubles are US$4.40/5.60 with private baths or US$4.20 without. Hot water is available. You can use the fridge and cook your own meals here, or hire a a TV for US$2.80.

On 12a Calle at the corner of 7a Avenida,

near the Transportes Norteños and Sáenz bus stations where you can get buses to San Pedro Sula, the *Condesa Inn* (☎ 377857) has small rooms without ventilation, but with private hot baths, for US$5.45/6.60.

If you're at the end of your economic rope there are plenty of other hotels that are a few cents cheaper, but most are a lot less pleasant.

Places to Eat

Comayagüela has plenty of Chinese restaurants where you can eat for US$2 or less; *Lean Chou* on the corner of 6a Avenida and 10a Calle has huge portions. A few blocks east is *Restaurant Lizeth*, where small portions are off-set by very low prices; breakfasts are around US$0.70 (or you could risk trying the 'Clud Sandwich'!).

Most of the good restaurants are on the Tegucigalpa side of the river. The *Restaurante Duncan Maya*, on Avenida Cristobal Colón a block west of the Parque Central, is a good, basic restaurant for all meals. It's open every day from 8 am to 10 pm. The 'plate of the day' is US$2.40; breakfasts, burgers, sandwiches and soups are all around US$1.40, and dinners are US$2.80 to US$4. Alcohol is served and it's a large, popular place.

In the next block west of the plaza is the upstairs *La Terraza de Don Pepe*, 'a tradition in Honduras' the sign announces. It, too, is very popular, with a family atmosphere and loud, live music in the evenings. Prices are excellent: US$1.50 for chicken, US$1.90 to US$4 for seafood and grilled meats, US$0.70 for burgers, sandwiches or enchiladas. There's also a bar. It's open every day from 9 am to 10 pm.

Directly behind the cathedral, the *Restaurante Al Natural* is lovely and relaxing, removed from the hubbub of the city, with tables set around a lush covered garden and a toucan at the door. The food is good and fresh; pasta, meat and seafood dinners are around US$2.20 to US$5, and there's a large menu to select from. English, French, Spanish and Portuguese are spoken. It's open Monday to Friday from 8 am to 7 pm, Satur-

day from 8.30 am to 3 pm, and closed Sunday.

For vegetarians there's the simple *Restaurante Vegetariano Todo Rico* on Avenida Miguel de Cervantes, between Calle El Telégrafo and Calle Morelos. Breakfast or the *plato del día* lunchtime meal is US$0.85, soups, enchiladas or tacos are US$0.40. Open hours are 7 am to 6 pm Monday to Friday, 7 am to 3 pm Saturday, closed Sunday.

A popular air-con *Pizza Hut* is on the corner of Avenida Cristobal Colón and Calle La Leona, half a block west of the Parque Central, open daily from 9 am to 10 pm. Opposite this is a *Dunkin' Donuts*. There are many branches of *Dunkin' Donuts* and *Burger Inn* all around Tegucigalpa.

Entertainment

Tegucigalpa has a couple of districts with lots of choice in nightlife (restaurants, discos etc). Boulevard Morazán is the 'night on the town' zone, with discos including *Sueños*, and *Chico Lara* where there's live music.

The other, newer nightlife zone is on Avenida Juan Pablo II, in the area around the Sheraton. Dancing is good at the *Tropical Port* disco, which has a Caribbean coast flavour (it's opposite the Las Gemelas drive-in); other nightspots in the same area are *Backstreet* and the *Encuentro* piano bar.

Check the offerings at the *Teatro Nacional Manuel Bonilla*. The national theatre hosts a variety of performing arts and it's a very enjoyable place to attend a performance.

The super-expensive *Hotel Honduras Maya* has a gambling casino (no dress code), restaurants, a bar and other entertainment. The area around the hotel, Colonia Palmira, is the upper-class district of Tegucigalpa, the area for fancy, expensive, excellent restaurants.

There are cinemas everywhere you turn in Tegucigalpa, and several on the Comayagüela side too. Most of the hotels mentioned under Places to Stay have at least one cinema nearby (entry around US$1). You can often find films in English, with Spanish subtitles, in the theatres. Check the

Prensa newspaper for movie listings, especially the Sunday edition. *Café Paradiso* on Avenida Barahona shows free films (sometimes in English) on Thursday evening and Saturday at 10 am and 4 pm; it also has a bookshop with political texts.

Things to Buy
Honduran handicrafts, including woodcarving, leatherwork, woven hats and bags, paintings and ceramics are sold at many places around town. You can buy in the streets if you stroll along some of the walking malls, especially Avenida Miguel P Barahona, between Parque Central and the post office.

Honduran paintings, typically depicting white adobe houses with red-tiled roofs in village scenes, are lined up along the northern wall outside the Cathedral; a shop opposite the Iglesia San Francisco plaza also has paintings and other handicrafts.

On the west side of the Los Dolores church plaza, on the corner of Avenida Jeréz, is a handicrafts shop with a good selection of leatherwork, woodcarvings, souvenirs etc. Best of all is their collection of handmade wooden musical instruments of all shapes and sizes. Most of the instruments are not expensive; you could get a resonant guitar or violin for as little as US$15.

In Comayagüela you can find just about anything in the sprawling blocks of the market, everything from vegetables to second-hand clothing to some excellent leatherwork shops.

Getting There & Away
Air Tan/Sahsa has domestic flights connecting Tegucigalpa with San Pedro Sula, La Ceiba, and the Bay Islands of Roatán and Guanaja.

Bus Excellent bus services connect Tegucigalpa with other parts of Honduras. However, the buses do not depart from a central bus station; each bus line has its own station. The tourist office can give you a complete list. See the introductory Getting

There & Away section for information on Tica Bus international services.

San Pedro Sula (four hours, 239 km, US$2).
Transportes El Rey, Danéry & San Cristobal (☎ 376609), corner 9a Calle and 6a Avenida, Comayagüela, has buses every half hour to an hour from 2.30 am to 7 pm.
Transportes Norteños (☎ 370706), 12a Calle between 6a and 7a Avenida, Comayagüela, has approximately hourly buses from 3 am to 6.15 pm.
Transportes Sáenz (☎ 376521), 12a Calle between 7a and 8a Avenida, Comayagüela, has buses at 2 am, 5 am, 7 am, then hourly until 5 pm.
Tela and La Ceiba (444 km, US$4.35).
Traliasa Transportes (☎ 377538), 12a Calle at 8a Avenida; buses at 6 and 9 am.
Trujillo (nine hours, 686 km, US$5.05). Cotraipbal (☎ 377538), 8a Avenida at 11a Calle. Buses at 5 am and noon.
Olancho & Juticalpa (three hours, 167 km, US$1.70). Lineas Terrestres Aurora (☎ 373647), 8a Calle between 6a and 7a Avenida, Comayagüela, has buses hourly from 4 am to 5 pm (serves entire Olancho department).
Choluteca (three hours, 137 km, US$1.55).
Mi Esperanza (☎ 382863), 6a Avenida, southern end (around 23a Calle), Comayagüela, has hourly buses from 4 am to 6.30 pm. Buses continue from here to the Nicaraguan border (San Marcos de Colón or Guasaule.)
Nicaraguan border, El Paraíso (2½ hours, 109 km, US$1.10).
Transportes Discua Litena (☎ 327939), Mercado Jacaleapa, in Colonia John F Kennedy, southern Tegucigalpa (take bus No 26 from Avenida Molina, or a colectivo for US$0.25 at Calle Adolfo Zuniga). Buses leave every half-hour from 5.30 am to 6.30 pm (take another bus, US$0.30, for the half-hour trip from El Paraíso to the border station).
El Salvador border, El Amatillo (2½ hours, 133 km, US$1.25).
Various companies do this route. Take a bus from Mercado Zonal Belén, 6a Avenida between 10a and 13a Calles, Comayagüela. There are frequent buses from 6 am to 5 pm.

Getting Around
To/From the Airport Toncontín international airport is 6½ km south of the centre of Tegucigalpa. Local 'Loarque' bus Nos 1 and 11 stop right outside the entrance to the airport, frequently every day from 5 am to 9 pm. The cost is the usual city bus fare, US$0.05. To go to the airport from the city

centre, catch the Loarque buses on Avenida Jeréz.

A taxi to the airport costs about US$4.50; from the airport to town, colectivo taxis are cheaper.

A new airport is to be built at El Pedregal lagoon but it won't open until around 1997.

Bus There's an excellent system of city buses, operating with frequent buses every day from 5 am to 9 pm. The cost is US$0.05. Many buses heading east stop on the north side of Parque Central; many other buses run westwards along Avenida Máximo Jeréz and turn south to Comayagüela by Parque Herrera.

Taxi Taxis cruise all over town, giving a little honk to advertise they're free. Cost for a ride in town is around US$1.80. You can phone for a taxi on ☎ 223304, 220533, 370418 or 223748.

Rental Cars At all the rental car companies you have the best chance of getting one of their cheapest cars if you reserve it about three days (or more) in advance. Avis (☎ 320888), Budget (☎ 335170) and Molinari (☎ 323191) all have offices at Hotel Honduras Maya and at Toncontín Airport. Others include Toyota Rent-a-Car (☎ 335210) and Tropical Car Rental (☎ 339449).

AROUND TEGUCIGALPA
Suyapa
The Virgen de Suyapa is the patron saint of Honduras. On the Suyapa hillside, about seven km south-east of the centre of Tegucigalpa, the huge Gothic **Basílica de Suyapa** dominates the landscape. The construction of the basilica, famous for its large, brilliant stained-glass windows, was begun in 1954, and finishing touches are still being added.

The Virgen de Suyapa herself is a tiny statue, only a few cm tall, believed to have performed hundreds of miracles. She is brought to the large basilica on holidays, especially for the annual Feria de Suyapa

beginning on the saint's day, 3 February, and continuing for a week; the celebrations attract pilgrims from all over Central America. Most of the time, however, the little statue is kept on the altar of the very simple old church of Suyapa, on the plaza a few hundred metres behind the basilica.

The basilica of Suyapa is just up the hill from **UNAH**, the Universidad Nacional Autónoma de Honduras. The campus is called Ciudad Universitaria.

Getting There & Away You can get from Tegucigalpa to Suyapa on the No 31 Suyapa-Mercado San Isidro bus, departing from the San Isidro market in Comayagüela, or there's a colectivo stop near the river (see map) where you can catch a colectivo taxi to the university (US$0.25) and walk the short distance from there.

Santa Lucía
Population 4,174

Santa Lucía is a charming old Spanish mining hill town, with lots of lanes and walkways winding around the hillside. The town has great views of the piney hills and Tegucigalpa away in the valley. The church, which has many old Spanish paintings and the Christ of Las Mercedes, given to Santa Lucía by King Philip II in 1572, is perched on a hillside and is especially beautiful.

Santa Lucía is an attractive and peaceful town for walking around in the fresh mountain air. There are many possible walks out of town in the hills where there are many farms, and they say that an old mule trail leads down to the capital, a couple of hours hiking downhill.

Getting There & Away Santa Lucía is 13 km east of Tegucigalpa, 2½ km off the road leading to Valle de Angeles and La Tigra. You can take the half-hourly Valle de Angeles bus from the stop on Avenida La Paz, get off at the crossroads and walk or hitch the 2½ km into town. A direct bus to Santa Lucía departs every 1½ hours from Mercado San Pablo in Colonia Reparto (US$0.25); bus route No 6, 'Carrizal-El

Sitio', departing from the Parque Central, goes to Mercado San Pablo.

Valle de Angeles
Population 6,761

About 11 km past Santa Lucía, Valle de Angeles is another old Spanish mining town. It's been declared a tourist zone and much of the town has been restored to its original 16th-century appearance. In front of the old church is an attractive shady plaza. The annual fair is held on 4 October.

There are many artisans' shops and souvenir emporiums in Valle de Angeles where you can find excellent Honduran artesanías that are marginally cheaper and of better quality than in Tegucigalpa. Woodcarving, basketry, ceramics, leatherwork, paintings, dolls, wicker and wood furniture, and other items are featured. Avoid the weekend crowds.

Places to Stay & Eat Valle de Angeles has a great number of small, simple restaurants. Half a block behind the church, on the road to your right as you face the church, the pleasant *Posada del Angel* (☎ 762233) has very clean single/double rooms with private hot bath for US$5.60/11.20 facing onto a lovely courtyard.

Getting There & Away A bus bound for Valle de Angeles departs every 30 minutes from a stop just off Avenida La Paz in Tegucigalpa, half a block south of the Hospital San Felipe; the cost is US$0.30. The Lomas and San Felipe buses departing from the north side of Parque Central will drop you at Hospital San Felipe.

San Juancito
About 11 km past Valle de Angeles, San Juancito is a small village nestled into a crevasse by an even smaller river, at the foot of a steep mountain. San Juancito is an historic mining town but there's not much to the town now; people mostly just pass through it on their way to La Tigra National Park, at the top of the mountain.

San Juancito has been declared an historic

place, and there are plans to establish museums, to build *balnearios* by the river, restore hotels and buildings to their colonial appearance, and build a funicular cable car from the town right up to El Rosario, the ghost town at the top of the mountain at the entrance to La Tigra. Nobody has put the money up yet, but it may happen one day.

Getting There & Away A direct bus service between Tegucigalpa and San Juancito does exist but it's inconvenient; a bus departs from Mercado San Pablo in Tegucigalpa at 3 pm, and from San Juancito for the return trip at around 6 am. Or, from the same place, you can take a bus (infrequent) heading for Cantarranas or San Juan de Flores and get off at the turnoff for San Juancito, leaving you a two km walk. Or you can take the bus to Valle de Angeles and hitch from there, continuing along the same road; just about any vehicle passing by will give you a lift.

La Tigra National Park & El Rosario
La Tigra National Park is one of the most beautiful places in Honduras, preserving a lush cloud forest. Only a short distance from Tegucigalpa, at an altitude of 2270 metres, the pristine 7482 hectare reserve was Honduras's first national park. The climate at La Tigra is fresh and brisk; in fact it's often quite cold – bring plenty of warm clothes with you. At night the temperature can drop to around 5°C. Even when it's not cloudy in a cloud forest, the sun never shines on the ground because of the canopy of trees.

The forest is home to a great abundance of wildlife – ocelots, pumas, monkeys, quetzal and other birdlife, and much more. It is also a botanist's delight, with lush trees, ferns and flowering plants. Trails have been cut through the forest and you are urged to stay on them – it is a very rugged, mountainous area, and the damp ground can give way unexpectedly off the trails.

There are two entrances to La Tigra. The eastern one is at El Rosario, a 'ghost town' mining settlement of old wooden houses about four km up the hill from San Juancito (see San Juancito for details about how to get there). It's a very steep climb up a dirt road from San Juancito to El Rosario; any passing vehicle would probably give you a lift up, but unless you go on a weekend, you may be the only person on the road.

At El Rosario there's a ranger station and park visitors' centre that has displays on the wildlife and plants in the park. A ranger is always there. You can stay for free in an empty house, courtesy of the visitors' centre, and you only need bring your food (there may not be a cooker), bedding and warm clothes. It's a supremely pleasant and relaxing place, and some foreigners have stayed for weeks. You can get simple meals at the white house at the bend, 300 metres down from the visitors' centre, but only up to about 6 pm.

If you're planning to stay overnight, you must first get a letter of permission from the Ministerio de Recursos Naturales on Boulevard Centroamerica, by Hondutel in Miraflores (take bus No 5 'Carrizal-Miraflores'). The office is open Monday to Friday from 8 am to 4.30 pm, and you need to see the DIGEPESCA department (☎ 328600).

The western entrance to the park, above Jutiapa, is a shorter distance from the capital. Here, too, there's a ranger station and visitors' centre, but you can't stay overnight. This entrance is reached by taking a turnoff from the top of El Picacho and passing through the villages of El Hatillo and Jutiapa. Frequent small buses depart from the north side of Parque Herrera in Tegucigalpa and go as far as Los Limones; from there it's about a 1½-hour walk, mostly uphill, to the park gates. If you don't fancy the walk, it's easy to hitch, and the odd bus does go nearer to the park gates. T1he last bus back leaves around 5 pm.

With your own vehicle you can easily see the park on a day trip from Tegucigalpa. By public transport you can just about do it in one day, with a very early start, but you're better off planning an overnight stay. You can walk from one entrance to the other in a couple of hours by the old disused road (no vehicles allowed), but you see more if you take the footpaths (about three to four hours minimum). Signs in the park are sometimes poor.

Ojojona
Population 6,644

Yet another attractive 16th-century Spanish mining town in the hills near Tegucigalpa, Ojojona has a couple of simple old churches with religious art; the main church has a painting said to be a Murillo. Ojojona is also the birthplace of the contemporary artist Pablo Zelaya Sierra, and the old Spanish adobe opposite the main church is now a museum of his paintings. The village is historically important as the home of General Francisco Morazán.

Getting There & Away The bus to Ojojona leaves half-hourly from the corner of 6a Avenida and 4a Calle in Comayagüela, diagonally opposite the Banco Atlántida (1¼ hours, US$0.30).

Western Honduras

Western Honduras is the most settled part of the country and holds some of Honduras's principal attractions, most notably the Maya ruins of Copán.

Other attractions include Honduras's principal lake, the Lago de Yojoa, a couple of national parks, and Comayagua, Honduras's historic first capital.

Also here is San Pedro Sula, second-largest city in the country. The road between San Pedro Sula and the capital is probably the most travelled in Honduras, connecting as it does the country's two major cities as well as the southern, western and northern regions.

TEGUCIGALPA TO SAN PEDRO SULA
It's 246 km along Honduras's Highway 1 from Tegucigalpa to San Pedro Sula, about a four-hour trip. The route passes Comayagua, Siguatepeque and the Lago de Yojoa.

COMAYAGUA

Population 60,720

Comayagua, 82 km north-west of Tegucigalpa, is the historic first capital of Honduras. There is still much evidence of the town's colonial past, and there are several fine old churches (including the famous cathedral), three plazas and two interesting museums.

History

Comayagua was founded as the capital of the colonial province of Honduras in 1537 by the Spanish captain Alonso de Cáceres, fulfilling the orders of the Spanish governor of Honduras to establish a new settlement in the geographic centre of the territory. The town was initially called Villa de Santa María de Comayagua, but in 1543 the name was changed to Villa de la Nueva Valladolid de Comayagua.

Comayagua was declared a city in 1557, and in 1561 the seat of the diocese of Honduras was moved from Trujillo to Comayagua for the more favourable conditions, central positioning and closer proximity to the silver and gold-mining regions that Comayagua afforded.

Comayagua was the centre for the political and religious administration of Honduras; it was the capital city for over three centuries, until the capital was shifted to Tegucigalpa in 1880.

Things to See

Churches The **cathedral** in the centre of town is a gem of colonial style. It was built over 30 years from 1685 to 1715, and is abundantly decorated. It contains much fine art, both inside and out. The altar is similar to that of the Tegucigalpa cathedral; both were made by the same artist.

The clock in the church tower is one of the oldest in the world, and is probably the oldest in the Americas. It was made over 800 years ago by the Moors for the palace of Alhambra in Seville, and was later donated to the town by King Philip II.

The first university in Central America was founded in 1632 in the **Casa Cural**, the building to the right of the cathedral, which now houses the Museo Colonial; priests have occupied this building since 1558. The university operated there for almost 200 years, until 1842.

Comayagua's first church was **La Merced**, built from 1550 to 1558. Other fine churches are **San Francisco** (1584) and **La Caridad** (1730). **San Sebastián** (1585) is further from the centre, on the south end of town. All are worth seeing. Another colonial church, San Juan de Dios (1590), was destroyed by an earthquake in 1750, but samples of its artwork, along with that of all the other churches, are on display in the Museo Colonial.

If you can read Spanish, look for a small book entitled *Las Iglesias Coloniales de la Ciudad de Comayagua*, which contains an interesting history of Comayagua and its churches.

Museums The **Museo Colonial**, in the Casa Cural, is small but remarkable. Totally renovated in 1990, it contains artwork and religious paraphernalia culled from all the five churches of Comayagua, spanning 400 years, from the 15th to the 18th centuries. In one salon is a display of jewels and ornaments that people gave to the statues in the churches, including pearls and emeralds the size of your thumbnail.

This museum, opened in 1962, was the first in Honduras; the well-informed curator can give you an interesting tour explaining (in Spanish) the history of each piece. The museum is open every day from 9 am to noon and 2 to 5 pm (admission US$0.45).

A block north of the cathedral, the **Museo Regional de Arqueología** has displays of Honduran archaeological discoveries. Opening hours are Wednesday to Friday from 8.30 am to noon and 1 to 4 pm; on Saturday and Sunday it opens half an hour later, and it's closed on Monday and Tuesday. Admission is US$1.40.

Places to Stay & Eat

The *Hotel Libertad* (☎ 720091) on the main plaza has a quiet courtyard with hammocks and plants. Single/double rooms, sharing a collective cold bath, are US$2.10 per person.

Hotel Quan (☎ 720070) is a little out of the way but has a variety of clean rooms, with hot water, parking, and air-conditioning available. Prices vary: singles/doubles with private bath start at US$3.80/4.50. There are also some cheaper rooms which have a shared bath.

Also clean is the *Hotel Luxemborgo*, on the road coming into Comayagua from the highway; rooms with private bath are US$2.80 per person. There's another inexpensive place next door.

There are restaurants and small eateries all around the main plaza, and from there heading towards the market. *Pollos Chalo 3* (no sign outside) between the plaza and the market is said to have the best grilled chicken in town, and it is indeed delicious; a lunch of a quarter-chicken, tortillas and a soda is US$0.85. There are many other small restaurants on the same block. *La Gran Hein Wong*, on the main plaza, is good for Chinese food for about US$2.80. *Restaurante Yadisma* is a popular place for steaks for under US$4. There's also a *Dunkin' Donuts* in the next block north.

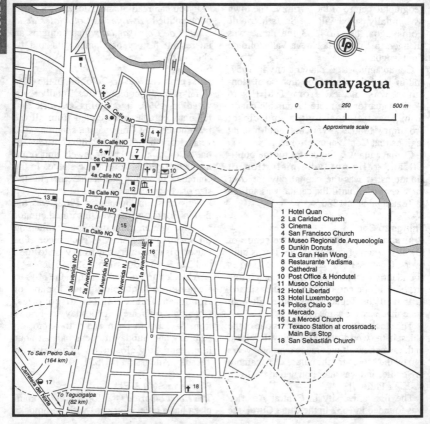

Comayagua

0   250   500 m

Approximate scale

1 Hotel Quan
2 La Caridad Church
3 Cinema
4 San Francisco Church
5 Museo Regional de Arqueología
6 Dunkin Donuts
7 La Gran Hein Wong
8 Restaurante Yadisma
9 Cathedral
10 Post Office & Hondutel
11 Museo Colonial
12 Hotel Libertad
13 Hotel Luxemborgo
14 Pollos Chalo 3
15 Mercado
16 La Merced Church
17 Texaco Station at crossroads;
   Main Bus Stop
18 San Sebastián Church

To San Pedro Sula (164 km)

Carretera del Norte

To Tegucigalpa (82 km)

Getting There & Away

Comayagua is about one km east of the Tegucigalpa-San Pedro Sula highway. Any Tegucigalpa-San Pedro Sula bus will drop or pick you up at the crossroads; you can walk the one km into town, or take a taxi for US$0.35.

To Tegucigalpa, express buses cost US$1.10, and take about 1½ hours; slower buses (US$0.85, two hours) drop and pick up at Comayagua's plaza or just south of the market.

SIGUATEPEQUE

Population 39,293

Siguatepeque is halfway between Tegucigalpa (114 km) and San Pedro Sula (132 km), about a two-hour drive from either place. There's no real reason to stop in Siguatepeque; south of the town is the turnoff for La Esperanza and Marcala. The annual festival days are 25 January and 18 to 27 April.

Places to Stay & Eat

The best place to stay in the centre is the *Hotel Gomez* (☎ 732868), Calle 21 de Junio, a clean, modern motel with courtyard parking and hot water. Singles/doubles are US$2.10/3.50 with shared bath or US$4.20/5.60 with private bath.

If that's full you might try the *Hotel Versalles* or the *Boarding House Central* (☎ 732108), beside one another on the main plaza.

Between and around the two plazas, and also in the market, are several *comedores* where you can get basic meals. The *Restaurante China Palace* is OK for Chinese and international food, with dishes for around US$3.

Getting There & Away

Any bus going between Tegucigalpa and San Pedro Sula will drop you at the crossroads at the entrance to Siguatepeque. From there you can walk the two km into town or take a taxi for US$0.35.

Empresas Unidas and Transportes Maribel operate direct buses between Tegucigalpa and Siguatepeque (two hours, US$1.25). In Siguatepeque the bus station is on the south side of the plaza near the basketball courts; in Tegucigalpa, both companies' bus stations are in Comayagüela near the intersection of 7a Avenida and 12a Calle.

LA ESPERANZA

Buses go from Siguatepeque to La Esperanza, 86 km to the south-west, a quiet colonial town with an attractive church and a Lenca Indian market on Sundays. The area is good for walks in the hills, and there are places to stay and eat.

There is a road from La Esperanza to Gracias and on to Santa Rosa de Copán; see Gracias for more on this route.

At Marcala, south-east of La Esperanza, is the Cormaca coffee cooperative that you can visit, and somewhere to stay overnight. Several buses per day run from Comayagua.

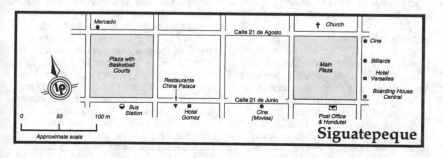

Siguatepeque

LAGO DE YOJOA

The Lago de Yojoa, about three hours north of Tegucigalpa and one hour south of San Pedro Sula, is a popular recreation area and highway stopover. The quality of the lake water is still quite good, but the dumping of toxic wastes into the streams that feed the lake will soon threaten flora & fauna. A visitors' centre in due to open near the main road in 1994.

Places to Stay & Eat

The highway passes by the lake, but there are only a few places with direct lake access. One of the more popular spots is the *Hotel Los Remos*, on the south side of the lake. They have rowboats for hire (US$3.45 per hour) and a restaurant overlooking the lake. Rooms cost US$5.60 per person, all with private bath. It's the most convenient place for lake access, and many people come just for the day. All the buses between Tegucigalpa and San Pedro Sula will stop there.

About one km north of the Hotel Los Remos, a row of about 30 restaurants and small comedores serving fried fish fresh from the lake stretches along the highway. The lake is famous for its black bass. A meal of fried fish, salad and tortillas will cost from US$1.40 to US$3, depending on the size and kind of fish.

On the north side of the lake, five km off the highway, is another, more expensive lakeside resort, the *Agua Azul* (☎ 517125), where cabins for two start at US$12. Boating and horse-riding are available. The restaurant *Only Bass*, 500 metres along the main road, has been recommended.

SANTA BÁRBARA

Population 23,207

About 35 km west of the Lago de Yojoa, Santa Bárbara, capital of the department of the same name, is a small town known for its woven *junco* handicrafts. There are places to stay and eat in Santa Bárbara.

Roads connect Santa Bárbara with the Tegucigalpa-San Pedro Sula highway, and also with the San Pedro Sula-Nueva Ocotepeque highway running along the western side of Honduras. You could get a bus directly from Tegucigalpa to Santa Bárbara, though the buses run infrequently. Buses run hourly between Santa Bárbara and San Pedro Sula (two hours, 90 km, US$1.45).

PULHAPANZÁK

Pulhapanzák, a magnificent 100-metre waterfall on the Río Lindo, can be visited as a stop along the route from Tegucigalpa to San Pedro Sula, or as a day trip from San Pedro. In the area of the waterfall is a very pleasant park and places to swim in the river. It's a popular spot that can be crowded on weekends and holidays.

From San Pedro, Pulhapanzák is about one hour south on the highway to Tegucigalpa, then another hour on an unpaved road heading west from the highway. By bus, take the Tirla bus going to Río Lindo all the way to the waterfall; the bus leaves every half-hour from 2a Avenida, between 5a & 6a Calle SE, starting at 6.50 am.

SAN PEDRO SULA

Population 325,900

Second-largest city in Honduras, San Pedro Sula (or just San Pedro) is the major industrial, commercial and business centre of the country. It is also the major centre for the agricultural products of the fertile lowlands in a wide region surrounding the city.

San Pedro is the transportation hub for the western half of Honduras and for travel to the north coast. The city doesn't have many sights or attractions for visitors, but there are always travellers passing through.

San Pedro is extremely hot and humid for much of the year; the town lies in a valley just 76 metres above sea level, with little movement of air. January and February are the coolest months; October to March may be bearable; but in the summer, from around April to September, San Pedro sizzles.

In the last week of June, San Pedro celebrates a large festival and fair in honour of its founding and the day of San Pedro.

History

San Pedro Sula was founded by Pedro de Alvarado in June 1536. The original name of the town was San Pedro de Puerto Caballos, and it was founded in the nearby Valle de Chooloma (Valle de los Pájaros, or Valley of the Birds). The Spaniards later moved the town to its present location, which was the site of an Indian village, Azula, beside the Río Las Piedras. The name San Pedro Sula is a mixture of the names of the two towns.

San Pedro has experienced various disasters, including fire and flooding; despite its long history there is nothing left to see of its colonial past.

Orientation

The centre of San Pedro is flat; avenidas run north-south and calles run east-west. Primera (1a) Avenida crosses 1a Calle, forming the beginning of the numbering system; from there, the numbered avenidas and calles extend out in every direction.

Every address in the centre is given in relation to a numbered calle and avenida, with the further identification of being in the north-east (noreste, or NE), north-west (noroeste, or NO), south-east (sureste, or SE) or south-west (suroeste, or SO) quadrant of the city.

The centre is surrounded by a bypassing highway, the Circunvalación, to reduce traffic in the centre. Nevertheless there is still a lot of traffic. Most streets in the centre are one-way streets.

There are a couple of supermarkets on 5a Avenida near 5a Calle. Banco Banffaa, by the cathedral, changes travellers' cheques, including American Express.

Information

The Instituto Hondureño de Turismo (☎ 523023/95) is three blocks north of the plaza on 4a Calle, on the 3rd floor of the building housing the DHL courier service on the ground floor. The office is open Monday to Friday from 8 am to 4 pm.

There's a selection of books and magazines in English, as well as the *Miami Herald*

newspaper, at the tobacco shop of the Gran Hotel Sula, on the north side of the plaza.

Post & Telecommunications The post office is on 9a Calle at 3a Avenida SO. It's open Monday to Friday from 7 am to 8 pm, and on Saturday from 7 am until noon. The Hondutel office is on the corner of 5a Calle and 4a Avenida SO.

Foreign Consulates All the foreign embassies in Honduras are in Tegucigalpa, but a number of foreign consulates are in San Pedro Sula. They include:

Costa Rica
  Edificio Martinez Valenzuela, 3rd floor, No 307 (☎ 533208)
El Salvador
  Edificio Rivera and CIA, 5th floor (☎ 534604)
Germany
  Berkling Industrial, Salida Puerto Cortés (☎ 531244)
Guatemala
  8a Calle, between 5a and 6a Avenida NO, No 38 (☎ 533560)
Mexico
  2a Calle, Colonia Rio de Piedras
UK
  Terminales Cortés 4A, 4a Calle NO (☎ 532600)

Travel Agencies There are many travel agencies in San Pedro, including:

Avia Tours
  Edificio Bolivar, 1a Calle SO, corner with 2a Avenida (☎ 531250, 532580)
Agencia de Viajes Brenda
  2a Calle, between 4a and 5a Avenida SO (☎ 530360)
Mundirama
  Edificio Martinez Valenzuela (☎ 523400); agent for American Express; will hold mail for six months for card and cheque users
Transmundo
  6a Avenida SO, No 15, between 3 and 2 Calle (☎ 531140, 534188)

Things to See & Do

The large **cathedral**, facing onto a large shady plaza, is the central feature of San Pedro Sula. It was built during the 1950s.

The **Mercado Guamilito** is on the north-west side of town on the block between 8a

HONDURAS

■ PLACES TO STAY	▼ PLACES TO EAT	3 Centro Cultural Sampedrano
5 Gran Hotel Sula & Café Skandia	4 Cafeteria & Pizzeria Italia, Mi Rinconcito	6 Train Station
11 Hotel El Nilo	5 Gran Hotel Sula & Café Skandia	7 Central Plaza
12 Hotel San Pedro & Restaurante Granada	9 Frap's	8 Cathedral
14 Hotel Terraza	12 Hotel San Pedro & Restaurante Granada	10 Mundirama (travel agent), Costa Rican Embassy & Banco Banffaa
17 Hotel Palmira	13 Cafeteria Mayan Way	
20 Hotel San Juan	15 Pizza Hut	16 Hondutel
21 Hotel Brisas del Occidente		18 Copan Ruinas Buses
22 Hotel El Parador	OTHER	19 El Progreso Buses
23 Hotel Brasilia		26 Mercado
24 Hotel El Castillo	1 Mercado Guamilito	27 Post Office
25 Hotel La Siesta	2 Tourism Office	

San Pedro Sula

and 9a Avenida, 6a and 7a Calle. In addition to the usual fruits, vegetables, household goods and comedores, it houses the **Asociación Nacional de Artesanos de Honduras**, which has a wide selection of arts and handicrafts from all over Honduras and some also from Guatemala and El Salvador. The market is open daily from 7 am to 5 pm (Sunday from 8 to 11.30 am).

The main **Mercado** is in the south-east section of town, in the block between 6a and 7a Calle, 4a and 5a Avenida. There are stalls in the streets spreading out for blocks around the market. This is a distribution centre and you can sometimes see metres-high piles of green bananas and other produce.

The **Centro Cultural Sampedrano**, two blocks north of the plaza on 3a Calle, between 3a and 4a Avenida NO, has an art gallery, a library with books, magazines and newspapers in English and Spanish, and a theatre where plays are presented. **Alliance Française** (☎ 531178), on 4a Calle, at 23a Avenida SO, has a borrowing library of books and magazines in French, and offers classes in French and occasional cultural events.

Beside the **Río Las Piedras** on the northern outskirts of town, the **Parque Presentación Centeno** is an attractive natural forest reserve and park.

Also on the outskirts of town, up on the mountain near the Coca-Cola sign, the **Mirador Bella Vista** offers a sweeping view of San Pedro and the surrounding region. There are no buses going up there, but you could take a taxi there and back for around US$3.50.

Otherwise, there's not much of attraction for visitors in San Pedro. You can, however, make a few interesting excursions from town; see Around San Pedro Sula.

Places to Stay

San Pedro has many good, clean, cheap places to stay. A favourite is the *Hotel San Pedro* (☎ 532655, 531513), on 3a Calle between 1a and 2a Avenida SO. It's large, with several types of rooms, and there's hot water in the showers. With shared bath, single rooms are US$2.40 to US$3.10, doubles are US$4.60. With private bath, prices start at US$3.80/5.60 for singles/doubles.

In the next block, on 3a Calle between 2a and 3a Avenida SO, the *Hotel El Nilo* (☎ 534689) has spacious, clean rooms with private cold bath and fan at US$4.20/5.60 for singles/doubles.

Another favourite, popular with Peace Corps volunteers, is the *Hotel Brisas del Occidente* (☎ 522309), on the corner of 5a Avenida and 7a Calle SO. The building is old but kept clean; rooms with shared bath are just US$2.10 per person. A block away, the *Hotel San Juan* (☎ 531488), on the corner of 5a Avenida and 6a Calle SO, has OK rooms (though the beds are a bit lumpy) with shared bath at US$4.20 for one or two people, or with private cold bath at US$5.20.

Hotel El Castillo (☎ 531490), on the corner of 6a Avenida and 8a Calle SO, has rooms with shared bath at US$2.50/3.50, often with a sink in the room, or US$3.90/4.90 with private bath. All the rooms come with fan.

The *Hotel El Parador* (☎ 576687), on the corner of 2a Avenida and 6a Calle SE, has rooms with private cold bath and fan at US$3.50/4.90. The old name sign fell down and they might not have put a new one up yet.

Hotel Brasilia (☎ 526765), nearby at the corner of 2a Avenida and 7a Calle SE, has rooms with private cold bath at US$4.20 with fan, or US$8.45 with air-con. Diagonally opposite, the *Hotel La Siesta* (☎ 522650), is another reasonable place. Rooms are US$2.95/5.05 with shared bath, or US$4.90/6.30 with private cold bath and fan. Other cheap hotels are nearby.

Hotel Terraza (☎ 533108), 6a Avenida SO between 4a and 5a Calle, has cable TV, a lift, and hot water in the morning. Good singles/doubles with private bath are US$5.20/6.70; a few have private TV.

Places to Eat

One of the most enjoyable places to eat or just hang out in San Pedro is the *Café*

Skandia, the cafeteria of the Gran Hotel Sula on the north side of the plaza. It's air-conditioned, open 24 hours, and not expensive; you can get breakfast, sandwiches or burgers for US$1.20. They also have lots of foods you don't normally see in Central America, like waffles, onion rings and apple pie. There are tables beside the swimming pool, and it's an easy place to meet foreigners or locals.

A block south of the plaza, the *Pizza Hut* is open every day from 10 am to 9 pm. Cheaper but good pizza (from US$2.40) can be had at the *Cafeteria & Pizzeria Italia*, two blocks west of the plaza on the corner of 1a Calle and 7a Avenida NO. A couple of doors back towards the plaza, *Mi Rinconcito* is a popular, cheap place with a good atmosphere, specialising in natural fruit drinks and meats from the charcoal grill. It has tables inside or on the patio behind. Its opening hours are Monday to Saturday from 8 am to 9.30 pm.

For typical Honduran dishes a good and inexpensive spot is the *Cafeteria Maya Way*, on 6a Avenida SO near 5a Calle SO. A choice of three lunch specials (including soup) is just US$1. The place is friendly and clean. Nearby on 6a Calle, the restaurant in the *Hotel Palmira* is cheap and great value. Breakfast and lunch is US$0.55 to US$1.55.

Also excellent for typical Honduran fare are the comedores at the two mercados, especially those on the south side (inside) of the general Mercado, on 7a Calle between 4a and 5a Avenida SE. Prices are low and there are long tables with lots of people eating; as markets go, this one is quite clean and well set up for dining. The even cleaner Mercado Guamilito also has dining.

Dunkin' Donuts has several locations around the city for that coffee and sugar fix.

The place to go for gourmet dining is the *Restaurante Granada*, upstairs in the Hotel San Pedro. They have occasional culinary themes and a sumptuous lunchtime buffet for US$5.60 (plus service and tax). The lunch buffet at *Frap's* on 3a Avenida SO is rather less lavish, but still good value at US$1.05 with meat or just US$0.50 without. Breakfasts are also not bad here.

Entertainment

San Pedro has many movie houses and discos, and the Centro Cultural Sampedrano usually has a play going on.

Getting There & Away

Air San Pedro Sula is a hub of air transport. There are daily direct flights from San Pedro to all the major cities in Central America; to New Orleans, Houston, Miami, New York, Los Angeles and San Francisco in the USA; and, within Honduras, to Tegucigalpa, La Ceiba and Roatán island.

Airlines serving San Pedro include Tan/Sahsa, Taca, Lacsa, American Airlines, Iberia and Continental.

There are black-market moneychangers and an exchange booth at the airport.

Bus San Pedro is also a hub of land transport; there are many bus lines and routes departing in all directions.

There are direct buses to La Ceiba on the north coast, but none to Tela, which is closer; you have to take a bus from San Pedro to El Progreso and transfer there to a bus going to Tela (very frequent buses).

Tegucigalpa (four hours, 239 km, US$2).
  Transportes El Rey, Danéry & San Cristobal, (☎ 534264, 534509), 7a Avenida, between 5a and 6a Calle SO, has buses every hour from 2.30 am to 7.30 am, then half-hourly from 7.30 am to 7 pm.
  Transportes Saenz (☎ 531829), 9a Avenida, between 9a and 10 Calle SO, has hourly buses from 1.30 am to 5.40 pm.
  Transportes Norteños (☎ 522145), 6a Calle, between 6a and 7a Avenida SO, has hourly buses from 6 am to 5 pm.
  Transportes Hedman y Alas (☎ 531361), 3a Calle between 7a and 8a Avenida NO, has eight buses daily; they're more expensive (US$2.55) but less crowded.
Puerto Cortés (one hour direct, US$1.10, 1½ hours with stops, US$0.85, 57 km).
  Transportes Impala (☎ 533111), 2a Avenida, between 4a and 5a Calle SO, and Transportes Citul (☎ 530070), 7a Calle SO, between 5a and 6a Avenida. Buses every 15 minutes or so from 6 am to 9 pm.
La Lima & El Progreso (to La Lima, 30 minutes, 14 km, US$0.15; to El Progreso, one hour, 28 km, US$0.30).

Transportes Catisa (☎ 531023), 2a Avenida between 5a and 6a Calle SO, has buses every five minutes, 4.30 am to 10 pm.

La Ceiba (3½ hours, 198 km, US$1.95).

Transportes Catisa, City & Tupsa (☎ 664030), 2a Avenida between 5a and 6a Calle SO, has buses hourly from 5.30 am to 7.30 pm.

Copán Ruinas (five hours, 198 km, US$1.80).

Transportes Etumi (☎ 533674), 6a Calle SO, between 6a and 7a Avenida, has two departures daily at 11 am and 1 pm.

Santa Rosa de Copán (four hours, 164 km, US$1.25).

Transportes Torito & Copanecos (☎ 534930, 531954), 6a Avenida, between 8a and 9a Calle SO, beside Hotel El Castillo, has buses every 35 minutes, 4.30 am to 5.15 pm.

Agua Caliente (seven hours, 270 km, US$2.80).

Transportes Congolón (☎ 531174), 8a Avenida, between 9a and 10a Calle SO, has a direct bus at midnight; others at 6.30 am, 10.30 am and 2.30 pm.

Santa Bárbara (two hours, 108 km, US$1.10).

Transportes Cotisbá (☎ 528889), 4a Avenida, between 9a and 10a Calle SO, has hourly buses from 6 am to 6 pm.

Train The railway station (☎ 533230, 534080) is in the centre of town, on the corner of 1a Calle and 1a Avenida. The train is slower but cheaper than the bus.

Trains to Puerto Cortés depart from San Pedro every morning at 6.45 am, arriving in Puerto Cortés around 9.30 or 10 am; cost is US$0.30.

To go by train to Tela, take the 6.45 am train from San Pedro Sula to Baracoa. Arriving at Baracoa at around 8 am, change trains there and continue on from Baracoa to Tela, arriving in Tela around 11 am. The fare from San Pedro Sula to Tela is US$0.45, but be sure to check the schedule first: trains between Baracoa and Tela may not run every day.

Getting Around

To/From the Airport The Villeda Morales airport is about 15 km east of town. There is no direct bus, but you can get on any El Progreso bus, alight at the airport turnoff, and walk for 10 minutes. Taxis cost about US$2.80 from the airport to town, but double that going the other way.

Bus There are local buses to the suburbs; cost is US$0.05.

Taxi The average taxi ride in town costs around US$0.75 per person. There are always lots of taxis cruising. You can phone for a taxi on ☎ 575122, 521160, 530404 or 521830.

Car Rental Blitz Rent-a-Car has offices in the Gran Hotel Sula on the north side of the plaza (☎ 522405) and at the airport (☎ 682471). Also with an office at the Gran Hotel Sula is Molinari Rent-a-Car (☎ 532639).

Other rental car companies in San Pedro include American Car Rental (☎ 527626, 562337), Budget Rent-a-Car (☎ 682267, at the airport), Martha Elena (☎ 534672) and Maya Rent-a-Car (☎ 522670 in town, 68-2463 at the airport).

AROUND SAN PEDRO SULA

Pulhapanzák waterfall, Lago de Yojoa and Puerto Cortés are easy excursions from San Pedro Sula: see the separate entries for these places earlier in this chapter. La Lima, 14 km east of San Pedro, is a banana 'company town' established by United Brands, where you can see the banana plantation and packing operations. The La Lima railroad office can give information and may provide you with a letter of introduction.

The Cusuco National Park, 20 km west of San Pedro, is a mountainous cloud forest, with the highest peak at 2242 metres. There is a visitors' centre: ask there about camping in the park. Information on the park is available at the Ministerio de Recursos Naturales (☎ 523202). Getting there is easiest with a private vehicle. The only buses from San Pedro go to Cofradia, a few km short of the park. They're run by Etica, 5a Avenida SO at 11a Calle, with departures half-hourly from 4.30 am to 10 pm.

SAN PEDRO SULA TO THE SOUTH-WEST

From San Pedro Sula, the Carretera de Occidente highway runs south-west, roughly

HONDURAS

parallel with the Guatemalan border though rather far into the Honduran side. At La Entrada, 127 km south-west of San Pedro Sula, the road forks and heads west to Copán Ruinas and the Guatemalan border, south to Santa Rosa de Copán, Nueva Ocotepeque and the two borders of Agua Caliente (Guatemala) and El Poy (El Salvador).

LA ENTRADA

La Entrada is a crossroads town with a small archaeological museum, several places to stay and eat, and lots of buses and traffic passing through, going north-east to San Pedro Sula, south to Santa Rosa de Copán and Nueva Ocotepeque, and south-west to Copán Ruinas. You never have to wait long for a bus in La Entrada. Roads are being improved here, which should shorten bus journey times.

COPÁN RUINAS

Population 22,270

The town of Copán Ruinas, also sometimes called simply Copán, is about one km from the famous Maya ruins of the same name. It is a beautiful little village; cobblestoned streets passing among typical white adobe buildings with red-tiled roofs, and a lovely colonial church on the plaza. This valley was inhabited by the Maya for around 2000 years and an aura of timeless peace fills the air. Copán has become a primary tourist destination, but this hasn't disrupted the peace to the extent one might expect.

The town's annual festival is from 15 to 20 March. Another annual fair, an Artisans' Fair with handicrafts and cultural presentations from all over Honduras, was begun in 1990; it runs from 15 to 21 December.

History

Copán must have had significant commercial activity since early times, though little archaeological evidence of this has been found.

Around 435 AD one princely family came to rule Copán, led by a mysterious king named Mah K'ina Yax K'uk' Mo' (Great Sun Lord Quetzal Macaw). The dynasty ruled throughout Copán's florescence during the Classic period (250 to 900 AD).

Of the early kings who ruled from about 435 to 628 we know little. Only a few names have been deciphered: Cu Ix, the fourth king, Waterlily Jaguar the seventh, Moon Jaguar the 10th, Butz' Chan the 11th.

Among the greatest of Copán's kings was Smoke Imix (Smoke Jaguar), the 12th king, who ruled from 628 to 695. Smoke Imix was wise, forceful and rich, and he built Copán into a major military and commercial power in the region. He may have taken over the nearby princedom of Quiriguá, as one of the famous stelae there bears his name and image. By the time he died in 695, Copán's population had grown significantly.

Smoke Imix was succeeded by 18 Rabbit (695-738), the 13th king, who willingly took the reigns of power and pursued further military conquest. In a war with his neighbour, King Cauac Sky, 18 Rabbit was captured and beheaded, to be succeeded by Smoke Monkey (738-49), the 14th king. Smoke Monkey's short reign left little mark on Copán.

In 749, Smoke Monkey was succeeded by his son Smoke Shell (749-63), one of Copán's greatest builders. He commissioned the construction of the city's most famous and important monument, the great Hieroglyphic Stairway, which immortalises the achievements of the dynasty from its establishment until 755, when the stairway was dedicated. It is the longest such inscription ever discovered in the Maya lands.

Yax Pac (Rising Sun, 763-820), Smoke Shell's successor and the 16th king of Copán, continued the beautification of Copán even though it seems that the dynasty's power was declining and its subjects had fallen on hard times. By the year 1200 or thereabouts even the farmers had departed, and the royal city of Copán was reclaimed by the jungle.

Visiting the Ruins

The archaeological site is open daily from 8 am to 4 pm. Admission costs US$4.20 and includes entry for the Las Sepulturas site and the Copán museum; the ticket is valid for two

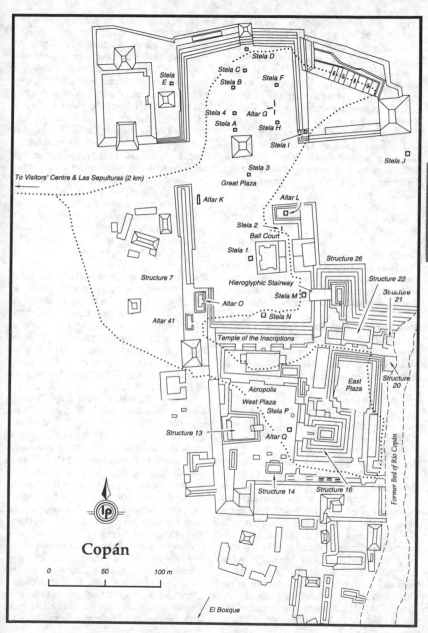

HONDURAS

Stela E

Stela D
Stela C
Stela B
Stela F
Stela 4
Altar G
Stela A
Stela H
Stela I
Stela J

To Visitors' Centre & Las Sepulturas (2 km)

Stela 3
Great Plaza

Altar K
Altar L
Stela 2
Ball Court
Stela 1
Structure 26
Structure 7
Hieroglyphic Stairway
Structure 22
Stela M
Structure 21
Altar O
Altar 41
Stela N
Temple of the Inscriptions
Structure 20
Acropolis
West Plaza
East Plaza
Stela P
Structure 13
Altar Q
Former Bed of Río Copán
Structure 14
Structure 16

Copán

0   50   100 m

El Bosque

days. The visitors' centre (centro de visitantes) building at the entrance to the ruins houses the ticket seller and a small exhibition about the site and its excavation. Nearby are a patio restaurant (La Cafetería) with a counter at which you can buy snacks and cold drinks, and there are souvenir and handicrafts shops in La Casa del Turista. There's also a tourist office desk here. Cheaper food is available across the road at the Comedor Mayapán. There's a picnic area along the path to the Principal Group of ruins. A nature trail (sendero natural) enters the forest several hundred metres from the visitors' centre.

You can camp at the ruins, outside the fence, using the water and toilets in the visitors' centre.

The Principal Group

The Principal Group of ruins is about 400 metres beyond the Visitors' Centre across well-kept lawns, through a gate in a strong fence and down shady avenues of trees.

Stelae of the Great Plaza The path leads to the Great Plaza and the huge, intricately carved stelae portraying the rulers of Copán. Most of Copán's best stelae date from 613 to 738, during the reigns of Smoke Imix (628-95) and 18 Rabbit (695-738). All seem to have originally been painted; a few traces of red paint survive on Stela C. Many stelae had vaults beneath or beside them in which sacrifices and offerings could be placed.

Many of the stelae on the Great Plaza portray King 18 Rabbit, including Stelae A, B and 4. Perhaps the most beautiful stela in the Great Plaza is Stela A (731 AD), now in danger of crumbling because of centuries of exposure to the elements. Nearby and almost equal in beauty are Stela 4 (731), Stela B (731), depicting 18 Rabbit upon his accession to the throne, and Stela C (782) with a turtle-shaped altar in front; this last stela has figures on both sides. Stela E (614), erected on top of Structure 1 on the west side of the Great Plaza, is among the oldest stelae.

Stela D (736), at the northern end of the Great Plaza at the base of Structure 2, also portrays King 18 Rabbit. On its back are two columns of hieroglyphs; at its base is an altar with fearsome representations of Chac, the rain god. In front of the altar is the burial place of Dr John Owen, an archaeologist with the expedition from Harvard's Peabody Museum who died during the work in 1893.

On the east side of the plaza is Stela F (721), which has a more lyrical design, with the robes of the main figure flowing around to the other side of the stone, where there are glyphs. Altar G (800), showing twin serpent heads, is among the last monuments carved at Copán. Stela H (730) may depict a queen or princess rather than a king. Stela 1 (692), on the structure which runs along the east side of the plaza, is of a person wearing a mask. Stela J, farther off to the east, resembles the stelae of Quiriguá in that it is covered in glyphs, not human figures.

Ball Court & Hieroglyphic Stairway South of the Great Plaza, across what is known as the Central Plaza, is the ball court (Juego de Pelota, 731), the second-largest in Central America. The one you see is the third one on this site; the other two smaller ones were buried by this construction. Note the macaw heads carved at the top of the sloping walls. The central marker in the court was the work of King 18 Rabbit.

South of the ball court is Copán's most famous monument, the Hieroglyphic Stairway (743), the work of King Smoke Shell. Today it's protected from the elements by a roof. This lessens the impact of its beauty, but you can still get an idea of how it looked. The flight of 63 steps bears a history – in several thousand glyphs – of the royal house of Copán; the steps are bordered by ramps inscribed with more reliefs and glyphs. The story inscribed on the steps is still not completely understood because the stairway was partially ruined and the stones jumbled.

At the base of the Hieroglyphic Stairway is Stela M (756), bearing a figure (probably King Smoke Shell) in a feathered cloak; glyphs tell of the solar eclipse in that year. The altar in front shows a plumed serpent with a human head emerging from its jaws.

Beside the stairway, a tunnel leads to the tomb of a nobleman, a royal scribe who may have been the son of King Smoke Imix. The tomb, discovered in June 1989, held a treasure trove of painted pottery and beautiful carved jade objects which are now in Honduran museums.

Acropolis The lofty flight of steps to the south of the Hieroglyphic Stairway is called the Temple of the Inscriptions. On top of the stairway, the walls are carved with groups of hieroglyphs. On the south side of the Temple of the Inscriptions are the East Plaza and West Plaza. In the West Plaza, be sure to see Altar Q (776), among the most famous sculptures here. Around its sides, carved in superb relief, are the 16 great kings of Copán, ending with its creator, Yax Pac. Behind the altar was a sacrificial vault in which archaeologists discovered the bones of 15 jaguars and several macaws which were probably sacrificed to the glory of Yax Pac and his ancestors.

The East Plaza also contains evidence of Yax Pac – his tomb, beneath Structure 18. Unfortunately, the tomb was discovered and looted long before archaeologists arrived. Both the East and West Plazas hold a variety of fascinating stelae and sculptured heads of humans and animals. To see the most elaborate relief carving, climb Structure 22 on the northern side of the East Plaza. Excavation and restoration is still under way.

El Bosque & Las Sepulturas
Excavations at El Bosque and Las Sepulturas have shed light on the daily life of the Maya of Copán during its golden age.

Las Sepulturas, once connected to the Great Plaza by a causeway, may have been the residential area where rich and powerful nobles lived. One huge, luxurious residential compound seems to have housed some 250 people in 40 or 50 buildings arranged around 11 courtyards. The principal structure, called the House of the Bacabs (officials), had outer walls carved with the full-sized figures of 10 males in fancy feathered headdresses; inside was a huge hieroglyphic bench.

To get to the site, you have to go back to the main road, turn right, then right again at the sign (two km).

Other Things to See & Do
The **Museo Regional de Arqueología Maya** on the town plaza is small but well worth a visit. It contains the original Stela B, portraying King 18 Rabbit; he was the great builder-king who unfortunately lost his head to the king of Quiriguá. Other exhibits of painted pottery, carved jade, Maya glyphs and the calendar round are also interesting and informative. The museum is open every day from 8 am to 4 pm; the admission ticket (US$4.20) includes entry to the archaeological sites.

About four blocks north of the plaza is the **Mirador El Cuartel**, the Old Jail, with a view over town.

There are some **hot springs** about an hour's drive or hitchhike from town; a trip to the hot springs and back will take you all day if you walk it. There are also **caves** in the area.

A few km from town (20 minutes by bus), on the road towards La Entrada, is **Santa Rita de Copán**, a lovely village built at the confluence of two rivers. Here, too, cobblestoned streets wind among adobe houses, with mud ovens standing alongside. The town has a beautiful little plaza and a simple, peaceful colonial church. Santa Rita is pleasant to walk around and it makes an enjoyable excursion from Copán Ruinas.

You can hire a **horse** in Copán Ruinas to go out to the ruins or make other excursions. A tour company in the block behind the church has horses for hire; you can probably find a horse for less if you just ask around town and do some bargaining. Many of the locals have horses.

Various tours, including adventure trips into the Mosquitia region, are operated from the Tunkul Bar; ask there for info.

Places to Stay
Copán is such a popular site that the hotels sometimes get full; try not to arrive late in the day.

The *Hotel Los Gemelos*, a block behind the plaza, is a favourite place to stay, with a garden patio, a place for washing clothes, and filtered water available. Doubles are US$4.20 with shared cold bath; if it's not busy you can get single occupancy for US$2.80. A block south is the cheap, basic, but neatly kept *Hotelito Copán*.

By the entrance to town, the *Hotel y Restaurante Paty* has rooms at US$2.80 per person with shared bath, or US$5.60 per person with private bath; rooms are being upgraded so expect a price hike. On the same crossroads, the *Hotel Honduras* is basic but not bad, with a courtyard and a mango tree. Rooms are US$2.10/3.50 with shared bath, or US$4.20/6.30 with private cold bath.

Nearby is the *Hotelito Brisas de Copán*, managed by a friendly Señora. A few rooms with shared cold bath cost US$2.10 per person; rooms with private bath are US$5.60/8.45, or a little more with air-con.

The *Hotel La Posada* near the plaza, is rather bare but cheap; rooms are US$2.10/2.80 with shared cold bath. It's across from the expensive and luxurious *Hotel Marina Copán* (☎ 983070).

If you want to camp out, you could camp

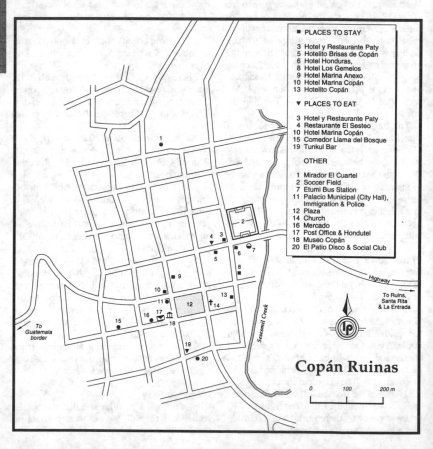

PLACES TO STAY
3   Hotel y Restaurante Paty
5   Hotelito Brisas de Copán
6   Hotel Honduras,
8   Hotel Los Gemelos
9   Hotel Marina Anexo
10 Hotel Marina Copán
13 Hotelito Copán

▼ PLACES TO EAT
3   Hotel y Restaurante Paty
4   Restaurante El Sesteo
10 Hotel Marina Copán
15 Comedor Llama del Bosque
19 Tunkul Bar

OTHER
1   Mirador El Cuartel
2   Soccer Field
7   Etumi Bus Station
11 Palacio Municipal (City Hall),
    Immigration & Police
12 Plaza
14 Church
16 Mercado
17 Post Office & Hondutel
18 Museo Copán
20 El Patio Disco & Social Club

To Guatemala border

To Ruins, Santa Rita & La Entrada

Highway

Sesesmil Creek

Copán Ruinas

0   100   200 m

at the ruins by the visitors' centre, outside the fence.

Places to Eat
The best place to eat is the very popular comedor *Llama del Bosque*, two blocks from the plaza. It has an attractive covered garden dining patio, a bar, and a good selection of inexpensive meals and snacks. It's open every day from 6 am to 9.30 pm.

Other restaurants in town include the restaurant at the *Hotel Marina Copán* on one corner of the plaza; it's a little more expensive but still popular. There's also the *Restaurante El Sesteo* at the entrance to town, with a good selection of typical Honduran food in an uninspiring environment; it's open daily from 6 am to 9 pm.

The *Tunkul Bar* is another good place to eat in Copán (see Entertainment). There are also a couple of cheap snack shacks in the centre, and most of the hotels have their own eateries.

Entertainment
The *Tunkul Bar* is the main gathering spot in town. It has good food, good music, good company, and a book exchange. The Tunkul is open every day from around 9 am to midnight; happy hour is from 6 to 7 pm.

On Saturday nights there's a dance at the *El Patio* social club and disco.

Getting There & Away
All the buses to and from Copán Ruinas depart from the tiny Etumi bus station, beside the Hotel Honduras at the entrance to town.

Direct buses to San Pedro Sula depart at 4 and 5 am (4½ hours, 198 km, US$1.80). If you don't want to get up so early you can easily take a bus to La Entrada (2½ hours, 60 km, US$1) and transfer there to a bus heading to San Pedro. The buses to La Entrada depart every 40 minutes from 4 am to 4.30 pm.

Copán Ruinas is about 12 km (45 minutes by bus) from the Guatemalan border at El Florido. Buses depart for the border from the Etumi bus station every 40 minutes through-out the day. Colectivos are inexpensive and also run to the border. From the border, regular buses leave for Chiquimula on the Guatemala side (58 km, 2½ hours, US$2). The border crossing is open daily from 7 am to 6 pm; allow about 45 minutes for the formalities.

If you are entering Honduras from Guatemala only to visit the ruins at Copán, read the section on El Florido in the Guatemala chapter.

SANTA ROSA DE COPÁN
Population 29,461
Santa Rosa de Copán is a small, cool, very Spanish mountain town, with cobbled streets and a lovely colonial church beside the plaza. The town is up on a hill, about one km from the bus station on the highway. There's no real reason to go out of your way to come to Santa Rosa, but if you happen to be in the area the town is a pleasant place for a stop-over or to spend the night. The annual festival day is 30 August.

Places to Stay & Eat
The *Hotel Mayaland* (☎ 620233) on the highway opposite the bus station is a clean and modern motel with rooms at US$5.30 per person, all with private bath and hot water, set around a grassy courtyard. The hotel has a restaurant and there are also many cheap comedores along this stretch of the highway near the bus station.

In town, the *Hotel Copán* (☎ 620265), at the corner of 1a Calle NE and 3a Avenida NE, has clean if small singles/doubles at US$1.95/2.90 or US$3.35/4.30 with private hot bath.

On Calle Real Centenario, east of the plaza at the corner of 6a Avenida NE, the *Hospedaje Calle Real* is also clean and decent, and one of the cheapest places in town. Rooms are US$1.40 with a single bed, US$1.70 with a double bed, or US$2.80 with two single beds, all sharing a cold bath.

The *Hotel Maya Central* (☎ 620073), on the corner of 3a Avenida NO and 1a Calle NO, has rooms at US$1.70 per person with private cold bath, or US$3.50 per person

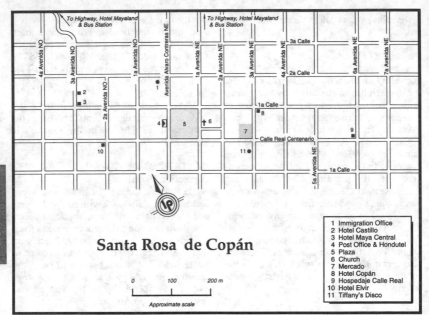

Santa Rosa de Copán

0   100   200 m

Approximate scale

1 Immigration Office
2 Hotel Castillo
3 Hotel Maya Central
4 Post Office & Hondutel
5 Plaza
6 Church
7 Mercado
8 Hotel Copán
9 Hospedaje Calle Real
10 Hotel Elvir
11 Tiffany's Disco

HONDURAS

with a hot shower. A couple of doors away, the *Hotel Castillo* (☎ 620368) has rooms per person at US$1.70 with shared cold bath or US$2.10 with private bath.

There are a number of small, typical comedores around town. The *Hotel Elvir* on the corner of 2a Avenida NO and Calle Real Centenario, two blocks west of the plaza, is a mid-price hotel (rooms from US$7.55/ 13.50), but its cafeteria is pleasant, clean, inexpensive, and it's open until 10 pm. The restaurant at the hotel opens at 6.30 am.

Getting There & Away
Buses from Santa Rosa de Copán come and go from the bus station on the main highway, about one km from the centre of town. Taxis wait at the station and cost US$0.40 for a ride into town.

Buses to San Pedro Sula (3½ hours, 164 km, US$1.25) depart every half-hour from 4 am until 5 pm. The same buses stop at La Entrada (28 km, US$0.40) one hour after

leaving Santa Rosa. At La Entrada you can transfer to a minibus heading to Copán Ruinas.

Buses head south-east to Gracias every 1½ hours from 7 am to 5 pm (1½ hours, 45 km, US$0.85).

GRACIAS & PARQUE NACIONAL CELAQUE
Gracias is a small, attractive mountain town, 45 km south-east of Santa Rosa de Copán. There's a good hot springs several km outside town; you could walk to the hot springs in about three hours, or get a ride from town and ask the driver to come back and pick you up.

Five km from Gracias is an entrance to the Parque Nacional Celaque. (Another entrance is at Belén Gualcho on the park's western side, with accommodation available in the town.)

Celaque is one of Honduras's most impressive national parks, containing the highest peak in the country (2849 metres) covered by a lush cloud forest. The park contains the headwaters of 10 rivers, a majestic waterfall seen from the entire valley, and some vertical cliffs which are a challenge to expert mountain climbers. The park is rich in plant and animal life, including several rare or endangered species: jaguars, pumas, ocelots, quetzals and much other wildlife can be seen.

It takes at least a day to climb to the top of the mountain. In the park is a visitors' centre with route information in English, and cabins where you can stay for US$0.70. Bring your own food (cooking facilities available) and bedding. It's a fairly easy walk from Gracias along the Río Arcagual up into the park; it takes around 1½ hours to the entrance and a further half hour to the visitors' centre.

More information on the park is available from any office of the Ministerio de Recursos Naturales or from the Cohdefor office in Gracias.

Places to Stay & Eat

There are several pleasant and inexpensive places to stay and eat in Gracias. The *Hotel Erick*, a block from the plaza, is clean, friendly and has singles/doubles for US$2.50/3.80. You can leave your luggage here if you stay overnight in the park.

Restaurant *La Fonda* has been recommended for its good food and pleasant courtyard.

Getting There & Away

Buses run between Gracias and Santa Rosa de Copán six times daily on a newly improved road (1½ hours, 45 km, US$0.85).

An unpaved road continues south-east from Gracias to La Esperanza, and from there north-east to Siguatepeque on the San Pedro Sula-Tegucigalpa highway. On the map this looks like a shortcut from Santa Rosa de Copán to Tegucigalpa, but the road is extremely bad and in reality it makes a very gruelling trip. Buses between Gracias and La Esperanza usually run only about every other day, but they may not run at all during the rainy season. Check whether transport and road conditions have improved before contemplating this route; if you do go this way, there are places to stay at La Esperanza and Siguatepeque.

NUEVA OCOTEPEQUE

In the south-west corner of Honduras, Nueva Ocotepeque is another crossroads town, with a lot of traffic to and from the nearby borders at Agua Caliente (Guatemala) and El Poy (El Salvador). There's not much to the town, but it's a convenient place to stay overnight before or after crossing the border.

Places to Stay & Eat

All the places to stay and eat in Nueva Ocotepeque are on or near the main highway through town, within about five blocks of one another.

Hospedaje San Antonio, a few doors from the main road, is basic but good value, with singles/doubles at US$1.40/2.80 with shared bath, or US$5.60 for doubles with private cold bath. Nearby, at the *Mini Hotel Turista*, rooms are US$1.70/3.35 with shared cold bath and US$2.80/5.60 for singles/doubles.

The *Hotel y Comedor Congolón*, on the main road past the plaza, has rooms for US$1.40 per person with shared bath, or US$4.20 per room with private cold bath. Unfortunately, service is poor and, as the Congolón buses to San Pedro Sula operate from here, it's noisy from buses and waiting passengers.

Opposite this, the *Mini Hotel* is quieter; singles/doubles with shared bath are US$2.10/2.80, or US$3.50/4.20 with private cold bath.

There are many simple restaurants on the main road in the blocks near the bus station. Try *Comedor Gitano*, which has meals for US$1.10. *Cafeteria Sandoval*, just off the main road, is inexpensive and has a wider choice.

Getting There & Away

Frequent buses run between Nueva Ocotepeque and the borders at Agua Caliente (30 minutes, 22 km, US$0.40) and El Poy

(15 minutes, eight km, US$0.20). The buses operate all day until the borders close at around 5 or 6 pm. Colectivos to El Poy cost US$0.30.

Heading north to San Pedro Sula, buses depart at 9 and 11 am, 1 and 3 pm, and midnight (six hours, 248 km, US$1.95). Two companies make the trip; Congolón buses go one day, Impala buses the next. The road to San Pedro Sula is an excellent paved road all the way.

You could take one of the San Pedro Sula buses if you're going to Santa Rosa de Copán or to La Entrada. To Santa Rosa de Copán, however, there are more frequent buses; they depart from Nueva Ocotepeque every 45 minutes, from 6 am until 3 pm (3½ hours, 95 km, US$1). From Santa Rosa, buses depart every half-hour or so heading north to La Entrada and San Pedro Sula.

Northern Honduras

The Caribbean coast of Honduras is for the most part a narrow coastal plain backed by mountains; another large plain in the area is the Ulua River valley, with Honduras's second-largest city, San Pedro Sula (see the Western Honduras section). These plains are among Honduras's most fertile and productive agricultural areas: it is here that Standard and United Fruit grow bananas and pineapples for export to the USA. The two companies own a large part of northern Honduras, and several of the towns, ports, railways, roads, banks etc in the area were put there by the banana companies.

The Caribbean coast has an interesting mixture of races. In addition to the mestizos found everywhere in Honduras, there are many Black people descended from Jamaicans and other West Indians who came during the years when the British occupied the Caribbean coast.

A very interesting north-coast people are the Garífuna, a mixture of African and Carib Indian peoples, brought by the British from the island of St Vincent to the island of

Roatán in the late 18th century. From Roatán they spread out along the coast and now have small coastal fishing and agricultural villages all the way from Belize to Nicaragua. Their language, Garífuna, has a strong West African sound and is a mixture of several languages – Arawak, French, Yoruba, and perhaps others as well. The Garífuna have their own religion, music, dance and other cultural patterns.

The principal towns of the north coast are Puerto Cortés (Honduras's major port), Tela, La Ceiba and Trujillo. All of them have their attractions, but probably the two most enjoyable for travellers are Tela and Trujillo. La Ceiba is the usual jumping-off point for travel to the Bay Islands, with air and boat transport to all of the islands departing from there.

The attractions of the Caribbean beach towns are just about what you'd expect: lovely beaches lined by coconut palms, and delicious fresh seafood (try the coconut bread and the seafood soups made with coconut). All of these towns have interesting places to visit nearby, and many km of beaches good for walking and exploring. It is generally a safe area, but in all the beach towns the local women will warn you that it's not safe for a woman alone to walk on the beach at night.

The coast fills up with tourists during Semana Santa, when Hondurans have their one week of holiday, beach-going and merry-making. If you're on the coast at this time, make sure you've secured a place to stay in advance. Hotels fill up for this week and prices double. The rest of the time, you won't usually see too many tourists.

It can rain on the Caribbean coast any time of year, but the most rain occurs from around September to January (mostly after around November). Sometimes there are floods at this time, making the roads impassable.

PUERTO CORTÉS
Population 32,500
Puerto Cortés, 57 km north of San Pedro Sula, is the westernmost Caribbean town in Honduras. It is also the country's most

important port: the only port in the country which can handle big cargo containers. Puerto Cortés handles over half of Honduras's export shipping trade. It's just a two-day sail from the USA, with frequent cargo ships sailing to New Orleans and Miami laden with bananas, pineapples and other produce. The docks, right in the town, are the town's focal point and raison d'être.

There are no good beaches in Puerto Cortés, but there are several within a short distance, easily accessible by bus; the Spanish fortress at Omoa is a half-hour bus ride from town. It takes only an hour by bus to Puerto Cortés from San Pedro Sula, and the beaches around the area – Omoa, Baja Mar and Travesía – are popular day trips for visitors from San Pedro.

Puerto Cortés' annual fair is held on 15 August.

Places to Stay & Eat

Most people visit Puerto Cortés as a day trip from San Pedro Sula, but there are some cheap lodgings if you want to stay over. The *Hotel Formosa* (☎ 550853), on 3a Avenida, three blocks west of the plaza, has singles/doubles with fan at US$2.10/3.50 with shared bath, US$3.50/4.90 with private bath.

On the plaza, *Hotel Tuek-San* is a little run-down, but the rooms are very big and all have private bath: US$2.80/4.90 with fan or US$5.60/9.85 with air-con. Its restaurant is OK for Chinese food.

By the docks is the *Hotel & Restaurante Las Vegas* (☎ 550163). Rooms for one or two people are US$3.50 but the place seems to operate as a pick-up joint for sailors.

There are lots of restaurants around the plaza. *Café Viena* has good food, especially the red snapper for US$2.80. The waterfront area also has restaurants, as well as seedy bars. *Burger Boy's*, east of the plaza, is a popular place for burgers from US$0.60, and it has music videos on a giant screen.

Getting There & Away

Bus Buses run frequently between Puerto Cortés and San Pedro Sula, a one-hour trip. The two bus companies that make the trip, Transportes Impala and Citul, both have their depots on 3a Avenida in the block west of the plaza.

See 'Around Puerto Cortés' for info on local buses.

Train A train runs daily between Puerto Cortés and San Pedro Sula, departing Puerto Cortés at 3.15 pm and arriving in San Pedro at around 6.30 or 7 pm. The cost is US$0.25.

You can also take the train from Puerto Cortés to Tela, departing on the same train bound for San Pedro and changing trains at Baracoa; the ride to Tela takes about four hours. If you're going to Tela, be sure to check the schedule; the train from Baracos to Tela may go only three or four times a week.

Boat There are no regularly scheduled passenger boats from Puerto Cortés, but it's possible to come and go by cargo or fishing boat if you're prepared to wait a few days. Ask around at the docks for info. If you are entering or leaving the country by boat, be sure to stop at the immigration office to get your entrance or exit stamp; there is an office in Puerto Cortés on the north-east side of the plaza.

Boats go between Puerto Cortés and other Honduran ports, especially La Ceiba and Roatán. The trip to Roatán takes about 10 hours and there's usually a boat leaving weekly. The *Utila Express* leaves every second weekend, stops for a day or so in Utila then continues to Roatán. The *Bay Islands Express* has a two-weekly cycle, taking in Roatán, Puerto Cortés, Tampa and New Orleans.

Boats to Guatemala are not very frequent. To Dangriga in Belize, what is described as a 'big canoe' departs every Wednesday and Saturday (weather permitting, US$22.50); the office is near the bridge on the isthmus: take local bus Ruta 1 and get off at the naval base.

HONDURAS

HONDURAS

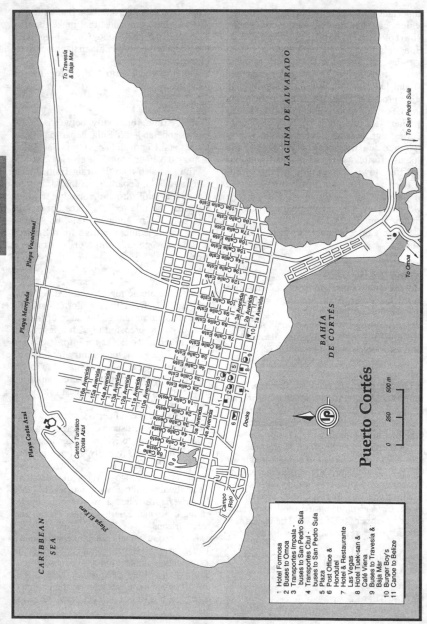

Puerto Cortés

1   Hotel Formosa
2   Buses to Omoa
3   Transportes Impala -
    buses to San Pedro Sula
4   Transportes Citul -
    buses to San Pedro Sula
5   Plaza
6   Post Office &
    Hondutel
7   Hotel & Restaurante
    Las Vegas
8   Hotel Tuek-san &
    Café Viena
9   Buses to Travesía &
    Baja Mar
10 Burger Boy's
11 Canoe to Belize

CARIBBEAN SEA

Playa El Faro
Playa Costa Azul
Centro Turístico Costa Azul
Playa Marejada
Playa Vacacional
To Travesía & Baja Mar

LAGUNA DE ALVARADO
To San Pedro Sula
To Omoa

BAHÍA DE CORTÉS

Campo Rojo
Docks

0   250   500 m

AROUND PUERTO CORTÉS

Omoa

At Omoa, by the sea 15 km west of Puerto Cortés, is an old Spanish fortress, the Fortaleza de San Fernando de Omoa. It was built between 1759 and 1777 under orders from King Fernando of Spain, to protect the coast from the rampant piracy, but in 1779 the fortress was captured by the British after only a four-day battle.

The fort is still in good shape, maintained by the Instituto Hondureño de Antropología e Historia. It is open daily from 8 am to 4 pm, admission US$1.40.

Omoa also has a decent beach, popular on weekends. Along the waterfront are many little seafood restaurants. The beach is at the end of the paved road, a few blocks' walk from the fortress. Omoa's annual festival is held on 30 May.

Buses to Omoa depart from Puerto Cortés every half-hour from the depot on 2a Calle Este, one block west of the plaza. It's a 30-minute ride and costs US$0.20. They let you off on the highway, a short walk from the fort.

Travesía & Baja Mar

To the east of Puerto Cortés, Travesía and Baja Mar are two seaside Garífuna villages with good beaches and lots of palm trees. The road from Puerto Cortés runs along the seaside, first through Travesía and on into Baja Mar; the two villages form a continuous row of wooden houses beside the sea, with small fishing boats lining the shore. The beach is lovely along the whole stretch. There are one or two restaurants in each village for beachgoers.

The bus from Puerto Cortés to Travesía and Baja Mar departs from the block southeast of the plaza. It takes about 45 minutes to go all the way to the end of the bus line at Baja Mar, passing through Travesía; the cost is US$0.20. It may not run on a Sunday, in which case you can take local bus Ruta 2, get off where it swings round for the return leg (at Comaguey), and walk along the coast road for 20 minutes.

TELA

Population 24,000

Tela is many travellers' favourite Honduran Caribbean beach town; it's a small, quiet town with superb seafood, several good places to stay, and some of the most beautiful beaches on the north coast. This is a great place for relaxing on the beach and enjoying the simple life.

Large cargo ships come and go from the pier, carrying bananas away for export; bananas and other tropical fruits are cultivated in the area surrounding Tela. Standard Fruit once had quite a 'company town' here, but it is now converted to a luxury resort, the Hotel Villas Telamar.

Tela is somnolent most of the year, but it's quite another story during Semana Santa, when the town fills up with holiday-makers. Hotel rates double, advance bookings are essential if you want to get a room, and the beaches are full of campers. The annual fiesta day is 13 June.

Expect big changes here in the next couple of years. US$24.5 million is being pumped into the Tela Bay Development Project, intended to boost tourism in the region (and no doubt prices, too).

Orientation & Information

Tela is divided into two sections: Tela Vieja, the 'old town', on the east bank where the Río Tela meets the sea, and Tela Nueva, on the west side of the river, where the Hotel Villas Telamar hugs some of the best stretch of beach.

The post office and Hondutel are beside one another on 4a Avenida NE. A block away on the same street is a laundromat, the *Lavandería El Centro* (US$2.10 per load).

Jimmy's, by the beach, has simple food but also an excellent and extensive book exchange (US$0.15 per swap). It's open daily from 10 am to 11 pm.

Things to See & Do

Tela's main attraction is its magnificent beaches which stretch around the bay for several km on either side of the town. The beach right in front of the town is not bad,

HONDURAS

but the one just over the bridge in Tela Nueva, in front of the Hotel Villas Telamar, is much better; its pale, powdery sand and a shady grove of coconut trees and lawn just behind it are kept clean.

The Hotel Villas Telamar is very expensive to stay in, but you can pay US$2 per day for the use of its services, including the large swimming pool, sauna and jacuzzi. The café by the pool is not too expensive. There is a golf course and tennis courts, and you can play bingo at weekends. The Club Telamar, east of the pool, has a bar and various indoor games such as billiards. The hotel rents horses and bicycles for US$2 per hour.

There are several very pleasant excursions you can make just a few km from town (see Around Tela).

Places to Stay

Tela has a number of places to stay right on the beach; everywhere is within a few blocks of it.

The best of the cheapest places is the Hotel Preluna, near the bus station, where basic but clean singles/doubles with a fan are just US$2.10. Nearby, Hotel Robert is similar and costs US$2.10/4.20, and has some rooms with private bath for US$5.60. It can get noisy from the next-door bars. Hotel Miramar is above a weekend disco and has large, bare rooms for US$2.80/4.20.

The Boarding House Sara (☎ 482108) on 11a Calle NE, is a big old house by the beach; lots of backpacking foreigners stay here. Singles/doubles sharing cold bath are US$2.10/4.20: comparatively expensive for what they are, but the sociable atmosphere more than compensates. Hammocks are strung up on the balcony. If you ask, the owners will cook an excellent meal for guests at just US$1.10 per person. There are also several fully equipped three-bedroom houses starting at US$18.25 per night (negotiate for a good rate). The owner speaks fluent English.

Also on 11a Calle NE by the beach are several other hotels. The Hotel Marazul, at the corner of 4a Avenida NE, has slightly bare rooms for two/three people with private bath and fan at US$5.60/8.45. Singles are US$4.20 with shared bath. The Hotel Playa has rooms with private bath at US$2.80/5.60 with one or two beds, purified water and a place to do your laundry; they offer a discount if you stay a few days.

In town, three blocks from the beach, Mini Hotel La Posada del Sol has singles/doubles with private bath for US$3.90/6.80 and a garden courtyard, but it's not a friendly place.

A bit more expensive, the Hotel Tela (☎ 482150) has a rooftop terrace and clean, spacious rooms with private cold bath for US$6/11.25. The Gran Hotel Presidente (☎ 482821), new in 1991 and right on the plaza, has small but very clean rooms with private hot water bath for US$6.70/11.25; doubles for US$15 have air-con and cable TV. There is room service.

The Gran Hotel Puerto Rico (☎ 482413), built in 1988, is right on the beach. It has rooms with private bath, cable TV and air-con for US$17.50, or US$21 with fridge, beach view and balcony. The sea-view bar/restaurant here is open 24 hours. A couple of blocks west, the Hotel Sherwood has comparable rooms (but no TV) for US$14. Try negotiating in both these places.

At the rock-bottom level are several very cheap hotels near the train tracks which the locals refer to as hoteles de la mala muerte! The Hotel Paradise, 15 minutes' walk beyond Hotel Villas Telemar, has some inexpensive cabañas for rent by the beach; it's near the San Juan bus route.

Places to Eat

Seafood is plentiful, delicious and inexpensive around Tela. Seafood soups are a particular delicacy of the town; fish, shrimp, lobster and caracol (conch) are all found in many restaurants.

Half a block back from the beach, Luces del Norte is popular with foreign backpackers and has a casual atmosphere. It's open every day from 7 am to 10 pm. Breakfasts are good, but it serves any meal anytime, plus alcohol.

Along the beach there are several cheap

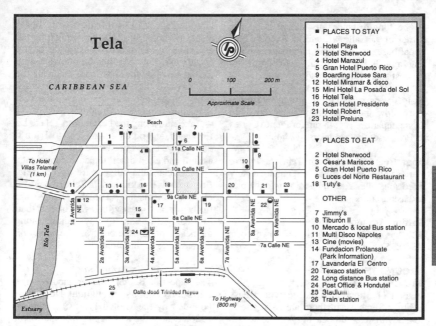

comedores and some reasonably priced better restaurants. *Hotel Sherwood* is an attractive bar/restaurant with wood decor and a deck with palm trees, right on the beach, open daily from 7 am to 11 pm. Opposite, *Cesar's Mariscos* is another attractive open-air bar/restaurant, slightly cheaper, and with great seafood soups for around US$2.25. Also on the beach, the open-air bar/restaurant at the *Gran Hotel Puerto Rico* is open 24 hours and has good seafood.

Back from the beach, on 9a Calle, there are several places to eat, including a good Chinese restaurant. Near the plaza, *Tuty's* is a pleasant, clean, inexpensive little place for pastries, simple meals, and a variety of fruit cocktails, fruit drinks and ice cream. The licuados for US$0.35 are excellent. It's open every day from 6 am to 11 pm.

Entertainment
The *Hotel Villas Telamar* has a disco on Friday and Saturday nights, with a minimal admission charge. Other discos in town include *Multi Disco Napoles* and the disco below the *Hotel Miramar*, both near the bridge where 9a Calle NE crosses to Tela Nueva. There's a cinema *(cine)* on 9a Calle NE, three blocks west of the plaza.

The favourite backpackers' evening hangout is *Tiburón II*, opposite Boarding House Sara, for beers, socialising, and playing pool.

Getting There & Away
Bus Buses depart from Tela bound for La Ceiba every half hour from 4.30 am to 6 pm (105 km, 2½ hours, US$0.80).

There are no direct buses between Tela and San Pedro Sula; you have to change buses at El Progreso. Buses leave Tela for El Progreso half-hourly from 4.30 am until 6 pm (63 km, 2½ hours, US$0.70). From El Progreso to San Pedro Sula it's another hour's ride; the buses leave about every five minutes, with the last bus at 9 pm.

The long-distance bus station is on the corner of 9a Calle NE and 9a Avenida NE. Local buses to the Garífuna villages of San Juan and El Triunfo de la Cruz depart from the east side of the Mercado.

Train The passenger train serving Tela is old, rusty, slow and very cheap. Every day there is one departure at 1.45 pm for Puerto Cortés *or* Progreso; the trip takes 4¼ hours.

Boat Boats depart from Tela for Puerto Cortés and other destinations, but not on any fixed schedule. You can go down to the pier and ask around.

Getting Around
Tela has many taxis; a ride in town costs US$0.35.

AROUND TELA
Garífuna Villages
Several Garífuna villages are within easy reach of Tela. All of them are right on the coast, with splendid beaches, simple houses shaded by coconut trees, fishing canoes resting on the sand, and tiny restaurants serving delicious Garífuna food; the specialities are seafood soups and fish cooked in coconut. You can spend some idyllic days walking along the beaches from Tela and visiting the coastal villages.

The larger villages may hold dances on the weekends; a Garífuna dance is a great experience. San Juan and El Triunfo de la Cruz have cultural dance troupes which have performed in many places.

The closest village is **La Ensenada**, a three-km (45-minute) walk east along the arc of the beach from Tela, just before you reach the point, Punta Triunfo, crowned by the Cerro El Triunfo de la Cruz. Along the way you need to ford a river up to one metre deep. La Ensenada is a lovely little village with seafood restaurants (although most are only open on the weekend), places for a drink, and a great beach.

Rocks prevent you walking around the point, but you can keep walking on the inland road for another 1½ to two km and reach the larger village of **El Triunfo de la Cruz**; buses also come here from Tela, departing from the corner on the east side of the Mercado, or you could take any bus heading towards La Ceiba, get off at the crossroads and walk the 1½ km into the village. Another beautiful spot, this village was the site of the first Spanish settlement in Honduras.

Take care along the beach from Tela to La Ensenada, and on the inland road to Triunfo de la Cruz: a traveller wrote about a violent assault and cited other unpleasant incidents.

Other Garífuna villages are west of Tela. **San Juan** is five km west of Tela, a beautiful place worth visiting; Tornabé is three km further on, and other villages are on past that. You can get to San Juan by walking along the beach, or take the bus from the corner on the east side of the Mercado.

Lancetilla Jardín Botánica
The Lancetilla Botanic Garden and Research Centre is famous throughout Honduras. Founded by the United Fruit Company in 1926, Lancetilla was begun to experiment with the cultivation of various tropical plants in Central America; some of the plants that were first planted there are now important crops in Central America. Of its 694 hectares, some protecting natural forest forming the watershed for Tela, only 53 hectares are accessible to the visitor.

The garden contains fruit trees from every continent, cacao, fine timber plantings, nuts and palms, and a long tunnel formed by an arch of bamboo. A wonderfully cool swimming hole is on the Río Lancetilla at the far end of the park, about 1½ km from the visitors' centre. Another attraction of the park is its birdlife; the various plantings have created habitats for over 200 recorded species of birds, and a bird checklist for birdwatchers is available at the visitors' centre.

The park has dormitory accommodation with space for 32 people, with four to six beds in a room; cost is US$2 a night, sheets and bedding included. Sometimes the dorms are full when a group of students come to study in the park, but usually there is space available. The dorms don't have kitchens, but food and refreshments are sold in the park.

Lancetilla is about five km south-west of the centre of Tela; there's a ticket kiosk on the highway to El Progreso about two km from Tela, and the park is another 3½ km inland. You can usually hitch a lift with any passing vehicle past the ticket booth entrance. There's a visitors' information centre where the park begins, and an explanatory map in English is available.

Lancetilla is open every day from 7.30 am to 3.30 pm; admission is US$1. Free guided tours are available for groups of five or more persons (which is not difficult to come up with on weekends).

Parque Nacional Marino Punta Sal

Standing on the beach at Tela, you can look out and see a long arc of land curving out to the west to a point almost in front of you. This point, Punta Sal, is the site of the Parque Nacional Marino Punta Sal.

Within this national marine park are various habitats, including mangrove forests and swamps between the mouth of the Río Ulua and the Laguna de los Micos, plus a small tropical forest, offshore reefs and the rocky point itself.

This area is completely unspoilt and undeveloped so you need to take your own food and a tent or hammock.

Getting there along the coast is an adventure in itself: it takes about two days by a combination of bus, truck, boat and walking; hiring a boat right across the bay would still take several hours and be very expensive.

Access to the park will soon improve, as the area between Punta Sal and Tornabe is the proposed site of tourist developments under the Tela Bay Development Project. The likely affect on flora & fauna in the park has not been calculated, but it's unlikely to be beneficial.

Find out more about Punta Sal from Fundacion Prolansate (☎ 482042), the park information office by Tela's cinema.

LA CEIBA
Population 77,100

La Ceiba is the largest of Honduras's Caribbean port towns, though Puerto Cortés actually takes the lead as the busiest port. Situated on the narrow coastal plain between the towering Cordillera Nombre de Dios mountain range and the Caribbean, it's surrounded by pineapple and banana plantations, which are mostly owned by Standard Fruit, and is rich both in fishing and agriculture.

La Ceiba is not a particularly attractive town and there's not much to see in the town itself, but some interesting excursions can be made in the surrounding area (see Around La Ceiba). The main reason travellers stay there is that it's the jumping-off point for visits to the Bay Islands.

La Ceiba attracts visitors from far and wide for its annual Carnaval, held during the third week in May; it lasts for two weeks but the big Carnaval day is the third Saturday in May. People dress up in costumes and masks and dance themselves silly, and it's a great time. There's a saying in Honduras: 'Tegucigalpa piensa, San Pedro Sula trabaja, y La Ceiba se divierte' (Tegucigalpa thinks, San Pedro Sula works, and La Ceiba has fun). At Carnaval it's no mystery why La Ceiba is known for having fun.

La Ceiba got its name from a very large ceiba tree that used to stand on the coast near where the pier is now. Boats would pull in near this spot, and people would congregate to meet, buy and sell in the shade of the big tree.

Orientation

The heart of La Ceiba is its attractive, shady central plaza. Avenida San Isidro, running from the east side of the plaza to the sea, is La Ceiba's 'main drag'. Avenida La República, running to the sea from the opposite side of the plaza, has railway tracks down its centre, which were used to transport fruit and cargo to the pier at the foot of this street. There are lots of cheap hotels along Avenida La República.

If you go along 1a Calle and cross the

bridge over the estuary, you're in Barrio La Isla. Many Garífuna people live on this side, and there are a couple of places to stay along the beach here, many simple restaurants and several popular discos. Farther east, about one km from the centre of town where the Río Cangrejal meets the sea in several sandbars, there are pleasant beaches that are cleaner than those in the centre.

Information

Tourist Office The Instituto Hondureño de Turismo has an information kiosk on the west side of the central plaza, open Monday to Friday from 8 to 11 am and 2 to 5 pm, and Saturday from 8 to 11 am.

Post & Telecommunications Hondutel is back from the road on Avenida Ramón Rosa, between 5a Calle and 7a Calle, and is open 24 hours every day. The post office is south of the central plaza, on the corner of 13a Calle and Avenida Morazan; it's open Monday to Friday, 8 am to 5 pm, and Saturday, 8 am to noon.

Travel Agencies At the Gran Hotel Paris there are two travel agencies, Transmundo (☎ 432820) and Ecotours (☎ 432391). Other recommended places include:

Caribbean Travel
    Avenida San Isidro, near the Gran Hotel Ceiba
    and Hotel Iberia (☎ 431360)
Hondu-Tours
    Corner of 9a Calle and Avenida 14 de Julio
    (☎ 420569, 430457; fax 431853)
Agencia de Viajes Atlántida
    Boulevard 15 de Septiembre, by Banco Conti-
    nental (☎ 430337)

Other It's difficult to find postcards anywhere on the north coast, but Souvenirs El Buen Amigo, a souvenir shop on Avenida 14 de Julio between 8a and 9a Calle, has a good selection.

There's a laundry on Avenida Victor Hugo in front of the stadium where it costs US$1.80 for a minimum 13-pound (6-kg) load.

Things to See & Do

There's not much to do in town, though the central plaza is relaxing and it has a crocodile and turtle enclosure.

The sea water is none too clean at La Ceiba, so better beaches are either side of the centre: Playa La Barra, near the sandbars where the Río Cangrejal meets the sea, and Playa Miramar, about one km in the opposite direction. There are plenty of good, cleaner beaches a few km from town. Some beaches are said to be dangerous at night, particularly around Barrio La Isla.

The public can swim at the pool at the Hotel Partenon Beach or the Gran Hotel Paris; each charges US$1.80 per day.

There's a view of La Ceiba, the coastline and all the way out to the Bay Islands from Colonia La Merced; go up the road that ascends the hill behind the golf course, about an hour's walk. Alternatively, take the 'La Merced' bus from near the south-west corner of the central plaza. A taxi from town costs US$0.35. Bring binoculars if you have them.

Places to Stay

There are a great number of cheap places to stay in La Ceiba, though some are of very low quality.

In the centre of town, the pick of the cheapies is the *Hotel San Carlos* (☎ 430330), on Avenida San Isidro. Good, clean singles/doubles with overhead fan and private cold bath are just US$2.10/2.80.

Hotel Royal (☎ 430723) on Avenida 14 de Julio is old but reasonably clean, the rooms have windows and purified water is available. Rooms for one or two people are US$2.25 with shared bath, or US$3.65 with private bath. Two-bed rooms cost US$4.35.

Hotel California (☎ 420303) is OK, with singles/doubles for US$3 with shared bath, or US$4.50 with private bath. The *Hotel Principe* (☎ 430516) on 7a Calle is cheap enough, with rooms on the same basis for US$3.35/5.05, but a traveller reported that the management weren't particularly helpful when he had his camera stolen from his hotel room.

The *Hotel Las 5 Rosas* (☎ 420725) on 8a

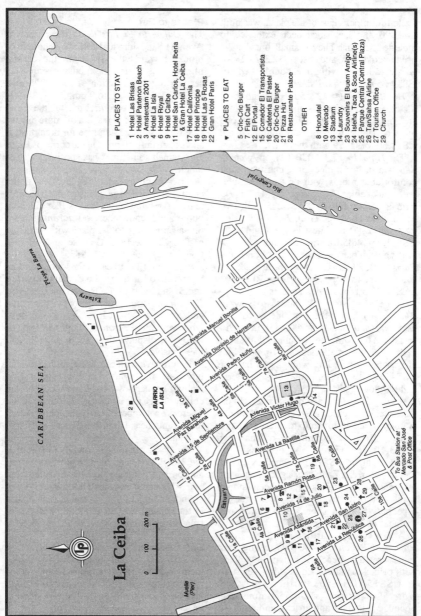

La Ceiba

CARIBBEAN SEA

Muelle (Pier)

Playa La Barra

Estuary

BARRIO LA ISLA

Río Cangrejal

HONDURAS

■ PLACES TO STAY

1 Hotel Las Brisas
2 Hotel Partenon Beach
4 Amsterdam 2001
6 Hotel La Isla
9 Hotel Royal
11 Hotel Caribe
 Hotel San Carlos, Hotel Iberia & Gran Hotel La Ceiba
17 Hotel California
18 Hotel Principe
19 Hotel Las 5 Rosas
22 Gran Hotel Paris

▼ PLACES TO EAT

5 Cric-Cric Burger
7 Fish Cart
12 El Portal
15 Comedor El Transportista
16 Cafeteria El Pastel
20 Cric-Chic Burger
21 Pizza Hut
28 Restaurante Palace

OTHER

8 Hondutel
10 Mercado
13 Stadium
14 Laundry
23 Souvenirs El Buem Amigo
24 Isleña, Taca & Sosa Airline(s)
25 Parque Central (Central Plaza)
26 Tan/Sahsa Airline
27 Tourism Office
29 Church

Calle four blocks east of the plaza, was built in 1990 and has since been extended to include 35 rooms. They're small, but all have private cold bath, and cost US$2.35/3.25 for singles/doubles with one double bed, or US$4.55 with two beds.

Hotel Caribe (☎ 422550) is also not bad; it's clean and the rooms up on the 3rd floor are quite spacious and sunny. Rooms for one or two people with private cold bath are US$4.50, or US$9 with two beds.

The *Hotel Iberia* (☎ 430401), on Avenida San Isidro, has a nice inner courtyard and comfortable rooms with private hot water bath and cable TV. Rooms are US$11.95 with a double bed or US$16.85 with two beds. Next door, the *Gran Hotel La Ceiba* (☎ 432737/47) is almost as good and costs US$11.25/14.05 for singles/doubles.

If you can pay even more, the *Gran Hotel Paris* (☎ 432371/91) on the central plaza has loads of facilities; prices start at US$18/22.50 for singles/doubles.

There are also a few places to stay in Barrio La Isla, on the east side across the estuary. *Hotel La Isla* (☎ 432835), in Barrio La Isla on the corner of 4a Calle and Avenida Pedro Nuño, is small, clean and friendly, and has rooms at US$3.50 with shared bath or US$4.20 with private bath, plus a cafeteria and bar downstairs.

Amsterdam 2001, a simple place right on the beach at Avenida Miguel Paz Barahona, is overpriced compared to places in the centre. Beds in communal rooms cost US$3.10 per person, and doubles with private bath are US$7. It's owned by an old Dutch sailor, Jan Zaal; he's a good source of information and stories but has been known to be abrupt or even offensive to guests, especially women. There's a restaurant and bar next door.

A few blocks further east, the *Hotel Partenon Beach* (☎ 430404), along this same stretch of beach, is a luxurious place with prices to match; singles/doubles start at US$15.10/17.55. Farther east, the *Hotel Las Brisas* is not recommended because it is dark and airless, and rents its rooms by the hour.

Places to Eat

The *Cafeteria El Pastel*, on the corner of Avenida San Isidro and 6a Calle, a couple of blocks towards the sea from the central plaza, is a basic, inexpensive cafeteria serving a good selection of food. It's open every day from 7 am to 9 pm.

The air-con *Le Petit Cafe*, at the Gran Hotel Paris on the plaza, is a bit more expensive but it's not a bad place for breakfast; it stays open until 10 pm. On the corner is *Pizza Hut*, which sometimes has special deals for lunch.

Cric-Cric Burger has two locations in the centre; both are large, pleasant open-air restaurants serving basic snacks like chicken, burgers and sandwiches. *Restaurante Palace* on 9a Calle is a popular place with an inside and a patio section. Chinese and international meals are around US$3.

You can find cheap comedores almost everywhere you turn in La Ceiba, both in the centre and in Barrio La Isla. At the *Comedor El Transportista*, on the corner of 7a Avenida and Avenida Ramón Rosa, you can choose whatever you like from the large selection of foods on display; their food is good and inexpensive.

If you have a place to prepare it, you can buy fresh fish every morning from a little ice-cart further down the same block, on the corner of 5a Calle and Avenida Ramón Rosa. There are a number of fairly inexpensive fish restaurants near Hotel Las Brisas in Barrio La Isla.

The best restaurant in town is *El Portal* in the Hotel El Colonial. It has plush decor, air-con and good service; the excellent and extensive menu includes Thai cuisine. Prices are not as high as you'd expect, with dishes in the range US$2.50 to US$8: well worth splashing out for.

Entertainment

La Ceiba has several popular discos, most of them in Barrio La Isla, on the east side of town past the estuary. These include *D'Lido* and *La Kosta*, both on 1a Calle beside the beach, and *Black and White*, on Calle La Barra. Other discos include *Central Park* in the centre and *Leonardo's* in Barrio La Julia, or there's the *Garibaldi Night Club* at the foot of Avenida San Isidro, on 1a Calle.

Cinemas in La Ceiba include the *Cine Maya* on 8a Calle between Avenida San Isidro and Avenida 14 de Julio, and *Cine Luis* also at 8a Calle and Avenida 14 de Julio.

Getting There & Away

Air Tan/Sahsa, Taca, Isleña and Sosa airlines all have their offices on the main plaza. Fares quoted are one-way (double for return). Flights from La Ceiba include:

Tan/Sahsa (☎ 432030)
> Daily flight leaving at 6 am, calling at Roatán (US$11.55), San Pedro Sula (US$12.95) and Tegucigalpa (US$15.85). Daily connection to Miami.

Taca (☎ 431912)
> Flights to Los Angeles, San Francisco, Guatemala City, San José and Panama City connect through San Pedro Sula and San Salvador. Flights to Miami connect directly from San Pedro Sula.

Isleña (☎ 430179)
> to Roatán (five flights daily, US$11.55)
> to Utila (daily except Sunday, 6 am and 4 pm, US$7.10)
> to Guanaja (daily except Sunday, 6 am and 4 pm, US$14.45)
> to Palacios (daily except Sunday, 7 am, US$21.61)
> to Puerto Lempira (Monday, Tuesday, Thursday and Saturday, 7 am, US$36.60)

Sosa (☎ 431399)
> to Utila (daily except Sunday, 6 am & 3.30 pm, US$7.10)
> to Brus Laguna, Ahuas or Puerto Lempira (Tuesday, Thursday and Saturday, US$36.60)

To go to the Bay Islands you usually only need reserve your flight one day in advance; you might reserve it earlier if coming at a busy time of year (like Semana Santa).

Bus The bus station is at Mercado San Jose, about two km from the centre of La Ceiba. A local bus goes between the bus station and the central plaza for US$0.05, or you can take a taxi for US$0.40.

There are bus services from La Ceiba to:

Trujillo (242 km, 3½ hours, US$2.10)
Tela (105 km, 2½ hours, US$0.80)
San Pedro Sula (198 km, three hours, US$1.95)
Tegucigalpa (444 km, 6½ hours, US$4.35)
Nueva Armenia (40 km, two hours, US$0.70)
La Unión (via El Porvenir) (20 km, 1½ hours, US$0.35)
Corozal (10 km, 40 minutes, US$0.20)
Sambo Creek (16 km, 40 minutes, US$0.20)

Train Cargo trains transport freight and produce in the area, but there are no passenger trains.

Boat Boats run from La Ceiba to all the Bay Islands; current information on their sailing schedules is available in the downstairs cafeteria of the Hotel San Carlos, on Avenida San Isidro. Passage can be uncomfortable, boats infrequent, and you don't save much compared to flying. Destinations include:

Roatán (four or five hours, US$6.30). Several boats a week but no set schedule.
Utila (two to three hours, US$4.20). The *Starfish* departs every Tuesday between 10 am and noon. Other boats depart irregularly.
Guanaja (seven hours, US$9). Very occasional boats.
Cayos Cochinos (2½ hours, US$3.65). Small motor launches occasionally do the crossing but it's easier to take a bus to Nueva Armenia and then take a boat from there.

Fishing and cargo boats also depart from La Ceiba bound for many other destinations. Ask around at the docks.

Getting Around

To/From the Airport La Ceiba's airport, the Aeropuerto Internacional Golosón, is about seven km west of La Ceiba, on the highway to Tela. A slow local bus goes from the central plaza to near the airport; taking a colectivo from the south-west corner of the plaza is a more reliable option (US$0.40). A normal taxi costs about US$2.80; if coming *from* the airport, it's cheaper to flag one down once on the main road.

Taxi There are lots of taxis in La Ceiba; a taxi ride in town costs US$0.40.

Car Rental Try Molinari Rent-a-Car (☎ 420055) in the Gran Hotel Paris, Aries (☎ 430524) in Hotel Iberia, or American (☎ 431368) in Hotel La Ceiba.

Bicycle Rental You can hire bicycles cheaply from Renta Bicicletas, on 13a Calle between Avenida San Isidro and Avenida 14 de Julio.

AROUND LA CEIBA
Beaches
A number of good beaches are found a few km from La Ceiba. Heading east towards Trujillo there's **Boca Vieja**, five km from La Ceiba and two km from the highway; the popular **Playa Peru**, six km from La Ceiba and one km from the highway; and **Cuyamel**, 14 km from La Ceiba, where there's a small admission fee and you can have barbecued fish by the beach and the river, especially on Sundays. (See also the Garífuna Villages entry following.)

Heading west towards Tela, **Dantio** is six km from La Ceiba, with a beach, estuary, and fresh fish for sale; **El Porvenir** is 15 km from La Ceiba, with a beach, river and typical food.

Garífuna Villages
Corozal, 10 km east of La Ceiba, and **Sambo Creek**, six km further east, are two seaside Garífuna fishing villages that are easy to reach from La Ceiba. They are enjoyable places, with good beaches and fresh fish to eat.

Both villages have Garífuna musical groups with the traditional large drums, conch shell and song; dances are held on weekend nights, with the traditional Garífuna dances. Try to attend a Garífuna dance some time during your stay on the north coast of Honduras: it's a memorable experience (and easy to see if you're going to Trujillo).

The annual fair at Corozal, held from around 6 to 18 January, is a big event that attracts people from far and wide, especially on the weekends of the fair when there is dancing, partying, games and competitions.

lots of fun on the beach, and good seafood. The annual fair at Sambo Creek is held in June.

Places to Stay & Eat
At Sambo Creek, the *Hotel Hermanos Avila*, built in 1991, is opposite the beach, at the end of the main beach road by the Río Sambo, at the end of the bus line. It has 12 clean rooms with fan and shared bath at US$4.20 for one, two or three people. They also have a small restaurant where fried fish or seafood soup costs US$1.40, and chicken or pork chops slightly more. You can probably hire a dugout *cayuca* (canoe) for exploring on the river. You can also arrange a motorboat ride out to the Cayos Cochinos from Sambo Creek; the crossing takes about an hour.

At Corozal, the *Glorieta Modelo* on the entrance road, opposite the soccer field, is a good place to eat, as is the *Glorieta Marleny*, on the road along the beach.

Balnearios
On the **Río Maria**, seven km east of La Ceiba on the highway to Trujillo, about eight blocks from the highway, is a freshwater balneario with pools in the tropical forest, a waterfall, and a viewpoint from which you can see the Bay Islands.

Los Chorros, 10 km east of La Ceiba along the road to Trujillo, is another pleasant balneario.

There are some other balnearios and riverside beaches on the Paseo Río Cangrejal.

Paseo Río Cangrejal
An attractive scenic drive can be done along the Río Cangrejal, starting about three km from La Ceiba on the highway to Trujillo. This is the Old Highway to Olanchito (Antigua Carretera a Olanchito), also called La Culebra because it is such a snakelike, winding road.

The road passes waterfalls, rapids and several balnearios including Playa de Venado, eight km from La Ceiba; Playa de los Lobos, two km further on; and Balneario Las Mangas, 16 km from La Ceiba, with its iron bridge. The route passes through a lovely forest of precious woods and has some good views.

Buses depart hourly from La Ceiba bus terminal (US$0.30) and go as far as Balneario Las Mangas. Bring your lunch along, as there's nowhere to buy food out here; fishing is also good.

There is said to be an important archaeological site in this area, at La Colorada. It is unexcavated as yet but there are around 60 mounds; experts speculate that the site may one day rank among the important Maya ruins.

Reserva Natural Cuero y Salado

On the coast about 20 km west of La Ceiba, the Cuero y Salado Nature Reserve takes its name from two rivers, the Cuero and Salado, that meet at the coast in a large estuary. This estuary is a protected reserve for its varied wildlife including manatees, howler monkeys, iguanas, boa constrictors, herons and other birds, sharks and fish.

To get to the reserve, take a bus or drive from La Ceiba to La Unión, past El Porvenir. At La Unión the road meets some old railway tracks. From this point, you take a *burra*, a small rail car propelled by poles, half an hour out to the reserve; if you walk along the railway tracks it takes 1½ hours to reach the reserve at a brisk pace.

When you reach the reserve there is an entry fee of US$7 per visit. Inside are houses and offices belonging to FUSCA, which runs the nature reserve, and to Standard Fruit. You can tour the reserve by canoe or motorboat, and there's excellent fishing on the estuary; you're allowed to fish with a hook and line, but not with a net.

Cuero y Salado can be visited from La Ceiba in one day, but only with a lot of luck and a very early start; the last bus leaves La Unión to return to La Ceiba at around 4 pm. It's better to allow a couple of days for a leisurely visit, especially given the high entry fee. FUCSA offers rooms (two beds) for US$3.50; take some candles as there's only electricity for two hours per day. Meals are available but it's a good idea to bring some food along too. Standard Fruit can also accommodate visitors for a low cost: bring your own bedding and food.

You can get more information from FUCSA's office (☎ 430329) in Edificio Reyes, Calle San Isidro, La Ceiba; look for the iron gate by the large 'Carrion' store. FUCSA can organise all-in tours to the reserve.

Parque Nacional Pico Bonito

Pico Bonito, a few km behind La Ceiba, is one of Honduras's best-known national parks, with an unexplored core area of 500 sq km. It was already the largest national park in Honduras when further forest territory was included in July 1992. It has magnificent forests of several different types at different elevations, rivers and waterfalls, and abundant wildlife including jaguars, armadillos, wild pigs, tepescuintes, squirrels, monkeys, doves, toucans, insects and plenty more.

The peak itself, at 2435 metres, is very difficult to climb, requiring ropes and mountain climbing experience; few groups have succeeded in climbing it and the ascent and descent would take several days.

However, easier walks around the fringes of the park are possible to do. The easiest way to enter the park is to walk up the next river east of the Río Danto; about 10 km from La Ceiba on the highway to Tela, opposite the Posta de Tránsito, you can walk through La Piñera, the Standard Fruit pineapple plantation, to the river. It could be done as a day hike but you could see more of the forest if you allowed two days or more, one for the ascent and one for the descent.

For more information on the park, contact COHDEFOR (Honduran Corporation for Forest Development; ☎ 431033).

Cayos Cochinos

Cayos Cochinos (the Hog Islands), 29 km from La Ceiba and just 17 km from the shore, can be visited as a day trip or camping trip from La Ceiba. See the Bay Islands section later in this chapter.

HONDURAS

TRUJILLO

Population 27,077

Capital of the department of Colón, Trujillo sits on the wide arc of the Bahía de Trujillo and is famed for its lovely beaches with coconut palms and gentle seas. Though it's known as one of Honduras's most attractive Caribbean coastal towns, it is not usually full of tourists, except at Semana Santa and during the annual fair of the town's patron saint, San Juan Bautista, in the last week of June (24 June is the exact day, but the festival goes on for a week).

History

Trujillo is not a large place but it has played an important part in the history of Central America. It was near Trujillo, on 14 August 1502, that Columbus first set foot on the American mainland, having sailed from Jamaica on his fourth (and final) voyage. The first mass on American mainland soil was said on the spot where they landed.

Founded on 18 May 1525, Trujillo was one of the earliest Spanish settlements in Central America. It was the first Spanish town in the colonial province of Honduras, and was the capital of the province until the seat was shifted to Comayagua in 1537. The Catholic bishop's see remained in Trujillo until 1561, when it too was moved to Comayagua.

The Spanish used the port at Trujillo to ship out gold and silver from the interior of Honduras, attracting pirates to the bay. The Bay of Trujillo was the scene of several great battles when the town was attacked by pirates, including van Horn and Aury Morgan.

The Spanish built several fortresses, the ruins of which are still standing; the ruins of the fort of Santa Bárbara can be seen near the plaza in town. Despite the fortifications, the buccaneers prevailed and after a sacking by Dutch pirates in 1643, the town lay in ruins for over a century until it was resettled in 1787.

William Walker (see his story under Nicaragua) made his final attack on Central America at Trujillo; he was captured and executed here on 12 September 1860. His grave can be seen in the old cemetery in town.

Things to See & Do

Trujillo is best known for its attractive white sand beaches, but there are also several other interesting places to visit in and near town.

The ruins of the 17th-century Spanish fortress, properly named the Fortaleza Santa Bárbara de Trujillo but usually called **El Castillo**, are in the centre of town, near the plaza, behind the basketball courts and overlooking the sea. The fort offers several old cannons and other relics, a plaque marking the place where Walker was executed, and an excellent view along the coast. Operated by the Instituto Hondureño de Antropología e Historia, the ruins are open every day from 8 am to noon and from 1 to 4 pm; admission is US$0.15.

William Walker's grave is in the Cementario Viejo (Old Cemetery), a few blocks from the plaza. On the plaza itself is a historic church.

The **Museo Arqueológico**, by the Río Cristales, has a fascinating collection: interesting archaeological relics and historical objects are arrayed alongside clapped-out household junk (seemingly selected on the basis of 'if it's old and rusty, display it'!) Exhibits range from Maya carvings to mangled typewriters; there's even the remains of an aircraft wrecked in the bay in 1985. It is open Friday to Sunday from 8 am to 6 pm. The US$0.35 admission includes entry to the **Piscina Rivera del Pedregal** at the rear, comprising a couple of open-air swimming pools, a rope bridge and picnic areas. Food and drink are not always available.

Trujillo's white sand **beaches** are the major attraction of the town. They stretch for several km around the bay – you can walk along the beach in either direction from town and just pick your spot. Five km east of Trujillo, out past the airstrip and the Río Negro, is the **Laguna Guaymoreto**, a large lagoon with a natural passageway onto the bay. The lagoon, about six km by nine km, is home to abundant animal, bird and plant

HONDURAS

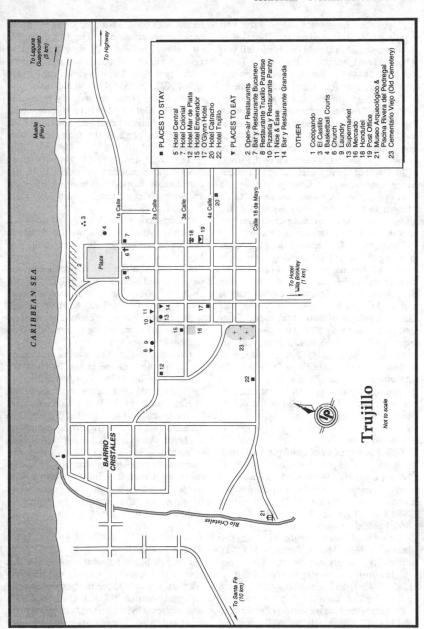

Trujillo

Not to scale

CARIBBEAN SEA

To Laguna Guaymoreto (5 km)

To Highway

Muelle (Pier)

Plaza

1a Calle

2a Calle

3a Calle

4a Calle

Calle 18 de Mayo

To Hotel Villa Brinkley (1 km)

BARRIO CRISTALES

Río Cristales

To Santa Fe (10 km)

■ PLACES TO STAY

5 Hotel Central
7 Hotel Colonial
12 Hotel Mar de Plata
15 Hotel Emperador
17 O'Glynn Hotel
20 Hotel Catracho
22 Hotel Trujillo

▼ PLACES TO EAT

2 Open-air Restaurants
7 Bar y Restaurante Bucanero
8 Restaurante Trujillo Paradise
10 Pizzeria y Restaurante Pantry
11 Nice & Ease
14 Bar y Restaurante Granada

OTHER

1 Cocopando
3 El Castillo
4 Basketball Courts
6 Church
9 Laundry
13 Supermarket
16 Mercado
18 Hondutel
19 Post Office
21 Museo Arqueológico &
   Piscina Rivera del Pedregal
23 Cementario Viejo (Old Cemetery)

life; you can hire someone to take you boating. Near the airstrip, the Bar y Restaurante Bahía should be able to tell you where to hire boats to tour the lagoon. Turtle Tours (☎ 444444) in the Hotel Villa Brinkley organises trips to the lagoon and elsewhere.

Further east from Trujillo, around the bay, is **Puerto Castilla**, the port on the inward arm of the Cabo de Honduras, which forms the bay. This is one of Honduras's major ports, shipping fruit and other products from Honduras to the Caribbean ports of the USA.

Just west of town, where the Río Cristales flows into the sea, is **Cocopando**, in the Garífuna barrio of Cristales on the west side of town. In the daytime you can stop here for a soda or beer; in the evening, this is the best spot in Trujillo for dancing and music.

You can walk further west along the coast, crossing the Río Grande and several other rivers and streams; the beach is bordered by coconut palms the whole way. Ten km along the coast is the Garífuna village of **Santa Fe**, and a couple of km further on, the smaller Garífuna villages of **San Antonio** and **Guadalupe**. A dirt road runs out to these villages from Trujillo, and there is an infrequent bus service (except Sunday). There is supposed to be a bus from Santa Fe to Trujillo in the late afternoon, but if there aren't enough people who want to go, it may not run; you can walk back along the road or the beach. Santa Fe's annual fair is on 16 July.

Places to Stay
Trujillo has a number of good places to stay. At Semana Santa you should book.

Hotel Catracho (☎ 444438), 4a Calle, has a row of wooden rooms built in the garden. Each has a private bath and costs US$2.80/4.20 for one/two people. There's also a bar and restaurant.

A couple of blocks up the hill from the plaza is the *Hotel Mar de Plata* (☎ 444458), a friendly, family-run place. There are singles/doubles with shared bath at US$2.80/4.90, and six more with private bath for US$3.50/6.30.

Closer to the plaza is the *Hotel Emperador* (☎ 444446), with small but well-equipped

rooms with private bath for US$4.90, more expensive with air-con. The *Hotel Trujillo* (☎ 444202) on Calle 18 de Mayo is also good, with very clean rooms with private bath, fan, and TV; singles/doubles are US$4.90/7, or US$8.45 with two beds.

Beside the plaza, the recently renovated *Hotel Colonial* (☎ 444610) has rooms with air-con and private cold bath for US$11.40. Also on the plaza is the rather miserable *Hotel Central*.

The *O'Glynn Hotel* (☎ 444592), three blocks from the plaza and built in 1993, has comfortable singles/doubles for US$11.25/15 with air-conditioning and hot bath. Triples are US$21.

The deluxe *Villa Brinkley* (☎ 444444), perched on the hill about one km from the centre of town, enjoys a fine view of the bay. Prices start at US$15/19.65 for singles/doubles; or you can pay US$43 per person for room and three meals. Children 17 and under are free. There are several larger rooms, with up to four beds, and many amenities including hot-water baths, a bar and two restaurants, swimming pool, recreation room and books in English.

Even higher-class hotels are now opening up in Trujillo near the airport, such as the *Trujillo Bay Resort Hotel* (☎ 444732).

You can find more casual accommodation at Cocopando, in the Barrio Cristales right by the beach, and at Santa Fe, the Garífuna village 10 km west of Trujillo, again right on the beach. It may be difficult to find anything available during Semana Santa, when the place is enormously popular, but the rest of the time you can often find a house or a room to rent by asking around. The prices won't be expensive and it would be especially pleasant for a longer stay.

Places to Eat
On the beach, just below the plaza, there's a row of thatch-roofed open-air seafood restaurants. Prices here are the best in town for fish and shellfish (US$2), shrimp (US$3) and lobster (US$9), served with fried plantains and salad. These restaurants are open

all day and late into the evening. Eating is also cheap and good in Cocopando.

There are several good inexpensive restaurants in town. Try the *Granada*, the *Pantry* or the *Bucanero*; all have bars and serve much the same selection of seafood, meats, soups, sandwiches and burgers, breakfasts etc at much the same prices. Granada is marginally the cheapest, the Pantry is air-conditioned and also serves pizza. *Nice and Ease* is the place for fruit drinks and pastries.

Otherwise there are several cheap comedores on the entrance road into town, and you can always find fresh food at the Mercado.

For elegant atmosphere, the restaurants at the *Villa Brinkley* up on the hill are most enjoyable, with that excellent view. They serve simple lunches, and more elaborate dinners. The menu is varied and includes seafood prepared in many styles; the average main course costs around US$5.

Another fine restaurant is the *Bar y Restaurante Bahía*, by the beach near the airstrip. They have the usual menu at the usual prices, plus a great stretch of beach.

If you go to Santa Fe, eat at *Comedor Caballero*. Meals start at US$1.70, but as Señor Caballero is thought by many to be the best cook in Honduras, it's worth splashing out on his 'especial carte', where dishes are US$4.20 or more. The restaurant looks basic but the food really is something special; some people visit the village solely to eat at his place. He speaks English.

Entertainment

In Barrio Cristales, where the Garífuna people live, dances are held at least four times a week, on Thursday to Sunday nights. On the road heading to Cocopando are a couple of discos with recorded music, attracting a mostly young crowd. Weekend nights are very lively.

At Cocopando, the *Los Menudos* nightclub has live Garífuna music and dancing. The band is the traditional Garífuna combination of three large drums, some maracas and a big conch shell, producing throbbing,

haunting rhythms and melodies. The chanted words are like a litany, with responses often taken up by the audience. The dance is the *punta*, a Garífuna dance with a lot of hip movement. At Los Menudos and the discos there's an admission charge of US$0.40 to US$0.70.

Some restaurants, such as Truxillo Paradise, Bucanero and Pantry, have cable TV showing English-language films.

Getting There & Away

Air Trujillo has a small airstrip, but so far no regularly scheduled flights. Isleña is expected to start daily flights when the expensive hotels near the airport are up and running. Charter and private planes can use the strip.

Bus Buses arrive and depart from the central plaza. Daily buses depart Trujillo for La Ceiba at 2, 4, 5, 6 and 10 am and 2 pm (242 km, 3½ hours, US$2.10). Minibuses to Tocoa, along the way to La Ceiba, depart frequently.

There are two inland routes to Tegucigalpa. A direct bus departs daily at 4 am and goes over the mountains via La Unión, taking about nine hours. Another bus departs on the same route at 9 am, though you have to change buses in the mountains. The longer route is via Juticalpa: a bus departs daily at 4 am from outside the Hotel Catracho (270 km, eight hours, US$4.20); from Juticalpa you can continue on to Tegucigalpa.

Local buses go from Trujillo to the Garífuna villages of Santa Fe, San Antonio and Guadalupe to the west, and to Puerto Castilla across the bay. You'll have to ask when they're leaving, and watch to see you don't miss the bus; they don't go on any regular schedule, but depart whenever they're full.

Boat Getting a boat is largely a matter of luck, as departures to any one place aren't particularly frequent.

Boats depart from the *muelle* (pier) at Trujillo for various points including the Bay

Islands, the Nicaraguan coast, some Caribbean islands (including the Cayman Islands and Jamaica) and the USA (usually New Orleans, four days away by boat). None of these are scheduled departures; you just have to walk down to the pier, see what boats are there, where they're going and when. They are usually fishing or cargo boats, but you can often pay passage and go along.

Also check Puerto Castilla, round the Bay; there's more chance from here of getting a boat to the Mosquitia or Guanaja.

LIMÓN

A couple of hours east of Trujillo is Limón, a Garífuna village by the sea, at the mouth of the Río Limón. From the village you can go upriver by canoe and see plenty of wildlife. There are many birds, including toucans and parrots, and monkeys coming to the river early in the morning. There are also good beaches around Limón.

Limón has a basic hospedaje where you can stay, and places to eat.

Getting There & Away

Limón is at the end of the bus line (buses depart from Trujillo) and is as far east as you can go by bus on the north coast of Honduras; east of Limón is the beginning of the sparsely inhabited Mosquitia region.

The road from Trujillo is paved as far as the crossroads at Corocito, but after that it's a dirt road, which could become impassable in rainy weather. There are occasionally boats going from Trujillo or Puerto Castilla to Limón, though it's easier to take the bus.

Bay Islands

The three Bay Islands (Islas de la Bahía) about 50 km off the north coast of Honduras – Roatán, Guanaja and Utila – are prime attractions for visitors to Honduras. Their extensive coral reefs are a continuation of the Belize reefs (second-largest barrier reef in the world after Australia's Great Barrier

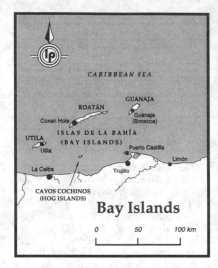

Bay Islands

Reef) and the islands are great for diving and snorkelling.

The island economy is based mostly on fishing and shrimp and lobster catching. Many islanders also work as merchant seafarers; all the island settlements hug the sea, and the culture is as much oriented towards the sea as towards land. Tourism is an increasingly significant factor in the economy of the islands. Utila retains low-key tourist facilities; Roatán is gradually catching Guanaja as a more up-market retreat. Even so, a stay on any of the three main islands needn't be expensive.

Snorkelling and scuba diving are the activities that lure many visitors. The Bay Islands – particularly Utila – are one of the cheapest places in the world to take a PADI scuba-diving course.

History

Maya ruins on the Bay Islands indicate that they were inhabited well before the Europeans arrived; there are also caves which are believed to have provided shelter for groups of Paya Indians.

Christopher Columbus, on his fourth and final voyage to the New World, landed on the island of Guanaja on 30 July 1502. He encountered a fairly large population of Indians, whom he believed to be cannibals. The Spanish enslaved the islanders, and sent them to work on the plantations of Cuba and in the gold and silver mines of Mexico. By 1528 the islands were completely depopulated.

They didn't stay empty for long, however; English, French and Dutch pirates established settlements on the islands, and raided the cumbersome cargo vessels of the Spanish that were laden with gold and other treasures from the New World. The English buccaneer Henry Morgan established his base at Port Royal on Roatán Island in the mid-17th century, and at that time as many as 5000 pirates were ensconced on the island.

In March 1782, after many vain attempts, the Spanish waged a successful land attack against Port Royal, killing most of the pirates and selling the rest off as slaves. Once again, the islands were left uninhabited, and once again they didn't stay that way for long.

In 1795 the Garífuna uprising on the Caribbean island of St Vincent was quickly put down by British troops. The survivors were rounded up, and those that didn't die of fever were shipped by the British to Roatán; some 3000 were dumped at Port Royal on 12 April 1797. From Roatán the Garífuna migrated to the mainland, eventually setting up small fishing and agricultural villages along the coast all the way from Belize to Nicaragua, but mostly along the north coast of Honduras. There is still one settlement of Garífuna people on Roatán, at Punta Gorda, but the rest are on the mainland.

The Bay Islands, along with the large Mosquitia territory in north-eastern Honduras, remained in the hands of the British until 1859, when Great Britain signed a treaty ceding the Bay Islands and the Mosquitia to Honduras. Only in the last few decades, however, when the Honduran school system decided that Spanish must be spoken in all the country's schools, did the islanders begin to speak Spanish. English, spoken with a broad Caribbean accent, remains the preferred language of the islands.

The orientation of the islands is still, in many ways, more towards England and the USA than towards the Honduran mainland just 50 km away; many islanders are more likely to have visited the USA than their own capital, Tegucigalpa, and many have relatives in the USA.

Population

The population of the Bay Islands is a very mixed bag. The Isleñas are Black people whose heritage is African mixed with Carib Indians, Europeans and other races. English is spoken, with Spanish as a second language. On Roatán there is a Garífuna settlement at Punta Gorda, where Garífuna, English and Spanish are spoken.

There are still some White descendants of early British settlers; you'll probably meet people who look like they just got off the boat from England, Scotland or Ireland, though actually their ancestors came hundreds of years ago.

More recently, there has been an influx of Latinos from the mainland, especially on Roatán, which, because it is economically better off than the mainland, attracts Hondurans looking for work. There is also a small population of foreign Whites, mostly from Europe and the USA.

Information

The Instituto Hondureño de Turismo office in La Ceiba has some information on the islands, and there is a tourist office in Roatán.

Costs

The Bay Islands are reputed on the mainland to be expensive, but it's quite possible to visit them cheaply. It costs nothing to swim in the sea or lie on the beach. Scuba diving is a comparatively expensive activity, but prices here are among the lowest in the world, and many travellers budget for taking some sort of course (see Activities).

All the islands have inexpensive places to stay; Guanaja tends to be the most expensive of the three, followed by Roatán. Food is a little more expensive than on the mainland, but only marginally so in Utila.

Climate

The rainy season on the islands is roughly from October or November to February. March and August are the hottest months; at other times the sea breezes temper the heat. Tropical storms are possible in September.

Dangers & Annoyances

The islands are generally safer than the mainland, but the mosquitoes and sandflies are voracious, especially during the rainy season. Be sure to bring plenty of repellent. Some people say that a heavy application of coconut oil and salad oil is more effective against sandflies than repellent.

In the water, keep an eye out for spiny sea urchins on the coral reefs. Don't walk or stand on coral: it damages the reef and will probably cut open your feet.

When swimming or snorkelling, don't leave unattended valuables on the beach; there have been reports of thefts from West Bay in Roatán and from the airport beach in Utila.

Activities

Popular activities on the islands are diving, snorkelling, hiking, swimming, fishing, lazing on the beach and meeting the locals and other travellers.

Diving Dive shops have proliferated on the Bay Islands in the last few years. Prices have come down and it's now one of the cheapest places in the world to get a diving qualification. Most dive shops offer a range of options, from an introductory resort course (basic instruction plus a couple of dives) to a full PADI certification course allowing you to dive as a qualified diver worldwide. A PADI course lasts around four days and usually includes two confined water and four open-water dives. Advanced courses are also available. Despite the low cost, safety and equipment standards are reasonable.

In 1993 Utila was the cheapest island for PADI courses and scuba diving in general, though competition is fierce and prices can fluctuate. When comparing diving prices, check whether tax and the certificate are included. Prices for Roatán are usually inclusive of the PADI certificate; in Utila you might have to add from US$14 to US$20 depending upon the place.

But don't select a course purely on the basis of price: assess the experiences of other travellers, talk to the instructors, and enquire about the structure of the course, the size of the class (the smaller the better) and the standard of the equipment.

Qualified divers also have plenty of options, including night dives, deep dives, wreck diving and tailor-made dive charters. As well as coral walls and caves, there is a great variety of fish to be seen. The water between Roatán and Utila is one of the best places in the world to view whale sharks (approximately from May to September).

Equipment for dives is invariably provided by the dive shops. If you have your own gear you might be able to negotiate a small discount.

Getting There & Away

Air Planes fly to all the islands from La Ceiba; see the La Ceiba section for details. To and from Roatán there are also daily flights with Tan/Sahsa to San Pedro Sula and Tegucigalpa. Through these two cities, flights connect with all the other major Central American airports, the USA (New York, Los Angeles and San Francisco) and with other international destinations. It's quite easy to come from the USA and be in the Bay Islands in a few hours.

Tan/Sahsa also has one direct flight a week to Roatán from Miami (Tuesday), New Orleans (Friday) and Houston (Saturday). American Airlines is expected to start flying to Roatán in 1994.

Boat You can get to any of the Bay Islands by boat from the mainland, or go by boat between the islands; see each island, and the La Ceiba section, for details.

Getting Around

There are daily direct flights between Roatán and Guanaja (see Roatán for details); from Utila to one of the other islands you have to fly via La Ceiba. Boats go fairly frequently between the islands.

ROATÁN
Population 10,565
Roatán is the largest and most popular of the Bay Islands. It is about 50 km off the coast of Honduras at La Ceiba; about 50 km long and just two to four km wide, it is surrounded by over 100 km of living reef, making it a paradise for diving and snorkelling. Parts of Roatán, especially the West End and West Bay beach, are as idyllic as the most tempting tourist brochure, with clear turquoise water, colourful tropical fish, powdery white sand and coconut palms.

Orientation
Coxen Hole is Roatán's principal town. The airport is about a 10-minute drive from Coxen Hole. The best place to stay on the island is probably West End village, with nearby Sandy Bay a good second option, but there are also other possibilities.

Information
The Instituto Hondureño de Turismo (☎ 451559) has an office in the centre of Coxen Hole by the tiny park.

Close by in Coxen Hole is the Bay Islands Tour & Travel Centre (☎ 451146) beside the Tan/Sahsa airline office. Tan/Sahsa (☎ 451093) is open for the usual business hours during the week and on Saturday.

Dangers and Annoyances
When swimming, beware of rip tides that can pull you out to sea (see Swimming Safety in the Facts for the Visitor chapter), especially at West End.

A traveller wrote to warn that taxi drivers in Roatán are a bit shifty: they have been known to drive off with people's gear on board, or may claim they have no change. When taking you from the airport to Coxen Hole they'll probably say the bus no longer runs to West End.

Things to See & Do
Diving, snorkelling, swimming, boating,

fishing, hiking and just lazing around on the beach are all popular activities on Roatán.

In Sandy Bay, the Institute for Marine Sciences and the small Roatán Museum are worth a visit. The eastern side of the island, from Punta Gorda in the north around to Port Royal in the south, including the islands of Morat, Barbareta, Santa Helena and the mangrove swamps, has been declared a National Marine Park.

There are a number of very expensive resorts you can visit. Fantasy Island resort, three km past French Harbour, is about the most luxurious; it has a superb location, and you can partake of all kinds of water sports. Anthony's Key Resort in Sandy Bay specialises in diving, and there are others.

Coxen Hole
Coxen Hole is only a small town, but it's the largest town on Roatán island. The government and shipping offices are here, the post office and Hondutel, and people come here from around the island to go to the supermarket, HB Warren, which has the island's lowest food prices. There are a couple of discos, the *Harbour View* and the *Paragua*. Otherwise, Coxen Hole is not an attractive town – it's rather small and dusty, and though it's right beside the sea there is no beach here. It can also be unsafe at night, and the Paragua disco has the odd violent incident.

Places to Stay On the west side of town, about a five-minute walk west down the main seaside road and 300 metres past the bridge, is *Hotel Allen* (☎ 451243). Rooms (some with private WC) sharing common bath are US$4.20 for one or two people. Mr Allen is an interesting character and will talk you under the table on any subject you care to name: ask his views on colonialism and the monarchy. He also cooks great food.

On the main road in town, the *Hotel Coral* (☎ 451080) has singles/doubles at US$4.20/8.40, again with shared bath. Nearby, the *Hotel El Paso* (☎ 451059) has rooms with shared bath at US$7, and a restaurant looking out over the water. The *Hotel Cay View*

HONDURAS

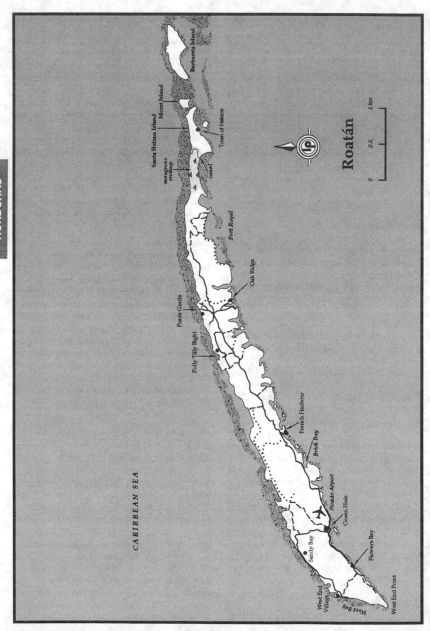

(☎ 451202) is more luxurious, starting at US$21.80/26.70.

Places to Eat The cafeteria in the *HB Warren supermarket* has low prices, a selection of meals and snacks, great ice cream and some of the best fried chicken on the island. The cafeteria and the supermarket are open Monday to Saturday from 7 am to 6 pm.

Hotel Allen (see Places to Stay) has a tiny comedor with good, cheap food. The tasty, filling soup costs US$0.70. Mr Allen only cooks in the early evening until about 7 pm, though you can drink there a little later.

The bar/restaurant at the *Hotel El Paso* has a pleasant patio looking over the water to the palm-covered cay nearby. It's open daily and the meal of the day costs US$2.10, although other dishes are twice that. There are several other cheap eateries around Coxen Hole.

French Harbour

French Harbour is the second-largest town on Roatán. It is an important port town, home of a large fishing, shrimp and lobster fleet. At the entrance to the town is the *French Harbour Yacht Club* (☎ 451478) with good food, very comfortable rooms (singles/doubles from US$31/36), and a fine view of the marina. It's a good place to ask around if you want to hitch a ride on a boat. From here, a path leads down to Long John's Off The Wall Divers (same telephone) on the marina; it has a good reputation, though it's more expensive than the West End dive shops.

French Harbour has a disco and several cheap comedores. The cheapest budget rooms are at the shabby *Hotelito Brooks*, where it's US$3.50 for one or two people. Opposite the expensive *Buccaneer Inn* and beside the medicine shop is a nameless place with a couple of rooms for US$4.90. You could also try the *Hotel Isabel* (US$8.50) or the *Hotel Dixon Plaza* (from US$12/14).

Oak Ridge

Another port town, Oak Ridge, on Roatán's eastern side, is a more attractive town than French Harbour or Coxen Hole; with old-fashioned wooden houses all nestled around the sea, it looks like it could be on Cape Cod as easily as on the Caribbean. The tiny town consists of the port facilities and lots of colourful boats, a long row of wooden houses stretching in an arc around a point of land, and a town on a small cay just a two-minute motorboat ride from shore. Water taxis cost one or two lempira.

On the cay, ask at the Reef House or the Road House about boat trips. The Road House also serves food.

Also on the cay, the small *Hotel San José* is a good place to stay, costing US$5.60 per person. Or *Miss Alice*, who lives on the finger of land stretching out to sea after you go over the arching footbridge and past the Baptist church, also has rooms for rent. Here, as on much of the island, you can often find a place to stay by asking around among the locals; a fishing and travelling people, the islanders often have a spare room.

West End

On the west end of the island, West End village is probably the most beautiful part of the island. It's only a small village, but it is exceptionally lovely, on a turquoise bay laced with coconut palms.

West End is the area to which most backpacking travellers flock. Unfortunately, cheap accommodation is very limited, and most places are now geared to tourists with more money to spend.

If you're in West End, be sure to also check out Sandy Bay, a long walk but a short bus ride away.

Snorkelling There's good snorkelling just offshore at West End. Jimmy Miller has free snorkelling gear for the guests at his lodge. He can show you the best snorkelling spots; 'the channel' in front of the restaurant is especially fine. Some of the dive shops in West End rent snorkelling gear, particularly Ocean Divers.

Diving West End has several dive shops offering a variety of dives and courses. The three places mentioned below each offer a PADI course for US$150, and boat dives at

US\$15 per tank; West End Divers (☎ 451531) is a little more expensive.

Seagrape Plantation Dive Centre (☎ 451428) has shore diving for just US\$10 per tank and good quality equipment. It's in the northern end of West End beyond the road to Coxen Hole.

Tyll Sass, in front of Chino's restaurant (☎ 451314), has a long-established dive shop, although recent reports have been mixed. He is, however, willing to undertake customised dive and boat trips, including to local shipwrecks.

Roatán Divers (☎ 451255) also offer a rival to the PADI course, a three-day PDIC course, costing US\$125 to US\$150, depending on the number in the group.

Beaches & Hikes The beach at West Bay, about four km south of West End village, is known as the most beautiful on Roatán. It's a lovely stroll down the beach from West End, or you can take a motorboat from Foster & Vivian's restaurant or Jimmy's Lodge for US\$1.80 return. There's good snorkelling at West Bay.

The beach is currently fringed by palm trees. However, progress (if you can call it that) marches on. The land adjoining West Bay has been partitioned up and there are plans underway to build numerous luxury cabins (commanding prices of around US\$40,000 each!). Work has already started in the northern portion of the beach. It's not inconceivable that one day West Bay will be private access only; it certainly won't remain an isolated paradise for very long.

You can hike across the island from West End to Flowers Bay, about a three-km walk; when you reach the ridge, you can look out over both sides of the island. A round trip from West End to Flowers Bay, then south almost to the tip of the island, over the ridge to West Bay and back up the beach to West End makes a good five or six-hour hike; the Flowers Bay side of the island on this walk looks quite different from the West Bay side. Be sure to bring fresh water, and adequate repellent against the numerous ticks.

There are other trails to some Maya ruins on this end of the island. Jimmy Miller sometimes takes people on trips out into the jungle. Carambola Botanic Gardens, on the road between West End and Sandy Bay, is another place with hiking and nature trails.

Other Activities Belvedere's Island Watersports, behind D & D Market, has windsurfers at US\$5 per hour, plus lessons on the beach or in the water; there's also a glass-bottomed boat and sailing.

Jimmy Miller (see Places to Stay) has horses for rent from US\$5 per hour.

Places to Stay If it wasn't for the Miller family, budget travellers would be all but priced out of West End. Jimmy Miller runs *Jimmy's Lodge*, on the far (south) end of town. Dozens of travellers crowd into an open area upstairs where there are mattresses on the floor and hammocks strung from the beams. The cost is US\$2.10. It's friendly and sociable but extremely basic, with just one outside shower and no electricity. Jimmy provides snorkelling gear free for guests, and expects soon to offer private rooms for US\$3.50 per person.

Jimmy's older brother Sam has a restaurant next door; he has a total of 10 basic rooms available for US\$2.80 to US\$4.90 per person, with electricity. The Millers' sister Zoey also has rooms on the south end of town, behind the Church of God. There are two double rooms standing alone, costing US\$8.45 with electricity or US\$7 without. Zoey is in the house just behind (☎ 451335), where three more rooms are available.

Inland from Yoly's restaurant there are three rooms with shared bathroom for US\$4.20; Ask for Kenny or Sammy at the restaurant. *Sunset Inn* (☎ 451005) has six double rooms for US\$12.65 – expensive, as the bathroom is down the hall.

The only other option for budget travellers in West End is to try to get a room in a family home. There are very few of these. At the house by the sign for Half Moon Cabins (on the way to Seagrape Plantation) the family has one spare room for US\$2.80 per person.

Other accommodation in West End is a big

step up in both price and comfort. *Robert's Hill Hotel* (☎ 451176), opposite Foster's restaurant, has double rooms with private bath for US$20 to US$25. The nearby *Lost Paradise Inn* (☎ 451306) has doubles for US$20 with private bath, and more expensive cabins.

Free-standing wooden cabins, with a veranda and private bath is a common, albeit expensive, option in West End. *Chino's Restaurant* (☎ 451314) has some cabins right by the sea for US$20. *Foster & Vivian's Restaurant* (☎ 451008, 451124) has bungalows which start at US$35 but can hold several people, and they also have more expensive bungalows down the coast at West Bay Beach (they actually own most of the land round there).

Keiffito's Plantation Retreat, about 10 minutes along the beach towards West Bay, has good cabins for US$25/30 for two/three people, and a good, inexpensive restaurant.

Burke's Place (☎ 451252), in the north of the village beyond the Coxen Hole road, has two double cabins for US$20/25 with kitchen. A little farther on is the plusher *Seagrape Plantation* (☎ 451428) where singles/doubles are US$25/35.

Places to Eat The place where backpackers eat and drink is Sam Miller's *New York Restaurant*. Chicken or fish dinners cost US$2.10; it's an amenable place to linger, which is just as well because the food takes ages to arrive. Along the beach to the south is *Bite on the Beach*, also popular. The hosts are very friendly and tasty meals cost around US$2.80 to US$5.60.

Other travellers' haunts include *Restaurant Yoly's* and *Chino's Restaurant*; both are small and inexpensive. The place for breakfast is *Rudy's Coffee Stop*. Good banana pancakes ('the best in the world' Rudy exclaims modestly) cost US$0.85. He always has a welcoming smile and he'll make local phone calls for you for US$0.30.

Foster & Vivian's Restaurant built on stilts out over the water, is good if fairly expensive (from around US$5). The nearby *Bamboo Hut* only has snacks in the evening, but

shows a film at 7.30 pm on Tuesday, Thursday and Saturday.

You can eat at the *Lost Paradise Inn* resort even if you're not staying there. They have a big breakfast (US$2.80) which you can just show up for; if you want to come for dinner, you should let them know a few hours in advance. The restaurant at *Keiffito's Plantation* is also worth investigating.

Sandy Bay

About four km before you reach West End is Sandy Bay, another lovely little town on the sea, though it's not as developed as West End. The beach here is not as good as that at West End or West Bay, and it's a little shallow for swimming. The Sandy Bay community passed an ordinance protecting its reef as a nature reserve, so it's an excellent place to snorkel, with lots of marine life. There's a nature trail on nearby Bailey's Cay, which also has good snorkelling. Anthony's Key Resort is one of the major diving resorts on the island, with facilities for diving, underwater photography etc, but it's an expensive place.

In Sandy Bay is the **Institute for Marine Sciences** (☎ 451327), a research and educational facility working with dolphins. There are several dolphin training demonstrations daily; you could also go for a swim with the dolphins but this is expensive. On site is the small Museum of Roatán, which has Maya artefacts found on the island, plus a classroom with videos and educational material about dolphins, coral reefs and other sea life. The Institute is open daily except Wednesday from 8.30 am to 6 pm; admission is US$2.80 (US$4 if you pay in dollars).

Places to Stay & Eat North-east of Anthony's Key Resort is *Beth's Hostel* (☎ 451266), on a hill overlooking Sandy Bay not far from the sea. Two single and two double rooms face onto a comfortable kitchen-dining-sitting room, and rates are US$8 per person, or US$50 per week; half price for Peace Corps or other volunteers. Only nonsmokers may stay. Snorkelling gear is available at US$4 per day. The Bahai Library of Roatán is also at the hostel.

Continuing north-east is *Sandy Bay Sea Food Restaurant and Minni Hotel*. There are three rooms with private bath from US$7 (negotiable) and the food is inexpensive.

Farther north-east, beyond the small bridge, is *Miss Effie* (☎ 451233), with two apartments by the sea: US$20 for one double room, or US$30 for two rooms with a cooker and fridge. Also ask for Chuck (☎ 451123) in Sandy Bay: he has cabins for US$15.

South-west of Anthony's Key Resort is *Oceanside Inn* (☎ 451552), with rooms for US$25/40 and fairly expensive food, and *Yadira*, a basic but cheap comedor.

Other Towns

There are various other towns around Roatán, including Punta Gorda, a Garífuna village on the north shore of the island, and Polly Tilly Bight, a small settlement also on the north shore. You pass both of these on the bus from French Harbour to Oak Ridge, and there are a few other villages around the island's coast. At most of them, if you liked them enough to stay, you could probably ask around among the locals and come up with some accommodation.

The small island of Santa Helena, on the east end of Roatán, is a beautiful place with good diving. You can eat well and cheaply in Santa Helena town, and there are almost always some houses for rent. Tyll Sass in West End makes charter boat and dive trips to Santa Helena island.

Getting There & Away

Air Tan/Sahsa, Isleña and Lansa all have daily flights between La Ceiba and Roatán; see the La Ceiba section for schedules and fares. It takes only 10 minutes to fly from La Ceiba to Roatán. Utila is reached via La Ceiba; it's cheaper to buy one straight-through ticket instead of one for each leg.

Sosa flies daily to Guanaja, departing from Roatán at 9.30 am and returning at 10 am; on Friday, Saturday and Sunday another plane goes at 4 pm and returns at 4.30 pm. The fare is US$10.85.

Boat Most boats don't leave on any set schedule as itineraries depend on cargo requirements, and not all of them can legally take passengers. You can get current information on boats to and from Roatán at the helpful office of the Capitania de Puerto, in the Gobernación Política building by the wharf in Coxen Hole; the office faces the tiny park beside the supermarket.

Boats usually leave Roatán for La Ceiba every second day or so; it takes around five hours and cost US$6.30. Boats between Roatán and Guanaja depart only about every week or 10 days; it takes three hours and costs about US$7. Most fishing boats to Guanaja are based at French Harbour.

There's a boat, the *Utila Express*, running every two weeks between Roatán, Utila and Puerto Cortés, a 12-hour journey. The only other boat between Utila and Roatán that regularly takes passengers is the *Utila Clipper*, which also goes to/from La Ceiba. The *Bay Islands Express* cargo ship goes from Roatán to Tampa, via Puerto Cortés, but it may not take passengers.

Also bi-weekly is the *Painkira*, which sails to Puerto Lempira in the Mosquitia.

Getting Around

To/From the Airport Bus Route 1 stops at the airport. The cost is US$0.55 from the airport to Coxen Hole; in a taxi it's not much different, at US$0.70. If you're arriving at the airport and going to the west end of the island, go to Coxen Hole (10 minutes from the airport) and catch a bus from there; a taxi from the airport to West End costs about US$5.60.

Bus Roatán has two minibus routes, both originating from Coxen Hole.

Route 1 goes east from Coxen Hole past the airport to French Harbour, past Polly Tilly Bight, through Punta Gorda and on to Oak Ridge. It departs every half-hour from 6 am to 6 pm; the cost is US$0.55 to French Harbour, US$1.10 to Oak Ridge. It takes about 10 minutes from Coxen Hole to the airport, another 15 minutes to French

Harbour, and a further 35 minutes to Oak Ridge.

Route 2 goes west from Coxen Hole, through Sandy Bay to West End. The cost is US$0.70 to West End, a 25-minute ride on a good road.

The buses run from around 7 am to 5 pm, Monday to Saturday, but there are no buses on Sunday.

Taxi There are plenty of taxis based at Coxen Hole. Fares are US$5.50 to West End or French Harbour, and US$4.50 to Sandy Bay. Some taxis operate as colectivos during the day and don't charge much more than buses.

Car Rental Main roads west of Punta Gorda are paved and in good condition. Amigo Rent-a-Car, opposite Roatán airport (☎ 451428) charges upwards of US$40 per 24 hours depending upon the condition of the car. Toyota (☎ 451166), also at the airport, is more expensive but has better cars. With either firm, be clear about your liability in the event of an accident.

Hitching Hitching is easy on Roatán in the daytime. It's much more difficult to get a ride at night.

Boat The settlements on Roatán all hug the seashore, and the islanders are very much a sea-oriented people. Anywhere there are people, someone will have a boat. You can easily hire someone to take you in a motorboat almost anywhere you could want to go.

UTILA
Population 1523

Utila is a welcoming place, where the locals always have time to shout a friendly greeting. It's a small island, about 13 km long and five km wide, with several tiny cays on the south side. It is the closest island to La Ceiba, just 32 km away. Utila is practically flat, with only one small hill. The population lives almost entirely in one settlement on a curving bay; another small settlement is on a cay, about a 20-minute boat ride away.

Utila is the cheapest to visit of the three Bay Islands; the big spenders go to Roatán or Guanaja. The pace of life on the island is very slow; it's a good place for just relaxing and taking it easy, but most people come to dive.

Be sure to bring plenty of insect repellent, especially if you come during the rainy season; the mosquitoes and sandflies (*jejenes*) on the island are voracious.

Orientation & Information
There's only one town on Utila, and it has only one main road. On one end of the main road is the airport, just a few hundred metres from the 'centre' of town. Along this road are houses, several places to stay, restaurants, bars, small food shops, a disco, the post office and a bank (Bancahsa).

From the corner by the bank, another road takes off inland. About a block away is the Bucket of Blood Bar. Near it are several more places to stay. The road soon forks; a few doors along the left turn is Gunter's Gran View Gallerie.

The road west of the bank leads to the Sosa office and the post office. Next door to the post office is the office of the Capitania de Puerto, which has boat information; Rose supermarket opposite is also knowledgeable about boats.

Electricity shuts off in Utila from midnight to 6 am.

Things to See & Do
Diving There are several excellent diving spots around Utila, and several diving operators to help you explore them. The north shore is said to have the best dive sites, though the shore near the cays is also good. PADI courses cost around US$125, or even less during price wars. Some operators throw in four nights' free accommodation or extra dives, so it pays to shop around. Somebody is starting a course just about every day of the week. Always ask if the PADI certificate costs extra.

Advanced courses and speciality trips such as cave dives, night dives and deep dives are also offered. Dive trips cost about

US$12.50 per tank, going down to US$10 per tank if you buy several at once.

Gunter of Gunter's Gran View Gallerie (☎ 453113) has opened a new school opposite the Seaside Inn, west of the bank. All the other dive operators are on the road between the bank and the airport, and we've received good reports about all of them. Ronald Janssen at Cross Creek (☎ 453134), and Utila Diver Centre are the longest-established schools, though also check Underwater Vision and the Sea Eye Centre, right by the airport.

Snorkelling There's excellent snorkelling on the reef by the airport. The easiest approach to the coral is from the east end of the runway. Another good spot is on the south side of Water Cay, about a half-hour boat ride from town. Dive shops rent snorkelling gear for about US$2.50 per day.

Other Most of Utila's coast is rocky, but there's a sandy beach on Pumpkin Hill Bay, about a three-km walk across the island from town. Nearby, Pumpkin Hill has some caves; one is supposed to have been a hideout for the pirate Henry Morgan. Shelby McNab (☎ 453223) is a good source of stories and history of Utila; he sometimes offers guided tours of historical places. You can also visit Gunter's Gran View Gallerie, up past the Bucket of Blood Bar.

Windsurfers, motorboats and glass-bottomed boats are available for hire; just ask around.

Places to Stay
Utila has some great deals for cheap accommodation. There are other good possibilities beside those listed below, and it doesn't take long to walk around and find something that suits you.

On the inland road is *Blueberry Hill*, run by a friendly old couple, Norma and Will. They have basic cabins with a cooker, sleeping three, for just US$4.20, plus singles/doubles for US$1.40/2.80.

A little farther along the same road are two wooden houses called *Monkey's Tail*

(☎ 453155), with rooms at US$1.40/12.80 for singles/doubles. Enquire in the store opposite. On the road to the airport, the *Blue Room Store* has rooms for the same price, but they're very basic and claustrophobic.

Also on the airport road, *Cooper's Inn* (☎ 453184) has new singles/doubles with mosquito netting for US$2.80/4.20, sharing common bath. Nearby is *Palm Villa* (☎ 453219), with singles/doubles with shared bath for US$2.10/4.20, and larger doubles with private bath for US$7. There's also a fully equipped house costing US$7 per day for two people or US$11.25 for four.

The *Hotel Spencer* (☎ 453161/2) in the Bancahsa bank building has rooms with two single beds and private bath for US$4.20. Enquire in the Hunter & Morgan Store opposite. About 10 minutes farther along the western road is the *Seaside Inn* (☎ 453150), run by a friendly, talkative couple. It's great value, with a range of singles/doubles from US$2.10/2.80 with shared bath to US$4.90/7 with private bath.

Places to Eat
There's a good choice of eating places for such a small settlement, including people's homes where they might offer only one speciality (eg pizza or lasagna). There are many places on the airport road; *Cooper's Inn* serves a good pizza. You can eat well for under US$3.

On the western road, *Seaside Inn* serves great seafood (try the camarones) and cold beers.

On the inland road, the food is good in the *Tropical Sunset Restaurant*. On the same road, *Thompson's Bakery* is a fine place for breakfast for about US$1, and it also has a book exchange. Farther along, opposite the Bucket of Blood Bar, the *Jade Seahorse Café* has good, big licuados for US$0.50.

Entertainment
The bar opposite the bank is where the whole village goes dancing on Saturday night. The music blares out long after the rest of the island has lost its electricity.

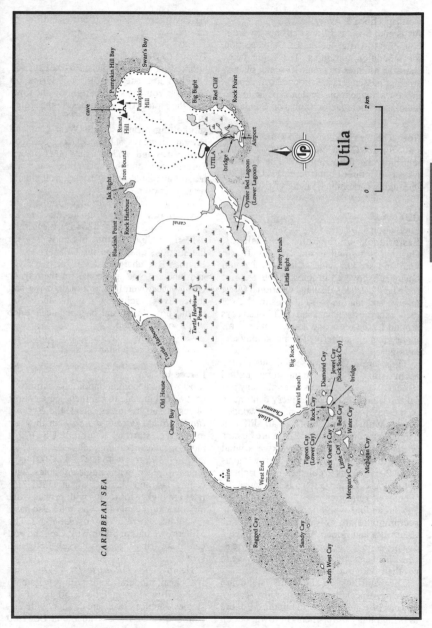

Getting There & Away

Air Isleña, Sosa and Lansa airlines fly from La Ceiba to Utila; see the La Ceiba section for schedules and fares. The flight takes about 15 minutes on small 10-seater planes; arriving passengers are dropped off, departing ones loaded on, and it's back to the mainland. There are no flights on Sundays.

Boat The *Starfish*, based on Utila, usually sails for La Ceiba on Mondays at 4 am, returning the following day. The crossing takes two or three hours; the cost is US$4.20. In rough weather the boat doesn't sail.

GUANAJA

Population 4155

Easternmost of the three Bay Islands, Guanaja is a small island, roughly 18 km long and six km wide at its widest point. Guanaja is covered in forest; about 90% of the island has been declared a national forest reserve and marine park. Many km of coral reefs encircle the island and the 15 or so cays around it; the reefs and some sunken ships make Guanaja attractive for snorkelling and diving.

There are a few tiny settlements on the main island, but Guanaja town, called 'Bonacca' by the locals, is on a small cay just off the island's east coast. Every centimetre of the cay has been built on, with wooden houses with sloping roofs at all different heights, standing on stilts. There are no cars on the cay, and no roads; walkways wind around among the houses, and narrow canals allow the residents to pull their boats right up to the house. Guanaja town is known as the 'Venice of Honduras'.

You can find everything you need in town: accommodation, restaurants, two banks (Bancahsa and Banco Atlántida) and even a disco. As on the other Bay Islands, the residents here can speak Spanish if they have to but their preferred language is English.

The sandflies on the main island are amazing, especially during the rainy season; you can be eaten alive in 15 minutes. Be sure to bring plenty of repellent. In town, out on the cay, there are few, if any, sandflies or mosquitoes.

Things to See & Do

Snorkelling, diving and visits to the cays and beaches are the popular activities on Guanaja. You can snorkel right off the town cay; the Hotel Alexander, beside the water, is a good place to start. There's good snorkelling around South West Cay and several other cays, at Michael Rock beach on the main island, and at many other places. Surprisingly, though, snorkelling gear is not readily available on the island; you should bring your own.

Diving trips can be arranged through the Bayman Bay Diving Club (contact in La Ceiba: Hondu-Tours (☎ 430457), the Posada del Sol, or Club Nautilus in Sandy Bay, on the main island opposite Guanaja town. Bayman Bay charges US$50 for two dives and lunch, if you just come for the day, or US$100 for overnight accommodation and three dives, including a night dive. You should be able to find cheaper deals once you're on the island.

On weekend evenings, the Mountain View disco is a popular hot spot.

Places to Stay

Most of the accommodation and activity is centred in Guanaja town; there are a couple of resorts on the main island, the *Bayman Bay Club* and *Posada del Sol*, but they are expensive, starting at around US$100 a night, meals and diving included.

Hotel Miller (☎ 454327, 454202) is a pleasant place with singles/doubles with ceiling fan and shared bath at US$11/15; rates are higher for rooms with private bath, air-con and/or cable TV. The hotel also has a restaurant, where meals cost US$3.65. The Millers own half of South West Cay, and you can make trips there to snorkel, BBQ and swim.

Nearby, *Hotel Rosario* (☎ 454240) has five clean, modern rooms with private bath and ceiling fan at US$15.50/16.80 for singles/doubles; rates are higher with air-con, and cable TV is available at US$1.80

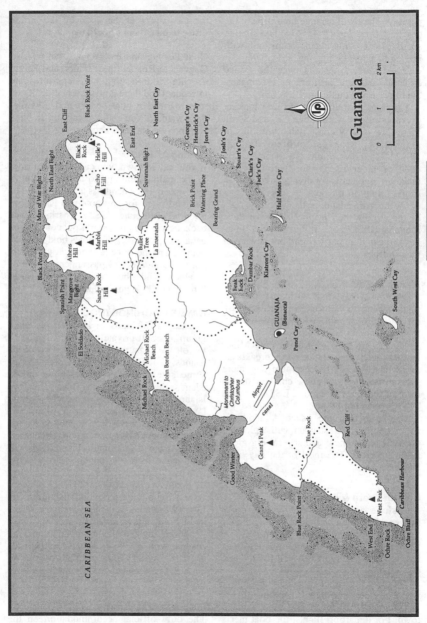

per day. They will arrange boat trips to the beaches. *Days Inn* (☎ 454174) is a similar, small place, with clean rooms, all with private bath and ceiling fan, at US$7/8.45.

Hotel Carter, upstairs over the Banco Atlántida and Tan/Sahsa offices, is comparable in price and quality to Days Inn.

The *Hotel Alexander* (☎ 454326), looking over the water towards Pond Cay and South West Cay, is very comfortable with lots of amenities. Singles/doubles start at US$25/35; larger rooms are available and children under 12 stay for free. They can make arrangements for diving, and you can snorkel right off the dock.

On the main island, on the waterside right by the airport, the *Airport Hillton* has three rooms at US$17 each. It's convenient if you have to catch an early flight, but beware of the sandflies.

Places to Eat

There are several small, inexpensive restaurants around town; some of the bars also serve food. As it's such a small place it's easy to explore.

The *TKO Restaurant* near the Hotel Miller is small and pleasant, serving breakfasts, sandwiches, burgers, ice cream and more substantial meals; steaks, chicken or the meal of the day cost around US$2 or more. TKO is open until 9 pm.

The Nest, near the Banco Atlántida, is another enjoyable restaurant, with a pleasant open-air atmosphere and several big green talking parrots. The meal of the day costs US$1.80.

Getting There & Away

Air Isleña and Lansa airlines fly daily between La Ceiba and Guanaja; see the La Ceiba entry for schedules and fares. The flight from La Ceiba takes 25 minutes. Sosa has daily direct flights between Roatán and Guanaja (see the Roatán entry).

There's a little dock right near the airport, where a motorboat meets incoming flights and charges US$1 for the five-minute ride to town. For departing flights, the boat meets the passengers at the dock by the airline office to take them back to the airport.

Boat Fishing and cargo boats sail to/from Guanaja to Roatán (three hours) and Puerto Castilla (four hours), but departures are infrequent and there is no set schedule. If you want to travel by boat, be prepared to 'waste' days waiting. You could always try to hitch with private yacht owners.

Getting Around

If you stay in town, you can take boat rides to the main island and to the cays; almost everyone on the island has a motorboat. The standard price for any boat trip is not low, however, at around US$20 per trip out and back. Economically it works out better if you get a group together; the boats hold up to 10 people, and the price is charged by the trip, not by the number of passengers. You may be able to find a boatman to take you for as little as US$8, if you're lucky.

CAYOS COCHINOS (HOG ISLANDS)

The Cayos Cochinos, or Hog Islands, are a group of small privately owned islands, 17 km off the coast near La Ceiba. Two of the islands, though small, are forested and of some size, and can properly be called islands; the others are tiny cays. The Hog Islands can be seen from the beaches at both La Ceiba and Trujillo.

The islands were once inhabited by the Maya; ancient Maya pottery, ornaments and statues have been found. The islands got their name from the conquistador Cortés, who tried farming on the islands. In addition to Spanish conquerors, the islands were visited by pirates including the infamous Henry Morgan. Today the islands are inhabited by only a few private owners.

Snorkelling and diving is good around the islands, with black coral reefs, wall diving and cave diving. You can hire a boat to go out to the cays, and there are some interesting walks.

Places to Stay & Eat

The only official accommodation on the

islands is the *Plantation Beach Resort* on the smaller island, expensive at US$750 a week, although this does include three meals a day and diving. Contact Hondu-Tours in La Ceiba for details. Otherwise, you should be able to camp on the small cays, but ask permission of the owners first. Bring your own food and water.

Getting There & Away

To get to the Hog Islands, take a bus from the bus station at La Ceiba heading east to Nueva Armenia (40 km, two hours, US$0.70). From there you can hire a motorboat to take you to the islands (17 km, 50 minutes, US$21 for a boat carrying up to 15 people). You could also hire a boat at Sambo Creek if you happen to be there, but Nueva Armenia is the usual landing for boats to the islands.

With an early start, you could visit the islands in a day trip from La Ceiba, but you'll have a more leisurely visit if you plan to stay overnight on the islands or in Nueva Armenia. It's good to make the sea crossing early in the morning, when the sea is calm, as the boats may not make the trip if the sea is too rough.

Eastern Honduras

The eastern part of Honduras, including all the department of Gracias a Dios and the eastern sides of Olancho and Colón, is a vast, sparsely inhabited area of rivers and forests. The easternmost part of Honduras is known as the Mosquitia, where there is just one minor road.

The only major road to traverse the area north-east of Tegucigalpa is the road from Tegucigalpa to Juticalpa, with another turning north and on to Trujillo on the north coast. On this route between Trujillo and Tegucigalpa you have to change buses and may have to overnight in Juticalpa. However, there is a route between Tegucigalpa and Trujillo that climbs the mountains west of Juticalpa and can be

crossed the same day in one hop; see Tegucigalpa or Trujillo for details.

JUTICALPA

Population 73,823

The only major town in north-eastern Honduras is Juticalpa, capital of the department of Olancho. There's nothing much to see but it's a pleasant, friendly town to spend a night. The annual festival is held on 8 December.

Places to Stay

On the corner of 1a Avenida NE and 6a Calle SO, between the bus station and the central plaza, the *Hotel El Paso* (☎ 952311) is quiet, spacious and clean, with enclosed parking and rooms around a grassy courtyard. It has a small shop, and there are restaurants in the same block. Singles/doubles, all with private bath, overhead fan and wood decor, are US$5.60/7.75.

Hotel Las Vegas (☎ 952116), in the block beside the plaza, has clean rooms, all with private bath and fan, at US$4.20/7, with a cafeteria downstairs.

The *Hotel Antúñez* (☎ 952250), a block from the plaza, is a large hotel with various types of rooms priced from US$2.60 to US$7 per person, depending on what amenities you choose. The *Hotel Antúñez Anexo* (☎ 952034), half a block away, is simple but clean and has rooms with shared or private bath from US$2.95 to US$3.80 per person.

Places to Eat

As usual, there are several simple comedores around the plaza.

Around behind the church, the *Restaurante El Rancho* is a covered, outdoor patio with wooden picnic tables and a good selection of food, open daily from 9 am to 11.30 pm.

Four blocks from the plaza, on the entrance road into town, the *Restaurant El Tablado* is a fancier restaurant with a bar; meat and seafood meals are US$2.50 to US$4.

Getting There & Away

The bus station is about two km from town,

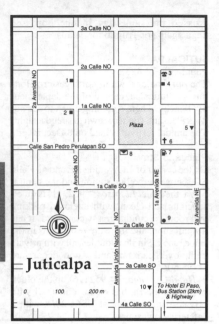

Juticalpa

0   100   200 m

■ PLACES TO STAY

1   Hotel Antuñez Anexo
2   Hotel Antuñez
4   Hotel Las Vegas
12   Hotel El Paso

▼ PLACES TO EAT

5   Restaurante El Rancho
10   Restaurante El Tablado

OTHER

3   Hondutel
6   Church
7   Texaco station
8   Post Office
9   Cine (movies)

Tegucigalpa (167 km, three hours, US$1.80). The first bus leaves Juticalpa at 3.30 am, the last at 6 pm.

The road between Juticalpa and Trujillo is a full day's journey, passing from pine-forested mountains down to the coastal lowlands covered in jungle and coconut palms. Along the way are cattle ranches and lots of cowboys.

There is one direct bus a day from Juticalpa to Trujillo, departing at 4 am (270 km, nine hours, US$4.20). If you don't want to get up so early, it's possible to do this journey via bus and minibus with changes at San Esteban and Tocoa, though you may have to overnight at San Esteban.

CATACAMAS
Population 53,775
Catacamas, 50 km north-east of Juticalpa (about 45 minutes by bus), is a more attractive town than Juticalpa and it's the end of the line for buses coming from Tegucigalpa; all the Tegucigalpa-Juticalpa buses continue to Catacamas, and additional buses go just between these two towns. There are places to stay in Catacamas. From Catacamas, other buses traverse the dirt road to the small town of Dulce Nombre de Culmí.

THE MOSQUITIA
The Mosquitia region, comprising the entire north-east portion of the country, is very different from the rest of Honduras. There are no roads going through the vast area, and most of the region is uninhabited. Those people who do live there – mostly Miskito Indians, with isolated groups of Paya and Sumo Indians in the interior – have their own distinct culture.

The settlements of the Mosquitia are remote and a little backward; if you go there, don't expect city life. The Mosquitia is mainly worth visiting for its pristine natural beauty. Manatees and much other wildlife live in the eastern lagoons; monkeys can be seen in the forested areas along the rivers early in the morning; and there is abundant birdlife, with parrots, egrets, herons, pico oros and many others. Alligators can be seen

on the entrance road in from the highway. Plenty of taxis run between town and the station, costing around US$0.35.

Buses run hourly between Juticalpa and

in many of the waters, especially at night, and especially in the mangrove-lined rivers; if you're travelling by water, keep your hands inside the boat!

Most travellers who have made it to the region have been highly enthusiastic about what they found there. All the towns mentioned have inexpensive accommodation for visitors (and somewhere to eat), whether in formal hospedajes or with families who rent rooms; some provision will always be made. You can also camp out.

Fish is magnificent in the Mosquitia; other food has to be imported into the region and can be scarce or expensive. If you intend to get really off the beaten track bring as much food with you as you can, as you'll end up sharing meals with families. Be sure to take water purification tablets.

Mosquitoes and sandflies are a major irritation; bring insect repellent, a mosquito net, and anti-malaria pills. It can rain anytime, so rain gear is a good idea, as is a torch (flash light) since many places have no electricity.

As the place is so remote, and accommodation and transport are relatively unstructured, a working knowledge of Spanish is more important here than elsewhere in Honduras. Such enforced interaction with the locals makes a visit all the more of an adventure.

Some travel companies undertake organised tours, an easy if expensive way to get a taste of the Mosquitia. La Moskitia Ecoaventuras (☎ 379398), based in Tegucigalpa, is a specialist in the region.

Puerto Lempira
Population 5600

Puerto Lempira, the largest town in the Mosquitia, is situated on the inland side of the Laguna de Caratasca. The lagoon is very large, with several sub-lagoons, but not deep; its average depth is about three metres, with deeper pockets in a few places.

Because the depth clearance over the sandbar forming the entrance to the lagoon is only about two metres, large vessels cannot enter the lagoon, and only small boats ply the waters. There is a lot of small boat traffic, especially between Puerto Lempira and Cauquira, a village on the lagoon's north side, from where you can easily walk to the sea.

Manatees, birds, fish and other wildlife are found in the lagoon. Mopawi has a water buffalo farm outside of town, which you can ask permission to visit.

Palacios & the Río Plátano Nature Reserve

The Río Plátano Nature Reserve is probably the most magnificent nature reserve in Honduras. The reserve, established jointly in 1980 by Honduras and the United Nations, is home to abundant bird, mammal and aquatic life, including a number of exotic and endangered species in the river and surrounding jungle. However, there's nowhere for humans to stay or eat.

Palacios, a small town with only about 100 houses, is the most accessible place from which to visit the Río Plátano, with regular flights coming in from La Ceiba. From Palacios you can easily arrange boat trips on the river, or across the lagoon to the Garífuna village of Batalla.

Palacios has a good hospedaje (no name), and a restaurant (also without a name) where you can eat for US$0.55.

Ahuas

Ahuas, another small town with a population of under 1000, is inland from the coast, about two hour's walk from the Río Patuca. You can take boat trips upriver to the village of Wampu Sirpi, or downriver to Brus Laguna, from Ahuas. At certain times of year, however, the river may not be navigable, whether from too much water (rainy season) or too little (dry season). Check current conditions before you go.

Brus Laguna

Beside the lagoon of the same name, at the mouth where the Río Patuca meets the lagoon, Brus Laguna is another small Mosquitia town. There is a friendly hospedaje where you can cook if you have your own food.

HONDURAS

Getting There & Away

Air La Ceiba is the main takeoff point for flights to the Mosquitia, with services to Puerto Lempira, Palacios, Ahuas, and Brus Laguna. See the La Ceiba section for details.

From Tegucigalpa, Setco (☎ 331711/2) has flights to Puerto Lempira twice a week; the cost is US$63.65 one way (double for return).

Land It may seem tempting to get into Nicaragua through the Mosquitia and avoid backtracking to Tegucigalpa. However, Paul Roos (Netherlands) reported the following experience taking the crossing used by locals called 'Lemuch', 40 km south of Puerto Lempira:

After acquiring his exit stamp at the Puerto Lempira migration office he took the thrice-weekly pick-up (US$4) to the small village at the border crossing. The police officer on the Nicaraguan side had no entry stamp. Continuing to Puerto Cabezas was straightforward, but at the Migration office there he was told he had entered illegally and a payment of US$200 was demanded. This was eventually reduced to US$80 (all the money he had) for the entry stamp – but only after hours of negotiation and threats.

Boat There are no regularly scheduled boats to the Mosquitia, but cargo and fishing boats go from La Ceiba, Roatán and Guanaja, and may take passengers.

Getting Around

Air The air route into the Mosquitia begins at La Ceiba, with stops at Puerto Lempira, Palacios, Brus Laguna, and Ahuas, so you can fly between these places.

Alas airline, a small enterprise in the Mosquitia for missionaries and hospitals, will take passengers, but space is not always available. They serve the mission hospital in Ahuas and several other places; fares are around US$25.

Land There is a thrice-weekly pick-up running along the road south-west from Puerto Lempira. The only other land transport is by foot or mule.

Boat Ground-level transport is almost entirely by boat, on the lagoons and rivers as well as the sea, though prices can be high. Cayucas are the principal transport, propelled by poles, paddles, or small engines. The motorised canoes are called 'tuk-tuks', taking their name from their sound. They can be very unstable.

The rainy season in the Mosquitia is from June to December. Too much water (sometimes to the point of flooding) and flotsam in the water during the rainy season can occasionally impede navigation of rivers at this time; during the dry season, some waterways can become too shallow to navigate. Most of the time, though, there is no problem getting around by boat.

Southern Honduras

Honduras touches the Pacific with a 124-km coastline on the Golfo de Fonseca. Bordered by the Golfo de Fonseca on the seaward side and by hills on the land side, the strip of lowland here is part of the hot coastal plain that extends down the Pacific side of Central America through several countries. It's a fertile agricultural and fishing region; much of Tegucigalpa's fish, shrimp, rice, sugar cane, and hot-weather fruits (like watermelon) come from this area. Honduras's Pacific port is at San Lorenzo.

Southern Honduras is a much-travelled region; it is where the Interamerican Highway crosses Honduras, carrying all the north and southbound traffic of Central America, and also where the highway branches north from the Interamerican Highway towards the rest of Honduras.

TEGUCIGALPA TO EL PARAÍSO

The most direct route from Tegucigalpa to Managua is via El Paraíso. It's only 132 km from Tegucigalpa to the border going this way (2½ hours by bus, US$1.25). You can make it from Tegucigalpa to Managua in a day if you get an early start.

The border crossing is at Las Manos, near

El Paraíso. Coming from Tegucigalpa, take a bus to El Paraíso and then change buses to continue on the half-hour journey to the border station (US$0.30). Like the other Honduran border stations, Las Manos is open every day from 7 am to 5 pm.

There are several interesting stopovers along this route. About 40 km east of the capital at Zamorano, there's a turnoff for San Antonio de Oriente, an attractive old Spanish mining village about five km north off the highway.

Further east is a turnoff south to Yuscarán, 77 km from Tegucigalpa. Capital of the department of El Paraíso, it is another pleasant old Spanish colonial mining village. Its annual fair is held on 8 December.

Danlí (population 98,830), 108 km east of Tegucigalpa and 23 km from El Paraíso, is the largest town along this route. An attractive town, Danlí is the centre of an agricultural area producing sugar cane and tobacco; the town has several cigar factories where you can buy good hand-rolled cigars. The annual festival at Danlí, the Fiesta del Maíz in the last weekend in August, is a big event and attracts people from far and wide. There are several places to stay and eat at Danlí. El Paraíso also has accommodation.

TEGUCIGALPA TO THE PACIFIC
Highway CA 5 heads south about 95 km from Tegucigalpa until it meets the Interamerican Highway (CA 1) at Jícaro Galán, winding down from the pine-covered hills around the capital to the hot coastal plain. From the crossroads at Jícaro Galán it's 41 km west to the border with El Salvador at El Amatillo, passing through the town of Nacaome six km west of Jícaro Galán; or 115 km east to the Nicaraguan border at El Espino, passing through Choluteca 50 km from Jícaro Galán.

If you are travelling along the Interamerican Highway, crossing only this part of Honduras in transit between El Salvador and Nicaragua, you can easily make the entire crossing in a day; from border to border it's only 148 km (three hours by bus).

If, however, you want to stop off, there are a few possibilities. The border stations close at 5 pm, so if you can't make it by that time you'll have to spend the night and start off again in the morning.

GOLFO DE FONSECA
The shores of Honduras, El Salvador and Nicaragua all touch the Golfo de Fonseca; Honduras has the middle and largest share, with 124 km of coastline and jurisdiction over nearly all of the 30-plus islands in the gulf. A ruling of the International Court of Justice in September 1992 eased previous tensions by ruling that sovereignty in the gulf must be shared by the three nations, barring a three-mile maritime belt around the coast. Of the islands in the gulf, sovereignty was disputed by Honduras and El Salvador in three cases. The court found in favour of Honduras in respect of the island of El Tigre, while El Salvador prevailed on Meanguera and Meanguerita. The Golfo de Fonseca is an extremely hot region.

The European discovery of the Golfo de Fonseca was made in 1522 by Andrés Niño, who named the gulf in honour of his benefactor, Bishop Juan Rodríguez de Fonseca. In 1578 the buccaneer Sir Francis Drake occupied the gulf, using El Tigre as a base as he made raids as far afield as Peru and Baja California. There is still speculation that Drake may have left a hidden treasure, but it has never been found.

El Salvador has a major town on the Gulf, La Unión, but Honduras doesn't; on the Honduras part of the coastline there are only small settlements, and the highway never meets the sea except on the outskirts of San Lorenzo.

San Lorenzo
The only place where the Interamerican Highway touches the Golfo de Fonseca is on the outskirts of San Lorenzo. San Lorenzo is the Pacific port town of Honduras but there's not much to the town, which is small, sleepy and hot. San Lorenzo is in a deep inlet, the Bahía de San Lorenzo, so although you can get to the water and jump in for a swim, there's no view out into the gulf.

From the bus stop on the highway, it's about 10 blocks to the water, passing the market, the church and the plaza. At the end, beside the shrimp packing plant, the *Hotel Miramar* (☎ 812138) has a restaurant and bar, with a large deck hanging over the water. Meals, mostly seafood, are about US$3 to US$5. Canoes and small boats pass by in the channel and there's a small beach beside the hotel. Buses passing along the Interamerican Highway all stop at San Lorenzo, some at the bus stop on the highway, some coming the few blocks into town to the market.

Cedeño & Punta Ratón

These are the two principal swimming beaches on the Golfo de Fonseca. Cedeño is the more popular; it has very basic places to stay and eat. Buses come from Choluteca and San Lorenzo, but only a few times a day; it takes about one to 1½ hours to get to the beaches from either town. There are also buses that run directly between Cedeño and Tegucigalpa.

Amapala

Amapala is a quiet fishing village of about 8000 souls on the island of El Tigre, an inactive volcanic island 783 metres high. It was once Honduras's Pacific port town, before the port was moved to the mainland at San Lorenzo. Visitors come here for holidays during Semana Santa, but otherwise the place is very quiet.

There are a few places to stay and eat in Amapala, and some good hikes around the island; from El Vijia, about 100 metres up, there's a good view of the gulf and its islands. El Tigre also has a couple of good beaches: Playa Grande (with the Cueva de la Sirena, or Mermaid Cave) and Playa Negra, with tranquil shores. Other beaches are Caracolito and El Caracol. Seafood is an attraction of the island.

To get to Amapala, small boats and a car ferry depart from Coyolito, 30 km from the Interamerican Highway. Buses go to Coyolito infrequently from San Lorenzo, or you could hitch. There are no overnight facilities at Coyolito.

CHOLUTECA

Population 63,000

Choluteca, capital of the department of the same name, is the largest town in southern Honduras. It's built near the Río Choluteca, the same river that runs through Tegucigalpa.

There's not much to do in Choluteca; it's principally a commercial centre for the agricultural region and a stopping-off point between the borders. It is a pleasant, though very hot, town. The annual festival day is 8 December, the day of the Virgen de la Concepción.

Orientation

The streets in Choluteca are very well signposted. Unfortunately you often see two different signs together; eg Calle 3a is also Calle Vincente Williams, and Calle 4a is also Calle Franklin D Roosevelt.

But it's still easy to find your way around. The old market *(mercado viejo)*, San Antonio, is the centre of activity and practically everything you need is near it. The new market *(mercado nuevo)*, La Concepción, is five blocks south. The bus stations are nine blocks east on Boulevard Carranza, the main road heading east, which runs two blocks south of the old market.

Places to Stay

The quiet, clean and pleasant *Hotel Pacífico* (☎ 820838) is on 4a Avenida NE, one block south of Boulevard Choluteca, in the residential neighbourhood near the bus stations. There's a courtyard with hammocks, and cable TV in the tiny lounge area. All rooms have private bath and fan; singles/doubles are US$3.50/5.60.

Most of the places to stay in Choluteca are near the old market, which in Choluteca is a fine area, not somewhere to be avoided as in some other cities.

The *Hotel Lisboa* (☎ 820355), facing the old market on the western side, is comfortable and clean. All the rooms have private bath, overhead fan, and face onto a colourful courtyard full of plants and hammocks. They cost US$3.50/7/10.55 for singles/doubles/triples.

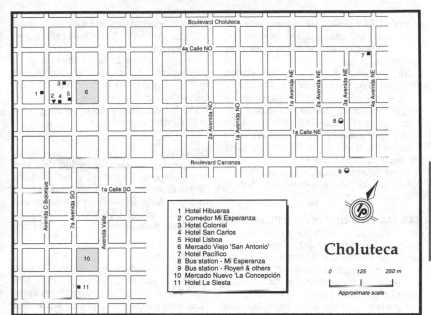

1 Hotel Hibueras
2 Comedor Mi Esperanza
3 Hotel Colonial
4 Hotel San Carlos
5 Hotel Lisboa
6 Mercado Viejo 'San Antonio'
7 Hotel Pacífico
8 Bus station - Mi Esperanza
9 Bus station - Royeri & others
10 Mercado Nuevo 'La Concepción
11 Hotel La Siesta

Choluteca

0   125   250 m

Approximate scale

HONDURAS

Around the corner to the south is the *Hotel San Carlos* (☎ 820885). It is nearly as good and prices are slightly cheaper; rooms are US$2.95/5.15/7. There's parking in the courtyard.

Around the next corner, the *Hotel Hibueras* (☎ 820512) on Avenida C Bojorque is also in a similar style; it is a bit more run-down than the other two, but cheaper, at US$2.50/4.75 (plus tax) for singles/doubles. Also nearby, the equally run-down *Hotel Colonial* is even cheaper, at US$2.10/4.20, yet rooms still have a private bath.

Half a block south of the new market, *Hotel La Siesta* is a simple and friendly family-run place, with enclosed parking and spacious rooms with private bath. Singles/doubles are around US$2.80/3.50, and some have a big hammock.

Places to Eat

There are lots of small comedores in the streets bordering the old market, with good, inexpensive, basic meals, such as *Comedor Mi Esperanza* where dishes start at US$0.85. The new market has a cheap eating area in the centre.

The Hotel Pacífico has a café opposite, and there's a good open-air burger place nearby on 4a Calle NE.

Getting There & Away

Frequent buses connect Choluteca with Tegucigalpa (142 km, three hours, US$1.40), San Marcos de Colón near the Nicaraguan border (60 km, one hour, US$0.56), and El Amatillo at the Salvadoran border (85 km, two hours, US$1.25). The buses generally start running at around 4 or 5 am, and finish at around 5 or 6 pm. Buses run hourly, but as there are several companies, you shouldn't have to wait long for a bus.

Royeri and several other companies share a bus station on Boulevard Carranza, at the corner of 3a Avenida NE. There are small comedores and shops in the bus station. Some buses stop by the old market after leaving the station.

Mi Esperanza has its own bus station (☎ 820841) on 3a Avenida NE, 1½ blocks north of the other station. Mi Esperanza is one of the main companies doing the Tegucigalpa-Choluteca-San Marcos de Colón route and their buses are more comfortable than some of the others (and marginally more expensive).

Local buses connect Choluteca with other places in the south, around the Bay of Fonseca.

SAN MARCOS DE COLÓN & EL ESPINO
San Marcos de Colón is the closest town to the Nicaraguan border at El Espino. It is a small, pleasant mountain town, cool at night, with several places to stay and eat. Some families here offer comfortable accommodation in private homes; you may be approached by their children at the bus station. It's easy to change money in San Marcos.

Honduran buses to the border go only as far as San Marcos. From San Marcos, taxis will take you the 12 km to the border station at El Espino (open daily from 7 am to 5 pm). If you need a visa for either country, be sure you already have it before you reach the border.

If it's getting late in the day, you may want to stay in Choluteca or San Marcos before crossing the border, and make the crossing the following day. The choice of accommo-

dation is better there than on the Nicaraguan side near the border. There is no place to stay at El Espino.

Crossing the border in the other direction, you can catch direct buses from San Marcos to Tegucigalpa (196 km, four hours, US$1.65) and Choluteca (60 km, one hour, US$0.56). Choluteca has connecting buses to El Amatillo.

GUASAULE
This border crossing reopened in 1992 after the European Community repaired the bridge there. It's open the usual hours, 7 am to 5 pm daily. Buses from Choluteca take 1½ hours and cost US$0.50. On the Nicaraguan side, buses go to Chinandega and Leon.

EL AMATILLO
El Amatillo, the border crossing between Honduras and El Salvador, is open daily from 7 am to 5 pm. It is a relaxed border post; Honduran *campesinos* cross the border here every day to go to market in Santa Rosa de Lima, 18 km from the border on the El Salvador side. There are places to stay at Santa Rosa de Lima, or you could press on to San Miguel or La Unión, each a two-hour bus ride from El Amatillo. There's also a basic hospedaje at El Amatillo on the Honduran side.

From El Amatillo into Honduras, buses leave frequently for Tegucigalpa (137 km, three hours, US$1.25) and Choluteca (85 km, two hours, US$0.70). At Choluteca you can continue to the Nicaraguan border.

EL SALVADOR

El Salvador

The smallest and most densely populated of the Central American countries, El Salvador is richly fertile, a land of volcanoes and agriculture.

Civil war raged in El Salvador throughout the 1980s, making headlines around the world and cutting the flow of visitors to a trickle. With the signing of the peace accords in January 1992 the country began to welcome tourists again. Entry requirements are being eased all the time and the local people are for the most part welcoming and friendly. A visit to the former zones of conflict provides a unique opportunity to see small communities engaged in the task of rebuilding war-torn lives. However, El Salvador's problems are far from over and the UN-brokered peace is a fragile one.

El Salvador is also physically a beautiful country, offering impressive volcanoes, rolling hills and verdant valleys. Surfers are attracted by the huge waves on the Pacific coast.

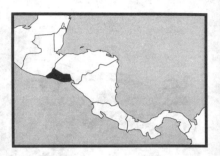

Facts about the Country

HISTORY

Its volcanic soil makes El Salvador very fertile, and people have lived here since prehistoric times. The Olmec people, whose culture was already long established in Mexico, lived in El Salvador at least as early as 2000 BC. The Olmec Boulder, a stone sculpture of a giant head found near Chalchuapa in western El Salvador, shows an early Olmec presence or influence.

The step pyramid ruins at Tazumal and San Andrés, among others, testify to a Maya presence in western El Salvador that lasted over 1000 years. Archaeologists have found evidence that it was well connected with the rest of the Maya Empire and with other settlements from Mexico to Panama.

When the Spanish arrived in the 16th century, the country was dominated by the Pipil, descendants of Nahuatl-speaking Toltec and Aztecs both Mexican tribes. The Pipil probably came to central El Salvador in the 11th century. Their culture was similar to that of the Aztec, with heavy Maya influences and a maize-based agricultural economy that supported several cities and a complex culture including hieroglyphic writing, astronomy and mathematics. Their language, Nahua, a dialect related to Nahuatl, is still heard in some Indian villages. Other tribes included the Lempa, Pokoman and Matagalpa.

Spanish Conquest & Independence

Pedro de Alvarado, the murderous conquistador, had been with Cortés in Mexico, then conquered Guatemala before he arrived on the coast of El Salvador near Acajutla in June 1524. The resident warriors put up a fierce fight, but by 1540 the region was under Spanish control. It was designated a province of Nueva España and placed under the direct rule of Guatemala. It was in San Salvador in 1811 that Father José Matías Delgado raised the first cry for Central American independence from Spain.

Independence from Spain came on 15 September 1821. On 1 July 1823 El Salvador joined Honduras, Guatemala, Nicaragua and Costa Rica to form the Provincias Unidas del

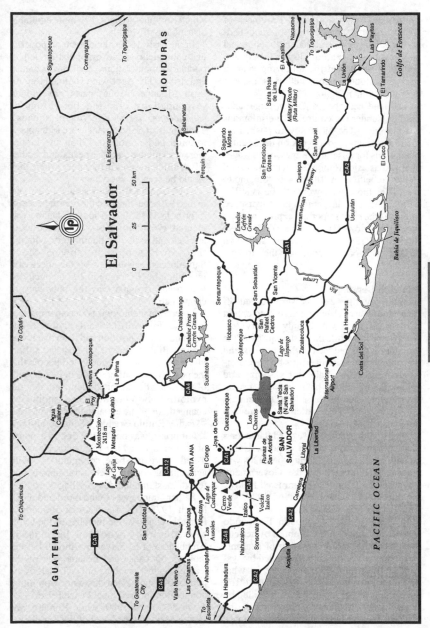

EL SALVADOR

EL SALVADOR

Centro de América (United Provinces of Central America, or Central American Federation). However, regional and ideological conflicts beset the union. It was finally dissolved in 1840, and the following year El Salvador adopted a constitution as a sovereign independent nation.

The land had been settled in large landholdings under the control of the infamous '14 families'. The Indians were pushed off their land and forced to work on the Spanish plantations for miserable wages, or no wages at all. Anastasio Aquino led an unsuccessful Indian rebellion in 1833, with the motto 'Land for those who work it'; he is still a national hero. Today, coffee has superseded indigo as the most important export crop, but working conditions are otherwise unchanged; 2% of the people still own around 60% of the land, and the struggle continues.

The 20th Century

Increasingly, the peasants were pushed off their land. It was then turned over to export cash crops from which only a very few reaped a profit, while the vast majority of the population was reduced to dire poverty and discontent. Intermittent efforts by the majority to redress El Salvador's social and economic injustices have been met with severe repression by those keen to maintain the status quo. This pattern still prevails today.

By the 20th century, 95% of El Salvador's income came from coffee exports. Union activity in the industry during the 1920s was vigorously repressed by the Government. But when coffee prices plummeted following the stock market crash of 1929, the situation became unbearable.

In January 1932, Augustín Farabundo Martí, a founder of the Central American Socialist party, led an uprising of peasants and Indians. The military responded by systematically killing 30,000 people in what became known as La Matanza ('the massacre'). Martí was arrested and killed by firing squad. His name is preserved by the FMLN (Frente Martí Liberacion Nacional),

which continues to fight for a more equitable distribution of wealth.

In the early 1970s, landlessness, poverty, unemployment and overpopulation led to popular demonstrations, civil disobedience and strikes. The right-wing National Republican Alliance (Arena) party government responded by creating the infamous *esquadrones de muerte* (death squads). Thousands of Salvadorans were kidnapped, tortured and murdered. Often the bodies were decapitated and the heads and bodies left in different spots in the street, where they would be seen by everyone.

This, combined with fraudulent elections in the 1970s, put the lie to the idea of peaceful reform. In 1972, José Napoleon Duarte was elected president. He was immediately arrested and exiled by the military, who put their own people in power. Many Salvadorans, encouraged by the successful revolution in Nicaragua in 1979, concluded that armed struggle was the only way to create a change.

Liberation theology was also an important influence in the drift towards civil war. The standard church position had been that it was God's will that there be poverty and suffering. Radical priests began to tell people that the poverty they suffered was in fact the will of the rich who exploited them, and that the exploitive system could and should be changed, for all are equal in the sight of God.

Father Rutilio Grande, a Salvadoran-born Jesuit priest, was one of the first to espouse liberation theology in El Salvador. He established 'Christian base communities', with agricultural cooperatives, rural unions and federations, in hundreds of villages.

Father Grande was found murdered on 12 March 1977. His friend Oscar Romero, a formerly conservative member of the Catholic hierarchy who had been made Archbishop of El Salvador a month before, took up his cause and became one of the leading figures speaking out on behalf of the poor and dispossessed; his work won him a nomination for the Nobel Peace Prize.

On 24 March 1980, while Romero was saying Mass in the chapel of the San Salvador Divine Providence Cancer Hospital, an assassin drove up and fired through the doorway at the altar, killing Romero with a single bullet in front of the entire congregation. Romero's blood-spattered vestments and his room can still be viewed in the hospital. The murder of the beloved archbishop, champion of the people's cause, ignited an armed insurrection the same year.

The US government, unnerved by the success of Nicaragua's socialist revolution, pumped huge amounts of money into the Salvadoran military to fight the guerrilla FMLN. 'Advisors' were stationed in Honduras, just over the Salvadoran border, to train the Salvadoran military. This influx of money (see Economy) made the military a power to be reckoned with – one that came to rival the landholding aristocratic elite.

In 1984 Duarte was brought back and made president. However, the military was still in control of the country, and the violence and repression did not stop

Recent Political Developments

In March 1989 Alfredo Cristiani, a wealthy businessman of the Arena party that had made 'death squads' a household word, was elected President. On 16 November 1989 the military murdered six Jesuit priests, their housekeeper and her little daughter. This outrage intensified the war: the FMLN launched an offensive attack against military and strategic targets all over the country and the government responded with a major counter-offensive in which 4000 people are believed to have been killed.

After 11 years of conflict it became increasingly clear that neither side could defeat the other by force. Negotiations between the two sides, the government and the FMLN, mediated by the United Nations, began in April 1990. The negotiations were stalemated many times. One of the first agreements was a human rights accord signed by both parties in July 1990, but violations occurred practically as soon as the ink was dry. Violent deaths actually increased in 1991, the year that a United

Nations mission arrived in the country to monitor human rights.

Finally, on 16 January 1992, the agreement which ended the war was signed. It was a compromise in which no side was the clear winner. The ceasefire took effect on 1 February. The FLMN became an opposition party, and the government agreed to various reforms, including dismantling paramilitary groups and death squads and replacing them with a national civil police force.

As part of the peace accords, a UN-appointed Truth Commission was set up to investigate past human rights violations in El Salvador. Information on around 22,000 victims was collected (95% attributed to the military or death squads), but only 30 cases could be followed up in detail. The Commission published its report in March 1993. A key recommendation was that all military and judicial officials named in the report should be removed from office. The recommendations of the report are binding on the government, but it responded by immediately passing the General Amnesty Law for the Consolidation of Peace, which was specifically designed to protect those responsible for human rights abuses. Many other terms of the peace accords were yet to be implemented by the end of 1993.

During the course of the 12-year war, an estimated 75,000 people were killed. Over the same period the USA gave a staggering US$6000 million to the Salvadoran government's war effort, despite the fact that the USA had held documents (declassified in November 1993) implicating various government members in the operation of the death squads. The USA had also ignored evidence of atrocities carried out by the military, such the massacre of the village of El Mozote in 1981 (where eyewitnesses report that soldiers slit children's throats, hung them from trees, and threw a baby into the air and bayoneted it). Now many Salvadorans believe that the USA has an obligation to pump a similar sum into reconstruction. The USA currently does give more money than the whole of the European Union, but it can't resist trying to attach conditions to the funds (eg money for land transfers initially had the stipulation that no land was to go to co-operatives).

Despite the peace, the political situation in El Salvador remains volatile. In October 1993 the UN reported that the death squads had started up again, and several prominent FLMN people were murdered. Victims included Francisco Velis, member of the FMLN National Council, who was shot on 25 October while taking his one-year-old daughter to a creche, and Justa Victoria Orellana Cortéz, a former FMLN combatant, shot at close range two days later while she was breast-feeding her child.

On 8 November 1993 UN observers arrived in the country to investigate the recent killings; within hours two more bodies were discovered which bore all the hallmarks of death-squad killings.

Political killings and threats continued right up to the March 1994 election. In those elections the Arena party failed to achieve an overall majority in the National Assembly, but was expected to finalise an alliance that would help it to retain power. Calderón Sol, the Arena presidential candidate, also narrowly failed to gain the outright majority which was necessary to win on the first vote. A new round of voting took place in April, after which he was elected.

The elections were not conducted without problems: there were allegations of technical fraud, and according to one report, 40,000 dead people voted!

GEOGRAPHY

El Salvador is the smallest country in Central America, with a total area of 20,752 sq km. It is bordered by Guatemala to the west, Honduras to the north and east, and the Pacific Ocean to the south. The coastline is about 320 km long.

In most of the country you are always within sight of a volcano. The largest ones are the San Salvador, San Vicente, Santa Ana, and San Miguel – each with a city or town of the same name at its foot – but there are plenty of others.

The volcanic soil of El Salvador is incredibly fertile, especially on the slopes of the volcanoes themselves. Though it seems that the foot of a large volcano would be a very precarious place to establish a city, these were the places that supported the most abundant agriculture, and thus, in time, the major population centres grew there.

GOVERNMENT

El Salvador's government has three divisions. Executive power is held by a president, elected by popular vote to a five-year term. Legislative power is vested in a National Assembly, with 60 members elected to a three-year term. The 13-member Supreme Court is elected by the National Assembly. The country is divided into 14 departments.

Calderón Sol, of the right-wing National Republican Alliance (Arena) party, was elected president in 1994 for a four-year term. The other main parties are the Frente Farabundo Martí Liberación Nacional (FMLN), the Christian Democratic Party (PDC), the Convergencia Democratia, and the National Conciliation Party.

ECONOMY

Agriculture accounts for about 25% of the GNP and 75% of exports, and employs about 40% of the labour force. The main crops are coffee, cotton, maize and sugar cane. Other important primary industries are cattle raising, commercial fishing, and balsam for medicine and perfume-making: El Salvador was once the world's primary source of balsam. Manufacturing is the second-largest sector of the economy, contributing 15% to the GNP and employing 22% of the workforce.

Coffee is by far the most important crop, even though both coffee and sugar production suffered during the civil war. The Salvadorean Coffee Company, sugar exports and the banking system are being privatised.

El Salvador has traditionally been ruled by the '14 families', who formed a landholding oligarchy. In this century, the 14 have expanded to around 250 families, whose wealth derives not only from land but also business and manufacturing. Export wealth goes into the hands of these few, rather than circulating through the economy. It is estimated that only 2% of the population could be described as upper class, with the relatively new middle class (mostly in the towns) accounting for another 8%. Everyone else is poor. Unemployment is around 50% and those who do work often earn just a couple of dollars – barely enough to survive. Since the war ended the Salvadoran economy has improved, and in 1993 inflation was estimated at 15%.

Despite the evident poverty, El Salvador is not a very poor country overall: income per capita is US$1102 – twice that of Nicaragua. While the majority of the population lives in mud huts, the wealthy families typically have homes in the capital, in the countryside, by the lakes and at the seashore, drive expensive cars and holiday in Miami.

POPULATION & PEOPLE
Government figures in 1992 put the population at 5,047,925, though more recent estimates place the total some 250,000 higher. The people of El Salvador are 90% *mestizo* – a mixture of Spanish and Indian. About 5% are Indians, descendants of the Pipil, and 5% have European ancestry.

El Salvador is not only the smallest, but also the most densely populated country in Central America, with an average of about 265 people per sq km. Most of the land is devoted to agriculture; there is little wilderness land unaffected by people.

ARTS
Poetry is very popular in El Salvador. Many people write poetry and people from whom you would least expect it may surprise you by quoting a poem. They will tell you the poetry movement in El Salvador was first inspired by Rubén Darío, the Nicaraguan poet, but now El Salvador has its own popular movement of poetry and literature.

Most of the music you hear on the radio comes from the USA, Mexico or other parts of Latin America and is standard pop. However, there is a small underground movement of *canción popular* or folk music, telling of the life and current events among the people of El Salvador. Music festivals include folk singers with guitars, flutes and percussive instruments, singing about everything that is going on in El Salvador today, as well as traditional Salvadoran folk music. Groups playing music of the Andes are also popular at festivals and outdoor occasions, where popular theatre is also presented.

The village of La Palma, in the Chalatenango region of northern El Salvador, has become famous for a school of art started by Fernando Llort. Characterised by images of rural daily life in El Salvador – peasants, farm animals, white adobe buildings with red-tiled roofs, churches, and so on – painted in bright colours with childlike simplicity, this style of art is used on wood, jewellery, textiles, and many other objects. La Palma has many workshops which welcome visitors; Fernando Llort also maintains his own gallery, Arbol de Dios, in San Salvador.

El Salvador produces various traditional handicrafts including textile arts, ceramics, woodwork, masks and basketry. Several villages are famous for their own handicraft specialities, among them Ilobasco for its ceramics and San Sebastián for textile arts.

RELIGION
El Salvador is predominantly Roman Catholic. A number of other churches are also represented, including Baptists, Mormons, Seventh-Day Adventists, Jehovah's Witnesses, and Evangelicals and Pentecostals, as well as Bahais.

LANGUAGE
Spanish is the national language. The indigenous languages have died out in daily use. There is now some academic interest in preserving the old Nahua language of the Pipils, but you won't hear Nahua spoken in the streets, except in a few Indian villages.

Facts for the Visitor

VISAS & EMBASSIES
Visa requirements to enter El Salvador are gradually easing, so check with a Salvadoran embassy or consulate to find out whether you need one. If you do need one it must be obtained before you arrive. At the time of writing, citizens of the USA, Canada, Australia and New Zealand needed a visa; citizens of the UK and most of Western Europe did not. The visa stamp is good for a single entry to the country within 90 days of issue. Visas can be free (e.g. for US citizens) or cost up to US$30 depending upon your nationality and in which country you acquire the visa. No vaccinations are required unless you are coming from an area infected by yellow fever.

The immigration official at the point of entry has the authority to decides whether to admit you or not (even if you have a valid visa). The same official has the power to decide how much time you will get in El Salvador. You can get a maximum of 30 days with a visa, or 90 days if you don't need a visa, but in either case the official may decide to give you less.

Visas can be extended twice, for a total stay of three months. After that, if you want to stay longer you must apply for a temporary resident's permit. Visas can be extended in San Salvador at the Office of Immigration (☎ 212111) on the 2nd floor of the federal building in the Centro Gobierno. The office is open Monday to Friday from 8 am to noon and 1.30 to 4 pm.

El Salvadoran Embassies
If your nationality requires a visa, you must obtain it from a Salvadoran embassy or consulate before you arrive. In the USA, El Salvador has consulates in Houston, Los Angeles, Miami, New Orleans, New York and San Francisco, in addition to its embassy in Washington DC.

Other Salvadoran embassies include:

Belize
    11 Handyside St, Belize City (☎ 02-78158)
Canada
    209 Kent St, Ottawa, Ontario K2P 1Z8
    (☎ 613-238-2939)
Colombia
    Carrera 9, No 8015, Oficina 503, Bogotá
    (☎ 212-5932, 211-0012)
Costa Rica
    Avenida 10, Calle 33 & 35, Los Yoses, San José
    (☎ 224-9034)
Guatemala
    12 Calle 5-43, Zona 9, Guatemala City
    (☎ 325848, 326421)
Honduras
    2a Avenida Norte, No 205, Colonia San Carlos,
    1 block from Blvd Morazán, Tegucigalpa
    (☎ 325045, 321344)
Mexico
    Avenida las Palmas, No 1903, Lomas de
    Chapultepec, Mexico DF 11000 (☎ 596-7366)
New Zealand
    24 Seccombes Rd, Epsom, Auckland 3
    (☎ 549376)
Nicaragua
    Pasaje Los Cerros, Avenida del Campo, No 142,
    Las Colinas (☎ 74892)
Panama
    Via España, Edificio Citibank, 4th floor, Panama
    City (☎ 233020)
UK
    5 Great James St, London WC1N 3DA
    (☎ 071-430-2141)
USA
    2308 California NW, Washington DC 20008
    (☎ 202-265-9671)

Foreign Embassies in El Salvador
There are a great many embassies and consulates in San Salvador. The tourist office keeps a current listing, with many more than are mentioned here. Some of the most often used ones are:

Belize
    Condominio Médico B, Local 5, 2nd floor,
    Tutunichapa, Urbanización La Esperanza
    (☎ 263588)
Colombia
    Calle El Mirador, No 5120, Colonia Escalón
    (☎ 793290/04)
Costa Rica
    3107 Alameda Roosevelt, Centroamericana
    Building, 3rd floor (☎ 790303)
Guatemala
    15a Avenida Norte, No 135, at Calle Arce
    (consulate ☎ 222903; embassy ☎ 712225)

Honduras
67a Avenida Sur, No 530, Colonia Flor Blanca
(☎ 712139, 212234)
Mexico
Pasaje 12 and Avenida Circunvalación, Colonia
San Benito (☎ 981079, 781084)
Nicaragua
71a Avenida Norte and 1a Calle Poniente, No 164
(☎ 237729, 240970)
Panama
Alameda Roosevelt and 55a Avenida Norte, No
2838 (☎ 980884)
UK
4828 Paseo General Escalón (☎ 981763)
USA
Boulevard Santa Elena, Antiguo Cuscatlán
(☎ 784444)

CUSTOMS
Given the broad discretionary powers of the immigration official who admits you into the country, it is best to present yourself as a clean, financially solvent, conservative, respectable tourist. Most visitors are shooed through with no problem. As in most Central American countries, you can expect less investigation at the airport than if you arrive overland, since people arriving by plane are presumed to have money.

Importation of fruit, vegetables, plant and animal products is restricted, and questionable articles may be confiscated or fumigated. You can bring in three cartons of cigarettes or one kg of tobacco, and two bottles of liquor.

MONEY
El Salvador's currency is the colón; the symbol is a cent sign (¢) in front of the number. There are 100 centavos in a colón. Coins are of one, three, five, 10, 25 and 50 centavos value. Notes are in denominations of ¢5, ¢10, ¢25, ¢50 and ¢100.

Foreign		El Salvador
A$1	=	¢6.25
C$1	=	¢6.40
DM1	=	¢5.20
NZ$1	=	¢5.05
UK£	=	¢13.20
US$1	=	¢8.75

VAT (IVA) of 10% should apply on all goods and services in El Salvador; make sure you know whether this is already included in prices, or to be added on later. At the lower end of the market the tax is invariably included; either that, or they simply don't bother to collect or charge it.

When leaving El Salvador, change your extra colones before you go. They can be changed at the borders or at the airport, up to a maximum of US$40. Once you are into neighbouring countries you may have to resort to the black market to change Salvadoran currency.

CLIMATE
El Salvador's principal seasons are the wet season (invierno or winter, May to October) and the dry season (verano or summer, November to April). During the wet season, there is usually a rain (often a downpour) every evening, just after sundown. Normally it's an hour's refreshing rain, but sometimes it goes on all night. The rest of the year is quite dry and dusty.

The temperature doesn't vary much throughout the year: in San Salvador, maximum temperature varies from 30°C in November to 34°C in March and April; minimum night-time temperatures are between 16°C and 19°C all year round. The coastal lowlands are much hotter than the rest of the country. San Salvador, at a medium elevation (680 metres above sea level), has a comparatively moderate climate.

TOURIST OFFICES
The main office of the Instituto Salvadoreño de Turismo (ISTU) (☎ 228000, 223241) is in the centre of San Salvador at 619 Calle Rubén Darío, between 9a and 11a Avenida Sur. It is open Monday to Friday from 8 am to 4 p and Saturday from 8 am to noon.

There's another branch of ISTU at the international airport (☎ 399454), open every day from 8 am to 5.30 pm.

There are also ISTU offices at the borders at El Amatillo (in the east, on the Honduran border) and Las Chinamas (in the west, on

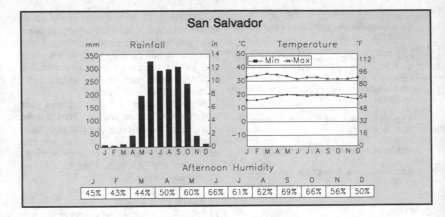

the Guatemalan border). They are open the same hours as the border stations (see Getting There & Away).

BUSINESS HOURS & HOLIDAYS

Normal business hours are Monday to Friday from 8 am to noon and from 2 pm until 4 or 5 pm. Banks are open Monday to Friday from 9 am to 4 pm. Shopping hours are longer, usually from 8 am to 6 pm, and Saturday mornings until noon.

The festival day of El Salvador del Mundo, patron of El Salvador, is 6 August. Celebrations, including a fair and a big parade, are held in San Salvador on this day and during the week preceding it. Other celebrations are held during Semana Santa (Holy Week) and on 12 December, the day of the Virgen de Guadalupe. Each city, village and town has a festival for its patron saint sometime during the year.

Public holidays are:

1 January
   New Year's Day
March-April
   Holy Thursday, Good Friday, Easter Saturday and *Sunday (Semana Santa)*
1 May
   Labour Day
3 to 6 August
   Festival of El Salvador del Mundo

15 September
   Independence Day (1821)
12 October
   Columbus Day
2 November
   All Souls' Day
5 November
   Anniversary of First Call for Independence (1811)
25 to 31 December
   Christmas

POST & TELECOMMUNICATIONS
Post

There are three rates for sending mail: surface, air mail, and express mail. Rates and transit time for mail sent from El Salvador are:

To the USA

air mail	US$.25	8 days
express mail	US$0.55 extra	5 days

To Europe or Australia

air mail	US$0.35	12 days
express mail	US$0.55 extra	10 days

Poste restante mail should be addressed to Lista de Correos. Be sure to conclude the address with 'República de El Salvador, Central America', to prevent it being sent to any other El Salvador in any other part of the world.

Telecommunications
Telephone boxes are found in many public places, including petrol stations and parks. Local calls require a 10-centavo coin for three minutes. Put in more coins if you want to talk longer, or you'll get cut off.

Long-distance phone calls, telegraphs, telex and fax can be sent from Antel offices. Every city, town and village has an Antel office. National phone calls are inexpensive. The country code when calling El Salvador from abroad is 503.

TIME
El Salvador is six hours behind Greenwich Mean Time.

WEIGHTS & MEASURES
The metric system is used in El Salvador. Some US measures are also used, including gallons for fuel, and you may hear occasional use of the *libra* (a pound weight, 0.48 kg) in addition to the kg. There is also a variety of purely local measurements but if you ask, someone can always translate them into their metric equivalents.

BOOKS & MAPS
Books
Various books shed light on happenings in El Salvador. *El Salvador: The Face of Revolution* by Robert Armstrong & Janet Shenk (2nd edition, South End Press, Boston, 1982) is a very readable history of the country, focusing on the roots, reasons and development of the current conflict. It also comments on Honduras, Nicaragua, Guatemala, and the role of the USA in the region.

Witness to War: An American Doctor in El Salvador by Charles Clements MD (Bantam Books, Toronto, 1984), the personal story of a Quaker American doctor who worked in the war zone of Chalatenango in 1982-83, has become a classic; a film was made from the book.

Other books about the war in El Salvador include:

El Salvador: The Other War by Tom Barry & Deb Preusch (Resource Center, 1986, paperback).

El Salvador in Crisis by Philip L Russell (Colorado River Press, 1984, paperback).

El Salvador at War: An Oral History edited by Max G Manwarring & Court Prisk (National Defense University Press, 1988, paperback).

El Salvador Notes 1989 (NARMIC/American Friends Service Committee, 1989, paperback).

The American Connection, Volume 1: State Terror and Popular Resistance in El Salvador (Zed Books, London, 1985, paperback).

Rebel Radio by José Ignacio López Vigil (Latin America Bureau, 1994, paperback), the story of the FLMN's Radio Venceremos and its broadcasts during the war.

There are good sections on El Salvador in several of the books on Central America mentioned in the Facts for the Visitor chapter. Patrick Marnham's impressions of San Salvador in *So Far From God* (Penguin Books, New York, 1985) are especially memorable.

Manlio Argueta, novelist and poet, is one of El Salvador's finest writers. His novel *One Day of Life* (Vintage Books, Random House, New York, 1983), a translation of *Un Dia en la Vida*, is a down-to-earth portrayal of peasant life in El Salvador. The book was banned in El Salvador (though it is now available there, in Spanish) and the author exiled. His novel *Cuscatlán* has also been translated into English.

Life For Those Who Come After by Francisco Rodriguez is available in Central America in English or Spanish. It is a simple but moving account by a Salvadoran refugee who saw five members of his family murdered by the military (three hacked to death by machete). He was nine at the time.

Poetry is an important social artform in El Salvador. Roque Dalton is a revolutionary poet whose many works include *Poemas Clandestinas* ('Clandestine Poems').

Salvador Salazar Arrué, writing under the pen name of Salarué, is one of El Salvador's famous older writers. His *Cuentos de Barro*

('Tales of Mud'), published in 1934, is said to mark the beginning of the modern Central American short story genre.

Maps

Free mimeographed maps of El Salvador and San Salvador are available from the tourist offices. Some Esso petrol stations sell an excellent map. Good maps are also available from Budget Rent-A-Car, which has offices in San Salvador and at the airport. Some Texaco petrol stations also sell maps but these have very small, almost unreadable print.

See the San Salvador section for more details on where to obtain maps in the city.

MEDIA
Newspapers & Magazines

San Salvador has five daily newspapers. *La Prensa*, *El Diario de Hoy* and *La Noticia* all appear in the morning; *El Mundo* and *Diario Latino* are afternoon papers. All are privately owned. *Diario Latino* is the only one with a leftist slant.

La Prensa and *Diario de Hoy* are possibly best for day-to-day news events; check the Saturday paper for cinema and entertainment listings. It's sold in Café Teatro, La Luna, Centro Cultural and other places.

The capital also has the *News Gazette* a weekly bilingual paper (English and Spanish) with a useful 'Stepping Out' guide to places and events.

Radio & TV

There are six TV stations and about 60 radio stations. Radio Venceremos (FM 100.5 MHz) was the voice of the FMLN during the war and still has an FMLN slant.

FILM & PHOTOGRAPHY

Film and photographic supplies are readily available, especially in San Salvador where there are several film and camera shops. They may be harder to come by outside the capital.

HEALTH

Foreigners must pay for all medical treat-

ment. It's best to assume that tap water in El Salvador is unsafe to drink; US$100 million has been pumped into the River Lempa Project to ensure a clean supply of drinking water, but this aim hadn't been achieved by the end of 1993.

DANGERS & ANNOYANCES

The ubiquity of firearms during the war has left its legacy; youths with guns are a growing problem on the streets of many towns and cities. During daylight you should be safe enough, but take care after dark. Try to seek local advice about when and where it's safe to walk around, and take a taxi if in doubt.

Take normal precautions against theft: bag-slashing, bag-snatching, jewellery-snatching and all the other forms of thievery are common, especially in the capital.

Some women have reported problems on crowded buses, with importunate males pressing against them.

HIGHLIGHTS
Volcanoes

The San Salvador volcano towering over the capital, affectionately called Boquerón, makes a good day trip from the city, with fine views and good walks around the top and right down into the crater.

Izalco, the 'lighthouse of the Pacific', is another notable volcano. You can hike to it from the nearby Parque Nacional Cerro Verde, a reserve on an even higher volcano nearby; there's an excellent view of Lago de Coatepeque below. El Salvador has plenty of other giant volcanoes, which you'll see as large cones on the landscape.

Montecristo Cloud Forest (El Trifinio)

Montecristo, also called El Trifinio, is one of Central America's largest and most magnificent cloud forests.

The summit of the 2418-metre Montecristo marks the point where the borders of El Salvador, Guatemala and Honduras converge, and this nature reserve is cooperatively protected by all three countries. It contains a variety of microclimates and habitats, and possibly the greatest diversity of wildlife in all Central America.

The forest is quite remote and a bit of a challenge to reach; this is one reason the animals, many of them rare species, have survived there. The reserve can be visited only from October to March, outside the animals' breeding season.

Maya Ruins & National Museum

El Salvador's Maya ruins do not quite compare to some of the more famous ones in Guatemala and Honduras. There are some significant ruins, however, especially the step pyramids at Tuxmal and La Campana de San Andrés, which are both in the western part of the country. Joya de Ceren is a recently discovered site.

The Museo Nacional Davíd J Guzmán, El Salvador's national museum in San Salvador, contains several of the most notable and unusual finds from the ruins.

Turicentros

El Salvador has 14 Turicentros spread across the country. These are recreational and camping parks set up at beaches, lakes or spring-fed natural pools, with basic facilities and low entrance fees – ideal for budget travellers. Los Chorros, half an hour west of the capital, is many people's favourite.

Cultural Events

You can spend some very pleasant times in El Salvador participating in the cultural events of the people. As everywhere in Central America, each town in El Salvador has its annual festival days, and some are celebrated with costumes, masks, processions, music and dancing in the streets. The anniversary dates of the communities repopulated since the war are also marked by a festival.

In the capital, the lush, turn-of-the-century Teatro Nacionál hosts many types of presentations, and there are several other good centres for the arts. Sometimes wandering outdoor musicians play at Parque Balboa, outside the capital, on Sundays, and there are other music festivals there.

There's an annual pilgrimage to the Virgen de Fátima grotto near Cojutepeque around 13 May every year, but the grotto is a quietly impressive place to visit any time, attracting visitors and pilgrims all year round.

Politics

Internationalists, volunteers and many people of a political bent are attracted to El Salvador by its much publicised troubles. Dozens of political and cultural groups flourish in San Salvador; they can provide information on particular aspects of the country, and may even help you organise trips to the repopulated communities. Groups to contact in the following fields are: repopulation – CCR (☎ 745604); development – ASDI (☎ 712465); women's rights – DIGNAS (☎ 986002); human rights – PDH (☎ 221604); environment – CESTA (☎ 256746); Christian base communities – CEBES (☎ 260888).

Handcrafts

A number of distinctive *artesanías* are produced in El Salvador, including textile arts, ceramics and woodwork. A distinctive art style has made the northern village of La Palma famous. You can see and buy Salvadoran handmade arts in the capital at the Mercado Ex-Cuartel or the Mercado Nacional de Artesanías, or visit the villages where they are made, and buy direct from the craftspeople. Several villages have specialized in one or other handicraft for over a century.

ACCOMMODATION

In general, accommodation is reasonable value, but the best deal of all for visitors is at government workers' centres (*obreros*), where tourists can stay free of charge. These are at Lago de Coatepeque, El Tamarindo, and just outside La Libertad. You can stay as long as you like (within reason), subject to availability. Bring your own bedding. The only drawback is you have to get written permission in advance, but this is only a formality. Apply in person at the Ministerio de Trabajo, behind the Productos de Café

EL SALVADOR

(coffee factory) in San Bartolo, east San Salvador. Take bus No 29 from the city centre.

FOOD

The ubiquitous *pupusa* is a small, thick, corn tortilla with a filling of sausage, cheese or beans. Pupusas cost about US$0.25 each; a few pupusas and a cold drink make an excellent meal. Small *pupuserías* are everywhere in El Salvador. Otherwise there's the typical beans, rice, salad etc.

DRINKS

The most common cold drinks are *frescos* (mixtures of fruit juice, water and sugar) and *gaseosas* (sodas).

With all the coffee grown in El Salvador, you might think the average cup of coffee would be rich and delicious. Not so. A cup of coffee in El Salvador is usually weak and not very flavourful, whether it is boiled grounds or instant. In fact, people often drink coffee that is not even pure, but diluted with barley or something similar.

On the alcoholic side, beer and spirits are made in El Salvador and are heartily consumed by the populace. Beer is especially popular: most widely drunk is Pilsener, followed by Suprema, made by the same Salvadoran brewery but slightly more expensive.

Much stronger are Tic-Tack ('el licor nacional de los Salvadoreños') and Torito, a similar brew. They look like vodka and have an even higher alcohol content: genuine firewater made from Salvadoran sugar cane.

THINGS TO BUY

El Salvador produces some distinctive handicrafts. You can go to the villages and see how they are made, but just about everything of interest is also sold in the capital.

Sorpresas (surprises) are tiny ceramic figures hidden in egg-shaped shells about the size of walnuts; when you pick up the top of a sorpresa you'll find a finely detailed scene inside. There are also nativity scenes inside tiny churches. These and other ceramics are made in the village of Ilobasco (see Around San Salvador).

Woven textiles are made in San Sebastián (see also Around San Salvador). Many kinds of hammock, from cheap utilitarian ones to art quality, and many other woven and textile objects are made there. Colourful embroidered clothing and pillowcases, decorated with human and animal figures, are attractive.

The village of La Palma, north of San Salvador in the Chalatenango province, produces brightly painted wooden artwork that has become famous throughout El Salvador. Painting is also done on seeds, with a fineness of detail similar to the sorpresas. These are worn as pendants.

Nahuizalco, a few km to the north of the town of Sonsonate, is a Pipil Indian village specialising in traditional basketry.

Getting There & Away

AIR

El Salvador is a hub of air travel in Central America. It is served by a number of airlines including American, Copa, Continental, Eastern, Emerald, Lacsa, Taca, and Tan/Sahsa. Taca is the national airline.

Flights go to and from all the major points in Central America (Belize City, Guatemala City, Tegucigalpa, San Pedro Sula, Managua, San José, Panama City) and North America (New York, Miami, Houston, Dallas, San Francisco, Los Angeles, Mexico City).

Some airlines use El Salvador as a connecting airport, so you may be able to make free stopovers in El Salvador on your way to and from other destinations. Most of Taca's flights to and from points within Central and North America are routed through El Salvador but it no longer permits free stopovers.

LAND

Bus

To/From Guatemala International buses operate between Guatemala City and San

Salvador. It is a trip of about five hours, with a brief stop at the border. Puerto Bus (☎ 222158) has a new bus terminal in San Salvador, on Alameda Juan Pablo II at 19a Avenida Norte, with frequent departures from 3.30 am (6.30 am on Sunday) until 4 pm, and the fare is US$5.15. Also in San Salvador, Tica Bus (☎ 224808) has an office in the Hotel San Carlos, Calle Concepción, with departures daily at 6 am; the cost is US$8. Services to Guatemala City can also be picked up in Santa Ana.

National buses bound for the Guatemalan border leave from San Salvador's Terminal de Occidente. At the border you can transfer to a Guatemalan bus. Coming into El Salvador from Guatemala, it is about half an hour by bus from the Las Chinamas border post to Ahuachapán, and 1½ to two hours to Santa Ana.

To/From Honduras International buses from San Salvador to Tegucigalpa take about nine hours. The Puerto Bus service departs at 6 am and 1 pm and costs US$12.60, and Tica Bus leaves at 5 am and costs US$15. The Tica bus then continues to Managua (US$35), on to San José (US$50) after an overnight stop, and finally to Panama (US$75; the second night is spent on the bus).

A cheaper option to Honduras is to take an ordinary bus to the border. Departing from San Salvador's Terminal de Oriente, bus No 119 takes about four hours to reach the northern El Poy border crossing (US$0.90). You can then walk across the border, pick up a colectivo to Nueva Ocotepeque, and continue by bus from there. The eastern border crossing is at El Amatillo, where, after crossing the border, you can transfer directly onto a bus to Tegucigalpa or Choluteca. Buses to El Amatillo arrive and depart from San Salvador at the Terminal de Oriente; they leave San Salvador five times a day, with the last bus at 12.30 pm. The ride to El Amatillo is five hours from San Salvador, two hours from San Miguel or La Unión, or about half an hour from Santa Rosa de Lima.

Driving
If you drive into El Salvador you must show a driving licence (an International Driving Permit is accepted) and proof that you own the car. There are extensive forms to fill out. Car insurance is available and advisable but not required. Vehicles may remain in El Salvador for 30 days, with extensions possible for a further 60 days.

Border Crossings
The tourist office (ISTU) has an office at the principal crossing with Guatemala, Las Chinamas. Other Guatemalan crossings are at Hachadura, San Cristóbal and Anguiatú. The main border crossings to Honduras are at El Amatillo, where ISTU has an office, and at El Poy. The crossing at Sabanetas, north of Perquín, should become fully operational in 1994 but there are currently no buses running up there.

At any border crossing you should avoid arriving late in the afternoon if you're using public transport, as services can end early. The last bus south from El Poy, for example, leaves at around 3 pm. The official opening times from El Salvadoran border posts are from 8 am to about 5 pm daily. However, if you have your own transport you should be able to pass through later, as the guards live at the post (though they will charge a fee).

SEA
Boats on the Golfo de Fonseca between El Salvador, Honduras and Nicaragua were discontinued while the countries were squabbling about their respective rights there. The International Court of Justice settled the matter in 1992, so boat travel should now be more viable in the gulf. Don't expect to find scheduled services; instead, ask around the ports to get a ride.

LEAVING EL SALVADOR
There's a US$17 departure tax at the airport if you're flying out. Going overland, you have to pay US$0.60 to the border guards to enter or leave the country. Sometimes, such as when departing at El Amatillo, you may find yourself having to pay this twice.

EL SALVADOR

Getting Around

Street names are usually clearly displayed in towns. If you can't see a sign, look at the kerb at the corner of the road junction – the name is sometimes painted there.

AIR

Transportes Aéreos de El Salvador (TAES) (☎ 270314, 272046) has daily flights from the Ilopango airport, 13 km east of San Salvador, to San Miguel, Santa Rosa de Lima, San Francisco Gotera, La Unión and Usulután. Charter flights can also be arranged. The TAES office in San Salvador is in the Edificio Plaza, at 5a Avenida Norte and 19a Calle Poniente. TAES also provides transport to the airport.

BUS

El Salvador has an excellent bus system. Buses are often crowded but they do run very frequently. Between major towns (San Salvador to Santa Ana, for example, or Santa Ana to Sonsonate) they may depart every five or 10 minutes; many long-distance buses depart every half-hour. They are also cheap; to ride from San Salvador to Santa Ana, a 1½ to two-hour ride, costs about US$0.50.

The last bus of the day will usually depart in time to reach its destination at or soon after dark. A couple of buses run later – the one between Santa Tecla and San Salvador, for example, runs until 9 pm – but it's a very good idea to be sure you know the departure time of the last bus when making any travel plans.

TRAIN

There are railway lines but no conventional passenger trains in El Salvador.

TAXI

Most towns in El Salvador have taxis, all of them painted a bright yellow. You will see them cruising around everywhere in San Salvador and most other large towns, or you can

phone for them. A typical fare in any town would be about US$1.25, but negotiate the fare before you get into the cab.

CAR & MOTORBIKE
Road Safety

Driving in El Salvador presents no special problems. Car insurance is, of course, a good idea but it is not required. Motorbike helmets are also not required but likewise recommended. Roads are usually maintained, at least reasonably. In the capital city traffic moves very fast and erratically. People run red lights whenever they think they can get away with it and make liberal use of the horn.

Car Rental

There are a number of car rental agencies in San Salvador. Avis, Budget and Hertz have offices at the international airport as well as in town, but their prices are high (Hertz US$50 per day, Avis US$58 per day, Budget US$53 per day for unlimited km).

Cheaper companies include Sure Rent (☎ 251810) on Boulevard de los Héroes at 23a Calle Poniente, with cars at US$23 per day for one to three days, US$20.60 per day for four to six days, or US$18.30 per day (US$128 per week) if you keep the car from seven to 15 days. Superior (☎ 229111, 210453), on the corner of 3a Calle Poniente and 15a Avenida Norte, has similar rates.

Other local car rental companies in San Salvador include IMOSA (☎ 246082), at the intersection of 49 Avenida Norte and Alameda Juan Pablo II; Renta Autos (☎ 237397), at 73a Avenida Norte, No 330, Colonia Escalón; and Dollar Rent (☎ 233108) at Calle Arce, No 2226, by 3a Avenida Norte.

Be sure to check carefully for differences in unlimited km vs per km rates. It pays to shop around. Always ask about your liability in the event of an accident or breakdown; some prices (eg Budget) include insurance, others (eg Hertz) don't.

HITCHING

Use discretion when hitching in El Salvador. It is not the local custom so much as in other

Central American countries and can be unsafe on the main highways. Hitching to get between the repopulated communities is safer and quite easy.

San Salvador

Population 422,570

The capital city of El Salvador, San Salvador, lies in the Valle de las Hamacas ('valley of the hammocks'), at the foot of the large San Salvador volcano, which was called Quetzaltepec ('mountain of quetzal birds') in Nahua. The valley is 680 metres above sea level and forms a pocket which tends to trap air pollution. It's not as hot here as it is on the coast, but when the oily black clouds roaring out from the buses and traffic engulf you and mix with the sweat trickling down every part of your body, the feeling is quite unforgettable.

San Salvador is the largest city in El Salvador and the principal centre for the entire country. It only takes a few hours to get from the capital to anywhere in the country, so it makes a convenient base.

The declining economy during the war set off an internal migration of people from the countryside, and the city expanded with new urban poor. The last couple of years since the war has seen some of these people move back to the countryside. But unemployment is still high in the city – around 50% – and people do whatever they can to get by. Everywhere there are people with something to sell, be it lottery tickets, armloads of T-shirts, pieces of fruit – anything at all. Some districts, such as San Benito and Colonia Escalón, are as luxurious as any of the well-to-do neighbourhoods of industrialised countries, while other areas of the city are large colonies of shacks made of cardboard, tin and mud.

The earthquake of 10 October 1986 caused considerable damage in San Salvador, destroying many buildings in the centre, killing over 1000 people and leaving thousands homeless. The city is mostly back in shape now but reconstruction is still going on; the elegant Palacio Nacional, for example, is still being repaired. The annual fair for the patron saint of San Salvador is on 6 August, with big celebrations in the preceding week.

History

San Salvador was founded in 1525 by the Spanish conqueror Pedro de Alvarado about 30 km to the north-east of where it now stands, near Suchitoto. Three years later it was moved to its present site; it was declared a city in 1546.

San Salvador was the capital of the colonial province of Cuscatlán. It was here, in 1811, that Father José Matías Delgado made the first call for the independence of Central America. From 1834 to 1839 San Salvador was the capital of the United Provinces of Central America. It has been the capital of El Salvador since 1839.

Despite its long history, there are no old buildings to see. The city has been destroyed several times – by earthquakes in 1854 and 1873; by the most recent eruption of the San Salvador volcano in 1917; and yet again by floods in 1934. Further earthquakes, including that in 1986, have caused extensive damage.

Orientation

Once you understand how the streets are numbered in San Salvador's central area, it's very easy to find your way around.

Avenidas (avenues) run north-south; calles (streets) run east-west. The central avenue and central street form the hub of the system, with all the other roads numbered out from them. The central avenue is called Avenida España north of the point where it intersects with the central street, and Avenida Cuscatlán south of it. The street is called Calle Delgado on the east side of the intersection, and Calle Arce on the west side.

Avenidas on the west side of Avenida Cuscatlán/Avenida España, are named by sequential odd numbers (1a, 3a, 5a etc) which increase as they move further out. On

EL SALVADOR

EL SALVADOR

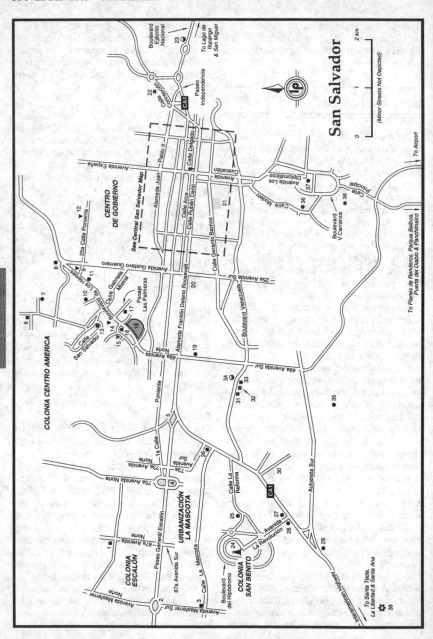

San Salvador

(Minor Streets Not Depicted)

0   1   2 km

To Airport

To Santa Tecla,
La Libertad & Santa Ana

To Planes de Renderos, Parque Balboa,
Puerta del Diablo & Panchimalco

To Lago de
Ilopango
& San Miguel

■ PLACES TO STAY		OTHER		26	El Salvador Travel Service (American Express)
1	Hotel Sheraton	2	Plaza Masferrer	27	Feria Internacional de El Salvador
6	Casa de Huéspedes Clementina	3	El Arbol de Dios Gallery	28	Museo Nacional Davíd J Guzmán
13	Ximena's Guest House	4	Parque Beethoven	29	Ceiba de Guadalupe Shrine
16	Hotel Camino Real	5	Plaza de las Américas	30	Parque Nacional de Béisbol
17	Florida Guest House	6	Café Libre		
22	Hotel Imperial, Hotel Izalco & others	7	Centro Sur	34	Terminal de Occidente bus station
31	Hotel Roma	8	University of El Salvador		
32	Hotel Pasadena	10	La Luna	35	Estadio Cuscutlán (Soccer Stadium)
33	Hotel Occidental	11	Sure Rent (Car Rental)	36	Parque Zoológico (Zoo)
▼ PLACES TO EAT		18	Metrocentro shopping mall	37	Casa Presidencial
		19	Estadio Nacional (National Stadium)	38	Parque Saburo Hirao, Museo de Historia Natural
9	Restaurante Entremeses de Federico	20	Parque Cuscatlán		
12	Felipe's	21	Mercado Central	39	Jardín Botánico La Laguna
14	Pizza Hut	23	Terminal de Oriente bus station		
15	Many restaurants behind Hotel Camino Real	24	Monumento a la Revolución		
		25	Zona Rosa		

the east side they carry even numbers (2a, 4a, 6a etc). Similarly, the calles are numbered in sequence by odds on the north side of Calle Arce/Calle Delgado, and by evens on the south side.

The avenidas are all 'Norte' on the north side of Calle Arce/Calle Delgado, and 'Sur' on the south side of it. Similarly, all the calles are 'Poniente' on the west side of Avenida España/Avenida Cuscatlán, and 'Oriente' on the east side of it.

A few other major roads (Boulevard de los Héroes, Paseo General Escalón) are mentioned in this chapter. An interesting one is Alameda Juan Pablo II (formerly 7a Calle), so renamed because Pope John Paul II walked along it when he visited San Salvador in 1983.

Information

Tourist Office The Instituto Salvadoreño de Turismo (ISTU) (☎ 228000, 223241) is in the centre at 619 Calle Rubén Darío, between 9a and 11a Avenida Sur. It is open Monday to Friday from 8 am to 4 pm, and Saturday from 8 am to noon. It has free maps and plenty of tourist information, including printed literature in English and Spanish, and the helpful staff can answer most questions.

There is also a branch of the tourist office at the airport (☎ 399454/64), open every day from 8 am to 5.30 pm.

Post The central post office is in the Centro Gobierno complex. It's open Monday to Friday from 7.30 am to 5.30 pm, and on Saturday from 8 am to noon. Poste Restante may be addressed to:

Lista de Correos
Correos Centro Gobierno
San Salvador
República de El Salvador
Centro América.

Also at the post office is an EMS international courier office. There are smaller branch post offices in the Mercado Central at Local No 3; on Plaza Morazán, fronting the Teatro Nacional on 2a Avenida Norte, on the 1st floor over the PHL stationery shop; at Metrocentro, on the Boulevard de los

Héroes; and at Centro Comercial Gigante in Colonia Escalón.

Telecommunications Long-distance telephone, telegraph, telex and fax services are available at Antel. The main Antel office is in the centre, on the corner of Calle Rubén Darío and 5a Avenida Sur. The office is open daily from 6 am to 10 pm. This office is very busy.

A smaller branch office of Antel is in the Torre Roble, in the Metrocentro shopping mall on Boulevard de los Héroes, opposite the Hotel Camino Real. It offers the same services and it is a smaller and easier place to get anything done. It is open Monday to Saturday, 7 am to 6 pm, closed Sunday. Antel's large building in the Centro Gobierno complex is a business office only. You have to go to one of the other two to make phone calls.

Local telephone calls can be made from coin boxes; the cost is 10 centavos.

Money Money can be changed at banks and at *casas de cambio*. There are several casas de cambio in the centre, and another in the Torre Roble at Metrocentro on Boulevard de los Héroes. There's one at the airport too but you'll get better rates in town. You can change US dollars and the currencies of Mexico, Honduras, Guatemala, and some other Central American countries. Some travellers have found banks reluctant to change travellers' cheques, but it can be done with a minimum of fuss at Banco Salvadoreño, a block from the tourist office, and at Banco Hipotecario on Plaza Barrios. The latter also gives Visa or MasterCard advances (no commission charge) in either colones or US dollars.

The black-market moneychangers operate outside the post office. Nearby, on the south side of the Parque Infantil, is a cluster of casas de cambio and more money-changers. Black-market money-changers are also sometimes found at the bus terminals, near where the international buses depart; money-changers pay about the same (or less!) as the banks, and some accept travellers' cheques.

American Express El Salvador Travel Service (☎ 230177), Centro Comercial Mascota, Calle La Mascota, is an American Express agent and will hold mail for card and cheque holders.

Immigration Office Visa renewal and other immigration matters are handled at the Immigration Office (☎ 212111) in the federal building at the Centro Gobierno. The office is open Monday to Friday from 8 am to noon and 1.30 to 4 pm.

Foreign Embassies See the Facts for the Visitor section at the start of this chapter for details of foreign embassies in San Salvador.

Bookshops There are a number of bookshops in the area around the Teatro Nacional, especially in 4a Avenida Norte. Others are on Calle Arce. It's rare to see books in English; bring your own reading material, or take the opportunity to practise reading in Spanish. Shaw's, a coffee shop in Metrocentro, has some English-language books and magazines, including the local *News Gazette*.

Maps The tourist office hands out free city and country maps which are small, mimeographed and not particularly clear, although certainly better than nothing. Their separate, more detailed map of the city centre, however, is the best around.

A few Esso petrol stations sell an excellent map that has small print but is very useful; the Texaco maps of the city are practically unreadable.

Budget Rent-A-Car (☎ 231668, 242802) has good city and country maps, but to get one you have to get to their office at 79a Avenida Sur, No 6, near the corner of Calle La Mascota in the Urbanización La Mascota on the west side of the city. If you arrive by air, pick one up from the Budget counter at the airport. Some other car-rental places (like Avis) also have maps.

Dangers & Annoyances As in most other cities in El Salvador, crime is a big and growing problem, especially crime involving the use of firearms. Locals will warn you against carrying a cloth day pack (could be slit by a razor blade) or wearing any sort of jewellery (could be snatched from your body). The central area, in particular, is considered unsafe for walking after around 8 pm. Other more well-to-do districts are safer, but it's still wise to get a taxi if you're out late at night.

Things to See
City Centre Walking Tour Look for the large, tall dome of the **Catedral Metropolitana**. You can use this as a landmark from anywhere in the centre. The cathedral is in the block at the corner of the '0' intersection – Avenida Cuscatlán/ Avenida España, and Calle Arce/Calle Delgado.

The cathedral entrance is on 2a Calle Oriente, facing onto **Plaza Barrios**, the city's large principal plaza. Also on this plaza is the Palacio Nacional, where the government met before the devastation of the 1986 earthquake. Both the palace and the cathedral are still undergoing reconstruction and the buildings are not yet open, but the workmen might let you in to view Romero's tomb in the cathedral crypt.

At the rear of the cathedral and one street over, on the corner of Calle Delgado and 2a Avenida Sur, the **Teatro Nacional** is worth seeing. You can go in any time for a look; check the performance schedule for plays, dance and music concerts etc. The theatre was built in 1917 in an opulent style, with ornate golden boxes and trimmings, lots of lush red velvet and a sensuous ceiling mural. There's a companion ceiling mural in the **Teatro Café**, around the corner at the rear of the building, on 2a Avenida Sur. (See Entertainment for more on the Teatro Café.) The theatre faces onto the small **Plaza Morazán**.

Two blocks east of Plaza Barrios is the equally large **Plaza Libertad**, with a winged statue of Liberty facing an unusual church, **El Rosario**. This is a modern church built on the site of a demolished older one. It holds the grave of Father Delgado, the father of Central American independence, and religious imagery in modern art sculptures.

There are two principal markets in the centre. **Mercado Ex-Cuartel** is the market for artesanías and traditional handicrafts, with the largest selection and cheapest prices in town. Be sure to bargain. It covers one city block, bordered by Calle Delgado and 1a Calle Oriente, 8a and 10a Avenida Sur – three blocks east of the Teatro Nacional on Calle Delgado.

The huge **Mercado Central** is a few blocks south-east, in the area of 10a and 12a Calle Poniente, Calle Gerardo Barrios, and 5a Avenida Sur. Here are food, household goods, clothing, and all the ordinary stuff of everyday life.

West of the Centre One block south of Calle Arce is the parallel Calle Rubén Darío, the street with the tourist office between 9a and 11a Avenida Sur. Heading west, Calle Rubén Darío becomes one of San Salvador's main thoroughfares, changing names a couple of times and bringing you to the large and pleasant Parque Cuscatlán. It soon becomes Alameda Franklin Delano Roosevelt; keep on going all the way to 65a Avenida and you come to the **Plaza de las Américas**, with the famous statue, **El Salvador del Mundo**, symbol of the country, with Jesus standing on top of the world. This new statue was erected in 1990 to replace one in the same location.

Continuing west past this plaza the road changes name again to Paseo General Escalón. It passes through the upper-class **Colonia Escalón**, and along it are many restaurants, cinemas and nightclubs – it's one of San Salvador's better nightlife and residential districts.

At 75a Avenida you come to the small **Parque Beethoven**. About 12 long blocks further west, at Avenida Masferrer, is the **Plaza Masferrer**, another good spot for nightlife (see Entertainment). You can take bus No 52 down the entire length of this boulevard, from the centre all the way to Plaza Masferrer.

Once at Plaza Masferrer, you could turn south onto Avenida Masferrer and walk about four long blocks to **El Arbol de Dios**,

EL SALVADOR

the gallery of the famous La Palma artist Fernando Llort. This gallery houses an extensive collection of his work, with excellent sculptures and canvas paintings that are very different from his simpler and better-known wood paintings. The gallery's opening hours are Monday to Saturday from 9 am to 6 or 6.30 pm.

South-West of the Centre If you turn south at Plaza de las Américas and head south-west on the Interamerican Highway (Carretera Panamericana) as if you were leaving the city, you come to some other interesting sights. (Bus No 34 comes this way from the centre; you can catch it at the corner of 4a Calle Poniente and 7a Avenida Sur.)

The first thing you'll come to on your right as you head out of the city is the **Feria Internacional de El Salvador**. The large fairground is home to an international fair in November each even-numbered year; other events are also held here, including the festival of El Salvador's patron saint, El Salvador del Mundo, every August.

All year round, the fairground is the site of the **Mercado Nacional de Artesanías**, or national artisans' market. This is another good place to buy traditional Salvadoran handicrafts (see Things to Buy earlier in this chapter).

You'll see a lot of soldiers in this area; a little north of the fairground is the **Cuartel**, the place where El Salvador's military is trained. Beside it is the **Parque Nacional de Béisbol**, the national baseball stadium.

Opposite the Feria Internacional on Avenida la Revolución, almost at the corner of the Interamerican Highway, is the national museum, the **Museo Nacional Davíd J Guzmán**. This small but interesting museum holds most of El Salvador's notable archaeological finds, including an eerie life-size statue of an ancient priest wearing the inside-out skin of a sacrificial victim. Other noteworthy exhibits include the Great Stella of Tazumal, the Chac-Mool of Casa Blanca (Chalchuapa) and the Solar Disc of Cara Sucia (Ahuachapán). The museum is open every day except Monday, from 9 am to noon and from 2 to 5 pm, admission free.

A little further south-west on the Interamerican Highway is an elegant white shrine, **La Ceiba de Guadalupe**, which attracts many pilgrims.

If you continue up Avenida la Revolución past the museum, you come to the small Plaza Italia, at the entrance to the upper-class Colonia San Benito. The **Zona Rosa**, San Salvador's ritziest and most exclusive restaurant and nightlife district, is on the Boulevard del Hipódromo, which crosses the Plaza Italia. Continuing up Avenida la Revolución from this tiny plaza is the large, modernist **Monumento a la Revolución**.

The **Jardín Botánico La Laguna**, also called Plan de La Laguna, is an attractive botanical garden of nearly three hectares on a site that was once a swamp at the bottom of a volcanic crater. Walkways wind around through a forest of thousands of species of tropical plants from around the world, shady and cool even on a hot day, with a pleasant cafeteria beside a lily-pad pond. The garden is open every day except Monday, 9 am to 6 pm, admission US$0.18. It is near Antiguo Cuscatlán on the outskirts of San Salvador. Take bus No 44 from the centre; the bus driver will let you off at the right spot, from where it's a further one km downhill walk to the garden.

North-West of the Centre From the centre, you can go north on either 29a Avenida Norte or 49a Avenida Norte to reach the **Boulevard de los Héroes**, or take bus No 30 from the centre (you can catch it on Calle Arce, between 11a and 13a Avenida Norte). Along here are restaurants and music in the evening (see Entertainment) and the Hotel Camino Real.

Also on this boulevard, opposite the Hotel Camino Real, is **Metrocentro**, a large, modern shopping mall, with its twin just to the south, **Metrosur**. Prices are higher here than elsewhere but you can find anything you need, including a supermarket, many restaurants (see Places to Eat), a bank and casa de cambio, Antel for long-distance telecommunications, a post office branch, and more.

South of the Centre Heading south from the centre on Avenida Cuscatlán, turn right (west) onto Calle Modelo and in a few blocks you will come to the **Parque Zoológico** – the zoo. It's open Wednesday to Sunday from 9 am to 5 pm, admission US$0.12. This is a fine zoo and a popular place for families on weekends.

About 350 metres south of the zoo (follow the signs) is the **Parque Saburo Hirao**, open Wednesday to Sunday from 9 am to 4 pm. The park contains some children's playgrounds and the **Museo de Historia Natural**, which has some interesting exhibits on coral snakes and other reptiles, butterflies, whales and so on, but is nothing world-class.

Bus No 2 goes to the zoo, leaving from Avenida Cuscatlán between Calle Arce and Calle Rubén Darío.

If you head straight south on Avenida Cuscatlán, without turning off for the zoo, you pass the **Casa Presidencial**, the presidential palace. Continue south on Calle Principal to go to the **Planes de Renderos, Parque Balboa, Puerta del Diablo** and **Panchimalco** (see Around San Salvador).

Check with the tourist office to see if the **Teleférico de San Jacinto** is running again. It was one of San Salvador's primary attractions, with Swiss cable cars climbing high up to a popular amusement park at the upper San Jacinto terminal. It has been closed for years but there are rumours that it may be put back into operation if the money can be raised.

Activities

Sports are popular in El Salvador, with soccer inspiring the wildest enthusiasm of all. Soccer games are held in the Estadio Nacional (on 49a Avenida Sur) and other stadia such as the Estadio Cuscutlán (just off Autopista Sur). Entry is around US$1.70. The tourist office may know current times, or check the newspapers.

The Parque Nacional de Béisbol, the national baseball stadium, is on the Inter-american Highway south-west of the centre, not far from the fairgrounds where the Feria Internacional takes place.

Spanish Courses

The Salvador Miranda Escuela de Español (☎ 221352) is at 5a Calle Oriente, No 819, by 12a Avenida Norte. The school offers 20 hours of tuition per week for US$75 and can arrange food and board with a local family for a further US$50 per week (reductions for volunteers and internationalists). They also organise trips and cultural programmes and can give a revealing insight into the country's political problems.

Places to Stay

There are plenty of good places to stay in San Salvador. Basically they are found in four areas: in the centre; on Calle Concepción near the Terminal de Oriente (eastern) bus station and just a few blocks from the centre; on Boulevard Venezuela near the Terminal de Occidente (western) bus station; and in a couple of more suburban areas a short walk or bus ride from the centre. These last ones tend to be the most pleasant.

In the Centre There are several options if you want to stay smack dab in the bustling centre of the city. Do be aware, though, that it's a very loud, crowded, traffic-congested, dirty area, and that it's considered unsafe to walk here at night.

However, if braving the *centro* is for you, there are several possibilities. One of the best deals in terms of price is *Hotel Internacional Custodio* at 10a Avenida Sur, No 109. It's clean and centrally located, albeit rather large and impersonal. Single/double rooms are US$4/5.75, or with private bath US$6.30/8.

Hotel Nuevo Panamericano (☎ 222959) at 8a Avenida Sur, No 113, is a smaller place, with 18 rather dark rooms arranged around a central courtyard/parking area. Rates are US$6.90/8 for rooms with a private bath behind a wall reaching only halfway to the ceiling. The rooms without a bath cost US$4.60/5.75.

EL SALVADOR

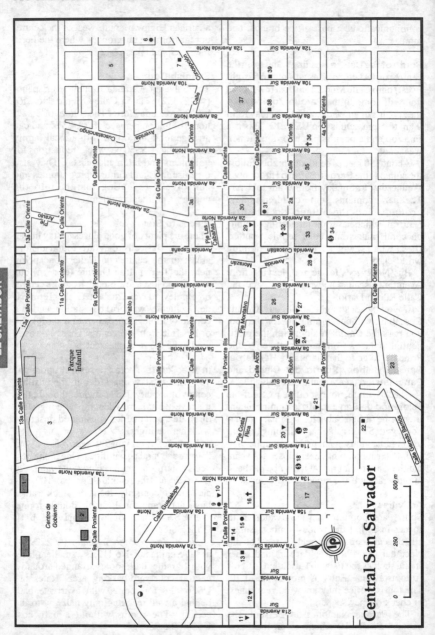

Central San Salvador

Hotel San Carlos (☎ 224808, 228975) at 121 Calle Concepción, between 10a and 12a Avenida Norte, is more comfortable inside than you'd expect from looking at the neighbourhood around it. Being a couple of blocks from the commercial area puts it outside the general street tumult. The 33 rooms are small and clean, all with private bath, and cost US\$6.30/11.50 for singles/doubles.

The *Hotel Centro* (☎ 715045) at 9a Avenida Sur, No 410 is modern and clean, in contrast to the dusty market sprawl nearby. All the rooms have TV, telephone and private bath and cost US\$8.05 from 5 pm to 9 am or US\$13.80 for 24 hours. They also have a rate for two hours – and you can order condoms by room service!

Near the Terminal de Oriente About a 10-minute walk from the Terminal de Oriente (eastern) bus station or the centre is a cluster of cheap hotels on Calle Concepción, near the traffic circle at 24a Avenida Norte. The area is a little seedy so be careful at night.

One of the best of these is the *Hotel Imperial* (☎ 224920, 225159) at 659 Calle Concepción, a large, three-floor hotel with rather ordinary meals served in the central courtyard. Single/double rooms are US\$4/8.05, or US\$5.75/10.30 with private bath. Bus No 4 runs to the town centre.

There are several other simple hotels in this part of Calle Concepción which are cheaper and very good value:

Hospedaje Santa Rosa, No 672 (☎ 229290) – US\$2.30/4.60 for singles/doubles, with private bath US\$2.90/5.75.
Hotel Yucatán, No 673 (☎ 212585) – US\$1.70/3.40, private bath US\$2.50/5.05.
Hospedaje Emperador, No 665 (☎ 227572) – US\$3.65, private bath US\$4.60.
Hotel Cuscatlán, No 675 (☎ 223298) – US\$5.75, all with private bath and TV.
Hospedaje Figueroa, No 653 (☎ 221541) – US\$2.90/4, private bath US\$6.90. Not the friendliest of places.

Near the Terminal de Occidente Near the Terminal de Occidente (western) bus station are a number of tiny, very basic guesthouses, all in the same block as the bus station on Boulevard Venezuela.

Across the road from the bus station and 100 metres to the west (turn right as you exit the station) is the *Hotel Occidental* (☎ 243648) at 3077 Boulevard Venezuela. Rooms cost US\$4, all with shared bath,

EL SALVADOR

■	PLACES TO STAY	12	Restaurante La Zanahoria	15	Guatemalan Embassy
				16	Basilica del Sagrado
7	Hotel San Carlos	20	Hong Kong		Corazón
8	Family Guest Home	21	Restaurante Koradi	17	Parque Bolívar
13	American Guest House	23	Mercado Central	18	Banco Salvadoreño
14	Hotel Fenix	25	McDonald's	19	Tourist Office (ISTU)
22	Hotel Centro	27	Pollo Campero	23	Mercado Central
38	Hotel Nuevo Panamericano	29	McDonald's	24	Antel
39	Hotel Internacional Custodio	37	Mercado Ex-Cuartel	26	Plaza Hula Hula
				28	Palacio Nacional
			OTHER	30	Plaza Morazán
▼	PLACES TO EAT			31	Teatro Nacional
		1	Central Post Office	32	Catedral Metropolitana
10	Actoteatro, Restaurante Entremeses de Federico	2	Office of Immigration	33	Plaza Barrios
		3	Palacio de los Deportes	34	Banco Hipotecario
		4	Puerto Bus Terminal	35	Plaza Libertad
11	Restaurante Arbol de Vida	5	Parque Centenario	36	El Rosario church
		6	Salvador Miranda Escuela Español	37	Mercado Ex-Cuartel
		9	Quinto Sol		

though some have private WC. It's open 24 hours.

About 100 metres farther west is the *Hotel Pasadena* (☎ 236627) at No 3093, another simple place with single/double rooms at US\$4.60/8.60, all with private bath. The rooms are big and the best of the bunch round here. Another few doors west on Boulevard Venezuela is *Hotel Roma* (☎ 240256) with rooms with shared or private bath at US\$4.60/5.75.

Suburban Guesthouses Only about five minutes' walking distance from the centre, but in a residential avenue, the *American Guest House* (☎ 710224) is at 17a Avenida Norte, No 119, between Calle Arce and 1a Calle Poniente. It is clean, pleasant and comfortable, built in the Spanish style. Rooms with private hot bath are US\$14.90/17.25 for singles/doubles, and some larger group rooms are available. They accept American Express, Visa and MasterCard credit cards, and there's a café upstairs.

Around the corner on 1a Calle Poniente is the *Hotel Fenix* (☎ 711269) where rooms with TV and hot-water bath are US\$14.30/17.25, and cheap breakfasts are available.

Nearby is the *Family Guest Home* (☎ 221902, 212349) at 1a Calle Poniente Bis, No 925, a tiny side street half a block north of 1a Calle Poniente between 15a and 17a Avenida Norte. Single/double rooms, again with private hot bath, are US\$13.80/17.25, and there are also several larger rooms sleeping four to 12 people at US\$5.20 each. There are a few rooms without bath for US\$6.30/7.50, and meals can be ordered.

Near the wide Boulevard de los Héroes, with its restaurants and nightlife, are two small, clean and quiet guesthouses. *Ximena's Guest House* (☎ 269268) at 202A Calle San Salvador in the Colonia Centro América charges US\$12.10/16.70 for singles/doubles with private bath. Rooms with shared bath are US\$10.30/14.90.

Nearby, also just a couple of blocks from Boulevard de los Héroes, the *Florida Guest House* (☎ 261858) is small, quiet and clean, with single/double rooms at US\$10.30/17.25, all with private bath. The address is 115 Pasaje Los Almendros, Urbanización La Florida: to find it, walk down Pasaje Las Palmeras from Boulevard de los Héroes for two short blocks and turn right into a tiny cul-de-sac.

This area around the Boulevard de los Héroes is safe for walking at night and it's pleasant to walk out and hear the mariachis in the evening. Bus Nos 29 and 30 run frequently between here and the centre.

About one km farther north is *Casa de Huéspedes Clementina* (☎ 255962), 34 Avenida Morazán (39a Avenida Norte). It's a good place to meet people interested in political issues and has four-bed rooms (they mix-and-match) for US\$6.30 per person, doubles for US\$8.30 per person and singles for US\$11.50. There's a garden area with hammocks, and meals are available.

Places to Eat
See also Entertainment for other suggestions on where to eat.

In the Centre There are cheap places to eat wherever you turn in this city. Pupuserías, where you can sample the typical Salvadoran snack, the pupusa, are everywhere. A few pupusas and a cold drink make a meal. Many simple restaurants serve a set lunch (almuerzo del dia) for as little as US\$1. *Hong Kong*, opposite the tourist office, is one of several inexpensive Chinese restaurants in the centre.

Good, cheap food is sold at the stands in the Mercado Central and at the Mercado Ex-Cuartel. Various fast food chains have branches around the city, including *Pollo Campero*, *Dunkin' Donuts* and *McDonald's*.

The pleasant *Teatro Café* is in the Teatro Nacional building, to the rear around the corner from the main entrance. It's open every day from 9 am to 6.30 pm and serves light meals. There's often a guitarist/singer (see Entertainment).

A few blocks west of the centre on 1a Calle Poniente, No 822, between 13a and 15a

Avenida Norte, the *Restaurante Entremeses de Federico* in the Actoteatro building is a good place for lunch, with an ample buffet and patio dining. It is open only from noon to 2 pm, Monday to Saturday. A meal will cost around US$1.50 to US$2.50.

Boulevard de los Héroes Away from the centre, a few other areas of town are noted for their many restaurants and for nightlife (see Entertainment). Along Boulevard de los Héroes, in the blocks near the Hotel Camino Real, there are many inexpensive restaurants, including several pizzerías. A cluster of popular restaurants is hidden away behind the parking lot of the Hotel Camino Real.

Across the boulevard, Metrocentro has several eating places including a *Pollo Campero*, a *Pizza Hut* and *Mister Donut*. In the Metrosur section of Metrocentro, south of Avenida Los Andes, is a large open-air café. The dining area is surrounded by a variety of takeaway counters where you can get everything from tacos to Chinese food to cream puffs. Most of the restaurants in Metrocentro are air-conditioned.

The *Restaurant Entremeses de Federico* has another branch half a block south of the boulevard, at 25a Calle Poniente, No 1144, behind the Bloom Hospital, with a similar lunchtime buffet to the one in the centre. It's open from 11 am to 2 pm Monday to Saturday.

About ten minutes' walk east of the boulevard is *Felipe's* (☎ 265453), 27a Calle Poniente on the corner of 13a Avenida Norte. It's a very popular place for Mexican food for about US$2.30 to US$4.

Vegetarian You can eat healthily and cheaply at any of several vegetarian restaurants in San Salvador. Most items will cost around US$0.25 to US$0.75.

Right in the centre, on 9a Avenida Sur near the corner of 4a Calle Poniente, *Koradi* is a tiny, basic vegetarian restaurant and health food store, open weekdays from 8 am to 6.30 pm, Saturday 8 am to 3 pm.

About a 10-minute walk from the centre, heading west on Calle Arce, are two other popular vegetarian restaurants. *La Zanahoria*, at 1144 Calle Arce between 19a and 21a Avenida Norte, is a large open-air restaurant and café, open weekdays from 8 am to 7 pm, Saturday 8 am to 2 pm. Around the corner, *Arbol de Vida* is on 21a Avenida Norte near Calle Arce, downstairs in the Condominio Plaza Real; the sign is visible on the street. The restaurant also sells a small variety of whole-grain baked goods, bulk natural foods, vitamins and incense.

Entertainment
Three sections of the city – the Zona Rosa, Colonia Escalón, and Boulevard de los Héroes – are centres for night-time entertainment. All are safe for walking at night.

One place for good entertainment is the *Teatro Nacional*, on the corner of Calle Delgado and 2a Avenida Sur. Check the theatre for its current offerings, which may include music performances, dance, theatre and other performing arts. The theatre itself is a work of art and it's a great place to enjoy any performance.

Teatro Café, around to the side of the Teatro Nacional building, has a singer/guitarist on weekdays from 12.30 to 2 pm and from 4.30 to 6 pm. Sometimes there are other cultural events, such as a musical or literary *peña*, with scheduled readings of poetry, literature and sometimes theatre performances. Teatro Café is very popular with students.

You can visit the Boulevard de los Héroes any night, though most of the action is on Friday and Saturday nights. There are lots of good, inexpensive restaurants but the boulevard is mostly known for its mariachis.

In the block north of the Hotel Camino Real, on the opposite side of the boulevard, mariachis gather every evening from around 8.30 pm. They hang around this particular footpath for a good reason: they are ready to work. Customers drive up here, hear a song or two, and whisk the groups off to parties and celebrations. They play up and down in several restaurants along the boulevard, strolling for customers. You can come across these musicians all over town; another place specially known for them is Plaza El Trovador, south of Boulevard Venezuela on Avenida Cuscutlán.

You can also hear mariachis and *conjuntos* (musical groups) at the Plaza Masferrer. All around the plaza lawn are open-air cafés and pupuserías. The musicians stroll around, the air is warm and the cafés stay open practically all night.

North of Boulevard de los Héroes are several good places fairly close to each other. *La Luna* (☎ 254987), 228 Calle Berlin, is a great venue, creatively decorated and with food menus painted on old LPs (records, not guidebooks!). There's something going on every day of the week, ranging from dance and cinema to live jazz or rock. A similar place is *Centro Sur* (☎ 263968), on the corner of Calle Las Roses and Avenida Central. Also good is *Café Libre* (☎ 255581), Calle Avenida Washington No 50, round the corner from Casa de Huéspedes Clementina. It serves up food, music and various cultural events.

The Zona Rosa is the best-known (and most expensive) place for a night out in San Salvador, with lots of upper-class restaurants and nightclubs. *Mario's* is a popular nightclub, with good entertainment, and there are plenty of others.

Most of the expensive hotels have nightly entertainment. The *Hotel Camino Real* (☎ 793888), for example, on Boulevard de los Héroes, has live bar music every night except Sunday, dining music in its Restaurant Escorial, and a poolside buffet with mariachi music for US$10.30 every Wednesday and Friday evening. The plush *Hotel El Salvador* (☎ 790777) offers various entertainment, such as a dinner and dance on Friday and Saturday.

Colonia Escalón, on Paseo General Escalón around the Parque Beethoven and in the blocks west of it, is another good area for restaurants, cinema, and nightclubs. This is another of San Salvador's ritzier districts.

Not far from the centre is *Quinto Sol*, an inexpensive restaurant and dancing venue with live music two to three times a week. Cover is US$1.15 to US$2.30 and things only get lively after about 10 pm. It's on the corner of 1a Calle Poniente and 15a Avenida Norte.

Things to Buy

Handicrafts can be found at Mercado Ex-Cuartel, in the centre on the block between Calle Delgado and 1a Calle Oriente, between 8a and 10a Avenida Norte. It has dozens of tiny stalls and the lowest prices in the city. Be sure to bargain for a good price.

The Mercado Nacional de Artesanías is in the grounds of the Feria Internacional, on the Interamerican Highway south-west of the centre, at the entrance to the city. Prices are higher here, but they have good quality merchandise. There are other arts and crafts shops around the city but their prices will be higher.

Getting There & Away

Air See the Getting There & Away section and the Getting Around section, early in this chapter, for information on international and domestic flights.

Bus San Salvador has three main terminals for long-distance buses. See the chapter introduction for information on international buses.

Buses serving all points east, including Honduras and the CA-4 highway, arrive and depart from the Terminal de Oriente, on the eastern side of the city, where Alameda Juan Pablo II becomes the Boulevard Ejército Nacional. City bus Nos 7, 29 and 33 stop near the terminal.

Buses serving all points west, including Guatemala, arrive and depart from the Terminal de Occidente, on the corner of Boulevard Venezuela and 49a Avenida Sur. City bus Nos 4, 27 and 34 stop near the terminal.

Bus Terminal San Marcos, in the south of the city, serves destinations towards the Pacific, such as Costa del Sol and Zacatecoluca. Buses also depart there for La Libertad, but it's easier to pick one up in the city centre. To get to San Marcos take either bus A or 11B from Calle Rubén Darío.

Buses going shorter distances may depart from places in town rather than from the long-distance bus terminals: for example, those to La Libertad, Santa Tecla and Los Chorros.

Getting Around
To/From the Airport
The international airport is near the coast, about 44 km from San Salvador at Comalapa. It is about a 45-minute drive on a well-maintained highway.

Taxis Acacya (☎ 714937/8), on the corner of 19a Avenida Norte and 3a Calle Poniente, runs colectivo vans between the airport and the capital. They depart from San Salvador daily at 6 am, 7 am, noon and 3 pm, and from the airport whenever they fill up with passengers. It costs US$2.90 for the one-way trip. A taxi to or from the airport costs about US$10 to US$14.

The old airport at Ilopango, 14 km east of the city, is now used mainly as a military airport and for domestic flights. If you take a domestic flight from the Ilopango airport, a ride to the airport will be arranged when you reserve your flight.

Bus
Most people in San Salvador get around on buses and there's an extensive network of buses running frequently to just about anywhere you'd want to go. You pay US$0.07 on the regular blue buses, or US$0.12 on red *preferencial* buses, which run on the same routes but are better maintained and less crowded.

A fleet of microbus vans running on roughly the same routes also cost US$0.12.

Buses run daily from 5 am to 7.30 pm with a frequent service; on Sunday they run during the same hours, but less frequently (50% service). Between around 7.30 and 8.30 pm the buses become less frequent and finally stop; the microbuses run later, until around 9 pm. After 9 pm you'll have to take a taxi or walk.

Taxi
Taxis are plentiful in San Salvador. A ride in town costs about US$1.15 to US$2.30 (depending on distance) during the day; late at night the rates are higher, about half as much again. Taxis are not metered, so negotiate an acceptable price before you climb in.

If you don't spot a taxi passing by at the moment you want one, which would be unusual, you can always phone for one. Taxis Acacya (☎ 714937/8), Acontaxis (☎ 223361, 223268), Taxis Dos Pinos (☎ 211285/6) and Acosat (☎ 254015, 254140) all have radio taxis.

Around San Salvador

Many places near San Salvador make interesting excursions from the city. With a vehicle, you could combine many in the same day. This could also be done by bus with a bit more planning. La Libertad (see Western El Salvador) is also an easy day-trip from San Salvador.

EAST OF SAN SALVADOR
Lago de Ilopango
About 15 km east of San Salvador, just past the Ilopango airport, the Lago de Ilopango is the largest lake in El Salvador, about 15 km long, eight km wide and 248 metres deep. The lake is in a giant volcanic crater; warm and pleasant, it is a popular spot for swimming, boating and fishing.

A violent volcanic explosion, probably in the 2nd century, covered large parts of central and western El Salvador with layers of white ash. Near the present lake, the ash was up to 50 metres thick. It is thought that after the explosion there was a massive migration of people up into the highlands of Guatemala and Mexico. Later the ground sank and the lake was formed. The most recent eruption, in early 1880, threw up the Cerros Quemados (Burnt Hills) islands in the middle of the lake.

The best place to visit on the lake is at the village of Apulo, where there is a government Turicentro (admission US$0.60) with good swimming, lots of shady trees, picnic tables and restaurants. You can take boat rides at the Turicentro or with the village fishermen – either rowing boats or motor-boats.

There are lots of restaurants in the village. Several are right on the lake, with sundecks projecting over the water. Fresh lake fish and crayfish are the local speciality (despite the fact that the lake is said to be polluted by heavy metals discharged from the enterprise zone on the shore). There are a few simple hotels in Apulo including the *Hotel Colonial* (US$4.60 a night) and the *Hotel Las Malvinas* (US$9.20 a night).

To come from the city, take bus No 15 from 3a Avenida Sur at Plaza Hula Hula.

Cojutepeque

Cojutepeque, 32 km east of San Salvador, is a small town best known for the Cerro de las Pavas (Hill of the Turkeys), a large park on a hill about a one-km walk up from the centre of town, with excellent views of volcanoes and Lago de Ilopango below. The summit has a fenced-off communications complex, but you can ask permission of the guards to enter and see the best panorama (but be careful about where you point your camera).

Within the park is an outdoor shrine to the Virgen de Fátima, who appeared to three shepherd children on 13 May 1917 near Fátima, Portugal. The statue here was brought here from Fátima in 1949. The site was already holy: lights and visions had been seen here. The shrine attracts ordinary visitors and religious pilgrims from near and far, especially on Sundays and during May; 13 May is the Virgin's day.

Bus No 113 comes from the Terminal de Oriente in San Salvador; it's about an hour's ride.

Ilobasco

Ilobasco is one of El Salvador's foremost traditional crafts villages. You can see the famous ceramics of Ilobasco in San Salvador at the Mercado Ex-Cuartel and the Mercado Nacional de Artesanías.

Free tours to see how the ceramics are made are given at the Centro Artesanal de Cerámica Ilobasco Banafi, open Monday to Saturday from 8 am to noon and from 1 to 5 pm, and at the Taller y Escuela de Cerámicas Kiko, open the same hours. Both are on Avenida Carlos Bonilla, the road into town. The Escuela is the first one you get to, on the right just after the road splits, and has the better tour.

The intricate process involves everything from making the clay to the final painting. Best of all are the famous sorpresas: tiny, detailed scenes and figures in little egg-shaped shells about the size of walnuts.

In Nahua, Ilobasco means 'the place of tortillas made from young corn'. The annual fair is held on 29 September.

Ilobasco is 54 km from San Salvador (about 1½ hours) or 22 km from Cojutepeque, on a road branching north from the Interamerican Highway. Take bus No 111 from the Terminal de Oriente in San Salvador, or from Cojutepeque.

San Sebastián

This is another town with an economy based on traditional handicrafts. Textile arts have been the speciality here for well over 100 years. Walking around town you can see hammocks, bedspreads, tablecloths, fabrics, and other woven goods being made on large, handmade wooden looms, and skeins of colourful dyed yarn drying in the sun in front of many houses. You can buy the textiles here direct from the people who make them. The annual fair is held on 20 January, with a festival in the week preceding it.

San Sebastián is 50 km from San Salvador. Bus No 110 departs from the Terminal de Oriente in San Salvador, and there are buses from Cojutepeque.

San Vicente

San Vicente is an attractively situated town, 59 km east of San Salvador. It sits in the Valle Jiboa by the Río Alchuapa at the foot of the tall, twin-peaked San Vicente volcano, also called Chinchontepec. On the approach from San Salvador the town is a lovely sight, with the tall white church spire rising above the town. San Vicente is most noted for its fine colonial church, El Pilar, built in the 1760s.

There is also a pleasant, shady square. The town festival is held on 1 November.

Bus No 116 runs frequently from the Terminal de Oriente in San Salvador.

About two km out of town is Amapulapa, a relaxing Turicentro with large swimming pools, restaurants, lots of trees and a large park area. Entrance is US$0.60. Bus No 171 runs frequently from San Vicente. Also near San Vicente is Lago Apastapeque, a small but beautiful lake.

Zacatecoluca
Fifty-seven km south-east of San Salvador and 19 km south of San Vicente, Zacatecoluca is an average town, but it is the home of Ichanmichen, the largest Turicentro in El Salvador. This is a wooded area of several hectares with many natural springs, pools, fish, flowers, and trails. Look for the Piscina Sihuanaba (pool of the Sihuanaba), beside the statue of the Sihuanaba: a mythical figure in Salvadoran folklore, she is a beautiful woman beside a pool who lures people (especially men) with her beauty, then changes herself into an ugly witch. Other pools are dedicated to other folkloric characters – you could ask the locals to tell you their stories. There are lots of small restaurants around the park. The park doesn't close at night. Admission is US$0.60, and cabañas (beach huts) cost US$3.40.

Bus No 133 runs to Zacatecoluca from the Terminal San Marcos in San Salvador; there are also buses from San Vicente. From the centre of Zacatecoluca you can take the local bus No 92 to Ichanmichen, or walk the one km from town.

WEST OF SAN SALVADOR
Boquerón
The San Salvador (Quetzaltepec) volcano, towering above the city of San Salvador, has two peaks. The higher peak, at 1960 metres, is called Picacho; the other, which has a giant crater, is 1893 metres high and is affectionately known as Boquerón ('big mouth'). You can hike up the volcano for spectacular views over the city and the Valle de las Hamacas, looking towards Puerta del Diablo

on the opposite mountain, and the twin peaks of Volcán Chinchontepec towering over San Vicente. On a clear day you can see all the way out to the coast.

Boquerón is a good place for hiking. You can hike around the rim of the crater, 1½ km across, in two or three hours, or follow a trail down 543 metres into the crater itself. The paths can be steep and narrow in places. The main crater contains a second, smaller crater, 45 metres high and perfectly symmetrical, which was formed by the volcano's most recent eruption in 1917, when an earthquake following the eruption destroyed most of the city.

By bus to Boquerón from San Salvador takes a couple of hours. First, take bus No 101 to Santa Tecla, departing every few minutes from the stop on 1a Calle Poniente at 3a Avenida Norte. From Santa Tecla, bus No 103 departs two-hourly from 6a Avenida Sur, two blocks west of the second (western) plaza; pick-ups depart from the same place. It's an 11-km trip uphill to the village of Boquerón, from where it's a one-km walk up to the crater. Try and get a bus going all the way to the top; some go only go as far as the crossroads, a 30-minute walk below the village. Be sure to check the times of the last buses returning to the city.

Los Chorros
The park at Los Chorros is a shady and relaxing escape from San Salvador. It is within easy reach of the city, but it feels like it's in another world. Cool, clear water springs forth from fern-covered volcanic cliffs and cascades into three large swimming pools at different levels. There is also a separate children's pool. Trails wind upwards around the cliffs overlooking the pools, and there's an abundance of tropical plants, flowers, ferns and brightly coloured butterflies.

At the restaurant a BBQ chicken or beef lunch costs about US$1.80, or you could bring a picnic or eat in the comedores outside. Entrance is US$0.60. Los Chorros is open daily, 7 am to 5 pm. It is most pleasant on weekdays; on weekends and holidays it can get crowded.

Opposite Los Chorros, the *Hotel Monteverde* (☎ 282314) mainly takes groups on religious seminars, but may have a few rooms spare. Rooms are US$6.90 per person, or US$10.30 including three meals.

Los Chorros is 18 km west of San Salvador, right on the Interamerican Highway and beyond Santa Tecla. Bus No 79 leaves frequently from the stop at 11a Avenida Sur and Calle Rubén Darío.

Ruinas de San Andrés

The ruins of San Andrés are also sometimes called the 'Ruinas de la Campana de San Andrés'; the unexcavated pyramids are shaped like bells *(campanas* in Spanish).

The site, 33 km west of San Salvador in the Valle Zapotitan, has been inhabited by Maya, Aztec and Pipil. A step pyramid and large courtyard, with a subterranean section below the courtyard, were unearthed in 1977; there are other, smaller structures, and about 15 mounds yet to be excavated.

Pottery, grinding stones, flint and other artefacts were found at the ruins and are housed in the tiny museum at the site and at the Museo Nacional Davíd J Guzmán. The site is open Tuesday to Sunday, 9 am to noon and 2 to 5 pm, admission free.

The ruins are just a few metres north of the highway, 33 km west of San Salvador. You can take any bus heading west from San Salvador at the Terminal de Occidente, get off at Km 33 just past the Río Sucio where there's a sign for the ruins, turn right (north) and walk the few metres to the ruins.

Joya de Ceren

This Maya farmhouse settlement was buried under five metres of volcanic ash by an eruption of the Laguna Caldera volcano in 600. It was discovered in 1976 during the construction of silos and is still being excavated. So far, 12 buildings have been uncovered of the 17 identified. The compounds are closed off but you can overlook two of them from viewing areas. Volcanic soil still towers over the ancient dwellings and, together with the

adjoining modern silos, gives a real sense that the ancient past is all around us, waiting to be uncovered. A museum on site tells the story of the find and subsequent discoveries, using models, drawings and photos, plus retrieved objects and carbonised remnants.

The tourist office has some notes in English on Joya de Ceren; enquire there about the new admission price and opening times. The site is 36 km west of San Salvador; take bus No 108 from the Terminal de Occidente and get off when you see the silos on your left.

Lago de Coatepeque & Cerro Verde

Lake Coatepeque and Cerro Verde are closer to Santa Ana or Sonsonate than they are to San Salvador (see later in this chapter), but they can be visited as a day trip from the capital, especially if you have a vehicle for the trip.

SOUTH OF SAN SALVADOR
Parque Balboa

This popular 28-hectare park is 12 km from the centre of San Salvador, on a high hill in the Planes de Renderos district. Trails meander among forests and gardens; the many birds and animals include rabbits, sloths and agoutis. The park also has sports fields, some fine pre-Columbian-style stone sculptures, a skating rink, shady picnic areas and a great number of outdoor cafés specialising in pupusas. Admission is US$0.60.

From San Salvador take the No 12 'Mil Cumbres' bus from the east side of the Mercado Central, at 12a Calle Poniente. If you're driving, head out past the zoo on Boulevard V Carranza.

Puerta del Diablo

A couple of km past Parque Balboa, Puerta del Diablo ('the devil's door') is formed by two huge, towering boulders, reputedly once a single stone that split in two, at the summit of Cerro Chulo. Trails that wind up and around the boulders give an excellent view of the region, with its many volcanoes, the city and Panchimalco, the village at the foot of the mountain.

Take the same No 12 'Mil Cumbres' bus that goes to Parque Balboa for Puerta del Diablo.

Panchimalco

This village of Pancho Indians, descendants of the Pipil, is on the far side of the Planes de Renderos from San Salvador; from San Salvador you can look up the hill to Puerta del Diablo, and from there you can look down the other side to Panchimalco.

There's not much to do in Panchimalco apart from look at the attractive white church, stroll in the cobblestone lanes winding around the hilly village, and head back to town. The dearth of visitors to El Salvador in recent years has meant that tourist attractions have been allowed to wind down.

Bus No 17 to Panchimalco departs from 12a Calle Poniente, beside the Mercado Central in San Salvador.

Costa del Sol

Costa del Sol is a beachside resort area with a stretch of broad white sand beach, several km long. It is much hotter than La Libertad (see Western El Salvador), being on the coastal plain, and at 67 km from the city it's somewhat further away.

There are several big luxury resorts along the coast here, but no places to stay for shoestring travellers, unless you want to camp at the Turicentro or along the coast. The Turicentro Costa del Sol, right on the beach, has a swimming pool, sports and picnic areas, and several small restaurants. Entrance is US$0.60, cabañas US$3.40. The beach clubs have better facilities and fewer crowds and cost US$4 for the day.

Bus No 495 goes to Costa del Sol from the Terminal San Marcos. The trip takes 2½ hours each way so you need an early start to make it viable as a day trip. The last bus back to the city leaves at 3 pm.

NORTH OF SAN SALVADOR
Toma de Quetzaltepeque

This is another of El Salvador's Turicentros, with large natural swimming pools, sports

and forest areas, and restaurants. It is 25 km north of San Salvador, on the north-west side of the town of Quetzaltepeque. Entrance costs US$0.60, cabañas are US$3.40. Take bus No 109 from the Terminal de Oriente.

Western El Salvador

LA LIBERTAD
Population 32,075

This small seaside fishing town, 37 km south-west of San Salvador, is the closest beach to the capital and a popular resort on weekends and holidays. The rest of the time it is slow and peaceful, with only the local folk about. The black sand beach curves out to a point on the west side which marks the edge of town. La Libertad is nothing luxurious but it's a relaxing, enjoyable spot.

Activities

Swimming is good, with large, regularly formed waves, though at times there's a very strong current. Take special care in the shallows: as at most of the other beaches on this stretch of the coast, there are rocks and stones under the waterline, which can be hazardous in the powerful waves. Surfing is good in town, and around past the western point. Zunzal, about eight km west, is one of the best surfing beaches in Central America; international surfing competitions are held there during Semana Santa.

Swimming, surfing, lazing around on the sand, walking on the beach and out on the pier, and lounging around one of the many open-air seaside restaurants are the main activities in La Libertad.

Places to Stay

Some hotels in La Libertad charge for 12 hours at a time. So if you just want to spend one night, you check in during the afternoon and out again in the morning. If you're staying the entire 24 hours, the price may be double! Be sure you're clear on what you're paying for at the time you check in. If you don't mind being out of the centre, head for

EL SALVADOR

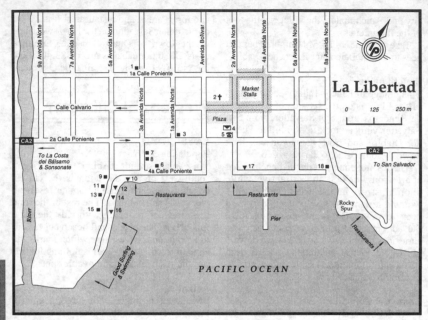

La Libertad

0   125   250 m

PACIFIC OCEAN

Good Surfing & Swimming

River

To La Costa del Bálsamo & Sonsonate

To San Salvador

Rocky Spur

Restaurants

Pier

Restaurants

Restaurants

■ PLACES TO STAY

1   Hospedaje Nuevo Amanecer
3   Hotel Porto Bello
6   Hotel Amor y Paz
7   Comedor Margoth
8   La Posada Familiar
9   Hotel El Retiro Familiar
11   Motel Rick
13   La Posada de Don Lito
15   La Hacienda de Don Rodrigo
18   El Malecón de Don Lito

▼ PLACES TO EAT

7   Comedor Margoth
10   Restaurante Nuevo Alta Mar
12   Restaurante Punta Roca
14   Restaurante Rancho Mar El Delfín
16   Restaurante Vista al Mar
17   Pentagonal Restaurant

     OTHER

2   Church
4   Post Office
5   Antel

the free government workers' centre (see La Costa del Balsamo).

Hospedaje Nuevo Amanecer, 1a Calle Poniente, has solid brick rooms with fan for US$3.40, arranged round a central courtyard. Another cheapie is *Comedor Margoth* on 3a Avenida Norte. It's a little rundown but the rooms have a bed and a hammock, and cost US$3.40 for one person or US$4 for two (24 hours). Next door is *La Posada Familiar* (☎ 353252), where hammocks are slung round a large, grassy courtyard. Negotiate for a good price: if it's not busy you should be able to get a double room for US$6.90 for 24 hours.

Hotel Amor y Paz (☎ 353187), on 4a Calle Poniente, is very basic, but some rooms are directly over the beach. Singles/doubles with camp bed and use of hammock are US$4.60/6.90 (24 hours). It's also probably the friendliest place in town, with a welcoming host and hostess who have sheltered many international travellers and surfers.

Ask them to tell you the story of how the place got its name ('love and peace').

A block behind this and a block back from the sea, on the corner of 2a Calle Poniente and 1a Avenida Norte, the *Hotel Porto Bello* (☎ 353013) is a clean place with 25 rooms. Rates for 24 hours start at US$4.60/6.30. More expensive rooms have an outdoor terrace and private bath. It's on the main road through town and so lacks some of the charm of the places on the beach front. A traveller wrote in to say that this place is unsafe for women (but didn't explain why).

If you have more money to spend, there are several good places right by the sea. *Motel Rick* (☎ 353033), behind the Restaurante Punta Roca, looks like a US -style motel from the outside. The rooms are simple but clean, all with private bath. Cost is US$8.05/11.50 for 24 hours.

Next door are *La Posada de Don Lito* and *La Hacienda de Don Rodrigo* (☎ 353166, 353201). These are fancier seaside hotels, with private bath, more space, swimming pools, and verandas with tables, chairs and big hammocks. Rates are US$13.80 from 6 pm to 9 am, but double that for 24 hours. Air-conditioned rooms are available. *El Malecón de Don Lito* (☎ 352001), on the east side of town, is under the same management and is a comparable deal.

Other places to stay are a few km west of town; see La Costa del Bálsamo, later in this chapter.

Places to Eat

There are dozens of open-air restaurants along the beach in La Libertad, all specialising (naturally) in seafood. Unfortunately they have got used to catering for wealthy visitors from San Salvador and abroad, so the prices are depressingly high. If you have a place to cook, buy some fish out on the pier – they sell it live, fresh, or dried. Here, prices are very cheap: a tuna large enough to feed 12 people costs less than a dollar. Buy fresh fruit and other ingredients for a meal at the outdoor market in town, in the streets near the church. Otherwise, the cheapest eating is at small comedores away from the seashore, like *Comedor Margoth*.

Of the seaside restaurants, the cheapest are the cluster of places in front of the pier. A good, nameless, open-air place has tables grouped round a blue/green pentagonal kitchen. A fish meal here will cost around US$2.70 and their ham omelettes (US$0.90) are unusual but tasty.

Another row of restaurants is at the east end of town, but this side is considered less safe in the evening. It is, however, the liveliest stretch: on weekend afternoons almost all of them have live music of one kind or another. Most fish meals are US$4.50 to US$9. There's another group of equally expensive restaurants at the west end of town. In this batch, both the *Restaurante Punta Roca* and the *Restaurante Nuevo Alta Mar* are good. Bear in mind that some places (eg Punta Roca) shut as early as 7 pm.

Getting There & Away

Bus No 102 comes from San Salvador, a 1¼-hour ride; it costs US$0.45. In San Salvador, catch it on 4a Calle Poniente at 13a Avenida Sur, beside the Parque Bolívar. If you're driving from San Salvador, go to Santa Tecla and turn left (south) at 5a Avenida Sur, which leads to La Libertad.

Bus No 192 runs from La Libertad to the west down the La Costa del Bálsamo as far as La Perla, beyond El Zonte. From here, bus No 261 continues to Sonsonate (you may have to change again in Mizata). Allow four hours for the 76-km trip. Alternatively, a direct bus (No 287) runs from La Libertad to Sonsonate at 6 am. Another (probably quicker) option is to go to Santa Tecla (bus No 102) and take a frequent Sonsonate bus from there. But that way you miss the scenic coastal road – this passes many fine beaches that make good day trips from La Libertad, including Conchalio (five km west), Zunzal (eight km), El Zonte (16 km), Mizata (40 km) and Sihuapilapa (43 km).

Three km east of La Libertad is San Diego beach; take bus No 80-B from town, which also goes west goes as far as Zunzal.

All buses leave from near the intersection of 4a Avenida Norte and 2a Calle Poniente.

LA COSTA DEL BÁLSAMO

Between La Libertad and Acajutla, 72 km to the west, is la Costa del Bálsamo (the Balsam Coast). This region was once the source of much of the world's balsam; now only a few balsam trees are left.

The route along the Balsam Coast is pleasant and picturesque. Much of El Salvador's coastline is bounded by a hot lowland plain, but here the hills drop down to a rocky coast with many sheltered coves and sandy beaches (most are private access). The highway is cut into the cliffs above the sea. Zunzal is the most famous of the beaches here but there are many others.

See the La Libertad Getting There & Away entry for information on buses along the coast.

Places to Stay

About half a km west of La Libertad, *Hotel Los Arcos* (☎ 353490) is a fancy hotel with a fountain and swimming pool in the courtyard and (sometimes) poolside music on Sundays. All the rooms have air-con, TV, telephone and private bath; MasterCard and Visa are accepted. The rates are US$23 a night with one bed, US$28.75 with two.

A little farther west is a government workers' centre, *Centro Obrero Dr Humberto Romero Alvergue*, with cabins, a canteen and swimming pool. Tourists can stay free of charge, but only with prior written permission from the Ministerio de Trabajo in San Salvador.

Three km west of La Libertad, *La Cabaña de Don Chepe* (☎ 711313, 710933) is set back from the highway, a 100-metre walk from the beach. Guests receive friendly attention and it's tranquil and peaceful most of the time, filling up with Salvadoran families on weekends and holidays. There's a small swimming pool in the courtyard, and hammocks you can take to the beach; meals are served for US$2.90. Double rooms cost US$8.60 with shared bath or US$14.40 with

private bath. There's a couple of pokey singles for US$7.50 with private bath.

Six km west of La Libertad is a sign pointing inland to *El Bosque*. About half a km inland, this a family-style tourist park in a pleasant forest with swimming pools, a small lake with canoes, and lots of play area for children. It is mostly visited in the daytime, but there are a couple of basic cabins available for US$4.60 per night (12 hours), or you can camp out. Big investments and higher prices are planned for this place – the owners want to make it more exclusive.

Beyond El Bosque, by the turnoff for Zunzal, there's a little sign saying *Sealquila Habitaciones*. Two double rooms are available, each with camp beds: one costs US$2.90 and the other costs US$4.

Another four km west down the coast brings you to the *Atami Beach Club* (☎ 239000, 237698) a lovely, private beach club. It's an expensive place to stay overnight, but you can pay US$4.60 to enter for the day and enjoy the facilities. Its restaurant is closed on Monday.

LAGO DE COATEPEQUE

On the eastern slope of the Santa Ana volcano, Lago de Coatepeque is a lovely, clean, sparkling blue volcanic crater lake, six km wide and 120 metres deep, surrounded by steep green slopes rising 250 to 500 metres above it. Cerro Verde looms 1290 metres above the lake. Swimming, fishing, boating and general holiday-making are popular on weekends and holidays; during the week it is quiet.

Access to the lake is obstructed by private homes and boat docks, but there are a number of waterfront *balnearios* you can enter for about US$1. The hotels, of course, also have lake access.

Places to Stay & Eat

The best deal on the lake is the *Balneario Los Obreros*, where you can stay for free if you get written permission in advance from the Ministerio de Trabajo in San Salvador – you just have to ask for it. It's a pleasant holiday resort for government workers, with extensive grounds, lake access, a fishing pier, a swimming pool, and a restaurant serving all meals. Accommodation is in cabins complete with beds, showers and private kitchens. It is on the right, shortly after the bus loops round to circle the lake in a clockwise direction.

A couple of km farther on is the *Amacuilco Guest House*, a friendly place with meals and interesting art objects. It's overpriced but still the cheapest hotel: rooms with shared shower are US$11.50 or US$14.40.

Another 500 metres brings you to the *Hotel Torremolinos* (☎ 411859). It has ample, clean singles/doubles with private bath at US$14.40/20.10, or a three-bed room is US$23. There's a swimming pool, and an expensive restaurant overhangs the water; you can eat in any of many small comedores (eating places) nearby.

The *Hotel del Lago* (☎ 469511) is another 1½ km round the lake, near where the bus terminates. Spanish-style rooms with high ceilings and wooden shutters are US$20.10. More modern rooms cost US$33.30; these have nicer bathrooms but aren't worth the extra. There's an elegant terrace overlooking the lake, a sandy beach and a swimming pool. Meals are available but expensive.

Aside from the hotel restaurants, there are many small comedores near the lake, where you can eat quite reasonably. Lake crabs and fish, especially guapote, are the local speciality.

Getting There & Away
Bus No 220, 'El Lago', comes hourly from Santa Ana, 16 km away. The last bus back to the city leaves the lake at 4.30 pm. If you are coming from San Salvador, 55 km away, take any bus heading west towards Santa Ana and get off at El Congo, five km from the lake. Here you can meet the No 220 bus coming from Santa Ana, without having to go all the way to Santa Ana to catch it.

CERRO VERDE & VOLCÁN IZALCO
High above Lake Coatepeque is Cerro Verde, a hilltop national park atop an old volcano. It has a large forest area with hiking trails,

native birds and wildlife, camping and a fine hotel, and great views of the lake below and of the nearby Izalco volcano.

This volcano has a famous history. Until February 1770, there was nothing where Izalco now stands but a column of black sulphuric smoke rising from a hole in the earth. Then a cone began to form where the smoke fumed. Within a short time the cone had grown to prodigious size – today it stands 1870 metres high. Izalco continued to erupt into this century, sending out smoke, boulders and flames: an impressive sight by night or day. The volcano could be seen from far out to sea, and was known as 'the lighthouse of the Pacific'.

Then, in 1957, after erupting continuously for 187 years, Izalco's activity stopped. The small eruption in 1966 is the only time it's been heard from since, although it's still classified as active. Today it is a disquieting sight in the landscape: a perfect cone, black and bare, devoid of life in an otherwise incredibly fertile land.

Things to Do
You could spend some enjoyable days hiking around Cerro Verde and the Izalco volcano, perhaps taking a day trip the few km down to the lake. To enter Cerro Verde there's a US$0.60 fee and parking costs a further US$0.60. A short, 40-minute circular trail gives views of the lake and Santa Ana volcano, and a path branches off to the top of Santa Ana volcano (three hours return).

You can also climb Izalco; a marked path starts near the Cerro Verde car park and takes about two or three hours return. If you just want to look, the best viewpoint is from Cerro Verde, which at 2030 metres above sea level allows you to look down on Izalco. The view of Izalco from the Hotel de Montaña at Cerro Verde is probably the most famous view in El Salvador.

Places to Stay & Eat
You can camp out in Cerro Verde, at no charge apart from the entrance fee.

The *Hotel de Montaña* (☎ 712434) at Cerro Verde has an interesting story. Built to take maximum advantage of the view of the erupting Izalco, the hotel was nearing completion in 1957 when the volcanic activity unexpectedly ceased. With its raison d'être gone, construction stopped and the hotel sat unfinished for years. Now, however, it has been completed and opened. It's a most enjoyable place – all the 20 large rooms (10 with forest view, 10 with volcano view) have a sitting area, fireplace, TV, and a private hot water bath with tub. Cost is US$25.30 for one or two people from Monday to Thursday. The rest of the week it's US$30.50 for forest view or US$35.50 for volcano view. The charge for additional people is US$9.40. You should reserve in advance (especially for weekends) at the San Salvador tourist office. The hotel has a bar, a cafeteria, and a restaurant with that great view of Izalco.

Getting There & Away
Bus No 248 departs from Santa Ana for Cerro Verde three times a day, at 8.40 am, 10.20 am and 3.25 pm. The last bus back is at 5.30 pm. As with Lago de Coatepeque, if you're coming from San Salvador you could get off the bus at El Congo on the Interamerican Highway and meet the Cerro Verde bus there, saving yourself the extra trip into Santa Ana.

Some of the Santa Ana-Sonsonate buses (they're marked 'Cerro Verde') skirt the lake, so you can get off at the Cerro Verde turnoff and hitch the 14 km uphill from there.

Cerro Verde is 37 km from Santa Ana and 44 km from Sonsonate. Coming from San Salvador, it is 67 km if you come by the CA-8 route (the road to Sonsonate), or 77 km by the more scenic Interamerican Highway route (the road to Santa Ana).

CARRETERA PANORÁMICA
The scenic road between the Interamerican Highway and CA-8 is known as the Carretera Panorámica ('panoramic highway') for its marvellous views. It passes along a narrow ridge that drops off sharply to either side, with Lago de Coatepeque sparkling in its volcanic crater on one side and a broad, fertile valley stretching away on the other.

You will pass along here if you go to Cerro Verde from the Interamerican Highway (Santa Ana) side.

SANTA ANA
Population 202,337
Santa Ana is the second-largest city in El Salvador, capital of the department of the same name, and the principal centre for the western part of the country. It's a pleasant place but there's not much to do; its atmosphere is definitely that of an oversized country town rather than a city.

Being 63 km from San Salvador (1½ hours by bus), 16 km from Lake Coatepeque, 37 km from Cerro Verde, 13 km from the Ruins of Tazumal at Chalchuapa, and 57 km from the Guatemalan border, Santa Ana can make a convenient base.

The original name of Santa Ana was Cihuatehuacán, meaning in Nahua, 'place of holy women'.

Things to See & Do
The most notable sight in Santa Ana is its large Gothic **cathedral**. Pigeons lodge among the ornate carvings that cover the entire front of the church, and the inside has that characteristic sense of high-arched spaciousness and peace.

On the square in front of the cathedral is another notable edifice, the **Teatro de Santa Ana**, which is being restored.

On the outskirts of Santa Ana is **Sihuatehuacán**, a Turicentro with trees, gardens, swimming pools and a children's pool, sports areas, restaurants and a large open-air theatre. Admission is US$0.60. Take local bus No 51 from the plaza in front of the cathedral.

Places to Stay
There are many basic and cheap hotels in Santa Ana, built in the Spanish style, with dark rooms that have no windows – only wooden doors opening onto a central courtyard.

The best of these is the *Hospedaje San Miguel* (☎ 413465) at 126 Avenida José Matías Delgado Sur. Mattresses are thin but at least the rooms are clean. With shared bath, rates are US$2.30 for a room with one bed, or US$3.40 with two beds; with private bath it's US$4. The beds are more comfortable in the *Hotel Lívingston* (☎ 411702) at 10a Avenida Sur, No 17-A. Rooms are US$3.75/6.30 with shared/private bath.

Hospedaje Tikal on 10a Avenida Norte costs US$3.40 for one or two people in rooms that vary in size – some are fairly big. It's quite friendly and there's a convenient place to wash clothes.

The *Hotel La Libertad* (☎ 412358), one block around the corner from the cathedral at 4a Calle Oriente, No 2, on the corner of 1a Avenida Norte, is clean and pleasant. It costs US$6.90 for a room with one double bed, US$10.30 with two double beds, all with private bath and fan.

The *Internacional Inn* (☎ 400804/10), on the corner of 25a Calle Poniente and 10a Avenida Sur, is modern, clean and comfortable, but it is on an extremely loud and busy corner; if you stay here, try to get a room away from the street. All the rooms have private bath, TV and fan; rooms are US$10.30 with one double bed, US$17.25 with two beds. The meals are served in the restaurant.

Places to Eat

You can get good, cheap meals in the Mercado, in the block between 1a and 3a Calle Poniente, and 6a and 8a Avenida Sur. Inexpensive meals are also served at the restaurants in the bus station; outside the bus station is a market area with open-air stalls. There are also the usual comedores scattered around town – *Comedor Gloria* on 10a Avenida Sur isn't bad. Along 8a and 10a Avenidas Norte are many *pastelerias* where a pastry and a coffee make a good breakfast.

There's a *Pollo Campero* near the centre. The pizzas are OK at *Bambino's Pizza* and fairly cheap (from US$2.90).

Getting There & Away

Santa Ana is the transport hub for western El Salvador. Buses from Santa Ana include those to: San Salvador (63 km, 1½ hours,

bus No 201); Las Chinamas border crossing (57 km, 1½ hours, bus No 236); Ahuachapán (34 km, one hour, bus Nos 202 and 210); Sonsonate (40 km, 1½ hours, bus Nos 209 and 216); the ruins of Tazumal, Chalchuapa (13 km, 20 minutes, bus No 218); Lago de Coatepeque (16 km, one hour, bus No 220); Cerro Verde (37 km, 1½ hours, bus No 248); and Metapán (45 km, two hours, bus Nos 201A and 235). There are also direct buses between Santa Ana and Guatemala City: they don't leave from the terminal but from the stop on 25a Calle Poniente near the Internacional Inn.

MONTECRISTO CLOUD FOREST

The Montecristo cloud forest is 14 km northeast of Metapán, a town 45 km north of Santa Ana. The forest is an international nature reserve protected by three countries; the borders of El Salvador, Guatemala and Honduras converge at **El Trifinio**, at the 2418-metre summit of Montecristo.

The cloud forest only begins at 2100 metres above sea level. It is by far the most humid region in the country, with 2000 mm annual precipitation and 100% average relative humidity – the forest is always soaking wet, even during the dry season. The oak and laurel trees grow to 30 metres, and their leaves intertwine at the top to make a canopy impenetrable to sunlight. The forest floor provides a habitat for abundant exotic plant life including orchids, mushrooms, lichens and mosses, and the numerous ferns include tree ferns growing up to eight metres high. The temperature averages between 10°C and 15°C.

The diversity of microclimates and habitats harbours the most varied wildlife in all Central America, with many rare and protected plant, animal and bird species. Animals include spider monkeys, two-fingered anteaters, porcupines, spotted and hooded skunks, pumas, red and grey squirrels, wild pigs, opossums, coyotes, agoutis and many others.

The forest is also home to at least 87 species of bird, including quetzals, green toucans, woodpeckers, hummingbirds,

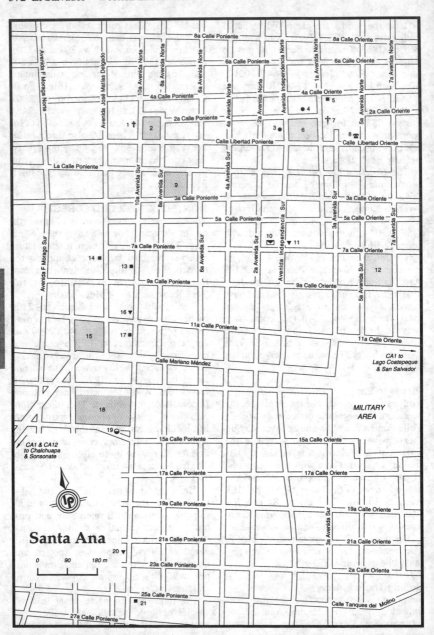

Santa Ana

0   90   180 m

EL SALVADOR

nightingales, white-faced quail, striped owls and many more.

You can visit the forest, but only from October to March; as a protected nature reserve, it is closed to the public from 1 April to 30 September, the animals' breeding season. To visit the forest you must obtain permission in advance from the Department of National Parks at the Ministry of Agriculture in San Salvador (☎ 770622). The office is in Calle Al Matazano in Colonia Santa Lucia (bus No 33A from the city centre). Getting permission is usually no problem, except for weekends.

Getting to Montecristo is a bit of a challenge. You can take a bus to Metapán from Santa Ana (1½ hours), but beyond that there is no public transport. You need a 4WD vehicle to negotiate the road up to the forest, and it can be difficult to hire someone to take you. You could always walk the 14-km trail from Metapán; if you start very early you may be able to hitch a ride with park workers.

You can camp in the forest once you have obtained permission to visit it; a ranger may be there to meet you.

LAGO DE GUIGA
On the way from Santa Ana to Montecristo, before you reach Metapán, is the Lago de Guiga. Straddling the border between El Salvador and Guatemala, it is reputed to be El Salvador's most beautiful lake, with ancient ruins and rock carvings found around its shore and islands. The lake is difficult to get to from the El Salvador side; a road serves it from Guatemala.

CHALCHUAPA & RUINAS DE TAZUMAL
The Maya ruins of Tazumal, considered the most important in El Salvador, are in the town of Chalchuapa, 13 km west of Santa Ana and on the way to Ahuachapán. The name Tazumal means, in the Quiché language, 'pyramid where the victims were burned'.

The excavated ruins on display here are only one part of a vast archaeological zone covering about 10 sq km, much of it buried under the present-day town of Chalchuapa. This zone has been inhabited more or less continuously for many centuries – certainly since 1200 BC, with some estimates placing the first settlements at around 5000 BC – and excavated structures date from a period spanning over 1000 years.

Part of the significance of the ruins at Tazumal is that the things found here – 400 clay vessels, hundreds of ritual ornaments, sculptures and much more – are evidence of an ancient and active trade between Tazumal and other places as far away as Panama and Mexico, involving cultural and trading contacts among dozens of important ancient cities.

At the site is a restored step pyramid and other excavated structures including a playing field for ball games. Some of the restoration was done in drab concrete, but at least there's a good view from the top.

Many interesting artefacts are on display in the museum (some signs in English); others are now housed at the Museo Nacio-

EL SALVADOR

nal Davíd G Guzmán in San Salvador, including the famous Estela de Tazumal, a basalt monolith 2.65 metres high and 1.16 metres wide that represents a notable person. Its sides are inscribed with hieroglyphics.

Tazumal is open Tuesday to Sunday from 9 am to 5 pm, admission free. Bus No 218 comes from Santa Ana, 13 km (20 minutes) away; a sign on the main road through town points towards the ruins, about a five-minute walk from the highway.

AHUACHAPÁN
Population 83,885
There is not much of interest in Ahuachapán, a small, quiet town that is capital of the department of the same name, but it is the closest town to the Las Chinamas border 16 km away. If you have just crossed the border from Guatemala you might want to spend the night here; otherwise you could forge on to Santa Ana, 34 km to the east.

The most notable sight in the area of Ahuachapán is **Los Ausoles** ('the cauldrons'), a geothermal area of boiling mud pools, hot springs, geysers and steaming earth. It is possible to walk among the ausoles even though the area is tapped for geothermal power. There is no public transport to the ausoles but the 'El Barro' bus from Ahuachapán will take you to within five km.

En route to/from Chalchuapa you could stop off in **Atiquizaya** to look at the gallery of Alfredo Melara Farfán, at the junction with the main road. He makes interesting sculptures using old bits of metal: Don Quixote is a favourite theme.

Places to Stay & Eat
The best place in town is the *Boarding House Casa Blanca* (☎ 431505) at 102 Calle Gerardo Barrios, on the corner of 2a Avenida Norte. It is clean and pleasant, Spanish-style, and has only four rooms, each with a private hot bath. Rates are US$9.20/14.40 for singles/doubles. They are planning to build extra rooms and bar/café.

Hospedaje Granada, is on 8a Calle Poniente between 4a and 6a Avenida Norte, a couple of blocks from El Calvario church.

It's nothing fancy, with rather dark rooms and shared bath, but it's clean and family-run. Prices for rooms are US$3.40 with one double bed, US$5.75 with two beds, or US$8.60 with three beds. You could also try *Hotel San José*, overlooking Plaza Menendez, where rooms are US$4.60/9.20.

There is cheap eating in the large indoor market, completed in 1990, beside the Plaza Menendez a block from the bus station. Or there are several little restaurants and snack stands around the Plaza Concordia; *La Estrella* is good, and has a *plato del día* for US$1.05.

Getting There & Away
Bus Nos 202 and 210 run between Ahuachapán and Santa Ana (34 km, one hour). Bus No 263 comes from the border at Las Chinamas (16 km, half an hour). There are also buses to Sonsonate, 36 km to the south-east.

SONSONATE
Population 76,200
The town of Sonsonate, the centre of an agricultural district, is not of much interest in itself (though there are a couple of churches worth glancing at if you have time), but it is a crossroads to other more interesting places.

Nahuizalco, a few km to the north, is a Pipil Indian village specialising in traditional basketry.

The village of **Izalco**, eight km to the north-east, is at the foot of the Izalco volcano. Nearby is **Atecozol**, a government Turicentro on the slopes of the volcano, with a large swimming pool, shaded grounds, gardens, cabañas and little restaurants. At Atecozol are several interesting monuments, including one to Atonatl, the Indian who shot an arrow through the leg of the conquistador Pedro de Alvarado here in 1524; one to Tlaloc, the god of rain; and one to a frog found here, which led to the discovery of water. Entrance is US$0.60, cabañas US$3.40.

Places to Stay & Eat

Near the bus station are many small hotels. Cleanest and best of the lot is the *Hotel Florida* (☎ 510967). Rooms with one bed are US$2.90/3.40 with shared/private bath; US$6.90 with two beds or US$8.60 with three. It's on 18 Avenida Sur: turn right as you leave the bus station then take the first right.

For the centre of town, turn left from the bus station. This road becomes Calle Obispo Marraquin; near the intersection with 8a Avenida Norte is *Hospedaje Teresita*, where rooms are US$2.90 for one or two people.

In the centre, the *Hotel Centroamericana* on the corner of Calle Alberto Masferrer and 6a Avenida Norte has rooms at US$4.60/5.75 with shared/private bath. Or there's the fancier US-motel-style *Hotel Orbe* (☎ 511416, 511517) on the corner of 4a Calle Oriente and 2a Avenida Sur. Clean single/double rooms, all with private bath, are US$6.90/10,50, or US$10.30/13.80 with air-conditioning.

There are the usual comedores around Sonsonate.

Getting There & Away

Bus No 53D goes to Nahuizalco, bus No 53A to Izalco, and bus No 209 to Santa Ana (40 km, 1½ hours). Bus No 261 goes east along la Costa del Bálsamo to La Perla, from where No 192 continues to La Libertad. There are also frequent buses to the border at La Hachadura (59 km), to the beaches at Metalío (bus No 259) and Los Cobanos (bus No 257), and to Acajutla, 20 km away.

ACAJUTLA

Acajutla is El Salvador's principal port and one of the most modern in Central America. A large part of El Salvador's coffee and other exports are shipped through this port. The port and the town are separated; for security reasons, entrance to the port side is restricted.

The town side of Acajutla, a fishing town and beach resort, is very small, little more than a double line of buildings strung along the seaside. The large, curving beach attracts plenty of beachgoers on weekends and holi-

days; the rest of the time it is quiet. Surfing is reputed to be good here in summer.

Places to Stay & Eat

The classiest place to stay, though still quite basic, is the *Motel Miramar* (☎ 523183), where simple rooms with private bath are US$5.75 a night. The swimming pool is filled for holidays, and there is an attractive covered dining patio by the sea, complete with tables, hammocks and coconut palms.

There are a number of run-down *hospedajes* in town but they are nothing to write home about, often small, dark and dirty. You might try the rooms behind the *Tienda/Neveria La Campana* (☎ 523003). They are very basic rooms with a shared bath for US$2.90/4.60 per single/double, the owners are friendly and meals are served.

Otherwise, there are a few families that take in guests. Opposite the taxi station and right on the beach is the family home of Lillian Padilla (☎ 523776), where a few simple rooms off to one side of the courtyard, with shared bath, are US$3.40.

Being a beach resort, the beachside at Acajutla is packed with restaurants, specialising in seafood – of course!

Getting There & Away

Buses run frequently between Acajutla and Sonsonate, 20 km away. The border station at La Hachadura is 48 km from Acajutla; buses run frequently between La Hachadura and Sonsonate but do not turn into Acajutla. You might have to go into Sonsonate to catch the bus, or you could meet it at the cross-roads.

Eastern El Salvador

The Interamerican Highway goes east from San Salvador to San Miguel, on to La Unión and to the border at El Amatillo. Highway CA-7, known as the Ruta Militar, is a shorter, more direct connection between San Miguel and El Amatillo.

The Carretera del Litorál, Highway CA-2,

runs from San Salvador south-east through Zacatecoluca and Usulután, eventually coming to a crossroads with routes heading north to San Miguel and south to the Pacific Coast.

SAN MIGUEL
Population 182,817
San Miguel, El Salvador's third-largest city, was founded in 1530 and is the principal town in the eastern half of the country. It is the capital of the department of the same name. People come from all over the surrounding countryside to buy and sell in the lively market streets. There are also some attractive churches and parks. San Miguel is an old, slow, pleasant town.

The town sits at the foot of the 2130-metre San Miguel volcano, also called Chaparrastique, a large, lone, conical volcano that dominates the landscape around it. The volcano is still active: it has erupted at least 10 times in this century, most recently in 1976.

Information
There's an Office of Immigration on 1a Avenida Norte, between 2a and 4a Calle Poniente.

Locals will warn you that the central district is unsafe after about 8 pm at night.

Things to See & Do
There's a big, attractive outdoor swimming pool at **Altos de la Cueva**, one km north of town. At the grounds are an outdoor restaurant under the trees, cabañas, and gardens. Admission is US$0.60, cabañas US$3.40. Take local bus No 94 from the plaza in front of the cathedral.

There are some ruins, the **Ruinas de Quelepa**, a half-hour bus ride from San Miguel; take local bus No 90. **Playa El Cuco**, an attractive volcanic black-sand beach, is 37 km south of San Miguel, about a two-hour ride on bus No 320 from the main bus terminal. It is the closest beach to San Miguel and therefore attracts many beachgoers on weekends and holidays. There are places to stay.

The **cathedral** in San Miguel dates from the 18th century. Around the corner behind it is the **Antiguo Teatro Nacional**, an elegant edifice which is being restored.

Places to Stay
There are many good, inexpensive places to stay in San Miguel, particularly near the bus station. The *Hotel Migueleño* on 4a Calle Oriente, No 610, is in a two-storey building built in 1990 and it's excellent value at US$3.40 for a good room with one double bed, US$4.60 with two beds; all rooms have private bath and overhead fan.

Hotel San Rafael (☎ 614113) at 6a Calle Oriente, No 704, is in the block east of the bus station and is also fine. The rates are US$4.45/6.30 for singles/doubles in rooms with private bath, one or two beds and a big hammock. Air-conditioned rooms cost US$8.80.

El Motelito (☎ 613748) at 10a Avenida Norte, No 104, is around the corner to the west of the bus station. It is a popular family place. The rooms are simple but clean, all with private bath; rates are US$2.90 with one double bed, US$5.80 with two beds.

If all these places are full, you could try the *Hospedaje Hawai* (☎ 613743), at 10a Avenida Norte, No 206, even though it's more run-down than the other places. It costs US$2.90 for a room with one double bed and a hammock, or US$4 with two double beds and a hammock, all with shared bath. They may initially quote higher prices.

There are a number of motels on the highway, but they are overpriced compared to the places in town, and no better. Between the highway and the town are a couple of decent places in a quiet residential district. *Hospedaje Modelo* (☎ 613122) is on 17a Calle Poniente, No 208. Large, clean rooms, some with high ceilings and all with private bath, overhead fan, a double bed and a big hammock, cost $5.75; they are set around spacious grounds with lots of trees and ample parking areas.

A couple of blocks further south, *Boarding House Diana* (☎ 613314) at the corner of 21a Calle Poniente and 3a Avenida Sur,

EL SALVADOR

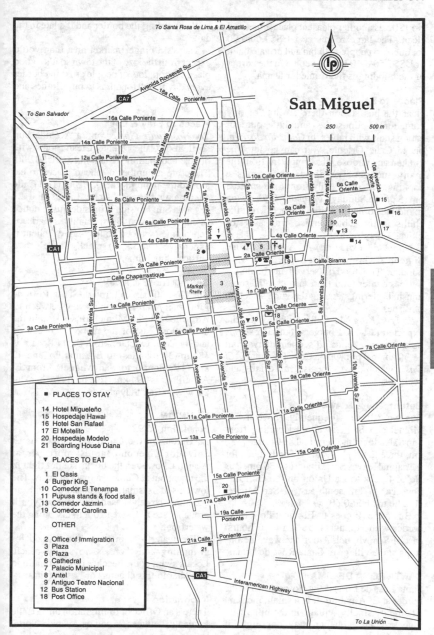

San Miguel

0   250   500 m

To Santa Rosa de Lima & El Amatillo

To San Salvador

To La Unión

Interamerican Highway

Market Stalls

- ■ PLACES TO STAY
  - 14 Hotel Migueleño
  - 15 Hospedaje Hawai
  - 16 Hotel San Rafael
  - 17 El Motelito
  - 20 Hospedaje Modelo
  - 21 Boarding House Diana

- ▼ PLACES TO EAT
  - 1 El Oasis
  - 4 Burger King
  - 10 Comedor El Tenampa
  - 11 Pupusa stands & food stalls
  - 13 Comedor Jazmin
  - 19 Comedor Carolina

  OTHER
  - 2 Office of Immigration
  - 3 Plaza
  - 5 Plaza
  - 6 Cathedral
  - 7 Palacio Municipal
  - 8 Antel
  - 9 Antiguo Teatro Nacional
  - 12 Bus Station
  - 18 Post Office

No 1202, is another pleasant place, quiet and clean. The large rooms cost US$4.60/6.90 for one/two people with fan and private bath, or US$7.50/8.60 with air-con. On the corner of the building is the Comedor Diana.

Places to Eat

Near the bus station there are lots of tiny comedores, pupuserías and little outdoor eating stalls with tables. In *Comedor Jazmin*, on 4a Calle Oriente, you can go into the kitchen and choose what you want from the many inexpensive dishes you can see cooking. It is open daily from 6.30 am to 8 pm (5 pm on Sunday). *Comedor El Tenampa* round the corner is a similar place. Treat the chillis in the table garnish with asbestos gloves – they're hot!

Comedor Carolina on Avenida José Simeón Cañas is rather bigger and very popular. The food is served up behind a buffet counter, and there are usually some unusual offerings among the wide selection of dishes.

Burger King, 4a Calle Oriente, has the expected fast-food burgers, but also serves pizza on weekends. It's open daily from 11.30 am to 9 pm. On 4a Calle Poniente is *El Oasis* which serves meals, fruit drinks and cocktails.

Getting There & Away

Bus No 301 runs frequently between San Miguel and San Salvador, departing from San Salvador at the Terminal de Oriente (136 km, three hours, US$1.45). The last bus for the capital leaves San Miguel at 4.30 pm. Bus No 324 goes to La Unión on the Golfo de Fonseca, 47 km south-east of San Miguel (1¼ hours, US$0.60).

Bus No 330 goes to El Amatillo, on the border with Honduras, 58 km (two hours) east of San Miguel. Along the way, the bus stops at the village of Santa Rosa de Lima.

SANTA ROSA DE LIMA

Santa Rosa de Lima is the closest town to the border at El Amatillo. It is a small, pleasant (if slightly smelly) village in the hills, with places where you can stay overnight if

you're crossing the border and it's late in the day.

There's a bigger market area than you'd expect from the size of the town so it's a good place to shop; lots of people cross the border every day from Honduras to buy clothes and food.

Places to Stay & Eat

Try *Hospedaje Gomez* on 2a Avenida Sur, south of 6a Calle Oriente. Clean rooms with double bed, hammock and fan are US$2.50. There are a number of cheap places to eat around the main plaza. *La Pema* is on Calle 4a Oriente between Calle Larios and 2a Avenida Sur. No sign is outside, just a notice saying 'Sale Carro'. Its speciality is mariscos consommé (seafood soup) – an excellent if expensive (US$5.75) meal. There's live music at lunchtime.

Getting There & Away

Bus No 330 passes through Santa Rosa de Lima every half hour on its way between El Amatillo and San Miguel. Buses stop in the bus station, east of the market between 6a and 4a Calle Oriente. From Santa Rosa it is 18 km (30 minutes) to El Amatillo, and 40 km (1¼ hours) to San Miguel. From El Amatillo it is 194 km (five hours by bus) all the way to San Salvador.

LA UNIÓN

Population 36,927

La Unión, on the Golfo de Fonseca, is El Salvador's second-largest port. As at Acajutla, however, the docks are not right in the town, but at Cutuco, a few km away. The town itself is small and peaceful, with an economy largely based on fishing; you'll probably see fish spread out to dry along the waterfront.

The waterfront in town is not good for swimming and there is no sandy beach. Locals swim at the beaches of El Tamarindo (see later in this chapter) or Las Playitas.

Information

There's an Office of Immigration on 3a Calle Poniente, between 2a and 4a Avenida Norte.

La Unión

Golfo de Fonseca

■ PLACES TO STAY

5 Hotel Centroamericano
10 Hospedaje Anexo Santa Marta
11 Hotel San Francisco
13 Hospedaje Nigth and Day

▼ PLACES TO EAT

2 Cafetín El Asador
4 Cafetín El Marinero
12 Comedor Mayra
14 Restaurante Miramar
15 Restaurante Amanacer Marino
16 Restaurante Rancho Alegre

OTHER

1 Bus Station
3 Office of Immigration
6 Market Stalls
7 Church
8 Post Office
9 Antel

EL SALVADOR

Places to Stay

There are several good places to stay in La Unión. The *Hotel San Francisco* (☎ 644159) on Calle Generál Menéndez, No 6-3, between 9a and 11a Avenida Sur, has 29 large, clean and sunny rooms at US$4.60 with one double bed and a big hammock, or US$9.20 with air-con and two double beds.

The *Hotel Centroamericano* (☎ 644029) is a large hotel, clean and well kept, covering the entire block between 2a and 4a Calle Oriente, 1a and 3a Avenida Sur. It has an older section and a newer one; the older section has large rooms with high Spanish

ceilings, and a pleasant sitting area in the covered central courtyard. The rooms in the newer addition are smaller but OK. Single/double rates for rooms sharing a bath are US$2.90/5.75 with an overhead fan; rooms with private bath are US$4/8 with overhead fan, or US$5.20/10.40 with air-conditioning.

Hospedaje Anexo Santa Marta (☎ 644238), near the corner of Calle Generál Menéndez and 7a Avenida Norte, is a family-run place, with 11 small, clean but scruffy rooms on one side of a dirt courtyard with trees. All the rooms have private bath, one double bed and a big hammock, and some have air-con for the same price. They cost is US$4 per night, or US$4.60 to include the day.

Finally at 11a Avenida Sur, No 7-1, there's the *Hospedaje Nigth and Day* – you can call it the 'Noche y Dia' or the 'Night and Day', but the sign says 'Nigth and Day'! It's small and family-run, with 14 rooms, all with private bath, one double bed and a hammock, at US$3.20.

Places to Eat

There are lots of snack stands around the plaza in front of the church, and a couple of good inexpensive restaurants patronised by the locals. *Comedor Mayra*, opposite the Hotel San Francisco, is cheap and not bad.

Cafetín El Marinero, on the corner of Avenida General Cabañas and 3a Calle Poniente, one block from the plaza, is a bit more expensive. It's an enjoyable little place, with tables set out on a terrace. Or there's the *Cafetín El Asador* on the corner of 1a Calle Poniente and 4a Avenida Norte, another local favourite and with similar prices.

Down by the sea are several seafood restaurants where fish meals start at around US$3: *Rancho Alegre*, *Amanacer Marino* and *Miramar*.

Getting There & Away

Bus No 324 operates between La Unión and San Miguel (47 km, 1¼ hours). Bus No 353 connects La Unión with El Amatillo on the Honduras border (41 km, two hours). Bus No 383 goes to the beaches and fishing village of El Tamarindo (1½ hours), and bus No 418 goes to the beach at Las Playitas (one hour).

EL TAMARINDO

This small fishing village is less than 1½ hours by bus from La Unión. At the northern end there are colourful scenes with the villagers tending fishing boats or cleaning the catch; to the east is a fine sandy beach that curves round the bay and is often all but empty. The sea is gentle, and there is also an estuary that attracts many species of birds.

Places to Stay & Eat

Stay free of charge at *Centre Obrero Dr Miguel Felix Charlaix*, about 800 metres before you get to the main village. It's more basic than other government workers' centres in that you have to draw water from the well, the cabins are musty and there's nowhere to eat, but it's still a bargain for nothing. You must get permission to stay in advance from the Ministerio de Trabajo in San Salvador. Otherwise, there's one other place to stay in the village, but it's described as 'basura' (rubbish) by locals.

Comedor Viajero halfway towards the centre from the workers' centre, is a good place to eat. At *Comedor y Pupuseria Janeth*, in the main village, the meat and cheese pupusas (US$0.15) are tasty, and the beers cold.

Getting There & Away

Many buses run to/from La Unión. Two a day go direct to El Cuco beach (one hour). There are three a day to San Miguel (three hours), departing at around 9 am, 3.15 and 4.30 pm.

Northern El Salvador

The districts of Chalatenango and Morazán were the principal areas of warfare between the government army and the FMLN guerrillas. The people who evacuated the villages have now returned, and such places provide a fascinating opportunity to witness the process of reconstruction, talk to the people about their war experiences, and maybe even join in their folk dances. There's rarely anywhere to stay in the smaller places, though you may be able to stay overnight in a family home if you ask around. If there are any Western volunteers around they're normally happy to help. Food is basic, too, and public transport fairly infrequent.

The north has some of the best scenery in the country: attractive rivers, valleys, and hills that seem to roll on forever.

EL SALVADOR

CHALATENANGO
Population 27,600
Capital of the district of the same name, Chalatenango was in the hands of the government during the war, and the military are still to be seen around the main plaza.

Things to See & Do
The main street, running east-west, is Calle José Maria San Martin, and is the location of the market. Beside this road at 3a Avenida Sur is the **church**, interesting for the many hand-written notes of thanks for various miracles *(miralgo)*.

Follow Calle José Maria San Martin 400 metres to the east and you reach a sign pointing 500 metres north for the government Turicentro, **Agua Fria**. It's like all the others, with swimming and picnic areas, and a US$0.60 entry fee.

Chalatenango makes a good base for exploring the nearby repopulated communities which were evacuated during the war. **San Antonio Los Ranchos**, to the southeast, and **San José Las Flores**, to the east, have been recommended. San José has a church with murals of Bishop Romero.

Places to Stay
There are only two places to stay in Chalatenango. *Hospedaje el Nuevo Amanecer*, behind the market on 1a Calle Oriente, has clean rooms with good beds for US$2.90 for one person or US$3.40 for two. The doors close at 9 pm and there's a ridiculous 7 am check-out time; they also don't give you a room key, but unlock the door for you. Somebody should tell them that this makes guests feel like prison inmates.

West of the church, right opposite Antel, is a nameless place, identified by a small 'pilsner' sign outside. There are six basic rooms for US$2.90 per person, with thin mattresses. The place also serves food.

Places to Eat
There are plenty of cheap places to eat in and around the market. Either side of Hospedaje el Nuevo Amanecer are *Comedor Karlita* and *Comedor Campesino*, both of which are busy and good.

Getting There & Away
Bus No 125 runs regularly from San Salvador, a 2¼-hour trip, and terminates near the church. Just beyond the Agua Fria sign is the stop for the bus going to San Antonio Los Ranchos and then to San José Las Flores, where it terminates. It departs at 11 am and returns the next day at 6 am. In between times, cars and trucks on these dirt roads usually stop to pick up hitchers.

LA PALMA
La Palma is 84 km north of San Salvador and is famous for its artesanías. The village was held by the FMLN during the war.

Things to See & Do
La Palma is known primarily as a centre for producing brightly painted images on wood, mostly depicting rural and religious scenes (see Arts and Things to Buy in the chapter introduction). Simply wandering around the centre you'll come across many small **workshops** producing such items. Some are proper studios, others are simply a designated area in a private house. Either way, you're welcome to enter and look around.

All around La Palma is beautiful mountain scenery; ask the locals to recommend **hikes**. The Río Nunuapa (in the Nahua language the name means 'silent river') is about a 40-minute hike to the south.

Places to Stay & Eat
Hotel La Palma (☎ 359012) has no name outside: it's behind the building with the square, white, crenellated tower. There are a few rooms available in the house for US$2.30 per person, or rooms with private bath in the annexe built in 1993 cost US$8.60 per person.

On the main road, Calle Gerardo Barrios, are several places to eat, including a cheap pupusería. *Cafeteria La Estancia* has burgers, snacks, and meals for around US$1.80.

EL SALVADOR

Getting There & Away

Bus No 119 runs hourly from San Salvador to the El Poy border with Honduras, and takes four hours. It stops at La Palma. The northern section of the road is paved but in poor condition; La Palma is only about 12 km south of the border yet it's a 50-minute bus trip. Although the border closes at 5 pm, the last bus south from El Poy leaves around 3 pm.

PERQUÍN

Perquín, in the district of Morazán, was the headquarters of the FLMN guerillas during the war, so it is fitting that the village now has the **Museo de la Revolucíon**. It charts the causes and progress of the armed struggle using photos, posters, weapons and histories of those who died in action. Weapons range from hi-tech hardware to home-made bombs and mines. There's also the remains of a helicopter and exhibits on Radio Venceremos, the voice of the FLMN. The museum is open Tuesday to Sunday from 9 am to 5 pm and entry costs US$1.15.

Opposite and to the north of the museum is a hill; it only takes 10 minutes to climb to the top for a fine view of the village and surrounding hills. The San Miguel volcano is clearly visible.

Places to Stay & Eat

The only place to stay is *Casa de Huépedes El Gigante*, down the turnoff to the left before you reach the village sign (when heading north). It's really just a big barn, separated into cubicles by two-metre-high boards, with space for little else except the bed. Cost for singles/doubles is US$2.30/2.85 overnight or US$2.85/3.45 for 24 hours.

Eat in the village centre by the church: it's an open-air place under an octagonal roof. There's a buffet counter where you can choose from very cheap food. There's also a small comedor by the village sign that's sometimes open, but it's not as good.

Getting There & Away

Bus No 332 runs from San Miguel and takes three hours (US$0.95); departures are only every one to two hours. There are no buses from Perquín to Sabanetas, on the border.

SEGUNDO MONTES

This repopulated community is named after one of the six Jesuit priests murdered by the military in 1989. It's an interesting community to visit as it's one of the best organised, with several local cooperatives and programmes covering health, culture, education and conservation. Its education programmes are particularly important in the context of a national illiteracy rate of 68.1% in 1985, up from 30.5% in 1980.

Get information from the Centro Cultural in the main settlement of San Luis. There are good views and hikes close to the village.

Places to Stay & Eat

At the Centro Cultural there are four-bed dorms for US$2.90 per person; the office is open weekdays and Saturday morning. Nearby, on the main road, is the intriguingly named comedor, *La Guacamaya Subversiva*, a supermarket, and other places to eat.

About three km north, up the hill, is the settlement called Quebrachos; enquire in *Comedor Los Samnelitos* about basic rooms for US$1.70.

Getting There & Away

Buses to/from Perquín stop at Segundo Montes. It's also easy to hitch.

NICARAGUA

Nicaragua

The largest of the Central American countries, Nicaragua has been the scene of dynamic events in the past couple of decades, making headlines all over the world. But no matter how much you might have heard about Nicaragua, being there yourself is guaranteed to teach you things you didn't know. A visit to Nicaragua is an illuminating and memorable experience.

The country has three distinct regions, all of them worth visiting. The world's only freshwater sharks live in Lago de Nicaragua, Central America's largest lake, and there are plenty of noteworthy natural features including islands, volcanoes, and navigable rivers.

The most interesting aspect, though, may be just to be there – to see how this post-revolutionary society is operating and to talk to the people who have lived through it all.

Facts about the Country

HISTORY
Early History
The earliest traces of human habitation in Nicaragua are the Footprints of Acahualinca, a 10,000-year-old archaeological site within the city of Managua. Here you can see the footprints of humans and animals running towards Lago de Managua. Apparently they were fleeing an ancient volcanic eruption when they were buried, and their footprints were preserved by volcanic ash.

Around the 10th century AD, indigenous people from Mexico migrated to Nicaragua's Pacific lowlands. There are ancient stone statues and carvings on many islands in Lago de Nicaragua. Many Nicaraguan places have Nahuatl names, a legacy of Aztec migrations around the 15th century.

European Arrival
The first contact with Europeans was in

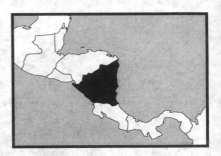

1502, when Columbus sailed down the Caribbean coast.

The first Spanish exploratory mission, led by Gil González de Avila, came north from the Spanish settlement at Panama and reached Nicaragua in 1522. It found the southern shores of Lago de Nicaragua heavily populated by Indians. The Spanish derived the name Nicaragua from their chief, Nicarao. The population under Nicarao interacted peacefully with the Spanish and were among the first indigenous Americans to voluntarily convert to Christianity.

A couple of years later the Spanish were back to colonise the region, led this time by Francisco Hernández de Córdoba, who founded first the city of Granada, and then the city of León, in 1524. Both cities were established near indigenous settlements, and the Indians were subjugated by the Spanish. The land around Managua was also densely populated by an agricultural, hunting and fishing people. They put up fierce resistance to the Spanish and their city was destroyed. For the next three centuries, Managua was but a village.

Colonial Settlement
The gold which had initially attracted the Spanish settlers to Nicaragua soon gave out, but Granada and León remained. Granada, on the north shore of Lago de Nicaragua,

became a comparatively rich colonial city, its wealth due not only to surrounding agriculture but also to its importance as a trading centre. The navigable Río San Juan, flowing out of Lago de Nicaragua, gave Granada a direct shipping connection to the Caribbean, and thence to Europe.

León was originally founded on the shore of Lago de Managua. The city was destroyed by earthquake in 1610 and a new city was established near the Indian village of Subtiava. It was poorer than Granada, but the Spanish made it the capital of the colonial province.

The difference in wealth between the two cities, and the political supremacy of the poorer one, led to conflicts that raged for more than a century, at times amounting to civil war.

León became the centre for radical clerics and intellectuals, the Liberal Party, support for the unification of Central America, and reforms based on those of the French and American revolutions. Granada, with a wealthier business class, became the centre for the Conservative Party, favouring traditional Spanish values of monarchy and Catholic authority.

Differing explanations have been advanced for this factional divide. León, as the centre of colonial administration and religious authority, might have been expected to be more conservative, but was surprisingly more open to liberal influences, in governance and in theology, that also swept the mother country, Spain. In addition, León was an area in which conflicts between Spanish-born administrators and the locally-born elite, as well as between the local residents and the clerical class, stirred resentments expressed through liberalism.

Granada, a wealthy merchant centre, might have been expected to embrace liberalism, given its greater cosmopolitanism. It, however, chose to express its local identity by embracing conservatism, apparently in the hope that by proving its political loyalty to the crown it could gain status over León.

Another explanation for the split between the two cities holds that it was a perpetuation of tribal rivalries existing before the European conquest. In any case, continual fighting between the two led the government to eventually move the capital to Managua.

While the Spanish were settling the Pacific lowlands, the English, who were becoming a major power in the Caribbean, were the dominant influence on the Caribbean side of Nicaragua. English, French and Dutch pirates plied the Caribbean waters, and Granada was attacked repeatedly by pirates in the 17th century.

Early Independence

Along with the rest of Central America, Nicaragua gained independence from Spain in 1821, was part of Mexico for a brief time, then part of the Central American Federation, and finally achieved complete independence in 1838. León and Granada continued to feud.

After independence, not only the liberals and conservatives were vying for power. With the Spanish out of the picture, Britain and the USA both became extremely interested in Nicaragua and its strategically important passage from Lago de Nicaragua to the Caribbean. Both powers wanted to put a canal somewhere in Central America to connect the Atlantic and Pacific oceans, and Nicaragua looked like the spot.

In 1848 the British seized the Caribbean port of San Juan del Norte, at the mouth of the Río San Juan, and renamed it Greytown. Meanwhile, the California gold rush had added fire to the quest for an interoceanic passage. Spurred by the sudden flood of passengers wanting to reach California by the quickest means possible, Cornelius Vanderbilt established the Accessory Transit Company to take passengers from San Juan del Norte (Greytown), up the Río San Juan, across Lago de Nicaragua to the port at San Jorge (near Rivas), then 20 km by stagecoach to the Pacific port at San Juan del Sur, where they boarded ships bound for California.

William Walker

The growing US interest in Nicaragua took a new twist in the person of William Walker. Born in Nashville, Tennessee (USA) in 1824, Walker graduated from university in 1838, received his medical degree in 1843, and then became a lawyer. The early 1850s found him working as a journalist in the California gold rush boom town of San Francisco.

An opportunistic fellow, Walker became a filibuster, intent on taking over Latin American territory. In 1853 he led a small party to attack Mexico, where he declared himself president of 'independent' Baja California and the state of Sonora before he was ignominiously driven out.

A couple of years later, in 1855, the liberals of León asked Walker to come and help them seize power from the conservatives, based in Granada. Walker entered Nicaragua with 56 followers, attacked Granada, and prevailed.

Within a year of taking Granada, Walker had himself elected president of Nicaragua. The USA recognised his government almost immediately. Three months after gaining the presidency he instituted slavery in Nicaragua, a country where almost the entire population was non-White, in order to gain favour with the southern states of the USA.

He declared English the official language of Nicaragua, seized Vanderbilt's transport company, and took out a large loan, putting the territory of Nicaragua up as collateral.

Walker then adopted the slogan 'five or none', and announced his intention to take over the remaining Central American countries. These countries united to drive Walker out, supported by Cornelius Vanderbilt. In May 1857 Walker was defeated at Rivas and surrendered to the US navy, to avoid capture by the Central American forces. They evacuated him back to the USA.

Walker did not give up, however. Six months later, he sailed from Mobile, Alabama with another invading party. He landed at San Juan del Norte (Greytown), only to be arrested and returned once again to the USA.

In 1860, the erstwhile president of Nicaragua sailed from Mobile on yet another attempt to conquer Central America. Landing near Trujillo, on the coast of Honduras, he was captured by the British navy, who turned him over to the Honduran authorities. He was tried and executed by firing squad on 12 September 1860; his grave is in Trujillo's Old Cemetery.

Late 19th Century
When William Walker was defeated in 1857, the Liberal Party, which had invited him into the country, lost power to the conservatives. In the same year the capital was transferred from León to Managua, in an attempt to quell the rivalry between Granada and León. Managua was chosen largely because it lay between the two cities; it was then little more than a village.

In 1860 the British signed a treaty ceding the Caribbean region, called the the Mosquito Coast (Costa de Miskitos) or Mosquitia, to the now independent governments of Honduras and Nicaragua. The Nicaraguan section remained an autonomous region until the 1890s.

The conservatives ruled Nicaragua from the new capital at Managua in relative peace from 1857 until 1893.

Zelaya & the Marines
In 1893 a liberal leader, José Santos Zelaya, deposed the conservative president and became dictator. A nationalist, Zelaya soon antagonised the USA. In 1909 the US government forced his resignation. In 1911, the US responded to further conflict by sending 350 marines to Nicaragua.

For the next few years the USA controlled politics in Nicaragua, installing presidents it favoured and ousting ones it didn't like, using the leverage of its occupying force of marines. In 1914 the Bryan-Chamorro Treaty was signed, giving the USA exclusive rights to build a canal in Nicaragua, and to establish US naval bases there.

In 1925, a new cycle of violence began with a conservative coup. The marine guard at the US embassy was withdrawn but more political turmoil ensued and in 1926 the marines returned.

Augusto C Sandino & the Somoza Era
The conservative regime was opposed by a group of liberal rebels including Juan Bautista Sacasa, General José María Moncada, and, most importantly in the long run, Augusto C Sandino, 'General of Free Men.' Moncada and Sacasa attained power with US support.

Sandino, however, fought on, inspiring rebels throughout the Hispanic world. Moncada was president from 1928 to 1933, Sacasa from 1933 to 1936. In 1931 the marines withdrew from Nicaragua, but left behind a new Nicaraguan Guardia Nacional (National Guard), which they had set up and trained. It was led by Anastasio Somoza García.

In February 1934 Somoza engineered the assassination of Sandino. A couple of years later he overthrew Sacasa. Fraudulent elections were held and Somoza became president himself in January 1937. Somoza created a new constitution to give himself more power, set up a faction of the liberals as a state party, and ruled Nicaragua as an internationally notorious dictator for the next 20 years, sometimes as president and at other times from behind a puppet president.

NICARAGUA

Somoza amassed huge personal wealth by vicious means. The Somoza landholdings grew to the size of El Salvador: Nicaragua was virtually the personal possession of the Somozas and their friends.

The Somozas were educated in the USA, and supported by the US government. On 21 September 1956, the day after Somoza had been nominated for another presidential term by his party, a celebration was held by dignitaries in León. Rigoberto López Pérez, a radical young poet and journalist, arrived dressed as a waiter and shot Somoza. It was a suicide mission and López Pérez was killed on the spot, becoming a national hero. Somoza died eight days later in Panama. You can see the place in León where this happened; a plaque outside proclaims that the event marked the 'beginning of the end' of the Somoza dictatorship.

Somoza was succeeded by his elder son, Luis Somoza Debayle, and the Somoza family, with the help of the Guardia Nacional, continued to rule Nicaragua for many more years. In 1967 Luis died, and his younger brother, Anastasio Somoza Debayle, assumed the presidency.

But the opposition gained pace. In 1961, Carlos Fonseca Amador, a prominent figure in the student movement that had opposed the Somoza regime in the 1950s, joined forces with an old fighting partner of Sandino, Colonel Santos López, and some other activists, to found the Frente Sandinista de Liberación Nacional (Sandinista National Liberation Front), or FSLN.

The 1970s

On 23 December 1972, at around midnight, an earthquake devastated Managua, levelling over 250 city blocks, killing 6000 people and leaving 300,000 homeless. International aid that poured into Nicaragua was diverted to the Somozas and their associates, while the people who needed it suffered and died. This obvious abuse increased opposition to Anastasio Somoza among all classes of Nicaraguans.

Anastasio Somoza was then the commander of the Guardia Nacional,

constitutionally unable to serve a second term as president. When the earthquake struck, he made himself head of a national emergency committee to gain direct access to the aid coming into the country. In 1974, a new constitution, the 10th since independence, made it possible for him to run for president again, and in rigged elections (normal practice by then) he became president once more.

By 1974 opposition to Somoza was widespread. Two groups were widely recognised – the FSLN (also called Sandinistas) led by Carlos Fonseca, and the Unión Democrática de Liberación (UDEL) led by Pedro Joaquín Chamorro, owner and editor of the Managua newspaper La Prensa, which printed articles critical of the Somoza regime.

In December 1974, the FSLN kidnapped several leading members of the Somoza regime, and gained ransoms and the release of political prisoners in exchange for the release of Somoza hostages. The Somoza government responded with a campaign of systematic killings over the following 2½ years. It was in 1976 that Carlos Fonseca was assassinated.

Revolution & the FSLN

In January 1978, the popular newspaper publisher Pedro Joaquín Chamorro was assassinated. This was the last straw for the Nicaraguan public. The people erupted in violence and declared a general strike, and the former moderates joined with the FSLN in their efforts to oust the Somoza dictatorship by whatever means necessary.

On 22 August 1978 the FSLN occupied the Palacio Nacional, took 1000 hostages and held them for two days. The government acceded to the FSLN's demands and the hostages were released. The revolt spread, and another general strike was called.

The FSLN staged its final offensive in June 1979. The FSLN forces won city after city, with the support of thousands of civilians fighting on their side. On 17 July, as the revolutionary forces had won everywhere and were preparing to march on Managua, Somoza resigned the presidency and fled the country. (A year later, on 17 September 1980, he was assassinated in Asunción, Paraguay.) The Sandinistas marched victorious into Managua on 19 July 1979.

The day after they entered Managua, the FSLN and a Government of National Reconstruction set up a five-member junta to administer the country. The 1974 constitution was suspended, the national congress dissolved, and the Somoza Guardia Nacional was dissolved and replaced by the Sandinista People's Army. Many of the people were mobilised as a civil militia.

In May 1980 a 47-member Council of State was appointed to act as an interim legislature. In 1981 the ruling junta was reduced from five members to three, with revolutionary commander Daniel Ortega Saavedra appointed coordinator, and the Council of State was increased to 51 members.

The Sandinistas inherited a country in a shambles of poverty, homelessness, illiteracy, insufficient health care, and many other problems. An estimated 30,000 people had been killed in the revolutionary struggle, and half a million left homeless.

The new government nationalised the lands of the Somozas and their supporters, now gone, and established farming cooperatives. They waged a massive education campaign which reduced illiteracy from 50% to 13%. An immunisation programme eliminated polio, and reduced infant mortality to a third of the rate it had been before the revolution.

Idealism ran high after the victory of the revolution. There were many problems to iron out, and disagreements arose about what to do and by what means. But, in general, Nicaragua was a country full of hope.

Nicaragua's 'Good Neighbour'

It wasn't long, though, before the country encountered serious problems from its 'Good Neighbour' to the north.

The USA had supported 'their' Somoza dynasty all the way up until the final year, when its impending fall was unavoidable. A successful popular revolution against a government supported by the USA was not what the US government wanted at all. The news was out in Central America that this impoverished people had thrown off a powerful US-supported dictatorship, were now running their own country and were making rapid social gains for the common people. It was a dangerous example to the region.

In 1981, the year Ronald Reagan became US president, relations between Nicaragua and the USA took a turn for the worse. Three months after Reagan took office, the USA announced that it was suspending aid to Nicaragua, and began putting pressure on international aid agencies and banks, including the World Bank and the Inter-American Development Bank, not to lend to Nicaragua, which was already struggling to meet payments on a US$1.6 billion debt left by Somoza.

In the same year the USA allocated US$10 million for the organisation and funding of the counter-revolutionary military groups known as Contras, operating out of Honduras. Later, the Contras operated out of Costa Rica as well, so that Nicaragua was under attack from both its borders. Some of the original Contras were ex-soldiers of Somoza's Guardia Nacional, although disaffected local people later joined as well.

The USA escalated its war effort against Nicaragua throughout the 1980s, the Contras acting as its proxy army. Honduras was heavily militarised during this period; large-scale joint manoeuvres were carried out, apparently in preparation for a military invasion of Nicaragua. Contra camps were established along both Nicaraguan borders as bases from which attacks were launched.

1984 Elections

In January 1984 the FSLN announced that elections would be held in the following November. The elections, closely supervised by neutral international observers, were declared to be fair and just, although they were marred by accusations of discrimination against the opposition candidates. Daniel Ortega, head of the ruling junta, was elected president with 67% of the vote, and the FSLN won 61 of the 96 seats in the new National Assembly, which was to draft a new constitution within two years of its election. The new government took office in January 1985.

President Reagan, however, who had justified attacking Nicaragua on the grounds that its government was not elected and was not 'democratic', now maintained that the democratically elected government was not valid because the election was a sham. The USA continued its attacks on Nicaragua.

The Late 1980s

In May 1985, the USA implemented an embargo on trade with Nicaragua, and pressured other countries under its influence to do the same. The economic embargo lasted for the next five years and helped to strangle Nicaragua's economy.

US intervention in Nicaragua grabbed world newspaper headlines throughout the 1980s. Scandal succeeded scandal. It was known that the USA continued to fund the Contras, largely covertly through the CIA. The US Congress passed the 'Boland Amendment' and other bills, setting limits or calling for an end to US funding of the Contras. The US leadership and the CIA secretly continued funding, but the details leaked out in a series of revelations. The infamous 'Iran-Contra Affair' blew up when it was discovered that the CIA had sold weapons illegally to Iran at inflated prices, and used the money to fund the Contras.

Various peace plans were proposed by other countries throughout the years of conflict, but no agreement could be reached. The Costa Rican president, Oscar Arias Sánchez, finally came up with a peace plan that was signed in August 1988 by the presidents of Costa Rica, El Salvador, Nicaragua, Guatemala and Honduras. It was hailed as a great stride forward, but it was never fully implemented.

The 1990 Election

The next elections were scheduled for February 1990. By then, Nicaragua had been virtually crushed by the pressures of war and a collapsing economy. Much of what people remember about the late 1980s is hardship: shortages, food rationing, buses that could not be fixed for lack of spare parts, inflation up to 30,000% in 1988. The government, unsure of who was a Contra and who wasn't, carried out unwise acts of repression and maintained conscription, which was extremely unpopular, to fight the war which resulted in so many deaths.

The Unión Nacional Opositora (UNO), a broad coalition of 14 parties opposing the Sandinista government, was formed in 1989. As the 1990 elections approached, UNO had the backing and financing of the USA. The USA and leaders of the reforming (now former) Soviet Union began joint efforts to end the Central American conflict, and the USA also promised to lift the trade embargo, and give hundreds of millions of dollars in economic aid to Nicaragua if UNO won.

The UNO presidential candidate was Violeta Barrios de Chamorro, widow of the martyred *La Prensa* newspaper editor, Pedro Joaquín Chamorro, whose murder set off the revolution.

Elections were held on 25 February 1990. Chamorro won 55% of the vote for president, to Daniel Ortega's 41%. In the National Assembly, UNO won 51 seats, and the FSLN 39 seats. Though a minority, the FSLN's seats were enough to prevent UNO from having the 60% majority needed to change the constitution which had been put into effect under the FSLN government in January 1987.

Chamorro took office on 25 April 1990. The Contras stopped fighting at the end of June with a symbolic and heavily publicised turning-in of their weapons. Isolated skirmishes still occurred, but the all-out war was over.

The economic progress Chamorro had promised was slower in coming. In March 1990, before Chamorro even took office, the USA lifted its five-year trade embargo. But the expected economic aid was delayed; it was not until a year later that Nicaragua received aid from the USA, which, however, soon encountered new obstacles raised by an ultraconservative Washington politician, Republican Senator Jesse Helms.

Chamorro faced a tricky balancing act in trying to reunify the country and satisfy all interests. The FSLN, no longer in control, experienced some disintegration and division into hard-line and moderate factions; the radical wing, mainly based on the Sandinista unions, remained a potent political and social force.

GEOGRAPHY
Nicaragua, with 30,700 sq km, is the largest country in Central America. It is bordered on the north by Honduras, on the south by Costa Rica, on the east by the Caribbean Sea, and on the west by the Pacific Ocean.

The country has three distinct geographical regions: the Pacific lowlands, the north-central mountains, and the Caribbean lowlands, also called the Mosquito Coast or Mosquitia.

Pacific Lowlands
The Pacific coastal region is a broad, hot, fertile lowland plain, broken by about 40 volcanoes. Some of the largest are San Cristóbal (1745 metres), north-east of Chinandega; Concepción (1610 metres), on Isla de Ometepe in Lago de Nicaragua; Momotombo (1280 metres) on the north shore of Lago de Managua; and Masaya, also known as Santiago (1363 metres), which is protected as a national park.

The fertile volcanic soil, and the hot climate with its distinct rainy and dry seasons (191 cm annual rainfall), make these Pacific lowlands the most productive agricultural area in the country. The three major cities, Managua, León and Granada, are all in the Pacific lowlands, and most of Nicaragua's population lives here. The Pacific lowlands are also notable for their lakes. Lago de Nicaragua, also known by its indigenous name Cocibolca, or 'the sweet sea,' has a surface area of 8157 sq km. It is the largest lake in Central America, and the 10th-largest freshwater lake in the world. In it live the earth's only freshwater sharks, and other unusual life forms; scientists say this is because the lake was part of the Pacific Ocean until the volcanoes and rising land isolated it from the sea. The lake has over 400 islands. Forty-five rivers flow into Lago de Nicaragua, and one, the Río San Juan, flows out of it to the Caribbean.

Much smaller, at 644 sq km, Lago de Managua, or Xolotlán, is nevertheless a large lake. Eight rivers flow into it and one, the Río Tipitapa, flows from it into Lago de Nicaragua. There are many smaller lakes in volcanic craters.

North-Central Mountains
The north-central region, with its high mountains and valleys, is cooler than the Pacific lowlands and also very fertile. About 25% of the country's agriculture takes place here. The region is not as heavily populated as the lowlands but there are several major towns, including Estelí and Matagalpa. The highest point in the country, Pico Mogotón (2103 metres) is near the Honduran border, in the region around Ocotal. Lago de Apanás, an artificial reservoir on the Río Tuma near Jinotega, provides much of Nicaragua's electricity.

Mosquito Coast
The Caribbean region, or Mosquito Coast, occupies about half of Nicaragua's area. It is the widest lowland plain in Central America, averaging around 100 km in width. The 541-km coastline is broken by many large lagoons, river mouths and deltas; 23 rivers, some of them very big, flow from the central mountains into the Caribbean. Some of the most notable are the Río Coco (685 km long), Nicaragua's longest river, which forms much of the border between Nicaragua and Honduras; the Río Grande Matagalpa (430 km), the second-longest river, with its source near Matagalpa; and the Río San Juan (200 km), which flows from Lago de Nicaragua and defines much of the border between Nicaragua and Costa Rica.

The Caribbean region is hot, though not quite as hot as the Pacific side, and gets an immense rainfall, averaging from 330 to 635 cm annually. The region is very sparsely

NICARAGUA

populated, and is covered by tropical rain-forest and pine savanna. The largest towns in this region are Bluefields and Puerto Cabezas, both coastal ports.

There are a number of small islands off the Caribbean coast, surrounded by coral reefs. The largest islands, though even they are small, are the Islas del Maíz (Corn Islands) about 70 km off the coast.

CONSERVATION

Nicaragua has developed a serious environmental movement based in the government's Ministry of Environment & Natural Resources (Marena). Another important entity is the Fundación Nicaragüense para la Conservación y Desarrollo (FUNCOD) or the Nicaraguan Conservation & Development Foundation, which is active in campaigns to clean beaches.

There are also Municipal Ecological Brigades (Brigadas Ecológicas Municipales) which monitor the cleanliness of restaurants, and the national Colegio de Biólogos y Ecólogos (College of Biologists & Ecologists) which is a professional body and not a college in the educational sense. The Nicaraguan government is also committed to the environmental protection of the Río San Juan through projects described in that section of the guide.

CLIMATE

Different regions of Nicaragua have different climates, largely depending on altitude. The entire Pacific lowland zone, including Managua, is very hot. In the rainy season from May to November, the countryside is green and the air fresh, though humid. During the dry season from December to April, the plains become parched and brown, and when the wind blows, clouds of dust turn the air brown too. March and April are the hottest months.

The mountainous northern regions, around Matagalpa and Estelí, are much cooler than the lowlands. Even in the dry season, it's not as dusty there.

The Caribbean coastal lowlands are hot and wet, with an annual rainfall anywhere

between 330 and 635 cm. It can rain heavily even during the brief regional dry season, which lasts only from March to May.

GOVERNMENT

The government is divided into executive and legislative branches. The executive is headed by a president, elected by popular vote to a six-year term, assisted by a vice-president and an appointed cabinet. Violeta Barrios de Chamorro, of the UNO party, was elected president in the election of February 1990. The legislative branch consists of a 96-member National Constituent Assembly, also elected to a six-year term, by popular vote on a proportional representation basis.

The Sandinista government divided the country into six regions, but the Chamorro administration reverted to the long-standing system of 15 'departments', adding two autonomous regions on the Atlantic coast to split the former Zelaya department.

Since independence from Spain, Nicaragua has had 11 constitutions. The current one was approved by the National Assembly in 1986 and came into effect in January 1987.

ECONOMY

Agriculture is the basis of the Nicaraguan economy, accounting for around a quarter of the national income and employing around 35% of the labour force. Important crops include sugar cane, maize, beans, sorghum, bananas, oranges, coffee, cocoa, rice, wheat, sesame, and tobacco; livestock, shrimp and lobster are also important. The principal export crop is coffee; the cotton industry, formerly of importance, has fallen into decline. Beef, bananas and gold are also exported. Gold is the only mineral product. Nicaragua has great natural resources, including timber, metals and fishing, which have not been exploited.

Manufacturing, the second-largest sector of the economy (20% of national income), employs only 8% of the workforce. Unemployment rates are high, with estimates in 1993 at no less than 50% of the overall workforce.

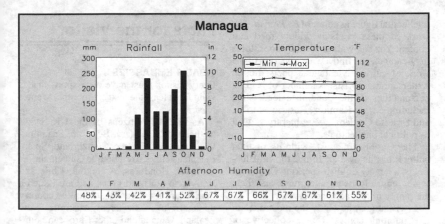

POPULATION & PEOPLE

Government statistics estimate that, in 1992, the population of Nicaragua was almost four million. *Mestizos*, of mixed Spanish and Indian ancestry, form the majority with 77% of the population. Other groups include Spanish and other Europeans, 10%; Blacks, 9%; and Indians, 4%.

The great majority of the population, around 90%, live in the Pacific lowland belt. The Caribbean region is very sparsely populated; it makes up half the country's land area, but has only 6% of its population.

There are about six ethnic groups in the Caribbean region. Indians include the Miskitos, Sumos and Ramas. There are two groups of Black people: those of West Indian (often Jamaican) descent, who are often English-speaking, and a small number of Garífunas (see the Honduras chapter for more on Garífuna people); and then there are mestizos, who often have come from other parts of Nicaragua, either recently or in the past. There has been a lot of mixing, so population grouping estimates are rather fuzzy.

The drift of people within Nicaragua from rural to urban areas has swollen the cities; although agriculture is important to the economy, 60% of the population is urban. People are also moving out of the country altogether. In the 1980s many refugees and exiles fled Nicaragua, mostly to Honduras and the USA. Perhaps as many as 20% of the people left. Since the change of government and the end of the war, some of these people have been returning to Nicaragua.

Nicaragua is a nation of young people: 74% of the population is under 30 years old, and 46% of the population is under 15.

ARTS

Poetry is one of Nicaragua's most important and beloved arts. Hispanic scholars count the country with Spain, Mexico, Argentina, and Cuba as a leader in the development of literary models and achievements, and no other Central American nation can match Nicaragua's literary output. Rubén Darío (1867-1916), a poet who lived in León, was known as the 'Prince of Spanish-American literature'. His writings inspired poetry movements and literary currents throughout the Latin world.

Three outstanding writers emerged soon after Darío, and their works are still popular: Azarías Pallais (1884-1954), Salomón de la Selva, and Alfonso Cortés. In the 1930s an experimental group, the 'Vanguardia' movement, came on the scene, led by José Coronel Urtecho, Pablo Antonio Cuadra, Joaquín Pasos, and Manolo Cuadra. The latter two, each brilliant in his own way, died early, but Pablo Antonio Cuadra remains a national

NICARAGUA

intellectual figure as editor of *La Prensa*. The work of these poets is widely read and quoted. You can walk into many bookstores in Nicaragua and find a wide selection of the work of current Nicaraguan poets, fiction writers, and essayists. A number of leading personalities in the Sandinista leadership, including Sergio Ramírez, Rosario Murillo, and Ernesto Cardenal, were literary as well as political intellectuals.

The Caribbean coast, with its distinct culture, has its own art forms, too. In Bluefields, a largely English-speaking Caribbean town, reggae is the popular music and there are plenty of reggae dance clubs.

In visual arts, probably the most distinctive painting comes from a collective of artists in the Archipiélago de Solentiname, in the south of Lago de Nicaragua. Ernesto Cardenal established a commune of artists, poets, craftspeople and other creative types. The area has since become well known for its colourful, primitivist style of painting.

Many *artesanías* (handicrafts) are produced in Nicaragua, some of them traditional arts, some of more modern origin. See the Things to Buy section later in this chapter for more details on handicrafts and where to find them.

RELIGION

Roman Catholicism is the dominant religion in Nicaragua, claiming almost 90% of the population. There is freedom of religion, however, and a number of Protestant sects also exist; notable among these are Pentecostals and Baptists.

The Moravian church, a Protestant sect that was introduced by missionaries in the days of the British, is important on the Caribbean coast.

LANGUAGE

Spanish is the language of Nicaragua. On the Caribbean coast, which was under British influence for over a century, English is also spoken, as are various Indian languages. English is the language of the Islas del Maíz.

Facts for the Visitor

VISAS & EMBASSIES

Every visitor must have a passport, that is valid for at least the next six months, to enter Nicaragua.

As of 1993, citizens of the UK, USA, Netherlands, Hungary, Belgium, Scandinavian countries, Greece, Switzerland, Spain, Liechtenstein, Luxembourg, Guatemala, El Salvador, Honduras, Argentina, Chile and Bolivia do not need visas, and are issued a tourist card for 30 days' stay in the country upon arrival. Citizens of Australia, New Zealand, Canada and other European countries do need visas, and these are good for 30 days from the date of issue, for entry and for 30 days after actual entry into the country.

However, border and airport practice is reportedly inconsistent in this area, so the best thing is to check with the Nicaraguan embassy in your country of origin. Tourist cards are officially available through airlines. Visa requirements may change, so you should check the current requirements before you go.

Visas can be extended twice, for 30 days each time, for a total stay of three months. Visas can only be extended at the Migración (immigration) office in Managua, which is at Km 7, Carretera Sur (☎ 650014/20). If you want to stay after the second extension runs out, you must leave the country and re-enter.

Nicaragua has, on paper, an onward ticket requirement, but it seems to be rarely enforced.

Nicaraguan Embassies

Visas can be obtained from a Nicaraguan embassy or consulate before reaching Nicaragua. In the USA, Nicaragua has consulates in Houston, Los Angeles, Miami, New York and San Francisco, in addition to its embassy in Washington DC.

Nicaraguan embassies in other countries include the following:

Canada
170 Laurier Ave West, Ottawa, Ontario KIP 5V5
(☎ (613) 234-9361/2, fax (613) 238-7666)
Colombia
Carrera 4a No 75-73, Bogotá (☎ 217-7680,
217-0391, fax 217-0509)
Costa Rica
Avenida Central No 2540, Barrio La California,
San José (☎ 333479, 338747, fax 215481)
El Salvador
71 Avenida Norte & 1a Calle Poniente, No 164,
San Salvador (☎ 246662, fax 241223)
Guatemala
10 Avenida, 14-72, Zona 10, Guatemala City
(☎ 374264, fax 357648)
Honduras
Colonia Lomas del Tepeyac, Bloque M-1,
Tegucigalpa (☎ 324290, 309025, fax 311412)
Mexico
Payo de Rivera 120, Lomas de Chapultepec, CP
11000, México DF (☎ 520-4421)
Panama
Calle 50 & Avenida Federico Boyd, Panama City
(☎ 696721, 230981)
UK
8 Gloucester Rd, London SW7 4PP
(☎ (071) 5813430)
USA
1627 New Hampshire Ave NW, Washington DC
20009 (☎ (202) 939-6570)

Foreign Embassies in Nicaragua

See the Managua section for details on
foreign embassies in Nicaragua.

CUSTOMS

Customs regulations are the usual 200 cigarettes or half-kg of tobacco, and three litres
of alcohol.

MONEY

During the Sandinista period, the country
sought hard currency, and most hotels in
Nicaragua, particularly those in Managua,
required payment in US dollars. However,
one economic goal the Chamorro administration has fulfilled is the establishment of a
stable national currency, the *córdoba*.
Payment in dollars is no longer required
anywhere in the country. Most hotels will
readily accept and change travellers'
cheques.

The Chamorro government has also facil-
itated reopening and expansion of the private

banking system, and travellers' cheques may
be exchanged at any bank as well as at *casas
de cambio*. Nicaragua is the only country in
Central America that does not have an American Express office.

In addition to MasterCard and Diners'
Club cards, Visa cards are now widely
accepted.

Note that Nicaraguan currency cannot
readily be changed in any other country. Be
sure to spend your córdobas before you leave
the country: once you cross the border, they
may only be good for souvenirs, though
black-market transactions are possible elsewhere in Central America, with rates better
at border stops than in the bigger cities. This
may change in the future.

During the 1980s, travellers were required
to change at least US$60 into córdobas upon
entering Nicaragua, but this requirement has
now been lifted.

Currency

The córdoba is divided into 100 centavos.
Bank notes come in denominations of one,
five, 10, 20, 50 and 100 córdobas. There are
smaller notes for 10 and 25 centavos, and
regular-sized notes bearing the fraction '½'
for half a córdoba (50 centavos). There are
no coins.

You may hear prices given in *pesos*,
another name for the córdoba.

Foreign		Nicaragua
A$1	=	4.7 córdobas
C$1	=	4.8 córdobas
DM1	=	3.95 córdobas
NZ$	=	3.8 córdobas
UK£1	=	9.95 córdobas
US$1	=	6.6 córdobas

Costs

You can usually find a cheap hotel room for
around US$3 to US$5 per person and an
inexpensive meal for around US$2 to US$4;
it costs around US$1.50 for a 100-km bus
ride. But these prices can vary quite a bit,
depending on where you are. Some places,

NICARAGUA

such as the Caribbean coast, are a bit more expensive.

Tipping
Most Nicaraguans do not leave tips in cheap restaurants. In good restaurants you could leave some change, or up to 10% of the bill in top-end places. Some restaurants include a service charge with the bill.

Bargaining
As usual, be certain to bargain in large outdoor markets, especially when buying artesanías. In small indoor grocery stores, known as *pulperías*, you don't bargain.

WHAT TO BRING
Most of Nicaragua is hot, especially the western lowlands around Managua; you probably won't need warm clothes unless you go to places in the mountains, like Matagalpa or Estelí. Take an umbrella if you are travelling during the rainy season or planning to visit the wet Caribbean coast.

Bring a torch (flashlight) for power failures. When travelling, carry your own toilet paper, as you normally won't find it in public facilities including bus stations.

Pharmacies are now opening all over Managua, and most standard medical supplies and medicines are widely available, including the antimalarial medication, chloroquine, necessary since malaria is endemic in Nicaragua.

You can find almost anything that is available in Nicaragua at the large Mercado Central (formerly named after Roberto Huembes) in Managua.

TOURIST OFFICES
Mintur, the ministry of tourism, has an office in Managua, a block from the Intercontinental Hotel, and an office in the Augusto C Sandino international airport. See the Managua section for details. Mintur also has offices in Nicaragua's main towns, and the people there are very helpful.

BUSINESS HOURS & HOLIDAYS
Business and government office hours are from 8 am to noon and 2 to 4 or 5 pm, Monday to Friday. Some businesses are also open on Saturday from 8 am to noon. Banks may be open shorter hours, from only around 9 am to 1 pm.

Public holidays include:

1 January
  New Year's Day
March/April
  Semana Santa (Holy Week) – Thursday, Friday and Saturday before Easter Sunday
1 May
  Labour Day
19 July
  Liberation Day (anniversary of 1979 revolution) – no longer an official holiday, but still observed with large commemorative events by the Sandinistas
1-10 August
  Festival of Santo Domingo (Managua only)
14 September
  Battle of San Jacinto
15 September
  Independence Day
2 November
  Día de los Muertos (All Souls' Day)
8 December
  Inmaculada Concepción (Immaculate Conception)
25 December
  Navidad (Christmas)

CULTURAL EVENTS
Each town and city in Nicaragua has annual celebrations for its patron saint. Two of the most famous of these celebrations occur in January and July, when the towns of Diriamba, Jinotepe, and San Marcos, in the department of Carazo south of Managua, celebrate St Sebastian's and St James' (Santiago) Days. These celebrations, known as Toro Guaco, include distinctive masked processions and mock battles involving folkloric figures satirising the Spanish conquistadors. Another Toro Guaco festival – the term covers a number of Nicaraguan folkloric celebrations – is held in honor of St Jerome (San Jerónimo) in the city of León.

POST & TELECOMMUNICATIONS
Post, telephone and telecommunications ser-

vices are provided at Telcor offices in every city and town in Nicaragua.

You can receive poste restante mail at any Telcor office by having it addressed to:

(name)
Lista de Correos
Telcor
(town name)
(department name)
Nicaragua

It will usually be held for one month, though sometimes only for a week or two.

The basic mailing charge for a postcard from Nicaragua to the USA (air mail) is four córdobas or US$0.64, and delivery time can be anywhere between seven to 21 days. Rates to Europe and Australia are about 30% to 50% higher, with much longer delays. Travellers in Nicaragua are strongly urged to register any important mail.

Long-distance domestic or international telephone calls can be made from Telcor offices, though access to direct dial and Sprint services are available from private phones. It may not be possible to make collect (reverse-charge) calls from every office, or to every country. In Managua, fax services are available in dozens of photocopying/camera shops as well as in many Telcor offices.

When dialling Nicaragua, remember that Managua's city code is (2). When dialling internally in Nicaragua, remember that each city has its own area code. When dialling from city to city, add a 0, so that, for example, calling Managua from Granada one would first dial (02). Numbers in Managua may be of five or six digits.

The following is a list of the area codes for Nicaraguan towns and cities:

Bluefields	082
Chinandega	0341
Estelí	071
Granada	055
Jinotega	063
Jinotepe	041
Juigalpa	081
León	0311
Masaya	052
Matagalpa	061
Ocotal	073
Poneloya	032
Rama	083
Rivas	0461
San Juan del Sur	0466
Somoto	072

TIME

Nicaragua is five hours behind GMT/UTC. Standard time is the equivalent of Eastern Standard Time in the USA. This is one hour ahead of both Honduras and Costa Rica.

WEIGHTS & MEASURES

The metric system is standard for weights and measures. Various other measures are also used, including the US gallon for petrol, and the *vara* (0.825 metres, or 33 inches) for distance.

BOOKS

Political events and developments in Nicaragua have inspired a flood of books about the country. Some informative or insightful ones include:

History & Politics

Una Tragedia Campesina (UCA, Managua, 1991, paperback), by Alejandro Bendaña (a prominent Sandinista), is an insightful account of the impact of the Contra war on Nicaraguan society.

Así es Nicaragua (Inturismo, Managua, 1989, paperback), by Dr Jaime Incer, Dr Francisco J Olivas & Guillermo Rothschuh Tablada, is an official guidebook published under the Sandinistas, and is useful for cultural data.

Comandos: The CIA & Nicaragua's Contra Rebels (Holt, New York, 1992, paperback), by Sam Dillon, is a detailed analysis of the Contra war by a leading US newspaper correspondent.

Culture & Politics in Nicaragua (Lumen Books, New York, 1986), by Steven White, has fascinating interviews and related material on the link between literature and revolution in Nicaragua.

Fire from the Mountain: The Making of a Sandinista (Crown, New York, 1985), by Omar Cabezas, is the classic account of the Sandinista guerrilla experience.

Nicaragua: Revolution in the Family (Vintage, New York, 1986), by Shirley Christian, is a historical narrative of the 1979 revolution by the leading US journalist on the ground at that time.

Nicaragua (WW Norton & Co, New York, 1989), by

NICARAGUA

William Frank Gentile, is a paperback of colour photographs.

Sandino (Monthly Review Press, New York, 1981), by Gregorio Selser, is an authoritative biography of Nicaragua's outstanding revolutionary.

The War in Nicaragua (University of Arizona Press, 1985), is William Walker's own account of his actions in Nicaragua. It was first published in 1860, the year he was shot by firing squad in Honduras.

Poetry

Useful collections of Nicaraguan poetry, which will offer the traveller many insights into the national culture, include:

Poets of Nicaragua, 1918-1979 (Unicorn Press, Greensboro, NC, 1982), by Steven White, is a useful bilingual anthology.

The Birth of the Sun: Selected Poems (Unicorn Press, Greensboro, NC, 1988), by Pablo Antonio Cuadra, is a judicious selection from the work of Nicaragua's outstanding contemporary writer.

Antología General de la Poesía Nicaraguense (Ediciones Distribuidora Cultural, Managua, 1984), by Jorge Eduardo Arellano, is an excellent anthology of Nicaraguan poetry.

MAPS

Mintur publishes *Mapa Turístico de Nicaragua*, with a Nicaraguan country map on one side and a city map of Managua on the other. It is sold for US$4 at the Mintur offices in Managua and at the airport.

MEDIA

Four daily newspapers are published in Managua. *La Prensa*, long established as the leading national daily, is owned by the Chamorro family and was extremely critical of the Sandinistas, but has followed an independent editorial line since the election of her government. *Barricada* and *El Nuevo Diario* are run by the Sandinistas. A new daily, *La Tribuna*, emphasizes business and foreign reporting, but also includes useful event listings. Generally, *La Prensa* and *Barricada* are available throughout the country. There are also several weeklies, as well as radio and TV stations.

The newspaper *Barricada* also created an international monthly magazine, *Barricada Internacional*, with Spanish, English and German editions. It costs US$35 per year for a regular subscription, US$25 per year for low-income earners, or US$18 for six months. For information or subscriptions, contact its offices at the following addresses:

Nicaragua
  Apartado 4461, Managua
UK
  23 Bevenden St, London N1 6BH
Canada
  PO Box 398, Station E Toronto, Ontario M6H 4E3
USA
  PO Box 410150, San Francisco, CA 94141 (☎ (415) 621-8981)

FILM & PHOTOGRAPHY

Film is available everywhere. Try photocopying/fax shops, often labelled *librerías* or bookstores although they often do not sell books, as well as pharmacies and pulperías (grocery stores). A roll of 36 colour-print film costs about US$7.

Opinions vary on whether it is wise to have your film processed in Nicaragua; you may want to keep it until you get to a country where the processing quality is likely to be more reliable. On the other hand, computerised, one-hour processing is now widely available throughout the world, including in Nicaragua.

HEALTH

Tap water is usually safe to drink in all but the smallest rural places. This is reportedly thanks to a joint USA-Somoza government potable water project, carried out years ago. Managuan tap water tastes unpleasantly of chlorine and other chemicals, but it shouldn't hurt you as long as it's running fresh from the tap. In some other cities the water tastes much better and is still safe to drink. You should still exercise the usual care about eating unpeeled raw foods, salads, meats and food from unsanitary street stalls.

Be sure to take precautions against malaria. Malaria-carrying mosquitoes are a problem in this country, especially during the rainy season. Chloroquine is available in pharmacies. But it's always a good idea to bring anything you think you might need with you.

WOMEN TRAVELLERS

The national Sandinista women's organisation, formerly called AMNLAE (Asociación de Mujeres Nicaraguenses Luisa Amanda Espinosa), is now known as IXCHEN. Some cities and towns around the country have an IXCHEN women's centre *(casa de la mujer)*, mainly featuring community and women's health clinics, as well as legal and family services. In San Juan del Sur, on the Pacific coast, the association operates a popular restaurant, La Soya. Visiting women are welcome to drop in at any IXCHEN women's centre.

There are no special dangers for women travelling in Nicaragua, but the same advice applies as for the rest of Central America about dress and so on (see the Women Travellers section in the introductory Facts about the Region chapter).

DANGERS & ANNOYANCES

Fortunately, the Contra war is over, so this is no longer a danger. However, violent demonstrations and outbreaks of kidnapping and other bandit-like activities by rearmed former Contras (known as *recontras)* and former Sandinista soldiers (similarly dubbed *recompas)* have taken place. Regions where travel was once prohibited or restricted, like the Caribbean coast, are now open and no special permits are required to travel there.

Crime, on the other hand, is getting worse as the economy remains in crisis and many families do not have even enough to eat. Most of it is sneak theft like pickpocketing and bag-slashing in crowded places. Pickpockets on buses, especially on the Managua city buses but also on the long-distance buses and trains, are notorious.

Expect at least one attempt during your visit, and protect yourself in advance. Wear a day pack on your chest rather than your back, don't wear jewellery, and do not allow yourself to be distracted in public places. You will probably never find yourself in any physical danger, and you certainly don't need to be paranoid, but you should be alert and aware, especially in Managua.

Robberies while leaving banks and casas de cambio have also increased.

Remember also that most of Nicaragua's freshwater lakes, including Lago de Managua, Laguna de Masaya and Lago de Nicaragua, are seriously polluted.

WORK

During the 1980s, *internacionalistas* from around the world came to Nicaragua to help the Sandinista effort, volunteering their labour for building projects, health projects, education, coffee picking, and more. With the defeat of the FSLN in the 1990 election, international volunteers suddenly dried up. A few international volunteer organisations still operate in Nicaragua (one of the better known ones, Habitat, constructs houses), but the country is not as full of idealistic volunteers as it once was.

Nonetheless, there is still plenty of need in the country. The FSLN still exists and 'the revolution continues', as the motto goes, and there are still opportunities for involvement if you want to volunteer. The best sources of such information are still the monthly foreign-language editions of *Barricada Internacional*.

Although it no longer runs extensive volunteer programs, you might inquire at the Central Sandinista de Trabajadores José Benito Escobar, near the north-western corner of the Barrio Martha Quezada in Managua. They may be able to use people in education or related areas. If you volunteered, you would be able to live in Nicaragua, learn much about the country and its people, improve your Spanish, and make a contribution to a people who can certainly use whatever help they can get, but you wouldn't get rich.

You probably won't find any paid work either. Teaching English, the old stand-by, might be an option, though even this might be hard to find.

NICARAGUA

ACTIVITIES
Hiking

Hiking is good in the Selva Negra forest, near Matagalpa, and in the surrounding mountains of the north; on Isla de Ometepe and the Archipiélago de Solentiname in Lago de Nicaragua; around the Volcán Masaya National Park; and the Laguna de Masaya lake just below it, to name a few places.

On the islands in Lago de Nicaragua – Ometepe, the Solentiname archipelago, and Zapatera – there are ancient petroglyphs (rock carvings), left by the Indians, which make good destinations for hikes.

Volcanoes are another good excuse for hiking; the Volcán Masaya and the two volcanoes on Isla de Ometepe (Concepción and Madera) are obvious spots, but there are many others in western Nicaragua.

Water Sports

Nicaragua has various possibilities for water sports. The Islas del Maíz offer swimming, snorkelling and diving; there's said to be an old Spanish galleon under about 20 metres of water about two km off the coast of the Isla de Maíz Grande, and there are various interesting caves and rocks full of marine life for exploring.

Fishing is good on Lago de Nicaragua, in other lakes and rivers, and in the sea. Surfing is popular at Poneloya beach, near León, as well as at Playa Popoyo in the department of Rivas. Beginning surfing instruction is to be offered at Montelimar.

There is good swimming at any of these beaches, and in various lagunas (volcanic crater lakes), including some in and near Managua. The Pacific coast resorts at Pochomil and San Juan del Sur are also very popular. The Laguna de Xiloá, 20 km from Managua, is most people's favourite for lake swimming, and unlike most Nicaraguan lakes it's clean.

HIGHLIGHTS
Regions

If you just rush through the country on the Interamerican Highway, you'll be missing something. Take the time to see and feel something of the variety of regions in Nicaragua.

The country's important cities and towns, including Managua, León, Granada and Masaya, are in the western lowlands. The mountainous, rural region to the north is cooler and fresher. Then there's the Caribbean region, most of it impenetrable tropical rainforest, where English is still spoken by a mixture of Indian and West Indian ethnic groups. The Islas del Maíz or Corn Islands, just 70 km offshore, are small, idyllic Caribbean islands with white sandy beaches and palm trees, surrounded by coral reefs.

You can make some interesting journeys while exploring Nicaragua's different regions: by boat down the Río Escondido from Rama to Bluefields on the Caribbean coast, by boat down the Río San Juan from San Carlos to El Castillo, by bus through some beautiful mountains and valleys between Matagalpa and Jinotega, or by a slow train clattering over the plains from Granada to León.

Colonial Cities

León and Granada were Nicaragua's two principal colonial cities. Both were founded in the 1520s and retain their Spanish colonial architecture.

The highlights of León include the magnificent cathedral, the largest in Central America, and the cathedral plaza with its lion statues, the unusual façade of the Church of La Recolección, and the Museo Rubén Darío, in the famous poet's boyhood home. Highlights in Granada include similarly distinctive churches and other buildings, a ride through the old city to the lake in one of the horse-drawn carriages still used as taxis, and a day trip to Las Isletas and Isla Zapatera just offshore. In both towns, simply walking around through the streets is interesting.

Masaya, another old city, has the most famous handicrafts market in the country. The town sits beside a volcanic crater lake, the Laguna de Masaya, over which towers the Volcán Masaya. The volcano is a national park, with a road going all the way to the top of the giant crater, and is also certainly worth seeing.

Managua, the capital, is much more recent, and most of the few old buildings it did have have been destroyed by earthquake. However, there's one old building in Managua that's hauntingly memorable: the ruins of the cathedral, standing eerily silent beside the lake.

Jinotega, half an hour from Matagalpa in the mountainous north, is not as old as some of the other old towns but the church there is one of the most beautiful in all Central America.

Islands

There are over 400 islands in Lago de Nicaragua, the largest lake in Central America. You might not get around to all 400 of them, but there are some especially worth seeing.

Ometepe, the largest island, has two volcanoes (one with a remote volcanic lake), good beaches, plenty of walks, and places to stay. Las Isletas, a group of 356 small islands, are just offshore from Granada and can be visited as a day trip. So can Isla Zapatera, known for its archaeological finds. The Archipiélago de Solentiname in the south of the lake is a haven for artists, poets and artisans.

Petroglyphs, ancient Indian rock carvings, as well as statuary and pottery, are found on Zapatera, Ometepe, and the Solentiname islands.

The Islas del Maíz or Corn Islands, off the Caribbean coast, are as idyllic as Caribbean islands are supposed to be.

Conversation

Nicaragua has been the scene of some of the most profound political developments in the world in the last 20 years. The people of Nicaragua have a lot to say. If you express interest, ask questions, and let them tell you about living through the years of dictatorship, the revolution and all that happened since, you'll hear many points of view and many remarkable things. A few weeks spent doing this can teach you more than years of reading newspapers.

ACCOMMODATION

Most budget accommodation in Nicaragua is in small, family-operated *hospedajes* or hotels. Usual costs are around US$3 to US$5 per person for a room with shared bath, which will almost certainly have cold water only; hot water is very rare. Normal hotel accomodation is widely available for US$7 to US$15 per person per night.

FOOD

A basic *plato típico* meal in Nicaragua is much like that anywhere else in Central America, consisting of eggs or meat (usually chicken, beef, pork or fish), beans and rice, salad (cabbage and tomatoes), tortillas, and fruit in season.

Under the free-enterprise-oriented Chamorro regime the restaurant sector has exploded in Nicaragua, and virtually every kind of food is available, ranging from cheap meals at street stands and in small restaurants to international cuisine, as well as pizza, Chinese food, and the ubiquitous *hamburguesas* (burgers).

Most common of all Nicaraguan foods is *gallo pinto*, a blend of rice and beans, with cooking water from the beans added to colour the rice. It is often served with eggs for breakfast. Another favourite breakfast dish is the *nacatamal* or sweet tamale made with ground corn. *Tajaditas*, crisp, fried banana chips, are also sometimes sold on the streets. Although Nicaraguans are rather proud of their beef, and it is a mainstay of many restaurants, vegetarians will be met with respect and hospitality.

DRINKS

Soft drinks such as Coca-Cola and Pepsi are found everywhere in Nicaragua. Fresh fruit drinks are usually safe to drink, even when mixed with water and ice, except in those few places where tap water is not safe to drink. Nicaraguan beers include Toña and Victoria. Rum is also produced in Nicaragua; the two major brands are Flor de Caña and Ron Plata. Many connoisseurs of rum consider Flor de Caña superior to Cuban, Haitian, and other expensive brands.

NICARAGUA

THINGS TO BUY

A wide variety of handicrafts are produced in Nicaragua. Some are particular to certain towns or villages. Distinctive Nicaraguan artesanías include quality cotton hammocks, basketry, ceramics, *junco* and other woven mats, ropes, threads, twines, weavings and textile arts, woodcarving, jewellery, paintings, carved and painted gourds and leatherwork.

Two large markets specialise in artesanías, selling arts & crafts from all over Nicaragua. The most famous handicrafts market in the country is at Masaya, 26 km from Managua. It's well worth visiting, and there are other places around Masaya where you can see crafts made and displayed.

Nicaragua's other well-known artesanías market is in one section of Mercado Central/Roberto Huembes in Managua, but the selection is not quite as wide as at Masaya.

You can also go to other towns where handicrafts are produced, see how they're made, and buy them there. Some of the towns known for ceramics are San Juan de Oriente (near Masaya), La Paz Centro (between Managua and León), and Somoto (near the Honduran border).

The village of Camoapa, in the Boaco department, is known for its woven hats and purses.

The islands of the Archipiélago de Solentiname, in the south of the Lago de Nicaragua, are known for a unique primitivist style of painting.

Other handicrafts are more widespread within regions. Large baskets of bamboo or cane, for example, are made in the Masaya department as a whole, as are *petate* mats (made of *tule*, a species of junco). The Centro de Artesanías in Masaya has a large map showing the regions where the various types of handicrafts are made.

Authentic pre-Columbian pottery, including burial urns, is apparently offered for sale on the island of Ometepe. However, it may be illegal to take such artifacts out of Nicaragua and/or illegal to import them into your home country.

Getting There & Away

AIR

Nicaragua's international airport, the Augusto C Sandino airport, is 12 km east of Managua. Nica is the national airline; in 1993, it only offered international flights to/from Miami, as well as a couple of domestic routes within Nicaragua.

Other airlines with international flights to/from Nicaragua include Aviateca, Tan/Sahsa, Lacsa, Copa, Caal, Cubana, American, Continental, Iberia and Aeroflot. Various other airlines (Taca, SAM, KLM, Lufthansa, British Airways and others) also have offices in Managua and offer flights that connect with Managua through other places.

Aeroflot, the Russian airline, long offered the cheapest regular direct flight between Central America and Europe. Although the end of the Soviet Union has also brought changes in Aeroflot business practices, you may want to inquire as to its fare offerings – bearing in mind its deteriorating safety record. It has one weekly flight from Moscow to/from Managua; see the Getting There & Away chapter for more information. In Nicaragua, the Aeroflot office is in the Edificio Málaga, Plaza España, Managua (☎ 660162, 660565).

LAND

Nicaragua has four overland border stations: three at the Honduran border and one at the Costa Rican border. All of them are open every day from around 8 am to 5 pm. Extensive international bus services are now available to, from, and through Nicaragua. Tica Bus operates to Tegucigalpa, San Salvador and Guatemala City from Managua, in addition to its services to Panama City through San José from Managua.

In Managua, the Tica Bus station (☎ 26094) is two blocks east of the Cine Dorado, in the Barrio Martha Quezada district where the budget hotels are found. (There's no sign on the building, but it's right on the corner.) All Tica Bus fares are payable in either córdobas or dollars except on the San José to Panama City leg, which must be paid in dollars (US$50).

Sirca bus tickets are generally cheaper: US$20 one-way or US$40 return, but their buses are somewhat older and in worse repair than the Tica buses.

The Sirca bus office (☎ 73833, 75726) is in the southern part of Managua, on Avenida Eduardo Delgado in the Altamira district, behind the Plaza de Compras.

To/From Honduras

The three border crossings between Nicaragua and Honduras are at Las Manos (near Ocotal), El Espino (near Somoto), and Guasaule between El Triunfo (Honduras) and Somotillo (Nicaragua). The latter crossing was closed after a flood washed the bridge away in 1982, but is now reopened. Buses go to all three border crossings.

Tica Bus services to Tegucigalpa cost US$20 one way and US$40 return, leaving Managua at 7 am and arriving at 4 pm.

To/From Costa Rica

The Nicaraguan side of the main border crossing between Nicaragua and Costa Rica, formerly at Peñas Blancas, seems to have moved down the road to Sapoá, several km inside the Nicaraguan border. Another border station at Los Chiles is reachable by boat from San Carlos on the Río San Juan (see that section later in the chapter for details).

Remember that Costa Rica has an onward ticket requirement, although it seems not to be rigorously enforced for non-Central American residents. Two bus companies, Tica Bus and Sirca, operate international buses between Managua and San José. Tica Bus advises that Nicaraguans, at least, may not be allowed across the border into Costa Rica unless in possession of an outward-bound ticket. This can be either an air or bus ticket. However, Tica Bus also advises that its bus drivers will sell passengers a return ticket if one is demanded by zealous border personnel. To be completely secure, you could buy a one-way ticket out of San José, either back to Managua (available from both companies) or on to Panama City (available from Tica Bus) to satisfy the requirement. (If you are driving your own vehicle into Costa Rica, of course no onward ticket will be required.)

A much cheaper option is to take a regular Nicaraguan bus up to the border, go across, and continue on the other side on a Costa Rican bus. You may still need your onward ticket from Costa Rica to cross the border, but you could buy a one-way ticket out of San José from one of the international operators in Nicaragua. Local buses to the border depart frequently from Rivas.

Tica buses leave Managua daily at 7 am, arriving in San José at around 4 pm and cost 180 córdobas (about US$30) one way or US$60 return. Officially such tickets are only sold to Nicaraguan citizens, with foreigners obliged to purchase a ticket through San José to Panama City, for US$40 one way and US$80 return.

Sirca buses leave Managua on Monday, Wednesday and Friday at 5 am, and are generally cheaper at US$20 one way or US$40 return. They make a stop at Rivas at about 9.30 am before reaching the border, so you can board Sirca buses at Rivas, or just buy an onward ticket there as well as in Managua. Unlike Tica, Sirca do not sell tickets at the border itself – so if you arrive at the border without an onward ticket and one is demanded by border personnel, you'll have to buy the more expensive Tica Bus ticket.

To/From Other Central American Countries

The Tica buses which leave Managua daily at 7 am (arriving in San José at around 4 pm) continue on to Panama the next day at 10 am, arriving there at 5 pm.

The Tica service to San Salvador costs US$35 one way (US$70 return) via Tegucigalpa. Buses leave Managua at 7 am, arrive in Tegucigalpa at 4 pm, then leave immediately to reach the Salvadoran capital by 6 pm.

The service to Guatemala City, via Tegucigalpa and San Salvador, costs US$43 one way and US$86 return. It leaves Managua at 7 am and stays overnight in San Salvador, where the rider is obliged to pay for his own hotel, arriving in Guatemala City at 11 am the next day.

SEA

Nicaragua's major Caribbean ports are Bluefields and, less importantly, Puerto Cabezas. On the Pacific coast, the main ports are Corinto, Puerto Sandino, and San Juan del Sur, in that order of importance.

There are no organised passenger boat services to these places, but fishing and cargo boats are always coming and going on the Caribbean side, especially at Bluefields, (the port is actually at Bluff, just offshore). You may be able to hitch a ride to another Central American port or island or some other Caribbean destination. Ask around and try your luck. The Pacific coast does not have as much small-boat traffic.

RIVER

Rivers define much of the border between Nicaragua and Honduras (the Río Coco, also called Río Segovia), while the Río San Juan forms much of the border with Costa Rica. The major border crossings, however, are not over these rivers. Both of these borders were dangerous zones of conflict during the Contra war, and it's still unlikely you'll be crossing into or out of Nicaragua by river. There is a border crossing between Nicaragua and Costa Rica at Los Chiles, reachable by boat from San Carlos.

LEAVING NICARAGUA

There's a US$12 tax on departing flights.

Getting Around

AIR

Nica (formerly Aeronica) operates two domestic air routes. One goes five times a week between Managua and Bluefields, and costs US$45 one way, US$91 return. The other goes seven days a week between Managua and Puerto Cabezas, costing US$58 one way, US$115 return. Reservations must be confirmed 24 hours before departure.

Nica at one time was the only commercial domestic airline in Nicaragua. It also operated a Managua-Bluefields-Islas del Maíz route, which may begin again.

Another company, VIG Aeroservicios (☎ 631070), now offers a Managua to Puerto Cabezas flight on Monday, Wednesday and Friday for US$54 one way. There are also services to Bluefields on Tuesday and Thursday (US$47 one way) and to the Islas de Maíz the same days (US$60 one way). The same company flies to the mining villages of Rosita, Bonanza and Siuna for US$53 to US$63 return, depending on the destination.

A new air service, run by La Costeña (☎ 631228/81), is open between Managua and the Atlantic coast. Daily flights are available from Managua to Buefields, Puerto Cabezas, Islas del Maíz, Waspaán and some mining villages (where foreigners almost never go).

BUS

There are buses to most cities, towns and villages in Nicaragua. During the US embargo in the 1980s, local bus services were in a mess, but now buses are regular and frequent, albeit very crowded. Bus services usually start very early in the morning, and finish in the late afternoon.

Nicaraguan buses are famous for their pickpockets. Expect someone to try to pickpocket you on every journey, and take appropriate precautions. If you have luggage which must be put into the storage compartment or on the roof, watch it whenever there would be any possibility of someone either taking off with it or going through it.

Nicaraguan buses often charge an extra fare for your baggage: in fact, you may have to pay the same fare for your pack to ride the bus as for yourself – or sometimes even more. You can haggle over this, but usually you will have to pay. Many travellers stash their baggage somewhere safe and use only a day pack to carry essentials while travelling within the country, avoiding the extra fare and the problem of guarding belongings every minute. Just about any hotel will store baggage for you while you travel.

Yellow former US school buses now operate on many interurban lines in Nicaragua. They are not school buses even though they have not been repainted.

TRAIN

Nicaragua's only major rail line, the Ferrocarril del Pacífico de Nicaragua (Nicaragua Pacific Railroad) operates from Managua north to León and further, and south to Granada, with the latter service stopping at Masaya.

Trains from Managua to León leave at 8 am, 1 and 6 pm daily and take two hours (US$0. 85 one way). The 1 pm service continues north to Sauce, Malpaisillo, and Río Grande, where it remains overnight. Returning from León to Managua there are trains daily at 5, 6 and 8 am.

There's also a 1st-class service (tren grande), on Monday and Thursday only, which departs Managua at 7.30 am (arriving 2 pm) and returns the same day (US$1 return).

Trains from Managua to Granada depart daily at 8 am, take 1½ hours and cost US$0.85 one way. There is also a 6 pm service (arriving at 8 pm) which remains overnight in Granada. Returning from Granada to Managua there are trains daily at 5, 10 and 11.30 am.

For further information, call the rail company (☎ 24337) in Managua. Watch out for pickpockets on trains, just as on buses.

TAXI

Taxis operate in all the major towns and cities of Nicaragua. They're not metered; be sure to negotiate the fare before getting in.

CAR RENTAL

There are several car rental agencies in Managua; see that section for details.

BICYCLE

There's no reason why you couldn't bicycle through Nicaragua, except that it is uncomfortably hot. Bring any spare parts you might need with you. We heard of one bicycle rental shop in Managua (see the Bicycle Rental section), but didn't find it open; you might check it out.

HITCHING

Hitching is a common and accepted practice in Nicaragua. As elsewhere in Central America, it's polite to offer a little money when you're given a ride.

BOAT

Boats are the only way to get to some places in Nicaragua. On the Caribbean coast, boats go down the Río Escondido from Rama to Bluefields; from Bluefields to the Islas del Maíz; and from Bluefields to other places along the coast, including Laguna de Perlas.

Regularly scheduled boat services on Lago de Nicaragua include three routes from Granada: to Isla de Ometepe, to San Carlos via Isla de Ometepe, and to San Carlos via a couple of villages on the eastern lakeshore. A quicker service goes several times daily between Isla de Ometepe and San Jorge, near Rivas, which takes only one hour compared with 3½ hours from Granada. Boats also depart from Granada for shorter day trips to explore Las Isletas and Isla Zapatera. The Archipiélago de Solentiname in the south of the lake is reached from San Carlos.

Trips down the Río San Juan to El Castillo, an old Spanish fortress, and to San Juan del Norte (Greytown) have resumed, departing from San Carlos. However these are not cheap. (See the relevant sections.)

TOURS

Nueva Tur-Nica in Managua offers a wide selection of tours, not only around Managua but all over the country. See the Managua section for details on Nueva Tur-Nica. You could also contact Mintur, the ministry of tourism, for information on tours.

NICARAGUA

Managua

Population 933,597

The capital of Nicaragua, Managua is a large city spread across the southern shore of the lake of the same name. The lake itself, which the Indians called Xolotlán, is about 58 km long and 25 km wide, and there are a number of other lakes in the craters of old volcanoes within and near the city.

More than a quarter of Nicaragua's people live in Managua, and more are migrating all the time from the countryside. The city is the commercial centre for the surrounding agricultural land as well as the national centre for business, commerce, manufacturing, higher education and government. It is always hot, being only 50 metres above sea level: daytime temperatures hover around 30°C to 32°C (86°F to 90°F) throughout the year.

History

The site of Managua has been inhabited for a very long time. The Huellas de Acahualinca archaeological site within the city limits, where footprints of men, women, children and animals running towards the lake were covered and preserved by cool volcanic mud, is estimated to be at least 10,000 years old.

At the time of the Spanish conquest, Managua was an Indian city. The settlement stretched along the south shore of the lake as far as Tipitapa, and the Indians who lived here practised agriculture, hunting and fishing. They put up a vigorous resistance to the Spanish, who consequently destroyed their city and established their own principal cities at León and Granada. Managua was only a village from then until the mid-19th century.

In 1811, when struggles for independence were spreading through Central America, the village of Managua was given the title of Villa Leal de Santiago de Managua ('loyal town of St James of Managua') by the Spanish king. In 1846, 25 years after independence, Managua was proclaimed a city.

It was declared the capital of Nicaragua in 1857, as part of a settlement between the fiercely liberal León (capital of Nicaragua since 1524) and the equally fiercely conservative Granada, after conflicts between the two had repeatedly erupted into civil war. Managua, midway between the two, was chosen as a compromise capital.

A number of natural disasters, including two major earthquakes this century, have racked the city. The colonial city was destroyed by earthquake in March 1931, and swept by fire five years later. It was completely rebuilt, only to be destroyed once again by another earthquake in 1972. Geologists found the site of the city to be riddled with faults, so that major earthquakes had to be expected from time to time. After the 1972 earthquake, the city centre was not rebuilt, but rather decentralised, with markets, commercial centres and residential districts built on the city's outskirts.

Orientation

Since the 1972 earthquake, Managua has had no 'centre' or downtown district. Much of what was formerly the city centre is still vacant land; in some parts of the old centre, people have constructed houses out of tin or cardboard cartons on the bare dirt. Only the ruins of the old municipal cathedral, the plaza in front of it and a few important buildings nearby, like the Palacio Nacional, testify to where the centre used to be.

Like other Nicaraguan cities and towns, Managua has very few street names. Only the major roads have names; ordinary streets have none. Some names have fluctuated according to the changing outlook of the political regime. People describe locations not by street addresses, but in relation to landmarks. Directions are given sometimes by cardinal points (north, south etc) but more often by a system in which *al lago* (to the lake) means north, *al sur* (to the south) means south, *arriba* (up) means east, and *abajo* (down) means west. Locations will be given in these directions, in relation to landmarks, and usually by blocks; for example, 'del Cine Dorado, una cuadra al sur y dos

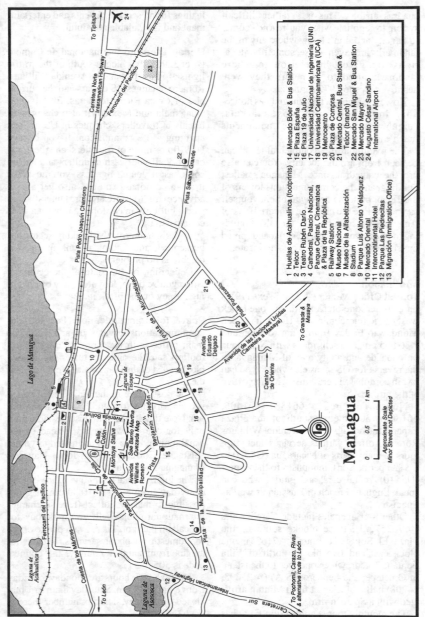

Managua

1   Huellas de Acahualinca (footprints)
2   Telcor
3   Teatro Rubén Darío
4   Cathedral, Palacio Nacional,
    Parque Central, Cinemateca
    & Plaza de la República
5   Railway Station
6   Museo Nacional
7   Museo de la Alfabetización
8   Stadium
9   Parque Luis Alfonso Velásquez
10 Mercado Oriental
11 Intercontinental Hotel
12 Parque Las Piedrecitas
13 Migración (Immigration Office)
14 Mercado Bóer & Bus Station
15 Plaza España
16 Plaza 19 de Julio
17 Universidad Nacional de Ingeniería (UNI)
18 Universidad Centroamericana (UCA)
19 Metrocentro
20 Plaza de Compras
21 Mercado Central, Bus Station &
    Telcor (branch)
22 Mercado San Miguel & Bus Station
23 Mercado Mayor
24 Augusto César Sandino
    International Airport

Approximate Scale
Minor Streets not Depicted

0   0.5   1 km

NICARAGUA

cuadras arriba'. This is a rather difficult system to negotiate when you're a newcomer to the city and don't know where any of the landmarks are; even worse, sometimes locations are given in relation to where landmarks used to be before they were destroyed by the 1972 earthquake.

However, signage in Managua has noticeably improved, with most markets, neighbourhoods, and public monuments much easier to find.

The pyramidal Intercontinental Hotel can be seen from around the city. You can also use the cathedral, once Managua's tallest building, and the communications towers of the Telcor building nearby to orient yourself as you explore the city. The modern Bank of America skyscraper is now the tallest building in Nicaragua. Managua is flat and spread out so these landmarks are easy to locate.

Information

Tourist Office Mintur (☎ 22498, ext 119) is on a corner, one block south and one block west of the Intercontinental Hotel. It is open Monday to Friday from 8 am to noon and 1.30 to 5 pm, and sells maps with Nicaragua on one side and a city map of Managua on the reverse for US$4; as elsewhere, you can pay in córdobas. There is also a Mintur office at the airport.

Nueva Tur-Nica (☎ 661387, 661406, 661306), 300 metres south of the Plaza España traffic lights on Avenida Williams Romero, offers various services including tours to many parts of Nicaragua (US$20 to US$35 per person), minibuses to the airport (US$10), rental cars, and guides who can speak English, French or Russian as well as Spanish.

Other tour agencies include Careli Tours (☎ 782572/3), three blocks south of the Plaza El Sol; ICN Tours (☎ 71694), one block east and two blocks north of Villa Fontana Telcor, which operates to the island of Ometepe; and Senderos (S A) (☎ 25693, 24208) half a block east from Mintur, affiliated with a Spanish firm.

The monthly tourist guide *Guía Fácil* has listings for all services, events and entertainment and is available at Mintur.

Money The Buro Internacional de Cambio (☎ 663296), two blocks south of the traffic lights at Plaza España on Avenida Williams Romero, changes US dollars and the currencies of Costa Rica, Honduras, El Salvador, Guatemala and Mexico. It also changes all brands of travellers' cheques in US dollars, charging a 3% commission. If you change US$100 or more of travellers' cheques, you can get half your cash in dollars and half in córdobas; if you change less, you must take it all in córdobas. You can also get a cash advance on MasterCard or Diners' Club cards, but only in córdobas and with a 12% commission.

Under Chamorro, the banking sector has burgeoned, and finding a bank or casa de cambio is no problem.

Depending on the state of the economy while you're there, 'coyotes' may be changing money on the black market.

Post & Telecommunications Post and telecommunications services are at Telcor. The main office is in the large building with a rooftop satellite antenna tower, about two blocks west of the Plaza de la República near the lake.

The post office in the main Telcor office is open Monday to Saturday from 8 am to 7 pm. Note that it will hold poste restante mail only for one or two weeks instead of the usual month. Have mail addressed to you at 'Lista de Correos, Telcor Jorge Navarro, Managua, Nicaragua'.

The international telephone office is open every day from 8 am to 10.30 pm. It is not possible to make a collect (reverse-charge) international phone call; you must pay for the call on the spot. There is a separate office for domestic telephone services. To call Nicaragua from another country, the country code is 505.

The fax office hours are Monday to Friday from 8 am to 10 pm, Saturday 8 am to 1 pm, closed on Sunday. The fax number there is (2) 62-4004/5.

Telcor has branch offices in various parts of the city, including one at the Mercado Central/Roberto Huembes, near the bus station.

Foreign Embassies The tourism office has a complete list of the many embassies and consulates in Managua. Embassies include:

Colombia
Reparto Los Robles, main entrance two blocks west and half a block north (☎ 78-0058)
Costa Rica
former IBM building, 2nd floor (☎ 62-5573)
Cuba
From principal (3rd) entrance of Las Colinas, 325 metres west, Km 8½, Carretera a Masaya (☎ 71182, 71392, 71203)
El Salvador
Pasaje Los Cerros, Avenida del Campo, Las Colinas, No 142 (☎ 71636, 71734)
Guatemala
Km 11½, Carretera a Masaya (☎ 79697)
Honduras
Planes de Altamira, No 29 (☎ 670182/3)
Mexico
Km 4½, Carretera a Masaya, beside Optica Matamoros (☎ 784919/21, 75886)
Panama
Pancasán No 61; from Hotel Colón, one block east, four blocks south and half a block north (☎ 78-3304)
UK
Entrada Principal de la Primera Etapa, Los Robles (☎ 78-0014/887)
USA
Km 4½, Carretera Sur (☎ 66-601/3/5)

Immigration The Migración office (☎ 65-0014, 65-0020) is at Km 7, Carretera Sur. It's open Monday to Friday from 8 am to noon and 2 to 4 pm. You must come here to extend your visa.

Travel Agencies Travel agencies in and near Plaza España include Viajes América (☎ 661130, 660684), Agencia de Viajes Fronteras (☎ 664134) and Aeromundo (☎ 663408).

Bookshops Librería Vanguardia (☎ 25944) is half a block east of the José Martí monument, at Paseo Tiscapa and Hispamer

(☎ 780825, 783216) is on the east side of the UCA in Reparto Tiscapa.

Pharmacies Pharmacies have opened all over Managua, with some operating 24 hours.

Emergency Emergency phone numbers in Managua are:

Police	71295, 71788,
	71245, 74130
Fire	651444
Red Cross (Cruz Roja)	51761, 51592

Things to See
Several of Managua's most notable buildings stand around the **Plaza de la República**, part of which is also called the **Parque Central**, near the lake.

The **municipal cathedral**, once a richly impressive edifice, was heavily damaged by the 1972 earthquake. But the ruin, still standing beside the lake, is one of Managua's most famous sights. You can go inside: the roof is gone, but the walls still stand.

Near the cathedral is the **Palacio Nacional**, one of the few colonial buildings that has not been demolished by earthquake. At the entrance there are two giant paintings, depicting Augusto C Sandino and Carlos Fonseca.

On the plaza itself is the **tomb of Carlos Fonseca**, and a monument to Rubén Darío, Nicaragua's best known and beloved poet. Behind the monument, near the lake, is the large, white, modern **Teatro Rubén Darío**. On the ground floor of the theatre is the **Teatro Experimental**.

On the other side of the plaza, opposite the theatre on the corner of Avenida Bolívar, there is a low, nondescript building: this is the **Cinemateca** theatre, which hosts excellent international films.

On the west side of the plaza, the communications antennae towering over the Telcor building make it visible from all over the city. Telcor is the centre for international and domestic telecommunications and postal services.

NICARAGUA

410 Nicaragua – Managua

A large *malecón*, or walkway, has been built at the lakeside by the city administration, but unfortunately the lake is too polluted for swimming.

Away from the city centre is the new **Cathedral of the Immaculate Conception**. Most of the money for its construction was provided by Tom Monaghan, owner of a chain of pizza restaurants. It is a modern but rather curious concrete structure; some say its many small domes make it resemble a mosque. Cardinal Miguel Obando y Bravo, who formerly served mass at a small colonial church at Santo Domingo de las Sierritas, now officiates at the new cathedral. It is located south of Tiscapa near the Metrocentro mall.

Museums Managua has a number of museums. The **Huellas de Acahualinca** museum preserves some of the most ancient evidence of human habitation in Central America: the footprints of men, women, children and animals running towards Lago de Managua. The footprints are believed to be around 10,000 years old and to have been made during a volcanic eruption, possibly of the Masaya volcano, that buried them under a layer of ash and mud. This preserved the prints until their discovery in 1874. The museum (☎ 25291) is open Monday to Friday from 8 am to noon and 1 to 4 pm and admission is US$1. To get there, take bus No 112 west from in front of the Cine González, near the Plaza de la República.

The **Museo Nacional** (☎ 25291), about one km east of the Plaza de la República on Pista Pedro Joaquín Chamorro, is open Monday to Friday from 9 am to noon and 1 to 4 pm; admission is US$0.40 for foreigners. To get there, take bus No 112 from the Cine González, near the Plaza de la República.

Another museum is the **Museo de la Revolución**, beside Mercado Central, which has interesting exhibits on the history of Nicaragua, with emphasis on the revolutionary struggle throughout this century. The **Museo de Alfabetización**, half a block north of the Parque Las Palmas, tells the story of Nicaragua's literacy campaign under the Sandinistas.

Markets Probably the most interesting of Managua's large outdoor markets is **Mercado Central**, formerly Mercado Roberto Huembes, which has a large section devoted to artesanías from all over the country. This is a huge market and almost anything available in Nicaragua can be found in it. The Eduardo Contreras complex beside the market includes a major bus station and a branch office of Telcor. Bus Nos 109 and 119 come to Mercado Central; No 109 departs from in front of the Intercontinental Hotel or from the Plaza de la República, while No 119 departs from Plaza España.

Other major outdoor markets include the Mercado Oriental, Mercado Bóer (formerly Israel Lewites), Mercado San Miguel (formerly called Ivan Montenegro or Oscar Benavides), and Mercado Mayor.

Lagunas Several lagunas, or volcanic crater lakes, lie within and just outside the city limits. Behind the Intercontinental Hotel is the **Laguna de Tiscapa**. On the western outskirts of the city, the **Laguna de Asososca**, with the **Parque de las Piedrecitas** on its shores, is a popular swimming spot. On the north-western outskirts of the city, near Lago de Managua, is the **Laguna de Acahualinca**. The favourite, though, is the **Laguna de Xiloá**, 20 km north-west of the city (see Around Managua).

Activities
Baseball is popular in Managua. Games are held several times weekly in the height of the baseball season (October to April) at the large stadium on Avenida Williams Romero near the Barrio Martha Quezada.

Festivals
The festival of Santo Domingo, Managua's patron saint, is held from 1 to 10 August, and features a carnival, bullfights, cockfights and other sports. A procession with music and

dancers takes the statue of the saint to its shrine at Sierritas de Managua, culminating in fireworks. Local holidays are observed on 1 and 10 August. International Women's Day (8 March), May Day (1 May), the anniversary of the 1979 Sandinista Revolution (19 July), and Independence Day (15 September) are also celebrated in Managua.

Places to Stay

Barrio Martha Quezada, a district about eight blocks by five blocks between the Intercontinental Hotel on the east side and the Cine Dorado on the west, is a residential district with many simple, cheap guesthouses and places to eat. International travellers long tended to congregate here, as it was about the only place in the city with budget accommodation. There are no street names in this district; directions are usually given in relation to the Cine Dorado.

Hospedaje Norma (☎ 23498), one block south and half a block east of the Cine Dorado, is well known and about the cheapest lodging in the district, charging US$2.30 per person for basic rooms with shared bath.

Guest House Santos (☎ 23713), a block north and half a block east of the Cine Dorado, is a more pleasant place, with a courtyard area where travellers gather. Meals are served from the kitchen off to one side. Rooms cost US$3 per person and have windows and fans.

A block east on the same street, *Hospedaje Quintana* has double rooms at US$5 per person, with fan and shared bath; there's a sitting area and they will prepare breakfast if you want. Another block further east, still on the same street, *Hospedaje Meza* (☎ 22046) has rooms at US$4 per person for one or two people in a private room, or US$3 per person in a shared room with four beds.

Around the corner, *Hospedaje Carlos* (☎ 22554, 27946) has no sign outside except for the house number (No 735). It's clean and more up-market than most places in the area, in that all the rooms come with private bath, and costs US$5 per person. It is half a block north of the Tica bus terminal.

On the road running directly east from the Cine Dorado are three more hospedajes. In the first block in front of the movie house, *Hospedaje Dorado* (☎ 26012) has rooms at US$4 per person. Two blocks east, at the end of the block on the corner, *Hospedaje Molinito* (☎ 664431) has no sign, but it has rooms at US$2.50 per person.

In the same block, *Pensión Azul* has no sign either, but you can recognise it by its tall blue fence. This is a family home with just a couple of very pleasant rooms; the price is negotiable, depending how long you plan to stay, but is usually around US$4 per person. You can cook in the kitchen and wash your clothes, and the family is friendly.

There are also a few more expensive (and better quality) places to stay in this area. The *Jardines de Italia* (☎ 27967) charges US$15 per room for any number of people. All the rooms are clean, come with private bath and fan (air-conditioning is US$5 extra), and there's a TV, sitting area, a house restaurant and bar.

The *Hotel El Colibrí* (☎ 27420), beside the Hospedaje Norma, has double rooms with private bath and fan at US$10. Two blocks east on the same street, the *Tres Laureles* (☎ 24440) is an excellent small guesthouse with singles/doubles for US$16/24. Budget lodgings in other parts of the city include the *Hotel Chepito*, a few blocks from Plaza España, and the *Hotel Royal*, near the Museo Nacional.

B&B arrangements in private homes have now made an appearance in Managua with some success, but they are not necessarily cheap. *Señora Sandra Velez* (☎ 22243), across from La Primerísima radio, three blocks north and one east of the Cine Dorado, charges US$25 per day.

Small hotels have also opened in the Barrio Bolonia, including *El Portal* (☎ 662558), across from the San Francisco church, which has six rooms with private baths from US$6 to US$15. If you're planning a longer stay in Managua, check the newspapers' classified ads because there are often advertisements for rooms and houses for rent.

NICARAGUA

PLACES TO STAY			
6	Guest House Santos	22	Tres Laureles Guest House
7	Refugio Los Quelites	28	Intercontinental Hotel
8	Hospedaje Dorado		
10	Hotel El Colibri	▼	PLACES TO EAT
11	Hospedaje Norma		
13	Hospedaje Quintana	12	Cafetin Mirna
14	Hospedaje Meza	19	Comedor Sara
15	Hospedaje Carlos	21	La Bambu Vegetarian Breakfasts
16	Hotel Jardines de Italia	24	Cafetin Gloria
17	Hospedaje El Molinito	25	Restaurante El Cipitio
20	Pension Azul		

OTHER	
1	Stadium
2	Bus Stop
3	Central Sandinista de Trabajadores
4	Bus Stop
5	Bus Stop
9	Cine Dorado
18	Tica Bus Station
23	Cine Cabrera
26	Mintur (Tourist Office)
27	Bus Stop

Places to Eat

With the growth of the restaurant sector in Managua, travellers will have no trouble finding cheap places to eat. Pizza and pasta are available everywhere.

Ananda (☎ 662451) which is across from the Montoya statue, is a popular vegetarian restaurant.

There are several inexpensive places to eat in the Barrio Martha Quezada. Most of them are good places to meet other travellers.

Cafetín Mirna has no sign, but it's the first house around the corner from the Hospedaje Norma. It is an excellent place for breakfast or lunch: both cost around US$2. Mirna and her husband have put several big tables in what was the sitting room of the house; the food is well prepared and the service is fast and friendly. It's open every day from 7 am to 2 pm.

Another good place for breakfast is *La Bambú*, which has a sign out front saying 'Vegetarian Breakfasts'. It has four standard breakfasts to choose from, all at US$2; it's open Monday to Saturday, from 7 to 10 am.

The *Comedor Sara* and *Comedor Gloria* both open at around noon and stay open until the last diners have left in the evening. Both serve a typical lunch or dinner (meat, beans, rice, salad, tortillas, soft drink) for around US$2.

Los Antojitos, a Mexican restaurant on the eastern edge of Barrio Martha Quezada opposite the Intercontinental Hotel, is more expensive still. Most meals are around US$10; it's open for lunch and dinner. The restaurants at the *Hotel Intercontinental* are also fairly expensive.

Entertainment
On weekend nights there's music and a public party with dancing at La Piñata, beside Plaza 19 de Julio, opposite the Universidad Centroamericana on the Pista de la Municipalidad; it is popular with students. There are several places to eat around the plaza.

Discos include Lobo Jack's and El Infinito, both on the Camino de Oriente, and both expensive. Nicaraguans from the Caribbean coast patronise the Bambi, El Pinguino and Reggae Mansion nightclubs, which feature reggae and other coastal and Caribbean music.

Concerts, dance, theatre and other performances are presented at the Teatro Rubén Darío (☎ 23630/1/2), on the Plaza de la República. On the ground floor is a second, separate theatre, the Teatro Experimental.

Managua has a number of movie houses which present the usual fare (violence, kung fu, sex etc) but Cinemateca, on the south side of the Plaza de la República on the corner of Avenida Bolívar, frequently presents excellent films from particular countries and films by women. The building is inconspicuous:

look for the schedule of current films posted outside the door or printed, along with other event announcements, in *La Tribuna*.

Things to Buy
The best place in the city for Nicaraguan artesanías is Mercado Central, with a large section devoted to Nicaraguan and other Central American arts & crafts.

Getting There & Away
Air For information on domestic air services, see the introductory Getting Around section earlier in this chapter.

Bus The major bus stations for long-distance routes are at large outdoor markets. Only the major routes are mentioned here; there are many other bus services to smaller towns. Intercity bus fares in Nicaragua are generally US$1 to US$2 one way, and only rarely higher. You can phone ENABIN (☎ 52138) for information on intercity bus routes.

The principal bus stations are: Mercado Central/Roberto Huembes; Mercado San Miguel/Iván Montenegro and Mercado Bóer/Israel Lewites.

Mercado Central From here buses run:

to Masaya – buses leave every 15 mins, 5 am to 9 pm (26 km, 45 mins).
to Granada – buses leave every 20 mins, 5.20 am to 8 pm (44 km, 1 hr).
to Rivas – buses leave every 30 mins, 5 am to 6 pm (109 km, 2½ hrs).
to San Juan del Sur – take bus to Rivas and transfer there (total 138 km, 3½ hrs).
to Matagalpa – buses leave every 40 mins, 4.20 am to 3 pm (129 km, 3 hrs).
to Estelí – buses leave every 40 mins, 4 am to 4 pm (149 km, 3¼ hrs).
to Somoto – same bus as for Estelí (217 km, 4½ hrs).
to Ocotal – buses leave at 5 am & 4 pm (227 km, 5 hrs).

From the Mercado San Miguel, buses run to Rama every hour from 5 am to 8 am (292 km, seven hours, US$3). On Tuesday, Thursday, Saturday and Sunday, express buses depart Managua at 2 and 3 am to connect

NICARAGUA

with the morning ferry to Bluefields. If you miss the direct bus to Rama, take a bus to Juigalpa (137 km, three hours) and hitchhike or transfer there to another bus for Rama. The last bus from Juigalpa to Rama leaves at 2 pm. Buses also leave here for Nueva Guinea and Boaco.

From Mercado Bóer/Israel Lewites, buses run to León every hour from 5 am to 5 pm (90 km, two hours) and to Pochomil and Masachapa hourly from 7 am to 5 pm (65 km, 1½ hours). Buses also leave here for Chinandega, the Carazo pueblos, and areas close to Managua.

The Tica and Sirca bus companies run direct buses between Managua and San José (Costa Rica) as well as to Panama City, Tegucigalpa, and San Salvador. The Tica bus station (☎ 26094) is in the Managua's Barrio Martha Quezada, two blocks east of the Cine Dorado. The Sirca bus station (☎ 73-833, 75726) is in the Altamira district in the south of the city, on Avenida Eduardo Delgado behind the Plaza de Compras. For information on international buses, see the introductory Getting There & Away section of this chapter.

Train Managua's railway station is near the lake, a couple of blocks east of the Plaza de la República.

Two train routes depart from Managua: one to Granada, passing through Masaya on the way, and one to León. For departure times and costs, see the earlier introductory section on Getting Around.

Hitching As always, it's best to take a local bus to the outskirts of Managua before you start hitching along the major routes heading out of town. To hitch to León, take bus No 118 to Parque Las Piedrecitas. To hitch to Masaya and Granada, take bus No 119 to the Camino de Oriente, near the Colonia Centro América.

To hitch to Rivas, take bus No 118 or 114 to Km 7, Carretera Sur. To hitch to Estelí or Matagalpa, take bus No 112 along the Carretera Norte; get off when it turns off the main road and take bus No 105 to the outskirts.

Getting Around
To/From the Airport The Augusto C Sandino international airport is 12 km east of the city, near the lake. To get there, take bus No 112, 116, 118 or 119 from the Intercontinental Hotel to Mercado San Miguel/Iván Montenegro, change there to a bus heading for Tipitapa, and get off at the airport.

A shuttle to the airport is available for US$6 (☎ 670047).

Taxis at the airport charge US$20 for the ride into town. This is an outrageous price but all the airport taxi drivers have agreed on it, so you can rarely bargain them down. You may get one to take you for US$10, but you are more likely to find one at this price if you walk out of the airport and hail a passing taxi on the highway; these drivers are not part of the airport clique. To take a taxi from town to the airport should also cost US$10, as does the airport minibus operated by Nueva Tur-Nica (☎ 661387, 660406/306). Always bargain with taxi drivers.

Bus Most people get around by bus in Managua. Buses are frequent, very crowded, and justly famous for their professional pickpockets, so be alert.

Bus services have improved in Managua, not least thanks to a donation of 100 buses from the Spanish government. On all the city bus routes, the buses run every 10 minutes from 4.45 am to 6 pm, and then every 15 minutes from 6 pm until 10.15 pm. They cost US$0.15 if you pay cash, but vendors at bus stops sell bus tokens (outdated one córdoba coins) that come out a little cheaper. Ring ENABUS (☎ 44506) for city bus information.

Camionetas or pick-up trucks, which you will see loaded with passengers, are a cheap but adventurous way to travel around the city. Standing and waving is the normal method for getting aboard; fares are cheap.

Some of the bus routes you might have occasion to use are:

No 109 – Plaza de la República to Mercado Central/Roberto Huembes, stopping en route at the Intercontinental Hotel

No 118 – Intercontinental Hotel to Mercado Bóer/Israel Lewites

No 116, 118 & 119 – Intercontinental Hotel to Mercado San Miguel/Iván Montenegro or Oscar Benavides

No 119 – Plaza España to Mercado Central/Roberto Huembes; Plaza España to Linda Vista

No 112 – runs along Carretera Norte, by the lake, past the Plaza de la República (catch it at Cine González on the corner of Avenida Bolívar), the Museo Nacional, and on towards the airport

Taxi The average taxi ride in town costs around US$1. Taxi drivers' cooperatives decide fares and other policies, so rates are usually pretty standard, but it still never hurts to bargain. It's surprising what different rates the drivers will quote to go to the same place.

You can phone for a taxi: ☎ 24872 for the P J Chamorro Cooperative; ☎ 31577 for the Nicaragua Libre Cooperative, ☎ 23469 at the Intercontinental; or ☎ 22734 for the Carlos Fonseca Cooperative.

Car Rental Car rental agencies in Managua include:

Budget
    Intercontinental Hotel (☎ 23530, ext 148)
    Montoya, one block south & one block west (☎ 666226)
Hertz
    Intercontinental Hotel (airport), one block south of Ferretería Lang (☎ 668399)
Lugo
    two blocks south, one block west from the Cine Dorado (☎ 664477, 665240)
Targa
    Intercontinental Hotel (☎ 24881/2)
    Central Office, Avenida Sandino No 606 (☎ 24875)
    Airport (☎ 31576)
Toyota
    Hotel Camino Real (☎ 31411, ext 627)
    Casa Pellas (☎ 663620)

Bicycle Rental There is a bicycle-rental place two blocks north and 1½ blocks west of the Montoya statue. Try ringing (☎ 660235) and see if they answer before you go there.

Around Managua

There are several places worth visiting within a short distance of Managua. Probably the most notable is the Volcán Masaya National Park, but even Nicaragua's other principal cities are close enough to Managua to be comfortably visited in day trips from the capital. Masaya is only 45 minutes away by bus, Granada an hour away, and León two hours. Trains also run to all of these cities, but take longer.

In Managua's hot climate, it's natural that some of the favourite places to visit are places to swim and cool off. Some of the most popular are the crater lakes in and near the capital, especially the beautiful Laguna de Xiloá, but there are several popular Pacific beaches too.

VOLCÁN MASAYA NATIONAL PARK

The Volcán Masaya National Park has been established to protect one of Nicaragua's most interesting features, the Volcán Masaya, also known as Volcán Santiago. (Santiago is the name of the principal crater.) This large volcano is still classified as active, and you may find it smoking and steaming – activity comes and goes. In the area around it, on the way from the highway to the top, you will pass several tiny smoking volcanoes, and places where there are thermal waters and hot earth.

This volcano has had an important role in the history of both the Indians and the Spanish. Legends say that the Indians used to throw young women into the boiling lava at the bottom of the crater to appease Chaciutique, the goddess of fire, and skeletons of these human sacrifices have been found in lava tunnels near the volcano.

You can walk up to the summit of the volcano, where there now stands a cross; it is said the Spanish first placed a cross because they believed the volcano was an entrance to hell, inhabited by devils. The entrance to the national park is just 23 km from Managua, on the road to Masaya. You

NICARAGUA

can get there on any bus heading for Masaya or Granada. You pay around US$0.30 admission at the entrance gate; from there it's seven km of paved road to the top of the crater. There's no public transport, but it's easy to hitch a ride.

Two km from the gate you reach a visitors' centre and museum. From the top of the volcano you get a wide view of the surrounding countryside, including the Laguna de Masaya and the town of Masaya beside it.

The park gate is open Tuesday to Sunday, from 8 am to 5 pm (closed Monday). You must enter the park before 5 pm, but you don't have to leave at any particular time; the restaurant is open until 10 pm, and you can stay in the park as long as you like. The town of Masaya is six km along the highway, on the far side of the laguna.

VOLCÁN MOMOTOMBO
Volcán Momotombo is right on the shores of Lago de Managua, clearly visible to the west of the city. It is a symbol of Nicaragua and the subject of a notable poem by Darío.

To climb the volcano you must obtain special permission from the office of the Instituto Nicaraguense de Energía (INE) in Managua. There is a geothermal power plant which you must cross to get onto the volcano; if you arrive without permission, they will not allow you to proceed any further.

LEÓN VIEJO
At the foot of Momotombo are the ruins of León Viejo. Founded in 1524, this was one of the first Spanish settlements in Nicaragua, and one of the most important. Old León was the capital of the Spanish colonial province of Nicaragua until 1610, when it was destroyed by an earthquake caused by Momotombo. The city was then moved to its present site, and the old city was buried under layers of volcanic ash by subsequent eruptions of Momotombo, until archaeologists unearthed it this century.

León Viejo is now being excavated, and there are a number of interesting things to see, including the cathedral, and the historic plaza in front of it. It was here that the city's founder, Hernández de Córdoba, was beheaded. Later, 18 Indians were dismembered here after a rebellion against the Spanish. Along the main street of the town are private homes and the church and convent of La Merced, where the tomb of Pedrarias stands. Father Bartolomé de las Casas, Protector of the Indians, resided for a time in León Viejo in the 1530s.

To get to León Viejo, head towards León and turn off the highway at La Paz Centro, about 40 km north-west of Managua. Buses to La Paz Centro depart hourly from Managua's Mercado Bóer/Israel Lewites bus station, or you can take the León bus and get off at La Paz Centro. From La Paz Centro, it's about 16 km down a dirt road to León Viejo and Momotombo village. There is an infrequent bus, or it is easy to hitch. You can hitch out again at 5 pm when the workers from the geothermal plant get off work. If you want to stay the night, there's a hospedaje in Momotombo village.

LAGUNAS & BALNEARIOS
Besides the crater lakes in Managua, there are also several popular bathing spots a short distance from the city.

The **Laguna de Xiloá** is a beautiful crater lake about 20 km north-west of Managua off the road to León. It has clean, clear water and picnic areas and restaurants around the shore, and is good for swimming and boating. It is crowded on weekends, but quite peaceful the rest of the week, when you could probably camp here without a hassle.

At **El Trapiche**, a balneario 17 km from Managua in the other direction, east off the old road to Tipitapa, water from natural springs has been channelled into large outdoor pools surrounded by gardens and restaurants. Nearby, in **Tipitapa**, there are medicinal hot sulphur pools that were once open to the public; you could check to see if they have reopened. Buses to Tipitapa depart from the Mercado San Miguel/Iván Montenegro; it's about a 45-minute trip.

Somewhat further away is the **Laguna de Apoyo**, off the Managua-Granada highway.

Like the other swimming places, it is crowded on weekends but not during the week. There is no public transport to the lake, but on weekends you could hitch in from the highway. Otherwise, from the highway, it's about a 1½-hour walk from the turnoff at Km 38.

POCHOMIL

Pochomil is a clean and beautiful swimming beach about an hour's drive (65 km) from Managua. It has recently seen improvement of its services, which is appropriate considering its popularity with Nicaraguans. It now has several hotels and a variety of restaurants, comedores and bars, as well as beachside picnic areas with running water and wash-up and toilet facilities.

The hotel and restaurant *El Pelicano* has six rooms that rent by the weekend for US$37.50 each, and offers big meals for US$10. *Hotel Bajamar* has 20 rooms at US$40 with air-con or US$28 with fan. Restaurants in Pochomil serve mainly seafood for around US$2 to US$4.

Note that there is no telephone service in Pochomil at the time of writing; the closest is in nearby Masachapa. Note also that theft is a problem, so watch your belongings while luxuriating on the beach.

OTHER BEACHES

Several other pleasant Pacific beaches, about an hour's drive or 1½ hours' bus ride from the capital, are popular on weekends.

Two km before Pochomil is **Masachapa**; this beach is not quite as clean as Pochomil but there is a small fishing village there with basic places to stay. The same bus goes to both beaches from Managua, departing hourly from the Mercado Bóer/Israel Lewites bus station. The trip takes 1½ hours and costs US$1.20.

About five km north up the coast from Pochomil, **Montelimar** is the former beach house of dictator Somoza. It was expanded as a resort during the Sandinista period, and has been refurbished by the Spanish firm Barceló and is now open. Daily rates in this luxurious place are US$50. People interested

in a package to Montelimar can contact Careli Tours in Managua (☎ 284132/3).

Further north, off the old road to León, are two more good beaches: **El Velero** and **El Tránsito**. Buses to El Tránsito depart from the Mercado Bóer/Israel Lewites bus station in Managua, but only infrequently.

Heading south down the coast, the **La Boquita** beach is 72 km from Managua, but to get there by bus you must take one bus to the town of Diriamba, then change for La Boquita. A little south of La Boquita is **Casares**, with lots of shells and not so many people. Another few km south is the beach at **Huehuete**.

All of these beaches are most frequently visited on weekends during the dry season (from December to April) and especially during Semana Santa, when all Central America goes on holiday. At other times, you'll have the beaches almost to yourself.

North of Managua

From Managua, the Interamerican Highway runs north to the departments of Matagalpa, Estelí and Madriz, highland regions with mountains and fertile valleys rich with crops and livestock. The climate here is cooler and fresher than in the lowlands, and this part of Nicaragua has its own distinct character. Many people like this part best.

Estelí is the principal town between Managua and the border. South of Estelí, at Sébaco, there's a turnoff for Matagalpa and Jinotega; both are pleasant towns and worth visiting. North of Estelí the road forks to different points on the Honduran border. The Interamerican Highway route goes through Somoto, crosses the border at El Espino into the southern lowlands of Honduras, and goes on to El Salvador. The other road leads through Ocotal to the border crossing at Las Manos, and continues through the mountains to Tegucigalpa the capital of Honduras.

Another route between this highland region and the Nicaraguan lowlands runs between León, Nicaragua's second-largest city, and San Isidro, a tiny town at a cross-roads on the Interamerican Highway.

MATAGALPA
Population 26,986

The capital of the department of the same name, Matagalpa is a quiet, pleasant mountain town beside a river. Its climate is refreshingly cool. The Spanish conquistadores found three indigenous communities here: Matagalpa itself, which was Nahuatl-speaking; Molaguina or Laborio; and Guanuca, made up of Sumo Indians brought to the area. One tradition traces the name to the Nahuatl, as Matlatlcallipan ('house of nets'). Coffee is grown and cattle raised in the surrounding area. The nearby Selva Negra ('black forest') is one of Nicaragua's best walking areas.

The Río Grande Matagalpa is only small here, but by the time it reaches the Caribbean it is one of Nicaragua's largest rivers, and the second-longest after the Río Coco.

Matagalpa is famous as the birthplace of Carlos Fonseca, father of the Sandinista revolution; the house where he was born, one block off the Parque Darío plaza, is now a museum.

Orientation & Information
Matagalpa has two plazas at opposite ends of the town. Parque Morazán, at the northern end of town beside the big cathedral, is the larger. Parque Darío is at the southern end, beside the church of San José. Near this plaza are various places to stay and eat. The Mercado and bus station are together, about a 10-block walk south-west of this plaza and beside the river.

Telcor, the combined telecommunications and post office, is one block east of the cathedral. The local tourism office number is
☎ 3773.

Matagalpa's annual festival is on 24 September, the Día de la Virgen de las Mercedes.

Things to See & Do
Matagalpa is not a large town but it's a pleasant place to walk around. The **Museo Casa Cuna Carlos Fonseca**, birthplace of

the revolutionary, is open Monday to Friday from 9 am to noon and 2 to 5 pm. For nightlife, there's a disco and two cinemas.

The **Casa de la Cultura**, one block north of the cathedral, offers language and cultural classes for children. Matagalpa also has a women's centre, the **Casa de la Mujer Nora Hawkins**, half a block east of Parque Darío.

The **Selva Negra Hotel**, about 15 km north of town, is one of Nicaragua's most famous hotels. It is pricey, with cabins around US$45, but the owners have been known to rent rooms to individual guests at US$15 a night. The emphasis is Bavarian (the place is also known as Schwarzwald or Black Forest), and features a beer garden, restaurant, a small lake, and many km of hiking trails through the Selva Negra forest. The forest near here is full of wildlife, including congo (howler) monkeys, spider monkeys and others, ocelots, sloths and many other animals. It is especially known for its birdlife. Bird-watching is best early in the morning or late in the afternoon; among the many you might see are quetzals, toucans, woodpeckers, hummingbirds, wrens and hawks. To get there, take any bus heading north from Matagalpa and get off where an old military tank marks the turnoff for the hotel.

A visit to Jinotega, 34 km north of Matagalpa, makes a very enjoyable day trip from Matagalpa (see Jinotega for details). The ride there takes you through one of the most scenic parts of Nicaragua, and Jinotega itself is a pleasant town with one of the most beautiful churches in Central America.

The town of Sébaco, southwest of Matagalpa, in a valley of the same name, has an interesting history. Sébaco was an important ceremonial center for the Chorotega, a powerful indigenous community. Its name is traced to Cihuacuatl ('serpent mother') the Chorotega goddess of the earth and reproduction. In the nearby lagoon of Tecomapa are the remains of a ruined temple to the goddess.

Places to Stay
There are various inexpensive places to stay

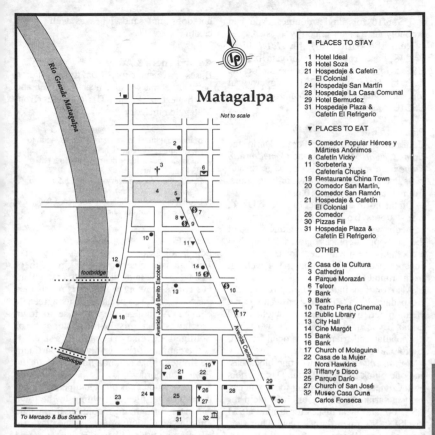

Matagalpa

Not to scale

■ PLACES TO STAY

1 Hotel Ideal
18 Hotel Soza
21 Hospedaje & Cafetín
   El Colonial
24 Hospedaje San Martín
28 Hospedaje La Casa Comunal
29 Hotel Bermudez
31 Hospedaje Plaza &
   Cafetín El Refrigerio

▼ PLACES TO EAT

5 Comedor Popular Héroes y
   Mártires Anónimos
8 Cafetín Vicky
11 Sorbetería y
   Cafetería Chupis
19 Restaurante China Town
20 Comedor San Martín,
   Comedor San Ramón
21 Hospedaje & Cafetín
   El Colonial
26 Comedor
30 Pizzas Fili
31 Hospedaje Plaza &
   Cafetín El Refrigerio

OTHER

2 Casa de la Cultura
3 Cathedral
4 Parque Morazán
6 Telcor
7 Bank
9 Bank
10 Teatro Perla (Cinema)
12 Public Library
13 City Hall
14 Cine Margót
15 Bank
16 Bank
17 Church of Molaguina
22 Casa de la Mujer
   Nora Hawkins
23 Tiffany's Disco
25 Parque Darío
27 Church of San José
32 Museo Casa Cuna
   Carlos Fonseca

around the Parque Darío. The best deal in town for the price – just US$0.60 per person – is *La Casa Comunal* (☎ 2695), a round, brick building a block east of Parque Darío. It has seven large rooms, each with several metal-framed bunk beds that can sleep up to 10 people in a room, though once you have taken a room it's yours and they won't put any more people in with you. Men's and women's rooms are separate – couples cannot stay together – and there are separate communal bathrooms for men and women.

Hospedaje Plaza, on the south side of the plaza, is nothing fancy but it's one of the better places in town and the price is OK. Upstairs rooms with shared bath, are US$2.40; downstairs rooms with private bath are US$3.20.

Also on the plaza, the *Hospedaje San Martín* (☎ 3737) is another basic place, with rooms with shared bath at US$4/6 for singles/doubles. The *Hospedaje El Colonial*, opposite the Hospedaje Plaza, has rooms with shared bath at US$2.40/4.80 for singles/doubles but it is very run-down. One block east of the plaza, the *Hotel Bermudez* (☎ 3439) is a more pleasant place and in better condition, but it's also more expensive at US$8/16 for singles/doubles. You can probably get a better price if you ask.

Near the cathedral, the *Hotel Ideal* (☎ 2483) has rooms with private bath at US$15 for one or two people. Beside the river, the *Hotel Soza* (☎ 2818) is overpriced for what you get, with rooms starting at US$10 for singles.

Places to Eat

Half a block north of the Parque Darío, the *Comedor San Martín* and the *Comedor San Ramón* are a couple of good, basic restaurants that are open every day for long hours, from around 6.30 am to 10 pm.

On the north-east corner of Parque Darío, a few doors from the church, there is a comedor with no name or sign that is one of the most popular places in town. You can get a good, big meal with meat for US$1.40, or cheaper meals. It's open only in the evening, from around 6 to 10 pm.

Also on the Parque Darío, beside the Hospedaje Plaza, *El Refrigerio* is a simple, clean place that serves sandwiches and drinks. Even though it only has two tables it's popular and friendly. It is open from 10 am to 9.30 pm.

Restaurante China Town, one block east and one block north of Parque Darío, offers both Chinese and Nicaraguan food; you can get vegetarian chop suey or chow mein for US$1.60, and meat dishes for around US$3 to US$4. It's open daily except Thursday, from noon to 10 pm.

Pizzas Fili, two blocks east of Parque Darío near the Hotel Bermudez, is a more expensive restaurant with a range of foods including pizza, steaks and other meats, Chinese dishes, burgers, sandwiches and Lipton's tea.

Around the Parque Morazán are several other places to eat. In the plaza itself, the *Comedor Popular Héroes y Mártires Anónimos* is open all day from 6 am to 5 pm. *Cafetín Vicky*, half a block south, specializes in pancakes for breakfast and a *comida corrida* at lunch time; it's open only from 7 am to 1 pm. In the next block south, the *Sorbetería y Cafetería Chupis* has burgers, hot dogs and sandwiches as well as ice cream.

Getting There & Away

Buses arrive and depart from the bus station beside the market and near the river and south-west of Parque Darío. Buses from Matagalpa include:

to Managua – buses leave every 40 mins, 4 am to 4.40 pm (129 km, three hrs).
to Jinotega – buses leave hourly, 6 am to 5 pm (34 km, two hrs).
to Estelí – buses leave every 40 mins, 5.50 am to 6 pm (70 km, two hrs).
to León – take the Estelí bus to San Isidro & change (146 km, four hrs).

JINOTEGA

Population 14,088

Jinotega is a quiet town 34 km north of Matagalpa, set in a valley amid a mountainous coffee-growing region. It is nicknamed the 'city of mists' because of its agreeable climate. A sign at the entrance to town proclaims that this is the sister city of Solingen, Germany. Though it is small, it is the capital of the very large department of Jinotega that extends north-east to the Honduran border.

Today, Jinotega is quiet and peaceful, but there was very heavy fighting in the town and in the surrounding mountains during and after the revolution; murals on the plaza are a testimony to these years. Having suffered enormous casualties, the townspeople will tell you that now they are very, very tired of violence, and only want peace.

The road from Matagalpa to Jinotega is one of the most beautiful in Nicaragua. Even at the end of the dry season, when the rest of the country is parched and brown, these mountains, some of them 1500 metres above sea level, are green and cool.

Roadside stands set up outside farms sell carrots, beets, cabbages, lettuce, tomatoes, bananas, flowers and more – a colourful sight that refreshes the spirit, especially if you've been in Managua a while. It's worth coming to Jinotega for the day from

Matagalpa, just to ride on this road, visit the little town and see Jinotega's famous church.

Jinotega's tourist office number is ☎ 441.

Things to See & Do
Church The church at Jinotega is one of the most beautiful in Central America. It doesn't look so remarkable from the outside, though it's noticeably large for such a small town. When you get inside, though, there is much magnificent religious art, statuary and hundreds of details; the architecture, too, is notable, with excellent natural lighting and acoustics. Among the most famous statues is the Black Christ of Esquipulas, but there are many that are equally fine.

It's taken a long time for this church to achieve its present peaceful splendour. The first church was built on the site in 1805; it was remodelled in 1882, and rebuilt in 1952 and 1958.

Plaza On the plaza in front of the church are some reminders of the revolutionary years in Jinotega. A large, colourful mural showing coffee pickers with rifles on their backs has been painted on the old Somoza jail, now a youth centre, on the south side of the plaza. Another depicts young people at war. On the plaza itself there is a mural of Carlos Fonseca.

Places to Stay
Jinotega is off the 'tourist trail' and there aren't many good places to stay. This makes it all the more surprising to find the *Hotel Sollentuna Hem* (☎ 334), a few blocks north of the church. Its name comes from Sollentuna, a suburb of Stockholm, where the owner lived for 15 years – 'Sollentuna Hem' is 'Sollentuna Home' in Swedish. English, Spanish and Swedish are spoken. The hotel is exceptionally clean and pleasant, with unusual touches like Chinese hand-embroidered bedclothes. A variety of rooms, with private or shared bath, cost around US$10 per person. There's an enclosed garage for cars and meals are served on request.

Other lodgings in Jinotega include the *Hospedaje Primavera* (☎ 400), four blocks north of the Esso gas station, with 20 rooms at around US$10, and the *Hospedaje El Tico* (☎ 530), near the Colegio La Salle, which is a bit less expensive.

Places to Eat
Jinotega has several good places to eat. On the north side of the plaza is the pleasant little *Cafetería Trebol*, open from 8.30 am to 4 pm.

There are more places to eat in the block behind the church. A nameless comedor beside the Super Tienda Las Brumas is recommended by locals. The *Sorbetería Eskimo* ice cream parlour serves sandwiches and burgers as well as ice cream, or there's the fancier *Restaurant McGarry*, with meals from about US$4 to US$6.

Restaurante Oriental, 1½ blocks north of the plaza, is an attractive patio restaurant serving both Chinese and regular food. It's one of the best restaurants in Jinotega but it's also a bit expensive, with most meals around US$5 to US$7.

Getting There & Away
The bus station in Jinotega is on the outskirts of town. Buses to Matagalpa depart hourly from 5.30 am until the last bus at 4.20 pm (34 km, two hours). Express buses to Managua depart in the morning.

AROUND JINOTEGA
Lago de Apanás
About 10 km from Jinotega, the large Lago de Apanás is a popular place for fishing and swimming, especially on weekends. Buses to the lake leave from beside the Mercado.

ESTELÍ
Population 26,892
Estelí, the main centre between Managua and the Honduran border, is a quiet, pleasant, friendly town in a valley between the mountains, and is a good stopover on the way to or from the border.

Capital of the department of the same name, Estelí is the centre for the surrounding agricultural area where tobacco, cotton, grains, sesame, potatoes, many other vegetables and fruits, and also livestock and cheese are produced. During the Sandinista years many farming collectives were established in the region around Estelí, and many internacionalistas came here. There was a popular Spanish-language school here for several years.

There was heavy fighting in Estelí during the revolution, and the town continued to be one of strongest support bases for the Sandinistas. Estelí, along with León, was one of only two important cities where the FSLN won a majority in the 1990 election.

As the major city between Managua and the Honduran border, and the capital of a large department, Estelí has a large number of places to stay and eat.

Orientation & Information

Avenida Bolívar, the main street in Estelí, runs north to south for about 25 blocks. Most of the town's commerce, and many hospedajes and restaurants, are found along it. Avenida Bolívar crosses the river at the northern end of town; at the southern end, it curves east to join the Interamerican Highway. There are many petrol stations and restaurants along the highway to serve the traffic heading north to Honduras and south to Managua. The bus station and Mercado are together, a block west of Avenida Bolívar at the southern end of town.

There are two Telcor (post and telephone) offices in Estelí. The main one is about a block from the plaza, and there is a smaller branch office three blocks north of the bus station. There are plenty of banks. A good bookshop, Librería Rufo Marín, is to be found half a block from the north-west corner of the plaza, and there are plenty of other bookshops, all with books in Spanish, around town.

The tourism office number is ☎ 2382. The IXCHEN, formerly AMNLAE women's centre, Casa de la Mujer Mercedes Rosales (☎ 2696), is on the corner of Calle Peru and the Interamerican Highway.

Things to See & Do

On the main plaza, Estelí has a big, new, modern **cathedral**. On the south side of the plaza, on the footpath in front of the Centro Recreativo Juveníl La Segovia, are several boulders with prehistoric carvings of human, animal and bird movement on them. They come from Las Pintadas, an archaeological site about eight km to the west.

The **Centro Recreativo Juveníl La Segovia**, the youth centre Estelí, is on the south side of the plaza and open to people of all ages. It has table tennis, billiards, a basketball court and music, and sells inexpensive snacks, such as tacos and enchiladas, and soft drinks. It's open every day from 2 to 10 pm. Beside it is the **Cine Estelí**; there are several other cinemas around town.

Around the corner, half a block south of the cathedral, is the **Galería de Héroes y Mártires**, a museum and gallery devoted to the memory of the town's revolutionary heroes and martyrs. It has murals around the outside. Beside it is the **public library**.

Around the corner again there is the **Casa de Cultura**, which sponsors many interesting activities. Every Saturday evening, from around 6 to 9 pm, there's a *peña cultural* with music, song, dance, folklore and so on; it's free and you can just show up. The centre also has art exhibits and an artesanías shop, and offers classes in art, music, dance and English. Best of all on a hot day, the centre has a swimming pool, open from 8 am to 6 pm. There's a charge of US$0.60 to use the pool.

Places to Stay

Estelí has a number of good places to stay. The *Hotel Mariella*, near the bus station, is a fine choice, simple but very clean, with rooms with shared bath at US$3/5 for singles/doubles.

Three blocks south, beside Cine Nancy's on Avenida Bolívar, the *Hotel Chalet* is clean and quite good, with singles/doubles at US$4/6, all with private bath.

Along Avenida Bolívar are a number of simple hospedajes. *Hospedaje Chepito*, 3½ blocks north of the bus station, is simple but clean, with rooms with shared bath at US$3/5 for singles/doubles. In the next

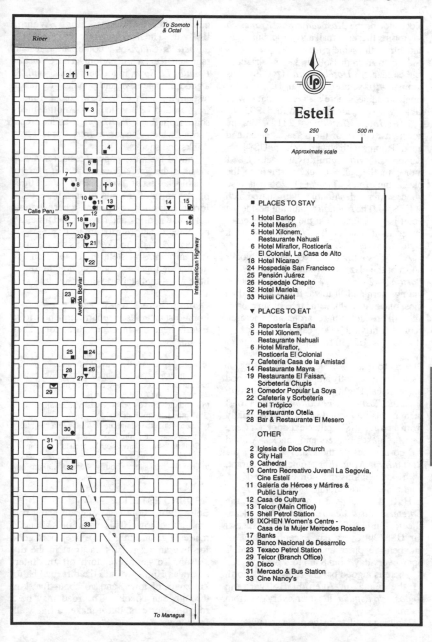

Estelí

0   250   500 m

Approximate scale

NICARAGUA

■ PLACES TO STAY

1 Hotel Barlop
4 Hotel Mesón
5 Hotel Xilonem,
  Restaurante Nahuali
6 Hotel Miraflor, Rosticería
  El Colonial, La Casa de Alto
18 Hotel Nicarao
24 Hospedaje San Francisco
25 Pensión Juárez
26 Hospedaje Chepito
32 Hotel Mariela
33 Hotel Chalet

▼ PLACES TO EAT

3 Repostería España
5 Hotel Xilonem,
  Restaurante Nahuali
6 Hotel Miraflor,
  Rosticería El Colonial
7 Cafetería Casa de la Amistad
14 Restaurante Mayra
19 Restaurante El Faisan,
  Sorbetería Chupis
21 Comedor Popular La Soya
22 Cafetería y Sorbetería
  Del Trópico
27 Restaurante Otelia
28 Bar & Restaurante El Mesero

OTHER

2 Iglesia de Dios Church
8 City Hall
9 Cathedral
10 Centro Recreativo Juvenil La Segovia,
  Cine Estelí
11 Galería de Héroes y Mártires &
  Public Library
12 Casa de Cultura
13 Telcor (Main Office)
15 Shell Petrol Station
16 IXCHEN Women's Centre -
  Casa de la Mujer Mercedes Rosales
17 Banks
20 Banco Nacional de Desarrollo
23 Texaco Petrol Station
29 Telcor (Branch Office)
30 Disco
31 Mercado & Bus Station
33 Cine Nancy's

block north, the *Hospedaje San Francisco* has rooms that are small and basic, but clean enough, at the same price.

Also on Avenida Bolívar, 1½ blocks south of the plaza, the *Hotel Nicarao* (☎ 2490) has rooms with shared bath at US$3/6 for singles/doubles; there's a central patio with tables where meals are served for US$2.

The *Hotel Miraflor* (☎ 2312), on the north-east corner of the plaza, is clean and good. Rooms with shared bath are US$4 per person, or with semi-private bath US$1 more. In the same block, north from the plaza, the *Hotel Xilonem* (☎ 2660) is also good, with singles/doubles with shared bath at US$3/4. The *Nahuali* restaurant beside the hotel is quite fancy. On the opposite corner is yet another hotel, the *Hotel Mesón*, with eight rooms at US$10.

A block south of the river, and six blocks north of the plaza on Avenida Bolívar, *Hotel Barlop* (☎ 2486) is in a residential district at the northern end of town. It is classier than most places in town, with large, clean rooms, all with private bath, set around an enclosed central courtyard where cars can be parked. Rooms cost US$10 for one or two people.

Places to Eat

Estelí has an equally ample selection of good places to eat. Right on the plaza, on the north side, the *Rostería El Colonial* serves roast meat meals for around US$4; it's open daily from 11 am until 10 pm. Next door, *La Casa de Alto* makes burgers and snacks. Around the corner, beside the Hotel Xilonem, the *Restaurante Nahuali* is a fancier restaurant, with cloth napkins and more elaborate décor, where meals cost around US$5.

Half a block west of the plaza, the *Cafetería Casa de la Amistad* is a clean, cheerful little café. It serves a lunch special for US$1.40 every day except Sunday, or inexpensive pizza and snacks; the café is open every day from 8 am to 8 pm.

There is a good bakery four blocks north of the plaza on Avenida Bolívar; the *Repostería España*. It's open every day from 6 am.

Walking south from the plaza you will find many other restaurants along Avenida Bolívar. The *Restaurante El Faisan y Sorbetería Chupis* is a combination restaurant and ice cream parlour. The *Comedor Popular La Soya*, in the next block south, is a good, inexpensive and popular vegetarian restaurant, open every day except Sunday from around 7.30 am to 5 pm. Another block south from that is *Del Trópico*, an ice cream parlour which also serves fresh tropical fruit drinks and snacks.

One of the more popular restaurants with locals is the *Bar & Restaurante El Mesero*, one block west of Avenida Bolívar and three blocks north of the bus station. It's a comfortable family restaurant where people come to eat, drink and have a good time. It's open every day from 10 am to 10 pm.

As always, the market offers the cheapest fare in town. In Estelí, the bus station and market are together; there's a double row of little restaurant stalls on the east side.

Getting There & Away

Long-distance buses depart frequently from Estelí, heading in every direction. They include:

to Managua – buses leave every 40 mins,
    4 am to 5.30 pm (149 km, 3¼ hrs).
to Matagalpa – buses leave every 40 mins, 5.50 am
    to 3.50 pm (70 km, two hrs).
to Jinotega – two direct buses daily, 8.30 am &
    1 pm (104 km, four hrs).
to León – take the Managua or Matagalpa bus and
    change at San Isidro (about four hrs).
to Somoto – buses leave hourly, 5.30 am to 6 pm
    (67 km, two hrs).
to Ocotal – buses leave hourly, 4 am to 5.30 pm
    (78 km, 2¼ hrs).

AROUND ESTELÍ

Salta Estanzuela is a waterfall about five km south of town. This waterfall is about 25 metres high and falls into a deep pool good for swimming; it isn't so great in the dry season. To get there, turn off the Interamerican Highway onto the dirt road half a km south of town, and go about five km, through San Nicolás. The road may be a rough go for cars, but it makes a fine walk from town.

Puente La Sirena, on the river north of town, is another good swimming spot.

NORTH TO HONDURAS

There are two ways north to Honduras. The shortest way to Tegucigalpa in Honduras is through Ocotal and on to the border crossing at Las Manos. On the Honduran side, you will go through Danlí on your way to Tegucigalpa; it's 132 km (2½ hours by bus) from the border to Tegucigalpa.

If, on the other hand, you want to continue on the Interamerican Highway into southern Honduras, take the highway to the town of Somoto, then to the El Espino border crossing, and on into Honduras, passing through the village of San Marcos de Colón on your way to Choluteca, the principal city in the southern Honduran lowlands. San Marcos is just a few km from the border; to Choluteca it's 60 km (one hour by bus). If you're continuing through to El Salvador on the Interamerican Highway, you can cross the southern part of Honduras and be at the Salvadoran border in three hours (plus waiting time for a connecting bus at Choluteca).

Whichever way you go to Honduras, if you're going by bus you will have to take one bus to the border, go through, and take another bus on the other side. The border stations are open from around 8 am to 4.30 or 5 pm.

Ocotal

Population 3863

The closest town to the Honduran border at Las Manos, Ocotal is about two hours north of Estelí. The capital of the department of Nueva Segovia, Ocotal is a small town, with a typical church and a plaza with a few blocks around it.

Orientation & Information The bus station is in the centre of town, 1½ blocks north of the plaza. Telcor, the post and telephone office, is beside the bus station, and the IXCHEN/AMNLAE women's centre, Casa de la Mujer Luisa Amelia Sierra, is beside that. There's a small artesanías shop just off

the plaza, on the south side. The tourist office number is ☎ 366.

Places to Stay & Eat The best place to stay is the *Pensión Segovia*, opposite the bus station. It's a basic hospedaje with small rooms, but it's clean and well cared for, and the price is great at just US$0.80 per person.

About five long blocks west from the centre of town, *Hospedaje Centroamericana* (☎ 340) is more expensive, with rooms with shared bath at US$3 per person. It's one of the best hotels in town, though still nothing fancy. It's half a block west of the highway, opposite the Shell station and the *Hotel Frontera* (☎ 461), which has rooms at US$5.

The *Hotel El Portal*, a block north of the bus station and around the corner, is an option if other places are full; it's quite run-down and the rooms cost US$3 per person.

As for places to eat, the *Comedor Occidental* is on the north-west corner of the plaza, opposite the church. One block north, on the corner near the bus station, *Soda Caprí* serves sandwiches, ice cream and drinks. At the bus station itself there are several small restaurant stalls. The Mercado is around the corner from the bus station and one block to the west.

Getting There & Away Buses to Estelí depart hourly from 4 am to 5 pm (78 km, 2¼ hours). Direct buses to Managua leave twice daily at 5 am and 3.30 pm (227 km, five hours). There are also hourly buses to Somoto from 5.45 am to 4 pm (33 km, one hour) and to Las Manos between 5 am and 3.30 pm (25 km, one hour).

Somoto

Population 29,843

Somoto, 20 km from the Honduran border at El Espino, is a small, quiet mountain town and capital of the department of Madriz. The colonial church on the plaza is one of the oldest in Nicaragua.

If you're crossing the border and it's late in the day, you might want to spend the night in Somoto. There's a good, inexpensive

NICARAGUA

hospedaje right on the plaza. The tourist office number is ☎ 364.

Getting There & Away The bus station at Somoto is on the main highway, a short walk from the centre of town. Buses depart hourly for the border (20 km, 30 minutes) and for Estelí (67 km, two hours). Direct buses bound for Managua (217 km, five hours) depart twice a day.

North-West of Managua

The area north-west of Managua, extending along the south-west shore of Lago de Managua all the way to the Golfo de Fonseca, is rich agricultural country. These are lowlands and, like Managua, very hot.

The major city in this region, and the only one much visited by travellers, is historic León. It was the capital of Nicaragua for about three centuries and today is Nicaragua's second-largest city. The other towns in the region are Chinandega, a much smaller agricultural centre, and Corinto, Nicaragua's principal Pacific port. Puerto Sandino, further south towards Managua, is being developed as another port.

LEÓN
Population 81,647
One of Nicaragua's oldest cities, León was founded in 1524 by Hernández de Córdoba, at the site of an indigenous village, Imbita. The location at the foot of the Momotombo volcano, on the shore of Lago de Managua, is 32 km from where León stands today. In 1610 the volcano's activity brought about an earthquake that destroyed the city. León's present site, at the indigenous community of Yococayoguas, was chosen for the reconstruction because it was close to the existing Indian capital, Subtiava.

León was the capital of Nicaragua throughout the colonial period and well after independence, until Managua became the capital in 1857. It was also the ecclesiastical capital for the bishop of Nicaragua and Costa Rica. It has many fine colonial buildings, including the cathedral, which is the largest in Central America. As befits a city named León, there are a number of lion statues around the cathedral and in the plaza. The Universidad Autónoma de Nicaragua, the country's first university, was founded here in 1812; the city streets are lined with old Spanish-style houses, with white adobe walls, red-tiled roofs, big thick wooden doors, and cool interior garden patios.

León is traditionally the most liberal of Nicaraguan cities and today remains the radical and intellectual centre of the country. A large majority of the population supports the FSLN. During the revolution, virtually the entire town fought against Somoza; in the 1990 election, the only major cities where the Sandinistas won were León and Estelí.

The agricultural area around León is principally devoted to maize, cotton, sugar cane and rice, though many other crops are also grown, and livestock is raised.

Information
The Telcor office is on the north-west corner of the plaza. For some reason, it can be cheaper to make international phone calls from here than from Managua. The tourist office number is ☎ 3682.

Festival days in León include 24 September, 1 November and 20 June, the anniversary of the date the Sandinistas defeated Somoza's soldiers in León.

Things to See & Do
León's **cathedral** is the largest in Central America. Its construction began in 1746 and took more than 100 years to complete. Local legend holds that the original plans for the structure were so sumptuous that the city's leaders feared they would be turned down by the Spanish imperial authorities, and they therefore sent a more modest but phoney set of plans to Spain. The cathedral's magnificent artworks include huge paintings of the *Stations of the Cross* by Antonio Sarria, that have been called masterpieces of Spanish colonial religious art.

The cathedral is also a kind of Pantheon

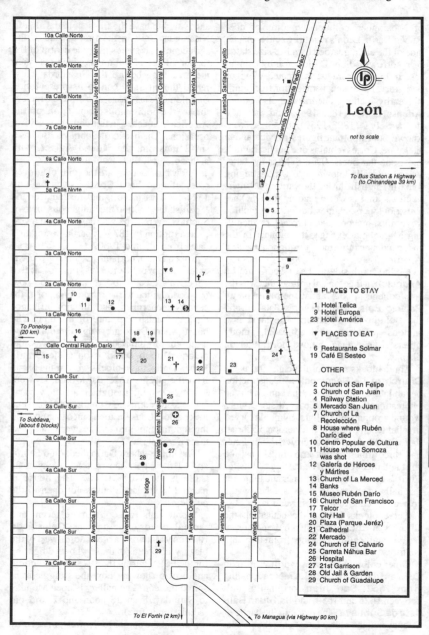

León

not to scale

To Bus Station & Highway
(to Chinandega 39 km)

To Poneloya
(20 km)

To Subtiava,
(about 6 blocks)

To El Fortín (2 km)

To Managua (via Highway 90 km)

■ PLACES TO STAY

1 Hotel Telica
9 Hotel Europa
23 Hotel América

▼ PLACES TO EAT

6 Restaurante Solmar
19 Café El Sesteo

OTHER

2 Church of San Felipe
3 Church of San Juan
4 Railway Station
5 Mercado San Juan
7 Church of La
  Recolección
8 House where Rubén
  Darío died
10 Centro Popular de Cultura
11 House where Somoza
  was shot
12 Galería de Héroes
  y Mártires
13 Church of La Merced
14 Banks
15 Museo Rubén Darío
16 Church of San Francisco
17 Telcor
18 City Hall
20 Plaza (Parque Jeréz)
21 Cathedral
22 Mercado
24 Church of El Calvario
25 Carreta Náhua Bar
26 Hospital
27 21st Garrison
28 Old Jail & Garden
29 Church of Guadalupe

NICARAGUA

of Nicaraguan culture: the tomb of poet Rubén Darío, León's favourite son, is on one side of the altar, guarded by a life-size statue of a sorrowful lion. Darío's tomb bears an inscription: 'Nicaragua is created of vigor and glory, Nicaragua is made for freedom.'

Nearby in the cathedral are also buried Alfonso Cortés (1893-1969) and Salomón de la Selva (1893-1959), two less well known but important figures in Nicaraguan literature. Cortés remains one of Nicaragua's most popular poets. 'Don Sal,' as the latter was universally known, also wrote stinging verse in English, during the various US interventions, that is worth reading today. Other illustrious personalities buried here include governors, bishops, and chroniclers, including Miguel Larreynaga, the pioneer of the independence movement throughout Central America.

On the south side of the cathedral are **La Asunción**, a theological college that was the first college in Nicaragua; the rather pretty **Palacio Episcopal** (Bishop's Palace); and the **Colegio San Ramón**. The latter is a famous institution that educated, among others, Larreynaga, whose portrait is on display.

Three blocks north of the cathedral is the **Church of La Recolección**. Construction began in the 18th century; the church has an interesting façade, with carved stone vines wound around stone pillars. Symbols carved in relief recall events in the Passion of Christ: there is the rooster that crowed after Peter had three times denied knowing Jesus; the shirt and dice refers to the casting of lots for Christ's cloak; a spike, hammer and tongs for the nails used on the cross are below the crowning scene of the Resurrection.

Three blocks behind the cathedral, the **Church of El Calvario** also has an unusual façade and ceiling, dating from the 18th century.

Other colonial churches worth visiting in León are the churches of **La Merced**, dating from 1662; **San Juan**, originally built between 1625 and 1650; and **San Juan Bautista de Subtiava**. The latter, in the barrio of Subtiava, is the oldest intact church in León,

and is said to have the finest colonial altar in Nicaragua. Built in the first decade of the 18th century, it stands near the centre of the Indian village of Subtiava, which occupied the area long before the Spaniards transferred the city of León to its present site. Bartolomé de las Casas, apostle and benefactor to the indigenous population of the Americas, preached in this church on several occasions. The barrio of Subtiava also has a small museum, the **Museo Adiact**, with archaeological finds from the area.

A few blocks away are the ruins of an even older church, **Vera Cruz**. It was built in 1524-1600 as the original nucleus for the 'Spanish city' within the indigenous town of Subtiava. Vera Cruz was destroyed in a volcanic eruption in 1835. A partial restoration dates from the mid-1960s.

Rubén Darío, born on 18 January 1867, is esteemed worldwide as one of Latin America's greatest poets, and, as the poet most committed to the introduction of 19th-century modernism, had a major influence on the Spanish literature of his time. The house where Darío grew up in León is now a museum to the poet's life and works: the **Museo Rubén Darío** is on Calle Central Rubén Darío, three blocks west of the plaza. It is officially open Monday to Saturday from 9 am to 5 pm, though hours may vary. There's no admission charge but you can make a donation. An attendant can guide you through the museum and answer your questions if you wish.

The house where Darío died, on 6 February 1916, is near the railroad tracks at 2a Calle Norte, No 410-412. The house is marked by a plaque but is not open to the public.

Monuments to León's more recent and radical history include the **Galería de Héroes y Mártires**, a block north-west of the plaza, with photos of those who died fighting for the FSLN during the 1978-79 revolution, and a map showing how the struggle transpired in León. The gallery is open Monday to Saturday, 8 am to noon and 2 to 5 pm (admission is free).

Around the corner to the west, marked by

a large plaque, is the house where Anastasio Somoza García, father of the dictator Anastasio Somoza Debayle, was assassinated by Rigoberto López Pérez on 21 September 1956. López Pérez, a poet and journalist, dressed as a waiter to gain entry to a party for dignitaries; he was also killed and became a national hero. The plaque outside the house says that his action marked the 'beginning of the end' of the Somoza dictatorship.

Several places where Somoza's Guardia Nacional were overpowered by the revolutionary fighters are now commemorated, including the **Old Jail** on 4a Calle Sur (now a garden); the **21st Garrison** around the corner to the east; and **El Fortín**, the Guardia Nacional's last holdout in León. El Fortín can be seen from town on a hill about two km to the south; you can walk there or take a taxi, which doesn't cost much.

The **Centro Popular de Cultura** has art exhibits that change twice a month; it also offers art classes and hosts occasional presentations of music, dance, and theatre.

León has three open mercados: one behind the cathedral, the Mercado San Juan near the railway station, and another on the outskirts of town, past the bus station.

Places to Stay
The classiest place to stay in León is the comfortable *Hotel Europa* (☎ 2596, 6040) on 3a Calle, north-east of 4a Avenida and near the railway tracks, where rooms are US$7 per person with shared bath, or US$10/15 a single/double with private bath. It's clean and well kept, with a restaurant serving breakfast and snacks, a house bar, and sitting areas among the plants on the patio.

Two blocks behind the cathedral on 2a Avenida Oriente near the corner of 1a Calle Sur, the *Hotel América* (☎ 5533) is a bit more worn but still pleasant, with plants and hammocks around the interior patio. Rooms with private bath and fan start at US$10.

The *Hotel Telica* (☎ 2136), on Avenida Comandante Pedro Aráuz near the railroad tracks, is a longer walk from town, though rooms are cheaper at US$4 for one or two people with shared bath, US$6 with private bath.

Hospedaje Primavera (☎ 4216) is even further from the centre of town, about 10 very long blocks north and three blocks east of the cathedral; the street has no name, and the hotel has no sign, but it's house No 305 and half a block west of the Hermita Dolores church. Rooms are set around a grassy court and cost US$1.60 for one or two people with private shower and hand basin, or US$2 with private toilet as well; all of the rooms come with fan.

Places to Eat
There are several comedores on the edges of the Mercado behind the cathedral. On the south-western corner of the Mercado, opposite the petrol station, the *Comedor Popular Raul Cabezas L* is nothing fancy but you can get a good, big breakfast or lunch for under US$1. It's open every day from around 6.30 or 7 am to around 6 pm.

On the plaza, the *Café El Sesteo* is a pleasant café with tables outside; it's open every day from 7 am to 10 pm. In the evening, tables are set up in the central plaza, selling the usual rice and beans, fried bananas, soft drinks and so on. It's open until about midnight.

Restaurante Solmar, three blocks north of the cathedral on Avenida Central Noreste, is a fancier restaurant, with patio dining and original art on display. Meat and seafood meals cost around US$4 to US$6, with drinks extra; it's open every day except Wednesday, from noon to 10 pm.

Entertainment
The Carreta Náhua, a block south of the cathedral on Avenida Central, is a quiet place for a beer, with an art gallery and a collection of books.

The Centro Popular de Cultura sometimes offers performances in the evening. León also has cinemas and a couple of discos.

Getting There & Away
Bus The bus terminal is about two km from

the centre of town, on 6a Calle Norte. Local buses run between the terminal and the centre, or you can take a taxi for around US$0.80.

Buses to Managua depart every 20 minutes from 5 am to 5 pm (90 km, two hours). The bus to Chinandega and Corinto also departs every 20 minutes, from 4.30 am and 6 pm; it's one hour to Chinandega (39 km), and two hours to Corinto (58 km).

An express bus to Matagalpa departs once a day at 4.30 am (four hours, 146 km). Alternatively, you could take a bus to San Isidro (three hours) and change buses there to continue to Matagalpa. You can also change there to go to Estelí and on to the Honduran border at Guasaule: there is an irregular bus service to Guasaule, inquire locally for details.

See Around León for information on getting to/from Poneloya.

Train Altogether, three trains depart daily for Managua, at 5, 6 and 8 am. You could inquire if an express, which formerly left at 3 pm, is also scheduled for the day. The trip costs US$0.85 and takes two hours.

Note that the first train of the day may be either an extra train, which will leave at 4.30 am, or a scheduled service at 5 am. You can't know which one it will be on any particular day, so get there before 4.30 am to be sure of catching it.

You can change in Managua for Masaya and Granada. You will have to wait at least an hour in between: the Granada trains leave Managua at 8 am and 6 pm.

Hitching Take a local bus to the outskirts to hitch from León to Managua. University students often hitch this route so it's usually easy to get a ride.

Getting Around
León has plenty of taxis; the fare within town is about US$0.80. There are also local buses.

AROUND LEÓN
Poneloya
The beach at Poneloya, 20 km west of León, is one of Nicaragua's finest. It has two sides: Las Peñitas and Poneloya. The beach is practically deserted on weekdays but lots of people come here on weekends and during Semana Santa.

Be very careful about swimming here. People have drowned in Poneloya's large waves and strong currents. You can hire a small boat to take you to the island offshore.

The *Hotel Lacayo* (☎ (032) 1) on the Poneloya side charges US$3 per person, with shared bath; it's a pleasant old wooden place with balconies and some sea-view rooms. Camping on the beach is also no problem, especially on weekdays. There are many little seafood restaurants.

A bus to Poneloya departs hourly from near the Subtiava church plaza. It's very easy to hitch between León and Poneloya on weekends, when many people are going; the trip takes about 30 to 45 minutes.

NORTH-WEST FROM LEÓN
A few km north of León, near Telica, a road turns off for San Isidro, on the Interamerican Highway. It's 104 km (about three hours) from León to San Isidro, where you can catch buses to Matagalpa, or to Estelí and on to the Honduran border.

The main road continues 39 km north-west from León to Chinandega, the centre of an agricultural region where cotton, bananas and sugar cane are the principal crops.

Chinandega has a tourist office (☎ 2809).

The area is known for its spiritual fervor. Nearby **El Viejo** is the focus of several annual religious pilgrimages. **Chichigalpa**, further south, is the home of the Ingenio San Antonio, the largest sugar mill in Central America, and of the Flor de Caña rum factory. In Chinandega, the *Hotel Glomar* (☎ 2562), a block south of the market, has 12 rooms for US$9 per person.

From Chinandega roads branch out in several directions: to Puerto Morazán and Potosí on the Golfo de Fonseca; to Corinto, Nicaragua's principal Pacific port, 19 km away; and to the Honduran border at Guasaule, a few km past Somotillo. The border here was closed but is now reopened;

the bridge over the river was destroyed by floods in the early 1980s but has been rebuilt.

South of Managua

The area south of Managua includes some of Nicaragua's most significant agricultural country and most important towns and cities, including Masaya, famous for its traditional handicrafts, and Granada, the third-largest city in Nicaragua and, together with León, one of its two important colonial cities. Masaya and Granada can both easily be visited as day trips from Managua, but both also have places to stay. Near Masaya is the Volcán Masaya National Park, which is well worth visiting. (See the Around Managua section for more details.)

There are many small farming villages around Masaya and Granada. Due south of Managua are the towns of Jinotepe, Diriamba, and San Marcos, site of the religious and folkloric celebration known as Toro Guaco. Continuing south towards the border, the only major town is Rivas, and even it is small. San Jorge, the port for ferries to Isla de Ometepe in Lago de Nicaragua, is near Rivas. So is the turnoff to San Juan del Sur, a fishing village and one of Nicaragua's favourite small, inexpensive beach resort towns. The trip from Managua to the Costa Rican border takes from 3½ to four hours, not counting stops.

MASAYA
Population 47,276
Masaya, known as 'the city of flowers,' is popular with visitors to Nicaragua; it's just 26 km (45 minutes by bus) from Managua. Granada is another 18 km down the road. Masaya is famous for its artesanías, some of the best produced in Nicaragua. As a handicrafts centre, its markets also sell work from all over the country.

Masaya sits at the edge of the crater lake, Laguna de Masaya. On the lake's opposite side, Masaya volcano towers over the town.

The tourist office number is ☎ 2936.

Things to See & Do
Artesanías There are several places around town where you can see Masaya's famous artesanías. By far the most extensive selection is to be found at the large **Mercado de Artesanías**, at the eastern end of town, just beyond the bridge. It includes excellent-quality cotton hammocks, colourful basketry and woven mats, charming cotton dolls of all sizes, carved and painted gourds, woodcarvings, paintings, ceramics and pottery, marimbas, coral jewellery, leatherwork and (if looking at them, let alone buying them, doesn't disgust you) goods made of reptile skins (crocodile, snake, iguana and frog), and stuffed alligators and frogs. It's a busy, colourful market, and well worth visiting. Be sure to bargain.

The **Centro de Artesanías de Masaya** (Cecapi) is at the other end of town, on the malecón overlooking the lake. The crafts are very good quality, but much more expensive than at the Mercado and there is not nearly as much here. It's worth coming, though, if for no other reason than to see the wall-sized country map that shows where all the various artesanías of Nicaragua are produced. The centre is open Monday to Saturday from 8 am to noon and 2 to 5 pm, and Sunday in the morning only.

A block behind the centre, away from the lake, are a couple of other artesanías shops, including Los Tapices de Luis and Rincón de las Artesanías, and there are others around town.

Some of the best artesanías in Nicaragua are produced in **Monimbó**, an Indian suburb of Masaya. The church of Magdalena in this barrio is worth a visit; there are artesanías shops around the church. You can also visit the many local workshops and see how the hammocks, woodcarvings, tapestries, masks and so on are made.

Malecón & Laguna de Masaya On the western side of town, the malecón, or lake-side walk, offers an excellent view over the Laguna de Masaya and to the Volcán Masaya (Santiago) behind it. From up here the lake

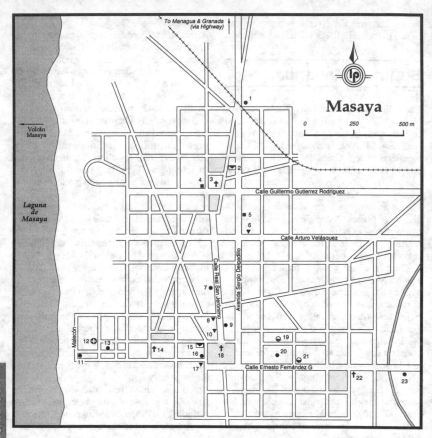

Masaya

To Managua & Granada
(via Highway)

Volcán
Masaya

Laguna
de
Masaya

Calle Guillermo Gutierrez Rodriguez

Calle Arturo Velásquez

Calle Real San Jerónimo

Avenida Sergio Delgadillo

Malecón

Calle Ernesto Fernández G

appears crystalline blue, but it is reported to be too polluted for swimming.

The Masaya volcano has been declared a national park; the park entrance is six km back down the road towards Managua from Masaya. A paved road runs all the way to the top of the volcano. (See the Around Managua section for more on this national park.)

Churches & Plazas Masaya has several old colonial churches, including the **Church of San Jerónimo**, on the northern side of town between two large plazas, and the **Church of La Asunción**, on the southern plaza (Parque

17 de Octubre), built in 1833. These are the two largest ones, but there are also the **Church of San Miguel**, the **Church of San Juan**, and the **Magdalena** church, which is in the Monimbó section of town.

Other Attractions Half a block north of the Parque 17 de Octubre is the local women's centre, the **Casa de la Mujer Silvia Marlene Ramirez**. In the next block north is the Palacio Municipal (city hall), which houses the **Museo y Galería de Héroes y Mártires**. The museum tells the story of Masaya's part in the Sandinista revolution; there are similar

■	PLACES TO STAY	3	Church of San Jerónimo	15	Telcor (Main Office)
				16	Cine Masaya
4	Hospedaje Josefina	7	Junta Municipal (City	18	Church of La
5	Hotel Regis		Hall) & Museo		Asunción,
			y Galería de		Parque 17 de
▼	PLACES TO EAT		Héroes y Mártires		Octubre
		9	Casa de la Mujer	19	Bus Stop (Long-
6	Nuevo Bar Chegris &		Silvia Marlene		Distance Buses)
	Restaurante		Ramirez	20	Mercado Viejo
8	Restaurante Alegría	11	Centro de Artesanías	21	Bus Stop (Local
10	Pizzas Jazz &		de Masaya		Buses)
	Sorbetería Chupis		(Cecapi)	22	Church of San Miguel
17	Restaurante Sándalo	12	Hospital Rafael	23	Mercado de
			Padilla		Artesanías
	OTHER	13	Los Tapices de Luis &		
			Rincón de las		
1	Train station		Artesanías		
2	Telcor (Branch)	14	Church of San Juan		

museums in other Nicaraguan cities. It is open Monday to Friday, from 8 am to noon and 2 to 4 pm.

Festivals

Masaya's patron saint is San Jerónimo. On the saint's day, 30 September, a large procession of people carrying flowers escorts a statue of the saint through the streets. The ensuing festival, featuring Indian dances in costume, lasts a week. Another important festival day is 16 March, when statues of the Virgen de Masaya and Cristo de Milagros of Nindirí, a village near Masaya, are taken by a procession to the lake for a blessing of the waters.

Places to Stay

The *Hotel Regis* (☎ 2300), at No 448-B Avenida Sergio Delgadillo, is a fine place, clean and well cared for, with rooms from US$8 with fan and shared bath. The owner is especially friendly and helpful, has been in Masaya for a long time and can tell you many interesting things about the town. If you plan to arrive after 10 pm, telephone ahead and let them know.

If the Regis is full you could try the *Hospedaje Josefina* or the *Hospedaje Rex*, both of which charge around US$1/1.50 for singles/doubles, but they are dives. The *Hotel Cailagua* (☎ 4435) at Km 29½ on the highway to Granada, has 15 rooms from around US$14.

Places to Eat

If you're just in Masaya to go to the Mercado de Artesanías, you can eat there, the market has several restaurant stalls serving basic Nicaraguan food.

The *Nuevo Bar Chegris* has a bar, as the name implies, but is also a good, very popular restaurant. It has a selection of meats and seafood, and is inexpensive, with most meals around US$2. Chegris is open every day from 10 am to 10 pm.

There are several good restaurants near the southern plaza. On the south-west corner, the *Restaurante Sándalo* is one of Masaya's fancier restaurants. It serves Chinese and regular food, with dining on the patio; meals are around US$2 to US$4. It's open every day except Wednesday, from 11 am to 10 pm.

A block north of this plaza, on the corner, the *Restaurante Alegría* restaurant is a good, basic restaurant, open daily from 11 am to 9 pm, with the usual meat and seafood meals and pizza. Between here and the southern plaza are the *Sorbetería* Chupis ice cream parlour and *Pizzas Jazz*.

Getting There & Away

Bus Buses arrive and depart from beside the Mercado Viejo. There are frequent buses to Managua (26 km, 45 minutes) and Granada

NICARAGUA

(18 km, 20 minutes), which start running around 4 am. The last bus to Granada leaves at around 5 pm, the last bus to Managua around 6 pm.

Train Trains between Managua and Granada stop at Masaya. Trains from Granada to Managua reach Masaya at around 5.45 am, 10.45 am, and 12.15 pm, then it's 45 minutes to Managua (US$0.20). Going in the other direction, from Managua to Granada, trains stop at Masaya around 8.45 am and 6.45 pm; it's an hour's ride from Masaya to Granada (US$0.40).

Getting Around
Horse-drawn carriages are one way to get around in Masaya; there are also plenty of taxis. Both charge around US$0.60 for a ride in town.

AROUND MASAYA
Coyotepe
On a hill just outside of town, overlooking the Managua-Granada highway, Coyotepe is an abandoned fortress. It was the last stand of the 1912 hero of resistance to US intervention, Benjamín Zeledón. You can hike up to it, but given the grim events with which it has been associated, it's said to be a rather spooky place.

Nindirí
The village of Nindirí is just a few km from Masaya (about 15 minutes by bus); the turnoff is at the 26 Km marker on the Managua-Granada highway, between Masaya and the national park entrance.

Nindirí has a small but interesting museum, the **Museo Tenderi**, which contains ancient Indian artefacts found around this region such as stone carvings, large burial jars, and musical instruments; there are still some caves in the area with prehistoric artwork. The museum is two blocks west of the Santa Ana church. The colonial church, built in 1798, contains some religious pieces that predate the church itself.

San Juan del Oriente & Catarina
San Juan del Oriente, not far from Masaya, is a colonial village famous for its pottery and ceramics. You can stop in at the well-known school of ceramics, and at a number of pottery workshops on the main road.

The nearby village of Catarina has a lookout, known as the **Mirador de Catarina**, that offers a spectacular view of the Laguna de Apoyo, Lago de Nicaragua, and the city of Granada. It is said to have been a favourite spot for youthful meditation by Augusto C Sandino, who was born nearby, This is appropriate since Catarina is also the site of the grave of Benjamín Zeledón, whose burial Sandino witnessed.

Niquinohomo
Augusto C Sandino was born and grew up in the village of Niquinohomo. His boyhood home, in the house opposite the church on the main plaza, is now a bookshop. The name of the town, interestingly enough, means 'valley of the warriors'.

Jinotepe, Diriamba & San Marcos
South-west of Masaya, in Carazo department, are the towns of Jinotepe and Diriamba, known as 'twin cities,' and San Marcos. Jinotepe has a tourist office (☎ 997) serving the whole department of Carazo.

These three towns, set in an area known for coffee, citrus and other fruit-tree cultivation, are the site of a distinctive Nicaraguan religious and folklore celebration, Toro Guaco.

Toro Guaco is a complex of festivals in which the Nahuatl town of Jinotepe and the Chorotega town of Diriamba, traditional rivals before the arrival of Europeans, commemorate their relationship. Jinotepe's patron is St James (Santiago), whose day is 25 July; Diriamba's is St Sebastian (20 January). The two towns and San Marcos carry out ceremonial visits to each other, involving dances, mock battles, and plays that also satirise the Spanish invaders. The pantomime figure of 'El Gueguense' is a symbol of Nicaraguan identity. The costumes, masks, and processions are striking.

The area is not very prepossessing, and does not get much tourist traffic. The *Hotel Jinotepe* (☎ 22978) is a remodelled, government-owned facility with rooms beginning at US$20 per person.

GRANADA
Population 56,232

Granada, nicknamed 'La Gran Sultana', Nicaragua's oldest Spanish city and now the third-largest city after Managua and León, was founded in 1523 by Francisco Hernández de Córdoba. It stands at the foot of Volcán Mombacho on the north-western shore of Lago de Nicaragua. The site lay between the indigenous town of Xalteva and the lake shore.

As León was colonial Nicaragua's liberal centre, so was Granada its conservative stronghold. Throughout the colonial period, Granada was rich. It was not only Nicaragua's principal trading city – the Río San Juan, entering Lago de Nicaragua at its south-eastern corner, provided access from Granada to the Caribbean and thence to Europe – but also gained wealth from the surrounding agricultural region.

Its wealth and strategic importance made Granada a target for English and French pirates during the 17th century. It also suffered serious damage in the 1850s when it was the scene of fighting in civil war, then was sacked and burned by William Walker in 1856.

Nevertheless, Granada retains its basic Spanish colonial character. Like León, its streets are lined with Spanish-style houses, with white adobe walls and large wooden doors opening onto cool interior patios. A number of the old colonial churches have survived, though some were damaged during turbulent episodes in the city's history and have been restored or rebuilt.

Granada has been designated a museum city by the Nicaraguan government and is a wonderful discovery for walkers. As the home of Nicaragua's 'Vanguardia' poets, including Joaquín Pasos and Pablo Antonio Cuadra, Granada is also a major literary city.

Orientation & Information
The cathedral and the plaza in front of it form the centre of the city, and there are several buildings of interest on or near the plaza. Telcor, the telephone and post office, is near its north-eastern corner. The neoclassic

NICARAGUA

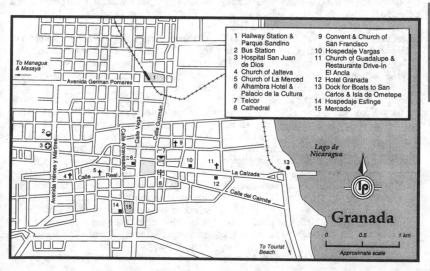

1 Railway Station & Parque Sandino	9 Convent & Church of San Francisco
2 Bus Station	10 Hospedaje Vargas
3 Hospital San Juan de Dios	11 Church of Guadalupe & Restaurante Drive-in El Ancla
4 Church of Jalteva	12 Hotel Granada
5 Church of La Merced	13 Dock for Boats to San Carlos & Isla de Ometepe
6 Alhambra Hotel & Palacio de la Cultura	14 Hospedaje Esfinge
7 Telcor	15 Mercado
8 Cathedral	

Granada

Mercado, built in 1890, is three blocks to the south; the railway station (also neoclassic and dating from 1888) is about six long blocks north of it, and the bus station about six long blocks to the west.

Lago de Nicaragua is on the eastern side of town. The main road leading from the plaza to the lake is called **La Calzada** (The Causeway). It's more than a km from the plaza to the lakeside park, a very pleasant ride in a horse-drawn carriage. A malecón is due to be constructed at the foot of La Calzada, to be named after the poet Pablo Antonio Cuadra. In the park there are picnic areas and restaurants next to a swimming beach. Boats for day trips to the islands on the lake depart from the far (southern) end of the beach.

Granada's tourist office (☎ 2801, 3313) is next to the Hotel Alhambra, and its staff are extremely helpful. Like other Nicaraguan towns, Granada has very few street signs.

Things to See & Do
The City The **cathedral** is on the east side of the central park and **Plaza de la Independencia**; nearby buildings of interest include the **Palacio Municipal** (city hall) on the south side of the plaza and the **Palacio Episcopal** (Bishop's Palace), which shows the influence of the New Orleans neoclassical architectural style.

Opposite the cathedral is the **Palacio de la Cultura Joaquín Pasos**. Pasos (1914-47) was the author of *Canto de Guerra de las Cosas* (War Song of Things), a surrealist masterpiece and one of the glories of 20th-century Spanish verse. He also wrote fascinating poetry in a curious English he claimed not to be able to speak. The Palacio was once the city's elite social club and has been beautifully restored. It has an art gallery and hosts special events including presentations of music, dance, poetry and theatre. Also on this side of the plaza is the fancy Alhambra Hotel.

North of the central park and plaza is the **Plazuela de los Leones**. The plazuela exhibits a stone portal which is all that remains of the original Casa de los Leones

which stood at the same site and was burned when Walker torched the city. The portal shows two lions, with the arms of the Montiel family, which included a governor of Costa Rica, and the motto 'Viva Don Fernan VII 1809,' referring to the Spanish king ruling in the year of the portal's placement.

The beautiful casa itself, constructed many decades before the installation of the portal in 1809, was destroyed by Walker, rebuilt and is now being refurbished with funds from the Austrian government. The declaration of loyalty to the crown in the motto reflects Granada's conservative tradition. However Diego de Montiel, who installed the portal, did not keep faith with this pledge; he joined the revolutionary movement against the Spanish and ended up imprisoned in Guatemala.

Granada has several other fine old colonial churches besides the cathedral. The **Convent & Church of San Francisco**, a couple of blocks north-east of the cathedral, was rebuilt in 1867-68 after Walker's incendiary attack. The convent was founded in 1524. Bartolomé de las Casas, benefactor and apostle to the Indians, has a significant history here. He preached in the convent and church, and from Granada, on 15 October 1535, Las Casas penned a letter of protest to the Spanish court denouncing the conversion of the indigenous people to Christianity by violent means. The complex is being completely rebuilt with Swedish government support.

In the past the convent housed the University of Granada, officially styled the Universidad (later Instituto) de Mediodía y Oriente. This academic institution long embodied the city's intellectual aspirations. It was shut down by dictator Anastasio Somoza García in 1951, as a reprisal for Granada's opposition to the dictatorship, and has yet to reopen. Many Granadinos feel the absence of a university, and plans for its reestablishment have been announced by the municipal authorities, with possible support from Chile.

Perhaps appropriately, given Las Casas'

history here, the last remnant of the Universidad's activity is a magnificent collection, sheltered in the Convent, of some 30 pieces of pre-Columbian stone statuary from Isla Zapatera in Lago de Nicaragua. Known as the 'Squier Collection' after the 19th-century US diplomat, Ephraim G Squier, who first called attention to 15 of the statues located at Jiquilito on Zapatera, it is well worth a special visit.

The statues are black basalt, and have been dated to the period 800-1200 AD. They depict human, animal and combined human-animal forms. They are ascribed to the Chorotega culture and may represent divinities, sacred dancers, or religious or clan leaders. Admission to the collection is free although a small donation, for the reconstruction of the overall site, will be welcomed.

The **Church of La Merced**, three blocks west of the plaza, also has an eventful history. Completed in early 1783, it was damaged in fighting in 1854, then restored and remodelled in 1862. Other notable colonial churches include the **Church of Jalteva**, a couple of blocks west of La Merced, and the **Church of Guadalupe** on La Calzada. The latter was used as a stronghold by William Walker.

The Lake At the lake there is a large park, the **Centro Turístico**, with trees, grassy picnic areas, restaurants, and a long swimming beach. If you drive in to the centre, there's an admission charge of US$1.60. Boats depart for day trips to the nearby islands from the Asese dock, at the southern end of the beach, or from some of the beachside restaurants. You can make a very enjoyable trip to Las Isletas and to Isla Zapatera. See the Around Granada section for more on these islands close to Granada, and the Lago de Nicaragua section for more on the islands further away: Isla de Ometepe, and the Archipiélago de Solentiname.

Festivals
Granada celebrates festivals at Semana Santa, Christmas, and at the feast of La Asunción de la Virgen, held during the last two weeks of August.

Places to Stay
Good budget hotels are scarce in Granada. *Hospedaje Vargas* (☎ 2897) on La Calzada is probably the best of the limited number of options; rooms with shared bath are US$2.50 per person. *Hospedaje Esfinge* (☎ 2267), opposite the Mercado, has rooms with private bath at US$8, or some other, dark rooms divided only by partitions for US$6.

Otherwise, the *Hotel Granada* (☎ 2974) on La Calzada is much more expensive with singles starting at US$30. The *Hotel Alhambra* (☎ 4486) on the plaza was slightly cheaper with rooms from US$25.

One good bit of news from Granada is that the Ministry of Tourism is encouraging owners of colonial homes to offer B&B service. Inquire at the tourist office.

Places to Eat
On La Calzada, opposite the Hotel Granada, the *Drive-In El Ancla* restaurant is good, clean and inexpensive, open from early until late, serving all meals and snacks.

There are many restaurants in the park along the lakeshore, selling meals or snacks. The *Rancho Colomer* has meals for around US$2 to US$4. In town, the Mercado also has cheap comedores that open the same hours as the Mercado: daily from 7 am to 4 pm except on Sunday, when they close early at 2 pm.

Getting There & Away
Bus Buses to Managua (18 km, 20 minutes) and Masaya (44 km, one hour) depart every 20 minutes from the bus station, beside the large Hospital San Juan de Dios on the south side of town. The first bus goes at around 4 am, the last at around 6 pm.

Buses to Rivas depart from another bus stop, near the Mercado, at 5.40, 6.40 and 9.30 am, and at 12.40 and 3 pm. The trip to Rivas takes two hours (65 km). However, if you miss one of these direct buses, you can take a bus from the same stop to the crossroads at Nandaime and catch any bus heading south from there to Rivas.

Train Trains to Managua and Masaya depart from Granada at 5, 10 and 11.30 am. They pass through Masaya first, an hour after leaving Granada, and arrive in Managua around 45 minutes later. The fare is US$0.20 to Masaya, US$0.85 to Managua.

Boat Boats depart from Granada's dock at the foot of La Calzada for different places around the lake every Monday, Thursday and Saturday.

On Monday and Thursday, a boat departs at 3 pm for Isla de Ometepe and San Carlos. It stops first at Altagracia, then Moyogalpa, and finally at San Carlos. It takes about 3½ hours to reach Isla de Ometepe; the fares are US$1.10 to Altagracia and US$1.50 to Moyogalpa. From Granada all the way to San Carlos takes nine hours and costs US$2. Also on Monday and Thursday, another boat leaves at 5 pm for Morrito, San Miguelito and San Carlos.

These boats return to Granada by the same routes on the Tuesday and Friday. On Saturday, a boat leaves at noon for Isla de Ometepe (Moyogalpa and Altagracia). It takes the same 3½ hours to get there, for the same fares.

It's probably a good idea to stop by the ticket office here to confirm the schedule if you're planning to travel on these boats. On the days the boats go, people wait around the dock all day long, and snacks and meals are served at tables set up under the trees.

Another option for getting to Isla de Ometepe is to take a *lancha* (small motorboat). These depart on Monday, Wednesday and Friday at around 9.30 or 10 am. They take longer to reach Ometepe (five hours), and are also more expensive (US$1.40) than the larger boats.

Getting Around
Horse-drawn carriages are a pleasant way to get around in Granada, and they're cheaper than the taxis. They cost US$0.20 to the centre of town, or US$0.40 all the way to the lakeside park.

AROUND GRANADA
Las Isletas & Isla Zapatera
Las Isletas is a group of 356 small islands just offshore from Granada; they can be reached by motorboat in about 15 minutes and are well worth visiting.

The islands were formed by volcanic activity. Most are covered with vegetation, and some are inhabited by people who make a living by fishing and growing tropical fruits such as mangoes and coconuts. Some wealthy Nicaraguans have also built homes here. There is a remarkable variety of wildlife, especially birds such as herons, cranes, egrets and many others. Early in the morning and late in the afternoon are the best times to watch them.

The island of **San Pablo**, the furthest of Las Isletas from Granada, has a small fortress built by the Spanish in the mid-18th century to protect Granada from attack by British pirates. The historic fortress, still with its cannons, has been restored and is open to visitors.

The larger Isla Zapatera is further from Granada, about an hour away by motorboat. Protected as a national park, this island is one of Nicaragua's most important archaeological areas. Giant stone statues erected by Indians in pre-Columbian times have been moved elsewhere (most notably, to Granada where they are on display at the Convent & Church of San Francisco), but you can see where the statues stood, and visit other ancient constructions and tombs. There are more tombs and some good rock carvings on **Isla del Muerto**, separated from Zapatera by a canal.

You can visit all these islands by hiring a boat from the tourist beach in Granada; some of the beachfront restaurants organise trips on the lake, or you can take a boat from the dock at Asese, at the southern end of the beach. Prices vary, so try to get the best deal you can. One restaurant, the Rincon Criollo (☎ 4317), was offering boats for all-day trips to at least 10 different islands, including

Zapatera and Isla del Muerto, at US$20 for a boat capable of holding 20 people.

Other islands in the lake are much further from Granada. Isla de Ometepe is 3½ hours away on the large boat and five hours by smaller boat, but only an hour from the nearer port of San Jorge, near Rivas. The Archipiélago de Solentiname is accessible by small boats from San Carlos. These more distant islands are covered in the Lago de Nicaragua section.

RIVAS
Population 21,000

Rivas is a small crossroads town and a hub for buses. Buses go from here to the Costa Rican border at Peñas Blancas, to the Pacific town of San Juan del Sur, to Granada and to Managua, and to San Jorge, the small port on the Lago de Nicaragua where boats depart for Isla de Ometepe. (You can see the cone of Ometepe's Concepción volcano towering in the east from Rivas.)

Most of Rivas is concentrated in a few blocks on the west side of the highway. The places to stay are mostly on or near the highway.

From the highway, it's worth walking the six blocks or so into town to see the old colonial church on the plaza. Among its curious artworks is a fresco in the cupola showing a battle at sea, with Communism, Protestantism and Secularism as burning hulks, Masonry as a dead warrior on the rocks, and Petrus (St Peter, the 'rock' on which the Christian Church was built) as a victorious ship entering the harbour.

Rivas is small, but it has had its moments of importance since its establishment in 1736. Some significant battles have been fought here, and during the California gold rush Rivas was an important stop on Cornelius Vanderbilt's overland stagecoach route taking fortune-seekers across Nicaragua to San Juan del Sur on the Pacific coast. Today Rivas is the capital of the department of the same name, and the centre for an agricultural region where maize, beans, rice, sugarcane, coffee, cacao and tobacco are grown, and livestock is raised.

The nearest tourist office is in San Jorge (☎ 35).

Places to Stay

The best place to stay is the *Hospedaje & Comedor Lidia*, half a block behind the Texaco station on the main highway. It's a clean, family-run place where rooms are US$4 per person, with shared bath and laundry. Meals are served, but these are expensive: for example, breakfast is US$4.

On the highway are three very basic hospedajes: the *Internacional*, the *Coco* and the *Primavera*. These are cheaper at US$2 per person, but they are all quite run-down.

Places to Eat

There is a small but pleasant Mercado in Rivas, several blocks west of the highway; beside it is the open lot where the buses pull in. The comedores inside the market are the cheapest places in town to eat: you can get a big breakfast or lunch, including a drink, for around US$1.50.

There are other places to eat, but these are significantly more expensive. The open-air *Rinconcito Salvadoreño*, on the plaza in front of the church, has a pleasant atmosphere. Also on the plaza, the *Restaurante Chop Suey* serves both Chinese and regular Nicaraguan food; most meals are around US$4 to US$5. It's a friendly place.

Out on the highway are a few simple comedores.

Getting There & Away

Buses from Rivas, with the exception of those to San Jorge, depart from the Mercado, about 10 blocks west of the highway. They also stop at the Texaco station on the highway before leaving town, but it's best to walk the extra distance to the Mercado if you want to get a seat.

The buses to San Jorge leave from the stop near the Shell station on the highway. It doesn't matter so much if you have to stand on this bus as it's only a four-km trip. A taxi from Rivas to San Jorge costs US$0.80.

If you miss the direct bus to Granada, you can take a bus heading for Managua, get off at the crossroads at Nandaime (45 km from Rivas), and take another bus or hitch the next 20 km to Granada. Buses from Rivas include:

to Managua – buses leave half-hourly, 4 am to 5 pm (109 km, 2½ hrs).
to Granada – buses leave at 6, 8 and 10.30 am and at noon (65 km, two hrs).
to San Juan del Sur – buses leave hourly, 6 am to 5 pm (29 km, one hr).
to San Jorge – buses leave half-hourly, 6 am to 5 pm (four km, 15 mins).
to Peñas Blancas – buses leave at 5.30, 7, 9.30 and 11 am, 12.45 and 2.30 pm (35 km, one hr).

RIVAS TO COSTA RICA
Getting to Peñas Blancas, the border crossing between Nicaragua and Costa Rica, is simply a one-hour bus ride. Alternatively, it's an easy hitch. The Nicaraguan border post seems to have moved a few km down the road to Sapoá.

Remember that you may have to show a ticket out of Costa Rica when you arrive at the border crossing. See the introductory Getting There & Away section for information on satisfying this requirement.

If you are in Rivas and still do not have your onward ticket from Costa Rica, you can buy one from the Sirca bus company, based at the Hospedaje & Comedor Internacional on the main highway through town. You can only buy a ticket between Managua and San José and it costs the same price here as in Managua: US$20 one way, US$40 return. The cheapest option is to buy a one-way ticket to bring you back to Managua from San José, which will fulfil the ticket requirement.

The Sirca buses leave Managua on Monday, Wednesday and Friday at 5 am and pass through Rivas at about 9.30 am. Another bus company, Tica Bus, runs buses between Managua and San José, but is more expensive (US$30 one way, US$60 return.) The Tica buses do not stop in Rivas on their way to the border, though they will stop there to let you off if you are coming into Nicaragua from Costa Rica.

The border station at Peñas Blancas is open daily from 8 am to 5 pm.

SAN JUAN DEL SUR
Population 16,020
San Juan del Sur is a fishing village on a pretty little cove with mountains rising behind it.

The town was once important as the terminus of Cornelius Vanderbilt's transport company, established in 1848 during the gold rush in California. Steamboats brought passengers from the Caribbean up the Río San Juan to Lago de Nicaragua; they then travelled 20 km by coach to the port at San Juan del Sur. From here, boats took them on to California.

More recently, the town became popular again during the Sandinista years, when this was a favourite refuge for internacionalistas taking a break by the sea. Today the town remains a leading beach resort, and is a beautiful spot, typically quiet except for the holidays at Semana Santa.

San Juan del Sur is also known for its annual procession to La Virgen del Carmen, patron of the port's mariners, on July 16.

If you come to San Juan del Sur, you may need protection against mosquitoes – insect repellent, coils, mosquito net, or whatever you prefer. Some of the hospedajes (such as the Joxi) have screens to keep the many mosquitoes out, but several places don't.

Places to Stay
San Juan del Sur has quite a selection of places to stay.

Casa 28, one block from the beach, is a long-standing favourite with backpackers and internacionalistas, not because it's fancy but because of the immensely warm hospitality of its owners, who provide everything to make you feel at home. You can wash your clothes here and use the kitchen to cook your meals, or they will cook meals if you like. It costs US$5 per person for rooms with shared bath.

Three blocks from the beach, the *Hospedaje Irazú* (☎ 371), run by a Costa

To Hospedaje, Bar &
Restaurante Gallo de Oro

PACIFIC OCEAN

San Juan del Sur

0   50   100 m

Approximate scale

1 Banco Nacional de Desarrollo
2 Restaurante La Soya
3 Casa 28
4 Hospedaje El Buen Gusto
5 Hotel Estrella
6 Casa Internacional Joxi
7 Restaurante Rancho Mira Valle
8 Hospedaje Irazú
9 Mercado & Bus Stop
10 La Fogata Bar & Restaurant
11 Church

Rican family, has good, clean rooms with private bath and fan, also at US$5 per person.

On the town's sea front there is the *Hotel Estrella* and opposite it, the *Hospedaje & Comedor El Buen Gusto*. The *El Buen Gusto* (☎ 304) asks US$12 per person, breakfast included.

The *Hotel Estrella* (☎ 82210) looks great from the outside, but inside the rooms are divided only by partitions. Several locals warned us that the Estrella also had a bad reputation for theft from the rooms, too much noise and abundant mosquitoes. It costs US$7 per person.

If you want to stay by the sea, you could try the *Hospedaje, Bar & Restaurante Gallo de Oro* (☎ 240), a couple of blocks north of town, beside the sea and the estuary. It's a very simple place that charges US$5 per person.

Casa Internacional Joxi (☎ 348), half a block from the beach between the Hotel Estrella and the Mercado, is a good, clean, new hotel operated by a friendly Norwegian-Nicaraguan couple. The most economical rooms have four bunks, fan and shared bath and cost US$8 per person. Other rooms, with private bath and air-con, are US$15 per

person, and they will make meals if you wish. Sailboat charters may also be arranged through the Joxi.

Places to Eat

Fresh fish and seafood are, of course, the specialities of the town, and they are delicious.

A good place to eat is the *Restaurante La Soya*, one block from the beach. It is operated by the Nicaraguan women's association IXCHEN, formerly AMNLAE, and is open every day from around 7 am to 8 pm. A basic meal of fish, rice, beans, cheese, salad and tortillas costs US$1.20 here; the same meal at the restaurants along the beach costs around US$3. There are quite a number of restaurants along the beach which, though they cost more, are good for their fine views of the cove.

As everywhere in Nicaragua, you can also dine economically in the Mercado.

Other restaurants include the bar and restaurant *La Fogata*, opposite the Mercado, which offers music on Saturday nights and has a hospedaje at the back, and the *Restaurante Rancho Mira Valle*, on a corner between the Mercado and the beach. Several

NICARAGUA

of the hotels also have restaurants or will make meals if you ask.

Getting There & Away
Buses come and go from beside the Mercado, three blocks from the beach. Buses to Rivas depart hourly, from 5 am to 3.30 pm (29 km, one hour). From Rivas you can transfer onto buses for many other places.

Lago de Nicaragua

Lago de Nicaragua, also known as Cocibolca, its indigenous name, and as La Mar Dulce ('the sweet sea') is the largest lake in Central America and the 10th-largest freshwater lake in the world: it is 177 km long by an average 58 km wide, covers 8157 sq km and is around 60 metres deep at its deepest point.

Forty-five rivers flow into the lake, including the Río Tipitapa that flows down from Lago de Managua. One large river, the Río San Juan, flows from Lago de Nicaragua to the Caribbean. This river has been navigated for centuries and was once an important sea link between Granada, on the lake's northern shore, the Caribbean and the route to Europe.

The world's only freshwater sharks live in Lago de Nicaragua. Although they are big – about three metres long – they are very rarely seen. Many other unusual fish are found in the lake, including freshwater swordfish, sawfish, tarpon and many others.

This strange aquatic life reflects the way the lake was formed. It is believed that both Lago de Nicaragua and Lago de Managua were originally part of a large Pacific bay, but that they were cut off from the ocean by volcanic eruptions that created lava flows and an uplift in the earth's crust. Isolated from the sea, the salt water very gradually became fresh, and the sea creatures trapped in the new lakes adapted as the water changed. The lake supports not only abundant underwater life, but birdlife as well.

An ancient Indian story relates how the Chorotega and Nahuatl peoples were overpowered by the Olmecs in Mexico, and thus forced to embark upon a massive migration south. Consulting their oracles, they were told that they would find a place to settle near a freshwater sea, where they would see an island with two high mountains. Some say that the lake also experiences tides, though others attribute the fluctuations in the water level to other causes.

There is ample evidence of ancient human habitation on the lake's 400 islands. Over 350 of these are in the group called Las Isletas, just offshore from Granada. Zapatera, the second-largest island in the lake, is just to the south of this group. The Archipiélago de Solentiname, on the south end of the lake, is another big group. The largest of all the islands, Ometepe, is formed by two massive volcanoes. Lago de Nicaragua is, indeed, just as the oracle described it.

Ancient Indian artefacts found on the islands, particularly on Zapatera, Ometepe, and the Solentiname group, include statues of people and animals, and petroglyphs with images of people, mammals, birds, and geometric shapes. Many tombs have been found too, notably on Zapatera and the Isla del Muerto beside it; apparently these islands were used as cemeteries.

The link created by the lake and the Río San Juan between Granada and the Caribbean was exploited for centuries by French, British and other pirates bent on attacking Granada and Léon. But the possibility of using this link as part of a trans-isthmian sea crossing also lent the lake strategic importance, firing imperial imaginations from the early 16th century to this day. Lago de Nicaragua, its islands, and the people who inhabit them are memorialized in Pablo Antonio Cuadra's *Cantos de Cífar*, one of the most famous works of contemporary Nicaraguan literature.

ISLA DE OMETEPE
Ometepe ('between two hills' in Nahuatl) is the largest island in Lago de Nicaragua. It is formed by two large volcanoes: Volcán Concepción, which rises 1610 metres from

the lake in an almost perfect cone, and Volcán Madera, which is smaller at 1340 metres high. Concepción is still active: it erupted most recently in 1983. Lava flowing from the two volcanoes created an isthmus between them to make a single island.

People are dotted in small settlements around the island's edges and live by fishing and growing bananas, citrus fruits, watermelon, maize, sesame, tobacco, coffee, cotton and cacao, among other crops; Ometepe's volcanic soil is very fertile. Parts of the island are still covered in forest where you can see abundant wildlife including white-faced monkeys, congo (howler) monkeys, green parrots and many other animals and birds.

Like Zapatera, Ometepe is famous for its ancient stone statues and petroglyphs, also made by the Chorotega people, and depicting people, animals, birds, and geometric shapes, especially spirals. They have been found all over the island, but there are many on Volcán Madera, between Santa Cruz and La Palma, about 800 metres back from the shore. Several ancient stone statues are displayed in Altagracia on the footpath in front of the church.

At Moyogalpa you may find pre-Columbian pottery, including funerary urns, for sale. The pieces are apparently authentic but prospective purchasers are counselled to investigate Nicaraguan laws and those in their home countries, governing purchase and exportation or importation of artefacts that may be considered part of Nicaragua's cultural heritage.

A road goes all round the part of the island formed by Volcán Concepción; at the isthmus it connects to a road that goes around the Volcán Madera side as far as Balgue on the north coast and Mérida on the south. However, people do live all around Madera and it is all accessible on foot, on horseback or in a small boat.

The island's two major villages are Altagracia and Moyogalpa. Both towns are very small, but they do have places to stay. They are connected to the mainland by ferries.

Books

Ometepe: Isla de Círculos y Espirales (1973, Hildeberto María), by Joaquín Matilló Vila, is an excellent illustrated book about the petroglyphs and other ancient evidence of civilisation found on the island. It may be difficult to find in shops, but Señor Ramón Castillo, owner of the Hospedaje Castillo in Altagracia, has a copy (in Spanish) which he keeps to share with visitors.

Things to See & Do

Ometepe does not have 'big city' attractions, but it's great for walking and exploring. You can get an excellent view just by walking for half an hour up the Volcán Concepción behind either Moyogalpa or Altagracia. If you're hardier and more determined you could hike all the way to the top.

There are some fine walks on the Madera side of the island, through forests full of wildlife. Locals recommend visiting the laguna on Madera, said to be an exquisitely beautiful crater lake. It is quite 'off the beaten track' but there is a way through to it that starts near Balgue.

The coast south of Altagracia has some lovely beaches, with clear water for swimming. You could walk down this stretch and catch the bus back from Balgue or Santa Cruz to Altagracia in the afternoon. The beach area of Santo Domingo, accessible via a two-km side road that begins about five km south of Altagracia, now features a small and modest hotel, the *Finca Santo Domingo*, with clean rooms, food and drink, and great serenity at around US$2 to US$3 per person per night.

Of course, there are plenty of hikes to see petroglyphs. Señor Castillo at the Hospedaje Castillo in Altagracia, the best source of information on the island, can arrange a guide and horses if you want to make an excursion to some of the more remote petroglyphs.

An enjoyable and less strenuous way to see the island is simply to ride on the bus, which goes all the way around Volcán Concepción, across the isthmus and down to Balgue on the Madera side, passing through

NICARAGUA

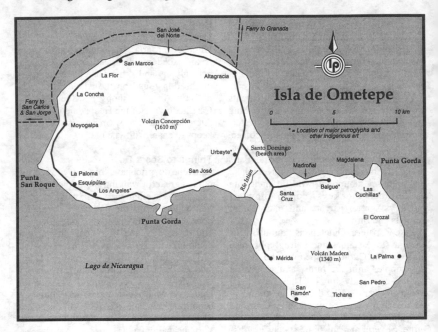

Isla de Ometepe

0   5   10 km

* = Location of major petroglyphs and
other indigenous art

NICARAGUA

many small villages and varied farming
country. It is a good way to orient yourself.
The gorgeous blue-tailed birds seen everywhere on the island are called *urracas*.

Moyogalpa
Population 9913

Moyogalpa is the principal village on the
west side of the island; ferries run several
times daily between Moyogalpa and the
mainland at San Jorge, near Rivas. The trip
takes only an hour and is the easiest and
fastest crossing to Ometepe. Though
Altagracia is the larger town, Moyogalpa has
more hotels.

Places to Stay & Eat On the road coming
up the hill from the ferry dock are two simple
but clean hospedajes, both with restaurants
and rooms with shared bath. The *Hospedaje
y Restaurante Moyogalpa* beside the port is
the first building you come to when you get
off the ferry. Rooms here cost US$1.60 per

person; the restaurant is popular and serves
breakfast for US$1.50, and lunch and dinner
for around US$3.

A little further up the same road, the
Hospedaje y Restaurante Aly has rooms
around a peaceful, attractive central patio
with tables, hammocks and lots of plants.
Rooms with shared bath are US$2.40 per
person. On the wall in the foyer is a large map
of the island. Meals begin at US$2.50.

If both these places are full, you could try
the *Hospedaje Omey*, one block from the
road leading up from the dock. It has no sign,
but it's on a corner and anyone can direct you
to it. Rooms here, also around a central patio,
are US$1 per person, and they also serve
meals.

El Pirata (☎ 23), nearby, has 12 rooms,
three with private bath, beginning at
US$5.75, and a restaurant. The owner,
Douglas Céspedes, will also rent Toyota
4WD vehicles, which are pricey at US$25 to
US$50 with driver but may be fun for those

who wish to brave the island's hair-raising roads. Señor Céspedes will also prepare box lunches for picnickers in addition to serving meals at the restaurant.

There are several restaurants in Moyogalpa besides those in the hotels. All are easy to find as the town is so small. The town also has a branch of the Banco Nacional de Desarrollo.

Altagracia
Population 15,603

Altagracia is not very big, but it is the largest town on Isla de Ometepe. The dock is a short distance out of town; from here, the ferry runs several times weekly to Granada (3½ hours) and to San Carlos (five hours). There is not much to see in Altagracia besides the ancient stone statues on the footpath in front of the church, which are quite fine, but it's a good starting point for walks.

Places to Stay & Eat
The only place to stay in Altagracia is the *Hospedaje Castillo*, one block south and half a block west from the church. The owner, Señor Ramón Castillo, is exceptionally friendly and helpful. He can tell you all the good things to see and do on Ometepe, and can arrange a guide if you want to hike around the island and see the ancient rock statues on its farther reaches. The hospedaje is somewhat crude; rooms with shared bath cost US$2.50 per person, US$4 with meals, served on the patio.

The patio of the Castillo is the only 'restaurant' in Altagracia, but the food is good and not too expensive. You can come here to eat and to talk to Señor Castillo whether or not you're a guest at the hospedaje.

A block from the Castillo, the *Hospedaje El Esfuerzo* has four rooms which are sometimes rented out.

Getting There & Away
To/From Granada & San Carlos The boat from Granada to San Carlos departs from the dock at Granada on Monday and Thursday at 3 pm. It arrives in Altagracia at around 6 or 6.30 pm, then goes around the island to stop at Moyogalpa, and takes off from there for San Carlos, on the south side of the lake. It costs US$1.10 from Granada to Altagracia, US$1.50 to Moyogalpa. The whole trip from Granada to San Carlos takes nine hours and costs US$2. On Saturdays, another boat goes from Granada just to Ometepe.

The boat returns to Granada from the dock at Altagracia on Tuesday and Friday at 10 pm, and on Sundays at 10 am, taking 3½ hours to make the trip.

To/From San Jorge The *El Diamante* ferry runs several times a day between San Jorge (near Rivas) and Moyogalpa. It operates seven days per week, departing from the dock in Moyogalpa at 8 am and 5 pm and reaching San Jorge an hour later. From San Jorge, it departs at 10 am and 6 pm. The trip costs US$2.50.

Travellers are urged to check with the office of the Empresa Nacional de Puertos (ENAP), the Nicaraguan national port authority, on the Moyogalpa dock, to confirm the departure time for the last boat. Service can be unreliable, with the last boat departing ahead of scheduled time. However, the ferry will make unscheduled trips in emergencies.

Getting Around
Buses go all the way around the side of the island formed by Volcán Concepción, and from Altagracia across the isthmus and down to Balgue on the Madera side. Ask for the bus schedule when you arrive on the island. The trip from Moyagalpa to Altagracia takes 1½ hours (US$0.70) and from Altagracia to Balgue takes another hour.

You can make a very enjoyable day trip from Moyogalpa by taking the 6 or 7 am bus to Altagracia, passing around the south side of Volcán Concepción on the way; the 9.30 am bus from Altagracia across the isthmus to Balgue; the return bus from Balgue back to Altagracia either at noon or at 3 pm; and another bus from Altagracia somewhere between 4.15 and 5 pm to return to

Moyogalpa, this time via the north side of Volcán Concepción.

There are also 4WD vehicles which are available for rent.

ARCHIPIÉLAGO DE SOLENTINAME

The Archipiélago de Solentiname, in the southern part of the Lago de Nicaragua, is composed of a number of islands; the largest ones are Mancarrón, San Fernando and La Venada.

The Solentiname islands are a sort of haven for artists. The Nicaraguan poet Ernesto Cardenal established a communal society here for artists, poets and crafts-people, and the islands are now known for their distinctive school of colourful primitiv-ist painting, with a characteristic style of charming simplicity.

The islands are great for hiking, fishing and taking it easy. Here, as on other islands in the lake, petroglyphs and stone carvings testify to ancient human settlement.

The *Hospedaje Solentiname*, on San Fer-nando island, has rooms for US$8 per person, with meals for US$5 to US$7. You could also come for the day. Boats to the islands depart from San Carlos. The charge for a same-day return trio in a 48 hp boat is US$80, or US$90 with an overnight stay.

SAN CARLOS

Population 1500

San Carlos is a small town on the south-eastern corner of Lago de Nicaragua, beside the Río San Juan. Boats go from here down the river as well as to Archipiélago de Solentiname.

People visit San Carlos mainly because of its proximity to other places, including the border with Costa Rica. But the town does have the ruins of an old fortress built by the Spanish to fight off pirates coming up the river and trying to enter the lake, and there are places to stay and to eat.

Getting There & Away

Boats leave from Granada for San Carlos on Monday and Thursday afternoons. There are two boats taking different routes: one stops off at Isla de Ometepe, while the other stops at Morrito and San Miguelito, two villages on the eastern lakeshore. San Miguelito is also the terminus of an unpaved but usable road from Juigalpa.

The boats leave San Carlos on Tuesday and Friday to return to Granada. The trip between San Carlos and Granada takes 10 to 12 hours and costs US$2.

There may also be buses to San Miguelito, with boat service (costing up to US$50) on to San Carlos. There are two hospedajes in San Carlos, *Hospedaje El Madroño* and *Hospedaje Peña*, both with rooms at about US$2.50.

Boats also leave San Carlos for the border station at Los Chiles.

RÍO SAN JUAN & EL CASTILLO

The Río San Juan flows 180 km through deep rainforest from Lago de Nicaragua to the Caribbean, where it meets the coast at the port of San Juan del Norte (formerly called Greytown). For much of its length, the river serves as the border between Nicaragua and Costa Rica.

As a part of a major Río San Juan Integral Development Project, El Castillo de la Inmaculada Concepción (also called El Castillo de la Concepción, El Castillo Viejo or simply El Castillo) is being rehabilitated with funding from the Spanish government. The fortress was built by the Spanish in 1675 at a strategic point on the river to try to block English, French and other pirates from coming up the river to attack Granada and León. It was one of several fortifications designed for this purpose, including those at San Carlos, and on San Pablo Island, near Granada.

Bitter battles were fought at El Castillo against flotillas of assailants. In 1762 there was a fierce battle to repel a 2000-strong force on 50 British ships, led by Henry Morgan. The fort was subsequently captured and briefly held by the British in 1780. Their intention was to annex the strategic trans-isthmian route, seize rich Granada and León, and divide the Spanish territory. A museum detailing the fort's turbulent history (Horatio

Nelson was also present) is to form part of the restoration project.

Boat trips on the Río San Juan were once a major attraction for visitors to Nicaragua, but travel on the river was suspended during the war against the Contras. Now that the war is over, trips have resumed, with service taking five hours, in regular motorboats. Boats depart San Carlos for El Castillo on Monday and Thursday at 2 pm and Tuesday and Friday at 9 am. Return trips from El Castillo to San Carlos depart on Monday and Thursday at 5 am.

Boat fares from San Carlos down the river, including as far as San Juan del Norte (Greytown) may be very expensive. Service from San Carlos to Los Chiles (a seldom-used entry station for Costa Rica) costs US$50, with the price to El Castillo at US$200 and to San Juan del Norte at US$750. (A sales tax may also be added!)

The Nicaraguan government has set aside a large area between El Castillo and San Juan del Norte (Greytown), as the Río Indio/Río Maíz Biological Preserve.

In Castillo, the *Albergue El Castillo* (☎ (055) 4635, ext 3) has been opened, with capacity for 25 people at US$10 to US$15 per person. Meals are available in town for around US$5.

Some 20 km further downriver from El Castillo, *Refugio Bartola* has been opened in connection with the Guises Montaña Experimental Research Station. It offers eight rooms at around US$15. For more information, write to the Refugio Bartola, Apartado 2715, or fax 2-97924 in Managua. Boat service to Bartola is cheaper than other Río San Juan services at US$40.

The Caribbean Coast

The Caribbean coast of Nicaragua is a long (541 km), wide, flat coastal plain covered in tropical rainforest. In many places the virgin jungle is so thick that it is practically impenetrable, and it provides a home to abundant wildlife. Some of the forest was destroyed by Hurricane Joan in 1988, but it is now growing back. The coast is hot and gets much more rain than the Pacific and inland regions: anywhere between 3300 and 6350 mm annually. Even during the short 'dry' season from March to May, rain is possible at any time.

The Caribbean coast of Nicaragua is part of the larger Mosquitia region that extends well into Honduras. The Río Coco, which forms the border between present-day Honduras and Nicaragua, runs right through the traditional Mosquitia region, and the Miskito Indians, today numbering around 70,000, live on both sides of it.

Other ethnic groups in the region include the Sumo and Rama Indian tribes, the Black Creoles originally brought from other parts of the Caribbean by the British, a small number of other Black people known as Garífunas (see the Honduras chapter), and mestizos from other parts of Nicaragua. The races have mingled a good deal over the centuries.

Unlike the rest of Nicaragua, the Mosquitia was never colonised by Spain. In the 18th century, leaders of the Mosquitia requested that it be made a British protectorate, as a defence against the Spanish. It remained British for over a century, with a capital at Bluefields, where the Miskito kings were crowned in the Protestant church.

The British signed treaties handing the Mosquitia over to the independent governments of Honduras and Nicaragua in 1859 and 1860. In Nicaragua, the region retained its autonomy until the 1890s, when it was brought under direct Nicaraguan government control.

The English language, and the Protestant religion brought by British missionaries, persist as important aspects of the regional culture.

Timber, shrimp and lobster are exported from the Caribbean coast to other parts of Nicaragua and to other countries. Fishing is mostly for local and domestic consumption. Bananas and coconuts were important before the hurricane struck, and have been replanted.

NICARAGUA

The only part of the coast much visited by international travellers is the city of Bluefields, as it is relatively easy to reach by air or by a combination of bus and boat. From Bluefields, boats depart for the Islas del Maíz (Corn Islands) off the coast.

MANAGUA TO THE CARIBBEAN

The trip from Managua to Bluefields has long been a favourite with travellers. At some times during the Contra war, entry to the area was forbidden; at other times, you could travel there but only with a special permit. Since the war ended, the trip has been both possible and safe, and no special permit is required any more.

The easiest way to get from Managua to Bluefields is to fly, but the journey overland is what many people like best about visiting the coast.

To go overland from Managua to Bluefields involves travelling 292 km to Rama at the end of the highway, a journey of six to seven hours, then taking a boat down the Río Escondido to Bluefields on the coast, a further five hours. Most people find it a tiring but very enjoyable journey. You could conceivably make the trip in one big push, departing Managua on the 2 or 3 am bus and arriving in Rama just in time to transfer to the boat, but it's much more pleasant to go to Rama, spend the night there, and then take the boat the following day.

The road from Managua to Rama has a few attractions. The town of **Juigalpa**, capital of the department of Chontales, has a tourist office (☎ (081) 2307). It has an archaeological museum with numerous pieces excavated in the area. The museum is half a block east of the Alcaldía or city hall, named after the local scholar Gregorio Aguilar Barea. Juigalpa is also interesting as a centre of Catholic *comunidades de base* ('popular communities'); its bishop, Monseñor Pablo Antonio Vega, is nationally known as a defender of the disadvantaged.

RAMA

Population 36,312

Rama is at the end of the highway heading east from Managua. There's not much to it – the town is just a few blocks square – and there's nothing in particular to do, but it's a peaceful enough place to spend the night while waiting for the boat to the coast. The simple, tropical-style church, with its stained glass and patterned decorations, is worth a visit. Rama is at the confluence of two rivers, the Río Síquia and the Río Rama. From here to the coast, the river is called the Río Escondido.

Places to Stay & Eat

All the places to stay in Rama are old wooden buildings offering rooms with shared bath. The *Hotel Amy*, beside the dock, has rooms for US$1.20 per person, plus a bar and restaurant with tables on a terrace overlooking the river. *Hotel Johanna*, a couple of blocks away, has rooms from US$2 per person. The *Ramada Inn* is nothing like the better known chain bearing its name (or is it the other way around?), but a smaller family-run hotel with rooms at US$3 per person. The *Cafetín Syham* is a clean, pleasant little restaurant open every day from 7 am to 9 pm. There is also the bar/restaurant at the Hotel Amy, and at the rear of the Mercado there's a simple restaurant stall.

Getting There & Away

Bus Buses take six to seven hours to travel between Managua and Rama (292 km, US$3.20). In Managua, they leave from the terminal at the Mercado San Miguel/Iván Montenegro hourly from around 5 to 8 am, with possibly one more bus departing at around 11 am, every day. On the days when the ferry runs from Rama to Bluefields, express buses depart from Managua at 2 and 3 am to connect with it; the same buses wait at the dock in Rama to meet the boat coming back from Bluefields, then leave immediately the passengers are on board for the return trip to Managua.

If for some reason you miss the direct bus from Managua to Rama, you could take another bus halfway, from Managua to Juigalpa (137 km, three hours), and take a second bus or hitch the rest of the way from

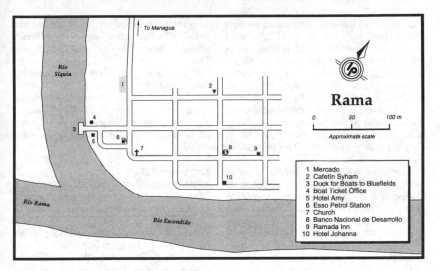

Rama

0   50   100 m

Approximate scale

1 Mercado
2 Cafetín Syham
3 Dock for Boats to Bluefields
4 Boat Ticket Office
5 Hotel Amy
6 Esso Petrol Station
7 Church
8 Banco Nacional de Desarrollo
9 Ramada Inn
10 Hotel Johanna

Juigalpa to Rama. The last bus leaves Juigalpa for Rama at 2 pm, but it's a very easy hitch. The road gets progressively worse as you get closer to Rama; the last hour of the journey will leave you with a sore bum and very delighted to arrive.

Boat The boat from Rama to Bluefields departs from Rama at 10.30 am on Tuesday, Thursday, Saturday and Sunday. Tickets go on sale at 9 am, but it's a good idea to get there earlier to try to claim a good spot on the boat, which is often crowded. Tickets cost US$5 and the trip takes five hours.

Food and drinks are sold at the dock before the boat departs; take some with you as there is nothing available on the journey.

BLUEFIELDS
Population 18,252
Bluefields is Nicaragua's principal Caribbean port, but the port itself is actually at Bluff, across the bay. The town was destroyed by Hurricane Joan in October 1988, but has now been rebuilt. Bluefields' economy is based on shrimp, lobster and deep-water fish; other food and merchandise

is brought in from Managua and is consequently more expensive than in the capital.

Bluefields has no swimming beaches – the water here is murky, anyway – and it's not a particularly attractive town, but it's an interesting place. There's a mix of ethnic groups including Indians (Miskitos, Ramas and Sumos), Black people (including Caribbean Creoles and a small number of Garífunas) and mestizos from the rest of Nicaragua. The people of Bluefields like to have a good time and there are several reggae clubs here and plenty of dancing on weekends. In May there's a week-long festival, with a maypole, music and dance.

Bluefields gets its English-sounding name not from any nearby blue fields (guess again), but from the Dutch pirate, Blewfeldt, who made a base here in the mid-17th century.

Places to Stay
Try to find a place to stay as soon as you get off the boat: all the arriving tourists make a mad dash from the dock to the hotels, and whoever gets there first grabs the available rooms.

The *Hotel Cueto* (☎ 567) is clean, with a

balcony facing the sea. Singles/doubles with shared bath are US$4/6, or US$5/8 with private bath. Breakfast, lunch or dinner costs US$2. Opposite the Cueto, the *Hotel Hollywood* (☎ 282) is another clean hotel with a sea-view balcony. Rooms with shared bath and fan are US$5/7, or US$8 with two beds.

Around the corner by the Mercado, the *Hotel Marda Maus* (☎ 429) has 11 rooms with shared bath and no ventilation at US$6 for one or two people, US$10 for a room with two beds.

The *Hotel Dorado* (☎ 365/6), a block behind the Hotel Cueto, has rooms with shared bath at US$5 per person. The *Mini-Hotel y Cafetín* (☎ 362) has 10 rooms from around US$6. The *Hotel y Restaurante Costa Sur* (☎ 452) has slightly more expensive rooms from around US$7; the restaurant is for guests only.

Places to Eat

Bluefields has plenty of restaurants and comedores, but none is particularly special. Prices are higher here than in other parts of Nicaragua. Even seafood is more expensive than you would expect, despite the fact that fishing is the town's main industry. You won't find seafood in every restaurant, either, although when you do it makes a pleasant change from the usual Nicaraguan fare.

Restaurants you might try include the *Restaurante Los Pepitos*, or the *Country's Customs*. Otherwise, the *Restaurante/Bar Caribbean* (expensive), the *Comedor Esperanza*, and the *Restaurante Tropical* can all be found near one another in the same block.

Entertainment

There are a number of bars and nightspots in Bluefields with dancing at weekends. Reggae is the town's favourite music. The popular dancing spots are the DB Disco (locals call it the 'Dibi Dibi') and Lego Lego, both walking distance from the centre in Barrio Olbak. There's also the cinema by the plaza, and Soda Palace, beside the Chez Marcel restaurant. Other spots include El Hotelito, the Tropicana, the Caimito and the Incognita.

Getting There & Away

Air Nica has flights between Managua and Bluefields every weekday. Tickets cost

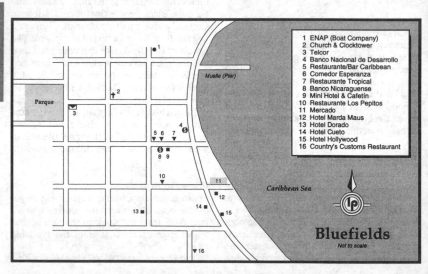

1 ENAP (Boat Company)
2 Church & Clocktower
3 Telcor
4 Banco Nacional de Desarrollo
5 Restaurante/Bar Caribbean
6 Comedor Esperanza
7 Restaurante Tropical
8 Banco Nicaraguense
9 Mini Hotel & Cafetín
10 Restaurante Los Pepitos
11 Mercado
12 Hotel Marda Maus
13 Hotel Dorado
14 Hotel Cueto
15 Hotel Hollywood
16 Country's Customs Restaurant

Muelle (Pier)

Parque

Caribbean Sea

Bluefields
Not to scale

US$45/91 one way/return. The Nica office in Bluefields is at the airport, about two or three km south of town. A taxi to the airport costs US$0.60.

Aeronica used to offer flights between Managua, Bluefields and the Islas del Maíz. You could check to see if it has started up again. VIG Aeroservicios (☎ (2) 631070 in Managua) offers a service to the Islas de Maíz.

Boat The boat from Bluefields to Rama departs at 4 am on Tuesday, Thursday, Saturday and Sunday; the five-hour trip costs US$5.

Buses wait at the dock in Rama to meet the arriving boats to take passengers direct to Managua. If you want to take one, try to be first off the boat and make a flying run for a seat. Even though there will be more than one bus waiting, there will probably be more people than seats. The locals all know this and will be making a dash for it as well.

Boats depart from Bluefields for other places along the Caribbean coast, including Laguna de Perlas, Puerto Cabezas, and many other smaller places, as well as to other parts of the Caribbean. Ask around at the wharf in Bluefields, or take a small motorboat (*panga*) over to the port at Bluff and ask around there.

See the Islas del Maíz section for details on getting to/from these islands off the coast.

LAGUNA DE PERLAS

The Laguna de Perlas (Pearl Lagoon), formed where the Río Kurinwas meets the sea about 80 km north of Bluefields, is large – about 50 km long and very wide in places. Miskitos living in the villages around the lagoon make a living from the abundant fish, shrimp and lobster.

Places to Stay & Eat

The only organised accommodation at the lagoon is *Miss Ingrid's*, at Laguna de Perlas village, which consists of about 30 or 40 houses. The hospedaje is just a few rooms added onto the family home; these cost US$3 per person. There are no restaurants in the village; it's a good idea to bring your own food, as extra food is in short supply. You can probably arrange to eat with a local family but even if you do, any contributions to the meal would be welcome. If you stay around the lagoon for a while you will soon meet other people and come up with other places to stay. Don't hesitate to ask around.

Getting There & Away

Ask at the wharf in Bluefields about boats to the lagoon. The trip takes around five hours and costs around US$4. Boats usually go early in the morning.

PUERTO CABEZAS

Population 30,720

Puerto Cabezas, on the north-east coast of Nicaragua, is the country's second most important Caribbean port. It's mainly a fishing town and there's nothing there of much interest to travellers, unless you happen to be coming by on a boat. There are various places to stay and eat.

Getting There & Away

Air Nica has flights seven days per week between Managua and Puerto Cabezas. Tickets cost US$58 one way and US$115 return.

Boat Fishing boats coming south from Honduras or north from Bluefields often stop at Puerto Cabezas. If you're hitching a ride on a fishing boat, you may stop here; otherwise it's pretty out of the way.

ISLAS DEL MAÍZ

Population 5600

The Islas del Maíz (Corn Islands), about 70 km off the coast from Bluefields, are made up of two islands, one larger (Isla del Maíz Grande) and one smaller (Isla del Maíz Pequeña). Even the larger island is only about six sq km, and the other island, 18 km away, is only about 1½ sq km.

Like other islands near the Caribbean coast, the Islas del Maíz were once a haven for buccaneers. Now, the larger island is a

NICARAGUA

popular holiday spot, with clear turquoise water, white sandy beaches fringed with coconut palms, excellent fishing, coral reefs good for snorkelling and diving, a mountain for hiking, and an unhurried, peaceful pace of life. You can visit the small island from the larger one, but it has no facilities for visitors.

People on the islands are of British West Indian descent and speak English. Most live on the larger island, making a living from fishing, particularly lobster fishing. Before the 1988 hurricane coconut oil manufacture was one of the islands' major industries; many coconut trees were damaged by the hurricane, but have now been replanted.

Places to Stay & Eat

The larger island has a number of places to stay. The *Hotel Morgan* charges US$6 per person, and the *Playa Coco* charges US$10. There are several little restaurants; some of the hospedajes also serve meals.

There's a bank where you can change money, but US dollars are accepted everywhere. You may want to bring along some of your own food, as food prices here are higher than on the mainland, reaching double the cost, according to recent visitors.

Getting There & Away

Aeronica, which used to operate flights to the islands from Managua and Bluefields, had discontinued the service. You could ask to see if it's started up again through its successor company, Nica.

A new air service, run by La Costeña (☎ 631228/81), is open between Managua and the Atlantic coast. Daily flights are available from Managua to Buefields, Puerto Cabezas, Islas del Maíz, Waspaán and some mining villages (where foreigners almost never go).

VIG Aeroservicios (☎ (2) 631070 in Managua) is offering flights on Tuesday and Thursday for US$60 one way.

An excellent boat service that was operating every day between Bluefields and the islands also appears to have been discontinued. Empresa Nacional de Puertos (ENAP) (☎ 668) may run passenger boats to the islands (four hours, US$3.75). Another possibility is to take a cheap panga to Bluff and ask around there to see if any fishing boats are going to the islands.

COSTA RICA

Costa Rica

Facts about the Country

HISTORY

Costa Rica has been strongly influenced by the Spanish conquest. The pre-Columbian cultures offered little resistance to the Spanish and few archaeological monuments remain, so our knowledge of the pre-Columbian history of Costa Rica is scanty. Despite this, a visit to see pre-Columbian artefacts at San José's Museo de Jade or Museo del Oro Precolombino is worthwhile.

The Spanish Conquest

The first European arrival was Christopher Columbus himself, who landed near present-day Puerto Limón on 18 September 1502 during his fourth (and last) voyage to the Americas. During his 17-day stay, he noted that some of the natives wore gold decorations. Because of this, the area was dubbed 'costa rica' (the rich coast) by the Europeans, who imagined that there must be a rich empire lying further inland.

The Spanish king, Ferdinand, appointed Diego de Nicuesa as governor of the region, and sent him to colonise it in 1506. The colonisers were hampered by the jungle, by tropical diseases, and by the small bands of Indians who used guerrilla tactics to fight off the invaders. About half the colonisers died and the rest returned home, unsuccessful.

Further expeditions followed, but they were unable to form a permanent colony, and many Spaniards died of hunger and disease. Meanwhile, the Indian population was decimated by European diseases to which the natives had no resistance. In 1562 Juan Vásquez de Coronado arrived as governor and decided to found a colony in the central highlands. Cartago was founded in 1563, and the healthy climate and fertile volcanic soil enabled the colony to survive.

For the next 150 years the colony remained a forgotten backwater, isolated from the coast and the major trading routes, and surviving only by dint of hard work and the generosity and friendliness which were to become the hallmarks of the Costa Rican character.

Eventually, in the early 18th century, the colony began to spread and change. Settlements became established throughout the fertile central highlands, including San José in 1737 and Alajuela in 1782. Much of Cartago was destroyed in an eruption of Irazú in 1723, but the survivors rebuilt the town. This expansion reflected slow growth from within Costa Rica, but the colony remained one of the poorest in the Spanish Empire.

Independence

Central America became independent from Spain on 15 September 1821. Costa Rica was briefly a part of Iturbide's Mexican Empire, and then it became a state within the United Provinces of Central America. The first elected head of state, from 1824 to 1833, was Juan Mora Fernández.

Coffee was introduced from Cuba in 1808, and was first exported during Juan Mora's term in office. The rest of the 19th century saw a steady increase in coffee exports, which improved Costa Rica's economy. Some of the coffee growers became rich and a class structure began to emerge. In 1849, a coffee grower, Juan Rafael Mora, became president and governed for 10 years.

Juan Rafael Mora's presidency is remembered both for economic and cultural growth, and for a somewhat bizarre military incident which has earned a place in every Costa Rican child's history books. In June 1855, the American filibuster, William Walker, arrived in Nicaragua to conquer Central America, convert it into slaving territory and then use the slaves to build a Nicaraguan canal to join the Atlantic and Pacific. (A filibuster, from the Spanish *filibustero*, is an irregular military adventurer, a freebooter.) Walker defeated the Nicaraguans and marched south.

Costa Rica had no army, so Mora organised 9000 civilians to gather what arms they could and, in February 1856, they marched north. In a short but determined battle at Santa Rosa, the Costa Ricans defeated Walker, who retreated to Rivas in Nicaragua, followed by the victorious Costa Ricans. Walker made a stand in a wooden fort and Juan Santamaría, a drummer boy from Alajuela, volunteered to torch the building, thus forcing Walker to flee. Santamaría was killed in this action, and is now remembered as one of Costa Rica's favourite national heroes.

Despite his defeat, Walker returned to Central America several more times, unsuccessfully, before finally being captured and shot in Honduras in 1860. Meanwhile, Mora lost favour in his country and was deposed in 1859. In 1860 he led a coup against the government. The coup failed, and Mora was executed.

Democracy

The next three decades were characterised by power struggles among members of the coffee-growing elite. In 1889 the first democratic elections were held, although women and Blacks were not allowed to vote. Democracy has been a hallmark of Costa Rican politics since then, with few lapses. One was between 1917 and 1919 when the Minister of War, Frederico Tinoco, overthrew the democratically elected president and formed a dictatorship. After opposition from both the rest of Costa Rica and the US government, the dictatorship was ended and Tinoco was exiled.

In 1940, Rafael Angel Calderón Guardia became president. His presidency was marked by reforms which were supported by the poor but criticised by the rich. These reforms included a recognition of workers' rights to organise and the introduction of minimum wages and a social security system. To further widen his power base, Calderón allied himself, strangely, with both the Catholic church and the communist party to form the United Christian Socialist Party. This further alienated him from the conservatives, the intellectuals and the upper classes.

Calderón was succeeded in 1944 by Teodoro Picado, a United Christian Socialist who was a supporter of Calderón's policies, but the conservative opposition claimed the elections were a fraud. In 1948, Calderón again ran for the presidency, against Otilio Ulate. The election was won by Ulate but Calderón claimed fraud because some of the ballots had been destroyed. Picado's government did not recognise Ulate's victory and the tense situation escalated into civil war.

Calderón and Picado were opposed by José (Pepe) Figueres Ferrer. After several weeks of civil warfare over 2000 people had been killed, and Figueres emerged victorious. He took over an interim government and in 1949 handed over the presidency to Otilio Ulate of the Partido Liberación Nacional (PLN – National Liberation Party). The year marked the formation of the Costa Rican constitution, which is still in effect. Women and Blacks received the vote, the army was abolished, presidents were not allowed to run for successive terms, and a neutral electoral tribunal was established to guarantee free and fair elections.

Although there are over a dozen political parties, since 1949 the PLN has dominated, usually being elected every other four years. Figueres continued to be popular, and was

COSTA RICA

456 Costa Rica – Facts about the Country

returned to two more terms of office (in 1954 and 1970). Another famous PLN president was Oscar Arias, who governed from 1986 to 1990. For his work in attempting to spread peace through Central America, Arias received the 1987 Nobel Peace Prize.

The Christian Socialists have continued to be the favoured party of the poor and working classes, and Calderón's son, Rafael Angel Calderón Fournier, has played a large role in that party, running for president three times. After two losses, he was finally elected president, and succeeded Oscar Arias in 1990.

The next presidential elections are slated for 1994 and will be between PLN candidate José María Figueres (son of Don Pepe Figueres) and Miguel Angel Rodriguez of the Partido Unidad Social Cristiana (PUSC – Social Christian Unity Party).

GEOGRAPHY

Costa Rica is bordered to the north by Nicaragua, to the north-east by the Caribbean, to the south-east by Panama, and to the west and south-west by the Pacific Ocean. Costa Rica is an extremely varied country despite its tiny size of 50,100 sq km.

A series of volcanic mountain chains runs from the Nicaraguan border in the north-west to the Panamanian border in the south-east, thus splitting the country in two. The highlands reach 3820 metres, and changing altitudes play an important part in determining geographical and ecological variation. In the centre of the highlands lies a plain called the *Meseta Central*, between about 1000 and 1500 metres high, which contains four of Costa Rica's five largest cities, including the capital, San José. Over half of the population lives on this plain, which contains fertile volcanic soils. Most of the mountains are volcanoes, some of which are active.

On either side of the volcanic central highlands lie coastal lowlands which differ greatly in character. The smooth Caribbean coastline is 212 km long and is characterised by year-round rainfall, mangroves, swamps, an intracoastal waterway and sandy beaches.

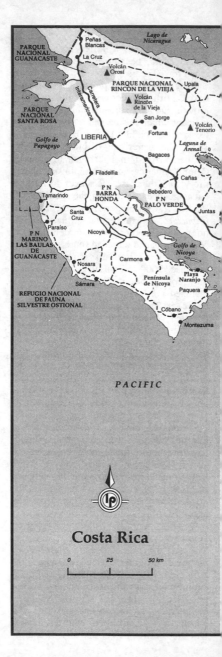

Costa Rica

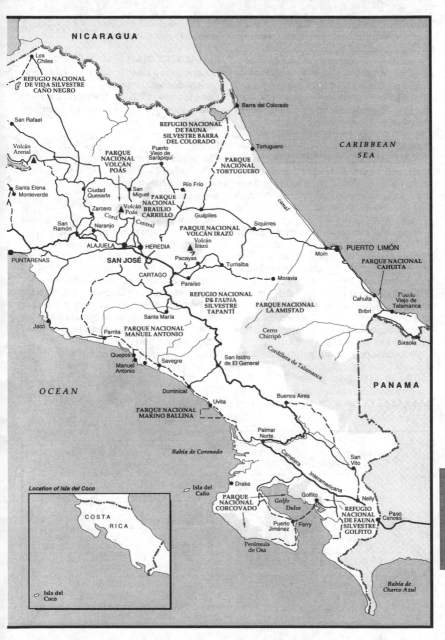

Tidal variations are small. The Pacific coast is much more rugged and rocky, and the tortuous coastline is 1016 km long with numerous gulfs and peninsulas. It is bordered by tropical dry forests which receive almost no rain for several months each year, as well as by mangroves, swamps and beaches. The tidal variation is quite large, and there are many offshore islands.

CLIMATE
The dry season is from late December to April and is called *verano* (summer) by Costa Ricans – contrary to most northern hemisphere terminology. The rest of the year tends to be wet, and is called *invierno* (winter) by the locals.

The Caribbean region is wetter than the rest of the country and the dry season has rainy days mixed with spells of fine weather. In the highlands the dry season really is dry, with only one or two rainy days per month. The north and central Pacific coastal regions tend to have the same rain pattern as the highlands, whilst the southern Pacific coast can experience rain year-round, but with less falling in the dry season.

Temperature is mainly influenced by altitude. San José has average lows of 15°C and average highs of 26°C. The coasts are much hotter, with the Caribbean averaging 21°C at night and 30°C during the day, and the Pacific coast averaging about 3°C more than that.

FLORA & FAUNA
Costa Rica is a small country, yet its diverse habitats harbour some of the richest flora & fauna in the world. This biodiversity attracts nature-loving visitors from all over the world.

Birds
The primary attraction for many naturalists is the birds, of which some 850 species have been recorded – more than in any one of the continents of North America, Australia, or Europe. Many birders want to see the resplendent quetzal – Monteverde is a good place to see them in season.

Over 50 species of hummingbirds have been recorded from Costa Rica. Other tropical birds include scarlet macaws and 15 other parrot species; six different toucans with their incredibly large and hollow bills; the huge and very rare harpy eagle, which is capable of snatching monkeys and sloths off branches as it flies past; and a large array of other tropical birds such as flycatchers (75 species), tanagers (45 species), antbirds (29 species) and cotingas (19 species).

Mammals
Costa Rica has over 200 species of mammals.

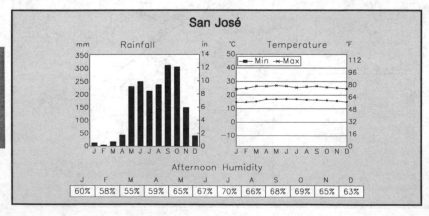

Visitors are likely to see some of the four monkey species found here. Other tropical specialities include sloths, armadillos, agoutis (large rodents), peccaries (wild pigs), kinkajous, raccoons, skunks, otters, foxes, squirrels and bats. Mammals such as ocelots, jaguars and tapirs are extremely hard to glimpse.

Insects
At least 35,000 species of insects from Costa Rica have been described, and many thousands remain unnamed. There are thousands of butterflies, including the dazzling morphos with 15-cm wingspans and electric-blue upper wings. There are many ant species – a favourite is the leafcutter ants (genus Atta), seen marching in columns along the forest floor, carrying pieces of leaves into their underground colony. The leaves rot and support a fungus which the ants eat.

Amphibians
The approximately 150 species of amphibians include red, black, blue or yellow poison-arrow frogs. They have skin glands which can exude a toxin capable of causing paralysis and death in many animals if it is introduced into the bloodstream.

Reptiles
Over 200 species of reptiles are found in Costa Rica. About half are snakes, which are much talked about but seldom seen. Bright green basilisk lizards live near water – the males have huge crests along their head, body and tail, and reach almost a metre in length. The young are nicknamed Jesus Christ lizards for their ability to run across water. There are 14 species of marine and freshwater turtles. Marine turtles nest in large numbers on sandy beaches – a spectacular sight. The largest marine turtles are the leatherbacks, whose carapace (shell) can reach 160 cm in length and which average a stunning 360 kg in weight. The smaller olive ridley turtles practise synchronous nesting when thousands of females emerge from the sea on a single night.

Plants
Some 10,000 species of vascular plants have been described and more are added every year. Orchids alone account for some 1200 species, and about 1400 tree species have been recorded.

Three-quarters of Costa Rica was forested in the late 1940s; by the late 1980s, barely a quarter of the country remained covered by forest. To try and control this deforestation and protect its wildlife, Costa Rica has instigated the most progressive national park system in the New World.

National Parks
The national park system began in the 1960s. There are now about three dozen national parks and other protected areas in Costa Rica – almost 12% of the land area. In addition, various buffer zones and forest reserves boost the total area of protected land to about 27%, but these buffer zones allow farming, logging, and other exploitation, and are not fully protected. Also, there are some two dozen privately owned lodges, reserves, and haciendas which are set up to protect the land.

National parks information is provided by the public information office of the Servicio de Parques Nacionales (SPN) (☎ 257-0922), Calle 25, Avenidas 8 and 10, San José from 8 am to 4 pm, Monday to Friday. SPN headquarters (☎ 233-4118, 233-4246, fax 223-6963; Apartado 10104-1000, San José) is also here.

Some parks and refuges provide basic camping facilities or food and accommodation in ranger stations. Arrange this beforehand through the SPN radio communications office (☎ 233-4160) which is in radio contact with all parks and refuges – it helps if you speak Spanish. Most national parks charge an entrance fee of US$1.50 per day plus US$2.25 for overnight camping per person.

You can volunteer to work in the national parks – jobs vary from office work in cities to helping in remote areas. Volunteers pay US$5 to US$7 per day towards costs and make a two-month commitment. For an application, write or fax Stanley Arguedas at the SPN address above or go in person.

GOVERNMENT

Government is based on the constitution of 7 November 1949. The president wields executive power, assisted by two vice-presidents and a cabinet of 18 ministers. Elections are held every four years and an incumbent cannot be re-elected.

There are seven provinces, each with a governor appointed by the president. Provinces are divided into 81 *cantóns* (counties) and subdivided into 429 districts. For every 30,000 people in each province, a congressman/woman is elected to the Legislative Assembly every four years. This is where much of the power of government lies.

The Legislative Assembly appoints 22 Supreme Court judges for eight-year terms. The Supreme Court selects judges for the lower courts. The idea behind these three power structures is to prevent any one person or group from having too much control, thus ensuring a real democracy.

Although there are about a dozen political parties, only two groups have been in power since 1949; the National Liberation Party or one of the Christian Socialist parties. Since 1990, the Social Christian Unity Party has been in power under the presidency of Rafael Angel Calderón Fournier.

In February 1994, José María Figueres narrowly won the national election and became Costa Rica's 51st president on 8 May 1994. At 39, he is Costa Rica's youngest president ever. The vote is mandatory for all citizens over 18.

There is no army. Instead, there is a 5000-strong Civil Guard which is really a form of police force. There are also rural and municipal police forces.

ECONOMY

Until the mid-19th century, Costa Rica was a very poor country with an economy based on subsistence agriculture. Then the introduction of coffee provided a product suitable for export. This was followed by bananas, and today these two crops generate the most export income for the country. Beef and sugar are also traditional agricultural exports and, in recent years, non-traditional products such as ornamental plants, pharmaceuticals, textiles, tyres, furniture and others have become increasingly important. In 1991, exports were worth US$1598 million and imports cost US$1877 million.

Recently, tourism has had an unprecedented boom in Costa Rica. The number of foreign tourists visiting the country rose from 376,000 in 1989 to 610,000 in 1992. The value of revenues from tourism in 1992 was US$421 million, making tourism a contender for the position of the single most important earner of foreign currency. In 1993 the sector continued to grow, with as many as 690,000 tourists according to early figures.

This boom has led to much controversy over which way this rapidly growing industry should develop. There are those who want to bring in mass tourism and build huge hotels – a sort of cut-rate Cancún. Critics of this approach point out that Costa Rica is simply not capable of handling any more tourists and that mass tourism would lead to severe environmental and cultural degradation, spoiling the Costa Rica which people were flocking to see. Haphazard building and development is occurring without adequate controls and the country lacks a master plan for the development of environmentally sensitive tourism. The debate continues to rage at all levels.

Inflation has been dropping steadily over the past few years (16.9% in 1992). This is less than what it was in the 1980s, but is still higher than in the 1960s and 1970s. The government says that its aim is to reduce inflation to 12%. The national debt is about US$4 billion. The standard of living is the second highest in Central America (after Panama). The economic growth of the country in 1992 was 7.3%, the highest total in almost a decade. In 1992, the Gross National Product grew by 4.9% over the 1991 figure of US$1806 per inhabitant – the highest such growth in 14 years. Unemployment runs between 5% and 6%. Average wages are under US$200 per month and the government claims that 22.2% of families live below the poverty level, which is a significant improvement over past years.

POPULATION & PEOPLE

As of July 1992, the population of Costa Rica was nearly 3.2 million. About 60% of the people live in the highlands and the annual population growth rate is 2.5%. The population density is about 62 people per sq km. Literacy is over 90% – among the best in Latin America.

Most people are of Spanish descent. Less than 2% of the population is Black, living mostly in the Caribbean region and tracing its ancestry to either the early days of slavery in Costa Rica or immigration from Jamaica to build the railroads and work the banana plantations in the late19th century. Many Blacks speak a dated form of English. They were actively discriminated against in the early 20th century, but since the 1949 constitution have legally won equal rights.

Indians make up much less than 1% of the population. Small tribes include the Bribri from the Talamanca area in the south-east and the Borucas in the southern Pacific coastal areas.

Costa Ricans call themselves *ticos* (males) or *ticas* (females). Visitors are constantly surprised at the warmth and friendliness of the people.

ARTS & CULTURE

There is very little indigenous cultural influence. Cultural activities have blossomed only in the last 100 years. Ticos consider San José to be the cultural centre of the country. It is here that the most important museums are found.

There are many theatres, and acting is one of the favourite cultural activities. The Teatro Nacional (National Theatre) in the heart of San José is the venue for plays, performances by the National Symphony, ballet, opera, poetry readings and other cultural events. The Teatro Nacional building is also an architectural attraction in its own right, and a highlight of any city tour of San José.

RELIGION

Over 80% of the population is Roman Catholic, at least in principle. Religious processions on holy days are less fervent and less colourful than in other Latin American countries. Semana Santa (Holy Week) is a national holiday, and everything, including the bus system, stops from lunchtime on Thursday until mid-Saturday. Buses run again on Saturday afternoon and Easter Sunday, but banks and many other businesses stay closed till Monday.

The Blacks on the Caribbean tend to be Protestants, and most other Christian denominations have a church in or around San José. There is a small Jewish community.

LANGUAGE

Spanish is the official language but English is understood in many hotels, airline offices, tourist agencies and along much of the Caribbean. Spanish courses are available in San José.

The following colloquialisms and slang are used in Costa Rica:

Adios!
  Hi! (used when passing a friend in the street, or anyone in remote rural areas; also means 'Farewell' but only when leaving for a long time)
bomba
  petrol (gas) station
buena nota
  OK, excellent (literally 'good note')
¿Hay campo?
  Is there space? (on a bus)
cien metros
  one city block (literally 100 metres)
maje
  buddy (used by young men to close friends)
mi amor
  my love (used by both sexes as a friendly form of address)

COSTA RICA

pulpería
    corner grocery store
pura vida
    super, far out (literally 'pure life', can be
    used as an expression of approval or even
    as a greeting)
salado
    too bad, tough luck
soda
    café or lunch counter
Upe!
    Anybody home? (used mainly in the coun-
    tryside at people's houses, instead of
    knocking)
vos
    you (informal, equivalent to 'tu')

Facts for the Visitor

VISAS & EMBASSIES
Passport-carrying nationals of the following
countries are allowed a 90-day stay with no
visa: Most Western European countries,
Argentina, Canada, Colombia, Israel, Japan,
Panama, Romania, South Korea, UK, USA,
Uruguay and Yugoslavia.

Passport-carrying nationals of the following countries are allowed a 30-day stay with
no visa: Most Eastern European countries,
Australia, Belgium, Brazil, Ecuador, Guatemala, Honduras, Iceland, Ireland (Eire),
Liechtenstein, Mexico, Monaco, New
Zealand, Sweden, Switzerland, Vatican and
Venezuela. Others require a US$20 visa from
a Costa Rican consulate.

Travellers officially need a ticket out of
Costa Rica before they are allowed to enter.
Most airlines will not let you board unless
you have a return or onward ticket, or an
MCO. Overland travellers can buy a Tica bus
ticket from Managua or Panama City.
Onward tickets are not always asked for,
however. Sometimes a show of cash is
required – US$300 to US$400 per month is
sufficient.

The law requires that you have your passport at all times. A photocopy of the pages
bearing your photo, passport number, and
entry stamp will suffice for most purposes,
but the passport should be in the hotel you
are staying at, not in San José.

Visa Extensions
Extending your stay beyond the authorised
90 or 30 days is a time-consuming hassle. It
is easier to leave the country for 72 hours or
more and then re-enter. Otherwise go to the
Migración office in San José. Many travel
agents in San José will take care of the red
tape for you for a small fee.

Requirements for stay extensions include
three passport photos, a ticket out of the
country, sufficient funds to support yourself,
and maybe even a blood test to prove you
don't have AIDS. Requirements change –
allow several working days. It really is easier
to cross the border to Panama or Nicaragua
for a couple of days.

If you overstay your 30 or 90 days, you
need an exit visa from Migración to leave the
country. They require a form from the
Tribunales de Justicia on Calle 17, Avenidas
6 and 8, San José, stating that you aren't
leaving dependants in the country. You pay
a US$4 fine for each month that you have
overstayed your visa, plus a US$12 fee if you
leave by air or US$40 if you leave by land.
The exit visa is valid for 30 days, and is not
required by travellers who have not overstayed their 30 or 90-day allowance.

Children (under 18) are not allowed to
stay for more than 30 days unless *both* their
parents request permission from the
Patronato Nacional de la Infancia (National
Child Protection Agency) on Calle 19 at
Avenida 6 in San José. If a child is planning
a stay of more than 30 days and will not be
travelling with both parents, then obtain a
notarised permit from the Costa Rican consulate of the child's home country.

Costa Rican Embassies
Canada
    135 York St No 208, Ottawa K1N 5T4
    (☎ (613) 562-2855)
France
    74 avenue Paul-Doumer, 75016 Paris
    (☎ (1) 45 04 50 93)

Germany
   5300 Bonn 1, Borsigallee 2 (☎ (0228) 252940)
Guatemala
   Avenida La Reforma 8-60, Zona 9, Edificio
   Galerías Reforma No 902, 01009 Guatemala
   City (☎ (02) 319604)
Honduras
   Blvd Morazán, Costado Oeste de Reasa,
   Apartado 512, Tegucigalpa (☎ 321768)
Israel
   13 Diskin St No 1, Jerusalem 91012
   (☎ (02) 666197)
Nicaragua
   Centro Comercial Camino de Oriente, contiguo
   a Nica, Managua JR
Panama
   Edificio Regency No 2, Apartado 8963, Panama
   (☎ 642980)
Spain
   Paseo de la Castellana 166, No 5, 28046, Madrid
   (☎ 250-9398)
UK
   36 Upper Brook St, London, W1 Y 1PE
   (☎ (071) 495-3985)
USA
   1825 Connecticut Ave, NW, No 211, Washington
   DC 20009 (☎ (202) 234-2945; 234-2947)

Other countries with Costa Rican embassies
or consulates include Argentina, Barbados,
Belgium, Belize, Bolivia, Brazil, Canada,
Chile, Colombia, Czechoslovakia,
Denmark, Dominican Republic, El Salva-
dor, Hungary, Italy, Jamaica, Japan, Kenya,
Korea (South), Mexico, Norway, Paraguay,
Poland, Portugal, Romania, Russia, Switzer-
land, Taiwan, Uruguay, Vatican and
Venezuela.

Foreign Embassies in Costa Rica
Most European countries and many non-
European countries have embassies in San
José. The smaller embassies seem to change
address quite often, so phone first. They're
listed in the phone book.

Canada
   Calle 3, Avenidas Central & 1; Edificio Cronos
   (☎ 255-3522, 228-5154, fax 223-2395)
Colombia
   Calle 29, Avenida 1 (☎ 221-0725, 255-0937)
E l Salvador
   Avenida 10, Calles 33 & 35, Los Yoses
   (☎ 224-9034)

France
   200 metres south, 25 metres west of the Indoor
   Club, Carretera a Curridabat (☎ 225-0733)
Germany
   200 metres north, 75 metres east of the Oscar
   Arias residence, Rohrmoser (☎ 232-5533)
Guatemala
   (☎ 232-6645, 231-6654)
Honduras
   300 metres east, 200 metres north of ITAN, Los
   Yoses Sur (☎ 234-9502)
Nicaragua
   Avenida Central, Calles 25 & 27 (☎ 233-3479)
Panama
   600 metres south of El Antiguo Higueron, San
   Pedro (☎ 225-3401, 225-0667)
UK
   Paseo Colón, Calles 38 & 40, Edificio Centro
   Colón (☎ 221-5566, 221-5816, fax 233-9938)
USA
   Carretera Pavas frente de Centro Commercial
   (☎ 220-3939, fax 220-2305)

CUSTOMS
Three litres of wine or spirits and 500 cigarettes or 500 grams of tobacco are allowed
duty free. Officially, you are limited to six
rolls of film, but this is rarely checked or
enforced. There's rarely a problem in bringing in items for personal use.

MONEY
Currency
The Costa Rican currency is the *colón*, plural
colones. There are 1, 2, 5, 10 and 20 colón
coins and 50, 100, 500, 1000 and 5000 colón
notes. Colones are normally written as ¢.

Exchange Rates
For years the exchange rate has dropped
steadily against the US dollar, although
occasionally the value of the colón may rise
sharply against the dollar. Prices are therefore given in US dollars throughout this
chapter. Some major currencies can be
changed into colones in San José but rates
are poor and by far the easiest to change will
be US dollars, so bring your money in US
currency if you can. It is difficult to change
currencies other than US dollars outside the
capital. Travellers' cheques are usually
exchanged at one or two colones lower than
the rate for cash, so plan accordingly. Buying

colones with US dollars outside Costa Rica results in poor rates (a loss of 20% or more) so wait until you arrive.

Foreign		Costa Rica
A$1	=	215¢
C$1	=	220¢
DM1	=	180¢
NZ$1	=	175¢
UK£1	=	455¢
US$1	=	155¢

Banks can be slow in changing money. You stand in one line to have your transaction approved, then in a second line to actually get your money. Some banks will take only certain kinds of travellers' cheques. American Express is usually good.

Banking hours are from 9 am to 3 pm, Monday to Friday. You'll need your passport when changing money. Several travellers have reported that, when changing travellers' cheques, they have been asked to show proof of purchase, so carry a copy of the receipt with you. Private banks (eg Banco Lyon, Banex or Banco Mercantil) are often faster than national banks (eg Banco Nacional, Banco de Costa Rica) though the latter may have branches open later. In San José, banks may remain open until 4 pm, and the Banco Nacional, Avenida 3, Calles 2 & 4, or the Banco de Costa Rica, Avenida Central, Calles 4 & 6, may be open longer still. The bank at the international airport is open from 6.30 am to 5 pm on weekdays, and from 7 am to 1 pm on weekends and holidays. Banks are closed on national holidays.

I found one *casa de cambio* in San José which gave the same rates as the bank and which provided faster service.

Street changers are found in San José and at the land borders. They have paid as much as 10% more than banks in the past, though in 1993 offered an advantage of only about 1%. They are mainly interested in US cash dollars, though travellers' cheques can be negotiated. Street changing is technically illegal, but the authorities turn a blind eye. Count your money carefully before handing over your dollars. Rip-offs are common so

many travellers prefer to change money legally at a slightly lower rate to avoid any hassle.

If visiting small towns, change enough money beforehand. Changing large colones bills can be difficult in rural areas.

You can change excess colones back into dollars at the banks and the airport, but you may need to show your exit ticket and an exchange receipt before you can buy back dollars. A maximum of US$50 can be bought back.

In May 1993, police broke up a counterfeiting ring which made false 5000 colones bills, but there are believed to be millions of colones worth of false 5000s out there. Police say the false 5000s can be identified by the absence of a watermark above the 5000 to the right of the official signature – the watermark can be seen in normal light. Also, counterfeits lack the fine gridlines in the blue section, and the fake blue is brighter than the normal blue.

Credit-card holders can buy colones, but not dollars, in banks. Visa and MasterCard are both widely accepted, though not in budget places. They charge the normal bank rates of exchange, and commissions are low. Card holders can buy Amex travellers' cheques in US dollars. The American Express office is at TAM travel agency at Calle 1, Avenidas Central and 1, in San José.

If you need money sent from home, you'll find the main branches of San José banks will accept cash transfers but charge a commission. Shop around for the best deal.

Costs

Travel costs are higher here than in most Central American countries, but less than in the USA or Europe. San José and the most popular tourist areas are more expensive than the rest of the country, and the dry season (December to April) is more expensive.

Budget travellers will find the cheapest hotels start at about US$3 per person for a box with a bed. Fairly decent hotels with private bathrooms, hot water, and maybe air-con are US$10 per person and up. Meals cost from about US$2 and up. The cheaper set lunches offered in many restaurants cost around US$2. The counter-lunch places, called *sodas*, have cheap meals. A beer will cost US$0.70 to US$2.50. Movie theatres charge about US$2.50.

Transport is also cheap, with the longest bus journeys, from San José to the Panamanian border for example, costing about US$7. A taxi, particularly when you're in a group, isn't expensive and costs US$1 to US$2 for short but convenient rides.

A budget traveller economising hard can get by on US$10 to US$20 per day. If you want rooms with private baths, meals other than set meals, expect to spend about twice that amount.

Tipping

Better restaurants add 13% tax and 10% tip to the bill. Cheaper restaurants might not do this. Taxi drivers are not normally tipped. If you take a guided tour, a tip of about US$2 per person per day is about right (if the guide does a good job!)

WHEN TO GO

The dry season is considered the best time to visit Costa Rica. During this time beach resorts are busy, and often full at weekends and holidays, especially Easter week which is booked months ahead. School vacations are from December to February. Travel in the wet season may be difficult on the poorer roads, but there are fewer visitors and hotel prices may be lower, especially at the better ones.

WHAT TO BRING

Clothes of all sizes are available in San José, but shoes in sizes larger than 43 (10½ US) are hard to find. Tampons are available in Costa Rica but imported items are heavily taxed, so women should bring their favourite brand from home. The same applies to contraceptives. Bring strong sunblock lotion as only moderate blocking lotions (SPF 4 or 8) are easily found. For wildlife viewing, binoculars and field guides are useful.

TOURIST INFORMATION

In the USA contact the Costa Rican National Tourist Bureau, 1101 Bricknel Avenue, BIV Tower, Suite 801, Miami, FL 33131 (☎ (305) 358-2150 or toll-free (800) 327-7033). Note that their info is of a very general nature – they don't have hotel prices etc.

Citizens of other countries can contact their Costa Rican consulate for tourist information. Or you can write to Instituto Costarricense de Turismo (ICT), Apartado 777, San José, Costa Rica.

The South American Explorers Club (☎ (607) 277-0488), 126 Indian Creek Rd, Ithaca, NY 14850, USA, is an information centre for travellers, adventurers, scientific expeditions etc. They have club houses in Lima, Peru and Quito, Ecuador and are evaluating the possibility of opening a club house in Costa Rica. (See Useful Organisations in the Facts for the Visitor chapter.)

BUSINESS HOURS & HOLIDAYS

Government offices are open from 8 am to 4 pm, Monday to Friday, but often close for lunch between about 11.30 am and 1 pm. Stores are open from 8 am to 6 or 7 pm, Monday to Saturday, but a two-hour lunch break is normal.

Banks, public offices and many stores close on national holidays. There are no buses at all on the Thursday afternoon and Friday before Easter and many businesses are closed during the week before Easter. From Thursday to Easter Sunday all bars are closed and alcohol sales are prohibited. Book hotels well in advance for this period.

1 January
  New Year's Day
19 March
  Saint Joseph's Day (patron saint of San José)
March or April
  Semana Santa (Holy Week, Thursday and Friday before Easter)
11 April
  Juan Santamaría's Day (national hero at Battle of Rivas against William Walker in 1856)
1 May
  Labor Day
29 June
  Saint Peter & Saint Paul's Day

25 July
> *Guanacaste Day* (annexation of Guanacaste Province, formerly part of Nicaragua) (

2 August
> *Virgin of Los Angeles Day* (patron saint of Costa Rica)

15 August
> *Mother's Day* (coincides with Catholic feast of the Assumption)

15 September
> *Independence Day*

12 October
> *Columbus Day* (discovery of America, locally called 'Día de la Raza')

8 December
> *Immaculate Conception*

25 December
> *Christmas Day*

In addition, various towns have celebrations for their own particular day. The week between Christmas and New Year's Day tends to be an unofficial holiday, especially in San José.

POST & TELECOMMUNICATIONS

Air-mail letters to the USA are about US$0.32 for the first 20 grams and a little more to Europe or Australia. Parcels can be mailed from the post office, but are expensive.

Have mail sent to you c/o Lista de Correos, Correos Central, San José, Costa Rica – letters usually arrive within a week from North America, a little longer from more distant places. There is a US$0.10 fee per letter received. Avoid having parcels sent to you, as they are held in customs and cannot be retrieved until you have paid a duty equivalent to the value of the gift plus the value of the mailing cost.

Public phones are found all over Costa Rica, marked with a telephone symbol. They accept coins of 5, 10 and 20 colones. Telephone numbers have seven digits, and you can call anywhere in the country from a public booth for under US$0.50 per three minutes. There are no area codes. In remote areas, operator-assisted radio telephones are used.

To call internationally, dial ☎ 116 on any phone to get an English-speaking international operator and ask for a collect (reverse charges) call. Some countries (eg the USA) with reciprocal agreements will accept collect calls, some won't. The party you call can call you back at the telephone you are calling from. To pay for an international call, go to a Radiográfica or ICE office, or an operator-assisted telephone facility such as a hotel telephone. Costs of calls per minute from Costa Rica are approximately US$2 to US$3 to North America, US$3 to US$4 to Europe, and US$5 to Australia. Cheaper rates are from 8 pm to 7 am and during weekends.

Some countries can be reached on a dial-direct system where a three-digit number will connect you to an operator in that country, after which you can call collect or use your credit card.

Canada	161
Germany	168
Italy	169
Spain	164
UK	167
USA, AT&T	114
USA, MCI	162
USA, Sprint	163

If you are calling Costa Rica from abroad, use the international code (506) before the seven-digit Costa Rican telephone number.

Radiográfica and ICE offices also have telex and fax machines for use by the public.

TIME

Costa Rica is six hours behind Greenwich Mean Time (GMT), the same as Central Time in the USA. There is no daylight saving time.

LAUNDRY

There are a few self-service laundry machines in San José, charging about US$4 a load for washing and drying. Many cheap hotels will do your laundry for about US$1 for a change of clothes. Allow two or three days if it's raining and they can't be dried. If you want to wash clothes yourself, ask the hotel staff where to do it.

BOOKS & MAPS

There are several guidebooks to Costa Rica; look for Lonely Planet's *Costa Rica – a travel survival kit* by Rob Rachowiecki.

Birders will need the excellent and thorough *A Guide to the Birds of Costa Rica* by F Gary Stiles & Alexander F Skutch (Cornell University Press, 1989). Louise H Emmons' *Neotropical Rainforest Mammals – A Field Guide* (University of Chicago Press, 1990) describes and illustrates rainforest mammals throughout Latin America. *The Butterflies of Costa Rica and Their Natural History* by Philip J DeVries (Princeton University Press, 1987) is recommended for lepidopterists.

A book with a historical perspective on politics and social change in Costa Rica is *The Costa Ricans* by Richard Biesanz et al (Waveland Press, Illinois, reissued 1988 with update). Two books written by former Peace Corps volunteer Paula Palmer about the people of the south Caribbean coast of Costa Rica are *What Happen: A Folk History of Costa Rica's Talamanca Coast* (Ecodesarollos, San José, 1977, reprinted 1993), and *Wa'apin Man* (Editorial Costa Rica, 1986). *Taking Care of Sibö's Gifts* by Paula Palmer, Juanita Sánchez & Gloria Mayorga (Asociación de Desarrollo Integral de la Reserva Indígena Cocles/KéköLdi, San José, 1991). Subtitled 'An Environmental Treatise from Costa Rica's KéköLdi Indigenous Reserve', this excellent booklet discusses the traditional Bribri lifestyle from the point of view of their natural surroundings. Book profits go to indigenous conservation and educational programmes. Look for these last three in Costa Rica.

La Loca de Gandoca by Anacristina Rossi (EDUCA, San José, 3rd edition, February 1993), describes the struggle of a local conservationist trying to halt the development of a hotel in a protected area of the Caribbean coast, and problems with corruption at various levels of government. Although the characters are imaginary and any similarity to reality is coincidental, local cognoscenti will tell you that remarkably similar events happened here recently. It's available locally and only in Spanish, but is short and simply written so it makes a good choice for someone who is interested in local conservation issues, even if their Spanish is limited.

Costa Rica – A Traveler's Literary Companion edited by Barbara Ras (Whereabouts Press, California, 1994) is a fine collection of 26 short stories by modern Costa Rican writers.

Pura Vida: Gay & Lesbian Costa Rica by Joseph Itiel (Orchid House, California, 1993) is a source for gay and lesbian travellers.

The best map is the very detailed 1:500,000 sheet published by and available from International Travel Map Productions (ITM), PO Box 2290, Vancouver, BC, V6B 3W5, Canada. In Europe write to Bradt Publications, 41 Nortoft Road, Chalfont St Peter, Bucks, SL9 0LA, UK. The second edition of this map was published in 1994.

The Instituto Geográfico de Costa Rica publishes a single sheet 1:500,000 map of Costa Rica. There is a nine-sheet 1:200,000 map set covering the country in detail. Most of the country is also covered by 1:50,000 scale topographical maps. The Costa Rican National Tourist Bureau has, in the past, published free maps of San José and Costa Rica, although these were unavailable recently.

MEDIA

The best local daily newspapers are *La Nación* and *La República*. The weekly English-language newspaper, *The Tico Times*, is published every Friday and is recommended. Major bookstores in San José carry some US and other newspapers (two or three days late) and magazines such as *Time* or *Newsweek*.

There are six local TV stations and many of the better hotels also receive cable TV from the USA. There are many AM/FM radio stations.

HEALTH

Costa Rica has among the highest standards of health care and hygiene in Latin America. The authorities do not, at present, require anyone to have a current international vaccination card to enter the country, though you

COSTA RICA

should make sure that your vaccinations are up to date.

You can drink tap water in San José and the major towns. In out-of-the-way places you should boil it first, or purify it with commercially available tablets. Bring purifying tablets with you as they are not readily available in Costa Rica. The lowlands are the most likely places to find unsafe drinking water. Bottled mineral water, soft drinks and beer are easily found alternatives. Uncooked fruits and vegetables are best avoided unless they are peeled.

The social security hospitals in the major cities provide free emergency services to everyone, including foreigners. Private clinics are also available. For emergencies in San José, call the Paramedics (☎ 118, no coin needed). Outside San José, call the Guardia (☎ 127). Medical care is less expensive than it is in most First World countries.

Most prescription drugs are available in Costa Rica, some of which are sold over the counter. For minor ailments and illnesses, pharmacists will often advise and prescribe for you.

WOMEN TRAVELLERS

Women are traditionally respected in Costa Rica (Mother's Day is a national holiday!) and recently women have made gains in the workplace. A woman vice-president (Victoria Garrón) was elected in 1986; Margarita Penon ran as presidential candidate in 1993; and women routinely occupy roles in the political, legal, scientific and medical professions, which used to be overwhelmingly dominated by men.

Despite this, Costa Rican men generally consider *gringas* (women from outside Latin America) to have looser morals and to be easier 'conquests' than ticas. They will often make flirtatious comments to single women, both local and foreign. A woman travelling with another woman is not exempt from this; women travelling with men are less likely to receive attention. Comments are rarely blatantly rude; the usual thing is a smiling 'Mi amor' or an appreciative hiss. The best way to deal with this is to do what the ticas do, ignore the comments completely and not look at the man making them.

Neither men nor women wear shorts in the highlands (unless actively jogging etc).

FILM & PHOTOGRAPHY

Camera gear is expensive in Costa Rica and film choice is limited, so your favourite type of film may be unavailable. Film processing is not very good – although it's OK for simple snapshots.

In the rainforest you will need high-speed film, flash, or a tripod. The light penetrating the layers of vegetation is surprisingly dim.

If you're making an international flight through San José airport, carry your films by hand, or use a lead bag. The X-ray machine there is vicious.

ACCOMMODATION

Call ahead during dry season weekends when hotels can be full. Sometimes it's difficult to find single rooms. Rooms, often in hotels called *cabinas*, may have four to six beds and are a cheap per person choice if you are travelling with a small group. Rates are lower in the wet season.

The cheap hotels often lack hot water. Many hotels have electric showers which are not as dangerous as they appear! Hotels will advertise hot water – but if supplied by an electric shower, tepid is normally the best you can expect. Note that (in common with many cheap Central American hotels) used toilet paper should be placed in the receptacle provided – the plumbing cannot handle the paper.

There is a small youth hostel system which charges US$6 per night at the main hostel in San José and more elsewhere. Cheap camping facilities are available in some national parks.

B&Bs are a recent and rapidly growing phenomenon in Costa Rica. The cheapest start at about US$25 and so are beyond most shoestring travellers, who will economise by staying in conventional hotels.

FOOD

The *casado* offered in most restaurants at lunch time is cheap. Also try the cheap luncheon counters called sodas. There are reasonably priced Chinese and Italian restaurants in most towns. Better restaurants add a 13% tax plus 10% service to the bill – the cheapest don't.

Costa Rican specialities include:

gallo pinto – a mixture of rice and black beans that is traditionally served for breakfast, sometimes with *natilla* (sour cream) or fried eggs. This dish is lightly spiced with herbs and is filling and tasty.

tortillas – either Mexican-style corn pancakes or omelettes, depending on what kind of meal you're having

casado – a filling and economical set meal of rice, black beans, fried plantain, beef (or other meat or fish), chopped cabbage, and maybe an egg or an avocado

palmitos – hearts of palm, usually served in a salad with vinegar dressing

pejibaye – a rather starchy-tasting palm fruit also eaten as a salad

arroz con pollo – a basic dish of rice and chicken

elote – corn on the cob

Traditional desserts include:

mazamorra – a pudding made from corn starch

queque seco – pound cake

dulce de leche – milk and sugar boiled to make a thick syrup which may be used in a layered cake called *torta chilena*

cajeta – similar to dulce de leche, but thicker, like fudge

flan – a cold caramel custard

The following are snacks, often obtained in sodas:

arreglados – little puff pastries stuffed with beef, chicken, or cheese

enchiladas – heavier pastries stuffed with potatoes and cheese, and maybe meat

empanadas – Chilean-style turnovers stuffed with meat or cheese and raisins

pupusas – El Salvadoran-style fried corn and cheese cakes

gallos – tortilla sandwiches containing meat, beans, or cheese

ceviche – seafood marinated with lemon, onion, garlic, sweet red peppers, and coriander. It can be made with *corvina* (a white sea bass), or *langostinos* (shrimps), or even *conchas* (shellfish).

patacones – a Caribbean speciality consisting of slices of plantain deep-fried like French-fried potatoes

tamales – boiled cornmeal pasties, usually wrapped in a banana leaf (you don't eat the leaf). At Christmas they traditionally come stuffed with chicken or pork, at other times of year they may be stuffed with corn and wrapped in a corn leaf. *Tamales asado* are sweet cornmeal cakes.

DRINKS

Coffee, tea, and herbal tea are easily found. The usual soft drinks are available. *Refrescos* are drinks made with local fruits. *Pipas* are green coconuts with a straw stuck in to drink the coconut 'milk' – a slightly bitter but refreshing and filling drink. *Agua dulce* is boiled water mixed with brown sugar, and *horchata* is a corn meal drink flavoured with cinnamon.

Alcohol

Costa Ricans like to drink, though they don't like drunks. Most restaurants serve a variety of alcoholic drinks. Imported drinks are expensive, local ones are quite cheap. There are five local beers which are all good. Local wines are cheap, taste cheap, and provide a memorable hangover. Distilled liquor is made from sugar cane which is grown in Costa Rica. The cheapest is *guaro* – the local firewater, drunk by the shot. Also inexpensive and good is local rum, usually drunk as a *cuba libre* (rum and Coke). A locally made coffee liqueur is Café Rica.

Many bars traditionally serve *bocas*. These are little savoury side dishes designed to make your drink more pleasurable – maybe you'll have another one! If you had several rounds, you'd eat enough bocas to make a very light meal. Some bars charge a small amount extra for them and a few don't have them at all.

THINGS TO BUY

Coffee is excellent and cheap; many visitors take some freshly roasted coffee beans back home.

Wood and leather crafts are well made and inexpensive. Wood items include salad bowls, plates, carving boards and other

COSTA RICA

kitchen utensils, jewellery boxes, and a variety of carvings and ornaments. Leatherwork includes the usual wallets and purses, handbags and briefcases.

Ceramics and jewellery are popular souvenirs. Some ceramics are replicas of pre-Columbian artefacts. Colourful posters and T-shirts with wildlife, national park and ecological themes are also popular.

Getting There & Away

AIR
Juan Santamaría international airport is 17 km outside San José and is the main international airport.

The national Costa Rican airlines are LACSA and Aero Costa Rica. They fly from the USA to Costa Rica and other Central American countries. Because Houston, New Orleans and Miami are roughly north of the Central American republics, they make good gateway cities to Costa Rica. See the Facts for the Visitor chapter for more details.

A local agency specialising in student and youth fares is OTEC (☎ 222-0866, fax 233-2321), Calle 3, Avenida 3, San José.

LAND
Costa Rica has land borders with Nicaragua and Panama. There are no problems crossing these borders, provided your papers are in order.

To/From Nicaragua
There are a couple of crossing points between Nicaragua and Costa Rica.

Via Peñas Blancas The main border post is at Peñas Blancas in Costa Rica – see Peñas Blancas in the North-Western Costa Rica section.

Via Los Chiles Officially, there is a border crossing here, but it is rarely used by foreign travellers. See Los Chiles in the North-Western Costa Rica section.

To/From Panama
There are also a couple of crossings between Costa Rica and Panama.

Via Paso Canoas This crossing is on the Interamerican Highway, and is the most frequently used entry and exit point with Panama. See Paso Canoas in the Southern Costa Rica section.

If you are entering Panama, you may need a visa or tourist card – see the Panama chapter. Regulations are subject to change, so you should check at the Panamanian consulate in San José about current requirements. Visas are not obtainable at the border, and tourist cards may not be available either.

Via Sixaola/Guabito This crossing is on the Caribbean coast. For details, see Sixaola in the Caribbean Lowlands section.

There is a Costa Rican consulate in David. Almirante is the first (or last) place in Panama with a selection of reasonably priced accommodation.

SEA
Several cruise lines make stops in Costa Rican ports and enable passengers to make a quick foray into the country. Most cruises are, however, geared to shipboard life and ocean travel, and so passengers can expect no more than a brief glimpse of Costa Rica – perhaps a day or so. Freighters also arrive in Costa Rica but most are for cargo only. Some of them may take a few, occasional passengers.

LEAVING COSTA RICA
There is a US$7.25 departure tax (depending on the exchange rate) on international flights from San José. This is payable in US dollars cash, or in colones.

Getting Around

AIR

Costa Rica's domestic airlines are SANSA and Travelair.

SANSA flies from the domestic terminal of Juan Santamaría airport. Services are with small aircraft (32-passenger DC3s and similar) and passenger demand is high, so book well in advance. Baggage allowance is 12 kg. SANSA flies between San José and Quepos, Golfito, Palmar, Coto 47, Tamarindo, Nosara, Sámara, and Barra Colorado.

Travelair flies from Tobías Bolaños airport in the San José suburb of Pavas, about five km from the city centre. It uses smaller aircraft for flights between San José and Quepos, Palmar, Golfito, Puerto Jiménez, Tamarindo, Nosara, Carrillo, Tambor, Barra Colorado and Tortuguero.

SANSA demands full payment at one of its offices before a reservation can be confirmed. It has a reputation for delays and cancelled flights but have been improving in 1993. Travelair can be booked through any travel agent and has a better record for on-time flights, but it's a little more expensive. Telephone numbers, flight and fare details are given under the appropriate towns.

Tobías Bolaños also has light planes (three to five passengers) for charter to anywhere in Costa Rica for about US$250 per hour.

BUS

San José is the transportation centre for the whole country. There is no central bus terminal in the capital, though some smaller towns have one. Larger companies with terminals sell tickets in advance. Smaller companies with just a bus stop expect you to queue for the next bus, but normally there is room for everyone. The exception is the days before and after a major holiday, especially Easter, when buses are ridiculously full. I have resorted to hitching in these cases. Friday nights and Saturday mornings out of San José can be very crowded, as can Sunday afternoons and evenings coming back.

Buses are of two types: *directo*, and *normal* or *corriente*. The direct buses are faster and about a quarter more expensive. Luggage space is limited, so leave what you don't need in San José. If you have to check luggage, watch that it gets loaded on the bus and that it doesn't 'accidentally' get given to the wrong passenger at intermediate stops. Trips over four hours have a rest stop – there are no toilets on buses.

The ICT tourist office in San José has a current listing of many bus departures.

TRAIN

Trains between San José and the two coasts were suspended indefinitely in 1991. There are four short train rides operating: between the San Pedro suburb of San José and Heredia – about 14 km away; between San José and Cartago – about 21 km; between Puerto Limón and the Río Estrella area – a 90-minute ride; and an expensive 'banana train' operated by tour companies.

TAXI

Taxis go to remote parts of the country, as well as on city streets. Most small towns have 4WD taxis to surrounding areas. Public buses do not go to all national parks – a taxi for a day trip is about US$40 to US$50.

CAR & MOTORBIKE

Most car rental agencies are in San José. Car rental is expensive, at least US$250 per week during the high season for the smallest car with no air-con. This includes insurance and unlimited mileage. Expect to pay US$300 to US$400 for a car with air-con, and US$450 to US$500 for a van or 4WD jeep. The insurance usually requires you to pay for the first US$750 of any damage – to be fully covered costs US$3 more per day. Rental agencies insist you rent a 4WD vehicle to drive on dirt roads in the wet season.

To rent a car you need a valid driver's licence, a major credit card and your passport. Your driver's licence from home is acceptable for up to 90 days. Most companies won't rent to drivers under 25. (Ada Rent-a-Car claims to have a minimum of 18 years;

Pilot claims 21 years; and Adobe 23 years – there may be others). Some companies take a $700 deposit instead of a credit card.

Carefully inspect rented cars for minor damage and ensure it is noted on the rental agreement. Never leave valuables in sight even when you briefly leave the car, and never park the car on the street overnight. Use a guarded parking lot and remove all your luggage.

Motorbikes can be rented in San José and along the coast – they cost about US$200 a week.

Petrol costs about US$0.40 per litre (US$1.50 per US gallon) and costs the same at all petrol stations.

Driving in San José is not recommended because of the crowded one-way system on narrow streets. Outside the capital, roads are narrow, steep and winding – drive very carefully. Speed limits are 80 km/h on primary roads and 60 km/h on others. Traffic police use radar and enforce speed limits. It is illegal to drive without using seat belts.

BICYCLE
There are no bike lanes and traffic can be hazardous on the narrow, steep, and winding roads. Touring cyclists report that locals are very friendly. There are bike shops in San José.

HITCHING
Hitching is not common, especially on main roads which have frequent buses. On minor rural roads, hitching is possible. Vehicles pass infrequently and you should wave them down in a friendly fashion and ask for a ride. (Watch how the locals do it.) If you get a ride, offer to pay for it when you arrive: *Cuanto le debo?* (How much do I owe you?). Your offer may be waved aside or you may be asked to help with money for *gasolina* (gasoline, petrol).

I haven't heard a negative story about single women hitching, but nevertheless, discretion is urged. Talk to the occupants of the car and get an idea if they seem OK; hitch from somewhere (a gas station, store, restaurant, police post) where you can retreat to if you don't like the look of your prospective ride. Hitch with a friend.

BOAT
Two ferries from Puntarenas cross the Gulf of Nicoya. A car ferry leaves twice a day for Playa Naranjo, and a small passenger ferry crosses to Paquera twice a day.

A daily passenger ferry links Golfito with Puerto Jiménez on the Osa Peninsula. This ferry is subject to cancellation.

Boats ply the inland waterway from Moín (near Limón) to Tortuguero. Dugout canoes go from Puerto Viejo de Sarapiquí down the Río Sarapiquí towards the Nicaraguan border and from Los Chiles up the Río Frío to the Refugio Caño Negro.

Costa Rica has first-class river rafting on the Ríos Pacuare and Reventazón, among others. Outfitters in San José sell whitewater rafting trips.

LOCAL TRANSPORT
Taxis from the International Airport to San José cost US$10. Buses from Alajuela to San José pass the airport several times an hour from 5 am to 9 pm, and often have room for passengers. Fares are US$0.40.

Local buses serve urban and suburban areas, but routes can be difficult to figure out. Many towns are small enough that it's easier to walk where you want to go.

Taxi cabs are red and have a small 'TAXI' sticker in the windshield. In San José, taxis have meters (*marías*) which should be used. Elsewhere, fares are agreed in advance. San José drivers may try to overcharge tourists by saying the meter is broken. Outside the capital taxi drivers are less likely to overcharge you. Within San José, a short ride costs about US$1. A ride across town is about US$2.

San José

Compared with other Central American capitals, San José is more cosmopolitan, even North American in character. There are department stores and shopping malls, fast-food restaurants and blue jeans. It takes a day or two to start getting the real tico feel of the city. Perhaps the first sign of being in Costa Rica is the friendliness of the people. Asking someone the way will often result in a smile and a genuine attempt to help you out.

The city was founded in 1737, but little remains of the colonial era. Until the Teatro Nacional was built in the 1890s, San José was not a notable city. Today the capital boasts several excellent museums, good restaurants and a fine climate, which are San José's main attractions. Costa Rica's road system radiates from San José, and the capital is a good base from which to visit the rest of the country.

The city stands at 1150 metres in a wide and fertile valley called the Meseta Central. The population of the city is 287,535 (1989 census), but the surrounding suburbs boost the number to about 885,000. Inhabitants of San José are called *joséfinos*.

Orientation

The city centre is arranged in a grid. The streets are numbered in a logical fashion, and you should learn the system because all street addresses rely on it. *Avenidas* run east to west and *calles* run north to south. Avenidas south of Avenida Central have even numbers (Avenida 2, Avenida 4 etc), while avenidas north of Avenida Central have odd numbers. Calles west of Calle Central have even numbers while calles east of Calle Central have odd numbers.

Street addresses are given by the nearest street intersection. Thus the address of the ICT tourist office is Calle 5, between Avenidas Central & 2. This is often abbreviated to C5, A Ctl/2, or C5, A 0/2. This system is used in many other Costa Rican towns.

Avenida Central becomes Paseo Colón west of Calle 14. The building on the north side of Paseo Colón, Calles 38 & 40, is known as Centro Colón and is a local landmark. Ticos use local landmarks to give directions or even addresses – an address

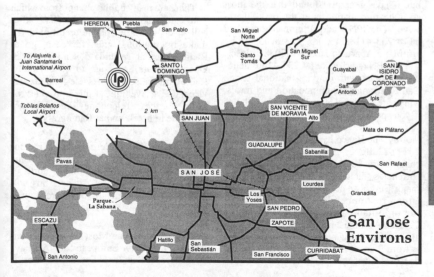

San José Environs

may be 200 metres south and 150 metres east of a church, pulpería or radio station. Sometimes the landmark no longer exists, but because it has been used for so long it's known by all the locals. A good example is the Coca-Cola bus terminal – it used to be a Coke bottling plant. A city block is called *cien metros*, literally 100 metres, so if someone says '250 metros al sur' they mean 2½ blocks south regardless of the actual distance.

Information
Tourist Office The ICT, or Instituto Costarricense de Turismo (☎ 222-1090), is on Calle 5, Avenidas Central & 2. Opening hours are 9 am to 5 pm from Monday to Friday and 9 am to 1 pm on Saturday. They answer questions (in English) and are also helpful with bus information.

Servicio de Parques Nacionales The public information office (☎ 257-0922) of the SPN is in the headquarters building at Calle 25, Avenidas 8 & 10. Opening hours are 8 am to 4 pm, Monday to Friday. You can obtain information and make reservations for places like the mountain hut on Chirripó, but I have generally found that the most accurate information is at the parks themselves. The SPN headquarters can be reached on ☎ 233-4118/246, fax 223-6963, or by writing to Apartado 10104-1000, San José.

The SPN radio office (☎ 233-4160) maintains contact with outlying national parks. Call to arrange accommodation and meals, which are provided by park rangers. (It helps if you speak Spanish.)

Money The Banco Lyon (☎ 222-7137, 221-2611) Calle 2, Avenidas Central & 1, changes travellers' cheques in a variety of currencies, including Canadian dollars and major European currencies, at official rates. Other recommended banks are Banco Metropolitano (☎ 233-8111) at Calle Central, Avenida 2 and Banex (☎ 257-0522) at Calle Central, Avenida 1. Normal banking is from 9 am to 3 pm. The Banco Nacional de Costa Rica, at Avenida 1, Calle 7, is open

from 8 am to 6 pm from Monday to Friday. The bank at the airport is open from 6.30 am to 5 pm from Monday to Friday, and from 7 am to 1 pm on weekends and holidays, but changes colones back to US dollars only between 9 am and 2 pm, Monday to Friday.

Valorinsa (☎ 257-1010, 257-2002) Calle 9, Avenidas Central & 2, is an exchange house giving good rates. Opening hours are 9 am to 5 pm, Monday to Friday.

At other times, street moneychangers can be found hanging out around Avenida Central, Calle 2. Rip-offs occur and street changing is not recommended – if you need to do it, be careful and go with a friend.

The American Express office is in the TAM travel agency (☎ 233-0044, after hours 223-0116), Calle 1, Avenidas Central & 1. Visa (☎ 257-1357, 222-4611, 223-2211) is in the Galería La Paz, Avenida 2, Calles 2 & 4. MasterCard (☎ 253-2155) is in San Pedro – call for directions.

Post & Telecommunications The Correo Central (central post office) is on Calle 2, Avenidas 1 & 3. Opening hours are 7 am to 6 pm from Monday to Friday and 7 am to noon on Saturday.

There are many public phones from which you can make international calls, either collect or with a telephone credit card. To make international calls for cash, go to Radiográfica at Avenida 5, Calles 1 & 3. Opening hours are 7 am to 10 pm daily. Radiográfica also provides telex and fax services. ICE at Avenida 2, Calle 1 provides the same services. Telephone directories are available in hotels and at Radiográfica.

Immigration The *Migraciones* office for visa extensions or exit visas is opposite the Hospital Mexico, about four km north of Parque La Sabana. Any Alajuela bus will drop you nearby. Opening hours are 8 am to 4 pm from Monday to Friday.

Foreign Embassies Most European countries and many non-European countries have embassies in San José. See under Visas &

Embassies in the Facts for the Visitor section earlier in this chapter for a list of embassies.

Travel & Tour Agencies Tours are expensive – about US$40 to US$100 for a full day tour, depending on the destination. Half-day tours for about US$20 to US$30 are better value. Swiss Travel (☎ 231-4055), which has offices in the major hotels, deals with airline tickets and standard tours. Costa Rica Expeditions (☎ 257-0766), Calle Central, Avenida 3, sells nature tours and river running trips. River running trips are also sold by Ríos Tropicales (☎ 233-6455), Calle 32, Avenida 2, and Aventuras Naturales (☎ 225-3939), Avenida Central, Calles 33 & 36. Tikal (☎ 223-2811), Avenida 2, Calle 7, does nature tours, airline tickets, and helps with visa problems. Companies doing the cheaper tours to Tortuguero include Cotur (☎ 233-0155), Calle 38, Paseo Colón & Avenida 1, and Mitur (☎ 255-2031), Paseo Colón, Calles 20 & 22.

Bookshops The Bookshop, on Avenida 1, Calles 1 & 3, has the best selection of books and magazines in English (including Lonely Planet guidebooks), but they charge twice the US price because of import taxes. The Travelers Store, Calle Central, Avenida 3, sells guidebooks including *Costa Rica – a travel survival kit.* Lehmann's, on Avenida Central, Calles 1 & 3, has some books, magazines and newspapers in English and a good selection of Costa Rican maps. The Librería Francesa, on Calle 3, Avenidas Central & 1, has books in French. Book Traders, Avenida 1, Calles 3 & 5, sells and exchanges used books in English.

Medical The free Hospital San Juan de Dios (☎ 222-0166) is centrally located at Paseo Colón, Calle 14. The best private clinic is the Clínica Bíblica (☎ 223-6422, 257-0466 for emergencies), on Avenida 14, Calles Central & 1. It has some English-speaking staff and is open 24 hours for emergencies. It carries out laboratory tests. For an ambulance, call the Cruz Roja (Red Cross) on ☎ 221-5818.

Things to See
Museo de Jade This is Costa Rica's most famous museum, housing the world's largest collection of American jade. Many pieces are mounted with a backlight so that the exquisite translucent quality of the gemstone can

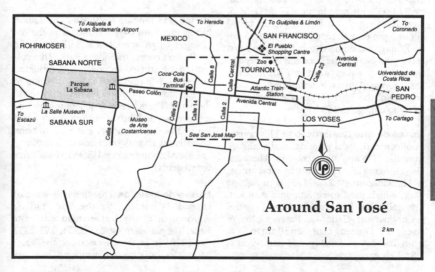

Around San José

0   1   2 km

COSTA RICA

be fully appreciated. There are also archaeological exhibits of ceramics, stonework and gold, arranged by cultural regions.

The museum (☎ 223-5800, ext 2581) is on the 11th floor of the Instituto Nacional de Seguros at Calle 9, Avenida 7. Opening hours are 9 am to 3 pm, Monday to Friday, and admission is free.

There is a good city view from the 11th floor – bring your camera.

Museo Nacional Housed in the Bellavista Fortress, the old army headquarters on Calle 17, Avenidas Central & 2, this museum (☎ 257-1433) shows Costa Rican archaeology, some jade and gold, colonial furniture and costumes, colonial and religious art, historical exhibits and natural history displays. Some pieces are labelled in English as well as Spanish. There is a garden with cannons; some of the walls are pockmarked with bullet holes from the 1948 civil war. There's a gift shop. Opening hours are 9 am to 5 pm, Tuesday to Sunday. Admission is US$0.75.

Museo de Oro Precolombino This houses a dazzling collection of pre-Columbian gold. There is a small numismatic museum and a display of Costa Rican art. The museum (☎ 223-0528) is next to the ICT on Calle 5, Avenidas Central & 2. Opening hours are 10 am to 5 pm on weekends and 1 pm to 5 pm on Friday, and admission is free. You must leave your bags at the door and may need to show your passport to get in. (The museum has reopened after a temporary closure because of the 1991 earthquake – hours are likely to change in 1994.)

Museo de Arte Costarricense This houses a collection of local paintings and sculpture from the 19th and 20th centuries. There are also changing shows of work by local artists.

The museum (☎ 222-7155) is in Sabana Park, which used to be San José's airport. The collection is housed in the old control tower just off Calle 42, Paseo Colón & Avenida 2. Opening hours are 10 am to 5 pm from Tuesday to Sunday, and admission is US$0.75, except on Sunday when it's free.

Galería Nacional de Arte Contemporaneo This houses changing exhibits of work by contemporary Costa Rican artists. The museum is next to the National Library on Calle 15, Avenidas 3 & 5. Opening hours are 10 am to 1 pm and 1.45 to 5 pm, from Monday to Saturday. Admission is free.

Serpentario This exhibits live snakes and poison-arrow frogs. A bilingual biologist will explain the collection and there is a small gift shop. The serpentarium (☎ 255-4210) is on Avenida 1, Calles 9 & 11. Opening hours are 10 am to 7 pm daily. Admission is US$1.50.

Parque Zoológico Simón Bolívar This small national zoo (☎ 233-6701) is in the park of the same name. Many of Costa Rica's animals can be seen, along with a few exotics. Some visitors have not been impressed with the conditions in which the animals are kept. The gate is at Avenida 11, Calles 7 & 9 (go north on Calle 7 to get there). Opening hours are from 8.30 am to 3.30 pm from Tuesday to Friday, 9 am to 4 pm on weekends, closed Monday. Admission is US$0.50.

Museo de Ciencias Naturales The natural history museum (☎ 232-1306) is in the old Colegio (high school) La Salle near the south-west corner of Sabana Park. This collection of stuffed animals and mounted butterflies is a resource to those wishing to identify some of the species they may see in the wild. There are also paleontology and archaeology exhibits. Opening hours are 8 am to 3 pm on weekdays and 8 am to noon on Saturday (it may be closed on Saturday – call ahead); admission is US$0.75 (half price for students).

Museo de Insectos This fine collection of insects is curated by the Facultad de Agronomía at the Universidad de Costa Rica. The museum (☎ 253-5323, 253-3253 ext 5318) is in the basement of the Artes Musicales building on campus. There are signs, or ask. Opening hours are 1 to 4.45 pm on weekdays, and admission is US$0.75.

Spirogyra Jardín de Mariposas This butterfly garden (not to be confused with the large Butterfly Farm in La Guacima) offers close-up looks at Costa Rican butterflies in a garden setting close to the city centre. The garden is 100 metres east and 150 metres south of Centro Comercial El Pueblo. Spirogyra (☎ 222-2937) is open daily except Tuesday from 9 am to 4 pm; the last guided tour starts at 3.30 pm. Admission is US$4.

Museo Postal, Telegráfico, y Filatélico de Costa Rica This museum (☎ 223-9766, ext 269) is upstairs in the central post office, Calle 2, Avenidas 1 & 3. Opening hours are 8 am to 4 pm from Monday to Friday; admission is free.

Museo de Criminología The stated objective of the Criminological Museum (☎ 223-0666, ext 2378) is the prevention of crime through the presentation of exhibits of criminal acts. The display reportedly includes such niceties as limbs which have been separated from their rightful owners by machete-wielding criminals. The museum is in the Supreme Court of Justice, Calle 17, Avenida 6, open from 1 to 4 pm on Monday, Wednesday and Thursday.

Museo Nacional de Ferrocarril See the first locomotive serving the San José-Limón run, as well as a model railway, old photographs and railroad paraphernalia. The museum is in the old Atlantic railway station at Avenida 3, Calle 19 and is open from 8 am to 4 pm daily except Monday. Admission is US$0.75.

Museo de Fotos This privately owned collection of many thousands of photographs gives a glimpse of life in Costa Rica during the early 20th century. The museum is on Calle 7, Avenidas Central & 1, and is open from 8.30 to 11.15 am from Monday to Saturday and 1.30 to 5 pm from Monday to Friday. Admission is US$2.25.

Teatro Nacional This is considered San José's most impressive public building. Built in the 1890s, it is the centre of Costa Rican culture. The outside is not particularly impressive: a columned facade, and statues of Beethoven and Calderón de la Barca (a 17th-century Spanish dramatist) flanking the entrance. Inside there are some paintings of Costa Rica, of which the most famous is a huge canvas showing coffee harvesting and export. The marble staircases, gilded ceilings, and parquet floors of local hardwoods are worth seeing. These are being restored after the 1991 earthquake.

Performances are held frequently and this is the best way to see the inside of the building. Otherwise, it is open from 10 am to noon and 2 to 6 pm, Monday to Friday, and costs US$1.80 to visit.

Mercado Central This is interesting to visit, although a little tame compared to the markets of other Central American countries. It is at Avenidas Central & 1, Calles 6 & 8. A block away is the similar **Mercado Borbón**, at Avenida 3 and Calle 8. Beware of pickpockets in these areas.

Parks & Plazas The pleasant and shady **Parque Nacional** is between Avenidas 1 & 3 and Calles 15 & 19. In the park centre is the Monumento Nacional showing the Central American nations driving out William Walker. Opposite the south-west corner is a statue of national hero, Juan Santamaría. Important buildings surrounding the national park include the Asemblea Legislativa (Congress Building) to the south, the Biblioteca Nacional to the north, and the Fábrica Nacional de Licores (founded in 1856 but no longer used for making liquor) to the north-west.

The small **Parque de España** has the tallest trees in San José. It is a riot of birdsong just before sunset. There is an outdoor art market on Sunday. The park is between Avenidas 3 & 7 and Calles 9 & 11. To the north is the Museo de Jade in the INS building fronted by a huge statue of 'The Family'.

COSTA RICA

COSTA RICA

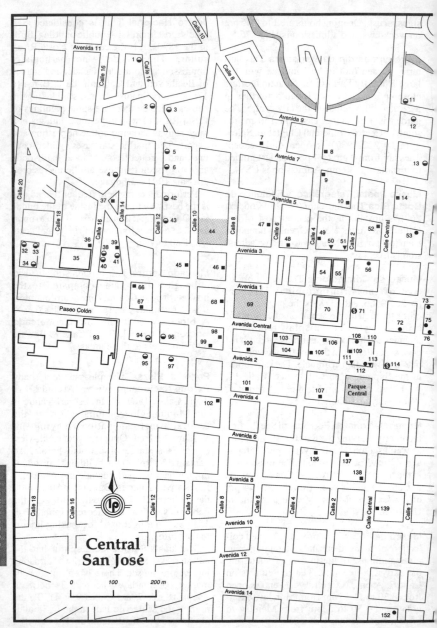

Central
San José

0   100   200 m

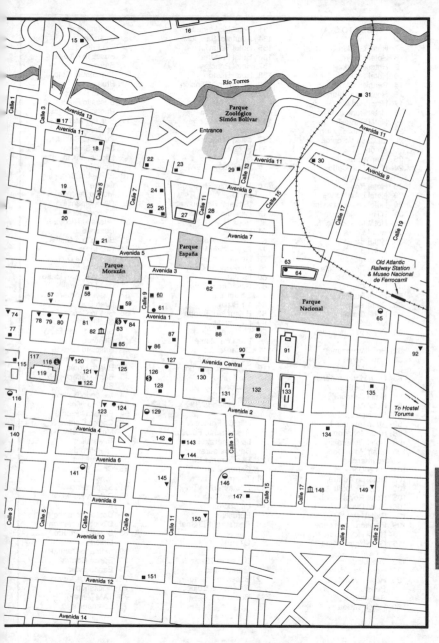

■ PLACES TO STAY

7 Hotel Garden Court
8 Hotel Marlyn
9 Hotel América
10 Hotel Rialto
14 Pensión Otoya
15 Hotel Villa Tournón
17 Hotel Hilda
18 Hotel Dunn Inn
20 Hotel Santo Tomás
21 Aurola Holiday Inn
22 La Casa Verde de Amón
23 Hemingway Inn
24 Hotel Don Carlos
25 Hotel Astoria
26 Hotel Rey
29 Hotel L'Ambiance
30 Hotel La Amistad Inn
31 D'Raya Vida
36 Hotel Musoc
37 Hotel Cocorí
39 Hotel Boruca
45 Hotel Bienvenido
46 Hotel Moderno
47 Hotel Compostela
48 Hotel Central
49 Hotel Capital
52 Hotel Europa
58 Diana's Inn
59 Hotel Amstel Morazán
60 Pensión Costa Rica Inn
62 Hotel Morazán
66 Hotel Roma
67 Hotel Alameda
68 Gran Hotel Imperial
77 Hotel La Gran Via
85 Hotel Balmoral
87 Hotel Asia
88 Pensión La Cuesta
89 Apartamentos Lamm
98 Hotel Johnson
99 Hotel Generaleño
100 Gran Hotel Centroamericano
101 Hotel Doral
102 Hotel La Aurora
103 Hotel Diplomat
105 Hotel Royal Dutch
106 Hotel Plaza
107 Park Hotel
109 Pensión Americana
110 Hotel Royal Garden
115 Gran Hotel Costa Rica
122 Tica Linda
125 Hotel Presidente
128 Hotel Avenida 2; Pensión Salamanca
130 Hotel Galilea

131 Hotel Nicaragua
134 Apartotel San José
135 Hotel Bellavista
136 Hotel Fortuna
137 Hotel Príncipe
138 Hotel Boston
139 Hotel Ritz; Pensión Centro Continental
140 Casa El Paso
143 Gran Hotel Doña Inés
147 Casa Ridgeway
151 Hotel La Gema

▼ PLACES TO EAT

16 El Pueblo Shopping Centre (Several Restaurants)
19 Restaurant Poás
50 Soda Nini
51 Lido Bar
57 Soda Central
74 Restaurant Vishnu
78 Restaurante Marisquería Omni
80 La Vasconia
81 Restaurant Goya & Chalet Suizo
84 Mr Pizza
86 Balcon de Europa
90 La Fogata
92 El Cuartel de la Boca de Monte
111 Soda Palace
113 Soda La Perla
119 Café Ruisenor (in the Teatro Nacional)
120 Soda B&B
121 La Hacienda Steak House, L'Ile de France & Restaurante Fulusu
122 La Esmeralda Bar/Restaurant
123 Restaurante El Campesino
144 Tommy's Ribs
145 Restaurantes Tin-jo & Don Wang
149 La Cocina de Bordolino
150 Restaurant El Shakti

OTHER

1 Buses to Tilarán & Monteverde
2 Buses to Puerto Jiménez & Bejuco
3 Buses to Puntarenas, Guápiles, Río Frio
4 Buses to Nicoya, Sámana, Tamarindo, Coto Brus
5 Bus to Bejuco
6 Buses to Playas Panamá, Hermosa
11 Bus to Puerto Viejo de Sarapiquí
12 Buses to Cahuita, Bribri, Sixaola
13 Microbuses to Heredia
16 El Pueblo Shopping Centre
27 Museo de Jade
28 Casa Amarilla (Yellow House)
32 Buses to Nicoya & Beaches
33 Bus to Los Chiles
34 Bus to Pavas
35 Coca-Cola Bus Terminal
36 Buses to San Isidro de El General
37 Buses to Nicaraguan Border
38 Bus to Cañas, Santa Cecilia, Upala & San Isidro de El General
40 Buses to Escazú
41 Buses to Liberia
42 Bus to Upala
43 Bus to Guápiles & Siquirres
44 Mercado Borbón
53 Radiográfica
54 Banco Nacional
55 Correo Central & Museo Postal, Telegráfico y Filatélico de Costa Rica
56 Costa Rica Expeditions
61 Serpentario
63 Galería Nacional de Arte Contemporaneo
64 Biblioteca Nacional
65 Buses to Puerto Limón
69 Mercado Central
70 Banco Central
71 Banco Lyon
72 Libería Universal
73 Bookshop
75 TAM (Amex)
76 Lehmann's

79	Book Traders	108	Churrería Manolos	127	Churrería Manolos
82	Museo de Fotos	112	Teatro Melico	129	TICA Bus
83	Banco Nacional de		Salazar		(International)
	Costa Rica	114	Banco Metropolitano	132	Plaza de La
91	Legislative Assembly	116	Bus to Irazú		Democracia
92	El Cuartel de la	117	Plaza de La Cultura	133	Museo Nacional
	Boca de Monte	118	ICT Tourism	141	Sirca (International
93	San Juan de Dios		Information Office		Buses)
	Hospital		& Museo de Oro	142	Mercado Nacional
94	Buses to Alajuela		Precolombino		de Artesanía
95	Bus to Poás	119	Teatro Nacional	146	Buses to Turrialba
96	Buses to Alajuela	124	Lavandería Sixaola	148	Museo de
97	Bus to Heredia	126	Valorinsa		Criminología
104	Banco de Costa Rica		(Money Exchange)	152	Clínica Bíblica

To the north-east is the Casa Amarilla which houses the Ministry of Foreign Affairs.

Parque Morazán covers four city blocks and is graced in the centre by the dome-roofed Templo de Musica. The north-east quarter of the park has a small Japanese garden and a children's playground.

The **Plaza de la Cultura** is the site of the Teatro Nacional, Museo de Oro and ICT office. The west side of the plaza is an open-air market of arts & crafts – it's very busy just before Christmas. Young people hang out here and check out what everyone else is doing.

Parque Central is between busy Avenidas 2 & 4 and Calles Central & 2. This is the place to catch many of the local city buses. To the east is the fairly modern and not very interesting Catedral Metropolitana.

Spanish Courses
There are good (if pricey) Spanish language schools in San José. Tuition is usually intensive, with class sizes from two to five per teacher and individual tuition available. Classes are for several hours every weekday. Students are encouraged to stay with a Costa Rican family to immerse themselves in the language. Family homestays are arranged by the schools, and so are the necessary visa extensions.

Costs range from US$375 to US$1300 per month depending on group size, number of hours and whether family homestays and cultural field trips are offered. Many schools advertise in *The Tico Times* every week.

Costa Rica – a travel survival kit gives an extensive listing of language schools.

Places to Stay
Hotels Budget hotels are found west of Calle Central. The area around the Coca-Cola bus terminal, Mercado Central and Parque Central has had reports of occasional thefts and a mugging. I've stayed in this area and haven't had any problems, but travellers should keep their eyes open and use taxis if arriving at night.

The basic *Gran Hotel Imperial* (☎ 222-7899), Calle 8, Avenidas Central & 1, is currently popular with shoestringers. This cavernous hotel provides security, reasonably clean beds, rather grungy showers that have hot water once in a while, and one of the best value cheap restaurants in town. Rooms are US$2.75 per person (few singles) and they'll hold a room until the afternoon if you call ahead.

Another popular place is the (poorly signed) *Tica Linda* (☎ 233-0528), Avenida 2, # 553, Calles 5 & 7, next door to the La Esmeralda Bar (where mariachis play late into the night). Ring the bell to get in. Cramped rooms sleeping four are US$3.30 per person; a private little box is US$4.50 a single. The place is noisy but friendly and secure, and has laundry facilities.

Other basic places include the *Hotel Nicaragua* (☎ 223-0292), Avenida 2, No 1167, Calle 13. It is family-run, reasonably clean, friendly and secure. There are only cold water showers and rooms are US$2.20 per

COSTA RICA

person. Nearby is the basic but clean and OK *Hotel Avenida 2* (☎ 222-0260), Avenida 2, Calles 9 & 11, which has hot showers and charges US$4.40 per person. On the same block is the more basic *Pensión Salamanca* which costs US$2.20 per person in box-like rooms and has cold showers only. The *Hotel Moderno* (☎ 221-2572), Calle 8, Avenidas 1 & 3, is a basic cold-water hotel charging US$2.60/3.70 for a single/double (one bed) or US$5.10 for a double (two beds).

The *Hotel Rialto* (☎ 221-7456), Calle 2, Avenida 5, is decent, has hot water in the mornings and charges US$4.40/5.10 for a single/double, or US$6.60 with a private washbasin and toilet. The *Hotel América* (☎ 221-4116), Calle 4, Avenida 7, is clean but lacks hot water – rooms are US$7.30 double. The very secure *Hotel Marlyn* (☎ 233-3212), Calle 4, Avenidas 7 & 9, charges US$5.50 for a small single or double with communal cold showers, or US$10 with private bath and (usually) hot water. The basic but secure *Hotel Asia* (☎ 223-3893), Calle 11, Avenidas Central & 1, charges US$5.25/7.50 for a single/double in small but clean rooms and has hot water in the communal showers. The *Hotel Generaleño* (☎ 233-7877), Avenida 2, Calles 8 & 10, is large, clean, but basic, and has cold showers only for US$3.70 per person.

The *Hotel Boruca* (☎ 223-0016), Calle 14, Avenidas 1 & 3, is convenient for buses but some rooms are noisy because of them. It is family-run, friendly, secure, clean and has hot water some of the time. Small rooms are US$4.40 per person. Nearby is the similarly priced *Hotel Roma* (☎ 223-2179), Calle 14, Avenidas Central & 1. It is adequate, clean and secure, but spartan and has cold water only.

The *Hotel Central* (☎ 222-3509, 221-2767), Avenida 3, Calles 6 & 8, has large clean rooms for US$11.75/15.50 single/double with private bath and tepid water. Four people can share a room for US$20.50. The upstairs rooms are the nicest. The *Hotel Astoria* (☎ 221-2174, fax 221-8497), Avenida 7, Calles 7 & 9, is often full.

A few very basic and grim rooms are US$5 per person and better rooms with private bath and hot water are US$18 double. The *Pensión Americana* (☎ 221-4171, 221-9799), Calle 2, Avenidas Central & 2, charges US$5.10 per person in large but dark rooms, though there is a TV room and the management is friendly. Communal showers are cold. The *Hotel Boston* (☎ 221-0563), Avenida 8, Calles Central & 2, has large rooms with slightly dank private baths and tepid water for US$9.50/12.50 single/double. The management is friendly. Ask for an inside room to avoid street noise.

The *Hotel Morazán* (☎ 221-9083), Avenida 3, Calles 11 & 15, has large, clean, bare rooms, and is secure. I was quoted US$7.25 for a single with communal cold shower and US$14.50 a double with hot water in March (high season), but in September (low season) it's about half this price. The *Pensión Otoya* (☎ 221-3925), Calle Central, Avenidas 5 & 7, is clean, friendly, and is often full. Decent rooms are US$7/12 or US$10/14 with private bath and hot water. The *Hotel Príncipe* (☎ 222-7983, 223-1589), Avenida 6, Calles Central & 2, is secure and has good rooms with tepid showers for US$10/14.50 a single/double.

The secure *Hotel Compostela* (☎ 221-0694), Calle 6, Avenidas 3 & 5, charges US$12.50 for very clean single or double rooms, each with a private hot bath across the corridor. They also have small rooms for US$5.10 per person with communal cold showers. The *Hotel La Aurora* (☎ 222-1463), Calle 8, Avenida 4, is reasonably clean and has rooms with private hot showers – those on the outside suffer from street noise. Rooms are US$10 (single/double, one bed) or US$18.50 (two beds).

The *Pensión Centro Continental* (☎ 222-4103), Calle Central, Avenidas 8 & 10, is clean, friendly and popular. There are kitchen facilities and tepid electric communal showers. Rooms are US$7/12.20 for singles/doubles and US$3.70 per extra person, up to five people. The *Hotel Musoc* (☎ 222-9437, fax 255-0031), Apartado 1049-1000, San José, Calle 16, Avenidas 1

& 3, is convenient for the Coca-Cola bus terminal. The hotel is clean, has English-speaking staff and accepts credit cards – but I have received criticisms of their left-luggage facility. They charge US$10/16 for singles/doubles and US$12/17.50 in rooms with private hot showers. The *Hotel Cocorí* (☎ 233-0081, 233-2188), Calle 16, Avenida 3, is also near the Coca-Cola bus terminal. Clean rooms with private hot showers are US$13/17.50 for single/double, or US$11.25/14.25 in rooms with communal cold showers.

The friendly *Casa Leo* (☎ 222-9725), Avenida 6 bis, Calles 13 & 15, is US$8 per person in dormitories and US$10 in private rooms. Hot showers, kitchen privileges and tourist information are available. The *Hotel Johnson* (☎ 223-7633/827, fax 222-3683; Apartado 6638-1000, San José), Calle 8, Avenidas Central & 2, accepts credit cards and reservations, has hot water in the private showers, and reasonably sized rooms with telephone and fax facilities. Rates are US$13/16.25 for singles/doubles. Some rooms will take up to five people for about US$22. The *Hotel Bienvenido* (☎ 221-1872, 233-2161; Apartado 389-2200, San José), Calle 10, Avenidas 1 & 3, is secure, has helpful staff and good clean rooms with hot water sometimes. Rates are US$15/18.50 for singles/doubles.

Hostels The *Hostel Toruma* (☎/fax 224-4085, ☎ 253-6588; Apartado 1355-1002, San José), Avenida Central, Calles 29 & 31, is associated with the YHA. Bunks in segregated dormitories are US$6.15 for YHA members, US$7.90 for nonmembers. (The hostel has recently been remodelled and may raise its prices.) Hot showers are sometimes available and inexpensive meals are served in the cafeteria. There are laundry facilities, a message board and information and reservations for other Costa Rican hostels can be made here. (Note that the San José hostel is by far the cheapest.)

The *Casa Ridgeway* (☎ 233-6168), Calle 15, Avenida 6 bis, No 1336, is operated by Quakers. There is a small library and the centre is staffed mainly by volunteers. Accommodation is US$10 per person in one single and four double rooms; there are basic kitchen facilities and communal hot showers.

Places to Eat
Sodas These inexpensive snack bars are rather featureless, but popular with ticos looking for a cheap meal. They cater to students and working people, and some close at weekends.

A popular one is the *Soda Central* (☎ 221-9085), Avenida 1, Calles 3 & 5, where the empanadas are good and you can have a gallo pinto with egg for just over US$1. The *Soda Nini* (☎ 233-7771), Avenida 3, Calles 2 & 4, has both tico and Chinese food and is cheap. The *Soda Magaly*, Avenida Central, Calle 23, has a good variety of meals under US$2. The *Soda Pulpería La Luz*, Avenida Central, Calle 33, is a an old local landmark near the youth hostel. The *Soda Palace*, Avenida 2, Calle 2, and the *Soda La Perla*, Avenida 2, Calle Central, are open 24 hours. The Palace is a classic tico joint, particularly at night, and the Perla serves good food – these last two are a little pricier than the others.

Vegetarian This isn't big in Costa Rica, but there are a few decent vegetarian restaurants. One is the *Vishnu* chain, of which the one at Avenida 1, Calles 1 & 3 serves a set lunch for about US$2.50 and is currently popular. You have to ask the waiter for prices. Other *Vishnus* are at Calle 3, Avenidas Central & 1, and Calle 14, Avenidas Central & 2. Others which have been recommended include *El Shakti*, Avenida 8, Calle 13, and *El Eden* Avenida 5, Calles Central & 2.

For lunches only, but good value, try *Don Sol*, Avenida 7 bis, Calles 13 & 15. Two more up-market macrobiotic restaurants (meals US$4 to US$8) are *Restaurant Mordisco* (☎ 255-2448), Paseo Colón, Avenidas 24 & 26, and *La Mazorca* (☎ 224-8069), 100 metres north and 25 metres west of the Banco Anglo in San Pedro.

COSTA RICA

Budget The *Mercado Central* has several cheapish eateries inside. Nearby on Avenida are a variety of other cheap places. The area around the market is not dangerous, but it is a little rough and women may prefer not to go there alone.

The *Restaurant El Campesino* (☎ 255-1438, 222-1170), Calle 7, Avenida 2, is a pleasant place with a homey atmosphere. It serves roasted (not fried) chicken, at about US$1.50 for a quarter, as well as Chinese dishes. The ex-owner has just opened an equally good place at *Pollos Gallo Pinto* (☎ 257-4437), Calle 17, Avenidas 2 & 6. The chicken is roasted over coffee roots and served with tortillas – delicious. *La Fogata*, Avenida Central, Calle 13, also serves a quarter chicken for US$1.50.

La Vasconia, Avenida 1, Calle 5, is a cheap but decent place – I like it. The clean *Restaurante Marisquería Omni*, Avenida 1, Calles 3 & 5, serves a good set lunch from 11.30 am to 1.30 pm for under US$2. Another cheap possibility is the *Lido Bar*, Calle 2, Avenida 3, which is less of a bar and more of a cheap lunch place, at least during the middle of the day. Ticos like to drink (in moderation), and see nothing surprising about eating in a bar. *La Cocina de Bordelino*, Calle 21, Avenidas 6 & 8, is a small place serving Argentine empanadas for under US$1.

Cafés & Coffee Shops These are good places for journal or letter writing. Prices are not necessarily cheap, but you don't have to buy much and can sit for hours. A favourite place is the pavement café of the up-market *Gran Hotel Costa Rica*, Calle 3, Avenida 2, where you get a good view of the comings and goings in the Plaza de la Cultura. The Teatro Nacional has an elegant but simple little coffee shop, *Café Ruisneor*. Both are well recommended. A homey little pastelería called *La Miel*, Avenida 6, Calles 13 & 15, serves delicious desserts to local office workers.

Other A good and reasonably priced pizza restaurant is *Mr Pizza* (☎ 223-1221),

Avenida 1, Calles 7 & 9, which is reputedly the nation's oldest pizzería. *Chosa del Indio*, in the north-eastern suburb of Sabanilla, 100 metres east of the church, serves typical Costa Rican food in rustic surroundings. There are also plenty of US-style fast-food places.

Entertainment
Bars & Discotheques The free weekly leaflet *Info-Spectacles* has information on live music. Issued on Tuesdays, it's available at many of the places mentioned here and at the ICT information office.

El Cuartel de la Boca del Monte (☎ 221-0327), Avenida 1, Calles 21 & 23, is a popular nightspot for young people. The music is sometimes recorded, sometimes live (on Wednesdays especially), but always loud. The packed back room has a small dance floor – a good place to meet young ticos.

Contravía (☎ 253-6989), 100 metres south of the Banco Popular in San Pedro, is popular with politically aware students for it's Nueva Trova music and *peñas*. *Baleares* (☎ 253-4577), 100 metres west of the Mas x Menos Supermercado in San Pedro, features Latin music some nights. The *Akelare* (☎ 223-0345), Calle 21, Avenidas 2 & 6, is in a huge mansion with a variety of bands playing a few nights a week. *Catastrofe Bar* (☎ 225-1043), Avenida Central and Calle 35 at the beginning of Los Yoses, features rock.

The well-known *La Esmeralda* (☎ 221-0530), Avenida 2, Calles 5 & 7, open all day and night (except Sunday), is the centre of the city's mariachi tradition. At night there are dozens of strolling musicians around. A few blocks west is the bright *Soda Palace*, Avenida 2, Calle 2, another 24-hour joint. It is open to the street – watch the street action and see who comes in. Musicians wander in later in the evening.

The El Pueblo Shopping Centre has a variety of pricey restaurants and nightspots – wander around on Friday or Saturday night and take your pick; some spots are cheaper than others. Several discotheques charge

US$4 to get in – but usually provide at least the first drink free.

Discotheques downtown include *El Tunel de Tiempo*, Avenida Central, Calles 7 & 9, with flashing lights and disco music; and *Dynasty*, in the Centro Comercial del Sur near the Puntarenas railway station, with soul, reggae, calypso, and even rap music. Both have covers of about US$2. Cheaper is the *Salsa 54*, Calle 3, Avenidas 1 & 3, with Latin music. Slightly more expensive is the *La Torre*, Calle 7, Avenidas Central & 1, with a mostly gay clientele. In San Pedro, *Club Crocodrilo*, Calle Central opposite the Banco Anglo, is a large bar with dance floor and videos, popular with students.

Theatre Theatres advertise in the local newspapers, including *The Tico Times*. Many performances are in Spanish, but prices are moderate.

The most important theatre is the Teatro Nacional – the season is April to November, when there are National Symphony Orchestra concerts and other events every few days. There are fewer performances out of season. Tickets are cheap by US/European standards. There are several other theatres featuring music, dance and drama. Buy tickets as early as possible. Theatres rarely have performances on Monday.

Cinemas Cinemas advertise in *The Tico Times* and local newspapers. Recent Hollywood films with Spanish subtitles and English sound are about US$2.

Sport The national sport is soccer. Costa Rica qualified for the World Cup in 1990. International and national games are played in the Estadio Nacional in Parque La Sabana. The soccer season is May to October.

La Sabana also has tennis, volleyball, and basketball courts, baseball areas and jogging paths. There's an Olympic-sized swimming pool, but it's only open from noon to 2 pm and it costs US$3 to swim there. Many ticos prefer the excursion to the Ojo de Agua pool (near Alajuela, frequent buses), where swimming costs about US$0.50 for the whole day.

Things to Buy
A recommended souvenir shop is in the Hotel Don Carlos, Calle 9, Avenida 9. The prices are good and the selection is wide. Other reasonably priced stores with good selections include the government-organised crafts cooperatives, such as CANAPI, Calle 11, Avenida 1, and Mercado Nacional de Artesanía, Calle 11, Avenidas 2 & 4. Also reasonably priced are Arte Rica, Avenida 2, Calles Central & 2, specialising in folk art, and ANDA, Avenida Central, Calles 5 & 7, specialising in pottery and gourd crafts produced by the few local Indians.

La Casona, Calle Central, Avenidas Central & 1, is a complex with a wide selection of items, including imports from other Central American countries. Malety, Avenida 1, Calles 1 & 3, specialises in leather goods, especially cases, handbags and wallets.

The Mercado Central, Avenidas Central & 1, Calles 6 & 8, has a small selection of handicrafts, and it's also the best place to buy fresh coffee beans at a fraction of the price you'd pay at home.

Getting There & Away
Air SANSA (☎ 221-9414, 233-3258, fax 255-2176) flies from Juan Santamaría airport in San José to Golfito (one or two flights daily except Sunday, US$26), Quepos (two or three flights daily, US$15), Nosara (Monday, Wednesday and Friday, US$33), Palmar (Monday, Wednesday and Friday, US$26), Coto 47 (daily except Sunday, US$26), Tamarindo and Samara (daily, US$33), and Barra Colorado (Tuesday, Thursday and Saturday, US$26).

SANSA can check you in at its city office (Calle 24, Paseo de Colón & Avenida 1), and provide transportation to the airport's domestic terminal, a few hundred metres to the right of the international terminal. SANSA reservations must be paid for before they will confirm the booking. You should reconfirm several times – delayed, cancelled or oversold flights are common.

Travelair (☎ 232-7883, 220-3054, fax 220-0413) is a newer, more expensive domestic airline. It has a better service record and flies from Tobias Bolaños airport. You can buy a Travelair ticket from any travel agent or from the Travelair desk at the Tobias Bolaños airport. A taxi is about US$3 from the city centre – no buses.

Travelair flies from San José to Quepos (three flights daily, US$37/64 one way/return), Barra Colorado and Tortuguero (daily, US$54/93), Golfito and Puerto Jiménez (daily, US$70/121, Palmar Sur (daily, US$61/106), Nosara and Samará/Carrillo (daily, US$61/106), Tamarindo (twice daily, US$70/121), and Tambor (twice daily, US$48/85).

Charter flights are available on request from Tobias Bolaños airport.

Juan Santamaría International Airport
    Alajuela, Airport Information (☎ 441-0744)
Tobías Bolaños Airport
    Pavas, Information (☎ 232-8049, 232-2820)

The following international airlines have flights to/from San José. Other airlines are listed in the telephone directory:

Aero Costa Rica
    San Pedro (☎ 253-4753)
American Airlines (USA)
    Paseo Colón, Calles 26 & 28
    (☎ 257-1266, 222-0786)
Aviateca (Guatemala)
    Calle 1, Avenida 3 (☎ 233-8390, 255-4949)
British Airways
    Calle 1, Avenida 5 (☎ 221-7315)
    Calle 32, Paseo Colón & Avenida 2 (☎ 223-5648)
Continental Airlines (USA)
    Calle 19, Avenida 2 (☎ 233-0266)
COPA (Panama)
    Calle 1, Avenida 5 (☎ 223-7033, 221-5596)
Iberia (Spain)
    Paseo Colón, Calle 40 (☎ 221-3311/411)
KLM (Holland)
    Sabana Sur (☎ 220 4111/2/3)
LACSA (Costa Rica)
    Calle 1, Avenida 5 (☎ 231-0033, 221-7315)
LTU (Germany)
    Avenida 9, Calles 1 & 3 (☎ 257-2990)
Mexicana
    Calle 38, Avenidas 3 & 5
    (☎ 222-1711, 233-6597, 222-7147))
Nica (Nicaragua)
    Avenida 1, Calles 11 & 13
    (☎ 223-7243, 255-0515)

SAHSA (Honduras)
    Avenida 5, Calles 1 & 3 (☎ 221-5774/561)
SAM (Avianca) (Colombia)
    Avenida 7, Calles 5 & 7 (☎ 233-3066)
TACA (El Salvador)
    Calle 1, Avenidas 1 & 3 (☎ 222-1790/44)
United (USA)
    Sabana Sur (☎ 220-4844, 220-1665)
Varig (Brazil)
    Avenida 5, Calles 3 & 5 (☎ 221-3087, 221-4004)

Train Since the 1991 earthquake, train services to both coasts have been cancelled indefinitely.

Intertren (☎ 226-0011) has trains from San José to Heredia, leaving from near the UCR (Universidad de Costa Rica) in San Pedro at 5.45 am, noon and 5.15 pm, Monday to Friday, via the old Estación Atlántico in San José (Avenida 3, Calles 21 & 23) en route to the south side of Heredia, near the Universidad Nacional (45 minutes). Sunday trains are at 10 am and noon. Buses from Avenida 2, Calles 5 & 7 in San José go near the railway station – get off at the Iglesia (church) in San Pedro.

Trains for Cartago (50 minutes) leave from the old Estación Atlántico via the UCR in San Pedro at 5 am, 7.15 am, 1.45 pm and 5.30 pm, Monday to Friday. Sunday trains leave at 9 am, 11.30 am and 1.50 pm.

Bus The Coca-Cola, Avenida 1, Calles 16 & 18, is a well-known landmark in San José. Many companies have buses leaving from within three or four blocks of the Coca-Cola, so this is an area to know. It is not in the best part of town; watch for pickpockets. The area is reasonably safe, although late at night you might take a taxi.

To/From Nicaragua & Panama Two international bus companies go to/from Managua (Nicaragua) and Panama City. They are used to dealing with border procedures and will wait for passengers who are delayed by the formalities. They are a bit more expensive than taking a regular public bus to the border, but they're convenient and worthwhile.

Tica bus (☎ 221-8954), Calle 9, Avenidas 2 & 4, has daily buses to Managua at 7 am

(11 hours, US$9; though it has reportedly been twice that in the past). Cheaper but less reliable service is provided by Sirca (☎ 222-5541, 223-1464), Calle 7, Avenidas 6 & 8. Buses go to Managua on Monday, Wednesday, Friday, and Sunday at 6 am (11 hours, US$8.50). Tica has a daily service to Panama City (20 hours, US$18) – departure times have varied from early morning to early evening, so ask.

TRACOPA (☎ 221-4214, 223-7685), Avenida 18, Calle 4, has daily directo buses at 7.30 am to David in Panama (nine hours, US$7.50). Tica also has service to David.

To/From Southern Costa Rica TRACOPA (see earlier) has five daily buses to Ciudad Neily (eight hours, US$5.50) and on to the Panamanian border at Paso Canoas. TRACOPA also has six daily buses to Palmar Norte, three daily buses to Golfito (eight hours, US$4.75) and a bus to San Vito (direct, five hours, US$6.50; normal, six hours, US$5.50).

Buses to Coto Brus, en route to San Vito, leave four times a day from Empresa Alfaro (☎ 222-2750, 223-8361), Calle 14, Avenidas 3 & 5.

There are many buses to San Isidro de El General (three hours, US$3) with Transportes Musoc (☎ 223-0686, 222-2422), Calle 16, Avenidas 1 & 3, next to the Coca-Cola terminal. Opposite, TUASUR (☎ 222-9763) also serves San Isidro.

Autotransportes Blanco (☎ 771-2550), opposite the big Puntarenas bus terminal at Calle 12, Avenida 9, has buses for Puerto Jiménez at 6 am and noon.

To/From Meseta Central Buses to Cartago (US$0.40) leave several times an hour from SACSA (☎ 233-5350), Calle 5, Avenida 18. Some buses continue to Turrialba, but more Turrialba buses leave from TRANSTUSA (☎ 222-4464), Avenida 6, Calle 13 (two hours, about US$1). Buses to Heredia (☎ 233-8392) leave several times an hour from Calle 1, Avenidas 7 & 9 (30 minutes, US$0.30). Buses for Alajuela leave every few minutes from TUASA (☎ 222-5325),

Avenida 2, Calle 12 – many of these buses stop at the international airport. Across the street from here, there are buses leaving for Heredia. Buses to Grecia (one hour, US$0.40), and on to Sarchí (US$0.50) leave about once an hour from the Coca-Cola terminal. Buses for San Ramón, halfway to Puntarenas, leave several times an hour from Calle 16, Avenidas 1 & 3, across the street from the Hotel Musoc.

To/From the Pacific Coast Buses for Quepos and Manuel Antonio leave from the Coca-Cola terminal with Transportes Morales (☎ 223-5567). Direct buses to Manuel Antonio, with reserved seats, leave at 6 am, noon and 6 pm (3½ hours, US$5). Slower, cheaper buses to Quepos leave five times a day. Other buses (☎ 232-1829) go to Jacó at 7.15 am and 3.30 pm. Slower, indirect buses (☎ 223-1109) leave at 7.30 am, 10.30 am and 3.30 pm. Empresarios Unidos de Puntarenas (☎ 222-0064) have buses for Puntarenas twice an hour during the day from Calle 12, Avenida 9 (two hours, about US$2.50).

To/From the Península Nicoya Buses for the Península Nicoya either use the Río Tempisque ferry or take the longer route through Liberia. Thus bus times can vary. Empresa Alfaro (see To/From Southern Costa Rica above) has seven daily buses to Nicoya (five hours, US$3), also going to Santa Cruz and Filadelfia. They also have daily buses for beaches at Sámara (noon) and Tamarindo (3.30 pm), as well as a bus to Quebrada Honda, Mansión, and Hojancha (2.30 pm). At Calle 12, Avenidas 7 & 9 (opposite the Puntarenas terminal), is a small office with afternoon buses to Jicaral and the beaches at Bejuco and Islita (five hours, US$5.50). TRALAPA (☎ 221-7202), Calle 20, Avenida 3, has daily buses to Playa Flamingo (8 am and 10.30 am) and Junquillal (2 pm), Tamarindo (4 pm) and Santa Cruz (six daily, US$4.50). The Pulmitan bus station (☎ 222-1650), Calle 14, Avenidas 1 & 3, has a daily bus to Playas del Coco at 10 am (US$3.50). Buses for Playas Panamá and Hermosa leave daily from the stop in front of Los Rodgriguez store, Calle 12, Avenidas 5 & 7. (These are dry season schedules – during the wet season services may be curtailed.)

To/From North-Western Costa Rica Buses to Monteverde leave from the Tilarán terminal (☎ 222-3854), Calle 14, Avenidas 9 & 11. Buses leave at 6.30 am on Saturday and at 2.30 pm from Monday to Thursday; advance ticket purchase is recommended (four hours, US$4 – there may be fewer departures in the wet season). Buses for Tilarán leave at 7.30 am, 12.45 pm, 3.45 pm and 6.30 pm. The ticket office is closed from 12.30 to 2 pm.

Buses for Cañas with Transportes La Cañera (☎ 222-3006) leave six times a day from Calle 16, Avenidas 1 & 3. La Cañera has buses for La Cruz and Santa Cecilia at 2.45 am and Upala at 6.30 am (6 am on Saturday). Upala buses also leave from Calle 12, Avenidas 3 & 5, at 3 and 3.45 pm daily.

Buses for Liberia leave eight times a day from Pulmitan (see above, 4½ hours, US$3). There are three buses daily to the Nicaraguan border at Peñas Blancas (six hours, US$4), with stops at the entrance to Santa Rosa National Park and La Cruz. The office (☎ 224-1968) is next to the Hotel Cocorí, Calle 16, Avenidas 3 & 5.

To/From Northern Costa Rica Buses to Ciudad Quesada (☎ 255-4318; two hours, US$2) via Zarcero (one hour) leave every hour from the Coca-Cola terminal. Direct buses to Puerto Viejo de Sarapiquí (3½ hours, US$3) leave from Avenida 11, Calles Central & 1 six times a day. Some of these buses go via Río Frío and Horquetas (for Rara Avis) and return to San José via Varablanca and Heredia; some do the route in reverse. Buses for Puerto Viejo via Heredia leave at 6 am and noon from the Coca-Cola terminal. Buses for Los Chiles leave from Avenida 3, Calles 18 & 20.

To/From the Caribbean Coast Buses for Puerto Limón (☎ 223-7811; 2½ hours, US$3) leave from Avenida 3, Calles 19 & 21,

with hourly departures via Guápiles. For buses direct to Cahuita, Bribri, and Sixaola, Autotransportes MEPE (☎ 221-0524), Avenida 11, Calles Central & 1, has three departures a day – schedules change. The fare is US$5.75 to Sixaola and US$4.75 to Cahuita (four hours). Some MEPE buses will detour to Puerto Viejo de Talamanca en route to Sixaola; there is a direct bus to Puerto Viejo at 3.30 pm. In front of the Puntarenas bus terminal is a stop with frequent departures to Guápiles, with a few buses continuing to Río Frío. For buses to Siquirres, go to the stop on Calle 12, Avenidas 3 & 5 on the east side.

Getting Around
Local buses are useful to get into the suburbs and surrounding villages, or to the airport. They have set routes and leave regularly from particular bus stops downtown. Buses run from 5 am to 10 pm and cost from US$0.05 to US$0.30. There are too many to list here – ask at ICT.

The Central Valley & Highlands

The local name for this area is La Meseta Central. Historically and geographically it is the heart of Costa Rica. To the north, east and south the region is bounded by mountain ranges containing several volcanoes, including the famous Poás and Irazú. To the west, the Central Valley drops to the Pacific. Four of Costa Rica's seven provinces have fingers of land within the Central Valley, and all four have their political capitals there. About 60% of Costa Rica's population lives in the region.

Many visitors use San José as a base for day trips to the other cities and attractions of the area. Travellers pass through attractive, rolling agricultural countryside that is covered with the shiny-leaved green plants bearing the berries that made Costa Rica famous – coffee.

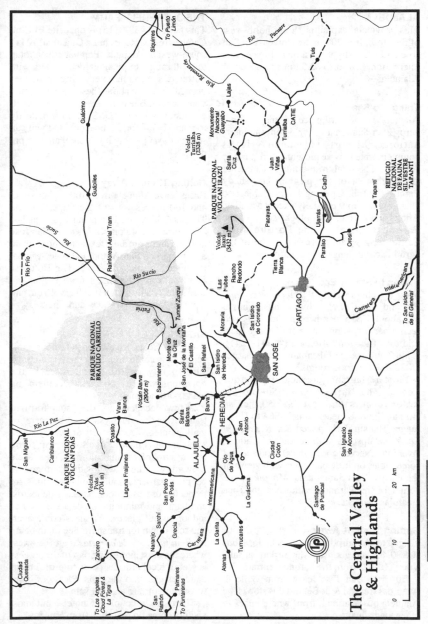

The Central Valley & Highlands

COSTA RICA

ALAJUELA

This provincial capital is 18 km north-west of San José. It is 200 metres lower than San José and has a slightly warmer climate. The international airport is 2.5 km south-east of Alajuela.

Things to See

Alajuela is the birthplace of the national hero, Juan Santamaría, for whom the international airport is named. He is commemorated by a museum and park in Alajuela. The small **museum** is in a former jail north-west of the pleasant and shady Parque Central. Opening hours (subject to change) are 2 to 9 pm daily except Monday. Admission is free. Two blocks south of the Parque Central is the **Parque Juan Santamaría** where there is a statue of the hero in action flanked by cannons.

Places to Stay & Eat

Most travellers stay in San José. The *Hotel Rex* and *Hotel El Real* by the bus terminal are about US$5 per person, but not well recommended – 'much street life' as a local told me. The *Hotel Alajuela* (☎ 441-1241), Calle 2, just south of the main plaza, charges US$24/30 for good rooms.

Most restaurants are near the Parque Central. The *Marisquería La Sirenita* has seafood dinners starting at US$3.50; the *Kun Wa* has Chinese meals in the US$4 to US$6 range. The similarly priced *Bar Restaurant La Jarra*, upstairs at the corner of Calle 2, Avenida 2, serves good typical food and has some tables on little balconies with views of the Parque Juan Santamaría. *Mönpik* on the corner of the Parque Central has good ice cream and snacks.

Getting There & Away

To get to the airport, take a San José bus (US$0.40) and get off at the airport, or take a taxi (US$2) from the Parque Central.

Buses to San José leave from Calle 8, Avenidas Central & 1. Behind this stop is the Alajuela bus terminal, from where buses to other towns leave.

THE BUTTERFLY FARM

This farm (☎ 438-0115) is opposite El Club Campestre Los Reyes in La Guácima, 12 km south-west of Alajuela. Popular educational tours through tropical gardens filled with butterflies explain everything you ever wanted to know about these insects. Bring your camera. Bee tours are also given. Adult admission is a pricey US$11 for the butterfly tour and US$8 for the bee tour, and you can stay all day. Opening hours are 9 am to 5 pm daily.

Getting There & Away

Buses leave Alajuela from 100 metres south and 100 metres west of the Supermercado Tikal at 6.45, 9 and 11 am and 1 pm; the last bus returns at 5.45 pm. Buses leave San José at 11 am and 2 pm daily, except Sunday, from a stop marked San Antonio/Ojo de Agua at Avenida 1, Calles 20 & 22. The Butterfly Farm collects passengers from major San José hotels on its own bus at 8 am, 10 am and 2 pm on Monday, Tuesday and Thursday.

SARCHÍ

Sarchí is Costa Rica's most famous craft centre. It is commercial but there is no pressure to buy anything and there is the opportunity to see wooden handcrafts being made – ask around.

A few decades ago, the usual form of transport in the countryside was by *carretas*, gaily painted wooden carts drawn by oxen. The carreta is now a traditional craft form, and a symbol of agricultural Costa Rica. Nowadays, they are used to decorate people's gardens, scaled-down versions are made for use as indoor tables, sideboards, and bars, and miniature models are used as indoor accent pieces. All sizes come apart and fold down for transport. See them being made in *fábricas de carretas* (cart factories) where the most interesting part of the process is seeing local artisans paint colourful mandalic designs onto the carts. Plenty of other wooden items are also for sale.

There are a couple of hotels, but most visitors come on day trips from San José.

Getting There & Away

Buses for Sarchí leave from the Coca-Cola in San José and the bus terminal in Alajuela. From San José it is often quicker to take a bus to Grecia and connect from there.

PARQUE NACIONAL VOLCÁN POÁS

This popular park lies 37 km north of Alajuela by road. The centrepiece is the active Volcán Poás (2704 metres). The park was closed briefly in 1989 after a minor eruption sent volcanic ash over a km into the air. Now the bubbling and steaming crater poses no imminent threat – though check with the SPN (☎ 257 0922) for current conditions. The crater is 1½ km across and 300 metres deep. Small eruptions take place periodically, with peaceful interludes lasting minutes or weeks. This park is a 'must' for anyone wanting to see an active volcano.

A dwarf cloud forest near the crater has bromeliads, lichens and mosses clinging to the curiously shaped and twisted trees. Birds abound, especially hummingbirds. One of the nature trails leads through this forest to an extinct nearby crater containing a pretty lake.

Information

Opening hours are 8 am to 3 pm daily except Monday. Entrance is US$1.50. There is a ranger station and small museum. There's a snack bar, but bringing your own food is a good idea. There are picnicking areas with drinking water, but there are no hotels or camping areas. The park is crowded on Sundays, when there are often slide shows in the museum auditorium, but it's quieter in the middle of the week.

The best time to go is in the dry season, especially early in the morning before the clouds roll in and obscure the view. It may be windy and cold during the day.

Getting There & Away

A crowded Sunday morning bus leaves San José at 8.30 am from Calle 12, Avenidas 2 & 4. Get there early. The round-trip fare is US$3.50 and the bus returns at 2.30 pm. Another bus leaves Alajuela on Sunday at 8 am from opposite the Restaurant El Cencerro on the Parque Central.

One or two buses a day go from Alajuela to Poásito (no hotels) from where it's a 10-km walk. Hitching is possible but there's little traffic.

Taxis from Alajuela cost about US$20 return, allowing an hour to visit the volcano. Four people could share the cab.

Many companies in San José advertise tours (US$20 to US$70 per person) which arrive at the volcano about 10 am. Some tours spend little time at the crater, so ask.

HEREDIA

This small provincial capital is 11 km north of San José. The city was founded in 1706 and retains some of its colonial character. The **Parque Central** is the best place to see the older buildings. To the east of the park is **La Inmaculada Concepción** church, built in 1797 and still in use. Its squat, thick-walled construction has withstood the earthquakes which have damaged most of the other colonial buildings in Costa Rica. To the north of the park is a colonial fortress called simply **El Fortín**. The area is a national historic site. The Universidad Nacional (National University) on the east side of town contains the **Museo Zoo Marino** (☎ 237-6363, ext 2240 for more information).

Places to Stay

Most travellers stay in San José. In Heredia, the basic *Pensión Herediana* (☎ 237-3217), Calle Central, Avenidas 4 & 6, is family-run and has a nice courtyard. Rooms are US$3.75 per person. The *Hotel Colónial* (☎ 237-5258), Avenida 4, Calles 4 & 6, is clean and family-run and charges US$4.50 per person. If these are full, try the similarly priced basic *Hotel El Parqueo* (☎ 238-2882), Calle 4, Avenidas 6 & 8. The clean *Hotel Verano* (☎ 237-1616), Calle 4, Avenida 6, charges US$11/18 for rooms with private electric showers. The *Casa de Huespedes* (☎ 238-3829) has hot showers and charges US$7.25 or US$9 per person, depending whether you have a private bath.

COSTA RICA

Places to Eat

A decent seafood restaurant is *Restaurant San Antonio*, Avenida 4, Calle 6. The *Bar & Restaurant El Candil* at Calle 4, Avenidas 2 & 4, has good casados for US$2.50. There is a *Pizza Hut* where students hang out, and there are some student bars and cafés near the university: the *El Bulevar* and *La Choza* have been recommended. *Yerba Buena* and *Natura* are vegetarian restaurants near the university.

Getting There & Away

Buses to San José leave from Calle Central, Avenida 4. The half-hour ride costs US$0.30.

Buses north for Barva leave from in front of the Cruz Roja on Calle Central, Avenidas 1 & 3. Buses to San José de la Montaña leave every hour from Avenida 8, Calles 2 & 4. At 5, 6.30 and 11.30 am these buses continue past San Pedro towards Sacramento for access to the Volcán Barva in the Parque Nacional Braulio Carrillo.

Trains leave Heredia at 6.30 am, 1 pm and 6 pm for San José.

BARVA

This colonial village, 2½ km north of Heredia, is a historic monument. It has a pleasant old-world ambience and is fun to stroll around in. To the south-west is **Café Britt** (☎ 260-2748) which has 'coffeetours' for US$11 per person, including a visit to a finca, a bilingual multi-media presentation using actors to describe the historical importance of coffee, and a tasting session. Tours are at 9 am, 11 am and 3 pm from November to April, and at 10 am for the rest of the year (but closed in September).

PARQUE NACIONAL BRAULIO CARRILLO

This national park protects the virgin rainforest which was threatened by the new highway between San José and Puerto Limón. The pristine areas on either side of the highway support many plants and animals.

Most people see the park by driving

through on one of the frequent buses between San José and Limón. The difference between this highway and other roads in the Central Valley is marked. Instead of small villages and large coffee plantations, the panorama is one of rolling hills clothed with thick mountain rainforest. This is the way much of Costa Rica looked in the 1940s. One reason why there is such a huge variety of plant and animal life in Braulio Carrillo is the large range of elevations within the park, from 2906 metres at the top of Volcán Barva to less than 50 metres in the Caribbean lowlands.

Hiking

You can take short hikes from the new San José-Limón road, but it's difficult to get to the area without a tour or a car. If going by car, be sure to park at one of the ranger stations near either entrance to the park on the San José-Limón road. Frequent thefts occur from cars parked elsewhere.

Visiting the park from the Sacramento entrance near San José de la Montaña is the best way to go if you want to climb Volcán Barva. Buses leave from Heredia. Ask the driver where to get off for Volcán Barva.

From the road the signed track climbs to the summit of Barva (about four or five hours round trip at a leisurely pace). The trail goes from Paso Llano (Porrosatí) to Barva's summit (about nine km) and returns to Sacramento if you want to make a round trip of it. From Sacramento back to Paso Llano is about a further five km. There is a ranger station near Sacramento; check with the information office in San José to see when it may be open. Sometimes the rangers will take you up to the top; it's about four km one way. Near the summit there are several lakes. Camping is allowed anywhere you can pitch a tent, but no facilities are provided so you must be self-sufficient. The best time to go is supposedly the 'dry' season (December to April), but it is liable to rain then too. Night temperatures can be below freezing.

Rainforest Aerial Tram

This new project is on the right of the San

José-Limón road, just after leaving the national park. A two to three-km dirt road leads to the 1.7-km tram, which has 20 cars each holding six passengers. The ride is designed to go silently through the rainforest canopy and provide a unique view of the rainforest. The tram was designed by one of the pioneers of canopy research, biologist Don Perry, and is planned to open in mid-1994. The trip will take 45 minutes in each direction and will cost US$47.50. An information centre and viewing platform is planned. Call ☎ 225-8869 for more information.

Next door to the tram is **Don Perry Aventuras** (fax 267-7254 for information). Here, in November 1993, Perry erected his famous Automated Web for Canopy Exploration (formerly at Rara Avis and described in his book *Life Above the Jungle Floor*). A day tour including transfer from San José, breakfast and lunch, a guided hike and orientation lecture and a 20-minute canopy ride on the web costs US$80 per person. Walk-in visitors can get the orientation lecture and web ride for US$40. Day tours which involve guided climbs of tall rainforest trees (using ropes and safety equipment) cost US$110.

Organised Tours
Several travel companies in San José offer guided day tours to Braulio Carrillo and Volcán Barva for about US$75. Cheaper tours are offered by Project Shelter International (☎ 221-9132, fax 257 2273; Apartado 3153-1000, San José). You stay in a basic shelter with cooking facilities next to the Río Corinto, by the eastern boundaries of the national park. Mattresses are provided, bring a sleeping bag. Washing facilities are in the river, there are trails nearby and you should bring food. There is a soda about one km away. Guided tours leave on Monday for two nights – US$35 per person including breakfast; transportation is by public bus.

CORONADO
This is the general name for several villages centred on San Isidro de Coronado, about 15 km north-east of San José. It is a popular destination during the dry season for joséfinos looking for an escape from the city. There are some simple restaurants but no accommodation. The village has an annual fiesta on 15 May.

Instituto Clodomiro Picado
This is a snake 'farm' at Dulce Nombre, about one km from San Isidro de Coronado. The university-run institute has a selection of local poisonous snakes on display. On Friday afternoons visitors can see the snakes being 'milked' for their poison, which is then used to make antivenin. Opening hours are 9 am to 4 pm, Monday to Friday; entry is free.

Getting There & Away
Buses for Coronado leave from Avenida 3, Calles 3 & 5 in San José. From San Isidro it's about a km back to the institute – ask the bus driver.

CARTAGO
Cartago was founded in 1563 and was the capital of the colony until the 1820s but major earthquakes in 1841 and 1910 ruined almost all the old buildings. The city is the capital of Cartago province, and lies at an elevation of 1435 metres, between the Cordillera Central and the Cordillera de Talamanca. Volcán Irazú looms nearby. The city is 22 km south-east of San José, with which it is connected by a good road and rail system.

Things to See & Do – In Cartago
The church at Avenida 2, Calle 2, was destroyed by the 1910 earthquake, and **Las Ruinas** now house a pretty garden. East of the town centre, at Avenida 2, Calle 16, is the most famous church of the Central Valley – **La Basílica de Nuestra Señora de los Angeles**. The story goes that a statue of the virgin was discovered on the site on 2 August 1635, and miraculously reappeared after being removed. A shrine was built on the spot, and today the statue, La Negrita, represents the patron saint of Costa Rica. La Negrita has miraculous healing powers attributed to her, and every year on 2 August

pilgrims arrive on foot from San José, 22 km away. Inside the Basilica is a chapel dedicated to La Negrita, where gifts from cured pilgrims can be seen. Most of the gifts are metal models of parts of the human body which have been miraculously healed. The Basilica was destroyed in the 1926 earthquake and rebuilt in Byzantine style.

Things to See & Do – Around Cartago
Lankester Gardens Six km east of Cartago, the university-run Lankester Gardens (☎ 551-9877) feature an extensive orchid collection and other plants. Catch a Paraíso bus and ask for the turnoff for the gardens. From the turnoff, walk one km to the entrance. Opening hours are 8 am to 3 pm daily; admission is about US$2.50. All year is good, but February, March and April are best for orchids. Free guided tours are sometimes given.

Río Orosi Valley This extends south-east of Cartago and is a popular day trip. There are pretty views, colonial buildings, hot springs, a lake and a wildlife refuge. Many San José companies offer day tours to the valley, but you can visit cheaply by public bus from Cartago. The first village is **Paraíso**, eight km east of Cartago, with decent restaurants. Seven km east of Paraíso is **Ujarrás**, flooded and abandoned in 1833. The ruined 17th-century church and other buildings are interesting to see. A short distance above Ujarrás is a lookout point for the artificial **Lago de Cachí**, formed by a hydroelectric dam.

Six km south of Paraíso is the village of **Orosi** named after a 16th-century Huetar Indian chief and now the centre of an important coffee-growing region. Orosi boasts an early 18th-century church – one of the oldest still in use in Costa Rica. A couple of km south is **Orosi Coffee Adventure** (☎ 533-3030, fax 533 3212) which offers a variety of half-day tours to visit the coffee fincas and other areas of interest – prices are from US$13 to US$30.

About 11 km south of Paraíso is the **Refugio Nacional de Fauna Silvestre**

Tapantí which is good for birdwatching – though very wet. Go in the dry season.

Parque Nacional Volcán Irazú This is the highest active volcano in Costa Rica (3432 metres). A major eruption on 19 March 1963 covered San José and most of the Central Valley with several cm of volcanic ash – it piled up over half a metre deep in places. Since then Irazú's activity has been limited to gently smoking fumaroles in a bare landscape of volcanic ash and craters.

A paved road leads to the summit – there is a car park and a small information centre, open from 9 am to 4 pm. There is no overnight accommodation, camping facilities or food. The entrance fee is US$1.50. From the summit it is possible to see both coasts, but it is rarely clear enough to do so. The best chance is in the early morning during the dry season (January to April). It tends to be cold and cloudy on the summit, so bring warm clothes.

Places to Stay & Eat
There are two cheap and basic flophouses by the railway station, if you're desperate. It's better to stay in San José. There are restaurants in town along Avenidas 2 & 4.

Getting There & Away
Bus Buses arrive from San José on Avenida 2, go as far as the Basilica, then return along Avenida 4. Buses returning to San José leave from Avenida 4, Calles 2 & 4 several times an hour between 5 am and 11 pm (¾ hour, US$0.50).

Buses for Turrialba leave every hour from in front of the Tribunales de Justicia on Avenida 3, Calles 8 & 10 (1½ hours, US$0.90).

Volcán Irazú cannot be reached from Cartago by bus. From San José, Buses Metropolí (☎ 272-0651, 591-1138) has a bus leaving from across the Gran Hotel Costa Rica, Avenida 2, Calles 1 & 3, on Saturday and Sunday at 8 am, returning at 12.15 pm. The fare is US$4.50 and the schedule allows about two hours on the summit.

Train Trains leave Cartago for San José at 6.10 am, 8.20 am, 2.50 pm and 6.35 pm. The station is at Avenida 6, Calles 1 & 3.

Tours
Many tour agencies in San José offer Irazú trips for US$20 to US$60 – the expensive ones have bilingual guides and include visits to Lankester Gardens and the Orosi Valley.

Getting Around
For Paraíso and the Lankester Gardens, the bus leaves from Avenida 1, Calles 2 & 4. For Orosí, the bus leaves from Calle 4 near Avenida 1. These buses leave at least once every hour.

The taxi rank is on the plaza west of the ruined church. A taxi to Irazú is about US$25.

TURRIALBA
This pleasant, friendly and laid-back little town, near the headwaters of the Río Reventazón, is popular with river runners and kayakers. It is a good base for visiting the nearby archaeological monument and agricultural station.

Places to Stay & Eat
Three cheap hotels by the old railway station are the *Hotel Interamericano* (☎ 556-0142), *Hotel Central* and *Hotel Chamango*. The best is the Interamericano which charges US$4.50/7.25 for singles/doubles or US$7.25/11 for rooms with private cold showers. The other two are cheaper. The *Hospedaje Hotel Primavera* is OK at US$3 per person. The *Hotel La Roche* (☎ 556-1624) has clean rooms for US$5/8.50. The *Pensión Chelita* (☎ 556-0214) charges US$5 per person, or US$6.50 in rooms with private bath.

The *Restaurant Nuevo Hong Kong* has good Chinese food at reasonable prices; the *Pizzería Julian* and the *Restaurant La Garza* sell good meals for US$2 to US$5. All three are by the Parque Central.

Getting There & Away
Bus Buses to San José leave every hour from Avenida 4 near Calle 2. Buses for Siquirres leave every two hours from the same place.

The terminal at Avenida 2 and Calle 2 has buses for nearby villages, including Santa Teresita (close to Guayabo) at 10.30 am and 1.30 pm.

CATIE
CATIE stands for Centro Agronómico Tropical de Investigatión y Enseñanza (Centre for Tropical Agronomy Research & Education). The centre is the most important of its kind in Central America. There is an extensive library and research facility, and guided tours can be arranged in advance by calling ☎ 556-6431, 556-1149. Visitors not on a tour can walk around the grounds, which have pleasant paths and a pond which is a good place to see water birds. The centre is four km east of Turrialba on the road to Limón.

MONUMENTO NACIONAL GUAYABO
This is the most important archaeological site in Costa Rica, although it is not as impressive as the Maya sites of northern Central America. The area was occupied from about 1000 BC to 1400 AD and supported 10,000 inhabitants at its height. Archaeologists do not know the exact significance of the site nor why it was abandoned. The excavated area comprises about 10% of the monument.

Things to See & Do
Visitors can see stone-lined canals, mounds and carved stones. The remaining area is rainforest and there are short trails for birdwatching and wildlife observation.

The ruins are open from 8 am to 3 pm on weekends and holidays. Excavation work done during the week may cause parts of the site to be closed. Rangers are available at weekends to show you around. Entrance is US$1.50.

Places to Stay & Eat
Camping is permitted next to the information centre. There are latrines, drinking water and a picnic area.

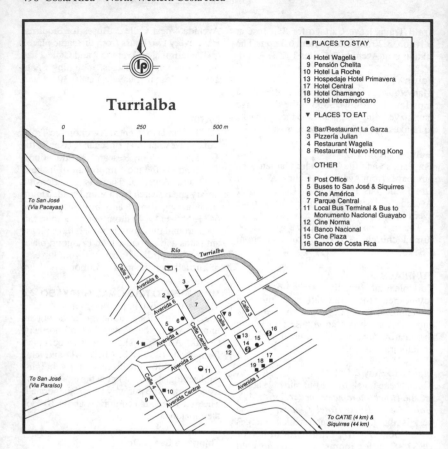

Turrialba

| 0 | 250 | 500 m |

■ PLACES TO STAY

4 Hotel Wagelia
9 Pensión Chelita
10 Hotel La Roche
13 Hospedaje Hotel Primavera
17 Hotel Central
18 Hotel Chamango
19 Hotel Interamericano

▼ PLACES TO EAT

2 Bar/Restaurant La Garza
3 Pizzería Julian
4 Restaurant Wagelia
8 Restaurant Nuevo Hong Kong

OTHER

1 Post Office
5 Buses to San José & Siquirres
6 Cine América
7 Parque Central
11 Local Bus Terminal & Bus to
    Monumento Nacional Guayabo
12 Cine Norma
14 Banco Nacional
15 Cine Plaza
16 Banco de Costa Rica

About one km from the monument is *Albergue La Calzada* (☎ 556-0465), which has a few simple rooms with shared bath at US$16 for singles or doubles. There is a restaurant selling local food. Be sure to call in advance.

Getting There & Away
The monument is 19 km north of Turrialba. There is a bus from Turrialba's main bus station on Sundays at 9 am, returning at 5 pm. Buses for Santa Teresita (also called Lajas) pass within four km of the monument. Taxis charge about US$15.

North-Western Costa Rica

North-west of the Cordillera Central lie two mountain chains, the Cordillera de Tilarán and the Cordillera de Guanacaste. The Cordillera de Tilarán has rolling mountains which used to be covered with cloud forest. The famous Monteverde reserve is a popular destination for those wishing to see this tropical habitat. Separating the two cordilleras is Laguna de Arenal and the nearby Volcán

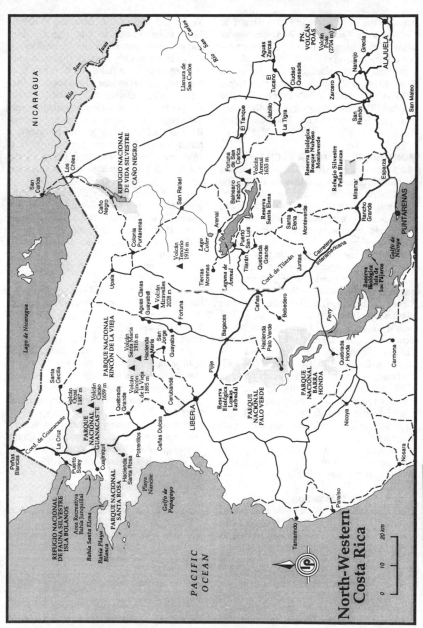

North-Western Costa Rica

Arenal – the most active in Costa Rica. The Cordillera de Guanacaste is a spectacular string of volcanoes, some of which are protected in national parks. West of the Cordillera de Guanacaste is the Peninsula Santa Elena with a rare, dry tropical forest habitat descending to remote Pacific beaches. This area is preserved in the beautiful and historic Parque Nacional Santa Rosa.

MONTEVERDE & SANTA ELENA

Monteverde is a small community founded by North American Quakers in 1951. The cloud forest reserve is just to the east of town. The Quakers bought about 1500 hectares and began dairy farming and cheese production. Today, Monteverde's cheese is sold throughout Costa Rica.

When the settlers arrived, they preserved a third of their property to protect the watershed above Monteverde. In 1972 about 2000 hectares were added – this became the Reserva Biológica Bosque Nuboso Monteverde (Monteverde Cloud Forest Biological Reserve), owned and operated by the Centro Científico Tropical (Tropical Science Centre) of San José. The Monteverde Conservation League (MCL), formed in 1985, continues to expand the protected area. In 1988 the MCL launched the International Children's Rainforest project, whereby school groups from all over the world raise money to save tropical rainforest adjacent to the reserve.

The Reserva Santa Elena was created in 1989 to relieve some of the heavy visitor pressure from Monteverde.

Information & Orientation

The community of Monteverde is scattered along several km of road which leads to the reserve. Several hotels are found along this road. Most of the budget hotels are in the village of Santa Elena, adjoining Monteverde and six km from the reserve.

The information office at the Monteverde reserve entrance is open daily from 7 am to 4 pm (closed on 6 and 7 October). Entrance is US$8 per day (but likely to increase) and

weekly or student discounts are available. The adjoining shop sells trail guides, bird and mammal lists, maps and souvenirs.

Trails are muddy (though the main ones have recently been stabilised with blocks to prevent erosion) and the cloud forest is dripping. Bring raingear and suitable boots. During the wet season some trails turn into quagmires, but there are fewer visitors. Because of the fragile environment, a maximum of 100 people are allowed in at any one time. Come first thing in the morning or you may have to wait for a few hours.

You'll stand a better chance of seeing wildlife if you hire a guide. Half-day guided hikes are arranged at the information office for US$13 per person (plus entrance fee). Night tours are also available. Some hotels can arrange for a local to guide you within the reserve or in the nearby surrounding areas.

Some hotels accept US dollars. There is a bank and small clinic in Santa Elena village.

Things to See & Do

Both reserves have marked and maintained trails but no camping. **Birdwatching** is good both in and around the reserves. Over 400 species have been recorded but most visitors want to see the resplendent quetzal, most easily seen when it is nesting in March and April.

Outside the reserves there are several other trails, including the **Sendero Bajo del Tigre** operated by the MCL; hours are 8 am to 4 pm and admission is US$3. The **Reserva Sendero Tranquilo** (☎ 645-5010/154 for information) offers four-hour guided hikes for US$12.50 per person – group size is two to six people and no more than two groups are allowed on the trail at any time. A free hiking option is the track leaving from behind the Hotel Belmar and climbing up to **Cerro Amigos** (1842 metres) about three km away. Several places advertise **horseback tours** for US$6 to US$10 per hour.

In the community of Monteverde is the interesting **Butterfly Garden**, open from

9.30 am to 4 pm daily. Admission is US$5 and includes an informative tour of the butterfly-raising greenhouses, guided by a biologist – you can then stay all day and get good photos of butterflies.

The local women's **arts & crafts** cooperative, CASEM, sells embroidered and hand-painted blouses, handmade clothing and other souvenirs. Profits benefit the local community. The **Hummingbird Gallery**, near the reserve entrance, has feeders attracting several species of hummingbirds – great photo opportunities!

Tours of the **cheese factory** (La Fábrica) can be arranged between 9 am and 1 pm.

The **Reserva Santa Elena** is five km north-east of Santa Elena village. It is open from 7 am to 4 pm daily and costs US$5.50 to enter. There is a good trail system, you can see quetzals and other birds, and one trail leads to views (weather permitting) of Volcán Arenal. This is an excellent alternative to the Monteverde reserve.

Places to Stay

Most budget hotels are in Santa Elena. The *Hospedaje La Esperanza* (☎ 645-5068/166) is good value for US$4.50 per person, with hot water in the communal showers – ask in the store below. Nearby, the family-run *Pensión El Sueño* (☎ 645-5021) cooks meals on request. Basic rooms are US$3.70 per person, US$7.40 with private bath and hot water.

The *Pensión Santa Elena* (☎ 645-5051) is clean, friendly and has electric showers in the communal bathrooms. Small rooms are US$6 to US$9. Breakfasts (US$3) and casados (US$4.50) are served. Luigi will arrange horse rental etc. Opposite, the basic *Verdulería El Tauro* has rooms at US$3 per person – tepid water in the communal showers. Nearby, the small, clean and friendly *Pensión Colibrí* charges US$5 per person – there is a hot electric shower in the communal bathroom. Casados (US$3.50) are cooked on request and horse rental for US$6 an hour is available. The *Hospedaje El Banco*, behind the bank, is clean, friendly and charges about US$5 per person. The shared electric showers are warm and laundry service and meals are available on request.

The *Pensión Tucán* (☎ 645-5017) is also clean and has hot water in the shared bathrooms. Rooms are US$4 to US$6 per person. Good meals are available. Opposite, the very basic *Pensión El Imán* has horrible little boxes for US$3 per person – the electric showers give only cold water. The *Hotel El Imán* rooms are a little better for about US$6 per person – a restaurant is attached.

About half a km north of Santa Elena is the quiet *Cabinas Marlin*, which has clean rooms with communal bath and hot showers for US$5 per person. About six km north of Santa Elena, near San Gerardo Abajo, is the *El Gran Mirador* – a rustic lodge with good views of Arenal. Double rooms with private bath are US$14.70; dormitory-style rooms with shared baths are US$7.30 per person. Home-cooked meals are served. Guided hiking and horseriding tours are available. To get there you will need a 4WD in the dry season or a horse in the wet months. For information, call the Albergue Bellbird (☎ 645-5026) in Monteverde.

A couple of km south-east of Santa Elena is the friendly *Pensión Manakín* (☎ 645-5080) which charges US$5 per person in rooms with shared bathrooms. There is hot water. They have two rooms (a double and a triple) with private bath for US$20. Good breakfasts are US$3 to US$4 and dinners are US$3 to US$5.

The *Monteverde Inn* (☎ 645-5156) offers rooms with private bath and electric showers for US$20 double and the owners will pick you up at the bus stop if you have a reservation. The new *Albergue Bellbird* (☎ 645-5026) has friendy owners, a restaurant, and clean, decent rooms. Introductory 1993 rates (subject to increase) were US$12/20 for single/double in rooms with shared hot electric bath or US$25 for a double with private bath.

The *Pensión Flor Mar* (☎ 645-5009) is owned by Marvin Rockwell, one of the original Quaker settlers. Simple rooms with shared bath (electric showers) are US$22 per

COSTA RICA

COSTA RICA

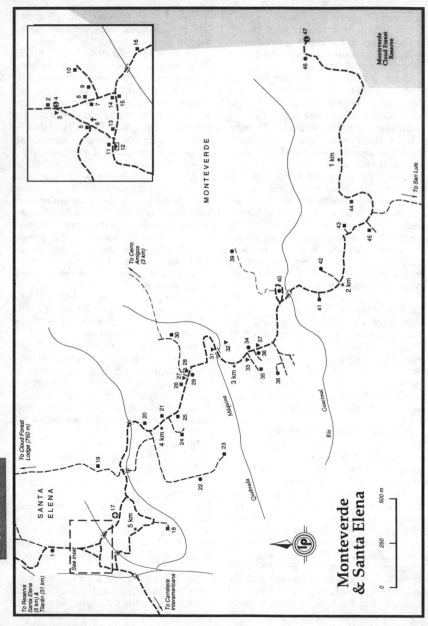

Monteverde
& Santa Elena

■ PLACES TO STAY		35	Cabinas El Bosque		OTHER
		41	Pensión Flor Mar		
2	Hospedaje El Banco	43	Cabinas Mariposa	1	School
5	Hotel El Imán	44	Hotel Villa Verde	4	Bank
7	Verdulería El Tauro	45	Hotel Fonda Vela	6	Church
8	Pensión Santa Elena			12	Post Office
9	Pensión Colibrí	▼	PLACES TO EAT	17	Clinic
10	Albergue Arco Iris			22	Butterfly Garden
	(Hotel &	3	Soda Central	28	Gas Station
	Restaurant)	5	Restaurant El Imán	29	Monteverde Conser-
11	Hospedaje La	10	Albergue Arco Iris		vation League
	Esperanza		(Restaurant &	34	Meg's Riding Stable
13	Pensión El Sueño		Hotel)	36	CASEM
14	Pensión Tucán	14	Soda Tucán	38	Entrance to Bajo El
15	Pensión El Imán	16	Restaurant Finca		Tigre
16	Hotel Finca Valverdes		Valverdes	39	Sarah Dowell's Art
18	Monteverde Lodge	19	El Sapo Dorado		Gallery
19	El Sapo Dorado	27	Soda Cerro Verde	40	La Lechería (Cheese
20	Hotel Heliconia	31	Soda Manantial		Factory)
21	Hotel El Establo	32	Restaurant La	42	Friends' Meeting
23	Monteverde Inn		Cascada		House & School
24	Pensión Manakín	33	Restaurant El Bosque	46	Hummingbird Gallery
25	Hotel de Montaña	37	Stella's Bakery	47	Reserve Entrance &
	Monteverde				Visitor Centre
26	Albergue Bellbird				
30	Hotel Belmar				

person; with private bath US$25 per person. This includes all three meals – they can make a sack lunch.

Camping Camping is permitted on the grounds of a few hotels – about US$1.50 per person includes use of a shower. These hotels include the *Pensión Flor y Mar*, *Cabinas El Bosque*, *Hotel Villa Verde* and *Hotel Fonda Vela* – ask around about other places.

Places to Eat
Budget travellers eat in Santa Elena, where a casado can be had for under US$3. Restaurants include the *Restaurant Imán* and the small *Soda Central* which puts out tasty local food. Also check out the restaurants associated with the *Pensión Tucan*, *Pensión Santa Elena* and *Albergue Arco Iris*.

For picnics, *Stella's Bakery* has homemade bread and rolls and *La Lechería* has fresh cheese. Or try the *Coope Santa Elena* grocery store next to CASEM.

The *El Bosque Restaurant* is a popular place serving good lunches and dinners for about US$4 to US$6 from noon to 9 pm daily. The similarly priced *Soda Cerro Verde*

has good food but the menu has no prices and I've heard that gringos get charged more than locals. Ask before you order. The *Soda Manantial* is another inexpensive choice in Monteverde.

The *Restaurant La Cascada* is popular, especially among young folks who hang around for the dancing afterwards. Good dinners (main courses for US$4 to US$8) are served from 6 to 9 pm. The disco/bar takes over from 9 pm to 1 am, Thursday to Sunday.

Getting There & Away
Buses to Monteverde leave San José from the Tilarán terminal (☎ 222-3854), Calle 14, Avenidas 9 & 11, at 6.30 am on Saturday and 2.30 pm from Monday to Thursday (five hours, US$4). Advance ticket purchase is recommended.

Most hotels in Monteverde/Santa Elena have bus information. Buses to San José go at 6.30 am, Tuesday to Thursday, and 3 pm Friday and Sunday.

In Monteverde, the last bus stop from San José is by La Lechería – ask to get off near your hotel. Buses return to San José from La Lechería.

COSTA RICA

A daily bus from Puntarenas to Santa Elena leaves from the beach between Calles 2 & 4 at 2.15 pm daily (3½ hours). The bus returns to Puntarenas at 6 am from next to the bank in Santa Elena.

A daily bus leaves Tilarán at noon for Santa Elena (three hours, US$2). From Santa Elena, the bus leaves for Tilarán from the *Hotel/Restaurant El Imán* at 7 am daily.

CAÑAS

This small, hot, lowland town is an agricultural centre which travellers use as a base for visits to the nearby Parque Nacional Palo Verde and for Corobicí river trips. Cañas is also the beginning/end of the Arenal back roads described later.

Organised Tours

Safaris Corobicí (☎/fax 669-1091; Apartado 99-5700, Cañas, Guanacaste) are five km north of Cañas on the Interamericana, just south of Hacienda La Pacífica. They offer daily trips on the Río Corobicí – a two-hour float is US$35 per person, a three-hour birdwatching float is US$43 per person, and a half-day saltwater estuary trip along the Bebedero and Tempisque rivers, bordering the Parque Nacional Palo Verde, costs US$50 per person, lunch included. The river float is gentle (Class I and II) and is good for wildlife watching.

Places to Stay & Eat

The *Hotel Guillén* (☎ 669-0070) and *Hotel Parque* are on the south-eastern side of the Parque Central. The Guillén is US$3 per person or US$3.75 with private bath; the marginally nicer Parque is US$3.50 per person.

The *Gran Hotel* on the north-western side of the parque is US$3 per person or US$9.50 for fairly basic double rooms with private bath. The *Cabinas Corobicí* (☎ 669-0241), Avenida 2 and Calle 5, are a little more pleasant and charge US$7 per person with private bath. None of these has hot showers.

The best place is the *Hotel Cañas* (☎ 669-0039; Apartado 61, Cañas, Guanacaste), Calle 2, Avenida 3. Rooms with private cold baths and fan are US$8.50/14.50 for a single/double; with air-con US$11/20. This hotel has a good restaurant and is very popular. Decent Chinese restaurants include the *Restaurant El Primero* on the parque and the *Restaurant Lei Tu* just off the parque on Avenida 1. Meals are US$2 to US$4.

Six km north of Cañas along the Interamericana is the *Rincón Corobicí* restaurant with good (though not cheap) food, outdoor dining, and an area where you can camp.

Getting There & Away

Buses from San José leave six times a day from Calle 16, Avenidas 1 & 3, opposite the Coca-Cola (3½ hours, US$2.50).

The new Cañas bus terminal and market is at Calle 1 and Avenida 11 – most buses leave from here. Some San José buses still leave from the La Cañera bus stop at Avenida Central and Calle 5. Eventually, all buses will leave from the new terminal. Buses for San José leave from the new terminal at 6 am, 9.15 am, 12.30 pm and 2.15 pm and from La Cañera stop at 4.30 am (except Sunday), 5.15, 6 and 9.15 am, and 2 pm.

The new terminal has seven daily buses to Liberia; seven daily to Tilarán; two daily to Las Juntas de Abangares; six daily to Bebedero (near Parque Nacional Palo Verde); five daily to Upala; and seven daily to Puntarenas. Not all buses originate in Cañas – many just stop here, such as the Liberia-Cañas-Puntarenas bus.

PARQUE NACIONAL PALO VERDE

This park on the north-eastern banks of the mouth of Río Tempisque, 30 km west of Cañas, is a major bird sanctuary. Several different habitats are found: swamps, marshes, mangroves, lagoons and a variety of seasonal grasslands and forests. Low limestone hills provide lookouts over the park. The December-March dry season is marked and much of the forest dries out. During other months, large areas are flooded.

September to March has a huge influx of migratory and endemic birds – one of the greatest concentrations of waterfowl and shorebirds in Central America. When the dry season begins, birds congregate in the lakes and marshes, trees lose their leaves and the massed flocks become easier to observe. December to February are the best months – bring binoculars.

Park admission is US$1.50 per day. Camping (US$2.25 per person) is permitted near the Palo Verde ranger station, where there are toilets and shower facilities. Rangers sometimes lead horse or boat trips for a fee.

Information is available from the Area de Conservación Tempisque (ACT) office (☎ 671-1062) run by the SPN in Bagaces (22 km north of Cañas on the Interamericana). Alternatively, call the SPN ranger station's radio telephone (☎ 233 4160) if you speak Spanish, and ask for Palo Verde.

The park is reached by a 28-km road leaving the Interamericana from in front of the ACT office. There are no buses.

RESERVA BIOLÓGICA LOMAS BARBUDAL

This reserve is just north of Palo Verde and until recently was a good example of tropical dry forest with riparian areas. Lomas Barbudal was locally famous for its abundance and variety of insects, including some 250 different species of bees – about a quarter of the world's bee species.

A devastating brushfire burnt 85% of the reserve in 1994. It will be years before the plant life recovers and longer before the animal life returns.

The reserve is administered by the SPN – information can be obtained from their ACT office in Bagaces. The Amigos de (Friends of) Lomas Barbudal (☎ 667-1069, fax 667 1203) also have a Bagaces office and sell bird checklists and trail guides, and provide information.

Entrance is US$1.50 and you can camp for US$2.25 per person. At the entrance is the *Casa de Patrimonio* – a museum and information centre run by the nearby community of San Rafael de Bagaces. If it is closed, ask at the Familia Rosales, less than a km to the

right. The reserve is on the other side of the Río Cabuyo behind the museum.

The turnoff to Lomas Barbudal from the Interamericana is at Pijije, 12 km north-west of Bagaces. The seven-km road to the reserve is signposted.

LIBERIA

Liberia, the capital of Guanacaste province and Costa Rica's most northerly important town, is a ranching centre and transport hub. It is a good base for visiting the nearby national parks.

Information

A tourist office (☎ 666-1606), in a 19th-century house on the corner of Avenida 6 and Calle 1, is open 9 am to noon and 1 pm to 6 pm from Tuesday to Saturday, and 9 am to 1 pm on Sunday.

Places to Stay & Eat

The *Hotel Liberia* (☎ 66-0161), south of the parque on Calle Central, has basic but adequate rooms for US$4.50 per person or US$11 double with private cold shower. The *Hotel Guanacaste* (☎ 666-2287, fax 666-0085) is affiliated with the youth hostels and has a restaurant. It is on Avenida 1, a block off the Interamericana, and is popular with Costa Rican truck drivers and families. Rooms vary – check in early for the best choice. Rates are US$11/16.50/22 for one to three people; add US$1.50 for a fan and US$5 for air-con. Other cheap and basic hotels include *Hotel Cortijo*, Avenida Central, Calles 3 & 5, and the *Hotel Rivas*, on the corner of the plaza.

On the west side of the plaza, *Las Tinajas* is a good place to sit outside with a cold drink and watch the unenergetic goings on. Meals are reasonably priced. There are several Chinese restaurants and sodas near the plaza. *La Casona Pizzería*, Calle 1 & Avenida 4, is in a nice 19th-century house and has a wood-burning oven and art gallery.

Getting There & Away

Pulmitan buses from San José (4½ hours, US$3) leave eight times a day from the

COSTA RICA

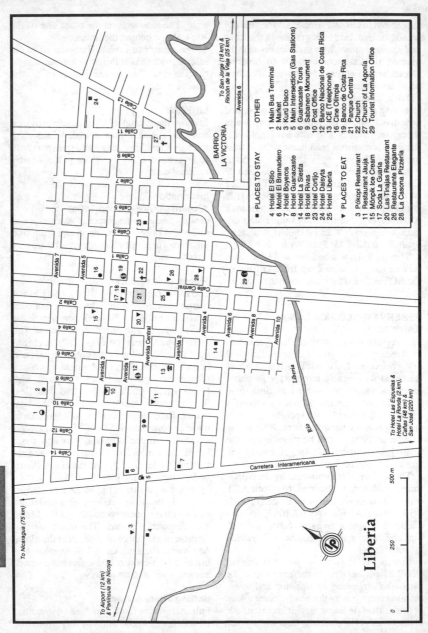

COSTA RICA

Liberia

■ PLACES TO STAY

4   Hotel El Sitio
6   Motel El Bramadero
7   Hotel Boyeros
8   Hotel Guanacaste
14 Hotel La Siesta
18 Hotel Rivas
23 Hotel Cortijo
24 Hotel Daisyta
25 Hotel Liberia

▼ PLACES TO EAT

3   Pokopi Restaurant
11 Restaurant Jauja
15 Mönpik Ice Cream
17 Soda La Guaria
20 Las Tinajas Restaurant
26 Restaurante Elegante
28 La Casona Pizzería

OTHER

1   Main Bus Terminal
2   Market
3   Kurú Disco
5   Main Intersection (Gas Stations)
6   Guanacaste Tours
9   Sabanero Monument
10 Post Office
12 Banco Nacional de Costa Rica
13 ICE (Telephone)
16 Cine Olimpia
19 Banco de Costa Rica
21 Parque Central
22 Church
27 Church of La Agonía
29 Tourist Information Office

To San Jorge (18 km) &
Rincón de la Vieja (25 km)

BARRIO
LA VICTORIA

Avenida 6

To Nicaragua (75 km)

To Airport (12 km)
& Peninsula de Nicoya

Carretera   Interamericana

To Hotel Las Espuelas &
Hotel La Ronda (2 km);
Cañas (46 km) &
San José (220 km)

Río   Liberia

terminal at Calle 14, Avenidas 1 & 3 (☎ 222-1650).

The Liberia bus terminal is on Avenida 7, a block from the Interamericana. Buses for San José leave at 6, 6.30 and 9 am and at 12.15 and 5 pm – others stop by en route from the Nicaraguan frontier. Filadelfia, Santa Cruz and Nicoya (US$1.25) are served on the hour from 5 am to 6 pm, plus other departures. Buses for Playas del Coco leave at 5.30 and 8.15 am and at 12.30, 2, 4.30 and 6.15 pm. Buses for Playa Hermosa and Playa Panamá leave at 11.30 am and 7 pm.

Buses for La Cruz and the Nicaraguan border leave eight times a day – they'll stop at the entrance to Parque Nacional Santa Rosa. Other buses go to local towns.

Buses go to Bagaces and Cañas at 5.45 am, 1.30 and 4.30 pm, and to Puntarenas at 5, 8.30, 10 and 11.15 am and 3.15 pm.

A taxi stand north-west of the plaza has cabs to Santa Rosa (US$15) and to Rincón de la Vieja (US$30 to US$40).

PARQUE NACIONAL RINCÓN DE LA VIEJA

The active Volcán Rincón de la Vieja (1895 metres) is the main attraction. Cones, craters and lagoons in the summit area can be visited on horseback or on foot. There are fumaroles and boiling mud pools, steam vents and sulphurous springs to explore.

Elevation changes result in a variety of different habitats and wildlife. Almost 300 species of birds have been recorded. Many mammals are present, including tapirs in the highlands. Insects include beautiful butterflies and annoying ticks (especially in grassy areas such as the meadow in front of the ranger station – long trousers tucked into boots and long-sleeved shirts are some protection). Plant life includes the orchid *Cattleya skinneri*, Costa Rica's national flower.

Information & Orientation

The park is 25 km north-east of Liberia by a poor road, and is not heavily visited. The park is in the Area de Conservación Guanacaste (ACG) administered by the SPN – information is available from the ACG headquarters at Santa Rosa (☎ 695-5598). Entrance is US$1.50 and camping is US$2.25 per person.

A short nature trail leads through the forests around the Santa María Ranger Station. From the station, a trail leads three km west to sulphurous hot springs with supposed therapeutic properties. A further three km takes you to the boiling mud pools of Las Pailas. Watch your step, because the edges are sometimes weak. From Las Pailas a trail leads north. After about two km, a fork to the left leads to Las Hornillas – sulphurous fumaroles about four km from the mud pools. There are waterfalls nearby. Continuing north from the fork takes you to the summit area. The highest point is about nine km beyond the mud pools.

Places to Stay

You can camp in most places if you are self-sufficient and prepared for cold and foggy weather. A compass is useful. The wet season is very wet, and there are lots of mosquitoes. You can sleep at the ranger station if you make arrangements with the park service in advance. There are a couple of old beds, or you can sleep on the wooden floor – bring your sleeping bag. Meals can be arranged for about US$2 or US$3 each, and horses can be hired.

The private *Hacienda Lodge Guachipelín* (☎ 441-6994/545, 441-4318, fax 442-1910) is near the southern boundary of the park. Dormitory rooms start at US$7 per person and more expensive accommodation is available. Five km further is the *Rincón de la Vieja Lodge* (☎ 666-2369, 233-7970, fax 666-0473) affiliated with the youth hostels. Dormitory rooms start at US$20 (HI members get a discount) and private rooms are available. Both lodges offer meals, tours, guides and horse rentals. The second lodge is two km from the mud pools and five km from the hot springs.

Getting There & Away

Hike to the ranger station, or take a taxi on the road that heads north-east out of Liberia through the Barrio La Victoria suburb. After 18 km the road passes San Jorge village and continues as far as the station. Call the ACG in Santa Rosa to ask if any SPN vehicles are going up – occasionally a ride can be arranged.

The Rincón de la Vieja Lodge is an eight-km hike from the ranger station. Alternatively, go five km north of Liberia on the Interamericana, turn right onto a gravel road 10 km to the village of Curubandé, then follow the blue arrows to Hacienda Lodge Guachipelín (six km) and on to the Rincón de la Vieja Lodge (five more km). The lodges can provide transport – otherwise you're on your own.

PARQUE NACIONAL SANTA ROSA
The park is named after Hacienda Santa Rosa, where a battle was fought in 1856 between Costa Rica and the invading forces of the US filibuster, William Walker. The park protects the last large stand of tropical dry forest in Central America, as well as important sea turtle nesting sites.

Information
The park entrance is on the west side of the Interamericana, 35 km north of Liberia. It is open from 7 am to 5 pm daily. Admission is US$1.50, and it costs US$2.25 per person to camp.

It is seven km (no transport) to the park (and ACG) headquarters (☎ 695-5598). Here are administrative offices, scientists' quarters, an information centre, camping ground, museum, and nature trail. The camping ground (one of the best-developed in the SPN) has drinking water, picnic benches, flush toilets, and cold showers. Large fig trees provide shade. A 4WD trail leads down to the coast, 12 km away. Campsites on the coast have drinking water and latrines, but no showers. Meals can be arranged in advance with the SPN, or bring your own food. Horses are available for hire and rangers may allow travellers to accompany them on their patrols.

The December to April dry season is the most comfortable time to visit, but the wet months of September and October are the best for watching sea turtles nesting.

Things to See & Do
The **museum** is in the historic Santa Rosa Hacienda. Exhibits explain the 1856 war and show Costa Rican life in the 19th century. There are antique firearms, furniture and tools. A display interpreting the ecological significance and wildlife of the park is also here.

Near the museum is a one km **nature trail**, with signs interpreting the ecological relationships between the plants, animals and weather patterns of Santa Rosa. You will see a variety of plants and birds and probably, if you move slowly and keep your eyes and ears open, monkeys, snakes, iguanas and other animals.

The best turtle beach is **Nancite**, and during September and October you may see as many as 8000 olive ridley turtles on the beach at once! Nancite beach is strictly protected and restricted, but permission can be obtained from the park service to see this spectacle.

Getting There & Away
Buses between Liberia and Peñas Blancas will stop at the entrance. The ranger has a timetable for buses passing the park to leave.

PARQUE NACIONAL GUANACASTE
This park is separated from Santa Rosa by the Interamericana and is an extension of Santa Rosa's habitats, but the terrain soon begins to climb towards Volcán Orosí (1487 metres) and Cacao (1659 metres). The park enables animals to range from the coast to the highlands, just as many of them have always done.

Places to Stay
Three biological stations in the park have dormitories for 30 to 40 people, and bathrooms with cold water. A bed and three meals cost about US$20 a day – if you can get in. Camping near the stations costs US$2.25 per night. Horses are available for hire. Make

arrangements at Santa Rosa headquarters (☎ 669-5598) or in San José to camp or stay.

PEÑAS BLANCAS
This is the border with Nicaragua, but there's nowhere to stay. The Costa Rican Oficina de Migraciones (☎ 666-9025) is next to the Restaurant La Frontera (☎ 666-9156/75). There are tourist information and bus ticket offices in this building. Opening hours are 8 am to 5 pm daily on the Costa Rican side, till 4 pm on the Nicaraguan side. Lunch is from noon to 1 pm. It is four km between the Costa Rican and Nicaraguan immigration offices – minibuses charge about US$1 and there are taxis. Exit fees are reportedly US$2 to leave Nicaragua and less than US$1 to leave Costa Rica.

Moneychangers at the Costa Rican post give good rates for US cash dollars, but travellers' cheques receive worse rates in the border bank. Both colones and córdobas are freely available. Excess córdobas or colones can be sold, but at a small loss.

There are four or five buses a day to the first Nicaraguan city, Rivas (37 km). Get to the border by early afternoon to get on a bus, and watch your luggage – many cases of pilfering on Nicaraguan buses have been reported. Recently, citizens of Canada, New Zealand, Australia and some European nations required a visa to enter Nicaragua – check with the Nicaraguan Embassy in San José.

Buses to Liberia and San José leave five times a day – the last in early afternoon. There are later buses to the first Costa Rican town, **La Cruz** (20 km). Here the best hotel is *Cabinas Santa Rita* (☎ 666-9062) which has clean doubles with private cold showers for US$14.50 – three other places are cheaper.

CIUDAD QUESADA
Locals call this town San Carlos. Quesada is not a major destination but it's a good place to spend the night en route to Arenal. Almost everything of importance is on the plaza, or close to it.

Places to Stay & Eat
The cheapest place to stay is the very basic and noisy *Hotel Terminal* (☎ 460-0301), in the bus terminal half a block from the parque. North of the parque, the first two blocks of Calle 2 have a street produce market and several cold-water-only hotels in the US$3 to US$6 per person price range. These include the *Ugalde* (☎ 460-0260), *Cristal* (☎ 460-0541), *Axel Alberto* (☎ 460-1423) and *Hotel Los Helechos*. They all look OK. A couple of better hotels on the parque are US$7 to US$12 per person.

The *Tonjibe* on the plaza is a good place for a meal, and there are others nearby.

Getting There & Away
Buses from San José leave the Coca-Cola terminal several times a day (two hours, US$1.50). It is an attractive ride over the western flanks of the Cordillera Central.

The Quesada terminal is half a block from the Parque Central. Buses return to San José about every hour during the day. Buses to Fortuna take two hours and leave six times a day. Buses to Tilarán take 4½ hours and leave at 6.30 am and 3 pm. There are five buses daily east to Venecia (one hour) and on to Puerto Viejo de Sarapiquí. Buses go to other nearby villages throughout the day.

FORTUNA & VOLCÁN ARENAL
Fortuna is the nearest village to the spectacular Volcán Arenal (1633 metres) which looms six km to the west. The volcano was dormant until 1968, when huge explosions triggered lava flows which killed several dozen people. Despite this massive eruption, the volcano retains its almost perfect conical shape and, with its continuing activity, Arenal is everyone's image of a typical volcano. The best night-time views are from the other (west) side of the volcano looking east at the red lava flows. The degree of activity varies from week to week; sometimes there is red-hot lava flowing and incandescent rocks flying through the air.

Many local hotels and tour operators arrange night tours to view the phenomenon – prices are around US$6 to US$8 per

COSTA RICA

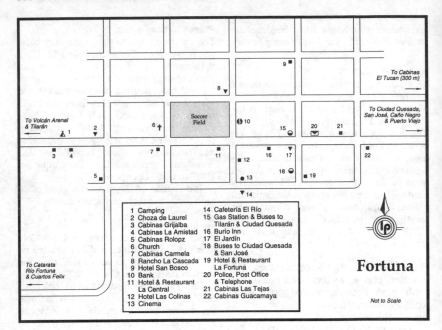

1 Camping
2 Choza de Laurel
3 Cabinas Grijalba
4 Cabinas La Amistad
5 Cabinas Rolopz
6 Church
7 Cabinas Carmela
8 Rancho La Cascada
9 Hotel San Bosco
10 Bank
11 Hotel & Restaurant
   La Central
12 Hotel Las Colinas
13 Cinema
14 Cafetería El Río
15 Gas Station & Buses to
   Tilarán & Ciudad Quesada
16 Burío Inn
17 El Jardín
18 Buses to Ciudad Quesada
   & San José
19 Hotel & Restaurant
   La Fortuna
20 Police, Post Office
   & Telephone
21 Cabinas Las Tejas
22 Cabinas Guacamaya

Fortuna

Not to Scale

person, and this is a very popular trip. Many of these tours include a dip in the Tabacón hot springs after the volcano visit. Other tours are available. This is a small town – ask around for what you need.

Places to Stay

The helpful *Hotel La Central* (☎ 479-9004, fax 479 9045) is basic but clean, and it's popular with budget travellers. There is a restaurant and US dollars can be exchanged. Rooms with shared showers are US$4.50 per person.

Many small, friendly, family-run hotels with shared electric showers have opened recently, charging about US$7 per person – but few singles. These include the *Cabinas Grijalba* (☎ 479-9129), *Cabinas Carmela* (☎ 479-9010), *Cabinas La Amistad* (☎ 479-9035) in town and *Cuartos Felix* about three km out of town towards the Catarata Río Fortuna.

Other cheap possibilities include *Cabinas Las Tejas* (☎ 479-9077) and *Cabinas Via Fortuna* (☎ 479-9139).

More up-market choices are the *Hotel La Fortuna* (☎ 479-9197), *Cabinas Rolopz* (☎ 478-8058) and *Cabinas Guacamaya* (☎ 479-9087) which charge US$15 to US$20 for doubles with private electric shower. There are more expensive places too.

Places to Eat

The most popular is *El Jardín* – budget travellers should stick with the casado for about US$2.50. Other inexpensive eateries include the restaurants in the hotels *Fortuna* and *Central* and the *Cafetería El Río*. Slightly more up-market is the attractive *Rancho La Cascada*.

Getting There & Away

Buses from San José's Coca-Cola leave at 6.15, 8.40 and 11.30 am – otherwise go to Quesada and change.

Fortuna has two bus stops – one in front of the gas station with buses for Tilarán; the other across from Hotel La Fortuna with buses for San José. Buses for Quesada leave from both stops. There are four buses daily to Quesada (all in the morning) and two afternoon buses to San José. There are also buses *de paso* which come through town on their way to somewhere else – ask about times.

ARENAL

This village, also called Nuevo Arenal, is the only town on Laguna de Arenal. There are a couple of stores and a bus stop near the plaza. A new botanical garden opened in 1993, about 4½ km south-east of the village.

Places to Stay

La Casona del Lago (☎ 231-4266) is 1½ km east of Arenal. It is affiliated withe IYHF and information is available in San José at the Toruma Youth Hostel. Overnight rates for IYHF members are US$15 including breakfast – nonmembers pay US$25.

Opposite the town's bus stop is *La Cage des Tigres* (☎ 695-5266, ext 112) with three rooms with private bath for US$15 a double. There are reportedly a couple of cheaper places.

Getting There & Away

Buses to Quesada leave at 8 am and 1.30 pm, and there are five buses daily to Tilarán.

TILARÁN

This small town, near the south-west end of Laguna de Arenal, is the centre of a ranching area. There's a rodeo here in the last weekend in April, and the hotels are often full at that time. There is another fiesta on 13 June. It is also the main windsurfing centre in Costa Rica – the nearby lake (five or six km away) has consistently high winds that attract experienced windsurfers.

Places to Stay & Eat

Cabinas Mary (☎ 695-5479), on the south side of the plaza, is good, clean, pleasant, and has a recommended reasonably priced restaurant. Rooms with private electric shower are US$6/11 for singles/doubles or US$4.50 per person with communal shower. The *Hotel Central* (☎ 695-5363), south-east of the church and 350 metres south of the main entrance road into town, has basic but clean rooms at US$4 per person, or cabins with private bath for US$10 a single or double. *Cabinas Lago Lindo* is a block from the parque and has clean rooms for US$6 per person. The basic *Hotel Grecia* on the parque charges US$5 per person.

There are two surfing resorts at the lakeshore – the best is *Hotel Tilawa Viento Surf* (☎ 695-5050, fax 695-5766) which charges US$600 per person for a complete eight-day package with all gear, transport and accommodation. Also try *Cabinas Puerto San Luis* (☎ 695-5750, fax 695-5387) which charges US$50 a double plus US$25 for windsurfing board rental.

Getting There & Away

Buses from San José (four hours, US$2.50) leave from Calle 14, Avenidas 9 & 11, four times a day.

In Tilarán the terminal is half a block from the parque. Buses to San José leave daily at 7 am, 7.45 am, 2 pm and 4.50 pm. The Sunday afternoon bus is usually sold out by Saturday. (These buses go via Cañas, not Fortuna.) Buses to Arenal leave at 10 am and 4 pm; to Quesada at 7 am and 12.30 pm; to Puntarenas at 6 am and 1 pm; and to Santa Elena (via Monteverde) at noon. Several small local towns are served by this terminal.

The Northern Lowlands

The original vegetation of the northern lowlands was mixed tropical forest, becoming increasingly evergreen towards the Caribbean. Now, much of this has been replaced by cattle pasture. The climate is wet and hot, and towards the Caribbean the dry season is shorter and not entirely dry. The population density is low, with a few small

COSTA RICA

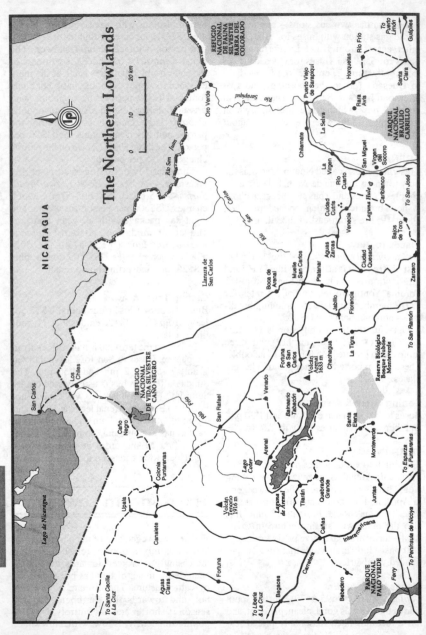

towns, a skeleton of roads, and limited tourist facilities.

LOS CHILES

This small town is on the Río Frío, three km from the Nicaraguan border. Its main interest is as an access to the Caño Negro refuge. It is rarely used by foreigners crossing into Nicaragua, although this is reportedly possible. The nearest Nicaraguan town is San Carlos on Lago de Nicaragua, which is connected to the rest of Nicaragua by a boat every two days. There is a Migraciones office open from 8 am to 4 pm, Monday to Friday.

Boat tours are offered from the Río Frío boat dock into the Caño Negro refuge – excellent bird and wildlife observation. Boats cost US$45 to US$80 to hire for half a day, so get a group together. Alternatively, hook up with a group in Fortuna.

Places to Stay & Eat

The best is the *Hotel Carolina* (☎ 471-1151, 471-1116) with basic rooms with a fan and cold shower for US$5.50 per person or less with shared shower. It is by the entrance to town. Nearby, the *Soda Sonia* offers reasonably priced tico food. Other cheap places near the parque include the *Hotel Río Frío* (☎ 471-1127), the *Hotel Central* and the *Restaurant El Parque*.

Getting There & Away

Boat A boat leaves daily at 8 am for San Carlos, Nicaragua, 14 km away. The fare is US$4.

Bus There are nine buses daily between Ciudad Quesada and Los Chiles – a 91-km drive on paved roads.

PUERTO VIEJO DE SARAPIQUÍ

Locally called Puerto Viejo, this shouldn't be confused with Puerto Viejo de Talamanca on the Caribbean. The town is at the confluence of the Río Puerto Viejo and the Río Sarapiquí, and used to be an important port on the trade route to the Caribbean. Today the region is known for its nearby, undisturbed premontane tropical wet forest, which extends out from the northern arm of Parque Nacional Braulio Carrillo. The easiest access to the rainforest is from the local lodges and research station – all expensive but good.

Places to Stay & Eat

Budget travellers stay on the main street. The *Cabinas Restaurant Monteverde* (☎ 766-6236) charges US$7/10 for singles/doubles with private cold bath. The restaurant is popular and reasonable. The *Restaurant Cabinas La Paz* (☎ 766-6257) has cheaper poor and old rooms and better new ones. The basic and run-down *Hotel Santa Marta* charges US$3 per person. There are several sodas and bars.

Getting There & Away

Buses from San José leave six times a day from a bus stop on Avenida 11, Calles Central & 1 (3½ hours, US$3). Most go via Río Frío and Horquetas; some go the other way. From Puerto Viejo to San José there are seven buses daily – the bus stop is on the main street. There are also five buses daily between Quesada and Puerto Viejo.

Motorised dugouts can be hired from the small port, and there is an 11 am boat daily down the Río Sarapiquí and on to the Río San Juan – US$2. Local lodges can arrange (expensive) boats to almost anywhere in north-eastern Costa Rica.

AROUND PUERTO VIEJO
La Selva

This biological station is five km south-east of Puerto Viejo, and is run by the Organisation of Tropical Studies (OTS) (☎ 240-9938, 240-6696, fax 240-6783). The place teems with researchers and grad students of tropical ecology. The many km of trails can be visited for US$17 per day or US$84 per day including meals and accommodation at the *Biological Station*. Reservations are required – sometimes months in advance.

Rara Avis

This is a remote private tropical rainforest reserve, 15 km west of Horquetas (which is

COSTA RICA

18 km south of Puerto Viejo). It's also an ecotourism lodge and is studying various methods of non-destructive profit from the forest – very interesting to those with a passion for tropical conservation. Trails offer excellent birdwatching.

There are two lodges. *El Plastico* is a ramshackle building with bunkbeds suitable for student groups. Accommodation is US$45 per day including meals – HI members are charged US$35. Three km further into the reserve is the attractive and comfortable (not luxurious) *Waterfall Lodge* where singles/doubles/triples cost US$85/150/195 including all meals and guided rainforest walks. Reservations are necessary. Contact Amos Bien (☎/fax 253-0844), Rara Avis, Apartado 8105, 1000 San José, Costa Rica.

Oro Verde

You can only reach this private reserve by boat along the Río Sarapiquí. Accommodation is spartan – student groups can stay in dormitory bunks for as little as US$15 per person per day, and kitchen facilities are provided. More expensive rooms and meals are also available – US$195 for three-day/two-night packages from San José, including everything. Make reservations at the Oro Verde office (☎ 233-6613, fax 223-7479), Avenida 2, Calles 17 & 19, San José.

Isla del Río

This is a lodge (☎ 710-6898, in San José ☎ 233-0366, fax 233 9671) nine km west of Puerto Viejo. There are three km of trails, and horseriding is available. Pleasant rooms start from US$30/44 a single/double with communal bathrooms – HI members receive a 20% to 33% discount if booking through the Hostal Toruma in San José.

Rancho Leona

This is a rustic, laid-back lodge (☎ 710-6312, 239-9410) 19 km west of Puerto Viejo. The focus is kayaking – two nights at the lodge combined with a day of kayaking with a guide is US$75 – no experience necessary.

The Caribbean Lowlands

The Caribbean coast is very different from the Pacific. Half of the Caribbean coast is protected, with two national parks and two national wildlife refuges. There is rain year round, though from February to March and September to October are less wet. The Caribbean is part of Limón province, which has 240,000 inhabitants, 30% of which are Blacks. Most live near the coast and speak some form of English, providing a cultural diversity that is missing in the rest of Costa Rica. Also, several thousand indigenous Bribri and Cabecar people survive in the south. The Caribbean coast has fewer roads and has been developed more slowly than the Pacific.

PUERTO LIMÓN

Puerto Limón is the capital of Limón province, and locals simply call the city Limón. It has a mainly Black population and is quite lively and busy, though not considered a tourist town. People spend a night here en route to somewhere else. Note that the locals don't use street names, but only local landmarks like the Municipalidad on Parque Vargas, or Radio Casino.

Things to See & Do

The main attraction is **Parque Vargas**, on the south-eastern corner of town by the waterfront. The park has tropical trees, flowers, birds, and sloths hanging out (literally) in the trees. From the park, walk north along the seawall for views of the rocky headland upon which the city is built. Another focal point is the colourful **public market**. Also check out the **Ethnography Museum**. The nearest beach is **Playa Bonita**, four km north-west of town, which is OK for bathing though nothing special.

Columbus landed at Uvita Island, one km east of Limón, and **Columbus Day** (12 October) is celebrated enthusiastically on most years. Thousands of ticos stream into

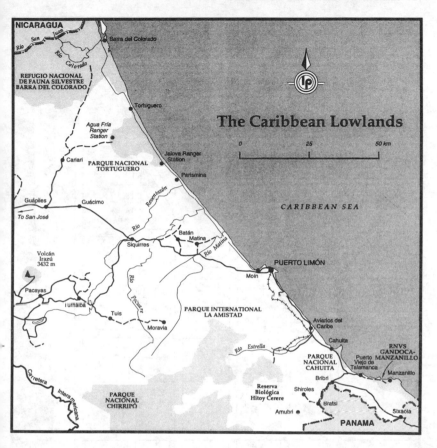

The Caribbean Lowlands

town for street parades: dancing, music, singing and drinking go on for some days. Hotels are booked in advance.

Warnings
Stick to the main, well-lit streets at night. Watch for pickpockets during the day.

Places to Stay
The basic *Pensión Los Angeles* charges US$3 per person but has few singles, and there is the similarly priced *Pensión El Sauce* – neither are particularly good. The *Hotel Río* looks OK and reasonably clean for US$3.60 per person – few singles. The *Cariari Hotel* (☎ 758-1395) has small, basic rooms with no fans for US$3.60 per person and has single rooms – it's OK. The *Hotel Venus* is similarly priced and reasonably clean, and the *Nuevo Hotel Oriental* (☎ 758-0117) charges US$7.20 a double and is OK. The basic *Hotel El Caño* (☎ 758-0894) is adequate at US$4.80 per person.

The *Hotel Ng* (☎ 758-2134) is busy midweek but less so at weekends. It seems clean and honest for US$5.50/9.50 single/double or US$7/11 with private cold shower. The *Hotel Fung* (☎ 758-3309) is also OK and

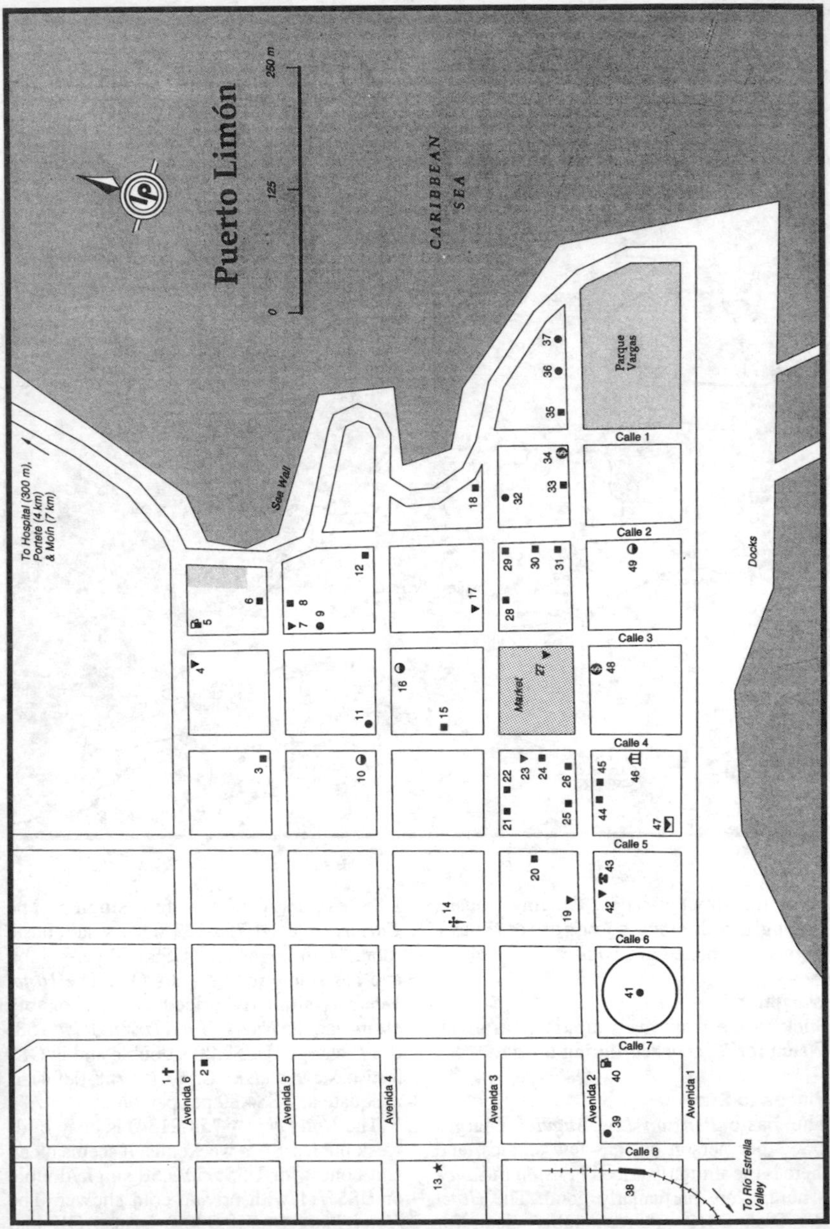

Puerto Limón

0   125   250 m

CARIBBEAN SEA

CARIBBEAN SEA

Parque Vargas

Sea Wall

To Hospital (300 m),
Portete (4 km)
& Moín (7 km)

Docks

Market

Calle 1
Calle 2
Calle 3
Calle 4
Calle 5
Calle 6
Calle 7
Calle 8

Avenida 6
Avenida 5
Avenida 4
Avenida 3
Avenida 2
Avenida 1

To Río Estrella
Valley

COSTA RICA

■	PLACES TO STAY	▼	PLACES TO EAT	14	Cathedral
				16	Bus to Cahuita,
2	Hotel Puerto	4	Restaurant Sien Kong		Puerto Viejo
3	Hotel Ng	7	Restaurant		& Sixaola
6	Hotel Lincoln		International	32	Fire Station
8	Nuevo Hotel Inter-	17	Mönpik		(Bomberos)
	nacional	19	Soda Restaurant Yans	34	Banco de Costa Rica
12	Hotel Venus	23	Restaurant Chong	36	Town Hall
15	Nuevo Hotel Oriental		Kong		(Municipalidad)
18	Park Hotel	27	Restaurant Doña Toda	37	Migración
20	Pensión El Sauce	35	American Bar	38	Railway Station
21	Pensión Los Angeles	42	Palacio Encantador	39	Bar Estadio
22	Hotel El Caño	48	Mares Soda Bar/Res-	40	Gas Station
24	Hotel Los Angeles		taurant	41	Baseball Stadium
25	Hotel Linda Vista			43	ICE Telephones
26	Hotel Fung		OTHER	46	Museo Etnohistorico
28	Hotel Acon				de Limón
29	Cariari Hotel	1	Church	47	Post Office
30	Hotel Palace	5	Gas Station	48	Banco Nacional de
31	Hotel Río	9	Helennik Souvenirs		Costa Rica
33	Hotel Las Palmeras		Shop	49	Buses to San José
35	Hotel Caribe	10	Bus to Moín		
44	Hotel Miami	11	Radio Casino		
45	Hotel King	13	Police		

charges US$5.75/10.25 with communal bath or US$11.50 a double with private cold shower. A good basic choice in this price range is the cheerful *Hotel King* (☎ 758-1033) at US$5.20 per person in rooms with communal bath and doubles with private cold shower for US$13.25. Most rooms have fans. Also reasonable for US$5.50 per person is the *Hotel Linda Vista* (☎ 758-3359). The old but interesting *Hotel Palace* (☎ 758-0419) charges US$6.25/11 for basic rooms with communal baths.

For something more up-market, try the clean *Hotel Miami* (☎ 758-0490, fax 758-1978) at US$11.25/17 with private cold shower and fan – more expensive for air-conditioning. There is a cafeteria. The newer *Hotel Puerto* (☎ 758-1095) has clean, quiet rooms with electric showers for about US$10 per person. The *Nuevo Hotel Internacional* (☎ 758-0662) has good, clean rooms with electric showers for US$12.50/17 with fans or US$26 a double with air-conditioning.

Places to Eat

There are snack bars and sodas around the market. One of the best is *Restaurant Doña Toda*, where simple meals start at US$2. On the west side of the market, *Restaurant Chong Kong* has Chinese meals for US$3 to US$5. The clean and popular *Mares Soda Bar Restaurant*, on the south side, is more up-market. Meals cost from US$3 to US$7. Two clean and reasonable Chinese restaurants a couple of blocks west of the market are the *Palacio Encantador* and the *Soda Restaurant Yans*.

Getting There & Away

Bus Buses from San José to Limón leave hourly from near the old Atlantic Railroad station. Buses returning to San José leave between 5 am and 8 pm from Calle 2, a block east of the market (three hours, US$3).

Buses to Sixaola leave at 5 am, 10 am, 1 pm and 4 pm, from the block north of the market. They stop at Cahuita (US$0.80), Puerto Viejo (US$1.20), Bribri (US$1.40), and Sixaola (three hours, US$2). The buses are crowded, so get a ticket in advance and show up early.

Buses to Moín leave from Calle 4, Avenida 4 several times an hour from 6 am, so you are able to get a boat for Tortuguero the same day.

COSTA RICA

Boat Boats to Tortuguero leave from Moín, 6½ km north-west of Limón.

PARQUE NACIONAL TORTUGUERO

This coastal park is the most important Caribbean breeding ground of the green sea turtle. The nesting season is from July to early October, with the highest numbers in late August. You can watch the turtles lay eggs or observe the eggs hatching – always check with park rangers or researchers working at the 'Casa Verde' centre for details. Smaller numbers of leatherback turtles nest from February to July, with a peak in April and May. Hawksbill turtles nest from July to October. Only the green sea turtle nests in large numbers.

Tortuguero has great opportunities for wildlife viewing and birdwatching, either from trails in the park or on boat trips. Apart from turtles, three species of monkey as well as sloths are frequently sighted, and many other mammals have been recorded. There are over 300 species of birds. Freshwater turtles line up on logs by the river bank, sunning themselves. Basilisk lizards look like little dinosaurs and can reach a metre in length. Young ones can run on water, hence the nickname 'Jesus Christ lizard'. Both the caiman and the crocodile can be seen here, as well as a variety of snakes and amphibians.

Information

Rain gear and insect repellent are useful – especially the latter!

The park headquarters (where there is information and a small exhibit room) is at the north end of the park, next to Tortuguero village. Camping here is US$2.25 per person, and drinking water and pit latrines are provided. Park entrance is US$1.50 per day – please don't try to avoid these fees, as the conservation of these parks relies on public contributions and entrance fees. There is a one-km nature trail and other trails in poor condition. Rangers give guided walks to see the turtles, starting at 8 pm during the season and costing US$5. Other hikes and boat trips can be arranged.

Watching hundreds of huge marine turtles nesting on the best nights of the season is a spectacular sight. So much so that the huge numbers of tourists admiring the spectacle have caused many of the turtles to leave and not lay their eggs – this is a serious problem. It is important to avoid harassing the turtles; the best way to do this (apart from not going) is to go with trained rangers or researchers and follow their instructions. Flash photos are particularly disturbing to the egg-laying.

The beaches are not suitable for swimming. The surf is very rough, the currents are strong and sharks regularly patrol the waters.

TORTUGUERO

This little village is at the north end of the national park. Several places have boats for hire. You can paddle your own dugout canoe for about US$1.50 per person per hour, or go with a guide for twice that. It is worth hiring a guide, at least for a few hours, because you are able to see so much more. In the village centre, the pulpería and adjoining Centro Social are good places for information and contacts.

Organised Tours

The cheapest tours are with Mitur (☎ 255-2031/262, fax 255-1846), on Paseo Colón, Calles 20 & 22, or Cotur (☎ 233-0155, 233-6579, fax 233-0778), Calle 36, Paseo Colón and Avenida 1. Both run three day/two night tours to Tortuguero for US$230/400 for a single/double – there are low-season discounts. All transport, guides, meals and accommodation are included. Day one includes a drive from San José to Moín, a five-hour boat ride to Tortuguero, and overnight in one of their lodges (rooms with private bath). The boat slows for photographs, and a bilingual guide is aboard. Day two has guided walks and boat tours of the area, and a night visit to the beach is added during the turtle nesting season. On day three you return by boat and bus. Their lodges are across the river from Tortuguero village, and boat visits can be arranged. More expensive tours with other companies are available.

Places to Stay & Eat

The family-run *Hospedaje Mariscal* has small rooms with shared bath and fans for US$10.50 a double. The clean *Cabinas Sabina* costs about the same in breezier upstairs rooms; downstairs rooms are US$4.50 per person. Food is available here. If these are full, ask around; you may be able to stay in someone's house. Another choice is the similarly priced *Cabinas Tatané* which is a five-minute boat ride away – the people at the pulpería may know where you can find the owner.

Restaurants charge about US$3 to US$4 for basic meals. Better meals are available by asking around and eating in private houses. A recommended cook is *Miss Juni* who will cook with a day's notice – US$2.50 for breakfast and US$4.75 for dinner. She is planning on building cabinas. *Las Brisas del Mar* is a local bar with cheap beers and cabins which looked closed down on my last visit. Other local places are opening up with the expansion of tourism.

Getting There & Away

Most people go to Tortuguero on a tour – getting there independently is difficult.

Air Travelair has daily flights to and from San José for US$54/93 one way/round trip. There is a Travelair office in Tortuguero village; the airport is four km north.

Boat It used to be possible to get to Tortuguero from Moín on cheaper public boats, but these don't run much any more – all foreigners are charged from about US$50 for the round trip. (See the Puerto Limón entry for details of buses from San José or Limón to Moín to connect with the boats.) Day trips for US$50 include lunch, but you can also be dropped off in Tortuguero and picked up another day. Boats usually leave between 7 and 8 am. You can make arrangements on the afternoon of the previous day or get there first thing in the morning. The trip takes about 2½ hours one way, but usually goes much slower to allow for wildlife observation and photography.

Other Routes A combination of asking around, hitching, luck, bus, boat, patience and time may get you to Tortuguero (and beyond to Barra del Colorado). Budget traveller Ursula Hoelzli from Canada described an unconventional trip she and a friend made in 1993.

There were no public boats from Moín so they hitched/bussed to Matina, where they found a very basic hotel for US$5 a double. Then a morning bus to Batán and from there another bus to San Rafael (locally called Freeman) near the mouth of the Río Pacuare. Locals told them a boat would be by at 2 pm; finally, at 5.30 pm a cargo boat passed by and gave them a ride to Parismina. They spent the following morning at the Parismina dock, got an afternoon ride to Tortuguero on a passing tourist boat (US$7.25 per person), and camped at Tortuguero for a few days. They met a man from Barra del Colorado who gave them a ride to his village, where they stayed with a family. They caught a daily 4.50 am boat to Puerto Lindo, 30 minutes away on the Río Colorado, connecting with a 6 am bus to Cariari (two hours, US$6.60 for boat and bus). From Cariari there are buses to Guápiles and on to San José.

CAHUITA

This village, 43 km south-east of Limón, is known for the attractive beaches in Parque Nacional Cahuita, immediately to the south. Although only three hours by car from San José, the area has a provincial and unhurried ambience.

Many of the 3500 inhabitants of the Cahuita district speak a Creole form of English. Much of the Creole culture remains for those who look for it, particularly in cooking, music and medicinal plants. Cahuita is expanding as a tourist destination.

Information

Telephone Cahuita has only one telephone number: call ☎ 758-1515 and the operator will connect you. The public telephone office is at the Soda Uvita. (The system is slated for expansion.)

Tours & Rentals These places provide tourist information as well as tours and rentals. They include Moray's (☎ ext 216), Cahuita Tours (☎ ext 232) and Lunazul Viajes

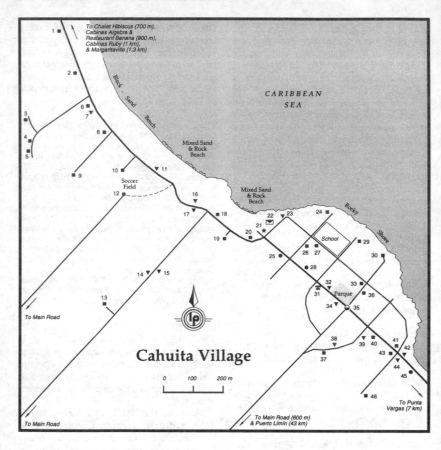

Cahuita Village

To Chalet Hibiscus (700 m),
Cabinas Algebra &
Restaurant Banana (900 m),
Cabinas Ruby (1 km),
& Margaritaville (1.3 km)

CARIBBEAN
SEA

Black - Sand Beach

Mixed Sand
& Rock Beach

Mixed Sand
& Rock Beach

Rocky Shore

Soccer
Field

School

Parque

To Main Road

To Main Road

To Main Road

To Punta
Vargas (7 km)

To Main Road (600 m)
& Puerto Limín (43 km)

0   100   200 m

(☎ ext 243) and may help with money changing. Sample day rentals are: mask, snorkel and fins US$5; bicycles US$5 to US$10; binoculars US$4.50; and surfboards US$10. Boat trips to the reef in a glass-bottomed boat, with snorkelling opportunities, are US$15 per person for three or four hours. Day trips to Tortuguero are about US$65.

Local hiking and horseriding trips are offered. Recommended local guides charging about US$15 per person for a three-hour tour include Carlos Mairena and José McCloud (☎ ext 288) and Walter Cunningham (☎ ext 229).

Warnings Don't leave your gear on the beach when swimming, don't walk the beaches alone at night, and be prudent if you enter some of the local bars. (I hear occasional complaints about local men who accuse tourists of being racist for not buying them drinks.) Some locals do take advantage of tourists, but this is not generally a major problem. Beware of drug sellers who may be in cahoots with the police.

Some single women travellers have been hassled by a few of the local men. Travelling with a friend may be a safer alternative to travelling alone. (I have also met single women travellers who have had a great time, but not everyone is so adept at avoiding unpleasant situations.)

'Safe sex' is rarely practised, but AIDS and other STDs are on the increase. If you are tempted by local sexual liaisons, bring your own condoms.

Nude bathing is not accepted. Wearing skimpy swimsuits in the villages is frowned upon. Wear a T-shirt and shorts.

Beaches At the north-west end of Cahuita is a long black-sand beach with good swimming. The white-sand beach at the eastern end of town is in the national park, and a trail in the jungle behind it leads to a third beach about six km away. These last two beaches are separated by a rocky headland with a small coral reef.

Places to Stay

Hotels are often full and not very cheap. Budget travellers can economise by renting rooms for two or more people – singles are at a premium.

Cabinas Bello Horizonte (☎ ext 206) has basic but clean rooms with communal bathrooms for US$5.50 per person and three cabins with private shower for US$25. *Cabinas Brigitte* has a few basic rooms for US$7.25/9 a single/double and they rent horses too. *Morays* (☎ ext 216) has very basic rooms for US$9 a double. A reader suggests *Erica's Cabinas* (near Cabinas Margarita) with two clean double rooms for US$7.25 per room – the shower is outside.

Cabinas Correoso (☎ ext 214) is clean and good for US$12.50/15 for a double/triple with bath and fan. *Cabinas Surfside* (☎ ext 246) has clean, concrete-block rooms with a fan and private bath for US$12 a double – there is a restaurant. They have better cabins a block away for US$17. *Cabinas Vaz* (☎ ext 218) has similar rooms for US$14.50/18.50 a single/double (some sleep up to five) – beware of loud music from the restaurant below. *Cabinas Rhode Island* (☎ ext 264) has clean small rooms for US$15.50 a double and larger rooms with

COSTA RICA

bath and fan for US$18.50/22 a double/triple.

Cabinas Algebra (message ☎ 582623) is 2.5 km north-west of town on the black beach road. Simple but adequate cabins with shower and fan are about US$20 and a restaurant is attached. About a hundred metres further out is the similarly priced *Cabinas Ruby*.

The clean and friendly *Cabinas Smith* has good rooms with electric showers and fans for US$22/26 a double/triple. *Cabinas Black Beach* (☎ ext 251) has nice rooms with balcony and private bath for US$21 a double or about US$30 for four. *Cabinas Margarita* (☎ ext 205) has clean rooms with cold water for US$21 and with hot water for US$26. *Cabinas Brisas del Mar* (☎ ext 267) charges US$22 for clean double rooms with cold showers. *Cabinas Sol y Mar* (☎ ext 237) has decent rooms with fan and shower for US$22. *Cabinas Jenny* (☎ ext 256) charges US$22 for the cheapest rooms; US$27 gets you a upstairs room with sea views and private bath.

Places to Eat & Drink

Most eateries are geared towards travellers and are not very cheap. *Miss Edith's* is traditionally popular and has recently expanded. Casados are about US$3, other dishes much pricier. Alcohol isn't served. *Restaurant Defi* is currently in vogue and features Caribbean music (occasionally live), and anything from creole cooking to Italian food (rasta pasta?). They open from early breakfast till late.

On a side road north-west of the town centre are the reasonably priced vegetarian *Cafeteria Vishnu* (breakfast/lunch only) and the *Pizzería El Cactus* which serves a US$5 pizza that will feed two if you're not starving (dinner only). Closer to the centre of town, the *Pizzería Revolución* serves local and vegetarian food as well as pizza.

Out towards the black-sand beach are *Las Rocas* and *Restaurant Las Brisas del Mar* – a couple of popular but slightly pricey beachfront restaurants. Nearby is the *Pastry Shop* – delicious bread, cakes and pies. *La Ancla Restaurant and Reggae Bar* (or

'Samwell's') has a limited menu, but it's a popular place for a beer with the rastas. *Restaurant Banana* by the Cabinas Algebra sells good local food. About 500 metres further north is the Canadian-run *Margaritaville* where you can get home-cooked dinners daily.

Restaurant Cahuita National Park by the entrance to the park is a little pricey but popular for all meals. *Restaurant Vista Del Mar* across the street serves seafood all day long. Nearby *Soda Sol y Mar* and *Restaurant Vaz*, attached to the cabinas of the same names, are both good. *Restaurant El Típico* has a variety of local food – budget travellers should order the casado for US$3. Local ladies may set up shop on the street and sell homemade stews and snacks direct from the pot.

Defi's and *Las Rocas* restaurants also have popular bars. *Hannias Bar* is a nice local bar. *Salon Vaz* is open all day and into the night, when the crowded back room pounds to the sounds of a Caribbean disco – be prepared for people bumming free drinks or offering ganga, coke or free love.

Getting There & Away

Autotransportes MEPE (☎ 221-0524) buses from San José to Sixaola stop at Cahuita three times a day (four hours, US$5.75). Buses return to San José at 6.30 and 9.30 am, and 4 pm, leaving from the crossroads in the middle of Cahuita. Buses to Limón (US$0.80) leave five times a day from the same place. Buses to Puerto Vargas, Puerto Viejo, Bribri, and Sixaola leave from here at 5.50 and 11 am, and 2 and 5 pm. Buses to Puerto Viejo and Manzanillo leave at 7 am and 3 pm.

PARQUE NACIONAL CAHUITA

This small park is one of the more frequently visited in Costa Rica. It has easy access, nearby hotels, attractive beaches, a coral reef, and a coastal rainforest, where you can easily observe many tropical species.

The main entrance is east of Cahuita village, through the Kelly Creek station. A two-km white-sand beach stretches to the east. The first 500 metres have warning signs about unsafe swimming, but beyond that the waves are gentle. The rocky Punta Cahuita (Point Cahuita) separates this beach from Vargas Beach, at the end of which is the Puerto Vargas ranger station, seven km from Kelly Creek. The two stations are linked by a trail through the coastal jungle behind the beach. A river near the end of the first beach can be thigh-deep at high tide. Many animals and birds can be seen by an observant hiker.

Information

The park stations are open daily from 8 am to 4 pm; entrance is US$1.50. You can get in and out after hours. You can camp at Vargas Beach, about one km from the Puerto Vargas ranger station. There are outdoor showers and pit latrines at the administration centre near the middle of the camping area. There is drinking water, and some sites have picnic tables. The area is rarely crowded. Camp close to the administration centre for greater security – it is safe if you don't leave your gear unattended. The daily camping fee is US$2.25 per person.

A good day hike is to take the 5.50 am Cahuita-Sixaola bus to the Puerto Vargas entrance road, walk one km to the coast, then seven more km back to Cahuita. Carry water, insect repellent and sunscreen.

PUERTO VIEJO DE TALAMANCA

Locally known as Puerto Viejo (don't confuse it with Puerto Viejo de Sarapiquí), this village is more tranquil than Cahuita. There is more influence from the local Bribri indigenous culture and less development. The surfing is good.

The village is 18 km south-east of Cahuita. The inhabitants traditionally lived by small-scale agriculture and fishing, although tourism is now becoming a minor industry. The mixture of Black and indigenous culture is interesting: you can buy Bribri handicrafts or listen to reggae; take horseriding trips or go fishing with the locals; and surf, swim, or hang out with the old-timers and talk. There's plenty to do, but things are very relaxed – take your time.

Information

ATEC The Asociación Talamanqueña de Ecoturismo y Conservación, headquartered in Puerto Viejo, is a nonprofit grassroots organisation promoting local tourism in ways that enhance nearby communities and provide a learning experience for visitors. Opening hours are noon to 6 pm. The president, Mauricio Salazar, is a Bribri local who knows the area very well. ATEC is an information centre about local issues, and can arrange homestays with locals and a variety of tours with an emphasis on native cultures, natural history and environmental issues. Tours are about US$12.50 for half a day and US$25 for a full day and involve a fair amount of hiking. Overnight trips are possible.

Telephone The Hotel Maritza (☎ 758-3844) and the Pulpería Manuel León (☎ 758-0854) have public phones. If you need to call someone at Puerto Viejo, call one of those and leave a phone number for them to call you back – this system works some of the time.

Surfing The waves are best from December to early March, with another season in June and July.

Horse & Bike Hire Several places rent horses and bikes – ask around.

Places to Stay

Most hotels provide mosquito netting or fans (a breeze helps keep mosquitoes away).

The friendly *Hostal Kiskadee*, a six or seven-minute walk south-east of the soccer field on a steep, unlit path, has dormitory-style accommodation for US$3.75 per person – add US$0.75 for kitchen privileges. The *Hotel Puerto Viejo* is the biggest place in town and is popular with surfers. Basic but clean upstairs rooms are US$5.20 per person; downstairs rooms aren't as good and are a little cheaper. Surfers also use the basic *Cabinas Manuel* (☎ 758-0854) which has a poor water supply. Rooms with private bath are about US$10 and some have four beds.

COSTA RICA

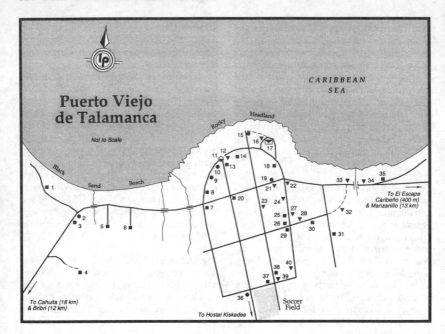

Another cheapie is the basic *Hotel Ritz* – US$6 for a double room with private bath. *Cabinas Jacaranda* has nice rooms with fans and mosquito nets at US$10.50 for singles and US$12 for doubles; doubles with a private bath cost US$15. *Cabinas Las Brisas* (also called 'Mister O'Conner's, over a km west of town) has four basic but decent rooms for US$7.25 per person. Still further west, the popular (and often full) *Cabinas*

Black Sands is thatched in the local Bribri style and set in a pleasant garden. Three basic rooms with mosquito nets are US$11/14 a single/double with communal kitchen and bathroom facilities.

The following are US$14.50 for one or two people: *Cabinas Diti* is decent and has private baths – ask at Taberna de Popo. *Cabinas Stanford* is also OK and has private baths and fans – ask at Stanfords restaurant. *Cabinas Salsa Brava* has basic rooms with private baths and good sea views.

The clean and attractive *Hotel Pura Vida* is US$13/17 for a single/double in rooms with fans and sinks but shared showers. Pleasant *Cabinas Casa Verde* has occasionally warm water in the communal bathroom – rates are US$12.50/18.50 for a single/double. *Cabinas Spence* has decent rooms with private bath for US$15.50 a single or double. The *Hotel Maritza* (☎ 758-3844) is US$18.50 for a double in nice cabins with fan, private bath and electric shower. They have a few very cheap and basic older rooms.

Cabinas Chimuri, run by ATEC president Mauricio Salazar and his European wife Colocha, has a few Bribri-style A-frame cabins for US$17/22 single/double (also one quadruple cabin). Communal kitchen and bathroom are simple. The cabins are set in a 20-hectare private reserve with trails and good birdwatching possibilities.

Places to Eat & Drink

Several small locally owned places serve typical meals and snacks – ask at ATEC for recommendations about these or about eating with a family. The bakery and soda at *Miss Sam* and *Soda Irma* are run by ladies who are long-term residents. *Doña Juanita* and *Doña Guillerma* cook out of their houses near the entrance to town. *Miss Dolly* sells baked goods and has a wide knowledge of local medicinal plants and herbs.

Bela Soda has cheap but good breakfasts. The *Restaurant Bambu* is inexpensive if you avoid the tourist menu, and it has a popular bar. *Jhonny's Place* has cheap, large Chinese meals. The *Café Pizzería Coral* has yoghurt,

granola, homemade wholewheat pancakes etc for breakfast and homemade pizzas at night. For breakfasts and snacks throughout the day, try the friendly *Soda Tamara*. *Soda Priscilla* has also been recommended.

Stanford's Restaurant Caribe is good for seafood and has a disco at weekends. *Restaurant Parquecito* is quite good and reasonably priced. The *Restaurant MexiTico* in the Hotel Puerto Viejo serves Mexican snacks and meals. The best in town is the recommended *Garden Restaurant*, serving Caribbean, Asian and vegetarian food – main courses begin around US$5.50.

La Taberna de Popo is a popular bar which sometimes has live entertainment.

Getting There & Away

Some buses continue to Sixaola and drop you at the intersection five km from Puerto Viejo – ask. Autotransportes MEPE (☎ 221-0524) has buses from San José. Buses leave Puerto Viejo at 6 am, 1 and 4 pm for Cahuita and Limón (no 1 pm bus on Sunday). A 7 am bus goes to San José. Buses to Manzanillo pass through at 7.30 am and 4 pm.

EAST OF PUERTO VIEJO

A 13-km dirt road heads east from Puerto Viejo along the coast, past sandy beaches and rocky points, through the small communities of Punta Uva and Manzanillo and sections of the Reserva Indigena Cocles/KéköLdi, and ending up in the Refugio Nacional de Vida Silvestre Gandoca-Manzanillo. There has been much discussion about the pros and cons of tourism in this remote area – talk to ATEC or read *La Loca de Gandoca* for some interesting perspectives.

Playa Cocles, two km east, has good surfing – surfers stay at *Cabinas & Soda Garibaldi*. Rooms with private bath and sea views are US$12. There are several houses with 'Rooms for Rent'. *Kapalapa* has music and videos and a few bottom-end rooms.

Near **Playa Chiquita**, five km east, is *Cabinas Dasa* (ring San José for reservations, ☎ 253-3431, 220-4089, or 236-2631). A room with shared bath is US$14/18 for a single/double, with private bath US$20 to

US$35 for two to four people, and a cabin with bath and kitchenette for up to six people is US$50. Nearby, *Maracú* (for reservations ring ☎ 225-6215) has two simple cabins with stove, two beds each, and shared bathroom for about US$7 per person. About a km beyond is *Restaurant Las Palmitas* with meals, simple cabins, and a camping area. Nearby, *Elena Brown's* is a nice local place to eat. Others are *Pinguin Soda* and *Soda Acuarius* – the latter bakes homemade bread and has a couple of basic rooms for rent as well as a rustic house for about US$300 per month. Several houses advertise 'Rooms for Rent'.

Punta Uva is seven km east. A sign advertises 'Caminata Guiada al Bosque'. Just beyond is the *Soda & Restaurant Naturales* on a hillside with good sea views, good seafood etc. Just beyond are *Selvin's Cabins* with basic rooms for US$10 double and a cabin with private bath for US$26 for four people. There is a restaurant (closed on Monday). About 200 metres further on is the reasonably cheap and popular *Walaba Cabinas* (☎ 225-8023) with basic rooms and dormitories. There are several other more expensive places to stay.

Manzanillo village is 12½ km east and within the Gandoca-Manzanillo wildlife refuge (it already existed when the refuge was established). The schoolmaster, Don German, is a fountain of local information. The road continues for about a km and then peters out. Footpaths continue around the coast through Gandoca-Manzanillo.

Near the bus stop in Manzanillo, the basic *Cabinas Maxi* are about US$8 per room. There is a restaurant. Local ladies prepare traditional meals in their homes – ask around.

The **Gandoca-Manzanillo** refuge continues south-east as far as Panamana. A coral reef is about 200 metres off-shore and snorkelling is possible. There is some rainforest and some of the most beautiful beaches on the Caribbean. A coastal trail leads 5½ km from Manzanillo to Punta Mona.

Florentino Grenald lives in Manzanillo

and acts as the reserve's administrator. He can recommend guides and provide information. Camping is permitted, but there are no organised facilities.

Getting There & Away

Buses leave Limón for Manzanillo (2½ hours, US$1.90) at 6 am and 2.30 pm, passing through Cahuita and Puerto Viejo. Return buses leaves Manzanillo at 8.30 am and 4.30 pm.

SIXAOLA

Sixaola is an unattractive border town with Panama. Most overlanders go via Paso Canoas on the Interamericana.

Places to Stay & Eat

There are two *Restaurants Central*, one of which has an extremely basic pensión attached. Other poor accommodation can be found by asking around. The best restaurant is the *El Siquerreno*.

Getting There & Away

There are three buses a day with Autotransportes MEPE from San José to Sixaola – the first one arrives by late morning. Buses return to San José at 5 and 8 am, and 2.30 pm (six hours, US$5.75). There are three buses a day to and from Limón.

Crossing the Border

The Panamanian town across the border from Sixaola is Guabito. There are no banks in Guabito, but stores accept colones, balboas and US dollars. Border hours are 7 to 11 am and 1 to 5 pm, but the guards sometimes take a few hours off at weekends! Frequent minibuses go from Guabito to Changuinola (16 km), which has a bank, an airport with daily flights to David, and buses to Almirante (30 km), where there are cheaper hotels. From Almirante continue into Panama by boat. Panama time is one hour ahead of Costa Rican time.

Southern Costa Rica

The Interamericana reaches its highest point near the 3491-metre mist-shrouded peak of Cerro de la Muerte, about 100 km south of San José. From there the road drops steeply to the town of San Isidro de El General (702 metres), the entry point to the nearby Parque Nacional Chirripó, which includes Costa Rica's highest mountains.

From San Isidro, the Interamericana continues south-east, through mainly agricultural lowlands, to Panama just over 200 km away. Towns are small but of interest to those wanting to see the Costa Rica off the main tourist trail. These towns provide access to some of the more remote protected areas in the country.

SAN ISIDRO DE EL GENERAL

San Isidro is the main town on the Interamericana Sur. The Río General valley is important for agriculture. A bustling, pleasant and fairly modern town, San Isidro is a transport hub and the commercial centre of the coffee fincas, cattle ranches and plant nurseries which dot the mountain slopes.

Southern
Costa Rica

COSTA RICA

San Isidro de El General

0   250   500 m

To San José (136 km)

Carretera Interamericana

Avenida 5

Avenida 3

Avenida 1

Avenida Central

Avenida 2

Avenida 4

Avenida 6

Calle 6

Calle 4

Calle 2

Calle Central

Calle 1

Calle 3

Río San Isidro

To Dominical (34 km)

To Hotel del Sur (6 km) & Panama (220 km approx)

■ PLACES TO STAY

4 Hotel Amaneli
5 Hotel Balboa
8 Hotel Iguazu
10 Hotel Lala
11 Hotel El Jardín
12 Hotel Astoria
20 Hotel Chirripó
25 Pensión Eiffel

▼ PLACES TO EAT

9 Restaurant El Tenedor
11 Restaurant El Jardín
14 Restaurant Hong Kong
20 Café & Restaurant Chirripó

OTHER

1 Reserva de la Biosfera La Amistad office
2 Gas Station
3 Musoc & TUASUR Buses to San José
6 Banco Nacional de Costa Rica
7 Museo Regional del Sur & Centro Cultural
13 Banco Anglo Costarricense
15 Texaco Gas Station & Buses to Puerto Jiménez
16 Parque Central
17 Cathedral
18 TRACOPA Bus Terminal
19 Banco de Costa Rica
21 Post Office & Telegrams
22 Mercado Municipal
23 New Bus Terminal
24 Buses to Dominical, Uvita & Quepos

Information

The bank on the Parque Central changes money. The small Museo Regional del Sur is at Calle 2 & Avenida 1. The annual agricultural fair is held at the beginning of February. San Isidro is the patron saint of farmers – animals are brought into town to be blessed on 15 May.

Places to Stay

Shoestringers use *Hotel El Jardín*, which has clean, basic rooms (US$3.30 per person) and a cheap restaurant. The more basic *Hotel Lala* (☎ 771-0291) charges US$2.20 per person or US$5.50 for a room with double bed and cold shower. The *Hotel Balboa* is also cheap. The *Hotel Astoria* (☎ 771-0914) has very basic boxes for US$2.75 per person, or slightly better boxes for about US$4 per person with private cold shower. The *Pensión Eiffel* (☎ 771-0230) is a cheap hotel near the new bus terminal.

The modern *Hotel Chirripó* (☎ 771-0529) costs US$4.75/8.50 for a single/double or US$7/11.50 in rooms with private electric shower. It has a decent restaurant. The clean and secure *Hotel Iguazu* (☎ 771-2571) is US$8.25/12 with private electric shower.

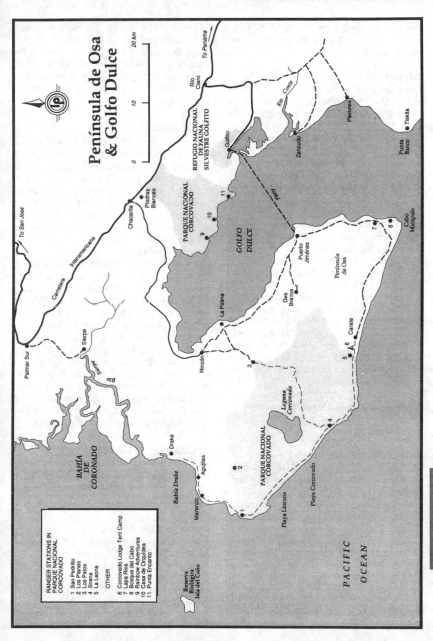

Península de Osa & Golfo Dulce

RANGER STATIONS IN
PARQUE NACIONAL
CORCOVADO
1 San Pedrillo
2 Los Planes
3 Los Patos
4 Sirena
5 La Leona

OTHER
6 Corcovado Lodge Tent Camp
7 Lapa Ríos
8 Bosque del Cabo
9 Rainbow Adventures
10 Casa de Orquídea
11 Punta Encanto

Reserva
Biológica
Isla del Caño

PACIFIC OCEAN

BAHÍA DE CORONADO

Bahía Drake

Marenco
Aguilitas
Drake

Palmar Sur

Carretera Interamericana

To San José

Sierpe

Río Sierpe

Rincón

La Palma

Chacarita

Piedras Blancas

PARQUE NACIONAL CORCOVADO

GOLFO DULCE

REFUGIO NACIONAL
DE FAUNA
SILVESTRE GOLFITO

Río Claro

To Panama

Río Coto Colorado

Río Conte

Golfito

Zancudo

Pavones

Punta Banco

Tiskita

Puerto Jiménez

Dos Brazos

Península de Osa

Carate

Cabo Matapalo

Playa Llorona

Playa Corcovado

Laguna Corcovado

COSTA RICA

The *Hotel Amaneli* (☎ 771-0352) is US$7 per person in rooms with private electric shower and fans.

Places to Eat

There are good sodas in the centre of town and in the market/bus terminal area. The *Hotel Restaurant El Jardín* is cheap and good. The *Hotel Chirripó Café* opens at 6 am and is cheap and popular. The *Restaurant El Tenedor* has a balcony overlooking a busy street – snacks and meals (including pizza) range from US$1 to US$5. The *Restaurant Hong Kong* is OK for Chinese food.

Getting There & Away

Buses from San José (three hours, US$3) leave often. Buses to San José leave from Calle 2 & the Interamericana.

A new bus terminal (see map) opened in late '93. Most buses will eventually leave from here – ask locally for details.

Buses for San Gerardo de Rivas (for Chirripó) leave at 5 am from the Parque Central and 2 pm from the new bus terminal. Buses leave for Quepos (via Dominical) at 7 am and 1.30 pm from Calle 1, Avenidas 4 & 6. Buses to Puerto Jiménez leave at 5.30 am and noon from near the petrol station on the Interamericana (six hours, US$4). Southbound buses stop here to pick up passengers. Several southern towns are served by TRACOPA on the corner of Calle 3 and the Interamericana.

SAN GERARDO DE RIVAS

This village is the base for climbing Chirripó. Three or four basic cabinas charge about US$3 per person. Simple meals are available. Buses from San Isidro stop outside the ranger station at the entrance to the village. Continue on foot past the various cabinas, the cheapest of which is *Cabinas Chirripó* about a km above the ranger station. Return buses to San Isidro leave from near the ranger station at 7 am and 4 pm (two hours).

PARQUE NACIONAL CHIRRIPÓ

This mountainous park is named for Cerro Chirripó (3819 metres), the highest peak in the country. The ranger station at San Gerardo is at 1350 metres, but most of the park is over 2000 metres above sea level. There are hiking trails and mountain huts near Chirripó's summit. Camping here is prohibited.

Information

During the busy dry-season weekends (especially Easter) the mountain huts may be full. The wet season is uncrowded, and it rarely rains before 1 pm. Officially, you need to make a reservation for one of the 40 sleeping spaces at the hut – in San José, the SPN may tell you there is a six-week waiting list, but at the San Gerardo ranger station space is often available within a day or two because of cancellations.

Pay fees (US$1.50 per day and US$3 per night at the hut) and obtain information at the San Gerardo ranger station. It is a steep 16-km climb on a good trail to the Chirripó summit area where there are two mountain huts with sleeping platforms – bring a warm sleeping bag and a camping stove. It can freeze at night. Allow seven to 16 hours for the climb – there is a small cave and a hut in poor condition along the way if you can't make it. Carry water – during the dry season there is only one place to get water before the huts. From the huts it is a further one to two hours hiking to the summit of Chirripó.

PALMAR NORTE & PALMAR SUR

This small town is used for reaching and leaving Parque Nacional Corcovado from the north. Palmar Norte has buses and hotels; Palmar Sur has the airport.

Places to Stay & Eat

On the Interamericana, *Cabinas Tico Aleman* (☎ 786-6232) have clean rooms with private bath and fan for US$7 per person, and *Cabinas & Restaurant Wah Lok* charge US$10.50 double with shower. In town, *Hotel Xenia* (☎ 786-6129) is slightly cheaper and *Cabinas Amarillas* (☎ 786-6251) is the best at US$10/15.

The *Chan Yeng* restaurant opposite the Supermercado Terraba is as good as any.

Getting There & Away

Air Travelair has daily flights from San José for US$61/106 one way/round trip. SANSA has less frequent service and is a bit cheaper.

Bus TRACOPA has seven buses a day (five on Sunday) to and from San José, four buses to San Isidro, and southbound buses on a space-available basis. Buses leave from the Supermercado Terraba five times a day to Sierpe.

SIERPE

This village on the Río Sierpe has boats to Bahía Drake from about US$15 per person (if there is a group). Ask at the dock next to the Las Vegas Bar/Restaurant. The *Hotel Margarita* has basic clean rooms for US$2.25 per person.

BAHÍA DRAKE

This community has several expensive lodges. The cheapest are the basic *Cabinas Cecilia* (☎ 771-2336) and leave a number where they can call you back) for US$25 per person including meals. The friendly *Albergue Jinetes de Osa* (for reservations ring San José, ☎ 253-6909) is US$30 per person including meals. The friendly and laid-back *Cocalito Lodge* (☎ 786-6150, fax 786-6291) is US$30 per person in nice rooms, or you can camp for US$7 each and use their facilities. Their restaurant is very good.

From Bahía Drake it's about a five-hour hike to the San Pedrillo ranger staion at the north end of Parque Nacional Corcovado (which is described below).

GOLFITO

Golfito is strung out along a coastal road backed by the steep forested hills of the **Refugio Nacional de Fauna Silvestre Golfito**. Boats and light planes cross the Golfo Dulce to Puerto Jiménez, which is the point of entry to the southern and eastern sides of Parque Nacional Corcovado.

The Golfito wildlife refuge administration is in town. Two km south of the town centre, a gravel road goes past a soccer field and up to some radio towers, seven km away and 486 metres above sea level. This is a good access road to the refuge. Another possibility is to continue north along the road past the airstrip – there are trails. Camping is permitted, but there are no facilities.

Places to Stay

The *Hotel Uno* (☎ 775-0061) has basic boxes without fans for US$1.75 per person. A better choice is the friendly *Cabinas Muzuren* (☎ 775-0058) with two rooms (shared bath) for US$3 per person and three rooms with private bath and fan for US$3.75 per person. The *Hotel Delfina* (☎ 775-0043) has basic rooms for US$3.75 per person or rooms with private baths and fan for US$14.50 a single or double. The *Hotel Golfito* (☎ 775-0047) has rooms with private bath and fan for US$9, single or double. The *Hotel Costa Rica Surf* (☎ 775-0034) has rooms with fan and shared bath for US$5.75/7.25 a single/double, or with a private bath for US$11/16. Many rooms lack windows.

In the quieter north end several families take guests. The friendly *Hospedaje Familiar* (☎ 775-0217) charges US$4.40 per person in airy rooms with fans and shared baths. The *Casa Blanca* (☎ 775-0124) has rooms with fans and private bath for US$8.75 a single or double. The *El Manglar* (☎ 775-0510) and *Cabinas Wilson* (☎ 775-0795) are similarly priced.

Other houses include the *Casa de Huespedes Felicia* (☎ 775-0539), the *Cabinas Marlin* (☎ 775-0191), the *Soda/Cabinas Santa Marta* (☎ 775-0508) and others – ask around. They charge US$2 to US$4.50 per person.

The friendly *Hotel del Cerro* (☎ 775-0006, fax 775-0551) has dormitories for US$5 per person ('Backpacker Rates') as well as rooms with fans and private bath for US$10/15. There is a restaurant.

Places to Eat

Inexpensive *Restaurant Uno* serves decent

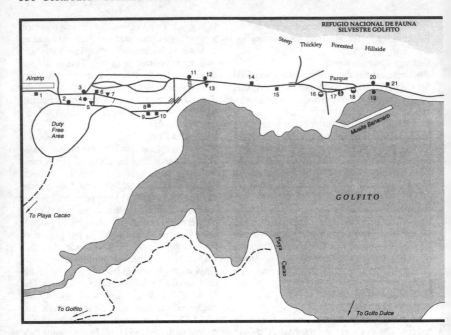

■	PLACES TO STAY		▼	PLACES TO EAT			Fauna Silvestre Golfito administration
1	Hotel Sierra		5	Bar Restaurant		12	School
6	Hotel Costa Sur			Cazuelita		16	Club Latino & Bus
8	Casa Blanca		7	Jardín Cervecero			Stop to Neily
9	Hospedaje Familiar		13	Soda Miriam		17	Banco Nacional de
10	El Manglar		23	Bar Restaurant Samoa			Costa Rica
14	Cabinas Wilson &		24	Hotel/Restaurant Uno		18	TRACOPA Bus
	Soda/Cabinas		27	Pequeño Restaurant			Terminal
	Santa Marta		28	El Jardín Restaurant		19	Taxi boats
15	Cabinas Princesa de		29	El Balcon Restaurant		20	ICE Building
	Golfo		32	La Eurakita		25	Muellecito
21	Hotel del Cerro			Restaurant		26	Banco de Costa Rica
22	Pensión Minerva						& Gas Station
24	Hotel/Restaurant Uno			OTHER		30	Laundry
26	Hotel Golfito					31	Post Office
29	Hotel Costa Rica Surf		2	Aero Costa Sol		33	Marea Baja Disco-
30	Cabinas Mazuren		3	Airport Terminal			theque
34	Hotel Delfina		4	Travelair		35	Eagle's Roost Marina
			11	Refugio Nacional de			

Chinese food and fish dinners. Luis Brenes's *Pequeño Restaurant* is popular and a good place for swapping information. *El Jardín Restaurant* is a friendly place and has a paperback book exchange. The *Soda Muellecito* is good for early breakfasts. The *Soda Miriam* and a couple of other cheap sodas are popular.

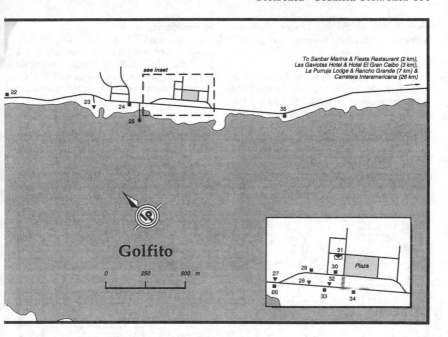

To Sanbar Marina & Fiesta Restaurant (2 km),
Las Gaviotas Hotel & Hotel El Gran Ceibo (3 km),
La Purruja Lodge & Rancho Grande (7 km) &
Carretera Interamericana (26 km)

see inset

Golfito

0   250   500 m

Plaza

Getting There & Away

Air Travelair has daily flights from San José for US$70/121 one way/round trip. They may have seasonal flights to Puerto Jiménez or Quepos. SANSA flies from San José every day except Sunday and is cheaper than Travelair.

Aeronaves and Aero Costa Sol have light aircraft to Puerto Jiménez for as little as US$12 – more expensive charter flights to any airstrip in the region are available.

The airport is four km north of the town centre.

Bus TRACOPA (in Golfito ☎ 775-0365) has three buses a day from San José to Golfito (eight hours). Return buses from Golfito leave at 5 am and 1 pm. Fares are US$4.75 to San José and US$3.50 to San Isidro.

Buses for Neily leave hourly from the north end of town. Buses for the surfing area of Pavones leave from the Puerto Jiménez boat dock – schedules vary.

Boat The daily passenger boat to Puerto Jiménez (1½ hours, US$2.50) leaves at 11.30 am – the service is sometimes suspended. There are boats to the nearby beaches – ask around.

Getting Around

Buses (US$0.15) and shared taxis (US$0.75) go up and down the main road of Golfito.

SOUTH OF GOLFITO

A good swimming beach, **Playa Zancudo**, 15 km south of Golfito, is popular with locals, especially in the dry season when buses may run; many people take a boat. Miguel 'Macarela' has boats to and from Golfito three times a week – about US$2 per person. Other boats are much pricier. There are several places to stay from about US$7 per person – single rooms are hard to find.

Pavones, 10 km south of Playa Zancudo, has good surfing – the best waves are from April to October. There is a daily bus to and

COSTA RICA

from Golfito – if the road is open. There are a few cheapish hotels where surfers hang.

PUERTO JIMÉNEZ

This is the main town on the Peninsula de Osa. It is 76 km (32 unpaved) from the Interamericana at Chacarita, or 20 km away from Golfito by boat. Gold mining and logging have made Puerto Jiménez fairly important and, with improved access, there is a burgeoning tourist industry. This is the main entry town to Parque Nacional Corcovado. The town is pleasant and friendly.

Information

The Corcovado information office (☎ 735-5036) is open from 8 am to noon and 1 to 4 pm daily. The adjoining Banco Central de Costa Rica buys dollars and gold. The Restaurant Carolina is an informal information centre.

Places to Stay & Eat

Hotels fill during dry-season weekends. The *Hotel Valentin* has clean but tiny, airless rooms for US$2.25 per person. The *Pensión Quintero* (☎ 735-5087) has bigger rooms for US$3.75 per person. The friendly *Cabinas*

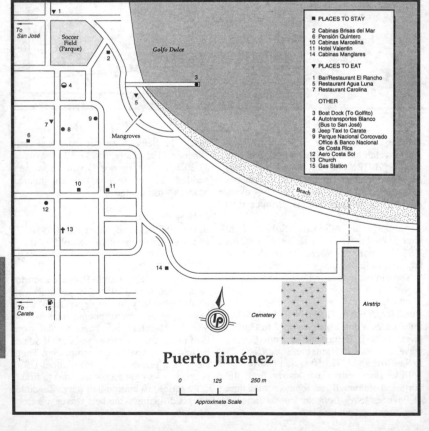

PLACES TO STAY
2 Cabinas Brisas del Mar
6 Pensión Quintero
10 Cabinas Marcelina
11 Hotel Valentin
14 Cabinas Manglares

PLACES TO EAT
1 Bar/Restaurant El Rancho
5 Restaurant Agua Luna
7 Restaurant Carolina

OTHER
3 Boat Dock (To Golfito)
4 Autotransportes Blanco (Bus to San José)
8 Jeep Taxi to Carate
9 Parque Nacional Corcovado Office & Banco Nacional de Costa Rica
12 Aero Costa Sol
13 Church
15 Gas Station

Puerto Jiménez

0   125   250 m

Approximate Scale

Marcelina (☎ 735-5007) has clean rooms with fan and bath for US$6/11.4 *Cabinas Brisas del Mar* (☎ 735-5012) has doubles with shower for US$15. Camping at *El Bambu*, 600 metres west of the soccer field, is about US$1.50.

Restaurant Carolina is popular. *Restaurant Agua Luna*, near the boat dock, has seafood and a sea view, and nearby *Bar/Restaurant El Rancho* serves meals and has a happy hour.

Getting There & Away

Air Aero Costa Sol (☎ 735-5017) has a daily flight to Golfito at 6 am for US$12. Travelair has dry-season flights to San José for US$70/121 at 11.55 am.

Bus Autotransportes Blanco leaves Calle 12, Avenida 9 in San José at 6 am and noon and returns from Puerto Jiménez, just south of the soccer field, at 5 and 11 am (nine hours, US$6.50).

Buses to Neily (US$2.50, four hours) leave at 5.30 am and 2 pm – catch one of these 23 km to La Palma for the eastern entry into Corcovado.

Truck A truck leaves from next to the Restaurant Carolina on Monday, Wednesday, Thursday and Saturday for Carate, at the south end of Corcovado (US$4).

Boat The passenger ferry to Golfito leaves at 6 am.

PARQUE NACIONAL CORCOVADO

This park has great biological diversity and has long attracted the attention of tropical ecologists. The park covers the southwestern corner of the Península de Osa and protects the best remaining Pacific coastal rainforest in Central America. Corcovado is home to Costa Rica's largest population of scarlet macaws and many other species of animals and plants.

Trails through the park lead to five ranger stations (see map). The trails are primitive, and the hiking is hot, humid and insect-ridden, but it's a good way to see the rainforest. It's more pleasant in the dry season (January to April).

Information

Four ranger stations are at the park boundaries, and a fifth is the headquarters at Sirena, in the middle of the park. Sirena offers food (US$10 per day for three meals), and basic accommodation if booked in advance. Camping is US$2.25 at any station, and meals can be arranged. Daily use fee is US$1.50. Make arrangements at the SPN office in San José or in Puerto Jiménez.

From Carate it is a 90-minute hike to La Leona ranger staion, from where it is six to seven hours to Sirena – check that the tides are low. From Sirena, hike inland for seven to eight hours to Los Patos ranger station, from where it is four hours to La Palma. Buses go from here to Puerto Jiménez – the last bus is at 2 pm. Alternatively, continue along the coast from Sirena to San Pedrillo ranger station (eight to 10 hours), then hike out to Bahía Drake (five hours).

NEILY

This hot but friendly agricultural centre, 17 km from Panama, is called 'Villa' locally. It is an important transport hub.

Information

Several banks change money.

Places to Stay & Eat

The basic but friendly *Pensión Elvira* (☎ 783-3057) is US$2.50 per person or US$3 with a fan – shared cold showers. Other cheap and basic places are the *Pensión Bulufer* (☎ 783-3216), *Hotel Las Vegas* (☎ 783-3205), *Pensión Familiar, Hotel El Viajero, Hotel Nohelia* and *Hotel Villa*.

The *Cabinas El Rancho* (☎ 783-3201/104/008/060) are OK for US$4.50 per person in simple rooms with bath and fans. The *Hotel Musuco* (☎ 783-3048) offers small basic rooms for US$4 per person, or US$5.50 with bath and fan. *Cabinas Andrea* (☎ 783-3784) has decent rooms with bath and fans for US$6 per person.

COSTA RICA

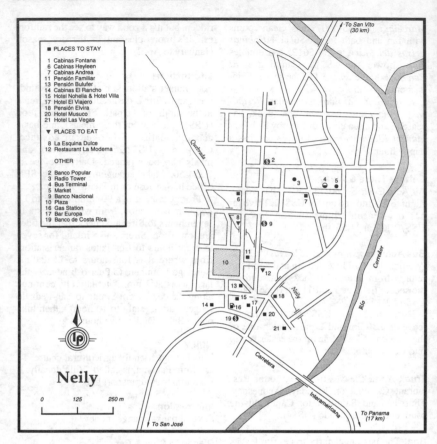

PLACES TO STAY

1 Cabinas Fontana
6 Cabinas Heyleen
7 Cabinas Andrea
11 Pensión Familiar
13 Pensión Bulufer
14 Cabinas El Rancho
15 Hotel Nohelia & Hotel Villa
17 Hotel El Viajero
18 Pensión Elvira
20 Hotel Musuco
21 Hotel Las Vegas

PLACES TO EAT

8 La Esquina Dulce
12 Restaurant La Moderna

OTHER

2 Banco Popular
3 Radio Tower
4 Bus Terminal
5 Market
9 Banco Nacional
10 Plaza
16 Gas Station
17 Bar Europa
19 Banco de Costa Rica

Neily

0   125   250 m

To San Vito (30 km)

To San José

To Panama (17 km)

Cabinas El Rancho has a decent restaurant attached. The *Restaurant La Moderna* has meals in the US$2 to US$5 range. *La Esquina Dulce* serves ice cream and snacks.

Getting There & Away

Air On most days SANSA has flights from San José to Coto 47, seven km south-west of Neily. Local buses pass the airport.

Bus The TRACOPA terminal is next to the market at the north-east end of town. There are five daily buses to San José (eight hours,

US$5.50); four daily to San Isidro; 19 daily to Paso Canoas; 13 daily to Golfito (1½ hours, US$0.55); four daily to San Vito (2½ hours, US$1.50); two daily to Puerto Jiménez.

SAN VITO

This pleasant town, 980 metres above sea level, offers respite from the heat of the nearby lowlands. The steep and winding drive up from Neily is scenic, as is the route from San José. The nearby botanical gardens are well worth a visit.

San Vito was founded by immigrants from

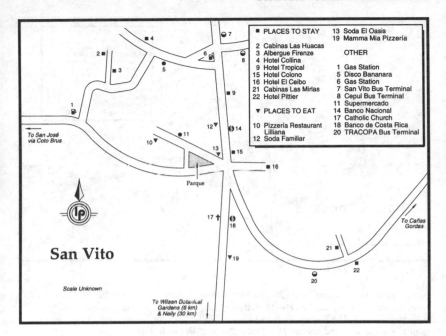

PLACES TO STAY

2 Cabinas Las Huacas
3 Albergue Firenze
4 Hotel Collina
9 Hotel Tropical
15 Hotel Colono
16 Hotel El Ceibo
21 Cabinas Las Mirlas
22 Hotel Pittier

PLACES TO EAT

10 Pizzería Restaurant Lilliana
12 Soda Familiar
13 Soda El Oasis
19 Mamma Mia Pizzería

OTHER

1 Gas Station
5 Disco Bananara
6 Gas Station
7 San Vito Bus Terminal
8 Cepul Bus Terminal
11 Supermercado
14 Banco Nacional
17 Catholic Church
18 Banco de Costa Rica
20 TRACOPA Bus Terminal

To San José
via Coto Brus

Parque

San Vito

Scale Unknown

To Cañas
Gordas

To Wilson Botanical
Gardens (6 km)
& Neily (30 km)

Italy in the early 1950s – you can still hear Italian spoken and eat Italian food.

Places to Stay & Eat

The *Hotel Tropical* is friendly and secure, though noisy. Basic rooms are US$2.50 per person. The *Hotel Colono* is another cheap and basic choice.

Clean and quiet *Cabinas Las Mirlas* (☎ 773-3054) charges US$5 per person and has private electric showers. The *Hotel Collina* is US$4.50/7.25 with private cold shower. The *Hotel Pittier* (☎ 773-3006) is about the same price but you need to call the owner to open it up. *Cabinas Las Huacas* (☎ 773-3115/517) has decent new rooms for US$6.25/11 with private electric showers. The *Albergue Firenze* (☎ 773-3206) is similar.

The *Hotel El Ceibo* (☎ 773-3025) is the best – US$6.75/11.75 with cold showers or US$10/18.25 in nicer rooms with electric showers. There is a reasonable restaurant.

Pizzería Restaurant Lilliana has Italian and local food for US$3 to US$4. The fancier *Mamma Mia Pizzería* is good. The *Soda El Oasis* and *Soda Familiar* have good cheap food.

Getting There & Away

The TRACOPA terminal (☎ 773-3410), at the south end of town, has four daily buses to San José (six hours, US$6.50) and two buses to San Isidro.

Two bus terminals near each other in the centre have local buses to Neily and other nearby villages.

WILSON BOTANICAL GARDENS

These attractive and well laid out gardens are 5.6 km south (uphill) from San Vito. Short but educational trails are named after the plants found alongside them, such as the Heliconia Loop Trail, the Bromeliad Walk etc. The gardens open daily (except 24-25 December) from 8 am to 6 pm. Foreigners

COSTA RICA

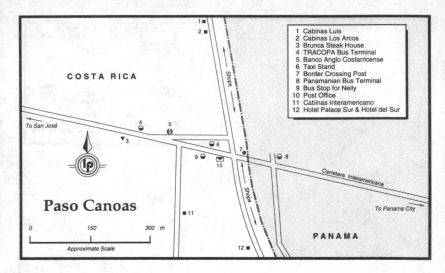

COSTA RICA

To San José

Paso Canoas

Shops

Shops

Carretera Interamericana

To Panama City

PANAMA

0   150   300 m

Approximate Scale

1 Cabinas Luis
2 Cabinas Los Arcos
3 Brunca Steak House
4 TRACOPA Bus Terminal
5 Banco Anglo Costarricense
6 Taxi Stand
7 Border Crossing Post
8 Panamanian Bus Terminal
9 Bus Stop for Neily
10 Post Office
11 Cabinas Interamericano
12 Hotel Palace Sur & Hotel del Sur

pay US$6 whilst ticos pay US$0.30 (to foster local interest in plant conservation). A trail map is provided. The money goes to maintaining the gardens and research facilities.

Places to Stay & Eat
The gardens are run by the OTS (☎ 240-6696, fax 240-6783). Overnight accommodation is US$58 (US$40 in the wet season), including meals.

Getting There & Away
Buses between San Vito and Neily pass the entrance to the gardens several times a day, but some buses to Neily take a different route – ask at the terminal. A taxi is US$2.50 – or walk.

PASO CANOAS
This small town on the Interamericana is the main port of entry between Costa Rica and Panama. Hotels are often full with tico bargain hunters during weekends and holidays. Most of the shops, hotels etc are on the Costa Rican side.

Information
Moneychangers hang out near the border and

give better rates than banks for cash US dollars. You can also change colones to dollars. Colones are hard to change further into Panama. Other currencies are harder to deal with. Travellers' cheques can be negotiated, but not as readily as cash. The banks are open weekdays during the morning.

Places to Stay & Eat
The basic *Hotel del Sur* and the *Hotel Palace Sur* next door are about US$3 per person. *Cabinas Interamericano* has clean rooms with private bath for US$4.75 per person. One of the better restaurants is attached. *Cabinas Los Arcos* is US$8.75 a double with private bath and fan. Next door is the *Cabinas Luis* in the same price range. There are several cheap sodas.

Getting There & Away
TRACOPA buses leave San José several times a day. The Friday night bus is full of weekend shoppers who return to San José on Sunday afternoon. Five daily buses leave Paso Canoas for San José (seven hours, US$6.50).

Buses for Neily leave the border every hour during the day.

Crossing the Border

Opening hours are 6 to 11 am and 1 to 10 pm – there are no buses after dark.

Citizens of the USA, Canada, New Zealand, Australia and some European countries require Panamanian visas (the cost varies from nothing to US$20). Visas are not available at the border. Check with the Panamanian consul in San José about current requirements. In Panama, a bus stop near the border has buses to David, about 1½ hours away. The last bus leaves at 7 pm.

If entering Costa Rica, you may be asked for a return or onward ticket. In David, you can buy a TRACOPA bus ticket for David to Paso Canoas and return, which is acceptable to the Costa Rican authorities. Apparently, you can't buy just the Paso Canoas to David section at the border. There is a Costa Rican consul in David, as well as in Panama City.

The Central Pacific Coast

The Pacific coast is more developed for tourism than the Caribbean coast, though you can still find deserted beaches, wildlife, and small coastal villages.

There are marked wet and dry seasons along this coast. The dry season is the high season, and hotel reservations are advised for weekends from December to April, especially for Easter week. During the wet season, ask about low-season discounts. High-season rates are given here.

PUNTARENAS

This city is the capital of the coastal province of Puntarenas. During the 19th century, Puntarenas was Costa Rica's major port. Now, Puerto Limón and the new port at Caldera, 18 km south-east of Puntarenas, take much of the shipping. Puntarenas remains a bustling place during the dry season, when tourists arrive. During the wet months it's much quieter.

The city is on the end of a sandy peninsula

almost eight km long but only 100 to 600 metres wide – arriving here is intriguing. You are always close to the ocean, but the beaches are too polluted for swimming. Puntarenas has traditionally been popular with ticos, but foreigners prefer destinations where they can swim. Many people come to Puntarenas to catch the ferry to the Península de Nicoya. It's a friendly port.

Information

Banks are found on Avenida 3 between Calles Central & 3. Beware of pickpockets along the beach.

Places to Stay

The basic, friendly *Hotel Río* (☎ 661-0331), Calle Central, Avenida 3, has rooms with fans for US$3.75/5.80 or with private shower for US$6.50/11.60. The area, by a dock and the market, is a little rough but not very dangerous.

The basic, friendly and clean *Pensión Cabezas* (☎ 661-1045), Avenida 1, Calles 2 & 4 is US$3.75 per person in small rooms with fans. Other similarly priced basic places include the clean and secure *Pensión Chinchilla* (☎ 661-0638), Calle 1, Avenidas Central & 2, and the *Pensión Montemar* (☎ 661-2771), Avenida 3, Calles 1 & 3. The *Pensión Juanita* (☎ 661-0096), Avenida Central, Calles Central & 1, has cramped rooms – fans are an extra US$1.50. The *Pensión El Nido* (☎ 661-2471), Avenida 1, Calles 4 & 6, has fans, and the *Pensión Gutierrez* around the corner looks the most basic.

Hotel Ayi Con (☎ 661 0164, 661-1477), Calle 2, Avenidas 1 & 3, has basic clean rooms with fans for US$4.50 per person, or US$6 with cold shower or US$7.25 with air-conditioning.

The Toruma Youth Hostel in San José makes reservations (strongly suggested) for members at *Cabinas San Isidro* (☎ 221-1225, 663-0031, fax 221-6822) for US$9 each (more for nonmembers). San Isidro is eight km east of the town centre – there are buses. The cabinas are near a beach, and

COSTA RICA

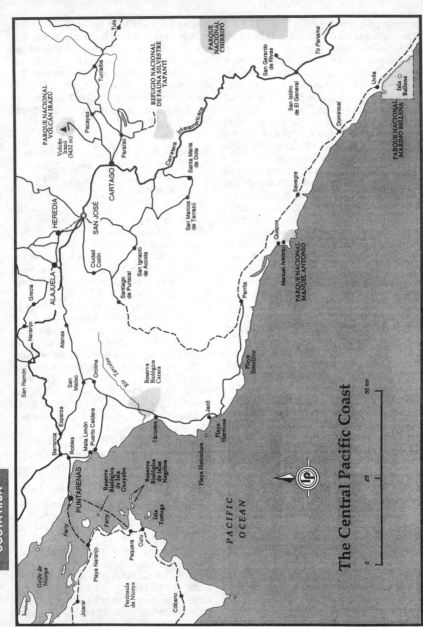

The Central Pacific Coast

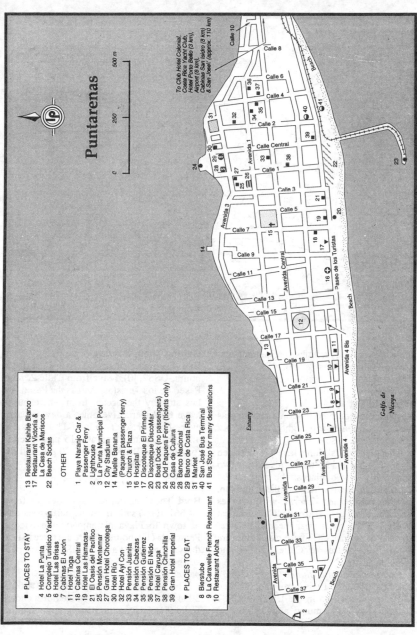

Puntarenas

0   250   500 m

PLACES TO STAY

4   Hotel La Punta
5   Complejo Turístico Yadran
6   Hotel Las Brisas
7   Cabinas El Jorón
11 Hotel Tioga
18 Cabinas Central
19 Hotel Las Hamacas
21 El Oasis del Pacífico
25 Pensión Montemar
27 Gran Hotel Chorotega
30 Hotel Río
32 Hotel Ayi Con
33 Pensión Juanita
34 Pensión Cabezas
35 Pensión Gutiérrez
36 Pensión El Nido
37 Hotel Cayuga
38 Pensión Chinchilla
39 Gran Hotel Imperial

▶ PLACES TO EAT

8   Bierstube
9   La Caravelle French Restaurant
10 Restaurant Aloha

13 Restaurant Kahite Blanco
17 Restaurant Victoria &
    La Casa de Mariscos
22 Beach Sodas

OTHER

1   Playa Naranjo Car &
    Passenger Ferry
2   Lighthouse
3   La Punta Municipal Pool
12 City Stadium
14 Muelle Banana
    (Paquera passenger ferry)
15 Church & Plaza
16 Hospital
17 Discoteque El Primero
20 Discoteque DiscoMar
23 Boat Dock (no passengers)
24 Old Paquera Ferry (tickets only)
26 Casa de Cultura
28 Banco Nacional
29 Banco de Costa Rica
31 Market
40 San José Bus Terminal
41 Bus Stop for many destinations

To Club Hotel Colonial,
Costa Rica Yacht Club,
Hotel Porto Bello (3 km),
Cabinas San Isidro (6 km),
Airport (6 km),
& San José* (approx. 110 km)

Estuary

Golfo de
Nicoya

COSTA RICA

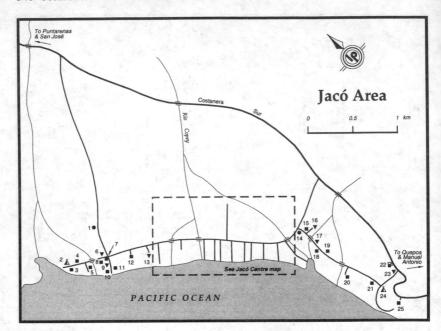

Jacó Area

To Puntarenas & San José

Costanera Sur

Río Copey

0   0.5   1 km

See Jacó Centre map

To Quepos & Manuel Antonio

PACIFIC OCEAN

there are cooking facilities, a restaurant, and a swimming pool.

Places to Eat

Restaurants along the Paseo de los Turistas are tourist oriented and slightly pricey – but not outrageously so.

Cheapish sodas along here are between Calles Central and 3; 300 metres east are two reasonably priced places: the popular *La Casa de Mariscos*, where English is spoken, and the *Restaurant Victoria*, which serves Chinese food and seafood. The cheapest food is in the sodas near the market area. Several inexpensive Chinese restaurants are within 200 metres of Calle Central and Avenida Central.

Restaurant Kahite Blanco (☎ 661-2093), Avenida 1 & Calle 19, is locally popular and serves good seafood in the US$3 to US$7 range. They have music and dancing at weekends.

Getting There & Away

Bus Frequent buses to San José (two hours, US$2.40), leave from Calle 2, near Paseo de los Turistas. Across the Paseo is a bus stop by the ocean, from where buses leave for Liberia five times a day, Esparza every hour or so, Tilarán at 11.30 am and 4.30 pm, Santa Elena at 2.15 pm, Quepos (passing Jacó) at 5 am and 2.30 pm, and for other local villages.

Boat The Conatramar car/passenger ferry (☎ 661-1069) sails from the north-west end of town to Playa Naranjo on the Nicoya Peninsula (1½ hours). There are three to five daily departures. Fares are US$1.10 for passengers and US$8.10 for cars. Foot passengers continue by bus to Nicoya.

The Paquera passenger ferry (☎ 661-3034, 661-2830) sails from the north end of Calle 9 at 6.15 am and 3 pm, with an extra sailing at 11 am in the high season (US$1.50,

1½ hours). Passengers continue to Montezuma by bus.

Getting Around
Buses marked 'Ferry' run up Avenida Central to the Playa Naranjo terminal, 1½ km from the centre of town.

JACÓ
Jacó is the closest developed beach resort to San José and is popular and crowded by Costa Rican standards. It is 2½ km off the coastal highway. Hotels and restaurants are scattered along the road which parallels the three-km-long beach. Jacó has a reputation as a 'party beach', but it is pretty sedate compared to North American 'party beaches'

like Daytona. The beaches are reasonably clean and safe for swimming, though you should be careful of rip currents. Jacó is popular with surfers.

Information
Several banks change money. Several places rent bikes for US$7.25 a day.

Places to Stay
Reservations are recommended during dry season. There are few single rooms and shoestringers won't find many bargains. Camping is an option. Low-season and surfer discounts are available.

Cabinas Calypso (☎ 643-3208) are US$14.50 a double – very basic with shared bath. The small *Cabinas Andrea* (☎ 643-3089) are similar. Fans are available. *Cabinas Las Brisas* (☎ 643-3074) have beaten-up rooms with bath and fan for US$11 a double, or US$22 a double for better rooms. This hotel is 'For Sale'.

Cabinas Bohío (☎ 643-3017) have basic cabins for US$18 sleeping three or four people (and nicer, pricier cabins). *Cabinas Cindy* are similarly priced. *Cabinas Supertica* (☎ 221-8136) has four basic cabins with kitchen, refrigerator, bath and fan – US$25 double or US$36 for six people. *Cabinas Emily* (☎ 643-3328) and *Cabinas García* (☎ 643-3191) have reasonable rooms with bath and fan for about US$22 a double; the Emily has some cheaper rooms with shared bath which are popular with shoestringers. The basic but friendly *Cabinas El Recreo* (☎ 643-3012) are about this price.

Cabinas Antonio (☎ 643-3043) have clean rooms with bath and fan for US$18 double. The *Hotel Mariott* charges US$22 for a basic room with bath but no fan – three people can stay. *Cabinas Garabito* are another cheap option.

Friendly *Camping El Hicaco* (☎ 643-3004) is US$1.80 per person and has a lock-up for your gear, picnic tables and bathrooms. The sandy campsites cut down on chiggers. For US$1.50 per person, try *Camping El Estero*, *Camping Madrigal* (☎ 643-3230), *Camping Garabito* and the

COSTA RICA

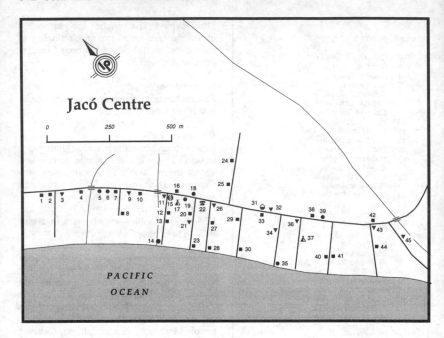

Jacó Centre

PACIFIC OCEAN

■ PLACES TO STAY

1 Jacó La Costa Condominiums
2 Cabinas García
4 Cabinas Emily
7 Cabinas La Sirena
8 Hotel Lido
10 Tangerí Chalets
12 Cabinas Mar de Plata
13 Los Ranchos
16 Cabinas Supertica
17 Camping Garabito
20 Cabinas Cindy
23 Cabinas Bohío
24 Cabinas Paraíso del Sol
25 Apartotel Gaviotas
27 Villas Miramar
28 Apartotel Flamboyant
29 Zabamar Resort
30 Hotel Cocal
33 Cabinas El Recreo
37 Camping El Hicaco
38 Cabinas Andrea
40 Cabinas Las Brisas
41 Cabinas Alice
42 Cabinas Marea Alta & Cabinas Calypso
44 Apartotel Sole d'Oro & Apartamentos El Mar

▼ PLACES TO EAT

3 Pura Vida
9 Killer Munchies Pizzería
11 La Ostra
21 Susie Q's
23 Restaurant El Bohío
26 Restaurant Flamboyant
32 Pizzería Guilloly & Soda Nenas
34 Restaurante Piccola
36 Pancho Villas
43 Restaurant Sen Ly
45 Soda Helen

OTHER

5 Unicornio Ranch
6 Nucleo de Turistas Bribri
14 Disco Papagayo
15 Banco de Costa Rica
18 ADA Car Rental
19 Fantasy Tours
22 Laundry; ICE phone & fax
31 Bus Stop & Supermercado
33 Banco Nacional
35 Disco La Central
39 Red Cross

COSTA RICA

lot outside the *Hotel Mariott* – all these are grassier.

Places to Eat

Eat cheaply at the *Restaurant El Verano* (fried chicken for US$2), the *Restaurant Doña Cecilia* (casados for US$2.50) and the *Restaurant Casita del Maíz* (casados for US$3).

Other cheap eats are the *Picnic Inn* for fried chicken and *Soda Nenas* for good casados. Also try the *Soda Helen*, open 7 am to 10 pm during the high season, and the sodas *Estrella del David* and *Perla del Mar*. *Pizzería Guilloly* has small individual pizzas for US$3 to US$6 depending on the toppings. They show surfing videos. There are many pricier restaurants.

Entertainment

The *Disco La Central* is the hip place for travellers. *Disco Papagayo* attracts a more local crowd. *Disco Upe* is a nice late-night place.

Getting There & Away

Direct buses leave the Coca-Cola in San José daily at 7.30 am and 3.30 pm (three hours, US$3).

Buses leave Jacó for San José at 5 am and 3 pm daily. Departures for Puntarenas are at 6.45 am, noon and 4 pm and for Quepos at 6.30 am and 4 pm. The bus stop is near the supermercado in Jacó.

QUEPOS

Quepos, once a major port, is now known as a sportfishing centre and the nearest town to the Parque Nacional Manuel Antonio.

Information

La Buena Nota (☎ 777-0345) at the entrance to town sells beach supplies and is an information centre. The owners plan to open a second store near the Manuel Antonio beach. The Banco Nacional de Costa Rica changes US dollars. The annual Fiesta del Mar takes place near the end of January, with processions and street dancing. The beaches are not recommended for swimming.

Places to Stay

The *Hotel Majestic* has basic boxes for US$3.75 per person. The *Hotel Luna* (☎ 777-0012) is equally basic at US$4.40 per person. The *Hospedaje La Macha* (☎ 777-0216) is basic but clean and has fans for US$5.50/10 a single/double. Other basic cheapies are the *Hospedaje Araya*, US$5.50 per person, and the *Hotel Linda Vista*, US$7.25/8.75.

Cabinas Kali has simple rooms with fans and private baths for US$7.25/11. *Cabinas Doña Alicia* (☎ 777-0419) has clean rooms with private bath and two double beds for US$14.50 for up to four people, or doubles for US$11.

The *Hotel Ipakarahi* (☎ 777-0392) has pleasant clean rooms with private bath and fan for US$14.50 double. *Cabinas Mary* (☎ 777-0128) is good at US$7.25 per person in clean rooms with private bath – but few rooms. *Cabinas El Cisne* (☎ 777-0522) is similar. Others with private bath for about US$7.25 per person include the *Hotel El Parque* (☎ 777-0063), the *Hotel Ramus* (☎ 777-0245) and the *Hotel Mar y Luna* (☎ 777-0394) – this last has rooms with shared baths for US$5.50 per person. The *Cabinas Villa Verano* (☎ 777-0236) has good clean rooms with private bath for US$11/14.50, as does the *Cabinas Horcones* (☎ 777-0090) for US$9 per person.

Places to Eat

Soda Nahomi has cheap snacks. The *Restaurant Ana* has casados for US$2.20. The *Bar Restaurant La Central* is inexpensive and the *Soda Isabel* is a little pricier but still good value. The market/bus station has cheap eateries such as the *Quepoa* on the south side, a no-name place at the south-east corner and the *Soda La Coquita* in the market. East of the market, *Pizza Gabriel* has good individual pizzas for US$3 to US$5.

George's American Bar & Grill is popular and crowded for breakfast, lunch and dinner. A sample meal: fried fish dinner for US$5.50. The *Marisquería Jiuberth* is similarly priced and is a good seafood place.

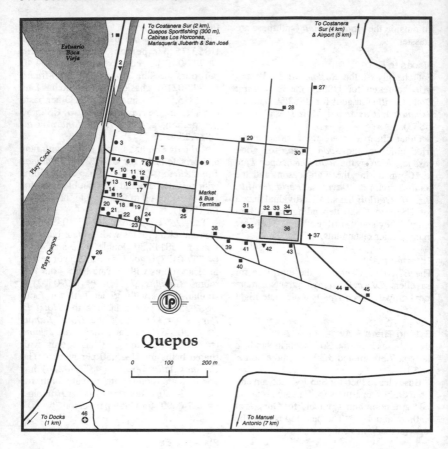

Quepos

0   100   200 m

To Docks
(1 km)

To Manuel
Antonio (7 km)

Entertainment

The *Arco Iris Riverboat Bar* (☎ 777-0449) has dancing at weekends. Opposite, the *Mirador Bahía Azul* has sea views and is a popular place for a beer, as is the *Gran Escape Bar*.

Getting There & Away

Air Travelair has one or more daily flights between San José and Quepos (US$37/64), some continuing to Palmar or Golfito, depending on the season. SANSA (☎ 777-0161) has one or more flights a day between San José and Quepos – fares are a little cheaper. Nahomi Travel makes air reservations and provides transfers for US$2.25 from anywhere in the area. The airport is five km from town and the airport tax is US$2.25.

Bus Direct buses from San José's Coca-Cola go to Manuel Antonio (3½ hours) at 6 am, noon and 6 pm, and normal buses go to Quepos (five hours) at 7 and 10 am and 2 and 4 pm.

The Quepos terminal sells tickets from 7 to 11 am and 1 to 5 pm daily except Sunday, when sales stop at 2 pm. Normal services to

■ PLACES TO STAY	40	Villas Cruz		OTHER
1 Hotel Viña del Mar	41	Hotel Quepos		
4 Hotel Linda Vista	43	Cabinas Mary	3	La Buena Nota,
6 Hotel Sirena	44	Apartotel Los Corales		Elegante Rent-a-
8 Hotel Paraíso	45	Hotel Voilá Voilá		Car & Sportfishing
10 Hotel Ramus				Agencies
12 Hotel Mar y Luna	▼	PLACES TO EAT	7	Banco Nacional de
14 Hotel Kamuk				Costa Rica
15 Hotel Luna	2	Arco Iris Riverboat	9	Town Hall
16 Hotel Malinche		Bar	11	Pico Motor Scooter
19 Hotel Majestic	5	Restaurant Ana &		Rental
20 Hotel El Parque		Gran Escape Bar	19	Banco de Costa Rica
22 Hospedaje Araya	13	Soda Isabel	21	Super Mas Grocery
27 Hotel Ipakarahi	17	Pizza Gabriel		Store
28 Cabinas Kali	18	Bar Restaurant La	23	Banco Popular
29 Cabinas Villa Verano		Central	25	Taxi Stand
30 Cabinas El Cisne	24	George's American	34	Post Office
31 Villas Morsol Inn		Bar & Grill	35	School
32 Cabinas Doña Alicia	26	Soda El Kiosko	36	Soccer Field
33 Hospedaje La Macha	42	Soda Nahomi	37	Church
38 Cabinas Helen			41	SANSA & Nahomi
39 Hotel Ceciliano				Travel
			46	Hospital

San José are at 5 and 8 am and 2 and 4 pm daily (US$3). Direct buses to San José leave three or four times a day from Manuel Antonio, and pick up passengers in Quepos (US$5). Buy tickets well in advance. Buses to Puntarenas (3½ hours, US$2.75) leave daily at 4.30 am and 3 pm, and to San Isidro at 5 am and 1.30 pm. Buses for Manuel Antonio leave 13 times a day US$0.30).

MANUEL ANTONIO

This village at the national park entrance is popular with younger international travellers. There is a good beach but swimmers should beware of rip currents. Don't leave your belongings unattended on any beach and keep your hotel room locked even when leaving for brief periods.

Places to Stay & Eat

Costa Linda (☎ 777-0304; affiliated with the Ticalinda in San José) is reasonably clean. Basic stuffy rooms with shared showers are US$5.50 per person. A bigger cabin sleeping up to six is US$36 with a private bath. Other basic cheapies are *Cabinas Grano de Oro* (☎ 777-0578), but they don't like to take phone reservations, and *Cabinas Anep*

(☎ 777-0565) which have some rooms with private (cold) bath. Both charge US$7.25/11 for singles/doubles.

Cabinas Irarosa have simple, clean rooms with fan and private cold bath for US$14.50/20. *Cabinas Ramírez* (☎ 777-0510) has dank rooms with private cold bath and fans for US$25 double or US$30 triple. For the same price, the *Cabinas Piscis* (☎ 777-0046) are a better alternative – they are close to the beach and have an inexpensive restaurant.

The *Restaurant Mar y Sombra* (☎ 777-0003) has casados and chicken and pasta plates for about US$3 and fish dinners for twice that. There are good sunset views. The *Restaurant y Soda Marlin* is often crowded and has meals for around US$3 to US$5. They serve breakfast. There are a number of other cheap sodas and roadside stands in the beach area – *Restaurant Las Olas* and *Pearl's Soda* have been recommended.

The *Discoteque Amor y Mar* (☎ 777-0510) serves cheapish meals, if you like the loud disco music – there is dancing here some nights. The *Bar del Mar* (☎ 777-0543) is a quiet place for a drink or snack, and you can rent surfboards and snorkels there.

Cabinas Manuel Antonio, a former

COSTA RICA

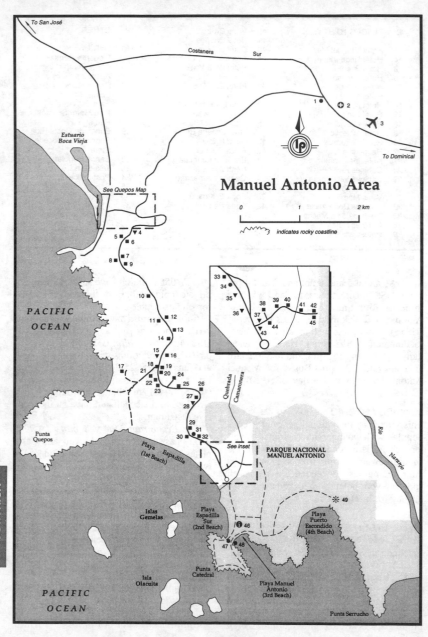

PACIFIC OCEAN

Estuario Boca Vieja

To San José

Costanera   Sur

To Dominical

Manuel Antonio Area

0   1   2 km

~~~ indicates rocky coastline

See Quepos Map

Punta Quepos

PACIFIC OCEAN

Playa Espadilla (1st Beach)

Quebrada Camaronera

Río Naranjo

PARQUE NACIONAL MANUEL ANTONIO

See inset

Islas Gemelas

Playa Espadilla Sur (2nd Beach)

Playa Puerto Escondido (4th Beach)

Isla Olocuita

Punta Catedral

Playa Manuel Antonio (3rd Beach)

Punta Serrucho

COSTA RICA

shoestringers' hangout, was ruined by the 1993 earthquake.

Getting There & Away
See the earlier Quepos entry. Buses leave from the end of the road leading to the national park. Buy your tickets in advance if possible, particularly at weekends. Call ☎ 777-0263 for bus reservations in Manuel Antonio. It is about US$1 cheaper to reach San José from Quepos than from Manuel Antonio.

PARQUE NACIONAL MANUEL ANTONIO
Manuel Antonio is the smallest national park but also one of the most popular ones. There are beautiful forest-backed tropical beaches, rocky headlands with ocean and island views, exotic wildlife, and a maintained trail system. This has led to intense pressure on both the park and the area – too many visitors, too many hotels, and too much impact on the wildlife and environment. There have been serious discussions about limiting the number of visitors to the park at any time – limits may be in effect when you arrive. If you are looking for solitude, this is not the place.

Cars are prohibited, and arriving on foot is a minor adventure – the estuary at the park entrance must be waded. The water is thigh deep at high tide. Trails lead to three beaches within an hour's walk. Another trail climbs a cliff with good views.

Most visitors who spend a day walking around will see monkeys. Sloths, agoutis, armadillos, coatimundis and raccoons are also sometimes seen. Over 350 bird species are reported for the park, and a variety of lizards, snakes, iguanas and other animals may be observed. There is a small coral reef off Manuel Antonio beach, but the water is rather cloudy and the visibility limited.

Information
The visitor information centre is near Manuel Antonio beach. Drinking water is available, and there are toilets nearby. The park is open from 7 am to 4 pm, and guards come round in the evening to make sure that

COSTA RICA

nobody is camping, which is prohibited. Carry plenty of drinking water, sun protection and insect repellent when visiting the park. Entrance costs US$1.50.

DOMINICAL

This quiet coastal village is 44 km south of Quepos – the road is gravelled but there are plans to pave it. It is 34 km from San Isidro by steep paved road. The long Dominical beach has strong rip currents, so be careful. Surfers hang out here and the area has a growing reputation as a place to get off the beaten track. A small ecotourism industry is developing and local operators, led by the owners of the Hacienda Barú, are banding together in an effort to promote the area without spoiling it.

Information

There are public phones outside the Soda Laura and Cabinas Coco. Selva Mar (tel/fax 771-1903) will pass on radio messages for the following local businesses if you leave a message: Hacienda Barú, Albergue Willdale, Cabinas Bellavista, Finca Brian & Milena and Cabañas Escondidas. Most of these are in radio contact with one another.

Places to Stay – in Dominical

In Dominical The following are on the main street. The basic but clean *Cabinas Coco* (☎ 771-2555) is US$7.25/11 for singles/doubles. The good *Albergue Willdale* (also called Cabinas Willy) has clean, spacious rooms with electric showers and fans for US$18/22/26 for singles/doubles/triples. Reserve rooms through Selva Mar. *La Residencia* charges US$22 for small, clean doubles with electric shower and fans. *Jungle Jim's* (☎ 771-2095) is similarly priced and has clean rooms with a communal shower.

Cabinas Nayarit (☎ 771-1878) is closer to the beach and charges US$22 for three people in rather grim rooms with bath and fan or cheaper rooms without bath. About one km south of town, the *Cabinas Roca Verde* is US$18 for three people in simple cabins with bath.

Around Dominical Hacienda Barú is in a 330-hectare private nature reserve covering several habitats in the steep coastal hills about 1½ km north of Dominical. Tours available include a rainforest hike with lunch (US$25), and an overnight in the rainforest with meals and comfortable camping (US$60). These prices are for one person – groups get discounts (maximum eight people). There are simple three-bedroom cabins with kitchen, refrigerator and electric shower for US$35 to US$70 (two to six people, high season). Make reservations with Selva Mar (☎/fax 71-1903), attention Jack or Diane Ewing, Apartado 215-8000, San Isidro de El General.

About three km south of Dominical, a sign points left to a rough road, locally called 'Escaleras' (Staircase), for *Cabinas Bellavista*. This is a revamped farmhouse at 500 metres above sea level – great views. Rustic but clean rooms are US$20/30/40 for one to three people; cold-water bathrooms are communal; meals are US$10 per day. Make reservations at Selva Mar – guests are picked up in Dominical for US$10 for the 4WD drive to this remote spot. Rainforest hikes and horse rental are available.

Also on the Escaleras road is the *Finca Brian y Milena*, Apartado 2-8000, San Isidro de El General, Costa Rica. This isolated working farm in the rainforest has a simple cabin (private bathroom) sleeping up to five (with portable cots). Rates are US$25 a single and US$15 per additional person. The tiny Birdhouse Cabin (shared bathroom) is US$15/25 for a single/double. Country-style meals are US$10 per day and a hot tub is available. If you don't have a 4WD, you can either hike (1½ hours) or ride a horse (US$7.50/hour) to get to their place. Rainforest/waterfall tours of one to five days (with optional camping or visits with campesino families) are available: a five-night trip starts at US$130 for one person and US$60 for each additional person including food and indigenous guides; horse rental etc is extra.

Seven km south of Dominical is *Cabañas Escondidas* (Apartado 364, San Isidro de El

General, or leave a message with Selva Mar). The cabins are in attractive gardens surrounded by 20 hectares of rainforest – very tranquil. The women running the place offer classes in tai chi and chi kung, give therapeutic massage, provide gourmet vegetarian meals, and arrange the usual guided rainforest hikes etc. It's a 10-minute walk to the beach. Cabins with ocean views and private baths are US$45 a double plus US$11 for additional people – breakfast included. Other meals are US$8 with advance notice. Two *ranchos* (simple sleeping platforms with thatched roofs and great views) are US$26 for two people.

Places to Eat

In Dominical, try the cheap *Soda Laura* and *Soda Nanyoa*. They open for breakfast and serve casados for about US$2. The pleasant tico-owned *Restaurant Maui* has decent meals ranging from US$2 to US$7. The US-owned *Jungle Jim's* has loud music, cable TV, bar and pricey hamburgers etc.

Getting There & Away

Quepos-San Isidro buses leave at 5 am and 1.30 pm, pass Dominical two hours later and continue 1½ hours to San Isidro. A bus leaves Uvita (near the Parque Nacional Marino Ballena) at 6.30 am, passes Dominical around 8 am and continues to San Isidro. Buses leave San Isidro at 7 am and 1.30 pm for Quepos and at 3 pm for Uvita, passing through Dominical about 1½ hours later. The Dominical bus stop is near the Soda Laura.

PARQUE NACIONAL MARINO BALLENA

This park protects coral and rock reefs in 4500 hectares of ocean around Isla Ballena, south of Uvita. The island has nesting seabird colonies and many green iguanas and basilisk lizards. Humpback whales migrate through the area from December to March. South-east of Punta Uvita the park includes 13 km of sandy and rocky beaches, mangrove swamps, river mouths and rocky headlands. Olive ridley and hawksbill turtles nest on sandy beaches from May to November, with a peak in September and October.

Information

The ranger station is in Bahía, on the sea three km from Uvita. Boats from Bahía to Isla Ballena can be hired for about US$15 to US$20 per hour; landing on the island and snorkelling is permitted. From the ranger station you can walk onto Punta Uvita and snorkel (best on a dropping/low tide). The park entrance fee is US$1.50. A campsite with pit toilets and water is planned near the ranger station – this will cost US$2.20 per person per night. Meanwhile, you can camp on the beach for free.

Getting There & Away

The daily Uvita-San Isidro bus begins and ends in Bahía – ask locally for the bus stop.

Península de Nicoya

This peninsula has few paved roads, but some of Costa Rica's major beach resorts are here, often remote and difficult to get to. There are several small and rarely visited wildlife reserves and parks, but for the most part people come here looking for beaches to relax on. Because of poor roads, public transport is not very convenient and travellers should allow plenty of time to get around. Hitching is a definite possibility. If you want to cook for yourself, bring food from inland. Stores are few and far between on the coast. Hotels tend to be expensive.

PLAYA DEL COCO

This beach area is 35 km west of Liberia and is the most easily accessible of the Península de Nicoya beaches, connected by good roads to San José. It is attractively set between two rocky headlands. There is a small village and some nightlife. It is a popular resort for ticos in particular, and foreign travellers to a lesser extent. The beach has strong rip currents and is somewhat shabby and littered because of the large number of visitors.

COSTA RICA

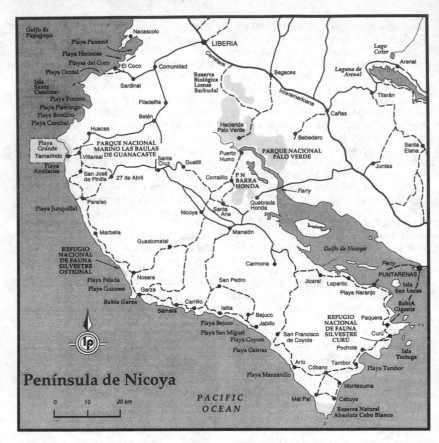

Golfo de Papagayo

Nacascolo

Playa Panamá

Playa Hermosa

Playas del Coco

El Coco   Comunidad

LIBERIA

Playa Ocotal

Isla Santa Catalina

Sardinal

Reserva Biológica Lomas Barbudal

Bagaces

Lago Coter

Arenal

Laguna de Arenal

Filadelfia

Playa Potrero

Playa Flamingo

Belén

Tilarán

Playa Brasilito

Playa Conchal

Huacas

Hacienda Palo Verde

Cañas

Bebedero

Santa Elena

Playa Grande

Tamarindo

PARQUE NACIONAL MARINO LAS BAULAS

Villareal

PARQUE NACIONAL DE GUANACASTE

Santa Cruz   Guaitil

Puerto Humo

PARQUE NACIONAL PALO VERDE

Juntas

Playa Avellanes

San José de Pinilla   27 de Abril

Corralillo

P N BARRA HONDA

Paraíso

Nicoya   Santa Ana

Quebrada Honda

Ferry

Playa Junquillal

Marbella

Guastomatal

Mansión

Golfo de Nicoya

REFUGIO NACIONAL DE FAUNA SILVESTRE OSTIONAL

Nosara

Carmona

Ferry

PUNTARENAS

Playa Pelada

San Pedro

Jicaral   Lepanto

Isla San Lucas

Playa Guiones

Garza

Playa Naranjo

BahíA Gigante

Bahía Garza

Carrillo

Islita

Sámara

Bejuco

Jabillo

REFUGIO NACIONAL DE FAUNA SILVESTRE CURÚ

Paquera

Curú

Playa Bejuco

San Francisco de Coyote

Pochote

Isla Tortuga

Playa San Miguel

Playa Coyote

Playa Caletas

Arío

Tambor

Playa Tambor

Cóbano

Península de Nicoya

Playa Manzanillo

Montezuma

0   10   20 km

PACIFIC OCEAN

Mal Paí

Cabuya

Reserva Natural Absoluta Cabo Blanco

Places to Stay & Eat

There is a campsite about 150 metres from the beach – follow the signs. The place is not very attractive, but seems secure and has bathrooms and showers. Rates are US$1.50 per person.

Cabinas El Coco (☎ 670-0110, 670-0276, fax 670-0167) is to the right as you arrive at the beach. Fairly basic rooms, all with private bath, are US$11.75/15 for a single/double at the back, more on the beach front. There is a mid-priced restaurant on the premises and a disco next door. *Cabinas Luna Tica* (☎ 670-0127, or annexe 670-

0279) has rooms with private bath and a double bed for US$20, or US$11/14.50 in the annexe. All rooms have a fan. The hotel is near the beach, but the annexe is set back from the beach and has nicer rooms. A restaurant is attached.

Other cheapies include the *Cabinas Las Brisas* (☎ 670-0155) just before the town plaza next to the Pronto Pizzería. An unsigned set of cabins is nearby. The *Pronto Pizzería* is popular for Italian food.

The *Cabinas Chale* (☎ 67-0036, 67-0303) is 600 metres to the right as you arrive (there are signs). Good rooms with private bath, fan and refrigerator are US$18/24. There is a big pool, and the staff are friendly.

Getting There & Away
Pulmitan (☎ 222-1650) has a bus from San José daily at 10 am (US$3.50). The return bus leaves Playa del Coco at 9.15 am. Buses to and from Liberia leave five times a day during the dry season, less frequently in the wet.

PLAYA TAMARINDO
There is a small community and a large and attractive beach here. Both surfing and windsurfing are good, and there is a wildlife refuge nearby. Parts of the beach have rip currents.

Tours & Rentals
Papagayo Excursions (☎/fax 680-0859) near the entrance of town arranges boat tours, snorkelling, horse rentals, visits to turtle nesting areas etc. Tamarindo Boutique, near the centre, rents surfboards, kayaks, snorkels and bikes. The friendly Iguana Surf Shop also rents kayaks and surfboards.

Places to Stay & Eat
Most places are not very cheap. It's hard to get single rates during the high season. At the entrance to town on the left, the *Hotel Pozo Azul* (☎ 654-4280; 680 0147 in Santa Cruz) has rooms with bath and some with kitchenette at US$21/27 for singles/doubles or US$34 with air-con. There is a pool. *Cabinas Rosa Mer* is in front of the rental and souvenir shops and is reportedly the cheapest place in town. In the centre, *Hotel Dolly* has rooms with fans and bath for US$22 a double. Opposite, *Cabinas Marielos* (☎ 441-4843) provides similar accommodation and prices.

At the end of the road, *Cabinas Zullymar*, (☎ 226-4732) has basic rooms with bath and fan at US$22/27 for doubles/triples or more expensive better rooms. Opposite, they have a good and reasonably priced restaurant. There are several other restaurants clustered around here. In the centre of town is the popular *Johann's Bakery* for fresh pastries, croissants etc. You can also get pizzas there.

Getting There & Away
Air Travelair flies twice daily from San José for US$70/121. SANSA has slightly cheaper daily flights. Some flights may stop at other peninsula airstrips: Carrillo, Nosara, Sámara and Tambor. The Travelair agent is the Hotel Pueblo Dorado and the SANSA agent is the Hotel Milagro.

Bus TRALAPA and Empresa Alfaro have daily afternoon buses from San José. TRALAPA buses leaves Santa Cruz at 6.45 am and 8.30 pm for Tamarindo.

PARQUE NACIONAL MARINO LAS BAULAS DE GUANACASTE
This includes Playa Grande, an important nesting site for the *baula* (leatherback turtle). This is the world's largest turtle and may weigh over 500 kg! Nesting season is October to March, and over 100 turtles may be seen laying their eggs during the course of a night.

The refuge is best visited by boat – ask at your hotel and they'll put you in contact with a boat owner.

PLAYA JUNQUILLAL
This is a wide and wild beach, with high surf, strong rip currents, and few people. The beach is two km long and has tide pools and pleasant walking. Sea turtles nest here, but in smaller numbers than at the refuges. There is no village to speak of.

Places to Stay
You can camp by the *Hotel Playa Junquillal* for about US$4 per night, or stay in one of their few basic cabins for about US$11 per person. You could probably camp almost anywhere along the beach if you had your own food and water.

Getting There & Away
TRALAPA has a daily bus from San José which takes six hours. There is also a daily TRALAPA bus from Santa Cruz. The bus may go only as far as Paraíso, which is four km by foot or taxi from the beach.

COSTA RICA

SANTA CRUZ

This small town, 57 km from Liberia, is a possible overnight stop for people visiting the peninsula. There is an annual rodeo and fiesta during the second week in January.

An interesting excursion is to the village of **Guaitil**, 12 km away, where local families make and sell attractive pottery in the pre-Columbian Chorotega style.

Places to Stay & Eat

The *Pensión Isabel* (☎ 680-0173), on the south-west corner of the Plaza de Los Mangos, has OK rooms for about US$4.50 per person. Cheap and basic wooden boxes are available at the *Pensión Pampera*, 100 metres west and 150 metres south of the Plaza de Los Mangos. Another cheapie is the *Hospedaje Amadita*, 250 metres north of the same plaza. Also try the family-run *Hospedaje y Restaurante Avellanas* (☎ 680-0808) which is 150 metres north of the Banco Anglo Costarricense.

Check out *La Fabrica de Tortillas*, 700 metres south of the Plaza de Los Mangos. They have good snacks, bread and tico-style meals, as well as tortillas, and they're not expensive.

Getting There & Away

Alfaro and TRALAPA have many buses a day from San José to Santa Cruz, some continuing to Nicoya. There are also buses about every hour from Liberia. There are daily buses for Tamarindo and Junquillal. There are six buses a day to Guaitil.

There are two bus terminals. One is on the Plaza de Los Mangos and a bigger one is 400 metres east of the centre. There are also bus stops for various destinations in other places – ask around.

NICOYA

Nicoya, 23 km south of Santa Cruz, is the most important town on the peninsula. It was named after the Chorotega Indian Chief Nicoya who welcomed the first Spaniards in 1523 – some locals are partly of Chorotega descent. The shining white church on the pleasant Parque Central dates to the mid-

17th century and is worth a look. Nicoya is now the commercial centre of the cattle industry as well as the political capital and the transport hub of the peninsula. Banks change US dollars.

Places to Stay & Eat

The *Hotel Ali* (☎ 685-5148) has basic rooms for US$3.25 per person. The *Hotel Venecia* (☎ 685-5325) charges US$7.25 for basic doubles with shared cold showers and US$14.50 double with private showers. The *Hotel Elegancia* (☎ 685-5159) is in the same price range. The clean and popular *Hotel Chorotega* (☎ 685-5245) has basic rooms with fans for US$3.75 per person and decent rooms with shower and fan for US$7.25 per person.

The *Hotel Las Tinajas* (☎ 685-5081/777, fax 685-5096) has decent rooms with bath and fans for US$11/15 single/double. Larger rooms with private bath sleeping six or seven people are US$6 per person. The *Hotel Jenny* (☎ 685-5050) is clean, popular and has bus information. Air-con rooms with bath and TV are US$14/21.

There are three or four Chinese restaurants in the centre. *Café Daniela* serves breakfasts, burgers, pizzas, and snacks and is popular. The *Bar/Restaurant Nicoya* is good for standard meals. Stands and sodas around the parque sell cheap snacks.

Getting There & Away

Alfaro has several buses a day from San José to Nicoya. There are frequent buses from the terminal in Liberia to Nicoya.

Most buses leave Nicoya from the bus terminal at the south end of Calle 5. Departures for Liberia leave 17 times a day from Transportes La Pampa at Avenida 1 and Calle 5, but they may move to the new terminal soon. There are six buses a day for San José, buses at 5.15 am and 1 pm for Playa Naranjo (connecting with the Puntarenas ferry), and daily service to Playa Sámara, Playa Nosara, Quebrada Honda, Santa Ana, Copal, and other local towns.

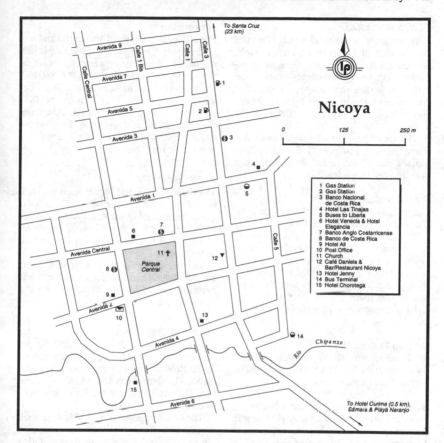

Nicoya

0   125   250 m

1   Gas Station
2   Gas Station
3   Banco Nacional
    de Costa Rica
4   Hotel Las Tinajas
5   Buses to Liberia
6   Hotel Venecia & Hotel
    Elegancia
7   Banco Anglo Costarricense
8   Banco de Costa Rica
9   Hotel Ali
10 Post Office
11 Church
12 Café Daniela &
    Bar/Restaurant Nicoya
13 Hotel Jenny
14 Bus Terminal
15 Hotel Chorotega

PARQUE NACIONAL BARRA HONDA

This park protects some of Costa Rica's most interesting caves, though they are hard to enter without caving gear.

Information

The ranger station at the south-west corner of the park provides information and takes the US$1.50 daily entrance fee. About 300 metres beyond the station is a camping area with latrines and water – US$2.20 per person. Trails lead to the top of nearby hills – carry plenty of water.

Just outside the park entance, the locals have organised *Proyecto Las Delicias*, which has a campsite (US$2.20 per person), simple restaurant and cabins for US$11 per person. Local guides with gear can be hired to descend into a cave – about US$50 per group.

Getting There & Away

There are no buses to the park, but buses go from Nicoya to Santa Ana, Corralillo and Nacaome, which are three, four and six-km walks respectively from the park.

PLAYA NOSARA

This attractive white-sand beach is backed by a pocket of luxuriant vegetation which attracts birds and wildlife. Foreign (especially North American) retirees live here year round. Note that the village and airport of Nosara are five km inland from the beach. Basic food supplies are available in the village.

The small beaches of Playa Pelada and Playa Guiones, a couple of km south of Playa Nosara, are attractive and worth visiting if you are spending a few days.

Places to Stay & Eat

Cheap hotels are in the village. The basic *Cabinas Chorotega* (☎ 680-0836) is US$7.25 per person. The clean *Cabinas Agnel* has rooms with private bath for US$8.75 per person. *Betty's Restaurant* serves Mexican food and *La Lechuza* is locally popular. Camping is possible on the beach and there are shelters and water. *Olga's Restaurant* on Playa Pelada has US$3 casados.

Getting There & Away

Air Travelair has daily flights from San José for US$61/106. SANSA has slightly cheaper flights three times a week.

Bus The 35-km dirt road from Nicoya to Nosara is poor, and buses may get stuck in the wet season. A daily bus leaves Nicoya at 1 pm and returns to Nicoya at 6 am. It's a two to five-hour trip.

REFUGIO NACIONAL DE FAUNA SILVESTRE OSTIONAL

This includes the coastal village of Ostional. The reserve is eight km long but only a few hundred metres wide. The main attraction is the annual nesting of the olive ridley sea turtle, from July to November with a peak from August to October.

Apart from turtles, there are iguanas, crabs, howler monkeys, coatimundis, and many birds to be seen. There is a small mangrove swamp, and the tide pools are teeming with life.

Information

The villagers of Ostional are helpful and will guide you to the best areas. Camping is permitted, but there are no camping facilities. Ostional has a small store (☎ 680-0467) where you can get basic food supplies. They also have a few basic rooms for rent at US$3 per person – bring mosquito coils. A bus runs from Santa Cruz at noon, depending on road conditions. Alternatively, walk eight km north-west from Nosara.

PLAYA SÁMARA

This beautiful, gentle, white-sand beach is one of the safest and prettiest in Costa Rica. Former president Oscar Arias has a vacation house near here. It is a favourite beach for tourists, and has an improving bus and air service.

The village has a general store, a disco, and a couple of basic hotels, restaurants, and bars. Pulpería Mileth has a public phone and bus information.

Places to Stay & Eat

Camp near *Soda Yuré* for US$1.50 per person or at *Coco's* for US$2.25 per person. *Soda Yuré* has typical food – casados for US$2.50, other plates around US$4, but no beer is served. Ask around for other places to camp.

The basic but popular *Hotel Playa Sámara* (☎ 680-0724) charges US$6 per person. A cheap soda and a disco are nearby. Other cheap places to try are the *Cabinas Sámara* (☎ 680-0222) with rooms with private baths, or the cheaper *Cabinas Magaly*. *Cabinas & Comedor Arenas* (☎ 680-0445) has rooms with bath and fan for US$29 double. The *Albergue Casa del Mar*, next to the Super Sámara store, charges US$20/30 for singles/doubles in spacious, clean and pleasant rooms with fans. The bathrooms are separate. Continental breakfast is included. Opposite, a house advertises rooms for rent.

About four km south-east of Sámara is the quiet **Playa Carrillo** where there are basic rooms offered by *Bar El Mago* and cabins rented by the *artesanía* store, next to the giant strangler fig by the beach. These rent for US$11 per person.

Getting There & Away
Air The airport is between Sámara and Carrillo and is also called Carrillo. Travelair has daily flights for US$61/106. SANSA has slightly cheaper flights on most days.

Bus Alfaro in San José has a daily noon bus to Sámara, taking six hours. It leaves Sámara at 4 am. Buses from Nicoya leave at 8 am and 3 pm (two hours, US$1.25).

PLAYA NARANJO
This village is the terminal for the Puntarenas ferry, and the beach is not very exciting. Most ferry passengers continue on to Nicoya, about 70 km to the north-west. There are no cheap hotels.

Getting There & Away
All transport is geared to Puntarenas ferry (☎ 661-1069), which departs five times a day. Buses meet incoming ferries and take passengers to Nicoya, three to four hours away.

If you want to go to the south part of the Península de Nicoya, don't come to Playa Naranjo – take the passenger ferry from Puntarenas to Paquera.

PAQUERA
This village is four km away from the Puntarenas-Paquera passenger ferry terminal. The passenger ferry leaves for Puntarenas at 8 am and 5 pm daily (plus another sailing at 12.30 pm in the high season). There is a snack bar at the Paquera ferry terminal, and a very crowded truck takes passengers into Paquera village, where there are a couple of basic pensiones. Most travellers take the bus from the ferry terminal to Montezuma (two hours, US$2.50). The bus is crowded – get off the ferry early to get a seat.

MONTEZUMA
This village, near the tip of the peninsula, has good beaches, friendly residents, a lovely waterfall and swimming hole nearby and a nature reserve a few km away. Montezuma is very popular with younger gringo travellers who enjoy the laid-back atmosphere and affordable prices.

Information
There is a central phone number (☎ 661-1122) with extensions to various hotels, houses and restaurants.

There are no banks, but you can change dollars at Chico's or the Sano Banano resturants – if they have enough colones.

Information booths in the centre of town help you find places to stay and connect you with rentals, tours etc. Bicycle rentals are US$7.25 per day. Horses are about US$20 for half a day. Snorkelling gear is US$3.75 for half a day, and kayaks are US$11 for half a day. All-day boat trips to Isla Tortuga are US$26 a person, – bring food, drink, sun hat and sunblock. It's 90 minutes to the island, where you can swim or snorkel. Boats carrying up to four passengers are US$22 per hour (per boat) for fishing, snorkelling or sightseeing, but you have to bring your own gear.

Places to Stay
The high season (December to April) is a difficult time to find rooms, especially if you arrive late afternoon. Single rooms are hard to find.

You can camp on a beach reasonably safely, though don't leave any gear inside your tent. Unfortunately, the already overstressed sewage disposal system precludes the building of toilet facilities, and campers are soiling the beaches.

The most famous budget place is *Cabinas Karen* – a white house with a couple of basic rooms near the entrance of town plus a pair of cabins 1½ km outside of town – no electricity, outside bathrooms, and a communal kitchen. The owner is a local conservationist (originally from Denmark) who has a 69-hectare private reserve surrounding the cabins – animals abound. The cabins are usually full and with a waiting list. Rates are about US$5 to US$10 per person.

Pensión Jenny has nice balcony views and

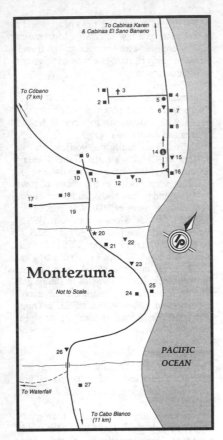

basic but clean rooms – a fair deal for US$5.50 per person in dormitories (four bunk beds) or US$11 for double rooms. All bathrooms are shared. Nearby, *Cabinas El Caracol* has large rooms with communal baths for US$7.25 per person; rooms with private bath are US$17.50 for a double. A cheap restaurant is attached.

Cabinas Tucan (☎ 661-1122, ext 284) is OK for US$14.50, single or double. It has an inexpensive restaurant. *Pensión Arenas* charges US$7.25 per person in shared rooms; private rooms are US$14.50/18 for singles/doubles. There's a family-run restau-

rant and people camp on the beach out front. *Pensión Lucy* (☎ 661-1122, ext 273) has ocean views – US$11 for an airy single or double room, and US$15.50 for a triple.

The *Hotel Moctezuma* (☎ 661-1122, ext 258) is central and has a restaurant and popular bar with music loud enough to wake light sleepers. Clean, large rooms with fans and shower cost US$14.50 a double; or US$11 in a few rooms with shared baths.

Cabinas Vilma charges US$14.50 for a single or double. Its rooms are clean and quiet, and it offers kitchen privileges. *Cabinas Capitan* has basic but clean rooms with three beds for US$22 a triple. The *Cabinas Mar y Cielo* (☎ 661-2472, 661-1122, ext 261) is also clean and charges about US$18 to US$26 double in rooms with private bath and fan. (Most rooms sleep three or four people.) The *Hotel La Aurora* has clean rooms with private bath, fans and mosquito nets for US$26 double or US$22 with shared bath. The *El Pargo Feliz* also has rooms with fans and private bath for US$22 to US$26 double.

Places to Eat

Chico's Bar is the traditional place to eat – not too expensive. Many places charge 21% tax on top of the bill. Ask first if you are on a budget. Cheap places which recently didn't add tax include the *Restaurant Tucan*, *Restaurante La Frescura*, *Soda La Gemelas* and *Restaurant El Parque*. A fish casado in these places is US$3.50, a little less with chicken or around US$5 for a full fish dinner. They don't sell alcohol, but you can bring your own. These places offer the best budget values and are very popular with young travellers – you should go by about 6 pm for the best choice of food and tables. The restaurant at *Cabinas El Caracol* is also similarly priced.

Other places which serve decent meals but are a little pricier include *El Pargo Feliz* which serves seafood, *Restaurant La Casacada* which is quiet and pleasant next to a stream, and the popular restaurant/bar in the *Hotel Moctezuma*. Next door to the Moctezuma is the *Pizzería del Sol*, which serves slices of pizza for US$1.20.

The *El Sano Banano* restaurant serves yoghurt, juices, fruit salads, vegetarian meals and pizzas. It has a big-screen TV and shows movies. The owners are a good source of information.

Getting There & Away

The Puntarenas-Paquera ferry connects with a bus to Montezuma. The 3 pm ferry gets you into Montezuma well after dark. Buses leave Montezuma at 5.30 am and 2 pm (plus 10 am in the dry season) for Paquera, connecting with the Puntarenas ferry.

RESERVA NATURAL ABSOLUTA CABO BLANCO

This beautiful reserve encompasses the southern tip of the peninsula. It is 11 km south of Montezuma by dirt road. The reserve has an evergreen forest, a couple of attractive beaches, and a host of birds and animals.

A trail leads to the beaches at the tip of the peninsula. The hike takes a couple of hours and you can return by a different trail. Look for seabirds such as boobies, pelicans and frigate birds.

A 4WD taxi (up to six passengers) from Montezuma to the park costs about US$15. There is a ranger station where you pay the US$1.50 entrance fee and can obtain information. Opening hours are 8 am to 4 pm. Camping is not permitted.

PANAMA

Panama

Some shoestring travellers try to whizz through Panama as fast as possible on the way between Central and South America. Others bypass it altogether.

They think it's expensive, and it's true that a hotel room which might cost US$6 for two people in Nicaragua or Guatemala might cost US$10 in Panama, and a meal that might cost US$1 there might cost US$2 here. However, in Panama more modern lodgings or better food may be available at lower prices than elsewhere in the region.

Or they say that Panama City is full of crime – but the poor districts in any city are risky at night, and many districts of Panama City are comparatively affluent and actually have less crime than some other Central American capitals. Images of the US invasion in 1989 don't help to make Panama seem inviting; but in the long history of US-Panama relations that was, in fact, a minor chapter.

Panama is an unknown delight. Unlike Costa Rica, it is politically less than stable, but also unlike its northern neighbours, it has a partying spirit. The diverse ethnic mixture of the Panamanian people creates an interesting cultural fabric. The capital city is not as dangerous as some people expect, and there are many things to do there and in the vicinity that cost only a few cents or nothing at all.

A few highlights from around the city include the Panama Canal's Miraflores Locks, the Summit Botanical Gardens & Zoo, the Sendero El Charco nature trail, the Parque Natural Metropolitano, and the Bahai Temple. In the city itself are the Casco Viejo district and the sea wall the Spanish built three centuries ago; good museums; good cheap restaurants; and first-run films from the USA with Spanish subtitles. Panama is notable for its enthusiasm for classical music and modern art and literatures.

Virtually everything in Panama is very cheap. A boat ride to the beautiful Isla Taboga, costs only US$5, and a visit to Isla

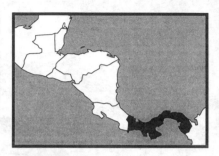

Barro Colorado in the Canal itself, with its famous Smithsonian Tropical Research Institute, costs US$12.

Panama seems to get more interesting the longer you stay and get into it. There are some travellers who stay a day or two, don't see much, say they don't like the place, and leave. To each their own.

Facts about the Country

HISTORY
Spanish Colonisation
When Europeans first arrived on the isthmus of Panama in the early 16th century, it was inhabited by various indigenous peoples including the Cuna, Chocó and Guaymí, among others. The population may have been as large then as it is now, but it was rapidly decimated by European diseases and Spanish swords.

The first European in the area was the Spanish explorer Rodrigo de Bastidas, who sailed along its Caribbean coast in 1501 with Vasco Nuñez de Balboa and Juan de la Cosa. The following year, Christopher Columbus sailed along part of this coast on his fourth and final New World voyage. Shortly thereafter, in 1510, the first Spanish settlement was founded at the mouth of the Río Chagres by another explorer, Diego de Nicuesa, and called Nombre de Dios.

Not far away, on the Gulf of Urabá in what is now Colombia, Alonso de Ojeda founded another settlement, San Sebastian de Urabá. This settlement was later moved to the Panamanian coast under the leadership of Vasco Nuñez de Balboa, and renamed Santa María la Antigua del Darién.

Indians told Balboa of a large sea and of a wealthy, gold-producing civilisation – almost certainly referring to the Inca empire of Peru – across the mountains of the isthmus. Balboa subsequently scaled the mountains and on 26 September 1513 'discovered' the Pacific Ocean, claiming it for the King of Spain.

In 1519 the settlement of Santa María was moved again, across the isthmus to the Pacific side, near where Panama City stands today. It was named Panamá (meaning 'abundance of fish') and became an important Spanish settlement, commercial centre and the springboard for further explorations, including the conquest of Peru and expeditions north into Central America.

The ruins of this old settlement, Panamá Viejo, are still there.

The Las Cruces Trail connected Panamá to Nombre de Dios on the Caribbean side. Goods were carried between the two ports until late in the century, when Nombre de Dios was destroyed by the English pirate Francis Drake. The small bay of Portobelo then became the chief Caribbean connection. Gold from Peru and other colonial products were brought there along El Camino Real (the king's highway) by mule train from Panamá. The treasure was then held for an annual trading fair, when Spanish galleons laden with goods from Europe would come to trade with the New World.

All this wealth concentrated in one small bay naturally attracted the English, French, Dutch and other pirates who were plying the Caribbean at the time. The Spanish built large stone fortresses to try to ward off attack: two of these, the fortresses at Portobelo and at Fort San Lorenzo at the mouth of the Río Chagres, can still be visited today.

They weren't enough, however. In 1671 the English pirate Henry Morgan overpowered Fort San Lorenzo, sailed up the Río Chagres and crossed the isthmus. His forces destroyed the city of Panamá, making off with its entire treasure and arriving back on the Caribbean coast with 200 mules loaded with loot. The town was rebuilt a few years later on a cape several km west of its original site, where the San Felipe district of Panama City is today.

After Portobelo was also destroyed in 1739, by the British Admiral Edward Vernon, the Spanish finally abandoned the Panamanian crossing in favour of sailing the long way around Cape Horn to the west coast of South America. Panama declined in importance and in that year was made a part of the Viceroyalty of Nueva Andalucia, later Nueva Granada, which was later to become Colombia.

Independence

In 1821 Colombia, including Panama, gained its independence from Spain. Panama joined Gran Colombia, which included Colombia, Venezuela, Ecuador, Peru and Bolivia: the united Latin American nation that Simón Bolívar had dreamed of. Later Gran Colombia split up, but Panama remained a province of Colombia.

The Panama Railroad

From the moment that it was discovered to be the narrowest point between the Atlantic and Pacific oceans, the isthmus of Panama attracted the interest of the world's major powers.

In 1846 Colombia signed a treaty to permit the USA to construct a railway across the isthmus. The treaty guaranteed the USA the right of free transit across the isthmus and the right to protect the line with military force. This was a time of great political turbulence in Panama. Construction began in 1850 and was completed in 1855; during that time Panama had 20 different governors.

The California gold rush of 1848 helped to make the railway a profitable venture. It also spurred efforts to construct an interoceanic canal across Central America.

The Panama Canal & the French

The idea of a canal across the isthmus was first mooted in 1524, when King Charles V of Spain ordered a survey to be made of the feasibility of constructing such a waterway. In 1878, the Colombian government awarded a contract to build a canal to Lucien N B Wyse, who sold the concession to the French diplomat Ferdinand de Lesseps, then basking in his success as the contractor-builder of the Suez Canal.

De Lesseps' Compagnie Universelle du Canal Interocéanique began work in 1880. De Lesseps was determined to build a sea-level canal alongside the interoceanic railway, but the project proved more difficult than anyone had expected. Yellow fever and malaria killed around 22,000 workers, there were insurmountable construction problems, and financial mismanagement drove the company bankrupt by 1889.

One of de Lesseps' chief engineers, Philippe Bunau-Varilla, formed a new canal company, but at the same time the USA was seriously considering putting its own canal

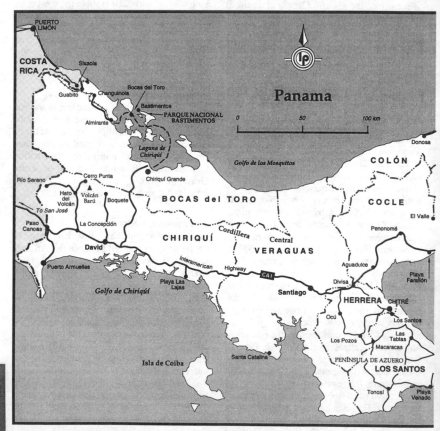

somewhere through Central America. Nicaragua seemed the most likely site (see the Nicaragua chapter) but taking over the canal in Panama was also a possibility. The French, unable to complete the canal, finally agreed to sell the concession to the USA. In 1903 Bunau-Varilla asked the Colombian government for leave to conclude the sale. Colombia refused.

Panama Becomes a Nation

Revolutionary sentiments had been brewing in Panama for many years, but repeated attempts to break away from Colombia had met with no success. In 1903 a civil war in Colombia was breeding fresh discontents, as Panamanians were drafted to fight and Panamanian property was seized by the Colombian government for the war effort.

When the Colombian government refused to allow the transfer of the canal treaty to the USA, it thwarted US and French interests as well as Panama's own. Bunau-Varilla, who had a lot to gain financially if the sale went through, approached the US government to back Panama if it declared its independence from Colombia.

A revolutionary junta declared Panama

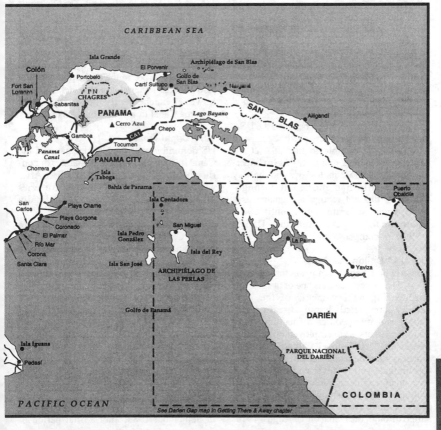

See Darien Gap map in Getting There & Away chapter

PANAMA

independent on 3 November 1903 with the support of the USA, which immediately recognised the new government. Colombia sent in troops to try to regain control of the province, but without success.

Canal Treaty

Fifteen days later, Bunau-Varilla, now Panamanian ambassador to the USA, signed a treaty with US Secretary of State John Hay. The Hay-Bunau-Varilla treaty, signed on 18 November, gave the USA far more than had been offered in the original treaty rejected by the Colombian government. Its 26 articles awarded the US 'sovereign rights in perpetuity over the Canal Zone', an area extending eight km on either side of the Canal, and a broad right of intervention in Panamanian affairs.

Bunau-Varilla had moved quickly to preempt the arrival of a delegation from Panama that was supposed to negotiate the treaty terms. By the time they arrived in Washington DC, the treaty was signed. It was ratified over their protests.

The treaty led to friction between the USA and Panama for decades, partly because it was overly favourable to the USA at the expense of Panama, and partly due to lingering questions about its legality and the way Bunau-Varilla had pushed it through. Colombia did not recognise Panama as a legitimately separate nation until 1921, when the USA paid Colombia US$25 million in 'compensation'.

The USA Builds the Canal

Construction began again on the canal in 1904. The project remains one of the greatest engineering achievements of the 20th century, completed despite disease, landslides, and many other difficulties. Over 75,000 workers were employed on it. Canal heroes included Colonel William Crawford Gorgas, who managed a massive campaign to eliminate yellow fever and malaria, and two chief engineers, John F Stevens and Colonel George Washington Goethals.

Construction took 10 years. The first ship sailed through the Canal on 15 August 1914.

Rise of the Military

The US military intervened repeatedly in Panama's political affairs until 1936, when the Hay-Bunau-Varilla treaty was replaced by the Hull-Alfaro treaty. The USA relinquished its rights to use its troops outside the Canal Zone and to seize land for Canal purposes, and the annual sum paid to Panama for use of the Canal Zone was increased.

With the new restrictions on US military activity, the Panamanian army grew more powerful. In 1968 the Guardia Nacional deposed the elected president and took control of the government; the constitution was suspended, the national assembly dissolved and the press censored. The Guardia's General Omar Torrijos Herrera emerged as the new leader.

Torrijos conducted public works programs on a grand scale, including a massive modernisation of Panama City, which won him the support of much of the populace but also plunged Panama into huge debt. He did, however, successfully negotiate a new Panama Canal treaty with the USA.

1977 Canal Treaty

US dominion over the Canal Zone, and the Canal itself, were continuing sources of conflict between Panama and the USA. After years of negotiation that foundered in a series of stalemates, a new treaty was finally accepted by both sides in 1977.

The new treaty provides that US control of the Canal will be gradually phased out, with Panama assuming complete ownership and control on 31 December 1999. It also provides for the phasing out of US military bases in Panama. A separate treaty ensures that the Canal shall remain open and neutral for all nations, during both peace and war. In 1978, the US Senate attached extenuating conditions that grant the US the right of limited intervention, and rights to defend the Canal, beyond the 1999 date. The treaty finally went into effect on 1 October 1979.

Manuel Noriega

Torrijos was killed in a plane crash in 1981. In September 1983, after a brief period of leadership by Colonel Paredes, Colonel Manuel Antonio Noriega Moreno took control of the Guardia Nacional and then of the country itself.

Noriega, a former head of Panama's secret police and a former CIA operative, quickly consolidated his power. He enlarged the Guardia Nacional and its powers, closed down all communications media that criticised him, and created a paramilitary 'Dignity Battalion' in every city, town and village, armed and ready to inform on any of their neighbours showing less than complete loyalty to the Noriega regime.

The first presidential election in 16 years was held in 1984. Although the count was challenged, Noriega's candidate, a respected economist, Nicolás Ardito Barletta, was declared the winner. A year later Ardito Barletta was removed by Noriega for insisting on a top-level investigation into the murder of a popular Panamanian political leader, Dr Hugo Spadafora.

In early 1987 Noriega became the focus of an international scandal. He was publicly accused of involvement in drug trafficking with Colombian drug cartels, murdering his opponents, and rigging elections. By February 1988, the US had indicted Noriega for drug trafficking and involvement in organised crime. In the same month, Barletta's successor as president, Eric Arturo Delvalle, attempted to dismiss him. But Noriega still held the reins of power, and it was Delvalle who ended up fleeing Panama after being deposed himself. Noriega appointed a substitute president.

Noriega's regime was now an international embarrassment. In March 1988 the USA imposed sanctions against Panama, ending a preferential trade agreement, freezing Panamanian assets, and refusing to pay Canal fees. Panama's international offshore banking industry, which the USA had asserted was deeply involved with international drug cartels and with laundering money for organised crime, buckled under the strain of the US sanctions.

A few days after the sanctions were imposed, there was an unsuccessful military coup. Noriega responded by stepping up the violent repression of his critics, including the increasing numbers of anti-government demonstrators.

Presidential elections were held once again in May 1989. This time, when Noriega's candidate failed to win, Noriega simply declared the entire election null and void. Guillermo Endara, the winning candidate, and his two vice-presidential running mates, were beaten bloody by Noriega's forces, live on national TV. Another attempted coup in October 1989 was followed by even more repressive measures.

On 15 December 1989, Noriega's legislature declared him president. At the same time, it was announced that Panama was at war with the USA. The following day, an unarmed US marine, dressed in civilian clothes, was killed by Panamanian soldiers.

'Operation Just Cause'

US reaction was swift. In the first hour of 20 December 1989, Panama City was attacked by aircraft, tanks and 26,000 US troops in an all-out mission called 'Operation Just Cause'. US President George Bush said the invasion had four objectives: to protect US lives, to maintain the security of the Panama Canal, to restore democracy to Panama, and to capture Noriega and bring him to justice.

Shortly before the invasion there had been an attempt to kidnap Noriega, but he had gone into hiding. Then on Christmas Day, the fifth day of the invasion, he went to the Vatican Embassy to request asylum. He remained there for 10 days. Outside, the US forces reinforced diplomatic pressure on the Vatican to expel him by setting up loudspeakers outside the embassy, blaring rock music (including the song 'You're No Good'), and the recorded sounds of helicopters and gunfire to wear down the nerves of those inside. Meanwhile, angry public riots near the blocked-off embassy urged Noriega's ousting.

The Vatican embassy chief finally persuaded Noriega to give himself up by threatening to cancel his asylum. Noriega surrendered to US forces on the evening of

PANAMA

3 January 1991. He was flown immediately to Miami, where he was tried on numerous criminal charges and convicted in April 1992. He remains a guest of the US penal authorities.

Post-Invasion Panama

Guillermo Endara, the legitimate winner of the 1989 election, was sworn in as president, and Panama City attempted to put itself back together. It had suffered damage not only from the invasion itself, but from widespread looting. Many residential blocks of the district of Chorrillo, near the Panama Defence Force headquarters, had been razed to the ground.

The death toll from the invasion remains a subject of controversy. Though the 'official' death toll was put at 540, a human rights commission later determined that at least 4000 Panamanians had been killed, and other sources gave estimates as high as 7000. Unknown numbers of bodies were buried in mass graves.

Panamanian opinion of the USA remains divided. On the one hand, many people are glad the USA got rid of Noriega, saying that the Panamanians themselves had been unable to do it. Some want to see the USA tried under international law for attacking Panama, and forced to comply with all treaties until the year 2000 when it is scheduled to transfer its ownership and control of the Canal to Panama. As that deadline approaches, relations between the USA and Panama may continue to be touchy; Panamanians see both gains and losses to be accrued from the transfer, since the Canal needs expensive technological upgrading, and salaries and other expenses have long been high, pegged to the US rather than the Panamanian national budget.

GEOGRAPHY

Panama is the southernmost of the Central American countries. It is a long, narrow country in the shape of an S, bordered on the west by Costa Rica, on the east by Colombia, on the north by a 1160-km Caribbean coastline, and on the south by a 1690-km Pacific coastline. The total land area is 77,082 sq km.

The isthmus of Panama is the narrowest land mass between the Atlantic and Pacific oceans. At the narrowest point it is less than 50 km (30 miles) across; the Panama Canal is around 80 km (50 miles) long. The Panama Canal effectively divides the country into eastern and western regions.

Two mountain chains run along Panama's spine, one in the east and one in the west. The highest point in the country is Volcán Barú, 3475 metres high, in the western Chitré province. Panama's only volcano, it is dormant, although hot springs around its flanks testify to continuing thermal activity underground.

Like all the Central American countries, Panama has large flat coastal lowlands. In some places these lowlands are covered in huge banana plantations.

There are around 500 rivers in Panama, and over 1600 islands near its shores. The two main island groups, both just off the Caribbean coast, are the San Blas and Bocas del Toro archipelagos, but most of the islands are in fact on the Pacific side. Even the Panama Canal has islands, including Isla Barro Colorado, which has a world-famous tropical rainforest research station operated by the Smithsonian Institution.

FLORA & FAUNA

Tropical rainforest is the dominant vegetation in the Canal area, along the Caribbean coast, and in most of the eastern half of the country. The Parque Nacional del Darién protects a large tropical rainforest wilderness region. Other vegetation zones include grasslands on the west coast, mountain forest in the highlands, alpine vegetation on the highest peaks, and mangrove forests on parts of the Caribbean coast.

Panama's position as a narrow land bridge between two huge continents has given it a remarkable variety of plant and animal life. Species migrating between the continents have gathered in Panama, so that there are South American armadillos, anteaters and sloths along with North American tapirs, jaguars and deer. With its wide variety of both native and migratory species, Panama is an interesting place for bird-watchers.

CLIMATE

Like the rest of Central America, Panama has two seasons. The dry season (summer, or 'verano') lasts from January to mid-April, the rainy season (winter, or 'invierno') from mid-April to December.

The rain patterns, however, are markedly different on the Caribbean and Pacific sides of the country. The mountains that extend almost all the way along the spine of the country form a barrier against the warm, moist trade winds blowing from the Caribbean. As the warm air rises against the mountains the moisture it holds falls, frequently and heavily, as rain. The coast gets around 1500 to 3500 mm a year; of course the rainy season is wetter, but downpours are possible at any time of year. There are lush tropical rainforests on the Caribbean side, along the Panama Canal, and in the Darién province.

Most people live on the Pacific side of the mountains. Here, the annual rainfall is only 1140 to 2290 mm. This is still no small amount, but the rains are confined almost entirely to the rainy season. This seasonal weather pattern does not support tropical rainforest; the Pacific coast is lined with broad grasslands, or savanna.

Temperatures are typically hot in the lowlands (day/night temperatures around 32°/21°C), and cool in the mountains (18°/10°C). These remain about the same all year. In Panama City, the heat is tempered by fresh sea breezes.

GOVERNMENT

Panama now has a constitutional democracy. The executive is led by a president, elected by popular vote to a five-year term, assisted by two elected vice-presidents and an appointed cabinet. The legislative assembly has 67 members, also elected by popular vote to five-year terms. The judiciary consists of a nine-member Supreme Court, appointed to 10-year terms by the president and approved by the legislature, and various lower courts.

Panama has nine provinces, plus the autonomous region of San Blas governed by the Cuna Indian tribal leaders *(caciques)*. Each province has a governor appointed by the president, and is divided into municipal districts.

ECONOMY

Panama is much better off economically than the other countries of Central America. Panama City, especially, with its tall skyscrapers and international banking and trade, is as modern as any capital city, though like other modern cities it also has its slums,

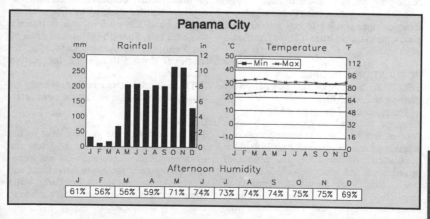

crime and unemployment – officially 11%, but probably much higher in fact.

Agriculture, including fishing, livestock and forestry, employs about 30% of the workforce, though it accounts for only 11% of the GNP. The principal crops are rice, maize, sugar cane, beans, bananas, and plantains. Cattle, pigs and poultry are farmed; sea products include fish, shrimp and lobster.

Bananas, produced primarily around the Bocas del Toro and Puerto Armuelles areas, account for 25% of Panama's exports; other important exports are shrimp (19%), coffee (5%), sugar (5%) and clothing (5%). The USA is Panama's main trading partner, taking 65% of its exports and providing 34% of its imports.

Other sectors of the labour force are engaged in trade (15%), services, public administration and defence (29%), and manufacturing (10%). The largest portion of the GNP is produced by transport and communications (29%), followed by finance and real estate (15%), public administration and defence (15%), and trade (10%).

The Colón Free Zone is the world's second most important duty-free trade zone after Hong Kong; business here includes manufacturing, warehousing and re-exporting. Panama has an important offshore banking industry. The Panama Canal brings in substantial revenue; in 1992 over 12,600 oceangoing vessels passed through it. The numbers of people crossing Panama in every direction, and coming to buy international goods, mean that tourism is also a significant industry.

POPULATION & PEOPLE

The 1990 census put the population of Panama at 2,329,329.

The majority of the population, 62%, are mestizos, of mixed indigenous and Spanish descent. But there are also a number of other sizeable groups. Blacks make up 14% of the population, Whites 10%, and people of mixed Black and White descent 5%.

The Blacks are mostly descendants of English-speaking West Indians such as Jamaicans, Bajuns and Trinidadians, who were brought to Panama as cheap labour on various projects. West Indians worked on banana plantations in the Bocas del Toro province, the trans-isthmian railway in the 1850s, the first French canal project in the 1870s and 1880s, and the US construction of the Canal in the early 20th century.

Indigenous Indians make up about 6% of the population. Panama has three major tribes: the Cuna on the San Blas islands and north-eastern Caribbean coast, the Chocó in the Darién region, and the Guaymí in western Panama. There are also several smaller indigenous groups in the western part of the country, the largest of which are the Teribe and the Bokota. Each of these groups maintains its own language and culture. The Cuna, who govern their ancestral territory as an autonomous region and send representatives to the legislature, are the most organised politically.

Panama City is a cosmopolitan crossroads of the world, and you can see people of just about every kind on earth there. The US military bases are like little US colonies.

ARTS

Panama's arts reflect its ethnic mix. Traditional products include woodcarving, weaving and textiles, ceramics, masks, straw goods, and many other handicrafts. Some of the more famous Panamanian handicrafts include *molas*, colourful hand-stitched appliqué textiles made by the Cuna Indian women, and the *pollera*, the intricately stitched, lacy, Spanish-influenced dress of the Península de Azuero, which is the 'national dress' of Panama for festive occasions.

There is also a magnificent variety of music, dance, theatre and all the other arts.

CULTURE

The Indian tribes, the various West Indian groups, the Spanish-Indian mestizos, the Chinese, Middle-Eastern, Swiss and Yugoslav immigrants, the North Americans and others all maintain their own cultures, while some elements of the cultures have mixed to make new combinations.

The cultures of different regions, homes to different ethnic groups, are as different as if they were on opposite sides of the planet. Many come together in Panama City, where there's as much international variety as anywhere on earth. To take music as an example, in one week in Panama City you could hear anything from salsa to calypso, symphony to jazz, heavy metal to reggae, traditional pan pipe music and much more besides. Panama's trade connections also mean that you can buy goods from anywhere in the world, on a scale unparallelled elsewhere in Central America.

RELIGION

Panama is predominantly Catholic, but other faiths are also represented. The major faiths are Roman Catholicism (84%), Protestant denominations (5%), Islam (5%) and Bahai (1%). There are also a small number of Hindus, Jews and other believers.

Religion is especially mixed in Panama City, home to immigrants from all over the world. The city has many Catholic and Protestant churches, a Jewish synagogue, and Hindu, Muslim and Bahai temples.

LANGUAGE

Spanish is the official language of Panama, but most of the descendants of the West Indian immigrants still speak their original Caribbean-accented English. English is also common as a second language among other ethnic groups, due to US influence in Panama City and the areas around the former Canal Zone, and Panama's role in international business.

The Indian groups still speak their own languages, and many immigrant groups do the same. You may hear Spanish, English, Cuna, Chinese, Serbo-Croat, Italian and Arabic spoken.

Panamanian Spanish is distinctive and may be difficult to understand at first. It has a lot of slang and unusual words and its own particular accent, and it is spoken very rapidly.

Facts for the Visitor

VISAS & EMBASSIES

Most nationalities need either a visa or a tourist card as well as a passport and an onward (or return) ticket to enter Panama. Travellers may also be asked to show a minimum of US$330 at the point of entry.

Visas must be obtained before entering the country by Australians, New Zealanders, Indians, Japanese and some other nationalities; they are issued at Panamanian embassies and consulates within 24 hours of application and cost around US$15, depending on the nationality of the applicant. It is probably easiest to tackle this at one of the many embassies or consulates in Central or North America. An onward ticket from Panama may be required before a visa will be issued.

Most other nationalities, including US and Canadian citizens, require only an onward or return ticket, and a US$5 tourist card, available from consulates, embassies and also from airlines, Tica bus or at the airport or border post upon entry. However, the Panamanian consulate-general in the UK advises that US and Canadian nationals would be advised to obtain a normal visa, even though it is not technically required, rather than risk being refused entry – if only because the border post has run out of tourist cards, which has happened. Visas and tourist cards are both good for 30 days and can be extended within Panama to 90 days.

Citizens of the UK, Spain, Switzerland, Germany and some Central American countries require neither a visa nor a tourist card to stay for up to three months. UK citizens do not need either an onward ticket or proof of sufficient funds at the border.

To extend your stay past the 30 days (or 90 days for UK citizens), go to an office of Migración y Naturalización in Panama City, David, Santiago or Chitré. You must bring two passport-size photos, your onward air or bus ticket, a letter to the director stating your reasons for wishing to extend your visit, and

US$11. You will then be issued a plastic photo ID card, good for another 60 days in the country. You may also have to show that you will continue to be solvent; a photocopy of your bank book or statement from home is recommended.

If you do extend your time, you then must obtain a permit when you want to leave the country (a *permiso de salida*). For this, bring your passport and a 'Paz y Salvo' form to the immigration office. Paz y Salvos are issued at the Ministerio de Hacienda y Tesoro, which simply requires that you bring in your passport, fill out a form and pay US$0.25.

Panamanian Embassies

If you need a visa, you can get one from a Panamanian embassy or consulate in another country. Some countries have several consulates; in the USA, Panama has consulates in Atlanta, Houston, Los Angeles, Miami, New Orleans, New York and San Francisco, in addition to its embassy in Washington DC. Panamanian diplomatic missions include:

Australia
    PO Box 276, Kenmore, Queensland 4069
Belize
    5481 Princess Margaret Drive, Belize City
    (PO Box 7, Belmopan) (☎ (2) 44232)
Colombia
    Calle 87, No 11A-64, Bogotá (☎ 256-8280, 257-5067, 257-5068)
Costa Rica
    del Higuerón de la Granja de San Pedro, 600 metres south and 25 metres east, Casa Esquinera, San José 1000 (☎ 225-3401, 225-0667)
El Salvador
    Alameda Roosevelt & 55a Avenida Norte, No 2838, San Salvador (☎ 98-0884)
Guatemala
    Vía 5, No 4-50, Zona 4, Edificio Maya, 7th floor, Guatemala City (☎ (2) 320763; fax 347161)
Honduras
    Colonia Palmira, Edificio Palmira, 2nd floor, opposite Hotel Honduras Maya, Tegucigalpa (☎ 31-5441)
Mexico
    Campos Elyseos, No 111, Dept 1, Colonia Polanco, México 5 DF (☎ 250-4229, 250-4259, 250-4245, 250-4246)
Nicaragua
    Pancasán No 61; from Hotel Colón, one block

east, four blocks south and half a block north, Managua (☎ 78-3304)
UK
    119 Crawford St, London W1H 1AF
    (☎ (071) 224 1140/0755)
USA
    2862 McGill Terrace NW, Washington DC 20008
    (☎ (202) 483-1407)

Foreign Embassies in Panama

Foreign embassies are in Panama City; see that section for details. Costa Rica has a consulate in David as well.

CUSTOMS

You may bring in 500 cigarettes, 500 grams of tobacco, and three bottles of alcoholic beverages.

MONEY

Panama uses the US dollar as its currency. The official name for it is the Balboa, but it's exactly the same bill, and in practice people use the terms *'dólar'* and 'Balboa' interchangeably.

Panamanian coins are of the same value, size and metal as US coins; both are used. Coins include one, five, 10, 25 and 50 centavos; there are 100 centavos to a Balboa.

Foreign		Panama
A$1	=	1.40 Balboas
C$1	=	1.45 Balboas
DM1	=	1.20 Balboas
NZ$	=	1.15 Balboas
UK£1	=	2.95 Balboas
US$1	=	1.00 Balboas

WHEN TO GO

You can go to Panama any time; the busiest tourist season, if Panama can be said to have one, is from September to April. The Darién Gap can be crossed only during the dry season, but other than that there are no particular seasonal difficulties. Rain in Panama, as elsewhere in the tropics, tends to come in sudden downpours that freshen the air and are followed by sunshine.

PANAMA

WHAT TO BRING

You can buy anything you are likely to need in Panama, and probably more cheaply than you can back home. But, depending which parts of Panama you'll be visiting, you may need to bring one or more kinds of anti-malarial medication. See the Health section in the introductory Facts for the Visitor chapter for recommendations.

TOURIST OFFICES

The Instituto Panameño de Turismo (IPAT), has offices in Panama City at the Atlapa Convention Centre and at the international airport at Tocumen. There are also offices in Colón, Portobelo, David, Santiago and Chitré. The staff can answer questions, and they have maps and plenty of printed information about the country, including the tourist magazine *Focus on Panama* with a fold-out map.

USEFUL ORGANISATIONS

The International Student Travel Confederation (ISTC) is represented in Panama City by APTE (Asociación Panameña de Turismo Estudiantil). Student discounts on airfares, tours, and many products and services within Panama are available through them.

For information on national parks, go to the Instituto de Recursos Naturales Renovables (Inrenare). The Asociación Nacional para la Conservación de la Naturaleza (Ancon), also has information on Panama's flora and fauna, and on some of the national parks and other areas.

All these organisations have offices in or near Panama City; see the Panama City section for details.

BUSINESS HOURS & HOLIDAYS

Business hours are normally Monday to Friday, 8 am to noon and 1.30 to 5 pm, and Saturday from 8 am to noon. Government offices are open Monday to Friday from 8 am until 3 or 4 pm, without closing for lunch. Banks are open Monday to Friday, from 8 or 9 am until 1 pm.

Public holidays are:

1 January
  New Year's Day
9 January
  Martyrs' Day
March-April
  Good Friday, Easter Sunday
1 May
  Labour Day
15 August
  Founding of Old Panama (in Panama City only)
12 October
  Hispanic Day
1 November
  National Anthem Day
2 November
  All Souls' Day
3 November
  Independence Day
10 November
  First Call for Independence
28 November
  Independence from Spain
8 December
  Mothers' Day
25 December
  Christmas Day

CULTURAL EVENTS

Carnaval, the Panamanian version of Mardi Gras, is celebrated on the four days before Ash Wednesday, the beginning of Lent. It is a major holiday in Panama City with costumes, music, dancing, general festivities, and a big parade on Shrove Tuesday, the final day. Carnaval is also celebrated on the Península de Azuero at Las Tablas, Chitré, Villa de Los Santos, and Parita. The celebrations in Panama City and Las Tablas are famous and well worth attending.

Over the next few years, Ash Wednesday will fall on:

1995	1 March
1996	21 February
1997	12 February
1998	25 February
1999	17 February

The Semana Santa (Easter week) celebrations at Villa de Los Santos, on the Península de Azuero, are also famous. Masked and costumed dancers representing angels, devils, imps and other figures enact dances, acrobatics and dramas. On Good Friday, religious processions are held all over the country.

The Península de Azuero has a number of other notable festivals; see the Península de Azuero section for details. The Black Christ celebration at Portobelo on 21 October attracts pilgrims from near and far. In Boquete there is the Feria de las Flores y del Café, held for one or two weeks around 11 April, the anniversary of the town's founding in 1911, and the celebration for the Virgen del Carmen on Isla Taboga on 16 July attracts crowds. Many other celebrations and cultural events take place around Panama.

Panama's many ethnic groups stage cultural events; the Cuna people and the descendants of West Indians and Spanish all have their own music and dance. If you get a chance to see some, don't miss it.

POST & TELECOMMUNICATIONS
Postal Rates
Mail to the USA takes five to six days and costs US$0.35; to Europe and Australia takes seven days and costs US$0.45.

Receiving Mail
Poste restante mail can be addressed to '(name), Entrega General, (town and province), República de Panamá'. Be sure the writer calls the country 'República de Panamá' rather than simply 'Panamá', or the mail may be sent back.

Telephone
Intel offices throughout Panama offer international telephone, telegraph, fax, and sometimes modem services. Telephone calls to anywhere within Panama can be made from phone boxes; they cost US$0.10 for three minutes. Panama's country code is 507 There are no local area codes.

TIME
Panama time is in line with New York and Miami: five hours behind GMT, and one hour ahead of the rest of Central America. If you're coming from Costa Rica, be sure to check the time when you cross the border.

WEIGHTS & MEASURES
The metric system is the official system for weights and measures, but the US system of pounds, gallons, miles etc is also used.

ELECTRICITY
Beware of variations in electrical currents in Panama (and in Honduras). An ordinary socket may be either 110 or 220 volts; find out which before you plug in your appliance! Many travel appliances such as hairdryers can be adjusted for different voltages.

BOOKS
Getting to Know Panama by Michele Labrut (Focus Publications, Aptdo 6-3287, El Dorado, Panamá, República de Panamá, 1993) is an up-to-date, thorough and lively introduction to the country, available everywhere.

The Path Between the Seas: The Creation of the Panama Canal by David McCullough (Simon & Shuster, New York, 1977) is a readable and exciting account of the building of the Panama Canal. It's 700 pages long and reads like a suspense novel. *The Impossible Dream: The Building of the Panama Canal* by Ian Cameron (William Morrow & Co, New York, 1972) is also good.

The Panama Canal: The Crisis in Historical Perspective by Walter LaFeber (Oxford University Press, New York, 1989 updated edition, paperback) is a good scholarly history of Panama and its relations with the USA.

The Sack of Panamá: Sir Henry Morgan's Adventures on the Spanish Main by Peter Earle (Viking Press, New York, 1981) is a vivid account of the British pirate's looting and destruction of Panama City in 1671.

On a more recent note, *Our Man in Panama: How General Noriega Used the United States and Made Millions in Drugs and Arms* by John Dinges (Random House, New York, 1990) tells the story of Manuel Noriega.

PANAMA

MAPS

The *Focus on Panama* tourist magazine, available free from IPAT tourist offices and other places, has a fold-out map of Panama, with inset maps of Panama City, David and Colón.

The Instituto Geográfico Nacional Tommy Guardia in Panama City sells a tourist map (US$2) with a good street map of Panama City on one side and a country map on the other. They also sell 1:50,000 topographical maps, nautical maps, city maps and others. See the Panama City section later in this chapter.

MEDIA

La Estrella de Panamá and *La República* are the major daily newspapers, but there are others: *La Prensa, Crítica Libre, El Siglo* and *El Panamá América*.

The local radio and TV stations include a TV channel broadcasting in English for US military personnel, with both local and US programmes.

English-language dailies including the *International Herald Tribune* and the *Financial Times* are available at Farmacia Arrocha branches. The *Miami Herald International Edition* is widely available.

FILM & PHOTOGRAPHY

All types of cameras and film are available in Panama, and may be cheaper than elsewhere because of the duty-free zone in Colón. Film processing in Panama City is as advanced as anywhere.

HEALTH

Tap water is safe to drink in all except the smallest, most remote towns. This means that washed raw vegetables and ice are OK too.

Malaria is not a problem in Panama City. The area east of the Canal, including the San Blas islands and Darién province, is the one part of Central America with a chloroquine-resistant strain of malaria. If you go there you should take special precautions; see the Health section in the introductory Facts for the Visitor chapter.

Always protect yourself against the sun's rays with a hat and long sleeves and a good sunscreen lotion. Panama is between 7° and 10° from the equator – Panama City is exactly 9° north – so the sun is very strong. Be sure to drink plenty of liquids, preferably water, to avoid becoming dehydrated.

DANGERS & ANNOYANCES

Crime is a problem in certain parts of Panama City. But the upper-class districts are in fact much safer here than in many other capitals: witness the all-night restaurants and activity on the streets at night. On the other hand, it is not safe to walk around at night in the Casco Viejo (San Felipe) district, where most of the cheap accommodation is found; you should be careful even in the daytime. Use common sense and stay where it's well lit and there are plenty of people around.

Colón is a sad slum and known for street crime. If you walk around there, even in the middle of the day, well-meaning residents will inform you that you are in danger. Be sure not to carry anything in your hands. You might want to avoid the city altogether.

Most other areas of Panama are rural, and quite safe.

WORK

You might be able to pick up some casual labour as a linehandler (deckhand) on a yacht going through the Panama Canal. This is hard, heavy work and the two-day trip pays around US$30. You can check for possibilities at the yacht clubs on both sides of the Canal. Larger ships are pulled through the locks by locomotives.

Teaching English is another possibility. However, English is widely spoken and teachers are not in short supply.

ACTIVITIES
Snorkelling & Diving

Probably the best place in Panama for snorkelling and diving is the Parque Nacional Bastimentos, around Bocas del Toro. This park, the only one in the country set aside to protect a marine environment, includes the islands of the Archipiélago de Bocas del Toro and coral reefs.

Almost any island offers snorkelling opportunities, however. The Archipiélago de San Blas and Isla Grande, both on the Caribbean coast east of the Canal, are recommended. Isla Taboga, off the coast of Panama City, is not known for its snorkelling but is in fact very interesting.

IPAT can put you in touch with diving operators. Snorkellers should bring their gear, as it's not always available for hire.

Fishing

Remember the name Panama means 'abundance of fish'. There are around 500 rivers, 1600 islands and over 2000 km of coast here, so there's no problem finding a fishing spot, but there are also other possibilities including deep-sea fishing, fishing for bass in Lago Gatún on the Panama Canal, and trout fishing in the rivers running down Volcán Barú near the towns of Boquete, Hato del Volcán, Bambito and Cerro Punta.

Surfing

There are surf beaches along the Pacific coast. The best three are Playa El Palmar, near San Carlos, about 1½ hours west of Panama City and easily accessible; Playa Venado, on the south end of the Península de Azuero and connected by bus to La Tablas; and the comparatively remote Santa Catalina further west, which can be reached by a long road turning off from Soná.

Hiking

Opportunities for hiking abound in Panama. From Boquete, you can hike to the top of Volcán Barú, Panama's highest peak and only volcano. There are plenty of other walks around Boquete, where the narrow roads wind up and down the slopes among the coffee plantations. Cerro Punta, on the other side of Volcán Barú, is also good for walking.

Near Panama City, on the shores of the Canal, Parque Nacional Soberanía has a section of the old Las Cruces trail used by the Spanish to cross between the coasts, and a nature trail, the Sendero El Charco,

signposted from the highway. A leaflet about the national parks is available from any office of Inrenare.

The Parque Natural Metropolitano, on the outskirts of Panama City, also has some good walks including a nature trail and a 'monkey trail'.

Of course, the most famous walk in Panama is the trek of a week or more through the Darién Gap, where the Interamerican Highway comes to a dead end and a wilderness of tropical rainforest stands between Panama and Colombia. This is the only overland route to South America; it can only be undertaken in the dry season and it is currently extremely dangerous. The trek is described in detail in the Getting There & Away chapter near the front of this book.

HIGHLIGHTS
Panama Canal

Thousands of visitors come to see this engineering wonder. An observation platform, with informative literature, a museum and a bilingual guide, has been set up at Miraflores Locks, near Panama City, or you can take a boat tour on the Canal itself.

Islands

Panama has 1600 islands; the more accessible ones are among the most interesting and enjoyable places in the country.

There is the Archipiélago de San Blas, with its traditional Cuna Indian culture; the Archipiélago de Bocas del Toro, protected by the Parque Nacional Bastimentos, and the tiny Isla Grande, just off the Caribbean coast near Portobelo.

On the Pacific side are Isla Taboga, near Panama City, and the Archipiélago de Perlas, further out in the Gulf of Panama.

Tropical Rainforest

Panama has some significant areas of tropical rainforest. The Parque Nacional del Darién, along the Colombian border, is Panama's largest and protects a large rainforest wilderness. Closer to civilisation, Isla Barro Colorado, in the Canal itself, and the Parque Nacional Soberanía, beside the

Canal, can be visited in a few hours from Panama City. Both provide nature trails and literature explaining the basics of tropical rainforest ecology.

Boquete & Volcán Barú

Boquete is a lovely little town on the slope of Volcán Barú in western Panama. Its 1060-metre elevation means it has a cool, fresh climate. You can enjoy good walks in the hills, visit coffee plantations or a natural hot spring, go bird-watching or trout-fishing, or scale the 3475-metre Volcán Barú.

Boquete's Feria de las Flores y del Café, held annually for a week or two in early April, attracts visitors from all over the country. Lodging may be difficult to find at that time.

Volcán Barú's slopes are very fertile; the combination of rich, dark volcanic soil and ideal climate makes Boquete excellent for agriculture.

Festivals & Celebrations

Many annual festivals are celebrated in Panama. Some are large, modern affairs, like Carnaval in Panama City; others preserve centuries-old traditions of folkloric dance, popular outdoor theatre, storytelling, music, costumes, masks and handicrafts.

The Península de Azuero is particularly known for its traditional festivals (see Cultural Events), but other parts of the country also have some notable celebrations: see the sections on Isla Taboga and Portobelo, for example, later in this chapter.

FOOD

In keeping with its international and ethnic character, Panama offers a variety of food.

Panama's national dish is *sancocho*, a spicy meat and vegetable stew. *Ropa vieja* ('old clothes'), a spicy shredded beef combination served over rice, is another common and tasty dish.

Seafood is excellent and abundant. On the Caribbean coast and islands, common everyday foods include lobster, shrimp, Caribbean king crab, fish such as corvina, a tender white fish with few bones, and octopus. Often the seafood is mixed with coconut sauce; coconut rice and coconut bread are other Caribbean treats.

The area around Volcán Barú is known for its mountain rainbow trout, coffee, Boquete navel oranges, and the many other fruits and vegetables grown there. You can buy excellent honey in the plaza in David.

In Panama City carts sell cones of shaved ice, with sweet fruit syrup and optional condensed milk poured over the top, for US$0.25. This is no world-class gourmet dish but on these hot streets it tastes like heaven.

DRINKS

Fresh fruit drinks, sweetened and mixed with water, are called *chicha* and are the commonest cold drinks in Panama. (There is no need to worry about the water here.) Soft drinks are called *sodas* and all the usual brands are available.

Beer and rum are made in Panama. The Carta Vieja rum distillery, between David and Concepción, gives free tours (see David later in this chapter).

ENTERTAINMENT

Panama City has plenty of nightlife, with everything from casinos and striptease shows to the symphonies and ballets at the opulent turn-of-the-century Teatro Nacional. You can also see presentations of Panamanian music and dance. Concerts, theatre and dance performances, and other events are presented in the huge, modern Atlapa Convention Centre. The IPAT tourist office is also at the Atlapa Centre and staff can tell you about coming events.

Panama City also has many cinemas, some showing the latest films from the USA. There are horse races and cockfights. But perhaps the most entertaining events are the festivals, ranging from the giant Carnaval celebrations in Panama City to small towns' celebrations of saints' days (see Cultural Events).

THINGS TO BUY

A remarkable variety of imported goods,

PANAMA

including cameras, electronic equipment and clothing, is sold in Panama, both in the Colón Free Zone and in Panama City. Shop around and bargain, as there's a lot of competition. The favourite handicraft souvenir from Panama is the mola, a colourful, intricate, multi-layered appliqué textile sewn by Cuna Indian women from the Archipiélago de San Blas. Small, simple souvenir molas can be bought from street stalls in Panama City for as little as US$2 or US$5, but the best ones are sold on the islands and can fetch several hundred dollars from serious collectors.

Other handicrafts include woodcarvings, masks, ceramics and clothing. See the section on the Península de Azuero for details of particular villages' specialities. All the Gran Morrison chain stores have handicraft and traditional art sections.

Getting There & Away

Panama calls itself 'the crossroads of the world': sea vessels from all over the Caribbean, Atlantic and Pacific go through the Canal, overland travellers pass through the country, and Panama is also a major hub for air travellers.

Air, land and sea travel between Panama and Colombia is covered in the Getting There & Away chapter.

AIR
Airlines connect Panama with all the other Central American countries, South America, North America and the Caribbean, and you can usually arrange a ticket with one or more free stopovers.

The main air connection points in North America for flights to and from Panama are Miami, Houston, New York, Washington DC, Dallas and Los Angeles. Miami is the principal one.

Fares from the US are competitive and may change seasonally. Continental have offered one-way fares from Miami to Panama City at US$371, from Houston at US$445.

Copa is Panama's national airline. Panama City has dozens of travel agents, including a branch of ISTC, represented in Panama City by APTE. They offer discounts to students with an ISIC card, but only on a few special flights. See the Panama City section for APTE's details.

LAND
To/From Costa Rica
There are three border crossings between Panama and Costa Rica. Paso Canoas, on the Interamerican Highway, is the one you will probably use to go to or from Panama City. The Río Sereno border crossing is rather remote and not as busy. The northernmost crossing at Guabito (Sixaola on the Costa Rican side) is the closest to Bocas del Toro, and an interesting option for overland travellers.

The border crossing at Paso Canoas is open from 7 am to 10 pm, with a couple of hours off for lunch and dinner. The one at Guabito/Sixaola is open from 7 am to 5 pm, with a couple of hours off for lunch.

Bus At either Guabito or Paso Canoas, you can take local buses up to the border on either side, cross, and continue on the next country's local bus. There are also daily direct buses operated by Tica between San José and Panama City and between San José and David; see the Panama City and David sections for details.

Panama and Costa Rica both have onward ticket requirements, meaning you must be able to show them you have an air or bus ticket out of the country before they will let you in. The cheapest way to satisfy this requirement, whichever way you are crossing the border, is to buy either a return or onward ticket with Tica Bus. The cheapest option is a return between San José and David for US$20; note that if you don't use the return portion, you will not get a refund at the other end. Another alternative if you are entering Costa Rica from Panama is to buy a ticket that will take you out the other side, from San José to Managua.

Driving If you cross the border in a private vehicle, no onward ticket is required.

SEA

Since Panama is one of the major shipping bottlenecks of the earth, you would think you could find a boat here to take you almost anywhere. However, the only regular passenger services are those to Colombia mentioned in the Getting There & Away chapter. The ships waiting to pass through the Canal do not usually berth, so you don't have a chance to ask the crews about going along.

Some cargo boats will take occasional passengers. Some will accept passengers accompanying their own freight, such as a car, but others will only take the freight itself and you have to make your own way to pick it up at the other end.

The idea of working your way into the sunset on a cargo boat is little more than a dream these days. In addition to the usual international maritime regulations, a Panamanian law states that only their own merchant mariners can sign on in Panama.

You could conceivably get a crewing spot on a private yacht. Your chances are considerably improved by such desirable qualities as having experience, but often yachties who need crew will take whoever looks a likely prospect at the time. You can ask around and post signs at the yacht clubs on both the Colón and the Panama City (Balboa) ends of the Canal.

LEAVING PANAMA

If you've been in Panama for over 30 days and have had your visa or tourist card renewed, remember you will need an official permit to leave the country. See the Visas section earlier in this chapter.

If you're heading to Costa Rica, Colombia or Venezuela, you'll need an onward ticket before boarding the plane or crossing the border.

There's a US$15 departure tax at the airport.

Getting Around

AIR

Panama has several domestic airlines:

Aeroperlas
> services to Panama City, Colón, David, Changuinola, Bocas del Toro, Isla Contadora and San Miguel

Alas Chiricanas
> services to Panama City, David, Changuinola and Bocas del Toro

Ansa
> services to Panama City, Archipiélago de San Blas and Puerto Obaldía

Chitreana de Aviación
> services between Panama City and Chitré

Parsa
> services between Panama City and Darién province (La Palma, Sambú, Garachine, El Real, Yaviza, Jaqué)

Transpasa
> services between Panama City and Archipiélago de San Blas; also charter flights anywhere in the country

Details on the flights are given in the appropriate sections.

BUS

There's a good bus system serving all the accessible parts of the country. Intercity fares are typically within the US$1 to $US4 range, except for long-distance routes, which run from US$7 to US$10.

TRAIN

The famous old passenger train that ran along the Canal between Panama City and Colón was destroyed during the 1989 invasion. It was supposed to start running again early in 1994, but repairs had yet to be completed at the time of writing. Check with IPAT to see if it's back in operation.

The train service between the port of Almirante and Guabito/Sixaola on the Costa Rican border is running again, after the 1991 earthquake in the area. For information, ring ☎ 78-3215.

The banana train serving Puerto Armuelles no longer carries passengers.

PANAMA

CAR & MOTORBIKE
Rental
Many agencies offer competitive rates on rental cars in Panama City; a couple of agencies also have offices in David. Average prices are around US$30 per day, but what with price wars, weekly discounts etc, you may be able to find something for as little as US$16 per day. If you can get a few people together to share the cost, this is a great deal.

Purchase
You can buy a car easily in Panama; prices here are lower than in many other parts of Central America.

Selling a car is another matter. Panamanian law makes it virtually impossible for a foreigner to drive a car into Panama and then sell it. The highway does reach a dead end at the Darién Gap, so the law-makers may have had visions of their country becoming overwhelmed by mountains of used cars – or maybe it has more to do with duties and taxes. In any case, don't expect to sell an imported car there.

Bringing Your Own
There's a great deal of paperwork involved in bringing a car into the country.

If you do want to take a vehicle between Central and South America, you will have to ship it around the Darién Gap. See the Getting There & Away chapter for suggestions on how to do this.

BICYCLE
You could cycle through Panama easily enough, but it's a very hot country. Panama doesn't have much cool mountainous terrain, as some other Central American countries do. The Interamerican Highway is narrow and overhung with jungle in places, leaving no room to move aside.

In Panama City bicycles are available for long or short-term rentals; see Panama City for details.

HITCHING
Hitching is not as widespread in Panama as elsewhere in the region; most people travel by bus, and foreigners would do best to follow suit.

BOAT
Boats are the principal means of transport in several parts of Panama, particularly between the islands of the San Blas and Bocas del Toro island archipelagos. Cuna Indian merchant boats carry cargo and passengers all along the San Blas coast, between Colón and Puerto Obaldía, stopping at up to 48 of the islands to load and unload passengers and cargo. See the Archipiélago de San Blas section and the Getting There & Away chapter for further details on this route.

Boat trips from Panama City include those to Isla Taboga just offshore, Isla Contadora further out in the gulf, Isla Barro Colorado in Lago Gatún in the Panama Canal, and a longer trip to El Real, in Darién province. River boats form important links in the overland route through the Darién Gap.

TOURS
Travel agents in Panama City offer many tours; IPAT can give you referrals. Reisa Tours (☎ 25-4721) has one of the most extensive operations, with tours around the city and to all parts of Panama; they are affiliated with APTE and offer substantial student discounts.

Panama City

Population 584,803

The capital of Panama is a modern, thriving centre for international banking, business, trade and transport, with a cosmopolitan feel. An almost constant sea breeze keeps the air comfortably fresh.

History
Panama City was founded on the site of an Indian fishing village by the Spanish governor Pedro Arias Dávila (Pedrarias) in 1519, not long after Balboa first saw the Pacific.

The Spanish settlement immediately became an important centre of government and church authority. It was from here, too, that the gold and other goods from the Pacific Spanish colonies were taken along El Camino Real (the royal highway) trail across the isthmus to the Caribbean.

This treasure made Panama City the target of many attacks over the years. In 1671 the city was ransacked and finally destroyed by the English pirate Henry Morgan, leaving only the stone ruins of Panamá Viejo that still stand today.

Two years later, the city was re-established about eight km to the west, down the coast at San Felipe. The Spanish believed the new site, on a small peninsula, would be easier to defend. The sea lapped the city on three sides; a moat was constructed on the land side and a massive stone wall ran around the whole city within these defences. It was never successfully attacked again.

The overland trade route, however, was attacked repeatedly and the principal Caribbean port at Portobelo was destroyed. In 1746 the Spanish stopped using the route altogether; Panama City subsequently declined in importance. It was not until the 1850s, when the Panama Railroad was completed and gold rushers on their way to California flooded across the isthmus by train, that Panama City returned to prominence.

Panama was declared independent of Colombia on 3 November 1903 in Panama City's Parque Catedral; the city then became the capital of the new nation. Since the Panama Canal was completed in 1914, the city has gained in importance as a centre for international business and trade.

Orientation

Panama City stretches about 10 km along the coast, from the Panama Canal at its western end to the ruins of Panamá Viejo to the east.

Near the Canal are the US Albrook Air Force Base, Fort Amador, and the wealthy Balboa and Ancón suburbs built for the US canal and military workers. The Bridge of the Americas arches gracefully over the Canal.

The colonial part of the city, called San Felipe or Casco Viejo, juts into the sea on the south-western side of town. Most of the low-cost hotels are in this district.

From San Felipe, two major roads head east through the city. The 'main drag' is Avenida Central, which runs past the cathedral in San Felipe, then Plaza Santa Ana and Plaza Cinco de Mayo. At a fork further on, it becomes Avenida Central España; the section that traverses the business and financial district is called Via España. The other side of the fork becomes Avenida 1 Norte José D Espinar, Avenida Simón Bolívar, and finally Via Transístmica as it heads out of town and across the isthmus towards Colón.

Avenida 6 Sur branches off Avenida Central, not far out of San Felipe, and undergoes several name changes; it is called Avenida Balboa as it curves around the edge of the bay to Paitilla, on the bay's eastern point opposite San Felipe; it then continues under various names past La Paitilla airport and the Atlapa convention centre to the ruins at Panama Viejo.

All three main roads are served by frequent buses.

Information

Tourist Office IPAT has an information counter at the Atlapa convention centre (☎ 26-7000) on Via Israel, open Monday to Friday from 8.30 am to 4.30 pm. There is also an IPAT counter at the international airport (☎ 38-4356), open every day from around 8 am to 11 pm. Both offices give out free city and country maps, and the free tourist booklet *Focus on Panama* with information on things to see and do. They also keep current listings of hotels and their prices and have information on tours and boat schedules.

Inrenare (☎ 32-4325) has maps and information on all Panama's national parks. Their current office is in Paraíso, a fair distance from the city centre; they are planning to move closer into town, so ring before you go out there. The Paraíso bus will drop you right outside their door. They are open Monday to Friday, 8 am to 4 pm.

Panama City

To Gamboa & Canal Area

Minor Streets Not Depicted

0   1   2 km

Panama Canal (Canal de Panamá)

Muelle 18 (Pier 18)

Carretera Diablo

Carretera Gaillard

CURUNDU

Ave Juan Pablo II

ALBROOK

Carretera Curundu

Bridge of the Americas (Puente de las Américas)

Carretera Balboa

BALBOA

Ave 1 Norte José D Espinar

Ave Manuel E Batista

Ave Simón

Via Argentina

LA BOCA

Cerro Ancon (Ancon Hill)

ANCÓN

LA CRESTA

EL CANGREJO

To David

Ave Central

Ave Central España

Avenida de los

Mártires

LA EXPOSICIÓN

BELLA VISTA

Via España

Balboa Yacht Club

Calle Amador

Ave 3 Sur (Justo Arosemena)

Ave Federico Boyd

Avenida 4 Sur

Avenida Balboa

CALIDONIA

Avenida

Ave Central

CHORIRRILLO

Ave 6 Sur

Amador

Bahía de Panamá

PUNTA PAITILLA

See San Felipe/Casco Viejo map

To Causeway

See Central Panama City map

Ancon (☎ 64-8100), on Calle 50 opposite the Floristería Marbella, works on environmental protection throughout the country and has information on most natural attractions. For detailed maps, go to the Instituto Geográfico Nacional Tommy Guardia (☎ 36-2444), on the Transístmica highway opposite the Universidad de Panamá. They have an excellent collection for sale, including detailed topographical maps, city maps, tourist maps and more.

Money In contrast to other Central American countries, you can change most currencies

here (but not those of Nicaragua, Cuba and Peru). Panacambios (☎ 23-1800) is on the ground floor of the Plaza Regency, 177 Via España, opposite the El Rey supermarket in the El Cangrejo banking district. Many banks have branches in Panama; most will exchange their home countries' currencies.

Since the US dollar is the official currency of Panama, it is easy to cash US dollar travellers' cheques. Chase Manhattan Bank and the Banco del Istmo sell and cash Visa travellers' cheques, and give cash advances on Visa and MasterCard credit cards. The American Express office (☎ 25-5858) is on

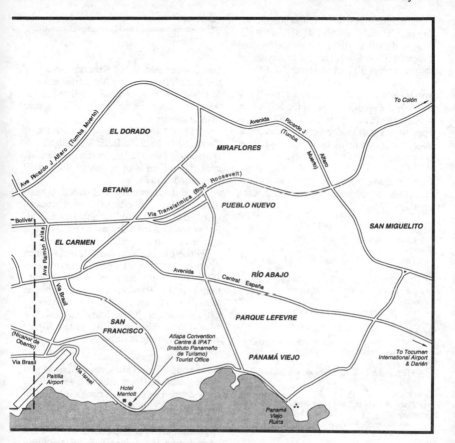

the 12th floor of the Union Bank building, 5 Avenida Samuel Lewis, a block from Via España.

Post The main post office is on the Parque Catedral in the San Felipe district, in a building that was once the headquarters for the French company that first set out to build the Panama Canal.

The post office is open Monday to Friday from 7 am to 5.45 pm, and Saturday from 7 am to 4.45 pm. Poste restante mail is held for one month and should be addressed in the following way:

(name)
Entrega General
Zona 1, Catedral
Panamá, República de Panamá

There are several smaller branch post offices in the districts around the city.

Telecommunications International telephone, telegraph, fax, and modem services, and communication with ships in the Atlantic and Pacific oceans, are available at Intel offices. There's an Intel office in the Edificio Di Lido on Calle Manuel María Icaza (☎ 64-8104), a

PANAMA

block behind the Hotel Continental on Via España. There's another in Balboa (☎ 62-0894) and another at the Tocumen international airport (☎ 38-4240). All are open every day of the year from 7.30 am to 10 pm.

Immigration On the corner of Calle 29 & Avenida 2 (Avenida Cuba) is the Migración y Naturalización office (☎ 27-1077). It is open Monday to Friday from 8 am to 3 pm. You can come here to extend your visa or get your permit to leave the country.

Foreign Embassies Over 50 countries have embassies or consulates in Panama City, including:

Belize
    Calle 50 & Calle 87 (☎ 26-4498)
Canada
    Calle Manuel María Icaza (☎ 64-7014, 64-2325)
Colombia
    Calle Manuel María Icaza, Edificio Grobman, 6th floor (☎ 64-9266, 64-9644)
Costa Rica
    Edificio Regency No 2, Apartado 8963 (☎ 64-2980)
Ecuador
    Calle Manuel María Icaza, Edificio Grobman, 3rd floor (☎ 64-7820)
El Salvador
    Via España, Edificio Citibank, 4th floor (☎ 23-3020)
France
    Plaza de Francia, San Felipe district (☎ 28-7835)
Germany
    Calle 50 & 53, Edificio Bank of America, 6th floor (☎ 63-7733)
Guatemala
    Calle 55, Condominio Abir, 6th floor, El Cangrejo (☎ 69-3475)
Honduras
    Avenida Justo Arosemena & Calle 31, Edificio Tapia, 2nd floor (☎ 25-8200)
Mexico
    Calle 50 & 53, Edificio Bank of America, 5th floor (☎ 63-5021)
Nicaragua
    Calle 50 & Avenida Federico Boyd (☎ 69-6721, 23-0981)
UK
    Calle 53, Edificio Swissbank, 4th floor, Marbella (☎ 69-0866)
USA
    Avenida Balboa & Calle 40, Edificio Macondo, 3rd floor (☎ 27-1777)

Venezuela
    Avenida Samuel Lewis, Edificio Banco Unión (☎ 69-1244)

Travel Agencies As befits the 'crossroads of the world', Panama City has a great number of travel agencies. Over 80 are listed in the telephone directory, and some of these have several offices.

APTE (☎ 25-2356) is at the corner of Calles 50 & 46 in the Bella Vista district. It is associated with ISTC, and issues the ISIC card. The office is open from 1.30 to 5.30 pm, Monday to Friday.

APTE distributes a list of over 100 businesses around the city offering discounts, some up to 50%, to ISIC cardholders, including everything from discos, cinemas, shops and restaurants to a dental clinic.

Working through the Reisa Travel Agency next door (☎ 25-4721), APTE also offers an ISIC student discount on certain international flights. When I asked, the discount was available only on Nica flights to Mexico City, Guatemala City, Managua and San José, Costa Rica, but discounted flights change from time to time.

Bookshops There are several Gran Morrison department stores around the city; they carry a small selection of books in English, including travel books.

Librería Argosy (☎ 23-5344) at Via Argentina and Via España, in the El Cangrejo district, is a regional cultural institution of no little importance. Its owner, Greek-born Gerasimos (Gerry) Kanelopulos, offers books in Spanish, English and French. The Argosy is a logical stopoff for intellectual travellers, but Señor Kanelopulos will help all and sundry in need of orientation.

Emergency Emergency phone numbers in Panama City are:

Police	104
Fire	103
Ambulance	25-1436, 28-2786/7
Hospital Santo Tomás	25-1436

Things to See & Do

Of course everybody's No 1 'thing to see' is the Canal, covered in the Around Panama City section. But there is also plenty to see and do in the city itself.

Walking Tour The colonial San Felipe district, also called Casco Viejo, is the budget hotel district and one of the more interesting parts of the city. You could start a walking tour in San Felipe at the **Paseo de las Bóvedas**, on the southern tip of the peninsula. A walkway runs along the top of the sea wall built by the Spanish to protect the city. From here you can see the ships lining up to enter the Canal, and the Bridge of the Americas arching over the Canal.

Below the wall, on the tip of the point, is the **Plaza de Francia**, where large stone tablets tell the story (in Spanish) of the Canal's construction and the role of the French. The plaza is dedicated to the memory of the 22,000 workers, most of them from France, Guadeloupe and Martinique, who died working on the Canal. Most were killed by yellow fever and malaria, and among the busts of the Frenchmen who played important parts in the Canal's construction is a monument to Carlos J Finlay, who discovered how mosquitoes transmit yellow fever. His work led to the eradication of the disease in Panama.

On one side of the plaza are some old **dungeons**. Although they now contain an art gallery and an expensive restaurant/piano bar, Las Bóvedas, you can still see the dungeons' original stonework. Also on the plaza are the Supreme Court of Panama and the French Embassy.

Leaving the plaza to walk up Avenida A, you soon come to the ruins of the **Iglesia y Convento de Santo Domingo** on the corner of Calle 3. Just inside the doorway is the **Arco Chato**, a long arch that has stood here, unsupported, for centuries. It reputedly played a part in the selection of Panama over Nicaragua as the site for the Canal: its stability was taken as evidence that the area was not subject to earthquakes. The **Museo de Arte Religioso** is now open again after seven years' restoration work.

Turning north along Calle 3, you pass the **Ministerio de Gobierno y Justicia** building, and behind it the **Teatro Nacional**, built in 1907. The ornate interior has been restored, and it boasts red and gold decorations, a ceiling mural, a big crystal chandelier and several tiers of seats. Performances are still held here; to find out about them, or just to have a look at the theatre, go around to the office door at the side of the building.

Opposite the theatre is the **Iglesia de San Francisco**, facing onto the **Parque Bolívar** plaza. In 1826 in a schoolroom opposite this plaza, Simón Bolívar held a meeting urging the union of the Latin American countries.

Around the block from this plaza, on Avenida Alfaro, is the presidential palace, called the **Palacio de las Garzas** for the herons kept there. The president of Panama lives on the upper floor; you can look at the ground floor if you ask permission and present identification. A few blocks further west are the **Port** and **Mercado**.

Two blocks south of the palace, at the centre of San Felipe, is the central plaza, **Parque Catedral**, also called the **Plaza de la Independencia**, fringed by several historic buildings. The **post office** was once the headquarters of the French company that first worked on the Canal; the Canal officials and other dignitaries stayed at the nearby **Hotel y Restaurante Central**, a very luxurious place in those days. Panamanian independence was declared in this plaza on 3 November 1903.

Beside the post office, the **Museo de Historia de Panamá** is on the top floor of the **Palacio Municipal** (city hall). The museum is open Monday to Friday from 8.30 am to 3.30 pm, admission US$0.25. Half a block south on Calle 7 are the ruins of another church, the **Iglesia y Convento de la Compañia de Jesus**. Walk to the end of the block to rejoin Avenida A, then walk a block west to arrive at the **Iglesia de San José**. There is a colourful story attached to its famous **Altar de Oro** (golden altar), about the only thing of value salvaged after Henry

San Felipe (Casco Viejo)

Morgan sacked Panamá Viejo in 1671. When word came of the pirate's impending attack, according to local tales, a priest painted the altar black – some say he covered it with mud – to disguise it. The priest allegedly told Morgan the famous altar had been stolen by another pirate, and even, according to legend, convinced Morgan to donate handsomely for its replacement! Morgan is said to have told the priest, 'I don't know why I think you are more of a pirate than I am.' Whatever the historical fact, the altar was later moved from its original church in the old city to this one, where it only just fits inside.

A block further on is another plaza, the **Parque Herrera**. A block north, on Avenida Central, two blocks behind the Cathedral, is the **Iglesia de La Merced**.

Walking out of the San Felipe district along Avenida Central, past the **Casa de la Municipalidad**, after a couple of blocks you come to the **Parque Santa Ana**, with its **Iglesia de Santa Ana**. Plaza Santa Ana marks the beginning of the Avenida Central shopping district; it is surrounded by restaurants and there are buses to the rest of the city.

Walk about five more blocks down Avenida Central, past all the big air-con

■ PLACES TO STAY		Refresquería Angélica Maria	14	Post Office
5	Pensión Panamericana	29 Restaurante & Piano Bar	15	Cathedral
6	Hotel y Restaurante Herrera	Las Bóvedas	16	Parque Catedral
8	Pensión Universal		19	Palacio de las Garzas (Palacio Presidencial)
10	Pensión Panamá	OTHER	21	Parque Bolívar
11	Hotel Foyo	1 Casa de la Municipalidad	22	Iglesia de San Francisco
17	Hotel y Restaurante Central	2 Port & Mercado (cargo boats to Colombia)	23	Teatro Nacional
20	Hotel Colonial	3 Iglesia de la Merced	24	Ministerio de Gobierno y Justicia
26	Pensión Vásquez	4 Parque Herrera	25	Iglesia y Convento de Santo Domingo (Ruins), Museo de Arte Colonial Religioso
▼ PLACES TO EAT		9 Iglesia de San José, Altar de Oro		
6	Hotel y Restaurante Herrera	12 Iglesia y Convento de la Compañia de Jesus (Ruins)	27	French Embassy
7	Restaurante La Victoria	13 Palacio Municipal, Museo de Historia de Panamá	28	Supreme Court
17	Hotel y Restaurante Central		29	Dungeons
18	Restaurante &		30	Paseo de las Bóvedas, Plaza de Francia

stores with hawkers outside, and you come to the large **Plaza Cinco de Mayo**. There are more restaurants here; there is also the **Museo Antropológico Reina Torres de Araúz**, which focuses on the anthropology and archaeology of Panama.

Plaza Cinco de Mayo is a major bus stop. Buses leave here for the Miraflores Locks, the Balboa Yacht Club and the Tocumen international airport. Any Via España bus will take you the rest of the way down the Avenida Central – which becomes the Via España – past the fancy French-Gothic-style **Iglesia del Carmen** and on to the business and banking district of **El Cangrejo**.

Panamá Viejo At the east end of the city, by the sea, are the ruins of the first city the Spanish built here. The ruins cover a large area and you can still see the cathedral with its stone tower, the plaza beside it, the Santo Domingo and San José convents, the San Juan de Dios hospital and the city hall. The bridge which marked the beginning of El Camino Real, on which the booty from Peru and other Pacific colonies was taken by mule train to the Atlantic side, is still standing.

The ruins are not fenced and you can visit them any time. The IPAT tourist office operates an artesanías shop nearby.

Museums A couple of museums have already been mentioned but there are several more. Here's a complete list:

Museo de Historia de Panamá (☎ 62-8089)
Palacio Municipal, on Parque Catedral, Calle 7, San Felipe; open Monday to Friday, 8.30 am to 3.30 pm; admission US$0.25. Exhibits on the history of Panama, mostly since its European discovery.
Museo de Arte Colonial Religioso
Avenida A & Calle 3, in the Santo Domingo chapel, next to the church and convent of the same name in the San Felipe district. Now open – after lengthy restoration – Monday to Friday, 9 am to 4 pm.
Museo Antropológico Reina Torres de Araúz (☎ 62-0415)
Plaza Cinco de Mayo, Avenida Central; phone for hours; admission US$0.25. Focuses on Panamanian anthropology, archaeology and pre-Columbian history; formerly called the Museum of Panamanian Man.
Museo de Arte Contemporaneo (☎ 62-8012)
Avenida de los Mártires, near Calle J, two blocks from Avenida Central; open Monday to Friday, 9 am to 4 pm, Saturday 9 am to noon; admission free. Permanent and changing exhibitions.
Museo Afro-Antilleano (☎ 62-5348)
Avenida Justo Arosemena & Calle 24; open

PANAMA

Monday to Friday, 10 am to 4 pm; admission US$0.25. Exhibits on the history of Panama's West Indian community.

Museo de Ciencas Naturales (☎ 25-0645)
Avenida Cuba, between Calle 29 & 30, behind Hotel Soloy; open Monday to Friday, 9 am to 4 pm; admission US$0.25. Natural sciences, flora, fauna, geology and palaeontology of Panama.

Causeway At the Pacific entrance to the Panama Canal, a *calzada* (causeway) connects the three small islands of Naos, Perico, and Flamenco to the Amador section of the city. Solidaridad, the beach on Naos, is one of the most popular in the area.

Many people come to the causeway in the early morning to jog, but you can also hire a bicycle at one of the booths at the entrance for US$1 per hour during the week, or US$1.50 per hour on weekends, and ride along it. It costs $0.25 to enter the causeway, and another $0.25 to go onto the beach itself. Snacks and drinks are sold there.

Parque Natural Metropolitano Up on a hill behind the city, this 265-hectare park protects a wild area of tropical forest within the city limits. There are two walking trails, the Nature Trail and the Tití Monkey Trail, which join to form one long loop, and a 150-metre-high lookout point affords a view over Panama City, the bay, and the Canal all the way to Miraflores Locks.

Mammals in the park include tití monkeys, anteaters, sloths and white-tailed deer; reptiles are represented by iguanas, turtles and tortoises. There are more than 200 species of birds including oropéndolas, woodpeckers, doves, owls, hawks and eagles. Fish, shrimp and turtles live in the Río Curundú which runs through the park.

An international team of scientists from the Smithsonian Institution has set up a crane in the park to study the forest canopy; there is a complete ecosystem 30 to 50 metres up, including many animals and birds that could never be studied from the ground.

The park is bordered on the west by Camino de la Amistad, on the east by Via Juan Pablo II and, further to the west, Tumba Muerto. The visitors' centre is on Via Juan

Pablo II. The rangers offer free one-hour tours with a slide show on some days; you can phone the visitors' centre (☎ 32-5516), any day except Monday between 9 am and 3 pm, to ask about the schedule.

Balboa Yacht Club Beside the Panama Canal at Fort Amador, the club (☎ 28-5794, 28-2313 or 28-5196) has a pleasant Canal-side bar/restaurant where you can sit and watch the ships glide under the Bridge of the Americas. The food here is expensive, but it's a fine place to go for a drink.

Activities

Organised Tours Latinsell (☎ 60-9127, 60-9235), the Panama Canal boat tour operators, also offer a number of other reasonably priced small boat tours, including a day tour of the Bahía de Panamá islands (Taboga and others) for US$25, salt and freshwater fishing tours for US$15 and up, sightseeing boat tours from US$5, and beach and jungle tours from US$8 (all prices per person). Hotel pick-up is included in all tours, repeat customers pay half-price, and they offer group discounts.

Servitur (☎ 64-3029, 64-3014) has a three-hour city tour, including a stop at the Miraflores Locks, for US$20 per person, and other tours outside the city. Reisa Tours (☎ 25-4721) offer 43 different tours; they are a bit more expensive but they do have student discounts. The tourist office has information on tours.

See the Panama Canal section for details on boat tours through the Canal, and to the Smithsonian nature reserve on Isla Barro Colorado in the Canal's Lago Gatún.

Sports Horse races, baseball, boxing, fishing, and water sports such as sailing and windsurfing are all popular in Panama City. The tourist office has all the details.

Festivals

Carnaval, on the four days preceding Ash Wednesday, is a magnificent holiday in Panama City. See the Cultural Events section for more details of the festival and Ash Wednesday dates for the next few years.

Places to Stay

San Felipe (Casco Viejo) San Felipe or Casco Viejo is where most of the low-priced hotels are found. Be careful about walking here at night.

Hotel y Restaurante Central (☎ 62-8044, 62-8096), on the plaza opposite the cathedral, was very grand around the turn of the century. The illustrious figures in the Canal's history lodged here in its early days. Now it is frayed around the edges, but it still has its high ceilings and arched French doors opening onto private balconies overlooking the plaza. It costs US$7/9 for singles/doubles with shared bath, US$1 extra for private bath. The hotel has its own restaurant on the plaza.

A block and a half from the cathedral, at 6 Calle, No 8-25, *Hotel Foyo* (☎ 62-8023) has rooms at US$5 for one or two people with shared bath, US$6 with sink in the room, US$7 with two beds, or US$11 with private bath. Some of the rooms of the same price are better than others; ask to see several.

Opposite the Foyo, the *Pensión Panamá* (☎ 62-8053) has single/double rooms with shared bath at US$4.50/6.

Pensión Vásquez (☎ 28-8453) at Avenida A, No 2-47, opposite the Museo de Arte Colonial Religioso and the ruins of the Iglesia y Convento de Santo Domingo, is a quiet, clean family pension. Single rooms with shared bath and fan are US$5.50 or US$6.60, doubles US$8.80. Some rooms have windows to the sea, and there's a laundry.

The large *Hotel Colonial* (☎ 62-3858) has no sign but you can't miss it on Calle 4 on Parque Bolívar. All the rooms have private bath, and many have balconies looking onto the plaza, with the sea a block away; they cost US$10/11 for singles/doubles.

On Parque Herrera, on 9 Calle, the *Hotel y Restaurante Herrera* (☎ 28-8994) has single/double rooms at US$4/8 with shared bath, or US$11 with private bath; rooms with air-conditioning, fridge and TV cost extra. The hotel restaurant is good and cheap. Also here on Parque Herrera is the *Pensión*

Panamericana, where rooms for one or two people are US$7 with shared bath, US$10 with private bath.

At Avenida Central No 8-16, in the block behind the cathedral, *Pensión Universal* (☎ 28-2796) has rooms with shared bath at US$5, or US$6 with fan.

Other Areas Most of the good cheap hotels are in San Felipe, but there are a few elsewhere. There are plenty in the Calidonia area, but it's not the best part of town at any time, and positively dangerous at night. These ones are in better districts.

Residencial Primavera (☎ 25-1195) is in a good location on Avenida Cuba near the corner of Calle 42, in a residential neighbourhood just a block from Vía España. All the rooms come with private bath and ceiling fans, and cost US$10 a night.

The *Residencial Turístico El Volcán* (☎ 25-5263) is on Calle 29, between Avenidas Cuba & Perú, opposite the Migración y Naturalización office. All the rooms have private bath; rates are US$12 with fan, US$14 with air-con if you get one double bed; add an extra US$2 if you want two beds.

Relatively inexpensive hotels are also opening up in the El Cangrejo business and banking district as well as other areas nearby. The *Bella Vista* (☎ 64-4029) on Vía España has rooms at US$24. The *Hotel California* (☎ 63-7844) at Vía España and Calle 43 is in the same range.

A luxurious but surprisingly economical alternative in Panama City is offered by the spreading phenomenon of 'suites' or 'aparthotels'. The *Aparthotel Las Vegas* (☎ 69-0722, fax 23-0047) is a modern, well-kept apartment/hotel with studio or suite apartments, all with private kitchens, hot-water bath, colour cable TV, telephone, and air-con. The rooms on the upper floors have a good view. The listed rate for studio apartments is US$55 per day – not a good deal – but if you stay for seven to 29 days the rate drops to US$25 per day, and it's US$20 per day if you stay by the month. If this is still too expensive, they may reduce the price for you. A 'mini-studio' without air-con costs

US$15/12/10 per day by the day/week/ month. The Las Vegas is in the El Cangrejo district at the corner of Calle 49 Oeste and Avenida Eusebio A Morales, two blocks from Via España and conveniently close to the 24-hour El Rey supermarket, banks, cinemas, a bus stop, and a number of decent restaurants (try the *Café Jimmy*).

Places to Eat

San Felipe (Casco Viejo) *Restaurante La Victoria*, on the corner of Avenida Central and Calle 9, has a Chinese and international menu so long that it makes a little booklet. The restaurant is air-conditioned, and the portions are large, cheap and good. It's open every day from 7 am to 11 pm and is also a popular place for takeaways or just a beer.

On the Parque Herrera, the *Hotel Herrera* restaurant has good, cheap food. On the Parque Catedral there's the restaurant in the *Hotel Central*, or the small *Restaurante & Refresquería Angélica María*, with good, inexpensive food and a comfortable atmosphere. There are several other cheap eateries near the Parque Catedral.

Parque Santa Ana A few blocks from the Casco Viejo district, at the corner of Avenida Central and Calle 12, the Parque Santa Ana has many inexpensive restaurants to choose from. Some are open-air, some air-con; the *Café Coca-Cola* on a far corner of the plaza is an old favourite, open every day from 7.30 am to 11.30 pm. You'll find plenty of other restaurants and cafés as you head down Avenida Central from this plaza, but beware of walking around this area at night.

Other Areas Panama City has hundreds of good places to eat, with everything from about 10 *McDonald's* to the fanciest gourmet restaurants. International restaurants include not only Chinese but also Japanese, French, Swiss, Cuban, Colombian, Mexican, Spanish, Argentine, Indian and vegetarian places. The tourist map available for US$1.50 at Tommy Guardia (see Information) shows about 100 restaurants and their

specialities; the tourist office also has information on restaurants.

The *Restaurante/Pizzeria Nápoli*, at the corner of Calle Estudiante and Calle 1, two blocks from Avenida Central and the Hotel Ideal, is great for Italian food. Good-sized pizzas start at US$1.50, pasta meals are US$1.50 to US$3, and they also have meat and seafood, Italian ice cream, and espresso. It's air-conditioned and open every day except Tuesday from 10 am to 11 pm.

La Cascada, near the corner of Avenida Balboa and Calle 25, is a good place for a pleasant evening out. It has a large garden dining patio and a bilingual menu with so many choices it may take you half an hour to read it. The meals are gigantic and very reasonably priced; for US$5 you can get an excellent steak or corvina fish.

If you want to spend up, *Las Tinajas*, at Calle 51, No 22, in the Bella Vista district, is one of the city's more famous places. It has a show with traditional music and dance performances on Tuesday, Thursday, Friday and Saturday nights at 9 pm; phone for reservations (☎ 69-3840). Dinners are around US$7 to US$10.

A splurge, but one well worth the price, is the nouvelle cuisine *Bon Profit*, at Via Argentina 5 (☎ 63-9667). The title, which means 'good eating' in Catalan, indicates the Catalan-Mallorcan background of the owner, who offers such delicacies as corvina in a spinach and garlic sauce, with dinners costing US$10-20 per person.

Entertainment

Panama City has plenty of nightlife.

The Teatro Nacional (☎ 62-3525) in the San Felipe district and the two theatres at the Atlapa convention centre (☎ 26-7000) present dance, music, theatre and other performing arts. Many air-con cinemas around the city show current US films (admission US$2.75).

Discotheques include Bacchus, on Via España, Disco 2000, on Via Brasil, Disco Magic, on Calle 50, and Patatus, in the Plaza New York.

Several of the larger hotels offer 'Noches

Central
Panama City

0   250   500 m

To Patilla
airport

Bahía de Panamá

ANCÓN

CALIDONIA

LA EXPOSICIÓN

BELLA VISTA

LA CRESTA

EL CANGREJO

Río Curundú

Carretera Curundú

To Parque Natural Metropolitano

Bus stop to San Felipe

PLACES TO STAY
3   Hotel Ideal
13 Residencial Turístico El Volcán
17 Bella Vista
18 Residencial Primavera
19 Hotel California
22 Aparthotel Las Vegas

PLACES TO EAT
2   Restaurante/Pizzería Napoli
11 Restaurante La Cascada
28 Restaurante Las Tinajas

OTHER
1   Museo de Arte Contemporáneo
3   Tica Bus Station
    (Buses to Costa Rica)
4   Parque Santa Ana
5   Plaza Cinco de Mayo
6   Museo Antropológico Reina
    Torres de Araúz
7   Bus Station (Buses to Interior)
8   Bus Station - Buses to
    Canal Area
9   Bus Station - Buses to Colón
10 Museo Afro-Antilleano
12 Migración y Naturalización
14 Museo de Ciencias Naturales
15 Monumento Vasco Núñez de Balboa
16 Club de Yates y Pesca
    (Yacht & Fishing Club)
20 Instituto Geográfico Nacional
    'Tommy Guardia'
21 Universidad de Panamá
23 Iglesia del Carmen
24 Panacambios (Casa de Cambio)
25 Librería Argosy
26 Discoteca Bacchus
27 Intel
29 Disco Magic
30 American Express

PANAMA

Típicas' with traditional Panamanian dancing and floor shows; the tourist office has current information. Traditional dancing is also presented at the Las Tinajas restaurant, and at the lottery draws on Wednesday and Sunday afternoons.

Gambling is legal; about 20 casinos, including some at the larger hotels, are listed in the telephone directory yellow pages.

Things to Buy

Merchandise from many countries is sold very cheaply in Panama. The Zona Libre (Free Zone) in Colón is famous for discounted prices, but you can often find bargains just as good on Avenida Central.

Some of the cheapest Panamanian artesanías in Panama City are the molas which the Cuna Indians sell on Avenida Central. Ask the prices at several stands; there's a lot of variation, but the molas will be cheaper here, bought directly from the Indians, than elsewhere in the city.

Gran Morrison department stores sell a variety of Panamanian handicrafts, including molas, ceramics, woodcarvings, woven hats, and basketry; they also sell postcards and travel books in English.

The tourist office operates an artesanías shop at the ruins of Panama Viejo; the handicrafts here are good quality but rather expensive. There are many other artesanías shops around Panama City; the tourist office has a complete list.

Getting There & Away

Air Several airlines provide services between Panama City and other parts of the country:

Aeroperlas (☎ 63-5663, 69-4555)
　　Colón, Monday to Friday, US$47 return
　　David, daily, US$92 return
　　Changuinola, daily, US$46 return
　　Bocas del Toro, Saturday and Sunday, $43 return
　　Isla Contadora, daily, US$44 return
　　San Miguel, Monday and Friday, US$34 return
Aerotaxi (☎ 64-8644)
　　El Porvenir, Archipiélago de San Blas, daily except Sunday, US$50 return
Alas Chiricanas (☎ 64-6448, 64-7759)

　　David, daily, US$100 return
　　Changuinola, daily, US$92 return
　　Bocas del Toro, US$86 return
Ansa (☎ 26-7891, 26-6898)
　　Porvenir, Archipiélago de San Blas, daily except Sunday, US$50 return
　　Puerto Obaldía, three times a week, US$42 return
Chitreana de Aviación (☎ 26-4116, 26-3069)
　　Chitré, daily except Sunday, US$53 return
Parsa (☎ 26-3803, 26-3883)
　　Darién province: La Palma, Sambú and Garachiné, daily, US$63 return
　　Yaviza and El Real de Santa María, three times a week, US$67 return
　　Jaqué, three times a week, US$75 return
Transpasa (☎ 26-0843)
　　Porvenir, Archipiélago de San Blas, daily, US$48 return

All domestic flights arrive and depart from La Paitilla airport, in the city.

International flights arrive and depart from the Omar Torrijos H airport at Tocumen, 25 km from the city centre. See the Getting There & Away section for information on international flights to and from Panama.

Bus Buses to most other parts of the country arrive and depart from the Interior bus station on Avenida Balboa. (Everything outside Panama City is referred to as the 'interior'.) On Avenida Balboa itself is the station for buses to David; directly behind this is the station for buses to other parts of the interior.

These are some of the major bus routes. There are also buses to many small towns.

to David (438 km)
　　regular bus, departs hourly from 7 am to 1 pm, then every 1½ hours until last bus at 7 pm (6½ to seven hours, around US$10); express bus, departs at midnight (5½ to six hours, US$15)
to Chitré and Los Santos (255 km, four hours)
　　hourly, 7 am to 9 pm
to Las Tablas (282 km, 4½ hours)
　　goes when bus is full (around every two hours), 6 am to 6 pm
to Darién
　　departs at 6.30, 8.30 and 10.30 am, and at noon; January to April it goes as far as Yaviza (10 hours, US$14); the rest of the year the rain makes the last part of the road impassable and the bus only goes as far as Canglón (eight hours, $11)

Buses departing from other locations include:

to Colón (76 km, 1¾ hours)
Departs from the corner of Avenida Central & Calle 26. Regular and express buses depart every 20 minutes from 5 am to 9 pm. The express bus is air-conditioned and costs US$0.50 extra, but doesn't get there much faster.

to Canal Zone
Buses to everywhere in the old Canal Zone (Miraflores and Pedro Miguel Locks, Gamboa etc) depart from the bus station at Plaza Cinco de Mayo, on Avenida Central.

to Costa Rica
Departs from Tica Bus office (☎ 62-2084, 62-6275) at Hotel Ideal, Calle 17, No 15-55, a block west of Avenida Central. Departs every day at 11 am, arriving in San José, Costa Rica, the following morning around 5 am. You must bring your passport when you reserve your ticket, at least one day in advance. It costs US$25 one way, US$50 return.

Train There are no longer any passenger trains serving Panama City. The train which used to take the famously scenic route to Colón along the Canal was damaged during the invasion. You could check with IPAT to see if it has been repaired.

Boat Passenger boats go from Panama City to the islands of Taboga and Contadora; tour boats go along part of the Panama Canal. See the Around Panama City section for details. Yachts cross the Canal on Tuesdays and Thursdays.

Cargo boats to Colombia depart from the docks near San Felipe; see the introductory Getting There & Away chapter for more information on boats to Colombia.

Getting Around
To/From the Airport The international airport Omar Torrijos is at Tucumen, 25 km north-east of the city centre. Local Tucumen buses depart every 15 minutes from the bus stop opposite the Plaza Cinco de Mayo; they cost US$0.35 and take an hour to reach the airport.

A taxi to the Tucumen airport costs US$20. Coming from the airport, it's cheaper (US$8 per person) to take a *colectivo* taxi.

La Paitilla airport, within the city, handles domestic flights. City bus No 2 that runs along Avenida Balboa stops there; the ride costs US$0.15.

Bus Panama City has an excellent network of local buses, which run every day from around 5 am to 11 pm. A ride costs US$0.15.

Taxi Taxis are plentiful. They are not metered but there is a list of standard fares which they are supposed to charge, measured by zones. The fare for one zone is the minimum of US$0.75; the maximum fare within the city is US$2. An average ride, crossing a couple of zones, would cost US$1 or US$1.50, plus US$0.25 for each additional passenger. Ask the driver to show you the zone map and agree on a fare before you get into the cab.

Watch out for unmarked, large-model US cars serving hotels as cabs. Their prices are up to four times that of regular street taxis.

You can phone for a taxi by calling Ama (☎ 21-1865), America (☎ 23-7694), El Parador (66-3111), Panamá (☎ 24-5436), San Cristóbal (☎ 21-8704) or Unico (☎ 21-4074).

Car Rental Rental car companies in Panama City include:

Agencias Giscombe
☎ 64-0111
Avis Rent-a-Car
☎ 64-0722, 63-5144; airport 38-4037
Barriga Rent-a-Car
☎ 69-0221
Budget Rent-a-Car
☎ 63-8777, 63-8474; airport 38-4069
Gold Rent-a-Car
☎ 64-1711
Hertz Rent-a-Car
☎ 64-1111, 63-6663; airport 38-4081, 38-4106
International Rent-a-Car
☎ 64-4540; airport 38-4404
National Car Rental
☎ 64-8277, 69-1921; airport 38-4144
Toyota Rent-a-Car
☎ 60-9916

As always, it pays to shop around to compare rates and special promotions. At the time of writing, rates ranged from US$30 to US$45 per day for the most economical cars, with insurance and unlimited km. Discount, Barriga, International, Agencias Giscombe, and Avis, in that order, had the lowest prices.

Bicycle Rental Alquiler de Bicicletas Moses (☎ 28-0116) has two shops in Panama City, both open every day. One, in the Balboa district by the entrance to the causeway, is open daily from 9 am to 7 pm; the other, by the Officers Club in Fuerte Amador, is open daily from 7 am to 7 pm. They hire bicycles for short or long term. Mountain bikes cost US$2 an hour, US$9.50 for 24 hours, and US$56 for a week; other bikes cost US$1 an hour, US$7.50 for 24 hours or US$40 for a week. Tandems are more expensive. Monthly rates are negotiable.

Around Panama City

There are many interesting places not far from Panama City. The Panama Canal, of course, is the first attraction for most visitors, and there are various places to visit around the Canal area. It is also easy to make a day trip across the isthmus to the Atlantic side, to visit Colón, Portobelo, the beaches between them, and Isla Grande on the east side of the Canal, and Fort San Lorenzo on the west side; all are only a couple of hours away by road.

Offshore in the Bahía de Panama, Isla Taboga and Isla Contadora are also just a short distance from the city.

THE PANAMA CANAL

The Canal is one of the most significant waterways on earth, and is truly an engineering marvel, stretching 80 km (50 miles) from Panama City on the Pacific side to Colón on the Atlantic side, cutting right through the Great Divide. In 1992, over 12,600 ocean-going vessels passed through the Canal; ships are crossing 24 hours a day, waiting in line in the ocean on both sides for their turn to go through. Ships worldwide are built with the dimensions of the Panama Canal's locks in mind: 305 metres (1000 feet) long and 33.5 metres (110 feet) wide.

The Canal has three sets of double locks: Miraflores and Pedro Miguel Locks on the Pacific side, and Gatun Locks on the Atlantic side. Between the locks, ships pass through a huge artificial lake, Lago Gatún, created by the Gatun Dam across the Río Chagres, which when they were created were the largest dam and the largest artificial lake on earth, and the Gaillard Cut, a 14-km cut through the rock and shale of the isthmian mountains. This cut was called the Culebra Cut, because of its snake-like appearance, before it was renamed for the engineer in charge of its construction. It was an extreme challenge – in the wet climate the loose soil was subject to horrendous landslides during construction, and even after the Canal opened.

The fees the ships pay for using the Canal bring millions of dollars into Panama every year. Ships pay according to their weight, with the average fee being around US$30,000 for commercial ships. The highest fee was US$117,285.51, in December 1989 for the *Queen Elizabeth II*; the lowest was 36 cents, in 1928 by Richard Halliburton, who swam through.

The more you learn about the Panama Canal, the more interesting it gets, both in terms of the monumental construction project, and the associated political intrigues.

Visiting the Canal
Miraflores Locks Probably the easiest and best way to visit the Canal is to go to the Miraflores Locks, the locks closest to Panama City, where a viewing platform gives you a good view of the locks in operation. A bilingual guide and bilingual illustrated pamphlets give information about the Canal, and there's a museum with a model and film about the Canal.

Entrance is free, every day from 9 am to 5 pm. To get there, take any Paraíso or Gamboa

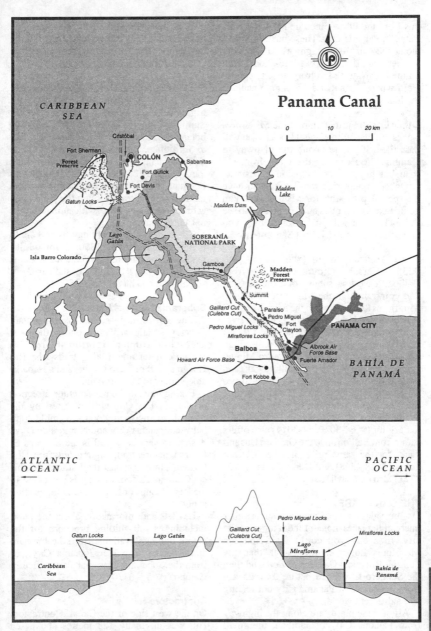

PANAMA

bus from the Plaza Cinco de Mayo bus terminal in Panama City. These buses, passing along the Canal-side highway to Gamboa, will let you off at the Miraflores Locks sign on the highway, 12 km from the city centre, from where it's about a 15-minute walk to the locks.

Other Locks Further on past the Miraflores Locks are the Pedro Miguel Locks. You will pass them if you're taking the highway to Gamboa. You can see the locks from the road, but they have no provision for visitors.

On the Atlantic side, the Gatun Locks have no special provision for visitors, but you could take a taxi or bus out from Colón to see the locks. You will pass over them if you cross the Canal to visit Fort San Lorenzo.

Canal Tours Latinsell (☎ 60- 9127, 60-9235) offers boat tours departing from Balboa, a western suburb of Panama City, and going through the Miraflores Locks to Miraflores Lake (between the Miraflores and Pedro Miguel Locks) and back, about a five-hour tour, for US$25 per person. Or, for US$10 more, you can continue on through Miraflores Lake, through the Pedro Miguel Locks, through part of the Gaillard Cut, and back to Balboa. These tours go several times a week, beginning at 8 am. They offer free hotel pick-up. A number of other tours are available.

Servitur (☎ 64-3029, 64-3014) also offers a tour from Balboa up to the Gaillard Cut and back, for the same price of US$35. Argo Tours (☎ 28-4348) and Reisa Tours (☎ 25-4721) also do Canal tours.

THE CANAL AREA
On the sides of the Canal are some other interesting places, none of them far from the city. In a day you could visit first the Miraflores Locks on the Canal, then the Summit Botanical Gardens & Zoo, and then the Sendero El Charco nature trail, 25 km from the centre of Panama City but feeling like a different world.

All of these places are along the highway from Panama City to Gamboa, the small

tropical town where the Río Chagres enters Lago Gatún. They can be reached by taking the Gamboa bus from the bus station at Plaza Cinco de Mayo in Panama City.

Summit Botanical Gardens & Zoo
Ten km past the Miraflores Locks, on the highway heading to Gamboa, are the Summit Botanical Gardens & Zoo. The botanical gardens were established in 1923 to introduce, propagate and disseminate tropical plants from around the world into Panama. They contain over 15,000 species of plant, with 50 of them numbered and marked along a trail through the park. Also at the park is a small zoo, with animals native to Central America.

The park is open every day from 8 am to 6 pm. Admission is US$0.25 for adults, US$0.10 for children, and includes some information and a trail map of the park.

The Gamboa bus stops here.

Soberanía National Park
A few km further on, the 22,104-hectare Soberanía National Park is one of the most accessible tropical rainforest areas in Panama. It features hiking trails, the Río Chagres, part of Lago Gatún, and a remarkable variety of flora & fauna.

Hiking trails in the park include a section of the old Las Cruces Trail, used by the Spanish to transport goods by mule train between Panama City and Nombre de Dios. A shorter, very easy trail is the Sendero El Charco nature trail, signposted from the highway, three km past the Summit Botanical Gardens & Zoo. Fishing is permitted in the Río Chagres or Lago Gatún, but hunting is not.

Leaflets and information about the park, including a self-guiding brochure for the nature trail, are available from the Inrenare and Ancon offices (see Panama City), or from the Soberanía National Park office in Gamboa (☎ 56- 6370).

Contractors Hill
On the west side of the Canal, Contractors Hill was originally 123 metres above sea

level. It was one of the highest points the Culebra (Gaillard) Cut had to cut through. There were landslides along the Cut, and Contractors Hill was reduced to its present height of 111 metres in 1954, in an effort to stabilise it.

Contractors Hill is one of the most accessible points from which to see the Gaillard Cut, but only if you have a private vehicle. The hill is pretty remote and is not served by public transport.

ISLA BARRO COLORADO
The Smithsonian Tropical Research Institute is Isla Barro Colorado, in the middle of Lago Gatún in the Panama Canal. A lush tropical rainforest, it is completely protected since only scientists and a limited number of visitors are allowed onto the island, and it makes an interesting day trip from the city, with a boat ride down a good part of the Canal, from Gamboa over Lago Gatún to the island. The institute is known worldwide, and some important scientific studies have been conducted here.

The island has over 40 km of trails, but visitors stay on a special 2.5-km nature trail, which has been marked with information about the forest. Self-guiding booklets are available. If you have time, the staff can show you other trails on the map.

Visitors are allowed on the island only on Tuesdays (individuals or groups of up to five people) and Saturdays (groups of 15 or more). Make a reservation as far in advance as possible – Tuesdays may be fully booked for three months ahead, Saturdays for over a year. They will try to squeeze you in if they can.

A visit to the island takes a full day. The Gamboa bus leaving Panama City at 6 or 6.15 am will connect you with the island boat which leaves the Gamboa pier at 7.25 am, arriving on the island an hour later. It costs US$12 per person fee to visit the island, including the boat ride there and back, and a good, all-you-can-eat lunch at the research station cafeteria. The boat leaves the island at 3.20 pm, arriving back in Gamboa at 4.30 pm. Children under 12 are not allowed on the

island. The island has many ticks so you should wear long pants, socks and closed shoes, and use insect repellent.

To arrange a visit to the island, you might contact the Smithsonian Tropical Research Institute (☎ 27- 6022, fax (507) 62-6084) at the Tapper Building, opposite the Legislative Palace, in the Ancón district of Panama City. The STRI has a research library that is open to the public, and a small bookstore which, in 1993, was only selling souvenirs and cards.

Tours to Barro Colorado, as well as across Darién and to similar sites, are also being offered by Eco-Tours (☎ 36- 3076, 36-4494, fax 36-3550).

CERRO AZUL
About an hour's drive east of Panama City is Cerro Azul, which is part of the Parque Nacional Chagres, a mountainous area of natural forest and mountain streams.

Within the park, Altos de Cerro Azul (☎ 60-4813, 60-0290) has built nature trails and other resources for visitors. The 1600-metre El Cantar nature trail passes through the forest and over streams; there's a free booklet on the trail.

Cerro Azul can't be reached by bus, but if you telephone, they may be able to help you get out there. If you have a vehicle, take the highway heading towards Tocumen and turn left at the intersection with the Hotel Riande.

BAHAI TEMPLE
On the outskirts of Panama City, 11 km from the city centre on the road to Colón, the white-domed Bahai Temple sits on the crest of a hill. It looks much like an egg from the outside but inside it is surprisingly beautiful, with a fresh breeze always blowing through. This is the Bahai House of Worship for all of Latin America. Information about the faith is available at the temple in English and Spanish.

It's open every day from 10 am to 6 pm. Any bus to Colón can let you off on the highway, but it's a long walk up the hill. A taxi from the centre costs US$4.45. The highway turnoff has a small, inconspicuous sign.

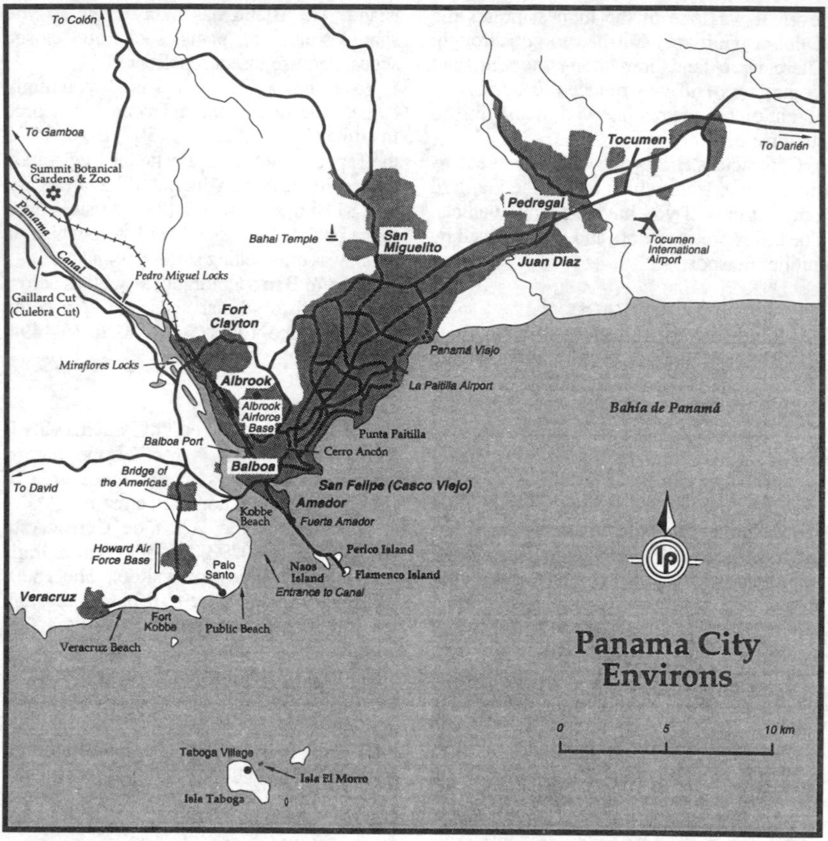

Panama City
Environs

0   5   10 km

HINDU TEMPLE
On the way to the Bahai Temple, also on a
hill, is the magnificent Hindu Temple. Services are held daily at 7.30 am and 7.30 pm.

BEACHES
Kobbe & Veracruz Beaches
Just across the Canal from Panama City,
Kobbe is a popular beach. Part of it is the
Kobbe Beach Club; at the entrance you pay
US$7 for coupons good for food and drink
at the beach. The beach is safe and protected,
and has lifeguards. Buses to Kobbe Beach
leave from the bus station at Plaza Cinco de

Mayo. If you're driving, go over the Bridge
of the Americas, take the first exit to your
left, and follow the signs to the beach. About
one km past the entrance to Kobbe Beach is
the signposted entrance to Veracruz, a free
public beach. Food is available, and it is a
popular beach, especially on weekends.

Beaches near San Carlos
A couple of hours' drive west of the city, a
strip of excellent beaches stretches along the
Pacific Coast from **Playa Chame** to **Playa
Farallón**.

About in the middle of this strip, 92 km

from Panama City, **San Carlos** is one of the best and most popular beaches in the country. Nearby, **Playa El Palmar** is one of the country's more famous surf breaks. Other good beaches along this part of the coast include **Playa Gorgona**, **Playa Coronado**, **Playa Río Mar**, **Playa Corona**, and **Playa Santa Clara**.

The Interamerican Highway runs near the coast along here, so it is easy to reach these beaches. From the Interior bus terminal, on Avenida Balboa in Panama City, you could take just about any bus heading west along this part of the coast.

EL VALLE

Just past San Carlos, a road takes off inland into the mountains. After 28 km winding up through the mountains, with good views back over the coastline, it reaches the small, pretty village of El Valle, known for its flora & fauna, including square-trunked trees and golden frogs. It's a good area for hiking in the mountain air, a refreshing change from the city and the lowlands. Every Sunday, Indians come down from the surrounding mountain villages to sell their wares and handicrafts in town.

From Panama City, buses to El Valle depart from the Interior bus station hourly from 7 am to 7 pm (123 km, 2½ hours). Or you can get to San Carlos on any bus heading west from Panama City, and take a bus up the hill from there (every half-hour from 6 am to 6.30 pm, 45 minutes).

ISLA TABOGA

About 20 km offshore and an hour's ferry ride from Panama City, Taboga is a small, peaceful island with a good beach and swimming, and an attractive village where a footpath is the only road. It is also known as the Island of Flowers, because at certain times of the year it is covered with sweet-smelling blossoms, the aroma filling the air. Taboga is a favourite retreat from the city.

Taboga has a long history. It was settled by the Spanish in 1515, just two years after Balboa first sighted the Pacific, and before Panama City was built. The village of

Taboga has a small church, said to be the second oldest in the western hemisphere; the island's graveyard dates back to the 16th century.

The island has a sheltered deep-water port and it was from here that Pizarro took off for Peru in 1524. Ships coming from South America anchored at this port during the colonial era; at that time, before the mainland port was built, the large tidal variations meant that ships could not anchor too close to the mainland.

Taboga also saw its share of piracy; Henry Morgan visited the island after sacking Panama City in 1671.

El Morro, the small island in front of the Hotel Taboga on one side of town, is joined to Isla Taboga at low tide. In the 1860s it was the headquarters of the Pacific Steamship Navigation Company. The ruins of some of the walls and the wharf can still be seen, though no buildings remain. Some of the company workers are buried in a small cemetery on the island.

Taboga's annual festival takes place on 16 July, the day of its patron saint, the Virgen del Carmen. A statue of the Virgin on a boat filled with flowers is sailed around the island, followed by a procession of fishing boats, motorboats, yachts and any other boats around at the time.

Information

Inrenare (☎ 50-2082) has an office on Taboga, near the ferry dock. It has information on the island's natural features, good snorkelling spots etc, and a big topographical map.

Taboga: Panama's Island of Flowers by Anita McAndrews & Alison Date (Focus Publications, Panama, 1984, paperback) covers the island's history, customs, and what can be found there today. It is sold on the island and in Panama City. It's lovingly written, illustrated and very informative.

Things to See & Do

On weekends, when most people visit Taboga, small boats will take you around the island to see it from all sides and to reach some good snorkelling spots. Bring your own gear. There are some caves on the island's west side, rumoured (of course) to hold golden treasure left there by pirates. During the week, when the small boats aren't taking people around, you can still snorkel around Isla El Morro, right in front of town, and see some large fish and other interesting things. Off the eastern side of El Morro there's something big in the water – it looks like the skeleton of a huge ship, but it could also be the remnants of a 19th-century wharf.

The **old church** in Taboga village is worth visiting. Even if it's closed, you can probably find someone to get the key for you. There's some beautiful old artwork inside.

Also interesting is the **shell house**, where the friendly old fisherman, shell diver and artist Jesús Heballo has spent years decorating the outside of his house with thousands of shells he collected when diving. There are some beautiful shells for sale, as well as the book *Taboga: Panama's Island of Flowers*, which has Jesús' artwork on the cover.

For a fine view of the island, you can walk up the hill, which has a cross on the top. You can also see the **pelican colony** on the island's far side. May is the height of the nesting season, but pelicans can be seen at any time from January to June. There are many other trails for walks around the island.

Places to Stay & Eat

There are two hotels on the island, but they are not cheap; most people just come over to the island for the day. The *Hotel Chu* (☎ 50-2035) has single/double rooms for around US$15/30; the *Hotel Taboga* (☎ 50-2122) is more expensive.

The Hotel Chu has a restaurant overlooking the sea, and there are many little shops and snack stands around town. The restaurant at the fancier Hotel Taboga is more expensive.

Getting There & Away

The one-hour boat trip to Taboga is part of the island's attraction. The ferry departs from Muelle (Pier) 18 in Balboa, passing under the Bridge of the Americas, along the Balboa port, and along the last part of the Panama Canal channel on its way out to sea, past the causeway linking Fuerte Amador to the three small offshore islands. On Monday, Thursday and Friday the ferry leaves Balboa at 8.30 am and 4 pm, departing Taboga for the return trip at 10 am and 6 pm. On Sunday and holidays it departs Balboa at 8.30 am, 11.30 am and 4 pm, and Taboga at 10 am, 3 pm and 6 pm. There's no service on Tuesday or Wednesday. It costs US$2.50 one way, US$5 return, half price for children. For more information or to check the schedule, contact Argo Tours (☎ 64-3549).

To get to Muelle 18, take one of the squat little buses leaving from the bus station at Plaza Cinco de Mayo.

ARCHIPIÉLAGO DE LAS PERLAS & ISLA CONTADORA

The archipelago, about 70 km out from Panama City, is named for the large pearls that were once found in its waters.

Contadora is the best-known island of the group and the easiest to get to. It is a lovely island devoted to luxury resorts, with white sand beaches, turquoise waters and excellent fishing.

Getting There & Away

The hotels on Contadora are very expensive, so if you want to visit Contadora you should make it a day trip. There may be a boat from Panama City: check with the tourist office. The journey takes three hours. Otherwise, you can fly to the island with Aeroperlas (☎ 63-5363, 69-4555), which has daily return flights for US$44.

Colón & Around

Colón is the capital of the large province of the same name, which extends over 200 km along the Caribbean coast from Veraguas province in the west to San Blas province in the east. Most of the region is undeveloped and inaccessible. It's probably best to avoid the city of Colón, but Portobelo and Fort San

Lorenzo, two historic Spanish fortresses, are worth seeing, and there are a couple of good beaches on the way to Portobelo, as well as Isla Grande, a tiny island just off the coast.

All of these places can easily be visited as day trips from Panama City, only a couple of hours away across the isthmus.

COLÓN
Population 59,832

On the Caribbean entrance to the Panama Canal, Colón is Panama's second largest city, the country's principal Caribbean port, the Atlantic gateway to the Panama Canal, and site of the Free Zone (Zona Libre), the world's second-largest duty-free port (after Hong Kong). Boats heading down the coast past the San Blas islands to Colombia depart from the Coco Solo pier near Colón.

Colón is a dangerous place and if you don't have a pressing reason to come here, you should give it a miss. Probably the only reason to come is the duty-free shopping, and many items will be just as cheap in Panama City.

The Gatun Locks, on the way to Fort San Lorenzo, are accessible by taxi or bus but have no special provision for visitors.

In the past Colón had some brighter times, but today it is a slum. Many of the wooden houses built at the turn of the century are now on the verge of collapsing, with people still living inside them.

Warning
Crime is a serious problem in Colón. It is not only possible but likely that you will get mugged. If you want to go to the Free Zone, take a taxi from the bus station, don't walk.

History
Colón was founded in 1850 as the Caribbean terminus of the Panama Railroad. It was originally called Aspinwall, after a builder who worked on the railway.

Around the turn of the century, when controversy over independence from Colombia was intense, the city was burned down in a political melee. It was rebuilt in a turn-of-the-century French style, similar to that of New Orleans, as the French were the dominant force in the area at that time. They were attempting to start construction on the Canal, and the port of Cristóbal was built to accommodate materials shipped in for the project.

Things to See & Do
The main reason travellers come to Colón is to go to the **Zona Libre** (Free Zone), a walled-off area of giant international stores selling things at duty-free prices. Most of them only deal in bulk merchandise but you can buy individual items at some stores. You're supposed to have the items either mailed directly out of the country, or delivered to the airport where you pick them up when you fly out.

The Free Zone is open Monday to Friday from 8 am to 5 pm; a few shops are open Saturday morning, and the whole Zone closes on Sunday. When you enter the Free Zone you must present your passport, or a tourist card with official identification, at the security office.

If you must walk around Colón, stick to the main streets.

The French-style **cathedral** on Calle 5 has an interesting altar, stained glass windows, and other details. It's open from 6.30 to 11.30 am and from 2 to 5.45 pm.

The **Hotel Washington**, by the sea on the north end of Avenida del Frente, is a relic of another era, a turn-of-the-century grand hotel with huge rooms and hallways, deep plush carpets, crystal chandeliers and other elegant touches. The hotel has a restaurant, bar and disco; and its cafeteria is a good place to come for a coffee, and to watch the ships lining up to enter the Canal.

Next door is the **de Lesseps residence**, former home of Ferdinand de Lesseps, the French contractor who built the Suez Canal and formed the first Panama Canal company.

Places to Stay
If you must stay overnight in Colón, there are several places where you'll be safe, as long as you don't venture out on the streets at night.

The best place to stay would be the *Hotel*

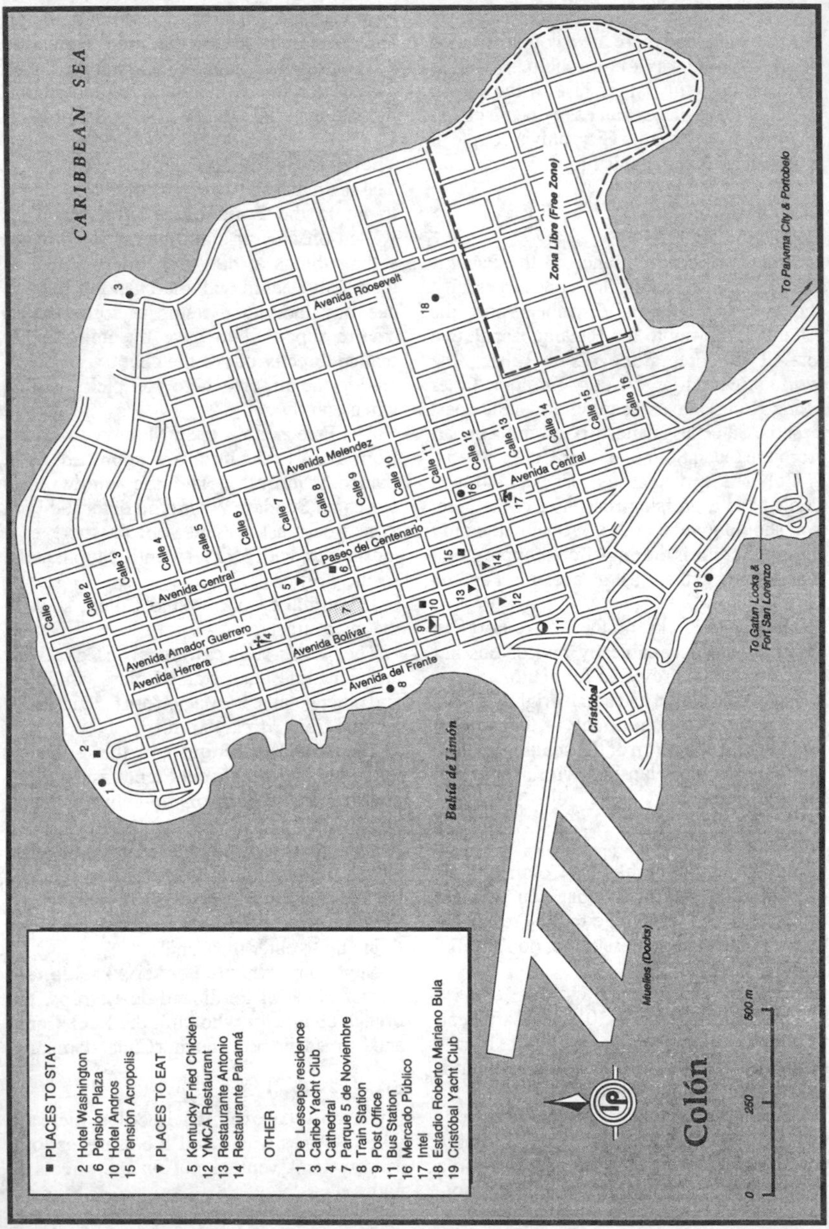

PANAMA

CARIBBEAN SEA

Colón

PLACES TO STAY
2 Hotel Washington
6 Pensión Plaza
10 Hotel Andros
15 Pensión Acropolis

PLACES TO EAT
5 Kentucky Fried Chicken
12 YMCA Restaurant
13 Restaurante Antonio
14 Restaurante Panamá

OTHER
1 De Lesseps residence
3 Caribe Yacht Club
4 Cathedral
7 Parque 5 de Noviembre
8 Train Station
9 Post Office
11 Bus Station
16 Mercado Público
17 Intel
18 Estadio Roberto Mariano Bula
19 Cristóbal Yacht Club

Avenida Roosevelt
Zona Libre (Free Zone)

Avenida Melendez
Avenida Central

Calle 1
Calle 2
Calle 3
Calle 4
Calle 5
Calle 6
Calle 7
Calle 8
Calle 9
Calle 10
Calle 11
Calle 12
Calle 13
Calle 14
Calle 15
Calle 16

Avenida Central
Avenida Amador Guerrero
Avenida Herrera
Paseo del Centenario
Avenida Bolívar
Avenida del Frente

Bahía de Limón
Muelles (Docks)

Cristóbal

To Panama City & Portobelo
To Gatún Locks & Fort San Lorenzo

0   250   500 m

Washington (☎ 41-7133), at the north end of Avenida del Frente. It's not cheap but it's probably one of the classiest places you'll ever stay in: large, high-ceilinged rooms with private hot-water bath, colour TV, deep carpet etc are US$25/31 for singles/doubles. The hotel has a cafeteria, restaurant, bar and disco, plus a fine sea view.

The *Pensión Acropolis* (☎ 41-1456), on Avenida Amador Guerrero near the corner of Calle 11, has rooms with shared bath and fan at US$6.50. The *Hotel Sotelo*, opposite the Acropolis, is more expensive. The *Pensión Plaza* (☎ 41-3216, 41-3624), on Paseo del Centenario between Calles 7 & 8, has rooms with shared bath at US$6, or private bath at US$8.50.

The *Hotel Andros* (☎ 41-0477), on Avenida Herrera between Calles 9 & 10, is a spotless, modern six-storey hotel, with rooms at US$17 with fan, or US$20 with air-con. All the rooms have private bath, hot water, colour cable TV and phone.

Places to Eat
The *cafeteria* in the Hotel Washington is air-conditioned and has a fine view of the sea.

The *YMCA Restaurant*, on Avenida Bolívar between Calles 11 & 12, serves mostly Chinese food. Most meals are a bit expensive, at around US$3 to US$8, but there's a special of the day for around US$2. Other restaurants, nothing fancy but recommended by locals as cheap, decent places to eat, are the *Restaurante Panamá* and the *Restaurante Antonio*, opposite one another at the intersection of Avenida Herrera and Calle 11. There's a *Kentucky Fried Chicken* on Paseo del Centenario between Calle 6 and 7.

Getting There & Away
Bus The bus station is on the corner of Avenida del Frente and Calle 12.

From Colón to Panama City (76 km) there are two buses, the regular and the express, but there's not much difference in travel time between the two. The regular buses depart every day, every 20 minutes from 4 am to 1 am (two hours). The express buses have air-con and depart every 20 minutes from 5

am to 9 pm Monday to Friday, hourly on Saturday; they don't run on Sunday (1¾ hours).

Buses to Portobelo depart every day, hourly from 6.30 am to 6 pm (44 km, one hour). These same buses can be boarded at Sabanitas, the turnoff for Portobelo.

Train A famous train once ran between Panama City and Colón, passing alongside the Canal and affording an excellent view of it. Though cargo trains still ply the route, the passenger train was destroyed during the 1989 invasion and had not been repaired at the time of writing. You could check with IPAT, the national tourist office, to see if it's been restarted.

PORTOBELO
Population 570
Portobelo, 44 km east of Colón, is one of Panama's most important historic places. The extensive ruins of Spanish stone fortresses erected centuries ago make for some interesting exploration.

In addition to the famous fort and line of cannons (featured on Panama's tourist literature) the site extends outward with stone walls and other ruins visible for some distance if you look for them. The present-day town of Portobelo is built among the ruins of the Spanish settlement. Yet more fortress ruins stand on either side of the harbour entrance.

The other notable feature of Portobelo is its large colonial church, built in 1776. It contains a famous life-size statue, the Black Christ, said to have miraculous powers. On 21 October each year, the Festival of the Black Christ attracts hundreds of pilgrims from near and far, many dressed in the same royal purple colour as the statue's clothes. The statue is paraded through the streets, people attach symbols to it in thanks for miracles performed, and the celebrations continue all day and all night.

There are no places to stay in Portobelo, but there are various little restaurants. It's probably best to come as a day trip from

Panama City, rather than risk staying in Colón.

On the way to Portobelo, the black sand Playa María Chiquita and the white sand Playa Langosta are two attractive beaches.

History

Portobelo, the 'beautiful port', was named by Columbus in 1502 when he stopped here on his fourth New World voyage. It was the principal Spanish Caribbean port in Central America for around 200 years, from the 16th to the 18th century. Gold and other treasure from Peru was shipped to Panama City and carried overland by mule trail to Portobelo. The goods were stored in fortresses at Portobelo until the annual trade fair, when galleons laden with goods from Spain arrived to trade for gold and other goods from the New World.

Naturally, all this wealth concentrated in one spot attracted the British and other pirates who roamed the Caribbean. They made repeated attacks on all the strategic points of the Spanish treasure route; in 1739 Portobelo was destroyed by an attack led by the British Admiral Edward Vernon. In 1746 the Spanish gave up and stopped using the overland Panama route altogether, instead sailing the long way around Cape Horn to and from the west coast of South America.

Portobelo was rebuilt a few years later, in 1751, but it never achieved its former importance. In time, it became a virtual ruin. Much of the outermost fortress was dismantled during construction of the Panama Canal, and the stones used in building the Gatún Locks. There are still considerable parts of the town and fortresses left, however, and today Portobelo is protected as a national park and historic place.

Getting There & Away

Buses run between Colón and Portobelo, hourly from 6.30 am to 6 pm (one hour).

If you're coming by bus from Panama City, you can get off at Sabanitas, 10 km before Colón, and catch the bus to Portobelo when it passes through. You don't have to go to Colón at all.

ISLA GRANDE

Past Portobelo, the road continues as a narrow dirt track until it reaches La Guayra, from where small boats go to Isla Grande, just offshore. This island, five km long and 1½ km wide, is remote and beautiful, with white sand beaches, palm trees and crystal-clear turquoise water.

About 300 people of African descent live on the island, making a living from fishing and producing coconuts. Seafood and coconut milk are the principal ingredients of the food on the island, which includes *fufu*, seafood soups, *ceviche*, Caribbean king crab, lobster, shrimp, octopus, sea turtle, shad and corvina. The island has several places to eat, and a couple of places to stay. Facilities are available for diving, snorkelling and fishing.

Visitors come to the island for a number of annual celebrations. San Juan Bautista is celebrated on 24 June, with swimming and canoe races. The day of the Virgen del Carmen is 16 July, with a land and sea procession, baptisms and masses. Carnaval is also celebrated in the days before Ash Wednesday; they dance the conga with ribbons and mirrors in their hair, the women wearing wide pollera dresses, and the men in ragged pants, inside out and tied at the waist with old sea rope. Together with the dancing there are actions and songs about current events, and a lot of joking in the Caribbean calypso tradition.

The French built a lighthouse here in 1893, which sent red, green and white light over 100 km out to sea. Today the lighthouse still functions, but with just a white light visible for only 70 km.

FORT SAN LORENZO

On a promontory to the west of the Canal, Fort San Lorenzo is perched at the mouth of the Río Chagres. It was on this river that the British pirate Henry Morgan gained access to the interior in 1671, enabling him to sack and destroy the original Panama City, today the ruins of Panamá Viejo.

Like the fortresses at Portobelo which date from the same period, the Spanish fortress here is built of stone and displays rows of old cannons. A British cannon among the Spanish ones is evidence of the times when British pirates overcame the fort. Much of the fort is very well preserved, including the moat, the cannons, and the arched stone rooms. The fort commands a wide view of the river and bay far below.

There is no public transport to Fort San Lorenzo. To get there, drive over the Gatun Locks and pass through the security gate of the US base, Fort Sherman, presenting identification to pass. The fort is in a military zone, about 10 km past Fort Sherman.

The Interamerican Highway

The Interamerican Highway (Carretera Interamericana, also called the Pan American Highway or Carretera Panamericana) stretches almost 500 km west from Panama City to Paso Canoas, where it crosses the border and continues into Costa Rica. Along the way it passes through highlands, lowlands, open grasslands used for grazing livestock, and places where the highway is only a narrow ribbon snaking its way through tropical jungle. Many travellers never see any more of western Panama than this highway, as they dash from Panama City to Costa Rica.

The three areas of western Panama with the most to see are the Península de Azuero, and the provinces of Chiriquí and Bocas del Toro. Bocas del Toro, on the Caribbean coast, is well off the Interamerican Highway and is more easily visited from Costa Rica. The Península de Azuero is reached by turning south from the highway at Divisa. Chiriquí is one of the most interesting areas of the country, and the Interamerican Highway passes right through it. These three areas are described in later sections; the following information is for those going straight through.

Westward on the Interamerican Highway

From Panama City, the first area of interest you come to is a stretch of Pacific beaches, starting at **Punta Chame** about 75 km from of the city, and extending about 50 km to **Playa Farallón**. Some of the notable beaches are **Nueva Gorgona, Coronado, San Carlos, El Palmar, Río Mar, Corona, Santa Clara** and **Farallón**. A few km past the town of San Carlos, a road leads 27 km north into the mountains to **El Valle**, a pleasant, cool mountain town. These places are only an hour or two from Panama City and are usually visited from there; see the Around Panama City section earlier in this chapter for details.

Continuing west, the highway cuts inland and passes through several small towns, including **Penonomé** and **Aguadulce**, before reaching **Divisa**, 214 km west of Panama City.

Divisa is a small crossroads town and it's here that you turn south if you're heading for the Península de Azuero (see the following section).

Thirty-five km west from Divisa, and 248 km from Panama City, is **Santiago**, Panama's fourth-largest city and capital of the large province of Veraguas – the only province with both Pacific and Caribbean coasts. Santiago is a pleasant town, but unremarkable. The town centre is about one km from the highway. Most of the town's commerce and services, including shops, banks, petrol stations, places to eat, and a few hotels, are along Avenida Central, the town's main drag.

Continuing west towards David you will start to see Guaymí people; the Guaymí women are easy to recognise, dressed in long, loose, brightly coloured dresses. Along the highway you'll pass roadside stands where these dresses are for sale, along with wide, beaded necklaces. The villages of **Tolé** and **San Félix**, each a km or two north off the highway, are home to many Guaymí people.

About seven hours (438 km) west of Panama City you come to **David**, Panama's third-largest city and capital of Chiriquí province. The border, at **Paso Canoas**, is 53 km away. David is an excellent spot for an overnight stay, and there are some lovely places to visit nearby (see the Chiriquí section later in this chapter).

Península de Azuero

The Península de Azuero hangs into the Pacific in a wide bulge. This area, settled by the Spanish in the 16th century, maintained many Spanish colonial traditions for centuries due to its relative isolation.

Today the region has an economy based on agriculture, but is primarily known for its many traditional festivals and handicrafts. The intricate *pollera* (the lacy, ruffled dress from the colonial era which is now a national costume and symbol of Panama) is produced in this region, as are other traditional handicrafts. The region is also known for its excellent beaches.

Parts of the peninsula are still as isolated as they ever were, but a paved road now serves much of the eastern and southern area. Turning south from the Interamerican Highway at Divisa, the road passes through Chitré, capital of Herrera province, and Las Tablas, capital of Los Santos province. If you want to stay on the peninsula, Chitré has the most facilities for travellers.

Many other small towns are dotted around the peninsula where they were founded by the Spanish four centuries ago, and not much bigger than they were then. Most still have their original, well-preserved colonial churches.

Festivals
Festivals on the Península de Azuero are famous throughout Panama for their traditional costumes and forms of celebration. Some have survived intact from centuries ago; the 'dance of the little devils', the 'penitent of the other life' and the 'peasant wedding' are dances and skits which show aspects of life in the times of the early Spaniards.

Some of the peninsula's best known festivals, attracting visitors from all over Panama, include:

20 January
    Festival of San Sebastián; in Ocú
February/March
    Carnaval; the four days before Ash Wednesday, in Las Tablas, Chitré, Villa de Los Santos and Parita.
March/April
    Semana Santa (Easter Week); in Villa de Los Santos and Pes
Late April/early May
    Feria de Azuero; in Villa de los Santos
May/June
    Fiesta de Corpus Christi; Thursday to Sunday, 40 days after Easter, in Villa de Los Santos; one of Panama's most famous celebrations, with medieval dances and traditional costumes
24 June
    Fiesta de San Juan Bautista; in Chitré
29 June
    Patronales de San Pablo; in Pedasí
20 July
    Fiesta de Santa Librada, Festival de la Pollera; in Las Tablas
15 August
    Festival del Manito; Fiesta Popular; Matrimonio Campesino; El Duelo del Tamarindo; El Penitente de la Otra Vida; all celebrated in Ocú with traditional costumes
24 September
    Festival de la Mejorana, Festival de la Virgen de las Mercedes; in Guararé with folkloric dance and music;
19 October
    Founding of District of Chitré (1848); parades, historical costumes and celebrations in Chitré
10 November
    First Cry for Independence (1821); in Villa de Los Santos

You can get details about these and other celebrations from any office of IPAT, the national tourist office.

Artesanías
The Península de Azuero is also known for its traditional handicrafts, some of which have been made in the same places for hundreds of years.

Some of the best known handicrafts, and the towns where they're made, include:

Polleras (dresses)
  Santo Domingo (near Las Tablas); La Enea (near Guararé)
Masks
  Parita; Villa de Los Santos
Musical instruments
  San José de Las Tablas (near Santo Domingo, which is near Las Tablas)
Ceramics
  La Arena (near Chitré)
Woven hats
  Ocú, Los Pozos
Woven Mats, Carpets and Wall Hangings
  Chitré (Galería Linares displays leather wall hangings and pictures by well-known leather artist Georgina Linares)

Beaches

There are dozens of good beaches around the peninsula. Some of the best are near Chitré; Playa Agallito where migratory birds are studied (see below), Playa Monagre and Playa El Rompío (both served by buses from town).

Another fine beach is Playa El Uverito, near Las Tablas. There's no bus to this one, but you can hitch or take a taxi from Las Tablas.

At the southern end of the peninsula, Playa Venado is famous for surfing. It's way off the beaten track. There are cabins at Playa Venado, costing around US$6 a night during the week, or US$17 for a weekend, or you could camp out. Playa Venado also has a bar and restaurant. A bus operates once a day between Playa Venado and Las Tablas; the trip takes two hours down a long dirt road; they say that it will take only 45 minutes when the new road goes through.

National Parks & Wildlife Refuges

The Humboldt Ecological Station, at Playa Agallito near Chitré, is a research centre specialising in migratory birds; you're welcome to visit.

In the north-east part of the peninsula, near Parita and Chitré, the Parque Nacional Sarigua protects an unusual tropical desert,

where a significant pre-Columbian archaeological site has been preserved.

On the south-east corner of the peninsula, the Refugio de Vida Silvestre Isla Iguana (Isla Iguana Wildlife Refuge) is an important reserve, not only for the iguanas the island is named for, but also for its forest and birdlife. The IPAT tourist office in Chitré can connect you with Señor René Chan, who does tours to the island.

The south-west corner of the peninsula is protected by the Parque Nacional Cerro Hoya. This is a remote area where roads have yet to penetrate.

CHITRÉ

Population 17,156
Capital of the province of Herrera, Chitré is the largest town on the peninsula, and it makes a convenient base. It's also the home of some of the area's best known festivals.

Information

The IPAT tourist office (☎ 96-4331) in Chitré is a bit out of the way, off the road to Los Santos on the outskirts of town, in the Ministerio de Comercio e Industria building, beside Seguro Social. Consequently, not many tourists drop in, but it has useful information, including an interesting booklet on festivals and things to see and do on the peninsula. They seem to be glad if a tourist comes in, and are happy to answer any questions. The office is open Monday to Friday, 8.30 am to noon and 12.45 to 4.30 pm.

Things to See & Do

Chitré has a fine **cathedral**, and an interesting little provincial museum, the **Museo de Herrera**, which is worth a visit. It's on Calle Manuel M Correa beside a little park; to find it, start from the cathedral, walk one block straight ahead, turn left and walk another three blocks. The museum is open Tuesday to Saturday from 8.30 am to noon and 1 to 4 pm, Sunday from 9 am to noon, closed Monday (admission US$0.25).

In the vicinity of Chitré are the Parque Nacional Sarigua, the Monagre and El Rompío beaches, the Humboldt Ecological

Station at Agallito beach and, a short walk or bus ride away, the village of La Arena where you can see ceramics being made. The town of Villa de los Santos, where some of the peninsula's most important festivals take place, is four km to the south.

Places to Stay & Eat

Halfway down the block directly in front of the cathedral, the *Hotel El Prado* (☎ 96-4620), at 3946 Avenida Herrera, is a clean, modern, well-kept hotel, with a 2nd-floor restaurant, sitting area and open balcony over the street, and an off-street car park. The rooms are back from the street so they're not too noisy. Single/double rooms with private bath cost US$10/16 with fan, or US$15/20 with air-conditioning.

Around the corner to the left heading away from the cathedral, the *Hotel Santa Rita* (☎ 96-4610), at the corner of Avenida Herrera and Calle Manuel M Correa, has a restaurant at street level serving Chinese and regular food, and clean, modern rooms upstairs for US$7.70/13.20 with overhead fan and private cold bath. There are more expensive rooms with air-conditioning, TV, hot water etc.

Pensión Herrerana (☎ 96-4356), 4072 Avenida Herrera, two blocks in front of the cathedral, is a clean but basic place where rooms with shared bath are US$4.40 per person, or US$5.50 per person with private bath.

In the same block as the museum, on Calle Manuel M Correa about three blocks from the cathedral, the *Pensión Colombia* (☎ 96-1856) has rooms with private bath and fan at US$10 for one or two people.

There are plenty of restaurants in the district around the cathedral. The Mercado is beside the cathedral.

Getting There & Away

Air Chitreana de Aviación (☎ 96-4430) operates flights between Chitré and Panama City twice daily, except Sunday. Cost is US$27 one way, US$54 return. A taxi to the airport costs around US$1.25.

Bus Chitré is a centre for bus transport in the region. There is no central bus station; buses leave from various corners near the cathedral. Anyone can tell you where the bus stops are situated.

Transporte Inazún (☎ 96-4177), at the corner of Calle Melitón and Calle San Pedro near the cathedral, has buses to Panama City leaving at 1 am, 4 am, and then hourly from 7.30 am to 5 pm. Nearby, also on Calle Melitón Martín, Tuasa (☎ 96-2661) has buses leaving for the capital at 4 am, and hourly from 7 am to 5 pm (251 km, four hours).

Other buses from Chitré include:

to La Arena (two km, five minutes)
to Villa de Los Santos (four km, 10 minutes)
to Playa El Aguillito, Playa Monagre, and
    Playa El Rompío (20 minutes)
to Las Tablas (31 km, 30 minutes)
to Tonosí (48 km, three hours)
to Ocú (one hour)
to Divisa (37 km, 30 minutes)
to Santiago (71 km, 1¼ hours)

VILLA DE LOS SANTOS

Villa de Los Santos (often just Los Santos) is four km south of Chitré.

This was where Colombia's first cry for independence from Spain was made, on 10 November 1821. The small **Museo de la Nacionalidad**, on the main road opposite Parque Simón Bolívar, has been established in the house where the Declaration of Independence was signed. The anniversary is celebrated in Los Santos on 10 November every year. Other notable festivals include Carnaval and Corpus Christi. The 18th-century Church of San Anastasio is also worth a visit.

GUARARÉ

The tiny town of Guararé, on the main road between Chitré and Las Tablas, is very small and there's nothing much to see. The single attraction is the **Museo Manuel F Zárate**. Zárate was a folklorist who appreciated and tried to conserve the traditions and folklore of the Azuero region. The museum, in his former home, contains pollera dresses, masks, *diablito* ('little devil') costumes and other exhibits. The museum is two blocks behind the church, about six short blocks from the main road (turn off at the Delta petrol station).

La Enea, a small village near Guararé, is known for the fine polleras made there.

LAS TABLAS
Population 5,230

Las Tablas is the capital of Los Santos province and has one of the finest colonial churches in the area. Santa Librada, with its ornate gold-painted altar, has been declared a national historical monument.

Another historic place is El Pausílipo, the former country estate of Belisario Porras, three times president of Panama. It's now being converted to a museum.

Las Tablas hosts annual festivals including Carnaval and the Fiesta de Santa Librada, with its accompanying Festival de la Pollera.

The small town of **Santo Domingo**, about 10 minutes from Las Tablas, is known for its fine pollera dresses; polleras are also made in the nearby towns of **San José, El Carate, La Tiza** and **El Cocal. Playa El Uverito** is the best beach in the vicinity.

Places to Stay & Eat

Las Tablas has several places to stay and eat; all are within a couple of blocks of Santa Librada church.

The *Hotel Piamonte* (☎ 94-6372), on Avenida Central, has single/double rooms at around US$15. Opposite the Piamonte, the *Pensión Mariela* is cheaper but it's quite run down. The best bet is probably to walk a couple of blocks to the *Pensión Marta*; it's in better shape than the Mariela and it's cheaper than the Piamonte.

Getting There & Away

Buses connect Las Tablas with Santo Domingo (10 minutes), Chitré (31 km, 30 minutes), Panama City (282 km, 4½ hours), Playa Venado (68 km, two hours), Tonosí (79 km, 2½ hours) and other places. There is no bus to Playa El Uverito; a taxi to the beach costs about US$4.

Chiriquí

Chiriquí is Panama's beautiful westernmost province.

The giant Volcán Barú, Panama's only volcano, is protected as a national park and at 3475 metres is the highest point in the country. The flanks of the volcano, with rich black volcanic soil and a cool mountain climate, have a number of farming communities including Boquete. There are also hot springs, beaches (Las Lajas is the best known) and opportunities for trout-fishing, hiking, mountain climbing and bird-watching. David, Panama's third largest city, is capital of the province. Both the highlands and lowlands of Chiriquí are fertile and productive. The province's most important products include coffee, citrus fruit, bananas, sugar cane, rum, vegetables, livestock, thoroughbred racehorses, and delicious rainbow trout.

Chiriquí province is home to the Guaymí Indian people. The Guaymí women are easily recognised, wearing full, long, brightly coloured dresses.

DAVID
Population 102,678

David is Panama's third-largest city, capital of Chiriquí province, and the centre of a rich agricultural region. It has a fine central plaza and plenty of places to stay and eat. The city's annual fair is held on 19 March.

Many travellers stop here overnight on their way to or from the Costa Rican border at Paso Canoas, 53 km away. It is also used as a base from which to visit Boquete or Hato del Volcán, near the Parque Nacional Volcán Barú. David is about halfway between San José (Costa Rica) and Panama City – about seven hours by road from either place.

Information

IPAT (☎ 75-4120), has a tourist information office on the corner of the central plaza, upstairs from the Fino Fino department store. It is open Monday to Friday from 8.30 am to

4.30 pm, and has information on the whole of Chiriquí province.

The post office is on Calle C Norte, a block behind the central plaza. Intel, for international phone calls, is a block away at the corner of Calle C Norte and Avenida Cincuentenario. It's open every day from 8 am to 9.30 pm. Calls to anywhere within Panama can be made from the telephone boxes on the footpath in front of the office.

There's a Costa Rican consulate (☎ 75-6194) on Avenida 2 Oeste, between Calles D & E Norte, where you can get a visa to enter Costa Rica. Office hours are Monday to Friday from 8 am to 1 pm.

Migración y Naturalización (☎ 75-4515), on Calle C Sur near the corner of Avenida Central, is the place to extend your Panamanian visa or get permission to leave Panama (if you need it because you've been in Panama for over 30 days). The office is open Monday to Friday from 8 am to 3.30 pm.

Things to See & Do

David's small history and art museum, the **Museo de Historia y de Arte José de Obaldía**, is in an old two-storey house on Avenida 8 Este, near the corner of Calle A Norte. It's in the former home of José de Obaldía Orejuela, founder of Chiriquí province.

The **cinema**, Cine Plaza, is half a block west of the plaza.

Otherwise there's not much to do in David itself, but there are many good places to visit within about an hour's drive, including Boquete, the Caldera Hot Springs, Hato del Volcán, Cerro Punta and the broad white sand beach at Playa Las Lajas. The **Carta Vieja rum distillery**, on the Interamerican Highway west of David, gives tours of the hacienda. Phone the office in David (☎ 75-2186) for information or just stop at the distillery.

Ask at the IPAT tourist office to see if the medicinal sulphur springs, **Pozo de Agua Sulfurosa**, on the outskirts of David, are open yet. The springs are off the road to the Universidad Santa María la Antigua (USMA).

Places to Stay

The *Hotel Saval* (☎ 75-3543), on Calle D Norte between Avenida Cincuentenario and Avenida 1 Este, is quiet and clean. It has rooms with up to six beds, a sitting area outdoors under a covered patio, and an economical little open-air restaurant in front selling breakfast and lunch. Rooms are US$7.70 per person with fan, US$9.90 with air-con, all with private bath.

Two blocks away, the *Pensión El Amanacer* (☎ 74-3922) is a small, quiet place with just a few rooms: US$7 with fan, US$10 with air-con, all with private bath. It has one entrance on Avenida 1 Oeste, between Calles D & E Norte, and another round the corner on Calle D Norte.

Pensión Costa Rica (☎ 75-1241), on Avenida 5 Este near the corner of Calle A Sur, is a larger place. Singles/doubles are US$4/7 with shared bath and no fan, or US$6/11 with fan and private bath. Buses to Costa Rica depart from the Tracopa office next door at 8.30 am.

Pensión Fanita (☎ 75-3718), on Calle B Norte two blocks south-east of the plaza, is a very basic place but it's cheap, with rooms with shared bath at US$2.75, with private bath at US$4.40, or with private bath and air-con at US$6.60. Near it are some other cheap places.

Pensión Clark (☎ 74-3452) is on Avenida Francisco Clark, about a km north-east of the plaza, the fourth house from the Avenida Cincuentenario corner. It's a small, clean place with just eight rooms, all with private bath, at US$7.70.

All of these places except the Fanita have areas for parking.

Places to Eat

David has a remarkable number of restaurants; you won't go hungry in this town.

There are several good restaurants just off the central plaza. On the north corner of the plaza is the *Restaurante y Cafetería Jimar*. Around the corner behind it are the *Café Ejecutivo* and the *Restaurante Parque*, and opposite these, the *Restaurante Salon Don Pedro*. All these places are air-conditioned,

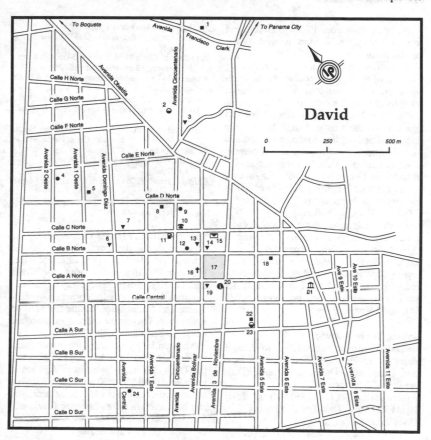

David

■ PLACES TO STAY

1 Pensión Clark
5 Pensión El Amanacer
8 Hotel Saval
18 Pensión Fanita
22 Pensión Costa Rica

▼ PLACES TO EAT

3 Frito's Café
6 Pizza House
7 Café Don Dicky
13 Restaurante Don
Pedro

14 Restaurante Jimar,
Restaurante
Parque, Café
Ejecutivo
19 Pollo Riko

OTHER

2 Bus Station
4 Costa Rican
Consulate
9 Mercado
10 Intel
11 24-hour Petrol Station
(Shell)

12 Cine Plaza
15 Post Office
16 Church
17 Central plaza
20 IPAT tourist office
21 Museo de Historia y
de Arte José de
Obaldía
23 Tracopa Buses to
Costa Rica
24 Migracíon

all are open from around 7 am to 10 pm, and several have Chinese food as well as the regular items.

Also on the plaza is *Pollo Riko*, with many varieties of chicken; or you can get inexpensive pizza at the small open-air *Pizza House*, three blocks north-west of the plaza.

Café Don Dicky on Calle C Norte is open 24 hours. From the front it looks like a cheap open-air diner, but they make good food and there's a more attractive dining area at the rear.

A pleasant little place for very inexpensive breakfast and lunch is the small open-air café in the front of the *Hotel Saval*. Service is friendly, and breakfast is US$1.25, lunch US$1.50, or soup US$0.50.

Near the bus station there are more places to eat. The *Restaurante América*, which is right in the bus station, is open daily from 5 am to midnight. Outside is a row of cafés; *Frito's Café* is clean, makes good waffles, and offers a typical meal at US$1.25 for lunch or dinner. It is open daily from around 7 am until 8 pm.

Getting There & Away
Air David's airport, the Aeropuerto Enrique Malek (☎ 75-2951), is about five km from town. There are no buses to the airport; taxi fare is US$2 per person.

Aeroperlas (☎ 75-4389) offers daily flights between David and Panama City (US$92 return).

Alas Chiricanas (☎ 75-0916) offers flights to Panama City (US$100 return), Bocas del Toro (US$21) and Changuinola (US$21); double these figures for return fares.

Bus The bus station is on Avenida Cincuentenario, about 600 metres north of the central plaza. It has a small office where you can leave luggage for US$0.25, and a restaurant open from 5 am to midnight. David is the hub of bus transport for western Panama and there are buses to many places, including:

Panama City
    Regular bus (438 km, 6½ to seven hours, around US$10); hourly, 7 am to 1 pm, then every 1½

hours until last bus at 7 pm.
    Express bus (five hours, US$15); one bus at midnight.
Paso Canoas, Costa Rican border (53 km, 1½ hours); buses every 10 minutes, 5 am to 7.30 pm.
Boquete (35 km, one hour); every half-hour, 6.15 am to 9 pm.
Caldera (20 km, 45 minutes); noon, 2, 4.30 and 6 pm.
Hato del Volcán (57 km, 1¾ hours); every half hour, 7 am to 6 pm.
Cerro Punta (79 km, 2¼ hours); the Hato del Volcán bus continues to Bambito Cerro Punta, half an hour further on.
Las Lajas (100 km, 1¾ hours); 11.45 am and 12.30 pm.
Chiriquí Grande (106 km, three hours); buses depart every 1½ hours, 6.30 am to 4 pm.
Puerto Armuelles (88 km, 2½ hours); every 15 minutes, 5 am to 8 pm.

To/From Costa Rica As well as the regular buses to the border town of Paso Canoas, Tracopa (☎ 75-0585) operates direct buses between David and San José, the Costa Rican capital. Buses depart every day at 8.30 am from their office at the corner of Avenida 5 Este and Calle A Sur, beside the Pensión Costa Rica. They arrive in San José at around 4.30 pm. The fare is US$10 one way.

You can buy your ticket when you show up for the bus, or up to two days in advance; the Tracopa office is open from 7.30 am to noon, and from 2 to 4.30 pm. Costa Rica has an onward or return ticket requirement; you can buy a return ticket between David and San José for US$20, but they won't refund the return portion in San José.

Getting Around
David has local buses and plenty of taxis. Taxi fares within the city are US$0.65.

Rental car companies in David include Budget (☎ 75-5597, 75-1667), Hertz (☎ 75-6828, 75-6829) and Mike's (☎ 75-4963).

BOQUETE
Population 2,831
Just 35 km (one hour by bus) from David, Boquete is so different it feels like it's in another country. Nestled into a craggy mountain valley at 1060 metres, with the rocky Río Caldera running through it, Boquete is known for its cool, fresh climate and pristine

natural environment. It's a fine place for walking, bird-watching, and enjoying a respite from the heat of the lowlands. It's claimed that several Boquete residents have lived to over 115 years of age.

Flowers, coffee, vegetables and citrus fruits are grown around Boquete. The town's annual festival, the Feria de las Flores y del Café, draws people from near and far. It is held for one or two weeks each April, some time around the 11th; Boquete was founded on 11 April 1911. Navel orange season, from November to February, is another popular time to visit Boquete – the oranges here are known for their fine flavour.

Things to See & Do

There is lots to see and do around Boquete. Several good paved roads lead out of town into the surrounding hills, passing coffee plantations, agricultural and cattle farms, gardens, and virgin forest. **Coffee plantations** include Café Sitton, Café Princesa Janca, Café Ruíz, and Highland Coffee. Café Sitton is one of the largest, with big processing barns. You can visit the plantations to see how the coffee is grown and processed.

Boquete is a great place for walking and hiking. You could walk around the roads and trails, up the river, or, for the ambitious, climb to the summit of 3475-metre Volcán Barú, in the nearby national park. There are several entrances to the park but the easiest access is from Boquete (see the section on Parque Nacional Volcán Barú).

Less strenuously, you can stroll around town and visit the central plaza, the **Parque de las Madres** with its flowers, fountain and children's playground, the fairgrounds, and the river.

Cockfights are held in the centre of town on Saturdays and Sundays. **Rodeos** are held from time to time in Boquete and other towns in the area, put together by a 'rodeo club' of local farmers and cattle ranchers. They welcome visitors.

Other activities include **bird-watching** (there are many species of birds here, including the quetzal), **trout fishing** in the river (bring your own tackle), and **horse riding**.

Plenty of people around Boquete have horses; you could ask the Coffee Bean Restaurant or the Pensión Marilós to put you in touch with someone with horses for hire. Further afield, you can visit the Caldera hot springs (see the next section).

At the entrance to town, where the 'Bienvenidos a Boquete' sign stretches over the highway, there's a statue of the Virgin, and a great view over the whole town and valley. Also here is the Coffee Bean Restaurant (☎ 70-1624), which offers a number of tours, including trips to the hot springs and coffee plantations, an all-day 4WD trip to the summit of Volcán Barú, camping trips on Volcán Barú, or longer trips by 4WD over the mountains to Chiriquí Grande or into the forest to see quetzals, monkeys and other wildlife.

Places to Stay

Pensión Marilós (☎ 70-1380), on the corner of Avenida A Este and Calle 6 Sur, is a great place to stay – family-run, clean and comfortable. Single/double rooms are US$6.60/ 9.90 with shared bath, or US$9.90/15.40 with private bath. Excellent 'all you can eat' meals are served in the dining room and cost US$1.50 for breakfast, US$2.50 for lunch or dinner.

Pensión Virginia (☎ 70-1260) on the central plaza is a good second choice, with singles/doubles at US$6.60/12 with shared bath, or US$8.80/16.50 with private bath. They have a restaurant downstairs, and a piano in the upstairs sitting room.

Several other places to stay in Boquete are a bit more expensive. Opposite the Pensión Marilós, the *Hotel Rebequet* (☎ 70-1365) has attractive rooms with private bath at US$15/20 for singles/doubles. *Hotel Fundadores* (☎ 70-1298) on the main road charges US$20 per room.

The *Hotel Panamonte* (☎ 70-1327, fax 70-1324) is more expensive, at US$38-50 for one or two people, but the owners, Mr and Mrs Collins, deal with many visiting naturalists and you could talk to them about camping on their land, which has a forest that

Around Boquete

is excellent for bird-watching (quetzals are often seen on their property).

Because of the cool climate, all the places to stay in Boquete have hot showers.

Places to Eat

Boquete has many inexpensive restaurants to choose from. *La Conquista*, on the main road near the plaza, has good typical food including local rainbow trout *(trucha)*. Opposite this, the *Pizzería La Volcánica* has pizza and Italian dishes. There's a Chinese restaurant on the corner of the plaza.

You can eat at the *Pensión Marilós*

whether or not you're staying there. They serve a big, family-style breakfast from 7 to 8.30 am (US$1.50), lunch from noon to 1 pm (US$2.50), and dinner from 6 to 7 pm (US$2.50). At lunch and dinner you can serve yourself all you can eat – it's an excellent deal and the food is delicious.

The *Coffee Bean Restaurant*, at the entrance to town where the 'Bienvenidos a Boquete' sign arches over the road, is a bit more expensive than other restaurants in town, but it's an attractive place with great atmosphere, good food, a splendid view of the town, and an English book exchange. A lion, Else, is kept in a cage at one side of the restaurant.

Getting There & Away

A bus runs between Boquete and David every half-hour from 6.15 am to 9 pm. The 35-km trip on a good paved road takes an hour and costs US$1.20.

Getting Around

Boquete is a small town and you can easily walk around the centre in a short time.

Walking is a great way to see the area, if you have plenty of time. The local 'urban' buses, winding around through the hills among coffee plantations, farms and forest, cost just US$0.50 and are a good way to get oriented. The folks at the Coffee Bean restaurant offer half-day local tours for US$15 per person, and some interesting longer trips. The owners of the Pensión Marilós can put you in touch with someone to take you around in a private car; if you get a group together, this is not expensive. There are also taxis.

Getting around on horseback is another option; see Things to See & Do.

CALDERA HOT SPRINGS

These natural hot springs ('Los Pozos de Caldera') are famous for their health-giving properties, especially for rheumatism sufferers. The springs are on private land near the town of Caldera, and have not been developed for visitors. The owners, the Collins family who own the Panamonte Hotel in Boquete, don't mind people visiting the springs, or even camping out there, as long as they respect the property, and take their rubbish out with them.

Getting There & Away

Caldera is about 14 km off the road from David to Boquete; a sign marks the turnoff. There's a bus from David to Caldera, or you could take any bus between David and Boquete, get off at the turnoff, and hitch the rest of the way (though there may not be much traffic).

The springs are about a 45-minute walk from Caldera, where the paved road passes through town. In a 4WD vehicle you can drive up to within about a 10-minute walk from the springs. You'll need to ask the way; there are no signs but all the locals know where they are. The people at the Coffee Bean restaurant in Boquete sometimes make trips there.

PARQUE NACIONAL VOLCÁN BARÚ

The giant Volcán Barú, Panama's only volcano, is the dominant geographical feature of western Panama. Its fertile volcanic soil and the temperate climate of its mid-altitude slopes support some of Panama's most productive agriculture, especially in the areas around Cerro Punta and Boquete. On the volcano's upper slopes, the large trees of the lower slopes give way to smaller plants, bushes, scrub and abundant alpine wildflowers.

Volcán Barú is no longer active and there is no record of its most recent eruption. It has not one but seven craters.

The 14,300-hectare Parque Nacional Volcán Barú provides ample possibilities for hiking, mountain-climbing and camping, with many walking trails. A climb to the top, though quite steep, is not technically difficult, and no special climbing equipment is required. The summit is the highest point in Panama and on a clear day it affords views to both the Pacific and the Caribbean coasts.

The park is home to abundant wildlife including puma, jaguar, tapir, and the spotted *conejo pintado*. It's also a good place for bird-watching.

The park has entrances on different sides of the volcano. The easiest access is from the town of Boquete, about 16 km from the summit, but it's a strenuous – some would say painful – uphill hike along a dirt road full of scree. One hiker suggested it would be better as a two-day trip. If you drive as far up as you can and then walk the rest of the way, it still takes about six hours to reach the summit from the park gate.

Another park entrance is just outside the town of Hato del Volcán, on the road to Cerro Punta. The road into the park here goes only to the foot of the volcano, not far off the main road. The view of the peaks from this entrance is impressive.

AROUND VOLCÁN BARÚ

A road branches off the Interamerican Highway at Concepción, and climbs steadily through the towns of Hato del Volcán (1500 metres) and Bambito until it stops at Cerro Punta (2130 metres), on the west side of Volcán Barú. It's a good, paved road as far as Hato del Volcán, but it becomes a rough dirt track before you reach Cerro Punta.

As in Boquete, the climate up here is cool and the air is brisk, fresh and invigorating. The agricultural lands around Cerro Punta also have rich, black volcanic soil and are very fertile. It is a great area for walking.

As you ascend towards Cerro Punta, everything starts to look more and more European, with meticulously tended agricultural plots and European-style houses with steep-pitched tin roofs. A Swiss colony was founded here (one farm is named 'Nueva Suiza'). Later immigrants included Yugoslavs, and you may still hear their language spoken in the area.

This area produces not only abundant cool-climate crops, including vegetables, fruits, strawberries, flowers and coffee, but also trout, livestock, and thoroughbred racehorses. You'll pass several stables (haras) where racehorses are bred, along the Cerro Punta road.

You can easily visit this area as a day trip from David; buses run frequently between David and Cerro Punta, via Hato del Volcán and Bambito. Or you could stay in Hato del Volcán, or camp in the national park.

Hato del Volcán

Coming from Concepción, Hato del Volcán, also known just as Volcán, is the first town you'll come to.

Three km before reaching the town, on the west side of the road, Arte Cruz is where the famous woodcarver José de la Cruz González makes furniture, carvings and other wood products known all over Panama. Visitors are welcome, and he is glad to demonstrate and explain his craft. There are small woodcarvings and glass and mirror etchings for sale.

Just past Hato del Volcán, on the way to Bambito, is one of the entrances to the Parque Nacional Volcán Barú. A rugged road goes up into the park, soon becoming too rough for anything but a 4WD vehicle. The view of the volcanic peaks from here is impressive.

Places to Stay & Eat The *Motel California* (☎ 71-4272), in town on the main road is run by a friendly old Yugoslav guy (who also speaks Spanish and English). Clean cabins with private hot bath are US$16.50 and up.

Just a little cheaper than the California, but much older and not as good, *Cabañas Señorial* (☎ 71-4239), on the main road, has cabins with private bath and two beds at US$14 per day.

Cabañas Reina (☎ 71-4338) is off the main road in a residential section of town; there's a sign at the turnoff, and they're planning to put up a sign at the place itself so it won't be so hard to find. There are several two-bedroom cabins, each with six beds, fully equipped kitchen, bathroom, sitting area and TV, set around a spacious lawn. Daily rates are US$27.50 for two.

In the centre of Hato del Volcán is a small food market and a number of restaurants.

Bambito

Bambito is barely a town at all. The only noticeable feature here is the large, expensive *Hotel Bambito*. Opposite this, the Truchapan rainbow trout farm is worth a stop, with thousands of trout being raised in outdoor ponds with frigid water from the nearby river surging through. You can buy fresh trout here, or hire some tackle and catch your own.

Cerro Punta

Cerro Punta is out in the boondocks; by the time you reach it the road is just a narrow dirt track, though it's still passable for buses. It's a beautiful area for walking among the meticulously tended farms and gardens, and enjoying the cool climate. There are no facilities here for visitors; you have to go back towards Hato del Volcán or David to find places to stay and eat. If you come for the day, bring lunch with you.

Getting There & Away
A bus runs from David to Cerro Punta every half hour from 7 am to 6 pm daily (79 km, 2¼ hours), stopping at Hato del Volcán (1¾ hours) and Bambito. You could catch this bus at Concepción if you're coming from Costa Rica.

RÍO SERENO
At Hato del Volcán a road turns off and heads west for 48 km to Río Sereno, on the Costa Rican border. This is not a major border crossing and doesn't seem to be served by any buses, but you could come this way if you have a private vehicle.

PUERTO ARMUELLES
Puerto Armuelles is Panama's second Pacific port, used mainly for loading bananas from the area's plantations. There are hotels and restaurants, but there's not much reason to come here. You can visit the banana plantations to see how the bananas are grown and packed for shipping. They're owned by the Chiriquí Land Company (☎ 70-7243, 75-6810), and cover much of the land around Puerto Armuelles.

A passenger train once operated between Puerto Armuelles and Concepción, but now the trains carry only bananas.

Buses go to Puerto Armuelles from David every 15 minutes or so, from 5 am to 8 pm (88 km, 2½ hours, US$2.65).

Bocas del Toro

Bocas del Toro, Panama's north-western province, is bordered by Costa Rica to the west, the Caribbean Sea to the north, and the Cordillera Central mountains to the south.

The main reason travellers go to Bocas is to visit the pristine islands of the Archipiélago de Bocas del Toro, Parque Nacional Bastimentos.

There are three ways to get to Bocas: by bus from David to Chiriquí Grande, and boat from there to the main island; from Costa Rica, via the border at Sixaola/Guabito to Almirante, and by boat from there; or by plane from either David or Panama City.

1991 Earthquake
In May 1991 Bocas del Toro was shaken by a major earthquake which destroyed buildings, water lines and roads, and left many people homeless and without the basics of life. That trauma was followed by major floods in the area. Most of the problems of shelter, fresh water, power and other services have been resolved, but travellers may still encounter inconveniences.

PARQUE NACIONAL BASTIMENTOS
Parque Nacional Bastimentos was established in 1988 as Panama's first marine park. Protecting various parts of the Archipiélago de Bocas del Toro, including parts of the large Isla Bastimentos (especially Playa Larga) and Cayo Zapatilla, the park is an important nature reserve for many species of Caribbean wildlife. Its beaches are used as a nesting ground by carey, canal and green turtles; the abundant coral reefs, great for snorkelling and diving, support countless species of fish, lobster, and other forms of sea life; lagoons are home to other wildlife including freshwater turtles and caymans; and there is still more wildlife in the forests.

You can get current park information from the ranger station (☎ 78-9244, 78-8967), the IPAT office in Bocas del Toro, or from any Inrenare office.

BOCAS DEL TORO
Population 2515
The town of Bocas del Toro, on the southeast tip of Isla Colón, is the principal town on the Archipiélago de Bocas del Toro and a pleasant and convenient base for exploring the Parque Nacional Bastimentos. (The town, the archipelago, and the province as a

whole all share the same name – Bocas del Toro.)

It's a peaceful little town of English-speaking Black people of West Indian descent. Bocas is a great place to hang out for a few days. There are great beaches, fringed by pipas and coconut palms, reefs etc. You can hire boats and snorkelling gear for explorations of the islands and coral reefs; ask at the Botel Thomas.

There's an IPAT tourist office in Bocas del Toro (☎ 78-9211).

Places to Stay & Eat

The *Pensión Peck* (☎ 78-9252), at the inland end of the main drag by the covered market (no sign), is highly recommended by travellers – they charge US$4.40 for immaculate rooms with fan, balcony etc. The *Botel Thomas* (☎ 78-9309, 78-9428), by the sea, and the *Bahía*, are more expensive, at US$10-15 for a double. Touts from various pensiónes will meet the boat when you arrive.

Eat in the market (breakfast and lunch), or try *Don Chicho's*, on the main street. Some of the places have turtle dishes on the menu – in the interests of wildlife conservation, please don't order them.

Getting There & Away

Air Daily flights operate between Bocas del Toro and Changuinola, Panama City and David. From David there are daily flights to either Bocas del Toro or Changuinola with Alas Chiricanas (US$21 one way, US$42 return). From Panama City, Aeroperlas has weekend flights to Bocas del Toro (US$86 return) and daily flights to Changuinola (US$92 return). Alas Chiricanas has flights from Panama City to both places, at the same fare.

To/From Costa Rica It takes just a few hours to reach Bocas del Toro from Costa Rica, so many people come this way. There are also boat and bus connections to David (see below), so you can make an interesting trip from Costa Rica to Panama via Bocas del Toro.

In Costa Rica, direct buses operate between San José or Limón and Sixaola on the border. Some travellers have reported that they were not asked for an onward ticket when they entered Panama at this crossing – but don't count on it.

A minibus runs from the border to Changuinola, where another leaves for the port of Almirante; it takes about 1½ hours to reach Almirante from the border. Almirante is a rather miserable port town; you can stay overnight at the *Hospedaje San Francisco* (US$7.50) if you have to wait for the morning ferry.

A daily ferry operates between Almirante and Chiriquí Grande, stopping at Bocas del Toro on the way. It departs from Almirante at 8 am, and arrives at Chiriquí Grande at 12.30 pm. It then departs Chiriquí Grande at 1.30 pm for the return trip, arriving at Almirante at 6.30 pm. On Sunday, another ferry leaves Almirante at 8 am, going only as far as Bocas del Toro, where it docks at 9.30 am and departs for the return trip at 10 am. Check for local information before making this trip; the service may be reduced to a few days a week. An alternative to the ferry is to charter a small motor boat; they cost about US$5 for the one or 1½-hour trip from Almirante to the island.

There is a train line running between Almirante and the border, which was disrupted for some time by an earthquake in 1991. For up-to-date information call ☎ 78-3215.

From David Buses depart from David for Chiriquí Grande every 1½ hours from 6.30 am to 4 pm (106 km, three hours, US$6). The coast-to-coast trip over the mountain range is a beautiful journey. From Chiriquí Grande, the ferry (see above) to Bocas del Toro departs at 1.30 pm. There are places to stay at Chiriquí Grande if you have to spend the night.

PARQUE INTERNACIONAL LA AMISTAD

Also in Bocas del Toro province is Panama's part of the international reserve of La Amistad, established jointly in 1988 by Panama and Costa Rica, in the Talamanca mountain range. It has some magnificent wildlife but it is quite difficult to reach.

Eastern Panama

Panama's eastern area is composed of two provinces. The San Blas province is a narrow, 200-km long strip on the Caribbean coast. The large Darién province covers all the rest of the eastern side of the country.

Eastern Panama is sparsely inhabited, has vast wilderness areas, and is not much visited by travellers, unless they're making the trip between Panama and Colombia through the area known as the Darién Gap, because there are no roads through the region. For information about travelling between Central and South America, including details about crossing the Darién Gap, see the Getting There & Away chapter early in this book.

The other big attraction of eastern Panama is the islands of the Archipiélago de San Blas.

ARCHIPIÉLAGO DE SAN BLAS
The islands of the San Blas archipelago are strung out along the coast of Panama from the Golfo de San Blas nearly all the way to the Colombian border. The tourist literature says there are 365 San Blas islands, one for every day of the year, but the Cuna Indians who live there say there are even more – 378 islands. They range in size from tiny, uninhabited sand cays, with just a few coconut palms, to islands with large villages of palm-thatched houses.

The islands are home to the Cuna Indians, who run San Blas as an autonomous province, with minimal interference from the national government, using their own system of governance, consultation and decision-making. They maintain their own economic system, language, customs, and culture, with distinctive dress, legends, music and dance. Given that their area has been in contact with Europeans ever since Columbus sailed along here in 1502, this is no mean achievement and has required remarkable tenacity, wisdom, foresight and practical organisation by the Cuna, who still jealously guard their traditional way of life.

The economy of the San Blas islands is based primarily on coconuts and fishing. No one knows why, but the coconuts from the San Blas islands are particularly good, and many are sold to Colombia. Seafoods include fish, lobster, shrimp, Caribbean king crab and octopus; these are not usually sold for cash, but are traded among the Cuna. Other food crops, including rice, yams, yucca, bananas and pineapples, are not grown on the islands themselves, but in plots on the mainland, a short distance away.

The Cuna women make the intricately hand-stitched, many-layered appliqué molas, the most famous of Panamanian traditional handicrafts. Buyers come here from many countries. It takes a long time and a lot of skill to make the best molas, so they are not cheap. You can find a tiny, simple souvenir mola for around US$5, but a high-quality mola can cost anywhere from US$50 to several hundred dollars. Molas are also sold on street stalls and in speciality shops in Panama City.

The Cuna women usually wear traditional dress: a colourful short-sleeved blouse with a red patterned mola sewn onto the front and back, a red and yellow printed scarf placed on the head but not tied, a colourful printed cloth tied around the waist to make a long skirt, dozens of bracelets on both arms and legs, and pure gold nose rings, earrings and sometimes necklaces. The heavy gold necklaces, which cover the whole chest, are not worn every day, but all the rest is daily attire. The women cut their shiny black hair short, and often have a black line tattooed down the middle of the nose. They are small people, but very striking in appearance. Cuna men usually wear Western dress, which in these warm islands often means shorts and a singlet.

Things to See & Do
Swimming and fishing are good on the islands, as are snorkelling and diving in some places. You may be able to hire snorkelling and diving gear, though serious snorkellers should bring their own. Diving conditions are fine except in April, May and June.

PANAMA

Some of the islands are uninhabited, while other islands have so many people that there's only enough room for their palm huts, and the narrow walkways between them.

In the area around El Porvenir, where the airport and the two main hotels are, some of the most interesting islands are Achutupu ('dog island'), which has a shipwreck offshore, and Kagantupu and Coco Blanco, with good beaches; all are good for snorkelling or diving. Or you can visit the island where the Smithsonian Institution operates a research station for marine and nature research.

If you want to take photos of people on the islands, bring plenty of small change. It is customary to pay Cuna Indians US$0.25 for each photo you take of them.

Places to Stay & Eat

There are only a couple of places to stay on the islands, and they provide all the meals for their guests. There are no restaurants or other places to eat. The meals are usually based on seafood, with lobster a speciality, but other food is available.

El Porvenir, a small island in the Golfo de San Blas, is the principal airport for the small planes coming from the mainland. It also has a post office and telephone station. Near Porvenir, the Hotel Anais (☎ 20-6546, 20-0746) on the island of Wichub-Wala has a swimming pool, and rooms with private bath, and costs US$75 per person per day. The price includes three meals and boat transport.

If you don't want to stay overnight, the hotel also offers one-day island tours. They pick you up at El Porvenir airport when the plane arrives at around 6.30 am, give you breakfast and lunch, take you to several different islands for exploring, swimming or snorkelling, and take you back to the airport for a 4 pm flight to Panama City. The day tours cost US$25 with the Hotel Anais.

The only other hotel in the archipelago is the Hotel Las Palmeras (☎ 22-3096) on the island of Ailigandí, halfway down the coast towards Colombia. It has accommodation for US$18 per night.

If you want to make some arrangement to stay on the islands, you will have to ask the Cuna elders. The Cuna are a kind people, but they are very particular about what outsiders do on their islands.

Getting There & Away

Air Several airlines operate small planes (10-seaters or so) between Panama City and the islands, including Ansa (☎ 26-7891, 26-6896), Aerotaxi (☎ 64-8644) and Transpasa (☎ 26-0843). All depart from Paitilla airport in Panama City at 6 am, arriving at the El Porvenir airport at 6.30 am. Return flights leave El Porvenir at 7 am, unless you've arranged a day tour leaving in the late afternoon. Though El Porvenir is the principal stop, several other islands in the archipelago have airports, and you may be able to stop at a number of them while they load and unload passengers or cargo.

It costs US$48-50 return between Panama City and El Porvenir, but it's best to get a one-way ticket, and buy your return ticket when you're ready to leave. Several flights depart El Porvenir airport every morning around 7 am, and if you haven't yet bought your return ticket, you can take whichever plane leaves first (there's always space when flying back to the mainland). If you have a return ticket, you're committed to one company and, if their flight is delayed, you won't be able to change your ticket for a more convenient one.

Sea Cuna merchant ships to the San Blas islands depart from Coco Solo Pier in Colón, and they act as the islands' merchant ships, buses and taxis. The boats usually depart from the pier at around midnight, to reach El Porvenir in the morning (eight hours, US$6.50 to US$10).

The boats continue east along the coast, stopping at about 48 islands along the way, until they reach Puerto Obaldía, near the Colombian border, where they turn around to come back. The trip from Colón all the way to Puerto Obaldía takes five days and costs US$25 including all meals. These boats are nothing luxurious, but they let you see the whole archipelago, and stop at many of the islands while goods and passengers are being loaded and unloaded. You might be able to stay on one or two of the islands along the way.

Car You can drive to Cartí Suitupo, on the coast of the Golfo San Blas, and take a boat from there. It takes about three hours on a rough road to reach Cartí from Panama City.

Until the road is improved there will be no bus along this route. A 4WD vehicle is needed to make the drive. Hitching to Cartí would be difficult because there's not much traffic.

From Cartí Suitupo you can hire a motorboat to take you to one of the islands. To El Porvenir, Nalunega or Wichub-Wala takes about 45 minutes and costs US$10 for the boat, which can take up to eight people.

Glossary

Abajo – down

Adiós – greeting used when passing someone in the street (Costa Rica); good-bye

Aguardiente – a clear liquor made from sugar cane, with an alcohol content even higher than that of vodka

Alfombra – carpet

Almacene – big store

Alquiler de automóviles – car hire

Antigeño – citizen of Antigua Guatemala

Apartado – post office box

Arriba – up

Artesanías – handcrafts

Bahía – bay

Baleada – filled tortilla (Honduras)

Balneario – public bathing or swimming spot

Barba amarilla – literally 'yellow beard'; the poisonous fer-de-lance snake

Barrio – neighbourhood

Bistec – grilled or fried beef

Bocas – little side dishes served with drinks

Bomba – petrol (gasoline) station

Cabaña – cabin

Cacique – Indian tribal elder; provincial warlord or strongman

Cafetería – literally 'coffee-shop'; any informal restaurant with waiter service, not a self-service place

Cafetín – small cafeteria

Calzada – causeway

Calzones – long baggy shorts

Cama matrimonial – double bed

Camarotes – smaller rooms

Camión – truck; bus

Caracol – seashell; snail

Carnet de passage – (French) literally 'card of passage'; official paper for vehicles going to South America

Carretera – highway

Casa de cambio – place to exchange money

Casa de huespedes – guesthouse

Casa de la mujer – women's centre

Casado – a cheap set meal, usually served at lunchtime

Cay, caye or **cayo** – small island of sand or coral fragments

Cayuca – dugout canoe

Cerro – hill

Cerveza – beer

Ceviche – seafood marinated in lime juice

Chamarras – thick, heavy woollen blankets (Guatemala)

Chapín – a citizen of Guatemala; Guatemalan

Chicha – fruit juice mixed with sugar and water (Panama)

Chuletas de puerco – pork chops

Churrasco – Guatemalan-style beef

Cine – movie theatre

Ciudad – city

Cocina – literally 'kitchen'; small, cheap cookshop of the kind found near markets

Cofradía – traditional religious brotherhood

Colón – Spanish spelling of Columbus; also the unit of currency in Costa Rica and El Salvador

Colectivo – van or minibus operating as a shared taxi

Comedor – a simple, cheap restaurant

Comida corrida – a set meal of several courses, usually offered at lunchtime

Comida corriente – a mixed plate of different foods typical of the local region

Comida típica – similar to a comida corriente

Completo – complete, booked out

Conjunto – combined; also an ensemble, a musical group

Conquistador – Spanish conqueror of Latin America

Contras – counter-revolutionaries fighting against the Sandinista government in Nicaragua in the 1980s

Cordillera – mountain range

Correo Aéreo – air mail

Costa – coast

Criollo – creole, born in Latin America of Spanish descent; on the Caribbean coast it refers to someone of mixed Black and European descent

Cuadra – city block

Cueva – cave

Día de los Muertos – Day of the Dead, or All Souls' Day, 1 November

Encomienda – Spanish colonial practice of putting Indians under the 'guardianship' of landowners, a form of serfdom

Enredo – a wraparound skirt

Esquadrones de muerte – death squads, supported by Somoza in El Salvador

Estación ferrocarril – railway station

Faja – waist sash, to bind the garments and to hold what we would put in pockets

Farmacia de turno – duty-chemist

Filibustero – filibuster, an irregular military adventurer, freebooter

Finca – plantation, ranch

Fresco – drink made of fruit juice, sugar and water

Frijoles con arroz – beans with rice

Galón, galones – US gallon (3.79 litres)

Gallo pinto – blend of rice and beans, with cooking water from the beans added; a common meal, especially in Nicaragua

Garífuna, plural **Garinagu** – also called Black Caribs, mixed-race descendants of Africans and Carib Indians from the Caribbean island of St Vincent, who came to Central America in the late 18th century

Gaseosa – soda, soft drink

Gibnut or **paca** – small, brown-spotted rodent similar to a guinea pig

Golfo – gulf

Gringo/gringa – non-Latin American, especially from the USA; sometimes, not always, derogatory

Guacamole – a salad of mashed or chopped avocadoes, onions and tomatoes

Guaro – the local firewater in Costa Rica

Guayabera – embroidered men's dress shirt, worn outside the pants

Hacienda – estate; also 'Treasury', as in

Departamento de Hacienda, Treasury Department

Hamburguesas – hamburgers

Hospedaje – guesthouse

Huipil – a long, woven, white sleeveless tunic from the Mayan regions, with intricate, colourful embroidery

Iglesia – church

Internacionalistas – volunteers from around the world who came to Nicaragua after the revolution to assist the Sandinistas

Invierno – winter; in Central America, the wet season, roughly from April to November

ISIC – International Student Identity Card, can be useful for obtaining student airfares or other discounts

IVA – the *impuesto al valour agregado,* or 'ee-vah', is a value-added tax

Jejenes – sandflies

Junco – type of basket weaving

Ladino – Indian or mestizo who speaks Spanish and lives a modern lifestyle

Lago – lake

Laguna – lagoon, lake

Lancha – small motorboat

Lempira Honduran unit of currency

Leng – colloquial Mayan term for coins (Guatemalan highlands)

Libra – pound weight, 0.45 kg

Licuado – fresh fruit drink, blended with milk or water

Lista de Correos – poste restante (general delivery)

Machismo – the exaggerated masculine pride of the Latin American male

Malecón – pier or jetty; waterside walkway

Manzana – literally 'apple', but also a term for a city block

Mar – sea

Mariachi – (adj & noun) traditional Mexican acoustic musical group

Mercado – market

Mestizo – person of mixed Spanish and Indian descent

Metate – flat stone on which corn is ground

Migración – immigration, office of an immigration department
Milla – mile (1.61 km)
Milpa – cornfield
Mirador – lookout
Mola – Cuna Indian fabric appliqué
Mordida – literally 'little bite'; a small bribe of the kind that keeps the wheels of bureaucracy turning
Morería – storehouse for the ceremonial masks, costumes and regalia used in religious festivals
Muchacho – boy; also used as 'mate' or 'pal'
Muelle – pier
Municipalidad – town hall

Navidad – Christmas
Nuevo/nueva – new

Oficina de Correos – post office
Onza – ounce (28 g)

Palacio de gobierno – colonial government headquarters
Palapa – roof thatched with palm leaves
Pan de coco – coconut bread
Panga – small motorboat
Panqueques – pancakes
Parque – park; sometimes also used for plaza
Pavo silvestre – wild turkey
Peña – a folkloric club; an evening of music, song and dance
Peso – nickname for Nicaraguan córdoba
Pensión – guesthouse
Petate – plant material used for basketry and mats (Nicaragua)
Pie, pies – foot, feet (0.3 metres)
Pisto – colloquial Mayan term for money, quetzals (Guatemalan highlands)
Playa – beach
Platillo chapín – dish of Guatemalan specialities
Plato típico – a mixed plate of various foods typical of a place or region
Pollera – lacy Panamanian national dress for women
Pollo asado – grilled chicken
Propina – tip (not a bribe)

Puente – bridge
Puerto – port, harbour
Punta – point; Garífuna dancing with much hip movement
Pupusa – a small, hot corn tortilla stuffed with meat, beans or cheese (El Salvador)
Pupusería – restaurant selling pupusas

Quebrada – ravine, brook
Quechiquémitl – a shoulder cape

Refresco – soda, soft drink
Río – river
Rockola – jukebox
Ropa vieja – literally 'old clothes'; spicy shredded beef and rice dish (Panama)
Rosticería – restaurant selling roast meats
Ruletero – jitney, public minibus

Sacbé – ceremonial limestone avenue between Maya cities
Salchichas – sausages, like hot dogs
Salsa – modern Latin dance music
Sancocho – spicy meat and vegetable stew, the national dish of Panama
Semana Santa – Holy Week, the week before Easter
Sendero – path
Servicios sanitarios – toilets
Sierra – mountain range; a saw
Soda – place that serves a counter lunch; soft drink (Panama)
Sorbetería – ice cream parlour
Sorpresa – literally 'surprise'; a tiny ceramic scene inside a ceramic cover
Supermercado – supermarket

Tajaditas – crisp, fried banana chips
Tamales – steamed corn dough rolls, perhaps with a meat or other stuffing
Teléfono monedero – coin-operated telephone
Temblor – earthquake
Tico/tica – inhabitant of Costa Rica
Tienda – small shop
Trucha – trout
Turicentro – literally 'tourist centre'; outdoor recreation centre with swimming, restaurants and camping (El Salvador)

Vegetariano – vegetarian
Venado – deer; venison
Ventanillas especiales – special teller windows for changing money
Verano – summer; in Central America, the dry season, roughly from November to April
Viajero/viajera – traveller

Viejo/vieja – old
Villa – village, settlement
Vinchuca – a bug which carries Chagas' Disease; a smooth, oval, brownish insect, with two antennae curving under the narrow conical head
Volcán – volcano

Index

TEXT

630

Thanks

Our thanks to the many readers and travellers who wrote in with information:

Roald Aavre (N), Dan Ahm (Dk), Rachel Marcus (UK), Kimberley Armstrong-Rossr (NZ), Dee Dee Arthur (USA), Marjorie Austin (USA), Catrionna Bain, Frank Bakker (NL), Michael Beller (USA), Tony Bennett (Aus), Rachel Biliski-Cohen (USA), Terrence Bishop (USA), Brigitte Blais (C), Sarah & Philippe Bonay (F), Will Bosch (C), David Brantley (USA), Leanne Broadbent (USA), Stuart Broderick (C), John Brox, Alison & Stefan Bruegger (C), John L Byrne (USA), Michael Carter (C), Sue Cartwright (NZ), Bernardo Castellanos, Samuel Charache (USA), Jeremy Chatowgy (UK), Capt John Clark, Marg & Michael Clark (Aus), Eddie Clements (UK), Stephen Colwell (USA), Elizabeth Corcoran (USA), Mark Crawford (UK), Cliff Cremer (NL), Elampini Danilo (I), Jay Davidson (USA), Gregory Dayman (Aus), M S de Jong (NL), Meriel de Vekey (UK), Tony Del Prete (USA), Carole Devine, Andrew Dinwoodie (UK), Larry Doffing (USA), Kate Dolby (UK), John Drever (USA), Laura Durand (USA), Louis Eby (USA), Kay & Beatrice Eggert (D), Sara Einus (D), Leonie Eiszele (Aus), James Farrell (UK), Chris Feierabend (USA), Malene Felsing (Dk), Kimberley Felton (USA), Samantha Francis (UK), Paul & Cari Francot (B), Paul Fretz (C), Matthias Frohlich (D), Peter Gedge (UK), M D Geuze (NL), Ben Gitterman (USA), Mark Goodwin (UK), Heinz Govlitz (D), John Grant (C), Giorgio Grazzini (I), Thomas Greig (UK), Kathy Griffiths (Aus), Kerrie Hall (Aus), Ray Halle (USA), Hank Heinekamp (NZ), B Henera (USA), Ingrid Henkle, Tom Henry (USA), Rolando I Herrera de Paz, John Hickey (C), Pat Hickey (USA), Nick Hubing (USA), Paol & Tess Huisman (NL), Bernard Huot (USA), Allen Johannesson (C), David Johnson (UK), J Zakariah Johnson (USA), Lindsay Johnston (UK), Gerallt Jones (UK), Chris Jones (USA), Soren Klippfjell (S), Ulrich Krueth (D), Julia Kushner (USA), Paul Lamann, Mark Laptin (UK), Gert Bue Larsen (Dk), Kathryn Licina (USA), Ann Liebau (C), Ted Lindland, Family Lomont-Cabral, Brian Lotimer (C), Cynthia Luce (USA), Laura Lund (USA), J Lynen (USA), Fergus Mahon (UK), Glenn Mair (Aus), Jerry Makransky (C), Pat Mallahan (USA), Linda Jo Malloy (C), A J M Markese, Laurent Mathez (S), Colin McKenzie (UK), F Timothy McNamara (USA), Aaron Mead (USA), Charles Meltmar (USA), Kim Meyer (USA), Paul Mills, Andrea Mull (USA), Mark Nedleman (USA), Nicoletta Negri (I), David Neville (Aus), Mikael Nilsson (S), Jim & Cindy Novelo, Elsa Nygren, Matthew O'Donnell (USA), Petra Offermann (D), Angela Orlando (USA), Bernadette Orr (USA), John Peluso (USA), Julie Perron, Anthony Peters (USA), Eugen Pfersich (D), Marc Philippe (F), Clive Porter (UK), Warren Post, Sheelah Powell (UK), Alberto Preti (I), Fred Prost, G F Pugsley (UK), Jan Rensen (NL), Keve Ribardo (USA), Beatrice Richards, Mai Riise (Dk), Alexandra Robak (UK), Gary Roberts (USA), Bruce Rogers (USA), Mitch Roman (USA), Paul Roos (NL), Thierry Roquet, Verma Samuels, Paul F Sargent (USA), I & A Schaefer (USA), Joel Schiavoni (USA), Elke Schreiber (D), Brian Sharrock (C), Mike Shawcross, Caesar Sherrard, Andy Shillaber (USA), Jill Simmons (USA), Anthony Slavin (Aus), Martin Spencer (Aus), David Steinke (D), Mark Stern (D), Penelope Stewarts (UK), A Stivland (UK), Duncan Stonehouse (UK), Baerbel Strauch (D), Maria Svenningsson (S), Stefan Svensson (S), Tom Taylor (USA), N Teasdale (Aus), Captain Terry, Steven Thomas (USA), Beth & Shaun Tierney (Aus), Craig Tower (USA), Ryan Trow (UK), Jim Tyra (USA), Donald Uber (USA), Sandra Urquieta (USA), Craig Vacovsky (USA), Souad von Allmen (CH), Kristopher Walmsley (S), Lee Ann Ward (USA), Simon Watson Taylor (UK), Susanne Wenk (CH), Peter Whitehead (UK), Helen Whitford, R Wiles, Michael Wilford (UK), Kent Williams (USA), Harriet Williamson (USA), Jason Wilson (UK), Cheri Wilson (UK), Carla Wolters (NL), Dan Workman (C), Jane Wright (UK), Jessica Wyatt (UK), Bruce Young (USA), Mathias Zab (D), Fennie Zwanepol (NL)

B – Belgium, C – Canada, CH – Switzerland, D – Germany, Dk – Denmark, F – France, I – Italy, N – Norway, NL – Netherlands, NZ – New Zealand, S – Sweden, UK – United Kingdom, USA – United States of America

PLANET TALK
Lonely Planet's FREE quarterly newsletter

We love hearing from you and think you'd like to hear from us.

When...*is the right time to see reindeer in Finland?*
Where...*can you hear the best palm-wine music in Ghana?*
How...*do you get from Asunción to Areguá by steam train?*
What...*is the best way to see India?*

For the answer to these and many other questions read PLANET TALK.

Every issue is packed with up-to-date travel news and advice including:

- *a letter from Lonely Planet founders Tony and Maureen Wheeler*
- *travel diary from a Lonely Planet author - find out what it's really like out on the road*
- *feature article on an important and topical travel issue*
- *a selection of recent letters from our readers*
- *the latest travel news from all over the world*
- *details on Lonely Planet's new and forthcoming releases*

To join our mailing list contact any Lonely Planet office (address below).

LONELY PLANET PUBLICATIONS
Australia: PO Box 617, Hawthorn 3122, Victoria (tel: 03-819 1877)
USA: Embarcadero West, 155 Filbert St, Suite 251, Oakland, CA 94607 (tel: 510-893 8555)
TOLL FREE: (800) 275-8555
UK: 10 Barley Mow Passage, Chiswick, London W4 4PH (tel: 081-742 3161)
France: 71 bis rue du Cardinal Lemoine – 75005 Paris (tel: 46 34 00 58)

Also available: Lonely Planet T-shirts. 100% heavyweight cotton (S, M, L, XL)

Guides to the Americas

Alaska – a travel survival kit
Jim DuFresne has travelled extensively through Alaska by foot, road, rail, barge and kayak, and tells how to make the most of one of the world's great wilderness areas.

Argentina, Uruguay & Paraguay – a travel survival kit
This guide gives independent travellers all the essential information on three of South America's lesser-known countries. Discover some of South America's most spectacular natural attractions in Argentina; friendly people and beautiful handicrafts in Paraguay; and Uruguay's wonderful beaches.

Baja California – a travel survival kit
For centuries, Mexico's Baja peninsula – with its beautiful coastline, raucous border towns and crumbling Spanish missions – has been a land of escapes and escapades. This book describes how and where to escape in Baja.

Bolivia – a travel survival kit
From lonely villages in the Andes to ancient ruined cities and the spectacular city of La Paz, Bolivia is a magnificent blend of everything that inspires travellers. Discover safe and intriguing travel options in this comprehensive guide.

Brazil – a travel survival kit
From the mad passion of Carnival to the Amazon – home of the richest ecosystem on earth – Brazil is a country of mythical proportions. This guide has all the essential travel information.

Canada – a travel survival kit
This comprehensive guidebook has all the facts on the USA's huge neighbour – the Rocky Mountains, Niagara Falls, ultramodern Toronto, remote villages in Nova Scotia, and much more.

Chile & Easter Island – a travel survival kit
Travel in Chile is easy and safe, with possibilities as varied as the countryside. This guide also gives detailed coverage of Chile's Pacific outpost, mysterious Easter Island.

Colombia – a travel survival kit
Colombia is a land of myths – from the ancient legends of El Dorado to the modern tales of Gabriel Garcia Marquez. The reality is beauty and violence, wealth and poverty, tradition and change. This guide shows how to travel independently and safely in this exotic country.

Costa Rica – a travel survival kit
Sun-drenched beaches, steamy jungles, smoking volcanoes, rugged mountains and dazzling birds and animals – Costa Rica has it all.

Eastern Caribbean – a travel survival kit
Powdery white sands, clear turquoise waters, lush jungle rainforest, balmy weather and a laid back pace, make the islands of the Eastern Caibbean an ideal destination for divers, hikers and sun-lovers. This guide will help you to decide which islands to visit to suit your interests and includes details on inter-island travel.

Ecuador & the Galápagos Islands – a travel survival kit
Ecuador offers a wide variety of travel experiences, from the high cordilleras to the Amazon plains – and 600 miles west, the fascinating Galápagos Islands. Everything you need to know about travelling around this enchanting country.

Guatemala, Belize & Yucatán: La Ruta Maya – a travel survival kit
Climb a volcano, explore the colourful highland villages or laze your time away on coral islands and Caribbean beaches. The lands of the Maya offer a fascinating journey into the past which will enhance appreciation of their dynamic contemporary cultures. An award winning guide to this exotic fregion.

Hawaii – a travel survival kit
Share in the delights of this island paradise – and avoid its high prices – both on and off the beaten track. Full details on Hawaii's best-known attractions, plus plenty of uncrowded sights and activities.

Mexico – a travel survival kit
A unique blend of Indian and Spanish culture, fascinating history, and hospitable people, make Mexico a travellers' paradise.

Peru – a travel survival kit
The lost city of Machu Picchu, the Andean altiplano and the magnificent Amazon rainforests are just some of Peru's many attractions. All the travel facts you'll need can be found in this comprehensive guide.

South America on a shoestring
This practical guide provides concise information for budget travellers and covers South America from the Darien Gap to Tierra del Fuego.

Trekking in the Patagonian Andes
The first detailed guide to this region gives complete information on 28 walks, and lists a number of other possibilities extending from the Araucanía and Lake District regions of Argentina and Chile to the remote icy tip of South America in Tierra del Fuego.

Also available:
Brazilian phrasebook, **Latin American Spanish** phrasebook and **Quechua** phrasebook.

Lonely Planet Guidebooks

Lonely Planet guidebooks cover every accessible part of Asia as well as Australia, the Pacific, South America, Africa, the Middle East, Europe and parts of North America. There are five series: *travel survival kits*, covering a country for a range of budgets; *shoestring guides* with compact information for low-budget travel in a major region; *walking guides*; *city guides* and *phrasebooks*.

Australia & the Pacific
Australia
Bushwalking in Australia
Islands of Australia's Great Barrier Reef
Fiji
Melbourne city guide
Micronesia
New Caledonia
New Zealand
Tramping in New Zealand
Papua New Guinea
Bushwalking in Papua New Guinea
Papua New Guinea phrasebook
Rarotonga & the Cook Islands
Samoa
Solomon Islands
Sydney city guide
Tahiti & French Polynesia
Tonga
Vanuatu
Victoria

South-East Asia
Bali & Lombok
Bangkok city guide
Cambodia
Indonesia
Indonesia phrasebook
Laos
Malaysia, Singapore & Brunei
Myanmar (Burma)
Burmese phrasebook
Philippines
Pilipino phrasebook
Singapore city guide
South-East Asia on a shoestring
Thailand
Thai phrasebook
Vietnam
Vietnamese phrasebook

North-East Asia
China
Beijing city guide
Cantonese phrasebook
Mandarin Chinese phrasebook
Hong Kong, Macau & Canton
Japan
Japanese phrasebook
Korea
Korean phrasebook
Mongolia
North-East Asia on a shoestring
Seoul city guide
Taiwan
Tibet
Tibet phrasebook
Tokyo city guide

Middle East
Arab Gulf States
Egypt & the Sudan
Arabic (Egyptian) phrasebook
Iran
Israel
Jordan & Syria
Middle East
Turkish phrasebook
Trekking in Turkey
Yemen

Indian Ocean
Madagascar & Comoros
Maldives & Islands of the East Indian Ocean
Mauritius, Réunion & Seychelles

Mail Order

Lonely Planet guidebooks are distributed worldwide.They are also available by mail order from Lonely Planet, so if you have difficulty finding a title please write to us. US and Canadian residents should write to Embarcadero West, 155 Filbert St, Suite 251, Oakland CA 94607, USA ; European residents should write to 10 Barley Mow Passage, Chiswick, London W4 4PH; and residents of other countries to PO Box 617, Hawthorn, Victoria 3122, Australia.

Indian Subcontinent
Bangladesh
India
Hindi/Urdu phrasebook
Trekking in the Indian Himalaya
Karakoram Highway
Kashmir, Ladakh & Zanskar
Nepal
Trekking in the Nepal Himalaya
Nepali phrasebook
Pakistan
Sri Lanka
Sri Lanka phrasebook

Africa
Africa on a shoestring
Central Africa
East Africa
Trekking in East Africa
Kenya
Swahili phrasebook
Morocco, Algeria & Tunisia
Arabic (Moroccan) phrasebook
South Africa, Lesotho & Swaziland
Zimbabwe, Botswana & Namibia
West Africa

Central America & the Caribbean
Baja California
Central America on a shoestring
Costa Rica
Eastern Caribbean
Guatemala, Belize & Yucatán: La Ruta Maya
Mexico

North America
Alaska
Canada
Hawaii

Europe
Baltic States & Kaliningrad
Dublin city guide
Eastern Europe on a shoestring
Eastern Europe phrasebook
Finland
France
Greece
Hungary
Iceland, Greenland & the Faroe Islands
Ireland
Italy
Mediterranean Europe on a shoestring
Mediterranean Europe phrasebook
Poland
Scandinavian & Baltic Europe on a shoestring
Scandinavian Europe phrasebook
Switzerland
Trekking in Spain
Trekking in Greece
USSR
Russian phrasebook
Western Europe on a shoestring
Western Europe phrasebook

South America
Argentina, Uruguay & Paraguay
Bolivia
Brazil
Brazilian phrasebook
Chile & Easter Island
Colombia
Ecuador & the Galápagos Islands
Latin American Spanish phrasebook
Peru
Quechua phrasebook
South America on a shoestring
Trekking in the Patagonian Andes

The Lonely Planet Story

Lonely Planet published its first book in 1973 in response to the numerous 'How did you do it?' questions Maureen and Tony Wheeler were asked after driving, bussing, hitching, sailing and railing their way from England to Australia.

Written at a kitchen table and hand collated, trimmed and stapled, *Across Asia on the Cheap* became an instant local bestseller, inspiring thoughts of another book.

Eighteen months in South-East Asia resulted in their second guide, *South-East Asia on a shoestring*, which they put together in a backstreet Chinese hotel in Singapore in 1975. The 'yellow bible' as it quickly became known to backpackers around the world, soon became *the* guide to the region. It has sold well over half a million copies and is now in its 7th edition, still retaining its familiar yellow cover.

Today there are over 130 Lonely Planet titles in print – books that have that same adventurous approach to travel as those early guides; books that 'assume you know how to get your luggage off the carousel' as one reviewer put it.

Although Lonely Planet initially specialised in guides to Asia, they now cover most regions of the world, including the Pacific, South America, Africa, the Middle East and Europe. The list of *walking guides* and *phrasebooks* (for 'unusual' languages such as Quechua, Swahili, Nepali and Egyptian Arabic) is also growing rapidly.

The emphasis continues to be on travel for independent travellers. Tony and Maureen still travel for several months of each year and play an active part in the writing, updating and quality control of Lonely Planet's guides.

They have been joined by over 50 authors, 60 staff – mainly editors, cartographers & designers – at our office in Melbourne, Australia, at our US office in Oakland, California and at our European office in Paris; another five at our office in London handle sales for Britain, Europe and Africa. Travellers themselves also make a valuable contribution to the guides through the feedback we receive in thousands of letters each year.

The people at Lonely Planet strongly believe that travellers can make a positive contribution to the countries they visit, both through their appreciation of the countries' culture, wildlife and natural features, and through the money they spend. In addition, the company makes a direct contribution to the countries and regions it covers. Since 1986 a percentage of the income from each book has been donated to ventures such as famine relief in Africa; aid projects in India; agricultural projects in Central America; Greenpeace's efforts to halt French nuclear testing in the Pacific and Amnesty International. In 1994 $100,000 was donated to such causes.

Lonely Planet's basic travel philosophy is summed up in Tony Wheeler's comment, 'Don't worry about whether your trip will work out. Just go!'.